Jay West

323-3126

AF718796

Brumbaugh Cs. Criminal 2nd Ed. UCB—1

University Casebook Series

March, 1991

ACCOUNTING AND THE LAW, Fourth Edition (1978), with Problems Pamphlet (Successor to Dohr, Phillips, Thompson & Warren)

George C. Thompson, Professor, Columbia University Graduate School of Business.
Robert Whitman, Professor of Law, University of Connecticut.
Ellis L. Phillips, Jr., Member of the New York Bar.
William C. Warren, Professor of Law Emeritus, Columbia University.

ACCOUNTING FOR LAWYERS, MATERIALS ON (1980)

David R. Herwitz, Professor of Law, Harvard University.

ADMINISTRATIVE LAW, Eighth Edition (1987), with 1989 Case Supplement and 1983 Problems Supplement (Supplement edited in association with Paul R. Verkuil, Dean and Professor of Law, Tulane University)

Walter Gellhorn, University Professor Emeritus, Columbia University.
Clark Byse, Professor of Law, Harvard University.
Peter L. Strauss, Professor of Law, Columbia University.
Todd D. Rakoff, Professor of Law, Harvard University.
Roy A. Schotland, Professor of Law, Georgetown University.

ADMIRALTY, Third Edition (1987), with Statute and Rule Supplement

Jo Desha Lucas, Professor of Law, University of Chicago.

ADVOCACY, see also Lawyering Process

AGENCY, see also Enterprise Organization

AGENCY—PARTNERSHIPS, Fourth Edition (1987)

Abridgement from Conard, Knauss & Siegel's Enterprise Organization, Fourth Edition.

AGENCY AND PARTNERSHIPS (1987)

Melvin A. Eisenberg, Professor of Law, University of California, Berkeley.

ANTITRUST: FREE ENTERPRISE AND ECONOMIC ORGANIZATION, Sixth Edition (1983), with 1983 Problems in Antitrust Supplement and 1990 Case Supplement

Louis B. Schwartz, Professor of Law, University of Pennsylvania.
John J. Flynn, Professor of Law, University of Utah.
Harry First, Professor of Law, New York University.

BANKRUPTCY, Second Edition (1989), with 1990 Case Supplement

Robert L. Jordan, Professor of Law, University of California, Los Angeles.
William D. Warren, Professor of Law, University of California, Los Angeles.

BANKRUPTCY AND DEBTOR-CREDITOR LAW, Second Edition (1988)

Theodore Eisenberg, Professor of Law, Cornell University.

BUSINESS CRIME (1990)

Harry First, Professor of Law, New York University.

BUSINESS ORGANIZATION, see also Enterprise Organization

BUSINESS PLANNING, Temporary Second Edition (1984)

David R. Herwitz, Professor of Law, Harvard University.

BUSINESS TORTS (1972)

Milton Handler, Professor of Law Emeritus, Columbia University.

CHILDREN IN THE LEGAL SYSTEM (1983) with 1990 Supplement (Supplement edited in association with Elizabeth S. Scott, Professor of Law, University of Virginia)

Walter Wadlington, Professor of Law, University of Virginia.
Charles H. Whitebread, Professor of Law, University of Southern California.
Samuel Davis, Professor of Law, University of Georgia.

CIVIL PROCEDURE, see Procedure

CIVIL RIGHTS ACTIONS (1988), with 1990 Supplement

Peter W. Low, Professor of Law, University of Virginia.
John C. Jeffries, Jr., Professor of Law, University of Virginia.

CLINIC, see also Lawyering Process

COMMERCIAL AND DEBTOR-CREDITOR LAW: SELECTED STATUTES, 1990 EDITION

COMMERCIAL LAW, Second Edition (1987)

Robert L. Jordan, Professor of Law, University of California, Los Angeles.
William D. Warren, Professor of Law, University of California, Los Angeles.

COMMERCIAL LAW, Fourth Edition (1985), with 1990 Case Supplement

E. Allan Farnsworth, Professor of Law, Columbia University.
John Honnold, Professor of Law, University of Pennsylvania.

COMMERCIAL PAPER, Third Edition (1984), with 1990 Case Supplement

E. Allan Farnsworth, Professor of Law, Columbia University.

COMMERCIAL PAPER, Second Edition (1987) (Reprinted from COMMERCIAL LAW, Second Edition (1987))

Robert L. Jordan, Professor of Law, University of California, Los Angeles.
William D. Warren, Professor of Law, University of California, Los Angeles.

COMMERCIAL PAPER AND BANK DEPOSITS AND COLLECTIONS (1967), with Statutory Supplement

William D. Hawkland, Professor of Law, University of Illinois.

COMMERCIAL TRANSACTIONS—Principles and Policies, Second Edition (1991)

Alan Schwartz, Professor of Law, Yale University.
Robert E. Scott, Professor of Law, University of Virginia.

COMPARATIVE LAW, Fifth Edition (1988)

Rudolf B. Schlesinger, Professor of Law, Hastings College of the Law.
Hans W. Baade, Professor of Law, University of Texas.
Mirjan P. Damaska, Professor of Law, Yale Law School.
Peter E. Herzog, Professor of Law, Syracuse University.

UNIVERSITY CASEBOOK SERIES—Continued

COMPETITIVE PROCESS, LEGAL REGULATION OF THE, Fourth Edition (1990), with 1989 Selected Statutes Supplement

Edmund W. Kitch, Professor of Law, University of Virginia.
Harvey S. Perlman, Dean of the Law School, University of Nebraska.

CONFLICT OF LAWS, Ninth Edition (1990)

Willis L. M. Reese, Professor of Law, Columbia University.
Maurice Rosenberg, Professor of Law, Columbia University.
Peter Hay, Professor of Law, University of Illinois.

CONSTITUTIONAL LAW, Eighth Edition (1989), with 1990 Case Supplement

Edward L. Barrett, Jr., Professor of Law, University of California, Davis.
William Cohen, Professor of Law, Stanford University.
Jonathan D. Varat, Professor of Law, University of California, Los Angeles.

CONSTITUTIONAL LAW, CIVIL LIBERTY AND INDIVIDUAL RIGHTS, Second Edition (1982), with 1989 Supplement

William Cohen, Professor of Law, Stanford University.
John Kaplan, Professor of Law, Stanford University.

CONSTITUTIONAL LAW, Eleventh Edition (1985), with 1990 Supplement (Supplement edited in association with Frederick F. Schauer, Professor, Harvard University)

Gerald Gunther, Professor of Law, Stanford University.

CONSTITUTIONAL LAW, INDIVIDUAL RIGHTS IN, Fourth Edition (1986), (Reprinted from CONSTITUTIONAL LAW, Eleventh Edition), with 1990 Supplement (Supplement edited in association with Frederick F. Schauer, Professor, Harvard University)

Gerald Gunther, Professor of Law, Stanford University.

CONSUMER TRANSACTIONS, Second Edition (1991), with Selected Statutes and Regulations Supplement

Michael M. Greenfield, Professor of Law, Washington University.

CONTRACT LAW AND ITS APPLICATION, Fourth Edition (1988)

Arthur Rosett, Professor of Law, University of California, Los Angeles.

CONTRACT LAW, STUDIES IN, Third Edition (1984)

Edward J. Murphy, Professor of Law, University of Notre Dame.
Richard E. Speidel, Professor of Law, Northwestern University.

CONTRACTS, Fifth Edition (1987)

John P. Dawson, late Professor of Law, Harvard University.
William Burnett Harvey, Professor of Law and Political Science, Boston University.
Stanley D. Henderson, Professor of Law, University of Virginia.

CONTRACTS, Fourth Edition (1988)

E. Allan Farnsworth, Professor of Law, Columbia University.
William F. Young, Professor of Law, Columbia University.

CONTRACTS, Selections on (statutory materials) (1988)

CONTRACTS, Second Edition (1978), with Statutory and Administrative Law Supplement (1978)

Ian R. Macneil, Professor of Law, Cornell University.

COPYRIGHT, PATENTS AND TRADEMARKS, see also Competitive Process; see also Selected Statutes and International Agreements

COPYRIGHT, PATENT, TRADEMARK AND RELATED STATE DOCTRINES, Third Edition (1990), with 1989 Selected Statutes Supplement and 1981 Problem Supplement

Paul Goldstein, Professor of Law, Stanford University.

COPYRIGHT, Unfair Competition, and Other Topics Bearing on the Protection of Literary, Musical, and Artistic Works, Fifth Edition (1990), with 1990 Statutory Supplement

Ralph S. Brown, Jr., Professor of Law, Yale University.
Robert C. Denicola, Professor of Law, University of Nebraska.

CORPORATE ACQUISITIONS, The Law and Finance of (1986), with 1990 Supplement

Ronald J. Gilson, Professor of Law, Stanford University.

CORPORATE FINANCE, Third Edition (1987)

Victor Brudney, Professor of Law, Harvard University.
Marvin A. Chirelstein, Professor of Law, Columbia University.

CORPORATION LAW, BASIC, Third Edition (1989), with Documentary Supplement

Detlev F. Vagts, Professor of Law, Harvard University.

CORPORATIONS, see also Enterprise Organization

CORPORATIONS, Sixth Edition—Concise (1988), with 1990 Case Supplement and 1990 Statutory Supplement

William L. Cary, late Professor of Law, Columbia University.
Melvin Aron Eisenberg, Professor of Law, University of California, Berkeley.

CORPORATIONS, Sixth Edition—Unabridged (1988), with 1990 Case Supplement and 1990 Statutory Supplement

William L. Cary, late Professor of Law, Columbia University.
Melvin Aron Eisenberg, Professor of Law, University of California, Berkeley.

CORPORATIONS AND BUSINESS ASSOCIATIONS—STATUTES, RULES, AND FORMS (1990)

CORRECTIONS, SEE SENTENCING

CREDITORS' RIGHTS, see also Debtor-Creditor Law

CRIMINAL JUSTICE ADMINISTRATION, Fourth Edition (1991)

Frank W. Miller, Professor of Law, Washington University.
Robert O. Dawson, Professor of Law, University of Texas.
George E. Dix, Professor of Law, University of Texas.
Raymond I. Parnas, Professor of Law, University of California, Davis.

CRIMINAL LAW, Fourth Edition (1987)

Fred E. Inbau, Professor of Law Emeritus, Northwestern University.
Andre A. Moenssens, Professor of Law, University of Richmond.
James R. Thompson, Professor of Law Emeritus, Northwestern University.

CRIMINAL LAW AND APPROACHES TO THE STUDY OF LAW Second Edition (1991)

John M. Brumbaugh, Professor of Law, University of Maryland.

UNIVERSITY CASEBOOK SERIES—Continued

CRIMINAL LAW, Second Edition (1986)

Peter W. Low, Professor of Law, University of Virginia.
John C. Jeffries, Jr., Professor of Law, University of Virginia.
Richard C. Bonnie, Professor of Law, University of Virginia.

CRIMINAL LAW, Fourth Edition (1986)

Lloyd L. Weinreb, Professor of Law, Harvard University.

CRIMINAL LAW AND PROCEDURE, Seventh Edition (1989)

Ronald N. Boyce, Professor of Law, University of Utah.
Rollin M. Perkins, Professor of Law Emeritus, University of California, Hastings College of the Law.

CRIMINAL PROCEDURE, Third Edition (1987), with 1990 Supplement

James B. Haddad, Professor of Law, Northwestern University.
James B. Zagel, Chief, Criminal Justice Division, Office of Attorney General of Illinois.
Gary L. Starkman, Assistant U. S. Attorney, Northern District of Illinois.
William J. Bauer, Chief Judge of the U.S. Court of Appeals, Seventh Circuit.

CRIMINAL PROCESS, Fourth Edition (1987), with 1990 Supplement

Lloyd L. Weinreb, Professor of Law, Harvard University.

DAMAGES, Second Edition (1952)

Charles T. McCormick, late Professor of Law, University of Texas.
William F. Fritz, late Professor of Law, University of Texas.

DECEDENTS' ESTATES AND TRUSTS, Seventh Edition (1988)

John Ritchie, late Professor of Law, University of Virginia.
Neill H. Alford, Jr., Professor of Law, University of Virginia.
Richard W. Effland, late Professor of Law, Arizona State University.

DISPUTE RESOLUTION, Processes of (1989)

John S. Murray, President and Executive Director of The Conflict Clinic, Inc., George Mason University.
Alan Scott Rau, Professor of Law, University of Texas.
Edward F. Sherman, Professor of Law, University of Texas.

DOMESTIC RELATIONS, see also Family Law

DOMESTIC RELATIONS, Second Edition (1990)

Walter Wadlington, Professor of Law, University of Virginia.

EMPLOYMENT DISCRIMINATION, Second Edition (1987), with 1990 Supplement

Joel W. Friedman, Professor of Law, Tulane University.
George M. Strickler, Professor of Law, Tulane University.

EMPLOYMENT LAW, Second Edition (1991), with Statutory Supplement

Mark A. Rothstein, Professor of Law, University of Houston.
Andria S. Knapp, Visiting Professor of Law, Golden Gate University.
Lance Liebman, Professor of Law, Harvard University.

ENERGY LAW (1983) with 1986 Case Supplement

Donald N. Zillman, Professor of Law, University of Utah.
Laurence Lattman, Dean of Mines and Engineering, University of Utah.

UNIVERSITY CASEBOOK SERIES—Continued

ENTERPRISE ORGANIZATION, Fourth Edition (1987), with 1987 Corporation and Partnership Statutes, Rules and Forms Supplement

Alfred F. Conard, Professor of Law, University of Michigan.
Robert L. Knauss, Dean of the Law School, University of Houston.
Stanley Siegel, Professor of Law, University of California, Los Angeles.

ENVIRONMENTAL POLICY LAW 1985 Edition, with 1985 Problems Supplement (Supplement in association with Ronald H. Rosenberg, Professor of Law, College of William and Mary)

Thomas J. Schoenbaum, Professor of Law, University of Georgia.

EQUITY, see also Remedies

EQUITY, RESTITUTION AND DAMAGES, Second Edition (1974)

Robert Childres, late Professor of Law, Northwestern University.
William F. Johnson, Jr., Professor of Law, New York University.

ESTATE PLANNING, Second Edition (1982), with 1985 Case, Text and Documentary Supplement

David Westfall, Professor of Law, Harvard University.

ETHICS, see Legal Profession, Professional Responsibility, and Social Responsibilities

ETHICS OF LAWYERING, THE LAW AND (1990)

Geoffrey C. Hazard, Jr., Professor of Law, Yale University.
Susan P. Koniak, Professor of Law, University of Pittsburgh.

ETHICS AND PROFESSIONAL RESPONSIBILITY (1981) (Reprinted from THE LAWYERING PROCESS)

Gary Bellow, Professor of Law, Harvard University.
Bea Moulton, Legal Services Corporation.

EVIDENCE, Sixth Edition (1988 Reprint), with 1990 Case Supplement (Supplement edited in association with Roger C. Park, Professor of Law, University of Minnesota)

John Kaplan, Professor of Law, Stanford University.
Jon R. Waltz, Professor of Law, Northwestern University.

EVIDENCE, Eighth Edition (1988), with Rules, Statute and Case Supplement (1990)

Jack B. Weinstein, Chief Judge, United States District Court.
John H. Mansfield, Professor of Law, Harvard University.
Norman Abrams, Professor of Law, University of California, Los Angeles.
Margaret Berger, Professor of Law, Brooklyn Law School.

FAMILY LAW, see also Domestic Relations

FAMILY LAW Second Edition (1985), with 1991 Supplement

Judith C. Areen, Professor of Law, Georgetown University.

FAMILY LAW AND CHILDREN IN THE LEGAL SYSTEM, STATUTORY MATERIALS (1981)

Walter Wadlington, Professor of Law, University of Virginia.

FEDERAL COURTS, Eighth Edition (1988), with 1990 Supplement

Charles T. McCormick, late Professor of Law, University of Texas.
James H. Chadbourn, late Professor of Law, Harvard University.
Charles Alan Wright, Professor of Law, University of Texas, Austin.

FEDERAL COURTS AND THE FEDERAL SYSTEM, Hart and Wechsler's Third Edition (1988), with 1989 Case Supplement, and the Judicial Code and Rules of Procedure in the Federal Courts (1989)

Paul M. Bator, Professor of Law, University of Chicago.
Daniel J. Meltzer, Professor of Law, Harvard University.
Paul J. Mishkin, Professor of Law, University of California, Berkeley.
David L. Shapiro, Professor of Law, Harvard University.

FEDERAL COURTS AND THE LAW OF FEDERAL-STATE RELATIONS, Second Edition (1989), with 1990 Supplement

Peter W. Low, Professor of Law, University of Virginia.
John C. Jeffries, Jr., Professor of Law, University of Virginia.

FEDERAL PUBLIC LAND AND RESOURCES LAW, Second Edition (1987), with 1990 Case Supplement and 1990 Statutory Supplement

George C. Coggins, Professor of Law, University of Kansas.
Charles F. Wilkinson, Professor of Law, University of Oregon.

FEDERAL RULES OF CIVIL PROCEDURE and Selected Other Procedural Provisions, 1990 Edition

FEDERAL TAXATION, see Taxation

FOOD AND DRUG LAW (1980), with Statutory Supplement

Richard A. Merrill, Dean of the School of Law, University of Virginia.
Peter Barton Hutt, Esq.

FUTURE INTERESTS (1970)

Howard R. Williams, Professor of Law, Stanford University.

FUTURE INTERESTS AND ESTATE PLANNING (1961), with 1962 Supplement

W. Barton Leach, late Professor of Law, Harvard University.
James K. Logan, formerly Dean of the Law School, University of Kansas.

GOVERNMENT CONTRACTS, FEDERAL, Successor Edition (1985), with 1989 Supplement

John W. Whelan, Professor of Law, Hastings College of the Law.

GOVERNMENT REGULATION: FREE ENTERPRISE AND ECONOMIC ORGANIZATION, Sixth Edition (1985)

Louis B. Schwartz, Professor of Law, Hastings College of the Law.
John J. Flynn, Professor of Law, University of Utah.
Harry First, Professor of Law, New York University.

HEALTH CARE LAW AND POLICY (1988)

Clark C. Havighurst, Professor of Law, Duke University.

HINCKLEY, JOHN W., JR., TRIAL OF: A Case Study of the Insanity Defense (1986)

Peter W. Low, Professor of Law, University of Virginia.
John C. Jeffries, Jr., Professor of Law, University of Virginia.
Richard C. Bonnie, Professor of Law, University of Virginia.

INJUNCTIONS, Second Edition (1984)

Owen M. Fiss, Professor of Law, Yale University.
Doug Rendleman, Professor of Law, College of William and Mary.

INSTITUTIONAL INVESTORS, (1978)

David L. Ratner, Professor of Law, Cornell University.

INSURANCE, Second Edition (1985)

William F. Young, Professor of Law, Columbia University.
Eric M. Holmes, Professor of Law, University of Georgia.

INSURANCE LAW AND REGULATION (1990)

Kenneth S. Abraham, University of Virginia.

INTERNATIONAL LAW, see also Transnational Legal Problems, Transnational Business Problems, and United Nations Law

INTERNATIONAL LAW IN CONTEMPORARY PERSPECTIVE (1981), with Essay Supplement

Myres S. McDougal, Professor of Law, Yale University.
W. Michael Reisman, Professor of Law, Yale University.

INTERNATIONAL LEGAL SYSTEM, Third Edition (1988), with Documentary Supplement

Joseph Modeste Sweeney, Professor of Law, University of California, Hastings.
Covey T. Oliver, Professor of Law, University of Pennsylvania.
Noyes E. Leech, Professor of Law Emeritus, University of Pennsylvania.

INTRODUCTION TO LAW, see also Legal Method, On Law in Courts, and Dynamics of American Law

INTRODUCTION TO THE STUDY OF LAW (1970)

E. Wayne Thode, late Professor of Law, University of Utah.
Leon Lebowitz, Professor of Law, University of Texas.
Lester J. Mazor, Professor of Law, University of Utah.

JUDICIAL CODE and Rules of Procedure in the Federal Courts, Students' Edition, 1989 Revision

Daniel J. Meltzer, Professor of Law, Harvard University.
David L. Shapiro, Professor of Law, Harvard University.

JURISPRUDENCE (Temporary Edition Hardbound) (1949)

Lon L. Fuller, late Professor of Law, Harvard University.

JUVENILE, see also Children

JUVENILE JUSTICE PROCESS, Third Edition (1985)

Frank W. Miller, Professor of Law, Washington University.
Robert O. Dawson, Professor of Law, University of Texas.
George E. Dix, Professor of Law, University of Texas.
Raymond I. Parnas, Professor of Law, University of California, Davis.

LABOR LAW, Eleventh Edition (1991), with 1991 Statutory Supplement

Archibald Cox, Professor of Law, Harvard University.
Derek C. Bok, President, Harvard University.
Robert A. Gorman, Professor of Law, University of Pennsylvania.
Matthew W. Finkin, Professor of Law, University of Illinois.

LABOR LAW, Second Edition (1982), with Statutory Supplement

Clyde W. Summers, Professor of Law, University of Pennsylvania.
Harry H. Wellington, Dean of the Law School, Yale University.
Alan Hyde, Professor of Law, Rutgers University.

UNIVERSITY CASEBOOK SERIES—Continued

LAND FINANCING, Third Edition (1985)

The late Norman Penney, Professor of Law, Cornell University.
Richard F. Broude, Member of the California Bar.
Roger Cunningham, Professor of Law, University of Michigan.

LAW AND MEDICINE (1980)

Walter Wadlington, Professor of Law and Professor of Legal Medicine, University of Virginia.
Jon R. Waltz, Professor of Law, Northwestern University.
Roger B. Dworkin, Professor of Law, Indiana University, and Professor of Biomedical History, University of Washington.

LAW, LANGUAGE AND ETHICS (1972)

William R. Bishin, Professor of Law, University of Southern California.
Christopher D. Stone, Professor of Law, University of Southern California.

LAW, SCIENCE AND MEDICINE (1984), with 1989 Supplement

Judith C. Areen, Professor of Law, Georgetown University.
Patricia A. King, Professor of Law, Georgetown University.
Steven P. Goldberg, Professor of Law, Georgetown University.
Alexander M. Capron, Professor of Law, University of Southern California.

LAWYERING PROCESS (1978), with Civil Problem Supplement and Criminal Problem Supplement

Gary Bellow, Professor of Law, Harvard University.
Bea Moulton, Professor of Law, Arizona State University.

LEGAL METHOD (1980)

Harry W. Jones, Professor of Law Emeritus, Columbia University.
John M. Kernochan, Professor of Law, Columbia University.
Arthur W. Murphy, Professor of Law, Columbia University.

LEGAL METHODS (1969)

Robert N. Covington, Professor of Law, Vanderbilt University.
E. Blythe Stason, late Professor of Law, Vanderbilt University.
John W. Wade, Professor of Law, Vanderbilt University.
Elliott E. Cheatham, late Professor of Law, Vanderbilt University.
Theodore A. Smedley, Professor of Law, Vanderbilt University.

LEGAL PROFESSION, THE, Responsibility and Regulation, Second Edition (1988)

Geoffrey C. Hazard, Jr., Professor of Law, Yale University.
Deborah L. Rhode, Professor of Law, Stanford University.

LEGISLATION, Fourth Edition (1982) (by Fordham)

Horace E. Read, late Vice President, Dalhousie University.
John W. MacDonald, Professor of Law Emeritus, Cornell Law School.
Jefferson B. Fordham, Professor of Law, University of Utah.
William J. Pierce, Professor of Law, University of Michigan.

LEGISLATIVE AND ADMINISTRATIVE PROCESSES, Second Edition (1981)

Hans A. Linde, Judge, Supreme Court of Oregon.
George Bunn, Professor of Law, University of Wisconsin.
Fredericka Paff, Professor of Law, University of Wisconsin.
W. Lawrence Church, Professor of Law, University of Wisconsin.

LOCAL GOVERNMENT LAW, Second Revised Edition (1986)

Jefferson B. Fordham, Professor of Law, University of Utah.

MASS MEDIA LAW, Fourth Edition (1990)

Marc A. Franklin, Professor of Law, Stanford University.
David A. Anderson, Professor of Law, University of Texas.

MUNICIPAL CORPORATIONS, see Local Government Law

NEGOTIABLE INSTRUMENTS, see Commercial Paper

NEGOTIATION (1981) (Reprinted from THE LAWYERING PROCESS)

Gary Bellow, Professor of Law, Harvard Law School.
Bea Moulton, Legal Services Corporation.

NEW YORK PRACTICE, Fourth Edition (1978)

Herbert Peterfreund, Professor of Law, New York University.
Joseph M. McLaughlin, Dean of the Law School, Fordham University.

OIL AND GAS, Fifth Edition (1987)

Howard R. Williams, Professor of Law, Stanford University.
Richard C. Maxwell, Professor of Law, University of California, Los Angeles.
Charles J. Meyers, late Dean of the Law School, Stanford University.
Stephen F. Williams, Judge of the United States Court of Appeals.

ON LAW IN COURTS (1965)

Paul J. Mishkin, Professor of Law, University of California, Berkeley.
Clarence Morris, Professor of Law Emeritus, University of Pennsylvania.

PENSION AND EMPLOYEE BENEFIT LAW (1990)

John H. Langbein, Professor of Law, University of Chicago.
Bruce A. Wolk, Professor of Law, University of California, Davis.

PLEADING AND PROCEDURE, see Procedure, Civil

POLICE FUNCTION, Fifth Edition (1991)

Reprint of Chapters 1–10 of Miller, Dawson, Dix and Parnas's CRIMINAL JUSTICE ADMINISTRATION, Fourth Edition.

PREPARING AND PRESENTING THE CASE (1981) (Reprinted from THE LAWYERING PROCESS)

Gary Bellow, Professor of Law, Harvard Law School.
Bea Moulton, Legal Services Corporation.

PROCEDURE (1988), with Procedure Supplement (1989)

Robert M. Cover, late Professor of Law, Yale Law School.
Owen M. Fiss, Professor of Law, Yale Law School.
Judith Resnik, Professor of Law, University of Southern California Law Center.

PROCEDURE—CIVIL PROCEDURE, Second Edition (1974), with 1979 Supplement

The late James H. Chadbourn, Professor of Law, Harvard University.
A. Leo Levin, Professor of Law, University of Pennsylvania.
Philip Shuchman, Professor of Law, Cornell University.

PROCEDURE—CIVIL PROCEDURE, Sixth Edition (1990)

Richard H. Field, late Professor of Law, Harvard University.
Benjamin Kaplan, Professor of Law Emeritus, Harvard University.
Kevin M. Clermont, Professor of Law, Cornell University.

UNIVERSITY CASEBOOK SERIES—Continued

PROCEDURE—CIVIL PROCEDURE, Fifth Edition (1990)

Maurice Rosenberg, Professor of Law, Columbia University.
Hans Smit, Professor of Law, Columbia University.
Rochelle C. Dreyfuss, Professor of Law, New York University.

PROCEDURE—PLEADING AND PROCEDURE: State and Federal, Sixth Edition (1989), with 1990 Case Supplement

David W. Louisell, late Professor of Law, University of California, Berkeley.
Geoffrey C. Hazard, Jr., Professor of Law, Yale University.
Colin C. Tait, Professor of Law, University of Connecticut.

PROCEDURE—FEDERAL RULES OF CIVIL PROCEDURE, 1990 Edition

PRODUCTS LIABILITY AND SAFETY, Second Edition, (1989), with 1989 Statutory Supplement

W. Page Keeton, Professor of Law, University of Texas.
David G. Owen, Professor of Law, University of South Carolina.
John E. Montgomery, Professor of Law, University of South Carolina.
Michael D. Green, Professor of Law, University of Iowa

PROFESSIONAL RESPONSIBILITY, Fifth Edition (1991), with 1991 Selected Standards on Professional Responsibility Supplement

Thomas D. Morgan, Professor of Law, George Washington University.
Ronald D. Rotunda, Professor of Law, University of Illinois.

PROPERTY, Sixth Edition (1990)

John E. Cribbet, Professor of Law, University of Illinois.
Corwin W. Johnson, Professor of Law, University of Texas.
Roger W. Findley, Professor of Law, University of Illinois.
Ernest E. Smith, Professor of Law, University of Texas.

PROPERTY—PERSONAL (1953)

S. Kenneth Skolfield, late Professor of Law Emeritus, Boston University.

PROPERTY—PERSONAL, Third Edition (1954)

Everett Fraser, late Dean of the Law School Emeritus, University of Minnesota.
Third Edition by Charles W. Taintor, late Professor of Law, University of Pittsburgh.

PROPERTY—INTRODUCTION, TO REAL PROPERTY, Third Edition (1954)

Everett Fraser, late Dean of the Law School Emeritus, University of Minnesota.

PROPERTY—FUNDAMENTALS OF MODERN REAL PROPERTY, Second Edition (1982), with 1985 Supplement

Edward H. Rabin, Professor of Law, University of California, Davis.

PROPERTY, REAL (1984), with 1988 Supplement

Paul Goldstein, Professor of Law, Stanford University.

PROSECUTION AND ADJUDICATION, Fourth Edition (1991)

Reprint of Chapters 11–26 of Miller, Dawson, Dix and Parnas's CRIMINAL JUSTICE ADMINISTRATION, Fourth Edition.

PSYCHIATRY AND LAW, see Mental Health, see also Hinckley, Trial of

PUBLIC UTILITY LAW, see Free Enterprise, also Regulated Industries

UNIVERSITY CASEBOOK SERIES—Continued

REAL ESTATE PLANNING, Third Edition (1989), with Revised Problem and Statutory Supplement (1991)

Norton L. Steuben, Professor of Law, University of Colorado.

REAL ESTATE TRANSACTIONS, Revised Second Edition (1988), with Statute, Form and Problem Supplement (1988)

Paul Goldstein, Professor of Law, Stanford University.

RECEIVERSHIP AND CORPORATE REORGANIZATION, see Creditors' Rights

REGULATED INDUSTRIES, Second Edition, (1976)

William K. Jones, Professor of Law, Columbia University.

REMEDIES, Second Edition (1987)

Edward D. Re, Chief Judge, U. S. Court of International Trade.

REMEDIES, (1989)

Elaine W. Shoben, Professor of Law, University of Illinois.
Wm. Murray Tabb, Professor of Law, Baylor University.

SALES, Second Edition (1986)

Marion W. Benfield, Jr., Professor of Law, University of Illinois.
William D. Hawkland, Chancellor, Louisiana State Law Center.

SALES AND SALES FINANCING, Fifth Edition (1984)

John Honnold, Professor of Law, University of Pennsylvania.

SALES LAW AND THE CONTRACTING PROCESS, Second Edition (1991)

(Reprinted from Commercial Transactions, Second Edition (1991)
Alan Schwartz, Professor of Law, Yale University.
Robert E. Scott, Professor of Law, University of Virginia.

SECURED TRANSACTIONS IN PERSONAL PROPERTY, Second Edition (1987) (Reprinted from COMMERCIAL LAW, Second Edition (1987))

Robert L. Jordan, Professor of Law, University of California, Los Angeles.
William D. Warren, Professor of Law, University of California, Los Angeles.

SECURITIES REGULATION, Sixth Edition (1987), with 1990 Selected Statutes, Rules and Forms Supplement and 1990 Cases and Releases Supplement

Richard W. Jennings, Professor of Law, University of California, Berkeley.
Harold Marsh, Jr., Member of California Bar.

SECURITIES REGULATION, Second Edition (1988), with Statute, Rule and Form Supplement (1988)

Larry D. Soderquist, Professor of Law, Vanderbilt University.

SECURITY INTERESTS IN PERSONAL PROPERTY, Second Edition (1987)

Douglas G. Baird, Professor of Law, University of Chicago.
Thomas H. Jackson, Dean of the Law School, University of Virginia.

SECURITY INTERESTS IN PERSONAL PROPERTY (1985) (Reprinted from Sales and Sales Financing, Fifth Edition)

John Honnold, Professor of Law, University of Pennsylvania.

SELECTED STANDARDS ON PROFESSIONAL RESPONSIBILITY, 1991 Edition

SELECTED STATUTES AND INTERNATIONAL AGREEMENTS ON UNFAIR COMPETITION, TRADEMARK, COPYRIGHT AND PATENT, 1989 Edition

SELECTED STATUTES ON TRUSTS AND ESTATES, 1991 Edition

SOCIAL RESPONSIBILITIES OF LAWYERS, Case Studies (1988)

Philip B. Heymann, Professor of Law, Harvard University.
Lance Liebman, Professor of Law, Harvard University.

SOCIAL SCIENCE IN LAW, Second Edition (1990)

John Monahan, Professor of Law, University of Virginia.
Laurens Walker, Professor of Law, University of Virginia.

TAXATION, FEDERAL INCOME (1989)

Stephen B. Cohen, Professor of Law, Georgetown University

TAXATION, FEDERAL INCOME, Second Edition (1988), with 1990 Supplement (Supplement edited in association with Deborah H. Schenk, Professor of Law, New York University)

Michael J. Graetz, Professor of Law, Yale University.

TAXATION, FEDERAL INCOME, Sixth Edition (1987)

James J. Freeland, Professor of Law, University of Florida.
Stephen A. Lind, Professor of Law, University of Florida and University of California, Hastings.
Richard B. Stephens, late Professor of Law Emeritus, University of Florida.

TAXATION, FEDERAL INCOME, Successor Edition (1986), with 1990 Legislative Supplement

Stanley S. Surrey, late Professor of Law, Harvard University.
Paul R. McDaniel, Professor of Law, Boston College.
Hugh J. Ault, Professor of Law, Boston College.
Stanley A. Koppelman, Professor of Law, Boston University.

TAXATION, FEDERAL INCOME, OF BUSINESS ORGANIZATIONS (1991)

Paul R. McDaniel, Professor of Law, Boston College.
Hugh J. Ault, Professor of Law, Boston College.
Martin J. McMahon, Jr., Professor of Law, University of Kentucky.
Daniel L. Simmons, Professor of Law, University of California, Davis.

TAXATION, FEDERAL INCOME, OF PARTNERSHIPS AND S CORPORATIONS (1991)

Paul R. McDaniel, Professor of Law, Boston College.
Hugh J. Ault, Professor of Law, Boston College.
Martin J. McMahon, Jr., Professor of Law, University of Kentucky.
Daniel L. Simmons, Professor of Law, University of California, Davis.

TAXATION, FEDERAL INCOME, OIL AND GAS, NATURAL RESOURCES TRANSACTIONS (1990)

Peter C. Maxfield, Professor of Law, University of Wyoming.
James L. Houghton, CPA, Partner, Ernst and Young.
James R. Gaar, CPA, Partner, Ernst and Young.

TAXATION, FEDERAL WEALTH TRANSFER, Successor Edition (1987)

Stanley S. Surrey, late Professor of Law, Harvard University.
Paul R. McDaniel, Professor of Law, Boston College.
Harry L. Gutman, Professor of Law, University of Pennsylvania.

TAXATION, FUNDAMENTALS OF CORPORATE, Second Edition (1987), with 1989 Supplement

Stephen A. Lind, Professor of Law, University of Florida and University of California, Hastings.
Stephen Schwarz, Professor of Law, University of California, Hastings.
Daniel J. Lathrope, Professor of Law, University of California, Hastings.
Joshua Rosenberg, Professor of Law, University of San Francisco.

TAXATION, FUNDAMENTALS OF PARTNERSHIP, Second Edition (1988)

Stephen A. Lind, Professor of Law, University of Florida and University of California, Hastings.
Stephen Schwarz, Professor of Law, University of California, Hastings.
Daniel J. Lathrope, Professor of Law, University of California, Hastings.
Joshua Rosenberg, Professor of Law, University of San Francisco.

TAXATION, PROBLEMS IN THE FEDERAL INCOME TAXATION OF PARTNERSHIPS AND CORPORATIONS, Second Edition (1986)

Norton L. Steuben, Professor of Law, University of Colorado.
William J. Turnier, Professor of Law, University of North Carolina.

TAXATION, PROBLEMS IN THE FUNDAMENTALS OF FEDERAL INCOME, Second Edition (1985)

Norton L. Steuben, Professor of Law, University of Colorado.
William J. Turnier, Professor of Law, University of North Carolina.

TORT LAW AND ALTERNATIVES, Fourth Edition (1987)

Marc A. Franklin, Professor of Law, Stanford University.
Robert L. Rabin, Professor of Law, Stanford University.

TORTS, Eighth Edition (1988)

William L. Prosser, late Professor of Law, University of California, Hastings.
John W. Wade, Professor of Law, Vanderbilt University.
Victor E. Schwartz, Adjunct Professor of Law, Georgetown University.

TORTS, Third Edition (1976)

Harry Shulman, late Dean of the Law School, Yale University.
Fleming James, Jr., Professor of Law Emeritus, Yale University.
Oscar S. Gray, Professor of Law, University of Maryland.

TRADE REGULATION, Third Edition (1990)

Milton Handler, Professor of Law Emeritus, Columbia University.
Harlan M. Blake, Professor of Law, Columbia University.
Robert Pitofsky, Professor of Law, Georgetown University.
Harvey J. Goldschmid, Professor of Law, Columbia University.

TRADE REGULATION, see Antitrust

TRANSNATIONAL BUSINESS PROBLEMS (1986)

Detlev F. Vagts, Professor of Law, Harvard University.

TRANSNATIONAL LEGAL PROBLEMS, Third Edition (1986) with 1991 Revised Edition of Documentary Supplement

Henry J. Steiner, Professor of Law, Harvard University.
Detlev F. Vagts, Professor of Law, Harvard University.

TRIAL, see also Evidence, Making the Record, Lawyering Process and Preparing and Presenting the Case

TRUSTS, Fifth Edition (1978)

George G. Bogert, late Professor of Law Emeritus, University of Chicago.
Dallin H. Oaks, President, Brigham Young University.

TRUSTS AND ESTATES, SELECTED STATUTES ON, 1991 Edition

TRUSTS AND SUCCESSION (Palmer's), Fourth Edition (1983)

Richard V. Wellman, Professor of Law, University of Georgia.
Lawrence W. Waggoner, Professor of Law, University of Michigan.
Olin L. Browder, Jr., Professor of Law, University of Michigan.

UNFAIR COMPETITION, see Competitive Process and Business Torts

WATER RESOURCE MANAGEMENT, Third Edition (1988)

The late Charles J. Meyers, formerly Dean, Stanford University Law School.
A. Dan Tarlock, Professor of Law, IIT Chicago-Kent College of Law.
James N. Corbridge, Jr., Chancellor, University of Colorado at Boulder, and Professor of Law, University of Colorado.
David H. Getches, Professor of Law, University of Colorado.

WILLS AND ADMINISTRATION, Fifth Edition (1961)

Philip Mechem, late Professor of Law, University of Pennsylvania.
Thomas E. Atkinson, late Professor of Law, New York University.

WRITING AND ANALYSIS IN THE LAW, Second Edition (1991)

Helene S. Shapo, Professor of Law, Northwestern University
Marilyn R. Walter, Professor of Law, Brooklyn Law School
Elizabeth Fajans, Writing Specialist, Brooklyn Law School

University Casebook Series

CASES AND MATERIALS

ON

CRIMINAL LAW AND APPROACHES TO THE STUDY OF LAW

SECOND EDITION

By

JOHN M. BRUMBAUGH
Professor of Law
University of Maryland School of Law

Westbury, New York
THE FOUNDATION PRESS, INC.
1991

615 Merrick Ave.
Westbury, N.Y. 11590

Printed in the United States of America

Library of Congress Cataloging-in-Publication Data

Brumbaugh, John M., 1927–
Cases and materials on criminal law and approaches to the study of law / by John M. Brumbaugh. — 2nd ed.
p. cm.
Includes index.
ISBN 0–88277–866–8
1. Criminal law—United States—Cases. I. Title.
KF9218.B78 1991
345.73—dc20
[347.305] 90–21409

Brumbaugh Cs. Criminal Law 2nd Ed. UCB

To Alice

*

PREFACE TO THE SECOND EDITION

The plan of the first edition has been retained, with very little in the way of rearrangement of materials. The order of topics at the beginning of Chapter V has been changed: material involving intent to injure only is taken up before provocation, and burden of persuasion on defenses is considered immediately before justification and excuse. Where I have found cases which seem better than the ones used originally, I have made substitutions.

There are two major and a number of minor additions. First, the material on rape and related offenses had been expanded. In the first edition, the topic of rape was used to illustrate the problem of mistake as to consent or age of the victim. It is retained for this purpose, but the new edition also focuses on rape itself, the plight of the victim, and the evolution of the crime over the years. Second, there is new material in the last chapter on vicarious liability and the liability of corporations, as to which there was very little in the first edition.

Some other new or expanded topics include the federal sentencing guidelines, impact of crime on victims, abortion policy, assault on children, various syndromes (for example, the battered child and post-traumatic stress syndromes), and the borderline area between justification and excuse.

The main text of the new edition is about the same length as the old. Some changes in type size may make it difficult to compare. To make room for added material, some of the longer cases have been re-edited. One of these, Commonwealth v. Barone, in the first edition, reappears in a streamlined version as one of the Ohypo cases, State v. Cross. These hypothetical cases have proved popular, efficient, and effective in teaching, and I have added one entirely new one on duress, State v. Tremulo.

To the useful sources noted in the original preface should be added an excellent new text, Dressler, Understanding Criminal Law (Matthew Bender 1987).

In addition to the thanks for the permissions granted for material used in the first edition, which I renew for material used in this edition, I wish to thank Mr. Paul Benzaquin, The Berkeley Women's Law Journal, Professor Lynne Henderson, and Mr. Hart Pomerantz, for permission to reproduce material. Specific acknowledgment is given in the text for each excerpt reproduced. As in the first edition, I have freely edited cases and other materials. Case and statute citations, as well as footnotes, of courts and commentators have been omitted without so specifying; numbered footnotes are from the original materials and retain the original numbering. Letters are reserved for my own footnotes, except for a few of the cases in which lettered footnotes were used in the English Reports.

I thank all of my colleagues at Maryland for the cooperative environment in which we work. I thank especially Ted Tomlinson, for some suggestions on editing cases, and Taunya Banks, Karen Czapanskiy, Alan Hornstein, Jana Singer, Marley Weiss, and Robin West, for advice as to revision of the rape and abortion materials. Apart from minor inconsistencies in this advice, I can probably safely divide it into a greater and a smaller portion: the greater, which I wisely adopted, and the smaller, which I will later wish I had adopted. Above all, I thank my wife and colleague, Alice Brumbaugh, for her continuing loving support, for many suggestions as to new cases and arrangement of materials, and for her proofreading assistance. In helping me to proofread the manuscript for the first edition, she became addicted to crime and has added criminal law to her teaching repertory.

I hope that users of the book will bring errors to my attention and let me know about changes they would welcome.

JOHN M. BRUMBAUGH

January, 1991

PREFACE

Since there are a number of good criminal law casebooks available, the production of a new entry in the field calls for some explanation. All of the good books set out the elements of the subject in a way designed to assist in the development of student powers of analysis and synthesis, but most of them stop there; they pay little attention to other goals of beginning law study: to impart a little fundamental jurisprudence, to introduce some legal history, to develop a sense of how to deal with common law and statute, for example. Perhaps these general objectives will be assigned primarily to a course in Legal Method, but all first year courses have some responsibility for them. This casebook is designed to bring such considerations into a criminal law course in a systematic way. No first year course more clearly presents problems of law intertwined with problems of morality and public policy.

I have not slighted the central elements of teaching the nuts and bolts of substantive criminal law and developing methods of legal thinking. The book is suited to a course devoted solely to the traditional ends. There is rather complete coverage of all of the usual major topics. A prime objective has been to find cases and materials which are interesting and illuminating and which work well in the classroom. I hope that I have provided a good mix of old warhorses and promising young entries.

I have tried to bring in some of the more general first year objectives in a more explicit and more organized fashion than is usual, by pairing areas of doctrine with particular non-doctrinal objectives with which they fit well. I have searched for materials with such a double aspect. Some of these combinations will be familiar; others will not.

The first chapter combines sentencing law and some basic constitutional restrictions affecting criminal law with background on procedure, punishment theory, and initial consideration of what the criminal law can and cannot accomplish. Chapter II takes up the theoretical anatomy of a criminal offense—the elements of *mens rea* and *actus reus*—and uses such crimes as assault and rape for the illumination of both the particular crimes and the theoretical models. The next chapter deals with theft and studies it primarily from the point of view of historical development of English common and statutory law, concluding with the problems of statutory consolidation. Chapter IV uses the law of arson, burglary, and kidnapping as a starting point for the examination of problems of statutory construction and drafting. There follows a long chapter on homicide, justification, excuse, and mitigation, in which the materials also focus on problems of public policy and the justice of the criminal law. The final chapter is on accomplices, attempt, and conspiracy, and it presents a number of difficult problems for which no resolution is yet in sight; the student is encouraged to live with the uncertainty of the law and to search for new methods which may resolve at least parts of the problems.

The presentation of the materials has been carefully worked out to provide an order which helps the beginning law student to understand the subject. Abrupt breaks are avoided within chapters, where possible, so that the student will find connections between neighboring sections and chapters. The book attempts to prepare the ground for complex problems (like the felony-murder situation) by dealing first with subsidiary problems (like the nature of the underlying felonies commonly involved), so the main lines of the problem can be followed without unnecessary digressions. While I strongly favor the arrangement chosen, I recognize that many teachers will prefer some different order.

Most teachers wish to or find it necessary to make cuts in any set of materials prepared by others. Those who want to deal mostly with "the general part" and with homicide can eliminate or reduce greatly the assignments in Chapters III and IV. Suggestions for cuts within chapters will be found in the Teacher's Manual.

Occasionally—usually, when I have not found cases to my liking—I have made up my own cases to present a point or a problem. In reading through the book, these phonies can be identified quickly by the "Ohypo" jurisdiction designation. They also appear in the Table of Cases under the names of the hypothetical defendants: Bangs, Berg, Burns, Chip, Fence, Lucifer, Parley, Roundsquare, and Verge. (I have used one hypothetical case prepared by others.) I hope that I will not be drummed out of the Society of the Friends of the Common Law Tradition for these lapses. Sometimes nature simply fails to imitate art in any adequate way.

This book does not attempt to be a reference work, complete with footnoted support for every proposition and strings of citations. The student should turn to a text for this sort of thing. Most of the book consists of cases, with questions for student study or class consideration and my own notes sprinkled among them. There is relatively little from other sources, except for the Model Penal Code. I am content to let the judges, for the most part, speak for themselves. I have freely edited cases and other materials. Case and statute citations, as well as footnotes, of courts and commentators have been omitted without so specifying; numbered footnotes are from the original materials and retain the original numbering. In a few of the English cases, where letters have been used to designate footnotes in the originals, I have substituted numbers. Letters are reserved for my own footnotes.

I have relied heavily on the work of The American Law Institute, both in direct quotation from the Model Penal Code and through cases which interpret it. The Code provides an inventive, constructive, and lucid approach to many of the problems of the course. Students will find helpful for further study both the text (largely reprinted here in an appendix taken from the Proposed Official Draft) and the comments, which should be available, for all sections, in the bound volumes of the official draft by the time this book appears.

Among many other useful sources for students are two texts, La Fave & Scott, Handbook on Criminal Law (1972), and Perkins & Boyce, Criminal Law (3d ed. 1982). Each has its virtues; I tend to prefer La Fave & Scott for theory and organization, and Perkins & Boyce for doctrinal detail. More theoretical than these, and very challenging, are Williams, Criminal Law: The General Part (1961), and Fletcher, Rethinking Criminal Law (1978).

I wish to thank the University of Maryland for a grant of sabbatical leave to complete the temporary edition of the book, and Dean Michael J. Kelly of the School of Law for his encouragement. I appreciate the permissions of The American Bar Association, The American Law Institute, The Cleveland State Law Review, The Criminal Law Quarterly, The Controller of Her Brittanic Majesty's Stationery Office, Policy Review, and The Selden Society, to reproduce material. Specific acknowledgment is given in the text for each excerpt reproduced. I acknowledge with gratitude the work of my research assistants, Cynthia Jessen Pyles, Nora T. Terres, and Frank B. Cahn, who found promising leads and checked many of the citations; of my secretary, Marilyn J. O'Neill, who typed most of the manuscript with far more efficiency and cheerfulness than I deserved; and of my wife, Alice, who is at once a loving and supportive companion and an eagle-eyed spotter of lapses and inconsistencies. For the vast residuum of error, muddle, and infelicity which I am sure that every reader will instantly recognize, I alone bear responsibility. I hope that users will let me know about this; suggestions for improvements will be gratefully received.

I hope that users of this book will learn in using it, as I have learned in making it, while enjoying themselves, as I have enjoyed myself, in working through the problems of legal study.

JOHN M. BRUMBAUGH

February, 1986

*

SUMMARY OF CONTENTS

CHAPTER VI. ACCOMPLICES AND VICARIOUS AND CORPORATE LIABILITY; ATTEMPTS AND CONSPIRACY; LIVING WITH INTRACTABLE LEGAL PROBLEMS

APPENDICES

TABLE OF CONTENTS

CHAPTER I. FRAMEWORK

CHAPTER II. ASSAULT, RAPE, BIGAMY, AND RELATED OFFENSES; *MENS REA* AND *ACTUS REUS*

CHAPTER III. THEFT; HISTORICAL DEVELOPMENT OF THE CRIMINAL LAW

CHAPTER IV. ARSON, BURGLARY, AND KIDNAPPING; PROBLEMS OF STATUTORY CONSTRUCTION

CHAPTER V. HOMICIDE; JUSTIFICATION, EXCUSE, AND MITIGATION; THE JUSTNESS AND MORALITY OF THE CRIMINAL LAW

CHAPTER VI. ACCOMPLICES AND VICARIOUS AND CORPORATE LIABILITY; ATTEMPTS AND CONSPIRACY; LIVING WITH INTRACTABLE LEGAL PROBLEMS

APPENDICES

*

TABLE OF CASES

Principal cases are in italic type. Non-principal cases are in roman type. References are to Pages.

*

TABLE OF SECONDARY AUTHORITIES

TABLE OF SECONDARY AUTHORITIES

CASES AND MATERIALS

ON

CRIMINAL LAW AND APPROACHES TO THE STUDY OF LAW

*

Chapter I

FRAMEWORK

A. INTRODUCTION

The purpose of this chapter is to provide a framework for your study of criminal law by furnishing basic information about some things which are important to the main subject matter of the course but a little apart from it.

First, there is a sketchy introduction to criminal procedure. In most law schools, criminal procedure is a separate course or a separate part of a course in criminal law and procedure, and, in either event, it is likely to be studied after criminal law. But you need a minimum understanding of procedure to gain some idea of how the criminal justice system works and to grasp the meaning, significance, and setting of the substantive law decisions. This minimum (and no more) is provided.

Every lawyer ought to have some knowledge of the ends of the criminal justice system. What is it meant to do? What does it actually accomplish? How does sentencing work? Full exploration of these problems must be assigned to other courses, but a beginning is made in this chapter's section on punishment. This section also considers the issue of what sort of conduct should be made criminal.

The chapter concludes with a look at some things which impede the "efficient" operation of the criminal process. Some are constitutional constraints, some are inherent in any system of rules. What policy ends do these impeding forces serve? We pay close attention to the requirement that the criminal law give fair warning to the prospective criminal that his conduct will be a crime.

This chapter leaves out many avenues of possible exploration and fails to note many exceptional situations. It is necessarily general in its approach and therefore not an adequate guide to full understanding of the material covered. But, if it sets the stage for what is to follow, it serves its purpose.

B. PROCEDURAL BACKGROUND

1. Note on Jurisdiction

Jurisdiction refers to the inherent power of a nation or state to subject an accused person to its criminal process. The nation or state must have both personal jurisdiction over the accused and subject matter jurisdiction over the offense. If it does not, courts of other jurisdictions and higher courts of the jurisdiction itself will generally give no recognition to convictions obtained.

Personal jurisdiction. Personal jurisdiction in criminal cases is based upon the presence of the accused in the jurisdiction. He must be brought before the court in order to be tried. Extradition among the states is governed by the federal extradition act, and in a majority of states by the Uniform Criminal Extradition

Act, which sets out procedures for returning the accused from the state where he is found to the demanding state. Extradition among nations is usually governed by treaty.

State subject matter jurisdiction. State criminal charges are based on alleged violation of penal statutes or of the common (judge made) law of crimes. Generally, the crime must have been committed, in some sense, within the territory of the state. The situs of the crime is usually the place in which the injury is inflicted. So, if A fires a gun in state X and hits B in state Y, and B staggers into state Z and dies there, state Y has the clearest claim to try A for murder. The injury in larceny has traditionally included both the taking and the immediate carrying away of the stolen property, and so, when stolen property is immediately taken across a state border, either state may be entitled to try the thief. By statute, states often extend their jurisdiction to cases in which any part of the crime is committed within their borders, or even to any crime which has some designated effect within their borders. For a broadly drawn statute on territorial jurisdiction, see Model Penal Code § 1.03.[a] Within each state there are rules of venue as to which political subdivision is the proper place of trial.

Federal subject matter jurisdiction. Federal criminal jurisdiction is based on powers granted the federal government by the Constitution. Federal territories or enclaves may be governed by federal criminal law. Areas over which the Constitution grants the federal government powers may be regulated by special criminal provisions. The federal power to regulate interstate commerce has produced a number of criminal statutes of this sort. While the federal government has no powers except those found in the Constitution to punish crimes, where it does have such powers and exercises them through legislation, such legislation takes precedence over state criminal law if such law is in conflict with the federal scheme.

Prosecution by more than one jurisdiction. If A steals a car in Ohio and drives it across the border into Pennsylvania, he might be prosecuted by any of three jurisdictions: Ohio or Pennsylvania, because the crime occurred in both states, and the United States, if it has an appropriate statute punishing the interstate transportation of stolen vehicles. Perhaps none of the criminal provisions is in conflict with any of the others; they all aim to punish theft. Does this mean that A can be punished three times? There does not seem to be a clear federal constitutional bar based on the double jeopardy clause of the Constitution to such multiple prosecutions by different sovereignties. However, as a matter of legislation or policy, a second or third prosecution is often declined. For the Model Penal Code recommendation as to such prosecutions see § 1.10. For more on double jeopardy see the note in Chapter IV, p. 367.

a. For this and other references to the Model Penal Code, see Appendix A.

2. The Criminal Justice System

THE CHALLENGE OF CRIME IN A FREE SOCIETY

A REPORT BY THE PRESIDENT'S COMMISSION ON LAW ENFORCEMENT AND ADMINISTRATION OF JUSTICE (1967), pp. 7–12

AMERICA'S SYSTEM OF CRIMINAL JUSTICE

The system of criminal justice America uses to deal with those crimes it cannot prevent and those criminals it cannot deter is not a monolithic, or even a consistent, system. It was not designed or built in one piece at one time. Its philosophic core is that a person may be punished by the Government if, and only if, it has been proved by an impartial and deliberate process that he has violated a specific law. Around that core layer upon layer of institutions and procedures, some carefully constructed and some improvised, some inspired by principle and some by expediency, have accumulated. Parts of the system—magistrates' courts, trial by jury, bail—are of great antiquity. Other parts—juvenile courts, probation and parole, professional policemen—are relatively new. The entire system represents an adaptation of the English common law to America's peculiar structure of government, which allows each local community to construct institutions that fill its special needs. Every village, town, county, city, and State has its own criminal justice system, and there is a Federal one as well. All of them operate somewhat alike. No two of them operate precisely alike.

Any criminal justice system is an apparatus society uses to enforce the standards of conduct necessary to protect individuals and the community. It operates by apprehending, prosecuting, convicting, and sentencing those members of the community who violate the basic rules of group existence. The action taken against lawbreakers is designed to serve three purposes beyond the immediately punitive one. It removes dangerous people from the community; it deters others from criminal behavior; and it gives society an opportunity to attempt to transform lawbreakers into law-abiding citizens. What most significantly distinguishes the system of one country from that of another is the extent and the form of the protections it offers individuals in the process of determining guilt and imposing punishment. Our system of justice deliberately sacrifices much in efficiency and even in effectiveness in order to preserve local autonomy and to protect the individual. Sometimes it may seem to sacrifice too much. For example, the American system was not designed with Cosa Nostra-type criminal organizations in mind, and it has been notably unsuccessful to date in preventing such organizations from preying on society.

The criminal justice system has three separately organized parts—the police, the courts, and corrections—and each has distinct tasks. However, these parts are by no means independent of each other. What each one does and how it does it has a direct effect on the work of the others. * * *

A general view of The Criminal Justice System

This chart seeks to present a simple yet comprehensive view of the movement of cases through the criminal justice system. Procedures in individual jurisdictions may vary from the pattern shown here. The differing weights of line indicate the relative volumes of cases disposed of at various points in the system, but this is only suggestive since no nationwide data of this sort exists.

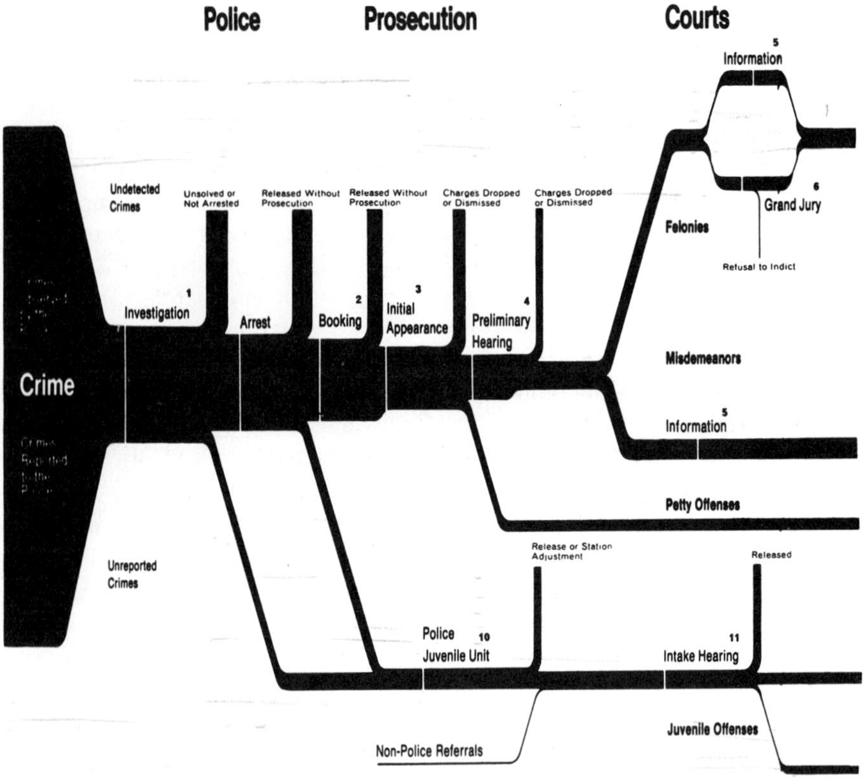

1 May continue until trial.

2 Administrative record of arrest. First step at which temporary release on bail may be available.

3 Before magistrate, commissioner, or justice of peace. Formal notice of charge, advice of rights. Bail set. Summary trials for petty offenses usually conducted here without further processing.

4 Preliminary testing of evidence against defendant. Charge may be reduced. No separate preliminary hearing for misdemeanors in some systems.

5 Charge filed by prosecutor on basis of information submitted by police or citizens. Alternative to grand jury indictment; often used in felonies, almost always in misdemeanors.

6 Reviews whether Government evidence sufficient to justify trial. Some States have no grand jury system; others seldom use it.

[D5956]

The chart * * * sets forth in simplified form the process of criminal administration and shows the many decision points along its course. Since felonies, misdemeanors, petty offenses, and juvenile cases generally follow quite different paths, they are shown separately.

The popular, or even the lawbook, theory of everyday criminal process oversimplifies in some respects and overcomplicates in others what usually happens. That theory is that when an infraction of the law occurs, a policeman finds, if he can, the probable offender, arrests him and brings him promptly before a magistrate. If the offense is minor, the magistrate disposes of it forthwith; if it is serious, he holds the defendant for further action and

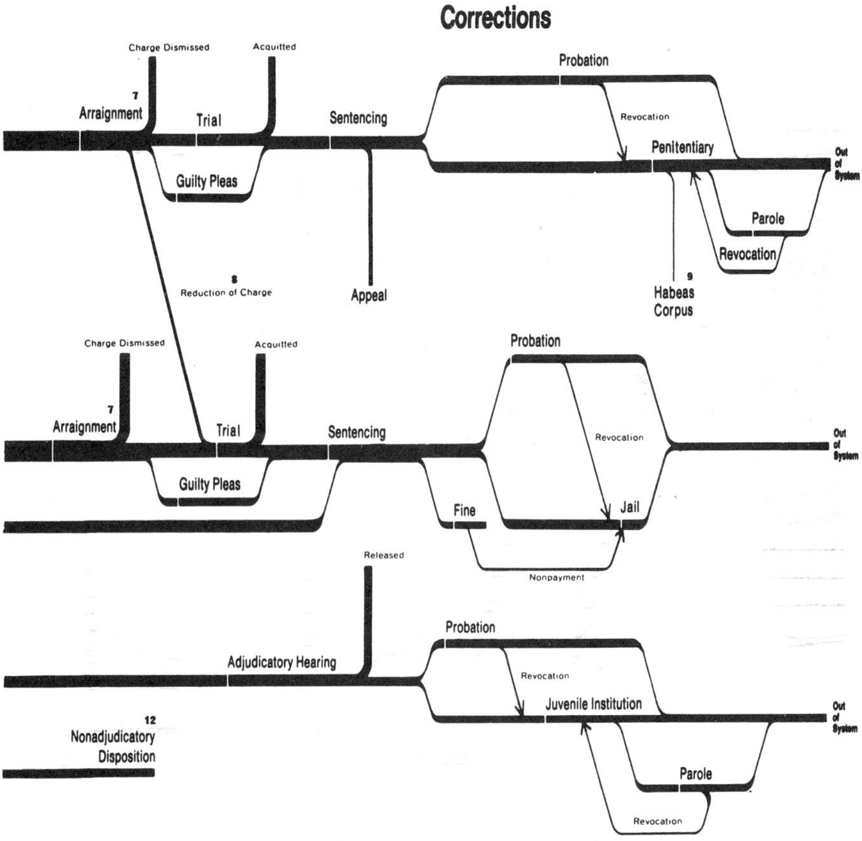

7 Appearance for plea; defendant elects trial by judge or jury (if available); counsel for indigent usually appointed here in felonies. Often not at all in other cases.

8 Charge may be reduced at any time prior to trial in return for plea of guilty or for other reasons.

9 Challenge on constitutional grounds to legality of detention. May be sought at any point in process.

10 Police often hold informal hearings, dismiss or adjust many cases without further processing.

11 Probation officer decides desirability of further court action.

12 Welfare agency, social services, counselling, medical care, etc., for cases where adjudicatory handling not needed.

[D5957]

admits him to bail. The case then is turned over to a prosecuting attorney who charges the defendant with a specific statutory crime. This charge is subject to review by a judge at a preliminary hearing of the evidence and in many places if the offense charged is a felony, by a grand jury that can dismiss the charge, or affirm it by delivering it to a judge in the form of an indictment. If the defendant pleads "not guilty" to the charge he comes to trial; the facts of his case are marshaled by prosecuting and defense attorneys and presented, under the supervision of a judge, through witnesses, to a jury. If the jury finds the defendant guilty, he is sentenced by the judge to a term in prison, where a systematic attempt to convert him into a law-abiding citizen is made, or to a term of probation, under which he is permitted to live in the community as long as he behaves himself.

Some cases do proceed much like that, especially those involving offenses that are generally considered "major": serious acts of violence or thefts of large amounts of property. However, not all major cases follow this course, and, in any event, the bulk of the daily business of the criminal justice system consists of offenses that are not major—of breaches of the peace, crimes of vice, petty thefts, assaults arising from domestic or street-corner or barroom disputes. These and most other cases are disposed of in much less formal and much less deliberate ways.

The theory of the juvenile court is that it is a "helping" social agency, designed to prescribe carefully individualized treatment to young people in trouble, and that its procedures are therefore nonadversary. Here again there is, in most places, a considerable difference between theory and practice. Many juvenile proceedings are no more individualized and no more therapeutic than adult ones.

What has evidently happened is that the transformation of America from a relatively relaxed rural society into a tumultuous urban one has presented the criminal justice system in the cities with a volume of cases too large to handle by traditional methods. One result of heavy caseloads is highly visible in city courts, which process many cases with excessive haste and many others with excessive slowness. In the interest both of effectiveness and of fairness to individuals, justice should be swift and certain; too often in city courts today it is, instead, hasty or faltering. Invisibly, the pressure of numbers has effected a series of adventitious changes in the criminal process. Informal shortcuts have been used. The decision making process has often become routinized. Throughout the system the importance of individual judgment and discretion, as distinguished from stated rules and procedures, has increased. In effect, much decision making is being done on an administrative rather than on a judicial basis. Thus, an examination of how the criminal justice system works and a consideration of the changes needed to make it more effective and fair must focus on the extent to which invisible, administrative procedures depart from visible, traditional ones, and on the desirability of that departure.

THE POLICE

At the very beginning of the process—or, more properly, before the process begins at all—something happens that is scarcely discussed in lawbooks and is seldom recognized by the public: law enforcement policy is made by the policeman. For policemen cannot and do not arrest all the offenders they encounter. It is doubtful that they arrest most of them. A criminal code, in practice, is not a set of specific instructions to policemen but a more or less rough map of the territory in which policemen work. How an individual policeman moves around that territory depends largely on his personal discretion.

That a policeman's duties compel him to exercise personal discretion many times every day is evident. Crime does not look the same on the street as it does in a legislative chamber. How much noise or profanity makes conduct "disorderly" within the meaning of the law? When must a quarrel be treated as a criminal assault: at the first threat or at the first shove or at the first blow, or after blood is drawn, or when a serious injury is inflicted? How suspicious must conduct be before there is "probable cause," the constitutional basis for an arrest? Every policeman, however complete or sketchy his education, is an interpreter of the law.

Every policeman, too, is an arbiter of social values, for he meets situation after situation in which invoking criminal sanctions is a questionable line of action. It is obvious that a boy throwing rocks at a school's windows is committing the statutory offense of vandalism, but it is often not at all obvious whether a policeman will better serve the interests of the community and of the boy by taking the boy home to his parents or by arresting him. Who are the boy's parents? Can they control him? Is he a frequent offender who has responded badly to leniency? Is vandalism so epidemic in the neighborhood that he should be made a cautionary example? With juveniles especially, the police exercise great discretion.

Finally, the manner in which a policeman works is influenced by practical matters: the legal strength of the available evidence, the willingness of victims to press charges and of witnesses to testify, the temper of the community, the time and information at the policeman's disposal. Much is at stake in how the policeman exercises this discretion. If he judges conduct not suspicious enough to justify intervention, the chance to prevent a robbery, rape, or murder may be lost. If he overestimates the seriousness of a situation or his actions are controlled by panic or prejudice, he may hurt or kill someone unnecessarily. His actions may even touch off a riot.

THE MAGISTRATE

In direct contrast to the policeman, the magistrate before whom a suspect is first brought usually exercises less discretion than the law allows him. He is entitled to inquire into the facts of the case, into whether there are grounds for holding the accused. He seldom does. He seldom can. The more promptly an arrested suspect is brought into magistrate's court, the less likelihood there is that much information about the arrest other than the arresting officer's statement will be available to the magistrate. Moreover many magistrates, especially in big cities, have such congested calendars that it is almost impossible for them to subject any case but an extraordinary one to prolonged scrutiny.

In practice the most important things, by far, that a magistrate does are to set the amount of a defendant's bail and in some jurisdictions to appoint counsel. Too seldom does either action get the careful attention it deserves. In many cases the magistrate accepts a waiver of counsel without insuring that the suspect knows the significance of legal representation.

Bail is a device to free an untried defendant and at the same time make sure he appears for trial. That is the sole stated legal purpose in America. The Eighth Amendment to the Constitution declares that it must not be "excessive." Appellate courts have declared that not just the seriousness of the charge against the defendant, but the suspect's personal, family, and employment situation, as they bear on the likelihood of his appearance, must be weighed before the amount of his bail is fixed. Yet more magistrates than not set bail according to standard rates: so and so many dollars for such and such an offense.

The persistence of money bail can best be explained not by its stated purpose but by the belief of police, prosecutors, and courts that the best way to keep a defendant from committing more crimes before trial is to set bail so high that he cannot obtain his release.

THE PROSECUTOR

The key administrative officer in the processing of cases is the prosecutor. Theoretically the examination of the evidence against a defendant by a judge at a preliminary hearing, and its reexamination by a grand jury, are important parts of the process. Practically they seldom are because a prosecutor seldom has any difficulty in making a prima facie case against a defendant. In fact most defendants waive their rights to preliminary hearings and much more often than not grand juries indict precisely as prosecutors ask them to. The prosecutor wields almost undisputed sway over the pretrial progress of most cases. He decides whether to press a case or drop it. He determines the specific charge against a defendant. When the charge is reduced, as it is in as many as two-thirds of all cases in some cities, the prosecutor is usually the official who reduces it.

* * *

THE PLEA AND THE SENTENCE

When a prosecutor reduces a charge it is ordinarily because there has been "plea bargaining" between him and a defense attorney. The issue at stake is how much the prosecutor will reduce his original charge or how lenient a sentence he will recommend, in return for a plea of guilty. There is no way of judging how many bargains reflect the prosecutor's belief that a lesser charge or sentence is justified and how many result from the fact that there may be in the system at any one time ten times as many cases as there are prosecutors or judges or courtrooms to handle them, should every one come to trial. In form, a plea bargain can be anything from a series of careful conferences to a hurried consultation in a courthouse corridor. In content it can be anything from a conscientious exploration of the facts and dispositional alternatives available and appropriate to a defendant, to a perfunctory deal. If the interests of a defendant are to be properly protected while his fate is being thus invisibly determined, he obviously needs just as good legal representation as the kind he needs at a public trial. Whether or not plea bargaining is a fair and effective method of disposing of criminal cases depends heavily on whether or not defendants are provided early with competent and conscientious counsel.

Plea bargaining is not only an invisible procedure but, in some jurisdictions, a theoretically unsanctioned one. In order to satisfy the court record, a defendant, his attorney, and the prosecutor will at the time of sentencing often ritually state to a judge that no bargain has been made. Plea bargaining may be a useful procedure, especially in congested urban jurisdictions, but neither the dignity of the law, nor the quality of justice, nor the protection of society from dangerous criminals is enhanced by its being conducted covertly.

* * *

An enormously consequential kind of decision is the sentencing decision of a judge. The law recognizes the importance of fitting sentences to individual defendants by giving judges, in most instances, considerable latitude. For example the recently adopted New York Penal Code, which will go into effect in autumn of 1967, empowers a judge to impose upon a man convicted of armed robbery any sentence between a 5-year term of probation and a 25-year term in prison. Even when a judge has presided over a trial during which the facts of a case have been carefully set forth and has been given a probation report that carefully discusses a defendant's character, background, and problems, he cannot find it easy to choose a sentence. In perhaps nine-tenths of all cases there is no trial; the defendants are self-confessedly guilty.

In the lower or misdemeanor courts, the courts that process most criminal cases, probation reports are a rarity. Under such circumstances judges have little to go on and many sentences are bound to be based on conjecture or intuition. When a sentence is part of a plea bargain, which an overworked judge ratifies perfunctorily, it may not even be his conjecture or intuition on which the sentence is based, but a prosecutor's or a defense counsel's. But perhaps the greatest lack judges suffer from when they pass sentence is not time or information, but correctional alternatives. Some lower courts do not have any probation officers, and in almost every court the caseloads of probation officers are so heavy that a sentence of probation means, in fact, releasing an offender into the community with almost no supervision. Few States have a sufficient variety of correctional institutions or treatment programs to inspire judges with the confidence that sentences will lead to rehabilitation.

Corrections

The correctional apparatus to which guilty defendants are delivered is in every respect the most isolated part of the criminal justice system. Much of it is physically isolated; its institutions usually have thick walls and locked doors, and often they are situated in rural areas, remote from the courts where the institutions' inmates were tried and from the communities where they lived. The correctional apparatus is isolated in the sense that its officials do not have everyday working relationships with officials from the system's other branches, like those that commonly exist between policemen and prosecutors, or prosecutors and judges. It is isolated in the sense that what it does with, to, or for the people under its supervision is seldom governed by any but the most broadly written statutes, and is almost never scrutinized by appellate courts. Finally, it is isolated from the public partly by its invisibility and physical remoteness; partly by the inherent lack of drama in most of its activities, but perhaps most importantly by the fact that the correctional apparatus is often used—or misused—by both the criminal justice system and the public as a rug under which disturbing problems and people can be swept.

The most striking fact about the correctional apparatus today is that, although the rehabilitation of criminals is presumably its major purpose, the custody of criminals is actually its major task. On any given day there are well over a million people being "corrected" in America, two-thirds of them on probation or parole and one-third of them in prisons or jails. However, prisons and jails are where four-fifths of correctional money is spent and where nine-tenths of correctional employees work. Furthermore, fewer than one-fifth of the people who work in State prisons and local jails have jobs that are not essentially either custodial or administrative in character. Many jails have nothing but custodial and administrative personnel. Of course many jails are crowded with defendants who have not been able to furnish bail and who are not considered by the law to be appropriate objects of rehabilitation because it has not yet been determined that they are criminals who need it.

What this emphasis on custody means in practice is that the enormous potential of the correctional apparatus for making creative decisions about its treatment of convicts is largely unfulfilled. This is true not only of offenders in custody but of offenders on probation and parole. Most authorities agree that while probationers and parolees need varying degrees and kinds of supervision, an average of no more than 35 cases per officer is necessary for effective attention; 97 percent of all officers handling adults have larger caseloads than that. * * *

Except for sentencing, no decision in the criminal process has more impact on the convicted offender than the parole decision, which determines how much of his maximum sentence a prisoner must serve. This again is an invisible administrative decision that is seldom open to attack or subject to review. It is made by parole board members who are often political appointees. Many are skilled and conscientious, but they generally are able to spend no more than a few minutes on a case. Parole decisions that are made in haste and on the basis of insufficient information, in the absence of parole machinery that can provide good supervision, are necessarily imperfect decisions. And since there is virtually no appeal from them, they can be made arbitrarily or discriminatorily. Just as carefully formulated and clearly stated law enforcement policies would help policemen, charge policies would help prosecutors and sentencing policies would help judges, so parole policies would help parole boards perform their delicate and important duties.

In sum, America's system of criminal justice is overcrowded and overworked, undermanned, underfinanced, and very often misunderstood. It needs more information and more knowledge. It needs more technical resources. It needs more coordination among its many parts. It needs more public support. It needs the help of community programs and institutions in dealing with offenders and potential offenders. It needs, above all, the willingness to reexamine old ways of doing things, to reform itself, to experiment, to run risks, to dare. It needs vision.

3. Note on Trial and Appeal in Criminal Cases

In petty criminal cases, where no more than six months imprisonment may be imposed, there is no established federal constitutional right to a jury trial and the accused may be tried by a judge sitting alone, unless the law of the trying jurisdiction provides otherwise. See Blanton v. City of North Las Vegas, Nev., 489 U.S. 538, 109 S.Ct. 1289, 103 L.Ed.2d 550 (1989). The accused may employ counsel, but indigent defendants are entitled (so far as the federal constitution is concerned) to free lawyers only in cases in which a sentence of imprisonment is actually imposed. The state may refuse free counsel if the punishment sought is to be something less. Trials of such petty offenses are more informal than trials of ordinary criminal cases, about to be described.

Courts of general criminal jurisdiction are likely to handle the most serious offenses and jury trials. First appeals from magistrates' courts may be to the courts of general criminal jurisdiction.

If the accused is entitled to and has elected a jury trial, a judge presides over the selection of the jury. Questions may be put to prospective jurors to elicit information which may show disqualification or bias. Both the prosecution and defense may challenge for cause, and usually each side is given a number of preemptory challenges, by which prospective jurors may be eliminated without specific grounds.

Trials proceed in much the same way whether the judge sits alone (in which case all questions of law and fact are determined by the judge) or sits with a jury (in which, generally, the judge decides issues of law and the jury decides issues of fact). The rules of evidence are more complex in jury trials, but the method and order of proof are the same. Usually the prosecutor begins by outlining the facts which can be established. Defense counsel may summarize the defense version of the case, either immediately afterwards or at the beginning of the presentation of defense evidence. The prosecutor calls witnesses and introduces other evidence. Defense counsel may object to the offering of particular evidence or to particular questions asked; the judge rules on admissibility. Defense counsel may cross-examine prosecution witnesses to bring out further details of the witness's account or to suggest that the witness may not be worthy of belief. When the prosecutor has presented the state's case, defense counsel may seek a directed verdict of acquittal; the judge must then decide whether, assuming the trier of fact believes the prosecution evidence, enough has been established to warrant a finding of guilty. If the motion is denied, the defense then presents its witnesses and other evidence, subject to objections and cross-examination by the prosecutor.

The prosecutor may not, because of an aspect of the constitutional privilege against self-incrimination, call the defendant as a witness or comment on the failure of the defendant to testify. If the defense calls the defendant, the prosecution may cross-examine him.

If the defense raises certain new matters of defense, which the prosecution is not bound to anticipate, the prosecution is allowed to present its own evidence on the new point in rebuttal. Throughout the proceedings, the trial judge acts as a kind of umpire, ruling on motions and objections of counsel, but usually not taking a more active part in the trial. The judge has power, however, to call witnesses and to ask questions of witnesses. This power is sometimes exercised, particularly to clarify a point which remains obscure. The judge must take care not to show partiality in such a case.

When the evidence is in, the defense and prosecutor make closing statements to the jury (or the judge, if the judge sits alone), and the judge instructs the jury on the law (or announces the legal principles which govern the decision). If the evidence is legally insufficient for conviction, the judge may direct a verdict of acquittal. From an acquittal, no appeal is allowed, though the prosecution may be permitted to appeal rulings of the judge made before trial (e.g., as to whether the indictment or information states an offense) or certain decisions as to sentencing. Following a conviction, the defendant may make motions, such as a motion for a new trial, based on alleged errors at the trial, or based on newly discovered evidence (usually only in certain narrowly defined circumstances). If these are denied, he is sentenced.

An appeal process is usually set out by statute. If federal constitutional error is claimed, appeals may proceed from state to federal courts. Once the defendant takes the initial appeal from a conviction, either side may appeal thereafter to higher courts until the appeal process is exhausted. An appeal is a direct attack on the conviction, appropriate for raising any question which by law is subject to review. These matters traditionally have not included the severity of sentence (so long as it is within limits set by the legislature or not attacked on constitutional grounds). Some jurisdictions now authorize full or limited review of the sentence imposed, often by special panels.

Certain kinds of indirect attack on the judgment may also be authorized, as in habeas corpus or coram nobis proceedings or statutory post-conviction proceedings. Grounds for relief here are usually narrowly limited.

It should be stressed that the foregoing is a general statement, omitting many details, that procedures differ considerably from one jurisdiction to another, and that this account may be slightly inaccurate for some states.

C. PUNISHMENT

1. Theories of Punishment

State v. Chip

Supreme Court of Ohypo, 1984.
304 Ohypo 106.

WYNKEN, C.J. This is one of the first cases to come before us under the Sentence Review Act of 1982 (27 Ohypo Rev.Code §§ 2980 ff.). The statute empowers this court to reduce, but not to increase, any sentence of imprisonment, where we find either that the sentencing judge has not followed proper principles of sentencing or that the judge has, in all of the circumstances, given an unreasonably severe sentence.

The defendant, Calvin Chip, is nineteen years of age and was, until he was recently expelled, a sophomore at Ohypo State University. Chip was not expelled for any deficiencies in scholarship. He has a brilliant high school record and stood third in a class of 3500 students at the end of his freshman year at Ohypo. He has no prior criminal or juvenile record, and he has not, in any ordinary sense, ever presented a disciplinary problem.

Chip was a precocious child, particularly in mathematics, and he soon became interested in and adept in the manipulation of computers. He has developed his skills as a hobby, and he planned to major in computer science. Using his own equipment, he found a way to break into the University's supposedly tamper-proof computer system and changed his records in two respects: (1) He erased the record of a $2000 loan, made to him as a freshman, and (2) He changed his grade in Ethics from an A minus (the only grade less than A he has received) to an A. Unfortunately for him, independent records of the loan and grade exist, and his tampering was discovered. He was expelled.

Under some broadly drawn theft statutes Chip might be guilty of grand larceny or attempted grand larceny for destroying the record of indebtedness; these offenses carry in our jurisdiction respectively maximum penalties of ten years and five years imprisonment. It is doubtful, however, that our own theft statute would reach such conduct, and Chip was charged only with two counts of tampering with public records, for which the maximum sentence is two years on each count.

Upon conviction on both counts—and he does not contest the correctness of the verdict—Chip was sentenced to serve the maximum sentence of imprisonment on each count, consecutively. Judge Bile, when he passed sentence, filed the following memorandum:

> I am convinced that you must receive the maximum sentence allowed by law. It is your good fortune that you were not convicted of at least attempted grand theft on the first count, for which I might have sentenced you to five years. Only because legislative draftsmanship has not caught up with the latest forms of computer thievery did you escape with a lesser charge. I find your acts particularly reprehensible. At a time when so much of our daily lives depends on the reliability of computer records and when public concern about the dangers of tampering with them is very great, you acted in such a way as to increase the anxiety of almost every member of society. We can lock up our money and jewels, but who can protect himself against computer fraud? Had you succeeded in wiping out the record of your debt, you would have responded to the generosity and trust imposed in you by the public by cheating your benefactors. Your grade tampering has cast doubt upon the entire system of academic records and devalued the records of those students who achieved their high grades honestly. The public outrage and concern you have caused and the contemptible character shown by your actions demand the severest possible sentence.

It may be questioned whether the sense of outrage and the thirst for revenge shown by Judge Bile are proper guidelines for sentencing. Most theorists do not regard revenge as an appropriate motive. Not only is it likely to disturb the detachment appropriate to the task of the sentencing judge, but society ought to be able to find a better reason than hatred of the offender for a long sentence. Some have maintained that more than simple retaliation is involved, that such a sentence is an important expression of community moral values, that it helps to form those moral bonds which assure a reasonable degree of social cohesion, or even that it acts as a safety valve to keep people from turning to vigilante justice. Indeed, what appears on the surface to be an action based on revenge may in fact be grounded on the more subtle theories advanced by members of this court. Whether or not revenge is ever an appropriate motive for sentencing, it hardly seems central here. The community is concerned about computer fraud, but it is not so concerned that there would be a severe rending of the social fabric if this defendant receives something less than the maximum sentence.

I would affirm the trial judge's sentence on an independent ground. The consecutive two year sentences will leave Chip eligible for probation in 32 months. Given the nonviolent nature of his crime and the space pressure in our prison system, he is almost certain to be released at the earliest possible time. I think it prudent to keep him out of circulation for a considerable period because the proof tended to show that Chip is something of a computer genius with very little moral sense. He is probably one of the few people in the state capable of tampering with a well-protected computer system and likely to do so when he gets the chance. If allowed to go free, he might well produce real havoc in, say, our banking system. By the time he is released we may hope either that he will have changed his ways or that he will have fallen far enough behind in computer technology to be significantly less of a public menace.

I agree with Judge Bile that had the legislature acted a bit faster, Chip might have been convicted of an offense carrying a five year maximum sentence, as well as the tampering charge for changing his grade. He is therefore lucky that his sentence is as low as it is. Had he been going to a private college, it is doubtful that he could have been convicted of any criminal offense, so the public is lucky, too.

To base my conclusions on the fairly simple idea that, while the convict is locked up he can't harm the public, may appear to ignore grander reasons of policy. But, I am afraid that my years on the bench have made me doubt the effectiveness of penal theories based on reform or deterrence. The deterrent effect of sentences remains speculative, and reform probably must begin with the inner determination of the convicted person to change his ways. This inner determination may or may not be fostered by confinement. Nobody knows.

BLYNKEN, J. With respect, I cannot agree with the approaches of the sentencing judge or of the Chief Justice in this case. Retaliation is never an adequate ground for sentencing; too much depends on the public passions of the moment. Nor can I believe that incapacitation of the accused is an important factor in the present circumstances. We are not dealing with a Bluebeard, and clever as Chip may be, there are doubtless at least a few others as dangerous as he to our public records and banking system who remain at large. Jailing him will not solve the problem of computer fraud.

Incapacitation as a punishment theory can be justified only if we can predict dangerousness with some degree of accuracy. Judges, psychiatrists, and parole boards do not have particularly good records in such predictions. We can never know how many of the long sentences imposed and served are really unnecessary to keep the convict from further crime, but surely there are a good many. We do know that large numbers of those serving light sentences are soon back before the criminal courts. Until we find better methods of prediction, we must usually rely on other theories than incapacitation to justify prison sentences. Even the idea that it does not hurt to err on the side of severity to protect the public will not withstand investigation. A prisoner may well be more of a public danger after serving a long sentence than he would be after serving a short one.

While, in themselves, revenge and incapacitation do not furnish solid grounds for sentencing, the need of the public to be reassured cannot be disregarded entirely. Where, as here, there has been considerable publicity given to a crime and much public concern about the problem, there is good reason for preferring some sentence of imprisonment.

Our major sentencing concern should be with the deterrent effect of the sentence on others. If we want to stop computer fraud, those who might be inclined to consider it must be discouraged, and the sentencing of those who do commit the crime to jail is as likely as anything to encourage honesty. A crime likely to be committed on the spur of the moment in hot blood is perhaps not capable of being stopped by the immediate threats of the criminal law, but the crime here under consideration requires careful planning and is ideally suited to a deterrent approach. It should be noted that deterrence may act more subtly than in the example in which one reads of a conviction in the morning newspaper and thereupon abandons a criminal scheme. One's general education in the mores of the community—formed in part by the actions of the criminal law—may be so influential over the long run that committing the crime is never seriously contemplated.

Of course, we must be concerned about reverse deterrence. An unduly harsh sentence may produce sympathy for the criminal rather than condemnation and a wish to avoid the crime.

It is well known that in the days when pickpockets might be hanged, they would often practice their trade in the crowds who came to watch the execution of a pickpocket. All this proves is that no theory of punishment is perfect; some will not be deterred by even the severest threats. The successes of deterrence are hidden; how do you count uncommitted crimes?

There is a better case for deterrence than for the theory of reformation advanced by my brother Nod. The threat of punishment is more effective for those not punished than the actual punishment is for those who go to jail. This is because jail does not really reform most prisoners; the forces working against rehabilitation in jail are all too often stronger than those working for it. Too many graduates of our prisons return for post-graduate courses in crime.

I conclude that a prison sentence is necessary to deter others, but that the sentence imposed is harsher than is necessary to achieve the maximum deterrent effect. I therefore vote to reduce the sentence imposed to one of one year's imprisonment.

NOD, J. I am astonished that any court would seriously contemplate a severe sentence for this defendant. When burglars with prior convictions are routinely sentenced to a few months in jail or even granted probation, it is proposed that this nineteen year old college student with no prior criminal record and no history of violence spend years in jail.

The mere fact of conviction will blight Chip's prospects and warn others of the risks of tampering with computers. We ought to be concerned primarily with salvaging what we can in human terms from this tragic situation. Why the Chief Justice is so concerned with Chip as a social menace mystifies me. Perhaps the concern is based on the testimony of Dr. Shrink at the sentencing hearing that Chip is a "borderline" psychopathic personality. A psychopathic personality is one who, though not insane, is not guided by any inner sense of conscience, morality, or decency; he is indeed likely to repeat crimes. But Dr. Shrink freely admitted that his diagnosis was so uncertain that he himself would not base any sentencing decision upon it, and three other equally eminent psychiatrists found no personality abnormality at all. It is therefore quite unwarranted to assume that Chip will continue to commit crimes on the basis of some supposed mental condition.

While deterrence is a matter to be considered in sentencing, it should not play the central role that Justice Blynken would give it. The theory pays no attention at all to the particular situation of the defendant. For one who believes in deterrence as the sole guide, it doesn't even matter whether or not the accused is in fact guilty of the crime, so long as his innocence will never be discovered and his fate can serve as a warning to others. Surely we need a philosophy which centers more on the person we are sentencing.

It is hard to see that imprisonment is likely to have any rehabilitative effect on Chip at all. The limited educational resources of the prison cannot help him. If our prisons were better places, there might be some merit in confining him for a limited period of time so that he could rethink his philosophy of life and become more mature. But the surroundings in our state prison are such that he will have to spend more time worrying about sexual attack than spiritual growth.

If I seem pessimistic about reform of the prisoner, I should make it clear that it is not the theory I doubt but the practice. Reform in prison has never really been given a fair trial. It cannot be expected to have a high success rate in the overcrowded and underfunded conditions of today's prisons. If we want most prisoners to leave prison less likely to commit crimes than when they came in, we need whole armies of physicians, social workers, psychologists, educators, and others to put to this task. How these can be funded when the legislature has so many demands from those with equal needs who have committed no crimes it is difficult to see. Even in the face of obstacles, prisons can and do rehabilitate some, but Chip does not appear to be a member of the class likely to be benefitted. He does not need to complete his high school education or to learn a trade.

He seems ideally suited for probation. There is no reason for confining him, as long as he can be given reasonable supervision. He may hope to continue his education or find work and become a valuable member of society. It is true that our probation system is as understaffed as our prisons, but it seems unlikely that Chip and the public will be in worse condition if Chip is placed on probation. I have been unable to persuade my colleagues of this course, and I must therefore reluctantly concur with my sister Blynken's vote for one year's imprisonment as at least better than a more extended period of confinement.

Sentence of imprisonment reduced to a period of one year.

United States v. Bergman

United States District Court, Southern District of New York, 1976.
416 F.Supp. 496.

SENTENCING MEMORANDUM

FRANKEL, DISTRICT JUDGE.

Defendant is being sentenced upon his plea of guilty to two counts of an 11-count indictment. The sentencing proceeding is unusual in some respects. It has been the subject of more extensive submissions, written and oral, than this court has ever received upon such an occasion. The court has studied some hundreds of pages of memoranda and exhibits, plus scores of volunteered letters. A broad array of issues has been addressed. Imaginative suggestions of law and penology have been tendered. A preliminary conversation with counsel, on the record, preceded the usual sentencing hearing. Having heard counsel again and the defendant speaking for himself, the court postponed the pronouncement of sentence for further reconsideration of thoughts generated during the days of studying the briefs and oral pleas. It seems fitting now to report in writing the reasons upon which the court concludes that defendant must be sentenced to a term of four months in prison.[1]

I. *Defendant and His Crimes*

Defendant appeared until the last couple of years to be a man of unimpeachably high character, attainments, and distinction. A doctor of divinity and an ordained rabbi, he has been acclaimed by people around the world for his works of public philanthropy, private charity, and leadership in educational enterprises. Scores of letters have come to the court from across this and other countries reporting debts of personal gratitude to him for numerous acts of extraordinary generosity. (The court has also received a kind of petition, with fifty-odd signatures, in which the signers, based upon learning acquired as newspaper readers, denounce the defendant and urge a severe sentence. Unlike the pleas for mercy, which appear to reflect

1. The court considered, and finally rejected, imposing a fine in addition to the prison term. Defendant seems destined to pay hundreds of thousands of dollars in restitution. The amount is being worked out in connection with a state criminal indictment. Apart from defendant's further liabilities for federal taxes, any additional money exaction is appropriately left for the state court.

unquestioned facts inviting compassion, this document should and will be disregarded.) In addition to his good works, defendant has managed to amass considerable wealth in the ownership and operation of nursing homes, in real estate ventures, and in a course of substantial investments.

Beginning about two years ago, investigations of nursing homes in this area, including questions of fraudulent claims for Medicaid funds, drew to a focus upon this defendant among several others. The results that concern us were the present indictment and two state indictments. After extensive pretrial proceedings, defendant embarked upon elaborate plea negotiations with both state and federal prosecutors. A state guilty plea and the instant plea were entered in March of this year. (Another state indictment is expected to be dismissed after defendant is sentenced on those to which he has pled guilty.) As part of the detailed plea arrangements, it is expected that the prison sentence imposed by this court will comprise the total covering the state as well as the federal convictions.

For purposes of the sentence now imposed, the precise details of the charges, and of defendant's carefully phrased admissions of guilt, are not matters of prime importance. Suffice it to say that the plea on Count One (carrying a maximum of five years in prison and a $10,000 fine) confesses defendant's knowing and wilful participation in a scheme to defraud the United States in various ways, including the presentation of wrongfully padded claims for payments under the Medicaid program to defendant's nursing homes. Count Three, for which the guilty plea carries a theoretical maximum of three more years in prison and another $5,000 fine, is a somewhat more "technical" charge. Here, defendant admits to having participated in the filing of a partnership return which was false and fraudulent in failing to list people who had bought partnership interests from him in one of his nursing homes, had paid for such interests, and had made certain capital withdrawals.

The conspiracy to defraud, as defendant has admitted it, is by no means the worst of its kind; it is by no means as flagrant or extensive as has been portrayed in the press; it is evidently less grave than other nursing-home wrongs for which others have been convicted or publicized. At the same time, the sentence, as defendant has acknowledged, is imposed for two federal felonies including, as the more important, a knowing and purposeful conspiracy to mislead and defraud the Federal Government.

II. *The Guiding Principles of Sentencing*

* * *

The court agrees that this defendant should not be sent to prison for "rehabilitation." Apart from the patent inappositeness of the concept to this individual, this court shares the growing understanding that no one should ever be sent to prison for *rehabilitation.* That is to say, nobody who would not otherwise be locked up should suffer that fate on the incongruous premise that it will be good for him or her. Imprisonment is punishment. Facing the simple reality should help us to be civilized. It is less agreeable to confine someone when we deem it an affliction rather than a benefaction. If someone must be imprisoned—for other, valid reasons—we should seek to make rehabilitative resources available to him or her. But the goal of rehabilitation cannot fairly serve in itself as grounds for the sentence to confinement.[3]

Equally clearly, this defendant should not be confined to incapacitate him. He is not dangerous. It is most improbable that he will commit similar, or any, offenses in the future. * * *

Contrary to counsel's submissions, however, two sentencing considerations demand a prison sentence in this case:

> *First,* the aim of *general deterrence,* the effort to discourage similar wrongdoing by others through a reminder that the law's warnings are real and that the grim consequence of imprisonment is likely to follow from crimes of deception for gain like those defendant has admitted.
>
> *Second,* the related, but not identical, concern that any lesser penalty would, in the words of the Model Penal Code, § 7.01(1)(c), "depreciate the seriousness of the defendant's crime."

Resisting the first of these propositions, defense counsel invoke Immanuel Kant's axiom that "one man ought never to be dealt with merely as a means subservient to the purposes of another." In a more novel, but equally futile, effort, counsel urge that a sentence for general deterrence "would violate the Eighth Amendment proscription against cruel and unusual punishment." Treating the latter point first, because it is a short subject, it may be observed simply that if general deterrence as a sentencing purpose were now to be outlawed, as against a near unanimity of views among state and federal jurists, the bolt would have to come from a place higher than this.

As for Dr. Kant, it may well be that defense counsel mistake his meaning in the present context. Whether or not that is so, and without pretending to authority on that score, we take the widely accepted stance that a criminal punished in the interest of general deterrence is not being employed "*merely* as a means * * *." Reading Kant to mean that every man must be deemed *more* than the instrument of others, and must "always be treated as an end in himself," the humane principle is not offended here. Each of us is served by the enforcement of the law—not least a person like the defendant in this case, whose wealth and privileges, so long enjoyed, are so much founded upon law. More broadly, we are driven regularly in our ultimate interests as members of the community to use ourselves and each other, in war and in peace, for social ends. One who has transgressed against the criminal laws is certainly among the more fitting candidates for a role of this nature. This is no arbitrary selection. Warned in advance of the prospect, the transgressor has chosen, in the law's premises, "between keeping the law required for society's protection or paying the penalty."

But the whole business, defendant argues further, is guesswork; we are by no means certain that deterrence "works." The position is somewhat

3. This important point, correcting misconceptions still widely prevalent, is developed more fully by Dean Norval Morris in *The Future of Imprisonment* (1974).

overstated; there is, in fact, some reasonably "scientific" evidence for the efficacy of criminal sanctions as deterrents, at least as against some kinds of crimes.[9] Moreover, the time is not yet here when all we can "know" must be quantifiable and digestible by computers. The shared wisdom of generations teaches meaningfully, if somewhat amorphously, that the utilitarians have a point; we do, indeed, lapse often into rationality and act to seek pleasure and avoid pain. It would be better, to be sure, if we had more certainty and precision. Lacking these comforts, we continue to include among our working hypotheses a belief (with some concrete evidence in its support) that crimes like those in this case—deliberate, purposeful, continuing, non-impulsive, and committed for profit—are among those most likely to be generally deterrable by sanctions most shunned by those exposed to temptation.[11]

The idea of avoiding depreciation of the seriousness of the offense implicates two or three thoughts, not always perfectly clear or universally agreed upon, beyond the idea of deterrence. It should be proclaimed by the court's judgment that the offenses are grave, not minor or purely technical. Some attention must be paid to the demand for equal justice; it will not do to leave the penalty of imprisonment a dead letter as against "privileged" violators while it is employed regularly, and with vigor, against others. There probably is in these conceptions an element of retributiveness, as counsel urge. And retribution, so denominated, is in some disfavor as a reason for punishment. It remains a factor, however, as Holmes perceived,[12] and as is known to anyone who talks to judges, lawyers, defendants, or people generally. It may become more palatable, and probably more humanely understood, under the rubric of "deserts" or "just deserts." [13] However the concept is formulated, we have not yet reached a state, supposing we ever should, in which the infliction of punishments for crime may be divorced generally from ideas of blameworthiness, recompense, and proportionality.

III. *An Alternative, "Behavioral Sanction"*

Resisting prison above all else, defense counsel included in their thorough memorandum on sentencing two proposals for what they call a "constructive," and therefore a "preferable" form of "behavioral sanction." * * *

* * *

* * * The seriousness of the crimes to which Dr. Bergman has pled guilty demands something more than "requiring" him to lend his talents and efforts to further philanthropic enterprises. It remains open to him, of course, to pursue the interesting suggestions later on as a matter of unforced personal choice.

9. See, e.g., F. Zimring and G. Hawkins, *Deterrence* 168–71, 282 (1973).

11. For some supporting evidence that "white-collar" offenses are somewhat specially deterrable, see Chambliss, *Types of Deviance and the Effectiveness of Legal Sanctions,* 1967 Wis.L.Rev. 703, 708–10.

12. See O. Holmes, *Common Law* 41–42, 45 (1881).

13. See A. von Hirsch, *Doing Justice* 45–55 (1976); see also N. Morris, *The Future of Imprisonment* 73–77 (1974).

IV. *"Measuring" the Sentence*

* * *

The criminal behavior, as has been noted, is blatant in character and unmitigated by any suggestion of necessitous circumstance or other pressures difficult to resist. * * * Viewed against the maxima Congress ordained, and against the run of sentences in other federal criminal cases, it calls for more than a token sentence.

On the other side are factors that take longer to enumerate. Defendant's illustrious public life and works are in his favor, though diminished, of course, by what this case discloses. This is a first, probably a last, conviction. Defendant is 64 years old and in imperfect health, though by no means so ill, from what the court is told, that he could be expected to suffer inordinately more than many others of advanced years who go to prison.

Defendant invokes an understandable, but somewhat unworkable, notion of "disparity." He says others involved in recent nursing home fraud cases have received relatively light sentences for behavior more culpable than his. He lays special emphasis upon one defendant whose frauds appear indeed to have involved larger amounts and who was sentenced to a maximum of six months' incarceration, to be confined for that time only on week nights, not on week days or weekends. This court has examined the minutes of that sentencing proceeding and finds the case distinguishable in material respects. But even if there were a threat of such disparity as defendant warns against, it could not be a major weight on the scales.

Our sentencing system, deeply flawed, is characterized by disparity. We are to seek to "individualize" sentences, but no clear or clearly agreed standards govern the individualization. The lack of meaningful criteria does indeed leave sentencing judges far too much at large. But the result, with its nagging burdens on conscience, cannot be meaningfully alleviated by allowing any handful of sentences in a short series to fetter later judgments. * * *

* * * We sit, to be sure, in a nation where prison sentences of extravagant length are more common than they are almost anywhere else. By that light, the term imposed today is not notably long. For this sentencing court, however, for a nonviolent first offense involving no direct assaults or invasions of others' security (as in bank robbery, narcotics, etc.), it is a stern sentence. For people like Dr. Bergman, who might be disposed to engage in similar wrongdoing, it should be sufficiently frightening to serve the major end of general deterrence. For all but the profoundly vengeful, it should not depreciate the seriousness of his offenses.

* * *

Note on Predicting Dangerousness

1. White, J., for the court, in Barefoot v. Estelle, 463 U.S. 880, 103 S.Ct. 3383, 3396–3398, 77 L.Ed.2d 1090, 1106–1109 (1983), rehearing denied 464 U.S. 874, 104 S.Ct. 209, 78 L.Ed.2d 185 (1983):

> The suggestion that no psychiatrist's testimony may be presented with respect to a defendant's future dangerousness is somewhat like asking us to

disinvent the wheel. In the first place, it is contrary to our cases. If the likelihood of a defendant committing further crimes is a constitutionally acceptable criterion for imposing the death penalty, which it is, Jurek v. Texas, 428 U.S. 262, 96 S.Ct. 2950, 49 L.Ed.2d 929 (1976), and if it is not impossible for even a lay person sensibly to arrive at that conclusion, it makes little sense, if any, to submit that psychiatrists, out of the entire universe of persons who might have an opinion on the issue, would know so little about the subject that they should not be permitted to testify. In *Jurek,* seven Justices rejected the claim that it was impossible to predict future behavior and that dangerousness was therefore an invalid consideration in imposing the death penalty. Justice STEVENS responded directly to the argument, 428 U.S., at 274–276, 96 S.Ct., at 2957–2958:

> "It is, of course, not easy to predict future behavior. The fact that such a determination is difficult, however, does not mean that it cannot be made. Indeed, prediction of future criminal conduct is an essential element in many of the decisions rendered throughout our criminal justice system. The decision whether to admit a defendant to bail, for instance, must often turn on a judge's prediction of the defendant's future conduct. Any sentencing authority must predict a convicted person's probable future conduct when it engages in the process of determining what punishment to impose. For those sentenced to prison, these same predictions must be made by parole authorities. The task that a Texas jury must perform in answering the statutory question in issue is thus basically no different from the task performed countless times each day throughout the American system of criminal justice. What is essential is that the jury have before it all possible relevant information about the individual defendant whose fate it must determine. Texas law clearly assures that all such evidence will be adduced."

Although there was only lay testimony with respect to dangerousness in *Jurek,* there was no suggestion by the Court that the testimony of doctors would be inadmissible. To the contrary, the Court said that the jury should be presented with all of the relevant information. Furthermore, in Estelle v. Smith, 451 U.S. 454, 473, 101 S.Ct. 1866, 1878, 68 L.Ed.2d 359 (1981), in the face of a submission very similar to that presented in this case with respect to psychiatric testimony, we approvingly repeated the above quotation from *Jurek* and went on to say that we were in "no sense disapproving the use of psychiatric testimony bearing on future dangerousness." * * *

In the second place, the rules of evidence generally extant at the federal and state levels anticipate that relevant, unprivileged evidence should be admitted and its weight left to the fact finder, who would have the benefit of cross examination and contrary evidence by the opposing party. Psychiatric testimony predicting dangerousness may be countered not only as erroneous in a particular case but as generally so unreliable that it should be ignored. If the jury may make up its mind about future dangerousness unaided by psychiatric testimony, jurors should not be barred from hearing the views of the State's psychiatrists along with opposing views of the defendant's doctors.

Third, petitioner's view mirrors the position expressed in the amicus brief of the American Psychiatric Association (APA). As indicated above, however, the same view was presented and rejected in Estelle v. Smith. We are no more convinced now that the view of the APA should be converted into a constitutional rule barring an entire category of expert testimony. We are not persuaded that such testimony is almost entirely unreliable and that the factfinder and the adversary system will not be competent to uncover, recognize, and take due account of its shortcomings.

The *amicus* does not suggest that there are not other views held by members of the Association or of the profession generally. Indeed, as this case and others indicate, there are those doctors who are quite willing to testify at the sentencing hearing, who think, and will say, that they know what they are talking about, and who expressly disagree with the Association's point of view.[7] Furthermore, their qualifications as experts are regularly accepted by the courts. If they are so obviously wrong and should be discredited, there should be no insuperable problem in doing so by calling members of the Association who are of that view and who confidently assert that opinion in their *amicus* brief. Neither petitioner nor the Association

7. At trial, Dr. Holbrook testified without contradiction that a psychiatrist could predict the future dangerousness of an individual, if given enough background information about the individual. Tr. Trial (T.Tr.) 2072–2073. Dr. Grigson obviously held a similar view. See T.Tr. 2110, 2134. At the District Court hearing on the habeas petition, the State called two expert witnesses, Dr. George Parker, a psychologist, and Dr. Richard Koons, a psychiatrist. Both of these doctors agreed that accurate predictions of future dangerousness can be made if enough information is provided; furthermore, they both deemed it highly likely that an individual fitting the characteristics of the one in the Barefoot hypothetical would commit future acts of violence. Tr. of Hearing (H.Tr.) 183–248.

Although Barefoot did not present any expert testimony at his trial, at the habeas hearing he called Dr. Fred Fason, a psychiatrist, and Dr. Wendell Dickerson, a psychologist. Dr. Fason did not dwell on the general ability of mental health professionals to predict future dangerousness. Instead, for the most part, he merely criticized the giving of a diagnosis based upon a hypothetical question, without an actual examination. He conceded that, if a medical student described a patient in the terms of the Barefoot hypothetical, his "highest order of suspicion," to the degree of 90%, would be that the patient had a sociopathic personality. H.Tr. 22. He insisted, however, that this was only an "initial impression," and that no doctor should give a firm "diagnosis" without a full examination and testing. H.Tr. 22, 29–30, 36. Dr. Dickerson, petitioner's other expert, was the only person to testify who suggested that no reliable psychiatric predictions of dangerousness could ever be made.

We are aware that many mental health professionals have questioned the usefulness of psychiatric predictions of future dangerousness in light of studies indicating that such predictions are often inaccurate. For example, at the habeas hearing, Dr. Dickerson, one of petitioner's expert witnesses, testified that psychiatric predictions of future dangerousness were wrong two out of three times. H.Tr. 97, 108. He conceded, however, that, despite the high error rate, one "excellently done" study had shown "some predictive validity for predicting violence." H.Tr. 96–97. Dr. John Monahan, upon whom one of the State's experts relied as "the leading thinker on this issue," H.Tr. 195, concluded that "the 'best' clinical research currently in existence indicates that *psychiatrists and psychologists are accurate in no more than one out of three predictions of violent behavior over a several-year period among institutionalized populations that had both committed violence in the past* * * * *and who were diagnosed as mentally ill.*" Monahan, The Clinical Prediction of Violent Behavior 47–49 (1981) (emphasis in original). However, although Dr. Monahan originally believed that it was impossible to predict violent behavior, by the time he had completed his monograph, he felt that "there may be circumstances in which prediction is both empirically possible and ethically appropriate," and he hoped that his work would improve the appropriateness and accuracy of clinical predictions. Id., at v.

All of these professional doubts about the usefulness of psychiatric predictions can be called to the attention of the jury. Petitioner's entire argument, as well as that of Justice Blackmun's dissent, is founded on the premise that a jury will not be able to separate the wheat from the chaff. We do not share in this low evaluation of the adversary process.

suggests that psychiatrists are always wrong with respect to future dangerousness, only most of the time. * * *

2. BLACKMUN, J., with BRENNAN and MARSHALL, JJ., dissenting in Barefoot v. Estelle, 463 U.S. 880, 103 S.Ct. 3383, 3408–3409, 3413, 77 L.Ed.2d 1090, 1121–1123, 1127 (1983), rehearing denied 464 U.S. 874, 104 S.Ct. 209, 78 L.Ed.2d 185 (1983):

> The American Psychiatric Association (APA), participating in this case as *amicus curiae,* informs us that "[t]he unreliability of psychiatric predictions of long-term future dangerousness is by now an established fact within the profession." Brief for American Psychiatric Association, as *Amicus Curiae,* 12 (APA Brief). The APA's best estimate is that *two out of three* predictions of long-term future violence made by psychiatrists are wrong. * * * Neither the Court nor the State of Texas has cited a single reputable scientific source contradicting the unanimous conclusion of professionals in this field that psychiatric predictions of long-term future violence are wrong more often than they are right.
>
> The APA also concludes, see APA Brief 9–16, as do researchers that have studied the issue, that psychiatrists simply have no expertise in predicting long-term future dangerousness. A layman with access to relevant statistics can do at least as well and possibly better; psychiatric training is not relevant to the factors that validly can be employed to make such predictions, and psychiatrists consistently err on the side of overpredicting violence. Thus, while Doctors Grigson and Holbrook were presented by the State and by self-proclamation as experts at predicting future dangerousness, the scientific literature makes crystal clear that they had no expertise whatever. Despite their claims that they were able to predict Barefoot's future behavior "within reasonable psychiatric certainty," or to a "one hundred percent and absolute" certainty, there was in fact no more than a one in three chance that they were correct.
>
> * * *
>
> Despite its recognition that the testimony at issue was probably wrong and certainly prejudicial, the Court holds this testimony admissible because the Court is "unconvinced * * * that the adversary process cannot be trusted to sort out the reliable from the unreliable evidence and opinion about future dangerousness." One can only wonder how juries are to separate valid from invalid expert opinions when the "experts" themselves are so obviously unable to do so. Indeed, the evidence suggests that juries are not effective at assessing the validity of scientific evidence.

Question

Might there be better ways to predict dangerousness than by way of expert psychiatric testimony?

A NOTE ON THE SENTENCING OF CRIMINALS *

Ernest van den Haag
1 Policy Review 107 (1977).

* * * Apart from incapacitation, the purpose of punishment must be to do justice: to punish those who by violating the criminal law deserved and have invited the punishment threatened by it. This is the threat or the promise of the law. As is any promise, that threat is a moral obligation that must be carried out regardless of usefulness. (There is a common misunderstanding here: it is believed that the obligation is to the criminal. It is not. It is to those who, perhaps because of the threat, did not commit crimes.) Further, if the threat is not carried out when the law is broken, it becomes incredible and, therefore, ineffective in restraining future lawbreakers. This would defeat the second purpose of the legal threat: to restrain prospective future lawbreakers from breaking the law.

Promises should be kept; threats should not be made unless one proposes to carry them out. Else they will be regarded as bluffs. If they are, threats cannot restrain or deter prospective law violators. Deterrence requires that the threats of the law be carried out by inflicting punishment—not rehabilitation—on those who volunteer to risk it, by breaking the law. Crime is deterred by the threat of punishment only as long as it remains credible. Thus, unlike Mr. Justice Black, I believe that the "dominant objective of criminal law" must be to do justice by punishing as threatened and thereby also to deter others. Rehabilitation, however desirable, cannot take the place of justice and deterrence. Moreover, attempts to achieve it lead to gross injustice and necessarily must fail, as indeed they have. Let us consider the distortions of justice that have occurred to accommodate these attempts.

On Mandatory Sentences

At the present time, considerable sentencing discretion is given to courts. After they have exercised it, parole boards determine what part of that sentence passed by the court is actually served. I oppose the discretion given judges and favor narrowing it to near zero. The law should mandate the sentence for each crime.[2] I propose further that parole and parole boards be abolished altogether.

Essentially sentencing discretion is left to courts because (a) the circumstances of each crime differ, and it is believed that the judge, familiar with the case, is the best person to adapt the sentence to those circumstances; (b) the personality of each criminal is different, and again it is believed that the judge is more able than the legislator to adapt the punishment to the individual

* "A Note on the Sentencing of Criminals", by Ernest van den Haag, is reprinted from *Policy Review*, Issue No. 1 (Summer, 1977). *Policy Review* is a publication of The Heritage Foundation, 214 Massachusetts Avenue, N.E., Washington, D.C. 20002.

2. The only penalty that I believe should not be mandatory is the death penalty. Courts should be able to choose between it and life imprisonment for the reasons that the Supreme Court has specified in recent decisions.

personality of the offender, to his degree of guilt, and to his chances for rehabilitation.

Certainly each crime is committed in different circumstances of an aggravating or extenuating nature, which legitimately ought to influence the sentence imposed by the court. However, these circumstances can be classified and listed in the law to a very large extent. Judges can be legally instructed to increase or decrease sentences accordingly. Thus, judicial discretion can be severely limited while aggravating or extenuating circumstances still can properly influence sentences. This limitation of judicial discretion is desirable, for without it elements of judgment (negatively expressed, of capriciousness) necessarily prevail. They give the appearance of injustice, at least of inequality, and sometimes the substance as well. Moreover, uncertainty about the sentence to be expected reduces the deterrent effect of punishment—crime becomes more of a gamble than it need be. Thus, I would make all sentences mandatory, allowing judges to increase or decrease the mandated sentence by no more than 10 percent for reasons (to be stated in passing sentence) beyond those specified in the law.[3]

Defendants differ, and this, too, is alleged to necessitate judicial discretion. Some, it is argued, have personalities more and others less susceptible to rehabilitation. This may be so. But, as has been noted, the purpose of a sentence is to punish those guilty of crime—rehabilitation is incidental to such punishment. Else, defendants not in need of rehabilitation could be released, guilty or not, and unrehabilitated offenders would have to be kept indefinitely. This would be unjust. Nor would it serve deterrence—it would indeed grant everybody immunity for at least one crime, provided he is found unlikely to commit other crimes.

At any rate, there is no evidence whatsoever that judges, even when aided by probation reports, or by psychologists, are able to gauge personality differences and to adapt sentences to them. * * *

Is Rehabilitation Possible?

The major purpose of parole has been to release from prison offenders who, in the opinion of the parole board, are rehabilitated. Since the parole board thus determines within a minimum and maximum the actual length of any sentence, it necessarily makes all sentences indeterminate. This practice is unjust; it leads to wholly capricious punishment; and, finally, it does not and cannot achieve its purpose of releasing the rehabilitated and keeping those who are not—regardless of whether that purpose itself is justifiable.

No one has ever shown that behavior within prison enables parole boards to infer anything about behavior upon release. Experience indicates that it does not. And why, indeed, should behavior in the very special conditions of prison tell us much about behavior outside? Yet all elements, other than behavior within prison, are already available at sentencing time and do not require a parole board to second-guess the sentencing judge.

3. S. 1437, a bill now before Congress, proposes a sentencing commission that would elaborate guidelines. This, if properly done, would have nearly the same effect as making sentences mandatory.

* * * In practical terms, no program has yet been discovered to effectively help rehabilitation.[4] Perhaps rehabilitative programs to help non-career criminals will be discovered and validated in the future. Although they may be added to it, they can never take the place of punishment as long as it is to be both just and a deterrent. At present, rehabilitative programs simply foster, abet and reward whatever histrionic and manipulative abilities prisoners possess. For, what is actually evaluated by parole boards is how well the prisoner gets along with the prison authorities and their notions of appropriate prison behavior, or of behavior indicating rehabilitation.

Somewhere between a quarter and a half of our prisoners are recidivists. (The data do not permit greater specification.) The rest are not. There is no evidence that any rehabilitation program here or abroad has ever made a difference in these proportions, in producing a change, in leading more people to be law-abiding upon release. It is quite possible that imprisonment itself does have effects, at least on the non-professional offenders, or that there are spontaneous changes. But there is no evidence that released offenders upon release commit either fewer or more crimes than they would have committed had they never been imprisoned. (Possibly the rehabilitative and criminalizing effects of imprisonment statistically offset each other.) Above all, there is no evidence that any specific treatment during confinement—any rehabilitation program—makes a difference.

The methods now used by parole boards do not ascertain the likely future behavior of a prisoner. Hence, there is no reason why the sentencing should not be left to the law and the judge. The parole board should be altogether abolished. Evidence abounds indicating that a disproportionate number of crimes are committed by previously incarcerated offenders, many released on parole. Among them are many career criminals whom parole boards believed rehabilitated.

Lest I be misunderstood, I do not necessarily advocate lengthier confinement for all offenders. I do advocate less arbitrary decisions on confinement and more equal sentences determined by law and by the courts, without any parole provisions whatever. I do not wish to eliminate "time off for good behavior" either. As long as it is a privilege and not a right, and left entirely to the prison administration to grant or withhold, "time off for good behavior" is a valuable tool of prison discipline. However, the maximum "time off" should never exceed 10 percent of the sentence being served. Else prison wardens gain excessive arbitrary power and sentences would no longer be determined by the law and by the courts. On the other hand, 10 percent of the sentence is enough incentive for proper conduct for any convict at all responsive to positive incentives.

To Limit the Powers of Parole Boards

It is frequently thought that our prisons would become over-crowded if parole boards did not release people. But if shorter effective sentences are

4. One must be careful to distinguish (1) rehabilitation brought about by the influence of extraordinary personalities—which, by definition, cannot be institutionalized; (2) rehabilitation by age, punishment, or other factors; (3) rehabilitation by a specific non-punitive program. It is the latter that nowhere has succeeded when institutionalized.

desired, this can be accomplished by reducing penalties judicially or legislatively. Parole boards are not needed to shorten time served.

However, if severe effective sentences do reduce the crime rate by reducing the number of crimes committed by those incapacitated—and that is likely, since many crimes are committed by a small number of "career criminals"—lengthy confinement would still cost less than release would. The additional crimes committed by the released convicts cost more to victims and to the criminal justice system than confinement does. Thus, if the prison population were to increase, investment in more prisons might be entirely worthwhile.

But such an increase of the prison population, though likely in the short run, is unlikely in the long run. If the punishment of offenders does deter others,[6] more severe and certain punishment would keep a greater proportion of offenders behind bars, but it also would reduce the total number of offenses by deterring prospective offenders. * * *

* * *

The Importance of Doing Justice

Legislators and judges and, not least, parole boards often appear to believe that offenders are to be confined not for the crimes they committed, but for the crimes they may or may not commit. Thus, they should be confined or released not on the basis of past behavior, including crime, but on the basis of predicted future behavior. The actual length of the sentence served is made to depend on whether criminal or law abiding behavior is predicted.

As indicated, there is no basis for making such predictions other than the kind of law abiding or law breaking behavior of which courts are made aware. * * * Criminal statutes threaten with punishment those who violate them. They do not threaten punishment to those who are believed likely to break the law in the future. However, unless carried out against the guilty, the threats of the law become incredible and ineffective. And the performance of anti-social acts is encouraged as the threat that was to deter them loses its credibility.

Justice consists in meting out the punishments threatened by law and deserved by guilt to those—and only to those—who voluntarily have run the risk of suffering them, regardless of predictions, or guesses, about their future behavior. By doing justice we also hope to deter others from offenses, as they see that offenders suffer the punishments threatened. Not all will be deterred, but it seems obvious that the deterrent effectiveness of punishment depends on the certainty and severity of punishment that can be expected by law-breakers—on the expected cost of law-breaking compared to the benefits expected by the law-breaker.[7]

6. There is ample evidence, experimental and statistical, for this effect. Some of it is presented in my *Punishing Criminals: Concerning a Very Old and Painful Question* (New York: Basic Books, 1975).

7. The idea that certainty alone matters, or matters more than severity, is true under some conditions (including mostly the present ones) and not others. E.g., certainty of mild punishment invites crime. There is an optimum

Before turning to the effectiveness of punishment, let me illustrate briefly why guilt, and guilt alone, must determine the actual sentence served. Suppose a man kills his wife. Quite often such a man need not be incapacitated—he is unlikely to kill anyone else. Further, the crime itself may have fully rehabilitated him: he wanted to kill this particular woman, his wife, and having done so he may be a good citizen in the future, he may even remarry, and if he does, live ever after happily with his new wife.

We punish such a person for the sake of justice—to carry out the threat of the law, to inflict the punishment deserved—and of deterrence. We feel, in Tolstoy's words, that the seeds of every crime are in everyone of us. Hence, other husbands need to be restrained from doing what may tempt them by seeing what happens to one who has done it. This way we keep most wives surviving. Or, for that matter, most husbands. Obviously, neither rehabilitation nor incapacitation is needed or relevant—anymore than they were needed for the "Watergate" criminals, for most white collar criminals or for most "crimes of passion." But justice and deterrence are indispensable.

The threat of punishment obviously has not deterred those who are guilty of crimes. Some, to be sure, are altogether undeterrable. Others are so committed to a criminal career that they are quite unlikely to be deterred or to be rehabilitated by any reasonable punishment. (This is often the case for minor professional criminals, e.g., pickpockets.) But the threat continues to deter most of us. Those who cannot be deterred, if guilty of crimes, must be incapacitated at least temporarily, to prevent them from committing the additional crimes they would commit if free and to deter others from entering a criminal career.

I do not advocate punishment of offenders for what they have yet to do. They can only be punished for their past crimes. I do suggest, however, that the law mandate courts to impose a much more severe sentence on second offenders than on first offenders who commit serious crimes. Anyone who has not learned from his first conviction and punishment is well on his way to a criminal career; whatever mitigates a first offense does not mitigate the second. Anyone who commits a third offense must be considered a career criminal. He should, if convicted, be incapacitated for a lengthy period if his crime was violent, or if, like burglary, it involves physical exertion. He should not be released before he reaches the age of forty. At that age resumption of his criminal career is unlikely. Few people commit violent crimes after 35. Age rehabilitates. Thus, contrary to present practice, youthfulness generally requires longer, while age permits shorter, confinement: the young career criminals are most likely to commit additional crimes, and least likely to be rehabilitated. Leniency toward young career criminals is based on the sentimental but demonstrably wrong premise that they are more likely to reform than older ones. The sentiment is generous but unrealistic. And the result is not generous as far as the victims of crime are concerned. While mandatory sentences should be determined by the gravity of the crime

combination of certainty and severity, and neither variable is in principle more important than the other, since deterrence is the product of these joint causes.

as defined by the law and by the courts, upon a third conviction the offender, particularly the violent offender, should not be released before reaching the age of forty. The law should take the habitual aspect of the criminal career into consideration.[8]

It is well known that career criminals commit a disproportionate number of all crimes. Nearly 50 percent of all violent crimes are committed by career criminals, many released on parole. The abolition of parole and the appropriate mandatory flat sentencing of career criminals alone are likely to reduce the crime rate by half, merely by incapacitation, quite apart from deterrent effects. Mandatory sentencing and the abolition of parole for *all* offenders, by incapacitation and by deterrence, would decrease the crime rate much further. * * *

ADDRESS *

THE DECLINE OF THE REHABILITATIVE IDEAL IN AMERICAN CRIMINAL JUSTICE **

Francis A. Allen
27 Clev.St.L.Rev. 147 (1978).

* * *

* * * Until the mid-sixties or even the early seventies, the rehabilitative ideal was, by all odds, the dominant American theory of penal treatment. The support in the public and on the bench was perhaps not as enthusiastic as in the academic halls, but there was a wide consensus that the objective of criminal justice, however infrequently attained, ought to be rehabilitation. There are various ways the dominance of the idea can be illustrated. Almost all of the characteristic innovations in criminal justice in the 20th century are related to the rehabilitative ideal: the juvenile court, systems of probation and parole, the indeterminate sentence, the promise (if not the reality) of therapeutic programs in the prisons. Moreover, the rehabilitative ideal dominated the research interests of scientific criminology in this country. Typically, criminology was not much interested in such issues as the definition of criminal behavior, or the procedures by which criminality is determined. The criminologist took the convicted offender as a given, and proceeded to think about how a different and better person could be made out of him. This is one of the interesting instances of how an over-arching ideology determines what kinds of questions will be researched. One of the consequences of this was that until the last decade there has been no comprehensive effort to research the question of the deterrent efficacy of legal sanctions. A good deal of work in this area is now being done, but most of it has its origins in the last decade.

8. Society obviously needs less protection from one who is at the end of his criminal career. Therefore, we can do with fewer years of incapacitation. Moreover, it is likely that a year in prison at forty is subjectively a greater loss than a year in prison at twenty.

* This Address was delivered as the Twelfth Cleveland-Marshall Fund Lecture, by Professor Allen on April 13, 1978, at the Cleveland-Marshall College of Law of the Cleveland State University.

We, today, suddenly find ourselves in a situation in which there has been a massive desertion from the rehabilitative ideal and its assumptions. The significant thing is not so much that the general public has abandoned the rehabilitative ideal, or that the media have, or that the politicians have. In this country about once every seven years, since the American Revolution, we suddenly discover that we have a crime problem. And each time we discover it we forget that it ever happened before. * * *

* * *

* * * There are sentencing statutes now being passed expressly stating that rehabilitative considerations shall not be taken into account with reference to certain kinds of sentencing. It is really inconceivable that such provisions could have been enacted as recently as ten years ago. There is a great impatience with discretion in sentencing; a great desire for something called certainty in sentencing; a great impatience with high levels of criminality; strong support for vigorous measures of law enforcement; strong support for the notion of mandatory minimum sentences; and strong support for the elimination of the parole function altogether. All these things are grist for the mill in the new age that has followed the dominance of the rehabilitative ideal.

* * *

At this point I am going to advance a proposition. It is an analytic proposition, not an empirical statement, and relates to what characteristics a society must possess in order to maintain a flourishing rehabilitative ideal. * * * First, you cannot have a flourishing rehabilitative ideal unless the society as a whole has a strong faith in the malleability of human behavior and human character. It ought not to be supposed that no society could exist without that faith. The Calvinist society of Geneva with beliefs in predestination and the fixity of behavior types might constitute one example. A society founded on the assumptions of the Italian School of criminology may provide a more modern possibility. Lombroso, the leader of that School, talked about "born criminals" and viewed crime as the product of basic biological constitutional factors. If one accepts those assumptions, then penal policy is likely to be largely incapacitative, not rehabilitative in character; and in fact members of the Italian School espoused extensive use of capital punishment. There is something inherently anti-rehabilitationist about capital punishment. * * *

* * * The second proposition is that there must be a sufficient consensus of values to permit practical agreement on what it means to be rehabilitated. An example is in order. The well-known psychiatrist, Eric Fromm puts this case in one of his books. A patient comes to a psychiatrist complaining of neurotic symptoms, and the therapist discovers a deep conflict in him. The patient has been educated as an architect and his dearest wish is to practice that profession. His father, however, insists that the young man enter the family business which is facing economic difficulties. And the son sacrifices his own inclinations and aspirations and gives up his profession. The question is, of what does the cure consist in this case? What does it mean to be rehabilitated? How do you distinguish the cure from the disease? Should the objective of therapy be to cause the young man to adapt to the

decision he has made in order that he can function effectively in the family business; or should the objective be to strengthen the resolve of the young man to break away from his family ties and proceed with the realization of his own ambitions?

There is a value choice to be made. Determining the ends of rehabilitation is surrounded by value choices. And the second condition for a flourishing rehabilitative ideal is, not unanimity of values in society, but a workable consensus on what it means to be rehabilitated.

* * *

The interesting question, of course, is whether those conditions are now satisfied in this society. If they are missing, this may give some clues about why the rehabilitative ideal has declined in these times. What are the institutions that we have traditionally relied on to change human nature for the better? The answer would certainly include the family, the schools, religion, and what might broadly be called therapy. This is not meant to be an exhaustive list. My gloomy conclusion is that in each of these areas there has been a precipitous loss of confidence in the capacity of the institution to make desirable changes in human character.

First, the family. We talk about family dissolution, violence within the family, child abuse, spousal violence. We note the fact, for it is a fact, that the family has suffered in importance because many of its functions have been taken over by other agencies, and quite deliberately so. The family has lost significance as an economic unit. There are not very many of us engaged in family farming these days, in an undertaking in which every member of the family has an economic role to play. We have delegated to public schools, to government, important aspects of the family—to adolescent peer groups, to self-styled experts on child-rearing and marital counseling. The paternalism of government is so pervasive that we almost forget that it occurs. * * *

* * *

What about the public school? It is the American tradition that public schools are a marvelous instrumentality for producing the kind of character that makes a democratic society possible. That faith begins at least with Thomas Jefferson and includes many 19th century reformers like Horace Mann. Is that the aspiration we hold for the public school today? One of the things most distressing today is not so much that citizens will not vote for schools levies, but the decline in our aspirations for the schools, the decline in our confidence in what the schools can accomplish. Instead of looking at the public schools as that great instrumentality for making the democratic way possible, the most we now demand, and that very tentatively, is that high school students shall have acquired basic literacy before graduating. And there are a great many public school people who say that that demand is too severe, and that all kinds of evil things can occur if you try to enforce it. * * * Time does not permit me to discuss religion. I am interested in the implications of the "born again" movement, but I shall not pause to talk about them.

What about therapy? This is a hard and complicated issue. It is certainly true that the kinds of therapy directed to making people adjust to their circumstances is not in great repute among young people in these times. On the other hand, we are afflicted by a kind of pervasive psychologism in this country which oozes out of television talk shows and situation comedies and in a whole literature of self-improvement, written, however, by persons other than the self to be improved. This psychologism performs the alchemy of transforming what are basically fundamental moral and ethical issues or basic issues of public policy into occasions for therapeutic manipulation. Despite the decline in the rehabilitative ideal, I see no corresponding decline in this pervasive psychologism. On the other hand, this kind of psychologism is directed to providing ease, comfort and excuse. It is not directed to bringing people together for the purpose of achieving major social objectives.

This does not present an inspiring view of the modern world. I am saying that there has, in fact, developed in this country a serious loss in the vibrancy of expectations about the capacity of our institutions to affect human character and behavior for the better. I also conclude that there has been a decline in the consensus of values relevant to the ends of rehabilitation, even though I shall not be able to develop that point in detail. Whatever the intellectual case against the rehabilitative ideal may be (and there is a case to be made) the decline in the rehabilitative ideal is not primarily the product of the case made. The decline is much more closely related to various cultural phenomena, most of which are not directly associated with criminal justice at all.

And so we enter a new era. It is an era in which we are very much concerned about granting discretion to public officials. This is one of the legacies of Viet Nam and Watergate. It is an era in which we are very much concerned in seeing that criminal sentences are certain, that criminal penalties are vigorously imposed. No doubt many of these tendencies are well justified by the circumstances of the times. But we need to understand that every stance that one takes toward a complex social issue has its own distinctive and peculiar pathologies. We ought not to think that in choosing a stance one can avoid fundamental difficulties. And the new stance in criminal justice today produces such difficulties. For example, if you say that it is a bad thing (and it is) to impose widely different penalties on two people who have done the same thing, one is recognizing a genuine problem of injustice that has caused deep concern, and properly so. But the other side of the coin is that there is another kind of injustice that results from providing the same penalty to persons who have done different things. * * * And one of the problems of present sentencing schemes is that in the effort to avoid disparities resulting from punishing people differently who have done the same thing, we may now tend to punish people the same way who have committed crimes in very different circumstances. The possibilities of legal definitions being made sufficiently precise to avoid that problem are very remote.

Maybe we don't know very much about how to make prisoners better—I think we don't. But the whole history of the prison indicates that we know a great deal about how to make them worse; so that even if the rehabilitative ideal is rejected, no sane society can avoid the problem of how to mitigate the harms created by its own penal efforts. We are going to have to worry about this unless we are simply blind. That means that some of the same concerns that were rampant during the dominance of the rehabilitative ideal will have to be considered again.

There is another thing, and with this I shall conclude. I was one of those who vigorously criticized the rehabilitative ideal, and I remain a critic of many of its modern manifestations. But one of the things the rehabilitative ideal did was to focus attention on the individual human being caught up in the system of criminal justice. The question is, if you forswear the rehabilitative ideal, where will the impetus come from to advance the essential decency of the system? * * * One of the consequences of the rehabilitative ideal was that there were compassionate people in institutions concerned about individual people. And even if they didn't succeed in affecting the recidivism rate, every so often they did useful things for individuals. Where is this impulse to come from in the future? I believe no matter how heinous the crime committed by the offender, we as a society cannot afford to deny him opportunities for self-improvement. I say those opportunities must be provided, that compassion and decency require that we do, and that this is true whether we embrace the rehabilitative ideal or not. I have a feeling too, that it would probably be a good thing if, now that we have become inoculated against the extravagant claims made on behalf of rehabilitation, we went back to the drawing board again and looked at some sorts of peripheral things like employment training to see if, just possibly, we might be able to accomplish something a little like rehabilitation in some cases. It may be possible in this way to succeed very modestly in rehabilitating the rehabilitative ideal.

Note on the Victim and the Criminal Law

The function of the criminal law is to settle accounts between society and the accused. Traditionally, the special interest of the victim is thought irrelevant; it is up to the law of torts or other civil law to provide relief to the individual. We surround the defendant with many constitutional protections in a criminal trial and pay little or no attention to the concerns of victims. The victim's wishes as to what charge to bring or whether to bring the charge at all carries little weight—except that, if the victim does not report the crime or cooperate with the prosecution, the prosecution may fail.

The accused person who testifies may be protected from damaging cross-examination about certain crimes he has committed in the past, while the victim as a witness may be required to respond about similar crimes he has committed. Upon conviction, the court may take no steps to help the victim recover any losses and is unlikely to consult the victim about the sentence. It may not even listen to the story of the disaster the accused has caused for the victim. If the accused is imprisoned, shouting threats against the victim, the victim may not even be informed when the accused is released on parole.

Many of these difficulties could be resolved or ameliorated, without unfairness to the accused, by legislation and a little extra effort by the authorities. Recent legislation has helped in a number of jurisdictions. Victim impact statements are often received at sentencing, though in capital cases their use is barred. See Booth v. Maryland, 482 U.S. 496, 107 S.Ct. 2529, 96 L.Ed.2d 440 (1987). Some states require notice to the victim upon release of the accused.

The federal Sentencing Guidelines (see Appendix B) provide for orders of restitution.

Imaginative uses of restitution provisions have sometimes been made. See, e.g., People v. Lopez, 139 Misc.2d 448, 528 N.Y.S.2d 748 (Sup.Ct.1988), where a major drug distributor was ordered to pay restitution to a drug rehabilitation agency, as representing the harm done to drug addicts by his conduct. The amount was calculated by taking the drugs seized (17,698 bags of heroin or the equivalent), and assuming that 20 bags would be distributed to each addict-customer. This meant 898 probable addicts would have received the drugs; this amount was multiplied by the minimum annual cost of treating one addict on an out-patient basis ($2,400) to produce a restitution figure of $2,155,000. (Five hundred thousand dollars was seized at the time of defendant's arrest.)

2. The Sentencing Decision

a. NOTE: WHO DECIDES AND WHAT ARE THE CHOICES?

There are at least three sets of issues with which those seeking to resolve the problem of sentencing must deal. First come the theoretical questions raised by the materials just studied: what are the proper grounds for punishing one convicted of crime?

The second group of issues deals with the question: what kind of punishment shall be imposed, once it is decided that punishment is appropriate? (The question of capital punishment is postponed until we study murder.) These issues are related to the first group. If the only purpose of punishment is isolation of a dangerous person, a well-guarded warehouse is what is needed. If you want to teach an offender to read and write, as part of a rehabilitation program, you need a school as a part of your program.

Our prisons are overcrowded; do we need to build more, or do we need to find more alternatives to prisons? How do we spend our limited resources? Should we concentrate on improving our probation and parole systems; on assisting the prisoner about to re-enter society through halfway houses, job assistance, or counseling; on improving diagnostic and social services within the prison; on improving the pay and status of prison guards; or what?

From the point of view of deterrence, most authorities believe that a great likelihood of being caught and being given some significant punishment is more likely to deter than severe sentences combined with a small likelihood of being caught and convicted. The size and the complex problems (especially in the cities) of our society overload our police departments and criminal courts. This is one reason why prison sentences in the United States tend to be longer than in most of the rest of the world, while a great many criminals remain unconvicted. Long sentences have the virtue of keeping criminals who might repeat out of action, but they also involve costs, not only in the dollars needed to keep the system running, but in the counterproductive effects which may be produced on the will and even on the capacity of the prisoner to function as a law-abiding member of society when released.

I have sometimes half seriously suggested to students that the greatest reform possible in punishment methods would be to return to the stocks as the principal method of punishing convicts who are neither to be warehoused for long periods because of their dangerousness nor released on probation. It cannot be denied that the stocks are cheap. Public demand that convicts suffer would be met, and a safety valve for public rage at crime would be provided in permitting garbage to be thrown at the prisoners. There would certainly be some measure of deterrent force. The discomfort and humiliation felt by the convicted might have as much of a reforming effect on the convict as prison, and a good many of the negative effects of prison would be eliminated. There would be no graduate school of crime, no brutal government by inmates, and a reduced likelihood of complete alienation from society; jobs and family relationships might be preserved. The world does not seem ready for so radical a proposal. But imaginative sentencing alternatives are constantly surfacing. A convict in a relatively stable social situation may be allowed to serve a sentence of imprisonment only on nights and weekends. A school vandal may be sentenced to assisting in school maintenance or repair work, or a white collar criminal to giving lectures on problems of morality in the corporate setting. Ask yourself to what extent these are good ideas.

Today, prisons differ according to whether they are maximum security institutions or designed for the less dangerous inmate. They might differ more. Perhaps a single sentence calls for different prison environments at different times. Suppose we sentenced all who were to go to prison (except those who were to be warehoused) to an initial six months in what might be characterized as an extreme marine boot camp environment: no visitors, no television, unappetizing food, etc. The purposes of this would be to make every prisoner resolve to avoid entering the prison system again and to satisfy public demand for punishment. At the end of the six month period, prisoners would be sent elsewhere, where the main emphasis would be rehabilitation and preparation for rejoining society.

Apart from decisions about the proper grounds of punishment and the kinds of punishment to be imposed we must decide the question: who makes the various decisions which determine what punishment is to be in each individual case? Today, in most jurisdictions, legislators, judges, and parole boards are involved, but the amount of responsibility in the hands of each varies considerably.

In a system in which the legislature takes a maximum role, the legislature may specify exact sentences for all crimes, leaving little or no discretion to judges, and it may abolish the parole board altogether. The legislative scheme might be a complex one, taking into account many factors relevant to sentencing. Different sentences might be specified for two persons, each of whom burned a warehouse in an attempt to defraud an insurance company. Sentencing specifications might take into account that A had a number of prior arson convictions and appeared to be a professional torch, while B was a first offender who had burned his own property, and that A had been indifferent to the risk to the life of a night watchman, while B had taken precautions to make sure that nobody was on the premises when the fire was started. The sentencing judge might be authorized to depart from the scheme to a limited extent if he found the existence of special circumstances not adequately taken into account in the scheme and if he provided a written memorandum of his reasons.

The advantage of such a plan is certainty and, in a sense, fairness. The punishment is made to fit the crime; sentences are predictable and understandable to those who are convicted; surface disparities are reduced to a minimum. Arguable disadvantages center about three points: (1) Is it possible for any scheme, no matter how elaborate, to think of everything relevant in advance? (2) Are we willing to abandon the idea of sentence reduction if the prisoner appears to be rehabilitated? (3) Will legislators respond to public fear and hatred of crime by locking us in to a system which makes them look good but is not necessarily effective—by simply providing high mandatory penalties for most crimes?

A system which gives maximum sentencing discretion to the judge would have the legislature provide wide ranges of permissible penalties for each offense, and would abolish the parole board, or limit its powers in the face of directions from the sentencing judge. The big advantage of such a plan is that the person who is in the best position to be aware of all relevant sentencing factors makes the decision. The judge has seen the defendant at the trial or at the time of the guilty plea and knows something of the crime and of the defendant's history. He may have the advantage of evidence introduced at a sentencing hearing or of a thorough pre-sentencing report prepared by the probation department. He can, however, only guess how well the defendant will do as a prisoner or probationer. A greater disadvantage is, at least in theory, wide disparity in sentencing from one judge to another. Judges may have eccentric ideas about particular crimes or particular classes of the criminal population. Two burglars may find themselves cellmates and discover that one of them is in for two years and the other for ten, though the circumstances of the two crimes appear to be similar. Of course, many of these apparent disparities are explained by actual, though not obvious, differences in the circumstances. To the extent that undesirable disparities exist, informal sentencing guidelines, required explanatory sentencing memoranda, or sentence review may reduce the scope of the problem.

Guidelines which are more than merely suggestions have been adopted for the federal system; substantial excerpts from these guidelines are reprinted in Appendix B to this casebook. The guidelines provide elaborate criteria for specifying the seriousness of the offense and the criminal history of the offender. They allow a sentencing judge to read from a grid the appropriate sentence, with only variations of a few months allowed. Departures from the guidelines are authorized in some situations. While many sentencing judges believe that they do not provide sufficient flexibility, the guidelines have been upheld against charges that they violate the separation of powers principle and constitute an excessive delegation of legislative powers. Mistretta v. United States, 488 U.S. 361, 109 S.Ct. 647, 102 L.Ed.2d 714 (1989).

Judges are apt to be more shielded from political pressures and public passions than legislators or members of parole boards. While judicial indifference to the feelings of society is not an unalloyed virtue, a certain degree of detachment works for justice.

Various ideas are advanced with the intention of improving the fairness or accuracy of the sentencing process. Some people, for example, see plea bargaining as a process which distorts the sentencing decision. While the bargain may reflect a more accurate assessment of the conduct of the accused than represented by the original charge, it is likely that pressures of time and numbers of cases or difficulties in producing evidence will induce the prosecutor to settle for something less than the defendant's conduct appears to warrant. A robber may be allowed to plead guilty to the less serious crime of grand larceny because of fears that the jury may not believe an identification witness or because the prosecutor's staff is heavily involved in more important cases. Sometimes a favorable sentencing recommendation will help to achieve a plea bargain. Some would encourage the judge to seek to determine the "real crime" and, if he finds it to be robbery rather than the grand larceny reflected in the plea, to sentence accordingly, so far as the statutes permit. At first consideration, this might appear to make sentencing more just and more accurate. Notice, however, that it creates problems for the effectiveness of the plea bargaining process, which may be necessary for the working of the system. It also permits the judge to act on what he suspects but has not been proved to him, and this raises serious questions of fairness and constitutionality. Finally, what happens as a practical matter when a judge is perceived to practice "real crime" sentencing? If the prosecutor wants a plea bargain, he will have to find a way to frustrate the intention of the judge. Perhaps he will accept a plea to petty larceny in the borderline robbery case, and the judge will be unable to impose a severe sentence. Perhaps the judge can be kept in the dark about the robbery possibilities. This paragraph is intended as an illustration of the difficulty of imposing "just" reforms on an imperfect working system which has built-in resistance to such reforms.

A third kind of sentencing scheme would leave major decisions, not to legislators or to judges, but to parole boards. Legislation might provide for judges to give indeterminate sentences for many offenses, with wide variation between the minimum and maximum sentence to be served. The real sentencing decision (once the judge decides upon prison) would be left until near the end of the term, when the parole board has information, not only about the prisoner's history and the nature of his crime, but also about how he has behaved in prison. For those who would stress rehabilitation, the parole board is likely to play an important role. (This is not necessarily the case. Some argue with force that the only rehabilitation which works rests on the inner motivation of the prisoner to reform himself; the prisoner should not be offered any inducement in the form of a lesser sentence to reform, but should simply be given opportunities to spend his fixed sentence in a profitable way.) Leaving the decision until the end has obvious attractions, but also presents serious difficulties. Parole boards generally do not have time to deal carefully with each prisoner; they must rely heavily on recommendations of prison officials and on their quick impressions of the prisoner. It is probably not hard for a moderately clever prisoner to deceive a parole board about his character and intentions, and even good behavior in prison may mean nothing more than the convict's recognition that obeying the rules is the fastest way out to the resumption of his criminal career. Finally, parole boards, along with able and conscientious members, may contain the kind of political appointees who add nothing and subtract a lot from the effectiveness and fairness of the board.

The safest generalization about the state of punishment for crime in a particular jurisdiction is that, no matter what theories and plans are being followed, a fair percentage of the population will think that the present system is among the worst possible, and a large number of people will be arguing for something which they believe will work better. Often such proposals are very similar to plans which have been abandoned in other places in the hope of finding a superior system. This is not to say that reform movements are pointless and that no plan is any better than another. It is to suggest that we are dealing with one of society's most difficult problems, and that no perfect solution is on the horizon. We cannot be sure what to do, how to do it, where we can get the resources for it, or how to make our actions fit in with other social goals. But we had better keep working on the problem—harder and more effectively than we have in the past.

The summary of the complicated and challenging problems of punishment provided in this section is by no means sufficient for the student who is seriously interested in the problem. Your school curriculum is likely to provide advanced courses in which more attention is given to the problems of punishment. Your library is certain to provide books and periodicals dealing with aspects of the problem.

Questions

1. How would one like Chip (page 12) be sentenced under the federal guidelines? (See Appendix B.) Assume that Chip was enrolled at West Point instead of Ohypo State and that federal law applies. Assume further that there is no federal statute relating specifically to the sort of computer fraud involved in Chip's case, and that he is convicted of the felony of record destruction as to the loan only, under a provision for which § 2F1.1 (*Fraud and Deceit*) provides the appropriate guideline.

2. D was convicted of a minor (non-sexual) assault in 1985 and given a sentence of six months probation. In August, 1986, he was convicted of selling obscene publications by mail and sentenced to twelve months in jail. In May, 1988, he got a job as janitor in a child day care center and committed a sexual assault on a six year old child. A week later, when not in any danger of arrest, he went to the police and confessed to this act and volunteered information which led to the conviction of a teacher at the day care center of twelve acts of sexual child abuse. He is in 1991 to be sentenced under the guidelines for the felony of criminal sexual abuse. What is his sentence?

3. D, wearing a mask, in a bank pointed a revolver which she had found in a trash can at a bank teller and demanded $5,000. The teller fainted, and D dropped the gun and ran away without getting any money. D repented her act, and for six years led a blameless life, holding a productive job and engaging in extensive community service. Her fingerprints were on file, and by chance they were matched with the fingerprints on the gun. She was convicted of the felony of attempted robbery, her first offense. What is her sentence under the guidelines?

b. PROPORTIONALITY

Solem v. Helm

Supreme Court of the United States, 1983.
463 U.S. 277, 103 S.Ct. 3001, 77 L.Ed.2d 637.

JUSTICE POWELL delivered the opinion of the Court.

The issue presented is whether the Eighth Amendment proscribes a life sentence without possibility of parole for a seventh nonviolent felony.

I

By 1975 the State of South Dakota had convicted respondent Jerry Helm of six nonviolent felonies. In 1964, 1966, and 1969 Helm was convicted of third-degree burglary. In 1972 he was convicted of obtaining money under false pretenses. In 1973 he was convicted of grand larceny. And in 1975 he was convicted of third-offense driving while intoxicated. The record contains no details about the circumstances of any of these offenses, except that they were all nonviolent, none was a crime against a person, and alcohol was a contributing factor in each case.

In 1979 Helm was charged with uttering a "no account" check for $100.

* * *

Ordinarily the maximum punishment for uttering a "no account" check would have been five years imprisonment in the state penitentiary and a $5,000 fine. See S.D.Comp.Laws Ann. § 22–6–1(6) (1967 ed., supp. 1978) (now codified at S.D.Codified Laws § 22–6–1(7) (Supp.1982)). As a result of his criminal record, however, Helm was subject to South Dakota's recidivist statute:

> "When a defendant has been convicted of at least three prior convictions [*sic*] in addition to the principal felony, the sentence for the principal felony shall be enhanced to the sentence for a Class 1 felony." S.D.Codified Laws § 22–7–8 (1979) (amended 1981).

The maximum penalty for a "Class 1 felony" was life imprisonment in the state penitentiary and a $25,000 fine. S.D.Comp.Laws Ann. § 22–6–1(2) (1967 ed., supp. 1978) (now codified at S.D.Codified Laws § 22–6–1(3) (Supp.1982)). Moreover, South Dakota law explicitly provides that parole is unavailable: "A person sentenced to life imprisonment is not eligible for parole by the board of pardons and paroles." S.D.Codified Laws § 24–15–4 (1979). The Governor is authorized to pardon prisoners, or to commute their sentences, S.D. Const., Art. IV, § 3, but no other relief from sentence is available even to a rehabilitated prisoner.

Immediately after accepting Helm's guilty plea, the South Dakota Circuit Court sentenced Helm to life imprisonment under § 22–7–8. * * * The South Dakota Supreme Court, in a 3–2 decision, affirmed the sentence despite Helm's argument that it violated the Eighth Amendment.

After Helm had served two years in the state penitentiary, he requested the Governor to commute his sentence to a fixed term of years. Such a commutation would have had the effect of making Helm eligible to be considered for parole when he had served three-fourths of his new sentence. See S.D. Codified Laws § 24–15–5(3) (1979). The Governor denied Helm's request in May 1981.

In November 1981, Helm sought habeas relief in the United States District Court for the District of South Dakota. Helm argued, among other things, that his sentence constituted cruel and unusual punishment under the Eighth and Fourteenth Amendments. Although the District Court recognized that the sentence was harsh, it concluded that this Court's recent decision in Rummel v. Estelle, 445 U.S. 263, 100 S.Ct. 1133, 63 L.Ed.2d 382 (1980), was dispositive. It therefore denied the writ.

The United States Court of Appeals for the Eighth Circuit reversed. 684 F.2d 582 (1982). * * *

We granted certiorari to consider the Eighth Amendment question presented by this case. We now affirm.

II

The Eighth Amendment declares: "Excessive bail shall not be required, nor excessive fines imposed, nor cruel and unusual punishments inflicted." The final clause prohibits not only barbaric punishments, but also sentences that are disproportionate to the crime committed.

A

The principle that a punishment should be proportionate to the crime is deeply rooted and frequently repeated in common-law jurisprudence. In 1215 three chapters of Magna Carta were devoted to the rule that "amercements"[8] may not be excessive. And the principle was repeated and extended in the First Statute of Westminster, 3 Edw. I, ch. 6 (1275). These were not hollow guarantees, for the royal courts relied on them to invalidate disproportionate punishments. See, e.g., Le Gras v. Bailiff of Bishop of Winchester, Y.B.Mich. 10 Edw. II, pl. 4 (C.P. 1316), reprinted in 52 Selden Society 3 (1934). When prison sentences became the normal criminal sanctions, the common law recognized that these, too, must be proportional. See, e.g., Hodges v. Humkin, 2 Bulst. 139, 140, 80 Eng.Rep. 1015, 1016 (K.B. 1615) (Croke, J.) ("imprisonment ought always to be according to the quality of the offence").

The English Bill of Rights repeated the principle of proportionality in language that was later adopted in the Eighth Amendment: "excessive Baile ought not to be required nor excessive Fines imposed nor cruell and unusuall Punishments inflicted." 1 W. & M., sess. 2, ch. 2 (1689). * * *

* * * Although the Framers may have intended the Eighth Amendment to go beyond the scope of its English counterpart, their use of the language of the English Bill of Rights is convincing proof that they intended to provide at least the same protection—including the right to be free from excessive punishments.

B

The constitutional principle of proportionality has been recognized explicitly in this Court for almost a century. In the leading case of Weems v. United States, 217 U.S. 349, 30 S.Ct. 544, 54 L.Ed. 793 (1910), the defendant had been convicted of falsifying a public document and sentenced to 15 years of "cadena temporal," a form of imprisonment that included hard labor in chains and permanent civil disabilities. The Court noted "that it is a precept of justice that punishment for crime should be graduated and proportioned to offense," id., at 367, 30 S.Ct., at 549, and held that the sentence violated the Eighth Amendment. The Court endorsed the principle of proportionality as a constitutional standard, see, e.g., id., at 372–373, 30 S.Ct., at 551, and determined that the sentence before it was "cruel in its

8. An amercement was similar to a modern-day fine. It was the most common criminal sanction in 13th century England. See 2 F. Pollock & F. Maitland, The History of English Law 513–515 (2d ed. 1909).

excess of imprisonment," id., at 377, 30 S.Ct., at 553, as well as in its shackles and restrictions.

The Court next applied the principle to invalidate a criminal sentence in Robinson v. California, 370 U.S. 660, 82 S.Ct. 1417, 8 L.Ed.2d 758 (1962). A 90-day sentence was found to be excessive for the crime of being "addicted to the use of narcotics." The Court explained that "imprisonment for ninety days is not, in the abstract, a punishment which is either cruel or unusual." Thus there was no question of an inherently barbaric punishment. "But the question cannot be considered in the abstract. Even one day in prison would be a cruel and unusual punishment for the 'crime' of having a common cold."

Most recently, the Court has applied the principle of proportionality to hold capital punishment excessive in certain circumstances. Enmund v. Florida, 458 U.S. 782, 102 S.Ct. 3368, 73 L.Ed.2d 1140 (1982) (death penalty excessive for felony murder when defendant did not take life, attempt to take life, or intend that a life be taken or that lethal force be used); Coker v. Georgia, 433 U.S. 584, 592, 97 S.Ct. 2861, 2866, 53 L.Ed.2d 982 (1977) (plurality opinion) ("sentence of death is grossly disproportionate and excessive punishment for the crime of rape"); id., at 601, 97 S.Ct., at 2870 (POWELL, J., concurring in the judgment in part and dissenting in part) ("ordinarily death is disproportionate punishment for the crime of raping an adult woman"). * * *

C

There is no basis for the State's assertion that the general principle of proportionality does not apply to felony prison sentences. The constitutional language itself suggests no exception for imprisonment. We have recognized that the Eighth Amendment imposes "parallel limitations" on bail, fines, and other punishments, Ingraham v. Wright, 430 U.S., at 664, 97 S.Ct., at 1408, and the text is explicit that bail and fines may not be excessive. It would be anomalous indeed if the lesser punishment of a fine and the greater punishment of death were both subject to proportionality analysis, but the intermediate punishment of imprisonment were not. There is also no historical support for such an exception. * * *

In sum, we hold as a matter of principle that a criminal sentence must be proportionate to the crime for which the defendant has been convicted. Reviewing courts, of course, should grant substantial deference to the broad authority that legislatures necessarily possess in determining the types and limits of punishments for crimes, as well as to the discretion that trial courts possess in sentencing convicted criminals.[16] But no penalty is *per se* constitu-

16. Contrary to the dissent's suggestions, * * * we do not adopt or imply approval of a general rule of appellate review of sentences. Absent specific authority, it is not the role of an appellate court to substitute its judgment for that of the sentencing court as to the appropriateness of a particular sentence; rather, in applying the Eighth Amendment the appellate court decides only whether the sentence under review is within constitutional limits. In view of the substantial deference that must be accorded legislatures and sentencing courts, a reviewing court rarely will be required to engage in extended analysis to determine that a sentence is not constitutionally disproportionate.

tional. As the Court noted in Robinson v. California, 370 U.S., at 667, 82 S.Ct., at 1420, a single day in prison may be unconstitutional in some circumstances.

III

A

When sentences are reviewed under the Eighth Amendment, courts should be guided by objective factors that our cases have recognized. First, we look to the gravity of the offense and the harshness of the penalty. In *Enmund,* for example, the Court examined the circumstances of the defendant's crime in great detail. In *Coker* the Court considered the seriousness of the crime of rape, and compared it to other crimes, such as murder. In *Robinson* the emphasis was placed on the nature of the "crime." And in *Weems,* the Court's opinion commented in two separate places on the pettiness of the offense. Of course, a court must consider the severity of the penalty in deciding whether it is disproportionate.

Second, it may be helpful to compare the sentences imposed on other criminals in the same jurisdiction. If more serious crimes are subject to the same penalty, or to less serious penalties, that is some indication that the punishment at issue may be excessive. Thus in *Enmund* the Court noted that all of the other felony murderers on death row in Florida were more culpable than the petitioner there. The *Weems* Court identified an impressive list of more serious crimes that were subject to less serious penalties.

Third, courts may find it useful to compare the sentences imposed for commission of the same crime in other jurisdictions. In *Enmund* the Court conducted an extensive review of capital punishment statutes and determined that "only about a third of American jurisdictions would ever permit a defendant [such as Enmund] to be sentenced to die." Even in those jurisdictions, however, the death penalty was almost never imposed under similar circumstances. The Court's review of foreign law also supported its conclusion. The analysis in *Coker* was essentially the same. And in *Weems* the Court relied on the fact that, under federal law, a similar crime was punishable by only two years' imprisonment and a fine.

In sum, a court's proportionality analysis under the Eighth Amendment should be guided by objective criteria, including (i) the gravity of the offense and the harshness of the penalty; (ii) the sentences imposed on other criminals in the same jurisdiction; and (iii) the sentences imposed for commission of the same crime in other jurisdictions.

B

Application of these factors assumes that courts are competent to judge the gravity of an offense, at least on a relative scale. In a broad sense this assumption is justified, and courts traditionally have made these judgments—just as legislatures must make them in the first instance. Comparisons can be made in light of the harm caused or threatened to the victim or society, and the culpability of the offender. Thus in *Enmund* the Court determined that the petitioner's conduct was not as serious as his accomplices' conduct. Indeed, there are widely shared views as to the relative seriousness of crimes. See Rossi, Waite, Bose & Berk, The Seriousness of Crimes: Normative Structure and Individual Differences, 39 Am.Soc.Rev. 224, 237 (1974). For example, as the criminal laws make clear, nonviolent crimes are less serious than crimes marked by violence or the threat of violence.

There are other accepted principles that courts may apply in measuring the harm caused or threatened to the victim or society. The absolute magnitude of the crime may be relevant. Stealing a million dollars is viewed as more serious than stealing a hundred dollars—a point recognized in statutes distinguishing petty theft from grand theft. See, e.g., S.D. Codified Laws § 22–30A–17 (Supp.1982). Few would dispute that a lesser included offense should not be punished more severely than the greater offense. Thus a court is justified in viewing assault with intent to murder as more serious than simple assault. It also is generally recognized that attempts are less serious than completed crimes. See, e.g., S.D. Codified Laws § 22–4–1 (1979); 4 Blackstone * 15. Similarly, an accessory after the fact should not be subject to a higher penalty than the principal.

Turning to the culpability of the offender, there are again clear distinctions that courts may recognize and apply. In *Enmund* the Court looked at the petitioner's lack of intent to kill in determining that he was less culpable than his accomplices. Most would agree that negligent conduct is less serious than intentional conduct. * * * A court, of course, is entitled to look at a defendant's motive in committing a crime. * * *

This list is by no means exhaustive. It simply illustrates that there are generally accepted criteria for comparing the severity of different crimes on a broad scale, despite the difficulties courts face in attempting to draw distinctions between similar crimes.

C

Application of the factors that we identify also assumes that courts are able to compare different sentences. This assumption, too, is justified. The easiest comparison, of course, is between capital punishment and noncapital punishments, for the death penalty is different from other punishments in kind rather than degree. For sentences of imprisonment, the problem is not so much one of ordering, but one of line-drawing. It is clear that a 25-year sentence generally is more severe than a 15-year sentence, but in most cases it would be difficult to decide that the former violates the Eighth Amendment while the latter does not. Decisions of this kind, although troubling, are not unique to this area. The courts are constantly called upon to draw similar lines in a variety of contexts.

* * *

IV

It remains to apply the analytical framework established by our prior decisions to the case before us. We first consider the relevant criteria, viewing Helm's sentence as life imprisonment without possibility of parole.

We then consider the State's argument that the possibility of commutation is sufficient to save an otherwise unconstitutional sentence.

A

Helm's crime was "one of the most passive felonies a person could commit." State v. Helm, 287 N.W.2d, at 501 (Henderson, J., dissenting). It involved neither violence nor threat of violence to any person. The $100 face value of Helm's "no account" check was not trivial, but neither was it a large amount. One hundred dollars was less than half the amount South Dakota required for a felonious theft. It is easy to see why such a crime is viewed by society as among the less serious offenses.

Helm, of course, was not charged simply with uttering a "no account" check, but also with being an habitual offender. And a State is justified in punishing a recidivist more severely than it punishes a first offender. Helm's status, however, cannot be considered in the abstract. His prior offenses, although classified as felonies, were all relatively minor. All were nonviolent and none was a crime against a person. Indeed, there was no minimum amount in either the burglary or the false pretenses statutes, and the minimum amount covered by the grand larceny statute was fairly small.

Helm's present sentence is life imprisonment without possibility of parole. Barring executive clemency, Helm will spend the rest of his life in the state penitentiary. This sentence is far more severe than the life sentence we considered in Rummel v. Estelle. Rummel was likely to have been eligible for parole within 12 years of his initial confinement, a fact on which the Court relied heavily. Helm's sentence is the most severe punishment that the State could have imposed on any criminal for any crime. Only capital punishment, a penalty not authorized in South Dakota when Helm was sentenced, exceeds it.

We next consider the sentences that could be imposed on other criminals in the same jurisdiction. * * *

* * *

In sum, there were a handful of crimes that were necessarily punished by life imprisonment: murder, and, on a second or third offense, treason, first degree manslaughter, first degree arson, and kidnapping. There was a larger group for which life imprisonment was authorized in the discretion of the sentencing judge, including: treason, first degree manslaughter, first degree arson, and kidnapping; attempted murder, placing an explosive device on an aircraft, and first degree rape on a second or third offense; and any felony after three prior offenses. Finally, there was a large group of very serious offenses for which life imprisonment was not authorized, including a third offense of heroin dealing or aggravated assault.

Criminals committing any of these offenses ordinarily would be thought more deserving of punishment than one uttering a "no account" check—even when the bad-check writer had already committed six minor felonies. Moreover, there is no indication in the record that any habitual offender other than Helm has ever been given the maximum sentence on the basis of comparable crimes. It is more likely that the possibility of life imprisonment under § 22–

7–8 generally is reserved for criminals such as fourth-time heroin dealers, while habitual bad-check writers receive more lenient treatment. In any event, Helm has been treated in the same manner as, or more severely than, criminals who have committed far more serious crimes.

Finally, we compare the sentences imposed for commission of the same crime in other jurisdictions. The Court of Appeals found that "Helm could have received a life sentence without parole for his offense in only one other state, Nevada," 684 F.2d, at 586, and we have no reason to doubt this finding. At the very least, therefore, it is clear that Helm could not have received such a severe sentence in 48 of the 50 States. But even under Nevada law, a life sentence without possibility of parole is merely authorized in these circumstances. See Nev.Rev.Stat. § 207.010(2) (1981). We are not advised that any defendant such as Helm, whose prior offenses were so minor, actually has received the maximum penalty in Nevada.

It appears that Helm was treated more severely than he would have been in any other State.

B

The State argues that the present case is essentially the same as *Rummel v. Estelle,* for the possibility of parole in that case is matched by the possibility of executive clemency here. The State reasons that the Governor could commute Helm's sentence to a term of years. We conclude, however, that the South Dakota commutation system is fundamentally different from the parole system that was before us in *Rummel.*

As a matter of law, parole and commutation are different concepts, despite some surface similarities. Parole is a regular part of the rehabilitative process. Assuming good behavior, it is the normal expectation in the vast majority of cases. The law generally specifies when a prisoner will be eligible to be considered for parole, and details the standards and procedures applicable at that time. See, e.g., Greenholtz v. Nebraska Penal Inmates, 442 U.S. 1, 99 S.Ct. 2100, 60 L.Ed.2d 668 (1979) (detailing Nebraska parole procedures); Morrissey v. Brewer, 408 U.S. 471, 477, 92 S.Ct. 2593, 2598, 33 L.Ed.2d 484 (1972) ("the practice of releasing prisoners on parole before the end of their sentences has become an integral part of the penological system"). Thus it is possible to predict, at least to some extent, when parole might be granted. Commutation, on the other hand, is an *ad hoc* exercise of executive clemency. A Governor may commute a sentence at any time for any reason without reference to any standards. See, e.g., Connecticut Board of Pardons v. Dumschat, 452 U.S. 458, 101 S.Ct. 2460, 69 L.Ed.2d 158 (1981).

* * *

The Texas and South Dakota systems in particular are very different. In *Rummel,* the Court did not rely simply on the existence of some system of parole. Rather it looked to the provisions of the system presented, including the fact that Texas had "a relatively liberal policy of granting 'good time' credits to its prisoners, a policy that historically has allowed a prisoner serving a life sentence to become eligible for parole in as little as 12 years." 445

U.S., at 280, 100 S.Ct., at 1142. A Texas prisoner became eligible for parole when his calendar time served plus "good conduct" time equaled one-third of the maximum sentence imposed or 20 years, whichever is less. Tex.Code Crim.Proc.Ann., Art. 42.12, § 15(b) (Vernon 1979). An entering prisoner earned 20 days good-time per 30 days served, Brief for Respondent in *Rummel,* O.T.1979, No. 78–6386, p. 16, and this could be increased to 30 days good-time per 30 days served, Tex.Rev.Civ.Stat.Ann., Art. 6181–1, §§ 2–3 (Vernon Supp.1982). Thus Rummel could have been eligible for parole in as few as 10 years, and could have expected to become eligible, in the normal course of events, in only 12 years.

In South Dakota commutation is more difficult to obtain than parole. For example, the board of pardons and paroles is authorized to make commutation recommendations to the Governor, but § 24–13–4 provides that "no recommendation for the commutation of * * * a life sentence, or for a pardon * * *, shall be made by less than the unanimous vote of all members of the board." In fact, no life sentence has been commuted in over eight years, while parole—where authorized—has been granted regularly during that period. Furthermore, even if Helm's sentence were commuted, he merely would be eligible to be considered for parole. Not only is there no guarantee that he would be paroled, but the South Dakota parole system is far more stringent than the one before us in *Rummel.* Helm would have to serve three-fourths of his revised sentence before he would be eligible for parole, § 24–15–5, and the provision for good-time credits is less generous, § 24–5–1.

The possibility of commutation is nothing more than a hope for "an *ad hoc* exercise of clemency." It is little different from the possibility of executive clemency that exists in every case in which a defendant challenges his sentence under the Eighth Amendment. Recognition of such a bare possibility would make judicial review under the Eighth Amendment meaningless.

V

The Constitution requires us to examine Helm's sentence to determine if it is proportionate to his crime. * * * We conclude that his sentence is significantly disproportionate to his crime, and is therefore prohibited by the Eighth Amendment. The judgment of the Court of Appeals is accordingly

Affirmed.

CHIEF JUSTICE BURGER, with whom JUSTICE WHITE, JUSTICE REHNQUIST, and JUSTICE O'CONNOR join, dissenting.

The controlling law governing this case is crystal clear, but today the Court blithely discards any concept of *stare decisis,* trespasses gravely on the authority of the States, and distorts the concept of proportionality of punishment by tearing it from its moorings in capital cases. Only two Terms ago, we held in Rummel v. Estelle, 445 U.S. 263, 100 S.Ct. 1133, 63 L.Ed.2d 382 (1980), that a life sentence imposed after only a *third* nonviolent felony conviction did not constitute cruel and unusual punishment under the Eighth Amendment. Today, the Court ignores its recent precedent and holds that a life sentence imposed after a *seventh* felony conviction constitutes cruel and unusual punishment under the Eighth Amendment. Moreover, I reject the fiction that all Helm's crimes were innocuous or nonviolent. Among his felonies were three burglaries and a third conviction for drunk driving. By comparison Rummel was a relatively "model citizen." Although today's holding cannot rationally be reconciled with *Rummel,* the Court does not purport to overrule *Rummel.* I therefore dissent.

I

* * *

B

* * *

Rummel, in this Court, advanced precisely the same arguments that respondent advances here; we rejected those arguments notwithstanding that his case was stronger than respondent's. The test in *Rummel* which we rejected would have required us to determine on an abstract moral scale whether Rummel had received his "just deserts" for his crimes. We declined that invitation; today the Court accepts it. Will the Court now recall Rummel's case so five justices will not be parties to "disproportionate" criminal justice?

* * *

The lesson the *Rummel* Court drew from *Weems* and from the capital punishment cases was that the Eighth Amendment did not authorize courts to review sentences of *imprisonment* to determine whether they were "proportional" to the crime. * * *

* * * The *Rummel* Court emphasized, as has every opinion in capital cases in the past decade, that it was possible to draw a "bright line" between "the punishment of death and the various other permutations and commutations of punishment short of that ultimate sanction"; similarly, a line could be drawn between the punishment in *Weems* and "more traditional forms of imprisonment imposed under the Anglo-Saxon system." However, the *Rummel* Court emphasized that drawing lines between different sentences of imprisonment would thrust the Court inevitably "into the basic line-drawing process that is pre-eminently the province of the legislature" and produce judgments that were no more than the visceral reactions of individual Justices.

* * *

In short, *Rummel* held that the length of a sentence of imprisonment is a matter of legislative discretion; this is so particularly for recidivist statutes. I simply cannot understand how the Court can square *Rummel* with its holding that "a criminal sentence must be proportionate to the crime for which the defendant has been convicted."

* * *

II

Although historians and scholars have disagreed about the Framers' original intentions, the more common view seems to be that the Framers viewed the Cruel and Unusual Punishments Clause as prohibiting the kind of torture meted out during the reign of the Stuarts. Moreover, it is clear that until 1892, over 100 years after the ratification of the Bill of Rights, not a single Justice of this Court even asserted the doctrine adopted for the first time by the Court today. The prevailing view up to now has been that the Eighth Amendment reaches only the *mode* of punishment and not the length of a sentence of imprisonment. In light of this history, it is disingenuous for the Court blandly to assert that "[t]he constitutional principle of proportionality has been recognized explicitly in this Court for almost a century." That statement seriously distorts history and our cases.

This Court has applied a proportionality test only in extraordinary cases, *Weems* being one example and the line of capital cases another. The Court's reading of the Eighth Amendment as restricting legislatures' authority to choose which crimes to punish by death rests on the finality of the death sentence. Such scrutiny is not required where a sentence of imprisonment is imposed after the State has identified a criminal offender whose record shows he will not conform to societal standards.

The Court's traditional abstention from reviewing sentences of imprisonment to ensure that punishment is "proportionate" to the crime is well founded in history, in prudential considerations, and in traditions of comity. Today's conclusion by five Justices that they are able to say that one offense has less "gravity" than another is nothing other than a bald substitution of individual subjective moral values for those of the legislature. Nor, as this case well illustrates, are we endowed with Solomonic wisdom that permits us to draw principled distinctions between sentences of different length for a chronic "repeater" who has demonstrated that he will not abide by the law.

* * *

By asserting the power to review sentences of imprisonment for excessiveness the Court launches into uncharted and unchartable waters. Today it holds that a sentence of life imprisonment, without the possibility of parole, is excessive punishment for a seventh allegedly "nonviolent" felony. How about the eighth "nonviolent" felony? The ninth? The twelfth? Suppose one offense was a simple assault? Or selling liquor to a minor? Or statutory rape? Or price-fixing? The permutations are endless and the Court's opinion is bankrupt of realistic guiding principles. Instead, it casually lists several allegedly "objective" factors and arbitrarily asserts that they show respondent's sentence to be "significantly disproportionate" to his crimes. Must all these factors be present in order to hold a sentence excessive under the Eighth Amendment? How are they to be weighed against each other? Suppose several States punish severely a crime that the Court views as trivial or petty? I can see no limiting principle in the Court's holding.

There is a real risk that this holding will flood the appellate courts with cases in which equally arbitrary lines must be drawn. It is no answer to say that appellate courts must review criminal convictions in any event; up to now, that review has been on the validity of the judgment, not the sentence. The vast majority of criminal cases are disposed of by pleas of guilty, and ordinarily there is no appellate review in such cases. To require appellate review of all sentences of imprisonment—as the Court's opinion necessarily does—will "administer the *coup de grace* to the courts of appeal as we know them." H. Friendly, Federal Jurisdiction: A General View 36 (1973). This is judicial usurpation with a vengeance; Congress has pondered for decades the concept of appellate review of sentences and has hesitated to act.

III

Even if I agreed that the Eighth Amendment prohibits imprisonment "disproportionate to the crime committed," I reject the notion that respondent's sentence is disproportionate to his crimes for, if we are to have a system of laws, not men, *Rummel* is controlling.

The differences between this case and *Rummel* are insubstantial. First, Rummel committed three truly nonviolent felonies, while respondent, as noted at the outset, committed seven felonies, four of which cannot fairly be characterized as "nonviolent." At the very least, respondent's burglaries and his third-offense drunk driving posed real risk of serious harm to others. It is sheer fortuity that the places respondent burglarized were unoccupied and that he killed no pedestrians while behind the wheel. What would have happened if a guard had been on duty during the burglaries is a matter of speculation, but the possibilities shatter the notion that respondent's crimes were innocuous, inconsequential, minor, or "nonviolent." Four of respondent's crimes, I repeat, had harsh potentialities for violence. Respondent, far more than Rummel, has demonstrated his inability to bring his conduct into conformity with the minimum standards of civilized society. Clearly, this difference demolishes any semblance of logic in the Court's conclusion that respondent's sentence constitutes cruel and unusual punishment although Rummel's did not.

* * *

3. What Should Be Punished?

Introduction

When we perceive, or think we perceive, a social evil, we are apt to conclude that "there ought to be a law," and by this we usually mean a criminal law. This section is concerned with investigation of this notion. Is the criminal law always an appropriate response to a social problem? If not, can we identify factors which tend to make it inappropriate?

One question which recurs in considering what conduct should be criminal is the relationship between the criminal law and morality. Few things are criminal which are not regarded as immoral by at least a large segment of society, and many believe that those few things should not be criminal. Some things which are immoral are not criminal. To lie is not criminal except in a few special situations (e.g., perjury or obtaining property by false pretenses). Some lies are not immoral, but many which are not reached by the criminal law would be regarded as immoral by most people. Suppose a motorist in the countryside asks for the shortest route to town, and a farmer, out of sheer hatred for strangers, deliberately gives him directions for a long and difficult route. This is very unlikely to be a crime. Why should it not be?

In our analysis we might consider three groups of questions:

1. What is the nature of the harm to the person, to property, and to the social fabric brought about by the practice?
   a. Are there physical, mental, or property injuries caused by the practice?
   b. What are the indirect costs, in terms of such things as social isolation of those who fear the practice, expenses of protective devices to guard against the practice, etc.?
   c. Is there harm to the social fabric either through the existence of the practice or because failure to criminalize the practice confuses the public about acceptable social and moral principles?
2. If the practice does cause serious social harm, is the criminal law a good weapon to use against it?
   a. What harms would be brought about by criminalization of the practice, in terms of loss of freedom and lessening of social diversity?
   b. Will the criminal law be effective? How does its probable effectiveness compare with the probable effectiveness of alternative approaches, such as persuasion, education, use of civil remedies, etc.?
   c. Is there such disagreement about the merits of the practice or the proper way to deal with it that criminalization might produce sympathy for the accused or disrespect for the law?
   d. Are there constitutional constraints to be concerned about in the use of the criminal law?
3. If the practice does cause serious social harm, what are the costs of using the criminal law to attack it?
   a. How much police and prosecution effort is required?
   b. Are police and prosecution resources unavailable or needed more elsewhere?

These questions and others that they may suggest should help our consideration of particular topics. If we are asking whether shoplifting should be a crime, for example, we can point to the plain social harm caused by theft of property, the costs of detection machinery, and the probable moral outrage and confusion if the legislature repealed the statutes making shoplifting a crime. These seem to outweigh the loss of freedom for the shoplifter and the questionable enrichment of his life because shoplifting occurs. The criminal law is certainly not wholly effective in preventing shoplifting. Are there better approaches? It would seem that the criminal courts are at least necessary as one of alternative methods of dealing with the practice. There is little public sympathy with shoplifters and little feeling that they are being victimized by being subjected to the criminal process. (It is possible that some detection methods may be disapproved by the public.) There are no special constitutional problems involved in treating shoplifting as a crime. Merchants do much of the detection work themselves; the police usually appear on the scene only after the shoplifter has been caught. Processing and prosecution of many petty offenders may create a significant burden on lawyers and courts. But, while there are more serious crimes to deal with, it is doubtful that there is much harmful diversion of resources involved in prosecuting shoplifters.

As you read the material from the Model Penal Code which follows, consider how the suggested analysis applies to criminalization or decriminalization (are different considerations involved?) of private, consensual, adult, homosexual relations.

MODEL PENAL CODE § 213.2, COMMENTS 1 AND 2 *

1. *Background.* The phrase "deviate sexual intercourse" as used by the Model Code covers a number of situations that were treated differently in older law. Chiefly, it refers to "sodomy," a generic term that in its broadest import includes anal intercourse with a male or female and copulation with an animal. The term "sodomy" is also used in an older and narrower sense to describe only anal intercourse between males, and it is from this usage in the context of male homosexual relations that sodomy derives the name "crime against nature." In ancient times, sodomy was not a crime but was subject to punishment by the ecclesiastical authorities. Early statutes, however, made sodomy a secular offense, so that it was received by the American colonies as a common-law felony.

The original English enactments proscribed only anal intercourse between males, and this limitation had several peculiar consequences under derivative statutes. For one thing, the exclusion of oral sex effectively excepted female homosexuality from the realm of the criminal law, even though copulation between males was punished as a very grave offense. Moreover, different kinds of sexual activity between males became subject to dramatically disparate sanctions. Anal intercourse might be punished by a maximum term of 20 years in prison, while oral intercourse between the same persons was not reached by the early sodomy laws and would therefore be subject only to the comparatively minor sanctions authorized for such crimes as lewd and lascivious behavior.

By the time the Model Penal Code was drafted, however, most states no longer observed the early limitation of sodomy to anal copulation. The pattern at that time was to punish fellatio (oral stimulation of the penis) and cunnilingus (oral stimulation of the vulva or clitoris) as well as anal intercourse and bestiality (copulation between human and animal). This expansion of coverage was accomplished by express statutory language, by judicial interpretation of such traditional phrases as "crime against nature," and in at least one state by enactment of a separate provision against oral copulation. * * *

* * *

2. *Deviate Sexual Intercourse Between Consenting Adults.* Section 213.2 of the Model Code makes a fundamental departure from prior law in excepting from criminal sanctions deviate sexual intercourse between con-

senting adults. This policy applies to the various styles of sexual intimacy between man and wife and to sexual relations between unmarried persons, regardless of gender. Of course, the exclusion from liability does not extend to sexual relations with a person who is underage or otherwise incapable of giving meaningful consent. Such conduct is proscribed in terms by this section. Additionally, the exclusion does not reach open display, which is covered by Section 251.1 of the Model Code, nor does the exclusion reach prostitution, which constitutes an offense under Section 251.2, nor public solicitation, which is proscribed by Section 251.3. But under the Model Code deviate sexual intercourse is not criminal where both participants consent, where each is of sufficient age and mental capacity to render consent effective, and where they conduct their relations in private and create no public nuisance.

Decriminalization of consensual sodomy reaches three situations commonly covered by pre-Model Code statutes. First, it excludes the prospect of penal sanctions for untraditional sexual practices between husband and wife. * * * While it is difficult to see that non-standard sexual intimacy between spouses occasions any harm of which the state properly might take cognizance, it is easy to identify criminal sanctions for such conduct as inconsistent with the societal goal of protecting the marital relationship against outside interference. Indeed, it seems likely that the newly enunciated constitutional right of marital privacy extends to all forms of consensual sexual activity between husband and wife. It is probable, therefore, that imposition of criminal punishment for such behavior is not only unwise, but is also constitutionally impermissible. The Model Code position on this point has proved decidedly influential. Many modern revision efforts and proposed codes have excluded criminal sanctions for any form of sexual intimacy between husband and wife.

The second situation excluded from coverage is consensual sodomy between male and female outside the marital relationship. This is distinguished from the first case only in that sexual intimacy out of wedlock is not affirmatively sanctioned by law. Acceptance of the proposition that the state has no good reason to try to suppress non-standard sexual practices between married persons puts this second situation in its proper perspective. * * * The Model Code includes no penal provision against adultery or fornication, for reasons which are explained in some detail in the Note on Adultery and Fornication following the commentary to Section 213.6. The point here is only to emphasize that there is no reason to distinguish among styles of sexual intimacy for the purpose of imposing criminal sanctions on relations out of wedlock. Whatever policy governs traditional heterosexual intercourse between unmarried persons should also extend to other forms of sexual gratification by those same persons.

The third and most controversial case of consensual sodomy is homosexual relations. Here articulation of a legitimate state interest in suppression of such conduct is arguably more plausible. Because ordinary genital copulation is not possible between persons of the same gender, homosexual relations typically involve some sort of deviate sexual intercourse as that term is defined in Section 213.0. The popular aversion to such conduct arises not so much from the physical characteristics of sexuality as from the fact of sexual gratification with a person of one's own gender. This type of sexual preference constitutes a far more dramatic contravention of societal norms and prevailing moral attitudes than is involved in either of the first two situations discussed above. Continued criminal punishment of homosexual relations may be advocated on the ground that such conduct threatens the moral fabric of society by undermining the viability of the family or on the supposition that permitting such behavior between consenting adults leads inevitably to the corruption of youth. Arguments of the former sort raise the broad issue of the proper relation of the criminal law to community morality—a matter that is discussed more fully below. The view that activity between consenting adults should be proscribed in order to protect young persons flounders on the absence of either empirical data or reasoned analysis to suggest that one leads to the other. Perhaps more important than either of these factors is the simple truth that homosexuality excites widespread and often violent emotional hostility. Its manifestation in sexual conduct is viewed by many persons with a deep antipathy. The origin of this reaction is as much aesthetic as moral, and its force is not diminished by the difficulty of specifying exactly what harm is occasioned thereby. The conviction that homosexual conduct is "bad" quickly translates into the conclusion that it therefore should be punished, and there is a corresponding fear that removing criminal sanctions would amount to implied endorsement of a kind of behavior that majoritarian sentiment finds abhorrent.

While these concerns may be dispositive to some, the Model Code takes the view that private homosexual conduct between consenting adults should not be punished as a crime. In part, this conclusion stems from uncertainty about the morality of such conduct. Without delving into the question of the causes of homosexuality, one can identify at least three ways of looking at the phenomenon. First, of course, it may be regarded as a sin. Most orthodox theologies take this position, though there are increasing challenges to this view even from sources within organized religion.

Second, homosexuality may be viewed as a disease. There are two lines of thought in the disease model of homosexuality. Some theorists have posited that homosexuality is a pathological condition, the result of abnormal genetic or hormonal influences. To date, however, studies designed to show a biological basis have been inconclusive at best. Modern authorities have abandoned the position that homosexuality is an inherited genetic trait. On the other hand, many scientists today have adopted a psychological theory of homosexuality, thus viewing it as an emotional or mental disorder. The common theory is that the homosexual's emotional disturbance is caused by childhood environment. Even if this view is correct, however, homosexuality is subject to no known cure, save perhaps as psychiatry or behavior modification may attempt restructuring of the individual personality. For purposes of the criminal law, the real significance of viewing homosexuality as an illness lies not in the realms of medicine and science, but rather in the normative implications conveyed by labelling the homosexual as "sick." On the one hand, the disease model concedes that homosexual behavior is deviate, abnormal, unwelcome, and unattractive. It postulates that homosexuality should not be encouraged and that a "cure" would be desirable if one could be found. On the other hand, describing homosexuality as a kind of illness avoids imputation of moral failing to the individual so afflicted. In other words, the individual who finds himself sexually attracted to persons of his own gender is not blameworthy in the sense with which the criminal law is concerned.

The third view of homosexuality is that it is neither a sin nor an abnormality but only a difference. The notion here is that homosexual conduct is simply a matter of personal preference and is devoid of any normative content whatever. This is the position of the gay rights movement, and it may be gaining support in the community at large.

* * * Only one of the three conceptions—i.e., the view that homosexual conduct is a sin—provides an appropriate starting point for imposition of penal sanctions. No principle is more broadly accepted than that the criminal law, involving as it does both punishment and condemnation, should be concerned with conduct that is morally reprehensible or culpable. To the extent that it seems inappropriate to regard homosexual relations as blameworthy—that is, as representative of moral failing by the actor—the essential premise for assigning criminal punishment is vitiated. Of course, many in the community view homosexual conduct as morally reprehensible, but it is equally clear that many do not. Given the absence of harm to the secular interests of the community occasioned by atypical sexuality between consenting adults, the problematical nature of the underlying ethical issue should suggest the need for caution in continuing criminal proscription of this kind of behavior.

The foregoing reasoning is supportive of the Model Code position on consensual sodomy, but not essential to its acceptance. Even if one starts from the proposition that homosexual conduct is a moral default for which the actor may justifiably be condemned, there are still sufficient reasons to withhold penal sanctions. The criminal law cannot encompass all behavior that the average citizen may regard as immoral or deviate. In every field of activity the ethical precepts of the community set standards higher than the law can expediently enforce. Verbal cruelty, lying, racial and religious biases in private relationships, and the kiss that betrays a marriage are but a few examples of reprehensible conduct that no sensible legislator would make into a crime. Some of the reasons why the penal law must stop well short of encompassing all immoral conduct are eminently practical. Economic resources are finite. The amount of money that may be spent on law enforcement is limited by the wealth of the community and by the competing demands of other social interests. It seems sensible, therefore, that the criminal justice system should concentrate on repressing murder, robbery, rape, theft, and other crimes that directly threaten security of person and property. Authorization of penalties for consensual sodomy suggests not only that such conduct is wrongful, but also that it is sufficiently important to warrant diversion of resources from other areas. Furthermore, any genuine effort to enforce such prohibitions will be extremely costly and difficult. Private sexual behavior between consenting adults has no victim. There is no one who can be counted on to complain to the police or to provide evidence against suspected offenders. The resulting difficulty of identifying and convicting violators usually leads police to forego any attempt to enforce laws against consensual sodomy except in the rare case that happens to come to their attention. Cases that do surface commonly involve violence, corruption of minors, public solicitation, or some other aggravating factor that would continue to be punished under the Model Code. To the extent, however, that laws against deviate sexual behavior are enforced against private conduct between consenting adults, the result is episodic and capricious selection of an infinitesimal fraction of offenders for severe punishment. This invitation to arbitrary enforcement not only offends notions of fairness and horizontal equity, but it also creates unwarranted opportunity for private blackmail and official extortion. There is also the point that the methods available to the police for enforcing such laws involve tactics which are often unseemly and which, by their very nature, stretch the limits of constitutionality. Moreover, these costs may be incurred without gaining any corresponding benefit, for there is every reason to believe that continued criminal proscription of private sexual relations would prove largely ineffective to deter or inhibit such conduct.

To these practical concerns must be added a broader objection to criminal punishment of atypical sexual behavior between consenting adults. Any exercise of the coercive power of the state against individual citizens diminishes freedom. Nowhere is this curtailment of liberty more pronounced than where the state, acting through the penal law, punishes by incarceration. No doubt such action is necessary to prevent injury to other individuals, to guard them in the secure possession of their property, and to further the interest of all citizens in the unobstructed workings of their government. Less clearly, criminal penalties may also be appropriate in some instances where the actor's behavior does not threaten directly to impair any of these interests. The usual justification for laws against such conduct is that, even though it does not injure any identifiable victim, it contributes to moral deterioration of society. One need not endorse wholesale repeal of all "victimless" crimes in order to recognize that legislating penal sanctions solely to maintain widely held concepts of morality and aesthetics is a costly enterprise. It sacrifices personal liberty, not because the actor's conduct results in harm to another citizen but only because it is inconsistent with the majoritarian notion of acceptable behavior. * * *

* * *

* * * In 1961, Illinois became the first American jurisdiction to adopt the Model Code position. A number of other states have taken this step in recent revisions, and decriminalization of consensual sodomy is also a feature of several recently drafted proposals. The impact of the Model Code is, however, more pervasive than this summary suggests, for even though many states still punish consensual sodomy, most modern revision efforts effect a substantial reduction in the gravity of sanctions authorized for such behavior. Thus, consensual sodomy, which traditionally constituted a serious felony, is only a misdemeanor in at least seven states and is so classified under at least two proposed codes. As a practical matter, moreover, many law enforce-

ment agencies decline to enforce applicable statutes unless there exists some aggravating factor such as use of force or corruption of minors.

Note on Abortion Policy

The powerfully felt central moral positions of those who dispute abortion policy are not likely to be affected by discussion in a law school classroom. For those who hold that the fetus is a human being, how can it be right to allow killing the unoffending unborn child? Their opponents generally do not believe that the fetus is fully a human being, entitled to all human rights, and this leaves moral room for another strong argument: that a woman, as an autonomous moral agent, should properly be allowed by society to weigh all claims and decide whether to carry the fetus to term. This note attempts to bypass, so far as it is possible to do so, the question of the full humanity of the fetus, and to look at other arguments which need consideration and may profit by classroom debate, whatever position one takes on this issue.

Those who believe that abortion is morally wrong because the fetus is fully human do not put an end to discussion if their position as to the fetus is granted. As we have seen in the reading on homosexual conduct just completed, not all moral wrongs are or should be punished by the criminal law. Whether or not to punish a moral wrong depends on considerations like those involved in the debate about punishing homosexual conduct. Even those who regard homosexual acts as wrong may be persuaded that something should be granted to those who think differently, that the criminal law would be ineffective, or that the costs of criminal enforcement would be too great. So it may be with those opposed in principle to abortion.

Such arguments are perhaps more difficult to accept in the case of abortion than in the case of homosexual acts, because the life of a human being—here granting the fetus full human status for purposes of argument—is an interest less subject to erosion by other important interests than whatever interest society may have in preventing homosexual conduct. But, even interests in life are not absolute for the law. Killing in self-defense is universally justified; we may demand the knowing sacrifice of a soldier's life in wartime; some jurisdictions exact capital punishment.

Also, there are arguments that even if abortion is the taking of life, it is in a category by itself, where special rules may apply. Until viability at least, the life of the fetus is wholly dependent upon the life of another, the mother-to-be, in a way which is not duplicated in other situations. Such dependency may cut both ways: it may impose special responsibilities; it may grant special rights to the pregnant woman. Mere continuation of the pregnancy may be a serious threat to the health or life of the mother. Even if this is not the case, any state intervention to protect the fetus would be likely to restrict the freedom of the mother in unique ways; it might require her to undergo a caesarean section,[a] to remain in bed for weeks, or to undergo drug or alcohol rehabilitation, for example. Even if we decide to penalize only actions [such as abortion] and not non-actions [such as failing to alter a mother's way of life to protect the fetus], problems remain if abortion is to be criminalized.

a. This was held not required in the circumstances presented in In re A.C., 573 A.2d 1235 (D.C.App.1990) (en banc).

Abortion is not easy to detect or prosecute as a crime. Many do not disapprove of it or do not think it should be a crime. Abortions seem certain to take place in large numbers, whether criminal or not. Criminalization may only increase the risks and mortality rate among women. If the decision as to abortion, under a constitutional right of privacy theory, does not continue to reside with the woman, at least during the early part of pregnancy when the vast number of abortions is performed, it will presumably become a matter for decision in each state, with differing rules. There would surely be escape from anti-abortion rules in states with restrictive laws, at least by those who can afford travel to a more permissive jurisdiction.

For some who oppose abortion on moral grounds, these arguments are sufficient for them to oppose criminalization of abortion. For other opponents of abortion they are objections of insufficient weight to meet the argument for criminalization.

There remain further questions for discussion for those who do not reject abortion on moral grounds. Does approved, or even tolerated, abortion blunt our sensibilities and trivialize human life in other contexts? Do we put in the scale, against this possibility, what may be improvement in the quality of life for the woman or others? What is the nature of the right of an individual to do what she likes with respect to her own body, to choose whether or not to have children, and, if she chooses to have them, when to have them?

If we hold that the fetus is not, at least fully, a human being and that a woman, with medical agreement, has a "right" to determine whether to have an abortion, it need not follow that the right is absolute. Rights are not always absolute. They express important interests, which, unfortunately, tend to conflict with other important interests. We must assess the possible interests and rights in competition. There may be interests or rights in bringing the fetus to term, as well as interests or rights in termination of a pregnancy.

There are many possible interests in bringing the fetus successfully to term. If the woman herself wants to do so, no question is likely to arise; nobody suggests, absent some such extraordinary circumstance as the need to destroy the fetus to preserve the woman's life, that there is anywhere a sufficient interest to allow its destruction without the woman's consent.

Does the fetus itself, even if it is not treated as a full human being, have interests which should be considered? We might maintain that the fetus, during all or part of the time between conception and birth, though not a human being, is still entitled to some potential human status. We might presume an interest in the fetus in survival and say, for example, that it is a crime to destroy the fetus, at least without some reason that we would label adequate—perhaps its serious physical or mental defect or its coming into existence as a result of rape or incest. This was essentially the position of the American Law Institute "prior to Roe v. Wade, 410 U.S. 113, 93 S.Ct. 705, 35 L.Ed.2d 147 (1973)", which found a constitutional right to an abortion, at least in the first trimester of pregnancy.[b] (If we favor criminalization, we might make its destruction a crime as serious as murder, or we might take the position of the common law, which called abortion a lesser crime than murder or manslaughter.)

b. Doe v. Bolton, 410 U.S. 179, 93 S.Ct. 739, 35 L.Ed.2d 201 (1973), found a Georgia statute largely based on the Model Penal Code to be in violation of the woman's constitutional right of privacy.

How much respect do we grant this supposed fetal interest in continuing life? Does it prevail when the child will be born seriously defective? When it would be economically difficult for the mother or the parents to raise the child? When the unwanted child would be a poor candidate for adoption? Is it proper to increase the legal protection of the fetus as it approaches birth, as the Supreme Court has done?

We may be reluctant to grant any kind of right to the fetus, now, for purposes of argument, not granted full human status. However, some of these arguable rights can be restated as protectable interests of society, which, after all, is, in an overriding way, concerned with preservation of human life, and perhaps also of potential human life. The interest of society in promoting respect for human life may justify restriction on the right to an abortion. Roe v. Wade, which conceded possible limits on the right to an abortion as the fetus approached full term, may be regarded as an exercise in attempting to give as much as possible to the right of the woman to decide, while giving some weight to the social interest in protecting potential human life. Are there public health interests which justify regulation of abortion providers? If so, what kind of regulation?

There may be interests in others than the woman, the fetus, or society in survival of the fetus. Perhaps, for example, the father-to-be, a grandparent, or some other family member wants the child. The parents of a pregnant adolescent may have an interest in participating in the adolescent's choice, or at least in being informed of the situation. How is this to be weighed against contrary wishes of the young woman?

What interests might exist in the destruction of the fetus? Most obviously, the mother-to-be may have such an interest. It is easy, at least for men, to overlook the full impact of pregnancy and child-rearing on a woman. Even if a child is desired, limitations are imposed during and usually for years after pregnancy upon the life of the mother. If a child is not wanted, the burden, physically, mentally, economically, and in terms of what the woman wants to do with her life, may be overwhelming. Putting aside the possible hardships of pregnancy itself, a man might try to imagine being required to give primary care to a helpless person for a period of years, under circumstances in which he could not afford to hire someone else to do it, could not at the same time hold a demanding and interesting full-time job, and could not be emotionally indifferent to the fate of his charge. Relatively few men are in such a position; many women are. These considerations, at the very least, must produce compassion for anyone undergoing an unwanted pregnancy.

Women, in our society, are assigned primary responsibility for decisions in family planning. It is hard to imagine that anyone would prefer to plan through abortion, but sometimes birth control is not employed or fails, and the woman is faced with the difficult choice of a life of unwanted difficulties and complications or having an abortion, itself a traumatic experience. Should her choice be burdened by legal bars to abortion? Does potentiality for attaining human life make enough difference to outweigh the needs of those already living? Does this depend in part on society's assessment of the importance of these needs, or should society defer to individual assessment?

There may also be more remote claims to consideration by the father-to-be and by siblings or other people. How much do we care that a father-to-be does not want or is unable to care for the child after birth, or that there is a handicapped child, needing constant attention and care, already in the family, or that a child-to-be could not be cared for by its parents and has poor adoption prospects?

The fetus itself, in some circumstances, may be thought to have an interest in not surviving: its prospects for a happy or meaningful life may be remote. Society may be interested in not being burdened with the care of an unwanted or defective child.

As this is written, there is uncertainty as to how far the constitutional right provided by Roe v. Wade will survive continued scrutiny by the Supreme Court. The theoretical questions raised here may become questions of practical politics, as citizens and legislators debate what should be done about abortion.

Questions

1. Is the Model Penal Code treatment of prostitution consistent with its approach in the comments above? (See Appendix A, § 251.2.)

2. Police, prosecutors, and social workers are often reluctant to treat domestic disputes, in which the husband beats up his wife, as ordinary instances of the crime of battery. Why is this? Are they right?

3. Suppose that intermediate corporate executives, perhaps on pressure from above, enter into improper price-fixing or rebate agreements to increase corporate profits. These agreements have the effect of increasing the bills to consumers of the utility service furnished by the corporation by a few cents a year each. Should the making of such agreements be criminal? If so, should the convicted executives get prison terms?

D. CONSTRAINTS

1. Introductory Note

Even when society agrees on what it wants to punish as criminal, it operates under certain constraints which impede the discovery of the truth and the punishment of the guilty. Most of these constraints are not mere unnecessary barriers, which might be removed with better planning or more money; they are grounded on policy considerations which rank in importance to society with those which support the punishment of crime. Accommodation of partially conflicting goals is called for.

One set of constraints arises out of the very method we use to bring the guilty to justice—the adversary system. This method produces something resembling the old trial by battle. The umpire-judge sits above the fray while the champions of the people and of the defendant have at the evidence and each other. Roughly stated, the job of each lawyer is to make the best possible honest case for the side represented. This is different from an objective search for the truth, although a prosecutor, as the people's representative, has some obligation of objectivity. The evidence presented is likely to be distorted. An impressive witness, whose ideas correspond well with those of the proponent, is more likely to be called than a merely accurate one. The witness with the most objective view may be called by neither side if the jury is apt to dislike or distrust him. Some areas of possible testimony may be avoided by both sides as too hot to handle; either side might suffer disaster if the area is explored. Skilled counsel may make the worse appear the better cause, especially if the other side is inadequately represented.

While reforms are possible, our traditions make it unlikely that the adversary system will be abolished or even significantly modified. Furthermore, there is a real question whether an improvement can be found in a different method of handling the cases. The chief rival of the Anglo-American adversary system is a kind of inquisitorial system. In France, for example, a magistrate is put in charge of a criminal investigation from the beginning. His job is to investigate, develop a theory of the case, and prepare the case for trial, if trial is warranted. At the trial, the judge is likely to be influenced by the official view and to do most of the questioning of witnesses; other counsel tend to play a subsidiary and muted role. This process is apt to produce a picture which is clear, consistent, and very often correct. There is, however, a danger that the magistrate or judge will form a theory of the case which happens to be wrong. When a human being has a theory, facts and witnesses consistent with the theory tend to be remembered, emphasized, and believed; inconvenient inconsistencies may be brushed aside, consciously or unconsciously. When the adversary system works properly, the trier of fact hears two sides, robustly presented. The truth may be more likely to emerge from a contest than from a more directed presentation.

Rules of evidence may get in the way of the truth. Many of them are designed to exclude evidence which might mislead the jury or excite prejudice, but, in keeping out the dangerous, they may keep out the relevant and helpful. A complicated trial cannot be conducted without evidentiary ground rules, and any general rule will sometimes work particular injustice. It is important to keep reexamining the rules of evidence to try to assure that they tend toward maximum accuracy, fairness, and efficiency.

The federal Constitution adds important constraints of its own. Study of these forms an important part of law school courses in criminal procedure and constitutional law, and most of them must be ignored or treated only briefly here. We will give more extended attention to three constitutional constraints in the concluding part of this chapter.

There is a constitutional right of an accused person to counsel.[a] This may be inconvenient for the prosecution, at least in the early stages of the investigation, but it is important for the protection of the defendant's rights. In the complex legal world of today it is rare that a person without legal training can protect himself adequately. The scope of the right to legal representation is a matter for criminal procedure. (Interesting questions as to the ethics of representation in criminal cases also arise and should be considered elsewhere in your legal studies.)

The accused has a constitutionally protected privilege against self-incrimination. One aspect of the privilege we have already met. A criminal defendant cannot be required to testify against himself. Further, a witness in any proceeding has a privilege to refuse to answer particular questions which might tend to incriminate him. (The criminal defendant substantially waives this privilege by electing to testify at his trial.) The privilege even applies in pre-trial investigations by the police and prosecutor. You will probably study the nature and scope of the privilege in courses in criminal procedure, evidence, or constitutional law.

a. See p. 11, supra.

The courses in constitutional law or criminal procedure will also bring you to a study of such broad-gauged constitutional requirements as that of due process of law. Very generally, due process in criminal cases requires that legal proceedings be carried out according to principles which help to assure fairness to the accused.

2. The Right of Privacy

Bowers v. Hardwick

Supreme Court of the United States, 1986.
478 U.S. 186, 106 S.Ct. 2841, 92 L.Ed.2d 140.

JUSTICE WHITE delivered the opinion of the Court.

In August 1982, respondent Hardwick (hereafter respondent) was charged with violating the Georgia statute criminalizing sodomy [1] by committing that act with another adult male in the bedroom of respondent's home. After a preliminary hearing, the District Attorney decided not to present the matter to the grand jury unless further evidence developed.

Respondent then brought suit in the Federal District Court, challenging the constitutionality of the statute insofar as it criminalized consensual sodomy. He asserted that he was a practicing homosexual, that the Georgia sodomy statute, as administered by the defendants, placed him in imminent danger of arrest, and that the statute for several reasons violates the Federal Constitution. The District Court granted the defendants' motion to dismiss for failure to state a claim * * *.

A divided panel of the Court of Appeals for the Eleventh Circuit reversed. * * *

Because other Courts of Appeals have arrived at judgments contrary to that of the Eleventh Circuit in this case, we granted the Attorney General's petition for certiorari questioning the holding that the sodomy statute violates the fundamental rights of homosexuals. We agree with petitioner that the Court of Appeals erred, and hence reverse its judgment.

This case does not require a judgment on whether laws against sodomy between consenting adults in general, or between homosexuals in particular, are wise or desirable. It raises no question about the right or propriety of state legislative decisions to repeal their laws that criminalize homosexual sodomy, or of state-court decisions invalidating those laws on state constitutional grounds. The issue presented is whether the Federal Constitution confers a fundamental right upon homosexuals to engage in sodomy and hence invalidates the laws of the many States that still make such conduct illegal and have done so for a very long time. The case also calls for some

1. Georgia Code Ann. § 16–6–2 (1984) provides, in pertinent part, as follows:

"(a) A person commits the offense of sodomy when he performs or submits to any sexual act involving the sex organs of one person and the mouth or anus of another. * * *

"(b) A person convicted of the offense of sodomy shall be punished by imprisonment for not less than one nor more than 20 years. * * * "

judgment about the limits of the Court's role in carrying out its constitutional mandate.

We first register our disagreement with the Court of Appeals and with respondent that the Court's prior cases have construed the Constitution to confer a right of privacy that extends to homosexual sodomy and for all intents and purposes have decided this case. The reach of this line of cases was sketched in Carey v. Population Services International, 431 U.S. 678, 685, 97 S.Ct. 2010, 2016, 52 L.Ed.2d 675 (1977). Pierce v. Society of Sisters, 268 U.S. 510, 45 S.Ct. 571, 69 L.Ed. 1070 (1925), and Meyer v. Nebraska, 262 U.S. 390, 43 S.Ct. 625, 67 L.Ed. 1042 (1923), were described as dealing with child rearing and education; Prince v. Massachusetts, 321 U.S. 158, 64 S.Ct. 438, 88 L.Ed. 645 (1944), with family relationships; Skinner v. Oklahoma ex rel. Williamson, 316 U.S. 535, 62 S.Ct. 1110, 86 L.Ed. 1655 (1942), with procreation; Loving v. Virginia, 388 U.S. 1, 87 S.Ct. 1817, 18 L.Ed.2d 1010 (1967), with marriage; Griswold v. Connecticut, supra, and Eisenstadt v. Baird, supra, with contraception; and Roe v. Wade, 410 U.S. 113, 93 S.Ct. 705, 35 L.Ed.2d 147 (1973), with abortion. The latter three cases were interpreted as construing the Due Process Clause of the Fourteenth Amendment to confer a fundamental individual right to decide whether or not to beget or bear a child. Carey v. Population Services International, supra, 431 U.S., at 688–689, 97 S.Ct., at 2017–2018.

Accepting the decisions in these cases and the above description of them, we think it evident that none of the rights announced in those cases bears any resemblance to the claimed constitutional right of homosexuals to engage in acts of sodomy that is asserted in this case. No connection between family, marriage, or procreation on the one hand and homosexual activity on the other has been demonstrated, either by the Court of Appeals or by respondent. * * *

Precedent aside, however, respondent would have us announce, as the Court of Appeals did, a fundamental right to engage in homosexual sodomy. This we are quite unwilling to do. * * *

Striving to assure itself and the public that announcing rights not readily identifiable in the Constitution's text involves much more than the imposition of the Justices' own choice of values on the States and the Federal Government, the Court has sought to identify the nature of the rights qualifying for heightened judicial protection. In Palko v. Connecticut, 302 U.S. 319, 325, 326, 58 S.Ct. 149, 151, 152, 82 L.Ed. 288 (1937), it was said that this category includes those fundamental liberties that are "implicit in the concept of ordered liberty," such that "neither liberty nor justice would exist if [they] were sacrificed." A different description of fundamental liberties appeared in Moore v. East Cleveland, 431 U.S. 494, 503, 97 S.Ct. 1932, 1937, 52 L.Ed. 2d 531 (1977) (opinion of POWELL, J.), where they are characterized as those liberties that are "deeply rooted in this Nation's history and tradition." Id., at 503, 97 S.Ct., at 1938 (POWELL, J.).

It is obvious to us that neither of these formulations would extend a fundamental right to homosexuals to engage in acts of consensual sodomy. Proscriptions against that conduct have ancient roots. Sodomy was a criminal offense at common law and was forbidden by the laws of the original thirteen States when they ratified the Bill of Rights. In 1868, when the Fourteenth Amendment was ratified, all but 5 of the 37 States in the Union had criminal sodomy laws. In fact, until 1961, all 50 States outlawed sodomy, and today, 24 States and the District of Columbia continue to provide criminal penalties for sodomy performed in private and between consenting adults. Against this background, to claim that a right to engage in such conduct is "deeply rooted in this Nation's history and tradition" or "implicit in the concept of ordered liberty" is, at best, facetious.

Nor are we inclined to take a more expansive view of our authority to discover new fundamental rights imbedded in the Due Process Clause. The Court is most vulnerable and comes nearest to illegitimacy when it deals with judge-made constitutional law having little or no cognizable roots in the language or design of the Constitution. * * *

Respondent, however, asserts that the result should be different where the homosexual conduct occurs in the privacy of the home. He relies on Stanley v. Georgia, 394 U.S. 557, 89 S.Ct. 1243, 22 L.Ed.2d 542 (1969), where the Court held that the First Amendment prevents conviction for possessing and reading obscene material in the privacy of one's home: "If the First Amendment means anything, it means that a State has no business telling a man, sitting alone in his house, what books he may read or what films he may watch." Id., at 565, 89 S.Ct., at 1248.

Stanley did protect conduct that would not have been protected outside the home, and it partially prevented the enforcement of state obscenity laws; but the decision was firmly grounded in the First Amendment. The right pressed upon us here has no similar support in the text of the Constitution, and it does not qualify for recognition under the prevailing principles for construing the Fourteenth Amendment. Its limits are also difficult to discern. Plainly enough, otherwise illegal conduct is not always immunized whenever it occurs in the home. Victimless crimes, such as the possession and use of illegal drugs, do not escape the law where they are committed at home. *Stanley* itself recognized that its holding offered no protection for the possession in the home of drugs, firearms, or stolen goods. And if respondent's submission is limited to the voluntary sexual conduct between consenting adults, it would be difficult, except by fiat, to limit the claimed right to homosexual conduct while leaving exposed to prosecution adultery, incest, and other sexual crimes even though they are committed in the home. We are unwilling to start down that road.

Even if the conduct at issue here is not a fundamental right, respondent asserts that there must be a rational basis for the law and that there is none in this case other than the presumed belief of a majority of the electorate in Georgia that homosexual sodomy is immoral and unacceptable. This is said to be an inadequate rationale to support the law. The law, however, is constantly based on notions of morality, and if all laws representing essentially moral choices are to be invalidated under the Due Process Clause, the courts will be very busy indeed. Even respondent makes no such claim, but insists that majority sentiments about the morality of homosexuality should be declared inadequate. We do not agree, and are unpersuaded that the sodomy laws of some 25 States should be invalidated on this basis.[8]

Accordingly, the judgment of the Court of Appeals is

Reversed.

[The concurring opinion of CHIEF JUSTICE BURGER is omitted.]

JUSTICE POWELL, concurring.

I join the opinion of the Court. I agree with the Court that there is no fundamental right—i.e., no substantive right under the Due Process Clause—such as that claimed by respondent Hardwick, and found to exist by the Court of Appeals. This is not to suggest, however, that respondent may not be protected by the Eighth Amendment of the Constitution. The Georgia statute at issue in this case, Ga.Code Ann. § 16–6–2 (1984), authorizes a court to imprison a person for up to 20 years for a single private, consensual act of sodomy. In my view, a prison sentence for such conduct—certainly a sentence of long duration—would create a serious Eighth Amendment issue. Under the Georgia statute a single act of sodomy, even in the private setting of a home, is a felony comparable in terms of the possible sentence imposed to serious felonies such as aggravated battery, § 16–5–24, first-degree arson, § 16–7–60, and robbery, § 16–8–40.[1]

In this case, however, respondent has not been tried, much less convicted and sentenced.[2] Moreover, respondent has not raised the Eighth Amendment issue below. For these reasons this constitutional argument is not before us.

8. Respondent does not defend the judgment below based on the Ninth Amendment, the Equal Protection Clause, or the Eighth Amendment.

1. Among those States that continue to make sodomy a crime, Georgia authorizes one of the longest possible sentences. See Ala. Code § 13A–6–65(a)(3) (1982) (1–year maximum); Ariz.Rev.Stat.Ann. §§ 13–1411, 13–1412 (West Supp.1985) (30 days); Ark.Stat. Ann. § 41–1813 (1977) (1–year maximum); D.C.Code § 22–3502 (1981) (10–year maximum); Fla.Stat. § 800.02 (1985) (60–day maximum); Ga.Code Ann. § 16–6–2 (1984) (1 to 20 years); Idaho Code § 18–6605 (1979) (5–year minimum); Kan.Stat.Ann. § 21–3505 (Supp.1985) (6–month maximum); Ky.Rev.Stat. § 510.100 (1985) (90 days to 12 months); La.Rev.Stat.Ann. § 14:89 (West 1986) (5–year maximum); Md.Ann.Code, Art. 27, §§ 553–554 (1982) (10–year maximum); Mich.Comp.Laws § 750.158 (1968) (15–year maximum), 750.338a–750.338b (1968) (5–year maximum); Minn.Stat. § 609.293 (1984) (1–year maximum); Miss.Code Ann. § 97–29–59 (1973) (10–year maximum); Mo.Rev. Stat. § 566.090 (Supp.1984) (1–year maximum); Mont.Code Ann. § 45–5–505 (1985) (10–year maximum); Nev.Rev.Stat. § 201.190 (1985) (6–year maximum); N.C.Gen.Stat. § 14–177 (1981) (10–year maximum); Okla. Stat., Tit. 21, § 886 (1981) (10–year maximum); R.I.Gen.Laws § 11–10–1 (1981) (7 to 20 years); S.C.Code § 16–15–120 (1985) (5–year maximum); Tenn.Code Ann. § 39–2–612 (1982) (5 to 15 years); Tex.Penal Code Ann. § 21.06 (1974) ($200 maximum fine); Utah Code Ann. § 76–5–403 (1978) (6–month maximum); Va.Code § 18.2–361 (1982) (5–year maximum).

2. It was conceded at oral argument that, prior to the complaint against respondent Hardwick, there had been no reported decision involving prosecution for private homosexual sodomy under this statute for several decades. See Thompson v. Aldredge, 187 Ga. 467, 200 S.E. 799 (1939). Moreover, the State has declined to present the criminal charge against Hardwick to a grand jury, and this is a suit for declaratory judgment brought by respondents challenging the validity of the statute. The history of nonenforcement suggests the moribund character today of laws criminalizing this type of private, consensual conduct. Some 26 States have repealed similar statutes. But the constitutional validity of the Georgia statute was put in issue by respondents, and for the reasons stated by the Court, I cannot say that conduct condemned for hundreds of years has now become a fundamental right.

JUSTICE BLACKMUN, with whom JUSTICE BRENNAN, JUSTICE MARSHALL, and JUSTICE STEVENS join, dissenting.

This case is no more about "a fundamental right to engage in homosexual sodomy," as the Court purports to declare, than Stanley v. Georgia, 394 U.S. 557, 89 S.Ct. 1243, 22 L.Ed.2d 542 (1969), was about a fundamental right to watch obscene movies, or Katz v. United States, 389 U.S. 347, 88 S.Ct. 507, 19 L.Ed.2d 576 (1967), was about a fundamental right to place interstate bets from a telephone booth. Rather, this case is about "the most comprehensive of rights and the right most valued by civilized men," namely, "the right to be let alone." Olmstead v. United States, 277 U.S. 438, 478, 48 S.Ct. 564, 572, 72 L.Ed. 944 (1928) (Brandeis, J., dissenting).

The statute at issue, Ga.Code Ann. § 16–6–2 (1984), denies individuals the right to decide for themselves whether to engage in particular forms of private, consensual sexual activity. The Court concludes that § 16–6–2 is valid essentially because "the laws of * * * many States * * * still make such conduct illegal and have done so for a very long time." But the fact that the moral judgments expressed by statutes like § 16–6–2 may be " 'natural and familiar * * * ought not to conclude our judgment upon the question whether statutes embodying them conflict with the Constitution of the United States.' " Roe v. Wade, 410 U.S. 113, 117, 93 S.Ct. 705, 709, 35 L.Ed.2d 147 (1973), quoting Lochner v. New York, 198 U.S. 45, 76, 25 S.Ct. 539, 547, 49 L.Ed. 937 (1905) (Holmes, J., dissenting). Like Justice Holmes, I believe that " [i]t is revolting to have no better reason for a rule of law than that so it was laid down in the time of Henry IV. It is still more revolting if the grounds upon which it was laid down have vanished long since, and the rule simply persists from blind imitation of the past." Holmes, The Path of the Law, 10 Harv.L.Rev. 457, 469 (1897). * * *

I

* * * A fair reading of the statute and of the complaint clearly reveals that the majority has distorted the question this case presents.

First, the Court's almost obsessive focus on homosexual activity is particularly hard to justify in light of the broad language Georgia has used. Unlike the Court, the Georgia Legislature has not proceeded on the assumption that homosexuals are so different from other citizens that their lives may be controlled in a way that would not be tolerated if it limited the choices of those other citizens. Rather, Georgia has provided that "[a] person commits the offense of sodomy when he performs or submits to any sexual act involving the sex organs of one person and the mouth or anus of another." Ga.Code Ann. § 16–6–2(a) (1984). The sex or status of the persons who engage in the act is irrelevant as a matter of state law. * * * Michael Hardwick's standing may rest in significant part on Georgia's apparent willingness to enforce against homosexuals a law it seems not to have any desire to enforce against heterosexuals. But his claim that § 16–6–2 involves an unconstitutional intrusion into his privacy and his right of intimate association does not depend in any way on his sexual orientation.

Second, I disagree with the Court's refusal to consider whether § 16–6–2 runs afoul of the Eighth or Ninth Amendments or the Equal Protection Clause of the Fourteenth Amendment. * * * I need not reach either the Eighth Amendment or the Equal Protection Clause issues because I believe that Hardwick has stated a cognizable claim that § 16–6–2 interferes with constitutionally protected interests in privacy and freedom of intimate association. But neither the Eighth Amendment nor the Equal Protection Clause is so clearly irrelevant that a claim resting on either provision should be peremptorily dismissed.

II

"Our cases long have recognized that the Constitution embodies a promise that a certain private sphere of individual liberty will be kept largely beyond the reach of government." Thornburgh v. American College of Obstetricians & Gynecologists, 476 U.S. 747, 772, 106 S.Ct. 2169, 2184, 90 L.Ed.2d 779 (1986). In construing the right to privacy, the Court has proceeded along two somewhat distinct, albeit complementary, lines. First, it has recognized a privacy interest with reference to certain *decisions* that are properly for the individual to make. Second, it has recognized a privacy interest with reference to certain *places* without regard for the particular activities in which the individuals who occupy them are engaged. The case before us implicates both the decisional and the spatial aspects of the right to privacy.

A

The Court concludes today that none of our prior cases dealing with various decisions that individuals are entitled to make free of governmental interference "bears any resemblance to the claimed constitutional right of homosexuals to engage in acts of sodomy that is asserted in this case." While it is true that these cases may be characterized by their connection to protection of the family, the Court's conclusion that they extend no further than this boundary ignores the warning in Moore v. East Cleveland, 431 U.S. 494, 501, 97 S.Ct. 1932, 1936, 52 L.Ed.2d 531 (1977) (plurality opinion), against "clos[ing] our eyes to the basic reasons why certain rights associated with the family have been accorded shelter under the Fourteenth Amendment's Due Process Clause." We protect those rights not because they contribute, in some direct and material way, to the general public welfare, but because they form so central a part of an individual's life. * * * And so we protect the decision whether to marry precisely because marriage "is an association that promotes a way of life, not causes; a harmony in living, not political faiths; a bilateral loyalty, not commercial or social projects." Griswold v. Connecticut, 381 U.S., at 486, 85 S.Ct., at 1682. We protect the decision whether to have a child because parenthood alters so dramatically an individual's self-definition, not because of demographic considerations or the Bible's command to be fruitful and multiply. * * *

Only the most willful blindness could obscure the fact that sexual intimacy is "a sensitive, key relationship of human existence, central to family life, community welfare, and the development of human personality," Paris Adult Theatre I v. Slaton, 413 U.S. 49, 63, 93 S.Ct. 2628, 2638, 37 L.Ed.2d 446 (1973); see also Carey v. Population Services International, 431 U.S. 678, 685, 97 S.Ct. 2010, 2016, 52 L.Ed.2d 675 (1977). The fact that individuals define themselves in a significant way through their intimate sexual relationships with others suggests, in a Nation as diverse as ours, that there may be many "right" ways of conducting those relationships, and that much of the richness of a relationship will come from the freedom an individual has to *choose* the form and nature of these intensely personal bonds. See Karst, The Freedom of Intimate Association, 89 Yale L.J. 624, 637 (1980).

* * * The Court claims that its decision today merely refuses to recognize a fundamental right to engage in homosexual sodomy; what the Court really has refused to recognize is the fundamental interest all individuals have in controlling the nature of their intimate associations with others.

B

The behavior for which Hardwick faces prosecution occurred in his own home, a place to which the Fourth Amendment attaches special significance. * * * Just as the right to privacy is more than the mere aggregation of a number of entitlements to engage in specific behavior, so too, protecting the physical integrity of the home is more than merely a means of protecting specific activities that often take place there. * * *

The Court's interpretation of the pivotal case of Stanley v. Georgia, 394 U.S. 557, 89 S.Ct. 1243, 22 L.Ed.2d 542 (1969), is entirely unconvincing. *Stanley* held that Georgia's undoubted power to punish the public distribution of constitutionally unprotected, obscene material did not permit the State to punish the private possession of such material. According to the majority here, *Stanley* relied entirely on the First Amendment, and thus, it is claimed, sheds no light on cases not involving printed materials. But that is not what *Stanley* said. Rather, the *Stanley* Court anchored its holding in the Fourth Amendment's special protection for the individual in his home:

> "'The makers of our Constitution undertook to secure conditions favorable to the pursuit of happiness. They recognized the significance of man's spiritual nature, of his feelings and of his intellect. They knew that only a part of the pain, pleasure and satisfactions of life are to be found in material things. They sought to protect Americans in their beliefs, their thoughts, their emotions and their sensations.'
>
> * * *
>
> "These are the rights that appellant is asserting in the case before us. He is asserting the right to read or observe what he pleases—the right to satisfy his intellectual and emotional needs in the privacy of his own home." 394 U.S., at 564–565, 89 S.Ct., at 1248, quoting Olmstead v. United States, 277 U.S., at 478, 48 S.Ct., at 572 (Brandeis, J., dissenting).

The central place that *Stanley* gives Justice Brandeis' dissent in *Olmstead,* a case raising *no* First Amendment claim, shows that *Stanley* rested as much on the Court's understanding of the Fourth Amendment as it did on the First. * * * Indeed, the right of an individual to conduct intimate relationships in the intimacy of his or her own home seems to me to be the heart of the Constitution's protection of privacy.

III

The Court's failure to comprehend the magnitude of the liberty interests at stake in this case leads it to slight the question whether petitioner, on behalf of the State, has justified Georgia's infringement on these interests. I believe that neither of the two general justifications for § 16–6–2 that petitioner has advanced warrants dismissing respondent's challenge for failure to state a claim.

First, petitioner asserts that the acts made criminal by the statute may have serious adverse consequences for "the general public health and welfare," such as spreading communicable diseases or fostering other criminal activity. Inasmuch as this case was dismissed by the District Court on the pleadings, it is not surprising that the record before us is barren of any evidence to support petitioner's claim. In light of the state of the record, I see no justification for the Court's attempt to equate the private, consensual sexual activity at issue here with the "possession in the home of drugs, firearms, or stolen goods," to which *Stanley* refused to extend its protection. None of the behavior so mentioned in *Stanley* can properly be viewed as "[v]ictimless," drugs and weapons are inherently dangerous, see, e.g., McLaughlin v. United States, 476 U.S. 16, 106 S.Ct. 1677, 90 L.Ed.2d 15 (1986), and for property to be "stolen," someone must have been wrongfully deprived of it. Nothing in the record before the Court provides any justification for finding the activity forbidden by § 16–6–2 to be physically dangerous, either to the persons engaged in it or to others.[4]

The core of petitioner's defense of § 16–6–2, however, is that respondent and others who engage in the conduct prohibited by § 16–6–2 interfere with Georgia's exercise of the " 'right of the Nation and of the States to maintain a decent society,' " Paris Adult Theatre I v. Slaton, 413 U.S., at 59–60, 93 S.Ct., at 2636, quoting Jacobellis v. Ohio, 378 U.S. 184, 199, 84 S.Ct. 1676, 1684, 12 L.Ed.2d 793 (1964) (Warren, C.J., dissenting). Essentially, petitioner argues, and the Court agrees, that the fact that the acts described in § 16–6–2 "for hundreds of years, if not thousands, have been uniformly

4. Although I do not think it necessary to decide today issues that are not even remotely before us, it does seem to me that a court could find simple, analytically sound distinctions between certain private, consensual sexual conduct, on the one hand, and adultery and incest (the only two vaguely specific "sexual crimes" to which the majority points, ante, at 2846), on the other. For example, marriage, in addition to its spiritual aspects, is a civil contract that entitles the contracting parties to a variety of governmentally provided benefits. A State might define the contractual commitment necessary to become eligible for these benefits to include a commitment of fidelity and then punish individuals for breaching that contract. Moreover, a State might conclude that adultery is likely to injure third persons, in particular, spouses and children of persons who engage in extramarital affairs. With respect to incest, a court might well agree with respondent that the nature of familial relationships renders true consent to incestuous activity sufficiently problematical that a blanket prohibition of such activity is warranted. See Tr. of Oral Arg. 21–22. Notably, the Court makes no effort to explain why it has chosen to group private, consensual homosexual activity with adultery and incest rather than with private, consensual heterosexual activity by unmarried persons or, indeed, with oral or anal sex within marriage.

condemned as immoral" is a sufficient reason to permit a State to ban them today.

I cannot agree that either the length of time a majority has held its convictions or the passions with which it defends them can withdraw legislation from this Court's scrutiny. As Justice Jackson wrote so eloquently for the Court in West Virginia Board of Education v. Barnette, 319 U.S. 624, 641–642, 63 S.Ct. 1178, 1187, 87 L.Ed. 1628 (1943), "we apply the limitations of the Constitution with no fear that freedom to be intellectually and spiritually diverse or even contrary will disintegrate the social organization. * * * [F]reedom to differ is not limited to things that do not matter much. That would be a mere shadow of freedom. The test of its substance is the right to differ as to things that touch the heart of the existing order." It is precisely because the issue raised by this case touches the heart of what makes individuals what they are that we should be especially sensitive to the rights of those whose choices upset the majority.

The assertion that "traditional Judeo–Christian values proscribe" the conduct involved cannot provide an adequate justification for § 16–6–2. * * * The legitimacy of secular legislation depends instead on whether the State can advance some justification for its law beyond its conformity to religious doctrine. Thus, far from buttressing his case, petitioner's invocation of Leviticus, Romans, St. Thomas Aquinas, and sodomy's heretical status during the Middle Ages undermines his suggestion that § 16–6–2 represents a legitimate use of secular coercive power.[6] A State can no more punish private behavior because of religious intolerance than it can punish such behavior because of racial animus. * * *

Nor can § 16–6–2 be justified as a "morally neutral" exercise of Georgia's power to "protect the public environment," *Paris Adult Theatre I*, 413 U.S., at 68–69, 93 S.Ct., at 2641. Certainly, some private behavior can affect the fabric of society as a whole. Reasonable people may differ about whether particular sexual acts are moral or immoral, but "we have ample evidence for believing that people will not abandon morality, will not think any better of murder, cruelty and dishonesty, merely because some private sexual practice which they abominate is not punished by the law." H.L.A. Hart, Immorality and Treason, reprinted in The Law as Literature 220, 225 (L. Blom–Cooper ed. 1961). Petitioner and the Court fail to see the difference between laws that protect public sensibilities and those that enforce private morality. Statutes banning public sexual activity are entirely consistent with protecting the individual's liberty interest in decisions concerning sexual relations: the same recognition that those decisions are intensely private

6. The theological nature of the origin of Anglo–American antisodomy statutes is patent. It was not until 1533 that sodomy was made a secular offense in England. 25 Hen. VIII, ch. 6. Until that time, the offense was, in Sir James Stephen's words, "merely ecclesiastical." 2 J. Stephen, A History of the Criminal Law of England 429–430 (1883). Pollock and Maitland similarly observed that "[t]he crime against nature * * * was so closely connected with heresy that the vulgar had but one name for both." 2 F. Pollock & F. Maitland, The History of English Law 554 (1895). The transfer of jurisdiction over prosecutions for sodomy to the secular courts seems primarily due to the alteration of ecclesiastical jurisdiction attendant on England's break with the Roman Catholic Church, rather than to any new understanding of the sovereign's interest in preventing or punishing the behavior involved. Cf. 6 E. Coke, Institutes, ch. 10 (4th ed. 1797).

which justifies protecting them from governmental interference can justify protecting individuals from unwilling exposure to the sexual activities of others. But the mere fact that intimate behavior may be punished when it takes place in public cannot dictate how States can regulate intimate behavior that occurs in intimate places.

This case involves no real interference with the rights of others, for the mere knowledge that other individuals do not adhere to one's value system cannot be a legally cognizable interest, let alone an interest that can justify invading the houses, hearts, and minds of citizens who choose to live their lives differently.

* * *

JUSTICE STEVENS, with whom JUSTICE BRENNAN and JUSTICE MARSHALL join, dissenting.

Like the statute that is challenged in this case, the rationale of the Court's opinion applies equally to the prohibited conduct regardless of whether the parties who engage in it are married or unmarried, or are of the same or different sexes. Sodomy was condemned as an odious and sinful type of behavior during the formative period of the common law. That condemnation was equally damning for heterosexual and homosexual sodomy. Moreover, it provided no special exemption for married couples. The license to cohabit and to produce legitimate offspring simply did not include any permission to engage in sexual conduct that was considered a "crime against nature."

The history of the Georgia statute before us clearly reveals this traditional prohibition of heterosexual, as well as homosexual, sodomy. Indeed, at one point in the 20th century, Georgia's law was construed to permit certain sexual conduct between homosexual women even though such conduct was prohibited between heterosexuals. The history of the statutes cited by the majority as proof for the proposition that sodomy is not constitutionally protected, ante, at 2844–2846, and nn. 5 and 6, similarly reveals a prohibition on heterosexual, as well as homosexual, sodomy.

Because the Georgia statute expresses the traditional view that sodomy is an immoral kind of conduct regardless of the identity of the persons who engage in it, I believe that a proper analysis of its constitutionality requires consideration of two questions: First, may a State totally prohibit the described conduct by means of a neutral law applying without exception to all persons subject to its jurisdiction? If not, may the State save the statute by announcing that it will only enforce the law against homosexuals? The two questions merit separate discussion.

I

Our prior cases make two propositions abundantly clear. First, the fact that the governing majority in a State has traditionally viewed a particular practice as immoral is not a sufficient reason for upholding a law prohibiting the practice; neither history nor tradition could save a law prohibiting miscegenation from constitutional attack. Second, individual decisions by married persons, concerning the intimacies of their physical relationship, even when not intended to produce offspring, are a form of "liberty" protected by the Due Process Clause of the Fourteenth Amendment. Griswold v. Connecticut, 381 U.S. 479, 85 S.Ct. 1678, 14 L.Ed.2d 510 (1965). Moreover, this protection extends to intimate choices by unmarried as well as married persons. Carey v. Population Services International, 431 U.S. 678, 97 S.Ct. 2010, 52 L.Ed.2d 675 (1977); Eisenstadt v. Baird, 405 U.S. 438, 92 S.Ct. 1029, 31 L.Ed.2d 349 (1972).

In consideration of claims of this kind, the Court has emphasized the individual interest in privacy, but its decisions have actually been animated by an even more fundamental concern. As I wrote some years ago:

> "These cases do not deal with the individual's interest in protection from unwarranted public attention, comment, or exploitation. They deal, rather, with the individual's right to make certain unusually important decisions that will affect his own, or his family's, destiny. The Court has referred to such decisions as implicating 'basic values,' as being 'fundamental,' and as being dignified by history and tradition. The character of the Court's language in these cases brings to mind the origins of the American heritage of freedom—the abiding interest in individual liberty that makes certain state intrusions on the citizen's right to decide how he will live his own life intolerable. Guided by history, our tradition of respect for the dignity of individual choice in matters of conscience and the restraints implicit in the federal system, federal judges have accepted the responsibility for recognition and protection of these rights in appropriate cases." Fitzgerald v. Porter Memorial Hospital, 523 F.2d 716, 719–720 (CA7 1975) (footnotes omitted), cert. denied, 425 U.S. 916, 96 S.Ct. 1518, 47 L.Ed.2d 768 (1976).

Society has every right to encourage its individual members to follow particular traditions in expressing affection for one another and in gratifying their personal desires. It, of course, may prohibit an individual from imposing his will on another to satisfy his own selfish interests. It also may prevent an individual from interfering with, or violating, a legally sanctioned and protected relationship, such as marriage. And it may explain the relative advantages and disadvantages of different forms of intimate expression. But when individual married couples are isolated from observation by others, the way in which they voluntarily choose to conduct their intimate relations is a matter for them—not the State—to decide.[10] The essential "liberty" that animated the development of the law in cases like *Griswold, Eisenstadt,* and *Carey* surely embraces the right to engage in nonreproductive, sexual conduct that others may consider offensive or immoral.

Paradoxical as it may seem, our prior cases thus establish that a State may not prohibit sodomy within "the sacred precincts of marital bedrooms," *Griswold,* 381 U.S., at 485, 85 S.Ct., at 1682, or, indeed, between unmarried heterosexual adults. *Eisenstadt,* 405 U.S., at 453, 92 S.Ct., at 1038. In all

10. Indeed, the Georgia Attorney General concedes that Georgia's statute would be unconstitutional if applied to a married couple. See Tr. of Oral Arg. 8 (stating that application of the statute to a married couple "would be unconstitutional" because of the "right of marital privacy as identified by the Court in Griswold"). Significantly, Georgia passed the current statute three years after the Court's decision in *Griswold.*

events, it is perfectly clear that the State of Georgia may not totally prohibit the conduct proscribed by § 16–6–2 of the Georgia Criminal Code.

II

If the Georgia statute cannot be enforced as it is written—if the conduct it seeks to prohibit is a protected form of liberty for the vast majority of Georgia's citizens—the State must assume the burden of justifying a selective application of its law. Either the persons to whom Georgia seeks to apply its statute do not have the same interest in "liberty" that others have, or there must be a reason why the State may be permitted to apply a generally applicable law to certain persons that it does not apply to others.

The first possibility is plainly unacceptable. Although the meaning of the principle that "all men are created equal" is not always clear, it surely must mean that every free citizen has the same interest in "liberty" that the members of the majority share. From the standpoint of the individual, the homosexual and the heterosexual have the same interest in deciding how he will live his own life, and, more narrowly, how he will conduct himself in his personal and voluntary associations with his companions. State intrusion into the private conduct of either is equally burdensome.

The second possibility is similarly unacceptable. A policy of selective application must be supported by a neutral and legitimate interest—something more substantial than a habitual dislike for, or ignorance about, the disfavored group. Neither the State nor the Court has identified any such interest in this case. The Court has posited as a justification for the Georgia statute "the presumed belief of a majority of the electorate in Georgia that homosexual sodomy is immoral and unacceptable." But the Georgia electorate has expressed no such belief—instead, its representatives enacted a law that presumably reflects the belief that *all sodomy* is immoral and unacceptable. Unless the Court is prepared to conclude that such a law is constitutional, it may not rely on the work product of the Georgia Legislature to support its holding. For the Georgia statute does not single out homosexuals as a separate class meriting special disfavored treatment.

Nor, indeed, does the Georgia prosecutor even believe that all homosexuals who violate this statute should be punished. This conclusion is evident from the fact that the respondent in this very case has formally acknowledged in his complaint and in court that he has engaged, and intends to continue to engage, in the prohibited conduct, yet the State has elected not to process criminal charges against him. As JUSTICE POWELL points out, moreover, Georgia's prohibition on private, consensual sodomy has not been enforced for decades. The record of nonenforcement, in this case and in the last several decades, belies the Attorney General's representations about the importance of the State's selective application of its generally applicable law.

Both the Georgia statute and the Georgia prosecutor thus completely fail to provide the Court with any support for the conclusion that homosexual sodomy, *simpliciter,* is considered unacceptable conduct in that State, and that the burden of justifying a selective application of the generally applicable law has been met.

III

The Court orders the dismissal of respondent's complaint even though the State's statute prohibits all sodomy; even though that prohibition is concededly unconstitutional with respect to heterosexuals; and even though the State's *post hoc* explanations for selective application are belied by the State's own actions. At the very least, I think it clear at this early stage of the litigation that respondent has alleged a constitutional claim sufficient to withstand a motion to dismiss.[13]

I respectfully dissent.

Notes

1. In Schochet v. State, 75 Md.App. 314, 541 A.2d 183 (1988), the court held (2–1), after *Bowers,* that the Maryland Unnatural and Perverted Sexual Practices statute constitutionally punished an act of private, consensual, heterosexual fellatio between unmarried adults. On appeal, two judges agreed with the majority below and one with the dissent below, but a majority of four construed the statute to be inapplicable to private, consensual heterosexual acts, thereby avoiding constitutional issues for the present. Schochet v. State, 320 Md. 714, 580 A.2d 176 (1990).

2. Probably the most famous of the right to privacy cases is Roe v. Wade, 410 U.S. 113, 93 S.Ct. 705, 35 L.Ed.2d 147 (1973), rehearing denied 410 U.S. 959, 93 S.Ct. 1409, 35 L.Ed.2d 694 (1973) in which the Supreme Court relied on the concept to find that a woman has the right to choose whether or not to terminate her own pregnancy during the first trimester. The opinion did not necessarily bar the application of state abortion laws or other forms of discouragement or regulation of birth termination in the later stages of pregnancy, when the State's interest in the health of the mother or in the potential human life of the fetus might outweigh the privacy interest of the mother.

In Webster v. Reproductive Health Services, 492 U.S. ——, 109 S.Ct. 3040, 106 L.Ed.2d 410 (1989), the Supreme Court upheld a state statute which barred use of public funds and facilities for non-therapeutic abortions. In the view of the Chief Justice and Justices White, Scalia, O'Connor, and Kennedy, this holding was not inconsistent with Roe v. Wade. Justice Scalia, however, would have overruled *Roe.* He and the others so far named, with the exception of Justice O'Connor, rejected the trimester approach of *Roe* and suggested that the *Roe* doctrine is subject to some not clearly defined modifications. Justice O'Connor saw no need to reconsider *Roe* on the present facts. Justices Blackmun, Brennan, Marshall, and Stevens dissented, finding the legislation inconsistent with Roe v. Wade and subsequent cases, and believing that it should be found to be an unconstitutional invasion of the constitutional right to privacy.

In decisions not purporting to disturb *Roe,* the court by divided votes upheld statutes requiring that in the case of a minor one or both parents be notified of the

13. Indeed, at this stage, it appears that the statute indiscriminately authorizes a policy of selective prosecution that is neither limited to the class of homosexual persons nor embraces all persons in that class, but rather applies to those who may be arbitrarily selected by the prosecutor for reasons that are not revealed either in the record of this case or in the text of the statute. If that is true, although the text of the statute is clear enough, its true meaning may be "so intolerably vague that evenhanded enforcement of the law is a virtual impossibility." Marks v. United States, 430 U.S. 188, 198, 97 S.Ct. 990, 996, 51 L.Ed.2d 260 (1977) (STEVENS, J., concurring in part and dissenting in part).

impending abortion, unless the minor goes through a "judicial bypass" proceeding, demonstrating to a judge that she is sufficiently mature to decide on her own or that the abortion is in her best interest. Hodgson v. Minnesota, 497 U.S. ___, 110 S.Ct. 2926, 111 L.Ed.2d 344 (1990); Ohio v. Akron Center for Reproductive Health, 497 U.S. ___, 110 S.Ct. 2972, 111 L.Ed.2d 405 (1990).

3. Proof Beyond a Reasonable Doubt

In re Winship

Supreme Court of the United States, 1970.
397 U.S. 358, 90 S.Ct. 1068, 25 L.Ed.2d 368.

MR. JUSTICE BRENNAN delivered the opinion of the Court.

* * *

I

* * *

Expressions in many opinions of this Court indicate that it has long been assumed that proof of a criminal charge beyond a reasonable doubt is constitutionally required. * * *

* * *

The reasonable-doubt standard plays a vital role in the American scheme of criminal procedure. It is a prime instrument for reducing the risk of convictions resting on factual error. The standard provides concrete substance for the presumption of innocence—that bedrock "axiomatic and elementary" principle whose "enforcement lies at the foundation of the administration of our criminal law." * * *

The requirement of proof beyond a reasonable doubt has this vital role in our criminal procedure for cogent reasons. The accused during a criminal prosecution has at stake interest of immense importance, both because of the possibility that he may lose his liberty upon conviction and because of the certainty that he would be stigmatized by the conviction. Accordingly, a society that values the good name and freedom of every individual should not condemn a man for commission of a crime when there is reasonable doubt about his guilt. As we said in Speiser v. Randall, supra, 357 U.S., at 525–526, 78 S.Ct., at 1342: "There is always in litigation a margin of error, representing error in factfinding, which both parties must take into account. Where one party has at stake an interest of transcending value—as a criminal defendant his liberty—this margin of error is reduced as to him by the process of placing on the other party the burden of * * * persuading the factfinder at the conclusion of the trial of his guilt beyond a reasonable doubt. Due process commands that no man shall lose his liberty unless the Government has borne the burden of * * * convincing the factfinder of his guilt." * * *

Moreover, use of the reasonable-doubt standard is indispensable to command the respect and confidence of the community in applications of the criminal law. It is critical that the moral force of the criminal law not be diluted by a standard of proof that leaves people in doubt whether innocent men are being condemned. It is also important in our free society that every individual going about his ordinary affairs have confidence that his government cannot adjudge him guilty of a criminal offense without convincing a proper factfinder of his guilt with utmost certainty.

Lest there remain any doubt about the constitutional stature of the reasonable-doubt standard, we explicitly hold that the Due Process Clause protects the accused against conviction except upon proof beyond a reasonable doubt of every fact necessary to constitute the crime with which he is charged.

* * *

MR. JUSTICE HARLAN, concurring.

* * *

Professor Wigmore, in discussing the various attempts by courts to define how convinced one must be to be convinced beyond a reasonable doubt, wryly observed: "The truth is that no one has yet invented or discovered a mode of measurement for the intensity of human belief. Hence there can be yet no successful method of communicating intelligibly * * * a sound method of self-analysis for one's belief," 9 J. Wigmore, Evidence 325 (3d ed. 1940).

Notwithstanding Professor Wigmore's skepticism, we have before us a case where the choice of the standard of proof has made a difference: the juvenile court judge below forthrightly acknowledged that he believed by a preponderance of the evidence, but was not convinced beyond a reasonable doubt, that appellant stole $112 from the complainant's pocketbook. Moreover, even though the labels used for alternative standards of proof are vague and not a very sure guide to decisionmaking, the choice of the standard for a particular variety of adjudication does, I think, reflect a very fundamental assessment of the comparative social costs of erroneous factual determinations.

To explain why I think this so, I begin by stating two propositions, neither of which I believe can be fairly disputed. First, in a judicial proceeding in which there is a dispute about the facts of some earlier event, the factfinder cannot acquire unassailably accurate knowledge of what happened. Instead, all the factfinder can acquire is a belief of what *probably* happened. The intensity of this belief—the degree to which a factfinder is convinced that a given act actually occurred—can, of course, vary. In this regard, a standard of proof represents an attempt to instruct the factfinder concerning the degree of confidence our society thinks he should have in the correctness of factual conclusions for a particular type of adjudication. Although the phrases "preponderance of the evidence" and "proof beyond a reasonable doubt" are quantitatively imprecise, they do communicate to the finder of fact different notions concerning the degree of confidence he is expected to have in the correctness of his factual conclusions.

A second proposition, which is really nothing more than a corollary of the first, is that the trier of fact will sometimes, despite his best efforts, be wrong in his factual conclusions. In a lawsuit between two parties, a factual error can make a difference in one of two ways. First, it can result in a judgment in favor of the plaintiff when the true facts warrant a judgment for the defendant. The analogue in a criminal case would be the conviction of an innocent man. On the other hand, an erroneous factual determination can result in a judgment for the defendant when the true facts justify a judgment in plaintiff's favor. The criminal analogue would be the acquittal of a guilty man.

The standard of proof influences the relative frequency of these two types of erroneous outcomes. If, for example, the standard of proof for a criminal trial were a preponderance of the evidence rather than proof beyond a reasonable doubt, there would be a smaller risk of factual errors that result in freeing guilty persons, but a far greater risk of factual errors that result in convicting the innocent. Because the standard of proof affects the comparative frequency of these two types of erroneous outcomes, the choice of the standard to be applied in a particular kind of litigation should, in a rational world, reflect an assessment of the comparative social disutility of each.

When one makes such an assessment, the reason for different standards of proof in civil as opposed to criminal litigation becomes apparent. In a civil suit between two private parties for money damages, for example, we view it as no more serious in general for there to be an erroneous verdict in the defendant's favor than for there to be an erroneous verdict in the plaintiff's favor. A preponderance of the evidence standard therefore seems peculiarly appropriate for, as explained most sensibly, it simply requires the trier of fact "to believe that the existence of a fact is more probable than its nonexistence before [he] may find in favor of the party who has the burden to persuade the [judge] of the fact's existence."

In a criminal case, on the other hand, we do not view the social disutility of convicting an innocent man as equivalent to the disutility of acquitting someone who is guilty. * * *

In this context, I view the requirement of proof beyond a reasonable doubt in a criminal case as bottomed on a fundamental value determination of our society that it is far worse to convict an innocent man than to let a guilty man go free. It is only because of the nearly complete and long-standing acceptance of the reasonable-doubt standard by the States in criminal trials that the Court has not before today had to hold explicitly that due process, as an expression of fundamental procedural fairness, requires a more stringent standard for criminal trials than for ordinary civil litigation.

* * *

MR. JUSTICE BLACK, dissenting.

* * *

I admit a strong, persuasive argument can be made for a standard of proof beyond a reasonable doubt in criminal cases—and the majority has made that argument well—but it is not for me as a judge to say for that reason that Congress or the States are without constitutional power to establish another standard that the Constitution does not otherwise forbid. It is quite true that proof beyond a reasonable doubt has long been required in federal criminal trials. It is also true that this requirement is almost universally found in the governing laws of the States. And as long as a particular jurisdiction requires proof beyond a reasonable doubt, then the Due Process Clause commands that every trial in that jurisdiction must adhere to that standard. See Turner v. United States, 396 U.S. 398, 430, 90 S.Ct. 642, 24 L.Ed.2d 610 (1970) (Black, J., dissenting). But when, as here, a State through its duly constituted legislative branch decides to apply a different standard, then that standard, unless it is otherwise unconstitutional, must be applied to insure that persons are treated according to the "law of the land." The State of New York has made such a decision, and in my view nothing in the Due Process Clause invalidates it.

Notes

1. Carr v. State, 23 Neb. 749, 37 N.W. 630, 631–632 (1888):

* * * We have not at hand the edition of Greenleaf's work on Evidence referred to, but upon an examination of the 14th edition, we are satisfied section 29, note 2, of that edition is the one referred to by the author. In the text Greenleaf says: "But in criminal trials the party accused is entitled to the benefit of the legal presumption in favor of innocence, which in doubtful cases is always sufficient to turn the scale in his favor. It is therefore a rule of criminal law that the guilt of the accused must be fully proved. Neither a mere preponderance of evidence, nor any weight of preponderant evidence, is sufficient for the purpose, unless it generate a full belief of the fact to the exclusion of all reasonable doubt." The note consists in part of an extract from the very able charge of Chief Justice Shaw, given to the jury on the trial in the case of Com. v. Webster, 5 Cush. 320, 52 Amer.Dec. 711, as well as a number of extracts from decisions in other cases. The quotation from the instruction is as follows: "Then what is a reasonable doubt? It is a term often used, probably pretty well understood, but not easily defined. It is not mere possible doubt; because everything relating to human affairs and depending on moral evidence is open to some possible or imaginary doubt. It is that state of the case which, after the entire comparison and consideration of all the evidence, leaves the minds of jurors in that condition that they cannot say they feel an abiding conviction to a moral certainty of the truth of the charge. The burden of proof is upon the prosecutor. All the presumptions of law, independent of evidence, are in favor of innocence; and every person is presumed to be innocent until he is proved guilty. If, upon such proof, there is reasonable doubt remaining, the accused is entitled to the benefit of it by an acquittal; for it is not sufficient to establish a probability, though a strong one, arising from the doctrine of chances, that the fact charged is more likely to be true than the contrary, but the evidence must establish the truth of the fact to a reasonable and moral certainty,—a certainty that convinces and directs the understanding, and satisfies the reason and judgment of those who are bound to act conscientiously upon it. This we take to be proof beyond a reasonable doubt; because if the law, which mostly depends upon considerations of a moral nature, should go further than this, and require absolute certainty, it would exclude circumstantial evidence altogether." While the rule stated by Chief Justice Shaw was applied to a case depending upon circumstantial evidence, yet in the main we think it is applicable to all cases where the issue of the guilt or innocence of the accused is presented. The reasonable doubt is "that state of the case which, after the entire comparison and consideration of all the evidence, leaves the minds of the jurors in that condition that they cannot say they feel an abiding conviction to a moral certainty of the truth of the charge." All presumptions of law, independent of evidence, are in favor of innocence. Every person is presumed to be innocent until he is proved guilty. The burden of proof is upon

the prosecution, not only to remove this presumption, but to satisfy the minds and consciences of the jurors, beyond all reasonable doubt, of the guilt of the accused, upon the whole case. They must feel satisfied to a moral certainty of his guilt, or they must acquit, at least of the degree wherein this want of certainty exists.

2. State v. Sauer, 38 Minn. 438, 439, 38 N.W. 355, 356 (1888):

* * * In his charge to the jury, the court, after instructing them that, to entitle the state to a verdict, the guilt of defendant must be proved beyond a reasonable doubt, added: "This does not mean beyond any doubt, but beyond a doubt for which you can give a reason." This is assigned as error. This definition is not without some authority to support it, (see Com. v. Harman, 4 Pa. St. 274;) and we are not prepared to say that it contains any error prejudicial to defendant. Like many other definitions of the term which have been given, it does not define, but itself requires definition. The most serious objection to it is that it is liable to be understood as meaning a doubt for which a juror could express or state a reason in words. A juror may, after a consideration and comparison of all the evidence, feel a reasonable doubt as to the guilt of a defendant, and yet find it difficult to state the reason for the doubt. The term "reasonable doubt" is almost incapable of any definition which will add much to what the words themselves imply. In fact it is easier to state what it is not than what it is; and it may be doubted whether any attempt to define it will not be more likely to confuse than to enlighten a jury. A man is the best judge of his own feelings, and he knows for himself whether he doubts better than any one else can tell him. Where any explanation of what is meant by a reasonable doubt is required, it is safer to adopt some definition which has already received the general approval of the authorities, especially those in our own state.

4. Fair Warning

Note on Common Law Crimes

Anthropologists may argue about whether a society has judges before it has legislatures. In the history of Anglo-American criminal law, the judges certainly played the predominant role until about a hundred and fifty years ago. They punished crime without much attention to statutes. In the first centuries after the Norman Conquest, Parliament met infrequently and irregularly. It occasionally had something to say about crime, but it usually concerned itself with penalties, not definitions. The judges decided criminal cases according to the "unwritten" law, compounded of vestiges of Roman law or other legal rules known by those who decided the cases, and principles of moral and practical conduct shared by the community. There was no felt impropriety in deciding cases where no legislation existed and little or no precedent could be found. As the years passed precedents were collected and texts produced, and development became more orderly. Gradually the English judges gave common law crimes their shape.

There was an early division of crimes into treason, felonies, and misdemeanors (sometimes called trespasses in the early days). High treason consisted of taking some action designed to lead towards the killing of the king, or levying war against the king by a subject, and of certain other acts of disloyalty. Petty treason, finally incorporated into the law of murder in 1828, was the killing of a husband by his wife, a master by his servant, or an ecclesiastical superior by his cleric. Treason was always punished with extreme severity, and followed special rules of procedure of its own. (In the United States, treason is defined in the federal Constitution.)

Felonies at common law entailed at least the possibility of the death penalty or mutilation, and the loss of all of the felon's property. The earliest common law felonies were criminal homicides, **rape** (unlawful carnal knowledge of a woman without her consent) **arson** (malicious burning of the dwelling house of another), **larceny** (certain kinds of theft), and **robbery** (certain thefts involving violence or intimidation). At first, all homicides were in theory criminal, but pardons were automatic if investigation showed accident or self-defense. Malicious killings came to be designated as **murder,** and other criminal killings as **manslaughter.** By the fourteenth century **burglary** (breaking and entering, at night, the dwelling house of another with intent to commit a felony therein) was recognized by the courts as a felony, as was **mayhem** (malicious infliction of certain serious injuries, as the loss of an arm or leg, resulting in loss of fighting ability) by statute early in the fifteenth century. Some **escapes,** as where a felon broke out of prison, were recognized as felonious at common law. **Sodomy** (anal intercourse, with or without consent) and some instances of **piracy** were made felonious by statutes early in the sixteenth century and are usually regarded as common law felonies. Later felonies are statutory. Other common law crimes than treason and the felonies just mentioned were misdemeanors, punishable until modern times by fine or by whipping. After the fourteenth century imprisonment became a common punishment for all crimes. (Transportation to the colonies was sometimes authorized for serious offenders in the eighteenth and first half of the nineteenth centuries.) Today in the United States, by statute, felonies and misdemeanors are often distinguished according to the maximum prison term permitted. A year and a day is a common dividing line. Imprisonment is provided for both felonies and misdemeanors, but the distinction has continuing importance in such matters as the felony-murder rule and certain principles of justification. Originally, prisons were primarily for holding accused persons awaiting trial. Lengthy sentences of imprisonment might have amounted to death sentences in the early days, when disease or starvation might easily be the lot of the prisoner.

While in early English times the death penalty was possible upon conviction of any felony, many in fact escaped the carrying out of the death sentence. Pardon was sometimes available, and in some situations was almost a matter of course.

Or the felon might reach sanctuary (an area under church protection, but usually available only for a limited period of time) and then agree to forfeiture of his property for permission to abjure the realm—and return only on pain of outlawry. (The outlaw was outside the law and could be killed on sight by anyone without penalty.) Makers of such bargains were sometimes a bit slow to depart. At one time they were expected to make for Dover or a near port, dressed in sackcloth and ashes, and to stop in one place no more than one night; if they could not immediately find a departing vessel on arrival at the port they were expected to wade out into the sea as a token of their good faith. Such practices fell into decay and the most common method of avoiding the death penalty became benefit of clergy. Originally this was a privilege extended to clerics; they were turned over to the church for ecclesiastical discipline rather than killed. Over the years, the benefit was extended to all who could read—the common test was the Neck Verse (Psalm 51, verse 1): "Have mercy upon me, O

God, according to thy loving kindness; according to the multitude of thy tender mercies blot out my transgressions."—and eventually to everyone. But this did not mean the abolition of the death penalty, because concurrently Parliament was limiting by statute the felonies which were clergiable, and providing that a person could claim benefit of clergy only once; branding was supposed to identify those who had once been granted the privilege. In the nineteenth century benefit of clergy was abolished and the death penalty dealt with more directly by statute.

By the nineteenth century most important crimes (and defenses thereto) seemed to have been identified and given reasonably full judicial definition. Instances of striking innovation decreased; Parliament began to take the lead in creation of new crimes and definition of some of the old ones; and it began the work of codification. The courts continued to play an important role, interpreting the language of the statutes and developing the law interstitially.

Today, when you see a reference to a "common law" rule or a "common law" decision, without mention of some former time when the decision was made, the meaning is probably only that rule or decision is not based on a statute. It is not necessarily one grounded on some ancient legal notion; it may be informed by the Model Penal Code and other current writing on criminal law. Even in a jurisdiction which has completely codified its law, in the sense that all crimes are defined by statute, it might be correct to call a decision a common law one if, for example, it is based on the meaning of a word used but undefined by the statute, but having a definition, relied upon in the opinion, developed at common law.

In America the colonists almost always followed the English common law, sometimes accepting English statutory modifications, to the extent suitable for their circumstances. The new states began with a mixed common law and statutory base, and as statutory modification continued, they often created codes of criminal law. Even in code states, common law crimes were sometimes retained as supplementary to the new codes. Where common law crimes are supplanted by statute, many of the terms retain their common law definitions, and the judges continue to interpret the criminal law. The American Law Institute's Model Penal Code, most of the text of which is printed as an appendix to this book, is the great inspiration for reform of the criminal law in modern times. It abolishes common law crimes and defenses and attempts complete definition of all crimes, retaining in express language so much of the common law plan and definition as it deems desirable. See § 1.05 and comment number one thereto.

Commonwealth v. Mochan

Superior Court of Pennsylvania, 1955.
177 Pa.Super. 454, 110 A.2d 788.

HIRT, JUDGE.

* * *

* * * Defendant was tried before a judge without a jury and was convicted on both charges and was sentenced. He has appealed from the refusal by the court en banc of his motions in arrest of judgment, on the ground advanced by him that the conduct charged in the indictments, concededly not a criminal offense in this State by any statute, does not constitute a misdemeanor at common law. In a number of States and

especially in the common law State of Pennsylvania the common law of England, as to crimes, is in force except in so far as it has been abrogated by statute. The indictments in these cases by their language, clearly purported to charge a common law crime not included in our Penal Code or elsewhere in our statutory law.

It is established by the testimony that the defendant over a period of more than one month early in 1953, on numerous occasions and on the specific dates laid in the indictments, telephoned one Louise Zivkovich, a stranger to him and a married woman of the highest character and repute. He called as often as three times each week and at any hour of the day or night. His language on these calls was obscene, lewd and filthy. He not only suggested intercourse with her but talked of sodomy as well, in the loathsome language of that criminal act, on a number of occasions. The calls were coming in from a four-party line. Through co-operation with the telephone company, the defendant was finally located and was arrested by the police at the telephone after the completion of his last call. * * * Mrs. Zivkovich recognized his voice, in a telephone conversation with him which was set up by the police.

It is of little importance that there is no precedent in our reports which decides the precise question here involved. The test is not whether precedents can be found in the books but whether the alleged crimes could have been prosecuted and the offenders punished under the common law. Commonwealth v. McHale, 97 Pa. 397, 408. In Commonwealth v. Miller, 94 Pa. Super. 499, 507, the controlling principles are thus stated: "The common law is sufficiently broad to punish as a misdemeanor, although there may be no exact precedent, any act which directly injures or tends to injure the public to such an extent as to require the state to interfere and punish the wrongdoer, as in the case of acts which injuriously affect public morality, or obstruct, or pervert public justice, or the administration of government. 16 Corpus Juris, Sec. 23, page 65, citing Respublica v. Teischer, 1 Dall. 335; Com. v. Sharpless, 2 Serg. & R. 91, and Barker v. Com., 19 Pa. 412." Cf. Commonwealth of Pennsylvania v. DeGrange, 97 Pa.Super. 181, in which it is said: " 'Whatever openly outrages decency and is injurious to public morals is a misdemeanor at common law': Russell on Crimes and Misdemeanors, 8th Ed., Vol. 1, p. 10; 4 Blackstone's Commentaries 65, note." Any act is indictable at common law which from its nature scandalously affects the morals or health of the community. 1 Wharton, Criminal Law, 12 Ed., § 23. Thus in Barker v. Commonwealth, 19 Pa. 412, a common law conviction based upon open obscenity was affirmed. * * *

To endeavor merely to persuade a married woman to commit adultery is not indictable. Smith v. Commonwealth, 54 Pa. 209. The present defendant's criminal intent was evidenced by a number of overt acts beyond the mere oral solicitation of adultery. The vile and disgusting suggestions of sodomy alone and the otherwise persistent lewd, immoral and filthy language used by the defendant, take these cases out of the principle of the Smith case. Moreover potentially at least, defendant's acts injuriously affected public morality. The operator or any one on defendant's four-party telephone line could have listened in on the conversations, and at least two other persons in

Mrs. Zivkovich's household heard some of defendant's immoral and obscene language over the telephone.

* * *

Judgments and sentences affirmed.

WOODSIDE, J., filed a dissenting opinion in which GUNTHER, J., joins.

WOODSIDE, JUDGE (dissenting).

Not unmindful of the reprehensible conduct of the appellant, I nevertheless cannot agree with the majority that what he did was a crime punishable under the laws of this Commonwealth.

The majority is declaring something to be a crime which was never before known to be a crime in this Commonwealth. They have done this by the application of such general principles as "it is a crime to do anything which injures or tends to injure the public to such an extent as to require the state to interfere and punish the wrongdoer;" and "whatever openly outrages decency and is injurious to public morals is a misdemeanor."

Not only have they declared it to be a crime to do an act "injuriously affecting public morality," but they have declared it to be a crime to do any act which has a "potentially" injurious effect on public morality.

Under the division of powers in our constitution it is for the legislature to determine what "injures or tends to injure the public."

One of the most important functions of a legislature is to determine what acts "require the state to interfere and punish the wrongdoer." There is no reason for the legislature to enact any criminal laws if the courts delegate to themselves the power to apply such general principles as are here applied to whatever conduct may seem to the courts to be injurious to the public.

There is no doubt that the common law is a part of the law of this Commonwealth, and we punish many acts under the common law. But after nearly two hundred years of constitutional government in which the legislature and not the courts have been charged by the people with the responsibility of deciding which acts do and which do not injure the public to the extent which requires punishment, it seems to me we are making an unwarranted invasion of the legislative field when we arrogate that responsibility to ourselves by declaring now, for the first time, that certain acts are a crime.

* * *

GUNTHER, J., joins in this dissent.

Note on New Common Law Crimes

The supposed power to discover previously unsuspected common law crimes is not much exercised today, either because codification has eliminated any crimes not defined in the code or because judges think it inappropriate for modern times. For other examples of the exercise of such power see The King v. Manley, [1933] 1 K.B. 529 (C.C.A.) (making false reports to the police) and Shaw v. Director of Public Prosecutions, [1962] A.C. 220 (H.L.) (conspiracy to corrupt public morals through publication of a directory of prostitutes). Most modern writers have opposed the judicial creation of crimes. See, e.g., 3 Stephen, A

History of the Criminal Law of England, pp. 358–360 (1883) and Model Penal Code § 1.05, comment 3.

Keeler v. Superior Court of Amador County

Supreme Court of California, En Banc, 1970.
2 Cal.3d 619, 87 Cal.Rptr. 481, 470 P.2d 617.

MOSK, JUSTICE.

In this proceeding for writ of prohibition we are called upon to decide whether an unborn but viable fetus is a "human being" within the meaning of the California statute defining murder (Pen.Code, § 187). We conclude that the Legislature did not intend such a meaning, and that for us to construe the statute to the contrary and apply it to this petitioner would exceed our judicial power and deny petitioner due process of law.

The evidence received at the preliminary examination may be summarized as follows: Petitioner and Teresa Keeler obtained an interlocutory decree of divorce on September 27, 1968. They had been married for 16 years. Unknown to petitioner, Mrs. Keeler was then pregnant by one Ernest Vogt, whom she had met earlier that summer. * * *

On February 23, 1969, Mrs. Keeler was driving on a narrow mountain road in Amador County * * *. She met petitioner driving in the opposite direction; he blocked the road with his car, and she pulled over to the side. He said, "I hear you're pregnant. If you are you had better stay away from the girls and from here." * * * Petitioner then looked at her abdomen and became "extremely upset." He said, "You sure are. I'm going to stomp it out of you." He pushed her against the car, shoved his knee into her abdomen, and struck her in the face with several blows. * * *

* * * A Caesarian section was performed and the fetus was examined *in utero*. Its head was found to be severely fractured, and it was delivered stillborn. The pathologist gave as his opinion that the cause of death was skull fracture with consequent cerebral hemorrhaging, that death would have been immediate, and that the injury could have been the result of force applied to the mother's abdomen. There was no air in the fetus' lungs, and the umbilical cord was intact.

Upon delivery the fetus weighed five pounds and was 18 inches in length. Both Mrs. Keeler and her obstetrician testified that fetal movements had been observed prior to February 23, 1969. The evidence was in conflict as to the estimated age of the fetus, the expert testimony on the point, however, concluded "with reasonable medical certainty" that the fetus had developed to the stage of viability, i.e., that in the event of premature birth on the date in question it would have had a 75 percent to 96 percent chance of survival.

An information was filed charging petitioner, in Count I, with committing the crime of murder (Pen.Code, § 187) in that he did "unlawfully kill a human being, to wit Baby Girl VOGT, with malice aforethought." * * * His motion to set aside the information for lack of probable cause (Pen.Code, § 995) was denied, and he now seeks a writ of prohibition * * *.

I

Penal Code section 187 provides: "Murder is the unlawful killing of a human being, with malice aforethought." The dispositive question is whether the fetus which petitioner is accused of killing was, on February 23, 1969, a "human being" within the meaning of this statute. If it was not, petitioner cannot be charged with its "murder" and prohibition will lie.

Section 187 was enacted as part of the Penal Code of 1872. Inasmuch as the provision has not been amended since that date, we must determine the intent of the Legislature at the time of its enactment. But section 187 was, in turn, taken verbatim from the first California statute defining murder, part of the Crimes and Punishments Act of 1850. (Stats.1850, ch. 99, § 19, p. 231.) Penal Code section 5 (also enacted in 1872) declares: "The provisions of this Code, so far as they are substantially the same as existing statutes, must be construed as continuations thereof, and not as new enactments." We begin, accordingly, by inquiring into the intent of the Legislature in 1850 when it first defined murder as the unlawful and malicious killing of a "human being."

It will be presumed, of course, that in enacting a statute the Legislature was familiar with the relevant rules of the common law, and, when it couches its enactment in common law language, that its intent was to continue those rules in statutory form. * * *

We therefore undertake a brief review of the origins and development of the common law of abortional homicide. * * * From that inquiry it appears that by the year 1850—the date with which we are concerned—an infant could not be the subject of homicide at common law *unless it had been born alive.* * * * In short, "By Coke's time, the common law regarded abortion as murder only if the foetus is (1) quickened, (2) born alive, (3) lives for a brief interval, and (4) then dies." * * *

Against this background, a series of infanticide prosecutions were brought in the English courts in mid-19th century. In each, a woman or her accomplice was charged with murdering a newborn child, and it was uniformly declared to be the law that a verdict of murder could not be returned unless it was proved the infant had been born alive. * * *

* * *

By the year 1850 this rule of the common law had long been accepted in the United States. * * *

While it was thus "well settled" in American case law that the killing of an unborn child was not homicide, a number of state legislatures in the first half of the 19th century undertook to modify the common law in this respect. The movement began when New York abandoned the common law of abortion in 1830. * * *

In the years between 1830 and 1850 at least five other states followed New York and enacted, as companion provisions, (1) a statute declaring feticide to be a crime, punishable as manslaughter, and (2) a statute prohibiting abortion. In California, however, the pattern was not repeated. Much of the Crimes and Punishments Act of 1850 was based on existing New York statute law; but although a section proscribing abortion was included in the new Act (§ 45), the Legislature declined to adopt any provision defining and punishing a special crime of feticide.

We conclude that in declaring murder to be the unlawful and malicious killing of a "human being" the Legislature of 1850 intended that term to have the settled common law meaning of a person who had been born alive, and did not intend the act of feticide—as distinguished from abortion—to be an offense under the laws of California.

Nothing occurred between the years 1850 and 1872 to suggest that in adopting the new Penal Code on the latter date the Legislature entertained any different intent. * * *

Any lingering doubt on this subject must be laid to rest by a consideration of the legislative history of the Penal Code of 1872. The Act establishing the California Code Commission required the commissioners to revise all statutes then in force, correct errors and omissions, and "recommend all such enactments as shall, in the judgment of the Commission, be necessary to supply the defects of and give completeness to the existing legislation of the State * * *." In discharging this duty the statutory schemes of our sister states were carefully examined, and we must assume the commissioners had knowledge of the feticide laws noted hereinabove. Yet the commissioners proposed no such law for California, and none has been adopted to this day.

That such an omission was not an oversight clearly appears, moreover, from the commissioners' explanatory notes to Penal Code section 187. After quoting the definitions of murder given by Coke, Blackstone, and Hawkins, the commissioners conclude: "A child within its mother's womb is not a 'human being' within the meaning of that term as used in defining murder. The rule is that it must be born.—Rex vs. Brain, 6 Car. & P., p. 349. That every part of it must have come from the mother before the killing of it will constitute a felonious homicide. * * *" * * *

* * *

It is the policy of this state to construe a penal statute as favorably to the defendant as its language and the circumstances of its application may reasonably permit; just as in the case of a question of fact, the defendant is entitled to the benefit of every reasonable doubt as to the true interpretation of words or the construction of language used in a statute. (Walsh v. Dept. of Alcoholic Bev. Control (1963) 59 Cal.2d 757, 764–765, 31 Cal.Rptr. 297, 382 P.2d 337, and cases cited.) We hold that in adopting the definition of murder in Penal Code section 187 the Legislature intended to exclude from its reach the act of killing an unborn fetus.

II

The People urge, however, that the sciences of obstetrics and pediatrics have greatly progressed since 1872, to the point where with proper medical care a normally developed fetus prematurely born at 28 weeks or more has an excellent chance of survivial, i.e., is "viable"; that the common law requirement of live birth to prove the fetus had become a "human being" who may be the victim of murder is no longer in accord with scientific fact, since an unborn but viable fetus is now fully capable of independent life; and that one who unlawfully and maliciously terminates such a life should therefore be liable to prosecution for murder under section 187. We may grant the premises of this argument; indeed, we neither deny nor denigrate the vast progress of medicine in the century since the enactment of the Penal Code. But we cannot join in the conclusion sought to be deduced: we cannot hold this petitioner to answer for murder by reason of his alleged act of killing an unborn—even though viable—fetus. To such a charge there are two insuperable obstacles, one "jurisdictional" and the other constitutional.

Penal Code section 6 declares in relevant part that "No act or omission" accomplished after the code has taken effect "is criminal or punishable, except as prescribed or authorized by this Code, or by some of the statutes which it specifies as continuing in force and as not affected by its provisions, or by some ordinance, municipal, county, or township regulation * * *." This section embodies a fundamental principle of our tripartite form of government, i.e., that subject to the constitutional prohibition against cruel and unusual punishment, the power to define crimes and fix penalties is vested exclusively in the legislative branch. Stated differently, there are no common law crimes in California. * * *

* * * Indeed, "Constructive crimes—crimes built up by courts with the aid of inference, implication, and strained interpretation—are repugnant to the spirit and letter of English and American criminal law." (Ex parte McNulty (1888) 77 Cal. 164, 168, 19 P. 237, 239.)

Applying these rules to the case at bar, we would undoubtedly act in excess of the judicial power if we were to adopt the People's proposed construction of section 187. * * * Whether to thus extend liability for murder in California is a determination solely within the province of the Legislature. * * *

The second obstacle to the proposed judicial enlargement of section 187 is the guarantee of due process of law. Assuming *arguendo* that we have the power to adopt the new construction of this statute as the law of California, such a ruling, by constitutional command, could operate only prospectively, and thus could not in any event reach the conduct of petitioner on February 23, 1969.

The first essential of due process is fair warning of the act which is made punishable as a crime. "That the terms of a penal statute creating a new offense must be sufficiently explicit to inform those who are subject to it what conduct on their part will render them liable to its penalties, is a well-recognized requirement, consonant alike with ordinary notions of fair play and the settled rules of law." (Connally v. General Constr. Co. (1926) 269 U.S. 385, 391, 46 S.Ct. 126, 127, 70 L.Ed. 322.) "No one may be required at peril of life, liberty or property to speculate as to the meaning of penal statutes. All are entitled to be informed as to what the State commands or forbids." (Lanzetta v. New Jersey (1939) 306 U.S. 451, 453, 59 S.Ct. 618, 619, 83 L.Ed. 888.) The law of California is in full accord. (In re Newbern

(1960) supra, 53 Cal.2d 786, 792, 3 Cal.Rptr. 364, 350 P.2d 116; In re Davis (1966) supra, 242 Cal.App.2d 645, 650–651, 51 Cal.Rptr. 702.)

This requirement of fair warning is reflected in the constitutional prohibition against the enactment of ex post facto laws (U.S. Const., art. I, §§ 9, 10; Cal. Const., art. I, § 16). When a new penal statute is applied retrospectively to make punishable an act which was not criminal at the time it was performed, the defendant has been given no advance notice consistent with due process. And precisely the same effect occurs when such an act is made punishable under a preexisting statute but by means of an unforeseeable *judicial* enlargement thereof. (Bouie v. City of Columbia (1964) 378 U.S. 347, 84 S.Ct. 1697, 12 L.Ed.2d 894.)

In *Bouie* two Negroes took seats in the restaurant section of a South Carolina drugstore; no notices were posted restricting the area to whites only. When the defendants refused to leave upon demand, they were arrested and convicted of violating a criminal trespass statute which prohibited entry on the property of another "after notice" forbidding such conduct. Prior South Carolina decisions had emphasized the necessity of proving such notice to support a conviction under the statute. The South Carolina Supreme Court nevertheless affirmed the convictions, construing the statute to prohibit not only the act of entering after notice not to do so but also the wholly different act of remaining on the property after receiving notice to leave.

The United States Supreme Court reversed the convictions, holding that the South Carolina court's ruling was "unforeseeable" and when an "unforeseeable state-court construction of a criminal statute is applied retroactively to subject a person to criminal liability for past conduct, the effect is to deprive him of due process of law in the sense of fair warning that his contemplated conduct constitutes a crime." (378 U.S. at pp. 354–355, 84 S.Ct. at p. 1703.) Analogizing to the prohibition against retrospective penal legislation, the high court reasoned "Indeed, an unforeseeable judicial enlargement of a criminal statute, applied retroactively, operates precisely like an *ex post facto* law, such as Art. I, § 10, of the Constitution forbids. An *ex post facto* law has been defined by this Court as one 'that makes an action done before the passing of the law, and which was *innocent* when done, criminal; and punishes such action,' or 'that *aggravates* a *crime,* or makes it *greater* than it was, when committed.' Calder v. Bull, 3 Dall. 386, 390, 1 L.Ed. 648. If a state legislature is barred by the *Ex Post Facto* Clause from passing such a law, it must follow that a State Supreme Court is barred by the Due Process Clause from achieving precisely the same result by judicial construction. Cf. Smith v. Cahoon, 283 U.S. 553, 565, 51 S.Ct. 582, 586, 75 L.Ed. 1264. The fundamental principle that 'the required criminal law must have existed when the conduct in issue occurred,' Hall, General Principles of Criminal Law (2d ed. 1960), at 58–59, must apply to bar retroactive criminal prohibitions emanating from courts as well as from legislatures. If a judicial construction of a criminal statute is 'unexpected and indefensible by reference to the law which had been expressed prior to the conduct in issue,' it must not be given retroactive effect. Id., at 61." (Fn. omitted.) (Id. at pp. 353–354, 84 S.Ct. at pp. 1702–1703.)

* * *

Turning to the case law, we find no reported decision of the California courts which should have given petitioner notice that the killing of an unborn but viable fetus was prohibited by section 187. * * *

Properly understood, the often cited case of People v. Chavez (1947) 77 Cal.App.2d 621, 176 P.2d 92, does not derogate from this rule. There the defendant was charged with the murder of her newborn child, and convicted of manslaughter. She testified that the baby dropped from her womb into the toilet bowl; that she picked it up two or three minutes later, and cut but did not tie the umbilical cord; that the baby was limp and made no cry; and that after 15 minutes she wrapped it in a newspaper and concealed it, where it was found dead the next day. The autopsy surgeon testified that the baby was a full-term, nine-month child, weighing six and one-half pounds and appearing normal in every respect; that the body had very little blood in it, indicating the child had bled to death through the untied umbilical cord; that such a process would have taken about an hour; and that in his opinion "the child was born alive, based on conditions he found and the fact that the lungs contained air and the blood was extravasated or pushed back into the tissues, indicating heart action." (Id. at p. 623, 176 P.2d at p. 93.)

* * *

Chavez thus stands for the proposition—to which we adhere—that a viable fetus "in the process of being born" is a human being within the meaning of the homicide statutes. But it stands for no more; in particular it does not hold that a fetus, however viable, which is *not* "in the process of being born" is nevertheless a "human being" in the law of homicide. On the contrary, the opinion is replete with references to the common law requirement that the child be "born alive," however that term is defined, and must accordingly be deemed to reaffirm that requirement as part of the law of California.

* * *

We conclude that the judicial enlargement of section 187 now urged upon us by the People would not have been foreseeable to this petitioner, and hence that its adoption at this time would deny him due process of law.

Let a peremptory writ of prohibition issue restraining respondent court from taking any further proceedings on Count I of the information, charging petitioner with the crime of murder.

McComb, Peters, and Tobriner, JJ., and Peek, J. pro tem., concur.

Burke, Acting Chief Justice (dissenting).

The majority hold that "Baby Girl" Vogt, who, according to medical testimony, had reached the 35th week of development, had a 96 percent chance of survival, and was "definitely" alive and viable at the time of her death, nevertheless was not a "human being" under California's homicide statutes. In my view, in so holding, the majority ignore significant common law precedents, frustrate the express intent of the Legislature, and defy reason, logic and common sense.

* * *

The majority cast a passing glance at the common law concept of quickening, but fail to explain the significance of that concept: At common law, the quickened fetus *was* considered to be a human being, a second life separate and apart from its mother. * * *

Modern scholars have confirmed this aspect of common law jurisprudence. As Means observes, "The common law itself prohibited abortion after quickening and hanging a pregnant felon after quickening, *because the life of a second human being would thereby be taken,* although it did not call the offense murder or manslaughter." (Italics added; Means, The Law of New York Concerning Abortion and the Status of the Foetus, 1664–1968: A Case of Cessation of Constitutionality (1968) 14 N.Y.L.F. 411, 504.)

This reasoning explains why the killing of a quickened child was considered "a great misprision," although the killing of an unquickened child was no crime at all at common law (Means, supra, at p. 420). Moreover, although the common law did not apply the labels of "murder" or "manslaughter" to the killing of a quickened fetus, it appears that at common law this "great misprision" was severely punished. * * *

* * *

In my view, we cannot assume that the Legislature intended a person such as defendant charged with the malicious slaying of a fully viable child, to suffer only the mild penalties imposed upon common abortionists who, ordinarily, procure only the miscarriage of a nonviable fetus or embryo. (See Comment, Model Penal Code, § 207.11, p. 149 (Tent.Draft No. 9, 1959).) To do so would completely ignore the important common law distinction between the quickened and unquickened child.

Of course, I do not suggest that we should interpret the term "human being" in our homicide statutes in terms of the common law concept of quickening. At one time, that concept had a value in differentiating, as accurately as was then scientifically possible, between life and nonlife. The analogous concept of viability is clearly more satisfactory, for it has a well defined and medically determinable meaning denoting the ability of the fetus to live or survive apart from its mother.

The majority opinion suggests that we are confined to common law concepts, and to the common law definition of murder or manslaughter. However, the Legislature, in Penal Code sections 187 and 192, has defined those offenses for us: homicide is the unlawful killing of a "human being." Those words need not be frozen in place as of any particular time, but must be fairly and reasonably interpreted by this court to promote justice and to carry out the evident purposes of the Legislature in adopting a homicide statute. * * *

* * *

We commonly conceive of human existence as a spectrum stretching from birth to death. However, if this court properly might expand the definition of "human being" at one end of that spectrum, we may do so at the other end. Consider the following example: All would agree that "Shooting or otherwise damaging a corpse is not homicide. * * *" (Perkins, Criminal Law (2d ed. 1969) ch. 2, § 1, p. 31.) In other words, a corpse is not considered to be a "human being" and thus cannot be the subject of a "killing" as those terms are used in homicide statutes. However, it is readily apparent that our concepts of what constitutes a "corpse" have been and are being continually modified by advances in the field of medicine, including new techniques for life revival, restoration and resuscitation such as artificial respiration, open heart massage, transfusions, transplants and a variety of life-restoring stimulants, drugs and new surgical methods. Would this court ignore these developments and exonerate the killer of an apparently "drowned" child merely because that child would have been pronounced dead in 1648 or 1850? Obviously not. Whether a homicide occurred in that case would be determined by medical testimony regarding the capability of the child to have survived prior to the defendant's act. And that is precisely the test which this court should adopt in the instant case.

The common law reluctance to characterize the killing of a quickened fetus as a homicide was based solely upon a presumption that the fetus would have been born dead. * * * However, as we approach the 21st century, it has become apparent that "This presumption is not only contrary to common experience and the ordinary course of nature, but it is contrary to the usual rule with respect to presumptions followed in this state."

* * *

The majority also suggest that such an interpretation of our homicide statutes would deny defendant "fair warning" that his act was punishable as a crime. Aside from the absurdity of the underlying premise that defendant consulted Coke, Blackstone or Hale before kicking Baby Girl Vogt to death, it is clear that defendant had adequate notice that his act could constitute homicide. Due process only precludes prosecution under a new statute insufficiently explicit regarding the specific conduct proscribed, or under a preexisting statute "by means of an unforeseeable *judicial* enlargement thereof."

Our homicide statutes have been in effect in this state since 1850. The fact that the California courts have not been called upon to determine the precise question before us does not render "unforeseeable" a decision which determines that a viable fetus is a "human being" under those statutes. Can defendant really claim surprise that a 5-pound, 18-inch, 34-week-old, living, viable child is considered to be a human being?

The fact is that the foregoing construction of our homicide statutes easily could have been anticipated from strong dicta in People v. Chavez, supra, 77 Cal.App.2d 621, 625–626, 176 P.2d 92 (hg. den. by Sup.Ct.), wherein the court reviewed common law precedents but disapproved their requirement that the child be born alive and completely separated from its mother. The court in *Chavez* held that a viable child killed during, but prior to completion of, the birth process, was a human being under the homicide statutes. However, the court did not hold that partial birth was a prerequisite, for the court expressly set forth its holding "Without drawing a line of distinction applicable to all cases * * *." (77 Cal.App.2d at p. 627, 176 P.2d at p. 95.) In dicta, the court discussed the question when an unborn infant becomes a human being under the homicide statutes, as follows: "There is not much change in the child itself between a moment before and a moment after its expulsion from the body of its mother, and normally, while still dependent upon its mother, the child for some time before it is born, has not only the possibility but a strong probability of an ability to live an independent life. * * * While before birth or removal it is in a sense dependent upon its mother for life, there is another sense in which it has started an independent existence after it has reached a state of development where it is capable of living and where it will, in the normal course of nature and with ordinary care, continue to live and grow as a separate being. While it may not be possible to draw an exact line applicable to all cases, the rules of law should recognize and make some attempt to follow the natural and scientific facts to which they relate. * * * [I]t would be a mere fiction to hold that a child is not a human being because the process of birth has not been fully completed, when it has reached that state of viability when the destruction of the life of its mother would not end its existence and when, if separated from the mother naturally or by artificial means, it will live and grow in the normal manner." (77 Cal.App.2d at pp. 625–626, 176 P.2d at pp. 94, 95.)

* * *

SULLIVAN, J., concurs.

Rehearing denied; BURKE and SULLIVAN, JJ., dissenting.

Notes

1. Compare People v. Sobiek, 30 Cal.App.3d 458, 106 Cal.Rptr. 519, 82 A.L.R.3d 804 (1973), cert. denied 414 U.S. 855, 94 S.Ct. 155, 38 L.Ed.2d 104 (1973), construing a California theft statute to permit conviction of stealing of partnership property by a partner, contrary to earlier cases, and finding this not an ex post facto violation.

2. *Criminal homicide.* Most decisions agree with *Keeler* that the destruction before birth of the fetus is not criminal homicide at common law. See, e.g., reviewing authorities, Meadows v. State, 291 Ark. 105, 722 S.W.2d 584 (1987). For a case reaching a contrary common law result in view of modern medical knowledge (after a prior case gave warning of the change), see Commonwealth v. Lawrence, 404 Mass. 378, 536 N.E.2d 571 (1989). It *is* criminal homicide at common law to inflict an injury on the fetus which causes it to die after being born alive. Williams v. State, 316 Md. 677, 561 A.2d 216 [case 2] (1989). Section 187 of the California Penal Code was amended in 1970 to make the malicious killing of a fetus without the mother's consent murder.

3. *Feticide.* There was no common law crime of feticide, but the destruction of the fetus, in some circumstances, was the misdemeanor of abortion. Note that in a state which follows this common law scheme, and which, after Roe v. Wade, 410 U.S. 113, 93 S.Ct. 705, 35 L.Ed.2d 147 (1973), repeals its abortion legislation, a Keeler who acts in the early months of pregnancy may be guilty of nothing more than an assault on the mother.

4. *Ex Post Facto Legislation.* A starting point for consideration of *ex post facto* legislation is the 1798 opinion of JUSTICE CHASE in Calder v. Bull, 3 U.S. (3 Dall.) 386, 1 L.Ed. 648 (1798), in which he said (at 390 of U.S. and 650 of L.Ed.):

> I will state what laws I consider *ex post facto* laws, within the words and the intent of the prohibition. 1st. Every law that makes an action done before the passing of the law; and which was innocent when done, criminal; and punishes such action. 2d. Every law that aggravates a crime, or makes it greater than it was, when committed. 3d. Every law that changes the punishment, and inflicts a

greater punishment, than the law annexed to the crime, when committed. 4th. Every law that alters the legal rules of evidence, and receives less, or different, testimony, than the law at the time of the commission of the offense, in order to convict the offender.

Statutes of limitations are provisions which require that the prosecution of a crime commence within a stated period after its commission. Suppose that at the time A commits a crime, the statute of limitations is two years. Subsequently, the legislature extends the period to five years. Would prosecution of A commencing four years after the crime violate the *ex post facto* prohibition? Compare Falter v. United States, 23 F.2d 420 (2d Cir.1928), with Moore v. State, 43 N.J.L. 203 (1881). Suppose that a convicted felon was incompetent as a witness at the time of the crime, but that the legislature removed the bar before the trial; may a convicted felon testify against the defendant? See Hopt v. Utah, 110 U.S. 574, 4 S.Ct. 202, 28 L.Ed. 262 (1884). For two cases, reaching different conclusions (on different facts) about changes in penalties, see Dobbert v. Florida, 432 U.S. 282, 97 S.Ct. 2290, 53 L.Ed.2d 344, (1977) rehearing denied 434 U.S. 882, 98 S.Ct. 246, 54 L.Ed.2d 166 (1977), and Weaver v. Graham, 450 U.S. 24, 101 S.Ct. 960, 67 L.Ed.2d 17 (1981). Application of revised sentencing guidelines to a crime committed before their effective date violates the *ex post facto* provision. Miller v. Florida, 482 U.S. 423, 107 S.Ct. 2446, 96 L.Ed.2d 351 (1987).

Question

The Year and a Day Rule. A common law rule barred prosecutions for criminal homicide where death occurred more than a year and a day (actually more than one year by modern methods of counting) after the infliction of the injury. This "year and a day rule" was probably based primarily on medical uncertainty as to cause of death, where death is long delayed. In Commonwealth v. Ladd, 402 Pa. 164, 166 A.2d 501 (1960), Pennsylvania abolished the rule judicially, allowing the conviction in the case before it to stand, on the ground that the rule was obsolete in the light of modern medical knowledge. Unconstitutional?

United States v. Powell

Supreme Court of the United States, 1975.
423 U.S. 87, 96 S.Ct. 316, 46 L.Ed.2d 228.

MR. JUSTICE REHNQUIST delivered the opinion for the Court.

The Court of Appeals in a brief *per curiam* opinion held that portion of an Act of Congress prohibiting the mailing of firearms "capable of being concealed on the person," 18 U.S.C. § 1715, to be unconstitutionally vague, and we granted certiorari to review this determination. 420 U.S. 971, 95 S.Ct. 1390, 43 L.Ed.2d 651 (1975). Respondent was found guilty of having violated the statute by a jury in the United States District Court for the Eastern District of Washington, and was sentenced by that court to a term of two years' imprisonment. * * *

* * *

Respondent was indicted on a single count of mailing a firearm capable of being concealed on the person (the sawed-off shotgun contained in the second package), in violation of 18 U.S.C. § 1715. At trial there was evidence that the weapon could be concealed on an average person. Respondent was convicted by a jury which was instructed that in order to return a guilty verdict it must find that she "knowingly caused to be delivered by mail a firearm capable of being concealed on the person."

She appealed her judgment of conviction to the Court of Appeals, and that court held that the portion of § 1715 proscribing the mailing of "other firearms capable of being concealed on the person" was so vague that it violated the Due Process Clause of the Fifth Amendment to the United States Constitution. 501 F.2d 1136 (1974). Citing Lanzetta v. New Jersey, 306 U.S. 451, 59 S.Ct. 618, 83 L.Ed. 888 (1939), the court held that, although it was clear that a pistol could be concealed on the person, "the statutory prohibition as it might relate to sawed-off shotguns is not so readily recognizable to persons of common experience and intelligence." 501 F.2d, at 1137.

* * *

We said last Term that "[i]t is well established that vagueness challenges to statutes which do not involve First Amendment freedoms must be examined in the light of the facts of the case at hand." United States v. Mazurie, 419 U.S. 544, 550, 95 S.Ct. 710, 714, 42 L.Ed.2d 706 (1975). The Court of Appeals dealt with the statute generally, rather than as applied to respondent in this case. It must necessarily have concluded, therefore, that the prohibition against mailing "firearms capable of being concealed on the person" proscribed no comprehensible course of conduct at all. It is well settled, of course, that such a statute may not constitutionally be applied to any set of facts. Lanzetta v. New Jersey, 306 U.S., at 453, 59 S.Ct., at 619; Connally v. General Const. Co., 269 U.S. 385, 391, 46 S.Ct. 126, 127, 70 L.Ed. 322 (1926).

An example of such a vague statute is found in United States v. Cohen Grocery Co., 255 U.S. 81, 89, 41 S.Ct. 298, 300, 65 L.Ed. 516 (1921). The statute there prohibited any person from "willfully * * * mak[ing] any unjust or unreasonable rate or charge in * * * dealing in or with any necessaries. * * *" So worded it "forbids no specific or definite act" and "leaves open * * * the widest conceivable inquiry, the scope of which no one can foresee and the result of which no one can foreshadow or adequately guard against." Ibid.

On the other hand, a statute which provides that certain oversized or heavy loads must be transported by the "shortest practicable route" is not unconstitutionally vague. Sproles v. Binford, 286 U.S. 374, 393, 52 S.Ct. 581, 587, 76 L.Ed. 1167 (1932). The carrier has been given clear notice that a reasonably ascertainable standard of conduct is mandated; it is for him to insure that his actions do not fall outside the legal limits. The sugar dealer in *Cohen,* to the contrary, could have had no idea in advance what an "unreasonable rate" would be because that would have been determined by the vagaries of supply and demand, factors over which he had no control. Engaged in a lawful business which Congress had in no way sought to proscribe, he could not have charged *any* price with the confidence that it would not be later found unreasonable.

But the challenged language of 18 U.S.C. § 1715 is quite different from that of the statute involved in *Cohen.* It intelligibly forbids a definite course of conduct: the mailing of concealable firearms. While doubts as to the applicability of the language in marginal fact situations may be conceived, we think that the statute gave respondent adequate warning that her mailing of a 22-inch-long sawed-off shotgun was a criminal offense. Even as to more doubtful cases than that of respondent, we have said that "the law is full of instances where a man's fate depends on his estimating rightly, that is, as the jury subsequently estimates it, some matter of degree." Nash v. United States, 229 U.S. 373, 377, 33 S.Ct. 780, 781, 57 L.Ed. 1232 (1913).

The Court of Appeals questioned whether the "person" referred to in the statute to measure capability of concealment was to be "the person mailing the firearm, the person receiving the firearm, or, perhaps, an average person, male or female, wearing whatever garb might be reasonably appropriate, wherever the place and whatever the season." 501 F.2d, at 1137. But we think it fair to attribute to Congress the commonsense meaning that such a person would be an average person garbed in a manner to aid, rather than hinder, concealment of the weapons. Such straining to inject doubt as to the meaning of words where no doubt would be felt by the normal reader is not required by the "void for vagueness" doctrine, and we will not indulge in it.

The Court of Appeals also observed that "[t]o require Congress to delimit the size of the firearms (other than pistols and revolvers) that it intends to declare unmailable is certainly to impose no insurmountable burden upon it * * *." Ibid. Had Congress chosen to delimit the size of the firearms intended to be declared unmailable, it would have written a different statute and in some respects a narrower one than it actually wrote. To the extent that it was intended to proscribe the mailing of *all* weapons capable of being concealed on the person, a statute so limited would have been less inclusive than the one Congress actually wrote.

But the more important disagreement we have with this observation of the Court of Appeals is that it seriously misconceives the "void for vagueness" doctrine. The fact that Congress might, without difficulty, have chosen "[c]learer and more precise language" equally capable of achieving the end which it sought does not mean that the statute which it in fact drafted is unconstitutionally vague. United States v. Petrillo, 332 U.S. 1, 7, 67 S.Ct. 1538, 1541, 91 L.Ed. 1877 (1947).

The judgment of the Court of Appeals is

Reversed.

[The opinion of MR. JUSTICE STEWART, to the effect that the rule of *ejusdem generis* (treated in Chapter IV of this book) requires a construction of the statute which would exclude sawed-off shotguns, as a matter of congressional intent, is omitted.]

Question

Is the following statute, punishing a violation by a fine not exceeding $10,000 or imprisonment not exceeding 20 years, or both, constitutional?

> Any person not engaged in any lawful occupation, known to be a member of any gang consisting of two or more persons, who has been convicted at least three times of being a disorderly person, or who has been convicted of any crime, in this or in any other State, is declared to be a gangster * * *.

Notes

1. *Words of Degree.* MR. JUSTICE HOLMES wrote in Nash v. United States, 229 U.S. 373, 376–377, 33 S.Ct. 780, 781, 57 L.Ed. 1232, 1235 (1913), with respect to the constitutionality of legislation which had been interpreted to punish contracts and combinations which unduly restricted competition or unduly obstructed the course of trade:

> * * * And thereupon it is said that the crime thus defined by the statute contains in its definition an element of degree as to which estimates may differ, with the result that a man might find himself in prison because his honest judgment did not anticipate that of a jury of less competent men. The kindred proposition that "the criminality of an act cannot depend upon whether a jury may think it reasonable or unreasonable. There must be some definiteness and certainty," is cited from the late Mr. Justice Brewer, sitting in the circuit court. Tozer v. United States, 4 Inters.Com.Rep. 245, 52 Fed. 917, 919.
>
> But, apart from the common law as to the restraint of trade thus taken up by the statute, the law is full of instances where a man's fate depends on his estimating rightly, that is, as the jury subsequently estimates it, some matter of degree. * * *

2. *The Void for Vagueness Doctrine.* Bowers v. State, 283 Md. 115, 120–123, 389 A.2d 341, 344–346 (1978):

> From a long line of Supreme Court decisions, certain basic and universally accepted principles have emerged concerning application of the void-for-vagueness doctrine. The cardinal requirement is that a penal statute "be sufficiently explicit to inform those who are subject to it what conduct on their part will render them liable to its penalties." "[A] statute which either forbids or requires the doing of an act in terms so vague that men of common intelligence must necessarily guess at its meaning and differ as to its application, violates the first essential of due process of law." The Fifth and Fourteenth Amendments guarantee that "[n]o one may be required at peril of life, liberty or property to speculate as to the meaning of penal statutes. All are entitled to be informed as to what the State commands or forbids."
>
> In assessing the constitutionality of a statute assailed as overly uncertain either in respect of the acts it purports to prohibit or the persons to whom it applies, courts typically consider two basic criteria. The first of these may be described as the fair notice principle and is grounded on the assumption that one should be free to choose between lawful and unlawful conduct. Due process commands that persons of ordinary intelligence and experience be afforded a reasonable opportunity to know what is prohibited, so that they may govern their behavior accordingly. This notion of fair warning does not presume that criminals frequently consult the statute books prior to embarking on an illicit course of action. * * *
>
> A statute may also be stricken for vagueness if it fails to provide legally fixed standards and adequate guidelines for police, judicial officers, triers of fact and others whose obligation it is to enforce, apply and administer the penal laws. * * *
>
> This is not to say, of course, that a criminal statute is void merely because it allows for the exercise of some discretion on the part of law enforcement and judicial officials. It is only where a statute is so broad as to be susceptible to

irrational and selective patterns of enforcement that it will be held unconstitutional under this second arm of the vagueness principle.

As a general rule, the constitutionality of a statutory provision under attack on void-for-vagueness grounds must be determined strictly on the basis of the statute's application to the particular facts at hand. Thus, it will usually be immaterial that the statute is of questionable applicability in foreseeable marginal situations, if a contested provision clearly applies to the conduct of the defendant in a specific case.

A different rule governs, however, where the statute in question appears to intrude upon fundamental constitutional liberties, particularly the First Amendment guarantees of free speech and assembly. In such cases, not only may the two vices of inadequate notice and insufficient adjudicative guidelines be present, but in addition the indefiniteness of the statute itself may inhibit the exercise of protected freedoms. * * *

On account of this "chilling effect" which vagueness can exert on First Amendment liberties, the Supreme Court has stated that whenever a criminal statute may, because of imprecise draftsmanship, impact upon free speech rights, the void-for-vagueness doctrine "demands a greater degree of specificity than in other contexts." Translated, this principle of strict specificity means that where First Amendment values are at least potentially involved, the statute is to be tested for vagueness *on its face*. So considered, the principle is essentially a rule of standing, permitting a defendant to challenge the validity of a statute as applied to marginal cases, even though the acts for which he has been charged may be squarely within the coverage of the statute. Once it is determined, however, that a strict specificity standard ought to apply in any given case, the criteria for measuring the validity of a statute under the vagueness doctrine are the same as in a non-First Amendment context: fair warning and adequate guidelines.

Papachristou v. Jacksonville

Supreme Court of the United States, 1972.
405 U.S. 156, 92 S.Ct. 839, 31 L.Ed.2d 110.

MR. JUSTICE DOUGLAS delivered the opinion of the Court.

This case involves eight defendants who were convicted in a Florida municipal court of violating a Jacksonville, Florida, vagrancy ordinance.[1] Their convictions, entailing fines and jail sentences (some of which were suspended), were affirmed by the Florida Circuit Court in a consolidated appeal, and their petition for certiorari was denied by the District Court of Appeal, 236 So.2d 141, on the authority of Johnson v. State, Fla., 202 So.2d

1. Jacksonville Ordinance Code § 26–57 provided at the time of these arrests and convictions as follows:

"Rogues and vagabonds, or dissolute persons who go about begging, common gamblers, persons who use juggling or unlawful games or plays, common drunkards, common night walkers, thieves, pilferers or pickpockets, traders in stolen property, lewd, wanton and lascivious persons, keepers of gambling places, common railers and brawlers, persons wandering or strolling around from place to place without any lawful purpose or object, habitual loafers, disorderly persons, persons neglecting all lawful business and habitually spending their time by frequenting houses of ill fame, gaming houses, or places where alcoholic beverages are sold or served, persons able to work but habitually living upon the earnings of their wives or minor children shall be deemed vagrants and, upon conviction in the Municipal Court shall be punished as provided for Class D offenses."

Class D offenses at the time of these arrests and convictions were punishable by 90 days' imprisonment, $500 fine, or both. Jacksonville Ordinance Code § 1–8 (1965). * * *

* * *

852. The case is here on a petition for certiorari, which we granted. 403 U.S. 917, 91 S.Ct. 2233, 29 L.Ed. 694. For reasons which will appear, we reverse.

* * *

The facts are stipulated. Papachristou and Calloway are white females. Melton and Johnson are black males. Papachristou was enrolled in a job-training program sponsored by the State Employment Service at Florida Junior College in Jacksonville. Calloway was a typing and shorthand teacher at a state mental institution located near Jacksonville. She was the owner of the automobile in which the four defendants were arrested. Melton was a Vietnam war veteran who had been released from the Navy after nine months in a veterans' hospital. On the date of his arrest he was a part-time computer helper while attending college as a full-time student in Jacksonville. Johnson was a tow-motor operator in a grocery chain warehouse and was a lifelong resident of Jacksonville.

At the time of their arrest the four of them were riding in Calloway's car on the main thoroughfare in Jacksonville. They had left a restaurant owned by Johnson's uncle where they had eaten and were on their way to a nightclub. The arresting officers denied that the racial mixture in the car played any part in the decision to make the arrest. The arrest, they said, was made because the defendants had stopped near a used-car lot which had been broken into several times. There was, however, no evidence of any breaking and entering on the night in question.

Of these four charged with "prowling by auto" none had been previously arrested except Papachristou who had once been convicted of a municipal offense.

Jimmy Lee Smith and Milton Henry (who is not a petitioner) were arrested between 9 and 10 a.m. on a weekday in downtown Jacksonville, while waiting for a friend who was to lend them a car so they could apply for a job at a produce company. Smith was a part-time produce worker and part-time organizer for a Negro political group. He had a common-law wife and three children supported by him and his wife. He had been arrested several times but convicted only once. Smith's companion, Henry, was an 18-year-old high school student with no previous record of arrest.

This morning it was cold, and Smith had no jacket, so they went briefly into a dry cleaning shop to wait, but left when requested to do so. They thereafter walked back and forth two or three times over a two-block stretch looking for their friend. The store owners, who apparently were wary of Smith and his companion, summoned two police officers who searched the men and found neither had a weapon. But they were arrested because the officers said they had no identification and because the officers did not believe their story.

* * *

Campbell was arrested as he reached his home very early one morning and was charged with "common thief." He was stopped by officers because he was traveling at a high rate of speed, yet no speeding charge was placed against him.

Brown was arrested when he was observed leaving a downtown Jacksonville hotel by a police officer seated in a cruiser. The police testified he was reputed to be a thief, narcotics pusher, and generally opprobrious character. The officer called Brown over to the car, intending at that time to arrest him unless he had a good explanation for being on the street. Brown walked over to the police cruiser, as commanded, and the officer began to search him, apparently preparatory to placing him in the car. In the process of the search he came on two small packets which were later found to contain heroin. When the officer touched the pocket where the packets were, Brown began to resist. He was charged with "disorderly loitering on street" and "disorderly conduct—resisting arrest with violence." While he was also charged with a narcotics violation, that charge was *nolled.*

Jacksonville's ordinance and Florida's statute were "derived from early English law," Johnson v. State, 202 So.2d, at 854, and employ "archaic language" in their definitions of vagrants. Id., at 855. The history is an often-told tale. The breakup of feudal estates in England led to labor shortages which in turn resulted in the Statutes of Laborers, designed to stabilize the labor force by prohibiting increases in wages and prohibiting the movement of workers from their home areas in search of improved conditions. Later vagrancy laws became criminal aspects of the poor laws. The series of laws passed in England on the subject became increasingly severe.[4]

* * *

This ordinance is void for vagueness, both in the sense that it "fails to give a person of ordinary intelligence fair notice that his contemplated conduct is forbidden by the statute," United States v. Harriss, 347 U.S. 612, 617, 74 S.Ct. 808, 812, 98 L.Ed. 989, and because it encourages arbitrary and erratic arrests and convictions. Thornhill v. Alabama, 310 U.S. 88, 60 S.Ct. 736, 84 L.Ed. 1093; Herndon v. Lowry, 301 U.S. 242, 57 S.Ct. 732, 81 L.Ed. 1066.

4. See 3 J. Stephen, History of the Criminal Law of England 203–206, 266–275; 4 W. Blackstone, Commentaries *169.

Ledwith v. Roberts, [1937] 1 K.B. 232, 271, gives the following summary:

"The early Vagrancy Acts came into being under peculiar conditions utterly different to those of the present time. From the time of the Black Death in the middle of the 14th century till the middle of the 17th century, and indeed, although in diminishing degree, right down to the reform of the Poor Law in the first half of the 19th century, the roads of England were crowded with masterless men and their families, who had lost their former employment through a variety of causes, had no means of livelihood and had taken to a vagrant life. The main causes were the gradual decay of the feudal system under which the labouring classes had been anchored to the soil, the economic slackening of the legal compulsion to work for fixed wages, the break up of the monasteries in the reign of Henry VIII, and the consequent disappearance of the religious orders which had previously administered a kind of 'public assistance' in the form of lodging, food and alms; and, lastly, the economic changes brought about by the Enclosure Acts. Some of these people were honest labourers who had fallen upon evil days, others were the 'wild rogues,' so common in Elizabethan times and literature, who had been born to a life of idleness and had no intention of following any other. It was they and their confederates who formed themselves into the notorious 'brotherhood of beggars' which flourished in the 16th and 17th centuries. They were a definite and serious menace to the community and it was chiefly against them and their kind that the harsher provisions of the vagrancy laws of the period were directed."

And see Sherry, Vagrants, Rogues and Vagabonds—Old Concepts in Need of Revision, 48 Calif.L.Rev. 557, 560–561 (1960); Note, The Vagrancy Concept Reconsidered: Problems and Abuses of Status Criminality, 37 N.Y.U.L.Rev. 102 (1962).

Living under a rule of law entails various suppositions, one of which is that "[all persons] are entitled to be informed as to what the State commands or forbids." Lanzetta v. New Jersey, 306 U.S. 451, 453, 59 S.Ct. 618, 619, 83 L.Ed. 888.

Lanzetta is one of a well-recognized group of cases insisting that the law give fair notice of the offending conduct. In the field of regulatory statutes governing business activities, where the acts limited are in a narrow category, greater leeway is allowed.

The poor among us, the minorities, the average householder are not in business and not alerted to the regulatory schemes of vagrancy laws; and we assume they would have no understanding of their meaning and impact if they read them. Nor are they protected from being caught in the vagrancy net by the necessity of having a specific intent to commit an unlawful act.

The Jacksonville ordinance makes criminal activities which by modern standards are normally innocent. "Nightwalking" is one. Florida construes the ordinance not to make criminal one night's wandering, Johnson v. State, 202 So.2d, at 855, only the "habitual" wanderer or, as the ordinance describes it, "common night walkers." We know, however, from experience that sleepless people often walk at night, perhaps hopeful that sleep-inducing relaxation will result.

Luis Munoz-Marin, former Governor of Puerto Rico, commented once that "loafing" was a national virtue in his Commonwealth and that it should be encouraged. It is, however, a crime in Jacksonville.

"[P]ersons able to work but habitually living upon the earnings of their wives or minor children"—like habitually living "without visible means of support"—might implicate unemployed pillars of the community who have married rich wives.

"[P]ersons able to work but habitually living upon the earnings of their wives or minor children" may also embrace unemployed people out of the labor market, by reason of a recession or disemployed by reason of technological or so-called structural displacements.

Persons "wandering or strolling" from place to place have been extolled by Walt Whitman and Vachel Lindsay. The qualification "without any lawful purpose or object" may be a trap for innocent acts. Persons "neglecting all lawful business and habitually spending their time by frequenting * * * places where alcoholic beverages are sold or served" would literally embrace many members of golf clubs and city clubs.

Walkers and strollers and wanderers may be going to or coming from a burglary. Loafers or loiterers may be "casing" a place for a holdup. Letting one's wife support him is an intra-family matter, and normally of no concern to the police. Yet it may, of course, be the setting for numerous crimes.

The difficulty is that these activities are historically part of the amenities of life as we have known them. They are not mentioned in the Constitution or in the Bill of Rights. These unwritten amenities have been in part responsible for giving our people the feeling of independence and self-confidence, the feeling of creativity. These amenities have dignified the right of dissent and have honored the right to be nonconformists and the right to defy submissiveness. They have encouraged lives of high spirits rather than hushed, suffocating silence.

* * *

This aspect of the vagrancy ordinance before us is suggested by what this Court said in 1876 about a broad criminal statute enacted by Congress: "It would certainly be dangerous if the legislature could set a net large enough to catch all possible offenders, and leave it to the courts to step inside and say who could be rightfully detained, and who should be set at large." United States v. Reese, 92 U.S. 214, 221, 23 L.Ed. 563.

While that was a federal case, the due process implications are equally applicable to the States and to this vagrancy ordinance. Here the net cast is large, not to give the courts the power to pick and choose but to increase the arsenal of the police. * * *

Where the list of crimes is so all-inclusive and generalized as the one in this ordinance, those convicted may be punished for no more than vindicating affronts to police authority. * * *

Another aspect of the ordinance's vagueness appears when we focus, not on the lack of notice given a potential offender, but on the effect of the unfettered discretion it places in the hands of the Jacksonville police. Caleb Foote, an early student of this subject, has called the vagrancy-type law as offering "punishment by analogy." Such crimes, though long common in Russia, are not compatible with our constitutional system. We allow our police to make arrests only on "probable cause," a Fourth and Fourteenth Amendment standard applicable to the States as well as to the Federal Government. Arresting a person on suspicion, like arresting a person for investigation, is foreign to our system, even when the arrest is for past criminality. Future criminality, however, is the common justification for the presence of vagrancy statutes. * * *

A direction by a legislature to the police to arrest all "suspicious" persons would not pass constitutional muster. A vagrancy prosecution may be merely the cloak for a conviction which could not be obtained on the real but undisclosed grounds for the arrest. * * *

Those generally implicated by the imprecise terms of the ordinance—poor people, nonconformists, dissenters, idlers—may be required to comport themselves according to the life style deemed appropriate by the Jacksonville police and the courts. Where, as here, there are no standards governing the exercise of the discretion granted by the ordinance, the scheme permits and encourages an arbitrary and discriminatory enforcement of the law. It furnishes a convenient tool for "harsh and discriminatory enforcement by local prosecuting officials, against particular groups deemed to merit their displeasure." Thornhill v. Alabama, 310 U.S. 88, 97–98, 60 S.Ct. 736, 742, 84 L.Ed. 1093. It results in a regime in which the poor and the unpopular are permitted to "stand on a public sidewalk * * * only at the whim of any police officer." * * *

A presumption that people who might walk or loaf or loiter or stroll or frequent houses where liquor is sold, or who are supported by their wives or who look suspicious to the police are to become future criminals is too precarious for a rule of law. The implicit presumption in these generalized vagrancy standards—that crime is being nipped in the bud—is too extravagant to deserve extended treatment. Of course, vagrancy statutes are useful to the police. Of course, they are nets making easy the roundup of so-called undesirables. But the rule of law implies equality and justice in its application. Vagrancy laws of the Jacksonville type teach that the scales of justice are so tipped that even-handed administration of the law is not possible. The rule of law, evenly applied to minorities as well as majorities, to the poor as well as the rich, is the great mucilage that holds society together.

The Jacksonville ordinance cannot be squared with our constitutional standards and is plainly unconstitutional.

Reversed.

MR. JUSTICE POWELL and MR. JUSTICE REHNQUIST took no part in the consideration or decision of this case.

MODEL PENAL CODE § 250.6, TEXT AND COMMENTS 3 AND 5 *

§ 250.6 Loitering or Prowling

A person commits a violation if he loiters or prowls in a place, at a time, or in a manner not usual for law-abiding individuals under circumstances that warrant alarm for the safety of persons or property in the vicinity. Among the circumstances which may be considered in determining whether such alarm is warranted is the fact that the actor takes flight upon appearance of a peace officer, refuses to identify himself, or manifestly endeavors to conceal himself or any object. Unless flight by the actor or other circumstance makes it impracticable, a peace officer shall prior to any arrest for an offense under this section afford the actor an opportunity to dispel any alarm which would otherwise be warranted, by requesting him to identify himself and explain his presence and conduct. No person shall be convicted of an offense under this Section if the peace officer did not comply with the preceding sentence, or if it appears at trial that the explanation given by the actor was true and, if believed by the peace officer at the time, would have dispelled the alarm.

* * *

3. *Rationale and Elements of the Model Code Offense.* Section 250.6 applies to one who "loiters or prowls in a place, at a time, or in a manner not usual for law-abiding individuals under circumstances that warrant alarm for the safety of persons or property in the vicinity." This provision differs from prior legislation in that it is narrowly designed to reach only alarming loitering. Typical situations covered would be the following: a known professional pickpocket is seen loitering in a crowded railroad station; a person not

recognized as a local resident is seen lurking in a doorway and furtively looking up and down the street to see if he is being watched; an unknown man is seen standing for some time in a dark alley where he has no apparent business. Perhaps an even better example comes from the leading New York case of *People v. Berck:*

> [T]he police had been advised that certain residential premises would be temporarily unoccupied. On patrol, they observed defendant standing behind a tree, at 1:00 a.m., seeming to be examining the unoccupied premises. When questioned by the police, he refused to explain his presence, but more important, even to identify himself. No other person was present and there was, of course, no indication of a tryst.[19]

None of these situations would be covered by the law of attempt, even under the expanded definition of that offense in Section 5.01 of the Model Code. In no case has there been a "substantial step in a course of conduct planned to culminate in [the] commission of the crime." Also, none of these situations involves possession of burglar's tools or other instruments of crime that would sustain a conviction under Section 5.06.

The major issue of policy is what response to make to such situations. At least five courses are open:

(i) Loitering or wandering "at unusual hours" or "without lawful business" may be punished as a completed offense. This is the approach characteristic of prior law.

(ii) The situation giving rise to alarm for persons or property may be treated as an occasion for police inquiry. Failure to explain oneself satisfactorily would constitute an offense.

(iii) The situation giving rise to alarm may be deemed a proper basis for detention and interrogation but not for criminal prosecution.

(iv) The situation might be dealt with only as a basis for police orders to "move on" and thus to remove the immediate alarm.

(v) Finally, the kind of situation described above might be viewed as giving rise to no legal consequence. An officer, of course, could make inquiry of suspicious persons, most of whom would answer voluntarily. Where the responses do not dissipate suspicion, the officer could make such observations as would facilitate later identification of the suspect if a crime did take place.

None of these alternatives is entirely satisfactory. The first authorizes criminal conviction without proof of anti-social behavior or inclination. Additionally, as Comment 5 infra explains in some detail, it is difficult to imagine a statute of this sort that could pass constitutional muster under current standards. The second option is no doubt better, but it still imposes liability for failure to identify oneself or to give a credible account of one's behavior

19. 32 N.Y.2d 567, 347 N.Y.S.2d 33, 300 N.E.2d 411, *cert. denied,* 414 U.S. 1093 (1973).

without further proof of anti-social purpose. Another trouble with this approach is that the plausible lie about one's identity or purposes will in all probability avoid liability, while an implausible truth at least leaves one open to arrest. Finally, as will be explained in Comment 5, this kind of statute is also not free from constitutional doubt. The third approach involves a controversial and possibly unconstitutional change in the law of arrest rather than the definition of a substantive offense within the scope of the Model Code. The fourth solution, the police order to "move on," hardly solves the problem of the individual who is bent on crime and at the same time confers a disturbingly unbounded discretion on the police. The last option—authorizing no police action other than voluntary questioning and visual observation—is perhaps most consistent with the ideal of the role of police and with general normative principles governing the proper use of penal sanctions. Nonetheless, this total abandonment of the traditional vagrancy concept would lead to a significant loss in effective law enforcement and would encounter justifiably serious political resistance.

Section 250.6 of the Model seeks to provide the least objectionable form of the second alternative discussed above, together with certain safeguards not usually found in prior legislation of this sort. As a threshold matter, the section requires at least some manifestation of aberrant behavior. Specifically, the actor must loiter or prowl "in a place, at a time, or in a manner not usual for law-abiding individuals." The circumstances must be such that this behavior warrants "alarm for the safety of persons or property in the vicinity." This formulation marks a change from the tentative-draft version of the offense, which was based on justifiable suspicion that the actor was engaged in, or was about to engage in, crime.[27] This change was thought desirable in order to save the section from attack and possible invalidation as a subterfuge for authorizing arrest without probable cause.

Although it is impossible to describe with precision all circumstances that warrant alarm for persons or property, the Model Code provision does list three such factors: flight by the actor upon appearance of a peace officer, refusal of the actor to identify himself, and a manifest effort by the actor to conceal himself or any object. Additionally, the section requires that prior to arrest the peace officer shall, unless the circumstances make it impracticable, "afford the actor an opportunity to dispel any alarm which would otherwise be warranted, by requesting him to identify himself and explain his presence and conduct." This provision also is a change from the tentative draft. Under prior drafts, failure to respond to police requests for identification and explanation were circumstances that might be taken into account in determining whether suspicion or alarm was warranted. But if there was enough without that to justify alarm, the policeman was entitled to arrest, and

27. The tentative draft read as follows:

A person who loiters or wanders without apparent reason or business in a place or manner not usual for law-abiding individuals and under circumstances which justify suspicion that he may be engaged or about to engage in a crime commits a violation if he refuses a request of a peace officer that he identify himself and give a reasonably credible account of the lawfulness of his conduct and purposes.

Section 250.12, T.D. 13, at 59 (1961).

therefore to conduct an incident search, even though a moment's delay for inquiry would have elicited a satisfactory explanation for the actor's conduct.

The last sentence of Section 250.6 forbids conviction where this procedure is not followed and also takes account of the case of a person who has a true but incredible explanation for loitering or prowling. An arrest may be justified, but when it subsequently appears that despite the circumstances of alarm and the incredible explanation, the actor in fact was engaged in lawful business, liability should not attach. Section 250.6 accomplishes this result by barring conviction "if it appears at trial that the explanation given by the actor was true and, if believed by the peace officer at the time, would have dispelled the alarm." Finally, it should be noted that Section 250.6 is only a violation and therefore carries no term of imprisonment.

* * *

5. *Constitutional Considerations.* * * *

* * *

As noted earlier, the invalidated New York statute followed the tentative draft of the Model Code offense. The *Berck* court found several improvements in the final version of the offense and strongly hinted that it would withstand constitutional scrutiny. * * *

Nonetheless, at least one court has disagreed with the implied validation of the Model Code provision by the New York Court. In City of Portland v. White,[51] an Oregon appellate court held void for vagueness a municipal ordinance substantially similar to Section 250.6 as it now stands. On the other hand, three state supreme courts have upheld statutes patterned closely after the Model Code offense,[52] as has one intermediate appellate court.[53]

As a matter of constitutional policy, abrogation of loitering statutes is arguably sound. There is irreducible indeterminancy in the definition of loitering, as there is necessarily discretion in the police to decide in the first instance what the "public safety demands" or whether the circumstances "justify suspicion" or "warrant alarm." It is worth pointing out, however, that the statutes discussed above are a far cry from the ordinance invalidated in *Papachristou.* If even the Model Code provision is unconstitutionally vague, as the Oregon decision suggests, then it seems likely that no general provision against loitering can be drafted to survive constitutional review. Of course, narrower proscriptions of loitering with specific purpose—e.g., to solicit deviate sexual relations—may continue to be valid, but there would be no provision to deal with the person who is obviously up to no good but whose precise intention cannot be ascertained. Most courts are willing to consider in a void-for-vagueness analysis the need for some provision and the impossibility of achieving greater precision. This factor cuts strongly in favor of the constitutionality of the Model Code provision.[a]

* * *

51. 9 Ore.App. 239, 495 P.2d 778 (1972).

52. State v. Ecker, 311 So.2d 104 (Fla.), cert. denied, 423 U.S. 1019 (1975); City of Seattle v. Drew, 70 Wash.2d 405, 423 P.2d 522 (1967); State v. Starks, 51 Wis.2d 256, 186 N.W.2d 245 (1971).

53. People v. Solomon, 33 Cal.App.3d 429, 108 Cal.Rptr. 867 (1973), cert. denied, 415 U.S. 951 (1974).

a. For more recent cases, see Fields v. City of Omaha, 810 F.2d 830 (8th Cir.1987), holding a loitering statute based on the Model

Questions

1. A statute made one who "has in his possession with intent to sell, lend, give away, distribute or show * * * any book, pamphlet, magazine, newspaper, or other printed paper devoted to the publication, and principally made up of criminal news, police reports, or accounts of criminal deeds, or pictures, or stories of deeds of bloodshed, lust or crime," guilty of a misdemeanor. Defendant bookseller had in his possession with intent to sell a number of crime magazines. "They contain a collection of crime stories which portray in vivid fashion tales of vice, murder and intrigue. The stories are embellished with pictures of fiendish and gruesome crimes, and are besprinkled with lurid photographs of victims and perpetrators. Featured articles bear such titles as 'Bargains in Bodies,' 'Girl Slave to a Love Cult,' and 'Girls Reformatory'; these suggest the pattern of the literature." Can the defendant properly be convicted?

2. What sort of criminal vagrancy or loitering provision, if any, do you favor?

Note on Riot and Disorderly Conduct

Riot. Another crime relating to public order and tranquility is riot. At common law there is a riot when at least three assembled persons, in a violent or tumultous manner, act together to carry out a crime or trespass (or a lawful purpose, if a breach of the peace results). Production of terror or alarm in a not unreasonably susceptible populace is sometimes said to be essential. An unlawful assembly is a meeting of at least three persons with a common plan, which, if carried out, would result in a riot. Those who have assembled unlawfully and are *en route* to a riot are guilty of rout. All three of these crimes are misdemeanors at common law.

Under a statute of 1714 (not received as a part of American common law) riot was made a felony when it involved twelve or more persons who failed to disperse within one hour after a magistrate ordered them to do so. The reading of this order was known as "reading the Riot Act." Today, extremes of public disorder or public disaster may be handled by special emergency provisions, governing such matters as curfews and looting, to be invoked by public officials in stated circumstances.

Disorderly Conduct. Disorderly conduct is commonly punished by statutes which may specify such things as creating unreasonable noise in public places, obstructing free passage in public areas, or overzealous solicitation of members of the public. Public drunkenness may be dealt with as disorderly conduct or by special provisions regulating drinking or drunken conduct in public places. Sometimes an effort is made to coordinate these provisions with those relating to alcoholism, so as to encourage rehabilitation rather than punishment.

Penal Code provision unconstitutionally vague, and City of Milwaukee v. Nelson, 149 Wis.2d 434, 439 N.W.2d 562 (1989), upholding a similar statute.

Chapter II

ASSAULT, RAPE, BIGAMY, AND RELATED OFFENSES; *MENS REA* AND *ACTUS REUS*

A. INTRODUCTION

We begin with examination of the crime of assault, looking at what it requires, both as to the conduct and the state of mind of the accused, and we examine one factor which may serve as a justifying defense to an assault charge.

Assault and related crimes often appear as examples as we move to a more detailed analysis of *mens rea* (guilty mind) and *actus reus* (guilty act).

After a look at a group of crimes which requires no *mens rea,* we finish the chapter with material on the relationship between *mens rea* and the accused's ignorance of or mistaken belief about the facts or the law, using the law of rape and related offenses to help illustrate the problem.

B. ASSAULT

United States v. Dupree

United States Court of Appeals, Ninth Circuit, 1976.
544 F.2d 1050.

Before BROWNING and SNEED, CIRCUIT JUDGES, and RICHEY, DISTRICT JUDGE.

PER CURIAM:

Defendant Leonard Dupree, an Indian person, was charged under 18 U.S.C. § 1153 with assault with a dangerous weapon in violation of 18 U.S.C. § 113(c). The alleged assault was committed upon another Indian and within the Indian country. The indictment was dismissed by the district court on the ground that 18 U.S.C. § 113(c) was unconstitutionally vague. We reverse.

Title 18, section 1153 of the United States Code confers federal jurisdiction over the offense of assault with a dangerous weapon when committed by an Indian within the Indian country. * * *

Title 18, section 113 of the United States Code states in pertinent part:

> "Whoever, within the special maritime and territorial jurisdiction of the United States, is guilty of an assault shall be punished as follows:
>
> * * *

(c) Assault with a dangerous weapon, with intent to do bodily harm, and without just cause or excuse, by fine of not more than $1,000 or imprisonment for not more than five years, or both."

The district court believed "assault" to be undefined, and therefore found section 113(c) unconstitutionally vague. We disagree.

* * *

Section 113(c) is not impermissibly indefinite. The common-law meaning of a common-law term used in a federal criminal statute provides a source from which statutory precision may be derived.

Assault had two meanings at common law. A criminal assault was an attempt to commit a battery. 1 W. Hawkins, Pleas of the Crown 110 (8th ed. 1824); R. Perkins, Criminal Law 114 (2d ed. 1969). A tortious assault was an act which put another in reasonable apprehension of immediate bodily harm. R. Perkins, id. at 114.

Both concepts of assault have become recognized as criminal assaults, R. Perkins, supra at 116–17; W. LaFave & A. Scott, Criminal Law, § 82 (1972), and are included under the federal definition of assault. Thus an assault is committed by either a willful attempt to inflict injury upon the person of another, or by a threat to inflict injury upon the person of another which, when coupled with an apparent present ability, causes a reasonable apprehension of immediate bodily harm.

Use of this common-law definition of assault will render 18 U.S.C. § 113(c) sufficiently certain to give a person of ordinary intelligence fair notice that his contemplated activity is forbidden.

Defendant buttresses his argument in support of the trial court's dismissal of the indictment by pointing out that under § 113(c) a defendant can be charged with assault even though the facts indicate that he committed a battery. This Circuit, as well as others, follows this practice. Thus in Hockenberry v. United States, 422 F.2d 171 (9th Cir.1970) the defendant was charged under § 113(c) when he stabbed the victim with a knife. This practice, contends the defendant, prevents the accused from knowing whether the statute prohibits assault, battery, or both. * * *

* * * As the hornbooks put it, an assault is an attempted battery and proof of a battery will support conviction of assault. R. Perkins, supra, at 106–107. * * *

* * * The defendant is given fair notice that if either (1) he willfully attempts to inflict injury upon the person of another by means of a dangerous weapon, or (2) willfully threatens to inflict such injury by such means which, when coupled with an apparent present ability, causes a reasonable apprehension of immediate-bodily harm, he is chargeable under § 113(c). Fair notice does not cease to be such merely because he remains so chargeable even if he inflicts the injury. To hold otherwise would, we suggest, appear strange indeed to "a person of ordinary intelligence." We reverse and remand for further proceedings not inconsistent with this opinion.

Reversed and Remanded.

Notes

1. *Mens Rea in Criminal Battery.* Medley v. State, 156 Ala. 78, 83, 47 So. 218, 220 (1909):

> The evidence is without dispute that Lokey was hit by a bullet fired from the rifle in the hands of defendant. The tendencies of the testimony support the following theories of the shooting: That defendant intentionally shot Lokey, or that he intentionally discharged the rifle at a place where it was likely some person would be hit, or that he intentionally pointed the rifle at Lokey in violation of section 4342 of the Criminal Code of 1896, or that he was grossly negligent in the handling of the rifle and that its discharge was the result of such negligent act, or that he discharged the rifle along or across a public road in violation of section 5354 of the Criminal Code of 1896. If the battery was the result of any one or of several of these acts combined, the defendant was guilty of the offense for which he was convicted.

2. *Civil Assault.* People v. Wood, 10 A.D.2d 231, 234–237, 199 N.Y.S.2d 342, 345–348 (1960):

> We have been unable to find any reported cases in this state and no case has been called to our attention, directly holding that the pointing of an unloaded gun at a person constitutes an assault. * * * The court in People v. McKenzie, 6 App.Div. 199, 39 N.Y.S. 951, while recognizing that there was dictum to the contrary in People v. Ryan, 55 Hun 214, 8 N.Y.S. 241, assumed that an assault could be committed with an unloaded gun.

> Where there is no proof that the gun was loaded, and the charge is that an assault was committed by the use of a gun in the manner of its usual purpose and design, not as a club, but by pointing it at another person, the holdings of the adjudicated cases are hopelessly divided. This is true in this country and also in England. Authors and commentators express a like difference of opinion. Those jurisdictions which hold that it does not constitute an assault base their decisions on the nonexistence of a present ability to cause harm, or that the intent to inflict a physical injury is absent. Other jurisdictions hold that pointing an unloaded gun at a person who does not know that it is unloaded, and putting him in fear of bodily harm because of the threatening manner in which it is used, constitutes an assault. Part of the conflict and confusion results because of the lack of unanimity of opinion by courts and text writers as to the definition of criminal assault. It is clear that in civil assault apparent ability to cause injury is sufficient because the reasonable apprehension or fear created in the mind of the assaulted person may constitute the tort, but it has been held in several jurisdictions that present ability is an essential element of criminal assault. Some states have statutes requiring present ability, and rule out assaults with an unloaded firearm used in its usual manner and not as a bludgeon. The correct rule as to criminal assault is far from clear. In an article entitled "The Misuse of the Tort Definition of Assault in a Criminal Action", 11 Rocky Mountain Law Review 104 (1939) the writer states that the correct and more generally accepted definition of criminal assault is "An attempt or offer with force or violence to do a corporal hurt to another." He calls attention to Bishop's definition which is "any unlawful physical force 'creating a reasonable apprehension of immediate physical injury' " (Bishop New Criminal Law [8th ed.] § 23) and states that the cases cited by Bishop to support this definition do not support it. Bishop cites several English cases which the note writer points out were overruled by Regina v. James, 1 Car. & K. 530 (1844) which held that the pointing of an unloaded gun is not a criminal

assault. He argues that since the American cases which hold it to be an assault all cite Bishop or the English cases they are therefore based on a case overruled in its own jurisdiction. He maintains that under Bishop's definition there is no distinction between civil and criminal assault and that this is wrong.

Professor Rollin Perkins in an article in 26 Boston University Law Review 119, 136 (1946) maintains that although there was originally a distinction between civil and criminal assault the criminal has tended to take over the tort concept. Thus under what he terms the modern rule an assault is made out from either an attempt to commit a battery or an unlawful act which places another in reasonable apprehension of receiving an immediate battery. * * *

3. *History.* The crime of assault began as an attempt to commit a criminal battery. An attempt, for present purposes, can be taken as a try which comes fairly close to success, but fails. A criminal battery was originally an intentional and unprivileged touching of another person. So, an attempted criminal battery existed when, for example, A made an unjustified threat and waved his fist in B's face, or swung at B and missed. The threat had to be an imminent one, and it had to be accompanied by some action tending toward the desired result, but failing to reach it.

It occasionally happened that one charged with an attempted criminal battery would defend on the ground that he had committed an actual battery and was therefore charged with the wrong offense. Magistrates were understandably unsympathetic to pleas of this sort, and, commonly, jurisdictions developed the rule that one charged with attempted criminal battery (assault) could be convicted of the offense even when the proof showed battery instead of the attempt. Hence the saying that every criminal battery is also a criminal assault. Assault became not only the attempted crime, but could be charged for the completed crime as well. In this sense, battery became a second form of the crime of assault.

It is easy to see that criminal batteries and criminal attempted batteries, while not always the most serious of offenses, would be dealt with by fairly primitive legal systems. Assaults became both torts and crimes. Tort law compensated those injured; actions for assault or battery were brought by those claiming injury. Criminal law actions came to be initiated by the state to punish and to preserve the public peace.

The crime of battery tended to expand. It came to include not only intentional unprivileged touchings (to which the tort of battery remained limited), but also unintentional touchings produced by the defendant's great lack of care. One who recklessly rode his horse at rapid speed through a crowd and unintentionally knocked someone down could be convicted of battery (or assault). In a few instances battery was found when one accidentally touched another while engaging in an act *malum in se* (evil in itself). A housebreaker who slipped and fell on top of a sleeping householder, without any intention to do so and even without any carelessness, might, at least in theory, commit a battery. These expansions applied only where there was an actual touching; if there was no touching, only intentional conduct was punished.

In modern times many jurisdictions have broadened the crime of assault still further. It includes, as stated in the *Dupree* case, not only criminal assaults and (through a procedural device) criminal batteries, but also civil or tort assaults. The crime of assault is therefore broader in coverage than the tort of the same name. For the tort, an actual unprivileged intention to touch is not necessary; an intention to frighten is an acceptable alternative. The victim must be put in fear by the attack. Frightening a person by aiming a gun you know to be unloaded at him may be the crime of assault today, as well as the tort.

The state of the law of assault in a particular jurisdiction is not always easy to determine. Assault, as *Dupree* notes, is a crime at common law and was often never given precise definition until the crime came to be codified by legislatures in relatively modern times. Judicial decisions and opinions might produce only sketchy indications of the boundaries of the crime, particularly since ordinary assaults are usually treated as petty offenses and rarely get into the higher appellate courts.

Question

(a) Saul sees Vic asleep in the woods and decides to frighten him by throwing a stone to hit the tree near Vic's head. The stone actually grazes Vic's hair without awakening him. (b) Saul then decides to practice to improve his aim by seeing how close he can come to Vic's head without actually hitting him. His second stone hits the tree near Vic's head, and the sound awakens him. Saul hides. Vic sees the two stones, believes that someone has attacked him and then run off, and is frightened by his narrow escape. (c) Saul then reappears and raises his arm as if to throw, but, in fact, unknown to Vic, has no stone in his hand. As Saul moves his hand in a throwing motion, Vic runs away to avoid being hit. (d) Saul picks up a third stone, throws it at the running Vic, and misses. Vic never realizes that this stone has been thrown. Is Saul guilty of assault?

State v. Dumlao

Appellate Court of Connecticut, 1985.
3 Conn.App. 607, 491 A.2d 404.

BORDEN, JUDGE.

The defendants, Paulino and Aurora Dumlao, were charged with the crimes of assault in the first degree in violation of General Statutes § 53a–59(a)(3) [1] and injury or risk of injury to a child in violation of General Statutes § 53–21,[2] and were tried together. The jury found each of them not guilty of the charge of assault but convicted them each of injury or risk of injury to a child. The defendants appeal separately from their convictions, claiming in large part that the court erred in admitting certain evidence and that the evidence was insufficient for conviction. We find no error.

The jury could reasonably have found the following facts: On March 7, 1983, the defendants' two year old daughter was hospitalized at Yale–New Haven Hospital after being transferred from the Naval Hospital in Groton where she was referred by a local pediatrician. The child, at the time the defendants took her to the pediatrician and she was hospitalized, was in pain, generally unresponsive to her environment, covered with abrasions and bruises, including an open lesion the size of a nickel under the left eye, severely dehydrated, and had internal abdominal injuries which were later

1. General Statutes § 53a–59(a)(3) provides: "A person is guilty of assault in the first degree when: * * * (3) under circumstances evincing an extreme indifference to human life he recklessly engages in conduct which creates a risk of death to another person, and thereby causes serious physical injury to another person."

2. General Statutes § 53–21 provides in pertinent part: "Any person who wilfully or unlawfully causes or permits any child under the age of sixteen years to be placed in such a situation that its life or limb is endangered, or its health is likely to be injured * * * or does any act likely to impair the health * * * of any such child, shall be fined not more than five hundred dollars or imprisoned not more than ten years or both."

diagnosed as a fractured spleen, pancreatitis and liver dysfunction. The child's overall symptoms were properly diagnosed as battered child syndrome. Because her injuries were life-threatening, she was placed in intensive care. She had to be fed intravenously for two weeks. The medical history given by the defendant Paulino to the doctors was inconsistent with the child's injuries. The injuries occurred within approximately seven days prior to the child's arrival at the hospital.

* * *

We first address the claims of the defendant Paulino Dumlao, beginning with his argument that the court improperly admitted expert testimony on the issue of the battered child syndrome. * * *

Expert testimony is permitted, in the court's discretion, " 'if the witness has a special skill or knowledge, beyond the ken of the average juror, that, as properly applied, would be helpful to the determination of an ultimate issue.' " Battered child syndrome has become a well established medical diagnosis. Expert medical testimony that a child suffered from battered child syndrome has consistently been held admissible in other jurisdictions. See, e.g., People v. Jackson, 18 Cal.App.3d 504, 95 Cal.Rptr. 919 (1971); annot., 98 A.L.R.3d 306.

"[T]he 'battered child syndrome' simply indicates that a child found with [certain types of injuries] has not suffered those injuries by accidental means. This conclusion is based upon an extensive study of the subject by medical science." People v. Jackson, supra, 18 Cal.App.3d at 507, 95 Cal.Rptr. 919. A diagnosis of battered child syndrome is often indicated when a child's injuries do not jibe with the history given by the parent. See McCoid, "The Battered Child and Other Assaults Upon the Family: Part One," 50 Minn.L. Rev. 1, 18–19 (1965). A properly qualified expert medical witness, therefore, may appropriately explain the syndrome to the jury and express his opinion that the victim suffers from it. * * *

The expert witness should not be permitted to testify whether "the battered child syndrome from which this victim suffered was in fact caused by any particular person or class of persons engaging in any particular activity or class of activities"; the purpose of this kind of testimony is "not accusatory" and has no bearing on the defendant's culpability. On the other hand, evidence of battered child syndrome, coupled with other proof, such as a continuing opportunity to inflict the injuries, may permit an inference not only that the injuries were not accidental but also that they were inflicted by one who regularly cares for the child.

William Hellenbrand, a physician at Yale–New Haven Hospital, testified in detail about the child's injuries. He stated that battered child syndrome is an accepted medical term that is diagnosed "when a child suffers an injury or injuries * * * because of physical trauma done to the child by another individual." He testified that his examination of the child, indicating inflammation of the pancreas, a fractured spleen, damage to the liver, hematoma or collection of blood within the abdomen, and multiple bruises, fit within the classic description of battered child syndrome. He further testified that the explanation given by the parents' medical history did not adequately explain the severity of the injuries.

* * *

The defendant's next argument involves the sufficiency of the evidence to convict him. Included in this argument is the claim that his conviction was improperly based on circumstantial evidence. This claim is without merit. "[Triers of fact] necessarily rely upon circumstantial evidence and are entitled to draw reasonable and logical inferences from all the facts. * * *

* * *

The jury was presented with the following facts: The defendants' child was taken to a local pediatrician, required hospitalization, and was transferred to the Naval Hospital and then to Yale–New Haven Hospital. The doctors who examined her found she was significantly dehydrated, had suffered severe internal, life-threatening injuries, and had multiple abrasions and bruises all over her body. The history was given to the doctors by Paulino. He said that his wife, the co-defendant, had told him that the child's fifteen month old brother had hit the child with a toy car causing the injuries. He also told the doctors the child had vomited three or four times in the past couple of days. The doctors found this medical history inconsistent with the child's injuries. The extent of the child's dehydration was more severe than was normal for a child who had vomited three or four times. The bruises and scrapes on her body, some of which were from fingernails dug into her skin, occurred within approximately seven days prior to the child's hospitalization, some within the previous twenty-four hours. She was diagnosed as suffering from battered child syndrome. During a visit to the hospital, the defendant asked a nurse, who had told him that he and his wife could not be left alone with the child, "[a]re you afraid I will injure the child again?" The defendant Aurora made a statement to the police reiterating that the injuries were due to the child's younger brother hitting the child with a toy car, and stating that she never corrected her children by hitting them and that she never used a babysitter to take care of her children. The defendant Paulino was employed by the Navy as a security guard and was at work a great deal of the time. He did not, however, work round-the-clock and could, from time to time, leave his job at the Naval Base during working hours.

* * *

* * * For as long as twelve to sixteen hours on some days during the week the injuries were claimed to be inflicted, the defendant was available to have inflicted these injuries on the child himself or to observe the child's condition and act prudently to do something about it. Contrary to the defendant's contention, the extent of the child's injuries indicates that the child would have appeared to be obviously injured even to an untrained eye.

* * *

Viewing the evidence in the light most favorable to sustaining the verdict, therefore, and recognizing that in a case relying on substantial circumstantial evidence, it is "the cumulative impact of a multitude of facts" which establishes guilt; we conclude that the evidence was sufficient to support the verdict of guilty of injury or risk of injury to a child.

* * *

The defendant Aurora Dumlao raises numerous claims on appeal, the first of which challenges the sufficiency of the evidence to convict her. We note first that the bill of particulars requested by this defendant stated that "the manner in which the defendant is alleged to have committed each of the offenses" was "[b]y inflicting a severe beating upon the victim either by use of the hands or other instruments." Her conviction, therefore, had to be based on that portion of the statute that prohibits "any *act* likely to impair the health" of the child. (Emphasis added.) General Statutes § 53–21; see footnote 2, supra. The evidence presented, therefore, had to show that this defendant affirmatively acted to injure the child or impair her health.

* * * This argument is without merit. The evidence was sufficient, not only to negate her statements that the child's fifteen month old brother caused the injuries; it was also sufficient to show that an adult, not another child, caused the injuries, that the defendants were the only adults with the opportunity to injure the child, and that she was the adult who beat the child as claimed in the state's bill of particulars. It is the jury's prerogative to accept or reject the state's version of the evidence; if accepted, there must be evidence to support that version beyond a reasonable doubt. The jury was entitled to conclude, beyond a reasonable doubt, that the defendant was the child's regular caretaker, that the child was primarily in her care and custody when the injuries were inflicted, and that she was the adult who inflicted the injuries. * * *

The defendant also argues that the failure by the prosecution to identify her, by direct evidence, as the culpable party demonstrates that the evidence was insufficient to allow the conviction. We disagree. This was a case substantially based on circumstantial evidence such that no one, including the pre-verbal two year old victim, could testify from first hand knowledge precisely how the injuries occurred. Circumstantial evidence may be used to prove all elements of a crime beyond a reasonable doubt. * * *

* * *

Notes

1. *Aggravated Assaults.* Even before codification, legislatures often dealt with assaults by adding some specified factor or factors to simple assaults and creating new statutory aggravated assault crimes, which were usually punished more severely than ordinary assaults. *Dupree* shows a common form: assault with a dangerous weapon. Such statutes can involve interesting problems of construction. For example, is an unloaded gun not a dangerous weapon because it cannot be fired, or is it a dangerous weapon because the victim believes it can be fired and reacts to it as he would to a loaded gun? At other times assaults with particular purposes, e.g., to murder, to rape, or to rob, are made aggravated offenses. We will consider such assaults further when we study rape later in this chapter. At still other times assaults on particular persons, e.g., children or police officers, are made aggravated offenses. A glance at Article 211 of the Model Penal Code will show a modern statutory attempt to grade various forms of assault.

2. *The battered child syndrome.* State v. Tanner, 675 P.2d 539, 541–543 (Utah 1983):

* * * The development of the medical-social concept of the battered child syndrome is traced in McCoid, "The Battered Child & Other Assaults Upon the Family: Part One" 50 Minn.L.Rev. 1 (1965). The author points out that the "development of the concept of the battered child syndrome has moved from an initial identification of physical phenomenon [sic] to concern with the causative factors outside of the body of the child." Early publications concentrated on the identification of the pattern of injuries observed, but in the 1950s, articles began to address the origins of the trauma, including the role of the parents. Increasingly, as attention and research focused on the problem and statistics were assembled, the medical profession became aware of the abusive character of the injuries and the grave danger to the helpless child in the custody of an abusive caretaker. Id. at 4–8. McCoid summarizes:

> From this review, it appears that by early 1965, there had come a recognition of a distinctive phenomenon called "the battered child syndrome" which, though it begins with a pattern of injuries to the child, is really descriptive of a pattern of conduct on the part of the parents or others who are to guard the welfare of the child. The medical description can perhaps best be summarized as multiple injuries in various stages of healing, primarily to the long bones and soft tissues and frequently coupled with poor hygiene and malnutrition, but peculiarly identified by the marked discrepancy between the clinical or physical findings and the historical data provided by the parents. Described in terms of the conduct of the parents or their characteristics, the studies seem to confirm that the abuser is likely to be an emotionally immature individual from almost any walk or stratum of society, a person who probably suffers from the pressures of marital difficulties or economic circumstances or other emotional pressures not directly related to the child himself, so that the child becomes merely a focus for generalized frustration or anger and an outlet for the poorly controlled aggressiveness of the parent.

Id. at 18–19.

Over the past fifteen years, cases discussing the use of battered child syndrome evidence have appeared with increasing frequency in the state reporters. The battered child syndrome has become a well-recognized medical diagnosis, which must be testified to by an expert witness:

> The diagnosis is dependent on inferences, not a matter of common knowledge, but within the area of expertise of physicians whose familiarity with numerous instances of injuries accidentally caused qualifies them to express with reasonable probability that a particular injury or group of injuries to a child is not accidental or is not consistent with the explanation offered therefor but is instead the result of physical abuse by a person of mature strength.

State v. Mulder, 29 Wash.App. 513, 629 P.2d 462, 463 (1981). * * *

* * *

Battered child syndrome evidence is most frequently cited as admissible to show absence of accident. It is relevant to claims of accidents by the child, *e.g.*, "She was clumsy and fell a lot," as well as accidents by the adult, "I tripped while I was carrying him." Expert testimony as to types of injuries, their size, location and severity, together with evidence of their varying age and progress in healing, allows the lifeless or preverbal victim to testify in the only way possible. We are satisfied that the concept of the battered child syndrome is grounded in scientific research and is widely accepted in the medical community. Our research shows that all courts which have addressed the question have affirmed the admission of expert medical testimony regarding the presence of the battered child syndrome. * * *

3. *The battering person.* State v. Loss, 295 Minn. 271, 204 N.W.2d 404 (Minn.1973):

> Dr. Venters further testified that there is associated with the term "battered child syndrome" the term "battering person." This type of person fits into various patterns. One pattern is that of an individual simply repeating the type of discipline or child management to which he was subjected as a child. A child who is frequently beaten while growing up may develop the same pattern of discipline for his or her own children in later life. A second pattern is frequently seen in an individual who, as a child, has been shunted from foster home to foster home and feels rejected. A third pattern involves a role reversal in which the individual exhibits an even more significant lack of identity and poor self-concept or self-image, and when a child is born, it usually is seen as a love object who returns love and provides love for the needy parent. The fourth category of patterns involves parents who are hostile, abusive, impetuous, and who lash out at insignificant things frequently and react in a hair-triggered manner. Another category of child-abusing individuals is in the field of sexual molestation, but that usually occurs with older children.

State v. Brown

Superior Court of New Jersey, Law Division, 1976.
143 N.J.Super. 571, 364 A.2d 27 (1976), affirmed 154 N.J.Super. 511, 381 A.2d 1231 (App.Div.1977).

BACHMAN, J.S.C.

* * *

[This opinion was filed by the trial judge, pursuant to N.J. Rule 2:5–1(b), to amplify a trial ruling for the benefit of the appellate court and counsel.]

Specifically, defendant contends that he is not guilty of the alleged atrocious assault and battery because he and Mrs. Brown, the victim, had an understanding to the effect that if she consumed any alcoholic beverages (and/or became intoxicated), he would punish her by physically assaulting her. The testimony revealed that the victim was an alcoholic. On the day of the alleged crime she indulged in some spirits, apparently to Mr. Brown's dissatisfaction. As per their agreement, defendant sought to punish Mrs. Brown by severely beating her with his hands and other objects.

* * *

Some courts have allowed the defense of consent in civil suits, while denying it in criminal prosecutions for battery (e.g., Wright v. Starr, 42 Nev. 441, 179 P. 877 (Sup.Ct.1919)). According to these courts, there are two different interests at stake. While criminal law is designed to protect the interests of society as a whole, the civil law is concerned with enforcing the rights of each individual within the society. So, while the consent of the victim may relieve defendant of liability in tort, this same consent has been held irrelevant in a criminal prosecution, where there is more at stake than a victim's rights. Love, "Criminal Law: Consent as a Defense to Criminal Battery—The Problem of Athletic Contests," 28 Okla.L.Rev. 840 (1975).

Because of the dearth of authority in New Jersey, it will be useful to examine the manner in which other jurisdictions have resolved the issue of consent to criminal assaults. Several of these courts have ruled on the issue of consent in criminal assault cases that did not have sexual overtones but did involve actual batteries. These courts have almost invariably taken the position that since the offense in question involved a breach of the public peace as well as an invasion of the victim's physical security, the victim's consent would not be recognized as a defense, especially where the battery is a substantial or severe one. Taylor v. State, 214 Md. 156, 133 A.2d 414, 65 A.L.R.2d 740 (Ct.App.1957). See generally, 58 A.L.R.3d, *Assault and Battery,* § 2 at 662. It was very early held to be a crime to cut off the hand of a person at his request and with his full consent. *Wright's Case* (Leicester Assizes 1604), reported in Beale, *Cases on Criminal Law* (3 ed. 1915), 209. Professor Beale explained that

> Homicide, mayhem and battery may be committed, though the individual injured consented to the injury. The reason for this is clear: The public has an interest in the personal safety of its citizens and is injured where the safety of any individual is threatened, whether by himself or another. [Beale, "Consent in the Criminal Law," 8 *Harv.L.Rev.* 317, 324 (1895)].

Atrocious assault and battery is a crime in this State, as it is in others. As noted by the court in Martin v. Commonwealth, 184 Va. 1009, 37 S.E.2d 43 (Sup.Ct.App.1946),

> Invitations and consent to the perpetration of a crime do not constitute defenses. * * *
>
> If the doing of a particular act is a crime regardless of the consent of anyone, consent is obviously no excuse * * * The right to life and security is not only sacred in the estimation of the common law, but it is inalienable.

This was the governing law in Vermont as far back as 1884, where the court in State v. Burnham, 56 Vt. 445, 48 Am.Rep. 801 (Sup.Ct.1884), held that defendant's consent to engage in assaultive conduct (sparring and boxing) constituting a breach of the peace was not determinative of the quality of the same in regard to guilt or innocence. The consent to acts prohibited by law (i.e., street boxing) does not give character to their acts and prevent their becoming a breach of the peace.

Such was the governing law in England as well. Regina v. Coney, 8 L.R. 534 (Q.B.1882). There, Cave, J., went to great length to say that "an assault, being a breach of the peace, and unlawful, the consent of the person is immaterial." Stephen, J., reiterated and expounded upon the rule in his concurring opinion:

> * * * the consent of the person who sustains the injury is no defense, if the injury is of such a nature, or if it is inflicted under such circumstances, that its infliction is injurious to the public as well as to the person injured.

As recently as 1934 it was held in England that if an act is unlawful in the sense of it being in itself a criminal act, it is plain that it cannot be rendered lawful because the person to whose detriment it is done consents to it. No person can license another to commit a crime. Regina v. Donovan, 2 K.B. 498, 507 (1934). In accord, People ex rel. Burke v. Steinberg, 190 Misc. 413, 73 N.Y.S.2d 475 (Magis.Ct.1947).

The reasoning and public interest that is of concern and served by this rule is that of peace, health and good order. An individual or victim cannot consent to a wrong that is committed against the public peace. The state, not the victim, punishes a person for fighting or inflicting assaults. As astutely noted in Wright v. Starr, supra, the court, citing with approval 1 *Cooley, Torts,* 283, "There are three parties involved in criminal assaults, one being the state, which for its own good does not suffer the others to deal on a basis of contract with the public." It has been stated, and perhaps rightly so, that the only true consent to a criminal act is that of the community. Hughes, "Criminal Law—Defense of Consent—Test to be Applied," 33 *Can.B.Rev.* 88, 92 (1955).

This is so because these acts (the physical assaults by defendant upon Mrs. Brown), even if done in private, have an impingement (whether direct or indirect) upon the community at large in that the very doing of them may tend to encourage their repetition and so to undermine public morals.

State v. Fransua, 85 N.M. 173, 510 P.2d 106, 58 A.L.R.3d 656 (App.Ct. 1973), bears further illustration and support for this court's holding, as it is a classic and recent case of an invitation and consent to an aggravated assault. There, as the result of an argument the victim, in compliance with defendant's wishes, produced a loaded pistol, laid it within defendant's reach and said: there's the gun, if you want to shoot me go ahead. The defendant picked up the pistol and shot the victim, wounding him seriously. In response to defendant's argument of consent on the part of the victim, the court wisely opined,

> We cannot agree. It is generally conceded that a state enacts criminal statutes making certain violent acts crimes for at least two reasons: One reason is to protect the persons of its citizens; the second, however, is to prevent a breach of the peace [citing] State v. Seal, 76 N.M. 461, 415 P.2d 845 (1966). While we entertain little sympathy for either the victim's absurd actions or the defendant's equally unjustified act of pulling the trigger, we will not permit the defense of consent to be raised in such cases. Whether the victims of crimes have so little regard for their own safety as to request injury, the public has a stronger and overriding interest in preventing and prohibiting acts such as these. [510 P.2d at 107]

Also in accord is People v. Gray, 224 Cal.App.2d 76, 36 Cal.Rptr. 263 (D.Ct. App.1964), where the court said flatly and without discussion that "it is no defense to assert that the victim consented to an assault upon her likely to produce great bodily harm." Nor is consent a justification for a physical beating when it is a matter that concerns the peace and dignity of the state.

State v. Roby, 83 Vt. 121, 74 A. 638 (Sup.Ct.1909); Banovitch v. Commonwealth, 196 Va. 210, 83 S.E.2d 369 (Sup.Ct.App.1964).

There are a few situations in which the consent of the victim (actual or implied) is a defense. These situations usually involve ordinary physical contact or blows incident to sports such as football, boxing, or wrestling. People v. Samuels, 250 Cal.App.2d 501, 58 Cal.Rptr. 439 (D.Ct.App.1967), cert. den. sub nom. Samuels v. California, 390 U.S. 1024, 88 S.Ct. 1404, 20 L.Ed.2d 281. But this is expected and understood by the participants. The state cannot later be heard to charge a participant with criminal assault upon another participant if the injury complained of resulted from activity that is reasonably within the rules and purview of the sports activity.

However this is not to be confused with sports activities that are not sanctioned by the state. Thus, street fighting which is disorderly and mischievous on many obvious grounds (even if for a purse and consented to), and encounters of that kind which tend to and have the specific objective of causing bodily harm, serve no useful purpose, but rather tend to breach the peace and thus are unlawful. * * *

As stated by this court in its ruling and by the court in People v. Samuels, supra, it is a matter of common knowledge that a normal person in full possession of his or her mental faculties does not freely and seriously consent to the use upon his or herself of force likely to produce great bodily harm. Those persons that do freely consent to such force and bodily injury no doubt require the enforcement of the very laws that were enacted to protect them and other humans. A general principle of law is that a person cannot contract out of protective legislation passed for his other benefit. Day v. Davies, 2 K.B. 74 (C.A.1938). "If an act be prohibited, it cannot be the subject of a valid contract." The laws of this State and others that have dealt with the question are simply and unequivocally clear that the defense of consent cannot be available to a defendant charged with any type of physical assault that causes appreciable injury. If the law were otherwise, it would not be conducive to a peaceful, orderly and healthy society.

* * *

Defendant in Banovitch v. Commonwealth, supra, certainly lacked a hostile or evil disposition or malice, but was denied the defense of consent to the charge of mayhem (atrocious assault and battery) on facts showing that he recklessly applied a corrosive chemical to the victim's person in purporting to treat her for cancer. Nor did defendant in People v. Samuels, supra, entertain any malice when he administered a beating to another while making a sadomasochistic film. Yet the defense of consent was unavailable to him. And certainly the court in Commonwealth v. Farrell, supra, did not require an evil or hostile disposition on the part of defendant in order to sustain a conviction for assault based on a sadistic burning with a cigarette. In fact, there was no evil or hostile disposition on the part of defendant. Defendant there simply had a perverted notion of branding his female victim by burning his initials on the private parts of her body in order that she would be "his and she would never cheat on him." Similarly, defendants in People v. Lenti, supra, displayed or harbored no evil or hostile disposition but were merely administering and inflicting a so-called initiation punishment as a requirement for induction of pledgees (victims) into a fraternal organization. Nor did any other case that this court studied require malice or hostile or evil disposition, as it is not an element of the crime of criminal atrocious assault and battery.

This court concludes that, as a matter of law, no one has the right to beat another even though that person may ask for it. Assault and battery cannot be consented to by a victim, for the State makes it unlawful and is not a party to any such agreement between the victim and perpetrator. To allow an otherwise criminal act to go unpunished because of the victim's consent would not only threaten the security of our society but also might tend to detract from the force of the moral principles underlying the criminal law. A major dissent to the view that the victim's consent may be a valid defense to a charge of assault has been voiced by the noted English jurist, Sir Patrick Devlin, who stated,

> It is not a defense to any form of criminal assault that the victim thought his punishment well deserved and consented to it. To make a good defense the accused must prove that the law gave him the right to chastise and that he exercised it reasonably. There are certain standards of behavior or moral principles which society requires to be observed; and the breach of them is an offense not merely against the person who is injured, but against society as a whole. [*Devlin, The Enforcement of Morals,* 6 (1965)]

Thus, for the reasons given, the State has an interest in protecting those persons who invite, consent to and permit others to assault and batter them. Not to enforce these laws which are geared to protect such people would seriously threaten the dignity, peace, health and security of our society.

Questions

1. Is a kiss a criminal battery? A surgical operation? A football tackle?

2. Can you think of matters other than consent which might make what would otherwise be a battery privileged?

Notes

1. *Legally Effective Consent.* Even when the law recognizes consent as a defense, not all assent is legally effective consent. Assent procured by duress or deception is generally ineffective, as is assent by one who is too mentally incapacitated or too immature to judge the nature or significance of the conduct. See Model Penal Code § 2.11(c). This idea is often invoked in cases of assaults of a sexual nature on children, where the child may assent, unaware of the nature or meaning of the act.

2. *Policy.* For some crimes, non-consent of the victim is a definitional element of the offense. In such crimes, which include rape, larceny, and burglary, if the victim consents, the crime is not committed. For other crimes, such as murder and manslaughter, consent is irrelevant on the question of guilt or innocence because the definition leaves it out of consideration. Can you develop a general policy rule about when the definition of an offense should make consent a defense? Should condonation (forgiveness by the victim after the event) be recognized as a defense? Whatever their effect on the question of guilt, consent or condonation may be an important

consideration in sentencing and even on the question whether a crime is discovered or prosecuted.

3. *Evidence of Accomplice.* In some jurisdictions consent may be important because of a rule of evidence. Where conviction may not be had on the uncorroborated evidence of an accomplice, the consent of the victim may make him an accomplice for purposes of the rule. Suppose, for example, that the jurisdiction punishes consensual homosexual conduct. It may be impossible to convict one of the parties if the only evidence comes from the other. In statutory rape, the willing participation of the underaged girl is no defense. Would you expect the accomplice rule to be applied here?

C. *MENS REA* AND *ACTUS REUS*

1. Introductory Note

For purposes of analysis and study, a crime may be conveniently divided into a mental part (*mens rea* or guilty mind) and a physical part (*actus reus* or guilty act). This chapter, in addition to teaching you the rudiments of assault, rape, bigamy, and some related offenses, will examine the basic anatomy of a crime, identifying elements which are common to all, or at least most, crimes, and dealing with many of these common elements in enough detail to form a basis for the better understanding of two major fields of crime, theft and criminal homicide.

The *actus reus* differs with each crime according to the nature of the definition of the offense. In murder or manslaughter it is (roughly) causing the death of a human being, in rape it is (roughly) having sexual intercourse with a woman without her consent. An account of the *actus reus* of an offense always deals expressly or by implication with some *conduct* of the accused: pulling the trigger of a gun (or putting poison in a cup, etc.) in criminal homicides, or engaging in sexual intercourse in rape. Such conduct can be reduced to performing certain physical actions (or, in some cases, failing to perform required physical actions). The definition of the *actus reus* may (or may not) also refer to the production of certain *consequences* by acting (or failing to act), for example, the causing of death in criminal homicides. It is not murder if the bullet misses the victim or if the victim is wounded and does not die; it may, as we have seen, be some other crime which does not require the consequence of death as part of its *actus reus.* The *actus reus* may (or may not) also refer to surrounding *circumstances,* without which the conduct does not meet the definition of the crime. The non-consent of the rape victim is a part of the *actus reus* of rape.

Without some conduct of the accused, there is no crime. Even in attempts and conspiracy, the accused must do something to carry forward his thinking in order to commit the offense. If the rule were otherwise, people could be punished for ideas and intentions alone. This would produce a criminal justice system at once tending towards tyranny (thought control, when an accused might never translate his speculations into harmful acts) and towards chaos (how do you police thought and prove your case when there has been no act?).

While the *actus reus* varies from one crime to another, it has three constant elements which can be studied profitably apart from intense concentration on particular crimes. Two of these three form the subject matter of section 2. The third, *causation,* can be dealt with more effectively in the context of criminal homicides, where most of the causation issues arise, and it will be postponed until that time.

Mens rea, or guilty mind, concerns the wrongful attitude of the accused which accompanies the *actus reus* of the offense. Where the act is done without any kind of fault, there is no *mens rea.* There is less variety in the significant wrongful mental states than in wrongful acts; many crimes have purpose or recklessness as a significant mental state. Consequently it is convenient to survey these commonly relevant mental states in this chapter, before we proceed to the study of theft and criminal homicide. This is done in section 3. It should be noted that different mental elements may be appropriate for different elements of the *actus reus* of the single crime, where the *actus reus* has more than a single element. A jurisdiction may require purpose to have sexual intercourse in rape, but may not require a purpose to act without the victim's consent; recklessness or negligence as to whether the victim consents may be sufficient for the defendant's mental state as to this element.

In some instances the *mens rea* requirement has been dropped with respect to some or all of the elements of the *actus reus.* One who engages in the forbidden act of selling adulterated butter may be criminally liable even if he did not know and could not have had reason to suspect that the butter was adulterated. We will examine these special cases in section 5.

The final section deals with the relationship between *mens rea* and the mistake of the accused about the facts or the law.

Other elements of *mens rea* are concerned in problems of criminal responsibility. An insane person, for example, might have a particular mental element (purpose to kill) appropriate to murder, but still be legally incapable of committing a crime because of his general mental condition. These questions will be considered in Chapter V.

Question: In assault, what belongs to *actus reus,* and what to *mens rea*?

2. *Actus Reus*

a. *OMISSIONS*

State v. Parley
State v. Ward

Supreme Court of Ohypo, 1984.
303 Ohypo 9.

PER CURIAM. Timothy Topple, a lawyer, and Prudence Parley, a psychologist, were engaged to be married. On June 25, 1983, they were spending the afternoon at Camp Carnivor, a private game preserve, to which visitors were admitted for a fee. A quarrel developed. Topple's practice was not particularly successful and he wished to return to an earlier calling, that of circus high wire performer. Dr. Parley felt that this was an unwise choice, which tended to show immaturity on the part of her betrothed.

The game park's five o'clock closing hour was approaching as they returned to the entrance. Nearby, Queenie, a lioness recovering from an illness, was confined in a cage, connected by a passageway to an enclosed exercise yard. The passageway was closed by a simple drop panel, easily operated by a rope from outside the enclosure. As the couple watched

Queenie, the preserve's public address system repeated an announcement that the park closed at 5:00 p.m. and the speaker added a note that it was then 4:58 p.m.

Parley said, "Let's go. I've got a suicidal patient, and I mustn't be late for the appointment." Topple replied, "Wait a minute. I want to show you I haven't lost any of my old skills on the high wire." In a fit of bravado, he then lifted the panel in Queenie's passageway, climbed the exercise yard fence, and began to walk along a narrow beam which went along the top of the fence. He called out to Parley, "Stand by to help in case I slip." Parley answered, "You've convinced me you're a complete idiot. Our engagement is off. I have to leave immediately for my appointment." Topple responded, "Stick around and watch the performance." At this point, Topple's foot slipped and he fell into the exercise yard, breaking an ankle.

"Quick, drop the panel," Topple called to Parley, but she, although she could easily, and without any danger to herself, have done so, did not. Instead, she said, "You're on your own," and left for her appointment.

The scene was observed by Walter Ward, Queenie's keeper, who had unsuccessfully ordered Topple to come down from the fence. As Topple fell, the five o'clock whistle blew, and Parley headed for the exit. Queenie came through the open passageway and Topple screamed for help. Ward ignored him. Queenie came over to Topple, sniffed at him, swiped at him once with her paw, and sauntered back to her cage. A passerby dropped the panel, and Topple was rescued, but his claw wound required 78 stitches.

Parley and Ward were separately charged with and convicted of battery on account of Queenie's blow. Their appeals were consolidated for hearing in this court. The judgments of conviction are reversed in each case by a vote of two to one. Chief Justice Wynken would affirm the conviction as to defendant Ward. Justice Blynken would affirm the conviction as to defendant Parley. The separate opinions of the justices follow.

WYNKEN, C.J. Usually, criminal liability is based on some affirmative act or acts of the accused, but it is perfectly clear that at common law (and our statutes make no change in the common law rule) liability, in a proper case, may also be based on failure to take action. So, for example, a parent who has the ability to save, but lets his infant starve to death or die for lack of medical attention, may be liable for criminal homicide. One who accidentally starts a fire, but fails to take reasonable steps to put it out because he wants to collect on his fire insurance, may be guilty of an arson offense because of his failure to act. There is no reason in principle why one cannot commit a battery by failing to prevent a lioness from mauling another.

However, the common law has never imposed liability for omissions in all circumstances. It is an ancient commonplace that a stranger may watch a baby drown in a gutter, though he could easily fish him out, and suffer no criminal penalty. Perhaps because inaction is inherently ambiguous with respect to the accused's state of mind, or because causal connection is harder to trace, or because it is difficult to define the nature and limits of a stranger's duty to intervene, or because the law does not want to encourage officious intervention in the affairs of strangers, the criminal law has always required some ascertainable legal duty to act on the part of the accused before criminal liability will be imposed. Such a duty might be imposed because something in the causal circumstances singles the actor out as one upon whom it is appropriate to impose a duty. Suppose Topple had been in the exercise yard with Queenie confined in the neighboring cage, and a passerby, accidentally and without any fault, had tripped over the rope controlling the gate and had opened it. He might well be found to have a duty to close the gate again, although others in the area would not have such a duty.

More commonly a duty is imposed because of a statutory requirement, a contractual obligation, or a personal relationship existing between the accused and the victim. No statute imposes a duty on wild animal attendants to aid persons endangered by their beasts, and Ward did not even know Topple at the time of the incident, but I believe the jury could find that Ward violated a contractual duty. At his trial, Ward testified that he regarded it as a part of his job to protect patrons of the park from the animals, at least where he could do safely, but that his job was over at five p.m., and nothing in his contract required him to perform any work after that hour. I think that this is a wholly unreasonable interpretation of his obligation. It may not have been part of his job to respond to requests for aid phoned to his home in the middle of the night, but here an emergency arose within seconds after the five o'clock whistle. Surely his obligation continues while he is still on the premises in a situation of this kind. There was time to drop the gate before Queenie left her cage. I think the jury properly based its verdict on his failure to act at this time. I need not consider whether, had there been no time to drop the gate, Ward would have been required to take steps to protect Topple, even at some possible risk to his own safety.

I conclude that the jury could, as it did, properly find Ward guilty of battery beyond a reasonable doubt. As a guard, responsible for the safety of patrons, he knowingly took an unreasonable risk that Topple would be injured when he walked away from the situation. His failure to intervene was an important cause of the mauling.

My sister Blynken doubts Ward's duty, but argues that Parley was under a duty to rescue Topple. This supposed obligation, based on their former relationship and a kind of possible implied understanding between Topple and Parley, is much less firm a basis for imposing an obligation than is Ward's contractual obligation. The psychology of the situation works against such an obligation. There had been a serious quarrel and an engagement broken. Both should have understood that Parley would want nothing to do with Topple thereafter, at least until cautious reconciliation might be attempted. Topple also knew that Parley had an obligation to a suicidal patient. How can we find her guilty for deciding that that duty overrode any she might otherwise have had to her ex-fiance? After his idiotic behavior and after observing Parley's reaction to it, Topple could not expect any help from her. On the other hand, he had every reason to suppose that the keeper would come to his assistance if he got in trouble.

BLYNKEN, J. I am in general agreement with Chief Justice Wynken's approach to this case, but I depart from his views on questions of actual criminal responsibility of the defendants. To affirm Ward's conviction would be to accept a rather dubious point of contract law, not likely to be known to Ward, as a basis for criminal conviction. No doubt there was a general understanding that guards were to come to the aid of patrons in situations of emergency, but Ward's obligation to act was hardly as clear as, for example, that of a lifeguard to rescue a swimmer in distress. He may have been heartless in this situation, but it can hardly be said that he is a criminal because he broke a vague contract for the benefit of a third person, particularly when his contractual duties, if any, were arguably over for the day. Ward's conviction should be reversed.

I have no such doubts about voting to affirm Parley's conviction. It is clear that the criminal law imposes a duty upon a member of a family to rescue another member of the same family from peril, when this can be done safely. This obligation should extend even to friends who embark on a course of action together. Certainly it applies to an engaged couple. Topple asked Parley to stand by in case of trouble, and a lover's quarrel, even though it resulted in a broken engagement, does not instantly dissolve the obligation. Surely, Parley understood that she ought to help in case of trouble—at least until the parties had gone their separate ways—and that she could not suddenly abdicate her responsibility. The claim that the suicidal patient excuses her abrupt departure cannot be taken seriously. It would have taken but a moment to close the passageway. The jury could properly convict of battery on the basis that Parley must have intended injury to Topple, and that her breach of duty to act was an important cause of the injury.

NOD, J. The two opinions of my respected colleagues illustrate the difficulties encountered in trying to apply an unworkable rule. Nobody is really happy with the principle that in general there is no duty in criminal law to act to prevent disaster to another. It goes against common morality. Consequently, courts have found more and more exceptional situations, in which a duty is recognized. Almost any kind of personal relationship is enough to impose the duty; one wonders whether the old case, in which a defendant, who allowed his mistress to die of self-administered poison, went free, would be decided the same way today. Statutes which require people to act in particular ways are likely to make them criminals when they fail to act and somebody gets hurt. Strict contract is not required for the duty. The courts do not ask about consideration or other technical matters when one has agreed or seemed to agree to come to the assistance of another in case of trouble. Even a fault-free causal relationship may be enough, as the Chief Justice indicates.

Those left with no duty to act under these theories are essentially "strangers"—passersby who have no characteristic which tends to make us pick them out of a crowd of onlookers and impose upon them some duty to aid. It is said that if the duty is imposed on such strangers, everyone on the beach at Coney Island is guilty of criminal homicide when a bather, unassisted, drowns, or that one who fails to relieve a starving begger may be a felon. These cases do impose difficulties of administration, but they are no greater than the problems of hairsplitting under the old rule, illustrated in the present case. The test should be one of reasonableness; the criminal law is quite used to resolving such issues, difficult as they are. Any dangers to and difficulties of the passerby would be taken into account by the jury in determining whether his inaction was unreasonable in all the circumstances.

I have no difficulty in concluding that both of these defendants acted wholly unreasonably in failing to close the door to the cage before Queenie could get out. They should be guilty of battery. However, I am unwilling to impose a new test of criminal liability on these defendants, who had no way of knowing that they would not be judged by old standards. And, I do not have the support of my colleagues in changing the law, even prospectively. The old rule uses an uncertain standard, and one which presents borderline issues in the case of each defendant. In the circumstances, I cannot vote to affirm either conviction.

Convictions reversed.

Notes

1. *Policy.* T.B. Macaulay, A Penal Code Prepared by the Indian Law Commissioners, Note M (1837), reprinted in 7 Works of Lord Macaulay 493–497 (Trevelyan ed. 1879):

> Early in the progress of the code it became necessary for us to consider the following question: When acts are made punishable on the ground that those acts produce, or are intended to produce, or are known to be likely to produce, certain evil effects, to what extent ought omissions which produce, which are intended to produce, or which are known to be likely to produce, the same evil effects to be made punishable?
>
> Two things we take to be evident; first, that some of these omissions ought to be punished in exactly the same manner in which acts are punished; secondly, that all these omissions ought not to be punished. It will hardly be disputed that a jailer who voluntarily causes the death of a prisoner by omitting to supply that prisoner with food, or a nurse who voluntarily causes the death of an infant entrusted to her care by omitting to take it out of a tub of water into which it has fallen, ought to be treated as guilty of murder. On the other hand, it will hardly be maintained that a man should be punished as a murderer because he omitted to relieve a beggar, even though there might be the clearest proof that the death of the beggar was the effect of this omission, and that the man who omitted to give the alms knew that the death of the beggar was likely to be the effect of the omission. It will hardly be maintained that a surgeon ought to be treated as a murderer for refusing to go from Calcutta to Meerut to perform an operation, although it should be absolutely certain that this surgeon was the only person in India who could perform it, and that if it were not performed, the person who required it would die. It is difficult to say whether a penal code which should put no omissions on the same footing with acts, or a penal code which should put all omissions on the same footing with acts, would produce consequences more absurd and revolting. There is no country in which either of these principles is adopted. Indeed, it is hard to conceive how, if either were adopted, society could be held together.
>
> * * *
>
> What we propose is this, that where acts are made punishable on the ground that they have caused, or have been intended to cause, or have been known to be likely to cause, a certain evil effect, omissions which have caused, which have been intended to cause, or which have been known to be likely to cause the

same effect, shall be punishable in the same manner, provided that such omissions were, on other grounds, illegal. An omission is illegal if it be an offence, if it be a breach of some direction of law, or if it be such a wrong as would be a good ground for a civil action.

We cannot defend this rule better than by giving a few illustrations of the way in which it will operate. A. omits to give Z. food, and by that omission voluntarily causes Z.'s death. Is this murder? Under our rule it is murder if A. was Z.'s gaoler, directed by the law to furnish Z. with food. It is murder if Z. was the infant child of A., and had therefore a legal right to sustenance, which right a Civil Court would enforce against A. It is murder if Z was a bedridden invalid, and A. a nurse hired to feed Z. It is murder if A. was detaining Z. in unlawful confinement, and had thus contracted a legal obligation to furnish Z., during the continuance of the confinement, with necessaries. It is not murder if Z. is a beggar, who has no other claim on A. than that of humanity.

A. omits to tell Z. that a river is swollen so high that Z. cannot safely attempt to ford it, and by this omission voluntarily causes Z.'s death. This is murder, if A. is a peon stationed by authority to warn travellers from attempting to ford the river. It is murder if A. is a guide who had contracted to conduct Z. It is not murder if A. is a person on whom Z. has no other claim than that of humanity.

A savage dog fastens on Z. A. omits to call off the dog, knowing that if the dog be not called off, it is likely that Z. will be killed. Z. is killed. This is murder in A., if the dog belonged to A., inasmuch as his omission to take proper order with the dog is illegal. But if A. be a mere passer-by, it is not murder.

We are sensible that in some of the cases which we have put, our rule may appear too lenient; but we do not think that it can be made more severe without disturbing the whole order of society. It is true that the man who, having abundance of wealth, suffers a fellow creature to die of hunger at his feet is a bad man, a worse man, probably, that many of those for whom we have provided very severe punishment. But we are unable to see where, if we make such a man legally punishable, we can draw the line. If the rich man who refuses to save a beggar's life at the cost of a little copper is a murderer, is the poor man just one degree above beggary also to be a murderer if he omits to invite the beggar to partake his hard-earned rice? Again, if the rich man is a murderer for refusing to save the beggar's life at the cost of a little copper, is he also to be a murderer if he refuses to save the beggar's life at the cost of a thousand rupees? Suppose A. to be fully convinced that nothing can save Z.'s life unless Z. leave Bengal and reside a year at the Cape; is A., however wealthy he may be, to be punished as a murderer because he will not, at his own expense, send Z. to the Cape? Surely not. Yet it will be difficult to say on what principle we can punish A. for not spending an anna to save Z.'s life, and leave him unpunished for not spending a thousand rupees to save Z.'s life. The distinction between a legal and an illegal omission is perfectly plain and intelligible; but the distinction between a large and a small sum of money is very far from being so, not to say that a sum which is small to one man is large to another.

The same argument holds good in the case of the ford. It is true that none but a very depraved man would suffer another to be drowned when he might prevent it by a word. But if we punish such a man, where are we to stop? How much exertion are we to require? Is a person to be a murderer if he does not go fifty yards through the sun of Bengal at noon in May in order to caution a traveller against a swollen river? Is he to be a murderer if he does not go a hundred yards?—if he does not go a mile?—if he does not go ten? What is the precise amount of trouble and inconvenience which he is to endure? The distinction between the guide who is bound to conduct the traveller as safely as he can, and a mere stranger, is a clear distinction. But the distinction between a stranger who will not give a halloo to save a man's life, and a stranger who will not run a mile to save a man's life, is very far from being equally clear.

It is, indeed, most highly desirable that men should not merely abstain from doing harm to their neighbours, but should render active services to their neighbours. In general, however, the penal law must content itself with keeping men from doing positive harm, and must leave to public opinion, and to the teachers of morality and religion, the office of furnishing men with motives for doing positive good. It is evident that to attempt to punish men by law for not rendering to others all the service which it is their duty to render to others would be preposterous. We must grant impunity to the vast majority of those omissions which a benevolent morality would pronounce reprehensible, and must content ourselves with punishing such omissions only when they are distinguished from the rest by some circumstance which marks them out as peculiarly fit objects of penal legislation * * *.

2. *Liability for Omissions.* Probably for reasons suggested in *Parley,* the common law and most statutory schemes in common law countries do not impose liability for omissions unless some special reason to do so appears. Sometimes a statute will expressly require an act and impose criminal liability for failure to perform it, e.g., willful failure to file an income tax return. 26 U.S.C.A. § 7203. Often such statutory liability for omissions is imposed on those who engage in particular activities or businesses and fail to keep records or do specified things which protect the public from harm. In the absence of statute, the common law imposed duties to act in cases of such protective relationships as parent and child, husband and wife, or master and servant, and in cases in which the accused had contracted to act. If one undertakes aid of another, though he has no legal obligation to do so, he may incur criminal liability if he recklessly abandons the undertaking in circumstances which leave the victim worse off than before. Reg. v. Nicholls, 13 Cox Crim.Cas. 75 (Stafford Assize Court 1874).

Questions

1. How and on what grounds should the principal case be decided?

2. In Reg. v. Instan, [1893] 1 Q.B. 450 (Cr.Cas.Res.) the accused lived alone with an elderly aunt, who paid all of the living expenses for the household. Unknown to anyone else but the accused, the aunt became too sick to care for herself or communicate with outsiders. The niece gave her no food, did not call a doctor, and notified nobody of the situation. Although she could easily have taken some step to aid her aunt or to notify others, she simply allowed her to die. Did Instan have a legal duty to act? If so, on what basis?

3. Is it always clear whether specific events are acts or omissions? Suppose that a penal statute requires milk sellers to maintain storage within a specified temperature range. Kool stores milk for sale in an electric refrigerator which maintains proper temperature until it breaks down. Kool does not bother to get it repaired. The temperature rises above the allowed range. Act or omission? Would it be different if Kool had simply pulled the plug to save on his electric bill? Is your reasoning applicable to a case in which a life support machine for a terminal comatose patient is turned off? See Barber v. Superior Court of the State of California, County of Los Angeles, 147 Cal.App.3d 1006, 195 Cal.Rptr. 484 (1983).

4. Mother and Lover live in an apartment with Mother's infant Child. Lover frequently beats Child severely. One of these beatings finally kills Child. Mother does not seek help at any point. Is Mother independently liable for Child's death?

5. In the *Dumlao* case, supra, p. 111 the father was convicted under a statute which punished his permitting the child to be endangered; this expressly allowed punishment for omission to act in protecting the child. Could he properly have been convicted of assault on the child?

6. Parent does not seek medical assistance for sick Child because of a religious belief in the efficacy of prayer. Child dies. Is Parent criminally liable?

b. VOLUNTARY CONDUCT

United States v. Coleman

United States District Court, Eastern District Pennsylvania, 1979.
475 F.Supp. 422, affirmed 620 F.2d 290 (3d Cir.1980), cert. denied 446 U.S. 955, 100 S.Ct. 2926, 64 L.Ed.2d 814 (1980).

POLLAK, DISTRICT JUDGE.

Tyrone Coleman was tried before Magistrate Powers and found guilty of violating 18 U.S.C. § 113(d) [1] which prohibits "striking, beating, or wounding" another "within the * * * territorial jurisdiction of the United States." Mr. Coleman now appeals from that conviction.

On July 16, 1978, at approximately 2:30 A.M., appellant Coleman, who had been drinking, cut his hand on a glass panel near the entrance to the United States Post Office at 30th and Chestnut Streets, Philadelphia. * * * Security Officer Charles L. Ebner was assigned to follow Mr. Coleman to the hospital and to report back on his condition.

Appellant and Officer Ebner never reached their destination. Appellant stopped his car at a light on Chestnut Street, near the Post Office, and refused to move on when the light turned green, thereby creating an obstacle for traffic. * * *

* * * A confrontation ensued in which Mr. Coleman, fist raised, cursed the officers and threatened violence. Still shouting obscenities, appellant walked toward the Post Office, apparently to speak with the two officers' supervisor. At the door to the Post Office, appellant was met by Sergeant Smith, who had previously given him first aid; Smith calmed appellant and persuaded him to go to the hospital in a Government car. Appellant then entered a Government car and, with Officer Ebner, waited for another security officer to accompany him to the hospital.

After a five-minute wait, Mr. Coleman got out of the Government car, announcing his intention to drive himself to the hospital. Officer Ebner radioed for instructions and was told to arrest Mr. Coleman. He did just that: he stopped appellant in the street, grabbed him by the arm, and led him to

1. That section provides:

Whoever, within the special maritime and territorial jurisdiction of the United States, is guilty of an assault shall be punished as follows:

(d) Assault by striking, beating, or wounding, by fine of not more than $500 or imprisonment for not more than six months, or both.

the Post Office. In the revolving door of the Post Office, appellant kicked Ebner in the shin—the assault for which he stands convicted.

Critical to this appeal is the fact that appellant was stopped on a public street outside the jurisdiction of the United States and then brought back onto federal property where the assault occurred.

II

Appellant Coleman's argument, most broadly stated, is that he was not voluntarily on federal property at the time he committed the assault and that a voluntary presence is an essential element of the crime for which he stands convicted. In support of this position, Mr. Coleman relies on Martin v. State, 31 Ala.App. 334, 17 So.2d 427 (App.Div.1944) and People v. Newton, 72 Misc.2d 646, 340 N.Y.S.2d 77 (Sup.Ct.1973).

In *Martin,* the defendant was drinking in his home when police officers seized him, took him onto a public highway, and then arrested him there under an Alabama statute punishing "[a]ny person who intoxicated or drunk * * * appears in any public place * * * and manifests a drunken condition." Martin's conviction was reversed by the Alabama Court of Appeals because his presence on the public highway was involuntary: "[u]nder the plain terms of the statute, a voluntary appearance is supposed." In *Newton,* the defendant, concealing a loaded revolver on his person, boarded an airplane bound from the Bahamas to Luxembourg. Although no stops in the United States were scheduled, the plane put down in New York, and defendant was arrested on board for possession of a loaded firearm in violation of New York law. The New York Court granted *habeas corpus,* finding that his involuntary presence precluded criminal liability.[5]

These decisions—properly decided as they very likely were—are not, however, compelling authority for the conclusion that Section 113 of Title 18 requires voluntary presence on federal property. Here, unlike *Martin* and *Newton,* involuntary presence was not the final ingredient without which criminal liability would not have attached. Rather, appellant was convicted for his voluntary conduct once he was within the territorial jurisdiction of the United States—that voluntary conduct being his assault on Officer Ebner. The assault itself constitutes the necessary voluntary act: the requirement is not that every aspect of wrongful behavior be volitional, but that liability be "based on conduct which includes a voluntary act." Model Penal Code § * * * [2.01(1)].

Appellant argues that voluntary presence is required because Section 113 "was designed * * * to deter those who would come upon Federal property to commit an assault." But there is nothing to suggest that Congress' purpose was so limited. Congress, it appears, sought to insure that all assaults committed on federal property could be prosecuted in a federal

5. See also Larsonneur, 24 Cr.App. 74, 149 L.T.R. 542 (1933). There, a French woman was arrested in the Irish Free State, brought to England, and turned over to the British police who charged her with the offense of being an alien "found" in the United Kingdom without permission of the government—a crime for which she was convicted. The comments to the Model Penal Code criticize that result. Comments § 2.01.

forum, thereby guaranteeing uniform and vigorous protection of federal interests.[6] Indeed, as the Government notes, appellant's restrictive interpretation would render Section 113 inapplicable to assaults committed by persons imprisoned in federal institutions. The cases applying Section 113 in such circumstances are legion, and it is hard to conceive that Congress intended otherwise.

* * *

Accordingly, appellant's conviction is affirmed.

State v. Flaherty

Supreme Judicial Court of Maine, 1979.
400 A.2d 363.

NICHOLS, JUSTICE.

The Defendant, Timothy F. Flaherty, appeals from a judgment of conviction of the crime of possession of a firearm by a felon (15 M.R.S.A. § 393 (Supp.1978)) entered on a jury verdict returned July 12, 1978 in Superior Court in Cumberland County. He asserts that portions of the applicable statutes were unconstitutionally vague and that the omission of a crucial jury instruction relating to the Defendant's awareness of his control and possession of the firearm, constituted manifest error.

We sustain the appeal.

By an indictment returned May 3, 1978, the Defendant and his wife, Christine R. Flaherty, were charged with the theft of a hunting rifle belonging to Everard Giles. The jury was unable to reach a verdict on these charges of theft and a motion to dismiss these charges was granted. In a separate count of the same indictment the Defendant, Timothy F. Flaherty, was charged with the offense of possession of a firearm by a felon. At trial he stipulated to his prior conviction of a felony. He and his wife contended, however, that they were not aware of the presence of the firearm in the car which the Defendant was driving until shortly before they were stopped and arrested by the police.

The evidence at the trial revealed essentially the following facts: On February 21, 1978, the Defendant and his wife spent the day in Portland and Gorham in the company of Jerry Tuttle and Everard Giles, the latter a 74-year-old retired Maine hunting guide. They were drinking various alcoholic beverages most of the day and into the evening.

* * *

6. Cf. United States v. Feola, 420 U.S. 671, 95 S.Ct. 1255, 43 L.Ed.2d 541 (1975). In *Feola,* the Court held that knowledge that one's intended victim is a federal officer is not a requisite for a conviction under 18 U.S.C. § 111. In interpreting Section 111, the Court relied heavily on a 1934 letter from Attorney General Homer Cummings urging passage of the legislation because "[t]he Federal Government should not be compelled to rely upon the courts of the States, however respectable and well disposed, for the protection of its investigative and law enforcement personnel." The legislative history of Section 113 also evinces a Congressional choice not to entrust to the States the sole responsibility for the interdiction of assaults. In 1940, for example, the assault provision (then 18 U.S.C. § 455 and 18 U.S.C. § 7) was expanded to extend federal criminal jurisdiction to property over which the United States exercised concurrent territorial jurisdiction. Then Attorney General (later Justice) Frank Murphy endorsed the extension as necessary "to enhance the effectiveness of the administration of the federal law."

* * * Giles showed the Defendant and his wife his new hunting rifle. Giles did not at any later time see the Defendant or his wife with the gun.

* * * The Defendant and his wife decided to leave and about 11:30 P.M. they did so. Giles testified that he had not moved the gun after initially showing it to them * * *. The Defendant and his wife stressed, while Giles denied, the extreme drunkenness of Giles at this point.

The Defendant and his wife stated that they drove to Portland where they picked up Mrs. Flaherty's cousin, Andrea Johnston. Upon getting into the compact car, Mrs. Johnston found the rifle in the back of the car. The Defendant asserted that this was the first time he knew the rifle was in the car. He testified that he promptly checked it to see that it was not loaded. The Defendant then started to drive back to Buxton to return the rifle to Giles.

The Defendant, his wife and Andrea Johnston had proceeded only a few blocks along Portland streets when the police stopped the car and ordered all the passengers out. The police removed the rifle which at that time was lodged along the hump between the two front seats of Tuttle's compact car.

The key factual question in the case appears to have been the manner in which the rifle reached the Tuttle car. The Defendant's testimony raised the inference that Giles in his drunken state had put the gun in the car and then forgotten his actions. Giles denied any such lapse of memory or any such actions.

* * *

The offense stated in 15 M.R.S.A. § 393 (Supp.1978) [1] forbids any felon to "own, have in his possession or under his control any firearm." Applicable to this crime through 17–A M.R.S.A. § 6 (Supp.1978) [2] is 17–A M.R.S.A. § 51 (Supp.1978),[3] which in § 51(1) declares that a "person commits a crime only if he engages in voluntary conduct," and in § 51(3) further states:

1. 15 M.R.S.A. § 393 (Supp.1978) states in relevant part:

> 1. No person who has been convicted of any crime, under the laws of the United States, the State of Maine or any other state, which is punishable by one year or more imprisonment or any other crime which was committed with the use of a dangerous weapon or of a firearm against a person, except for a violation of Title 12, chapter 319, subchapter III, shall own, have in his possession or under his control any firearm, unless such a person has obtained a permit under this section. For the purposes of this subsection, a person shall be deemed to have been convicted upon the acceptance of a plea of guilty or nolo contendere or a verdict or finding of guilty by a court of competent jurisdiction.

2. 17–A M.R.S.A. § 6 (Supp.1978) reads in relevant part:

> 1. The provisions of chapters 1, 3, 5, 7, 47, 49, 51 and 53 are applicable to crimes defined outside this code, unless the context of the statute defining the crime clearly requires otherwise.

3. 17–A M.R.S.A. § 51 (Supp.1978) reads in full:

> 1. A person commits a crime only if he engages in voluntary conduct, including a voluntary act, or the voluntary omission to perform an act of which he is physically capable.
>
> 2. A person who omits to perform an act does not commit a crime unless he has a legal duty to perform the act.
>
> 3. Possession is voluntary conduct only if the possessor knowingly procured or received the thing possessed or was aware of his control thereof for a sufficient period to have been able to terminate his possession.

This section is based on the New Hampshire Criminal Code 1973, § 626.1. It also tracks in large measure § 2.01 of the Model Penal Code. Subsection 3, especially, is similar to § 2.01(4) of the Model Penal Code.

> Possession is voluntary conduct only if the possessor knowingly procured or received the thing possessed or was aware of his control thereof for a sufficient period to have been able to terminate his possession.

The Defendant's basic claim of error was the absence of an instruction to the jury that the Defendant was not criminally liable for possession unless his possession was voluntary conduct, and that they must find the Defendant was aware of his control of the rifle for a sufficient period to have been able to terminate his possession. * * *

* * *

Had the jury found the Defendant and his wife guilty of the theft charge, we would have little trouble in upholding their verdict that the Defendant "possessed" the rifle within the meaning of 15 M.R.S.A. § 393. Here, however, the jury was unable to conclude that they had taken the rifle from Giles' camper. By failing to convict the Defendant and his wife of theft, there is a substantial possibility that some members of the jury believed their version of the events; that is, that they were unaware of the rifle in the automobile other than for the short period of time after Mrs. Johnston allegedly discovered it in the Tuttle car. The State produced no direct evidence that the Defendant was aware of his control of the rifle prior to the admitted discovery of it. Taken together, all these factors generate the real possibility that the jury found that the Defendant only became aware of the rifle when Mrs. Johnston discovered it, but concluded that the Defendant's admission that he had had the rifle in his control for a brief interlude thereafter was *ipso facto* possession or control sufficient to support a conviction under 15 M.R.S.A. § 393 (Supp.1978). Under an appropriate instruction in terms of § 51(3), which was never given,[4] however, the jury might reasonably have concluded that the Defendant had not been aware of his control of the rifle for a sufficient period to have been able to terminate his possession. To omit such an instruction was manifest error.

The Defendant next asserts that the term "a sufficient period" in § 51(3) is unconstitutionally vague. See Knowlton v. State, Me., 257 A.2d 409, 410 (1969). We conclude that the term is not unduly vague, but rather fixes a reasonable standard by which to evaluate the Defendant's actions in terminating his possession of the rifle.

The key word "sufficient" has been defined as "enough to meet the needs of a situation or a proposed end." *Webster's New Collegiate Dictionary* 1164 (1973). In the context of this statute the term requires an evaluation of the surrounding circumstances in order to determine whether the Defendant acted appropriately.

Even in the absence of a provision comparable to § 51(3), this result has been reached under statutes similar to 15 M.R.S.A. § 393 (Supp.1978). In People v. La Pella, 272 N.Y. 81, 4 N.E.2d 943 (1936) the defendant was held

4. The court's jury instruction in pertinent part stated only:

> No person who has been convicted of any crime * * * which was committed with the use of a dangerous weapon or a firearm against a person shall own, have in his possession or under his control any firearm unless such a person has obtained a permit under this section. That is the statute.

entitled to an instruction that temporary possession incidental to a lawful purpose was not proscribed by a statute prohibiting possession of a concealed weapon by a person previously convicted of a crime. The defendant claimed to have found such a weapon twenty minutes before turning it over to the police. See also People v. Stone, 80 Misc.2d 536, 364 N.Y.S.2d 739, 742–43 (1975).

We find these decisions instructive. They indicate that the "grace" period permitted by § 51(3) is designed to separate illegal possession from temporary control incidental to the lawful purpose of terminating possession. Thus a "sufficient period" is not always the absolute minimum time required to get rid of the contraband. So long as the Defendant's control of the contraband remains incidental to the lawful purpose of terminating his possession and, viewed under the circumstances, remains "temporary," it falls within the "sufficient period" permitted him by 17–A M.R.S.A. § 51(3) (Supp.1978).

The entry is:

Appeal sustained.

Judgment vacated.

Remanded for further proceedings consistent with the opinion herein.

WERNICK, J., did not sit.

Notes

1. *Involuntary act.* The *actus reus* requirement includes not only an act (or acceptable omission), but conduct which is voluntary. A bodily movement which is not willed or which is performed during an unconscious state is simply, by the orthodox view, not an act at all, for purposes of the criminal law. It therefore can have no criminal consequences for the person who moved. § 2.01(2) of the Model Penal Code (P.O.D.1962) lists the following as involuntary acts: a reflex, a convulsion, a bodily movement during unconsciousness or sleep, conduct during hypnosis or resulting from hypnotic suggestion, or a bodily movement otherwise not a product of the effort or determination of the actor, either conscious or habitual. For an old sleepwalking case, see Fain v. Commonwealth, 78 Ky. 183, 39 Am.Rep. 213 (1879). People v. Freeman, 61 Cal.App.2d 110, 142 P.2d 435 (1943) is an epilepsy case.

2. *Insanity and Intoxication.* Most acts done by insane or intoxicated persons are not treated as involuntary. The issue is rather one of responsibility, a question of *mens rea,* not *actus reus.* Is different treatment justified? We will see that the different treatment produces important consequences when we study insanity.

Questions

1. In People v. Decina, 2 N.Y.2d 133, 157 N.Y.S.2d 588, 138 N.E.2d 799 (1956), defendant was charged with violating a statute which provided that a "person who operates or drives any vehicle * * * in a reckless or culpably negligent manner, whereby a human being is killed is guilty" of an offense. It was claimed that, knowing that he was subject to a disorder which rendered him likely to lose consciousness for a considerable period of time, he operated his car, and while so doing, suffered such an attack, which produced reckless operation of the car and the deaths of four sidewalk pedestrians. Is an offense charged?

2. Reconsider the *Martin, Newton,* and *Larsonneur* cases, all discussed in *Coleman.* Are they all clearly involuntary act cases?

3. Is the Model Penal Code correct in including hypnotism cases in the involuntary act category? Why does it exclude acts produced by habit?

4. Grasp finds a package on the floor of a gas station rest room. He takes it out to his car, where he plans to open it to see what it contains. At this point he is arrested and charged with possession of a drug which the package contains. Does he have an involuntary act defense? Suppose an unknown person had stuffed the package into Grasp's pocket.

3. *Mens Rea*

Regina v. Cunningham

Court of Criminal Appeal, 1957.
[1957] 2 Q.B. 396.

BRYNE J. read the following judgment. The appellant was convicted at Leeds Assizes upon an indictment framed under section 23 of the Offences against the Person Act, 1861, which charged that he unlawfully and maliciously caused to be taken by Sarah Wade a certain noxious thing, namely, coal gas, so as thereby to endanger the life of the said Sarah Wade.

The facts were that the appellant was engaged to be married and his prospective mother-in-law was the tenant of a house, No. 7a, Bakes Street, Bradford, which was unoccupied but which was to be occupied by the appellant after his marriage. Mrs. Wade and her husband, an elderly couple, lived in the house next door. At one time the two houses had been one, but when the building was converted into two houses a wall had been erected to divide the cellars of the two houses, and that wall was composed of rubble loosely cemented.

On the evening of January 17 last the appellant went to the cellar of No. 7a, Bakes Street, wrenched the gas meter from the gas pipes and stole it, together with its contents, and in a second indictment he was charged with the larceny of the gas meter and its contents. To that indictment he pleaded Guilty and was sentenced to six months' imprisonment. In respect of that matter he does not appeal.

The facts were not really in dispute, and in a statement to a police officer the appellant said: "All right I will tell you. I was short of money, I had been off work for three days, I got eight shillings from the gas meter. I tore it off the wall and threw it away." Although there was a stop tap within two feet of the meter, the appellant did not turn off the gas, with the result that a very considerable volume of gas escaped, some of which seeped through the wall of the cellar and partially asphyxiated Mrs. Wade, who was asleep in her bedroom next door, with the result that her life was endangered.

At the close of the case for the prosecution Mr. Brodie, who appeared for the appellant at the trial and who has appeared for him again in this court, submitted that there was no case to go to the jury, but the learned judge, quite rightly in our opinion, rejected this submission. The appellant did not give evidence.

The act of the appellant was clearly unlawful and therefore the real question for the jury was whether it was also malicious within the meaning of section 23 of the Offences against the Person Act, 1861.

Section 23 provides as follows: "Whosoever shall unlawfully and maliciously administer to or cause to be administered to or taken by any other person any poison or other destructive or noxious thing, so as thereby to endanger the life of such person, or so as thereby to inflict upon such person any grievous bodily harm, shall be guilty of felony * * *."

* * *

We have considered * * * the following principle which was propounded by the late Professor C.S. Kenny in the first edition of his Outlines of Criminal Law, published in 1902, and repeated in the sixteenth edition edited by Mr. J.W. Cecil Turner and published in 1952: "In any statutory definition of a crime, malice must be taken not in the old vague sense of wickedness in general but as requiring either (1) An actual intention to do the particular kind of harm that in fact was done; or (2) Recklessness as to whether such harm should occur or not (i.e., the accused has foreseen that the particular kind of harm might be done and yet has gone on to take the risk of it). It is neither limited to nor does it indeed require any ill will towards the person injured." The same principle is repeated by Mr. Turner in his tenth edition of Russell on Crime at p. 1592.

We think that this is an accurate statement of the law * * *. In our opinion, the word "maliciously" in a statutory crime postulates foresight of consequences.

In his summing-up Oliver, J. directed the jury as follows: "You will observe that there is nothing there about 'with intention that that person should take it.' He has not got to intend that it should be taken; it is sufficient that by his unlawful and malicious act he causes it to be taken. What you have to decide here, then, is whether, when he loosed that frightful cloud of coal gas into the house which he shared with this old lady, he caused her to take it by his unlawful and malicious action. 'Unlawful' does not need any definition. It is something forbidden by law. What about 'malicious'? 'Malicious' for this purpose means wicked—something which he has no business to do and perfectly well knows it. 'Wicked' is as good a definition as any other which you would get.

"The facts which face you (and they are uncontradicted and undisputed; the prisoner has not gone into the box to seek to give any particular explanation) are these. Living in the house, which was now two houses but which had once been one and had been rather roughly divided, the prisoner quite deliberately, intending to steal the money that was in the meter—*there* it is (indicating Exhibit 1)—broke the gas meter away from the supply pipes and thus released the mains supply of gas at large into that house. When he did that he knew that this old lady and her husband were living next door to him. The gas meter was in a cellar. The wall which divided his cellar from the cellar next door was a kind of honeycomb wall through which gas could very well go, so that when he loosed that cloud of gas into that place he must have known perfectly well that gas would percolate all over the house. If it were part of this offence—which it is not—that he intended to poison the old lady, I should have left it to you to decide, and I should have told you that there was evidence on which you could find that he intended that, since he did an action which he must have known would result in that. As I have already told you, it is not necessary to prove that he intended to do it; it is quite enough that what he did was done unlawfully and maliciously."

With the utmost respect to the learned judge, we think it is incorrect to say that the word "malicious" in a statutory offence merely means wicked. We think the learned judge was in effect telling the jury that if they were satisfied that the appellant acted wickedly—and he had clearly acted wickedly in stealing the gas meter and its contents—they ought to find that he had acted maliciously in causing the gas to be taken by Mrs. Wade so as thereby to endanger her life.

In our view, it should have been left to the jury to decide whether, even if the appellant did not intend the injury to Mrs. Wade, he foresaw that the removal of the gas meter might cause injury to someone but nevertheless removed it. We are unable to say that a reasonable jury, properly directed as to the meaning of the word "maliciously" in the context of section 23, would without doubt have convicted.

In these circumstances this court has no alternative but to allow the appeal and quash the conviction.

MODEL PENAL CODE § 2.02, TEXT *

General Requirements of Culpability.

(1) *Minimum Requirements of Culpability.* Except as provided in Section 2.05, a person is not guilty of an offense unless he acted purposely, knowingly, recklessly or negligently, as the law may require, with respect to each material element of the offense.

(2) *Kinds of Culpability Defined.*

(a) Purposely.

A person acts purposely with respect to a material element of an offense when:

(i) if the element involves the nature of his conduct or a result thereof, it is his conscious object to engage in conduct of that nature or to cause such a result; and

(ii) if the element involves the attendant circumstances, he is aware of the existence of such circumstances or he believes or hopes that they exist.

(b) *Knowingly.*

A person acts knowingly with respect to a material element of an offense when:

(i) if the element involves the nature of his conduct or the attendant circumstances, he is aware that his conduct is of that nature or that such circumstances exist; and

(ii) if the element involves a result of his conduct, he is aware that it is practically certain that his conduct will cause such a result.

(c) *Recklessly.*

A person acts recklessly with respect to a material element of an offense when he consciously disregards a substantial and unjustifiable risk that the material element exists or will result from his conduct. The risk must be of such a nature and degree that, considering the nature and purpose of the actor's conduct and the circumstances known to him, its disregard involves a gross deviation from the standard of conduct that a law-abiding person would observe in the actor's situation.

(d) *Negligently.*

A person acts negligently with respect to a material element of an offense when he should be aware of a substantial and unjustifiable risk that the material element exists or will result from his conduct. The risk must be of such a nature and degree that the actor's failure to perceive it, considering the nature and purpose of his conduct and the circumstances known to him, involves a gross deviation from the standard of care that a reasonable person would observe in the actor's situation.

* * *

(5) *Substitutes for Negligence, Recklessness and Knowledge.* When the law provides that negligence suffices to establish an element of an offense, such element also is established if a person acts purposely, knowingly or recklessly. When recklessness suffices to establish an element, such element also is established if a person acts purposely or knowingly. When acting knowingly suffices to establish an element, such element also is established if a person acts purposely.

(6) *Requirement of Purpose Satisfied if Purpose Is Conditional.* When a particular purpose is an element of an offense, the element is established although such purpose is conditional, unless the condition negatives the harm or evil sought to be prevented by the law defining the offense.

(7) *Requirement of Knowledge Satisfied by Knowledge of High Probability.* When knowledge of the existence of a particular fact is an element of an offense, such knowledge is established if a person is aware of a high probability of its existence, unless he actually believes that it does not exist.

Liparota v. United States

Supreme Court of the United States, 1985.
471 U.S. 419, 105 S.Ct. 2084, 85 L.Ed. 434.

JUSTICE BRENNAN delivered the opinion of the Court.

The federal statute governing food stamp fraud provides that "whoever knowingly uses, transfers, acquires, alters, or possesses coupons or authorization cards in any manner not authorized by [the statute] or the regulations" is subject to a fine and imprisonment. 7 U.S.C. § 2024(b). The question presented is whether in a prosecution under this provision the Government must prove that the defendant knew that he was acting in a manner not authorized by statute or regulations.

* * *

II

* * * The Government argues that petitioner violated the statute if he knew that he acquired or possessed food stamps and if in fact that acquisition or possession was in a manner not authorized by statute or regulations. * * *

Petitioner claims that the Government's interpretation * * * dispenses with the only morally blameworthy element in the definition of the crime. To avoid this allegedly untoward result, he claims that an individual violates the statute if he knows that he has acquired or possessed food stamps *and* if he also knows that he has done so in an unauthorized manner.[5] Our task is to determine which meaning Congress intended.

The definition of the elements of a criminal offense is entrusted to the legislature, particularly in the case of federal crimes, which are solely creatures of statute. United States v. Hudson, 7 Cranch 32, 3 L.Ed. 259 (1812). With respect to the element at issue in this case, however, Congress has not explicitly spelled out the mental state required. Although Congress certainly intended by use of the word "knowingly" to require *some* mental state with respect to *some* element of the crime defined in § 2024(b), the interpretations proffered by both parties accord with congressional intent to this extent. Beyond this, the words themselves provide little guidance. Either interpretation would accord with ordinary usage.[7] The legislative history of the statute contains nothing that would clarify the congressional purpose on this point.

5. The required mental state may of course be different for different elements of a crime. United States v. Bailey, 444 U.S. 394, 405–406, 100 S.Ct. 624, 631–633, 62 L.Ed.2d 575 (1980); United States v. Freed, 401 U.S. 601, 612–614, 91 S.Ct. 1112, 1119–1121, 28 L.Ed. 2d 356 (1971) (BRENNAN, J., concurring in judgment). See generally Robinson & Grail, Element Analysis in Defining Criminal Liability: The Model Penal Code and Beyond, 35 Stan.L. Rev. 681 (1983). In this case, for instance, both parties agree that petitioner must have known that he acquired and possessed food stamps. They disagree over whether any mental element at all is required with respect to the unauthorized nature of that acquisition or possession.

* * * In this case, petitioner argues that with respect to the element at issue, knowledge is required. The Government contends that *no* mental state is required with respect to that element.

7. One treatise has aptly summed up the ambiguity in an analogous situation:

"Still further difficulty arises from the ambiguity which frequently exists concerning what the words or phrases in question modify. What,

Brumbaugh Cs. Criminal 2nd Ed. UCB—7

Absent indication of contrary purpose in the language or legislative history of the statute, we believe that § 2024(b) requires a showing that the defendant knew his conduct to be unauthorized by statute or regulations.[9] * * *

This construction is particularly appropriate where, as here, to interpret the statute otherwise would be to criminalize a broad range of apparently innocent conduct. For instance, § 2024(b) declares it criminal to use, transfer, acquire, alter, or possess food stamps in any manner not authorized by statute or regulations. The statute provides further that "[c]oupons issued to eligible households shall be used by them only to purchase food in retail food stores which have been approved for participation in the food stamp program *at prices prevailing in such stores.*" 7 U.S.C. § 2016(b) (emphasis added); see also 7 CFR § 274.10(a) (1984). This seems to be the *only* authorized use. A strict reading of the statute with no knowledge of illegality requirement would thus render criminal a food stamp recipient who, for example, used stamps to purchase food from a store that, unknown to him, charged higher than normal prices to food stamp program participants. * * *

* * *

III

We hold that in a prosecution for violation of § 2024(b), the Government must prove that the defendant knew that his acquisition or possession of food stamps was in a manner unauthorized by statute or regulations. This holding does not put an unduly heavy burden on the Government in prosecuting violators of § 2024(b). To prove that petitioner knew that his acquisition or possession of food stamps was unauthorized, for example, the Government need not show that he had knowledge of specific regulations

for instance, does 'knowingly' modify in a sentence from a 'blue sky' law criminal statute punishing one who 'knowingly sells a security without a permit' from the securities commissioner? To be guilty must the seller of a security without a permit know only that what he is doing constitutes a sale, or must he also know that the thing he sells is a security, or must he also know that he has no permit to sell the security he sells? As a matter of grammar the statute is ambiguous; it is not at all clear how far down the sentence the word 'knowingly' is intended to travel—whether it modifies 'sells,' or 'sells a security,' or 'sells a security without a permit.'" W. LaFave & A. Scott, Criminal Law § 27 (1972).

9. The Dissent repeatedly claims that our holding today creates a defense of "mistake of law." Our holding today no more creates a "mistake of law" defense than does a statute making knowing receipt of stolen goods unlawful. In both cases, there is a legal element in the definition of the offense. In the case of a receipt of stolen goods statute, the legal element is that the goods were stolen; in this case, the legal element is that the "use, transfer, acquisition," etc. were in a manner not authorized by statute or regulations. It is not a defense to a charge of receipt of stolen goods that one did not know that such receipt was illegal, and it is not a defense to a charge of a § 2024(b) violation that one did not know that possessing food stamps in a manner unauthorized by statute or regulations was illegal. It *is*, however, a defense to a charge of knowing receipt of stolen goods that one did not know that the goods were stolen, just as it is a defense to a charge of a § 2024(b) violation that one did not know that one's possession was unauthorized. See American Law Institute, Model Penal Code § 2.02, Comment 11, p. 131 (Tentative Draft No. 4, 1955); United States v. Freed, 401 U.S. 601, 614–615, 91 S.Ct. 1112, 1120–1121, 28 L.Ed.2d 356 (1971) (BRENNAN, J., concurring). Cf. United States v. Morissette, 342 U.S. 246, 72 S.Ct. 240, 96 L.Ed. 288 (1952) (holding that it is a defense to a charge of "knowingly converting" federal property that one did not know that what one was doing was a conversion).

governing food stamp acquisition or possession. Nor must the Government introduce any extraordinary evidence that would conclusively demonstrate petitioner's state of mind. Rather, as in any other criminal prosecution requiring *mens rea,* the Government may prove by reference to facts and circumstances surrounding the case that petitioner knew that his conduct was unauthorized or illegal.[17]

Reversed.

JUSTICE POWELL took no part in the consideration or decision of this case.

JUSTICE WHITE, with whom THE CHIEF JUSTICE joins, dissenting.

* * *

I

The Court views the statutory problem here as being how far down the sentence the term "knowingly" travels. Accepting for the moment that if "knowingly" does extend to the "in any manner" language today's holding would be correct—a position with which I take issue below—I doubt that it gets that far. The "in any manner" language is separated from the litany of verbs to which "knowingly" is directly connected by the intervening nouns.

* * *

In any event, I think that the premise of this approach is mistaken. Even accepting that "knowingly" does extend through the sentence, or at least that we should read § 2024(b) as if it does, the statute does not mean what the Court says it does. Rather, it requires only that the defendant be aware of the relevant aspects of his conduct. A requirement that the defendant know that he is acting in a particular manner, coupled with the fact that that manner is forbidden, does not establish a defense of ignorance of the law. It creates only a defense of ignorance or mistake of fact. Knowingly to do something that is unauthorized by law is not the same as doing something knowing that it is unauthorized by law.

This point is demonstrated by the hypothetical statute referred to by the majority, which punishes one who "knowingly sells a security without a permit." Even if "knowingly" does reach "without a permit," I would think that a defendant who knew that he did not have a permit, though not that a permit was required, could be convicted.

Section 2024(b) is an identical statute, except that instead of detailing the various legal requirements, it incorporates them by proscribing use of coupons "in any manner not authorized" by law. This shorthand approach to drafting does not transform knowledge of illegality into an element of the crime. As written, § 2024(b) is substantively no different than if it had been broken down into a collection of specific provisions making crimes of particular improper uses. For example, food stamps cannot be used to purchase

17. In this case, for instance, the Government introduced evidence that petitioner bought food stamps at a substantial discount from face value and that he conducted part of the transaction in a back room of his restaurant to avoid the presence of the other patrons. Moreover, the Government asserts that food stamps themselves are stamped "nontransferable." A jury could have inferred from this evidence that petitioner knew that his acquisition and possession of the stamps was unauthorized.

tobacco. The statute might have said, *inter alia,* that anyone "who knowingly uses coupons to purchase cigarettes" commits a crime. Under no plausible reading could a defendant then be acquitted because he did not know cigarettes are not "eligible food." But in fact, that is exactly what § 2024(b) does say, it just does not write it out longhand.

The Court's opinion provides another illustration of the general point: someone who used food stamps to purchase groceries at inflated prices without realizing he was overcharged. I agree that such a person may not be convicted, but not for the reason given by the majority. The purchaser did not "knowingly" use the stamps in the proscribed manner, for he was unaware of the circumstances of the transaction that made it illegal.

The majority and I would part company in result as well as rationale if the purchaser knew he was charged higher than normal prices but not that overcharging is prohibited. In such a case, he would have been aware of the nature of his actions, and therefore the purchase would have been "knowing." I would hold that such a mental state satisfies the statute. Under the Court's holding, as I understand it, that person could not be convicted because he did not know that his conduct was illegal.

* * *

II

The broad principles of the Court's opinion are easy to live with in a case such as this. But the application of its reasoning might not always be so benign. For example, § 2024(b) is little different from the basic federal prohibition on the manufacture and distribution of controlled substances. 21 U.S.C. § 841(a) provides:

> "Except as authorized by this subchapter, it shall be unlawful for any person knowingly or intentionally—
>
> "(1) to manufacture, distribute, or dispense, or possess with intent to manufacture, distribute or dispense, a controlled substance * * *."

I am sure that the members of the majority would agree that a defendant charged under this provision could not defend on the ground that he did not realize his manufacture was unauthorized or that the particular substance was controlled. See United States v. Balint, 258 U.S. 250, 42 S.Ct. 301, 66 L.Ed. 604 (1922). On the other hand, it would be a defense if he could prove he thought the substance was something other than what it was. By the same token, I think, someone in petitioner's position should not be heard to say that he did not know his purchase of food stamps was unauthorized, though he may certainly argue that he did not know he was buying food stamps. I would not stretch the term "knowingly" to require awareness of the absence of statutory authority in either of these provisions.

These provisions might be distinguished because of the different placements of the "except as authorized" and the "in any manner not authorized" clauses in the sentences. However, nothing in the majority's opinion indicates that this difference is relevant. Indeed, the logic of the Court's opinion would require knowledge of illegality for conviction under any statute making it a crime to do something "in any manner not authorized by law" or "unlawfully." I suspect that if a case arises in the future where such a result is unacceptable, the Court will manage to distinguish today's decision. But I will be interested to see how it does so.

* * *

Notes

1. *Meaning of Mens Rea.* State v. Savoie, 67 N.J. 439, 454–457, 341 A.2d 598, 607–608 (1975):

> Any rational approach to the specific issues presented requires recognition at the outset that the term *mens rea* is an undifferentiated lump-concept which has been loosely used by law writers and judges to embrace a number of different and distinct legally significant states of mind of an accused. Professor Sayre has cogently observed that for clarity of analysis "[t]he old conception of *mens rea* must be discarded and in its place must be substituted the new concept of *mentes* [plural] *rea.*" Sayre, "Mens Rea", 45 *Harv.L.Rev.* 974, 1026 (1932); and see Hall, General Principles of Criminal Law, 103 (1960).
>
> Thus, such states of mind include the ordinary intent or conscious volition to do the act forbidden (or to omit the act commanded); the awareness of all the circumstances material to the offense, or, put otherwise, absence of reasonable mistake as to fact or as to a legal relationship if made an element of the offense; absence of incapacity, actual or constructive, to form an intent or to understand the circumstances material to the offense such as insanity and infancy, or to act voluntarily, as in duress (at common law and some states). They also include such "specific intents" as premeditation in murder, intent to defraud as in obtaining money under false pretenses, receiving stolen goods knowing them to have been stolen and many others, usually specified in criminal statutes. Decisions exculpating defendants under the purported broad rubric of absence of *mens rea,* evil mind or consciousness of wrongdoing have almost invariably been based on the lack of one or another of the particular incriminatory states of mind enumerated above. * * *[2]
>
> * * *
>
> It has been authoritatively observed that the general concept of *mens rea* in its classic sense of evil mind may have developed, at least in part, because all the common-law felonies involved conduct morally reprehensible to the community as well as patently intentional. Sayre, op. cit. supra, 45 *Harv.L.Rev.* at 988–989; cf. Mueller, op. cit. supra (42 *Minn.L.Rev.* at 1058, 1101). * * *
>
> Leading British and American writers and judges in the modern era have fairly uniformly eschewed positing criminal liability on a guilty or evil mind but have rather conceived the "mental element" of criminality as "either intention to do the act or bring [ab]out the consequence or (in some crimes) recklessness as to that consequence", Glanville Williams, "Criminal Law" 28–29 (1953); or, as more comprehensively stated: "*Mens rea* consists of two elements. It consists first of all of the intent to do an act and secondly of the knowledge of the circumstances that makes that act a criminal offense". Devlin, Statutory Of-

2. Professor Mueller, by contrast, argues for the existence at common law of a unifying concept of *mens rea* that would in all cases exculpate the morally blameless. Mueller, "On Common Law Mens Rea", 42 *Minn.L. Rev.* 1043, *passim* (1958). He suggests "[a]bsolute criminal liability is beginning to end in America", *id.* at 1104, and that any statutes "attempting to abolish a universal *mens rea* requirement * * * are unconstitutional". Ibid. We do not share these latter views.

We do share the view that the criminal law should tend to exculpate the morally blameless * * *.

fenses, 4 *J. of Soc. Pub. Teachers of L.* 213 (1958), as quoted in Hall, op cit. supra, p. 71; and see ibid., passim pp. 70–77. Knowledge of the criminal law, however, is ordinarily no part of the circumstances as to which the accused is required to have awareness to be culpable. Glanville Williams, op cit. supra at 384–387.

2. *Significant mental states.* Model Penal Code, § 2.02, Comments 1, 2, 3, and 4: *

1. *Objective.* * * * The section further attempts the extremely difficult task of articulating the kinds of culpability that may be required for the establishment of liability. It delineates four levels of culpability: purpose, knowledge, recklessness and negligence. It requires that one of these levels of culpability must be proved with respect to each "material element" of the offense, which may involve (1) the nature of the forbidden conduct, (2) the attendant circumstances, or (3) the result of conduct. The question of which level of culpability suffices to establish liability must be addressed separately with respect to each material element, and will be resolved either by the particular definition of the offense or the general provisions of this section.

The purpose of articulating these distinctions in detail is to advance the clarity of draftsmanship in the delineation of the definitions of specific crimes, to provide a distinct framework against which those definitions may be tested, and to dispel the obscurity with which the culpability requirement is often treated when such concepts as "general criminal intent," "mens rea," "presumed intent," "malice," "wilfulness," "scienter" and the like have been employed. What Justice Jackson called "the variety, disparity and confusion" of judicial definitions of "the requisite but elusive mental element" [2] in crime should, insofar as possible, be rationalized by a criminal code.

* * *

2. *Purpose and Knowledge.* In defining the kinds of culpability, the Code draws a narrow distinction between acting purposely and knowingly, one of the elements of ambiguity in legal usage of the term "intent." Knowledge that the requisite external circumstances exist is a common element in both conceptions. But action is not purposive with respect to the nature or result of the actor's conduct unless it was his conscious object to perform an action of that nature or to cause such a result. It is meaningful to think of the actor's attitude as different if he is simply aware that his conduct is of the required nature or that the prohibited result is practically certain to follow from his conduct.

* * *

3. *Recklessness.* * * *

* * *

Ultimately, then, the jury is asked to perform two distinct functions. First, it is to examine the risk and the factors that are relevant to how substantial it was and to the justifications for taking it. In each instance, the question is asked from the point of view of the actor's perceptions, i.e., to what extent he was aware of risk, of factors relating to its substantiality and of factors relating to its unjustifiability. Second, the jury is to make the culpability judgment in terms of whether the defendant's conscious disregard of the risk justifies condemnation. Considering the nature and purpose of his conduct and the circumstances known to him, the question is whether the defendant's disregard of the risk involved a gross

2. Morissette v. United States, 342 U.S. 246, 252 (1952).

deviation from the standards of conduct that a law-abiding person would have observed in the actor's situation.

This approach is thought to be a substantial improvement over previous attempts to be precise about the concept of recklessness. The history of prior common law judicial references to the subject is typified by essentially epithetical attempts to describe "a degree of negligence which far transcends [civil] negligence," "the recklessly careless use of a loaded, deadly pistol," "reckless negligence," "reckless carelessness," and the like. No statutory definition of recklessness could be found that existed prior to the initial Code formulation in 1955, though at that time the proposed Wisconsin code contained a partial definition limited to cases where the risk created was of death or great bodily harm.

* * *

4. *Negligence.* * * *

As with recklessness, the jury is asked to perform two distinct functions. First, it is to examine the risk and the factors that are relevant to its substantiality and justifiability. In the case of negligence, these questions are asked not in terms of what the actor's perceptions actually were, but in terms of an objective view of the situation as it actually existed. Second, the jury is to make the culpability judgment, this time in terms of whether the failure of the defendant to perceive the risk justifies condemnation. Considering the nature and purpose of his conduct and the circumstances known to him, the question is whether the defendant's failure to perceive a risk involves a gross deviation from the standard of care that a reasonable person would observe in the actor's situation.[23]

Formulation of the standard in these terms is believed to be a substantial improvement over the traditional approach to defining negligence for purposes of criminal liability. A number of codes have traditionally included a definition of negligence drawn from the New York Penal Law as it stood before the modern revision. Rarely, if ever, however, has such a definition served in itself to measure liability, since the rule of liability ordinarily imports the crucial additional requirement that negligence be "criminal" or "culpable." Thus, under such statutes, as at common law, the concept of criminal negligence has been left to judicial definition, and the definitions vary greatly in their terms. As Jerome Hall has put it, the judicial "opinions run in terms of 'wanton and wilful negligence,' 'gross negligence,' and more illuminating yet, 'that degree of negligence that is more than the negligence required to impose tort liability.' The apex of this infelicity is 'wilful, wanton negligence,' which suggests a triple contradiction—'negligence' implying inadvertence; 'wilful,' intention; and 'wanton,' recklessness." Much of this confusion is dispelled by a clear-cut distinction between recklessness and negligence in terms of the actor's awareness of the risk involved. Clarity is also promoted by formulating the inquiry in terms of the specific factors to which attention is directed in the Model Code.

A further point in the Code's concept of negligence merits attention. The standard for ultimate judgment invites consideration of the "care that a reasonable person would observe in the actor's situation." There is an inevitable ambiguity in "situation." If the actor were blind or if he had just suffered a blow or

23. For discussion of the distinction between recklessness and negligence, see Fitzgerald, *Crime, Sin and Negligence,* 79 Law Q.Rev. 351 (1963); Fitzgerald & Williams, *Carelessness, Indifference and Recklessness: Two Replies,* 25 Mod.L.Rev. 49 (1962); Turpin, *Mens Rea in Manslaughter,* 1962 Camb. L.J. 200; White, *Carelessness and Recklessness—A Rejoinder,* 25 Mod.L.Rev. 437 (1962); White, *Carelessness, Indifference and Recklessness,* 24 Mod.L.Rev. 592 (1961).

experienced a heart attack, these would certainly be facts to be considered in a judgment involving criminal liability, as they would be under traditional law. But the heredity, intelligence or temperament of the actor would not be held material in judging negligence, and could not be without depriving the criterion of all its objectivity. The Code is not intended to displace discriminations of this kind, but rather to leave the issue to the courts.[27]

3. *Specific and general intent.* State v. Bridgeforth, 156 Ariz. 60, 62, 750 P.2d 3, 5 (1988):

At common law, crimes were classified as requiring either general intent or specific intent. United States v. Bailey, 444 U.S. 394, 403, 100 S.Ct. 624, 631, 62 L.Ed.2d 575 (1980). Numerous writers have commented on the ambiguity and confusion surrounding the use of these terms. LaFave and Scott have noted that the distinctions drawn between specific intent and general intent vary widely:

> Sometimes "general intent" is used in the same way as "criminal intent" to mean the general notion of *mens rea,* while "specific intent" is taken to mean the mental state required for a particular crime. Or, "general intent" may be used to encompass all forms of the mental state requirement, while "specific intent" is limited to the one mental state of intent. Another possibility is that "general intent" will be used to characterize an intent to do something on an undetermined occasion, and "specific intent" to denote an intent to do that thing at a particular time and place.
>
> *However, the most common usage of "specific intent" is to designate a special mental element which is required above and beyond any mental state required with respect to the actus reus of the crime.*

W. LaFave & A. Scott, *Handbook on Criminal Law* § 28, at 201–02 (1972) (emphasis added).

The confusion surrounding the common-law term "specific intent" is further evidenced by the conflicting statements by commentators on the relationship between specific intent and the other culpable mental states. Several authorities state that the common law concept of specific intent corresponds with "intent" or "purpose." *Bailey,* 444 U.S. at 405, 100 S.Ct. at 632 ("In a general sense, 'purpose' corresponds loosely with the common-law concept of specific intent, while 'knowledge' corresponds loosely with the concept of general intent."); MODEL PENAL CODE § 2.02 Comment at 124–25 (Tent. Draft No. 4, 1955) (same); *State v. Morse,* 127 Ariz. 25, 29–31, 617 P.2d 1141, 1145–46 (1980) (deletion of language concerning intent in statute indicates legislature intended to exclude specific intent as an element of receiving stolen property); Gerber, *Arizona's New Criminal Code: An Overview and a Critique,* 1977 ARIZ.ST.L.J. 483, 485 n. 17.

Because of the confusion that has attached to the terms specific and general intent, the drafters of the Model Penal Code and the revised Arizona Criminal Code abandoned use of these terms. MODEL PENAL CODE § 2.02 Comments at 230–31, 234 (1985); see also ARIZONA CRIMINAL CODE COMMISSION, ARIZONA REVISED CRIMINAL CODE, at vii (1975). Arizona has instead adopted the use of the four culpable mental states of intention, knowledge, recklessness, and criminal negligence, as defined in A.R.S. § 13–105(6). The four

27. There is a similar problem with recklessness. Though recklessness requires defendant's conscious disregard of risk, the determination whether he shall be held liable for disregarding a risk turns on whether the disregard involves a gross deviation from the standard of conduct of a law-abiding person "in the actor's situation." Section 2.02(2)(c) thus requires the same discriminations demanded by the standard of negligence.

culpable mental states are the only terms used by the Criminal Code and replace all previous mental states used in our criminal laws. * * *

4. *Malice.* Note that the "malice" required by the *Cunningham* statute is not identical to the "malice" we will meet in other contexts.

5. *Motive.* What is a motive? The criminal law is often said not to take account of motive in determining questions of guilt or innocence. Suppose one injures another to prevent the other's injuring him, and, in the circumstances, the criminal law acquits of battery on the ground of self-defense. Is self-defense a motive? It is generally agreed that motive may be significant on questions of sentencing and for evidentiary purposes. E.g., the prosecution may be allowed to show that the accused had a motive to do what he denies doing, and the accused may be allowed to show that he had no motive for doing what he is charged with doing, on the issue of whether he did it or not.

Questions

1. Suppose Cunningham had acted purposely, in Model Penal Code terms: what was his state of mind with respect to the *actus reus* of the offense charged? Suppose he acted "knowingly"? "recklessly"? "negligently"?

2. Suppose the Court of Criminal Appeal had tried to describe the culpability requirement for the *Cunningham* offense in Model Penal Code terms. How would that portion of the opinion read?

3. Does Model Penal Code "negligence" involve true *mens rea* or fault?

4. Suppose Nephew (1) squeezes the trigger of his revolver, (2) fires the bullet, (3) thereby kills Uncle, (4) inherits Uncle's fortune, (5) takes a luxurious round-the-world trip, and (6) thereby becomes a happier person, and that Nephew desired all of these things to happen from the beginning. What is Nephew's Model Penal Code "purpose"?

4. Concurrence of *Actus Reus* and *Mens Rea*

Regina v. Prince

Court for Crown Cases Reserved, 1875.
L.R. 2 Cr.Cas.Res. 154.

[The accused was charged with the statutory misdemeanor of abduction, in unlawfully taking an "unmarried girl, being under the age of sixteen, out of the possession of her father." The majority of the court held that it was no defense that the accused reasonably believed her to be eighteen years of age if she was in fact under sixteen. (This part of the case is considered infra, p. 165.) In the course of the opinions, the judges considered arguments based on related statutory provisions.] [a]

The following judgment (in which COCKBURN, C.J., MELLOR, LUSH, QUAIN, DENMAN, ARCHIBALD, FIELD, and LINDLEY, JJ., and POLLOCK, B., concurred) was delivered by

BLACKBURN, J. * * *

* * *

a. The order of the opinions has been changed.

Sect. 50 enacts, that whosoever shall "unlawfully and carnally know and abuse any girl under the age of ten years," shall be guilty of felony. Sect. 51, whoever shall "unlawfully and carnally know and abuse any girl being above the age of ten years, and under the age of twelve years," shall be guilty of a misdemeanor.

It seems impossible to suppose that the intention of the legislature in those two sections could have been to make the crime depend upon the knowledge of the prisoner of the girl's actual age. It would produce the monstrous result that a man who had carnal connection with a girl, in reality not quite ten years old, but whom he on reasonable grounds believed to be a little more than ten, was to escape altogether. He could not, in that view of the statute, be convicted of the felony, for he did not know her to be under ten. He could not be convicted of the misdemeanor, because she was in fact not above the age of ten. It seems to us that the intention of the legislature was to punish those who had connection with young girls, though with their consent, unless the girl was in fact old enough to give a valid consent. The man who has connection with a child, relying on her consent, does it at his peril, if she is below the statutable age.

* * *

BRETT, J. [dissenting].

* * *

Upon all the cases I think it is proved that there can be no conviction for crime in England in the absence of a criminal mind or mens rea.

Then comes the question, what is the true meaning of the phrase. I do not doubt that it exists where the prisoner knowingly does acts which would constitute a crime if the result were as he anticipated, but in which the result may not improbably end by bringing the offence within a more serious class of crime. As if a man strikes with a dangerous weapon, with intent to do grievous bodily harm, and kills, the result makes the crime murder. The prisoner has run the risk. So, if a prisoner do the prohibited acts, without caring to consider what the truth is as to facts—as if a prisoner were to abduct a girl under sixteen without caring to consider whether she was in truth under sixteen—he runs the risk. So if he without abduction defiles a girl who is in fact under ten years old, with a belief that she is between ten and twelve. If the facts were as he believed he would be committing the lesser crime. Then he runs the risk of his crime resulting in the greater crime. It is clear that ignorance of the law does not excuse. It seems to me to follow that the maxim as to *mens rea* applies whenever the facts which are present to the prisoner's mind, and which he has reasonable ground to believe, and does believe to be the facts, would, if true, make his acts no criminal offence at all.

Notes on Mismatches Between Mens Rea *and* Actus Reus

1. *Wrong mens rea.* There are several ways in which a mismatch between *mens rea* and *actus reus* might be handled. We have seen in *Cunningham* that the *mens rea* of theft and the *actus reus* of statutory assault do not combine to produce an assault conviction. The guilty mind must be one appropriate for the offense charged. To the same effect is Reg. v. Faulkner, 11 Ir.R.C.L. 8 (Cr.Cas.

Res.1877), where an intention to steal did not combine with the *actus reus* of statutory ship arson to produce guilt of arson when the accused accidentally set fire to a ship while trying to steal from a keg of rum in the hold. The unrelated *actus reus* cannot stand by itself to produce guilt. (Note however that Faulkner might have been convicted of attempted theft if he took sufficient action toward carrying out his intention, and that Cunningham was actually convicted of stealing from the gas meter.)

A more difficult problem arises in cases like those supposed by the *Prince* judges. There is no exact match between *actus reus* and *mens rea*, but there is a very near miss. The degree of guilt may depend on such a factor as the age of the victim (as in the situation suggested by Blackburn, J.), or the *actus reus* of the crime contemplated may be a portion of the *actus reus* of another offense, actually "committed" but not contemplated (as when one sets out to commit an assault, and accidentally goes further and kills the victim). As Brett, J., suggests, the usual common law view is that the accused can be found guilty of the related more serious offense if he commits its *actus reus* while having a *mens rea* appropriate for the less serious offense. He takes the risk that things may turn out worse than he expected. Suppose he is charged with knowingly possessing one type of drug, but the proof shows that he knowingly possessed another drug, punished in a different provision of the code? Here, it would seem that he cannot be convicted of the offense charged, but could be charged successfully under the second drug statute. Suppose he is charged with knowingly possessing drug A, forbidden by section one, and the proof shows that he believed that he possessed drug A, but actually instead possessed drug B, knowing possession of which is forbidden by section two? Absent some curative legislation, it seems that he cannot be convicted of possession of either drug.

One might take the position that in some or all of these instances, it would be proper to convict not of the greater (or equal) offense not contemplated, but of the lessor (or equal) offense the defendant thought he was committing. See, Model Penal Code § 2.04(2). Or, one might convict only of an attempt, or might limit the punishment to that allowed for the lesser offense.

When one aims at a greater related offense but only commits the *actus reus* of the lesser, there is substantial agreement that he should be convicted of the lesser offense or of an attempt to commit the greater. So, if I intend to kill, but only wound, I may be guilty of battery or attempted murder.

Suppose the conduct contemplated (though similar to that of a crime) would be no crime at all, but through some mistake, the *actus reus* of an offense is committed. The modern view is that because there is no *mens rea* there is no offense. Is this true even when the conduct contemplated (though no crime) would be regarded by most of society as morally wrong? Suppose a society which regards all extramarital sex as morally wrong. A sets out to commit fornication, which is not a crime, but, because, as he did not know and could not have been expected to know, his wife remains alive, he commits the *actus reus* of the crime of adultery. Is he guilty of adultery? This is similar to the problem in *Prince* to be considered later.

2. *Wrong victim.* Another kind of problem arises in "wrong victim" cases. Suppose A sets out to commit a battery on B but in fact commits a battery on C instead. This may be because C was mistaken for B or because the brick missed B and hit innocent bystander C. A is guilty of a battery upon the person he

actually hits. Suppose D is the public executioner, lawfully required to execute E, and that D actually does execute E, mistakenly believing that E is his enemy F. Suppose G, a soldier in wartime, fires in the midst of battle at a figure he supposes to be his sergeant H, intending to murder him, and hits his target, who turns out to be an enemy soldier J.

3. *Wrong Time.* The mismatch between *mens rea* and *actus reus* may be a temporal one. Obviously if I intend to kill X today, but think better of it, and I accidentally cause his death next month, I do not kill him intentionally. But consider the grisly case of Jackson v. Commonwealth, 100 Ky. 239, 38 S.W. 422 (1896), on denial of rehearing 100 Ky. 239, 38 S.W. 1091 (1897), where the defendant arguably tried unsuccessfully to kill the victim by poison in Cincinnati, and then, believing incorrectly that he had succeeded, took her across the river to Kentucky, where he cut off her head to make identification more difficult, it being the decapitation which actually caused her death. He argued that he did not commit intentional murder in either jurisdiction; there was no *actus reus* in Ohio and no *mens rea* in Kentucky. The court said on rehearing (38 S.W. 1092):

> * * * Reduced to its lowest terms, the claim of counsel is that an attempt to commit a murder in another state, supposed by the guilty party to have been there successful, but in reality completed in this state, though by an act not by him believed to be the consummation of his purpose, is not in this state punishable. Such is not, nor should it be, the law. By the law of this state a crime is punishable in the jurisdiction in which it has effect. Statutes in numbers have been passed by the general assembly of this commonwealth providing that jurisdiction should be had of crimes in the county in which the crime became effectual. St.Ky. c. 36, art. 2. Such we believe to have been the common law before such enactments. Assuming that what the jury found was true, in what state or district could the crime be punished? If not here, where? If we concede the claims of counsel for appellants, no serious crime was committed in Ohio. Nothing was there done but an ineffective attempt to murder. None was committed here. What was done in this jurisdiction was only the mutilation of a supposed corpse. And yet the fact, established by overwhelming testimony, remains that the crime has been committed. Not all the refinements of counsel can lead us from the conclusion that when a crime has been completed, the result of which is a death in this commonwealth, we can take jurisdiction of the offense.
>
> Not for a moment can we admit as law the logical conclusion of counsel's argument, namely, that there is a variety of murder which, by reason of error in its commission, is not anywhere in any jurisdiction punishable; not in Ohio, for the reason that the attempt there made was not successful; not in Kentucky, for the reason that the act there done, and which accomplished and completed the actual killing, was done upon the supposition that the murder had already been accomplished. One reliance of the defense upon petition for rehearing is that the indictment charges murder by cutting the throat, or decapitation, and that the instructions permit and require the jury to consider a previous attempt to kill in a foreign state, and by different means. But in our opinion it was not error in the instructions to present to the jury evidential facts which, if found to be true, showed the criminal nature of the act by which the offense was completed. We see no good reason why we should not consider the motive which

inspired an attempted crime in another sovereignty, and the circumstances of the attempt, with the view to determine the character, criminal or not, of the ultimate fact which took place in this sovereignty. * * *

5. Absolute Liability Offenses

United States v. Balint

Supreme Court of the United States, 1922.
258 U.S. 250, 42 S.Ct. 301, 66 L.Ed. 604.

MR. CHIEF JUSTICE TAFT delivered the opinion of the Court.

* * * Defendants in error were indicted for a violation of the Narcotic Act of December 17, 1914, 38 Stat. 785, 786 (Comp.St. §§ 6287g–6287q). The indictment charged them with unlawfully selling to another a certain amount of a derivative of opium and a certain amount of a derivative of coca leaves, not in pursuance of any written order on a form issued in blank for that purpose by the Commissioner of Internal Revenue, contrary to the provisions of section 2 of the act. (Comp.St. § 6287h). The defendants demurred to the indictment on the ground that it failed to charge that they had sold the inhibited drugs knowing them to be such. The statute does not make such knowledge an element of the offense. The District Court sustained the demurrer and quashed the indictment. The correctness of this ruling is the question before us.

While the general rule at common law was that the scienter was a necessary element in the indictment and proof of every crime, and this was followed in regard to statutory crimes even where the statutory definition did not in terms include it (Rex v. Sleep, 8 Cox, 472), there has been a modification of this view in respect to prosecutions under statutes the purpose of which would be obstructed by such a requirement. It is a question of legislative intent to be construed by the court. It has been objected that punishment of a person for an act in violation of law when ignorant of the facts making it so, is an absence of due process of law. But that objection is considered and overruled in Shevlin-Carpenter Co. v. Minnesota, 218 U.S. 57, 69, 70, 30 Sup.Ct. 663, 666 (54 L.Ed. 930), in which it was held that in the prohibition or punishment of particular acts, the state may in the maintenance of a public policy provide "that he who shall do them shall do them at his peril and will not be heard to plead in defense good faith or ignorance." Many instances of this are to be found in regulatory measures in the exercise of what is called the police power where the emphasis of the statute is evidently upon achievement of some social betterment rather than the punishment of the crimes as in cases of mala in se. * * * Again where one deals with others and his mere negligence may be dangerous to them, as in selling diseased food or poison, the policy of the law may, in order to stimulate proper care, require the punishment of the negligent person though he be ignorant of the noxious character of what he sells. Hobbs v. Winchester Corporation (1910) 2 K.B.Div. 471, 483.

The question before us, therefore, is one of the construction of the statute and of inference of the intent of Congress. The Narcotic Act has been held by this court to be a taxing act with the incidental purpose of minimizing the spread of addiction to the use of poisonous and demoralizing drugs.

Section 2 of the Narcotic Act (38 Stat. 786) we give in part in the margin.[1] It is very evident from a reading of it that the emphasis of the section is in securing a close supervision of the business of dealing in these dangerous drugs by the taxing officers of the Government and that it merely uses a criminal penalty to secure recorded evidence of the disposition of such drugs as a means of taxing and restraining the traffic. Its manifest purpose is to require every person dealing in drugs to ascertain at his peril whether that which he sells comes within the inhibition of the statute, and if he sells the inhibited drug in ignorance of its character, to penalize him. Congress weighed the possible injustice of subjecting an innocent seller to a penalty against the evil of exposing innocent purchasers to danger from the drug, and concluded that the latter was the result preferably to be avoided. Doubtless considerations as to the opportunity of the seller to find out the fact and the difficulty of proof of knowledge contributed to this conclusion. We think the demurrer to the indictment should have been overruled.

Judgment reversed.

MR. JUSTICE CLARKE took no part in this decision.

Notes

1. *Costs of the drug problem.* People v. Lopez, 139 Misc.2d 448, 450–451, 528 N.Y.S.2d 748, 750 (1988):

> * * * Because drug addiction is so destructive to a person's general well being, the medical and related costs incurred by the total number of addicts is an astronomical figure. For those who are treated by the most inexpensive method, that is, on an out-patient basis, the annual cost is $2,400. For the untreated and unconnected addict no one really knows the cost. The most modest estimates, however, result in enormous amounts. For example, it could be modestly assumed that any addict would face $500 of expenses in any year, as a result of either medical cost or loss resulting from his or her inability to maintain a job. Thus, over a five year period each of the thousands of addicts in any city would sustain, by this most modest estimate, individual losses of $2,500. The loss caused by drug traffickers becomes even more dramatic when it is recognized that the loss sustained by individual addicts, is only a small component of the total cost, that society, at large, faces as a result of the 200,000 heroin addicts, and even more cocaine users in the City of New York alone. For example, in 1985, the New York City Hospital system handled over 3,000 emergency room drug related episodes. Thirty percent of AIDS victims are intravenous drug users. In addition to these health costs, there is the enormous cost that flows from the relationship between drug addiction and violent crime. A 1983 study by the

1. Part of section 2 of an act entitled "An act to provide for the registration of, with collectors of internal revenue, and to impose a special tax upon all persons who produce, import, manufacture, compound, deal in, dispense, sell, distribute, or give away opium or coca leaves, their salts, derivatives, or preparations, and for other purposes," approved December 17, 1914, 38 Stat. 785, 786:

"Sec. 2. That it shall be unlawful for any person to sell, barter, exchange, or give away any of the aforesaid drugs except in pursuance of a written order of the person to whom such article is sold, bartered, exchanged, or given, on a form to be issued in blank for that purpose by the Commissioner of Internal Revenue. * * *."

Division of Substance Abuse Service of the State of New York found that a daily heroin user committed an average of more than 200 non-drug crimes a year, including 12 robberies and 34 burglaries. * * *

2. *Absolute Liability Offenses.* In Liparota v. United States, the food stamp fraud case which appears supra at p. 139, the Court noted, with respect to absolute liability offenses (sometimes called strict liability offenses or, in appropriate instances, public welfare offenses), at 471 U.S. 419, 432–433, 105 S.Ct. 2084, 2092, 85 L.Ed.2d 434, 444–445 (1985):

> Second, the Government contends that the § 2024(b) offense is a "public welfare" offense, which the Court defined in United States v. Morissette, 342 U.S., at 252–253, 72 S.Ct., at 244–245, to "depend on no mental element but consist only of forbidden acts or omissions." Yet the offense at issue here differs substantially from those "public welfare offenses" we have previously recognized. In most previous instances, Congress has rendered criminal a type of conduct that a reasonable person should know is subject to stringent public regulation and may seriously threaten the community's health or safety. Thus, in United States v. Freed, 401 U.S. 601, 91 S.Ct. 1112, 28 L.Ed.2d 356 (1971), we examined the federal statute making it illegal to receive or possess an unregistered firearm. In holding that the Government did not have to prove that the recipient of unregistered hand grenades knew that they were unregistered, we noted that "one would hardly be surprised to learn that possession of hand grenades is not an innocent act." Id., at 609, 91 S.Ct., at 1118. See also United States v. International Minerals & Chemical Corp., 402 U.S. 558, 564–565, 91 S.Ct. 1697, 1701–1702, 29 L.Ed.2d 178 (1971). Similarly, in United States v. Dotterweich, 320 U.S. 277, 284, 64 S.Ct. 134, 138, 88 L.Ed. 48 (1943), the Court held that a corporate officer could violate the Food and Drug Act when his firm shipped adulterated and misbranded drugs, even "though consciousness of wrongdoing be totally wanting." See also United States v. Balint, 258 U.S. 250, 42 S.Ct. 301, 66 L.Ed. 604 (1922). The distinctions between these cases and the instant case are clear. A food stamp can hardly be compared to a hand grenade, see *Freed,* nor can the unauthorized acquisition or possession of food stamps be compared to the selling of adulterated drugs, as in *Dotterweich.*

The dissent, in footnote 6, 471 U.S. at 442–443, 105 S.Ct. at 2097, 85 L.Ed.2d at 451, responded:

> The Court distinguishes these as "public welfare offense" cases involving inherently dangerous articles of commerce whose users should have assumed were subject to regulation. Apart from the fact that a reasonable person would also assume food stamps are heavily regulated and not subject to sale and exchange, this distinction is not related to the actual holdings in those cases. The Court's opinion in *Boyce* and the concurrence in *Freed* do not discuss this consideration. And the Court's references to the dangerousness of the goods in *International Minerals* were directed to possible due process challenges to convictions without notice of criminality. * * *

State v. Cross

Supreme Court of Ohypo, 1989.
315 Ohypo 711.

The accused appeals from a verdict of guilty of homicide by vehicle, consequent upon the trial court's refusal of a jury instruction to the effect that guilt under § 2886 of the Ohypo Motor Vehicle Code requires that the accused be at least negligent. Section 2886 provides:

> Any person who unintentionally causes the death of another person while engaged in the violation of any law of this State applying to the operation or use of a motor vehicle or to the regulation of traffic is guilty of homicide by vehicle, a misdemeanor, when the violation is the cause of death. This offense is punishable by imprisonment for not more than five years or a fine of not more than $500 or both * * *.

The relevant violation is of § 5342 of the Motor Vehicle Code, which provides in part:

> After having stopped [at a stop sign], the driver shall yield the right-of-way * * * to any vehicle * * * approaching on another roadway [having no stop sign at the intersection] so closely as to constitute a hazard during the time when the driver is moving across or within the intersection.

The facts are not in dispute. On September 12, 1986, Ms. Cross was driving to work during the morning rush hour. It was a clear, dry day. She came to a stop at the stop sign on Oak Road at its intersection with Northern Boulevard, a major thoroughfare, with heavy traffic—traffic which had the right of way. After waiting for about three minutes for an opportunity to cross the boulevard safely, she proceeded into the intersection, where her car was struck by a motorcycle traveling on Northern Boulevard at a high rate of speed; the motorcycle driver was killed. Ms. Cross apparently either failed to look to her right immediately before entering the intersection or misjudged the distance and speed of the motorcycle.

Ms. Cross was in violation of § 5342, which concededly does not require *mens rea.* One issue before the court is whether § 2886 does. While Ms. Cross may have been reckless or negligent, it is agreed that the jury, under the instructions, could have found her guilty, while believing that she was without any *mens rea* at all.

A majority of the court reverses the judgment of conviction, though there is no agreement on reasons for the reversal. We do unanimously agree that, in view of our disagreement, the proper course of action is to retry the defendant according to the standards proposed by the Chief Justice.

WYNKEN, C.J.: Section 2886 mentions no *mens rea* element, except that it expressly allows conviction when the act is done "unintentionally." This excludes a requirement of purpose, but not necessarily a requirement of knowledge, recklessness, or negligence. Does the legislative omission of an express *mens rea* requirement mean that none is required? Did the legislature inadvertently omit the requirement? Did the legislature mean to express something like "recklessly" or "negligently" by the word "unintentionally"?

Strict or absolute liability is very much the exceptional situation in criminal law. Normally, the common law required at least recklessness for criminal liability, although negligence in attitude toward some matters of defense might suffice. Strict liability might be found in a few of the older crimes, such as statutory rape or bigamy, but it did not become common until the modern age of business and social regulation, and then it tended to appear only in regulatory areas: traffic offenses, health and safety codes, and the like. Where the main thrust of the legislation was regulatory and not in the traditional sense criminal—and criminal penalties were merely ancillary, where a great volume of minor infractions was to be anticipated, where penalties were mostly fines, absolute liability tended to appear as a method of more efficiently handling the cases.

Not all legislation in such regulatory areas imposes absolute liability, of course; the legislative intent must be ascertained. Unfortunately, there is little in the legislative history of this section to assist us in finding *any* legislative intention. Section 2886 was enacted as part of a comprehensive revision of the Motor Vehicle Code, designed to comply with the federal Highway Safety Act of 1966, 23 U.S.C. § 401 et seq., the purpose of which was to have the states work toward uniform rules of the road throughout the nation. Similar provisions appear in a number of modern state highway codes. The federal legislation was designed to reduce highway accidents and delays caused by drivers from various jurisdictions and accustomed to different driving rules. Neither it nor the Ohypo revision seems to have been specially aimed at reduction of carnage on the roadways or strengthening involuntary manslaughter laws. The legislature probably gave little attention to the provisions of § 2886 when it passed the legislative package.

Section 205 of our Criminal Code provides that for all offenses, including those in the Motor Vehicle Code, culpability is required, "except insofar as a legislative purpose to impose absolute liability plainly appears." We can not see any such plainly appearing purpose as to § 2886, either from the omission of words of culpability, or the legislative history, or from our sense of what the legislature probably would have found proper. It would make no sense to punish a driver who may have acted reasonably and prudently under the circumstances.

It may be said that § 2886 is redundant if *mens rea* is required, because our criminal code provision for involuntary manslaughter requires recklessness and covers automobile cases, as well as other kinds of homicide. We note that the manslaughter statute imposes a maximum penalty of fifteen years imprisonment, ten years more than the maximum penalty under § 2886. This suggests that something less than the recklessness needed for manslaughter might have been intended by the legislature as the mental element of § 2886, and we believe that the construction which best fits the situation is to require negligence for guilt. Negligence differs from recklessness in not demanding awareness of the risk by the accused; it is enough that the reasonable person in her situation would have been aware of the risk. In either case the risk must be a substantial and unjustifiable one, and the departure from the realm of reasonableness must be great, going beyond ordinary tort negligence. The accused, on the facts shown, may or may not have been negligent. I would therefore reverse the judgment and submit the question of negligence to the jury.

It may be objected that a negligence requirement would still leave § 2886 an absolute liability offense; negligence need not imply blameworthiness, as where the accused does not perceive a risk that the ordinary person would perceive because the accused is stupid. While this is a possibility, more commonly negligence does involve fault. It usually means that one has been inattentive and failed to show the concern for possible harm to others that society demands, and this is something for which the criminal law may fairly impose penalties.

BLYNKEN, J. I cannot agree that it is proper to read a *mens rea* requirement—and I will assume that a negligence specification really is a *mens rea* requirement—into § 2886. I find no indication in the legislative history that either the proponents of the Highway Safety Act or our own legislators meant to impose such a requirement. On this point I agree with my Brother Nod's conclusion in the opinion which follows.

I believe that this conviction must be reversed because the omission of a *mens rea* requirement in § 2886 renders the section unconstitutional for violation of the due process of law requirement of the Ohypo and perhaps also the federal constitution. As to the federal rule, JUDGE SPAETH, in a concurring opinion in Commonwealth v. Barone, 276 Pa.Super. 282, 302–309, 419 A.2d 457, 468–472 (1980), a case remarkably similar to this one, summarized the situation well [the footnotes are JUDGE SPAETH'S]:

> "The existence of mens rea is the rule of, rather than the exception to, the principles of Anglo-American criminal jurisprudence." Dennis v. United States, 341 U.S. 494, 500, 71 S.Ct. 857, 862, 95 L.Ed. 1137 (1950). "The contention that an injury can amount to a crime only when inflicted by intention is no provincial or transient notion. It is as universal and persistent in mature systems of law as belief in freedom of the human will and a consequent ability and duty of the normal individual to choose between good and evil." [5] Morissette v. United States, 342 U.S. 246, 250, 72 S.Ct. 240, 243, 96 L.Ed. 288 (1951); see Lambert v. California, 355 U.S. 225, 78 S.Ct. 240, 2 L.Ed.2d 228 (1957). The concept of strict criminal liability is apparently of relatively recent origin in our system of law,[6] and has been the subject of Supreme Court scrutiny on only a very few occasions.[7] In only one case, *Morissette,*

5. In his chapter on the criminal law in The Common Law, Justice Holmes remarked that "[e]ven a dog distinguishes between being stumbled over and being kicked." Id. at p. 3.

6. See Sayre, Public Welfare Offenses, 33 Col.L.Rev. 55, 58–63 (1933). And see Morissette v. United States, supra, 342 U.S. at 250–57, 72 S.Ct. at 243–246.

7. The Court has consistently held that the legislature has the power to create strict liability crimes. As Mr. Justice Douglas stated in *Lambert:* "We do not go with Blackstone in saying that a 'vicious will' is necessary to constitute a crime, * * * for conduct alone without regard to the intent of the doer is often sufficient. There is wide latitude in lawmakers to declare an offense and exclude elements of knowledge and diligence from its definition." 355 U.S. at 228, 78 S.Ct. at 242. While wide, however, the legislature's latitude is not unbounded, and legislation creating a strict liability crime must comport with constitutional guarantees. See Smith v. California, 361 U.S. 147, 150, 80 S.Ct. 215, 217, 4 L.Ed.2d 205 (1959) (holding unconstitutional an ordinance making it a crime to possess an obscene book without regard to defendant's knowledge of book's contents). Lambert v. California, supra (holding unconstitutional an ordinance making it a crime not to register, even though no probability of defendant knowing of duty to register).

The first case where the issue of the constitutionality of a strict liability crime was addressed by the Court was Shevlin-Carpenter Co. v. Minnesota, 218 U.S. 57, 30 S.Ct. 663, 54 L.Ed. 930 (1910). There the Court in dictum said that due process was not violated by a state statute that imposed imprisonment for the violation of a strict liability crime. In United States v. Balint, 258 U.S. 250, 42 S.Ct. 301, 66 L.Ed. 604 (1922), and United States v. Behrman, 258 U.S. 280, 42 S.Ct. 303, 66 L.Ed. 619 (1922), the Court relied on the dictum in *Shevlin-Carpenter* in concluding that federal narcotics violations punishable by pris-

has the Court undertaken a full discussion of the problems presented by a statute creating, or arguably creating, a strict liability crime.

In *Morissette* the question before the Court was whether the statute creating the crime of converting government property should be construed to require proof of the defendant's intent to steal. Mr. Justice Jackson, speaking for the majority, discussed the origins of strict liability crimes and compared strict liability crimes to common law crimes. In the course of this discussion, he explained the Court's earlier decisions in *Balint* and *Behrman:*

> However, the *Balint* and *Behrman* offenses belong to a category of another character, with very different antecedents and origins. The crimes there involved depend on no mental element but consist only of forbidden acts or omissions. This while not expressed by the Court, is made clear from examination of a century-old but accelerating tendency, discernible both here and in England, to call into existence new duties and crimes which disregard any ingredient of intent. The industrial revolution multiplied the number of workmen exposed to injury from increasingly powerful and complex mechanisms, driven by freshly discovered sources of energy, requiring higher precautions by employers. Traffic of velocities, volumes and varieties unheard of came to subject the wayfarer to intolerable casualty risks if owners and drivers were not to observe new cares and uniformities of conduct. Congestion of cities and crowding of quarters called for health and welfare regulations undreamed of in simpler times. Wide distribution of goods became an instrument of

on terms could be sustained without proof of intent. In so holding in *Balint,* the Court stated that the offense before it was an example of a "regulatory measure[ ] in the exercise of what is called the police power where the emphasis of the statute is evidently upon achievement of some social betterment rather than the punishment of crimes." 258 U.S. at 252, 42 S.Ct. at 302. The Court concluded that in drafting the statute, "Congress weighed the possible injustice of subjecting an innocent seller to a penalty * * * or exposing innocent purchasers to danger from the drug, and concluded that the latter was the result preferably to be avoided." Id. at 254, 42 S.Ct. at 303. In United States v. Dotterweich, 320 U.S. 277 (1943), 64 S.Ct. 134, 88 L.Ed. 48, the Court, without extended discussion, relied on *Balint* and *Behrman* in concluding that a conviction for violation of a federal law concerning the misbranding of drugs could be sustained without proof of intent. The Court described the crime as an example of "a now familiar type of legislation whereby penalties serve as effective means of regulation. Such legislation dispenses with the conventional requirement for criminal conduct-awareness of some wrongdoing. In the interest of the larger good it puts the burden of acting at hazard upon a person otherwise innocent but standing in a responsible relation to a public danger." 320 U.S. at 280–81, 64 S.Ct. at 136. In United States v. Freed, 401 U.S. 601, 91 S.Ct. 1112, 28 L.Ed.2d 356 (1971), the Court concluded that no scienter need be proved to obtain a conviction for a violation of the National Firearms Act. The Court stated that the case was close to *Dotterweich* because it involved "a regulatory measure in the interest of public safety, which may well be premised on the theory that one would hardly be surprised to learn that possession of hand grenades is not an innocent act. They are highly dangerous offensive weapons, no less dangerous than the narcotics involved in [*Balint*]." 401 U.S. at 609, 91 S.Ct. at 1118 (footnote omitted). See also United States v. Park, 421 U.S. 658, 672, 95 S.Ct. 1903, 1911, 44 L.Ed. 2d 489 (1975) (conviction under pure food statute; "[t]he requirements of foresight and vigilance imposed on responsible corporate agents are * * * demanding * * *, but they are no more stringent than the public has a right to expect of those who voluntarily assume positions of authority in business enterprises whose services and products affect the health and well-being of the public that supports them.").

> wide distribution of harm when those who dispersed food, drink, drugs, and even securities, did not comply with reasonable standards of quality, integrity, disclosure and care. Such dangers have engendered increasingly numerous and detailed regulations which heighten the duties of those in control of particular industries, trades, properties or activities that affect public health, safety or welfare.

342 U.S. at 252–54, 72 S.Ct. at 245 (footnotes omitted).

He further explained:

> While many of these duties are sanctioned by a more strict civil liability, lawmakers, whether wisely or not, have sought to make such regulations more effective by invoking criminal sanctions to be applied by the familiar technique of criminal prosecutions and convictions. This has confronted the courts with a multitude of prosecutions, based on statutes or administrative regulations, for what have been aptly called "public welfare offenses." These cases do not fit neatly into any of such accepted classifications of common-law offenses, such as those against the state, the person, property, or public morals. Many of these offenses are not in the nature of positive aggressions or invasions, with which the common law so often dealt, but are in the nature of neglect where the law requires care, or in action where it imposes a duty. Many violations of such regulations result in no direct or immediate injury to person or property but merely create the danger or probability of it which the law seeks to minimize. While such offenses do not threaten the security of the state in the manner of treason, they may be regarded as offenses against its authority, for their occurrence impairs the efficiency of controls deemed essential to the social order as presently constituted. In this respect, whatever the intent of the violator, the injury is the same, and the consequences are injurious or not according to fortuity. Hence, legislation applicable to such offenses, as a matter of policy, does not specify intent as a necessary element. The accused, if he does not will the violation, usually is in a position to prevent it with no more care than society might reasonably expect and no more exertion than it might reasonably exact from one who assumed his responsibilities. Also, penalties commonly are relatively small, and conviction does no grave damage to an offender's reputation. Under such considerations, courts have turned to construing statutes and regulations which make no mention of intent as dispensing with it and holding that the guilty act alone makes out the crime. This has not, however, been without expressions of misgiving.
>
> 342 U.S. at 255–57, 72 S.Ct. at 245 (footnotes omitted).

After discussing the common law origins of the crime of theft, and concluding that the crime of converting government property had the crime of theft as a direct antecedent, Justice Jackson concluded that in creating the crime of converting government property, Congress intended to require proof of an intent to steal.

Two important principles may be derived from *Morissette;* it is these principles that render distinctive the analysis to be employed when examining a statute creating, or arguably creating, strict criminal liability. The first principle is that in determining whether the imposition of strict criminal liability is consistent with due process, several factors, including the policy and intent of the legislature, the origins of the offense, the reasonableness of the standards imposed, and the punishment and stigma attached to a conviction, must be considered. The second principle is that in considering these several factors, a court must shuttle back and forth, between the question whether the statute *can* be construed as not requiring proof of criminal intent, and the question whether, *if* so construed, the statute will violate due process; the answer to one of these questions will color, or affect, the answer to the other. Thus in *Morissette* the Court was persuaded to construe the statute as not creating strict criminal liability but instead as requiring proof of intent.

In Holdridge v. United States, 282 F.2d 302 (8th Cir.1960), Judge, now Mr. Justice, Blackmun, after discussing the cases, summarized this process of analysis as follows:

> From these cases emerges the proposition that where a federal criminal statute omits mention of intent and where it seems to involve what is basically a matter of policy, where the standard imposed is, under the circumstances, reasonable and adherence thereto properly expected of a person, where the penalty is relatively small, where conviction does not gravely besmirch, where the statutory crime is not one taken over from the common law, and where congressional purpose is supporting, the statute can be construed as one not requiring criminal intent. The elimination of this element is then not violative of the due process clause.
>
> Id. at 310.

Or, to state Justice Blackmun's formulation conversely: If the factors discussed in *Morissette* are otherwise—e.g., if the penalty is *not* relatively small, and the conviction *does* gravely besmirch—then the elimination of the element of criminal intent *may* be violative of the due process clause.

Justice Blackmun's formulation has been quoted with approval by one other Justice of the Supreme Court, see United States v. Freed, supra, 401 U.S. at 613 n. 4, 91 S.Ct. at 1120 (Brennan, J., concurring), and has been repeatedly applied by the federal courts. * * *

Sometimes it has been held that a requirement of intent may not be read into the statute, but that even when so construed, the relevant factors are such that the statute does not violate due process. Thus, in United States v. Avo-Gonzalez, supra, the Fifth Circuit applies the *Morissette-Holdridge* analysis to determine whether the Bartlett Act prohibited unintentional fishing incursions by foreign vessels in United States waters. After an extensive examination of the policy of the Act and its legislative history, the court concluded that no proof of intent was required to sustain a conviction. The court also concluded that this creation of strict criminal liability did not violate due process because the conviction did not invite moral stigma and the maximum sentence of one year imprisonment was not too severe. * * *

Other times it has been held that a requirement of intent may be read into the statute, if the result will be that then the statute will not violate due process. Thus, in United States v. Heller, supra, the Sixth Circuit concluded that to sustain a conviction under a federal statute making it a crime to transmit any demand or request for a ransom the prosecutor was required to prove that the defendant had an intent to extort. The court reached this conclusion after making the analysis prescribed in *Morissette* and *Holdridge.* Especially pertinent to the decision were the legislative history of the statute and the severity of the punishment.

Finally, other times it has been held that a requirement of intent may not be read into a statute, even though the result is that the statute will then violate due process. See Lambert v. California, supra. There the Court was precluded from reading in a requirement of intent because the California court had construed the legislation in question—a Los Angeles ordinance—as not including such a requirement. After considering the relevant factors (more fully discussed in *Morissette*), the Court held that the ordinance violated due process.

Ohypo has taken a stricter view of our own due process requirement. In State v. Stein, 254 Ohypo 844 (1970), the owner of a bar had been convicted of selling liquor to a person under the age of eighteen years, in violation of a statute which specified no *mens rea* requirement. The sale was made in the defendant's absence by his bartender, who failed to observe the precautions as to ascertaining the ages of patrons the defendant claimed to have ordered him to follow. The defendant was convicted, fined, and sentenced to three months imprisonment by the trial court. We reversed as to the sentence of imprisonment, holding that it violated the Ohypo due process provision, which would not permit a sentence of imprisonment in an absolute liability offense.

Most commentators agree that imprisonment is never appropriate in an absolute liability case. See Model Penal Code § 2.05, Comment 1; Wechsler, The Challenge of a Model Penal Code, 65 Harv.L.Rev. 1097, 1109 (1952); Sayre, Public Welfare Offenses, 33 Col.L.Rev. 55, 69–70 (1933). Crime, especially where it involves imprisonment, entails moral condemnation of the offender; there should be no penal sanction unless we can declare that the accused did wrong. Otherwise, the concept of crime is cheapened, and crime may be taken less seriously by the public, on the one hand, while on the other, some people may be wrongly stigmatized as criminals.

Federal law does not necessarily bar imprisonment for an absolute liability offense; it also weighs whether conviction would gravely besmirch the accused's reputation. Even if this standard is applied, the conviction appears unconstitutional. The offense punishes a kind of criminal homicide, and any homicide conviction is likely to be viewed by the community as a seriously detrimental factor in the convicted person's reputation.

Since I am unable to find a construction of § 2886 which would bring it into accord with due process requirements, I conclude that the judgment of conviction should be reversed and the charge against the defendant dismissed.

NOD, J. I would affirm the conviction. I believe that the legislature wished to make § 2886 an absolute liability offense and that it was constitutionally entitled to do so.

When the legislature enacted the section, it was aware that a number of states following the federal highway plan had added specific requirements of recklessness or negligence to the counterparts of § 2886 in their legislation. Our legislature chose not to do so. This may have been unwise, but it is not our function to substitute our own judgment for that of our legislature, so long as it acts constitutionally. The words of the section are quite clear, and they do not contain any *mens rea* requirement. Highway safety and the carnage on the highways are difficult and important matters for legislative policy. There are many cases of motorists who fail to abide by the enacted rules of the road, and in an overwhelming number of these cases, the motorist is negligent, at least. Negligence, however, is often difficult to prove, and the legislature determined to make criminal responsibility dependent on violation of the traffic law rather than on negligence.

This standard is not an unreasonable one for the legislature to adopt, given the seriousness of the problem facing it. Such a reasonable response to a problem is not a violation of due process. Federal law does not bar imprisonment for absolute liability offenses, and some federal cases have approved maximum penalties comparable to the one under consideration here. See United States v. Park, 421 U.S. 658, 95 S.Ct. 1903, 44 L.Ed.2d 489 (1975) (misbranded or adulterated drugs—$1,000 and/or one year for first offense, $10,000 and/or three years for subsequent offenses); United States v. Freed, 401 U.S. 601, 91 S.Ct. 1112, 28 L.Ed.2d 356 (1971) (possession of unregistered firearms—$10,000 and/or ten years); Williams v. North Carolina, 325 U.S. 226, 65 S.Ct. 1092, 89 L.Ed. 1577 (1945) (bigamy—ten years); United States v. Balint, 258 U.S. 250, 42 S.Ct. 301, 66 L.Ed. 604 (1922) (unlawful drug sale—five years); United States v. Ayo–Gonzalez, 536 F.2d 652 (5th Cir.1976) (fishing limit violation—$100,000 or one year). It is not a bar to absolute liability that an offense (here a migratory bird violation) is a felony. United States v. Engler, 806 F.2d 425 (3rd Cir.1986); contra, United States v. Wulff, 758 F.2d 1121 (6th Cir.1985). What we said earlier in a liquor sale case should not be translated uncritically to the far more serious social problem that § 2886 was designed to address.

Questions

1. Under what circumstances, if at all, should a legislature create absolute liability offenses?

2. *An acceptable alternative?* Is there an acceptable alternative—fair to prosecution and defense—to the absolute liability offense? In Sweet v. Parsley, [1970] A.C. 132, (H.L.1969) the House of Lords allowed the appeal of landlord Stephanie Sweet, who had been convicted under section 5 of the Dangerous Drugs Act of 1965, when,

without her knowledge, the tenants of her farmhouse had smoked cannabis on the premises. LORD REID, on the question of legislative choice whether to make an offense one of *mens rea* or of absolute liability, remarked (at pp. 150–152):

> The choice would be much more difficult if there were no other way open than either mens rea in the full sense or an absolute offence; for there are many kinds of case where putting on the prosecutor the full burden of proving *mens rea* creates great difficulties and may lead to many unjust acquittals. But there are at least two other possibilities. Parliament has not infrequently transferred the onus as regards mens rea to the accused, so that, once the necessary facts are proved, he must convince the jury that on balance of probabilities he is innocent of any criminal intention. I find it a little surprising that more use has not been made of this method: but one of the bad effects of the decision of this House in Woolmington v. Director of Public Prosecutions [1935] A.C. 462 may have been to discourage its use. The other method would be in effect to substitute in appropriate classes of cases gross negligence for *mens rea* in the full sense as the mental element necessary to constitute the crime. It would often be much easier to infer that Parliament must have meant that gross negligence should be the necessary mental element than to infer that Parliament intended to create an absolute offence. A variant of this would be to accept the view of Cave J. in Reg. v. Tolson (1889) 23 Q.B.D. 168, 181. This appears to have been done in Australia where authority appears to support what Dixon J. said in Proudman v. Dayman (1941) 67 C.L.R. 536, 540:
>
> > "As a general rule an honest and reasonable belief in a state of facts which, if they existed, would make the defendant's act innocent affords an excuse for doing what would otherwise be an offence."
>
> It may be that none of these methods is wholly satisfactory but at least the public scandal of convicting on a serious charge persons who are in no way blameworthy would be avoided.
>
> If this section means what the Divisional Court have held that it means, then hundreds of thousands of people who sublet part of their premises or take in lodgers or are concerned in the management of residential premises or institutions are daily incurring a risk of being convicted of a serious offence in circumstances where they are in no way to blame. For the greatest vigilance cannot prevent tenants, lodgers or inmates or guests whom they bring in from smoking cannabis cigarettes in their own rooms. It was suggested in argument that this appellant brought this conviction on herself because it is found as a fact that when the police searched the premises there were people there of the "beatnik fraternity." But surely it would be going a very long way to say that persons managing premises of any kind ought to safeguard themselves by refusing accommodation to all who are of slovenly or exotic appearance, or who bring in guests of that kind. And unfortunately drug taking is by no means confined to those of unusual appearance.
>
> Speaking from a rather long experience of membership of both Houses, I assert with confidence that no Parliament within my recollection would have agreed to make an offence of this kind an absolute offence if the matter had been fully explained to it. So, if the court ought only to hold an offence to be an absolute offence where it appears that that must have been the intention of Parliament, offences of this kind are very far removed from those which it is proper to hold to be absolute offences.
>
> I must now turn to the question what is the true meaning of section 5 of the 1965 Act. It provides:

"If a person—(a) being the occupier of any premises, permits those premises to be used for the purpose of smoking cannabis or cannabis resin or of dealing in cannabis or cannabis resin (whether by sale or otherwise); or (b) is concerned in the management of any premises used for any such purpose as aforesaid; he shall be guilty of an offence against this Act."

We are particularly concerned with paragraph (b), and the first question is what is meant by "used for any such purpose." Is the "purpose" the purpose of the smoker or the purpose of the management? * * * It would require strong reasons—and there are none—to justify giving this provision a new meaning in section 5 different from that which it had in the 1920 Act and now has in section 8 of the 1965 Act. I think that in section 8 it is clear that the purpose is the purpose of the management. The first purpose mentioned is the purpose of the preparation of opium for smoking which can only be a purpose of the management. I believe that opium cannot be smoked casually anywhere at any time as can a cannabis cigarette. The section is dealing with "opium dens" and the like when the use of opium is the main purpose for which the premises are used. But it is a somewhat strained use of language to say that an ordinary room in a house is "used for the purpose" of smoking cannabis when all that happens is that some visitor lights a cannabis cigarette there. * * * So if the purpose is the purpose of the management, the question whether the offence with regard to opium in 1920, and now with regard to cannabis, is absolute can hardly arise. It could only arise if, although the manager not only knew about cannabis smoking and conducted the premises for that purpose, some person concerned in the management had no knowledge of that. One would first have to decide whether a person who is not actually assisting in the management can be regarded as being "concerned in the management," although ignorant of the purpose for which the manager was using the premises. Even if such a person could be regarded as "concerned in the management," I am of opinion that, for the reasons which I have given, he could not be convicted without proof of mens rea.

LORD PEARCE said (at p. 157):

Parliament might, of course, have taken what was conceded in argument to be a fair and sensible course. It could have said, in appropriate words, that a person is to be liable unless he proves that he had no knowledge or guilty mind. Admittedly, if the prosecution have to prove a defendant's knowledge beyond reasonable doubt, it may be easy for the guilty to escape. But it would be very much harder for the guilty to escape if the burden of disproving *mens rea* or knowledge is thrown on the defendant. And if that were done, innocent people could satisfy a jury of their innocence on a balance of probabilities. It has been said that a jury might be confused by the different nature of the onus of satisfying "beyond reasonable doubt" which the prosecution have to discharge and the onus "on a balance of probabilities" which lies on a defendant in proving that he had no knowledge or guilt. I do not believe that this would be so in this kind of case. Most people can easily understand rules that express in greater detail that which their own hearts and minds already feel to be fair and sensible. What they find hard to understand is rules that go "against the grain" of their own common sense. If a judge on a drug case * * * had simply said that they must consider the facts and do their best with the charge, I believe that they would evolve their duty in some such form as this; "First, I suppose, we must make sure that there really *was* drug smoking on the premises" (or, "that he really *had* drugs on him" or whatever the charge may be) "and then it is up to the defendant to persuade us that he did not know, or was not guilty for some other good reason." If I am right in this surmise, any judicial elaboration of their own instinctive reactions would be quite easy for them to understand.

If it were possible in some so-called absolute offences to take this sensible half-way house, I think that the courts should do so.

Note

In State v. Buttrey, 293 Or. 575, 651 P.2d 1075 (1982), the court upheld against constitutional attack [cf. Martin v. Ohio, infra. p. 424] a statute making driving with a suspended license an absolute liability offense, but providing that the accused had a defense if he established by a preponderance of the evidence that he had not, under certain circumstances, received notice of his suspension.

People v. Shaughnessy

District Court, Nassau County, Third District, 1971.
66 Misc.2d 19, 319 N.Y.S.2d 626.

JOHN S. LOCKMAN, JUDGE.

On October 9th, 1970, shortly before 10:05 p.m., the Defendant in the company of her boy friend and two other youngsters proceeded by automobile to the vicinity of the St. Ignatius Retreat Home, Searingtown Road, Incorporated Village of North Hills, Nassau County, New York. The Defendant was a passenger and understood that she was headed for the Christopher Morley Park which is located across the street from the St. Ignatius Retreat Home and has a large illuminated sign, with letters approximately 8 inches high, which identifies the park. As indicated, on the other side of the street the St. Ignatius Retreat Home has two pillars at its entrance with a bronze sign on each pillar with 4 to 5 inch letters. The sign is not illuminated. The vehicle in which the Defendant was riding proceeded into the grounds of the Retreat House and was stopped by a watchman and the occupants including the Defendant waited approximately 20 minutes for a Policeman to arrive. The Defendant never left the automobile.

The Defendant is charged with violating Section 1 of the Ordinance prohibiting entry upon private property of the Incorporated Village of North Hills, which provides: "No person shall enter upon any privately owned piece, parcel or lot of real property in the Village of North Hills without the permission of the owner, lessee or occupant thereof. * * *"

* * *

The problem presented by the facts in this case brings up for review the primary elements that are required for criminal accountability and responsibility. It is only from an accused's voluntary overt acts that criminal responsibility can attach. An overt act or a specific omission to act must occur in order for the establishment of a criminal offense.

The physical element required has been designated as the *Actus Reus.* The mental element is of course better known as the *Mens Rea.* While the mental element may under certain circumstances not be required as in crimes that are designated as *Malum Prohibitum,* the *Actus Reus* is always necessary. It certainly can not be held to be the intent of the legislature to punish involuntary acts.

The principle which requires a voluntary act or omission to act had been codified in the Revised Penal Law, Section 15.10 * * *.

* * *

In the case at bar, the People have failed to establish any act on the part of the Defendant. She merely was a passenger in a vehicle. Any action taken by the vehicle was caused and guided by the driver thereof and not by the Defendant. If the Defendant were to be held guilty under these circumstances, it would dictate that she would be guilty if she had been unconscious or asleep at the time or even if she had been a prisoner in the automobile. There are many situations which can be envisioned and in which the trespass statute in question would be improperly applied to an involuntary act. One might conceive of a driver losing control of a vehicle through mechanical failure and the vehicle proceeding onto private property which is the subject of a trespass.

Although the Court need not pass on the question, it might very well be proper to hold the driver responsible for his act even though he was under the mistaken belief that he was on his way to Christopher Morley Park. The legislature has provided statutes which make mistakes of fact or lack of knowledge no excuse in a criminal action. However, if the driver had been a Defendant, the People could have established an act on the part of the Defendant driver, to wit, turning his vehicle into the private property.

In the case of the Defendant now before the Court, however, the very first and essential element in criminal responsibility is missing, an overt voluntary act or omission to act and, accordingly, the Defendant is found not guilty.

Question

On the *Shaughnessy* court's reasoning, should the driver of the car be convicted of violation of the statute if he had reasonably believed that he was entering a public park? If an unforeseeable brake failure had prevented him from stopping the car before it entered the grounds of the Home?

D. MISTAKE

1. Introduction; Abduction and Bigamy

Regina v. Prince

Court for Crown Cases Reserved, 1875.
L.R. 2 Cr.Cas.Res. 154.

The following judgment [a] (in which COCKBURN, C.J., MELLOR, LUSH, QUAIN, DENMAN, ARCHIBALD, FIELD, and LINDLEY, JJ., and POLLOCK, B., concurred) was delivered by

BLACKBURN, J. In this case we must take it as found by the jury that the prisoner took an unmarried girl out of the possession and against the will of her father, and that the girl was in fact under the age of sixteen, but that the

a. The order of the opinions has been changed.

prisoner bona fide, and on reasonable grounds, believed that she was above sixteen, viz., eighteen years old. * * *

The question, therefore, is reduced to this, whether the words in 24 & 25 Vict. c. 100, s. 55, that whosoever shall take "any unmarried girl, being under the age of sixteen, out of the possession of her father," are to be read as if they were "being under the age of sixteen, and he knowing she was under that age." No such words are contained in the statute, nor is there the word "maliciously," "knowingly," or any other word used that can be said to involve a similar meaning.

The argument in favour of the prisoner must therefore entirely proceed on the ground that, in general, a guilty mind is an essential ingredient in a crime, and that where a statute creates a crime, the intention of the legislature should be presumed to be to include "knowingly" in the definition of the crime, and the statute should be read as if that word were inserted, unless the contrary intention appears. We need not inquire at present whether the canon of construction goes quite so far as above stated, for we are of opinion that the intention of the legislature sufficiently appears to have been to punish the abduction, unless the girl, in fact, was of such an age as to make her consent an excuse, irrespective of whether he knew her to be too young to give an effectual consent, and to fix that age at sixteen. The section in question is one of a series of enactments, beginning with s. 48, and ending with s. 55, forming a code for the protection of women, and the guardians of young women. These enactments are taken with scarcely any alteration from the repealed statute, 9 Geo. 4, c. 31, which had collected them into a code from a variety of old statutes all repealed by it.

* * *

The preamble states, as the mischief aimed at, that female children, heiresses, and others having expectations, were, unawares of their friends, brought to contract marriages of disparagement, "to the great heaviness of their friends;" and then, to remedy this, enacts, by the 1st section, that it shall not be lawful for any one to take an unmarried girl, being under sixteen, out of the custody of the father, or the person to whom he, either by will or by act in his lifetime, gives the custody, unless it be bona fide done by or for the master or mistress of such child, or the guardian in chivalry, or in socage of such child. This recognizes a legal right to the possession of the child, depending on the real age of the child, and not on what appears. And the object of the legislature, being, as it appears by the preamble it was, to protect this legal right to the possession, would be baffled, if it was an excuse that the person guilty of the taking thought the child above sixteen. The words "unlawfully take," as used in the 3rd section of 4 & 5 Phil. & Mary, c. 8, means without the authority of the master or mistress, or guardian, mentioned in the immediately preceding section.

* * *

We think those rulings were right, and consequently that the conviction in the present case should stand.

The following judgment (in which KELLY, C.B., CLEASBY, POLLOCK, and AMPHLETT, BB., and GROVE, QUAIN, and DENMAN, JJ., concurred) was delivered by

BRAMWELL, B. * * * Now the word "unlawfully" means "not lawfully," "otherwise than lawfully," "without lawful cause," such as would exist, for instance, on a taking by a police officer on a charge of felony, or a taking by a father of his child from his school. The statute, therefore, may be read thus: "Whosoever shall take, &c., without lawful cause." Now the prisoner had no such cause, and consequently, except in so far as it helps the construction of the statute, the word "unlawfully" may in the present case be left out, and then the question is, has the prisoner taken an unmarried girl under the age of sixteen out of the possession of and against the will of her father? In fact, he has; but it is said not within the meaning of the statute, and that that must be read as though the word "knowingly," or some equivalent word, was in; and the reason given is, that as a rule the mens rea is necessary to make any act a crime or offence, and that if the facts necessary to constitute an offence are not known to the alleged offender, there can be no mens rea. * * *

* * * This introduces the necessity for reading the statute with some strange words introduced; as thus: "Whosoever shall take any unmarried girl, being under the age of sixteen, and not believing her to be over the age of sixteen, out of the possession," &c. Those words are not there, and the question is, whether we are bound to construe the statute as though they were, on account of the rule that the mens rea is necessary to make an act a crime. I am of opinion that we are not, nor as though the word "knowingly" was there, and for the following reasons: The act forbidden is wrong in itself, if without lawful cause; I do not say illegal, but wrong. * * *

Let us remember what is the case supposed by the statute. It supposes that there is a girl—it does not say a woman, but a girl—something between a child and a woman; it supposes she is in the *possession* of her father or mother, or other person having lawful *care or charge* of her; and it supposes there is a *taking,* and that that taking is *against the will* of the person in whose possession she is. It is, then, a *taking of a girl,* in the *possession* of some one, *against his will.* I say that done without lawful cause is wrong, and that the legislature meant it should be at the risk of the taker whether or no she was under sixteen. I do not say that taking a woman of fifty from her brother's or even father's house is wrong. She is at an age when she has a right to choose for herself; she is not a *girl,* nor of such tender age that she can be said to be in the *possession* or under the *care or charge* of anyone. I am asked where I draw the line; I answer at when the female is no longer a girl in anyone's possession.

But what the statute contemplates, and what I say is wrong, is the taking of a female of such tender years that she is properly called a *girl,* can be said to be in another's *possession,* and in that other's *care or charge.* No argument is necessary to prove this; it is enough to state the case. The legislature has enacted that if anyone does this wrong act, he does it at the risk of her turning out to be under sixteen. This opinion gives full scope to the doctrine of the mens rea. If the taker believed he had the father's consent, though wrongly, he would have no mens rea; so if he did not know she was in anyone's possession, nor in the care or charge of anyone. In those cases he would not know he was doing the act forbidden by the statute—an act which, if he knew she was in possession and in care or charge of anyone, he would know was a crime or not, according as she was under sixteen or not. He would not know he was doing an act wrong in itself, whatever was his intention, if done without lawful cause.

* * *

* * * I think the conviction should be affirmed.

BRETT, J.

* * *

It has been said that even if the facts had been as the prisoner believed them to be he would still have been doing a wrongful act. The first point, therefore, to be considered would seem to be, what would have been the legal position of the prisoner, if the facts had been as he believed them to be, that is to say, what is the legal position of a man who without force takes a girl of more than sixteen years of age, but less than twenty-one years of age, out of the possession of her father and against his will. * * * It follows from this review that if the facts had been as the prisoner, according to the findings of the jury, believed them to be, and had reasonable ground for believing them to be, he would have done no act which has ever been a criminal offence in England; he would have done no act in respect of which any civil action could have ever been maintained against him; he would have done no act for which, if done in the absence of the father, and done with the continuing consent of the girl, the father could have had any legal remedy.

* * *

From these considerations of the forms of criminal enactments, it would seem that the ultimate proof necessary to authorize a conviction is not altered by the presence or absence of the word "knowingly" * * * and it would seem that there must be proof to satisfy a jury ultimately that there was a criminal mind, or mens rea, in every offence really charged as a crime, and therefore in the indictments charging the committal of those crimes, the name of the crime imports that a mens rea must be proved, as in murder, burglary, &c. In some the mens rea is contained in the specific enactments as to the intent which is made a part of the crime. In some the word "feloniously" is used, and in such cases it has never been doubted but that a felonious mind must ultimately be found by the jury. In enactments in a similar form, but in which the prohibited acts are to be classed as a misdemeanor, the word "unlawfully" is used instead of the word "feloniously." What reason is there why, in like manner, a criminal mind, or mens rea, must not ultimately be found by the jury in order to justify a conviction, the distinction always being observed, that in some cases the proof of the committal of the acts may prima facie, either by reason of their own nature, or by reason of the form of the statute, import the proof of the mens rea? But even in those cases it is open to the prisoner to rebut the prima facie evidence, so that if, in the end, the jury are satisfied that there was no criminal mind, or mens rea, there cannot be a conviction in England for that which is by the law considered to be a crime.

* * *

* * * It seems to me to follow that the maxim as to mens rea applies whenever the facts which are present to the prisoner's mind, and which he has reasonable ground to believe, and does believe to be the facts, would, if true, make his acts no criminal offence at all.

It may be true to say that the meaning of the word "unlawfully" is, that the prohibited acts be done without justification or excuse; I, of course, agree that if there be a legal justification there can be no crime; but I come to the conclusion that a mistake of facts, on reasonable grounds, to the extent that if the facts were as believed the acts of the prisoner would make him guilty of no criminal offence at all, is an excuse, and that such excuse is implied in every criminal charge and every criminal enactment in England. I agree with Lord Kenyon that "such is our law," and with Cockburn, C.J., that "such is the foundation of all criminal procedure."

Question

Is abduction an absolute liability offense?

Note on Bigamy

The crime of bigamy involves a *mens rea* dispute. A leading case, representing the prevailing conclusion, is Commonwealth v. Mash, 48 Mass. (7 Metc.) 472 (1872), in which Mehitabel Mash's husband departed early one morning, saying that he would return for breakfast, and disappeared. After fruitless inquiries, Mrs. Mash concluded that he must be dead, and she remarried three years and five months later, only to have Mash show up a month afterward. The statute, with no mention of *mens rea,* imposed a penalty on one who, having a living spouse, married another, but created an exception (known as an *Enoch Arden* provision, from a situation depicted in a poem) when the missing spouse had voluntarily withdrawn and remained absent for seven years, the remaining spouse not knowing the other to be living within that time. The court affirmed the conviction. It reasoned, at 473–474:

> It appears to us, that in a matter of this importance, so essential to the peace of families and the good order of society, it was not the intention of the law to make the legality of a second marriage, whilst the former husband or wife is in fact living, depend upon ignorance of such absent party's being alive, or even upon an honest belief of such person's death. Such belief might arise after a very short absence. But it appears to us, that the legislature intended to prescribe a more exact rule, and to declare, as law, that no one should have a right, upon such ignorance that the other party is alive, or even upon such honest belief of his death, to take the risk of marrying again, unless such belief is confirmed by an absence of seven years, with ignorance of the absent party's being alive within that time. It is analogous to other provisions and rules of law, by which a continued absence of a person for seven years, without being heard of, will constitute a presumption of his death. Loring v. Steineman, 1 Met. 204. Greenl. on Ev. § 41.

* * *

It was urged in the argument, that where there is no criminal intent, there can be no guilt; and if the former husband was honestly believed to be dead, there could be no criminal intent. The proposition stated is undoubtedly correct in a general sense; but the conclusion drawn from it, in this case, by no means follows. Whatever one voluntarily does, he of course intends to do. If the statute has made it criminal to do any act under particular circumstances, the party voluntarily doing that act is chargeable with the criminal intent of doing it. On this subject, the law has deemed it so important to prohibit the crime of polygamy, and found it so difficult to prescribe what shall be sufficient evidence of the death of an absent person to warrant a belief of the fact, and as the same vague evidence might create a belief in one mind and not in another, the law has also deemed it wise to fix a definite period of seven years' continued absence, without knowledge of the contrary, to warrant a belief that the absent person is actually dead. One therefore who marries within that time, if the other party be actually living, whether the fact is believed or not, is chargeable with that criminal intent, by purposely doing that which the law expressly prohibits.

(Mrs. Mash was subsequently pardoned.) A contrary view is represented by The Queen v. Tolson, 23 Q.B.D. 168 (Cr.Cas.Res., 1889), under a statute similar to that of Massachusetts. Mrs. Tolson, believing a report that her husband had perished when a ship went down at sea, remarried within the seven year period, only to find that he was still alive. A majority of the court quashed her conviction (and reasoned the same way as to the conviction of another woman similarly situated), reading a *mens rea* requirement into the statute. The following passages are from the opinions of WILLS, J., and STEPHEN, J. (at pp. 174–178 and 191):

WILLS, J.

* * *

If identical language may thus be legitimately construed in two opposite senses, and is sometimes held to imply that there is and sometimes there is not an offence when the guilty mind is absent, it is obvious that assistance must be sought aliunde, and that all circumstances must be taken into consideration which tend to show that the one construction or the other is reasonable, and amongst such circumstances it is impossible to discard the consequences. * * *

Now in the present instance one consequence of holding that the offence is complete if the husband or wife is de facto alive at the time of the second marriage, although the defendant had at the time of the second marriage every reason to believe the contrary, would be that though the evidence of death should be sufficient to induce the Court of Probate to grant probate of the will or administration of the goods of the man supposed to be dead, or to prevail with the jury upon an action by the heir to recover possession of his real property, the wife of the person supposed to be dead who had married six years and eleven months after the last time that she had known him to be alive would be guilty of felony in case he should turn up twenty years afterwards. It would be scarcely less unreasonable to enact that those who had in the meantime distributed his personal estate should be guilty of larceny. It seems to me to be a case to which it would not be improper to apply the language of Lord Kenyon when dealing with a statute which literally interpreted led to what he considered an equally preposterous result, "I would adopt any construction of the statute that the words will bear in order to avoid such monstrous consequences."

Again, the nature and extent of the penalty attached to the offence may reasonably be considered. There is nothing that need shock any mind in the payment of a small pecuniary penalty by a person who has unwittingly done something detrimental to the public interest. To subject him, when what he has done has been nothing but what any well-disposed man would have been very likely to do under the circumstances, to the forfeiture of all his goods and chattels, which would have been one consequence of a conviction at the date of the Act of 24 & 25 Vict., to the loss of civil rights, to imprisonment with hard labour, or even to penal servitude, is a very different matter; and such a fate seems properly reserved for those who have transgressed morally as well as unintentionally done something prohibited by law. I am well aware that the mischiefs which may result from bigamous marriages, however innocently contracted, are great: but I cannot think that the appropriate way of preventing them is to expose to the danger of a cruel injustice persons whose only error may be that of acting upon the same evidence as has appeared perfectly satisfactory to a Court of Probate, a tribunal emphatically difficult to satisfy in such matters, and certain only to act upon what appears to be the most cogent evidence of death. It is, as it seems to me, undesirable in the highest degree without necessity to multiply instances in which people shall be liable to conviction upon very grave charges when the circumstances are such that no judge in the kingdom would think of pronouncing more than a nominal sentence.

It is said, however, in respect of the offence now under discussion, that the proviso in 24 & 25 Vict. c. 100, s. 57, that "nothing in the section shall extend to any person marrying a second time whose husband or wife shall have been continually absent from such person for seven years last past, and shall not have been known by such person to be living within that time," points out the sole excuse of which the Act allows. I cannot see what necessity there is for drawing any such inference. It seems to me that it merely specifies one particular case, and indicates what in that case shall be sufficient to exempt the party without any further inquiry from criminal liability * * *. * * *

STEPHEN, J.

* * * It could not be the object of parliament to treat the marriage of widows as an act to be if possible prevented as presumably immoral. The conduct of the women convicted was not in the smallest degree immoral, it was perfectly natural and legitimate. Assuming the facts to be as they supposed, the infliction of more than a nominal punishment on them would have been a scandal. Why, then, should the legislature be held to have wished to subject them to punishment at all.

If such a punishment is legal, the following amongst many other cases might occur. A number of men in a mine are killed, and their bodies are disfigured and mutiliated, by an explosion; one of the survivors secretly absconds, and it is supposed that one of the disfigured bodies is him. His wife sees his supposed remains buried; she marries again. I cannot believe

> that it can have been the intention of the legislature to make such a woman a criminal; the contracting of an invalid marriage is quite misfortune enough * * *.

See the Model Penal Code § 230.1 for a third view.

Part of the difficulty in interpreting bigamy statutes is that bigamy was never a common law crime. It was an ecclestiastical offense only, until punished by the statute 1 Jac. I, c. 11 (1603).

2. Rape and Related Offences

Introductory Note

This subsection first, in subdivision a, introduces the crime of rape and some related offenses. It then, in subdivision b, returning to our focus on problems of *mens rea,* examines one *mens rea* problem in the rape area: What mental state of the accused is required with respect to the victim's consent in rape or assault with intent to rape (or age in statutory rape)? This investigation of a mistake of fact problem prepares us for the final subsection in the chapter, which contrasts mistakes of fact with mistakes of law.

a. THE EVOLUTION OF THE CRIME OF RAPE

THE EXPERIENCE OF RAPE * **

Lynne N. Henderson.
3 Berkeley Women's Law Journal 193, 221–224 (1988).

* * *

Although five and a half years have passed since I was raped, it takes but a moment to remember the forty-five minutes of terror and horror of the event and the aftermath of guilt, shame, fury, and isolation. I was asleep in my bed, when I awoke to find a man on top of me. I struggled to get up; "what are *you* doing here," I demanded. "I'm going to fuck you" was the response. "The hell you are," was mine. In the brief struggle, I told myself, "look, look at everything so you can remember, so you can describe." His fist hit my face repeatedly; I felt nothing except pressure. It seemed clear to me that this was a battle I wouldn't win; I turned my head and thought "oh God, this *is* really happening." I noticed I was bleeding. Time to switch gears—I tried talking assertively. That didn't do any good. My cat started crying: he threatened her. On and on it went: "I'll kill you, I'll kill you." He had a weapon, a screwdriver. "Spread your legs! Spread your legs!" At some point, I realized he might very well kill me if I did not cooperate, and if he killed me, I would not live to "get him." "Better a 261 than a 187" was my weird formulation. I left my body but I didn't: I remember thinking how can something so beautiful be so horrible? After he was done, he started insistently asking where was my jewelry, stating over and over that he would kill me if I moved (something I did not have any doubt about). At some

* From Review Essay: What Makes Rape a Crime? (reviewing Susan Estrich, Real Rape (Harv.U.Press, 1987)). The author of the essay is Professor of Law at Indiana Law School, Bloomington.

point, my face was covered by a pillow. I could not hear well, but I took a chance, got up, and called the police. The only part of that call I remember was also the only time I encountered the legendary insensitivity of the system: the dispatcher asked "are you sure it was a rape?" "Look, it was a righteous 261. There was penetration." What else was I supposed to say? To this day, I hope that dispatcher caught "hell" for her incredible insensitivity.

I became properly hysterical for a moment after the police arrived; I then went into a controlled mode to do everything I could to catch the rapist. He was caught; he denied everything. I had to testify at the preliminary hearing and the trial. It was a "cold" case, a sure winner, and district attorneys were fighting for it. But if it were such a sure thing, why a trial? I suppose because there were no offers made. And there was an eyewitness identification issue. I "blew" the line-up: he had changed his appearance; *thirteen* other women were also there trying to identify men who had raped *them;* the cast had just been removed from my nose; and I was sick, frightened and acutely aware of the potential importance of a line-up (that in this case the forensic evidence made identification much less crucial was of no moment).

And maybe, just maybe, like the myth of all rape trials, the jury would not convict, but instead put me on trial. For what? Being asleep in my own bed? Having possibly too much wine that night with some friends at dinner? For not having bars on the windows? For having a house in disarray? For being stupid enough to live on the fringes of what passes for a ghetto on the San Francisco Peninsula?

I really have no complaints about the actors in the criminal justice system; other than the dispatcher's initial incredulity, they were all sensitive and non-sexist. Although the delay between the arrival of the police and getting treatment seemed forever, I guess I just understood that to catch the man who did this, I had to help. Two show-ups and a stop at the stationhouse later, I was taken to the emergency room. An officer called a victim advocate then stayed with me during the long wait at the hospital emergency room. The doctor who examined me held my hand when I became hysterical. The district attorney met with me, stayed in touch, and asked if I wanted to continue the prosecution at each new stage in the proceeding. The police officers worked long hours to "make" the case. The defense lawyer never hinted at my foibles or my sexual history. He apparently did have the temerity to suggest in his closing argument that because there were no internal injuries, there was no rape. A broken nose, a dislocated jaw, and bruises and cuts in the relevant external areas apparently were not enough. After the case was over, I learned from a law student that the district attorney had a picture of me, taken immediately after the police arrived, prominently displayed in his office—a trophy. I passed along a strong objection to this; who knows if he ever removed it. The jury did not take much time to come back with a guilty verdict and was hunting for additional charges on which to convict the offender. Perfect, right?

Well, yes and no. Many people, men and women, were kind, but many men I knew could not handle the rape at all. Subtle messages of blame, denial—believe it or not—*prurience,* snuck through. None of the nice, middle- and upper-middle class males I knew had apparently given rape much thought; certainly the man I was dating had not. Three weeks after the assault, and only one week after the cast was taken off my nose, he said irritably, "Why are you still so angry?" I was scared—at the least little noise I would jump and sometimes scream; I was in pain; I was furious with men and my vulnerability; I was in mourning. I never thought I would recover—at times I thought I was losing my mind. I had nightmares. I felt guilty because I had not resisted "enough." This was beyond denying—I had some close calls as a teenager and some scares as an adult, but only one had come close, and I'd bitten him and gotten away. Through a combination of forgetting, self-blame, and relief, I had handled those incidents. I had never confronted the utter helplessness of rape, of knowing that it just *did not matter* that I existed; that I did not want this; that I was a human being; not a thing to be invaded, punched, or possibly killed.

For a year, I did not get over a kind of perpetual state of panic—a state not helped, perhaps, by the prospect of testifying against the rapist in another case, frighteningly similar to my own, that fortunately settled. It took three years to get over the "anniversary" nightmares. It took two years of my life to get over my absolute fear and distrust of men, and yet more time to overcome occasional flashbacks. And all the time I tried to act normally—work, function, and rebuild. I remember—what a triumph!—the first night I was able to go alone to a friend's house for dinner, stay, and come home without absolutely panicking.

My experience was not atypical, I think. Based on the stories of rape I have heard from other survivors, the feelings are similar. I thought I'd die; I wish I *had* died; I'm scared; I was terrified; the world isn't safe; I can't trust; I have/had nightmares; I feel guilty; I felt ashamed.

My experience, however, was in some ways "different." I had been a public defender. (Indeed I had represented some men charged with sexual offenses and that undoubtedly took some of the fear out of testifying.) The courtroom was, after all, familiar turf. I manifested a great deal more anger than many survivors with whom I have talked. I am more likely to mention the assault than many survivors. I was also very "lucky"—the rapist was caught, convicted, and sent to prison for a long time. Unlike other survivors, I do not worry about him finding me (at least not for a long while), telephoning me, or being at the office every day.

Although my experience is in some ways "unrepresentative," the only story I can tell is my own, and there is nothing I have heard or read in the stories of others that makes me think mine rings false. And this is true whether their rape experiences fit the stereotypical circumstances of mine, or were acquaintance rapes or date rapes or wife rapes; whether they were physically bruised and bleeding or not. I feel the pain of women who spoke and were hushed by family or friends, even if my anger at their being silenced means I am inept in simply acknowledging their pain. I also recognize the pain of women who have received insensitive treatment from police or doctors, even if the insensitivity was not "outrageous" by some "objective" standards. (For example, an emergency room physician speaking, in a dismissive tone, to a badly injured survivor of an assault with intent to commit rape: "Is it going to bother you that I'm a man?"). I know there are countless women out there who have rape stories—terrible, tragic stories—that they have never told.

I do not think I can ever overcome the nasty rumors about me that were spread because I have been open about the assault. That may be the price you pay for speaking out, and I understand why other rape survivors find that price too high to pay. I know I felt a chill reading that Estrich gets occasional late-night harrassing phone calls. But we are doomed to stay in the traps of rape mythology unless we look at what rape really *is.* Women *and men* must confront the horror, not deny it, and do everything in their power to end it.

Note on Gender as Influencing Attitudes

Rape is a difficult topic to discuss in the classroom. One reason for this is that women and men—or at least many of those men who have not been affected by the rape of a family member or friend—tend to have different attitudes toward the crime. A man tends to think of rape, even what he may think of as "true rape," where the rapist is a stranger who uses overwhelming force on the victim, merely as another serious crime, meriting severe punishment, as arson or armed robbery or any aggravated assault would. For most women, such a reaction is outrageously inadequate on at least two grounds.

First, as Professor Henderson's story shows, the cruel contempt for the humanity and integrity of victims which accompanies rape can produce years of fear and cramped living in victims, to the extent of ruining lives completely, quite apart from any direct physical injuries inflicted. Second, women can be as truly raped by parents, husbands, employers, or "friends" as by strangers lurking in dark alleys, even though these rapists are perhaps somewhat less likely to kill or beat the victim up in the process.

Some men also have fears, though of a lesser order, that women should be aware of. They tend to regard themselves as easily manipulated by women, whose mental processes may be puzzling to them. They fear that a woman may cry rape falsely, perhaps to punish a man for some real or fancied shortcoming in a romantic relationship. Also, they may be confused about how much sexual aggression is permissible.

In the seventeenth century, Sir Matthew Hale, a humane and wise judge and writer on the criminal law, wrote, in the course of discussing what he thought were some near miscarriages of justice he had seen: "It is true that rape is a most detestable crime * * *; but it must be remembered, that it is an accusation easily to be made and hard to be proved, and harder to be defended by the party accused, tho never so innocent." [a] This statement often found its way into jury instructions; today, it is becoming much less common to instruct juries in these terms. However, since the time of Lord Hale, this idea has been influential in the development of the law of rape; after all, men have been running the legal system. They have thought it a good idea to be cautious about conviction of rape

a. 1 Hale, *Pleas of the Crown* 635 (1736). Hale's work was not published until many years after his death. Hale was of course subject to error and influenced by the assumptions of his time.

and to make sure that the woman really resisted or called for help, and complained as soon as she had the chance.

If classroom discussion is to be useful, men must try to understand how women feel about the crime of rape. A man might try to imagine his feelings if he were forcibly sodomized—and faced a skeptical world if he reported it. He might also try to rethink the question of what sort of response to threatened or offered intercourse ought to be required to allow a woman to claim successfully to be a rape victim. Note that she would not have to resist to the utmost or cry out to be considered a victim of robbery. A woman might try to understand that most men are not used to trying to see rape from a woman's point of view and may have grown up with conventional male attitudes and concerns, which, while they exaggerate the dangers of erroneous conviction, are not utterly groundless.[b]

Note: The Elements of Common Law Rape

Rape at common law was unlawful carnal knowledge of a woman by a man by force and without her consent.

Unlawful. There is curiously little authority on the *mens rea,* with respect to having sexual intercourse, required for common law rape. In Model Penal Code terms, it is probably purpose. See § 2.02, Comment 1, at page 232. As a practical matter, the question is seldom litigated, a purpose to have intercourse rarely being debatable if the act takes place. The intoxication of the accused may occasionally suggest a defense of inability to form purpose, but the courts are likely to assume that if the accused was sober enough to accomplish the act, he was not too drunk to have purpose to do so. We will see when we study intoxication that drunkenness is traditionally no defense to a rape charge. The *mens rea* required with respect to the issue of belief in the victim's consent is investigated in the cases in the next subdivision.

Carnal knowledge. Carnal knowledge at common law requires penetration of the female sexual organ by the male organ. The slightest penetration is said to be enough; by the prevailing view, emission of semen is not necessary. Note that at common law the actor must be a man and the victim a woman. Sexual imposition by a woman on a man, a woman on a woman, or a man on a man could be reached only as some other crime, perhaps assault, or, depending on the circumstances, sodomy.

By force and without her consent. The use of at least some force is a central element of rape, though no more force than is necessary to accomplish penetration is necessary in the case of an unconscious or mentally or physically incapacitated victim.

Rape is a crime for which consent is a defense; without such a provision for consent, sexual intercourse would generally be a crime. Consent means assent which is legally effective. Assent procured by fear of death or great bodily injury to the victim or another was and is not regarded as true consent. Intoxication, insanity, or youth may prevent assent from being meaningful, and therefore from being effective. The crime of statutory rape substitutes for the "without her consent" element a requirement that the victim be younger than a legislatively

b. There are false charges of rape, just as there are false charges of robbery or any other crime, but there is no evidence that they are more frequent or more likely to produce convictions than false charges of other offenses.

stated age; in effect, assent by a woman below the stated age, whether in fact able to exercise good judgment or not, is not legally effective consent.

A husband's sexual intercourse with his wife could not be rape at common law. This has variously been put on the ground that marital intercourse is not "unlawful," that the wife was virtually her husband's property, that the marriage ceremony was irrevocable consent, or that the criminal courts should not concern themselves with squabbles in the marital bed. Modern statutes have often allowed conviction when the spouses are living apart under a judicial decree of separation and sometimes have discarded the marital limitation altogether.

As has been suggested, the common law was much concerned that it be clear that the woman had not consented. If not physically or mentally handicapped, she was expected to resist to the utmost, unless perhaps excused from so doing by fear of imminent death or serious injury. If there was any prospect of help, she was expected to cry out for help, unless inhibited by similar fear. She was expected to make prompt complaint to the authorities, at least if she was adult and of full mental capacity. Any failure here was evidence of consent. Reputation and perhaps other evidence of her unchaste character might be received at the trial, as tending to show consent on the occasion in issue.

Questions

1. Why is the phrase "without her consent" more accurate than "against her will" in the definition of rape?

2. In Don Moran v. People, 25 Mich. 356 (1872), defendant physician falsely told the victim, his inexperienced adolescent patient, who was just above the age of consent, that her disease would kill her unless she had sexual intercourse. He offered this "treatment"—telling her she was free to refuse it and go home, to die, if she preferred. She submitted to him. In Reg. v. Flattery, 2 Q.B.D. 410 (Cr.Cas.Res. 1877), defendant physician accomplished penetration by surprise, in the course of a purported surgical procedure. Was either or both of these doctors guilty of common law rape?

3. Suppose defendant goes through a mock wedding ceremony with victim, who consents to intercourse because she believes them to be married. Rape?

4. Where in the following array of circumstances would you draw the line between rape and non-criminal intercourse?

a. Victim resists with all her strength, screaming for help, but is physically overcome. Rape

b. Victim puts up token physical resistance and then submits, as defendant knows, out of fear of death or serious injury. Rape

c. As defendant knows, victim would have resisted with all her strength, but for the well-grounded fear that he would kill or seriously injure her. She makes no actual physical resistance, but makes clear her objection. Rape

d. Victim is not afraid that she will be killed or seriously injured if she refuses. She fears lesser physical injury, or the possibility of pregnancy, or is worn down by argument with the defendant. Her state of mind is manifest to the defendant. No Rape - no threat of serious injury

e. Victim does not fear force or other harm from the defendant, and defendant has no intention to inflict any harm beyond the intercourse itself, but victim, while she does not resist, makes it clear that she objects.

No Rape - need to resist

f. Victim does not by words or acts manifest consent or non-consent, and defendant has no good reason to suppose anything about her consent, but no force beyond what is implicit in the act of intercourse is contemplated by either.

g. Victim does not by words or acts manifest consent or non-consent on this occasion, but she has previously freely consented to intercourse; neither party contemplates force.

h. Victim freely consents and so states.

Note that none of these situations supposes a misunderstanding between the parties. (In the cases you will later consider in subdivision b, the issues are complicated by claims of mistake.)

5. Suppose the marital exemption for rape is abolished, so that a husband's intercourse with his wife can be rape. Would this have any effect on your answer to question 4?

State v. Willis

Supreme Court of Nebraska, 1986.
223 Neb. 844, 394 N.W.2d 648.

HASTINGS, JUSTICE.

* * *

The defendant, Charles Willis, was charged with first degree sexual assault of Diana Willis. Defendant filed a plea in abatement. At the conclusion of the hearing the district court ruled that at common law a husband could not be found guilty of raping his wife and that the common law applied in Nebraska. Because Charles Willis was the victim's legal spouse at the time of the alleged sexual assault, the court quashed the information and abated the prosecution.

* * *

The defendant claims that at common law a husband could not be found guilty of raping his wife. * * *

* * *

* * * [W]e note that the foundation for the spousal exclusion is extremely weak. The rule apparently has as its origin the following extrajudicial statement made by Lord Hale: "But the husband cannot be guilty of a rape committed by himself upon his lawful wife, for by their mutual matrimonial consent and contract the wife hath given up herself in this kind unto her husband, which she cannot retract." 1 M. Hale, The History of the Pleas of the Crown 629 (T. Dogherty ed. 1800). See Com. v. Chretien, 383 Mass. 123, 417 N.E.2d 1203 (1981). We, however, agree with the Supreme Court of New Jersey when it stated:

> We believe that Hale's statements concerning the common law of spousal rape derived from the nature of marriage at a particular time in history. Hale stated the rule in terms of an implied matrimonial consent to intercourse which the wife could not retract. This reasoning may have been persuasive during Hale's time, when marriages were effectively permanent, ending only by death or an act of Parliament. [Citation omitted.] Since the matrimonial vow itself was not retractable, Hale may have believed that neither was the implied consent to conjugal rights. Consequently, he stated the rule in absolute terms, as if it were applicable

> without exception to all marriage relationships. In the years since Hale's formulation of the rule, attitudes towards the permanency of marriage have changed and divorce has become far easier to obtain. The rule, formulated under vastly different conditions, need not prevail when those conditions have changed.

State v. Smith, 85 N.J. 193, 201, 426 A.2d 38, 42 (1981).

Another theory supporting the origin of the spousal exclusion is that the rule was a "derivation of the ancient definition of rape as 'unlawful' carnal knowledge of a woman by a man without her consent; intercourse between husband and wife is not unlawful; therefore, it is reasoned, neither spouse may be prosecuted for what would otherwise be rape." Com. v. Chretien, supra 383 Mass. at 127, 417 N.E.2d at 1207. Nebraska's former rape statutes never defined rape as the "unlawful" carnal knowledge of a woman, therefore that basis for believing the spousal exclusion was the law in Nebraska is also without merit.

The final theories supporting the spousal exclusion are that a wife is a chattel of her husband and that they were one person after marriage. Both of these theories no longer support the spousal exclusion. "Nowhere in the common-law world—indeed in any modern society—is a woman regarded as chattel or demeaned by denial of a separate legal identity and the dignity associated with recognition as a whole human being." Trammel v. United States, 445 U.S. 40, 52, 100 S.Ct. 906, 63 L.Ed.2d 186 (1980). * * *

In light of the facts that no case has ever held that the common-law spousal exclusion is the law in Nebraska, that Nebraska's former rape statutes never defined rape as the "unlawful" carnal knowledge of a woman, and that none of the justifications for the exclusion have any merit in modern society, we decline at this time the defendant's invitation to declare that the spousal exclusion was part of Nebraska rape law.

We decline that invitation because the existence of a common-law spousal exclusion to a rape prosecution is now immaterial, as Nebraska no longer has a rape statute. The Nebraska Legislature repealed Neb.Rev.Stat. §§ 28–407 (Reissue 1964) and 28–408 in 1975 when it adopted the first degree sexual assault statute. The sexual assault statute was slightly reworded in 1977 as part of the adoption of the new criminal code, and the pertinent portion reads as follows: "Any person who subjects another person to sexual penetration and (a) overcomes the victim by force, threat of force, express or implied, coercion, or deception * * * is guilty of sexual assault in the first degree." Neb.Rev.Stat. § 28–319(1) (Reissue 1979). The defendant was charged under § 28–319(1) (Reissue 1985).

We hold that the differences between the former rape statutes and the present first degree sexual assault statute are "more than sufficient to abrogate any 'implied consent' upon which a common-law 'interspousal exception' to prosecution may be based." State v. Rider, 449 So.2d 903, 905 (Fla.App. 1984).

First, and most importantly, we note that the first degree sexual assault statute proscribes a crime of violence, not a crime of sex. First degree sexual assault is not a "sexual [act] of an ardent husband performed upon an initially apathetic wife, [it is an act] of violence that [is] accompanied with physical and mental abuse and often leave[s] the victim with physical and psychological damage that is almost always long lasting." Warren v. State, supra 255 Ga. at 151, 336 S.E.2d at 222.

Second, not only is nonconsensual sexual intercourse proscribed by the first degree sexual assault statute, as was true under the former rape statutes, but also proscribed is any form of sexual penetration as set out in Neb.Rev. Stat. § 28–318(6) (Reissue 1985).

Third, under the former rape statutes, the sexual intercourse must have been forcibly obtained. Under the first degree sexual assault statute, however, the victim can be overcome in many ways short of force. Threat of force, express or implied, coercion, or deception is sufficient. § 28–319(1)(a) (Reissue 1985).

Finally, unlike rape, first degree sexual assault can be committed either by a man or a woman, and the victim can be either a man or a woman. See State v. Country, 194 Neb. 570, 234 N.W.2d 593 (1975). As stated in State v. Smith, 401 So.2d 1126, 1129 (Fla.App.1981):

> While anatomical differences between the sexes limit the manner in which the offense of sexual battery can be perpetrated, it nonetheless follows that if there is an implied consent by a woman to such conduct by her husband there has to be an implied consent to similar conduct by the husband. In Hale's time, a man could not be a victim of rape, but under section 794.011, Florida Statutes, he can be. It is inconceivable that a husband would accept the argument that by marriage he consented to the conduct defined in the statute if inflicted upon him by force or violence.

The same reasoning applies to first degree sexual assault in Nebraska under § 28–319 (Reissue 1985). We hold that by repealing the rape statutes and enacting such a radically different first degree sexual assault statute, the Legislature intended to abrogate any common-law assumptions concerning the crime of rape.

The trial court was in error in sustaining the plea in abatement and quashing the information. The exception is sustained, and the cause is remanded for further proceedings consistent with this opinion.

* * *

Reissue Revised Statutes of Nebraska, 1943 (1985)[c]

28–317. *Sexual assault; legislative intent.* It is the intent of the Legislature to enact laws dealing with sexual assault and related criminal sexual offenses which will protect the dignity of the victim at all stages of judicial process, which will insure that the alleged offender in a criminal sexual offense case have preserved the constitutionally guaranteed due process of law procedures, and which will establish a system of investigation, prosecution, punishment, and rehabilitation for the welfare

c. Under §§ 28–105 and 28–106 a Class II felony carries a 1 to 50 year sentence of imprisonment, a Class III felony a 1 to 25 year sentence, a class IV felony a 0 to 5 years sentence, and a class I misdemeanor a 0 to 1 year sentence.

and benefit of the citizens of this state as such system is employed in the area of criminal sexual offenses.

28–318. *Terms, defined.* As used in sections 28–317 to 28–321, unless the context otherwise requires:

(1) Actor shall mean a person accused of sexual assault;

(2) Intimate parts shall mean the genital area, groin, inner thighs, buttocks, or breasts;

(3) Past sexual behavior shall mean sexual behavior other than the sexual behavior upon which the sexual assault is alleged;

(4) Serious personal injury shall mean great bodily injury or disfigurement, extreme mental anguish or mental trauma, pregnancy, disease, or loss or impairment of a sexual or reproductive organ;

(5) Sexual contact shall mean the intentional touching of the victim's sexual or intimate parts or the intentional touching of the victim's clothing covering the immediate area of the victim's sexual or intimate parts. Sexual contact shall also mean the touching by the victim of the actor's sexual or intimate parts or the clothing covering the immediate area of the actor's sexual or intimate parts when such touching is intentionally caused by the actor. Sexual contact shall include only such conduct which can be reasonably construed as being for the purpose of sexual arousal or gratification of either party;

(6) Sexual penetration shall mean sexual intercourse in its ordinary meaning, cunnilingus, fellatio, anal intercourse, or any intrusion, however slight, of any part of the actor's or victim's body or any object manipulated by the actor into the genital or anal openings of the victim's body which can be reasonably construed as being for nonmedical or nonhealth purposes. Sexual penetration shall not require emission of semen; and

(7) Victim shall mean the person alleging to have been sexually assaulted.

28–319. *Sexual assault; first degree; penalty.* (1) Any person who subjects another person to sexual penetration and (a) overcomes the victim by force, threat of force, express or implied, coercion, or deception, (b) knew or should have known that the victim was mentally or physically incapable of resisting or appraising the nature of his or her conduct, or (c) the actor is nineteen years of age or older and the victim is less than sixteen years of age is guilty of sexual assault in the first degree.

(2) Sexual assault in the first degree is a Class II felony. The sentencing judge shall consider whether the actor shall have caused serious personal injury to the victim in reaching his decision on the sentence.

(3) Any person who shall be found guilty of sexual assault in the first degree for a second time shall be sentenced to not less than twenty-five years and shall not be eligible for parole.

28–320. ***Sexual assault; second or third degree; penalty.*** **(1) Any person who subjects another person to sexual contact and (a) overcomes the victim by force, threat of force, express or implied, coercion, or deception, or (b) knew or should have known that the victim was physically or mentally incapable of resisting or appraising the nature of his or her conduct is guilty of sexual assault in either the second degree or third degree.**

(2) Sexual assault shall be in the second degree and is a Class III felony if the actor shall have caused serious personal injury to the victim.

(3) Sexual assault shall be in the third degree and is a Class I misdemeanor if the actor shall not have caused serious personal injury to the victim.

28–320.01. ***Sexual assault of a child; penalty.*** **(1) A person commits sexual assault of a child if he or she subjects another person fourteen years of age or younger to sexual contact and the actor is at least nineteen years of age or older.**

(2) Sexual assault of a child is a Class IV felony.

28–321. ***Sexual assault; evidence of past sexual behavior; when admissible; procedure.*** **(1) If the defendant intends to offer evidence of specific instances of the victim's past sexual behavior, notice of such intention shall be given to the prosecuting attorney and filed with the court not later than fifteen days before trial.**

(2) Upon motion to the court by either party in a prosecution in a case of sexual assault, an in camera hearing shall be conducted in the presence of the judge, under guidelines established by the judge, to determine the relevance of evidence of the victim's or the defendant's past sexual behavior. Evidence of a victim's past sexual behavior shall not be admissible unless such evidence is: (a) Evidence of past sexual behavior with persons other than the defendant, offered by the defendant upon the issue whether the defendant was or was not, with respect to the victim, the source of any physical evidence, including but not limited to, semen, injury, blood, saliva, and hair; or (b) evidence of past sexual behavior with the defendant when such evidence is offered by the defendant on the issue of whether the victim consented to the sexual behavior upon which the sexual assault is alleged if it is first established to the court that such activity shows such a relation to the conduct involved in the case and tends to establish a pattern of conduct or behavior on the part of the victim as to be relevant to the issue of consent.

Note

Like Nebraska, many states have revised their rape laws to produce a number of important changes in the common law. It is necessary to examine the statutes of a particular jurisdiction to see how far these go. Note the following changes made by the Nebraska legislation:

Division of rape and related offenses into degrees. Not only are there three named degrees of sexual assault in addition to sexual assault on a child, but sexual assault in the first degree is aggravated by a prior conviction for the same offense. In addition to the "serious personal injury" which aggravates sexual assault in Nebraska, such factors as the absence of any prior social relationship between accused and victim, the use of a weapon, or "gang" raping may be chosen by a legislature as aggravating factors.

Consolidation with sodomy and other related law. The crime of sexual assault in Nebraska includes not only rape, but also forcible sodomy and other non-consensual homosexual and heterosexual conduct involving penetration of vulva, anus, or mouth by parts of the body or other objects, as set out in § 28–318(6). Note that heterosexual and homosexual conduct are dealt with on equal terms; adult, private, consensual conduct is not prohibited. Both men and women may commit the crime. In some consolidation statutes, separate offenses of rape, sodomy, etc., are retained, but they are defined in parallel and given similar penalties.

Consolidation with statutory rape law. Section 28–319(c) deals with statutory rape, a crime in which the victim's non-consent is not required as an element of the offense if she is under the age fixed by the legislature—at least if the accused is substantially older. The idea is that a victim under the statutory age is incapable of giving consent. A defendant of about the same age may be excused on the theory that adolescent romances which get out of hand should not be dealt with in the criminal courts. There is further material on statutory rape in subdivision b.

Consolidation with certain assault law. Sexual assaults and batteries short of rape were treated as ordinary assaults at common law; here they are brought into relationship with other sex crimes, with which they more logically belong. See §§ 28–320 and 28–320.01.

Addition of special provision to make it clear that no threat or force is necessary in the case of a physically or mentally handicapped victim. This holds only if the accused knew or should have known the situation. See §§ 28–319(b) and 28–320(b).

Addition of fraud alternative to the force requirement. "Deception"—not defined—is enough for convictions of sexual assault in Nebraska. See §§ 28–319(1)(a) and 28–320(1)(a).

Abolition of the marital exemption. See the *Willis* case, and People v. Liberta, 64 N.Y.2d 152, 485 N.Y.S.2d 207, 474 N.E.2d 567 (1984), holding a marital exemption unconstitutional.

Rape shield provision. Section 28–321 is a so-called rape shield provision, designed to make sexual assault cases less of an ordeal for victims. The intention is to keep out of evidence most inquiry into the past sexual behavior of the victim. Where the issue is consent, the accused might at common law be allowed to introduce such evidence as, for example, that the victim had a bad reputation for chastity in her community, as tending to show that she consented on the occasion in issue. Such evidence might turn the inquiry into one about the conduct of the victim rather than the conduct of the accused, and thereby increase the reluctance of a victim to report a rape or cooperate in prosecution. The statute eliminates most such inquiries and provides for notice and a non-public hearing in advance of trial if the accused wants to try to get such material into evidence.

Note the two instances in which an inquiry into past sexual history is allowed: (1) Where the defense is, for example, that no intercourse took place between the parties, but the prosecution shows the presence of semen, the accused may show that the victim had recently had intercourse—consensual or not—with someone other than the accused. This is something different from an attempt to show that the victim is the sort of person likely to consent. (2) A pattern of sexual conduct between accused and victim which tends to show consent in the case in issue may be shown. This does bear on consent, but does not allow exploration of the victim's conduct with third persons, and it is apt to be far more compelling on the issue of consent than such conduct with others.

The statute may not cover all cases in which an accused is constitutionally entitled to explore the victim's sexual history. Suppose the accused denies any relations [or any non-consensual relations] with the victim, but a prosecution witness testifies that he witnessed the event the prosecution claims took place. In cross-examining the witness, the defense wants to show a past sexual relationship between the victim and the witness, of a nature which might indicate that the witness's testimony is distorted by bias for the victim or against the accused. The defendant's constitutional right to confront his accusers may entail a right to show such bias, no matter what the statute says. For a case exploring the constitutional issue, see State v. Pulizzano, 155 Wis.2d 633, 456 N.W.2d 325 (1990) (proving alternative of source of child's sexual knowledge).

Other rape shield statutes may adopt different views of exceptions. They may, for example, allow exploration of sexual history when the victim can be shown to have made false sexual charges against others. For the version of the rule adopted in the Federal Rules of Evidence, see FRE 412.

b. *MISTAKES AS TO THE VICTIM'S CONSENT OR AGE*

Regina v. Morgan [a]

House of Lords, 1976.
[1976] A.C. 182.

LORD HAILSHAM OF ST. MARYLEBONE. My Lords, in Reg. v. Hyam [1975] A.C. 55 this House discussed the mental element in murder. This appeal is concerned with the mental element in rape. It involves two questions at vastly different levels of importance but each strangely illustrative of the other, which were argued before us. The first is a question of great academic importance in the theory of English criminal law, certified for this House by the Court of Appeal, which also gave leave to appeal. The second, which arises only if the first is answered favourably to the appellants, is whether the House can be satisfied that no miscarriage of justice has taken place so as to compel them to apply the proviso to section 2(1) of the Criminal Appeal Act 1968.[b] As I propose to answer these two questions, as to the first favourably, and as the second, unfavourably to the appellants, and thus dismiss the appeals, I will begin this opinion with the facts.

* * *

The question arises, in the following way. The appellant Morgan and his three co-defendants, who were all members of the R.A.F., spent the evening of August 15, 1973, in one another's company. The appellant Morgan was significantly older than the other three, and considerably senior to them in rank. He was * * * married to the alleged victim, but not, it seems at the time habitually sleeping in the same bed. At this time, Mrs. Morgan occupied a single bed in the same room as her younger son aged about 11 years, and by the time the appellants arrived at Morgan's house, Mrs. Morgan was already in bed and asleep, until she was awoken by their presence.

a. The order of the opinions has been changed.

b. "Provided that the Court may, notwithstanding that they are of the opinion that the point raised in the appeal might be decided in favour of the appellant, dismiss the appeal if they consider that no miscarriage of justice has actually occurred."

According to the version of the facts which she gave in evidence, and which was evidently accepted by the jury, she was aroused from her sleep, frog-marched into another room where there was a double bed, held by each of her limbs, arms and legs apart, by the four appellants, while each of the three young appellants in turn had intercourse with her in the presence of the others, during which time the other two committed various lewd acts upon various parts of her body. When each had finished and had left the room, the appellant Morgan completed the series of incidents by having intercourse with her himself.

According to Mrs. Morgan she consented to none of this and made her opposition to what was being done very plain indeed. In her evidence to the court, she said that her husband was the first to seize her and pull her out of bed. She then "yelled" to the little boy who was sleeping with her to call the police, and later, when the elder boy came out on the landing, she called to him also to get the police, and "screamed." Her assailants, however, covered her face and pinched her nose, until she begged them to let her breathe. She was held, wrists and feet, "dragged" to the neighboring room, put on the bed where the various incidents occurred. At this stage she was overcome by fear of "being hit." There was never a time when her body was free from being held. When it was all over she grabbed her coat, ran out of the house, drove straight to the hospital and immediately complained to the staff of having been raped. This last fact was fully borne out by evidence from the hospital.

In their evidence in court, the appellants made various damaging admissions which certainly amounted to some corroboration of all this. They admitted that some degree of struggle took place in the bedroom, that Mrs. Morgan made some noise which was forcibly suppressed, and that she was carried out forcibly into the other bedroom, and that her arms and legs were separately held. In addition to this, Mrs. Morgan's evidence was far more fully corroborated by a number of statements (each, of course, admissible only against the maker) which virtually repeated Mrs. Morgan's own story but in far greater and more lurid detail. Of course, the appellants repudiated their statements in the witness box, saying that the words were put into their mouths by the police, even though at least one was written out in the hands of the makers of the statement. I think it likely to the extent of moral certainty that the jury accepted that these statements were made as alleged and contained the truth. But I need not rest my opinion upon this, since the undeniable fact is that the jury accepted, after an impeccable summing up and adequate corroboration, that Mrs. Morgan was telling the truth in her evidence. I mention all these details simply to show, that if, as I think plain, the jury accepted Mrs. Morgan's statement *in substance* there was no possibility whatever of any of the appellants holding any belief whatever, reasonable or otherwise, in their victim's consent to what was being done.

The primary "defence" was consent. I use the word "defence" in inverted commas, because, of course, in establishing the crime of rape, the prosecution must exclude consent in order to establish the essential ingredients of the crime. There is no burden at the outset on the accused to raise the issue. Nevertheless, at the close of the prosecution case the accused had a formidable case to answer, and they answered by going into the witness box and swearing to facts which, if accepted, would have meant, not merely that they reasonably believed that Mrs. Morgan had consented, but that, after she entered the bedroom where the acts of intercourse took place, she not merely consented but took an active and enthusiastic part in a sexual orgy which might have excited unfavourable comment in the court of Caligula or Nero.

All four defendants explained in the witness box that they had spent the evening together in Wolverhampton, and by the time of the alleged offences had had a good deal to drink. Their original intention had been to find some women in the town, but when this failed, Morgan made the surprising suggestion to the others that they should all return to his home and have sexual intercourse with his wife. According to the three younger appellants (but not according to Morgan who described this part of their story as "lying") Morgan told them that they must not be surprised if his wife struggled a bit, since she was "kinky" and this was the only way in which she could get "turned on." However this may be, it is clear that Morgan did invite his three companions home in order that they might have sexual intercourse with his wife, and, no doubt, he may well have led them in one way or another to believe that she would consent to their doing so. This however, would only be a matter predisposing them to believe that Mrs. Morgan consented, and would not in any way establish that, at the time, they believed she did consent whilst they were having intercourse.

* * *

The certified question arises because counsel for the appellants raised the question whether, even if the victim consented, the appellants may not have honestly believed that she did. [*sic*] As I have pointed out, the question was wholly unreal, because if there was reasonable doubt about belief, the same material must have given rise to reasonable doubt about consent, and vice versa. But, presumably because, at that stage, the jury's view of the matter had not been sought, the matter was left to them, as the appellants complain, in a form which implied that they could only acquit if the mistaken belief in consent was reasonable, and it was not enough that it should be honest. * * *

* * * An honest belief in consent, they contend, is enough. It matters not whether it be also reasonable. No doubt a defendant will wish to raise argument or lead evidence to show that his belief was reasonable, since this will support its honesty. No doubt the prosecution will seek to cross examine or raise arguments or adduce evidence to undermine the contention that the belief is reasonable, because, in the nature of the case, the fact that a belief cannot reasonably be held is a strong ground for saying that it was not in fact held honestly at all. Nonetheless, the appellants contend, the crux of the matter, the factum probandum, or rather the fact to be refuted by the prosecution, is honesty and not honesty plus reasonableness. In making reasonableness as well as honesty an ingredient in this "defence" the judge, say the appellants, was guilty of a misdirection.

* * *

* * * The prohibited act in rape is to have intercourse without the victim's consent. The minimum mens rea or guilty mind in most common law offences, including rape, is the intention to do the prohibited act * * *. * * *

* * *

* * * I believe that "mens rea" means "guilty or criminal mind," and if it be the case, as seems to be accepted here, that the mental element in rape is not knowledge but intent, to insist that a belief must be reasonable to excuse is to insist that either the accused is to be found guilty of intending to do that which in truth he did not intend to do, or that his state of mind, though innocent of evil intent, can convict him if it be honest but not rational. * * *

* * *

Once one has accepted, what seems to me abundantly clear, that the prohibited act in rape is non-consensual sexual intercourse, and that the guilty state of mind is an intention to commit it, it seems to me to follow as a matter of inexorable logic that there is no room either for a "defence" of honest belief or mistake, or of a defence of honest and reasonable belief or mistake. Either the prosecution proves that the accused had the requisite intent, or it does not. In the former case it succeeds, and in the latter it fails. Since honest belief clearly negatives intent, the reasonableness or otherwise of that belief can only be evidence for or against the view that the belief and therefore the intent was actually held * * *. * * *

* * *

LORD CROSS OF CHELSEA. * * *

* * * To have intercourse with a woman who is not your wife is, even today, not generally considered to be a course of conduct which the law ought positively to encourage and it can be argued with force that it is only fair to the woman and not in the least unfair to the man that he should be under a duty to take reasonable care to ascertain that she is consenting to the intercourse and be at the risk of a prosecution if he fails to take such care. * * *

But, as I have said, section 1 of the Act of 1956 does not say that a man who has sexual intercourse with a woman who does not consent to it commits an offense; it says that a man who rapes a woman commits an offence. Rape is not a word in the use of which lawyers have a monopoly and the first question to be answered in this case, as I see it, is whether according to the ordinary use of the English language a man can be said to have committed rape if he believed that the woman was consenting to the intercourse and would not have attempted to have it but for this belief, whatever his grounds for so believing. I do not think that he can. Rape, to my mind, imports at least indifference as to the woman's consent. * * * That being my view as to the meaning of the word "rape" in ordinary parlance, I next ask myself whether the law gives it a different meaning. There is very little English authority on the point but what there is—namely, the reported directions of several common law judges in the early and the middle years of the last century—accords with what I take to be the ordinary meaning of the word. * * *

* * * If the appellants when they came to give evidence had said that what Mrs. Morgan had said was perfectly true, that she had never at any stage given any sign that she was consenting to—let alone enjoying—the intercourse, but that they were so much influenced by what her husband had told them that they believed throughout that her manifestations of unwillingness were only play acting, then it is conceivable that a jury, on a proper direction, might have acquitted them. They might, that is to say, have said to themselves that though it was almost incredible that any young men could have been so stupid yet, having seen and heard them, they would give them the benefit of the doubt. But the appellants chose—most unwisely—to challenge the truth of Mrs. Morgan's evidence and to assert that although to start with she manifested some unwillingness when it came to the point she co-operated in the proceedings with evident relish. So, as the judge made clear at the outset of his summing up, the only real issue in the case was whether what took place in the Morgan's house that night was a multiple rape or a sexual orgy. The jury obviously considered that the appellants' evidence as to the part played by Mrs. Morgan was a pack of lies and one must assume that any other jury would take the same view as to the relative credibility of the parties. That any jury which thought that the grounds for a belief in consent put forward by the defendants, which if truly held would have been eminently reasonable, were in fact never entertained by them at all, should in the same breath hold that they may have had an honest belief in consent based on different and unreasonable grounds is inconceivable. So I would apply the proviso and dismiss the appeal.

LORD FRASER OF TULLYBELTON. * * *

* * *

* * * If the effect of the evidence as a whole is that the defendant believed, or may have believed, that the woman was consenting, then the Crown has not discharged the onus of proving commission of the offence as fully defined and, as it seems to me, no question can arise as to whether the belief was reasonable or not. Of course, the reasonableness or otherwise of the belief will be important as evidence tending to show whether it was really held by the defendant, but that is all.

The argument for the Crown in support of an affirmative answer to the question in this case was not supported by any English decision on rape. * * *

* * *

* * * I would therefore answer the question in the negative—that is in favour of the accused. But, for the reasons stated by my noble and learned friends, Lord Hailsham of St. Marylebone and Lord Edmund-Davies, I would apply the proviso to the Criminal Appeal Act 1968, section 2(1), and I would refuse the appeal.

LORD EDMUND-DAVIES. * * *

* * *

In the absence of contrary evidence, the accused may be presumed to have appreciated the significance of circumstances which must have come to his notice. * * * The presumption is not conclusive and, unless it emerges that there is a weight of authority compelling a different conclusion, I should have considered that the honest belief of an accused charged with rape that the woman was willing, being wholly inconsistent with the criminal intention necessary to constitute the crime, would call for his acquittal. The more unreasonable such a belief in the proved circumstances of the case, the slimmer the chances of the jury's thinking that it was ever entertained. Nevertheless, if, after hearing all the evidence (and, in most cases, particularly that of the accused himself), they did not reject out of hand the plea of honest belief, even though they were alive to its unreasonableness, I should have thought that they were duty bound to acquit. Honest belief, however foolishly formed, that the woman was willing seems to me incompatible with an intention to rape her. Here, as in any other crime where knowledge is an essential ingredient, this should connote actual knowledge and not merely what the accused ought to have known. * * *

* * *

In this country a long line of authorities and numerous dicta indicate that, when an accused challenges that he had the necessary mens rea involved in the offence charged by asserting that he committed the actus reus under a mistake of fact, his belief must have been based on reasonable grounds. Of these cases, the best known are those arising from charges of bigamy. It is true that in Reg. v. Turner (1862) 9 Cox C.C. 145, Martin B. directed the jury simply to consider whether the accused woman "had an honest belief that her first husband was dead," but although Cleasby B. purported in Reg. v. Horton, 11 Cox C.C. 670, 671 to be following Reg. v. Turner, he in fact made a vital addition by twice directing the jury that:

> "You must find the prisoner guilty unless you think that he had fair and reasonable grounds for believing, and did honestly believe, that his first wife was dead."

Reg. v. Tolson, 23 Q.B.D. 168 established the correctness of the latter direction and it has been applied in countless bigamy cases even since; for example, in Reg. v. King [1964] 1 Q.B. 285, where Lord Parker C.J. said, at p. 293: "Honest belief is not enough; there must be an honest belief on reasonable grounds." Reg. v. Tolson had earlier been followed in Australia in Thomas v. The King, 59 C.L.R. 279 and both were in their turn followed here in Reg. v. Gould [1968] 2 Q.B. 65 where Diplock L.J. pointed out at p. 76 that the offence of bigamy:

> "* * * is not an absolute one and that honest and reasonable belief in a fact affecting the matrimonial status of the defendant which, if true, would make his second marriage lawful and innocent can constitute a defence * * *."

Such an approach has been criticised. In America, for example, Professor Jerome Hall observed (1957) 33 Indiana Law Journal 5:

> "* * * Anglo-American criminal law restricts the scope of ignorantia facti in ways which constitute serious limitations. * * * An honest mistake of fact is not sufficient. 'The apprehension of danger must be bona fide and reasonable' (Hill v. State, 194 Ala. 11). * * * The plain consequence of this application of

objective liability to ignorantia facti is that persons who commit harms solely because they are mistaken regarding the material facts are nonetheless criminally liable, i.e., despite the complete lack of criminal intent * * * (p. 11). The elimination of 'reasonableness' as a substantive restriction of the doctrine of ignorantia facti would clarify the public mind regarding the nature of criminal conduct. It would facilitate analysis of the criminal law and stimulate a sounder administration of it."

In this country, Russell on Crime, 12th ed. (1964), vol. 1, p. 76, in the course of a discussion of mens rea, refers to "the ancient doctrine that the mistake must be reasonable" and adds:

"It is hardly necessary to point out that such a doctrine, based purely on an objective test, is out of keeping with the modern principle that the mens rea required by the common law is a subjective element."

And Professor Glanville Williams has commented (Criminal Law, 2nd ed. (1961), p. 177):

" * * * it is not true to say that the general run of crimes can be committed by inattention. * * * It is submitted that this is not the law. In the absence of words in the statute dispensing with proof of mens rea, it should be held that the crime can be committed only intentionally or recklessly. If a person charged with bigamy believed that he was legally free to marry again, it cannot be said that the crime was committed either intentionally or recklessly, and the question whether the belief was unreasonable is irrelevant."

And, after a discussion of reported cases, he concluded, at p. 204:

"Even if, as a result of decisions like this, it must now be conceded that unreasonable mistake is no defence in bigamy, this only means that bigamy can be committed negligently. It does not prove that other crimes can be committed negligently."

For myself, I am greatly impressed by these forceful passages and others of a like kind to be found in the textbooks of many modern writers on the criminal law. They give rise to two questions: (A) Are there any grounds for differentiating between bigamy and rape in this matter of mistaken belief? I can think of none, and, although counsel for the appellants understandably stressed that in Reg. v. Tolson, 23 Q.B.D. 168, Wills J. said, at p. 180, that "there can be no crime without a tainted mind," the rest of his judgment relates to a bona fide belief on reasonable grounds held at the time of the marriage ceremony that the spouse was dead. Counsel was unable to indicate any reason why the two offences should be differently treated * * *. (B) Are there any grounds for thinking that the established law in bigamy is out of step with other aspects of criminal jurisprudence and accordingly ought not to be applied to other cases and, in particular, is inapplicable to the present case?

As to that, while Tolson dealt with a statutory offence, the majority who favoured an acquittal clearly did not consider that in so concluding they were doing anything more than applying established and general principles of the criminal law. Thus Cave J. said, at p. 181:

> "At common law an honest and reasonable belief in the existence of circumstances, which, if true, would make the act for which a prisoner is indicted an innocent act has always been held to be a good defence. This doctrine is embodied in the somewhat uncouth maxim, 'actus non facit reum, nisi mens sit rea.' Honest and reasonable mistake stands in fact on the same footing as absence of the reasoning faculty, as in infancy, or perversion of that faculty, as in lunacy. Instances of the existence of this common law doctrine will readily occur to the mind."

Again, Stephen J. said, at p. 188:

> "Apart, indeed, from the present case, I think it may be laid down as a general rule that an alleged offender is deemed to have acted under that state of facts which he in good faith and on reasonable grounds believed to exist when he did the act alleged to be an offence. I am unable to suggest any real exception to this rule, nor has one ever been suggested to me."

A little later, citing the dissenting judgment of Brett J. in Reg. v. Prince, L.R. 2 C.C.R. 154, Stephen J. commented, at p. 190:

> "His judgment established at much length, and, as it appears to me, unanswerably, the principle above explained, which he states as follows: 'That a mistake of facts on reasonable grounds, to the extent that if the facts were as believed, the acts of the prisoner would make him guilty of no offence at all, is an excuse, and that such an excuse is implied in every criminal charge and every criminal enactment in England'."

Finally, having declared (p. 191) that, "the general principle is clearly in favour of the prisoners," Stephen J. proceeded to consider "how does the intention of the legislature appear to have been against them," and concluded that in reality it was not.

To my way of thinking, such weighty observations as these make it impossible to put bigamy into a special category or to regard Tolson as turning merely upon the wording of a particular statute. The majority view was founded on common law principles of general applicability in the field of criminal law for many years. * * *

* * *

Finally, in relation to the critical comments of Professor Glanville Williams that crimes requiring mens rea ought not to be capable of being committed by inattention, it is important to recall that in Sweet v. Parsley [1970] A.C. 132, Lord Diplock said in this House, at p. 163:

> " * * * the importance of the actual decision of the nine judges who constituted the majority in Reg. v. Tolson, * * * was that it laid down as a general principle of construction of any enactment, which creates a criminal offence, that, even where the words used to describe the prohibited conduct would not in any other context

connote the necessity for a particular mental element, they are nevertheless to be read as subject to the implication that a necessary element in the offence is the absence of a belief, held honestly and upon reasonable grounds, in the existence of facts which, if true, would make the act innocent. As was said by the Privy Council in Bank of New South Wales v. Piper [1897] A.C. 383, 389, 390, the absence of mens rea really consists in such a belief by the accused."

At pp. 164–165:

> "It has been objected that the requirement laid down in Reg. v. Tolson, 23 Q.B.D. 168 and the Bank of New South Wales v. Piper [1897] A.C. 383 that the mistaken belief should be based on reasonable grounds introduces an objective mental element into mens rea. This may be so, but there is nothing novel in this. The test of the mental element of provocation which distinguishes manslaughter from murder has always been at common law and now is by statute the objective one of the way in which a reasonable man would react to provocation. There is nothing unreasonable in requiring a citizen to take reasonable care to ascertain the facts relevant to his avoiding doing a prohibited act."

These words express the general approach of the criminal law adopted over a wide spectrum, by courts applying the common law both here and overseas, approved of to the extent already indicated by this House and by courts of inferior jurisdiction, and in respect of a variety of offences. What Professor Glanville Williams has described as "the hoary error that a mistake to afford a defence to a criminal charge must be reasonable" ((1951) 14 M.L.R. 485) is not only old but widely accepted. * * *

* * *

* * * [T]he conclusion I have come to is that the necessary course is to uphold, as being in accordance with established law, the direction given in this case by the learned trial judge as to the necessity for the mistake of fact urged to be based on reasonable grounds. The approach which I should have preferred must, I think, wait until the legislature reforms this part of the law * * *. * * *

I should, however, make it clear that, even had I felt free to hold that there had been a misdirection, I would have been for applying the proviso to section 2(1) of the Criminal Appeal Act 1968. * * *

In my judgment, in the light of all the evidence in this extraordinary case, no reasonable jury could have failed to convict all four accused even had they been directed as counsel for the appellants urges they should. Accordingly, even had I acceded to the submission that there was a misdirection, I should have held that no miscarriage of justice resulted in respect of any of the accused. I would therefore still have said, as I now do, that the appeals of all four should be dismissed.

LORD SIMON OF GLAISDALE. My Lords, I have had the advantage of reading in draft the speech prepared by my noble and learned friend, Lord Edmund-Davies. I concur with him that the authorities demand that the question certified for your Lordships' consideration should be answered, Yes.

But, agreeing as I do with the judgment of Bridge J. in the Court of Appeal, I feel no reluctance in coming to this conclusion, which seems to me to accord with legal principle and with good sense.

* * *

It remains to consider why the law requires, in such circumstances, that the belief in a state of affairs whereby the actus would not be reus must be held on reasonable grounds. One reason was given by Bridge J. in the Court of Appeal, ante, p. 191D–E:

> "The rationale of requiring reasonable grounds for the mistaken belief must lie in the law's consideration that a bald assertion of belief for which the accused can indicate no reasonable ground is evidence of insufficient substance to raise any issue requiring the jury's consideration."

I agree; but I think there is also another reason. The policy of the law in this regard could well derive from its concern to hold a fair balance between victim and accused. It would hardly seem just to fob off a victim of a savage assault with such comfort as he could derive from knowing that his injury was caused by a belief, however absurd, that he was about to attack the accused. A respectable woman who has been ravished would hardly feel that she was vindicated by being told that her assailant must go unpunished because he believed, quite unreasonably, that she was consenting to sexual intercourse with him. * * *

Appeals dismissed.

Questions

1. How, in a common law jurisdiction with the usual marital exemption, could Morgan be convicted of the rape of his wife?

2. What is the proper *mens rea* for common law rape? With which of the *Morgan* opinions do you agree? After *Morgan,* in the Sexual Offenses Act of 1976, § 1(1), Parliament amended the law to require for acquittal that the accused not be reckless with respect to his belief in the victim's consent. Most American jurisdictions allow conviction if the accused is reckless or negligent with respect to his belief in consent.

State v. Rusk

Court of Appeals of Maryland, 1981.
289 Md. 230, 424 A.2d 720.

Argued before MURPHY, C. J., and SMITH, DIGGES, ELDRIDGE, COLE, DAVIDSON and RODOWSKY, JJ.

MURPHY, CHIEF JUDGE.

Edward Rusk was found guilty by a jury in the Criminal Court of Baltimore (Karwacki, J. presiding) of second degree rape in violation of Maryland Code (1957, 1976 Repl.Vol., 1980 Cum.Supp.), Art. 27, § 463(a) (1), which provides in pertinent part:

> "A person is guilty of rape in the second degree if the person engages in vaginal intercourse with another person:

(1) By force or threat of force against the will and without the consent of the other person; * * *."

On appeal, the Court of Special Appeals, sitting en banc, reversed the conviction; it concluded by an 8–5 majority that in view of the prevailing law as set forth in Hazel v. State, 221 Md. 464, 157 A.2d 922 (1960), insufficient evidence of Rusk's guilt had been adduced at the trial to permit the case to go to the jury. Rusk v. State, 43 Md.App. 476, 406 A.2d 624 (1979). We granted certiorari to consider whether the Court of Special Appeals properly applied the principles of *Hazel* in determining that insufficient evidence had been produced to support Rusk's conviction.

At the trial, the 21-year-old prosecuting witness, Pat, testified that on the evening of September 21, 1977, she attended a high school alumnae meeting where she met a girl friend, Terry. After the meeting, Terry and Pat agreed to drive in their respective cars to Fells Point to have a few drinks. On the way, Pat stopped to telephone her mother, who was baby sitting for Pat's two-year-old son; she told her mother that she was going with Terry to Fells Point and would not be late in arriving home.

The women arrived in Fells Point about 9:45 p.m. They went to a bar where each had one drink. After staying approximately one hour, Pat and Terry walked several blocks to a second bar, where each of them had another drink. After about thirty minutes, they walked two blocks to a third bar known as E. J. Buggs. The bar was crowded and a band was playing in the back. Pat ordered another drink and as she and Terry were leaning against the wall, Rusk approached and said "hello" to Terry. Terry, who was then conversing with another individual, momentarily interrupted her conversation and said "Hi, Eddie." Rusk then began talking with Pat and during their conversation both of them acknowledged being separated from their respective spouses and having a child. Pat told Rusk that she had to go home because it was a week-night and she had to wake up with her baby early in the morning.

Rusk asked Pat the direction in which she was driving and after she responded, Rusk requested a ride to his apartment. Although Pat did not know Rusk, she thought that Terry knew him. She thereafter agreed to give him a ride. Pat cautioned Rusk on the way to the car that " 'I'm just giving a ride home, you know, as a friend, not anything to be, you know, thought of other than a ride;' " and he said, " 'Oh, okay.' " They left the bar between 12:00 and 12:20 a.m.

Pat testified that on the way to Rusk's apartment, they continued the general conversation that they had started in the bar. After a twenty-minute drive, they arrived at Rusk's apartment in the 3100 block of Guilford Avenue. Pat testified that she was totally unfamiliar with the neighborhood. She parked the car at the curb on the opposite side of the street from Rusk's apartment but left the engine running. Rusk asked Pat to come in, but she refused. He invited her again, and she again declined. She told Rusk that she could not go into his apartment even if she wanted to because she was separated from her husband and a detective could be observing her movements. Pat said that Rusk was fully aware that she did not want to accompany him to his room. Notwithstanding her repeated refusals, Pat testified that Rusk reached over and turned off the ignition to her car and took her car keys. He got out of the car, walked over to her side, opened the door and said, " 'Now, will you come up?' " Pat explained her subsequent actions:

> "At that point, because I was scared, because he had my car keys. I didn't know what to do. I was someplace I didn't even know where I was. It was in the city. I didn't know whether to run. I really didn't think at that point, what to do.
>
> "Now, I know that I should have blown the horn. I should have run. There were a million things I could have done. I was scared, at that point, and I didn't do any of them."

Pat testified that at this moment she feared that Rusk would rape her. She said: "[I]t was the way he looked at me, and said 'Come on up, come on up;' and when he took the keys, I knew that was wrong."

It was then about 1 a.m. Pat accompanied Rusk across the street into a totally dark house. She followed him up two flights of stairs. She neither saw nor heard anyone in the building. Once they ascended the stairs, Rusk unlocked the door to his one-room apartment, and turned on the light. According to Pat, he told her to sit down. She sat in a chair beside the bed. Rusk sat on the bed. After Rusk talked for a few minutes, he left the room for about one to five minutes. Pat remained seated in the chair. She made no noise and did not attempt to leave. She said that she did not notice a telephone in the room. When Rusk returned, he turned off the light and sat down on the bed. Pat asked if she could leave; she told him that she wanted to go home and "didn't want to come up." She said, " 'Now, [that] I came up, can I go?' " Rusk, who was still in possession of her car keys, said he wanted her to stay.

Rusk then asked Pat to get on the bed with him. He pulled her by the arms to the bed and began to undress her, removing her blouse and bra. He unzipped her slacks and she took them off after he told her to do so. Pat removed the rest of her clothing, and then removed Rusk's pants because "he asked me to do it." After they were both undressed Rusk started kissing Pat as she was lying on her back. Pat explained what happened next:

> "I was still begging him to please let, you know, let me leave. I said, 'you can get a lot of other girls down there, for what you want,' and he just kept saying, 'no'; and then I was really scared, because I can't describe, you know, what was said. It was more the look in his eyes; and I said, at that point—I didn't know what to say; and I said, 'If I do what you want, will you let me go without killing me?' Because I didn't know, at that point, what he was going to do; and I started to cry; and when I did, he put his hands on my throat, and started lightly to choke me; and I said, 'If I do what you want, will you let me go?' And he said, yes, and at that time, I proceeded to do what he wanted me to."

Pat testified that Rusk made her perform oral sex and then vaginal intercourse.

Immediately after the intercourse, Pat asked if she could leave. She testified that Rusk said, " 'Yes,' " after which she got up and got dressed and Rusk returned her car keys. She said that Rusk then "walked me to my car, and asked if he could see me again; and I said, 'Yes;' and he asked me for my telephone number; and I said, 'No, I'll see you down Fells Point sometime,' just so I could leave." Pat testified that she "had no intention of meeting him again." She asked him for directions out of the neighborhood and left.

On her way home, Pat stopped at a gas station, went to the ladies room, and then drove "pretty much straight home and pulled up and parked the car." At first she was not going to say anything about the incident. She explained her initial reaction not to report the incident: "I didn't want to go through what I'm going through now [at the trial]." As she sat in her car reflecting on the incident, Pat said she began to "wonder what would happen if I hadn't of done what he wanted me to do. So I thought the right thing to do was to go report it, and I went from there to Hillendale to find a police car." She reported the incident to the police at about 3:15 a.m. Subsequently, Pat took the police to Rusk's apartment, which she located without any great difficulty.

Pat's girlfriend Terry corroborated her testimony concerning the events which occurred up to the time that Pat left the bar with Rusk. Questioned about Pat's alcohol consumption, Terry said she was drinking screwdrivers that night but normally did not finish a drink. Terry testified about her acquaintanceship with Rusk: "I knew his face, and his first name, but I honestly couldn't tell you—apparently I ran into him sometime before. I couldn't tell you how I know him. I don't know him very well at all."

Officer Hammett of the Baltimore City Police Department acknowledged receiving Pat's rape complaint at 3:15 a.m. on September 22, 1977. He accompanied her to the 3100 block of Guilford Avenue where it took Pat several minutes to locate Rusk's apartment. Officer Hammett entered Rusk's multi-dwelling apartment house, which contained at least six apartments, and arrested Rusk in a room on the second floor.

Hammett testified that Pat was sober, and she was taken to City Hospital for an examination. The examination disclosed that seminal fluid and spermatozoa were detected in Pat's vagina, on her underpants, and on the bed sheets recovered from Rusk's bed.

* * *

Rusk, the 31-year-old defendant, testified that he was in the Buggs Tavern for about thirty minutes when he noticed Pat standing at the bar. Rusk said: "She looked at me, and she smiled. I walked over and said, hi, and started talking to her." He did not remember either knowing or speaking to Terry. When Pat mentioned that she was about to leave, Rusk asked her if she wanted to go home with him. In response, Pat said that she would like to, but could not because she had her car. Rusk then suggested that they take her car. Pat agreed and they left the bar arm-in-arm.

Rusk testified that during the drive to her apartment, he discussed with Pat their similar marital situations and talked about their children. He said that Pat asked him if he was going to rape her. When he inquired why she was asking, Pat said that she had been raped once before. Rusk expressed his sympathy for her. Pat then asked him if he planned to beat her. He inquired why she was asking and Pat explained that her husband used to beat her. Rusk again expressed his sympathy. He testified that at no time did Pat express a fear that she was being followed by her separated husband.

According to Rusk, when they arrived in front of his apartment Pat parked the car and turned the engine off. They sat for several minutes "petting each other." Rusk denied switching off the ignition and removing the keys. He said that they walked to the apartment house and proceeded up the stairs to his room. Rusk testified that Pat came willingly to his room and that at no time did he make threatening facial expressions. Once inside his room, Rusk left Pat alone for several minutes while he used the bathroom down the hall. Upon his return, he switched the light on but immediately turned it off because Pat, who was seated in the dark in a chair next to the bed, complained it was too bright. Rusk said that he sat on the bed across from Pat and reached out

> "and started to put my arms around her, and started kissing her; and we fell back into the bed, and she—we were petting, kissing, and she stuck her hand down in my pants and started playing with me; and I undid her blouse, and took off her bra; and then I sat up and I said 'Let's take our clothes off;' and she said, 'Okay;' and I took my clothes off, and she took her clothes off; and then we proceeded to have intercourse."

Rusk explained that after the intercourse, Pat "got uptight."

> "Well, she started to cry. She said that—she said, 'You guys are all alike,' she says, 'just out for,' you know, 'one thing.'
>
> "She started talking about—I don't know, she was crying and all. I tried to calm her down and all; and I said, 'What's the matter?' And she said, that she just wanted to leave; and I said, 'Well, okay;' and she walked out to the car. I walked out to the car. She got in the car and left."

Rusk denied placing his hands on Pat's throat or attempting to strangle her. He also denied using force or threats of force to get Pat to have intercourse with him.

In reversing Rusk's second degree rape conviction, the Court of Special Appeals, quoting from Hazel, 221 Md. at 469, 157 A.2d 922, noted that:

> "Force is an essential element of the crime [of rape] and to justify a conviction, the evidence must warrant a conclusion either that the victim resisted and her resistance was overcome by force or that she was prevented from resisting by threats to her safety."

Writing for the majority, Judge Thompson said:

> "In all of the victim's testimony we have been unable to see any resistance on her part to the sex acts and certainly can we see no fear as would overcome her attempt to resist or escape as required by *Hazel.* Possession of the keys by the accused may have deterred

> her vehicular escape but hardly a departure seeking help in the rooming house or in the street. We must say that 'the way he looked' fails utterly to support the fear required by *Hazel.*" 43 Md. App. at 480, 406 A.2d 624.

The Court of Special Appeals interpreted *Hazel* as requiring a showing of a reasonable apprehension of fear in instances where the prosecutrix did not resist. It concluded:

> "we find the evidence legally insufficient to warrant a conclusion that appellant's words or actions created in the mind of the victim a reasonable fear that if she resisted, he would have harmed her, or that faced with such resistance, he would have used force to overcome it. The prosecutrix stated that she was afraid, and submitted because of 'the look in his eyes.' After both were undressed and in the bed, and she pleaded to him that she wanted to leave, he started to lightly choke her. At oral argument it was brought out that the 'lightly choking' could have been a heavy caress. We do not believe that 'lightly choking' along with all the facts and circumstances in the case, were sufficient to cause a reasonable fear which overcame her ability to resist. In the absence of any other evidence showing force used by appellant, we find that the evidence was insufficient to convict appellant of rape." Id. at 484, 406 A.2d 624.

In argument before us on the merits of the case, the parties agreed that the issue was whether, in light of the principles of *Hazel,* there was evidence before the jury legally sufficient to prove beyond a reasonable doubt that the intercourse was "[b]y force or threat of force against the will and without the consent" of the victim in violation of Art. 27, § 463(a)(1). * * *

The vaginal intercourse once being established, the remaining elements of rape in the second degree under § 463(a)(1) are, as in a prosecution for common law rape (1) force—actual or constructive, and (2) lack of consent. The terms in § 463(a)(1)—"force," "threat of force," "against the will" and "without the consent"—are not defined in the statute, but are to be afforded their "judicially determined meaning" as applied in cases involving common law rape. See Art. 27, § 464E. * * *

* * *

As to the element of lack of consent, the Court said in *Hazel*:

> "[I]t is true, of course, that however reluctantly given, consent to the act at any time prior to penetration deprives the subsequent intercourse of its criminal character. There is, however, a wide difference between consent and a submission to the act. Consent may involve submission, but submission does not necessarily imply consent. Furthermore, submission to a compelling force, or as a result of being put in fear, is not consent." Id.

The Court noted that lack of consent is generally established through proof of resistance or by proof that the victim failed to resist because of fear. The degree of fear necessary to obviate the need to prove resistance, and thereby establish lack of consent, was defined in the following manner:

> "The kind of fear which would render resistance by a woman unnecessary to support a conviction of rape includes, but is not necessarily limited to, a fear of death or serious bodily harm, or a fear so extreme as to preclude resistance, or a fear which would well nigh render her mind incapable of continuing to resist, or a fear that so overpowers her that she does not dare resist." Id. at 470, 157 A.2d 922.

Hazel thus made it clear that lack of consent could be established through proof that the victim submitted as a result of fear of imminent death or serious bodily harm. In addition, if the actions and conduct of the defendant were reasonably calculated to induce this fear in the victim's mind, then the element of force is present. *Hazel* recognized, therefore, that the same kind of evidence may be used in establishing both force and non-consent, particularly when a threat rather than actual force is involved.

* * *

Hazel did not expressly determine whether the victim's fear must be "reasonable." Its only reference to reasonableness related to whether "the acts and threats of the defendant were reasonably calculated to create in the mind of the victim * * * a real apprehension, due to fear, of imminent bodily harm * * *." 221 Md. at 469, 157 A.2d 922. Manifestly, the Court was there referring to the calculations of the accused, not to the fear of the victim. While *Hazel* made it clear that the victim's fear had to be genuine, it did not pass upon whether a real but unreasonable fear of imminent death or serious bodily harm would suffice. The vast majority of jurisdictions have required that the victim's fear be reasonably grounded in order to obviate the need for either proof of actual force on the part of the assailant or physical resistance on the part of the victim. We think that, generally, this is the correct standard.

As earlier indicated, the Court of Special Appeals held that a showing of a reasonable apprehension of fear was essential under *Hazel* to establish the elements of the offense where the victim did not resist. The Court did not believe, however, that the evidence was legally sufficient to demonstrate the existence of "a reasonable fear" which overcame Pat's ability to resist. In support of the Court's conclusion, Rusk maintains that the evidence showed that Pat voluntarily entered his apartment without being subjected to a "single threat nor a scintilla of force"; that she made no effort to run away nor did she scream for help; that she never exhibited a will to resist; and that her subjective reaction of fear to the situation in which she had voluntarily placed herself was unreasonable and exaggerated. Rusk claims that his acts were not reasonably calculated to overcome a will to resist; that Pat's verbal resistance was not resistance within the contemplation of *Hazel*; that his alleged menacing look did not constitute a threat of force; and that even had he pulled Pat to the bed, and lightly choked her, as she claimed, these actions, viewed in the context of the entire incident—no prior threats having been made—would be insufficient to constitute force or a threat of force or render the intercourse non-consensual.

We think the reversal of Rusk's conviction by the Court of Special Appeals was in error for the fundamental reason so well expressed in the dissenting opinion by Judge Wilner when he observed that the majority had "trampled upon the first principle of appellate restraint * * * [because it had] substituted [its] own view of the evidence (and the inferences that may fairly be drawn from it) for that of the judge and jury * * * [and had thereby] improperly invaded the province allotted to those tribunals." 43 Md.App. at 484–85, 406 A.2d 624. In view of the evidence adduced at the trial, the reasonableness of Pat's apprehension of fear was plainly a question of fact for the jury to determine. * * * Of course, it was for the jury to observe the witnesses and their demeanor, and to judge their credibility and weigh their testimony. Quite obviously, the jury disbelieved Rusk and believed Pat's testimony. From her testimony, the jury could have reasonably concluded that the taking of her car keys was intended by Rusk to immobilize her alone, late at night, in a neighborhood with which she was not familiar; that after Pat had repeatedly refused to enter his apartment, Rusk commanded in firm tones that she do so; that Pat was badly frightened and feared that Rusk intended to rape her; that unable to think clearly and believing that she had no other choice in the circumstances, Pat entered Rusk's apartment; that once inside Pat asked permission to leave but Rusk told her to stay; that he then pulled Pat by the arms to the bed and undressed her; that Pat was afraid that Rusk would kill her unless she submitted; that she began to cry and Rusk then put his hands on her throat and began " 'lightly to choke' " her; that Pat asked him if he would let her go without killing her if she complied with his demands; that Rusk gave an affirmative response, after which she finally submitted.

Just where persuasion ends and force begins in cases like the present is essentially a factual issue, to be resolved in light of the controlling legal precepts. That threats of force need not be made in any particular manner in order to put a person in fear of bodily harm is well established. Indeed, conduct, rather than words, may convey the threat. That a victim did not scream out for help or attempt to escape, while bearing on the question of consent, is unnecessary where she is restrained by fear of violence.

Considering all of the evidence in the case, with particular focus upon the actual force applied by Rusk to Pat's neck, we conclude that the jury could rationally find that the essential elements of second degree rape had been established and that Rusk was guilty of that offense beyond a reasonable doubt.

JUDGMENT OF THE COURT OF SPECIAL APPEALS REVERSED; CASE REMANDED TO THAT COURT WITH DIRECTIONS THAT IT AFFIRM THE JUDGMENT OF THE CRIMINAL COURT OF BALTIMORE; COSTS TO BE PAID BY THE APPELLEE.

SMITH, DIGGES and COLE, JJ., dissent.

COLE, JUDGE, dissenting.

I agree with the Court of Special Appeals that the evidence adduced at the trial of Edward Salvatore Rusk was insufficient to convict him of rape. I, therefore, respectfully dissent.

The standard of appellate review in deciding a question of sufficiency, as the majority correctly notes, is "whether, after viewing the evidence in the light most favorable to the prosecution, *any* rational trier of fact could have found the essential elements of the crime beyond a reasonable doubt." Jackson v. Virginia, 443 U.S. 307, 319, 99 S.Ct. 2781, 2789, 61 L.Ed.2d 560 (1979) (emphasis in original); Tichnell v. State, 287 Md. 695, 415 A.2d 830 (1980). However, it is equally well settled that when one of the essential elements of a crime is not sustained by the evidence, the conviction of the defendant cannot stand as a matter of law.

The majority, in applying this standard, concludes that "[i]n view of the evidence adduced at the trial, the reasonableness of Pat's apprehension of fear was plainly a question of fact for the jury to determine." In so concluding, the majority has skipped over the crucial issue. It seems to me that whether the prosecutrix's fear is reasonable becomes a question only after the court determines that the defendant's conduct under the circumstances was reasonably calculated to give rise to a fear on her part to the extent that she was unable to resist. In other words, the fear must stem from his articulable conduct, and equally, if not more importantly, cannot be inconsistent with her own contemporaneous reaction to that conduct. The conduct of the defendant, in and of itself, must clearly indicate force or the threat of force such as to overpower the prosecutrix's ability to resist or will to resist. In my view, there is no evidence to support the majority's conclusion that the prosecutrix was forced to submit to sexual intercourse, certainly not fellatio.

* * *

* * * *Hazel* intended to require clear and cognizable evidence of force or the threat of force sufficient to overcome or prevent resistance by the female before there would arise a jury question of whether the prosecutrix had a reasonable apprehension of harm. The majority today departs from this requirement and places its imprimatur on the female's conclusory statements that she was in fear, as sufficient to support a conviction of rape.

It is significant to note that in each of the fourteen reported rape cases decided since *Hazel,* in which sufficiency of the evidence was the issue, the appellate courts of this State have adhered to the requirement that evidence of force or the threat of force overcoming or preventing resistance by the female must be demonstrated on the record to sustain a conviction. In two of those cases, Goldberg v. State, 41 Md.App. 58, 395 A.2d 1213, certiorari dismissed as improvidently granted, September 18, 1979, and Winegan v. State, 10 Md.App. 196, 268 A.2d 585 (1970), the convictions were reversed by the Court of Special Appeals. *Goldberg* concerned a student, professing to be a talent agent, who lured a young woman to an apartment upon the pretext of offering her a modeling job. She freely accompanied him, and though she protested verbally, she did not physically resist his advances. The Court of Special Appeals held:

> The prosecutrix swore that the reasons for her fear of being killed if she did not accede to appellant's advances were two-fold: (1) she was alone with the appellant in a house with no buildings close by

> and no one to help her if she resisted, and (2) the appellant was much larger than she was. In the complete absence of any threatening words or actions by the appellant, these two factors, as a matter of law, are simply not enough to have created a reasonable fear of harm so as to preclude resistance and be "the equivalent of force". (Hazel v. State, supra, [221 Md. 464], at 469, [157 A.2d 922].) Without proof of force, actual or constructive, evidenced by words or conduct of the defendant or those acting in consort with him, sexual intercourse is not rape. [41 Md.App. at 69, 395 A.2d 1213.] [Footnote omitted.]

In *Winegan,* the appellant's conviction was reversed because, although the prosecutrix accompanied him to a boarding house and had sexual intercourse only because she thought he had a gun, *he in fact had no gun nor at any time claimed to have one.* It was on this basis, coupled with the facts that (1) the complainant at no time made outcry and (2) *she followed him up the steps to his room,* that the court concluded that her fear, if actually present, was so unreasonable as to preclude a conviction for rape.

Of the other twelve cases, four from this Court, not one contains the paucity of evidence regarding force or threat of force which exists in the case *sub judice.* * * *

* * *

In each of the above 12 cases there was either physical violence or specific threatening words or conduct which were calculated to create a very real and specific fear of *immediate* physical injury to the victim if she did not comply, coupled with the apparent power to execute those threats in the event of non-submission.

While courts no longer require a female to resist to the utmost or to resist where resistance would be foolhardy, they do require her acquiescence in the act of intercourse to stem from fear generated by something of substance. She may not simply say, "I was really scared," and thereby transform consent or mere unwillingness into submission by force. These words do not transform a seducer into a rapist. She must follow the natural instinct of every proud female to resist, by more than mere words, the violation of her person by a stranger or an unwelcomed friend. She must make it plain that she regards such sexual acts as abhorrent and repugnant to her natural sense of pride. She must resist unless the defendant has objectively manifested his intent to use physical force to accomplish his purpose. The law regards rape as a crime of violence. The majority today attenuates this proposition. It declares the innocence of an at best distraught young woman. It does not demonstrate the defendant's guilt of the crime of rape.

My examination of the evidence in a light most favorable to the State reveals no conduct by the defendant reasonably calculated to cause the prosecutrix to be so fearful that she should fail to resist and thus, the element of force is lacking in the State's proof.

Here we have a full grown married woman who meets the defendant in a bar under friendly circumstances. They drink and talk together. She agrees to give him a ride home in her car. When they arrive at his house, located in an area with which she was unfamiliar but which was certainly not isolated, he invites her to come up to his apartment and she refuses. According to her testimony he takes her keys, walks around to her side of the car, and says "Now will you come up?" She answers, "yes." The majority suggests that "from her testimony the jury could have reasonably concluded that the taking of her keys was intended by Rusk to immobilize her alone, late at night, in a neighborhood with which she was unfamiliar * * *." But on what facts does the majority so conclude? There is no evidence descriptive of the tone of his voice; her testimony indicates only the bare statement quoted above. How can the majority extract from this conduct a threat reasonably calculated to create a fear of imminent bodily harm? There was no weapon, no threat to inflict physical injury.

She also testified that she was afraid of "the way he looked," and afraid of his statement, "come on up, come on up." But what can the majority conclude from this statement coupled with a "look" that remained undescribed? There is no evidence whatsoever to suggest that this was anything other than a pattern of conduct consistent with the ordinary seduction of a female acquaintance who at first suggests her disinclination.

After reaching the room she described what occurred as follows:

> I was still begging him to please let, you know, let me leave. I said, "you can get a lot of other girls down there, for what you want," and he just kept saying, "no," and then I was really scared, because I can't describe, you know, what was said. It was more the look in his eyes; and I said, at that point—I didn't know what to say; and I said, "If I do what you want, will you let me go without killing me?" Because I didn't know, at that point, what he was going to do; and I started to cry; and when I did, he put his hands on my throat and started lightly to choke me; and I said "If I do what you want, will you let me go?" And he said, yes, and at that time. I proceeded to do what he wanted me to.

The majority relies on the trial court's statement that the defendant responded affirmatively to her question "If I do what you want, will you let me go without killing me?" The majority further suggests that the jury could infer the defendant's affirmative response. The facts belie such inference since by the prosecutrix's own testimony the defendant made *no* response. *He said nothing!*

She then testified that she started to cry and he "started lightly to choke" her, whatever that means. Obviously, the choking was not of any persuasive significance. During this "choking" she was able to talk. She said "If I do what you want will you let me go?" It was at this point that the defendant said yes.

I find it incredible for the majority to conclude that on these facts, without more, a woman was *forced* to commit oral sex upon the defendant and then to engage in vaginal intercourse. In the absence of any verbal threat to do her grievous bodily harm or the display of any weapon and threat to use it, I find it difficult to understand how a victim could participate in these sexual activities and not be willing.

What was the nature and extent of her fear anyhow? She herself testified she was "fearful that maybe I had someone following me." She was afraid because she didn't know him and she was afraid he was going to "rape" her. But there are no acts or conduct on the part of the defendant to suggest that these fears were created by the defendant or that he made any objective, identifiable threats to her which would give rise to this woman's failure to flee, summon help, scream, or make physical resistance.

As the defendant well knew, this was not a child. This was a married woman with children, a woman familiar with the social setting in which these two actors met. It was an ordinary city street, not an isolated spot. He had not forced his way into her car; he had not taken advantage of a difference in years or any state of intoxication or mental or physical incapacity on her part. He did not grapple with her. She got out of the car, *walked with him* across the street and *followed* him up the stairs to his room. She certainly had to realize that they were not going upstairs to play *Scrabble*.

Once in the room she waited while he went to the bathroom where he stayed for five minutes. In his absence, the room was lighted but she did not seek a means of escape. She did not even "try the door" to determine if it was locked. She waited.

Upon his return, he turned off the lights and pulled her on the bed. There is no suggestion or inference to be drawn from her testimony that he yanked her on the bed or in any manner physically abused her by this conduct. As a matter of fact there is no suggestion by her that he bruised or hurt her in any manner, or that the "choking" was intended to be disabling.

He then proceeded to unbutton her blouse and her bra. He did not rip her clothes off or use any greater force than was necessary to unfasten her garments. He did not even complete this procedure but requested that she do it, which she did "because he asked me to." However, she not only removed her clothing but took his clothes off, too.

Then for a while they lay together on the bed kissing, though she says she did not return his kisses. However, without protest she then proceeded to perform oral sex and later submitted to vaginal intercourse. After these activities were completed, she asked to leave. They dressed and he walked her to her car and asked to see her again. She indicated that perhaps they might meet at Fells Point. He gave her directions home and returned to his apartment where the police found him later that morning.

The record does not disclose the basis for this young woman's misgivings about her experience with the defendant. The only substantive fear she had was that she would be late arriving home. The objective facts make it inherently improbable that the defendant's conduct generated any fear for her physical well-being.

In my judgment the State failed to prove the essential element of force beyond a reasonable doubt and, therefore, the judgment of conviction should be reversed.

JUDGES SMITH and DIGGES have authorized me to state that they concur in the views expressed herein.

Note: The Victim's Behavior

1. *The Rape Trauma Syndrome.* State v. Black, 109 Wn.2d 336, 346–346, 745 P.2d 12, 16–18 (1987):

> The term "rape trauma syndrome" was first coined by Ann Burgess and Lynda Holmstrom in the 1974 article * * * describing symptoms commonly experienced by victims of rape. Burgess & Holmstrom, *Rape Trauma Syndrome,* 131 Am.J. Psychiatry 981 (1974). The authors state at page 982:
>
>> Rape trauma syndrome is the acute phase and long-term reorganization process that occurs as a result of forcible rape or attempted forcible rape. This syndrome of behavioral, somatic, and psychological reactions is an acute stress reaction to a lifethreatening situation.
>
> Studies conducted by both Burgess and Holmstrom and other authors assert that victims of rape may display any of a wide ranging variety of symptoms. In the acute phase, (immediately after the rape) any or all of the following may be observed: physical trauma, tension headaches, sleep pattern disturbances, gastrointestinal irritability, humiliation, embarrassment, anger, revenge, and self-blame. In the "long-term reorganization process", victims may display a number of additional symptoms, including: nightmares, changing one's residence, changing one's phone number, fear of indoors, fear of outdoors, fear of being alone, fear of crowds, fear of men, and sexual fears.
>
> One overriding theme permeates the literature on this subject: namely, that there is no "typical" response to rape. One commentator explains,
>
>> [e]ach rape victim responds to and integrates the experience differently depending on her age, life situation, the circumstances of the rape, her specific personality style, and the responses of those from whom she seeks support.
>
> Notman & Nadelson, *The Rape Victim: Psychodynamic Considerations,* 133 Am.J. Psychiatry 408, 409 (1976). Thus, the symptoms displayed by victims occur in various combinations and sequences. Moreover, Burgess & Holmstrom concede that victims of rape may display one of two directly conflicting emotional manifestations which are referred to as "styles". Some women display an "expressed style" (outwardly emotional) while others display a "controlled style" (calm, composed and subdued). Among the latter group, some display no visible symptoms at all.
>
> Because the symptoms associated with "rape trauma syndrome" embrace such a broad spectrum of human behavior, the syndrome provides a highly questionable means of identifying victims of rape. Indeed, the American Psychiatric Association indicates that the stress and trauma associated with rape is merely one type of a larger phenomenon known as "post-traumatic stress disorder" (PTSD). Similar symptoms may be triggered by any psychologically traumatic event that is "generally outside the range of usual human experience", including simple bereavement, chronic illness, marital conflict, assault, military combat, natural disasters, automobile accidents, bombing, or torture. American Psychiatric Ass'n, *Diagnostic and Statistical Manual of Mental Disorders* 236–38 (3d ed. 1980); see also Horowitz, Wilner, Kaltreider, & Alvarez, *Signs and Symptoms of Posttrau-*

matic Stress Disorder, 37 Archives of Gen. Psychiatry 85 (1980). Even those symptoms more especially applicable to sexual experiences may not be caused by rape. Authorities indicate that they may be caused by any "sexually stressful experience". See Notman & Nadelson, at 408; Note, *Checking the Allure of Increased Conviction Rates: The Admissibility of Expert Testimony on Rape Trauma Syndrome in Criminal Proceedings,* 70 Va.L.Rev. 1657, 1696 (1984).

Several authors have also criticized the methodology of the studies which have been conducted to determine symptoms of rape victims. Among the shortcomings cited are the following: (1) differences in definitions and criteria for "rape"; (2) unrepresentative, biased, or inadequate sampling of victims; (3) inadequate means of eliciting information about victims; (4) lack of long-term assessments of victims; and (5) lack of a control group (i.e., a group of nonraped women) against which to compare the symptoms observed in rape victims. Ruch & Leon, *Type of Sexual Assault Trauma: A Multidimensional Analysis of a Shortterm Panel,* 8 Victimology 237, 238–39 (1983); Kilpatrick, Resick & Veronen, *Effects of a Rape Experience: A Longitudinal Study,* 37 J.Soc. Issues 105, 108–09 (1981); Kilpatrick, Veronen & Resick, *The Aftermath of Rape: Recent Empirical Findings,* 49 Am.J. of Orthopsychiatry 658, 658–59 (1979); S. Katz & M. Mazur, at 3–27; Note, 70 Va.L.Rev. at 1667–80. One commentator succinctly describes the inherent difficulties in conducting reliable studies:

> It is difficult to design a scientific study investigating the impact of sexual assault on survivors. A controlled study would require obtaining data from a large sample of women, following these women over time, and later reassessing the sample to determine the incidence and impact of sexual assault. However, such a study is not feasible.

J. Becker, L. Skinner, & G. Abel, *Sequelae of Sexual Assault: The Survivor's Perspective,* in *The Sexual Aggressor: Current Perspectives on Treatment* 263 (1983). Largely because of these methodological shortcomings, "available studies are inconsistent as to the length of recovery time and the variables affecting the dynamics of rape victimization." Ruch & Leon, at 239.

These findings cast grave doubt on the reliability of employing "rape trauma syndrome" to prove that an alleged victim was, in fact, raped. * * *

The admissibility of expert testimony on rape trauma syndrome has been considered in a number of other jurisdictions. The courts are sharply divided on the issue. Some have held such testimony inadmissible to prove that the alleged victim did not consent to intercourse and was, therefore, raped. State v. Saldana, 324 N.W.2d 227 (Minn.1982); State v. Taylor, 663 S.W.2d 235 (Mo.1984); People v. Bledsoe, 36 Cal.3d 236, 681 P.2d 291, 203 Cal. Rptr. 450 (1984). Others have held such testimony admissible for this purpose. State v. Marks, 231 Kan. 645, 647 P.2d 1292 (1982); State v. Liddell, [211] Mont. [180], 685 P.2d 918 (1984); State v. Huey, 145 Ariz. 59, 699 P.2d 1290 (1985); State v. Allewalt, 308 Md. 89, 517 A.2d 741 (1986) (5–to–2 opinion held testimony on "post-traumatic stress disorder" admissible in rape case to prove lack of consent).

We find the opinions which exclude the testimony persuasive. * * *

In *Bledsoe,* 36 Cal.3d at 250, 681 P.2d 291, 203 Cal.Rptr. 450, the California Supreme Court emphasized that rape trauma syndrome was not intended to be a forensic, fact-finding device. Rather, it is an " 'umbrella' concept reflecting the broad range of emotional trauma experienced by clients of rape counselors." The court cogently points out how rape trauma syndrome differs significantly from other seemingly similar methods of proof:

> There is, however, a fundamental difference between rape trauma syndrome and both the battered child syndrome and the other scientific methods of proof that have in the past been evaluated against the *Frye* standard of reliability. Unlike fingerprints, blood tests, lie detector tests, voiceprints or the battered child syndrome, rape trauma syndrome was not devised to determine the "truth" or "accuracy" of a particular past event—i.e., whether, in fact, a rape in the legal sense occurred—but rather was developed by professional rape counselors as a therapeutic tool, to help identify, predict and treat emotional problems experienced by the counselors' clients or patients. As the professional literature makes clear—and as the expert testimony in this case also reveals—because in the past women who have brought charges of rape have traditionally had their credibility or motives questioned by the police and others, rape counselors are taught to make a conscious effort to avoid judging the credibility of their clients. As one expert in the field recently wrote: "When a woman seeks services from a psychologist, she wants and deserves help for her problems, not judgment. *Judgment is appropriate for courtrooms, not for psychologists' offices* * * *."
>
> Thus, as a rule, rape counselors do not probe inconsistencies in their clients' descriptions of the facts of the incident, nor do they conduct independent investigations to determine whether other evidence corroborates or contradicts their clients' renditions. Because their function is to help their clients deal with the trauma they are experiencing, the historical accuracy of the clients' descriptions of the details of the traumatizing events is not vital in their task.
>
> (Footnotes and citation omitted.) *Bledsoe,* at 249–50, 681 P.2d 291, 203 Cal.Rptr. 450.

The *Bledsoe* court did think that expert testimony on the syndrome might be properly admitted to disabuse the jury of misconceptions about rape and rape victims, so that it could evaluate the evidence free of mythology, even if it was not admissible to show that a rape had occurred.

2. *Should the rape victim resist?* People v. Barnes, 42 Cal.3d 284, 299–301, 228 Cal.Rptr. 228, 237–238, 721 P.2d 110, 118–120 (1986):

> Recently * * * the entire concept of resistance to sexual assault has been called into question. (See generally Note, *Elimination of the Resistance Requirement and Other Rape Law Reforms: The New York Experience* (1983) 47 Alb.L.Rev. 871 [hereafter *Elimination of Resistance*]; Schwartz, *An Argument for the Elimination of the Resistance from the Definition of Forcible Rape* (1983) 16 Loyola L.A.L.Rev. 567 [hereafter *Resistance Requirement*].) It has been suggested that while the presence of resistance may well be probative on the issue of force or nonconsent, its absence may not.

For example, some studies have demonstrated that while some women respond to sexual assault with active resistance, others "freeze." (See Queen's Bench Foundation, Rape Prevention and Resistance (1976) p. 18 [hereafter *QBF*]; Symonds, *The Rape Victim: Psychological Patterns of Response* (1976) 36 Am.J.Psychoanalysis 27, 29–33; Amir, Patterns in Forcible Rape (1971) pp. 163–164; *Resistance Requirement, supra,* 16 Loyola L.A.L.Rev. at p. 577.) One researcher found that many women demonstrate "psychological infantilism"—a frozen fright response—in the face of sexual assault. (Symonds, supra, 26 Am.J.Psychoanalysis at p. 30; see also *QBF,* supra, at pp. 18–20 [reporting that some women "freeze" and become helpless from panic and numbing fear].) The "frozen fright" response resembles cooperative behavior. (Symonds, supra, 26 Am.J.Psychoanalysis at p. 30.) Indeed, as Symonds notes, the "victim may smile, even initiate acts, and may appear relaxed and calm." (Ibid.) Subjectively, however, she may be in a state of terror. (Ibid.) Symonds also reports that the victim may make submissive signs to her assailant and engage in propitiating behavior in an effort to inhibit further aggression. (Id., at pp. 30–31.) These findings belie the traditional notion that a woman who does not resist has consented. They suggest that lack of physical resistance may reflect a "profound primal terror" rather than consent. (Id., at p. 30; see also Note, *Shifting the Communication Burden: A Meaningful Consent Standard in Rape* (1983) 6 Harv. Women's L.J. 143, 148, fn. 29.)

Additionally, a growing body of authority holds that to resist in the face of sexual assault is to risk further injury. (*Elimination of Resistance,* supra, 47 Alb.L.Rev. at p. 872; United States Dept. of Justice, Forcible Rape: A National Survey of the Response by Prosecutors (1977) vol. 1, pp. 14–15 [reporting that the likelihood of receiving injuries requiring medical treatment nearly doubled when victims resisted assailants]; *Forcible Rape,* supra, 61 Va.L.Rev. at p. 1506 [resistance is inadvisable since it may provoke greater injury]; Amir, Patterns in Forcible Rape, supra, at pp. 164–165; [*Comment, Towards a*] Consent Standard [*in the Law of Rape* (1976)], 43 U.Chi.L.Rev. [613,] 626–627.)

In a 1976 study of rape victims and offenders, the Queen's Bench Foundation found that over half of the sexual assault offenders studied reported becoming more violent in response to victim resistance. (*QBF,* supra, at p. 85.) Injury as reported by victims correlated with some form of resistance, including verbal stalling, struggling and slapping. (Id., at p. 108.) Those victims who resisted during coitus suffered increased violence as the assailant forced compliance. (Id., at p. 84.) Victim resistance, whether passive or active, tended to precede an increase or intensification of the assailant's violence. (Id., at p. 85; accord Amir, Patterns in Forcible Rape, supra, at pp. 164–165, 169–171 [victim resistance in some instances serves to provoke more physical brutality and sexual humiliation].)

On the other hand, other findings indicate that resistance has a direct correlation with *deterring* sexual assault. (*QBF,* supra, at p. 105.) Of the 75 convicted rapists the Queen's Bench Foundation questioned, half believed that their sexual assaults could have been deterred by active victim resistance. (Id., at p. 109.) Brownmiller argues that submissive behavior is *not* necessarily helpful to a rape victim and suggests that strong resistance on the part of women can thwart rape. (Brownmiller, [Against Our Will, Men,

Women and Rape (1975)], at pp. 357, 360–361.) She suggests it would be well for women to undergo systematic training in self-defense in order to fight back against their attackers. (Id., at pp. 403–404.)

Reflecting the foregoing uncertainties about the advisability of resistance, the Queen's Bench Foundation concluded: "Overall, the research findings suggest that rape prevention is more possible through vigorous resistance[;] however, resistance incurs greater risk of injury. When confronted with attack, each woman must make a choice which is highly personal and may be affected by situational factors beyond her control." (*QBF,* supra, at p. 109.) These conclusions are also contained in a pamphlet for distribution to the general public in which the reader is advised that physical resistance may increase the danger or may thwart the attack; the woman must therefore evaluate the threat she faces and decide how to react based on the kind of person she is. (Rape (Queen's Bench Foundation, undated pamp.)[)]

* * *. * * *

Question

Upon what principles should the *Rusk* case be decided? What is the proper legal issue?

People v. Cash

Supreme Court of Michigan, 1984.
419 Mich. 230, 351 N.W.2d 822.

WILLIAMS, CHIEF JUSTICE.

* * *

On the evening of September 23, 1979, the complainant, who was one month shy of her 16th birthday, met the defendant at a Greyhound bus station in Detroit. The complainant was running away from home at the time. After talking with complainant for a couple of hours and gaining her trust, defendant persuaded complainant to accompany him on a drive in his car. They drove to a motel in Marshall, Michigan, where two separate acts of sexual intercourse took place. The complainant managed to leave the motel room undetected after defendant fell asleep, and awakened the person in charge of the motel, who in turn called the police. The defendant was charged with two counts of third-degree criminal sexual conduct, namely, engaging in sexual penetration with a person between the ages of 13 and 16 years. Documents found in the court file indicate that at the time of the offense, the defendant was 30 years old.

At the preliminary examination, complainant admitted that she told defendant that she was 17 years old. The defendant had also indicated to the police at the time of his arrest that the complainant told him she was 17. The complainant was described by defendant as being 5′ 8″ tall and weighing about 165 pounds.

* * *

The trial court instructed the jury that the defense theory was one of mistake of fact and that defendant reasonably believed that complainant had reached the age of consent. Over defendant's objection, the court later instructed the jury that "[i]t is no defense that the defendant believed that [the complainant] was 16 years old or older at the time of the alleged act".

The defendant was found guilty by the jury of third-degree criminal sexual conduct, M.C.L. § 750.520d(1)(a); M.S.A. § 28.788(4)(1)(a), and was sentenced to a term of from 5 to 15 years in prison. The Court of Appeals affirmed defendant's conviction in an unpublished per curiam opinion. * * *

This Court first stated that a good-faith or reasonable mistake as to the complainant's age is not a defense to a statutory rape charge in People v. Gengels, 218 Mich. 632, 188 N.W. 398 (1922), nearly 61 years ago. In that case, the defendant was convicted under the predecessor to the current criminal sexual conduct statute of carnally knowing a female child under 16 years of age. * * *

* * *

This Court for the first time has the opportunity to review the rule announced in *Gengels* and determine whether it is still viable under the successor provision of the third-degree criminal sexual conduct statute and, if so, whether it comports with a defendant's right to due process.

The statute reads, in relevant part:

> "(1) A person is guilty of criminal sexual conduct in the third degree if the person engages in sexual penetration with another person and if any of the following circumstances exists:
>
> "(a) That other person is at least 13 years of age and under 16 years of age." M.C.L. § 750.520d; M.S.A. § 28.788(4). * * *

In the present case, defendant directly attacks the constitutionality of the above statute on due process grounds for imposing criminal liability without requiring proof of specific criminal intent, *i.e.,* that the accused know that the victim is below the statutory age of consent. In particular, he argues that the crime of statutory rape is rooted in the common law and, as with other common-law offenses, the element of intent must be implied within the statutory definition of a crime, absent clear legislative language to the contrary: We are urged by defendant to construe the statute's silence with respect to the element of intent as not negating the defense of a reasonable mistake of fact as to the complainant's age.

In support of his argument, defendant relies primarily on two out-of-state cases which represent the minority view that, in a statutory rape prosecution, an accused's reasonable, though mistaken, belief that the complainant was of the age of consent is a valid defense.[5] People v. Hernandez, 61 Cal.2d 529, 39 Cal.Rptr. 361, 393 P.2d 673 (1964); State v. Guest, 583 P.2d 836 (Alas.,

5. See generally Anno: *Mistake or Lack of Information as to Victim's Age as Defense to Statutory Rape,* 8 A.L.R.3d 1100.

A few states have adopted, by statute, the reasonable-mistake-of-age defense in statutory rape cases. See, e.g., Alas.Rev.Stat. § 11.41.445(b); Ariz.Rev.Stat.Ann. § 13–1407(B); Ark.Stat.Ann. § 41–1802(3); Ill.Ann. Stat. ch. 38, § 11–4(c) (Smith–Hurd); Ky.Rev. Stat. § 510.030; Mont.Rev.Codes Ann. § 45–5–506(1); Wash.Rev.Code § 9A.44.030(2).

This defense has also been adopted in limited fashion in the 1962 Proposed Draft of the Model Penal Code § 213.6(1), which reads:

> "(1) *Mistake as to Age.* Whenever in this Article the criminality of conduct depends on a child's being below the age of 10, it is no defense that the actor did not

1978). In both these cases, the Court engrafted a *mens rea* element onto the statutes in question where they were otherwise silent as to any requisite criminal intent.

The vast majority of states, as well as the federal courts, which have considered this identical issue have rejected defendant's arguments and do not recognize the defense of a reasonable mistake of age to a statutory rape charge. For the reasons discussed below, we agree with the majority's position.

* * *

First, a general rule of statutory construction is that the Legislature is "presumed to know of and legislate in harmony with existing laws". People v. Harrison, 194 Mich. 363, 369, 160 N.W. 623 (1916). The Legislature must have been aware of our earlier decision rejecting the reasonable-mistake-of-age defense under the old statutory rape statute. Had the Legislature desired to revise the existing law by allowing for a reasonable-mistake-of-age defense, it could have done so, but it did not do so. * * *

Second, while the crime of statutory rape has its origins in the English common law,[9] Michigan's new criminal sexual conduct statute represents a major attempt by the Legislature to redefine the law of sexually assaultive crimes, including that of statutory rape. It is well established that the Legislature may, pursuant to its police powers, define criminal offenses without requiring proof of a specific criminal intent and so provide that the perpetrator proceed at his own peril regardless of his defense of ignorance or an honest mistake of fact. In the case of statutory rape, such legislation, in the nature of "strict liability" offenses, has been upheld as a matter of public policy because of the need to protect children below a specified age from sexual intercourse on the presumption that their immaturity and innocence prevents them from appreciating the full magnitude and consequences of their conduct.

* * *

One critic has argued that the exclusion of a reasonable-mistake-of-age defense in statutory rape cases is no longer justified given the increased age of consent,[11] the realities of modern society that young teens are more sexually mature, and the seriousness of the penalty as compared with other strict liability offenses.[12] We are not convinced that the policy behind the statutory rape laws of protecting children from sexual exploitation and possible physical or psychological harm from engaging in sexual intercourse is outmoded.

know the child's age, or reasonably believed the child to be older than 10. When criminality depends on the child's being below a critical age other than 10, it is a defense for the actor to prove that he reasonably believed the child to be above the critical age."

9. For a thorough discussion of the history of statutory rape law, tracing its development from thirteenth-century England, see Myers, *Reasonable Mistake of Age: A Needed Defense to Statutory Rape,* 64 Mich.L.Rev. 105, 109–111 (1965); see also Hall, General Principles of Criminal Law (2d ed), pp. 338–339, 373–376.

11. The statutory age of consent has gradually risen from the original age of 10 years old to 16 on up to 21, varying among the states. See Myers, fn. 9 supra, pp. 110–111, fn. 44.

12. See Myers, fn. 9 supra, pp. 125–127. The penalty for third-degree criminal sexual conduct is up to a maximum of 15 years imprisonment. M.C.L. § 750.520d(2); M.S.A. § 28.788(4)(2).

Indeed, the United States Supreme Court recently acknowledged the state's authority to regulate the sexual behavior of minors in order to promote their physical and mental well-being, even under a gender-based statutory rape law.[13]

Contrary to defendant's contention, the mistake-of-age defense, at least with regard to statutory rape crimes, is not constitutionally mandated. * * *

Moreover, given the already highly emotional setting of a statutory rape trial, the allowance of a mistake-of-age defense would only cause additional undue focus on the complainant by the jury's scrutinizing her appearance and any other visible signs of maturity. The obvious problem is that because early adolescents tend to grow at a rapid rate, by the time of trial a relatively undeveloped young girl or boy may have transformed into a young woman or man. A better procedure would be to permit any mitigating and ameliorating evidence in support of a defendant's mistaken belief as to the complainant's age to be considered by the trial judge at the time of sentencing.[14]

* * *

Accordingly, we affirm defendant's conviction.

BOYLE, CAVANAGH, BRICKLEY and RYAN, JJ., concur.

KAVANAGH, JUSTICE.

* * *

Disallowing a defense of reasonable mistake of fact obviates proof of *mens rea.* While this practice has been approved in misdemeanor cases, we are cited no case, nor has our research uncovered one, wherein this Court has sanctioned it in felony cases.

Recognizing the defense of a reasonable mistake of age to a charge of statutory rape, however, does not imply that the defendant must have in fact known the person was under age. Instead, when the defense is raised, the factfinder need only determine whether the defendant honestly believed that the prosecutrix was an adult and, if so, whether the belief was reasonable.

Reasonable mistake of age should not be confused with the rule that a person under the statutory age is legally incapable of consent. Consent of the underage person is not the issue here. It is the defendant's state of mind. The gravamen of the charged offense is voluntary intercourse with an underage person. Just as proof of coercion of a defendant would defeat the charge, so should defendant's reasonable mistake of the fact of age. In neither instance could there be *mens rea,* for in each case there would be no free election to do the thing forbidden.

LEVIN, J., concurs.

13. See Michael M. v. Superior Court of Sonoma County, 450 U.S. 464, 472, fn. 8, 101 S.Ct. 1200, 1209, fn. 8, 67 L.Ed.2d 437 (1981), wherein the court upheld, against an equal protection challenge, California's statutory rape law which exclusively punished male perpetrators.

14. See State v. Elton, 657 P.2d 1261, 1262 (Utah, 1982). For example, some mitigating factors which a trial judge may take into consideration in imposing a sentence are the relative ages and relationship of the parties involved. We note that a more sympathetic sentencing situation would have been presented than in the case at bar had a 17–year–old defendant been prosecuted for relations with his almost 16–year–old girlfriend.

Questions

1. W is of an age at which statutory rape would occur if D had sexual intercourse with her when they were not married, but they are validly married and such intercourse is not criminal. Unknown to D, W has an identical twin sister V, and D has sexual intercourse with V, reasonably believing her to be W. In a jurisdiction which follows *Cash,* is D guilty of statutory rape? Cf. Reg. v. Fotheringham, 88 Crim. App. 206 (Ct.App. (Crim.Div.) 1988), where the charge was rape, and the accused claimed to have been so drunk that he thought that his fourteen year old babysitter was his wife. The court was unsympathetic, but the mistake was unreasonable.

2. How should the policy questions raised in *Cash* be decided?

United States v. Short

United States Court of Military Appeals, 1954.
4 U.S.C.M.A. 437, 16 C.M.R. 11.

ROBERT E. QUINN, CHIEF JUDGE.

A general court-martial in Japan convicted the accused of assault with intent to commit rape, and sentenced him to dishonorable discharge, total forfeitures, and confinement at hard labor for ten years. The convening authority modified the sentence by reducing the period of confinement to five years. A board of review affirmed the conviction and the modified sentence. We granted review to consider the correctness of the law officer's general instructions and his denial of certain defense requests for specific instructions.

The events of this case took place on November 28, 1952, in Tokyo. At about 11:30 p.m., two Japanese girls, Yayoi Tomobe and Tokiko Okano, left the shop in which they worked to dispose of some waste paper in a public latrine located across the street. Apparently as the girls were crossing the street, they were approached from behind by the accused and his companion, Private O'Rourke. From their speech, Okano deduced that the "foreigners" were intoxicated. She was frightened. Calling out to Tomobe to run, Okano ran back to the shop. Tomobe, however, tripped over a stone. As she regained her balance, she was caught under her right arm by the accused. The accused spoke to her in English. Although she had learned some English in school, she was "so scared and * * * surprised" that she did not know what was said, except that there was mention of yen. She was then pulled to the front of the latrine and pushed in. The accused entered and closed the door.

Tomobe tried to get away from the accused, but he was "very big." She was "scared" and "had no strength to go out." While the accused did not punch, kick, or otherwise inflict bodily harm upon her, he fondled her person against her protests. She kept saying "No" in Japanese as loudly as she could. She pushed the accused away, but he was "so strong that [she] was unable to hold him away."

In the meantime, Okano, having seen Tomobe pulled into the latrine, reported to the manager of the shop. He immediately went to the latrine and opened the door. He heard Tomobe saying "No," and he saw the accused holding her. However, just then O'Rourke tapped him on the shoulder and he made no further effort to interfere. Instead, he went to a police box, located approximately forty feet from the latrine, and reported the matter to the Japanese policemen. They hastened to the latrine. One of the policemen opened the door, and in Japanese called out to the accused to stop. In the same language, the accused replied that it was all right. Then he was forcibly removed from the latrine, and taken to the police box.

At the trial, the accused admitted fondling Tomobe, as set out in the specification. However, he denied that he acted unlawfully. He testified that when he saw Tomobe, he thought she was a prostitute since the area was known to be frequented by them. He "propositioned" her, and after some negotiation they agreed on a price of 500 yen. Tomobe showed him the latrine; he previously did not know of its existence. Inside, Tomobe helped him in his efforts to "make love to her." Although he was "under the influence," he was generally aware of what he was doing. When the police entered the latrine, he thought that they wanted to arrest the girl as a prostitute. He told them that it was all right because he was anxious to protect her.

* * *

* * * Each counsel submitted requests for specific instructions. With some modification, one of the three offered by the prosecution was accepted; the two submitted by the defense were rejected. The defense requests are as follows:

> "The essential elements of non-consent, or that the act be against the woman's will, signifies that it be committed against the utmost reluctance and resistance which the woman is capable of making at the time.
>
> "In order to constitute an offense, the accused must think victim is not consenting because he must intend not only to have carnal knowledge of the woman but to do so by force.
>
> "The guilt or innocence of the accused depends on the circumstances as they appear to him."

* * *

* * * We assume for the purposes of this case that sufficient evidence appears in the record from which it may reasonably be inferred the accused believed that Tomobe consented to his "proposition." However, the question still to be answered is whether the instruction requested is legally correct. The accused stresses the similarity of the requested instruction to that in McQuirk v. State, 84 Ala 435, 4 So 775. In that case the accused was charged with rape. The evidence showed that the prosecutrix was weak-minded. The defendant maintained that he believed she had consented to the act. He requested the following instruction which was denied by the trial judge:

> "If the jury believe, from the evidence, that the conduct of the prosecutrix was such towards the defendant, at the time of the alleged rape, as to create in the mind of the defendant the honest and reasonable belief that she had consented, or was willing for

defendant to have connection with her, they must acquit the defendant."

On appeal the conviction was reversed because of the failure of the trial judge to give the requested instruction.

It is immediately apparent that the requested instruction in this case is markedly different from that in McQuirk. It fails to qualify the accused's belief by requiring that it be reasonable and honest. See also: 44 Am Jur, Rape, § 12, page 909; United States v. Perruccio, 4 USCMA 28, 15 CMR 28. This omission is substantial. The requested instruction also assumes too much. When consent is in issue, whether or not it was given is a question of fact for the court. It, not the accused, must determine whether the woman's conduct was such as to lead the accused to believe she had consented to his acts. The accused's personal evaluation of the circumstances is but one factor to be considered by the court; it is not conclusive. * * *

* * *

[The opinion of JUDGE LATIMER, concurring in the result is omitted.]

BROSMAN, JUDGE (concurring in part and dissenting in part).

* * *

II

* * * Here the evidence seems to me to have raised reasonably the possibility that the accused believed the prosecutrix was acceding to his overtures. The principal opinion suggests that such a belief, to be effective, must be both reasonable and honest. For this its author cites United States v. Perruccio, 4 USCMA 28, 15 CMR 28, where an unreasonable—and thus negligent—mistake of fact was deemed no defense to a prosecution for negligent homicide. On the other hand, a mistake of fact may be negligent and yet negate the intent or knowledge required for conviction of certain offenses. United States v. Lampkins, 4 USCMA 31, 15 CMR 31. Within which category do rape and assault with intent to commit rape fall?

Rape—like unpremeditated murder—has ordinarily been treated as requiring only a general criminal intent. Thus, drunkenness, even in excessive degree, would probably not constitute a defense to this crime—that is, as serving to belie the accused's necessary intent. However, assault with intent to commit rape would seem to occupy a quite different position—since the very designation of the offense indicates the requirement of a specific intent. Clearly, then, drunkenness could operate to negate the intent required for conviction of such an assault. An *unreasonable* mistake of fact could perhaps not serve to deny criminal liability for a consummated rape. But could it negative the prerequisites for a finding of guilt of assault with intent to commit rape—just as an unreasonable mistake of fact is said to destroy liability for larceny by false pretenses?

The Chief Judge seeks to distinguish rape from assault with intent to rape as a step in his holding that certain action by the law officer, which would have prejudiced the accused in a rape trial, could not have prejudiced him under the present charge. My concern is whether—as to the second requested defense instruction—this distinction operates in reverse?

III

Assault with intent to commit rape demands proof of an assault on the prosecutrix accompanied by an intent to have unlawful sexual intercourse by force and without her consent—a purpose to overcome any resistance by force. Manual for Courts-Martial, United States, 1951, paragraph 213*d*(1)(*c*). If the woman consents to the application of force to her body, there would presumably be no assault in the first instance. Of course, if she had consented to sexual intercourse—that is, if her "will" favored such a result—she would also ordinarily have consented to that fondling which frequently precedes the act of coition. Thus, acts like those before us here would not partake of their usual character of a battery. See Manual, supra, paragraph 207*a*, page 371.

Ignorance or mistake of fact—if reasonable—normally provides a defense to an accused. * * * I would suppose that the type of consent with which we are now dealing is "factual" in nature, and that a mistake as to the woman's attitude would constitute one of fact. Thus, if the accused believed reasonably that the Japanese girl here was consenting to his proposals, he would be exonerated, I should think, even from the crime of assault. On the other hand, an unreasonable mistake on his part would not affect his liability for assault, in violation of the Uniform Code, Article 128, 50 USC § 722.

But if an assault is to be found here—on the theory there was neither consent nor a reasonable mistake with regard thereto—does not the accused's mistake reenter the picture? One possibility is that the trier of fact may conclude that the girl did not consent, and that no reasonable man would have thought she did, but that the accused—because of drunkenness or some variety of mild sexual complex which destroyed his realism—genuinely believed that she was acquiescent. His purpose simply was to enjoy sexual relations with her under the circumstances presented to him. Those circumstances he unreasonably construed to amount to an invitation on her part. However, he did not intend coitus under any other circumstances. This might be because (a) he did not desire intercourse without full consent; or (b) because he was just not the sort of person who worries about hypothetical problems. When an accused fondles a woman against a background of the frame of mind just mentioned, I would suppose him to be wanting in that variety of criminal purpose required for assault with intent to rape. One may well lack an intention to overcome resistance when nothing is present which seems to suggest the possibility of its presence.

It may be regarded as anomalous to conclude that an accused may be exonerated from guilt of assault with intent to commit rape because of an unreasonable mistake, whereas he could have been convicted lawfully of rape had penetration been effected under the same misapprehension. It is to be observed, however, that the anomaly is no greater than that involved in holding that an assault with intent to murder requires a specific intent to kill, whereas the crime of murder may be made out with a lesser intent. See United States v. Woodson, 3 USCMA 372, 12 CMR 128. The fact of the matter is that a specific intent is, by definition, required for the present finding. The evidence, in my view, raised the possibility that a mistake of fact on the accused's part precluded that intent.

* * *

V

I would reverse the decision of the board of review and order a rehearing.

Questions

1. Judge Brosman states the prevailing view of the law. Given this, do you see an apparent tactical error on the part of the defense?

2. Is there any justification for a stricter *mens rea* requirement for assault with intent crimes than for the crimes intended?

3. Mistake of Fact and Mistake of Law

MODEL PENAL CODE, § 2.04, TEXT *

Section 2.04. Ignorance or Mistake.

(1) Ignorance or mistake as to a matter of fact or law is a defense if:

(a) the ignorance or mistake negatives the purpose, knowledge, belief, recklessness or negligence required to establish a material element of the offense; or

(b) the law provides that the state of mind established by such ignorance or mistake constitutes a defense.

(2) Although ignorance or mistake would otherwise afford a defense to the offense charged, the defense is not available if the defendant would be guilty of another offense had the situation been as he supposed. In such case, however, the ignorance or mistake of the defendant shall reduce the grade and degree of the offense of which he may be convicted to those of the offense of which he would be guilty had the situation been as he supposed.

(3) A belief that conduct does not legally constitute an offense is a defense to a prosecution for that offense based upon such conduct when:

(a) the statute or other enactment defining the offense is not known to the actor and has not been published or otherwise reasonably made available prior to the conduct alleged; or

(b) he acts in reasonable reliance upon an official statement of the law, afterward determined to be invalid or erroneous, contained in (i) a statute or other enactment; (ii) a judicial decision, opinion or judgment; (iii) an administrative order or grant of permission; or (iv) an official interpretation of the public officer or body charged by

law with responsibility for the interpretation, administration or enforcement of the law defining the offense.

(4) The defendant must prove a defense arising under Subsection (3) of this Section by a preponderance of evidence.

People v. Snyder

Supreme Court of California, 1982.
32 Cal.3d 590, 186 Cal.Rptr. 485, 652 P.2d 42.

RICHARDSON, JUSTICE.

Defendant Neva B. Snyder appeals from a judgment convicting her of possession of a concealable firearm by a convicted felon (Pen.Code, § 12021), based upon her 1973 conviction for sale of marijuana, a felony (former Health & Saf.Code, § 11531). Defendant contends that the trial court erred in excluding evidence of her mistaken belief that her prior conviction was only a misdemeanor. We will conclude that defendant's asserted mistake regarding her legal status as a convicted felon did not constitute a defense to the firearm possession charge. Accordingly, we will affirm the judgment.

At trial, defendant offered to prove the following facts supporting her theory of mistake: The marijuana possession charge resulted from a plea bargain not involving a jail or prison sentence. At the time the bargain was struck, defendant's attorney advised her that she was pleading guilty to a misdemeanor. Believing that she was not a felon, defendant thereafter had registered to vote, and had voted. On one prior occasion, police officers found a gun in her home but, after determining that it was registered to her husband, the officers filed no charges against defendant.

The trial court refused to admit any evidence of defendant's mistaken belief that her prior conviction was a misdemeanor and that she was not a felon. The court also rejected proposed instructions requiring proof of defendant's prior knowledge of her felony conviction as an element of the offense charged.

Penal Code section 12021, subdivision (a), provides: "Any person who has been convicted of a felony under the laws of the * * * State of California * * * who owns or has in his possession or under his custody or control any pistol, revolver, or other firearm capable of being concealed upon the person is guilty of a public offense, * * *[.]"

The elements of the offense proscribed by section 12021 are conviction of a felony and ownership, possession, custody or control of a firearm capable of being concealed on the person. No specific criminal intent is required, and a general intent to commit the proscribed act is sufficient to sustain a conviction. With respect to the elements of possession or custody, it has been held that knowledge is an element of the offense.

Does section 12021 also require knowledge of one's legal status as a convicted felon? No case has so held. Penal Code section 26 provides that a person is incapable of committing a crime if he acted under a "mistake of fact" which disproves criminal intent. In this regard, the cases have distinguished between mistakes of fact and mistakes of law. As we stated in an early case: "It is an emphatic postulate of both civil and penal law that ignorance of a law is no excuse for a violation thereof. Of course it is based on a fiction, because no man can know all the law, but it is a maxim which the law itself does not permit any one to gainsay * * *. The rule rests on public necessity; the welfare of society and the safety of the state depend upon its enforcement. If a person accused of a crime could shield himself behind the defense that he was ignorant of the law which he violated, immunity from punishment would in most cases result." (People v. O'Brien (1892) 96 Cal. 171, 176, 31 P. 45 * * *.) Accordingly, lack of actual knowledge of the provisions of Penal Code section 12021 is irrelevant; the crucial question is whether the defendant was aware that he was engaging in the conduct proscribed by that section.

In the present case, defendant was presumed to know that it is unlawful for a convicted felon to possess a concealable firearm. (Pen.Code, § 12021.) She was also charged with knowledge that the offense of which she was convicted (former Health & Saf. Code, § 11531) was, *as a matter of law,* a felony. That section had prescribed a state prison term of from five years to life, and the express statutory definition of a "felony" is "a crime which is punishable with death or by imprisonment in the state prison." (Pen.Code, § 17, subd. (a).)

Thus, regardless of what she reasonably believed, or what her attorney may have told her, defendant was deemed to know *under the law* that she was a convicted felon forbidden to possess concealable firearms. Her asserted mistake regarding her correct legal status was a mistake of law, not fact. It does not constitute a defense to section 12021.

None of the California cases relied on by defendant is apposite here. People v. Hernandez (1964) 61 Cal.2d 529, 39 Cal.Rptr. 361, 393 P.2d 673, and People v. Mayberry (1975) 15 Cal.3d 143, 125 Cal.Rptr. 745, 542 P.2d 1337, each involved mistakes of fact, not law. In *Hernandez,* the mistake concerned the age of the alleged victim of a statutory rape. In *Mayberry,* defendant erred in assuming that the adult victim of forcible rape consented to his acts. People v. Vogel (1956) 46 Cal.2d 798, 299 P.2d 850, involved the good faith belief of a defendant charged with bigamy that he is free to remarry. We were careful to explain that defendant's mistake was a factual one: "We have concluded that defendant is not guilty of bigamy, if he had a bona fide and reasonable belief that *facts* existed that left him free to remarry." (Id., at p. 801, 299 P.2d 850; italics added.) Moreover, *Vogel* characterized bigamy as a crime which "has been regarded for centuries as * * * involving moral turpitude, * * *" Obviously a bona fide belief that one is free to remarry nullifies the moral opprobrium attached to the charge. On the other hand, being an ex-felon in possession of a concealable firearm, while illegal, hardly stamps the person charged as a moral leper. His belief that he is not a felon thus does not affect the criminality of his conduct.

* * *

Defendant relies primarily upon People v. Bray, supra, 52 Cal.App.3d 494, 124 Cal.Rptr. 913, but that case is distinguishable. There defendant pleaded guilty in Kansas to being an accessory before the fact and was placed on two years' summary probation, which he successfully completed. When he subsequently sought to register to vote, he filled out an explanatory form referring to a Kansas offense, and indicating that he was uncertain whether he had been convicted of a felony. He was permitted to vote. Seeking employment as a security guard, he stated that he had not been convicted of a felony but described the circumstances of his arrest and probation. The Bureau of Collection and Investigative Services registered him as a guard. On several other job applications he indicated his uncertainty as to his status while fully setting forth the circumstances of his arrest and probation.

In *Bray,* the court concluded that under these unusual circumstances the trial court erred in refusing to instruct on mistake or ignorance of fact and knowledge of the facts which make the act unlawful. (52 Cal.App.3d, at p. 499, 124 Cal.Rptr. 913.) The court cautioned, however, that its decision "should not be interpreted to mean instructions on mistake or ignorance of fact and knowledge of the facts are required every time a defendant claims he did not know he was a felon * * *. It is only in very unusual circumstances such as these that the giving of these instructions is necessary." (Ibid.)

In the present case, unlike *Bray,* defendant made no attempt to inform government officials of the circumstances of her conviction or to seek their advice regarding her correct legal status. (Some authorities have suggested that reliance upon the erroneous advice of governmental authorities might constitute an exception to the general rule that a mistake of law is no defense. See Perkins on Criminal Law (2d ed. 1969) p. 938; A.L.I. Model Pen.Code (Proposed Official Draft 1962) § 2.04(3)(b).)

We conclude that the trial court properly excluded evidence of defendant's asserted mistake regarding her status as a convicted felon.

The judgment is affirmed.

BIRD, C.J., and MOSK and KAUS, JJ., concur.

BROUSSARD, JUSTICE, dissenting.

I dissent.

* * *

Penal Code section 26 provides generally that a person is incapable of committing a crime when the act was committed under a mistake of fact disproving any criminal intent. Section 20 of that code provides: "In every crime or public offense there must exist a union, or joint operation of act and intent, or criminal negligence.

"The word 'intent' in section 20 means 'wrongful intent.' (See People v. Vogel, 46 Cal.2d 798, 801, fn. 2, 299 P.2d 850.) 'So basic is this requirement [of a union of act and wrongful intent] that it is an invariable element of every crime unless excluded expressly or by necessary implication.' (Id., at p. 801, 299 P.2d 850.)" (People v. Mayberry (1975) 15 Cal. 3d 143, 154, 125 Cal.Rptr. 745, 542 P.2d 1337.)

At common law an honest and reasonable belief in circumstances which, if true, would make the defendant's conduct innocent was held to be a good defense. (People v. Hernandez (1964) 61 Cal.2d 529, 535, 39 Cal.Rptr. 361, 393 P.2d 673.) The concept of mens rea, the guilty mind, expresses the principle that it is not conduct alone but conduct accompanied by certain mental states which concerns, or should concern, the law. While in some cases, culpability had been completely eliminated as a necessary element of criminal conduct, the court has moved away from imposition of criminal liability in the absence of culpability where the governing statute, by implication or otherwise, expresses no legislative intent or policy to be served by strict liability. (Id., at pp. 532–533, 39 Cal.Rptr. 361, 393 P.2d 673.)

The elements of the offense proscribed by section 12021 are conviction of a felony and ownership, possession, custody or control of a firearm capable of being concealed on the person. * * *

There does not appear to be any provision in section 12021 by implication or otherwise indicating legislative intent or policy to be served by refusing to apply the general criminal intent requirement to both of the elements of the offense. The Attorney General argues that, because knowledge of possession or custody of the gun are essential to conviction, strict liability would not result from holding that knowledge of a felony conviction is irrelevant. While under such construction the offense would not involve strict liability as to those who were unaware that they possessed a handgun, it would impose strict liability upon those who were unaware of their felony convictions and could legally possess handguns in the absence of conviction. The language of section 12021 sets forth both elements of the offense in parallel construction, and there is no basis in the language or grammatical construction of the statute warranting a distinction between the two elements with respect to the mens rea requirement. In the absence of any provision reflecting legislative intent or policy to establish strict liability, the mens rea requirement is applicable to the felony conviction element of the offense as well as the possession and custody element.

To hold otherwise is contrary to the settled California rule that a mens rea requirement is an "invariable" element of every crime unless excluded expressly or by necessary implication. Having established the rule, we must assume the Legislature is aware of it and acting in accordance with it, and the absence of any provision to establish strict liability must be read as reflecting legislative intent to require wrongful intent.

* * *

In determining whether a defendant's mistaken belief disproves criminal intent pursuant to Penal Code section 26, the courts have drawn a distinction between mistakes of fact and mistakes of law. Criminal intent is the intent to do the prohibited act, not the intent to violate the law. * * * Accordingly, lack of knowledge of the provisions of Penal Code section 12021 is irrelevant; the crucial question is whether the defendant was aware that he was engaging in the conduct proscribed by that section.

While mistake as to whether the conduct is violative of a statute is not a defense, a mistaken impression as to the legal effect of a collateral matter may mean that a defendant does not understand the significance of his conduct and may negate criminal intent. When the victim's status is an element of the crime, a mistaken belief as to the status has been held a defense in several decisions by this court. In People v. Hernandez, supra, 61 Cal.2d 529, 532, et seq., 39 Cal.Rptr. 361, 393 P.2d 673, it was held that a reasonable and honest belief that the prosecutrix was 18 years or more of age would be a defense to a charge of statutory rape, negating the requisite mental intent. Similarly, in People v. Atchison (1978) 22 Cal.3d 181, 183, 148 Cal.Rptr. 881, 583 P.2d 735, it was held that a reasonable and honest belief that the victim was 19 years of age was a defense to charges of annoying or molesting a child under age 18 and of contributing to the delinquency of a minor. And in People v. Mayberry, supra, 15 Cal.3d 143, 153–158, 125 Cal.Rptr. 745, 542 P.2d 1337, it was held that a mistaken belief that the prosecutrix had consented would be a defense to a charge of forcible rape and kidnaping.

This court has also held that criminal intent may be negated by defendant's reasonable and bona fide but erroneous belief as to his status. In People v. Vogel, supra, 46 Cal.2d 798, 801, et seq., 299 P.2d 850, the defendant was prosecuted for bigamy, and it was held that the defendant's bona fide and reasonable belief that his first wife had divorced him and remarried would be a good defense. The court reasoned in part that it would not be reasonable to hold "that a person is guilty of bigamy who remarries in good faith in reliance on a judgment of divorce or annulment that is subsequently found not to be the 'judgment of a competent court' (Pen.Code, § 282), particularly when such a judgment is obtained by the former husband or wife of such person in any one of the numerous jurisdictions in which such judgments can be obtained. Since it is often difficult for laymen to know when a judgment is not that of a competent court, we cannot reasonably expect them always to have such knowledge and make them criminals if their bona fide belief proves to be erroneous." (46 Cal.2d, at p. 804, 299 P.2d 850; see People v. Roessler (1963) 217 Cal.App.2d 603, 604, 31 Cal.Rptr. 684 (defendant remarried after service of the interlocutory decree of divorce but before entry of final decree).) The court also pointed out that at common law an honest and reasonable belief in circumstances which, if true, would make the act for which the person is indicted an innocent act, has always been held to be a good defense. (46 Cal.2d, at p. 805, 299 P.2d 850.)

People v. Flumerfelt (1939) 35 Cal.App.2d 495, 497–498, 96 P.2d 190, also illustrates the distinction between mistake of fact and mistake of law. In that case, the defendant was charged with selling corporate securities without a permit. The defendant claimed that before she sold the securities, her attorney told her that a permit to sell had been obtained, and it was held that her honest but mistaken belief that a permit to sell had been issued constituted a defense. However, the court distinguished the situation where counsel erroneously advises that the instrument to be sold is not a security, pointing out that a mistake as to the legal consequences of the act which constitutes a violation of the statute would not be a defense. (35 Cal.App.2d at pp. 498–499, 96 P.2d 190; see 1 Witkin, Cal. Crimes, supra, § 151, p. 145.)

The * * * cases, read together, make clear that a mistake of law is one premised on ignorance of the terms of the statute which the defendant is charged with violating. However, when the defendant reasonably and honestly believes that the statute is not applicable to him or that he has complied with it, there is a mistake of fact. There is a mistake of fact even though the matter as to which the defendant is mistaken is a question of law. The questions of age in *Hernandez* and *Atchison* were matters resolved as a matter of law as was marital status in *Vogel* and the nonissuance of a permit in *Flumerfelt.*

The Court of Appeal has held that a mistaken belief that a conviction was not a felony conviction could negate criminal intent in a prosecution for violation of Penal Code section 12021. (People v. Bray, supra, 52 Cal.App. 3d 494, 497–499, 124 Cal.Rptr. 913.) *Bray* graphically illustrates the injustice which results from holding that a reasonable and good faith belief of lack of felony status is not a defense. * * *

* * *

The Court of Appeal stated that its decision should not be interpreted to mean instructions on mistake or ignorance of fact or knowledge of the facts are required every time a defendant claims he did not know he was a felon. (Id.) Relying on that statement, the majority concludes that *Bray* should be limited to situations where a state agency has misled the defendant. The statement relied upon merely reflects that only in rare cases will there be a basis for a *reasonable* belief that a felony conviction was a misdemeanor conviction. The reasoning in *Bray* applies to any case where there is a reasonable and good faith mistake and is in accord with the common law and our statutory rule. The *source* of the reasonable and good faith mistake does not affect the existence of criminal intent.[2]

Had the trial court in the instant case admitted the offered evidence and given the requested instruction, the jury could properly have concluded that defendant had a reasonable and good faith belief that her conviction was not a felony conviction. She was granted probation without jail or prison sentence. Her attorney had advised her that the offense was a misdemeanor,[3] and there were additional circumstances reflecting a good faith belief.

* * *

I would reverse the judgment.

NEWMAN and REYNOSO, JJ., concur.

Questions

1. Compare Liparota v. United States, supra, p. 139.

2. Which of the following states of mind of Snyder should prevent conviction if reasonable? Even if unreasonable?

a. Snyder did not know she had the weapon in her pocket; it had been put there secretly by a third person.

2. I am perplexed by the majority's apparent limitation of the mistake doctrine to would-be "moral leper[s]." The more heinous the crime the more reason to limit defenses, and the majority's suggested limitation appears to turn the usual relationship between law and morality upside down.

3. It has been held that advice of counsel that prohibited conduct is lawful is not a defense because it would place the advice of counsel above the law. (See 1 Witkin, Cal. Crimes, supra, § 150, pp. 143–144.) Counsel's advice in the instant case is relevant to establish good faith; it does not in and of itself establish a defense.

b. Snyder believed that what she possessed was a carving of a gun; she did not realize it was a real weapon.

c. Snyder did not know of the existence of a statute which prohibited possession of a concealed firearm by a convicted felon.

d. Snyder was charged on the basis of ownership, not possession, and she wrongly believed that one does not become the owner of a firearm until title is transferred in the State Firearms Registry; no such transfer had been made to her.

e. Snyder wrongly believed that the crime she had been convicted of was a misdemeanor, not a felony.

f. Snyder read and believed an erroneous opinion by the State Attorney-General, which stated that the possession statute applied only to those convicted of felonies involving violence, and her conviction did not in fact involve any violence.

3. Can the criminal law be stated just as well without talking about special rules of mistake?

4. In Lambert v. California, 355 U.S. 225, 78 S.Ct. 240, 2 L.Ed.2d 228 (1957), the Supreme Court reversed, on due process grounds, the conviction of a previously convicted felon who had not, on moving to Los Angeles, registered with the city authorities, as required by ordinance, the State courts having rejected the sufficiency of her defense that she did not know of the ordinance requiring the registration of convicted felons. Does this case properly have a bearing on cases like *Snyder?* Was *Lambert* properly decided?

United States v. Brady

United States District Court, D. Colorado, 1989.
710 F.Supp. 290.

MATSCH, JUDGE.

The defendant is charged with two firearms violations. Count I charges possession of an unregistered firearm under 26 U.S.C. § 5861(d) and 26 U.S.C. § 5871. Count II charges possession of a firearm by a convicted felon in violation of 18 U.S.C. § 922(g)(1). Trial was held to the court after a waiver of jury.

FINDINGS OF FACT

The defendant, Ora A. Brady (Brady), is a 61–year–old tree trimmer and concrete worker who traps animals in the winter when the weather makes working his other jobs impossible. Brady has lived in Baca County, Colorado for the past 40 years. On December 28, 1987, Brady was found in possession of a number of "coyote getters" which he had set out as animal traps.

A coyote getter is a device used to kill coyotes by propelling cyanide into their mouths when they pull on the bait. * * *

* * *

Brady pleaded guilty to an unrelated state offense in the District Court for Baca County in 1987 and was put on probation for two years. He was told he could possess a firearm in connection with his work. In September, 1988, permission to possess a weapon was revoked by the court because it was learned that possession might be in violation of federal law. A hearing on the issue was held on October 3, 1988. After some discussion, Judge Norman Arends concluded that "Mr. Brady can utilize a firearm specifically for hunting and trapping within the confines of his occupation." The judge was aware of 18 U.S.C. § 922. Colorado law required that the judge inform himself about Brady's prior record before putting him on probation. See Colo.Rev.Stat. § 16–11–102 (requiring investigation of past criminal record upon a plea of guilty); cf. Colo.Rev.Stat. § 16–11–203(1)(d) (prior record is factor in probation determination). The judge's statement was incorrect because Brady had two prior felony convictions.

When he was arrested by Alcohol, Tobacco and Firearms (ATF) agents on November 29, 1988, Brady had a loaded .22 caliber revolver in a holster on his person. Brady was standing by a pickup truck which had a dead bobcat in the back. Brady's possession of the revolver was for the purpose of pursuing his trapping vocation. Brady shot the bobcat shortly before the arrest.

* * *

CONCLUSIONS OF LAW

Count I.

* * *

This court concludes that the coyote getter is not * * * included within the definition of a firearm. Brady is acquitted of this Count because the government has failed to prove that he possessed a firearm. * * *

Count II.

Count II charges possession of a firearm by a convicted felon based on Brady's possession of the .22 caliber revolver. Counsel for the government correctly observes that the defenses to this charge are few. Under the law, it is immaterial whether Brady knew he was a convicted felon. It also is no defense that he did not know he was prohibited from possessing a firearm. All that the government needed to prove to make a prima facie case was that the defendant possessed a firearm, that the firearm travelled in interstate commerce, and that he had previously been convicted of a crime punishable by a year or more.

* * *

* * * [T]his is not a situation where a defendant relied on nothing more than his own research or advice of counsel. Here, a judge with criminal jurisdiction over Brady specifically told him that he could continue to possess a firearm when hunting and trapping. There is a difference between merely acting reasonably and in good faith, and acting under the affirmative advice of a judge. In this case, it would violate due process to convict Brady of this offense in light of the fact that the defendant's conduct conformed to the judge's statement of law.

Two Supreme Court cases illustrate the principle. In Raley v. Ohio, 360 U.S. 423, 79 S.Ct. 1257, 3 L.Ed.2d 1344 (1959) four people were convicted in state courts for refusing to answer questions of a legislative commission.

They were told by the legislators that they could refuse to answer the questions because of the state privilege against self-incrimination. This was not in fact the law of Ohio because there was a statute giving the witnesses immunity. Nonetheless, the court held that the witnesses could not be convicted. To permit such a conviction, said the Court, "would be to sanction an indefensible sort of entrapment by the State—convicting a citizen for exercising a privilege which the State had clearly told him was available to him." 360 U.S. at 426, 79 S.Ct. at 1260.

Importantly, the Court did not conclude that the witnesses had been actually entrapped, that is, intentionally misled to entice them to commit a crime. "[T]here is no suggestion that the Commission had any intent to deceive the appellants." 360 U.S. at 438, 79 S.Ct. at 1266. The Court presumed that the violation of law was caused by the erroneous advice of the officials. * * *

Similarly, in Cox v. Louisiana, 379 U.S. 559, 570–71, 85 S.Ct. 476, 483–84, 13 L.Ed.2d 487 (1965) the Court reversed a conviction for violating a statute that prohibited demonstrations near a courthouse because the picketers had been told by the local police chief that they could lawfully protest across the street from the courthouse. Many other cases underscore the point. See United States v. Pennsylvania Industrial Chemical Corp., 411 U.S. 655, 674, 93 S.Ct. 1804, 1816, 36 L.Ed.2d 567 (1973) ("traditional notions of fairness inherent in our system of criminal justice" prevent the government with proceeding with a prosecution under a statute when the defendant reasonably relied on regulations issued under authority of the statute permitting performance of the charged acts); United States v. Clegg, 846 F.2d 1221, 1223 (9th Cir.1988) (good faith reasonable reliance on the apparent authority of government officials is a defense); United States v. Durrani, 835 F.2d 410, 422 (2d Cir.1987) (legitimate reliance on an official interpretation of the law is a defense); United States v. Rosenthal, 793 F.2d 1214, 1235 (11th Cir.) (legitimate reliance on an official interpretation of the law is a defense), modified on other grounds, 801 F.2d 378 (11th Cir.), cert. denied, 480 U.S. 919, 107 S.Ct. 1377, 94 L.Ed.2d 692 (1987); United States v. Duggan, 743 F.2d 59, 83 (2d Cir.1984) (although there are few exceptions to the rule that ignorance of the law is no excuse, there "is an exception for legitimate reliance on official interpretation of the law"); United States v. Barker, 546 F.2d 940 (D.C.Cir.1976); see also Marks v. United States, 430 U.S. 188, 196, 97 S.Ct. 990, 995, 51 L.Ed.2d 260 (1977) (it would be violative of due process to convict publishers based on an obscenity standard that came into existence after they disseminated their materials, they were entitled to rely on the previous standard); Model Penal Code § 2.04(3)(b) (1985) (reasonable reliance on an official statement of the law by an official responsible for interpretation, administration or enforcement of the law is a defense to criminal conduct).

The case for allowing the due process defense when the advice is given by a judge is even more compelling. Because of the unique role of the judiciary in interpreting the law, many courts have recognized that it "would be an act of 'intolerable injustice' to hold criminally liable a person who had engaged in certain conduct in reasonable reliance on a judicial opinion instructing that such conduct is legal." Kratz v. Kratz, 477 F.Supp. 463, 481 (E.D.Pa.1979) (footnotes omitted) (quoting Wilson v. Goodin, 163 S.W.2d 309, 313 (Ky.1942)). Accord United States v. Albertini, 830 F.2d 985, 989 (9th Cir.1987) ("The doctrine is applied most often when an individual acts in reliance on a statute or an express decision by a competent court of general jurisdiction * * * "); United States v. Moore, 586 F.2d 1029, 1033 (4th Cir.1978) ("Of course, one ought not be punished if one reasonably relies on a judicial decision later held to have been erroneous"); United States v. Mancuso, 139 F.2d 90, 92 (3d Cir.1943) (while all persons are presumed to know the law, a layman is not expected to know more law than a judge); United States v. Ehrlichman, 376 F.Supp. 29, 35 (D.D.C.1974) ("Mistake of law may * * * excuse an act if it resulted from good faith reliance upon a court order or decision") (citations omitted).

* * * The state judge had more than mere authority to interpret and apply federal law, he had a constitutional duty to do so. Further, state judges have a role in regard to this particular statute because state convictions trigger the applicability of the law. The judge's errors, factually or legally, do not vitiate the effect of his advice.

An opinion of the Eleventh Circuit is to the contrary. In United States v. Bruscantini, 761 F.2d 640, 641–42 (11th Cir.), cert. denied, 474 U.S. 904, 106 S.Ct. 271, 88 L.Ed.2d 233 (1985) the court declined to apply *Raley* and *Cox* based on a state court judge's assertion that a nolo plea did not make the defendant a convicted felon. *Bruscantini* did not discuss the constitutional authority and duty of state courts to interpret federal law.

* * *

* * * The better view is that the defense is not based on the government being bound by the conduct of its agents, but rather, the fundamental unfairness of punishing a defendant for conforming his conduct to an erroneous interpretation of the law by a judge having the power to confine him. Since the United States has given the state and federal courts a joint role in applying the Constitution and laws of the United States, a person is entitled to rely on a state court's views of federal law. Accordingly, this court declines to follow *Bruscantini.*

The due process defense is available even for a crime like this where there is no requirement of proof that the defendant knew he was committing a crime. This defense does not merely negate intent, it negates the criminality of the act. * * *

Upon all of the foregoing, it is

ORDERED that Ora A. Brady is found not guilty of the offense charged in Count I of the indictment and it is

FURTHER ORDERED that Ora A. Brady is found not guilty of the offense charged in Count II of the indictment.

Note on Mistakes of Law Involving Superior Orders

In United States v. Barker, 546 F.2d 940 (D.C.Cir.1976) "footsoldiers" in the Watergate break-in of a psychiatrist's office were convicted in the trial court, the trial judge refusing their requested instruction that they should be acquitted if they acted in reasonable good faith reliance on the apparent authority of E. Howard Hunt to authorize their conduct. Hunt was a lieutenant of John Ehrlichman, a principal assistant to President Nixon. According to Barker's testimony, Hunt enlisted his aid in carrying out the break-in, meeting him in the Executive Office Building, giving him an unlisted White House number where he could be reached, and corresponding with him on White House stationery. Hunt told Barker that he was working for a White House organization with greater jurisdiction than the F.B.I. and the C.I.A., and asked him to break in to a psychiatrist's office to obtain information relating to national security on "a traitor * * * who was passing * * * classified information to the Soviet Embassy." Barker had previously worked for Hunt, then with the C.I.A., in connection with the Bay of Pigs invasion of Cuba. Hunt asked him to become "operational" again. From Barker's point of view, the practice followed here was normal in such an operation: no written authority was shown and Barker was told no more than he needed to know about the operation. Barker and the others were paid only expenses and nominal sums for lost income.

In the three judge panel of the Court of Appeals, Judge Wilkey voted to reverse the conviction: the trial judge should have instructed the jury that a reasonable belief that Hunt was authorized was a defense. Wilkey found that there was no clear law on whether the president could authorize such searches in national security matters, but that the theory that he could was plausible. The facts known to the defendants made for a persuasive defense if the legal theory was tenable. There should be an exception to the doctrine that mistake of law is no defense in extraordinary cases such as this if the mistake of the accused is reasonable.

Judge Merhige concurred in the vote to reverse on the ground that mistake of law is a defense when the accused reasonably relies on a statement of law by an official charged with its interpretation, administration, or enforcement, in accordance with the Model Penal Code. The judge believed that the jury could find that Ehrlichman was such an official, and that he authorized Hunt to authorize the footsoldiers to break in.

Judge Leventhal dissented on the ground that mistake of law is no defense, and that even the Model Penal Code would not grant a defense in a case like this; there was no showing that Barker relied on Ehrlichman, or that Ehrlichman was charged with duties to interpret, administer, or enforce the law. Liberties are endangered under a contrary interpretation of the mistake of law defense. Where, as here, the accused had no semblance of a legal obligation to involve themselves in the project, there is no reason to acquit them. Light punishment might be appropriate, of course, and the sentencing judge in fact gave a sentence of probation.

Question

Should Barker be treated differently from a soldier charged with crime because he follows an unlawful order given in wartime? From a policeman who makes an unlawful arrest because he mistakes the position of the county borderline, or (where he may arrest for a felony committed in his presence) who thinks wrongly that the goods stolen are worth enough to make the crime a felony, or who wrongly believes he is authorized to arrest without a warrant in particular circumstances? From a client who remarries in good faith upon the erroneous advice of his reputable lawyer that his divorce is valid?

Chapter III

THEFT; HISTORICAL DEVELOPMENT OF THE CRIMINAL LAW

A. INTRODUCTION

1. A Historical Approach to Theft

The major portion of this chapter traces the historical development of the central theft offenses prior to statutory consolidation, almost entirely through English cases and statutes. There are several reasons for dealing with one important area of the law historically and for picking theft for that area. (It is convenient to confine the principal cases to a single jurisdiction, and England is a good choice. All of the early law was formed there, and the history of theft prior to modern statutory consolidation of most theft offenses was much the same in England and America.)

It is especially true in theft that understanding of current law demands some knowledge of how the law got to its present state. If you look at a modern consolidated theft statute you can see much of the bone structure of the common law and of the old statutes beneath the skin. The Model Penal Code section on Theft of Property Lost, Mislaid, or Delivered by Mistake (§ 223.5), for example, is a response to a group of situations which could not be easily accommodated to the concept of common law larceny. The elaborate definition of deception in Model Penal Code § 223.3 reveals the judicial struggles to clarify the nature of a false pretense. Most of the Model Penal Code sections are updated versions of the common law and old statutory crimes.

The history of the law of theft demonstrates lawyers' responses to problems of society and to problems of legal development. The specific issues change over the years but the techniques of response remain much the same. As you read the Carrier's Case (1473) infra, p. 258, ask yourself how different in its nature the debate seems from the conversations with today's law students or judges attempting to formulate the essential legal principles in a new problem.

In the history of theft law you will find a typical model for legal development. The socially serious and obtrusive problems are dealt with first, often in summary fashion by the judges. Legal rules develop and are stretched by fictions to cover tempting situations not quite within the core principles. Legislation finally steps in to make major changes which judicial development is not capable of accomplishing. The judges continue to elaborate the old judicial and the new legislative ideas. Finally a unifying codification is attempted, solving some problems and leaving others for the continuing work of the courts and legislatures.

Enriching your understanding of the law of theft and giving you insight into how legal development may occur are not the only objectives of this chapter. You will also absorb a little of the legal culture of which you are the inheritor. Great cases and great lawyers of the past help put the issues of today in context and add color and life to legal study. Every lawyer should know something of the history of his or her calling.

2. A Note on the History of English Criminal Law

This note is designed to help you to put in procedural context and to understand the English cases you will be dealing with in the next section and elsewhere. It is short and it abounds in generalizations which a good historian would wish to correct, qualify, or elaborate. For further study you may wish to look at such good legal histories as Radcliffe and Cross, *The English Legal System* (Butterworths, 6th ed., 1977) and Baker, *An Introduction to English Legal History* (Butterworths, 2d ed., 1979). Holdsworth's sixteen volume *History of English Law* is the standard work.

Before the Norman Conquest in 1066 the legal system was largely uncentralized, though royal control tended to increase over the years. There was nothing resembling a modern police force or prosecutor's office; cases were prosecuted by the victim or his family with the object of obtaining bot or compensation for the wrong done. The appropriate bot for various kinds of injury was minutely regulated by custom and law, according to a schedule not unlike that to be found in a modern worker's compensation plan. Such a compensation plan grew out of attempts to prevent the blood feuds which would otherwise have been the major method of dealing with wrongs. If either of the parties refused to respond to social pressure to submit the dispute to judicial arbitration, the bot system failed; the feud was on and the wrongdoer was outlawed.

The bot served both tort (compensatory) and criminal (retributive and deterrent) functions. Some offenses also entailed payment of a fine to the king through his sheriff, and some of the most serious offenses were "botless"; compensation could not settle the matter. Here the offender was killed or mutilated and his property was forfeited to the king. These botless crimes gave rise to actions by the King which became known as Pleas of the Crown, a name later applied more generally to criminal prosecutions, and the old Pleas of the Crown were the forerunners of the felonies.

After the Norman Conquest, victims or their families continued the initiation of many criminal proceedings by actions known as appeals of felony, now commenced before royally designated judges. (Felonies were some of the most serious crimes, including murder, manslaughter, mayhem, rape, robbery, larceny, burglary, and arson.) If no compromise was reached, trial was by battle, and conviction of felony brought loss of all the felon's property to the overlord or king. The tort aspect of the proceeding thus had to be pursued by other methods, and there was less motivation for private parties to initiate "appeals," though they continued very occasionally to do so after medieval times, when dissatisfied with government prosecutions. The last English "appeal" of murder occurred early in the nineteenth century, but when the defendant offered trial by battle, the "appeal" was discontinued (Ashford v. Thornton, 1 B. & Ald. 405, 106 Eng.Rep. 149 (K.B.1818)).[a]

a. In 1985 two defendants, on a charge of armed robbery, sought trial by battle in Scotland, which has a distinct legal system. The queen's champion, who would have been required to fight them, was the Lord Advocate for Scotland, the chief public prosecutor. Probably the right to trial by battle no longer exists, even in Scotland; at any rate, the view was taken that any right had been forfeited by the failure of the accused to throw down a white glove in the presence of their accusers.

The private appeal of felony system was quickly superseded by royal prosecution. Coroners and local communities were charged with the duty of searching out felons and holding them for presentation by grand juries before the king's justices, who would ride circuit "on eyre" to hear charges. Trial was originally by ordeal, and when this was abolished, by petty juries. Initially the accused could not be tried by jury without his consent, and when this became the only lawful method of trial, he could not be tried at all without such consent. Refusal, however, was met by one of history's more interesting procedural devices, *peine forte et dure*. The accused was laid flat on the ground and heavy weights were piled upon him, increasing each day, until he either agreed to be tried by jury or expired. If he died, he remained unconvicted, and his property was not forfeited. In the eighteenth century, the system was replaced by the less colorful automatic plea.

Early criminal trials of misdemeanors and some relatively unimportant felonies were handled by local magnates who became justices of the peace or magistrates under the crown. These in relatively modern times handled only minor cases, though when sitting together in Quarter Sessions they had somewhat broader powers. Their work was supplemented by the assizes, at which justices of the King's Bench and others were specially commissioned to hear and determine (oyer and terminer) particular cases or to conduct general jail deliveries—to hear all current criminal cases. The assizes came to be held in county circuits four times a year (Michaelmas Term in November, Hilary Term in January, Easter or Paschal Term in April and May, and Trinity Term in June), and in London, Manchester and Liverpool on a more continuous basis. In London, sessions were at the Old Bailey or Central Criminal Court. In 1971 all of these courts were formed into the Crown Court, which together with the High Court of Justice and the Court of Appeal form the Supreme Court of Judicature.

The remote ancestor of the High Court and the Court of Appeal was the King's Council. In early times, judicial, administrative, and legislative functions were not clearly differentiated in practice, and the King and Council dealt with important matters informally as they arose. From the twelfth to the fourteenth centuries, three specialized courts broke off from the King's Council and assumed separate judicial identities. The Court of Common Pleas dealt mainly with private common law actions, and gradually lost some jurisdiction to the other two courts. The Court of the Exchequer specialized in revenue cases. The Court of King's (or Queen's) Bench (at first) followed the King (or Queen) about from place to place and heard, among other cases, criminal matters. It would sometimes remove a pending criminal case which dealt with an important matter from a single justice of assize or from the justices of the peace. By writ of error it could also correct on appeal technical mistakes apparent on the face of the record, but it was not like a modern appellate court because it could not consider other points. Appeal from the King's Bench ran to the House of Lords. From 1830 to 1875 a Court of Exchequer Chamber (one of several courts bearing the same name; all met in the same place), with similar limited powers, was interposed as an intermediate appellate court beneath the House of Lords. In 1873 the Courts of Queen's Bench, Common Pleas, Exchequer, and Exchequer Chamber, with others, were abolished and replaced by the High Court of Justice, which for a while maintained divisions continuing the names of the old common law courts. In 1881, the

See V. Kiernan, The Duel in European History 323 (Oxford U. Press 1988).

others were merged into the Queen's Bench Division, which continued to hear some appeals from magistrates, but had little criminal business as a court, although the individual judges often sat as trial judges.

The modern appeal system grew in a different way. Trial judges had long followed the practice of reserving difficult questions for consideration, discussion, and advice by their colleagues. There was no limitation to the technical record points. A number of the cases you will consider in this chapter report the results of such references to, e.g., the "Twelve Judges"—that is the judges of Common Pleas, Exchequer, and King's Bench. This practice was formalized in 1848 in the creation of the Court for Crown Cases Reserved, of which all the common law judges were members. This Court was replaced in 1907 by the Court of Criminal Appeal, a true appellate court, composed of King's Bench Division judges, which in turn became the Court of Appeal (Criminal Division) in 1966. Further appeal still lies, under certain circumstances, to the House of Lords.

The legal business of the House of Lords since 1876 has been conducted by the Lord Chancellor and Lords of Appeal in Ordinary: life peers, chosen from experienced judges and barristers. They usually sit in panels of five. The Court of Appeal (Criminal Division) sits in panels which are often presided over by the Lord Chief Justice of England and usually contain at least one Queen's Bench Division judge. It is also staffed by Lords Justices of Appeal—specially appointed Court of Appeal judges.

The Queen's Bench Division is presided over by the Lord Chief Justice of England and staffed by puisne justices—other High Court judges, who as required, may sit in other courts, including the Court of Appeal. Two of the older common law courts, King's Bench and Common Pleas, also consisted of Chief Justices and puisne justices. The Exchequer had a Chief Baron and other barons.

The Crown Courts are staffed by High Court judges and circuit judges and by part-time recorders; justices of the peace may sit in certain cases. In London's Old Bailey, the Recorder is the senior full-time judge; he is assisted by the Common Sergeant, additional judges of the Central Criminal Court, and assigned High Court judges.

B. THE CENTRAL THEFT CRIMES PRIOR TO STATUTORY CONSOLIDATION

1. Original Common Law Larceny

Section one presents the elements of the basic common law offense of larceny, without the embellishments furnished by the major systems of legal fictions which were added by the courts or the improvements added by Parliament. It sets the stage for the historical developments traced in section two.

a. *INTRODUCTION*

An Old Definition of Larceny

3 Stephen, *A History of the Criminal Law of England* 134–135 (1883), quoting from and commenting on the *Mirror of Justices* (circa 1289):

> " 'Larceny is the treacherously taking away from another moveable corporeal goods against the will of him to whom they do

> belong by evil getting of the possession or the use of them. It is said a taking, for bailing or delivery is not in the case; it is said of moveables corporeal, because of goods not moveables or not corporeal, as of land, rent, advowsons of churches, there can be no larceny; it is said treacherously, because that if the taker of them conceive the goods to be his own, and that he may well take them, in such case it is no offence, nor in case where one conceives that it pleases the owner of the goods that he take them.'

"This is, as far as it goes, a perfect definition of the offence of theft as it is still understood in this country."

Historical Notes

1. The *Mirror of Justices* is in part a legal text of uncertain origin and authority. Much of it is inaccurate. The passage quoted does show, however, how far back the central ideas in larceny can be traced. Portions of it are used to introduce topics in this and the next subsection.

2. Sir James Fitzjames Stephen (1829–1894) was a great Victorian authority on criminal law. He worked on codification in England and India and wrote digests of Criminal Law, Criminal Procedure, and Evidence, as well as his *History of Criminal Law* and the best contemporary response to Mill's *Essay on Liberty: Liberty, Equality, Fraternity* (1873). He was a judge of the Queen's Bench Division from 1879 to 1891. You will come upon one of his opinions in the *Ashwell* case in this chapter (p. 269) and another later when you study the felony-murder rule (Reg. v. Serné at p. 647). He was a member of the extraordinary Stephen family, the older brother of Leslie Stephen and uncle of Virginia Woolf. According to one theory, one of his sons, James Kenneth Stephen (1859–1892), tutor to Queen Victoria's grandson, the Duke of Clarence, was probably Jack the Ripper. The Stephens, father and son, suffered mental deterioration towards the ends of their lives. For the Ripper theories, see Michael Harrison, *Clarence* (W.H. Allen, 1972), pp. 156–189; but see also Stephen Knight, *Jack The Ripper: The Final Solution* (David McKay, 1976), which finds J.K. Stephen not implicated, but argues that the Ripper killings were the work of Freemasons, acting to suppress evidence of the Duke of Clarence's secret marriage to a Catholic, and led by Sir William Gull, physician to Victoria, other members of her family, and also to the Stephen family.

b. THE CONDUCT ELEMENT OF THE ACTUS REUS *IN LARCENY*

*"Larceny is the treacherously taking away from another moveable corporeal goods * * *."*

1 Hawkins, *Pleas of the Crown*, ch. 33, § 2 (1716).

As to the first Particular, *viz.* What shall be said to be a felonious and fraudulent Taking, it is to be observed, That all Felony includes Trespass, and that every Indictment of Larceny must have the Words *Felonicè cepit,* as well as *asportavit,* from whence it follows, That if the Party be guilty of no Trespass in taking the Goods, he can not be guilty of Felony in carrying them away.

Rex v. Walsh

168 Eng.Rep. 1166, 1 Mood. 14.
Central Criminal Court, 1824.

The prisoner was tried before Thomas Denman Esquire, Common Serjeant, at the Old Bailey Sessions, January 1824, on an indictment for stealing a leathern bag containing small parcels, the property of William Ray, the guard to the Exeter mail.

At the trial it appeared that the bag was placed in the front boot, and the prisoner, setting on the box, took hold of the upper end of the bag, and lifted it up from the bottom of the boot on which it rested. He handed the upper part of the bag to a person who stood beside the wheel on the pavement, and both had hold of it together, endeavouring to pull it out of the boot, with a common intent to steal it. Before they were able to obtain complete possession of the bag, and while they were so engaged in trying to draw it out, they were interrupted by the guard, and dropt the bag.

The prisoner was found guilty, but the facts above stated were specially found by the jury, in answer to questions put to them by the Common Serjeant.

The Common Serjeant, entertaining some doubts, whether the prisoner could be truly said to have "stolen, taken, and carried away" the bag, he respited the judgment, in order that the opinion of the Judges might be taken on the case.

In Easter Term 1824, The Judges met and considered this case. They held the conviction right, being of opinion that there was a complete asportation of the bag. (Vide East, P.C. 555, 556, 557; 1 Hale, 508, 527.)

Note: Asportation

Compare the following note to Rex v. Coslet, 1 Leach 236, 168 Eng.Rep. 220, 221 (1782):

> Mr. Baron Perryn, before whom the prisoner was tried, mentioned a case of one Cherry which had been reserved at the Oxford Lent Assizes 1781, by Mr. Justice Nares for the consideration of the Twelve Judges. The prisoner was indicted for stealing, taking and carrying away a wrapper and four pieces of linen cloth. This bale contained linen, packed up in the form of a long square; and was put into a waggon travelling the Acton Road; it laid lengthways in the waggon; the prisoner set it up on one end, for the greater conveniency of taking the linen out; and cut the cloth or wrapper all the way down with intent to take out the contents, but he was discovered and apprehended before he had taken any thing out of it. The Jury found the prisioner guilty, but the case was saved for the opinion of the Judges, whether this was a sufficient taking away to support the indictment. And on 2d May 1781, the whole twelve Judges were of opinion that it was not such a removal of the property as was necessary to constitute the offense of larceny.

Rex v. Pitman

Gloucester Assizes, 1826.
2 Car. & P. 423, 172 Eng.Rep. 192.

The prisoner was indicted for stealing a mare, the property of Jonathan Blanch.

It was proved, that the prisoner came to George Inn, at Sodbury, on the fair day, and directed the ostler to bring out his horse. The ostler said, he did not know which it was. The prisoner went into the stable, and pointing to the mare, said, "that is my horse, saddle him." The ostler did so, and the prisoner tried to mount the mare in the inn yard, but, from the noise made by some music, the mare would not stand still. The prisoner then directed the ostler to lead the mare out of the yard for him to mount. The ostler led the mare out, and before the prisoner had time to mount her, a person, who knew the mare, came up, and the prisoner was secured.

Watson, for the prisoner, objected, that this was not a felonious taking by the prisoner, as the mare was never in his possession. It all along remained in the possession of the ostler, who never parted with it; and if the mare was never in the possession of the prisoner, he could not be guilty of stealing it.

GARROW, B.—If the prisoner caused the mare to be brought out of the stable, intending to steal her, and the animal being disturbed by the music, the ostler led her out of the yard for his accommodation and by his procurement, that is a sufficient taking to constitute a felony.

The defence was, that the prisoner was drunk, and took the mare by mistake; and the Jury, on that ground, found him

Not guilty.

Rex v. Harvey

Chelmsford Assizes, 1787.
1 Leach 467, 168 Eng.Rep. 335.

The prosecutor had sent his servant with the horse to Harlowbush fair, in order to sell it. The prisoner met the prosecutor, to whom he was personally known. "I hear," says the prisoner, "you have a horse to sell. I think he will suit my purpose; and if you will let me have him a bargain, I will buy him." The prisoner and the prosecutor walked together into the fair; and upon a view of the horse, the prosecutor said to the prisoner, "You shall have the horse for eight pounds"; and calling to his servant, he ordered him to deliver the horse to the prisoner. The prisoner immediately mounted the horse, saying to the prosecutor that he would return immediately and pay him. The prosecutor replied, "Very well, very well." The prisoner rode away with the horse, and never returned.

THE COURT. It is impossible by any construction whatsoever to make this case a felony. The case in Kelynge's Reports, 82, where a man rides away with a horse which he had obtained on pretence of trying its paces, was a conditional delivery. * * * But in the present case the delivery was unconditional, and the contract was completed. It was a sale; and the property as well as the possession was entirely parted with. The prisoner has defrauded the prosecutor of the price of the horse, but not of the horse itself; and the only remedy the prosecutor has is by action to recover the eight pounds; but the prisoner cannot be indicted for a felony.

And the prisoner was accordingly discharged.

Regina v. Pratt

Court for Crown Cases Reserved, 1854.
Dears. 360, 169 Eng.Rep. 760.

The following case was stated by the Recorder of the borough of Birmingham.

The prisoner, David Pratt, was tried before me at the last January sessions for the borough of Birmingham, upon a charge of having feloniously stolen, taken, and carried away, on the 18th day of May, in the 16th year of our Sovereign Lady the Queen, one die lathe, the goods of Edward Barker and another; and, on the 19th day of May, in the same year, ten lathes, the property of the said Edward Barker and another, the goods and chattels of the prosecutors, and was found guilty.

The prisoner was a thimble maker and manufacturer, carrying on his business in two mills, one a thimble mill, and the other a rolling mill, in the borough of Birmingham; and, before the occurrences hereinafter mentioned, he was the owner and proprietor of the property mentioned in the indictment.

On the 14th May 1853, the prisoner, being in pecuniary difficulties, arranged with the prosecutors, Edward Barker, and William Wayte, creditors of the prisoner, and with Mr. Collis, an attorney-at-law, who acted on their behalf, to execute an assignment to trustees for the benefit of his creditors; and on the 18th May a deed of assignment was executed by him, whereby the prisoner assigned to the prosecutors as trustees, for the purposes therein mentioned, certain property by the description following:

"All and every the engines, lathes, rolls, boilers, furnaces, horses, carts, machinery, tools and implements of trade, the stock in trade, goods, wares, merchandize, household furniture, fixtures, plate, linen, china, books of account, debts, sum and sums of money, and all securities for money, vouchers, and other documents and writings, and all other the personal estate and effects whatsoever and wheresoever, save and except leasehold estates of the said David Pratt, in possession, reversion, remainder, or expectancy, together with full and free possession, right, and title of entry, in and to all and every of the mills, works, possessions or tenements and premises, wherein the said several effects and premises then were, to have and to hold the said engines and other the premises unto the said Edward Barker and William Wayte, their executors, administrators, and assigns, absolutely."

* * *

In the nights of Monday, the 16th of May, and of every other day during that week, the prisoner removed property conveyed by the deed, including the articles mentioned in the indictment, from the thimble and rolling mills (some of the heavier machines being taken to pieces for the purpose of removal), and hid them in the cellar and other parts of the house of one of his workmen. Some time afterwards, and after the sale by the trustees of the remainder of the property, a Mr. Walker, who had been a large purchaser at the sale, recommenced the business at the thimble and rolling mills, and the prisoner acted as his manager when the property, which formed the subject of the indictment, was by the prisoner's directions brought back at intervals to the mills.

No manual possession of the property was taken by the prosecutors prior to its removal from and back to the mills, but the prisoner remained in possession after the execution of the deed in the same manner as before.

I asked the jury three questions

1. Did the prisoner remove the property after the execution of the deed of assignment?

2. Did he so act with intent fraudulently to deprive the parties beneficially entitled under the deed of the goods?

3. Was he at the time of such removal in the care and custody of such goods as the agent of the trustees under the deed?

I put these three questions to the jury separately, and they answered them separately as follows:—

1. He did remove the property after the execution of the assignment.

2. He did so remove it with such fraudulent intent; and lastly,

3. He was not in the care and custody of the goods as the agent of the trustees, and thereupon (being of opinion that the two affirmative answers would support a conviction notwithstanding the third answer in the negative) I directed the jury to find the prisoner guilty, which they did.

The questions for the opinion of the Court are,

1. Whether the deed of assignment ought to have been received in evidence?

2. Whether my direction to the jury was correct?

And lastly. Whether the conviction is valid?

M.D. Hill, Recorder

This case was argued on 3rd June 1854, before LORD CAMPBELL C.J., ALDERSON B., COLERIDGE J., MARTIN B., and CROWDER J.

* * *

LORD CAMPBELL C.J.—The jury expressly find that the prisoner was not in the care and custody of the goods as the agent of the trustees. * * * The prisoner therefore being in lawful possession of the goods cannot be convicted of larceny.

The other learned Judges concurred.

Conviction quashed.

1 Hale, *Pleas of the Crown* 513 (1736).

Regularly a man cannot commit felony of the goods, wherein he hath a property.

* * *

Yet if A. bail goods to B. and afterwards *animo furandi* steals the goods from B. with design probably to charge him for them in an action of detinue, this is felony; *quod vide* 7 H. 6. 43. a. Co. P.C. p. 110. Stamf. P.C. p. 26. a.

Questions

1. A chooses a Christmas tree from among a number leaning on their cut ends against a fence. He offers B, standing beside the tree, $25 for it, and B accepts the money. A pushes the top of the tree until the tree is standing vertically, and then further until the top rests against the back of his hatchback car. He then slides the tree into the car and drives off. B is in fact a loiterer and has no connection with the trees. He is charged with larceny of the tree A removed. Can B be guilty? If so, what was the point at which there was a sufficient caption and asportation of the tree?

2. Why was the early common law willing to convict one who took his own property from a bailee or one who took already stolen goods from a thief, but unwilling to convict the likes of Harvey or Pratt? How would Harvey and Pratt fare under Model Penal Code § 223.2?

Historical Note

Sir Matthew Hale (1609–1676) and William Hawkins (1673–1746) were two early and authoritative writers of criminal law treatises. Hale was successively a judge of Common Pleas, Chief Baron of the Exchequer, and Chief Justice of the Court of King's Bench. His treatise was published posthumously in 1736. Hawkins was a barrister and serjeant-at-law, whose book was published in 1716. Serjeants-at-law from the Middle Ages were leading barristers, appointed by the Crown, and from whom judges were chosen. Until 1845 only serjeants could practice before the Court of Common Pleas. They were gradually supplanted by King's Counsel, a rank created in the sixteenth century, and which now roughly replaces the former serjeants. The order of serjeants was dissolved in 1877 and the last serjeant, Lord Lindley, died in 1921. A distinctive feature of the dress of a serjeant was a small cap or coif. The order was known as the Order of the Coif, and the American honorary legal society perpetuates the name. The Thomas Denman who presided in the *Walsh* case later became an able Chief Justice of the King's Bench (1832–1850). He was succeeded by Lord Campbell (1850–1859), the author of *Lives of the Chief Justices* (1849–1857), who delivered the judgment in *Pratt.*

c. *PROPERTY SUBJECT TO LARCENY*

*" * * * [I]t is said of moveables corporeal, because of goods not moveables or not corporeal, as of land, rent, advowsons of churches, there can be no larceny * * *."*

The Case of the Peacocks

Court of King's Bench, 1526.
Y.B. 18 Hen. 8, f. 9, pl. 11.

A question was put to all the justices by the CHANCELLOR. If a man feloniously steals peacocks which are tame and domestic, if it be felony or not. And by FITZHERBERT and ENGLEFIELD it was said that it is not felony, for they are *ferae naturae.* * * * And the law is the same as to a mastiff, a hound, or a spaniel, or a goshawk which is tamed, for they are more properly things for pleasure than for profit. And similarly the peacock is a bird more for pleasure than for profit. * * * And again it was agreed that taking away the apples from the orchard which were growing on the trees at the time of taking, or the trees which were growing at the time of taking, or reaping grain and carrying it away, is not felony, even if it was done with felonious intent, for at the time of taking, these things were part of the freehold. But if I cut my corn or reap my grain, and then another takes it away with felonious intent, this is felony. But FitzJames and the other justices said that peacocks are commonly of the same nature as hens or capons, geese or ducks, and that the owner has property in them. They have *animus revertendi* and they are not fowls of warren, like pheasant or partridge * * *, as to which taking, even with felonious intent, is not felony. And finally all the justices agreed that the taking of peacocks was felony for the reason aforesaid. * * *

Regina v. Perry

Taunton Assizes, 1845.
1 Car. & K. 725, 174 Eng.Rep. 1008.

Larceny.—The prisoner, in one count of the indictment, was charged, as a servant of the Great Western Railway Company, with stealing an order for the payment of money, to wit, an order for the payment of £13, 9s. 7d., the property of the Great Western Railway Company; in another count the thing stolen was described to be "one piece of paper of the value of one penny," of the goods and chattels of the Great Western Railway Company. In other counts, the property was laid in different ways.

It appeared that the Great Western Railway Company being indebted for poor-rates to the overseers of the parish of Taunton St. James in the sum of £13, 9s. 7d., a cheque for the amount was by the proper authority drawn at Paddington upon their London bankers, and then transmitted through the hands of various officers of the company to the superintendent at the Taunton station; he received it on Saturday, the 1st of March, and at the time when the prisoner, the chief clerk there, was going into the town to his dinner, placed it in his hands, ordering him to pay it to the overseer, and to bring him a stamped receipt on his return. On his return, the superintendent asked the prisoner if he had paid the overseer; he answered, "Yes"; and being asked for the receipt, said, that the overseer, not having one by him, had promised to forward it to a certain inn in the town for him. In truth, the prisoner had not paid it, and on Monday morning got it changed by a tradesman in Taunton, and applied the proceeds to his own use. [a]

* * *

W.C. Rowe and Edwards, for the prisoner, objected, that the cheque * * * was not a valuable security because of failure to comply with the Stamp Act.

COLERIDGE, J., overruled the objection, and reserved the case for the opinion of the fifteen judges.

Verdict—Guilty.

* * *

W.C. Rowe—I submit that this cheque was void, and that the prisoner could not be properly convicted of stealing it.

LORD DENMAN, C.J.—It is not a piece of paper of the value of one penny.

ALDERSON, B.—There is no difference in the offence of stealing a cheque and stealing a piece of paper, and the count which states this to be a piece of paper puts an end to all question.

W.C. Rowe. * * * Mr. Serjeant Hawkins, in treating of those things which are the subject of larceny, says (1 Hawk. P.C., Bk. 1, ch. 33, s. 22) "They ought to have some worth in themselves, and not to derive their whole value from the relation they bear to some other thing which cannot be stolen, as paper or parchment on which are written assurances concerning lands, or obligations, or covenants, or other securities for a debt, or other chose in action."

WIGHTMAN, J.—Not as valuable securities; but are they not pieces of paper?

CRESSWELL, J.—If a blank cheque had been stolen, would that be a larceny?

W.C. Rowe.—I think it would.

CRESSWELL, J.—Would it be worse for being filled up? Bankers' paid notes were held to be the subject of larceny of the stamps and paper, and I do not see how the stamps carry the thing further, except by making the paper of greater value.

TINDAL, C.J.—There are two charges here—the one a charge of stealing a valuable security, the other a charge of stealing a piece of paper. You may get rid of the first by its being a bad cheque, but how can you get rid of the other?

W.C. Rowe.—It appeared to me that the effect of converting the paper into a cheque was to make it valuable, if at all, as a security for money, and that, the moment the paper had a cheque written upon it, it became a chose in action, which is not the subject of larceny.

ALDERSON, B.—The nature of the paper is not so wholly absorbed in the chose in action as you put it.

a. A trespassory taking from the company could be found through the fiction of custody. See infra, pp. 248–250 ff.

W.C. Rowe.—If the paper is not wholly absorbed in the chose in action, I should submit that it was of so infinitesimal value as to fall within the rule *de minimis non curat lex.*

LORD DENMAN, C.J.—Your client got £13, 9s. 7d. for it.

* * *

The case was considered by the judges, who held the conviction right, as, at all events, there was a stealing of a piece of paper, which was sufficient to sustain a count for larceny.

Notes

1. *Grand and Petit Larceny.* Larceny was one of the common law felonies, and in theory the death penalty could be imposed for any larceny in early times. But a statute in 1275 lessened the penalty for petit larceny (now often petty larceny), where the value of the stolen property was twelve pence (then about the wages for eight days' work for a laborer) or less, to forfeiture of goods and corporal punishment. While the amount at the dividing line changed, the division was retained in England into the nineteenth century and in the United States commonly until the present day. Frequently, in the United States, petit larceny became a misdemeanor by statute. The Model Penal Code provides for a $500 dividing line; it also provides that thefts of certain articles (e.g., automobiles) and theft by receiving stolen property are always felonious. See § 223.1(2).

2. *Property Subject to Larceny.* Common law felonies dealt with conduct which presented obvious social problems. Real estate or intangibles cannot be carried off in the way that the blatant thief runs off with a wallet. This is probably a sufficient explanation for the original rule limiting the subject matter of larceny to tangible personal property. The judges were generally unwilling to expand coverage of larceny here by fiction. This was probably due in part to a reluctance to extend the death penalty before alternative punishments such as transportation or imprisonment came into common use. Eventually there was enacted a series of curative statutes adding growing crops, dogs and other animals, and various kinds of intangibles, including checks and similar instruments (see 2 Geo. 2, c. 25, s. 3 (1728); 9 Geo. 2, c. 18 (1735); 7 & 8 Geo. 4, c. 29, s. 5 (1827)), to the list of stealable things, sometimes with a lesser penalty attached. Even such things as gas and electricity were commonly included. Consolidating statutes passed in this century commonly have very broad definitions of property which can be stolen. See, e.g., Model Penal Code § 223.0(6) which includes "anything of value," and then, to be sure nothing is left out, goes on to mention some specific things which have not always traditionally been included.

3. *Theft of Use.* In People v. Ashworth, 220 App.Div. 498, 222 N.Y.S. 24 (1927), the defendants, without permission, spun their own wool into yarn on the victim's machinery. They were found not guilty of larceny on the ground that mere unauthorized use of property was not a taking of it.

4. *Theft of Services.* Most modern theft provisions include theft of certain services. See Model Penal Code § 223.7 for the variety of services covered and the methods of acquisition.

Historical Note

The Case of the Peacocks is taken from the Year Books, a series of notes on cases written in Norman French from the thirteenth century to 1535, prepared by anonymous reporters, some of whom may have been law students. More recent cases are conveniently collected in the English Reports (Full Reprint), and later in the modern Law Reports and other series of reports. FitzJames was Chief Justice of the King's Bench (1526–1539). Englefield was a judge of Common Pleas, as was Fitzherbert, whose *La Grande Abridgement* (1514), a summary, arranged by subject matter, of the Year Books up until his time, was the first systematic study of the English criminal law.

Question

In United States v. Bottone, 365 F.2d 389 (2d Cir.1966), cert. denied 385 U.S. 974, 87 S.Ct. 514, 17 L.Ed.2d 437 (1966), the defendants took valuable documents describing a secret process home, photocopied them, using their own equipment, returned the originals to the files, and then transported the copies they had made in interstate commerce in the course of selling the secret information. They were charged under a federal statute punishing such transportation of "goods, wares, merchandise, securities or money * * *, knowing the same to have been stolen * * *." Was conviction proper?

1 Hale, *Pleas of the Crown* 513 (1736)

The wife cannot commit felony of the goods of her husband, for they are one person in law, 21 H. 6 Corone 455. Co. P.C. p. 110, and therefore, if she take or steal the goods of her husband, and deliver them to B. who knowing it, carries them away, this seems no felony in B. for it is taken, *quasi* by the consent of her husband, yet trespass lies against B. for such taking, for it is a trespass, but *in favorum vitae* it shall not be adjudged a felony, and so I take the law to be, notwithstanding the various opinions.

2 East, *Pleas of the Crown* 558 (1803)

As to this offence in particular, it is to be noted that joint-tenants or tenants in common of the chattel cannot be guilty of stealing the same from each other, because the property and possession is in both.

Notes

1. *Interspousal Theft.* The law has changed to some extent since the days of Hale and East, but something of the old views lingers on. Modern law has done away with the principle that interspousal theft is impossible. Abandonment of the old fiction may lead to treating interspousal theft on the same footing as theft between strangers. But this is as unsatisfactory as the old view. Legal property rights may not be understood exactly by the spouses, even where a lawyer would be clear about who owns what. Minor family disputes about property may be better dealt with out of court—particularly the criminal court. The balance struck by Model Penal Code § 223.1(4) is to exempt from prosecution spousal theft of household and personal effects and property normally accessible to both spouses, while the parties are living together.

2. *Theft by Co-owner.* Spousal theft is related to the broader problem of theft by one who himself has an interest of some kind in the property. As we have seen, supra, p. 235 ff., if the interest included present possessory rights, such a person could not be guilty of larceny at common law. Joint tenants and tenants in common have equal undivided possessory rights in the whole property. Consequently, such a co-owner could not possibly steal the property at common law; the cheated co-owner was left to civil remedies. Again modern law, while leaving a co-owner some

freedom of action to deal with the property, makes criminal prosecution possible when his action is clearly beyond his proper authority. See Model Penal Code § 223.0(7). Some jurisdictions, including New York, continue to follow the common law rule that a partner can not commit larceny of partnership property. People v. Zinke, 76 N.Y.2d 8, 556 N.Y.S.2d 11, 555 N.E.2d 263 (1990).

Question

Suppose the defendant buys a refrigerator on credit, title being retained for security purposes by the seller until payments are completed. After making three of twenty payments, the defendant sells the refrigerator to someone who cannot be identified and ceases to make the agreed payments. Should the accused be guilty of theft of the refrigerator or of any other crime? Suppose the defendant completes payments on the refrigerator and then conceals it when he knows his creditors are about to force him into bankruptcy?

Historical Note

Sir Edward Hyde East (1764–1847) wrote his treatise on Pleas of the Crown in 1803. He was subsequently Chief Justice at Calcutta and a member of the Judicial Committee of the Privy Council, an appellate body roughly corresponding to the House of Lords, but hearing appeals from colonies and dependencies and certain other bodies rather than from ordinary United Kingdom Courts.

d. THE MENS REA *IN LARCENY*

" * * [I]t is said treacherously, because that if the taker of them conceive the goods to be his own, and that he may well take them, in such case it is no offence, nor in case where one conceives that it pleases the owner of the goods that he take them."*

Rex v. Crump

Worcester Assizes, 1825.
1 Car. & P. 658, 171 Eng.Rep. 1357.

This prisoner was indicted for stealing a horse, three bridles, two saddles, and a bag, the property of Henry Bateman.

It appeared that he got into the prosecutor's stable, and took away the horse and the other property all together; but that, when he had got to some distance, he turned the horse loose, and proceeded on foot to Tewkesbury, where he was stopped attempting to sell the saddles.

GARROW, B., left it to the jury to say, whether the prisoner had any intention of stealing the horse; for that, if he intended to steal the other articles, and only used the horse as a mode of carrying off the other plunder more conveniently, and, as it were, borrowed the horse for that purpose, he would not be, in point of law, guilty of stealing the horse.

Verdict—Not guilty of stealing the horse—Guilty of stealing the rest of the property.

Rex v. Cabbage

Lancaster Assizes, 1815.
Russ. & Ry. 292, 168 Eng.Rep. 809.

The prisoner was tried before Thomson C.B., at the Lent assizes for the county of Lancaster, in the year 1815, on an indictment for feloniously stealing, taking, and leading away a gelding, the property of John Camplin.

* * *

It appeared that the gelding in question was missed by the prosecutor from his stables on Monday, the 28th February, 1815. The stable door, it appeared, had been forced open. The prosecutor went the same day to a coalpit, about a mile from the stable where he saw the marks of a horse's feet. This pit had been worked out and had a fence round it, to prevent persons from falling in, one of the nails of this fence had been recently knocked off; a man was sent down into the pit, and he brought up a halter, which was proved to be the halter belonging to the gelding. In about three weeks after the finding of the halter, the gelding was drawn up from the coal-pit in the presence of the prosecutor, and who knew it to be him. The horse's forehead was very much bruised, and a bone stuck out of it. It appeared that at the time this gelding was destroyed, a person of the name of Howarth was in custody for having stolen it in August 1813, and that the prosecutor Camplin had recovered his gelding again about five weeks after it was taken. Howarth was about to take his trial for this offence when the gelding was destroyed in the manner stated. The prisoner Cabbage was taken into custody on the 29th March, 1815; and on his apprehension he said that he went in company with Anne Howarth (the wife of Howarth who was tried for stealing the said gelding), to Camplin's stable door, and that they together forced open the door, and brought the horse out. They then went along the road, till they came to the coal-pit before mentioned, and then they backed the horse into the pit.

It was objected by the prisoner's counsel, that the evidence in this case did not prove a larceny committed of the horse; that the taking appeared not to have been done with intention to convert it to the use of the taker, "animo furandi et lucri causa."

THOMSON C.B. overruled the objection, and the prisoner was convicted upon the first count of the indictment, for stealing the horse. Judgment was passed on him, but the learned Chief Baron respited the execution to take the opinion of the judges, as to the propriety of the conviction.

In Easter term, 1815, the judges met to consider this case, and the majority of the judges held the conviction right.

Regina v. Peters

Gloucester Assizes, 1843.
1 Car. & K. 245, 174 Eng.Rep. 795.

Larceny.—The prisoner was indicted for stealing a golden chain, one breast-pin, and one eye-glass and pin, the property of Henry Bulkeley.

It appeared that Mrs. Bulkeley went into her garden, adjoining to the house, to walk, and, on her return into the house, missed the articles in question, which had been upon her dress when she went out walking. The prisoner was employed about the premises on the day in question, and, by the direction of the prosecutor, had walked through the garden, in company with the gardener, immediately after Mrs. Bulkeley had returned into the house; and another gold ornament, missed at the same time with those included in the indictment, was found, upon search being made by Mr. Bulkeley at a spot in the garden by which the prisoner had passed. The prisoner made no mention to the gardener of having found anything, and as soon as he had finished the work Mr. Bulkeley had directed him to do, which occupied about a quarter of an hour, he went away from the house. Mr. Bulkeley caused the loss to be cried the same evening and the following morning, and offered £2 reward to any person who had found the articles. On the following morning, the prisoner went to the crier and stated, that he knew a person who had found the things, and took the crier to his house, fetched them down stairs and gave them to the crier, with directions to go to Mr. Bulkeley's with them, but not to deliver them up unless the reward of £2 was paid. His wife, in his presence, said that she found them in a street in Cheltenham, a quarter of a mile from the prosecutor's; and the prisoner, on two subsequent occasions, stated that he found them in two other places, neither being the garden. The crier went to the prosecutor's, and refused to deliver up the things, and afterwards the prisoner himself went and refused to deliver them unless the reward was paid, which Mr. Bulkeley refused, as he thought the prisoner ought to have brought them to the house, and had been guilty of stealing in taking them away. * * *

* * *

ROLFE, B.—If a man is possessed of a chattel, he does not lose the property in it because he places or drops it in a field. Nay, if he drop it in a street, it still remains his property. The only case where a party can be justified in converting it to his own use is, where it has fallen or dropped where a party may fairly say the owner has abandoned it; or if the party cannot be found to whom it belonged. * * * But it is perfectly well known that, if a person leave anything in a stage coach, if the owner can be found by inquiry, the party finding the thing, and appropriating it to his own use, is guilty of larceny. So, if it is found in a street, and there is any mark by which the owner can be discovered. So, in the case where a gold ornament is found at the door of a house, it is ridiculous to say that any person picking it up would not suppose that it belonged to the owner of the house. There are two questions here, first, did the prisoner pick the things up? Secondly, with what intention did he take up the chain, and take it to his own house? The picking it up might be the most innocent act in the world; but what does he do with it? He takes it home. Did he or not take it home with the intention of appropriating it to his own use; or did he take it home with the intention of finding the true owner? If the latter, he is not guilty. If he took it up, and did not immediately bring it to the prosecutor, in the hopes that, by coming next day, he would get a present of £5, perhaps it might not amount to a larceny. If he took it away with the intention to appropriate it, and only restored it because the reward was offered, it is clear that he is guilty of felony. Are you satisfied that he took it home, either intending to sell it, or to get a reward if one was offered? If so, he is guilty of larceny.

Verdict—Guilty.

Questions

1. The common law speaks of an intention to deprive the victim permanently of his property as necessary for larceny. Which of the following would be sufficient intention:

   a. To deprive V of his Stradivarius for ten years?

   b. To deprive V of his quart of milk for one month?

Cf. Model Penal Code §§ 223.2 and 223.0(1).

2. Suppose the defendant wanted to use the property for a short period of time and did not much care whether the victim recovered the property afterwards, and

   a. left it on a bench at a bus terminal?

   b. left it with the victim's next-door neighbor?

3. Suppose the defendant picks up a purse with the intention to keep the contents if and only if the purse contains cash, and it in fact contains no cash?

4. We have seen that unauthorized *use* of property is not larceny. If, without authority, A borrows B's automobile for a few hours, intending to return it, some crime other than common law larceny will have to be charged. Theft of use or "joyriding" statutes long antedate the automobile. They are often limited to specific classes of property (horses and buggies prominently among them) and carry lesser penalties. See, e.g., Model Penal Code § 223.9, which is limited to motor-propelled vehicles. Should theft of use be treated the same as larceny? Should it be limited to motor-propelled vehicles?

5. Suppose one steals for the purpose of giving the proceeds to a worthy charity. Can this be larceny?

Rex v. Hall

Gloucester Assizes, 1828.
3 Car. & P. 409, 172 Eng.Rep. 477.

Indictment for robbing John Green, a gamekeeper of Lord Ducie, of three hare wires and a pheasant. It appeared, that the prisoner had set three wires in a field belonging to Lord Ducie, in one of which this pheasant was caught; and that Green, the gamekeeper, seeing this, took up the wires and pheasant, and put them into his pocket; and it further appeared, that the prisoner, soon after this, came up and said: "Have you got my wires?" The gamekeeper replied, that he had, and a pheasant that was caught in one of them. The prisoner then asked the gamekeeper to give the pheasant and wires up to him, which the gamekeeper refused; whereupon the prisoner lifted up a large stick, and threatened to beat the gamekeeper's brains out if he did not give them up. The gamekeeper fearing violence did so.

Maclean, for the prosecution, contended, that, by law, the prisoner could have no property in either the wires or the pheasant; and, as the gamekeeper had seized them for the use of the lord of the manor, under the statute 5 Ann. c. 14, s. 4, it was a robbery [a] to take them from him by violence.

VAUGHAN, B.—I shall leave it to the Jury to say whether the prisoner acted on an impression that the wires and pheasant were his property; for, however, he might be liable to penalties for having them in his possession, yet, if the Jury think that he took them under a *bona fide* impression that he was only getting back the possession of his own property, there is no *animus furandi*, and I am of opinion that the prosecution must fail.

Verdict—Not guilty.

The Fisherman's Case

circa 1584.

2 East, Pleas of the Crown 661–662, 1803.

* * * A traveller met a fisherman with fish, who refused to sell him any; and he by force and putting in fear took away some of his fish, and threw him money much above the value of it; and judgment was respited, because of the doubt whether the intent were felonious on account of the money given. Such, however, seems properly to be questions for the consideration of the jury. And the circumstance of the party's offering the full value or more at the time ought to be left to them to show that his intention was not fraudulent, and so not felonious; for it does not necessarily follow as a conclusion of law, that if the value of the thing taken be offered to be paid at the time, the intent is therefore not felonious; though it is, I apprehend, pregnant evidence in the negative. * * *

Questions

1. A believes in the old adage, "Finders, keepers." Does this belief protect him from a charge of larceny if he commits what would otherwise be larceny of lost property? (For the nature of theft of lost property, see infra, p. 266). What is the policy behind a claim of right defense?

2. A prankster A writes B a letter promising B C's power lawn mower if B will cut C's grass all summer while C is away. He signs C's name, and B falls for the hoax. B cuts the grass and at the end of the summer takes C's lawn mower over C's protests. Assume that on these facts B would be acquitted of larceny. Would it make a difference if the letter had promised $100 for the services and B, having performed the services, had taken $100 from C, while C was counting his money? Suppose the letter had promised only "to pay" for the services, and B, regarding the going rate as $5 per hour, had taken $75 for 15 hours' work? In any of these cases, does it make a difference whether B takes the money openly or removes it from C's wallet when C is not around?

3. Model Penal Code § 223.2(1), which includes the old common law larceny, expressly requires a "purpose" to deprive and says nothing expressly about whether "purpose," "knowledge," or "recklessness" is required as to other elements of the offense: taking, exercising control, movable property, and absence of claim of right. What *mens rea* is required for these? On claim of right see § 223.1(3).

a. Robbery is an aggravated form of larceny; it includes larceny from the person by violence.

2. Extensions of Common Law Larceny and New Statutory Crimes

In this section we look at three strands in the history of the expansion of larceny. In subsection a we see larceny being extended to breaches of trust, which seem, at first, to lack the element of trespass. This is assisted by the fiction of custody, but it ultimately requires legislation: new statutory offenses in the nature of embezzlement. Subsection c traces development of theft law in the area of fraud, which again seems to involve no trespass. Here we meet common law larceny by trick and statutory obtaining property by false pretenses. Subsection b deals with the intermediate problem of theft by bailees and others similarly situated.

a. THEFT BY SERVANTS AND OTHER FIDUCIARIES; LARCENY, EMBEZZLEMENT, AND THE LIKE

*"Larceny is * * * taking * * * by evil getting of the possession or the use of them."*

Anon.

Surrey Assizes, 1353.
27 Lib.Ass., f. 137, pl. 39.

A man was arraigned who had been taken in possession of property he had stolen, he claimed benefit of clergy. And the jury found that he was the guest in the house of a rich man * * *, and that the next morning he took the sheets out of the bedchamber and carried them out into the hall; and that he then went out to the stable to get his horse, but the ostler laid hands upon him. And it was put to the jury whether he carried the sheets into the hall with the intent to steal them, to which they answered yes. For this he was adjudged a felon, but he was delivered to the Bishop because he was a clerk.

The Carrier's Case

Star Chamber and Exchequer Chamber, 1473.
Y.B. Pasch. 13 Edw. 4, f. 9, pl. 5.

But if a taverner serve a man with a cup, and he take it away, it is felony, for he did not have possession of this cup, for it was put on the table only to serve him to drink. And so it is of my butler or cook in my house; they are only ministers to serve me, and if they carry it off it is felony, for they did not have possession, for possession was all the while in me; but if things were bailed to the servants, perhaps it would be otherwise, for then they would be in possession of them and it would not be felony.

Note (Common Pleas 1487)

Y.B. Mich. 3 Hen. 7, f. 12, pl. 9.

HUSSEY [C.J., K.B.] put a question. If a shepherd steal the sheep which are in his charge, or a butler the plate which is in his charge, or servants other things in their charge, whether it should be called felony. And it seemed to him that it should. And he referred to a case in which a butler had stolen certain stuff in his charge and was hanged for it. HAUGH [J., C.P.] cited the case of Adam Goldsmith of London who had stolen certain stuff in his charge and was hanged for it. BRIAN [C.J., C.P.]: It can not be felony because he could not take it *vi & armis,* because he had charge of it. And the justices were of the same opinion. * * *

Note (King's Bench 1506)

Y.B. Hil. 21 Hen. 7, f. 14, pl. 21.

In the King's Bench, Cutler, Serjeant, and Pigot, apprentice-at-law. And Pigot asked this question of Cutler. If I deliver a bag of silver to my servant to keep, and he flees from me taking the bag, will this be a felony? Cutler replied, as long as he is in my house or in my service, whatever I have delivered to him is in my possession; so, if my butler, who has my plate in his custody, flees with it, this is felony. And the law is the same if one who has custody of my horse runs off; in such case it was always in my possession. * * * If I give him a bag to carry to London, or to pay someone, or to buy something, and he flees with it, it is not felony, for it is out of my possession, and he comes lawfully by it. * * *

21 Hen. 8, c. 7 (1529).

Where before this time divers, as well noblemen, as other the King's subjects, have upon confidence and trust delivered unto their servants their caskets, and other jewels, money, goods, and chattels, safely to be kept to the use of their said masters or mistresses, and after such delivery the said servants have withdrawn themselves, and gone away from their said masters or mistresses, with the said caskets, jewels, money, goods and chattels, or part thereof, to the intent to steal the same, and defraud their said masters or mistresses thereof, and sometime being with their said masters or mistresses, have converted the said jewels, money, and other chattels, or part thereof, to their own use, which misbehaviour so done was doubtful in the common law, whether it were felony or not; and by reason thereof the foresaid servants have been in great boldness to commit such or like offences:

Be it therefore enacted, ordained, and established by the King our sovereign lord, by the assent of the lords spiritual and temporal, and the commons, in this present parliament assembled, and by authority of the same, That all the singular such servants, to whom any such caskets, jewels, money, goods, or chattels, by his or their said masters or mistresses, shall from henceforth so be delivered to keep, that if any such servant or servants withdraw him or them from their said masters, and mistresses, and go away with the said caskets, jewels, money, goods, or other chattels, or any part thereof, to the intent to steal the same, and defraud his or their said masters or mistresses thereof, contrary to the trust and confidence to him or them put by his or their said masters or mistresses, * * * that if the said caskets, jewels, money, goods, or chattels, that any such servant shall so go away with, * * * be of the value of xl. s. or above, that then the same false, fraudulent, and untrue act or demeanour, from henceforth shall be deemed and adjudged

felony; and he or they so offending, to be punished, as other felons be punished for felonies committed, by the course of the common law. * * *

Rex v. Bass

Central Criminal Court, 1782.
1 Leach 251, 168 Eng.Rep. 228.

At the Old Bailey in May Session 1782, William Bass was convicted of stealing a quantity of goods, the property of John Gatfee.

The prisoner was servant and porter in the general employ of the prosecutor, a gause-weaver in Bishopsgate street. On the day laid in the indictment he was sent with a package of goods from his master's house, with directions to deliver them to a customer at a particular place. On his way he met two men who invited him into a public house to drink with them and then persuaded him to open the package and sell the goods to a person whom one of the men brought in, which he accordingly did, by taking them out of the package and putting them into the man's bag; and he received eight guineas of the produce to his own use.

It was referred to the consideration of the Twelve Judges, Whether from the above facts, the prisoner was guilty of a felonious taking.

MR. BARON HOTHAM in December Session 1782, delivered it as the unanimous opinion of all the Judges, That the conviction was proper; for the prisoner standing in the relation of a servant, the possession of the goods must be considered as remaining in the master * * *, until and as the time of the unlawful conversion of them by the prisoner. * * *

Rex v. Chisser

Court of King's Bench, 1678.
T. Raym. 275, 83 Eng.Rep. 142.

Upon a special verdict the jury find, that on the day, and at the place in the indictment mentioned, Abraham Chisser came to the shop of Anne Charteris spinster in the said indictment likewise named, and asked for to see two crevats in the indictment mentioned, which she shewed to him, and delivered them into his hands, and thereupon he asked the price of them, to which she answered 7s. whereupon the said Abraham Chisser offered her 3s. and immediately run out of the said shop, and took away the said goods openly in her sight; but whether this be felony, or not, is the question. And if it shall be adjudged felony, we find him guilty; and that the goods were of the value of 7s. and that he had no goods or chattels, &c. But if it be not adjudged felony, we find him not guilty, nor that he fled for the same.

And I am of opinion, that this act of Chisser is felony; for that * * *

2. Although these goods were delivered to Chisser by the owner, yet they were not out of her possession by such delivery, till the property should be altered by the perfection of the contract, which was but inchoated and never perfected between the parties; and when Chisser run away with the goods, it was as if he had taken them up, lying in the shop, and run away with them. * * *

Rex v. Bazeley

Central Criminal Court, 1799.
2 Leach 835, 168 Eng.Rep. 517.

At the Old Bailey in February Session 1799, Joseph Bazeley was tried before John Silvester, Esq. Common Serjeant of the city of London, for feloniously stealing on the 18th January preceding, a Bank-note of the value of one hundred pounds, the property of Peter Esdaile, Sir Benjamin Hammett, William Esdaile, and John Hammett.

The following facts appeared in evidence. The prisoner, Joseph Bazeley, was the principal teller at the house of Messrs. Esdaile's and Hammett's, bankers, in Lombard-street, at the salary of £100 a year, and his duty was to receive and pay money notes and bills at the counter. . . . The prisoner was treasurer to an association called "The Ding Dong Mining Company"; and in the course of the year had many bills drawn on him by the Company, and many bills drawn on other persons remitted to him by the Company. In the month of January 1799, the prisoner had accepted bills on account of the Company, to the amount of £112, 4s. 1d. and had in his possession a bill of £166, 7s. 3d. belonging to the Company, but which was not due until the 9th February. One of the bills, amounting to £100, which the prisoner had accepted, became due on 18th January. Mr. William Gilbert, a grocer, in the Surry-road, Black-friars, kept his cash at the banking-house of the prosecutors, and on the 19th January 1799, he sent his servant, George Cock, to pay in £137. This sum consisted of £122 in Bank-notes, and the rest in cash. One of these Bank-notes was the note which the prisoner was indicted for stealing. The prisoner received this money from George Cock, and after entering the £137 in Mr. Gilbert's Bank-book, entered the £15 cash in his own money-book, and put over the £22 in Bank-notes into the drawer behind him, keeping back the £100 Bank-note, which he put into his pocket, and afterwards paid to a banker's clerk the same day at a clearing-house in Lombard-street, in discharge of the £100 bill which he had accepted on account of the Ding Dong Mining Company. * * *

* * *

* * * [T]he Court left the facts of the case to the consideration of the Jury, and on their finding the prisoner Guilty, the case was reserved for the opinion of the Twelve Judges on a question, whether under the circumstances above stated, the taking of the Bank-note was in law a felonious taking, or only a fraudulent breach of trust.

The case was accordingly argued before nine of the Judges (Lord Kenyon, L.C.J.; C.J. Eyre, C.B. Macdonald, Mr. Baron Hotham, Mr. B. Perryn, Mr. Baron Thompson, Mr. J. Grose, Mr. J. Lawrence. Mr. J. Rooke) in the Exchequer Chamber, on Saturday, 27th April 1799, by Const for the prisoner, and by Fielding for the Crown.

Const, for the prisoner. * * *

* * *

First, That the prosecutors cannot, in contemplation of law, be said to have had a constructive possession of the Bank-note, at the time the prisoner is charged with having tortiously converted it to his own use.

Secondly, That supposing the prosecutors to have had the possession of this note, the prisoner, under the circumstances of this case, cannot be said to have tortiously taken it from that possession with a felonious intention to steal it.

Thirdly, That the relative situation of the prosecutors and the prisoner makes this transaction merely a breach of trust; and,

Fourthly, That this is not one of those breaches of trust which the Legislature had declared to be felony.

The first point, viz. That the prosecutor cannot, in contemplation of law, be said to have had a constructive possession of this Bank-note at the time the prisoner is charged with having tortiously converted it to his own use. To constitute the crime of larceny, the property must be taken from the possession of the owner; this possession must be either actual or constructive; it is clear that the prosecutor had not, upon the present occasion, the actual possession of the Bank-note, and therefore the inquiry must be, whether they had the constructive possession of it? or, in other words, whether the possession of the servant was, under the circumstances of this case, the possession of the master? * * * The prosecutors in the present case had only a right or title to possess the note, and not the absolute or even qualified possession of it. It was never in their custody or under their controul. * * * Suppose the prisoner had not parted with the note, but had merely kept it in his own custody, and refused, on any pretence whatever, to deliver it over to his employers, they could only have recovered it by means of an action of trover or detinue, the first of which presupposed the person against whom it is brought, to have obtained possession of the property by lawful means, as by delivery, or finding; and the second, that the right of property only, and not the possession of it, either really or constructively, is in the person bringing it. The prisoner received this note by the permission and consent of the prosecutors, while it was passing from the possession of Mr. Gilbert to the possession of Messrs. Esdaile's and Hammett's; and not having reached its destined goal, but having been thus intercepted in its transitory state, it is clear that it never came to the possession of the prosecutors. It was delivered into the possession of the prisoner, upon an implied confidence on the part of the prosecutors, that he would deliver it over into their possession, but which, from the pressure of temporary circumstances, he neglected to do; at the time therefore of the supposed conversion of this note, it was in the legal possession of the prisoner. To divest the prisoner of this possession, it certainly was not necessary that he should have delivered this note into the hands of the prosecutors, or of any other of their servants personally; for if he had deposited it in the drawer kept for the reception of this species of property, it would have been a delivery of it into the possession of his masters; but he made no such deposit; and instead of determining in any way his own possession of it, he conveyed it immediately from the hand of Mr. Gilbert's clerk into his own pocket. * * * After these determinations, it cannot be contended that the possession of the servant is the possession of the master; for, independently of these authorities, the rule, that the possession of the servant is the possession of the master, cannot be extended to a case in which the property never was in the master's possession, however it may be so construed in cases where the identical thing stolen is delivered by the master, or where the question is between the master and a third person. "If," says Sir Matthew Hale, "I deliver my servant a bond to receive money, or deliver goods to him to sell, and he receives the money upon the bond or goods, and go away with it, this is not felony; for though the bond or goods were delivered to him by the master, yet the money was not delivered to him by the master"; but he admits, that "if taken away from the servant by a trespasser, the master may have a general action of trespass"; which shows that the law, in a criminal case, will not, under such circumstances, consider the master to have a constructive possession of the property. Such a possession arises by mere implication of law; and it is an established rule, that no man's life shall be endangered by any intendment or implication whatsoever.

Secondly, Supposing the prosecutor to have had the possession of this note, yet the prisoner, under the circumstances of this case, cannot be said to have tortiously taken it from that possession with a felonious intent to steal it. * * * In the present case there was no evidence whatever to show that any such intention existed in his mind at the time the note came to his hands; * * * but if, at the very time he received the note, he had no intent to steal it, it is no felony; for Sir Edward Coke, and all the writers on Crown Law agree, that the intent to steal must be when the property comes to his hands or possession; and that if he have the possession of it once lawfully, though he hath the animus furandi afterwards, when he carrieth it away, it is no larceny.

But, Thirdly, the situation which the prisoner held, and the capacity in which he acted in the banking-house of the prosecutors, make this transaction only a breach of trust. It appears from the paragraph already cited from Hale's Pleas of the Crown, that in consequence of the relation between master and servant, the law makes a distinction between civil and criminal proceedings, that the servant may be liable to an action for wrongfully withholding the property he may have received to his master's use; but that he cannot be proceeded against criminally for detaining or converting to his own use such property as he may have received in trust for the use of his master. * * *

Fourthly, But a breach of trust is not, either by the Common Law or by Act of Parliament, in this case, felony. * * * Taking it, therefore, as a settled point, that a breach of trust cannot, by the rules of the common law, be converted into a felonious taking, the next and last inquiry will be, in what cases the Legislature has made this particular breach of trust felony? There are only four statutes upon this subject, vis. the 21 Hen. VIII. c. 7; the 15 Geo. II. c. 13, s. 12; the 5 Geo. III. c. 35, s. 17; and 7 Geo. III. c. 50. The two last Acts related entirely and exclusively to breaches of trust committed by servants employed in the business of the Post-Offices; and the second to breaches of trust committed by servants employed in the business of the Bank of England, and of course, cannot affect, in any manner whatever, the present case. Nor can the case of the prisoner be construed within the statute 21 Hen. VIII. c. 7 * * *; for it has been determined upon this statute, that it is strictly confined to such goods as are delivered by the master to the servant to keep. But this Bank-note, as has been already shown, was not in the possession of the master, and therefore it cannot have been delivered by him; it being impossible for a man to deliver, either by himself or his agent, a thing of which he is neither actually nor constructively possessed; but, even admitting that it had been in the master's possession, and delivered by him to the prisoner, it would not have been delivered to him to keep, but for the purpose of entering it faithfully in the bank, and handing it over to the Bank-note cashier. * * *

Fielding, for the Crown, argued the case entirely on the question, Whether the prosecutors, Esdaile and Hammett, had such a constructive possession of the Bank-note as to render the taking of it by the prisoner felony? He insisted, that in the case of personal chattels, the possession in law follows the right of property; and, that as Gilbert's clerk did not deposit the notes with Bazeley as a matter of trust to him; for they were paid at the counter, and in the banking-house of the prosecutors, of which Bazeley was merely one of the organs; and, therefore, the payment to him was in effect a payment to them, and his receipt of them vested the property eo instanter in their hands, and gave them the legal possession of it. * * *

The Judges, it is said, were of opinion, * * * that this Bank-note never was in the legal custody or possession of the prosecutors, Messrs. Esdaile and Hammett; but no opinion was ever publicly delivered [1]; and the prisoner was included in the Secretary of State's letter as a proper object for a pardon.

But in consequence of this case the statute 39 Geo. III. c. 85 was passed, entitled, "An Act to protect Masters and others against Embezzlement, by their Clerks or Servants." [2]

Note

Custody; Fictions. Prior to the statute of 1529, the common law courts came to agree that guests did not get possession of the host's household goods or of the innkeeper's cutlery. Following this theme, they later found that a customer did not get possession of goods handed to him for examination by a shopkeeper. After some wavering, they also decided that a servant who was handed goods by his master did not get possession of these goods, at least while the master remained in the vicinity. The statute of 1529 confirmed a trend to hold that the servant never gets possession of goods from his master, even if he is allowed to take them away from the place of

1. On consultation among the Judges, some doubt was at first entertained; but at least all assembled agreed that it was not felony, inasmuch as the note was never in the possession of the bankers, distinct from the possession of the prisoner; though it would have been otherwise if the prisoner had deposited it in the drawer, and had afterwards taken it. * * * That although to many purposes the note was in the actual possession of the masters, yet it was also in the actual possession of the servant, and that possession not to be impeached; for it was a lawful one. * * *

2. See also 52 Geo. III. c. 63, by which the offence of embezzlement is extended to bankers, merchants, brokers, attornies, agents, of any description whatsoever, as to certain descriptions of property entrusted to their care, and 50 Geo. III. c. 59, as to embezzlements by collectors of the public monies. * * *

employment and use discretion in dealing with them. In all these cases, the recipient was said to have custody or charge of the goods. Do you see an objective difference between custody and possession, or are we dealing with a purely fictional distinction? What policy is served by the concept of custody?

A legal fiction, wrote the legal historian Henry Sumner Maine, is "any assumption which conceals, or affects to conceal, the fact that a rule of law has undergone alteration, its letter remaining unchanged, its operation being modified." *Ancient Law* 25 (5th ed., 1873). Custody can be viewed in this light: it permits us to continue to state that one in possession cannot commit larceny, although those now called custodians—eligible to steal—might earlier have been thought ineligible possessors.

The earliest English legal fictions were jurisdictional in nature. For example, in theory the Court of King's Bench had jurisdiction only over causes of action arising in the county in which it sat (Middlesex, after its itinerant days were over). But a plaintiff could allege a fictitious bill of Middlesex, claiming that the defendant had committed a trespass against him in that county. Once the defendant was brought into court, the plaintiff could allege the true cause of action, which arose elsewhere, and drop the trespass claim. In this way, the King's Bench extended its jurisdiction. The forms of action involved other early fictions. The action of trover alleged that the defendant had found goods and later converted them to his own use, but it could be used for all sorts of conversion cases not involving a finding.

It has been noted that a fiction does not actually deceive, and may not be intended to deceive anyone. It is usually only a kind of metaphorical policy argument. One may argue that a corporation is a person, meaning only to assert that it is proper, for many purposes, to treat a corporation legally as though it were a person. Perhaps, to the extent that custody is a fiction, it is no more than a short way of arguing that servants ought to be treated as strangers in a theft situation. But note that this kind of approach is apt to obscure the real reasons for the rule. On fictions generally, see, for example, L. Fuller, *Legal Fictions,* 25 Ill.L.Rev. 363, 513, 877 (1930–31).

Questions

1. Why was the custody "fiction" not extended to cover Bazeley's Case? Would it have somehow been too big a step to take? Are big steps easier to take in early or later stages of legal development? Were policy considerations working for conviction weaker here than in the earlier situations where custody arguments were accepted?

2. Note that once the servant transfers possession to his master, the servant may retain custody and thereafter may be guilty of larceny. This explains Const's remark in arguing his first point in Bazeley's Case, that if Bazeley had deposited a bank note in his master's drawer, this would have divested him of possession.

(a) Suppose the defendant is sent to get straw, returns with it to his master's courtyard and puts it by the stable door while he goes to get someone to open the stable. When it is opened he puts part of the straw in the hay loft and appropriates the rest of it. Is this larceny? See Reg. v. Hayward, 1 Car. & K. 518, 174 Eng.Rep. 919 (Shropshire Assizes 1844).

(b) Suppose a bank clerk receives money from a customer for the bank, decides to appropriate it, but because he fears he is being watched, puts it into the cash drawer for a few minutes and then removes it when he believes the coast is clear? See Commonwealth v. Ryan, 155 Mass. 523, 30 N.E. 364 (1892). Cf. State v. Ward, 151 Vt. 448, 562 A.2d 1040 (1989), reversing an embezzlement conviction when a bartender took cash provided by the employer from the cash drawer; the employer had possession of the money, the bartender's crime, if any (there was an arguable claim of right), was larceny.

(c) Suppose the appropriating servant is one in a chain of receiving clerks, who receives money from one servant and passes it on to another after making bookkeeping entries. Is he guilty of larceny? Does it make any difference that the appropriating servant is a paying clerk who receives the money from his master's receiving clerk so that he may pay the master's bill? See Reg. v. Masters, 1 Den. 332, 169 Eng.Rep. 268 (Cr.Cas.Res., 1848).

Historical Note

The *Liber Assisarum* or Book of Assizes is a part of the Year Books covering cases from 1327–1377.

39 Geo. 3, c. 85 (1799).

Whereas, bankers, merchants, and others, are, in the course of their dealings and transactions, frequently obliged to entrust their Servants, clerks, and persons employed by them in the like capacity, with receiving, paying, negociating, exchanging, or transferring, money, goods, bonds, bills, notes, bankers drafts, and other valuable effects, and securities: and whereas doubts have been entertained whether the embezzling of the same by such servants, clerks and others, so employed by their masters, amounts to felony by the law of England, and it is expedient that such offences should be punished in the same manner in both parts of the united kingdom; be it enacted and declared by the King's most excellent majesty, by and with the advice and consent of the lords spiritual and temporal, and commons, in this present parliament assembled, and by the authority of the same, That if any servant or clerk, or any person employed for the purpose in the capacity of a servant or clerk, to any person or persons whomsoever, or to any body corporate or politick, shall, by virtue of such employment, receive or take into his possession any money, goods, bond, bill, note, banker's draft, or other valuable security, or effects, for or in the name or on the account of his master or masters, or employer or employers, and shall fraudulently embezzle, secrete, or make away with the same, or any part thereof, every such offender shall be deemed to have feloniously stolen the same from his master or masters, employer or employers, for whose use or in whose name or names, or on whose account the same was or were delivered to, or taken into the possession of such servant, clerk, or other person so employed, although such money, goods, bond, bill, note, banker's draft, or other valuable security, was or were not otherwise received into the possession of his or their servant, clerk, or other person so employed; and every such offender, his adviser, procurer, aider, or abettor, being thereof lawfully convicted or attainted, shall be liable to be transported to such parts beyond the seas as his Majesty, by and with the advice of his privy council, shall appoint, for any term not exceeding fourteen years, in the discretion of the court before whom such offender shall be convicted or adjudged.

Notes

1. *Embezzlement Statutes.* This statute, the first general embezzlement provision, was provoked by Bazeley's victory. Note that it is narrowly drawn and aimed at Bazeley's situation. What is expressed or implied in this one is usually at the core of an embezzlement statute:

a. The servant or clerk is in possession of the property to be embezzled at the time of the crime.

b. This possession is obtained lawfully from a third person. This means at least that there is no clear indication given at or before the moment the servant receives possession that the servant intends to appropriate the property. The wrongful intention is actually formed at least a moment later, or, at any rate, there is no clear indication to the contrary from the facts.

c. The accused is in a fiduciary relationship with the victim. That is, he is in a position of trust and confidence, in which his obligation to the victim is something more than is required by the ordinary ethics of the marketplace. A fiduciary is obliged, in the course of his job, to put his employer's interests in the transactions he undertakes ahead of his own. He has duties of candor and loyalty. Servants are fiduciaries; bailees are not fiduciaries merely because they are bailees.

d. The accused converts the property; that is, he intentionally performs an act with respect to the property which seriously interferes with the victim's rights. Refusal to hand over the property on proper demand or any unauthorized disposition—sale, gift, pledge, destruction or serious damage, using it up—is generally sufficient for a conversion. Mere caption and asportation may not be enough. (Some statutes, on the other hand, may make it sufficient to co-mingle the property with other property, particularly if the other property belongs wholly to the defendant). Just how much is necessary for a conversion is further considered infra, pp. 263–266 ff.

e. The property subject to embezzlement, if not specified in the statute, is generally held by the courts to be whatever property might be subject to larceny in the jurisdiction.

f. *Mens rea* for embezzlement also follows generally *mens rea* for larceny, at least as to the claim of right defense. The requirement of an intention to deprive permanently is less clear. It may be enough that there is a conversion, even though there is an intention to restore the property later. An intention to replace the property taken with an equivalent will clearly be of no help to the accused; if Bazeley parts with the embezzled funds in betting on a sure thing and repays the bank out of his winnings, he is still guilty of embezzlement.

2. *Expansion of Embezzlement.* Embezzlement statutes were broadened throughout the nineteenth century to include other fiduciaries: agents, brokers, trustees, and attorneys, e.g. Sometimes this was done by amending the original statute in a jurisdiction, but in other instances new statutes with new opportunities for errors in charges were provided. Suppose the 1799 statute is amended to include attorneys, as well as servants and clerks. A client then gives his lawyer $10,000 in cash with instructions to hand over this money as payment of a judgment against the client. The attorney appropriates the money. Can you see why the attorney is guilty neither of embezzlement nor of larceny? Further amendment of the embezzlement statute, or creation of still another statutory offense—sometimes called larceny after trust—was required to convict this malefactor. Sometimes a broad form of embezzle-

ment statute will be enacted in which the only requirement is wrongful appropriation by one in possession of property; these are often called fraudulent conversion statutes.

Questions

1. Defendant drove a truck for the Utah By-Products Company which picked up scrap fat, meat, and bones from restaurants, etc. The defendant ordinarily issued receipts for the number of pounds taken, and his employer issued checks to the seller on the basis of copies of the receipts. One of the sellers was an Air Force base which demanded cash payments, so for this seller the company issued checks payable to defendant for scrap turned in, and the defendant cashed the checks and paid the Air Force. On one occasion the defendant short-weighted several other sellers, turned in the extra poundage in scraps as Air Force sales, and cashed the resulting check for $84.25, keeping the proceeds. He was charged with embezzling $84.25 from his employer. Assume an embezzlement statute broad enough to include larceny after trust. Should the defendant be convicted? See State v. Taylor, 14 Utah 2d 107, 378 P.2d 352 (1963).

2. Why do you suppose the statute of 1799 did not merely broaden the definition of larceny to include Bazeley's acts? Cf. Model Penal Code § 223.2(1).

b. THEFT BY BAILEES, FINDERS, ETC.; LARCENY, LARCENY BY BAILEE, ETC.

> *"It is said a taking, for bailing or delivery is not in the case* * * *."

Introductory Note

In Reg. v. Thristle, 2 Car. & K. 842, 843, 175 Eng.Rep. 354, 355 [two cases] (Exchequer Chamber 1848), the accused made unauthorized disposition of watches bailed to him by the owners for repairs or regulation. In overturning the larceny convictions, BARON PARKE noted a principle which had been—in the usual sort of case—recognized for hundreds of years (at p. 844 of Car. & K. and 355 of Eng.Rep.):

> "We are of opinion that it is quite clear, that, unless the possession was obtained with a felonious intent, no subsequent appropriation will make it a larceny."

The Carrier's Case

Star Chamber and Exchequer Chamber, 1473.
Y.B. Pasch. 13 Edw. 4, f. 9, pl. 5.

In the Star Chamber before the King's Council such matter was shown and debated: Where one had with another to carry certain bales of woad [a] and other things to Southampton, he took and carried them to another place, and broke open the bales and took the goods contained therein feloniously, and converted them to his own use, and disposed of them suspiciously; if that could be called felony or not, that was the case.

a. Woad is a plant from which a blue dye can be extracted.

BRIAN, [C.J., C.P.]: I think not, for where he has the possession lawfully from the party by a bailing and delivery, it cannot after be called felony nor trespass, for no felony can be except with violence and *vi & armis,* and what he himself has he cannot take with *vi & armis,* nor *contra pacem.* * * *

Hussey (the King's Attorney): It is felony to claim the property feloniously without cause with intent to defraud him in whom the property is, *animo furandi,* and here, notwithstanding the bailment, * * * the property remained in the bailor; therefore this property can be feloniously claimed by the bailee, just as a stranger can. * * *

* * *

Molineux. * * *: A thing lawfully done may be called felony or trespass according to the intent * * *: so if a man comes into a tavern to drink that is lawful, but if he carries off the piece or does other trespass, then all is bad, etc. So, although the taking for the purpose of carriage was lawful * * *, yet when he took the goods to another place, he did not pursue the same end, and so by his later act it may be called felony or trespass according to the intent.

BRIAN: When a man does something of his own head, it can be made lawful in one case and not in another, according to his act afterwards, as in the cases you have put, for there his intent shall be judged according to his act; but where I have goods by your bailment, this case cannot be made bad afterwards by anything. * * *

Vavisour: Sir, it seems to me that our case is better than a bailment, for here the goods were not delivered to him, but there was a bargain that he should carry them to Southampton * * *; and then if he took them to take them there, he took them warrantably; * * * his demeanor after shows that he took them as a felon and with another intent than to carry them as above, in which case he took them without warrant and cause, for he did not pursue the cause, and so it is felony. * * *

CHOKE [J., C.P.]: It seems to me that where a man has goods in his possession by reason of a bailment, he cannot take them feloniously, being in possession, but again it seems to me that here there is felony, for here the things which were inside the bales were not bailed to him; only the bales as an entire thing were bailed * * *; in which case if he had given the bales or sold them * * * it is no felony; but when he broke them and took out of them what was inside, he did that without warrant, as if one bailed a tun of wine to carry, if he sells the tun it is not felony nor trespass, but if he took some of it out it is felony; and here the twenty pounds [the contents of the bales] were not bailed to him, and perhaps he knew not of them at the time of bailment. So is it if I bail the key to my chamber to one to guard my chamber, and he takes my goods from my chamber, it is felony for they were not bailed to him.

It was then moved by some to the Chancellor that this matter ought to be determined at common law and not here [in the Star Chamber].

THE CHANCELLOR: This suit is brought by an alien merchant who came here under safe conduct; and he is not bound to sue according to the law of the land nor to await the trial of twelve men and other formalities of the law of the land, but should sue here where it will be determined according to the law of nature in Chancery, and he can sue here from hour to hour and from day to day for the speeding of merchants. * * *

* * *

And after the matter of the felony was argued before the justices in the Exchequer Chamber, and there it was held by all but Needham [J., K.B.] that when goods are bailed to a man he cannot take them feloniously. * * *

And it was held that where a man has possession and that determines, he can then be felon of the things, as if I bail goods to one to carry to my house and he brings them to my house and then takes them out, this is felony, for his possession is determined when they are in my house. * * *

LAICON [J., K.B.]: There seems to me to be a difference between a bailment of goods and a bargain to take and carry them, for by the bailment he has possession delivered, but by the bargain he has no possession until he takes them. And, if he takes them to carry, then it is lawful, but if he takes them with another intent than to carry, so that he does not pursue the cause, then it seems to me that it may well be called felony. * * *

BRIAN: It seems to me it is all one, a bargain to carry them, or a bailment, for in both cases he has authority of the person in whom the property was, so that it cannot be called felony. In Michelmas 2 Edw. 3 in an indictment "quod felonicè abduxit unum equum" was bad, but it should have been "cêpit" * * *, and in this case the taking cannot be feloniously, because he had lawful possession, so then the breaking the bales is not felony. * * *

And because it appeared that he had possession before, the writ being *vi & armis* was challenged, and yet it was held good and he pleaded not guilty.

And then the justices made a report to the Chancellor in the Council that in the opinion of most of them it was felony.

[The judges went on to give their opinion that the King could not claim the goods as waif—stolen goods thrown away by the thief in flight, which belong to the King if seized on his behalf before the owner can recover them, the owner being entitled to reclaim them upon a showing that he has pursued the thief with due diligence, or has obtained his conviction—because of the King's grant of safe conduct, which carried an implication that the goods would be returned to the alien merchant without the need of showing diligence or his obtaining of the conviction.]

Notes

1. *Breaking Bulk.* The Exchequer Chamber suggestion of breaking bulk or determining (terminating) the bailment had a rich, if somewhat nonsensical, history. Does it make any difference that there is no package or bag to be broken? Suppose, for example, the bailee brings his own bushel basket and scoops up a bushel of corn from a pile in a grain elevator. Is this larceny? Suppose a corporation bails six automobiles to a garage for repainting in the corporate colors. The bailee sells one of the cars. Is this larceny?

2. *Case on Breaking Bulk.* Nichols v. People, 17 N.Y. 114 (1858), split, five judges to two, on a breaking bulk issue. The majority found that the facts showed breaking bulk and therefore common law larceny:

It appeared from the bill of exceptions that the prisoner, being captain and owner of a canal boat, took on board at Albany thirty-four tons of pig iron, which he agreed with the owner to transport to Buffalo. The iron was in bars, each of which weighed about one hundred pounds. On the passage to Buffalo, the prisoner stopped his boat at Whitesboro' in the night, and then put off from the boat one hundred bars of the iron of the value of $175. There was further evidence on the part of the people, tending to show that this removal of the iron was with a felonious intent. The remainder of the iron was delivered by the prisoner at Buffalo. * * *

* * *

In the case at bar it is insisted, on the part of the people, that the bailee can commit larceny only where he actually breaks a bale or package; that it is this breaking alone which can determine the privity of contract and render the asportation by the carrier a trespass. But this, I think, is too narrow construction of the rule, and one not sustained by the commentators and adjudications. Any separation of a part from the whole would seem to be as much a trespass as the breaking of a package. Indeed, it is the separation that constitutes the trespass. This seemed to be conceded upon the argument in regard to grains and things of that kind, but a distinction was attempted to be drawn between grain and iron in the form of pigs.

But I am unable to perceive the force of the distinction. What the rule might be in the case of articles having, as it were, a separate identity, like barrels of flour, saw logs and the like, it is not necessary to inquire. In this case, the iron was in a condition in which it is transferred in bulk by the hundred pounds or by the ton, and not by count. Although more readily separated by individual count than the kernels of grain, it is not a subject of trade or commerce by count any more than grain is; and a separation of part from the rest would seem to be just as much a trespass as the separation of a portion of a load, in bulk, or corn, apples or potatoes from the whole would be. It is this separation of any article conveyed in bulk, by a carrier, from the whole, which constitutes the distinction between larceny and embezzlement.

* * *

In Rex v. Howell (7 Carr. & Payne, 325), the prisoner was employed to land a boat load of staves from a ship, and he landed all but two which he secreted in the bottom of the boat, and one, which he landed, he carried to his mother's house. The court held, in the words of Patteson, J., that the non-delivery of the two was not larceny, "but the prisoner separating one of the articles from the rest, and taking it to a place different from its destination, was, if he did it with intent to appropriate it to his own use, equivalent to breaking bulk, and therefore would be sufficient to constitute larceny."

The learned judge who read the opinion in the court below suggested that the decision of this case might have been based upon the actual delivery of the staves at the place of destination and a subsequent asportation, which would constitute larceny within all the cases. It is enough that the court in that case did not put their ruling upon any such ground; and I assume, from the remarks of Justice Patteson, that the stave was taken directly from the boat to the place where it was found, notwithstanding the imperfect statement of the facts would indicate that it was first landed.

* * *

The case of Rex v. Madox (1 Russ. & Ry., 92), was cited in the court below as a case in point against the prisoner. In that case the prisoner, who was the master of a vessel, received two hundred and eighty casks of butter to carry in his ship; most of the casks were stowed in the hold and battened down, but some were put upon deck. The master disposed of thirteen of those upon deck upon the voyage. It was held that this was not larceny, although it seemed to be admitted by the court that if the prisoner had broken bulk, by taking the thirteen from those battened down, it would have been larceny. This case, it seems to me, is not in point at all. These casks were delivered to the master by count and not in bulk, and consequently there was clearly no breaking bulk, no taking part from the whole of the mass or bulk delivered, but it was a mere separation of a number of separate articles from the whole number. The casks were clearly what might be deemed separate packages, as they lay upon the deck. But it seemed to be conceded that if the master had taken them from those battened down it would be larceny.

* * *

In Rex v. Pratley (5 Carr. & Payne, 533), the prisoner was employed to carry in his cart three trusses of hay, and he took away one of them, which was found in his possession but not broken up. It was held not larceny. Here there was clearly no breaking bulk. The three trusses were three separate packages, and the conversion of one whole package was held by the court not to be larceny. If the pig iron had been put up in separate boxes, and the prisoner in the case at bar had been indicted for stealing one or more boxes, that case would have been in point.

The dissenting judges thought otherwise:

> These pigs or bars of iron were as distinct and separate as the casks of butter, or the trusses of hay. The act of taking away a portion of them was no more a breaking of bulk than the taking of one or more of a parcel of any articles resembling each other. They were not mixed, and were incapable of being mixed like the barilla, or like corn taken to a mill to grind.

The result of the case was that the defendant went free. He had already been acquitted of larceny and was not guilty of a statutory offense dealing with thefts by bailees because the statute was thought to deal only with conduct which was not common law larceny.

3. *Larceny by Bailee Statutes.* Where the bailee took all of the goods or where the bailment was not "determined," the courts were unable to find common law larceny. Eventually, statutes were enacted in most jurisdictions under the heading of larceny by bailee or appropriation by bailee to create still another offense. Sometimes the new statutes did not completely cover the ground. Sometimes they included Carrier's Case larceny. Sometimes you can't be sure what they did. Consider for example section 5 of Article 27 of the Annotated Code of Maryland:

> If a bailee for hire * * * shall wilfully appropriate and use * * * the property, or any part thereof, which is the subject matter of the bailment, without the consent of the owner or owners of such property, he shall be deemed guilty of a misdemeanor. * * *"

Such conduct is now included in Model Penal Code § 223.2(1).

4. *Embezzlement Compared.* The rules here as to property, *mens rea,* and conversion are similar to those noted in the embezzlement situation.

Historical Note

The Carrier's Case is an example of frontier law making. Chief Justice Brian represented the established position: a bailee by definition has possession, and he cannot be guilty of larceny of the goods bailed to him because he cannot take them and carry them away out of the possession of another. The other judges and lawyers were attempting to modify this rule or to find some factual distinction which would make this bailee case different from the other bailee cases. Make sure that you can identify the different arguments made for conviction.

This case was decided shortly after the end of the Wars of the Roses and not long before the Yorkists were in turn overthrown by Henry VII, the first of the Tudors. It is some comment on the stability of the legal system that several of the participants in the Carrier's Case survived in office well into Tudor times. Judge Choke practiced from as early as 1440 and served as judge under both Lancastrians and Yorkists until 1483. Needham had similar service on the bench from 1457 to 1479, and Judge Laicon (Laken) served on the King's Bench from 1465 to 1475. All died peacefully in office or shortly after retirement. Attorney General Hussey (or Huse) later became Chief Justice of the King's Bench and continued to serve under Henry VII until 1495. Vavisour (Vavasour) was appointed to the Court of Common Pleas by Henry VII in 1490. Chief Justice Brian (Bryan) served under Henry until Brian's death in 1500. The mystery figure (at least to your editor) is the unnamed Chancellor. In The Queen v. Ashwell (infra, p. 259) JUDGE STEPHEN remarks at 16 Q.B.D. 208, in the course of discussing the Carrier's Case:

> But it must be observed that the Chancellor in 1474 was Booth, then Bishop of Durham, of whom Lord Campbell says, "His appointment turned out a great failure; he was equally inefficient in the Court of Chancery and in Parliament. Except that he did not take bribes, he had every bad quality of a judge." He was, in a few months after this case, "dismissed from his office of Chancellor," on account of his incompetency.

The only difficulty is that modern authorities date the case 1473 rather than 1474. Booth became chancellor in July, 1473, after the Easter Term, in which the case was decided, was over. The previous chancellor, Stillington, may have been too ill to attend to business in Easter Term, 1473; he resigned for reasons of health in June of that year. He did recover; a loyal Yorkist, he made his peace with Henry, but eventually died his prisoner in 1491. See 1 Campbell, *Lives of the Lord Chancellors of England* (4th ed. 1874), at pp. 365–367.

Questions

1. The variety of reasons advanced for conviction in the Carrier's Case is to be expected when the law takes a great leap forward. Compare almost any case before the U.S. Supreme Court today in which the law is modified. The Supreme Court's business consists largely of difficult problems in which the Court is invited to reinterpret the law. If it is disposed to do so, the members are likely to disagree on the proper rationale. It is only after a series of decisions that a satisfactory reformulation and rationale is likely to emerge. In the Carrier's Case it took centuries before the implications of the Exchequer Chamber decision were worked out. What goes on when the Court knows its conclusion before it can give convincing reasons for it? Does it indicate a kind of result-oriented judicial dishonesty?

2. Assume a larceny by bailee statute. Is there any difference between these two cases? (a) A check room attendant, who you are to assume is a bailee, borrows a checked mink coat. (b) A vacationer rents a car, stating that she will drive it from Chicago to New York, where she will turn it in two weeks from the date of rental; she is found driving the car in Boston 23 days after the rental.

Regina v. Hassall

Court for Crown Cases Reserved, 1861.
Le. & Ca. 58, 169 Eng.Rep. 1302.

* * *

It was proved that the prisoner and a man named Richard Shaw agreed, early in January, 1860, to start a Money Club. * * * Shaw was secretary, the prisoner was treasurer; and they, together with one Bellhouse, formed the committee of management.

The Rules of the Club were as follows:—Each member had to deposit weekly a sum of not less than three pence halfpenny nor more than thirteen pence halfpenny. Members omitting any weekly payment to be subject to a small fine; the odd halfpence to be expended, 1st on a feast at the end of the year, and 2nd in payment of the services of Shaw, the prisoner and Bellhouse. The prisoner alone had the custody of all moneys paid in by members, and had authority to lend, out of the Club money in his hands, provided he first obtained the secretary's written consent to the loan, sums not exceeding £1, at the rate of 5 per cent, interest; and several sums were thus lent out to members within the year, and repaid with interest. The rule of the Club was that such loans could only be made to members.

On the evening of the 24th of December, 1860, the Club money, which amounted to £39, 13s. 1d., was to have been distributed amongst the members in this way. Each member was to receive back the exact amount he had paid in, less the odd halfpence and the amount of his fines, if any; he was also to receive, in addition to the sum he had deposited, an equal share of the total amount arising from fines and from interest on loans. The sum of £2, 14s. 1d. laid in the indictment was the exact amount paid by John Farrell, the prosecutor, into the prisoner's hands, no part of it being made up of interest or fines.

On the morning of the 24th of December, the day when the distribution of the Club money was to have taken place, the prisoner told Shaw that his house had been broken into and robbed of the money belonging to the Club and of some of his own. The prisoner attended the Club the same evening, and said that, if time was given him, he could pay twenty shillings in the pound. The result of an examination of the prisoner's house by the police was that he was given into custody on a charge of stealing the Club money.

On the above facts it was contended by the prisoner's counsel,

1st. That the prisoner was not a bailee of the sum of £2, 14s. 1d. within the meaning of the 20 & 21 Vict. c. 54, as this money had been paid into his hands by the prosecutor in small sums in silver and copper coins, which particular coins he was not bound to return.

* * *

I overruled the objections, and left the case to the jury, who found the prisoner guilty; whereupon he was sentenced to twelve months' imprisonment with hard labour, until the opinion of the Court for the Consideration of Crown Cases Reserved could be taken, whether on the above facts the prisoner was rightly convicted.

This case was argued, on 1st June, 1861, before COCKBURN C.J., POLLOCK C.B., CROMPTON, J., WILLES J. and WILDE B.

Campbell Foster for the prisoner.—The evidence does not bring the case within the 20 & 21 Vict. c. 54, s. 4 [1], which is a criminal enactment and must be construed strictly. * * *

* * *

WILLES J.—I have heard it laid down by Lord Wensleydale that there is a taking of specific coins in embezzlement; because a servant who receives money for his master is bound to hand over the very money he receives.

* * *

COCKBURN C.J.—Here the prisoner was not bound to return the specific coins he received. Does not the word, bailee, imply that the thing received is to be specifically returned? A bailee must return either the article received or something into which it has been converted in accordance with the terms of the bailment.

Hannay for the Crown. If that be so the bailment known as *commodatum,* or loan to use, cannot apply to money. Now, it is said in Pothier (vol. 4, p. 5, ed. 1835, tit. Prêt a usage, § 10) that *commodatum,* or loan to use, has most analogy with the *prêt de consomption* or *mutuum* of the civil law. * * *

CROMPTON J.—Does he say that a loan of money is a bailment?

Hannay. Perhaps not; but, unless this is held to be a bailment, there will be a failure of justice.

WILDE B.—Or, in other words, non-payment of debts, even if accompanied by fraud, is not criminal.

Hannay. It is impossible to use money unless it may be exchanged.

COCKBURN C.J.—This conviction cannot be sustained. The prisoner is indicted, under the 4th section of the 20 & 21 Vict. c. 54, for larceny as a bailee. The word bailment must there be understood in its legal acceptation, viz. a deposit of something to be returned in specie, and does not apply to the receipt of money with an obligation to return the amount where there is no obligation to return the identical coin. * * *

Conviction quashed.

Historical Note

Lord Chief Justice Cockburn was a great advocate before he became a judge. His eloquent and impressive defense of Daniel M'Naghten in 1843 secured an acquittal in a case which laid the foundation for insanity law for the next century. It was said that he flew better than he walked: he was not so good at the daily grind, but he rose to great occasions.

1. Sect. 4 of the 20 & 21 Vict. c. 54 is as follows:—If any person, being a bailee of any property, shall fraudulently take or convert the same to his own use, or the use of any person other than the owner thereof, although he shall not break bulk or otherwise determine the bailment, he shall be guilty of larceny.

Questions

1. Be sure that you understand the distinction between two situations, one of which is almost certain to be embezzlement or some related statutory crime and the other of which is not criminal: (a) A, upon B's agreement to follow A's instructions, hands B two fifty dollar bills and tells him to give the bills to C the following morning in payment of A's $100 debt to C. B squanders the money in riotous living and does not pay C. (b) D, on E's agreement to follow D's instructions, hands E five twenty dollar bills and tells him to pay D's $100 debt to F the next morning. E squanders the money in riotous living and does not pay F.

2. Employer A pays his employees weekly in cash. Some employees have charge accounts with a local grocer. One of these employees, when A is about to hand him his pay, says, "Please retain $150 of that money in your hand and use it to pay my grocery bill." A agrees, but never pays the bill. Has A committed a crime? Compare Commonwealth v. Mitchneck, 130 Pa.Super. 433, 198 A. 463 (1938), with Model Penal Code § 223.8.

3. What is the relationship between a bank and one with a checking account at the bank? Can the bank steal or embezzle funds in the account from the depositor? Can a joint depositor steal or embezzle from the account when he defrauds the other joint depositor?

4. D, a confidence man, received a sum of money from V, promising to invest what he received in specified ways on behalf of V. He also gave V a promissory note for the amount taken, on which he paid interest. He used the sum received for his own purposes, and was charged with an embezzlement-type offense. What result?

5. D, a used car dealer, borrowed from V Finance Company to get money to purchase used cars. The agreement between them provided that V had security title to the cars so purchased. Such borrowings continued for a number of years, D reselling the cars to customers and repaying the loans as they became due out of his general funds. When, in bad economic times, D was unable to repay the loans on four cars which he had sold to customers, he was charged with an embezzlement-type offense. What result?

Regina v. Riley

Court for Crown Cases Reserved, 1853.
Dears. 149, 169 Eng.Rep. 674.

At the General Quarter Sessions of the Peace for the county of Durham, held at the city of Durham before Rowland Burdon Esquire, chairman, on the 18th day of October, 1852, the prisoner was indicted for having on the 5th of October, 1852, stolen a lamb the property of John Burnside.

The prisoner pleaded not guilty.

On the trial it was proved that on Friday, the 1st day of October, 1852, John Burnside, the prosecutor, put ten white-faced lambs into a field in the occupation of John Clarke, situated near to the town of Darlington. On Monday, the 4th day of October, the prisoner went with a flock of twenty-nine black-faced lambs to John Clarke, and asked if he might put them into Clarke's field for a night's keep, and upon Clarke's agreeing to allow him to do so for one penny per head, the prisoner put his twenty-nine lambs into the same field with the prosecutor's lambs.

At half-past seven o'clock in the morning of Tuesday, the 5th day of October, the prosecutor went to Clarke's field, and in counting his lambs he missed one, and the prisoner's lambs were gone from the field also. Between eight and nine o'clock in the morning of the same day, the prisoner came to the farm of John Calvert, at Middleton Saint George, six miles east from Darlington, and asked him to buy twenty-nine lambs. Calvert agreed to do so and to give eight shillings a piece for them. Calvert then proceeded to count the lambs, and informed the prisoner that there were thirty instead of twenty-nine in the flock, and pointed out to him a white-faced lamb, upon which the prisoner said if you object to take thirty, I will draw one. Calvert, however, bought the whole of them, and paid the prisoner twelve pounds for them.

One of the lambs sold to Calvert was identified by the prosecutor as his property, and as the lamb missed by him from Clarke's field. It was a half-bred white-faced lamb, marked with the letter T; and similar to the other nine of the prosecutor's lambs.

The twenty-nine lambs belonging to the prisoner were black-faced lambs. On the 5th of October, in the afternoon, the prisoner stated to two of the witnesses that he never had put his lambs into Clarke's field, and had sold them on the previous afternoon for eleven pounds twelve shillings, to a person on the Barnardcastle Road, which road leads west from Darlington.

There was evidence in the case to shew that the prisoner must have taken the lambs from Clarke's field early in the morning, which was thick and rainy.

It was argued by the counsel for the prisoner, in his address to the jury, that the facts shewed that the original taking from Clarke's field was by mistake, and if the jury were of that opinion, then as the original taking was not done *animo furandi* the subsequent appropriation would not make it a larceny, and the prisoner must be acquitted. The Chairman, in summing up, told the jury that though they might be of opinion that the prisoner did not know that the lamb was in his flock until it was pointed out to him by Calvert, he should rule that in point of law the taking occurred when it was so pointed to the prisoner and sold by him to Calvert, and not at the time of leaving the field.

The jury returned the following verdict:—"The jury say that at the time of leaving the field the prisoner did not know that the lamb was in his flock, and that he was guilty of felony at the time it was pointed out to him."

The prisoner was then sentenced to six months' hard labour in the house of correction at Durham, and being unable to find bail was thereupon committed to prison until the opinion of this Court could be taken upon the question:—

Whether Charles Riley was properly convicted of larceny.

* * *

On the 22nd January, A.D. 1853, the case was argued before POLLOCK C.B., PARKE B., WILLIAMS J., TALFOURD J., and CROMPTON J.

* * *

POLLOCK C.B.—We are all of opinion that the conviction in this case is right. The distinction between this and the case of Reg. v. Thristle, 1 Den. C.C. 502, is this. If a man rightfully gets possession of an article without any intention at the time of stealing it, and afterwards misappropriates it, the law holds it not to be a felony. In that case a man had delivered his watch to a watchmaker to regulate it, and the watchmaker afterwards disposed of it for his own use. In the case of Reg. v. Thurborn, 1 Den.C.C. 388, where Parke B. delivered the considered judgment of the Judges, it was ruled that "if a man find goods that have been actually lost, or are reasonably supposed by him to have been lost, and appropriates them with intent to take the entire dominion over them, really believing, when he takes them, that the owner cannot be found, it is no larceny; but if he takes them with the like intent, though lost or reasonably supposed to be lost, but reasonably believing that the owner can be found, it is larceny." It may reasonably be said not to be a violation of any social duty for a man who finds a lost article to take it home for the purpose of finding out the true owner; and if he does this honestly in the first instance, and afterwards, though he may have discovered the true owner, is seduced into appropriating it to his own use, he is not guilty of larceny, though he does wrong. So in *Leigh's* case, 2 East, P.C. 694, it appeared that the prosecutor's house was on fire, and that the prisoner assisted in saving some of his goods, and took some of them home to her lodgings, but next morning denied that she had them in her possession. It was suggested that she originally took the goods with an honest intent, that of assisting in saving her neighbour's property from the fire. She was found guilty; but the Judges, as it appeared that she originally took the goods merely from a desire of saving them for and returning them to the prosecutor, and that she had no evil intention till afterwards, held that the conviction was wrong. There the original taking was not wrongful; indeed it was right, for she took possession of the goods under the authority of the true owner. * * * [T]he original possession of the lamb was from the beginning wrongful. Here the taking of the lamb from the field was a trespass; or if it be said that there was no taking at that time, then the moment he finds the lamb he appropriates it to his own use. The distinction between the cases is this: if the original possession be rightful, subsequent misappropriation does not make it a felony; but if the original possession be wrongful, though not felonious, and then a man disposes of the chattel, *animo furandi,* it is larceny.

PARKE B.—The original taking was not lawful. The prisoner being originally a trespasser, he continued a trespasser all along, just as at common law, a trespass begun in one county continued in another, and, being a trespasser, the moment he took the lamb with a felonious intent, he became a thief. He at first simply commits a trespass; but as soon as he entertains a felonious intent that becomes a felonious trespass. *Leigh's* case was altogether a different case from the present. There the original possession was lawful, with the assent of the true owner, the prisoner rendering charitable assistance in preserving the goods from fire. When she first took the goods into her possession, she was not a trespasser.

WILLIAMS J., TALFOURD J., and CROMPTON J. concurred.

Questions

1. As A is about to leave home for work, her doorbell rings and a deliveryman from a local store hands her a package with an umbrella handle protruding from one end. A assumes that someone is sending her a gift. But after the deliveryman has left, A notices that the name and address on the outside package are those of her next door neighbor. She decides to keep the umbrella (X) for herself. She carries it to work and takes it to a restaurant at lunch time, when she leaves it hanging on a coatrack. After lunch, as she is walking back to work she notices that she has accidentally picked up umbrella Y from the coatrack rather than umbrella X. Since Y is of better quality, she decides to keep it. Further along, she sees a folding umbrella (Z) with a broken wrist strap in the middle of the sidewalk. She picks this up and notices a silver name plate on the handle with the name "Prunella Z. Farzetta-Waldenheim" engraved on it. A keeps this one as a spare. Has she stolen any of the umbrellas?

2. What is the theoretical larceny problem involved in the *Riley* case and the cases cited therein? How is it resolved by the Model Penal Code?

Historical Note

Lord Chief Baron Pollock (see the *Riley* case) was known for his able opinions and sat on the bench until his eighty-third year. He had fifty-four grandchildren, one of whom was Sir Frederick Pollock, the great legal scholar and historian, co-author of Pollock and Maitland, *The History of English Law before the Time of Edward I,* and of the *Holmes-Pollock Letters,* his correspondence with Justice Oliver Wendell Holmes.

The Queen v. Ashwell

Court for Crown Cases Reserved, 1885.
16 Q.B.D. 190.

[Ashwell asked Keogh for the loan of a shilling, and Keogh handed over a coin which both believed to be a shilling, but which in fact was a more valuable coin, a sovereign. Some time later, Ashwell discovered the coin was a sovereign and appropriated it to his own use. By a tie vote of 7 to 7, the court affirmed his conviction of larceny. There were a number of opinions; the central arguments of the judges, the first for acquittal and the second for conviction, follow.]

STEPHEN, J.

* * *

* * * The rule that in every theft there must be a felonious taking, or in other words a trespass, and that a fraudulent conversion after an innocent taking is not theft, is laid down by every text-writer who has dealt with the subject,—Coke (3rd Institutes, 107), Hale (1 Hale's Pleas of the Crown, 504), Hawkins (book I., chap. 19), Foster (Criminal Law, 123), and others, down to our time,—and has been recognised by many statutes which make exceptions to it in the case of embezzlement by servants, misappropriation by agents, and especially in the case of larceny by bailees. Indeed, my only reason for going so fully into the matter is to shew how characteristic and well established a part of the law the proposition in question is.

The application of this principle to the present case appears to me direct and obvious. Ashwell received the sovereign innocently, though he dealt with it fraudulently an hour afterwards, when he became aware of its value. The inference that he committed no felony at common law appears to me to follow of necessity.

There are two ways in which it is sought to avoid this inference. It is said, first, that the delivery being made under a mistake, passed neither the property in the sovereign nor the right to a possession of it, and that the prisoner must be regarded as having taken it, not when he accepted it under a mistake as to its value, but when knowing its value he determined to appropriate it to himself, or when he did so appropriate it by getting it changed and keeping the change. It is also said that even if no offence at common law was committed, the prisoner was guilty of larceny as a bailee under the 3rd section of the Larceny Act. I am unable to concur with either of these views.

The first view is, I think, contrary to principle, because it evades by a legal fiction the principle that a fraudulent appropriation consequent upon an innocent taking is not larceny. The guilt of the prisoner would follow easily and immediately from the principle that such a taking is larceny, and this second principle is in effect substituted for the first by an artificial interpretation either of the word "possession," or of the word "taking." If the word "possession" is chosen to be interpreted, this is done by explaining it to mean something beyond actual control over the thing possessed, namely, control coupled with knowledge, which may or may not exist. If the word "taking" is chosen to be interpreted, it is in this case interpreted to mean not an actual physical taking, but a subsequent change of mind relating back to such physical taking. I know of no authority for either of these fictions. The word "possession" is indeed used in many senses, some of them highly artificial, but this is a bad reason for adding a new artificial meaning to it. Its plain meaning in this case is the reception of the coin by Ashwell from Keogh. The interpretation suggested appears to me to be one against which there is express authority, which I now proceed to examine.

The cases which set the matter in the clearest light are those which related to the finding of lost property, particularly those which have been decided in modern times. * * *

These cases taken together appear to me to establish, with the utmost possible clearness, the proposition that in order to justify a conviction for larceny, the original taking, in the ordinary sense of the word, must be felonious, that a fraudulent misappropriation after an innocent taking is not theft, and that a change of mind after an innocent taking does not relate back to the innocent taking and make it felonious.

* * *

These cases, no doubt, differ from the present in the circumstances that in all of them the prisoner got possession of the property by finding. Their bearing upon the present case is this: They all proceed upon the principle that in all larceny the actual physical taking must be felonious; and they decide the question whether this was so in particular cases of finding, by reference to the state of the prisoner's mind at the time of finding. They will be found to establish the following proposition:—If at the time of taking the lost property the finder intends to appropriate it to himself and either knows or has the means of knowing the owner, or of knowing that he can be found, and subsequently appropriates the property, he is guilty of larceny; but if at the time of finding he either does not intend to appropriate the property, or does so intend without the knowledge or means of knowledge aforesaid, he is not guilty of larceny because his original taking is not felonious.

The question, therefore, reduces itself to this: What difference was there between the taking by a finder and the reception by Ashwell of the coin given by Keogh? Whatever difference there was appears to me both in law and in common sense to be in Ashwell's favour. A finder must know that the property he finds is not his, whoever may be the owner of it. Ashwell for an hour after he received it reasonably believed that the coin which he received was his own. * * *

* * * It seems to me that if a bailee who appropriated the thing bailed was not at common law guilty of larceny, Ashwell was not guilty à fortiori. A bailee knows what is bailed to him; he is under a direct obligation to deal with it in a particular way; he knows also who, as against him, is the owner of the goods. Ashwell took the coin under a reasonable belief that it was intended to become his own property, and that he incurred no other obligation to the man who gave it to him than that of paying back its equivalent. His taking was as innocent as a bailee's taking, and it involved no such responsibility as is incumbent on a bailee.

I may here notice one point which was raised in argument. It was said that the actual time of taking could not be the point at which the guilt or innocence of a finder must be determined, because in most cases a short time must elapse between the actual taking of a note or coin, the discovery of its nature or value, and the determination consequent upon that discovery to appropriate it; and this, it was said, shews that the time to be considered is the time of acquiring knowledge of the property taken and not the time of taking. If a man picks up a purse containing money, some seconds must usually pass before he can open the purse and discover and determine to appropriate the money. I think, however, that for legal purposes it is neither possible nor desirable to attempt to go into such a refinement as this. If a man finds a purse, picks it up, opens it, finds money in it, and thereupon determines to keep it for himself, it appears to me that the whole process ought to be regarded as one action, taking place at one time, as for many purposes the fractional parts of a day are not regarded by the law. If the examination were delayed for a substantial time, I think the question for the juror would be whether at the time of the taking the prisoner intended to keep what he had found, conditionally upon its turning out upon examination to be worth his while to do so, and whether at the time of taking the goods he had the means of knowing the owner.

* * *

LORD COLERIDGE, C.J., * * *.

* * *

* * * I assume it to be now established law that where there has been no trespass, there can at common law be no larceny. I assume it also to be settled law that where there has been a delivery—in the sense in which I will explain in a moment—of a chattel from one person to another, subsequent misappropriation of that chattel by the person to whom it has been delivered will not make him guilty of larceny, except by statute, with which I am not now concerned. But then it seems to me very plain that delivery and receipt are acts into which mental intention enters, and that there is not in law any more than in sense a delivery and receipt, unless the giver and receiver intended to give and to receive respectively what is respectively given and received.' It is intelligent delivery, as I think, which the law speaks of, not a mere physical act from which intelligence and even consciousness are absent. I hope it is not laying down anything too broad or loose, if I say that all acts, to carry legal consequences must be acts of the mind; and to hold the contrary, to hold that a man did what in sense and reason he certainly did not, that a man did in law what he did not know he was doing and did not intend to do—to hold this is to expose the law to very just but wholly unnecessary ridicule and scorn. I agree with my Brother Stephen that fictions are objectionable, and I desire not to add to them, but it seems to me, with diffidence, that he creates the fiction who holds that a man does what he does not know he does and does not mean to do, not he who says that an act done by an intelligent being for which he is to be responsible is not an act of that being unless it is an act of his intelligence. If it had been so decided by authority which binds me, of course I should submit, but if it has not been so decided, I take the freedom to say that it is not law—at least yet. In this case, therefore, it seems to me, there was no delivery of the sovereign to the prisoner by Keogh, because there was no intention to deliver, and no knowledge that it had been delivered.

Applying the same principles of reasoning, it appears to me that the sovereign was received by the prisoner and misappropriated by him at one and the same instant of time. In good sense it seems to me he did not take it till he knew what he had got; and when he knew what he had got, that same instant he stole it. According to all the cases, if at the very moment of the receipt of a chattel the receiver intends to misappropriate it, he is guilty of larceny. * * *

* * *

Question

How do you think the *Ashwell* case should be decided? Is *Riley* authority in support of conviction? The *Ashwell* judges cited several "container" cases. In Merry v. Green, 7 M. & W. 623, 151 Eng.Rep. 916 (1841), a civil case, a bureau, in which there was a secret drawer containing money, was sold. Neither the seller nor the buyer knew the money was there until after delivery of the bureau, and the court said that delivery of the bureau did not give the buyer lawful possession of the money. Is this case authority in support of the conviction?

Historical Notes

1. Stephen has been mentioned before in connection with the Mirror of Justices at the beginning of the section. A sketch of Lord Chief Justice Coleridge in Vanity Fair, published two years after *Ashwell* [March 5, 1887], described him as "far too egoistic for a Judge. * * * If nature had intended anyone for anything, it intended the great nephew of Samuel Taylor Coleridge for an actor. * * * He is a wit, and plays to the gallery. * * * He is not so much a profound thinker as a palpable sophist." The judge seems to have shared the family literary tastes, better seen in The Queen v. Dudley and Stephens, which appears later in the homicide materials. It was a political family; both Coleridge's father and son were appointed to the Court of King's Bench.

2. Stephen's opinion in *Ashwell* cites Coke's Third *Institute* (1641). Sir Edward Coke (1552–1634) was much involved in disputes between King and Parliament and between the courts of common law and equity. Successively Attorney-General, Chief Justice of Common Pleas, Chief Justice of King's Bench, and Privy Councillor, he finally emerged as a leading opponent of royal authority. His *Institutes* is perhaps the greatest and most influential of the early works attempting to summarize virtually the whole of the law. The first of these great encyclopedists was Henry de Bracton (d. 1268), the author of *De Legibus et Consuetudinibus Angliae.* Others include Francis Bacon (1561–1626) the author, not only of philosophical and literary works, but also of *The Elements of the Common Lawes of England* (1630), and Sir William Blackstone (1723–1780), a judge and the first university teacher of law, whose *Commentaries on the Laws of England* (1765–1770) was immensely popular in both England and America.

c. THEFT BY DECEIT; LARCENY AND OBTAINING PROPERTY BY FALSE PRETENSES

*"Larceny is the treacherously taking * * * goods * * * against the will of him to whom they do belong * * *."*

i. Introduction

Rex v. Turvey

Court of Criminal Appeal, 1946.
31 Crim.App. 154.

THE LORD CHIEF JUSTICE: The Court is of the opinion that the conviction must be quashed. The appellant appeals only against his conviction on count one of the indictment, on which he was sentenced to eighteen months' imprisonment. * * *

The circumstances were these: He was charged that on December 12, 1945, being a servant of His Majesty's Minister of Works, he stole from the Minister a considerable number of table knives, spoons and so forth. The appellant, evidently a thoroughly dishonest person to be in the employ of the Minister of Works, had got into touch with some foreigner living at Newton Abbot, and found that that person would be a ready receiver of goods which could be stolen from the depot of the Minister at Torquay, of which the appellant was then in charge. A Mr. Ward, who was in charge of a depot at Exeter, and was a perfectly honest and reliable servant, was tempted by the appellant and also by the would-be receiver at Newton Abbot, who apparently had control of certain bottles of spirits which were handed as inducements to Mr. Ward, to steal the property of the Minister and hand it to the appellant, who would in turn hand it to the man at Newton Abbot. Mr. Ward did the honest thing and at once communicated with his superiors at Bristol, the persons who were really in control of the property, and told them of this plan which had been suggested to him. The officials of the Ministry decided that it would be a good thing to let this plan go on and catch the culprits at a suitable time, which would enable them to prosecute the appellant for stealing. They told Mr. Ward to hand over the property to the appellant, and Mr. Ward did so.

On those facts, the question arose whether or not the appellant could be convicted of stealing. * * * It is perfectly clear that if he stole the goods, he stole them at Exeter, but he did not take them there against the will of the owner because the owner handed them to him and meant to hand them to him. Mr. Malcolm Wright submitted no case, but the learned Chairman overruled the submission, and it appears that he decided principally on the authority of Egginton (1801), 2 Leach 913 [, 168 Eng.Rep. 555 (1801)] an old case, but perfectly good law, and also because he took a certain view with regard to the control which the owner was exercising over the goods.

Let us see what were the facts in Egginton. It was a case in which a servant told his master that some persons were going to rob the premises. "Very well", said the master, "let them rob the premises and we will catch them." In other words, to give a homely illustration, a man, knowing that somebody is going to break into his house, leaves the bolts drawn and so makes it easy for the man to come into the house, and when he comes in he catches him. A crime has in those circumstances been committed, and committed none the less because the servant has been told to make things easy. In this case, if Ward had been told by Mr. Brown, the person who really had control of these matters, "Let Turvey come in and take the goods", that would have been one thing, but he was told to take the goods and hand them to Turvey, and that makes all the difference.

* * *

* * * He did not carry away the goods against the will of the owner because the owner was willing that he should have the goods and gave them to him. In those circumstances, the conviction of larceny will be quashed, but the appellant will not be discharged because he is already undergoing sentence of six months' imprisonment on other charges.

Conviction quashed.

Question

D asked S, an employee of the V Packing Company, to leave three barrels of V's meat on the company loading platform, with the idea that D would steal the meat by pretending to be a customer. S informed V and was instructed to pretend to go along with the scheme and did so. K, the employee in charge of the loading platform, was told by V that the barrels were put there for a man who would call for them. When D appeared and claimed the barrels, K allowed him to load them in D's wagon and then helped D arrange the goods in the wagon. Is D guilty of larceny? See Topolewski v. State, 130 Wis. 244, 109 N.W. 1037 (1906).

Notes

1. *Consent in Burglary.* Note that in the *Egginton* case the nature of the consent of the owner was sufficient to prevent a burglary conviction, if not the conviction for larceny.

2. *Consent Obtained by Fraud.* The idea that for larceny the taking must be without the victim's consent is a part of the notion of a trespassory taking. It also looks like common sense. The criminal law has plenty to do, and it hardly seems urgent to intervene when the victim voluntarily parts with the property. The result is not so clear, however, when the victim is duped into handing it over. This is the problem of the cases which follow.

ii. Larceny by Trick and False Pretenses

Maud's Case

Bedfordshire Eyre, 1202.
Seldon Society 27 (Select Pleas of the Crown, 1988).*

Maud, wife of Hugh, was taken with a false gallon with which she sold beer, so that the keepers of the measures testify that they took her selling beer with it. And since she cannot defend this, it is considered that she be in mercy. She made fine with two marks, for which the pledges are William, son of Ascelin, William de Solar, Osbert, William's son, Ralph Clerk.

33 Hen. 8, c. 1 (1541).

FORASMUCH as many light and evil-disposed persons, not minding to get their livings by truth, according to the laws of this realm, but compassing and devising daily how they may unlawfully obtain and get into their hands and possession goods, chattels and jewels of other persons, for the maintenance of their unthrifty living, and also knowing that if they come to any of the same goods, chattels and jewels by stealth, that they, being thereof lawfully convicted according to the law of this realm, shall die therefore; have now of late falsely and deceitfully contrived, devised and imagined privy tokens, and counterfeit letters in other mens names, unto divers persons their special friends and acquaintances, for the obtaining of money, goods, chattels and jewels of the same persons, their friends and acquaintances, by colour whereof the said light and evil-disposed persons have deceitfully and unlawfully obtained and gotten great substance of money, goods, chattels and jewels unto their hands and possession, contrary to right and conscience:

II. For reformation whereof, be it ordained and enacted by authority of this present parliament, that if any person or persons, of what estate or degree so ever he or they be, at any time after the first day of April next coming, falsely and deceitfully obtain or get into his or their hands or possession, any money, goods, chattels, jewels, or other things of any other person or persons, by colour and means of any such false token or counterfeit letter made in any other man's name, as is afore-

* Reprinted by permission of The Selden Society.

said, that then every person and persons so offending, and being thereof lawfully convict, by witnesses taken before the lord chancellor of England for the time being, or by examination of witnesses, or confession taken in the star-chamber at Westminster before the King's most honourable council, or before the justices of peace within any part of the King's dominions in their general sessions, or by action in any of the King's courts of record, shall have and suffer such correction and punishment, by imprisonment of his body, setting upon the pillory, or otherwise by any corporal pain (except pains of death) as shall be unto him or them limited, adjudged or appointed by the person or persons before whom he shall be so convict of the said offences, or of any of them.

* * *

Regina v. Jones

Court of Queen's Bench, 1703.
1 Salkeld 379, 91 Eng.Rep. 330.

Mr. Parker moved to quash an indictment, which was, that the defendant came to A., pretending B. sent him, to receive 20£., and received it, whereas B. did not send him. ET PER CUR. It is not indictable unless he came with false tokens; we are not to indict one man for making a fool of another: let him bring his action.

30 Geo. 2, c. 24 (1757).

WHEREAS divers evil-disposed persons, to support their profligate way of life, have by various subtle strategems, threats and devices, fraudulently obtained divers sums of money, goods, wares and merchandizes, to the great injury of industrious families, and to the manifest prejudice of trade and credit; therefore for the punishing all such offenders, be it enacted by the King's most excellent majesty, by and with the advice and consent of the lords spiritual and temporal and commons in this present parliament assembled, and by the authority of the same, That from and after the twenty ninth day of September one thousand seven hundred and fifty seven, all persons who knowingly and designedly, by false pretence or pretences, shall obtain from any person or persons, money, goods, wares, or merchandizes, with intent to cheat or defraud any person or persons of the same; or shall knowingly send or deliver any letter or writing, with or without a name or names, subscribed thereto, or signed with a fictitious name or names, letter or letters, threatening to accuse any person of any crime punishable by law with death, transporation, pillory, or any other infamous punishment, with a view or intent to extort or gain money, goods, wares or merchandizes from the person or persons so threatened to be accused, shall be deemed offenders against law and the publick peace; and the court before whom such offender or offenders shall be tried, shall in case he, she or they shall be convicted of any of the said offences, order such offender or offenders to be fined and imprisoned, or to be put in the pillory, or publickly whipped, or to be transported, as soon as conve-

niently may be (according to the laws made for transportation of felons) to some of his Majesty's colonies or plantations in America, for the term of seven years, as the court in which any such offender or offenders shall be convicted shall think fit and order.

Rex v. Wheatly

Court of King's Bench, 1761.
2 Burr. 1125, 97 Eng.Rep. 746.

Mr. Norton, for the prosecutor, shewed cause why judgment should not be arrested; a rule for that purpose having been obtained, upon a motion made by Mr. Norton on Monday 26th January last, in arrest of judgment upon this indictment for knowingly selling amber-beer short of the due and just measure, (whereof the defendant had been convicted).

The charge in the indictment was, "that Thomas Wheatly late of the parish of St. Luke in the county of Middlesex brewer, being a person of evil name, fame and of dishonest conversation, and devising and intending to deceive and defraud one Richard Webb of his monies, on, &c. at &c. falsely, fraudulently and deceitfully did sell and deliver and cause to be sold and delivered to the said Richard Webb sixteen gallons and no more of a certain malt liquor commonly called amber, for and as eighteen gallons of the same liquor; which said liquor so as aforesaid sold and delivered did then and there want two gallons of the due and just measure of eighteen gallons, for which the same was sold and delivered as aforesaid; (the said Thomas Wheatly then and there well knowing the same liquor so by him sold and delivered to want two gallons of the due and just measure as aforesaid;) and he the said Thomas Wheatly did receive of the said Richard Webb the sum of fifteen shillings, &c. for eighteen gallons, &c. pretended to have been sold and delivered, &c. although there was only sixteen gallons so as aforesaid delivered: and he the said Thomas Wheatly him the said Richard Webb of two gallons of, &c. fraudulently and unlawfully did receive and defraud; to the great damage and fraud of the said Richard Webb, to the evil example of others in the like case offending, and against the peace of our Sovereign Lord the King his Crown and dignity."

* * *

LORD MANSFIELD—The question is, whether the fact here alledged be an indictable crime or not. * * *

* * *

Here, the fact is allowed; but the consequence is denied: the objection is, that the fact is not an offence indictable, though acknowledged to be true as charged.

And that the fact here charged should not be considered as an indictable offence, but left to a civil remedy by an action, is reasonable and right in the nature of the thing: because it is only an inconvenience and injury to a private person, arising from that private person's own negligence and carelessness in not measuring the liquor, upon receiving it, to see whether it held out the just measure or not.

The offence that is indictable must be such a one as affects the public. As if a man uses false weights and measures, and sells by them to all or to many of his customers, or uses them in the general course of his dealing: so, if a man defrauds another, under false tokens. For these are deceptions that common care and prudence are not sufficient to guard against. So, if there be a conspiracy to cheat: for ordinary care and caution is no guard against this.

Those cases are much more than mere private injuries: they are public offences. But here, it is a mere private imposition or deception: no false weights or measures are used; no false tokens given; no conspiracy; only an imposition upon the person he was dealing with, in delivering him a less quantity instead of a greater; which the other carelessly accepted. It is only a non-performance of his contract; for which non-performance, he may bring his action.

The selling an unsound horse, as and for a sound one, is not indictable: the buyer should be more upon his guard.

* * *

Therefore the law is clearly established and settled; and I think on right grounds: but on whatever grounds it might have been originally established, yet it ought to be adhered to, after it is established and settled.

Therefore, (though I may be sorry for it in the present case, as circumstanced;) the judgment must be arrested.

[The concurring opinion of DENISON, J., is omitted.]

Historical Notes

1. As *Maud* shows, the use of false weights and measures in sales to the public is an ancient common law misdemeanor. The prudent citizen could not easily guard against thirty-five and a half inch yardsticks and the like, and the standardization of weights and measures was an early concern of the central authority. But there do not appear to have been criminal penalties for other fraudulent conduct prior to the statute of Henry VIII, and this statute is narrowly drawn. It applies only to cases of false tokens or counterfeit letters, as where the accused pretends to be a collecting agent and shows a signet ring falsely purporting to be that of the creditor to get the debtor to part with the debt payment.

2. The Selden Society publishes a series of volumes of early documents in English legal history.

3. The judge in Reg. v. Jones was Lord Chief Justice Holt (1642–1710), one of the greatest of the common law judges. Prior to his time, judicial corruption and incompetence were not uncommon. He was a model for the time of learning, fairness, integrity, and independence. He was also known for the directness of his reasoning, as appears in *Jones.* He is the subject of many anecdotes. One of the most famous has him, while ill at home, and perhaps not in his most judicial frame of mind, imperiously visited by one Lacy, on behalf of John Atkins, a fellow member of a religious brotherhood, called the Prophets, who was being held for trial. Lacy: "I come to you a prophet from the Lord God, who has sent me to thee, and would have thee grant a *nolle prosequi* for John Atkins, his servant, whom thou has sent to prison." Holt, C.J.: "Thou art a false prophet and a lying knave. If the Lord God had sent thee, it would have been to the Attorney-General, for He knows that it belongeth

not to the Chief Justice to grant a *nolle prosequi:* but I, as Chief Justice, can grant a warrant to commit thee to bear him company." He did so.

4. The statute of George II is broader in terms than that of Henry VIII and resembles the more modern false pretenses statutes. But note the reaction of the *Wheatly* court.

5. Lord Mansfield, Chief Justice of the Court of King's Bench for thirty-two years (1756–1788), was another great common law judge. He was most famous for his decisions in commercial law. He was the first to decide that a slave, once brought into England, became free, and the first to allow non-Christians to be sworn as witnesses in English courts. When law students visited his court, he would invite them to sit on the bench with him and would interrupt the proceedings to explain points of law to them.

Rex v. Pear

Central Criminal Court, 1780.
1 Leach 212, 168 Eng.Rep. 208.

This case was reserved by MR. JUSTICE ASHHURST, at the Old Bailey in September Session 1779.

The prisoner was indicted for stealing a black horse, the property of Samuel Finch. It appeared in evidence that Samuel Finch was a Livery-Stable-keeper in the Borough; and that the prisoner, on the 2d of July 1779, hired the horse of him to go to Sutton, in the county of Surry, and back again, saying on being asked where he lived, that he lodged at No. 25 in Kingstreet, and should return about eight o'clock the same evening. He did not return; and it was proved that he had sold the horse on the very day he had hired it, to one William Hollist, in Smithfield Market; and that he had no lodging at the place to which he had given the prosecutor directions.

The learned Judge said: There had been different opinions on the law of this class of cases; * * * that in the present case the horse was hired to take a journey into Surry, and the prisoner sold him the same day, without taking any such journey; that there were also other circumstances which imported that at the time of the hiring the prisoner had it in intention to sell the horse, as his saying that he lodged at a place where in fact he was not known. He therefore left it with the Jury to consider, Whether the prisoner meant at the time of the hiring to take such journey, but was afterwards tempted to sell the horse? for if so he must be acquitted; but that if they were of opinion that at the time of the hiring the journey was a mere pretence to get the horse into his possession, and he had no intention to take such journey but intended to sell the horse, they would find that fact specially for the opinion of the Judges.

The Jury found that the facts above stated were true; and also that the prisoner had hired the horse with a fraudulent view and intention of selling it immediately.

The question was referred to the Judges, Whether the delivery of the horse by the prosecutor to the prisoner, had so far changed the possession of the property, as to render the subsequent conversion of it a mere breach of trust, or whether the conversion was felonious? * * *

The Judges differed greatly in opinion on this case; and delivered their opinions seriatim upon it at Lord Chief Justice De Grey's house on 4th February 1780 and on the 22nd of the same month MR. BARON PERRYN delivered their opinion on it. The majority of them thought, That the Question, as to the original intention of the prisoner in hiring the horse, had been properly left to the jury; and as they had found, that his view in so doing was fraudulent, the parting with the property had not changed the nature of the possession, but that it remained unaltered in the prosecutor at the time of the conversion; and that the prisoner was therefore guilty of felony.

Notes

1. *Another Version of Pear's Case.* 2 East, *Pleas of the Crown,* 686–689 (1803), adds the following about *Pear's* case:

"This case underwent a great deal of discussion: and the Judges delivered their opinion seriatim upon it, on the 4th February 1780, at Lord C.J. De Grey's house: and on the 22d of the same month MR. BARON PERRYN delivered their opinion at the Q.B. as follows. (After stating the indictment, evidence, and finding of the jury as above stated,) This case has been maturely considered by all the Judges, and eleven of them, who met for the purpose, delivered their opinions at large upon the subject: seven of them held the offence to be a clear felony; two of them were of opinion that it was not felony; and the other two entertained great doubts at the last; which doubts were founded upon two statutes which he should take notice of. Three out of the four dissenting Judges agreed with the seven, that by the principles of the common law this was felony. But the doubts and opinions of those four Judges were founded chiefly on the statutes 33 H. 8. and 30 G. 2. against obtaining goods by false tokens or false pretences. Two of the Judges thought that as the delivery of the mare was obtained from the owner by means of asserting that which was false, viz. that the prisoner wanted to go a journey which he never intended to take at all; and as the two statutes before mentioned had made the offence of obtaining goods by false tokens or false pretences, punishable as a misdemeanor only; and the stat. 33 H. 8. had distinguished the case of obtaining goods by false tokens from the case of obtaining goods by stealth; they were bound by those statutes to say, that the prisoner's offence was not felony. One of them also held that this was not felony by the common law; because there was no actual taking of the mare by the prisoner. But ten out of the eleven Judges held it to be clear that the offence would have been felony by the common law, if the statutes had never existed: and seven of them held that it was not within or at all affected by the statutes of H. 8. or Geo. 2. That larceny was defined by Lord Coke to mean a felonious and fraudulent taking and carrying away of the goods of another. But it was settled by old authorities, that the taking need not be by force. If a carrier or porter received goods to carry from one place to another, and he opened the pack and sold them; that was felony; yet in that case there was no taking by force, but on a delivery by the owner. That the reason assigned for the determination * * * was because opening and disposing of them declared that his intent originally was not to take the goods upon the agreement and contract of the party, but only with a design of stealing them. * * * So if a horse were upon sale, and the owner let the thief mount him in order to try him, and the thief rode away with him, it was felony. * * * So in the case of one Tunnard; tried at the Q.B. in October Sessions 1729, who was indicted for stealing a brown mare of Henry

Smith's: and upon the evidence it appeared, that Smith lived in the Isle of Ely, and lent Tunnard the mare to ride three miles; but he, instead of riding three miles only, rode her up to London and sold her: this was holden to be felony. And Lord C.J. Raymond, who tried the prisoner, left it to the jury to consider, Whether Tunnard rode away with her with an intent to steal her? and the jury found him guilty. That here the same directions were given to the jury by the learned Judge who tried the prisoner, and the jury had given the same verdict. * * * That in all these cases the intention was the thing chiefly regarded, and fraud supplied the place of force. That what was the intention was a fact, which in every case must be left upon the evidence to the sound judgment of a jury. And in this case the jury had found that at the time when the prisoner obtained the possession of the mare, he intended to steal her. That the obtaining the possession of the mare, and afterwards disposing of her in the manner stated, was in the construction of law such a taking as would have made the prisoner liable to an action of trespass at the suit of the owner, if he had not intended to steal her. For she was delivered to the prisoner for a special purpose only, viz. to go to Sutton, which he never intended to do, but immediately sold her. * * * That ten of the Judges out of the eleven, therefore, were of opinion, that if a person obtained the delivery of a thing by fraud and falsehood, intending at the time that he so obtained the delivery to steal it; upon the principle of the common law and the adjudged cases which had been mentioned, if the statutes had not existed, his offence would be felony. That the next question was, Whether this offence were within or at all affected by the statutes of H. 8. and Geo. 2.[1] Seven of the Judges were of opinion, that it was not. That the stat. of Hen. 8. was confined to the cases of obtaining goods in other men's names, by false tokens or counterfeit letters, made in any other man's name. The stat. of Geo. 2. extended that law to all cases where goods were obtained by false pretences of any kind. But both these statutes were confined to cases where credit was obtained in the name of a third person; and did not extend to cases where a man, on his own account, got goods with an intention to steal them. That besides, the seven Judges held that neither of those statutes were intended to mitigate the common law, or to make that a less offence which was a greater before. On the contrary, the Legislature, by those statutes, meant to inflict a severer punishment in the cases of fraud than the common law had done. That in many cases it was extremely difficult, and sometimes impossible to prove what the offender's original intention was. The circumstances evidencing a felonious intent, or the contrary, were so various, that Hale (509) says it is impossible to prescribe them: they must be left to the consideration of a Judge and jury. That where an original felonious intent appeared, the statutes did not apply. Where no such intent appeared, if the means mentioned in the statutes were made use of, the Legislature had made the offender answerable criminally, who before by the common law of the land was only answerable civilly. That in the prisoner's case the intention was apparent, and the jury had rightly found that it was felonious. The crime then was felony, and of a nature which the statute law had made punishable with death."

1. On the debate in this case, Eyre B., adverting to these statutes, said he doubted if there were not a distinction in this respect between the owner's parting with the possession and with the property in the thing delivered. That where goods were delivered upon a false token, and the owner meant to part with the property absolutely and never expected to have the goods returned again, it might be difficult to reach the case otherwise than through the statutes; aliter, where he parted with the possession only: for there if the possession were obtained by fraud, and not taken according to the agreement; it was on the whole a taking against the will of the owner; and if done animo furandi, it was felony. MS. Buller J.

2. *Larceny by Trick.* How persuasive are the precedents suggested by East's account in Note 1? If a new fiction was necessary to convict Pear, is it any more questionable than earlier custody fictions? If so, why? This case established a special branch of larceny: larceny by trick. While technically it is only common law larceny, clarity requires that it be referred to by its separate title. Does Pear's conduct fall under Model Penal Code § 223.2 or 223.3? Does it matter?

Question

Why could not Pear have been convicted of obtaining property by false pretenses? of embezzlement?

Young v. Rex

Court of King's Bench, 1789.
3 T.R. 98, 100 Eng.Rep. 475.

An indictment was preferred at the sessions at Bristol against the defendants on the 30 Geo. 2, c. 24, for obtaining money by false pretences. The first count in the indictment stated that the defendants, fraudulently intending to obtain of the honest subjects of our lord the King their monies, goods, wares, and merchandizes, by false colours and pretences, on the 23d of December, in the 28th year, &c. at, &c. unlawfully, knowingly, wilfully, and designedly, did falsely pretend to one Thomas, that Young had made a bet of 500 guineas on each side with a colonel in the army then at Bath that William Lewis would on the next day run on the high road leading from Gloucester to Bristol ten miles in length within one hour, and that Young and Mullins did go 200 guineas each of and in the said bet, and Randal did go the other 100 guineas, (meaning that, in case such pretended bet was lost, Young was to contribute and pay 210£. Mullins the like sum, and Randal the remaining 105£.) and did then and there under colour and pretence of such bet, &c. obtain from Thomas as a part of such pretended bet 20 guineas of the 500 guineas; by which said false pretences the defendants did then and there, to wit, on, &c. at, &c. unlawfully, knowingly, and designedly, obtain from the said Thomas the said 20 guineas with intent to cheat and defraud him thereof; whereas in truth and in fact no such bet had been made, &c. to the evil example, &c. against the peace, &c. and against the form of the statute, &c. * * * The defendants were found guilty, and sentenced to be transported for seven years. And afterwards they removed the indictment by writ of error into this Court, and assigned for error that the supposed false pretences * * * are neither contrary to the statute, 33 H.8., or 30 Geo. 2, or any other statute. * * *

* * *

LORD KENYON, CH.J. * * * said, undoubtedly this indictment, being founded on the statute of 30 Geo. 2, c. 24, is different from a common law indictment. When it passed, it was considered to extend to every case where a party had obtained money by falsely representing himself to be in a situation in which he was not, or any occurrence that had not happened, to which persons of ordinary caution might give credit. The statute of the 33 Hen. 8, c. 1, requires a false seal, or token, to be used in order to bring the person imposed upon into the confidence of the other; but that being found to be insufficient, the statute 30 Geo. 2, c. 24, introduced another offence, describing it in terms extremely general. It seems difficult to draw the line, and to say to what cases this statute shall extend; and therefore we must see whether each particular case, as it arises, comes within it. In the present case, four men came to the prosecutor representing a race as about to take place, that William Lewis should go a certain distance within a limited time; that they had betted upon the event, and they should probably win: he was perhaps too credulous, and gave confidence to them, and advanced his money; and afterwards the whole story proved to be an absolute fiction. Then the defendants, morally speaking, have been guilty of an offence. I admit that there are certain irregularities which are not the subject of criminal law. But when the criminal law happens to be auxiliary to the law of morality, I do not feel any inclination to explain it away. Now this offence is within the words of the Act; for the defendants have by false pretences fraudulently contrived to obtain money from the prosecutor; and I see no reason why it should not be held to be within the meaning of the statute. * * *

ASHHURST, J.—As to the first objection: Cases which happened before the passing of the 30 Geo. 2, c. 24, do not apply to this. For that statute created an offence which did not exist before, and I think it includes the present. The Legislature saw that all men were not equally prudent, and this statute was passed to protect the weaker part of mankind. The words of it are very general, "All persons who knowingly by false pretences shall obtain from any person money, goods, &c. with intent to cheat or defraud," &c.: and we have no power to restrain their operation. * * *

* * *

BULLER, J.—To make an offence indictable at common law, it must be public in its nature. And the distinction, which has been taken in the case of using false weights and measures, shews it more clearly than any other. If a person sell by false weights, though only to one person, it is an indictable offence: but if without false weights he sell to many persons a less quantity than he pretends to do, it is not indictable. But though the common law, as applicable to this subject, is as stated by the counsel, it is in this case necessary to consider both the stat. 33 Hen. 8, c. 1, and the 30 Geo. 2, c. 24. By the former of those the offence consists in obtaining money or goods by false tokens; and unless some token be used, the case does not come within that Act. Now suppose a token had been produced in this case, and that the defendants, after telling their story to the prosecutor, had said, "If you have any doubt, here is the colonel's gorget;" I think it would have fallen within the Statute of 33 Hen. 8. If it would, then let us consider what effect the 30 Geo. 2, c. 24, has on the case. The Legislature thought that the former statute was too limited; and therefore the 30 G. 2, c. 24, was passed, which enacts, that all persons who shall obtain money from others by false pretences with intent to cheat or defraud such persons, shall be deemed offenders against the public peace. The statute therefore clearly extends to cases which were not the subject of an indictment at common law. The ingredients of this offence are the obtaining money by false pretences, and with an intent to defraud. Barely asking another for a sum of money is not sufficient; but some pretence must be used, and that pretence false; and the intent is necessary to constitute the crime. If the intent be made out, and the false pretence used in order to effect it, it brings the case within this statute. * * *

[The concurring opinion of GROSE, J., is omitted.]

Rex v. Collins

Court of Criminal Appeal, 1922.
17 Crim.App. 42.

Appeal against conviction.

Appellant was convicted at the Norfolk Sessions on 11th October, 1922, before the Chairman, of larceny, and sentenced to six months' imprisonment with hard labour.

* * *

Gerald Dodson for the Crown. I submit that upon the facts appellant could be convicted of larceny by a trick. Russett, 1892, 2 Q.B.D. 312 * * *.

THE LORD CHIEF JUSTICE: The appellant in this case was convicted on an indictment which charged him with larceny of £1 6s. 6d., under s. 2 of the Larceny Act, 1916, 6 & 7 Geo. 5, c. 50. The facts of the case are a little important in view of the points raised before us. A Mrs. Holmes gave evidence that on June 8th appellant called upon her and showed her samples of some boots and shoes. She chose two pairs of shoes costing 17s. and 9s. 6d., and gave to appellant £1 6s. 6d., for which she was to receive two pairs of shoes, but she in fact received nothing. * * *

It appears that to some of the persons from whom he obtained the money referred to in these indictments he represented that he was in some way connected with a firm named Dougall and Hastings, and to Mrs. Holmes he said that he represented that firm, and she expected to get the shoes from that firm. Mr. Hastings gave evidence that the firm opened a cash account with appellant, and that if appellant gave orders and paid for them, the firm would send the shoes. Mr. Dougall said that the firm would have let appellant have the shoes, but that he must pay for them.

Appellant said that he considered that he was an agent of the firm. He admitted having received the money, and that he had handed it to his wife. He said that he expected Messrs. Dougall and Hastings to act as was usual in such circumstances, and that they did not expect cash payments. Upon the facts the jury convicted the appellant of larceny by a trick, but there is an obvious difficulty in upholding the conviction.

Attention has been called to *Russett* (above). It is important to see the facts in that case and what were the principles laid down. A.L. Smith J. stated the law in a few clear words. He said: "The difference between the two offences is this; if possession only of money or goods is given, and the property is not intended to pass, that may be larceny by a trick, the reason being that there is a taking of the chattel by the thief against the will of the owner; but if possession is given and it is intended by the owner that the property shall also pass, that is not larceny by a trick, but may be false pretences, because in that case there is no taking, but a handing over of the chattel by the owner. This case, therefore, comes to be one of fact, and we have to see whether there is evidence that, at the time the £8 was handed over, the prosecutor intended to pass to the prisoner the property in that sum, as well as to give possession."

In that case it was held that the £8 was a deposit, and that there was no passing of the property in the money. Now it is said that that decision governs the present case, but the only possible way in which such a contention could be true would be that applying the principles laid down to the circumstances would lead to a similar result.

But in this case there is no evidence to show that Mrs. Holmes paid the money by way of deposit, and no evidence to show that she did not intend to part with the property in as well as the possession of the money.

No doubt, upon the facts, if proper steps had been taken, the jury might probably have found the appellant guilty of obtaining the money by false pretences * * *. * * *

* * *

Conviction quashed.

Questions

1. We see here what is apt to happen when two offenses seem to occupy the same legal territory. Rather than drop one of them, the courts may divide the territory in half. Is there any good reason for treating obtaining property by false pretenses differently from larceny by trick? See Pearce, *Theft by False Promises,* 101 U.Pa.L. Rev. 967 (1953).

2. Assume that the accused is guilty either of larceny by trick or of false pretenses in each of the following situations. Which crime is it?

a. A ordered a gasoline station attendant B to fill up his tank with gasoline and then drove off without paying.

b. C, wishing to bribe a policeman, consulted unscrupulous lawyer D about the best way to do this. D pretended to negotiate with the officer and reported that the officer agreed to accept $2000 in cash as a bribe. C handed D the $2000 with instructions to deliver it to the officer. D kept the cash.

c. The facts are the same as in the last problem except that D reported that the officer agreed to accept D's motorcycle as a bribe, and D told C he would give the officer the motorcycle if C gave D $2000, which C did. D kept both the money and the motorcycle.

d. In a situation similar to that in (b), D reported that the officer agreed to accept C's television set as a bribe. C was making installment payments on the set, and the seller E still retained security title to it. Nevertheless, C gave the set to D for the bribe. D, the accused, kept it.

3. Is larceny by trick, minus the trick, a crime? Suppose, without any representation or trick by Pear, Finch had offered to rent the horse for the day to Pear for a sum to be paid on return, and Pear had leapt into the saddle and ridden for the hills, having intended to steal the horse from the beginning?

Historical Note

The King's Bench that decided *Young* was an interesting court. Ashhurst, the oldest and senior judge in service, had presided at the trial in *Pear's* case. He was kindly, impartial, careful, and urbane. Buller, only thirty-two when appointed, had been a pupil of Ashhurst's and was learned and able, and a strong ally of Lord Mansfield, the then Chief Justice. (The only stain upon his reputation may be unjustified; he was credited, probably wrongly, with the cruel dictum that a husband is privileged to beat his wife, so long as he uses a stick no thicker than his thumb.) Mansfield pushed Buller's appointment as his successor, but Lord Kenyon, previously Master of the Rolls, got the job instead. Kenyon was honest and able, but he was also unpleasant, rude, undignified, and miserly. Buller got himself transferred to Common Pleas after a few years. Grose, whose opinion is not reproduced, had an arguably unjustified reputation for stupidity.

iii. The Nature of a False Pretense

Rex v. Barnard

Oxford Assizes, 1837.
7 Car. & P. 784, 173 Eng.Rep. 342.

False pretences.—The indictment charged that the prisoner falsely pretended that he was an undergraduate of the university of Oxford, and a commoner of Magdalen college, by means of which he obtained a pair of boot-straps from John Samuel Vincent.

It appeared that Mr. Vincent was a boot-maker, carrying on business in High-street, Oxford; and that the prisoner came there, wearing a commoner's cap and gown, and ordered boots, which were not supplied him, and straps, which were sent to him. He stated he belonged to Magdalen college.

It was proved by one of the butlers of Magdalen college that the prisoner did not belong to that college, and that there are no commoners at Magdalen college.

BOLLAND, B. (in summing up).—If nothing had passed in words, I should have laid down that the fact of the prisoner's appearing in the cap and gown would have been pregnant evidence from which a jury should infer that he pretended he was a member of the university, and if so, would have been a sufficient false pretence to satisfy the statute. It clearly is so by analogy to the cases in which offering in payment the notes of a bank which has failed, knowing them to be so, has been held to be a false pretence, without any words being used.

Verdict—Guilty.

The Queen v. Ardley

Court for Crown Cases Reserved, 1871.
L.R. 1 Cr.Cas.Res. 301.

Case stated by the Chairman of Quarter Sessions for the County Palatine of Durham.

Indictment for obtaining 5£. and an Albert chain of the value of 7s. 6d. by false pretences.

The prisoner was tried on the 2d of January, 1871.

The material facts were as follows:—

The prisoner went into the shop of the prosecutor, who was a watchmaker and jeweller, and stated that he was a draper, and was 5£. short of the money required to make up a bill, and asked the prosecutor to buy an Albert chain which he (the prisoner) was then wearing. The prisoner said, "It is 15-carat fine gold, and you will see it stamped on every link. It was made for me and I paid nine guineas for it. The maker told me it was worth 5£. to sell as old gold." The prosecutor bought the chain, relying, as he said, on the prisoner's statement, but also examining the chain, and paid 5£. for it, and gave also to the prisoner in part payment a gold Albert chain valued at 7s. 6d. The prisoner's chain was marked "15 ct." on every link, and in a very short time afterwards he (the prisoner) was apprehended, and then wore another Albert chain of a character similar to that sold to the prosecutor, this also being marked "15 ct." on every link. It was proved that "15 ct." was a Hall-mark used in certain towns in England, and placed on articles made of gold of that quality, and that chains when assayed are generally found to be one grain less than the mark, exceptionally two grains. The chain bought by the prosecutor was assayed and found to be a quality of trifle better than 6-carat gold, and of the value in gold of 2£. 2s. 9d. It was proved that had it been 15-carat gold it would have been worth 5£. 10s. Adding the charge for what is called "fashion" or "make," and the price of a locket attached, the chain bought by the prosecutor would be sold for 3£. 0s. 3d., but had it been 15-carat it would have been sold for 9£. * * *

The chairman was asked by the counsel for the prisoner to stop the case, on the authority of Reg. v. Bryan, Dears. & B.C.C. 265, but declined to do so, and left the case to the jury, who found the prisoner guilty, and said they found that the prisoner knew that he was falsely representing the quality of the chain as 15-carat gold.

The question was, whether or not the prisoner was rightly convicted of obtaining money under false pretences.

The case was argued before Bovill, C.J., Willes and Byles, J.J., Channell and Pigott, BB.

* * *

Bovill, C.J.—The question which we have to consider in this case is, whether there was evidence to go to the jury on which they could find the prisoner guilty of obtaining money under false pretences. I think there clearly was evidence; and that it would have been quite impossible for the learned chairman with any propriety to stop the case. There were, in addition to the representations as to the quality of the gold, distinct statements of matters of fact, and there was evidence of the falsehood of these statements. The prisoner stated that he was a draper, and was 5£. short of the money required to make up a bill. But there were no drapery goods, nor anything connected with such trade, found on the prisoner, but when arrested he had in his possession a license to sell plate, two watches, two white metal watch-guards, and the chain obtained from the prisoner [sic]; and he wore another Albert chain of a character similar to that sold to the prosecutor, this also being marked 15-carat gold on every link. Looking, therefore, at the whole of the evidence, there is sufficient ground on which the finding of the jury may be supported and the conviction sustained.

But the jury have further found that the prisoner, when he represented the chain to be 15-carat gold, knew this representation to be false. And the question whether the conviction can be supported upon that finding alone stands upon a somewhat different footing. The cases have drawn nice distinctions between matters of fact and matters of opinion, statements of specific facts and mere exaggerated praise. It is difficult for us, sitting here as a Court, to determine conclusively what is fact and what is opinion, what is a specific statement and what exaggerated praise. These are questions for the jury to decide. And the prisoner has this additional security, that the jury have to consider not only whether the statements made are statements of fact, but also whether they are made with the intention to defraud.

The case which has been most pressed upon us is Reg. v. Bryan, Dears. & B.C.C. 265. The representation is that case was, that certain plated spoons were "equal to Elkington's A." Prima facie, that representation would seem to be a mere matter of opinion, and the Court held that it was not sufficient to support the conviction. But many of the judges expressed the opinion that there might well be cases in which misrepresentations, though as to quality, would be within the statute. Cockburn, C.J., says: "If the person had represented these articles as being of Elkington's manufacture, when in point of fact they were not, and he knew it, that would be an entirely different thing." Pollock, C.B., says: "I think if a tradesman or a merchant were to concoct an article of merchandise expressly for the purpose of deceit, and were to sell it as and for something very different even in quality from what it was, the statute would apply." It is plain that these learned judges considered that a specific representation of quality, if known to be false, would be within the statute. Coleridge, J., expressly concurs in the observations of Pollock, C.B., Erle, J., at the close of his judgment says: "No doubt it is difficult to draw the line between the substance of the contract and the praise of an article in respect of a matter of opinion; still it must be done, and the present case appears to me not to support a conviction, upon the ground that there is no affirmation of a definite triable fact in saying the goods were equal to Elkington's A., but the affirmation is of what is mere matter of opinion, and falls within the category of untrue praise in the course of a contract of sale, where the vendor has in substance the article contracted for, namely, plated spoons." Crompton, J. also considered that the statute applies "when the thing sold is of an entirely different description from what it is represented to be." Willes, J., who dissented from the judgment of the Court, goes the whole length of saying that a representation as to quality, if known to be false, is enough to support a conviction. And Bramwell, B., leans to the same opinion.

Applying these observations to the present case, the statement here made is not in form an expression of opinion or mere praise. It is a distinct statement, accompanied by other circumstances, that the chain was 15-carat gold. That statement was untrue, was known to be untrue, and was made with intent to defraud. How does that differ from the case of a man who makes a chain of one material and fraudulently represents it to be of another? Therefore, whether we look at the whole of the evidence, or only at that which goes to the quality of the chain, the conviction is good. The case differs from Reg. v. Bryan, Dears. & B.C.C. 265, because here there was a statement as to a specific fact within the actual knowledge of the prisoner, namely, the proportion of pure gold in the chain.

[The concurring opinions are omitted.]

Regina v. Jennison

Court for Crown Cases Reserved, 1862.
Le. & Ca. 157, 169 Eng.Rep. 1343.

The following case was reserved by COCKBURN C.J.

John Jennison was indicted and tried before me, at the last Assizes for the county of Derby, for obtaining £8 of one Ann Hayes by false pretences.

The prisoner, who had a wife living, had represented himself to the prosecutrix, who was a single woman in service, as an unmarried man, and, pretending that he was about to marry her, induced her to hand over to him a sum of £8 out of her wages received on leaving her service, representing that he would go to Liverpool and with the money furnish a house for them to live in, and that having done so he would return and marry her. Having obtained the money, the prisoner went away, and never returned.

The prosecutrix stated that she had been induced to part with her money on the faith of the representations of the prisoner that he was a single man, that he would furnish a house with the money, and would then marry her.

There was no doubt that these representations were false, and that, morally, the money had been obtained by false pretences. But it was contended on the part of the prisoner that, as the prosecutrix had been induced to part with her money by the joint operation of the three representations made by the prisoner—that he was unmarried, that he would furnish a house with the money, and that he would then marry her—and as only the first of these pretences had reference to a present existing fact, while the others related to things to be done *in futuro*, the indictment could not be maintained.

I reserved the point, and, the prisoner having been convicted, have now to request the decision of the Court upon the question.

This case was considered, on the 26th of April, 1862, by ERLE C.J., MARTIN B., CHANNELL B., BLACKBURN J. and KEATING J.

* * *

ERLE C.J.—In this case we are all of opinion that the prisoner was properly convicted. * * * Now it is clear that a false promise cannot be the subject of an indictment for obtaining money by false pretences. Here, however, we have the pretence that he was an unmarried man. This was false in fact, and was essential, for without it he would not have obtained the money. Then this false fact by which the money is obtained will sustain the indictment, although it is united with two false promises, neither of which alone would have supported the conviction.

Conviction affirmed.

Regina v. Gordon

Court for Crown Cases Reserved, 1889.
23 Q.B.D. 354.

Case stated by LORD COLERIDGE, C.J.

The prisoner was tried before the Lord Chief Justice at Worcester on an indictment of which the following is an abstract:

The charges were,—first, on June 5, 1889, with intent to defraud, obtaining from Richard Summers Brown 10s. 6d. by false pretences that he was prepared to advance 100£. to him "at lower interest than was charged to others," and that all advances were repayable by easy instalments, to suit applicants; * * * fourth count, same date, with like intent, inducing them to make said promissory note for 100£. by false pretence "that he was prepared to pay to them or one of them 100£." * * *.

The evidence was set out in the case. It was to the following effect, viz.: that the wife of the prosecutor, Richard Summers Brown, a farmer, saw, on December 27 the following advertisement in a newspaper:

"Cash immediately advanced from 5£. to 500£., at lower interest than charged by others, to farmers, &c., on their own security, without bondmen, on note of hand alone, repayable by easy instalments to suit applicants. * * *

"Mr. J. Gordon, 6, Bridge Street, Worcester. * * *"

She read this to her husband; they were in want of money, knew Gordon before, went to his office and asked for 100£., and he, after inquiring and being told what stock they had on the farm, said he should be very pleased to lend it, that there would be 10s. 6d. for expenses, that it would be necessary to inspect their stock, and that the interest would be 5 * * * per cent. She said that they would pay back the capital 20£. a year. He said that he did not stop the 5 per cent. interest, and would pay the whole 100£. down on Wednesday morning. The wife paid the 10s. 6d. The defendant's clerk went over and inspected the stock, which subsequently realized 300£., and on Wednesday morning R.S. Brown and his father, Richard Brown, went to the office and saw Gordon, who caused his clerk, Hughes, to make out two documents, which the defendant produced, and asked the Browns to sign, and they signed them. One was as follows:—

"January 9, 1889.

"We (I and my son) have this day borrowed and received of Mr. Gordon the sum of 60£., for which we have agreed to pay him back 100£. (40£. interest on 60£.) in four quarterly instalments, as set forth on the promissory note, which we read over and signed, and which we clearly understand. * * *

"Witness,

"Richard Brown.

"T.W. Hughes. "Richard Brown, junr."

This document was all in Hughes' handwriting, except the signature and the words "we read the above over," which were in the father's handwriting.

* * *

They did not read either of them over, nor were they read to them, although the defendant told the father to write down the words "We read the above over;" * * * Then the defendant gave him 60£. "We counted it," said R.S. Brown, in his evidence "and I told him it was 60£. only, and not 100£., which my wife had bargained for. He said that was what he charged—the 40£. That was all I should have. He said 'I don't do business that way'." The prosecutor did not agree, but went home to his wife, she found there was 60£. in a bag, and went to the magistrate's clerk and then to the defendant's office with it and offered the money back; it was refused, and she communicated with the police.

For the defence the defendant's clerk was called and said, inter alia, that he read both documents out quite loudly to the Browns. In cross-examination, he said he knew they expected 100£.; it was not usual to charge 40£ for 100£.

The LORD CHIEF JUSTICE, after setting out the evidence in the case, stated. "I told the jury that if they were of opinion that the prisoner obtained the promissory note for 100£. from the two Browns, or either of them, by falsely pretending to them that he was ready to pay and would then pay to them, or one of them, 100£. on their signing the note, they might find him guilty. * * *

* * *

LOCKWOOD, Q.C. (Harington, with him), for the defendant.

[THE COURT intimated that the argument might be limited to the fourth count.]

First, no false pretence of an existing fact is alleged in the fourth count. The meaning of it is only that the defendant said, "If you will give me a promissory note for 100£. I will lend you 100£."—that is a mere promise to do something in the future, such as would be in the case of a purchaser saying to a tradesman, "If you will send goods to my house I will pay for them."

[WILLS. J. Suppose the defendant said, "I have the intention of advancing 100£," and he, in fact, had no intention of the kind.]

That would not be a sufficient false pretence. It would be impossible to prove that his intention was not that stated at the time, although it might have been changed afterwards. The defendant was undoubtedly in a position and able to advance 100£., and therefore literally "was prepared to do so."

* * *

LORD COLERIDGE, C.J. The false pretence alleged in the fourth count is that the defendant "Isaac Gordon was prepared to pay to them or one of them the sum of one hundred pounds, by means of which said false pretence the said Isaac Gordon did then unlawfully and fraudulently induce the said Richard Summers Brown and Richard Brown to make a certain valuable security, to wit, a promissory note for one hundred pounds, with intent" to defraud. Two objections have been made. First, that we must interpret the allegation that he was prepared to advance 100£., as if it meant that he was ready to do so at some future time, and that it was a mere statement of his intention that at some time afterwards he would deliver the 100£. I do not think that is the true interpretation of the pretence which is stated to be false. I am far from saying that on more consideration much may not be found in the suggestion of my brother Wills in the course of the argument, but that has not been argued out, and I base my judgment on a broader and less refined ground. It appears to me that the ordinary meaning of the allegation is: "I am *now* prepared to give you 100£. if you will sign this paper. Here is 100£., and when you sign that paper, which you will do in a moment, the 100£. is yours." That, apart from all question of existing state of mind, seems to me to be a false pretence of an existing fact—the existing fact stated being that the money was ready for the prosecutors on their signing the paper. That was untrue, and untrue to the knowledge of the defendant, and it is clear that the promissory note was obtained by means of it. So the first objection to the fourth count fails. * * *

* * *

WILLS, J. I am glad that it is possible to support the conviction without venturing on the somewhat dangerous ground to which I referred in the course of the argument, and rendering it necessary to distinguish between a pretence to do something, and a statement of intention. I find it difficult to see why an allegation as to the present existence of a state of mind *may* not be under some circumstances as much an allegation of an existing fact as an allegation with respect to anything else. For example, suppose that by an arrangement for the settlement of litigation, a man was to pay a sum of money, and when the time came he said: "I shall not pay until I know that A. has the intention of acceding to this arrangement. I do not insist upon having his promise. I shall be content if I know what his present intention is. Otherwise I shall not pay." Suppose B., who was to get the money, then told him that A. had that intention, and he believed B. and paid the money upon the faith of B.'s assurance, and all the while B. knew that A.'s intention was exactly the contrary to what he had stated. I should have thought that the allegation as to A.'s intention was one of an existing fact, capable of supporting an indictment for obtaining money by false pretences. But I am very sensible that in such an inquiry there must always be a danger of confounding intention with a representation or a promise as to something future; and I am very glad that it is possible, for the reasons given by my Lord, to affirm this conviction without approaching any such debateable ground.

[The other concurring opinions are omitted.]

Conviction affirmed.

Notes

1. *Nature of a Pretense.* One senses the long shadow of Lord Chief Justice Holt in the *Jones* case over later false pretense cases. The law resisted extending eligible pretenses beyond statements of past or present fact (as opposed to opinion or local law), except where the accused was in a fiduciary relationship to the victim. Why bother protecting fools who would rely on anything but representations of solid fact? Note Lord Coleridge's somewhat strained interpretation of the representation in *Gordon;* it had the merit of enabling the court to by-pass the ingenious argument of Justice Wills that a state of mind may be an existing fact and therefore allow statements of intention to qualify.

2. *Bad check statutes.* When I write a check on my bank account and give it in payment for goods to another, what implied representation do I make? If I represent that I have enough in the account to pay the check, and this is false at the time of representation, I may be guilty of obtaining the goods by a false pretense. Most courts have held, however, that any representation is only that the check will be paid on presentation, and in jurisdictions in which representations as to the future are insufficient the crime is not committed unless other false representations can be found. This difficulty is one reason why most jurisdictions have special bad check statutes. Another is that it may be desirable to punish passing a bad check even though no property or service is obtained or can be proved to be obtained thereby. It may also be desirable to provide a special punishment scheme for writers of bad checks. Finally, it is convenient to provide for special presumptions in the case of passing a bad check: that the accused knew that the check would not be paid if he had no account with the bank when the check was issued or if the check, though presented promptly, was not paid because of insufficient funds and not thereafter promptly made good. See Model Penal Code § 224.5.

Questions

1. A has a charge account with B Department Store. He has just been fired from his job and his total assets are about $50. He purchases a $300 overcoat from B on credit, representing that he intends to pay when billed. He does not pay. Should he be convicted of obtaining the coat by false pretenses?

2. Suppose C purchases D's property under the mistaken impression, as D knows, that there is gold thereon. False pretenses? Suppose in selling stock, the material in E's prospectus is literally true, but creates a false impression of high value because it says nothing about other unfavorable facts. False pretenses? See Model Penal Code § 223.3 and R. v. Kylsant (Lord), [1932] 1 K.B. 442 (C.C.A.1931).

3. Why should courts be so particular about the nature of a false pretense when any old trick will do for larceny by trick?

iv. Reliance and Harm

Rex v. Clucas

Court of Criminal Appeal, 1949.
33 Cr.App. 136.

The two men induced bookmakers to bet with them by representing that they were acting on behalf of a large number of workmen who were making small bets on various horse races, whereas in fact they were making bets in considerable sums of money on their own account. Some of the bets proved to be winning bets, and in respect of these they received money from the bookmakers. One of the bookmakers refused to pay Revell on a winning bet, and Revell thereupon repeated the false allegation and invited the bookmaker to telephone to a certain number which he represented as being the number of the place of employment of the workmen in question, in order to obtain confirmation of Revell's story. The number in fact was that of a public telephone near which the appellant was waiting to answer if the call from the bookmaker came through to the number given.

F. Honig, for the appellant:

* * * The person alleged to have been defrauded must have been induced by the false representations to act to his own injury in a monetary sense. The effective cause of the payment of money by the bookmaker in the present case was the winning of the horse backed, which was outside the control of the appellant and Revell and could not have been affected by the false representations made. * * *

H.V. Boileau, for the Crown:

There was evidence of a continuity between the false pretence and the obtaining of the money, and it was for the jury to say whether such continuity existed. Button, [1900] 2 Q.B. 587, is indistinguishable in principle from the present case. By making false representations a chance to bet with the bookmaker was obtained, and such chance would not have been obtained but for the false representations. If there was a continuing false pretence which operated on the mind of the bookmaker, there was an obtaining by false pretences, and it was a question of fact for the jury whether there was such a continuing false pretence. * * *

THE LORD CHIEF JUSTICE:

* * *

The main point which arises in the case * * * can be stated in this way: Does a man who induces a bookmaker to bet with him by making false pretences as to his identity or as to the capacity in which he is putting on the bets obtain money by false pretences if he is fortunate enough, having made those pretences, to back a winning horse so that the bookmaker pays him?

* * *

In the opinion of the Court it is impossible to say that there was an obtaining of the money by the false pretences which were alleged, because the money was obtained not by reason of the fact that the prisoners falsely pretended that they were somebody or acting in some capacity which they were not, but because they backed a winning horse as a result of which the bookmaker paid the sums obtained. No doubt the bookmaker might never have opened an account with these men if he had known the true facts, but we must distinguish between one contributing cause and the effective cause which led the bookmaker to pay the money. The effective cause which led the bookmaker to pay the money was the fact that these men had backed a winning horse.

* * *

Mr. Boileau has called the attention of the Court to certain cases, and no doubt the nearest case to this one and the only one which I think it is necessary to mention is Button, [1900] 2 Q.B. 597. In that case the defendant, by representing that he was a person of the name of Sims, who was a very moderate performer in athletic sports and was not known as a likely winner of races, managed to obtain from the committee of some athletic sports which were to be held at Lincoln a very substantial handicap in a race. He was in fact a man who had won a great many races and if the truth had been known he would have received either no handicap at all or a very moderate handicap instead of the very substantial handicap which he obtained. The Court held that by falsely representing himself to be someone whom he was not, thereby obtaining the substantial handicap which he did obtain, he obtained the prize by false pretences, because the pretence in question was a matter directly connected with the winning or not winning of the prize. He obtained for himself a winning chance. He got the handicap which he would not otherwise have got, and thereby enabled himself to win the race. We think that that case on the facts is clearly distinguishable from this case.

* * *

Questions

1. Did Lord Chief Justice Goddard adequately distinguish the *Button* case?

2. A awakens one morning to see a stranger B pacing off the vacant property next door to A's pleasant rural retreat. Upon inquiry, B states that he has just purchased the property and plans to build a rendering plant on it. A persuades B to agree to sell him the property for $15,000, triple its market value. Con-man B then purchases the property from its real owner for $5,000 and signs it over to A at the closing for $15,000. Is B guilty of obtaining property by false pretenses?

3. Using an American Express card found on the street, A charges a purchase at a department store. Can you see why many cases say this cannot be the crime of obtaining goods by false pretenses?

4. A borrows $1,000 from B, pledging as security a piano worth $5,000. A represents that his interest in the piano is $4,500, since he has only two more $250 payments to make to the conditional seller before he gets clear title. In fact A has paid only $3,000 of the price. The piano is completely destroyed in an accidental fire and A cannot repay the loan. Is he guilty of obtaining the property by false pretenses?

Note

Nature of Property. In general, absent legislation, the property which is subject to false pretenses is the same property which is subject to common law larceny. Legislation has generally extended the idea of property in the same way as in larceny. There is one special problem however: obtaining real property by false pretenses factually is easily possible (Cf. question 2, supra.) A special statute is generally thought necessary to include obtaining real property as a crime.

Rex v. Carpenter

Central Criminal Court, 1911.
22 Cox Crim.Cas. 618.

* * *

It was proved in evidence that the defendant carried on business in London and other places in the United Kingdom under the style of the Charing Cross Bank, and published the following advertisement in the newspapers:—

THE CHARING CROSS BANK.

Established 1870

28, Bedford Street, Charing Cross, London, and 39, Bishopsgate Street Within, London, E.C.

Assets, 1,607,949£.; liabilities, 1,236,871£.; surplus, 371,078£.

Loans of 30£. to 10,000£. made on approved security. Current accounts opened. Stocks and shares bought and sold. Deposits of 10£. and upwards received as under:—

Subject to 3 months' notice of withdrawal 5% per annum.

* * *

The figures in the above advertisement were copies from a balance sheet prepared by the defendant in June, 1907, and were based entirely on his own estimates, unaided by reports or valuations of experts. The values which he placed upon his assets far exceeded the amounts expended by him upon the properties, which consisted of unproductive undertakings in Canada and South Africa, of the leases, fittings, and good will of the branches of the Charing Cross Bank, and of a patent tyre. By an arithmetical error in calculating the value of the leases the net surplus was overstated by £90,000, while the patent tyre, which he valued at £100,000 ceased after 1909 to possess any commercial value whatever. Thus, by the end of 1909, the assets, as published in the advertisement, were over-valued to the extent of £190,000, while the liabilities to depositors had substantially increased; but the defendant continued to publish the same figures in his advertisements in 1908, 1909, and 1910. From the 1st day of January to the 17th day of October, 1910, the total income received by the defendant from his business amounted to £16,226, while the expenses of the business during the same period amounted to £210,725, of which £155,724 consisted of interest paid on deposits. The defendant punctually paid interest to the depositors, but as the expenses of his business so greatly exceeded the receipts, such interest was paid out of fresh deposits.

* * * On the 18th day of August, [1910, a firm of chartered accountants] * * * pointed out to the defendant that he was insolvent, and that it had become imperative for him to inform the depositors without a moment's delay of the position of affairs. The defendant made no alteration in his practice in consequence of this advice, and on the 14th day of September the firm again wrote urging him to close the doors of his under-

taking and call his creditors together. The defendant replied that he had other large assets of which the firm knew nothing, that his business was earning enough to pay deposit interest, and that he was considering whether he should lower his rates of interest. The firm, after taking counsel's opinion, consulted the President of the Institute of Chartered Accountants, who communicated with the Director of Public Prosecutions. * * *

* * *

The defendant gave evidence in his own behalf, and maintained that the value of his Canadian properties had been greatly underestimated, and that if he had been allowed to continue trading a few more years he would have been able to realise his assets to such advantage as to repay his creditors in full, and to make a fortune for himself.

CHANNELL, J. (in the course of his summing up to the jury)—* * * What you have got to consider, therefore, in the present case is whether this money was obtained by false pretences of existing fact, false to the knowledge of the person making them, and made with intent to defraud. * * *

If the defendant made statements of fact which he knew to be untrue, and made them for the purpose of inducing persons to deposit with him money which he knew they would not deposit but for their belief in the truth of his statements, and if he was intending to use the money so obtained for purposes different from those for which he knew the depositors understood from his statements that he intended to use it, then, gentlemen, we have the intent to defraud, although he may have intended to repay the money if he could, and although he may have honestly believed, and may even have had good reason to believe, that he would be able to repay it. You see it is the fraud in the mode of getting the money, because you may by fraud get hold of money, even if you mean to repay it, and thoroughly believe that you can repay it—you are still defrauding the depositor. * * * It is, as Mr. Bodkin just put it to you, very like the case of the man who embezzles his master's money to put it upon a horse, or of the man who appropriates his client's money to speculate with it upon the Stock Exchange: it is similar to that, and his belief that he will make it all right does not excuse the fraud by means of which he gets hold of the money. That, therefore, is substantially the charge that is made against the defendant.

The learned Judge then passes on to deal with the facts of the case.

Verdict—guilty, with a recommendation to mercy on the ground of the age and optimistic temperament of the defendant.

Sentence, two years' imprisonment in the second division.

Question

Suppose Carpenter's optimistic temperament had proved justified in that his South African holdings had unexpectedly turned out to include a valuable diamond mine, and suppose that he had fully paid all of his investors the day before the trial. Would this affect his guilt?

Note

Mens Rea. The *mens rea* in false pretenses is similar to that in larceny. Of course any intention to return is unlikely if the defendant means to get full title. Claim of right is usually accepted as a defense.

C. OTHER THEFT OFFENSES

1. Robbery and Extortion

People v. Bartowsheski

Supreme Court of Colorado, En Banc, 1983.
661 P.2d 235.

QUINN, JUSTICE.

The defendant, Michael J. Bartowsheski, appeals from judgments entered in the Arapahoe County District Court on guilty verdicts to the charges of first degree murder after deliberation, first degree felony murder, and robbery, all of which involved a single victim. * * *

* * *

* * * In November of 1978 the defendant was hitchiking in Nevada and was given a ride by a young man named Boyd Tarwater who, like the defendant, had no specific destination. A friendship developed between the two men, and Tarwater agreed to accompany the defendant to Colorado, where Bartowsheski knew of possible employment prospects through a man who owed him money. The man that the defendant had in mind was Richard Talbott, who with his wife Nancy and their four children lived in a home in Kiowa, Colorado. When the defendant and Tarwater arrived in Kiowa in late November, Talbott did secure employment for them at his landscaping business and also permitted them to share a basement room in the Talbott home with their twelve year old son.

On the evening of Friday, December 15, 1978, the defendant and Tarwater decided to spend the evening visiting several bars. They left the Talbott home just as Richard Talbott was arriving. They asked him to join them and he refused. A short discussion followed between Talbott and the defendant concerning the money which each believed to be owing from the other. After Talbott suggested that they discuss the matter on the following morning, the defendant and Tarwater drove off.

The defendant and Tarwater spent the evening at several bars, where they played pool and drank beer. In the course of the evening they visited the Stagecoach Inn in Franktown, Colorado, where they experienced difficulties in starting Tarwater's pickup truck and were forced to secure the assistance of another bar patron who was able to "jump start" the vehicle. They eventually headed back to the Talbott home and decided on their way to leave Colorado in favor of a visit to Tarwater's relatives in Kansas. They also decided, in order to compensate for the money Talbott allegedly owed the defendant, to steal several guns owned by Talbott. They accordingly stopped at the Talbott home.

According to Tarwater, who testified as a prosecution witness, he remained in the truck to keep it running while the defendant went into the Talbott home to recover their possessions and the guns. When the defendant failed to return in five or ten minutes, Tarwater fell asleep. He was awakened by the defendant who was sitting on the passenger's seat wrapped in a blanket and tapping him on the arm. The defendant told him that they had to leave and they proceeded to drive towards Kansas.

Nancy Talbott awoke about 4:00 a.m. on December 16th. On her way to the bathroom she noticed that the upstairs closet door was open and that her husband's guns, usually kept in the closet, were missing. She descended to the basement, where she saw her son but did not see either the defendant or Tarwater. Returning to the living room, she noticed blood on a pillow on the couch where eight year old Michelle Talbott had been sleeping. Upon investigating more closely she discovered that Michelle had been subjected to a brutal attack and had bled profusely from several wounds. Mrs. Talbott awoke her husband and, after discovering that their telephone lines had been cut, drove to the sheriff's nearby house. The ensuing investigation by law enforcement officers revealed indications of blood on the doorknob to the upstairs closet, on a nearby piece of paper and wall plaque, and on the upstairs telephone. The telephone lines, which had been cut on both the upstairs and downstairs telephones, had been positioned in such a manner as to conceal the cutting. A number of items were missing from the house, including three guns from the upstairs closet, $283 in cash from the upstairs bathroom, two piggy banks, a penny jar and a green rug from the kitchen, a quilt and a blanket from the basement, and a single boot which apparently had been on the steps leading upstairs.

* * *

An autopsy performed on the victim by Dr. Ben Galloway, Deputy Coroner for the City and County of Denver, disclosed that Michelle had sustained eight wounds, each of which had been inflicted by a sharp cutting instrument. * * * The deputy coroner concluded from the autopsy that each of these four major wounds was capable of causing death. There were also two minor wounds on the victim's thumb.

* * *

The defendant claims there was insufficient evidence to support the crime of robbery and, therefore, his conviction for felony murder must fall. Section 18–4–301(1), C.R.S.1973 (1978 Repl.Vol. 8), defines robbery as follows: "A person who knowingly takes anything of value from the person or presence of another by the use of force, threats, or intimidation commits robbery." Conceding that there was evidence of an unlawful taking of property from the home, the defendant argues that the evidence failed to establish two essential elements of robbery. First, he asserts that the element of a taking from the "person or presence" of the robbery victim, Michelle Talbott, was not proven because the items taken were located in parts of the Talbott home other than the living room where Michelle was present, and, alternatively, because the evidence indicated that Michelle was asleep at the time the taking occurred. Second, the defendant contends that the taking was not accomplished by the use of force, as required for robbery, because there was no evidence that the killing occurred immediately prior to or at the same time as the taking. We find no merit in the defendant's arguments.

We are satisfied that the prosecution established a taking of property "from the presence" of the victim within the statutory proscription of robbery. It is quite obvious what the term "from the person of another" means within the context of the robbery statute. The limits of the term "from the presence of another," however, are not so clear.

It has been stated that "presence" in the context of robbery "is not so much a matter of eyesight as it is one of proximity and control: the property taken in the robbery must be close enough to the victim and sufficiently under [her] control that, had the latter not been subjected to violence or intimidation by the robber, [she] could have prevented the taking." W. LaFave and A. Scott, *Handbook on Criminal Law* § 94 at 696 (1972). The word "presence" has been construed to encompass the taking of property from a location different from but near the place where the force, threats, or intimidation was initially employed against the robbery victim. See, e.g., Cobern v. State, 273 Ala. 547, 142 So.2d 869 (1962) (robbery committed where victim attacked and killed in her home and car stolen from her front yard); State v. Atkins, 549 S.W.2d 927 (Mo.App.1977) (property taken from closet in another room within a victim's presence or control). We hold that property is taken from the "presence of another" when it is so within the victim's reach, inspection or observation that he or she would be able to retain control over the property but for the force, threats, or intimidation directed by the perpetrator against the victim. Any narrower construction would "invite would-be perpetrators to waylay their victims in one location and then as part of the same transaction, to take their property from another nearby location, thereby avoiding guilt of robbery, even if the other elements of the offense were present." State v. Thompson, 37 N.C.App. 651, 661, 247 S.E.2d 235, 240–41 (1978). In this case, the "presence" element is broad enough to encompass the situation where the victim of the robbery, against whom the force, threats, or intimidation is directed, is present in one room of a family home and the taking occurs within another room.

Nor do we agree with the defendant's argument that the property was not taken from the victim's "presence" because the evidence indicated that she was asleep when the taking occurred. In fact, there was circumstantial evidence that the victim was awake prior to the attack and that the attack occurred prior to the taking. In order to reach the upstairs closet to take the guns, it was necessary for the defendant to go through the living room where Michelle was sleeping. Dr. Galloway, the deputy coroner, testified that the two minor wounds inflicted on Michelle's thumb were indicative of defensive efforts on her part to ward off an attack, thus indicating that she was awake at the time the attack occurred. Furthermore, the presence of blood in the upstairs area of the home circumstantially supports the inference that the killing, or at least the attack, took place before the guns were taken. We conclude that there was ample evidence indicating that the property was taken "from the presence" of Michelle Talbott, the robbery victim.

Turning to the second prong of the defendant's argument, we are satisfied that the prosecution's evidence, when appropriately viewed, supports the conclusion that the taking of the property was accomplished by the use of force directed against Michelle Talbott. The gravamen of robbery is the application of physical force or intimidation against the victim at any time during the course of a transaction culminating in the taking of property from the victim's person or presence. There is no requirement that the application of force or intimidation must be virtually contemporaneous with the taking. Nor must the victim necessarily be aware of the taking. Indeed, where the application of force or intimidation is employed for the very purpose of making the victim unaware of the taking, and property is thereafter knowingly taken from the person or presence of the victim, the statutory components of the crime are satisfied.

The evidence, as previously noted, indicates, that the defendant entered the Talbott house to steal guns, that the victim was in his path and awake prior to the attack, and that the attack occurred sometime prior to the taking. The totality of the evidence provides a reasonable basis in fact to conclude that Michelle was the victim of physical violence perpetrated against her during the course of an unlawful taking of property from her presence. There being sufficient evidence of the defendant's commission of the predicate crime of robbery, his challenge to his conviction of felony murder on grounds of evidentiary insufficiency must be rejected.

* * *

Notes

1. *Violence when?* State v. Aldershof, 220 Kan. 798, 800–803, 556 P.2d 371, 373–375, 93 A.L.R.3d 634, 638–640 (1976):

> For centuries the rule followed in England and later in the United States has been that in order for the defendant to be guilty of robbery it is essential that the prosecution prove that the defendant took the property by means of force or violence or by putting the victim in fear. The force or intimidation employed is the gist of the offense. Furthermore, the general rule is that the violence or intimidation must precede or be concomitant or contemporaneous with the taking. Violence or intimidation by the thief *subsequent to the taking* will not render the act robbery. In 4 Bl.Comm. 243, Blackstone, to emphasize that for robbery the larceny must be accomplished by violence or intimidation, said:
>
> > " * * * the taking must be by force, or a previous putting in fear, which makes the violation of the person more atrocious than privately stealing. * * * For if one privately steals sixpence from the person of another, and afterward keeps it by putting him in fear, this is no robbery, for the fear is subsequent. * * * "
>
> The general rule is recognized with many cases cited in 77 C.J.S. Robbery § 11 and 67 Am.Jur.2d, Robbery, § 26. A comprehensive annotation on the subject may be found in 58 A.L.R. 656.
>
> * * *
>
> In Wharton's Criminal Law, 12th Ed., Robbery, § 559, the rule is stated that when the defendant is able to take possession of the property without the use of force or fear but then employs force or fear in order to keep the property or to effect his escape, it is generally held that his offense is not robbery. The author

points out that the conflict in the decisions of some states arises because of the uncertainty as to when the taking is completed. Some cases have held that the snatching of property from the presence of an owner or his agent and a use of force or intimidation in carrying it away constitutes robbery, usually on the theory that the taking was not effected until the property was carried away, and any violence used in making an escape after the snatching was in effect violence in the taking. It is suggested that the problem raised by these cases has been met in some jurisdictions by statutes which define robbery so as to include the use of force to resist the retaking of the property.

California has adopted a minority position that any force used prior to the escape of the robber to a place of temporary safety elevates the crime from theft to robbery. (People v. Anderson, 64 Cal.2d 633, 51 Cal.Rptr. 238, 414 P.2d 366; People v. Laursen, 8 Cal.3d 192, 104 Cal.Rptr. 425, 501 P.2d 1145; People v. Carroll, 1 Cal.3d 581, 83 Cal.Rptr. 176, 463 P.2d 400; People v. Milan, 9 Cal.3d 185, 107 Cal.Rptr. 68, 507 P.2d 956.) Recent cases from other jurisdictions hold that the element of force or intimidation is an essential ingredient of the offense of robbery, and no violence or excitation of fear resorted to merely for the purpose of retaining possession already acquired, or to effect escape, will, in point of time, supply that element. (Mason v. Commonwealth, 200 Va. 253, 105 S.E.2d 149; Hicks v. State, 232 Ga. 393, 207 S.E.2d 30; Gray v. State, 10 Md.App. 478, 271 A.2d 390; State v. Adams [Mo.], 406 S.W.2d 608.) Illinois has taken the position that to sustain a conviction for robbery the force or the threat of force must precede or be contemporaneous with the taking of the property. Nevertheless, although the taking of the property may be peaceful, the departure with the property may be forceful and thus constitute robbery. (People v. Heller, 131 Ill.App.2d 799, 267 N.E.2d 685.) In *Heller* the court held that the use of a dangerous weapon at any point of a robbery, so long as it can reasonably be said to be part of a single occurrence or incident—or put another way, a part of the "res gestae of the crime"—will constitute armed robbery.

2. *Model Penal Code Changes in Robbery.* The Model Penal Code provision on Robbery, § 222.1, suggests some substantial changes in common law robbery: (1) defendant may threaten or inflict bodily injury or threaten or commit one of a defined class of serious felonies; (2) the injury threatened or inflicted must be "serious"; (3) there is no requirement of common law larceny; any of the instances of consolidated theft will do as the basic included crime; (4) the theft need not be completed and the force or threat may be applied at any time during an attempt or in flight afterwards, as well as at the time of taking; (5) there is no requirement that the theft be from the person or in the presence of the victim.

Questions

1. Erroneously believing that the finance company had no right to repossess his car, D went to the company office and forced the manager to return it at gunpoint. Robbery?

2. D came upon a drunk lying unconscious on the street and removed his wristwatch by stretching the springs in the expansion watch band. Robbery?

3. In *Aldershof* (note 1) the court found no robbery when the accused took a purse from a table in a bar, was followed to the adjoining parking lot by the victim, and responded with violence when the victim grabbed him. The court noted that the local theft statute had abolished the asportation requirement and that the accused had already gained peaceable possession of the purse. In a later case in the same

jurisdiction, State v. Long, 234 Kan. 580, 675 P.2d 832 (1984), the victim entered the room as the accused was stuffing the stolen money into his pockets, barred his exit, and was overcome by force. Robbery in Kansas?

4. D accosted V in front of V's store, and said "Hand me your wallet or I will immediately smash in your glass window with this hammer and murder your sister tomorrow." V gave him the wallet. Robbery?

United States v. Jannotti

United States Court of Appeals, Third Circuit, 1981.
673 F.2d 578, cert. denied 457 U.S. 1106, 102 S.Ct. 2906, 73 L.Ed.2d 1315 (1982).

Argued June 10, 1981

Before ALDISERT, WEIS and SLOVITER, CIRCUIT JUDGES.

Reargued In Banc Nov. 23, 1981

Before SEITZ, CHIEF JUDGE, and ALDISERT, ADAMS, GIBBONS, HUNTER, WEIS, GARTH, HIGGINBOTHAM and SLOVITER, CIRCUIT JUDGES.

OPINION OF THE COURT

SLOVITER, CIRCUIT JUDGE.

On September 16, 1980, after a six-day trial, a jury found defendants Harry P. Jannotti and George X. Schwartz guilty of conspiring to obstruct interstate commerce, in violation of the Hobbs Act, 18 U.S.C. § 1951(a) * * *. At the time of the events charged in the indictment, Schwartz was president of the Philadelphia City Council and Jannotti was the Council's majority leader. Following the entry of the guilty verdicts, defendants renewed their requests for judgments of acquittal and dismissal of the indictment, on which the trial court had previously reserved decision. On November 26, 1980, the district court entered an order setting aside the verdict of the jury in its entirety, dismissing Count III of the indictment (the Hobbs Act count) for lack of jurisdiction, and granting the motions of defendants for judgment of acquittal. The Government appeals.

* * *

* * * We reverse the district court's order and direct reinstatement of the jury's verdict.

I

SUMMARY OF EVIDENCE

* * *

* * * The government operation, which has come to be known as ABSCAM, began some time in 1978. The basic nature of the plan was that F.B.I. agents posed as employees of Abdul Enterprises, a fictional multinational corporation whose principal, a fictional Arab Sheik, Yassir Habib of the Arab nation of Abu Dhabi, was represented as interested in investing large amounts of money in this country and in emigrating here. According to the government, the plan was "conceived to create opportunities for illicit conduct by public officials predisposed to political corruption." From the very beginning

the government utilized the services of Melvin Weinberg, accurately characterized by the district court as a "career swindler," who, with F.B.I. agents, "spread the word" that the Sheik was interested in meeting public officials who could facilitate his planned investments.

This basic plan evolved into various subparts, each with its own cast of participants, which were ultimately the subject of a series of indictments returned by grand juries sitting in various federal districts of the country. Thereafter, a number of local and federal public officials were tried on offenses arising out of their participation. We focus on the facts material to the prosecution of Jannotti and Schwartz in the Eastern District of Pennsylvania.

The Philadelphia phase began on January 11, 1980 when Weinberg called Howard Criden, a Philadelphia attorney, and told him that the Sheik was "looking to build a hotel" in Philadelphia. Criden, who had previously received money from the F.B.I. agents for arranging introductions to congressmen in connection with another phase of the ABSCAM operation, was told that two representatives of the Sheik would be coming to Philadelphia to begin discussions. * * *

* * *

Wald [a federal agent, passing as a representative of the Sheik,] asked Criden about the municipal setup, including city council. Criden explained that Philadelphia City Council is composed of 12 district councilmen and five at-large councilmen, that his "partner [Johanson is] a district councilman", and that the president of city council, Schwartz, "is a powerful guy" who had been "president of city council for maybe now ten, twelve years, already now. Has got power." Wald responded, "He's the man." * * * Wald then asked what the "tariff" would be for Johanson and Schwartz, and Criden replied "[t]wenty-five" for Johanson, and "[a]nother fifty" for Schwartz. Wald demurred at the latter figure, and Criden asked, "You wanta go thirty on this guy?" Wald asked, "will he bite at thirty? * * * I mean does that take care of him?" and Criden replied, "Let me try it * * *. I'll run it up the flagpole." * * *

* * *

On January 23, 1980, Criden and Schwartz visited Wald at the Barclay suite. This conversation was videotaped. Criden stated that he and Schwartz had "spoken at length" and that Schwartz knew that those persons whom Wald represented were "interested in building a hotel facility in Philadelphia that may amount to some 30 or 40 million dollars." * * *

> WALD: * * * Now we know that there are problems inherent in any major construction, uh, in this city and any other city. What I am trying to do is take care of any potential problems long before they exist. We're not breaking ground tomorrow morning. We can forsee certain problems such as, uh, uh, zoning and variances and this type of thing * * * municipal government, how it effects those various things, but we don't want to be faced with problems down the road.

Schwartz responded to this overture with a soliloquy on his own political power and importance. * * * The essence of Schwartz' representations of control was repeated shortly thereafter:

> WALD: All right. You're controlling the council at this point.
>
> SCHWARTZ: Right.
>
> * * *
>
> WALD: Should we have anything that comes up to a vote, that has to be done on a vote basis, the council is with you.
>
> SCHWARTZ: Yes.

* * *

Schwartz stated that although he could not promise that the hotel project would not have problems, those problems would not be "insurmountable" as long as the project "is a proper project." Wald stated, "I am not putting up a cathouse", Criden interjected, "It's going to be legitimate", and Schwartz responded, "That I take for granted, or I wouldn't be here." * * * After additional discussion which concerned local law firms that could be employed by the hotel project, the economic climate in Philadelphia, and the encouragement received by business from the city, Wald referred to Schwartz' compensation:

> WALD: Our time frame is growing short, but we don't have those type of problems. We don't have that built-in resentment. Ah * * * We've talked to Howard, you know, the figures, the dollars we're talking are in the right ballpark. We're * * *
>
> SCHWARTZ: That's not my prime concern. I'm interested in the City of Philadelphia. I'm interested in a good project. I'm interested in tax rateables. I want to see Center City develop. Especially Center City. There are a few parcels left. Well anything else that's going to add to the tax rateables of the city that's going to create jobs.
>
> * * *
>
> WALD: Okay, and the sums appropriate and we're in good shape. Okay.

Shortly thereafter as seen on the videotape, Wald opened his briefcase and, without discussion of the amount, handed Schwartz an envelope [containing $30,000 cash], which Schwartz placed in his jacket without counting. * * *

* * *

The next evening, January 24, 1980, following telephone arrangements, Jannotti and Criden arrived at the Barclay suite to meet with Wald * * *. Jannotti had been briefed by Criden and Schwartz earlier that day who had "explained the whole situation." With Jannotti, as with Schwartz, Wald explained "I'm only here for one reason, to bring back some assurances." He continued:

> WALD: [W]e are prepared to make a major investment in this city, alright, and, ah, we have incredible funding but it's still a major investment even for the people that I represent at this time. Ah, it's

not a drop in the bucket even for them. It's a fair amount of money and ah, the way these people do business, is somewhat different than the way we do business in this country, they don't think. They just can't tolerate nor can they put up with psychologically any problems that arise. Now these type of problems do arise but they can be handled, but the type of problems that would get back to my employer. Ahe, he can't deal with them, and he turns to me and says I thought we had all this settled in Philadelphia. So, that's why I'm here, simply to take care of any problems now.

* * *

JANNOTTI: First of all you, you're going to invest a substantial amount of money and, ah, what you'll be doing is bringing into the City of Philadelphia a substantial amount of money, and this will create jobs, will create a tax base and ah from what I gather everything that you want to do with be strictly, ah, on board. I mean there's nothing phony about it.

* * *

CRIDEN: Michael wants to be sure that he has a friend if he has a problem.

JANNOTTI: Oh certainly.

WALD: If something arises, if something arises that needs a City Council vote to be very specific, a City Council vote is needed on the thing, can I count on your vote?

JANNOTTI: Why sure * * *.

WALD: Let me give you a short insight into the Arab mind, that its ah, it's at times difficult to understand now, ah, I can appreciate it because I've had both worlds and I can relate, ah, you know, you folks are here, right, they, they think differently, they deal differently, their psychological process are alien to the way I understand exactly what you're saying. Ok. I'm coming up with something that's going to help the City of Philadelphia. Ah, it would help, as it would help any city. Ah, he does not look on it that way. They do business, differently. They pay the freight up front. They make friends * * *.

Wald and Jannotti discussed City Council politics, and Jannotti affirmed Criden's statement that Council "never had a vote on an issue that George and Harry wanted passed that they'd lost in the last two years." They then discussed the payment to Jannotti:

* * *

WALD: Ah, you've been in business all your life, you've as you said, you got an education 20 years behind the bar, I was sent to Philadelphia to pay for certain things because that is the psychology and that is the method of business that these people are use to, and that is how they conduct business, they conduct with everybody they do. * * *

JANNOTTI: Well, you know ah, just on the basics, of what you said and what they want to do, it's enough for me to get on the floor and argue. I don't have to, even care what else they want to come up with. My basic point is, the fact that, ah what's coming in here, and this has been our job, to bring as much business and and, and ah tax base and employment to the City of Philadelphia. If that's the way they want to do business, that's all right too.

* * *

Wald then took an envelope from his briefcase [containing $10,000 cash], handed it to Jannotti, and asked if "that amount is sufficient." Jannotti took the envelope, answering, "We've discussed it."

* * *

II

HOBBS ACT CONSPIRACY

* * *

The broad language of the Hobbs Act, covering anyone who "in any way or degree * * * affects commerce * * * by * * * extortion or attempts or conspires so to do * * *", 18 U.S.C. § 1951,[9] demonstrates Congress' intent to free interstate commerce from burdens of any kind caused by extortion. * * *

We begin the analysis of Congress' power to regulate interstate commerce with the now-accepted principle that the commerce clause reaches, *inter alia,* activities *affecting* interstate commerce. However, application of a federal criminal statute is not limited to those cases in which an actual interstate effect is shown. * * *

* * *

* * * The ultimate failure of the conspiracy may diminish, but does not eliminate, the threat it poses to social order; therefore, the illegality of the agreement does not depend on the achievement of its ends. It is similarly irrelevant that the ends of the conspiracy were from the very inception of the agreement objectively unattainable. In this case the defendants agreed to do acts which, had they been attainable, would have affected commerce. * * *

* * *

* * * [T]he jury found that the defendants conspired to violate the Hobbs Act by their acceptance of payments in return for their promises to expedite completion of an elaborate hotel project which, had it been constructed, would have entailed at least a $30 million expenditure. Had the project actually been planned as represented, defendants' actions would have violated the Hobbs Act even if unforeseen difficulties, such as the overthrow of the "sheik", prevented any further action on the project. The federal interest in protecting interstate commerce is no less under the factual situation presented in this case. The threat posed by defendants' actions is just as

9. The Hobbs Act reads in pertinent part as follows:

> Whoever in any way or degree obstructs, delays, or affects commerce or the movement of any article or commodity in commerce, by robbery or extortion or attempts or conspires so to do * * * shall be fined not more than $10,000 or imprisoned not more than twenty years, or both.

* * *

great. Since Congress has exercised the full scope of its commerce power in the Hobbs Act, we conclude that there was Hobbs Act jurisdiction.

* * * [T]he district court held that defendants' conduct did not constitute "extortion" under the Act because they, at most, "passive[ly]" accepted the bribes. 501 F.Supp. at 1185. The Act defines "extortion" as:

> the obtaining of property from another, with his consent, induced by wrongful use of actual or threatened force, violence, or fear, or under color of official right.

18 U.S.C. § 1951(b)(2).

The district court's holding is inconsistent with the rationale underlying the holdings of this court that the Act is disjunctive and proscribes the "obtaining of property from another * * * under color of official right," without proof of coercion by the defendant. We reaffirmed this principle in United States v. Mazzei, 521 F.2d 639 (3d Cir.) (en banc), cert. denied, 423 U.S. 1014, 96 S.Ct. 446, 46 L.Ed.2d 385 (1975), where we stated:

> A violation of the statute may be made out by showing that a public official through the wrongful use of office obtains property not due him or his office, even though his acts are not accompanied by the use of "force, violence or fear."

Id. at 645 (citations omitted). In *Mazzei,* we observed that "the 'under color of official right' language [of the Hobbs Act] 'repeats the common law definition of extortion.'" Id. (citation omitted). At common law, extortion was defined as "any officer's unlawfully taking, by color of his office, from any man, any money or thing of value that is not due to him." 4 W. Blackstone, *Commentaries* *141. The requirement that the money be taken "by color of his office" meant "simply that the officer must have taken money not due him for the performance of his official duties." State v. Weleck, 10 N.J. 355, 372, 91 A.2d 751, 759 (1952). Thus, "[i]f the [Hobbs] Act is read in full, the distinction between bribery and extortion becomes unnecessary where public officials are involved." More recently, in United States v. Cerilli, 603 F.2d 415 (3d Cir.1979), cert. denied, 444 U.S. 1043, 100 S.Ct. 728, 62 L.Ed.2d 728 (1980), we upheld the conviction of state officials who received bribes in return for conferring valuable state contracts, and approved the district court's charge that extortion under "[c]olor of official right is defined as the taking by a public official of money not due him or his office * * *."

The holding in our cases that the Hobbs Act covers the acceptance of bribes by public officials even when payment was not obtained by force, threats, or use of fear, and the further suggestion that there need be no inducement or prior request for such payments, accords with the view taken by other courts of appeals. * * *

* * *

Accordingly we hold that the district court erred in dismissing Count III of the indictment.

III

ENTRAPMENT

As Justice Harlan noted, the meaning, purpose, and application of the defense of entrapment in criminal cases are problems that have sharply divided the Court. See Lopez v. United States, 373 U.S. 427, 434, 83 S.Ct. 1381, 1385, 10 L.Ed.2d 462 (1963). See also United States v. Russell, 411 U.S. 423, 439–40, 93 S.Ct. 1637, 1646–47, 36 L.Ed.2d 366 (Stewart, J., dissenting) (1973). To a large extent, that division has centered on whether the controlling standard focuses on the conduct of the government (the objective test) or the predisposition of the defendant (the subjective test). The legal principles which determine the application of the entrapment defense in this case, however, are not in serious dispute. The parameters of the entrapment defense are largely to be found from the four principal cases in which the defense has been considered by the Supreme Court, Sorrells v. United States, 287 U.S. 435, 53 S.Ct. 210, 77 L.Ed. 413 (1932); Sherman v. United States, 356 U.S. 369, 78 S.Ct. 819, 2 L.Ed.2d 848 (1958); United States v. Russell, 411 U.S. 423, 93 S.Ct. 1637, 36 L.Ed.2d 366 (1973); and Hampton v. United States, 425 U.S. 484, 96 S.Ct. 1646, 48 L.Ed.2d 113 (1976).

In *Sorrells v. United States,* where the Court first recognized the defense of entrapment, the Court held the defendant was entitled to have the jury consider whether his acts of possessing and selling one-half gallon of whiskey in violation of the National Prohibition Act were instigated by the prohibition agent who implanted in the "mind of an innocent person the disposition to commit the alleged offense and induce its commission in order that [Government officials] may prosecute." 287 U.S. at 442, 53 S.Ct. at 212. The nature of the defense was outlined more fully when the Court next considered the defense a quarter of a century later in *Sherman v. United States.* Chief Justice Warren, writing for the majority of the Court, stated that "[t]o determine whether entrapment has been established, a line must be drawn between the trap for the unwary innocent and the trap for the unwary criminal." 356 U.S. at 372, 78 S.Ct. at 820. In concluding that entrapment had been established as a matter of law, the Court determined from the undisputed testimony of the prosecution's witnesses that the defendant was induced to sell narcotics by the government informer and that he was not predisposed, i.e., that he engaged in conduct he would not otherwise have attempted. The Court noted, "Entrapment occurs only when the criminal conduct was 'the product of the *creative* activity' of law-enforcement officials." Id. (emphasis in original).

In *United States v. Russell,* the Court expressly disapproved of the decisions of the lower federal courts which had expanded the entrapment defense beyond the Court's opinions in *Sorrells* and *Sherman.* Instead, the Court reiterated that the defense was not of constitutional dimension, and reaffirmed its prior opinions that established that entrapment is a "relatively limited defense", 411 U.S. at 435, 93 S.Ct. at 1644, which cannot be used by a predisposed defendant. Most recently, in *Hampton v. United States,* a majority of the Court, in two separate opinions, upheld defendant's conviction arising from his sales of heroin which had allegedly been procured from a government informant, reaffirming once again the unavailability of the entrapment defense to a predisposed defendant.

Emerging from these cases are the principles which guide our review of the evidence which defendants argue and the district court found established entrapment as a matter of law. As the Court stated in *Sorrells,* "It is well settled that the fact that officers or employees of the Government merely afford opportunities or facilities for the commission of the offense does not defeat the prosecution." 287 U.S. at 441, 53 S.Ct. at 212. Entrapment occurs when a defendant who was not predisposed to commit the crime does so as a result of the government's inducement. The entrapment defense thus focuses on "the intent or predisposition of the defendant to commit the crime." United States v. Russell, 411 U.S. at 429, 93 S.Ct. at 1641. As we have previously held, the government has the burden "to disprove the whole [entrapment] defense beyond a reasonable doubt," United States v. Watson, 489 F.2d 504, 510 (3d Cir.1973).

Finally, although there may be instances where the undisputed facts establish the entrapment defense as a matter of law, or where the evidence is simply insufficient to submit the issue to the jury, entrapment is generally a jury question. This court has held that a defendant is entitled to an entrapment instruction,

> however unreasonable the judge would consider a verdict in favor of the defendant to be, when the accused shows (1) evidence that the Government initiated the crime, regardless of the amount of pressure applied to the defendant, and (2) any evidence negating the defendant's propensity to commit the crime.

United States v. Watson, 489 F.2d at 509.

The district court in this case submitted the issue of entrapment to the jury following a jury charge on that issue which is not here challenged. After the jury decided that defendants were not entrapped, the district court reconsidered the propriety of such submission in ruling on defendants' motions for acquittal. The court summarized the government's evidence as relying exclusively upon the fact that each defendant did accept money from the agents. The district court agreed that "[i]n some situations * * * a defendant's ready acquiescence in the Government's suggestion may be enough to justify a finding of predisposition."

However, the district court overturned the jury's decision. Although the court remarked that, "No-one who has viewed the videotape evidence in this case could avoid feelings of distress and disgust at the crass behavior the tapes reveal," it gave judgment for the defendants because "[t]he evidence was, as a matter of law, insufficient to establish the defendants' predisposition beyond a reasonable doubt." In support of that decision, the district court relied on three factors.

> In my opinion, in their zeal to make sure that the defendants would accept the tendered payments, the government agents offered such *attractive inducements as to preclude any reliance upon the*

> *defendants' acceptance* of the money as proof of predisposition. In the first place, the amounts offered were *exceedingly generous.* Standing alone, the very amounts of the bribes were, to paraphrase the language of the court in Scriber v. U.S., [4 F.2d 97 (6th Cir. 1925)], "a substantial temptation to a first offense."
>
> In the second place, it was clear that the *defendants would not be asked or expected to do anything improper on behalf of the proposed hotel venture;* and they agreed to do nothing inconsistent with their obligations as members of the City Council, working for the benefit of their constituents.
>
> Finally, and most importantly, they were led *to believe that if they did not accept the money, the project would not come to Philadelphia.* In the context of the fiscal crises which beset all large cities these days, and in the context of the problems of urban blight and decay, the governmental inducement in this case was indeed calculated to overwhelm.

Id. (emphasis added).

Before turning to that evidence, it will be useful to reiterate briefly the applicable principles governing deference to the jury's findings. In ruling on a motion to overturn a jury's finding of predisposition the trial court must view the evidence in the light most favorable to the prosecution, and resolve all reasonable inferences therefrom in its favor. * * * Viewing the evidence in this light, the trial court must uphold the jury's verdict unless no reasonable jury could conclude beyond a reasonable doubt that the defendant was predisposed to commit the offense for which he was convicted. * * * Thus, we must independently examine the evidence on the three factors relied upon by the district court to determine whether it was as overwhelming for the defendants as the district court found. If not, it was error to withdraw the decision on the predisposition issue from the jury.

A

The size of the payments

The undisputed evidence shows that Schwartz, chairman of Philadelphia City Council, accepted a payment *in cash* of $30,000 from an F.B.I. agent posing as a representative of the sheik, that he looked inside the envelope, fingered the bills, and licked the envelope closed. The evidence also shows that Jannotti, a member of Philadelphia City Council, accepted a payment in cash of $10,000 from the same F.B.I. representative, that he placed the envelope in his pocket without opening it, and that he declined to discuss the amount of the payment, repeating several times "We won't even discuss it."

* * *

Even if the dollar amount offered were relevant to disprove predisposition, a question which we do not decide, we find nothing in the record to support the district court's conclusion that in today's inflationary times, city councilmen would view sums of $30,000 or $10,000 as so large or generous as to overcome an official's natural reluctance to accept a bribe. Certainly, the question of the generosity of the sums given must be viewed in relationship to the circumstances of the acceptors. What would be tempting to an office clerk would plainly not be enough to tempt a millionaire. Yet the record is almost bare of any evidence of the defendants' financial situations. What the record does disclose hardly suggests that either man was in dire straits financially. * * *

* * *

The jury was well aware of the amount of the bribes as well as the defendants' stations in life. Since there is nothing in the record to support the district court's conclusion that the amounts involved were, *as a matter of law,* so generous and enticing as to overcome any possible refusal by the defendants, the court's action in overturning the jury's resolution of this issue was plainly an intrusion on the jury's prerogative.

B

The "benignity" of the payments

The second of the three factors which the district court stressed in holding that the evidence was insufficient as a matter of law to establish that the defendants' acceptance of the money showed their predisposition was that "the defendants would not be asked or expected to do anything improper on behalf of the proposed hotel venture" and that "they agreed to do nothing inconsistent with their obligations as members of the City Council, working for the benefit of their constituents." * * *

* * * It may be that the district court, in stating that defendants agreed to do nothing "improper", was referring to the defendants' repeated statements on tape that they assumed that the hotel was to be a legitimate venture and their frequent comments that the project would be good for Philadelphia. However, as the district court acknowledged, the evidence permitted the inference that the payments represented "bribes" to elected public officials in return for the use of their official positions. We fail to see how any court anywhere under any circumstances can fail to characterize a public official's acceptance of payment to "pave the way for expeditious completion of the project" as "improper".

* * *

* * * In view of the jury's adverse determination that the payments were not for "friendship" but were to improperly influence defendants in the exercise of their official positions, the district court's substitution of its view of the evidence in deciding that *as a matter of law* there could be no predisposition represented an unfortunate usurpation of the jury's prerogative.

C

The "contingency" of the hotel project, i.e., "the Arab mind"

The final factor, and the one considered "most important" by the district court in its assessment of the "overwhelm[ing]" inducement offered by the F.B.I. agents posing as the sheik's representatives, was the fact, as described by the district court, that defendants were "led to believe that if they did not accept the money, the project would not come to Philadelphia." The district court, in reviewing the entire undercover operation which has come to be known as ABSCAM, stated: "Perhaps the crucial aspect of the undercover operation was its emphasis upon 'the Arab mind,' the 'Arab way of doing business.' A constant theme of *the agents' representations was that their principals would not undertake any project unless first assured of the 'friendship' of the persons* with whom they were dealing." Id. at 1194 (emphasis added).

This conclusion suffers from the failure to cite to evidence that any such representation was ever made to or communicated to defendant Schwartz. We have found no such evidence. * * *

* * *

With regard to Jannotti, there is no question that a reference to the "Arab mind" was made to him, and that Wald also represented that this "is the method of business that these people are use [sic] to, and that is how they conduct business * * *." * * *

Later in the meeting Wald reiterated that "Philadelphia has already been sold, to the man." Thus, even as to Jannotti, at most the evidence presents the basis for differing arguments to the jury as to the interpretation to be placed on the conversations.

* * *

D

Acceptance of the money by Schwartz and Jannotti

* * * Thus, we return to the initial proposition, that the acceptance of the money itself may be sufficient to show predisposition.

In certain types of crimes, it is often possible for the government to show predisposition by proof of the defendant's prior convictions or his or her participation in similar transactions. Such evidence would be extremely difficult to produce in the case of acceptance of a bribe by a public official. Because such officials are often intelligent, educated and worldly, it is unlikely that they will accept money from those to whom they have not had "safe" introductions and who, because they are also implicated, are unlikely to report to the authorities. In addition, because the crime has no direct victim, its occurrence leaves no public trail which cries for investigation. Since the ultimate factual determination is whether the defendant was "ready and willing to commit the crime if an opportunity should be presented," as distinguished from having been "corrupted by some overreaching or special inducement," the very acceptance of a bribe by a public official may be evidence of a predisposition to do so when the opportunity is presented.[13]

* * *

13. Researchers have found it difficult to locate a case in which the defense of entrapment has been successfully interposed in prosecutions of public officials for accepting, agreeing to receive, or soliciting bribes. *See* Annotation, Entrapment to Commit Bribery or Offer to Bribe, 69 A.L.R.2d 1397, 1431 (1960). Defendants have cited to no such case, nor has our independent investigation uncovered one. This is to be contrasted with the occasional successful entrapment defense by those persons who have been enticed by public officials to make the payments.

The facts of this case are unlike any of the few in which the entrapment defense has been successful. In United States v. Klosterman, 248 F.2d 191, 193 (3d Cir.1957), the government contacted a reluctant intermediary eleven times before he agreed to make the necessary introduction. The other defendant in *Klosterman* was, as the subject of an IRS investigation which had been continuing "for an unusual length of time," under anxiety and therefore "more susceptible" to the government's persuasion. Id. at 196. In Sorrells v. United States, the agent "lured" defendant by "repeated and persistent solicitation in which he succeeded by taking advantage of the sentiment aroused by reminiscences of their experiences as companions in arms in the World War." 287 U.S. at 441, 53 S.Ct. at 212. In Sherman v. United States, the defendant, after rebuffing numerous requests by the government agent, finally relented and sold drugs to the agent, who had played upon the defendant's sympathy by predicating his request upon his suffering from lack of narcotics. 356 U.S. at 373, 78 S.Ct. at 821. See Wall v. United States, 65 F.2d 993 (5th Cir.1933). The situation here is obviously not analogous. Defendants in this case point to no statements or gestures which indicate any reluctance whatsoever to accept the proffered payments.

* * *

* * * [D]efendants accepted the money readily, unprotestingly, even casually, without ever once attempting to use their consummate political skill to say, as diplomatically as the circumstances required, "Thanks, but no thanks."

The ultimate factual decisions in an entrapment case must be left to the jury. Where, as here, the jury was uniquely equipped to inquire into the calculus of human interaction, a court should not interfere with its conclusions. We conclude that in determining that defendants were entitled to a judgment of acquittal on the ground of entrapment as a matter of law the district court impermissibly substituted its own determination of the credibility of witnesses, the weight of the evidence and the inferences to be drawn from the evidence for that of the jury.

IV

DUE PROCESS

* * *

It is plain * * * that a successful due process defense must be predicated on intolerable government conduct which goes beyond that necessary to sustain an entrapment defense. * * * We must necessarily exercise scrupulous restraint before we denounce law enforcement conduct as constitutionally unacceptable; the ramifications are wider and more permanent than when only a statutory defense is implicated.

We must be careful not to undermine the Court's consistent rejection of the objective test of entrapment by permitting it to reemerge cloaked as a due process defense. While the lines between the objective test of entrapment favored by a minority of the Justices and the due process defense accepted by a majority of the Justices are indeed hazy, the majority of the Court has manifestly reserved for the constitutional defense only the most intolerable government conduct. * * *

* * *

Defendants argue that both the initiation of the Philadelphia phase of the investigation and the subsequent approach to them constituted "outrageous" conduct in that the government had no reasonable basis to believe that such tactics would uncover criminal activity. We find this unpersuasive * * *. * * * Where the conduct of the investigation itself does not offend due process, the mere fact that the investigation may have been commenced without probable cause does not bar the conviction of those who rise to its bait.

* * *

ALDISERT, CIRCUIT JUDGE, dissenting, with whom WEIS, CIRCUIT JUDGE, joins, with the exception of * * * [the statement about "color of official right"].

* * *

In my approach to this case, I acknowledge that transgressors must be punished for conduct that violates legal standards, but I place a restriction on this abstract theory: those who receive society's commission to go forth and capture transgressors may not themselves transgress. A free society can exist only to the extent that those charged with enforcing the law respect it themselves. * * * The law enforcers may themselves offer inducements to transgress *if, and only if,* the persons so induced were predisposed to violate the law and the offered inducements provided only the opportunity to act on their predispositions. A society cannot long remain free if we permit the law enforcer to offer more than opportunity for transgression; a free society cannot and will not endure if it permits law enforcers to select individuals arbitrarily, and then to proceed by deception to persuade, cajole, entice, and implant a law-breaking disposition that was not theretofore present. * * *

Federal public policy, and, indeed, basic social policy, dictate that it is better to let a technical transgressor go free than to allow federal law enforcement officials to manufacture crime that entraps the unwary innocent. The predicate of this public policy against entrapment is threefold. First, it recognizes the awesome power of the financial and personnel resources at the disposal of federal law enforcement authorities. Second, reflecting the Judeo-Christian understanding that weakness has inhered in mankind since the days of Adam, it appreciates that even the most morally scrupulous members of society can be persuaded to breach behavioral standards if presented with sufficiently tempting inducements. Third, it acknowledges that a line can be drawn that will permit the proper use of government resources to identify and prosecute the wrongdoer and at the same time serve as an instrument to prevent abuse of those resources. If the government presents temptations, small or large, but the defendant is predisposed to succumb to them, then the government's conduct is usually permissible; if the defendant is not predisposed, then the government's conduct is beyond the pale.

* * *

I refuse to proceed as if no important social issue were involved in this case which implicates both the wrongdoing of city public officials and the questionable activities of federal police officials. I believe that we are confronting an extremely sensitive intersection between morals and positive law, which demands that the judiciary assume rather than shirk responsibility. * * *

* * *

Let me clear the air as to what I perceive case law to regard as legitimate and, therefore, permissible, undercover police work, and that which goes beyond the pale. In the permissible category I put all undercover activity that searches out contemplated or ongoing criminal conduct and even results in actual participation in the illegal enterprise. In this same category I would justify an agent's inducement of others to engage in crime, so long as there is proof of predisposition by the others to participate in the illegal activity. Where, as here, there is absolutely no proof that the defendants had any disposition to commit an illegal act but for the government's inducement, however, then the government's actions are impermissible, and the defense of entrapment is available as a matter of law—and it is for a judge and not a jury to blow the whistle on the improper conduct.

* * *

* * * The crucial question, then, is whether the defendant was induced to commit the offense by agents of the government or predisposed to commit like offenses whenever the opportunity arose. We have recognized, however, that evidence of inducement may be highly probative of predisposition. * * *

Chief Justice Warren emphasized that the function of law enforcement is the prevention of crime and the apprehension of criminals, and "that function does not include the manufacturing of crime." Sherman, 356 U.S. at 372, 78 S.Ct. at 820. A review of the evidence in this case persuades me that the agents of the FBI were consummate manufacturers of crime. They built the plant, they designed the machinery, they operated it, and they covertly solicited the defendants to be customers of their product. It is difficult to conceive of a stronger case of inducement by the government. * * *

* * *

Given the evidence of overwhelming inducement, the government's evidentiary burden to prove predisposition was commensurately substantial. I need not attempt to delineate the outer limits of that burden here, because, in my view, the prosecution's proof fell far short of the requirement. The government's best case scenario shows that the defendants arrived at the Barclay at the government's invitation, discussed city government and hotel investments, and accepted unsolicited offers of money. The circumstances demonstrate that they were offered substantial sums for their "friendship," that they considered the project in the city's best interests, and that they were made to believe that the sheik would not invest in Philadelphia unless he were permitted to "buy friends." In essence, the government's case is that the defendants consummated the crime by accepting money for friendship. Receiving money under these circumstances, whatever its relevancy to prove extortion, was insufficient as a matter of law to prove predisposition. The government has demonstrated convincingly that it has massive resources to encourage and inveigle local officials to commit crimes; that if sufficiently attractive monetary and civic inducements are dangled, there are fish who will bite. It does not demonstrate that the fish were predisposed to take the bait.

* * *

* * * [T]he major discussion of this very important issue, set forth at great length in Part III of the majority opinion, consists only of a refutation of what is described as the district judge's three stated reasons for his post-trial decision. Having rebutted these reasons, albeit skillfully, the majority rest their case. At most, however, what the majority have done, incident to refuting the benignity of the payments, is to prove a theory of extortion. They have not demonstrated how the government met its burden of proving defendants' predisposition to commit the offense. I can accept every iota of the majority's analysis in Part III and still conclude that their analysis passes wide of the relevant mark. * * *

* * *

I turn now to the question of the district court's jurisdiction under the Hobbs Act. * * *

* * *

* * * The Hobbs Act contemplates conspiracies that have at least a realistic probability of affecting interstate commerce. A purely hypothetical effect, a fairy tale conjured by the FBI's answer to the Brothers Grimm, is not "a sufficient threat to [commerce] so as to give rise to federal jurisdiction." * * *

* * *

To avoid unduly prolonging an opinion that is already too lengthy, I will not discuss in detail the majority's treatment of the "extortion under color of official right" argument, set forth in Part IIB of the majority opinion, other than to assert my continued disagreement with both the majority's conclusion and its supporting reasoning. I adhere to the views set forth in United States v. Cerilli, 603 F.2d 415, 426 (3d Cir.1979), cert. denied, 444 U.S. 1043, 100 S.Ct. 728, 62 L.Ed.2d 728 (1980) (Aldisert, J., dissenting), where I identified and analyzed the serious error this court committed in United States v. Kenny, 462 F.2d 1205 (3d Cir.), cert. denied, 409 U.S. 914, 93 S.Ct. 233, 34 L.Ed.2d 176 (1972), in its revolutionary interpretation of the Hobbs Act. * * *

* * *

* * * Because I agree with the result reached by Judge Fullam, I would affirm the judgment of acquittal.

Notes

1. *Extension of Extortion.* The limited nature of common law extortion is explained in the following note. Legislatures commonly either expand this offense to cover most taking by threats which does not amount to robbery, or enact special blackmail statutes to cover other kinds of extortionate conduct. The Model Penal Code consolidates extortion into the general theft crime. See § 223.4. How do you distinguish permissible threats in economic competition from extortion? E.g., "I will drive you out of business unless you use my brand of widgets."

2. *Extortion, Bribery, and the Hobbs Act.* United States v. Cerilli, 603 F.2d 415, 433–435 (3d Cir.1979) (ALDISERT, CIRCUIT JUDGE, dissenting), cert. denied 444 U.S. 1043, 100 S.Ct. 728, 62 L.Ed.2d 728 (1980):

> I believe that the congressional intent underlying the Hobbs Act is clearly and unambiguously disclosed by its legislative history. Not only is there a total lack of specific congressional intent that the Act apply to state and local public officials in the absence of violence or coercion, but the legislative history indicates that Congress intended to rely on the New York law of extortion for its definition of the crime. * * *
>
> Extortion under color of official right under the New York schema must implicate (1) oppression, as therein defined, and not applicable in *Kenny* or here, (2) extortion in the sense of the original common law formulation, defined as a public officer's asking, receiving, or agreeing to receive a *fee* where no fee is authorized or in excess of that allowed by statute, or (3) extortion by wrongful use of force or fear. Unless money is received under a specific misrepresentation that it is an authorized fee, a public official cannot be guilty of extortion under New York law in the absence of duress.
>
> The salient feature of New York extortion law is the unusually clear distinction between the offenses of bribery and extortion. This is manifested in People v. Dioguardi, 8 N.Y.2d 260, 203 N.Y.S.2d 870, 168 N.E.2d 683 (1960), which held that bribery and extortion were "mutually exclusive crimes" and that a defendant charged with extortion was entitled to acquittal if the jury found that he had been bribed. The court reasoned that bribery "makes the payor equally as guilty as the payee, *which could never be the case with extortion,*" and that the *payee* could not be guilty of extortion if the *payor* were guilty of bribery, id. (emphasis added), relying on People v. Feld, 262 App.Div. 909, 28 N.Y.S.2d 796 (1941), and on Hornstein v. Paramount Pictures, 22 Misc.2d 996, 1003, 37 N.Y.S.2d 404, 412 (Sup.Ct.1942), aff'd 266 App.Div. 659, 41 N.Y.S.2d 210, aff'd, 292 N.Y. 468, 55 N.E.2d 740, both of which were decided well before the enactment of the Hobbs Act. The holding of *People v. Feld* was that bribery of a labor representative and extortion were mutually exclusive crimes; *Hornstein* held that "the essence of bribery is the *voluntary* giving of something of value to influence the performance of *official duty,* whereas the essence of extortion is duress."
>
> Although this nuance of New York law has been criticized as a "*unique* interpretation" which should not restrict federal courts applying the Hobbs Act, I believe it is totally consistent with the common law origins of the offenses. Moreover, congressional reliance on New York law demands adherence to that interpretation, however it may differ from the law of other states.
>
> * * *
>
> The historical basis of extortion, a common law misdemeanor, was the corrupt collection of an unlawful *fee* under color of public office. The requirement that the unlawful fee be associated with the office held by the recipient is central to an understanding of the traditional Blackstonian definition generally expressed in broader language. Professor Perkins advises:
>
>> A fee collected under color of office is unlawful if—(1) the law does not authorize a fee for the purpose for which this fee is collected, or (2) a fee is authorized but only in an amount smaller than that collected, or (3) a fee might be authorized but none was due at the time this fee was collected. For this reason Blackstone defined extortion as "an abuse of public justice, which consists in any officer's unlawfully taking, by colour of his office, from

any man, any money or thing of value that is not due to him, or more than is due, or before it is due." Since a fee is unlawful under any one of the three circumstances the simpler wording is preferred for purposes of definition.

* * *

On the other hand, the common law misdemeanor of bribery is an offense which may be committed both by the giver and the recipient. It originated as an offense which could only be committed by a judge or other person concerned with the administration of justice but was broadened in the eighteenth century to extend beyond the conduct of judicial officers. A bribe has been defined as "something given for the purpose of improperly influencing official action, and either giving or accepting a bribe constitutes bribery." [31]

There is an obvious correlation between the common law offenses of bribery and extortion. Nevertheless, in addition to the fact that both a bribe-giver and a bribe-taker are guilty of bribery whereas the victim of extortion is innocent, another distinction between the offenses is apparent. The later development of the crime of extortion, including blackmail, occurred "in order to plug a loophole in the robbery law by covering sundry threats which will not do for robbery. * * * [B]oth crimes equally require that the defendant's threats induce the victim to give up his property, something which he would not otherwise have done." [32] Thus, although both bribery and extortion originated as offenses related to performance of public office, bribery is a victimless crime whereas extortion developed along the lines of robbery.

At their tangent, the offenses of bribery and extortion may both arise out of the same nucleus of operative facts. A public official who corruptly accepts an unauthorized fee for the performance of his official duty may be guilty of both bribery and extortion. At the opposite extreme, however, the offenses bear little resemblance.

3. *Mens Rea in Extortion.* Does the mens rea requirement for extortion differ from that for other theft offenses with respect to a claim of right? There is authority that claim of right is not a defense in extortion. In People v. Fichtner, 281 App.Div. 159, 118 N.Y.S.2d 392 (1952), affirmed without opinion 305 N.Y. 864, 114 N.E.2d 212 (1953), defendant supermarket employees caught a shoplifter after, as they claimed, observing him steal on several occasions. He had taken a $.53 item on this occasion and conceded that he had previously taken a $.65 item. The defendants claimed to have seen him take various items worth $5.61 and to believe that he had taken at least $75 worth of merchandise. By threatening arrest and publicity they got the shoplifter to sign a statement admitting he had taken $50 worth of goods and agreeing to pay to the store $25 on account, with a promise of the rest later. The court held proper the refusal of an instruction that if defendants had believed the shoplifter owed approximately $50, they should be acquitted of extortion. A majority thought that it made no difference how much had been taken or what defendant believed—that it was extortion to try to collect a just debt by a threat of criminal prosecution, even if the crime had been committed. (Cf. the common law misdemeanor of compounding a crime, defined infra p. 319.) The New York legislature disagreed and amended the law to provide a defense of reasonable belief in truth of the charge, where the sole purpose is restitution. For the view that the common law claim of right defense is applicable to statutory extortion, see R. v. Bernhard, [1938] 26 Cr.App. 137 (C.C.A.), where the conviction of the former Hungarian mistress of the victim, who threatened her lover with publicity unless he continued to make promised

31. Perkins, supra note 26, at 468–69. *Accord* Wharton, supra, note 26, at 771–73.

32. LaFave & Scott, supra note 26, at 707.

support payments, was quashed after the trial judge had declined to give a claim of right charge. Accord, Model Penal Code § 223.4, which allows the defense where the threat is to accuse of crime, expose a secret, or take or withhold official action, and the property obtained is honestly (not, as in New York, reasonably) claimed as restitution or compensation.

4. *Entrapment.* Entrapment is not usually accepted as a defense in very serious crimes, such as robbery or murder. An agent of the government must be involved in the entrapping conduct.

Question

Why is entrapment recognized as a defense? Does it prevent adequate *mens rea* on the part of the accused?

2. Receiving Stolen Goods

State v. Fence

Supreme Court of Ohypo, 1978.
285 Ohypo 260.

TOVE, J.: Defendant, Dr. Florian Fence, is a Professor of Biology at Ohypo State University, and a leading opponent of "genetic engineering," a process by which new life forms may be created in the laboratory. Dr. Fence fears that such experimentation may produce dangerous species. His colleague, Dr. Celia Centaur, was a leading experimenter in the field, and her laboratory was in a building a few hundred yards from the defendant's office and laboratory.

According to the State's evidence, which Dr. Fence does not dispute, Arthur Aid, a thirteen year old child prodigy and one of Fence's graduate student assistants, who had a set of keys to Fence's laboratory, telephoned Fence at home at ten o'clock on the evening of December 3, 1977, and told Fence that he had been much impressed by Fence's lectures on the dangers of genetic engineering, that he was calling from Fence's laboratory, and that he needed Fence's advice as to what he should do with some laboratory notes of Dr. Centaur's which had come into his hands. Fence replied, "Burn them in my lab furnace. Anything you can do to impede her research is a gift to humanity." Aid did so.

Fence was charged with receiving stolen goods under our statute (Ohypo Rev.Code, Art. 27, § 550), which provides:

> Every person who shall receive any stolen property, knowing the same to be stolen, shall be guilty of the crime of receiving stolen property and shall be sentenced to imprisonment for not more than ten years or fined not more than ten thousand dollars, or both.

His motion for a directed verdict of acquittal was denied and the jury found him guilty. He appeals on the ground that the facts do not show that he committed the elements of the offense.

We think that the jury could find beyond a reasonable doubt that the prosecution established all of the elements of the offense.

It is first necessary to show that the notes were stolen property. There is no question that they qualify as property of some value under our statute, but Fence contends that there is no proof that they were stolen. Dr. Centaur died of a mysterious disease before trial, and, while her associates were able to identify the remains of the burned notes as hers, they were unable to say how Aid might have got hold of them. Aid did not testify at the trial. We think that the jury would have been justified in drawing the inference in the circumstances that Centaur would have guarded the notes carefully and would not have voluntarily put the notes in Aid's hands for any reason. It seems clear that one of three things happened: (1) Aid stole the notes himself, either from Centaur or from some member of her staff to whom she had entrusted them. In this case Aid committed an act of larceny and the goods were stolen. (2) An unknown staff member, to whom the goods were entrusted by Centaur, turned them over to Aid. In this case the goods were embezzled if the staff member was a colleague or taken by larceny if the staff member was a servant. Our statute has been construed to cover embezzled goods as well as goods taken by larceny, so they could have been received in any event. (3) An unknown third person committed larceny of the notes, in which case they retained the status of stolen goods, no matter how Aid acquired them.

Fence objects that since Aid was under the age of fourteen (when at common law there would have been a weak presumption of criminal incapacity), he could not, under our Juvenile Justice Code, be guilty of larceny himself, so that the state would have to establish a theft by someone else. It is true that the law requires that one of Aid's age be found a juvenile delinquent unless jurisdiction of the juvenile court is waived, on the basis of conduct which would be larceny in an adult (a point we need not consider), and that Aid could not technically be found guilty of a crime in juvenile court. But this provision exists solely to protect the child, and not to protect adult participants. For present purposes, if Aid did what in an adult would be larceny, this is enough. The Fagins of this world cannot take advantage of the youth of their suppliers.

But Fence denies that he ever received the property. His home was several miles from the campus, and the notes never left the campus. He certainly never came into physical possession of them, as would be normal in a receiver. However, it is well established that it is sufficient that the receiver obtain constructive possession. Fence assumed direction of the situation by telephone and his directions were followed. The jury could find that he "received" the notes.

Fence must also be shown to have known that the notes were stolen at the time he received them. The knowledge requirement means that he must have actually believed (certainty is not a realistic requirement) the goods to have been stolen. That he was put on notice, or that a reasonable person in his position would have known is not enough. But the jury is entitled to infer, if the proof does not suggest otherwise, that if a reasonable person would have believed the property to be stolen, Fence in all probability believed this. The natural inference from Aid's telephone conversation was that Aid took the notes himself. If a more cautious analysis is appropriate, Fence might have thought of the alternate possibilities we have noted, but, as we have seen, all of these lead to the same conclusion, that the notes were stolen. Knowledge was sufficiently established.

The only remaining requirement is that Fence be shown to have received the goods with intent to deprive the owner of them; if he had got hold of them with intent to restore them to Dr. Centaur, he would not be guilty. But he intended that they be destroyed, and this is as much an intent to deprive as if he had meant to keep them for himself.

Conviction affirmed.

Question

On the basis of your knowledge of theft law, do you find any problems with the argument of the *Fence* opinion?

Notes

1. *Receiving, Compounding, and Misprision.* The common law did not punish receiving stolen goods directly. The receiver was not regarded as a party to the theft merely because he bought the stolen goods; he was not an accessory after the fact because he did not receive, comfort, hide, etc., the thief, but only received the stolen property. But he might sometimes be punished for one of two common law misdemeanors:

(a) If he knew that a larceny had been committed but agreed not to report or prosecute it in return for something of value (say, a lower price for the goods), he was guilty of *compounding a crime*. Note that the victim of a crime may commit this offense. The Model Penal Code § 242.5 allows a defense where the actor believed the benefit he received was no greater than what would be justified as restitution for his loss. Of course, there is nothing wrong with the victim's trying to get his property back where this is not coupled with an agreement to refrain from prosecuting.

(b) In early common law times there was at least a theoretical obligation upon one who knew that a felony had been committed to make a timely report of the crime to the authorities. Failure to do so was known as *misprision of felony*. The crime has seldom been prosecuted in modern times and has not usually been received as a part of the common law in American jurisdictions. Misprision statutes usually require some conduct assisting the felon in addition to mere failure to report.

In 1691 a statute punished receiving as accessoryship, and later receiving was punished as a separate offense. Receiving has traditionally been punished less severely than larceny, but from the point of view of penal policy it should be punished as severely or more severely. Not much other than cash would be worth the professional thief's effort to steal unless he had a receiver to whom he could sell the goods, and the receiver is likely to profit more from the theft than the thief and perhaps even to encourage or direct a platoon of thieves. The Model Penal Code consolidates the offense into its general theft provision. See § 223.6.

2. *Model Penal Code Provisions.* The Model Penal Code consolidation helps resolve two problems in the prosecution of receivers:

(a) If the offenses are separate, how do you determine whether one in recent guilty possession of stolen goods is a thief or a receiver?

(b) Do separate receiving provisions apply to goods obtained by embezzlement or false pretenses?

3. *Stolen goods.* Proof that the goods are actually stolen may present more difficulties than are immediately apparent, especially if a cache of suspicious goods is found and ownership cannot be traced convincingly. Problems also arise when once stolen goods are returned to the owner or taken on his behalf and then offered to a suspected receiver. They may have lost their character as stolen goods. Even an *attempted* receiving charge may not stand in such a case. People v. Jaffe, 185 N.Y. 497, 78 N.E. 169 (1906). See the Model Penal Code solution in § 223.6(1).

4. *Knowledge and Presumptions.* Proof of knowledge may also be difficult. Many statutes carry presumptions which assist here, as for example where a dealer pays much less than the market value or has in his possession goods stolen from more than one source. See, e.g., Model Penal Code § 223.6(2). Note that there is a constitutional requirement that a presumption against a criminal defendant be based on a logically probable inference. See, e.g., Leary v. United States, 395 U.S. 6, 89 S.Ct. 1532, 23 L.Ed.2d 57 (1969).

3. Forgery

State v. Hamilton

Supreme Court of Oregon, En Banc, 1981.
291 Or. 283, 634 P.2d 208.

PETERSON, JUSTICE.

Defendant was convicted of five counts of forgery in the first degree (ORS 165.013) * * *. * * *

Defendant was employed at John Snyder Tool Co., Inc., as an assistant bookkeeper. The normal procedure for handling the deposit of checks was as follows: when checks were received in payment of accounts receivable at her employer's office, she stamped the checks with a restrictive endorsement ("for deposit only"), took them to the bank, and deposited them into her employer's account.

On six occasions over a twenty-day period, defendant crossed out the words "for deposit only," initialed the change, signed her own name, cashed the checks, and retained the proceeds. For illustration, the back of one such check is set forth below.

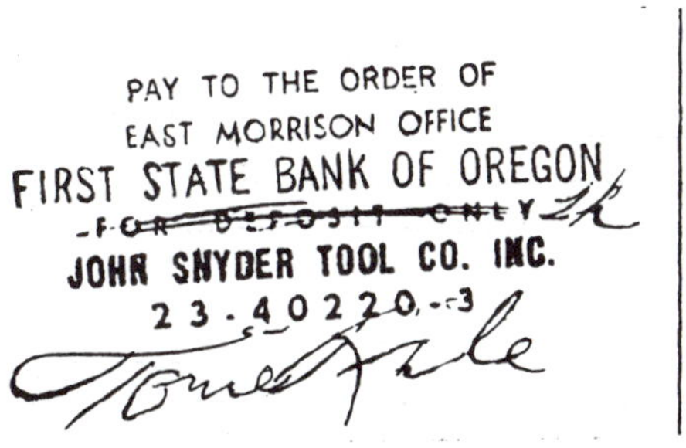
PAY TO THE ORDER OF
EAST MORRISON OFFICE
FIRST STATE BANK OF OREGON
~~FOR DEPOSIT ONLY~~
JOHN SNYDER TOOL CO. INC.
23-40220-3
Toni Kile 1

* * *

1. Defendant's true name at the time was Toni Jean Kile.

The crime of forgery in the first degree is defined in ORS 165.013. The crime is committed if one

> "* * * violates ORS 165.007 and the written instrument is or purports to be any of the following:
>
> "* * *.
>
> "(c) A deed, will, codicil, contract, assignment, commercial instrument or other document which does or may evidence, create, transfer, alter, terminate, or otherwise affect a legal right, interest, obligation or status * * *."

Second degree forgery is defined in ORS 165.007 and is committed if an actor

> "(1) * * * with intent to injure or defraud * * *
>
> "* * *.
>
> "(b) Utters a written instrument which he knows to be forged."

ORS 165.002(8) defines "forged instrument" as

> "* * * a written instrument which has been falsely made, completed or altered."

"Written instrument" is defined in ORS 165.002(1) as:

> "* * * any paper, document, instrument or article containing written or printed matter or the equivalent thereof, whether complete or incomplete, used for the purpose of reciting, embodying, conveying or recording information or constituting a symbol or evidence of value, right, privilege or identification, which is capable of being used to the advantage or disadvantage of some person."

ORS 165.002(6) concerns false alteration and provides:

> "(6) To 'falsely alter' a written instrument means to change, without authorization by anyone entitled to grant it, a written instrument, whether complete or incomplete, by means of erasure, obliteration, deletion, insertion of new matter, transposition of matter, or in any other manner, so that the instrument so altered falsely appears or purports to be in all respects an authentic creation of its ostensible maker or authorized by him."

* * *

The issue raised by the defendant is whether these checks were "falsely altered" under ORS 165.002(6) so that the instruments "* * * falsely appear[ed] or purport[ed] to be in all respects an authentic creation of [their] ostensible maker or authorized by him." The outcome of this case turns on the meaning of the term "ostensible maker," as used in ORS 165.002(6).

* * *

* * * [W]e believe that "maker" is to be understood in the broad sense, as "one who makes or executes." In this sense, an endorser is also a maker, since the endorser is executing the endorsement.

A provocative issue is raised by the defendant's contention that, because she signed her own name, "* * * there is nothing falsely stated on the checks themselves." She relies upon an article by Professor Harold G.

Hanbury entitled "Forgery and its Effects," The Jubilee Lectures of the Faculty of Law, University of Sheffield 29, 32–33 (O.R. Marshall ed. 1960), in which these statements appear:

"a) Only a writing or document can be forged.

"b) A writing is forged only when it *tells a lie about itself.*

"c) The offending statement must cause the *document itself* to seem other than what it is.

"d) The falsification must be of the *document itself;* forgery is not constituted by making false statements in or about it.

"e) There can be *no forgery by non-feasance.*

"f) The making of a false statement in the name of a fictitious person is forgery.

"g) The falsity must be *material.*

"h) The offence may be complete without any publication or uttering of the forged document." (Emphasis in original.)

* * *

Had defendant simply endorsed her name to the check, this case might come within the rule she espouses. But in addition to signing her name, the defendant also altered the check, changing the endorsement from a restrictive endorsement (ORS 73.2050(3)) to a special endorsement (ORS 73.2040(1)), in order to cash the checks.

True, there is evidence that, in addition to making the alterations, the defendant made representations to the bank tellers that the alterations were made to obtain petty cash for the business. The defendant contends that this is "the only falsehood" in the case. This argument requires us to ignore the alterations themselves.

That defendant's conduct may have created a foundation for guilt of other crimes does not establish her innocence of the crimes charged. In a very real sense, the endorsements, as altered, told a lie about themselves, making the documents seem to be other than they were. In making the alterations, the defendant intended to make it appear that the altered endorsements were authentic and that the alterations had been authorized by the ostensible maker.

Whatever the rule at common law under the authorities cited above, upon which defendant relies, the decision in this case turns on the meaning of Oregon's forgery statutes, specifically the definition of "falsely alter." When reduced to its simplest terms (so far as this case is concerned) the ORS 165.002(6) definition of "falsely alter" involves these factors:

1. Changing a written instrument
2. Without authorization
3. By means of insertion of new matter
4. So that the instrument purports to be either (a) an authentic creation of its ostensible maker or (b) authorized by the ostensible maker.

Without question, elements 1 through 3 are here present. As to the fourth element, there is substantial evidence, convincing beyond any reasonable doubt, that the checks, as altered, were believed to be authentic, were treated as authentic, were acted upon as being authentic, and that the instrument had been so altered that it purported to have been authorized by the employer. That defendant contemporaneously may have made representations in addition to the alterations does not require that we cloak her exclusively within those representations and exonerate her by saying that "forgery is not constituted by making false statements."

When the restrictive endorsement was originally stamped on the back of the check, the employer became the actual maker of the endorsement as well as the ostensible maker. As such, the check with its endorsement was what (to paraphrase ORS 165.002(6)) it appeared or purported to be—"an authentic creation of its ostensible maker or authorized by him." The trier of fact could find that, by virtue of defendant's employment, and after the alteration was made, the endorsement appeared or purported to be either (a) "an authentic creation of its ostensible maker" or (b) "authorized by him." But the altered endorsement was not that of its ostensible maker (the employer), nor had it been authorized by the employer.

* * *

Affirmed.

Questions

1. Is one who writes a check on a non-existent bank account or on one which has insufficient funds a forger?

2. Is one who signs another's check as his agent, knowing that he has no authority to do so, a forger?

3. Is one who makes a false duplicate original of the United States Constitution a forger? Does it make any difference whether it is a true copy to be sold as an antique or an altered copy to be used in an attempt to influence the result in a constitutional case? Is the fabricated signature of a United States president on a letter of endorsement for a candidate for public office a forgery? See Lewis v. Superior Court of the County of Sacramento, 217 Cal.App.3d 379, 265 Cal.Rptr. 855 (1990).

Notes

1. *Forgery and Uttering.* The misdemeanor of common law forgery required knowledge that the instrument was bad and an intention to defraud, but not the actual obtaining of anything through the forgery. The related common law misdemeanor of uttering is the asserting (usually by passing) of the validity of a forged instrument, knowing it to be forged.

2. *Model Penal Code.* See Model Penal Code § 224.1 for a forgery provision.

3. *Destruction of Records.* A number of statutory provisions deal with unauthorized making, alteration, concealment, or destruction of records. See, e.g., Model Penal Code §§ 224.3 (recordable instruments), 224.4 (records), and 241.8 (tampering with public records). These may have nothing to do with theft, of course.

D. CONSOLIDATION OF THE THEFT OFFENSES

As we have seen, when the common law judges were unable or unwilling to carry their fictions further into areas of stealing society wanted to deal with, it was usual for the legislature to act. In the early days at least, the legislature usually did not touch the common law definition of larceny. It simply created new crimes at the borderline to extend control over the new area. These new statutory crimes were in turn usually left alone in the next wave of reform; more offenses were created. The statutory crimes did not normally overlap common law larceny or each other; they were usually misdemeanors, even when material of great value was taken, and punishments were all over the lot, though less than for grand larceny.

In a jurisdiction with a wide array of statutes, many close borderline questions could be presented, for example:

1. Is the conduct common law larceny under the Carrier's Case or is it statutory larceny by bailee?

2. Is the conduct common law larceny by servant or is it embezzlement?

3. Is it embezzlement by a servant or embezzlement under a statute covering "agents" or other groups?

4. Is it embezzlement or larceny after trust?

5. Is it common law larceny by trick or is it obtaining property by false pretenses?

6. Is it larceny or receiving stolen goods?

7. Is it robbery or extortion (or, for that matter, bribery)?

Where you have not met cases presenting these borderline fact problems, it would be a good exercise to construct hypotheticals for yourself.

Where it is possible for the prosecutor to guess wrong about the offense committed, you are likely to have offenders escaping justice, or, at best, participating in lengthy and difficult proceedings. These pitfalls were often useful to the defense in plea bargaining; a prosecutor who could not be sure whether the offense was grand larceny or false pretenses might be willing to accept a guilty plea to petit larceny.

Of course, the State might charge all the possible offenses in separate indictment counts, but before going to the jury it might be required to elect only one court for jury consideration. Disagreements among prosecutor, trial judge, jury, and appellate court as to the appropriate charge might allow the accused to escape all charges.

Sometimes procedural relief would be available on appeal; the appellate court might be authorized to substitute a verdict, or deny an appeal if it thought the accused had been done substantial justice.

The English Larceny Act of 1916 and similar American statutes have tried to solve the problem of larceny by trick *versus* false pretenses by allowing conviction of false pretenses on a false pretenses charge even if the proof shows larceny. This is not intellectually satisfactory, but it is a device which can work and can be applied to other areas of doubt. One catch is that the penalties for the two offenses are apt to differ, and, if so, it is a conviction of the lesser offense which will be permitted, and the prosecution must be satisfied with the lesser penalty if it does not want to fight out the substantive issue.

A more thoroughgoing attempt at reform combines the common law and various statutory crimes into a single offense, usually called "larceny" or "theft," by listing the definitions of the various old offenses and providing that any of them is "theft." Often such statutes have been construed merely to provide a single penalty and to require specification of and proof of one of the old offenses. Where this happens, the old practical problems remain.

Finally, you may have a clear attempt at consolidation, as in the Model Penal Code. When this is well done, most of the problems of borderline disappear, though shadows of the seams may remain. These statutes still have the problem of the external shape of the pattern: what is included and excluded from the consolidated offense?

The problems which can arise in attempting to consolidate the theft offenses are well illustrated in the history of theft law in New York. An early case is Nichols v. People, 17 N.Y. 114 (1858), supra, p. 260, in which the trial court, at the close of the evidence, decided that a bailee's misappropriation of a portion of a shipment of iron bars was embezzlement, not common law larceny, the offense charged. (New York had an embezzlement statute broad enough to include appropriation by bailees.) When the larceny indictment was dismissed, Nichols was charged with and convicted of embezzlement. On appeal, a majority of the court thought that the offense was larceny, after all, and reversed the conviction. The accused, having been previously acquitted of larceny, could not, on double jeopardy grounds, be tried for the same offense on the same facts again, and he went free.

The statute provided that a carrier should be punished in the same manner for conversion, whether or not he broke bulk, but the court said that this did not create a single offense; it merely provided the same punishments for two different offenses, the proper one of which had to be charged and proved.

For many years, the New York decisions tended to frustrate legislative enactments which seemed to be designed to work towards consolidation. See, for example, People v. Noblett, 244 N.Y. 355, 155 N.E. 670 (1927), and People v. Karp, 298 N.Y. 213, 81 N.E.2d 817 (1948).

In 1967, inspired by the Model Penal Code, the legislature tried again. But instead of the complete new definitions provided in Article 223 of the Model Penal Code, New York enacted:

§ 155.05 Larceny; defined

1. A person steals property and commits larceny when, with intent to deprive another of property or to appropriate the same to himself or to a third person, he wrongfully takes, obtains or withholds such property from an owner thereof.

2. Larceny includes a wrongful taking, obtaining or withholding of another's property, with the intent prescribed in subdivision one of this section, committed in any of the following ways:

(a) By conduct heretofore defined or known as common law larceny by trespassory taking, common law larceny by trick, embezzlement, or obtaining property by false pretenses. * * *

While § 155.05(2)(d) creates a new kind of larceny by "false promise," as the Model Penal Code Comment to § 223.1 (note 8) observes, problems remain. If the Cheshire Cat has faded away, the smile lingers on.

Questions

1. Why do you suppose the 1967 New York provisions retained the old categories and by-passed the Model Penal Code definitions?

2. As a matter of policy, is it defensible to retain some of the old distinctions, despite the difficulties in pleading and proof they cause?

3. How do codifiers decide which theft offenses to consolidate and which to define separately? Why, for example, include extortion and exclude forgery and credit card offenses?

4. This chapter has frequently referred you to the Model Penal Code for modern treatments of the problems which arose in the development of the law of theft. You should, before leaving the problem of theft, view Article 223 of the Model Penal Code or the theft consolidation provisions of a jurisdiction you are interested in as a whole. Can you list some of the old problems which are solved? some which are not solved?

Chapter IV

ARSON, BURGLARY, AND KIDNAPPING; PROBLEMS OF STATUTORY CONSTRUCTION

A. INTRODUCTORY NOTE

In this chapter you will study three important areas of crime. Offenses in the arson and burglary area combine, commonly but not always, threats to property (especially dwelling houses), of a somewhat different nature than threats in the theft area, with some danger to the person, an area touched upon in Chapter II and to be explored further in the next chapter. Kidnapping brings us fully into the realm of danger to the person. These crimes are important for several reasons: (1) They are of fairly frequent occurrence, carrying serious consequences. (2) They are felonies which often form the basis for felony-murder prosecutions, or crimes which need to be understood in order to evaluate claims of justification or excuse (based, for example, on a claim that a householder killed a would-be burglar). (3) They raise interesting questions of public policy, particularly when they have undergone legislative expansion.

The crimes will be used as subject matter areas for an introduction to problems of statutory interpretation.

B. THE CRIMES OF ARSON, BURGLARY, AND KIDNAPPING

The two cases in this section introduce the common law crimes of arson and burglary. **To deal with them, you will have to read the appropriate chapters in Perkins & Boyce, *Criminal Law* 246–288 (3d ed., 1982), or the equivalent.** You will then be in a position to see that the analysis in the two cases is woefully inadequate and to prepare the outline of a careful dissenting or concurring opinion for each case. The notes following the cases will complete the picture and bring you up to date on statutory modifications of the common law crimes. The section concludes with a note on kidnapping. All of this will prepare you to deal with the statutory interpretation issues which follow.

State v. Burns

Supreme Court of Ohypo, 1963.
233 Ohypo 29.

WAMBLE, J.: Woodrow Burns appeals from conviction for common law arson on the ground that his motion for a directed verdict of acquittal at the close of the prosecution's case was erroneously denied.

The prosecution showed that Burns is the owner of Flashacre, a farm in Farenheit County. On the evening of March 15, 1962, he invited a number of friends to attend his fortieth birthday party. A highlight of the festivities was a fireworks display put on by the host. The setting off of fireworks without a permit—and concededly none was obtained by Burns—is a misdemeanor, punishable by imprisonment for not more than six months, or a fine of not more than $1,000, or both. A roman candle, ignited by Burns on his front porch, shot through the sky, across State Road 77, and came to rest on an outside handle of a winter storm shutter, in place at a window in Burns' remodeled barn, about 100 feet from its starting point. The shutter caught fire, and one of the guests called the volunteer fire department. By the time the fire was put out, part of the shutter had burned through and the fire had scorched the paint on the window frame. No further damage was done.

The barn had been converted into a barracks for itinerant workers, employed by Burns during the harvest season every autumn, and was unoccupied on March 15th. A few of the workers, who planned to return, had left behind, with Burns' permission, some articles of furniture, but the barn was otherwise empty, except for simple furnishings supplied by Burns.

The judgment of conviction of arson must be reversed. Common law arson is the malicious burning of the dwelling house of another. None of the requirements is met here.

First, what was burned was not a dwelling house. The building itself was never on fire; only the shutter was partially consumed. The shutter was removable and not part of the structure; the burning of personal property is not arson at common law.

Even if we assume a "burning," this structure was not the dwelling house of another. It was a reconverted barn, unoccupied during the period when the fire occurred. Such a building, when sometimes frequented by human beings and in the immediate vicinity or within the curtilage of a dwelling house, is subject to arson, but only if it is the building of another. Here, it was the accused's own barn.

Finally, even if we assume that Burns set fire to the dwelling house of another, his act was not malicious. Malice in arson requires a purposeful burning without justification or excuse. While Burns can claim no justification or excuse for his unlawful and careless action, what indication is there that he meant to set fire to the barn?

The law of arson was never meant to forbid conduct like this. Negligent or reckless starting of fires presents a public danger, but one far removed from the threat produced by the deliberate arsonist.

The judgment of conviction is reversed.

State v. Berg

Supreme Court of Ohypo, 1963.
233 Ohypo 984.

WAMBLE, J.: This is an appeal from the denial of a directed verdict of acquittal on a charge of common law burglary. The accused, Jimmy Berg, tried to interest a friend, Secundus Storey, in a kidnapping plan, which was to involve the abduction of Lotta Cash, the six year old daughter of a wealthy industrialist. While Storey was thinking the venture over, Berg left with him a ransom note, to be used in the scheme if Berg and Storey decided to go through with it. It was prepared by pasting printed letters from different periodicals on sheets of paper. On Saturday, June 23, 1962, Storey telephoned Berg to tell him that he was not interested in the idea and was thinking about turning the ransom note over to the police. Berg was unable to persuade him to cooperate, but told him he was determined to continue with the plan, alone if necessary.

Storey owns and operates a secondhand furniture store in a run down commercial area, and he lives alone on the second floor of the store. Berg knew that Storey would be away from home on Sunday, June 24th, and would not return until the store opened at 10 A.M. on Monday morning. At one A.M. on Monday morning Berg set out to recover the ransom note, which he knew to be in a desk drawer in Storey's second floor apartment. He decided to enter the building through an old-fashioned cellar door, which consisted of padlocked flimsy wooden panels, slanted from the rear wall of the building to the ground and covering concrete stairs, descending to the cellar. The neighborhood being deserted, he attacked one of the panels with a pickaxe he had brought along. The point of the axe had splintered the wood and dug into the concrete step below, when a police car approached and Berg fled, leaving the pickaxe still embedded in the wood and concrete.

Later, Berg tried again. The store remained open until 10:00 P.M. Monday night, June 25th. Sometime that evening, while Storey was busy with customers, Berg came into the store through a revolving door and hid behind a sofa until Storey had locked the store for the night and gone upstairs. At eleven-thirty P.M., apparently believing Storey to be asleep, Berg moved cautiously toward the stairway from the store to the living quarters, picking up a heavy glass ashtray along the way.

A squeaking floorboard alerted Storey, who immediately suspected the truth. Storey unlocked the door at the top of the stairs, quietly got his shotgun, and sat down in a living room chair, waiting to confront the intruder. Berg pushed his way through a beaded glass curtain at the foot of the stairs, climbed to the second floor, and opened the door outward onto the upstairs landing. He then saw Storey with the shotgun and threw the ashtray at him. It missed and shattered against the wall, as Berg ran past Storey and departed, amid another shower of glass, through a closed window onto a garage roof, where he was caught by the police.

This court has seldom had an easier case to decide. Common law burglary is the breaking and entering at night of the dwelling house of another, with intention to commit a felony. There are a number of breakings and enterings, any of which the jury may have relied on for its finding of guilt: the attack on the cellar door, the later return to the store and hiding behind the sofa, pushing past the beaded curtain, going into the upstairs apartment, and departing via the window. All of the activity was nocturnal and was directed at the dwelling house of another. Felonious intentions include kidnapping, assault with a dangerous weapon (a felony by statute), and two larcenies.

The conviction of burglary is affirmed.

Notes

1. *Statutory Expansion; Related Crimes.* Why, originally, were these crimes limited to "dwelling houses," and why did burglary have to be a nocturnal venture? The common law crimes of arson and burglary have undergone considerable statutory expansion. Commonly legislatures have extended the crimes to other structures, to most or all buildings outside the curtilage: commercial structures, public buildings, churches, and even bridges, but have provided lesser penalties in such cases. Even personal property is sometimes included: it may be a lesser form of burglary to break and enter a motor vehicle, and the burning of personal property of another of a certain value may be a form of arson. The modern statutory crimes may be aggravated according to the danger to the person of another contemplated or risked.

In modern arson statutes damage by explosion, even without "burning," is often covered. The requirement that the property be that of another is almost always eliminated, especially if insurance fraud is involved. Sometimes reckless burning or failure to report a fire is included.

Malicious destruction of real or personal property of another by means not amounting to arson was the common law misdemeanor of malicious mischief, a crime generally continued and redefined by statute. Model Penal Code § 220.3 penalizes reckless and even some negligent conduct. It also extends to purposely or recklessly causing pecuniary loss by deception or threat.

In burglary the breaking requirement is often eliminated entirely. Note that this might make an ordinary shoplifter who enters a department store in the usual way a statutory burglar. To eliminate such possibilities, the entry requirement may be stated as entering unlawfully, sometimes with the alternative of unlawfully remaining on premises. Daytime intrusions are included, with lesser penalties. The object crime often need not be a felony, and sometimes need not be contemplated until after the accused is inside. Breaking out may be an acceptable substitute for breaking in.

At common law housebreaking was a misdemeanor; this was common law burglary with the nocturnal element omitted and without a requirement of intent to commit any crime inside. This misdemeanor has generally been absorbed into the modern statutory scheme. Mere trespass to land was not ordinarily criminal unless a breach of the peace occurred. Today statutes often make some forms of intrusion on land criminal trespass. E.g., hunters on posted property, loiterers in public building, Peeping Toms who wander into back yards, and those who refuse to leave premises on demand may find that they have committed misdemeanors of the sort.

For examples of modern families of arson and burglary provisions, see the Model Penal Code provisions (Articles 220 and 221).

2. *Malice in Arson.* The common law required that the burning in arson be malicious. This means something more than recklessness; a purpose to burn, or something fairly close to this is required. But, there is an additional requirement for malice in arson. Because of insurance fraud problems and the general dangers from building fires, statutory arson usually extends to burning the insured's own house and his other buildings. Suppose, under such a statute, a crime is charged when the accused deliberately burns down his own isolated building, as the cheapest way to clear the land. No danger to the person or property of another and no insurance fraud is involved or contemplated. Does he have a defense? Brown v. State, 285 Md. 469, 403 A.2d 788 (1979) says that he does because malice is absent. What is the missing element? The case suggests that reckless disregard for the safety of others is implicit in the idea of malice. Perhaps this idea was suggested by the depraved heart murder cases, which, as you will see, find the required element of malice for

murder in a "depraved heart," or outrageous indifference to the safety of others, as where one heedlessly tosses a brick off a roof and kills a pedestrian in the crowded street below. The case also speaks in passing of justification, and this is probably a better approach. Malice usually involves an act done purposefully or with enormous heedlessness and without justification, excuse, or mitigating circumstances. Here, the justification would be that the threat of danger or harm to others (including insurance companies), normally present when a building is burned, is absent. Other circumstances of justification, excuse, or mitigation might include, in some contexts, consent of the property owner to the burning or burning necessary to create a fire-break.

Questions

1. How far does the Model Penal Code incorporate the common law idea of malice in arson? Of what crime, if any, would Burns be guilty if the Model Penal Code were law in the jurisdiction?

2. Suppose the accused approaches at night the dwelling house of another, intending to steal property in the house. He expects to enter through open french windows. In fact, there is a sheet of glass across the entry way which he does not notice and he crashes in through the glass. Is this common law burglary? What *mens rea*, if any, is required with respect to the breaking and entering elements? How does the Model Penal Code resolve this problem?

3. In early times the typical arson defendant was an angry neighbor who found it simpler to burn down a house than pursue a more peaceful method of redressing supposed grievances. His nearest modern counterpart is perhaps the teenage lout who, in burning an abandoned building, is simply in search of a little fun or excitement or perhaps engaging in social criticism. Sometimes the modern arson defendant is mentally disturbed. At other times he is a business man who prefers the insurance proceeds to his stock in trade.

Burglars often have long and peaceful careers, only rarely interrupted by a conviction or even an arrest. They may painstakingly wait for the occupants to leave before entering, choose their loot with discrimination, and never in their careers attack a human being.

What, if anything, do these considerations suggest about the proper definition and grading of these offenses and the general level of appropriate penalties?

A Note on Kidnapping [a]

A hundred years ago most jurisdictions had no crime closely corresponding to a modern kidnapping statute. There were two common law misdemeanors, sometimes given some legislative redefinition. One was false imprisonment. This was very similar to the corresponding tort. An intentional and unprivileged confinement of another is the gist of the matter.

The common law misdemeanor of kidnapping was a specialized offense. It was the forcible stealing of a person from his own country and taking him to another. One who shanghaied the innocent wanderer on the docks and took him unwillingly abroad as an able seaman was a kidnapper.

Abduction, the offense involved in the *Prince* case, supra, p. 165, was made a crime by Parliament in 1487. The more modern statutes vary, but generally they forbid the taking, enticing, or detaining of a female for some unlawful

a. Or "kidnaping." It is spelled both ways.

purpose related to the fact that she is female: to compel marriage or sexual relations, to force into prostitution, or merely, in the case of an infant, to deprive the lawful custodian of custody. Abduction of heiresses, followed by whirlwind courtships on the way to Gretna Green, where there was no waiting period for the marriage ceremony, was once a thriving and profitable occupation.

Child stealing was also commonly made a misdemeanor by statute. The taking of a child from parents or guardians was punished. Often an exception was made, or a reduced penalty provided, where the accused was the other parent of the stolen child.

Towards the end of the last century, kidnapping for ransom became more common and more daring, and the ransom demands, pursuing the new wealth of the victims' families, became more spectacular. The Lindbergh kidnapping in the nineteen-thirties, in which the baby of popular celebrity parents was taken and killed, is a prime example. Legislatures commonly responded by expanding liability and increasing penalties, usually redefining kidnapping until it absorbed or paralleled the other old offenses and went far beyond them.

Methods of expansion included some or all of the following:

1. Fraud or enticement were added as alternatives to force.

2. Confinement, secret confinement, detention, or taking to another place within the jurisdiction were added as alternatives to removing the victim from his own country (now in the United States, generally his own state).

3. Sometimes a taking with intent to do one or more of the forbidden things was all that was required; no actual confinement or removal needed to be shown.

The enlarged crime was generally made a felony with the death penalty (no longer applicable) or long periods of imprisonment attached. Sometimes the element of ransom or harm to the victim was made an aggravating factor. The "Lindbergh Law" made the interstate transportation of kidnap victims a federal crime and allowed federal authorities to join in the search when statutory presumptions that the victim had been so transported had been met.

The Model Penal Code provisions on kidnapping and related offenses will be found in Article 212. If they seem somewhat more narrowly drawn than you might expect, the reasons for this will appear later in the Chapter.

C. PROBLEMS OF STATUTORY CONSTRUCTION

1. Introductory Note: McBoyle v. United States

A judge may believe that the statute before him presents no problem of construction. If it has a single, clear meaning, no thought or explanation is necessary. The famous decision of MR. JUSTICE HOLMES in McBoyle v. United States, 283 U.S. 25, 51 S.Ct. 340, 75 L.Ed. 816 (1931) shows this attitude. In reading his words, ask yourself whether (1) Holmes really relies simply on the plain meaning of the statute or invokes other methods of construction, (2) the statute has a plain meaning with respect to the inclusion of airplanes, and (3) if it does, what that plain meaning is. Here, with minor omissions, is the opinion:

The petitioner was convicted of transporting from Ottawa, Illinois, to Guymon, Oklahoma, an airplane that he knew to have been stolen, and was sentenced to serve three years' imprisonment and to pay a fine of $2,000. The judgment was affirmed by the Circuit Court of Appeals for the Tenth Circuit. 43 F.(2d) 273. A writ of certiorari was granted by this Court on the question whether the National Motor Vehicle Theft Act applies to aircraft. Act of October 29, 1919, c. 89, 41 Stat. 324, U.S. Code, title 18, § 408 (18 USCA § 408). That Act provides: "Sec. 2. That when used in this Act: (a) The term 'motor vehicle' shall include an automobile, automobile truck, automobile wagon, motor cycle, or any other self-propelled vehicle not designed for running on rails. * * * Sec. 3. That whoever shall transport or cause to be transported in interstate or foreign commerce a motor vehicle, knowing the same to have been stolen, shall be punished by a fine of not more than $5,000, or by imprisonment of not more than five years, or both."

* * * The question is the meaning of the word "vehicle" in the phrase "any other self-propelled vehicle not designed for running on rails." No doubt etymologically it is possible to use the word to signify a conveyance working on land, water or air, and sometimes legislation extends the use in that direction, e.g., land and air, water being separately provided for, in the Tariff Act, September 21, 1922, c. 356, § 401(b), 42 Stat. 858, 948 (19 USCA § 231(b)). But in everyday speech "vehicle" calls up the picture of a thing moving on land. Thus in Rev.St. § 4 (1 USCA § 4) intended, the Government suggests, rather to enlarge than to restrict the definition, vehicle includes every contrivance capable of being used "as a means of transportation on land." And this is repeated, expressly excluding aircraft, in the Tariff Act, June 17, 1930, c. 497, § 401(b), 46 Stat. 590, 708 (19 USCA § 1401). So here, the phrase under discussion calls up the popular picture. For after including automobile truck, automobile wagon and motor cycle, the words "any other self-propelled vehicle not designed for running on rails" still indicate that a vehicle in the popular sense, that is a vehicle running on land is the theme. It is a vehicle that runs, not something, not commonly called a vehicle, that flies. Airplanes were well known in 1919 when this statute was passed, but it is admitted that they were not mentioned in the reports or in the debates in Congress. It is impossible to read words that so carefully enumerate the different forms of motor vehicles and have no reference of any kind to aircraft, as including airplanes under a term that usage more and more precisely confines to a different class. The counsel for the petitioner have shown that the phraseology of the statute as to motor vehicles follows that of earlier statutes of Connecticut, Delaware, Ohio, Michigan and Missouri, not to mention the late Regulations of Traffic for the District of Columbia, title 6, c. 9, § 242, none of which can be supposed to leave the earth.

Although it is not likely that a criminal will carefully consider the text of the law before he murders or steals, it is reasonable that a fair warning should be given to the world in language that the common world will understand, of what the law intends to do if a certain line is passed. To make the warning fair, so far as possible the line should be clear. When a rule of conduct is laid down in words that evoke in the common mind only the picture of vehicles moving on land, the statute should not be extended to aircraft simply because it may seem to us that a similar policy applies, or upon the speculation that if the legislature had thought of it, very likely broader words would have been used.

The material which follows explores the way in which courts construe statutes and the kinds of arguments they make when the plain meaning is not plain enough. We will not reconsider here construction arguments which are primarily grounded on constitutional considerations (for these see Chapter I, supra). After an introductory case, we will look first at problems of struggling with the meaning of words in context, through analysis and legislative history, to arrive at a meaning. We will then embark upon the hazardous search for broad legislative purpose and conclude with a bit of comic relief. Most of the materials will involve construction in the fields of kidnapping, arson, and burglary.

2. The Basic Rule of Statutory Construction

People v. Weiss

Court of Appeals of New York, 1938.
276 N.Y. 384, 12 N.E.2d 514, 114 A.L.R. 865.

O'BRIEN, JUDGE.

These appellants, without authority of law, seized and confined Paul H. Wendel, who was suspected or whom some pretended to suspect of the commission of a murder in New Jersey which had attracted attention throughout the country. They have been convicted of the crime of kidnapping as defined by section 1250 of the Penal Law, which provides: "A person who wilfully: 1. Seizes, confines, inveigles, or kidnaps another, with intent to cause him, without authority of law, to be secretly confined or imprisoned within this state, or to be sent out of the state or to be sold as a slave, or in any way held to service or kept or detained, against his will * * * is guilty of kidnapping."

The elements necessary to constitute the crime of kidnapping are different from those which are embraced within the torts of illegal arrest and false imprisonment. Where the detention is illegal, a civil action for damages will lie without regard to the innocence of the defendant in his intentions. Snead v. Bonnoil, 166 N.Y. 325, 328, 59 N.E. 899. In order to make out the crime of kidnapping, proof beyond a reasonable doubt must be produced that the defendant willfully intended, without authority of law, to confine or imprison another. To illustrate the difference: A reputable citizen is approached by a man, clothed in a police uniform and wearing a police shield, who requests him to assist in the arrest of one whom he describes as a murderer. The law-abiding citizen, in good faith and in the belief that he is performing his duty, assists the uniformed stranger and participates in the arrest of one who is entirely innocent. While the citizen may be answerable in damages in a civil action, he is not guilty of the crime of kidnapping, even though proof is later adduced that the uniformed stranger is an imposter and a kidnapper. In such a case, far from intending to seize or confine the prisoner without authority of law, he believed that his act was with such authority. In prosecutions for kidnapping, therefore, willful intent to seize a person without authority of law is the essential issue. Inferences of fact as to intent depend upon the degree of credibility accorded to witnesses by the jury and may be drawn from the defendant's disbelief or belief in the legality of his act. For the purpose of enabling the jury to draw its inference of fact, a defendant is entitled to the right of informing the jury in respect to his belief. His testimony may be of such a character as to fail to convince a jury, yet, nevertheless, he is entitled as a legal right to produce it for what it may be worth and to have it considered by the jury.

Appellant Schlossman testified that, prior to the seizure of Wendel, he had a conversation with appellant Weiss and with Ellis Parker, Jr., at a hotel in New York. His counsel attempted to introduce testimony in relation to statements by Parker, for the purpose of showing Schlossman's belief in his authority to act, but the offer was excluded and an exception taken. The following statement by Schlossman to Parker was, however, admitted: "I have got to have something to show that I am doing something within the law, helping you out this way, so he took out a badge, Secret Service of the State of New Jersey, and gave it to me and said he is hereby appointing me a special deputy to help him in the Lindbergh case." The questions, "Did you desire to help a detective solve any part of the Lindbergh mystery at that time?" and "Did you think at that time that you were taking part in some noble work?" were excluded and exceptions taken. * * * Exception was taken also to the ruling which sustained objection to this question directed to Weiss: "Did you believe that you were doing your Police work?"

Counsel for defendants requested: "That if the defendants, or either of them, acted in the honest belief that his act in seizing and confining Wendel was done with authority of law, even if they were mistaken in such belief, that they cannot be convicted of seizing, confining or kidnapping Wendel, with intent, to cause him without authority of law to be confined or imprisoned within the State and the jury must acquit such defendants or defendant." To this request the court replied: "I not only decline to charge that but I repeat that the question of good faith is no defense." The jury was also instructed that "even if they [defendants] did believe it, it is no defense in this case." If such interpretation is to prevail, then it must follow that in every instance where a defendant admits the fact that he intended to make the arrest and the courts later declare the arrest to have been made without authority of law, he must necessarily be convicted as a kidnapper, irrespective of his belief or his intentions to conform with the law. A peace officer, in the mistaken belief that he is acting with authority of law, makes an illegal arrest and later, in an effort to extort a confession, puts his prisoner through the third degree. He is guilty of the crime of assault or of official oppression but he is certainly not a kidnapper. * * *

* * *

No matter how doubtful the credibility of these defendants may be or how suspicious the circumstances may appear, we cannot say as matter of law that, even in so strong a case as this for the prosecution, the jury was not entitled to consider the question whether defendants in good faith believed that they were acting with authority of law. We are, therefore, constrained to reverse the judgment of conviction and order a new trial for the purpose of submitting that question of fact to the jury.

The judgments should be reversed and a new trial ordered.

CRANE, CHIEF JUDGE (dissenting).

* * *

* * * Of course, if there be legal authority, there is no crime, but the fact that the person mistakenly thought that they had authority does not lessen the crime. The charge of the court, in my judgment, was correct, in accordance with the authorities of this state. In People v. Camp, 139 N.Y. 87, 91, 34 N.E. 755, Judge Earl, writing in reference to the crime of kidnapping, as defined in the Revised Statutes, vol. 2, pt. 4, c. 1, tit. 2, § 28, p. 664, says: "Every person who shall without lawful authority forcibly seize and confine any other, * * * with intent * * * to cause such other person to be secretly confined or imprisoned in this state against his will," is guilty of kidnapping. This is the Revised Statutes, and you see at once that the intent has reference to the confining and to the seizing, and does not apply to the intent to do it contrary to law. Persons are supposed to know the law; and believing that the law gives them right to do things does not rob acts of criminal consequences. Judge Earl says that these words have now been carried over into the Penal Code, and so we find them in our Penal Law, § 1250.

* * *

LEHMAN, LOUGHRAN, and RIPPEY, JJ., concur with O'BRIEN, J.

CRANE, C.J., dissents in opinion, in which HUBBS and FINCH, JJ., concur.

Judgments reversed, etc.

Questions

1. What *is* the basic rule of statutory construction? Hint No. 1. Neither opinion in *Weiss* follows the basic rule very well. Hint No. 2. The basic rule for construing statutes resembles the basic rule for conducting almost any enterprise.

2. How should the issue in the *Weiss* case be resolved?

3. The Search for Meaning in Context and History

State v. Durant

Supreme Court of Utah, 1983.
674 P.2d 638.

DURHAM, JUSTICE:

In this case the defendant appeals from a conviction of aggravated arson, a second degree felony. In a statement to the police, the defendant admitted setting a house on fire, but claimed that he was acting under the direction of the owner of the house. In his appeal the defendant claims that under U.C.A., 1953, § 76–6–103 the owner could not have been convicted of aggravated arson for setting fire to his own home. Therefore, the defendant argues that he should not have been convicted of aggravated arson because he was acting as the owner's agent. We disagree and affirm the conviction.

The defendant's argument depends upon his assertion that an owner who sets fire to his own house cannot be convicted of aggravated arson. The statute reads as follows:

Aggravated arson.—(1) A person is guilty of aggravated arson if by means of fire or explosives he intentionally and unlawfully damages:

(a) A habitable structure; or

(b) Any structure or vehicle when any person not a participant in the offense is in the structure or vehicle.

(2) Aggravated arson is a felony of the second degree.

U.C.A., 1953, § 76–6–103 (1978 edition). The defendant points out that at common law it was not unlawful to burn one's own dwelling. The provisions of the Utah Criminal Code, however, supersede the common law. U.C.A., 1953, § 76–1–105 (1978 edition). The statute regarding aggravated arson is one of three sections that deal with arson. The previous section defines arson:

(1) A person is guilty of arson, if, under circumstances not amounting to aggravated arson, by means of fire or explosives, he unlawfully and intentionally damages:

(a) Any property with intention of defrauding an insurer; or

(b) The property of another.

(2) A violation of subsection (a) is a felony of the third degree. A violation of subsection (b) is a felony of the third degree if the damage caused exceeds $5,000 value; a class A misdemeanor if the damage exceeds $1,000 but is not more than $5,000 value; a class B misdemeanor if the damage caused exceeds $250 but is not more than $1,000; any other violation is a class C misdemeanor.

U.C.A., 1953, § 76–6–102 (1978 edition). Reckless burning is also defined:

(1) A person is guilty of reckless burning if he:

(a) Recklessly starts a fire or causes an explosion which endangers human life; or

(b) Having started a fire, whether recklessly or not, and knowing that it is spreading and will endanger the life or property of another, either fails to take reasonable measures to put out or control the fire or fails to give a prompt fire alarm; or

(c) Damages the property of another by reckless use of fire or causing an explosion.

(2) A violation of subsections (a) and (b) is a class A misdemeanor. A violation of subsection (c) is a class A misdemeanor if damage to property exceeds $1,000 value; a class B misdemeanor if the damage to property exceeds $500 value; and a class C misdemeanor if the damage to property exceeds $50 value. Any other violation under subsection (c) shall constitute an infraction.

U.C.A., 1953, § 76–6–104 (1978 edition). Both the arson and reckless burning statutes distinguish "the property of another" from other types of property. The aggravated arson statute makes no reference to ownership of property in proscribing damage by fire to "a habitable structure" or "any structure or vehicle" when it is occupied. Nevertheless, the defendant contends that the statute should be construed as if it read "the habitable structure of another." The defendant points to the word "unlawfully" in the statute and argues that the arson statute, § 76–6–102, defines what conduct is unlawful. Thus, the defendant incorporates the provisions of § 76–6–102, *Arson,* into § 76–6–103, *Aggravated Arson,* claiming that aggravated arson is simply arson, i.e., damage with the intent to defraud or to damage the property of another, when the property is habitable or occupied. The defendant cites no case law or legislative history to support this construction of the statute. Neither does the defendant explain why "unlawfully" in the arson statute should be internally defined, but the same word in the aggravated arson statute should be defined by the provisions of the arson statute. The defendant's only justification for this construction is that it preserves the common law concept of arson. However, a review of the statutes which preceded the current code indicates that our legislature did not intend to exclude the burning of one's own property from the statutes.

Under Utah's earliest statutes, as under the common law, arson was a crime against possession rather than ownership of property. * * *

Arson was defined as "the wilful and malicious burning of a building with intent to destroy it." Compiled Laws of Utah § 119–40–8248 (1917). "Maliciously burning in the night time an inhabited building in which there is, at the time, some human being, is arson in the first degree; all other kinds of arson are of the second degree." Compiled Laws of Utah, § 119–40–8254 (1917). Thus, even when the Utah statute closely followed the common law, ownership of the property was a secondary consideration. The primary concern was for danger to human life.

In 1931, the Utah legislature enacted new statutes that classified arson as first, second and third degree arson according to the likelihood of danger to human life. Rather than attempt a general definition of when and under what circumstances lives might be endangered by burning structures, this statutory scheme distinguished the three degrees of the offense by specifying the particular property burned. First degree arson was the willful and malicious burning of a dwelling or any other building "that is parcel thereof, or belonging to or adjoining thereto, *whether the property of himself or of another.*" U.C.A., 1943, § 103–6–1 (emphasis added). Second degree arson was even more explicit in penalizing the willful and malicious burning of "any church, meetinghouse, courthouse, school, jail or other public building, or any public bridge" as well as "any barn, stable, garage or other building, *whether the property of himself or of another,* not a parcel of a dwelling house; or any shop, storehouse, warehouse, factory, mill or other building, *whether the property of himself or another.*" U.C.A., 1943, § 103–6–2 (emphasis added). Section 103–6–3, third degree arson, dealt with the willful and malicious burning of various structures not considered to be buildings, crops in storage or in the field, piles of fuel or building materials, and various types of vehicles. The application of this statute, however, is specifically limited to property worth $25 or more that is the *property of another.* In summary, it is apparent that the most severe penalty was intended to reach those who burned structures likely to be occupied, regardless of ownership or actual occupancy, while the least severe penalty was imposed for damage to various kinds of personal property belonging to another.

This scheme was used in the Model Arson Law proposed by the National Board of Fire Underwriters in 1953. See Model Penal Code § 220.1 comment 1 at n. 15 (1980). However, a system of classification by type of property has a number of weaknesses.

> For example, the burning of an empty, isolated dwelling could lead to a 20–year sentence, while setting fire to a crowded church, theater, or jail was a lesser offense with a 10–year maximum. The destruction of a dam, factory, or public service facility was regarded as less serious than destruction of a private garage on the grounds of a suburban home. It also makes little sense to treat the burning of miscellaneous personal property, whether out of malice or to defraud insurers, as a special category of crime apart from the risks associated with burning. To destroy a valuable painting or manuscript by burning it in a hearth or furnace cannot be distinguished criminologically from any other method of property destruction. Moreover, the treatment of attempt as the same two-year felony no matter what the nature of the crime attempted seriously undercuts the grading scheme.

Id. at 8–9. In 1973, the Utah legislature revised the Criminal Code. By referring explicitly to "habitable structures" and the actual presence of a person, the current arson statutes preserve the classification of the offense according to degree of danger to human life while eliminating many of the inconsistencies associated with the previous method. The most severe penalty is still intended to reach those who burn structures likely to be occupied, regardless of ownership or actual occupancy. The absence of the words "property of another" from the aggravated arson statute is entirely consistent with the legislature's earlier treatment of the offense. There is no reason to assume that the omission of those words was inadvertent. Neither is there any necessity for contriving a definition of "unlawfully" in order to superimpose common law notions on the plain words of the statute. A fire poses unique hazards. As a means of destruction, it is difficult to control and may quickly spread to nearby buildings or fields. Firemen and policemen are endangered. Neighbors and passers-by, fearing that a structure is occupied, may attempt hazardous rescue efforts. It is the apparent intent of the legislature that persons who create these risks should suffer a heavy penalty.

This is not to say that the statute absolutely prohibits an owner from setting fire to his own property. Section 76–6–103 states that the person is guilty only if he acted "intentionally and unlawfully." * * * The word "unlawfully" also limits the reach of the aggravated arson statute. Although the term is not defined by statute, it appears often in the Criminal Code meaning without justification, license or privilege. See, e.g., U.C.A., 1953, § 76–6–201(3) (1978 edition). Many municipalities have fire safety regulations. See, e.g., Revised Ordinance of Salt Lake City, Utah § 15–1–10, *et seq.* (1974). If a property owner complied with such regulations, obtained any necessary permit, notified the fire department, warned the neighbors, obtained assistance in organizing safety precautions, or assured an adequate supply of water, an owner could demonstrate the lawful nature of his activity.[1]

* * *

In the instant case the defendant, who was in possession of the house, and his friend apparently fired some shots in the kitchen very late one night. The friend then left, and the defendant apparently used a fire accelerant to set the house on fire. There is no suggestion that the fire was accidental or that there was any justifiable or beneficial purpose for the fire that occured at approximately 1:50 a.m. The defendant intentionally created the risk that neighbors, firefighters and policemen would be exposed to danger, all without any demonstrated justification or lawful purpose.

It may be felt that the imposition of the penalty for a second degree felony is too harsh when no person was actually in the structure or actually injured by the fire.[2] However, the decision to extend broad protection to all habitable structures, in order to avoid the risk to human life posed by fire, is a policy decision that the legislature is competent to make. * * *

* * *

The judgment of the trial court was correct, and we affirm.

OAKS and HOWE, JJ., concur.

STEWART, JUSTICE (dissenting):

* * *

The aggravated arson statute, Section 76–6–103(1)(a), reads as follows:

> A person is guilty of aggravated arson if by means of fire or explosives he intentionally *and unlawfully* damages:
>
> (a) a habitable structure; * * *
>
> [Emphasis added.]

The term "habitable structure" is broadly defined by U.C.A., 1953, § 76–6–101(2) to mean "any building, vehicle, trailer, railway car, aircraft, or watercraft used for lodging or assembling persons or conducting business whether a person is actually present or not." This provision is part of an integrated statutory scheme which also makes it a crime to intentionally and unlawfully burn (1) *any* property with the intention of defrauding an insurer, § 76-6–102(1)(a) (arson to defraud); (2) the property of another, § 76–6–102(1)(b) (arson of another's property); (3) *any* structure when another person is inside, § 76–6–103(1)(b) (aggravated arson of a structure). Also, § 76–6–104 prohibits a reckless burning which endangers human life or the

1. The dissent argues that "unlawfully" is the equivalent of the word "maliciously," which requires that "the burning be done to injure another in the house or the property of another in the house." Section 103–6–1 of U.C.A., 1943, predecessor of the current aggravated arson statute, included the word "maliciously" as did the second degree arson statute. In 1973, the legislature deliberately omitted the term. The rest of the statute is consistent with this omission: (1) the "habitable structure" need not be occupied, U.C.A., 1953, § 76–6–101(2) (1978 edition), and (2) there is no requirement that the property be that of another. It is not the function of this Court to amend the legislature's revision.

2. The defendant was found guilty of aggravated arson, a second degree felony, but was sentenced to a third degree felony penalty under the provisions of U.C.A., 1953, § 76–3–402(1) (1978 edition). This statute allows the trial court to impose a sentence appropriate for the next lower category of offense if the circumstances as a whole warrant.

property of another, the concern which forms the basis of the majority holding. I think it clear that in the context of all the provisions, the aggravated arson statute may not be applied to an owner who burns his own habitation unless he intentionally threatens the life or the property of another.

The aggravated arson statute makes a burning a crime if a person *"intentionally and unlawfully"* damages a habitable structure. The burning in this case was intentional. The critical question in this case is the meaning of the term unlawful. That term implies a purpose of intending harm to another or to another's property. It does not include intent to defraud because that is covered by § 76–6–102.

Where criminal statutes are susceptible to different meanings, they should be construed in light of the common law. Continental National Bank & Trust Co. v. John H. Seely & Sons Co., 94 Utah 357, 77 P.2d 355 (1938). Where the language of a statute is subject to some doubt, reference to common-law principles may provide a valuable clue as to whether a particular situation is controlled by the statute. 2A C. Sands, *Sutherland Statutory Construction* § 50.01 (rev. 3rd ed. 1973). As Lord Coke stated, "To know what the common law was before the making of the statute is the very lock and key to set open the windows of the statute." State v. Pierson, 44 Ark. 265, 266 (1884). See also 3 *Wharton's Criminal Law* § 352 n. 66 (14th ed. 1980) and cases cited therein.

At common law, arson was the willful and malicious burning of the dwelling house of *another.* 4 W. Blackstone, *Commentaries* *220. It was an offense not against property, but against the habitation or occupancy of property. Id.; 3 *Wharton's Criminal Law,* supra, at § 345.

* * *

The word in § 76–6–103 which is the equivalent of "maliciously" is "unlawfully." The majority defines that word to mean "without justification, license or privilege." In the context of the aggravated arson statute that does not support the majority's interpretation. Indeed, it cuts strongly against it. Surely an attribute of ownership of property is the right to destroy it unless it is done for the purpose of defrauding or injuring another in his person or property. One who destroys his own habitation must surely be considered to have a "license or privilege"—indeed a right—to destroy it.

* * *

Of course it is a serious offense to burn another's habitation. The aggravated arson statute clearly covers that. But an innocent and harmless burning of one's own habitation was not intended to be a second degree felony. Cf. Brown v. State, 285 Md. 469, 403 A.2d 788 (1979). A burning rises to that level of culpability only if the fire was intended to harm others or their property. See, e.g., Voss v. State, 204 Wis. 432, 236 N.W. 128 (1931); People v. Ferlin, 203 Cal. 587, 265 P. 230 (1928) (owner's house was in possession of tenants). If one sets his habitation afire and fails to take reasonable measures to protect the lives and property of others—which seems to be the central concern of the majority—he is guilty of reckless arson under § 76–6–104.

In the present case, the state does not dispute the defendant's contention that he acted as the owner's agent. Nor does the state contend that the defendant intended to harm other persons or their property by the burning. The evidence only indicates that the owner intended to burn his own home. On these facts, I do not see how a conviction of aggravated arson of a habitable structure can be sustained.

If the real purpose of this prosecution were to punish the defendant for intent to defraud an insurer, he should have been prosecuted for arson to defraud under § 76–6–102(1)(a), which specifically applies to that offense, and includes intent to defraud as an element of that offense. The punishment under that statute, which is a third degree felony, is more commensurate with such a crime than the punishment for aggravated arson of a habitable structure, a second degree felony.

Under the construction which the Court places upon the aggravated arson statute, the State may now charge a person who commits arson for the purpose of defrauding an insurer under both the aggravated arson provision and under the arson to defraud provision. But as a practical matter such cases will always be brought under the aggravated arson statute if the structure is a habitation, as they frequently are, because the elements of the crime are far easier to prove and the punishment greater. The statutory provision outlawing arson with intent to defraud will largely be a nullity. The Legislature never intended such anomalous results.

HALL, C.J., concurs in the dissenting opinion of STEWART, J.

Gooch v. United States

Supreme Court of the United States, 1936.
297 U.S. 124, 56 S.Ct. 395, 80 L.Ed. 522.

MR. JUSTICE MCREYNOLDS delivered the opinion of the Court.

* * *

"* * * Gooch and Nix, while heavily armed, were accosted by the officers at Paris, Texas. To avoid arrest, Gooch and Nix resisted and disarmed the officers, unlawfully seized and kidnaped them and transported them by automobile from Texas to Oklahoma, and liberated them in the latter State. During the time Gooch and Nix were kidnaping the officers they inflicted serious bodily injury upon one of the officers, from which injury he was suffering at the time of such liberation in the State of Oklahoma."

The Act of June 22, 1932, c. 271, 47 Stat. 326, provided:

> "That whoever shall knowingly transport or cause to be transported, or aid or abet in transporting, in interstate or foreign commerce, any person who shall have been unlawfully seized, confined, inveigled, decoyed, kidnaped, abducted, or carried away by any means whatsoever and held for ransom or reward shall, upon conviction, be punished by imprisonment in the penitentiary for such term of years as the court, in its discretion, shall determine."

The amending Act of May 18, 1934, c. 301, 48 Stat. 781, 18 U.S.C.A. § 408a, declares:

> "Whoever shall knowingly transport or cause to be transported, or aid or abet in transporting, in interstate or foreign commerce, any person who shall have been unlawfully seized, confined, inveigled, decoyed, kidnaped, abducted, or carried away by any means whatsoever and held for ransom or reward *or otherwise, except, in the case of a minor, by a parent thereof,* shall, upon conviction, be punished (1) by death if the verdict of the jury shall so recommend, provided that the sentence of death shall not be imposed by the court if, prior to its imposition, the kidnaped person has been liberated unharmed, or (2) if the death penalty shall not apply nor be imposed the convicted person shall be punished by imprisonment in the penitentiary for such term of years as the court in its discretion shall determine."

Counsel for Gooch submit that the words "ransom or reward" import "some pecuniary consideration or payment of something of value"; that as the statute is criminal the familiar rule of ejusdem generis must be strictly applied; and finally, it cannot properly be said that a purpose to prevent arrest and one to obtain money or something of pecuniary value are similar in nature.

The original act (1932) required that the transported person should be held "for ransom or reward." It did not undertake to define the words and nothing indicates an intent to limit their meaning to benefits of pecuniary value. Generally, reward implies something given in return for good or evil done or received.

Informed by experience during two years, and for reasons satisfactory to itself, Congress undertook by the 1934 act to enlarge the earlier one and to clarify its purpose by inserting "or otherwise, except, in the case of a minor, by a parent thereof," immediately after "held for ransom or reward." The history of the enactment emphasized this view.

* * *

The House Judiciary Committee * * * said:

> "This bill, as amended, proposes three changes in the act known as the 'Federal Kidnaping Act.' First, it is proposed to add the words 'or otherwise, except, in the case of a minor, by a parent thereof.' This will extend Federal jurisdiction under the act to persons who have been kidnaped and held, not only for reward, but for any other reason, except that a kidnaping by a parent of his child is specifically exempted. * * * H.Rep.1457, 73d Cong., 2d Sess., May 3, 1934."

Evidently, Congress intended to prevent transportation in interstate or foreign commerce of persons who were being unlawfully restrained in order that the captor might secure some benefit to himself. And this is adequately expressed by the words of the enactment.

The rule of ejusdem generis, while firmly established, is only an instrumentality for ascertaining the correct meaning of words when there is uncertainty. Ordinarily, it limits general terms which follow specific ones to matters similar to those specified; but it may not be used to defeat the obvious purpose of legislation. And, while penal statutes are narrowly construed, this does not require rejection of that sense of the words which best harmonizes with the context and the end in view.

Holding an officer to prevent the captor's arrest is something done with the expectation of benefit to the transgressor. So also is kidnaping with purpose to secure money. These benefits, while not the same, are similar in their general nature and the desire to secure either of them may lead to kidnaping. If the word "reward," as commonly understood, is not itself broad enough to include benefits expected to follow the prevention of an arrest, they fall within the broad term, "otherwise."

The words "except, in the case of a minor, by a parent thereof" emphasize the intended result of the enactment. They indicate legislative understanding that in their absence a parent, who carried his child away because of affection, might subject himself to condemnation of the statute. Brown v. Maryland, 12 Wheat. 419, 438, 6 L.Ed. 678.

* * *

Commonwealth v. Krasner

Supreme Judicial Court of Massachusetts, 1971.
358 Mass. 727, 267 N.E.2d 208.

CUTTER, JUSTICE.

An indictment (see G.L. c. 266, § 49) charged that Krasner on January 15, 1970, at Cambridge, "did make an implement, to wit: a battering ram, adapted and designed for breaking open a room, and that such implement was used to break into the room of the President's office of Massachusetts Institute of Technology, to commit the crime of trespass knowing the same to be adapted and designed for the purpose aforesaid, with intent to use or employ or allow the same to be used or employed for such purpose." A Superior Court judge dismissed the indictment on the ground that it "does not set out a crime." The Commonwealth appealed under G.L. c. 278, § 28E (inserted by St.1967, c. 898, § 1).

General Laws c. 266, § 49 (as amended by St.1966, c. 269, § 1), provides: "Whoever makes * * * or knowingly has in his possession, an engine, machine, tool or *implement adapted* and *designed for* cutting through, forcing or *breaking open a building, room,* vault, safe or other depository, in order to steal therefrom money or other property, *or to commit any other crime,* knowing the same to be adapted and designed for the purpose aforesaid, *with intent to use* * * * or allow the same to be used * * * for such purpose * * * shall be punished by imprisonment in the state prison for not more than ten years or by a fine of not more than * * * [$1,000] and imprisonment in jail for not more than * * * [2½] years" (emphasis supplied). Trespass is made a criminal offence by G.L. c. 266, § 120 (as amended through St.1969, c. 463, § 2).[1]

The Commonwealth contends that the words "or to commit any other crime" include the crime of trespass. The trial judge ruled that the statute was designed "to prevent crimes of an acquisitive nature by punishing the making or possession of instruments designed and intended for use in the perpetration of such crimes." In addition, he concluded that in view of the heavy penalty permitted under § 49, as contrasted with the relatively light penalty provided by § 120, it was unlikely that the Legislature intended to impose severe punishment under § 49 for conduct designed to assist commission of a misdemeanor, such as trespass.

1. Chapter 266, § 49, was first enacted by St.1853, c. 194, entitled, "An Act concerning Implements of Burglary." The statute appears to have originated (1853 House Journal [vol. 75], p. 629, April 11) in an order "that the committee [on the judiciary] consider the expediency of providing for the punishment of persons making [b]urglar tools, or having such in their possession, *with intent that they shall be used*" (emphasis supplied). A bill, apparently in the form finally adopted, was reported from the Committee on the Judiciary and enacted in both Houses[2] without any mention in the Journals of amendments to the bill. In the Journals (see fn. 2) the bill consistently was described as the bill "Concerning Implements of Burglary," the title appearing on the statute itself. The original House order (as contrasted with the entry in the Journal) describes it as designed to "punish persons having burglar tools in their possession with intent to *use them unlawfully*" (emphasis supplied).[3]

2. A majority of the court are of opinion that the 1853 act was not confined to making or possession of tools of burglary by a person intending to

1. Section 120, as amended in 1969, reads: "Whoever, without right *enters or remains in or upon* the dwelling house, buildings * * * or enclosed land * * * of another, after having been forbidden so to do by the person who has the lawful control of said premises, either directly or by notice * * * shall be punished by a fine of not more than one hundred dollars or by imprisonment for not more than thirty days, or both. A person who is found committing such trespass may be arrested by a * * * police officer and kept in custody in a convenient place, not more than twenty-four hours, Sunday excepted, until a complaint can be made against him for the offence, and he be taken upon a warrant issued upon such complaint" (emphasis supplied).

2. See 1853 House Journal, pp. 680, 762; 1853 Senate Journal, pp. 529, 538, 549, 551.

3. In the manuscript engrossed version of the statute in the State Archives, the words "or to commit any other crime" have been inserted in the margin, in lettering smaller than that of the text, but in a hand apparently the same as that in the balance of the text. Also on the engrossed copy is a reference to Vermont, Compiled Stat. (1851), p. 546, § 6. Our 1853 statute appears to have been copied almost verbatim from the Vermont statute. The words "or to commit any other crime" do not appear in the Vermont statute. Although no reference to amendment of the bill appears in the Journals, this addition, at some stage (perhaps in committee) of the legislative process, indicates a definite and conscious legislative purpose that the "intent" aspect of the offence be broader than merely acquisitive crimes. So far as pertinent, the 1853 statute read, "Every person who shall make * * * or knowingly have in his possession, any engine, machine, tool or implement, adapted and designed for cutting through, forcing or breaking open any building, room, vault, safe, or other depository, in order to steal therefrom any money or other property, or to commit any other crime, knowing the same to be adapted and designed for the purpose aforesaid, with intent to use or employ or allow the same to be used or employed for the purpose aforesaid; shall be punished. * * *"

use them to commit theft or some other crime of an acquisitive nature. Because the language of the statute ("or to commit any other crime") is plain, it should be interpreted in accordance with the natural meaning of the words. See Johnson v. District Atty. for the No. Dist., 342 Mass. 212, 215, 172 N.E.2d 703. The words "any other crime" must be given their reasonable and normal effect or they will have no effect at all. Commonwealth v. Woods Hole, Martha's Vineyard & Nantucket S.S. Authy., 352 Mass. 617, 618, 227 N.E.2d 357. This interpretation gains some support from the legislative history outlined above.

There is no occasion to resort to canons of construction or to the title of the act as an aid to interpretation. The words "of burglary" in the 1853 title may be regarded as being merely descriptive of the prohibited tools and other instruments and not of their intended use. In any event the "title to * * * [a] statute * * * cannot limit its operation to a field more narrow * * * than that established by the statute itself." See Commonwealth v. Tilley, 306 Mass. 412, 417, 28 N.E.2d 245, 248.

The words describing the places to be entered, viz. "building, room, vault, safe, or other depository" do not indicate to us any legislative purpose to limit, to theft and other acquisitive crimes, the criminal intent proscribed by the statute. The quoted language refers not only to places where goods susceptible of theft may be found or deposited but also to places (buildings and rooms) which humans ordinarily occupy. Nothing in the 1853 statute or its history suggests that the Legislature was not as concerned about use of an implement (e.g. a battering ram) to enter an inhabited room to commit a misdemeanor (or even a more serious depredation or offence, e.g. arson, rape, or assault) as it was with situations where the prospective entrant's intention was to steal. The statutory language was not restricted. We see no basis for the application of the principle of ejusdem generis.[4]

One intending to break into a room merely to occupy the premises by a "sit-in" to the discomfort or exclusion of the usual occupant, or for more violent purposes (e.g. to destroy evidence, or to engage in some form of "protest"), is committing an offence within the term "any other crime," as fully as if a theft were his purpose. The perpetrator of such an offence, using or intending to use the tools of a burglar to commit it, must be held to know that he is violating a statute. The Legislature has said, we think plainly, that he may suffer the same consequences as those visited upon one who intends to be a burglar.

3. The trial judge suggested that the Legislature may have had no intent to impose the penalty stated in § 49 "for conduct designed to facilitate the commission of a petty misdemeanor such as trespass."[5] This suggestion runs

4. The words "or other depository" seem to us to have been inserted to broaden the word "safe" and not to limit the more general earlier words "building" and "room." Also, in view of the plain language of the statute ("or to commit any other crime"), the principle that criminal statutes are to be strictly construed has no application. See Lustwerk v. Lytron, Inc., 344 Mass. 647, 653, 183 N.E.2d 871.

5. The same contention may be made with respect to the misdemeanor defined in G.L. c. 266, § 16A, originally inserted by St.1945, c. 229, as amended by St.1966, c. 408 ("Whoever * * * breaks and enters a building * * * with intent to commit a misdemeanor shall be punished by a fine of not more than * * * [$200] or by imprisonment for not more than six months, or both"). Although

counter to the plain statutory language. The offence proscribed in effect is making or possession of burglar's instruments intended to be used for any crime. One fairly obvious evil of such an offence is the risk of violence implicit in the use of some of the tools and instrumentalities covered by § 49. The present case involves a battering ram designed to achieve an illegal entry. Certainly this was an implement "adapted * * * for * * * breaking open a * * * room." See Commonwealth v. Jones, 355 Mass. 170, 176–177, 243 N.E.2d 172. Making or possessing such an implement, with the intent to use it to invade the house, room, or office of a college president or any other citizen, or to violate his privacy, creates a risk of serious public disorder and is likely to lead to violent resistance. There is nothing improbable about a legislative determination that a serious penalty should be imposed for making or possessing instruments intended for use in committing either a then existing or future misdemeanor which may result in violence.[6]

4. We assume that, in the past, § 49 and its predecessors have been employed largely to prosecute those making or possessing burglar's equipment with a view to theft of some type. See e.g. Commonwealth v. Anderson, 245 Mass. 177, 184–185, 139 N.E. 436; Commonwealth v. Tilley, 306 Mass. 412, 414–417, 28 N.E.2d 245; Cortellesso v. Commonwealth, 354 Mass. 514, 516, 522, 238 N.E.2d 516. That, however, does not mean that § 49 must be confined to such cases. As was said in the *Tilley* case (306 Mass. at pp. 415–416, 28 N.E.2d at p. 247), "The object of a statute may be * * * so broad as to reach conditions fairly coming within its intent and sweep although such conditions did not come into existence until years after its enactment." Now that a case, which involves no theft, has arisen within the scope of the words "or to commit any other crime," we think that § 49 must be applied as broadly as the natural import of the words indicate the application should be.

* * *

6. The order dismissing the indictment is reversed. The case is to stand for further proceedings in the Superior Court.

So ordered.

SPALDING, JUSTICE (dissenting).

The court today remolds a statute, previously used only as a shield for the protection of the public against burglars, into a sword to be used against trespassers. In my view, neither the statutory language nor the legislative history supports this interpretation.

The majority rest their conclusion mainly on the premise that the meaning of the phrase "or to commit any other crime" as used in the statute is "plain" and therefore resort to canons of construction is unnecessary. I

§ 49 and § 16A appear in the same chapter, they were originally enacted at widely different times and cover somewhat different subject matter.

6. Of course, the entry alone is not the only trespass which may take place. Continued occupation by the invader, with its continuing risk of violence, would also be an intended trespass which could be proved under this indictment. Section 49 specifies only maximum punishments, so the Legislature probably considered that all circumstances would be taken into account in sentencing persons convicted under the section, including the nature of the intended crime.

disagree. The doctrine of ejusdem generis has been consistently applied by this court in similar situations to interpret statutes, and I would apply it here to limit the statute's reach, as the trial judge ruled, to crimes of an acquisitive nature.

A number of examples are illustrative. In Commonwealth v. Dejardin, 126 Mass. 46, the statute in question made it a criminal offence to publish, sell or distribute "any book, pamphlet, ballad, printed paper, *or other thing* * * * [which contains obscene matter]" (emphasis supplied). We said there that the maxim noscitur a sociis (the equivalent of ejusdem generis) should be applied to determine the meaning of "or other thing." In Babcock Davis Corp. v. Paine, 240 Mass. 438, 134 N.E. 342, the statute referred to "heating apparatus, plumbing goods, ranges or *other personal property*" (emphasis supplied). We held, at pp. 440–441, 134 N.E. 343, that ejusdem generis applied to limit the statute's application to items of personal property similar to those enumerated. In Wellesley College v. Attorney Gen., 313 Mass. 722, 727, 49 N.E.2d 220, 224, the question was raised by a statute that applied only to "trusts created by will or other written instrument." The phrase, "or other written instrument," had been added by amendment, and the question was as to the meaning of the amending words. We held that they "must be interpreted to mean written instruments of the same kind and nature." Other cases to the same effect are: Stetson v. Kempton, 13 Mass. 271, 278–280; Brailey v. Inhabitants of Southborough, 6 Cush. 141, 60 Mass. 141; Wall v. Platt, 169 Mass. 398, 406, 48 N.E. 270; Becker Transp. Co. v. Department of Pub. Util., 314 Mass. 522, 526, 50 N.E.2d 817; and Salvation Army of Mass., Inc. v. Board of Appeal of Boston, 346 Mass. 492, 495, 194 N.E.2d 99.

The purpose of the doctrine is to give meaning to *all* the words of the statute. In order to avoid treating the specific words as surplusage, effect is given to both the specific and general words by treating the specific words as indicating a class, and the general words as extending the provisions of the statute to everything embraced in that class. Sutherland on Statutory Construction (3d ed.) § 4909, pp. 395–400. The reasoning of the majority that the words "or to commit any other crime" were added to the text "in lettering smaller than that of the text," to vary it from its Vermont model, misses the point. If, as the majority hold, the Legislature meant to cover "any crime," it could have effectively done so by not only adding the language it did, but also by omitting the language, "to steal therefrom money or other property." Since the Legislature chose to leave this language in the statute, the doctrine of ejusdem generis should be applied; otherwise the specific words become surplusage.

It is settled law that criminal statutes are to be strictly construed. Commonwealth v. Paccia, 338 Mass. 4, 6, 153 N.E.2d 664. United States v. Boston & Maine R.R., 380 U.S. 157, 160, 85 S.Ct. 868, 13 L.Ed.2d 728. Application of the ejusdem generis principle, therefore, is especially appropriate here. See, for example, People v. Thomas, 25 Cal.2d 880, 899, 156 P.2d 7, where the Supreme Court of California observed that, "In construing criminal statutes the *ejusdem generis* rule of construction is applied with stringency." Consistent with the above interpretation also are both the use of the word "depository" and the title of the statute.

The majority reason further that the Legislature may well have intended to punish possession of instruments intended for use in committing a trespass. The short answer to this is that the crime of trespass in general did not appear on the Massachusetts statute books until almost ten years after the statute in question was passed, and it was almost thirty years later before trespass to buildings was made an offence.[1] The assertion that the Legislature could have had in mind the "crime" of trespass when it inserted the words "any other crime" seems to be, therefore, without foundation. Moreover, even if all other crimes were included, trespass itself would not be since it is not a separate crime committed after entry, but one committed by the very act of entry itself.

The judge below rested his decision in part on the ground that the Legislature could not have intended to prevent the commission of misdemeanors by making intent to use burglary tools to accomplish them a felony. I agree. As noted, there was no crime of trespass when the statute in question was passed. In 1890 the maximum penalty for the crime of trespass was a fine of $20. This remained the maximum penalty until 1969.[2] That the Legislature contemplated the prevention of a crime punishable with a $20 fine by a separate crime punishable by ten years in prison is hardly conceivable. Consistent with this conclusion is that no case has been called to our attention—and I have found none—in which the statute under consideration in its more than 115 years of existence has been applied to a crime of a non-acquisitive nature.

My belief in the correctness of this conclusion is reinforced by G.L. c. 266, § 16A, which provides that one who breaks and enters a building in the nighttime or daytime with the intent to commit a misdemeanor is guilty of no more than a misdemeanor. The punishment (six months imprisonment) is to be contrasted with the ten year penalty provided by the statute in question. While I recognize that § 16A was enacted much later than § 49, it nevertheless evinces a legislative pattern that would not treat the offence here involved as a felony.

I would affirm the action of the court below in dismissing the indictment for failure to state a crime.

Questions

1. Does the majority or the dissent have the better argument in the *Durant* case? In the *Krasner* case? Dissent in Krasner

1. A statute in form similar to the present trespass statute was St.1890, c. 410, which amended Pub.Sts. c. 203, § 99 (1882), to read: "Whoever without right enters upon or remains on or in the dwelling-house, buildings or improved or enclosed land of another, after being forbidden so to do * * * shall be punished by a fine not exceeding twenty dollars." Before 1882 the only trespass statute in Massachusetts concerned land under tillage and was first enacted in 1862 (St.1862, c. 89). "Forcible entry" was indictable at common law, but the elements are not charged in the indictment before us. Commonwealth v. Shattuck, 4 Cush. 141, 145, 58 Mass. 141.

2. Statute 1969, c. 463, § 2, increased the penalty to a fine of not more than $100 or imprisonment for not more than thirty days, or both.

2. To what extent do the courts in these cases appear to be applying the rules of construction in a neutral manner, and to what extent are they applying the rules to reach a desired result?

4. The Broader Search for Legislative Purpose

People v. Hope

Court of Appeals of New York, 1931.
257 N.Y. 147, 177 N.E. 402.

HUBBS, J.

About 1 o'clock in the morning of March 22, 1930, Lawrence McCarthy, a young boy, and his brother-in-law, Vincent Klemmer, were on Forty-Third street, New York City, in front of McCarthy's home. They were about to enter an automobile, a Buick coupé, to go on an errand. McCarthy entered the car and seated himself at the wheel. Klemmer took the seat beside him. At that time, three men, whom they did not know, stepped up to the car. They ordered McCarthy to get into the rumble seat, and Klemmer to drive the car. Two of the strangers got into the car and sat on the front seat with Klemmer and one on the rumble seat with McCarthy. One of the men placed a gun against Klemmer, and frightened him. He was ordered to drive ahead and keep his eyes forward or they would blow his head off. One of the men, referring to McCarthy, said, "If he moves, let him have it." They told Klemmer to drive to Long Island. He started the car and drove it about a mile when he saw a police booth at Columbus Circle. He gave the car a sudden turn and hit the booth and stopped the car. The three strangers jumped out and ran. The policeman in the booth saw the defendant sitting on the front seat of the car and succeeded in capturing him after he had jumped out and run a short distance. The other two strangers escaped. The defendant was indicted for kidnapping and has been convicted.

* * * The only question which we deem it necessary to consider is whether there is any evidence which sustains the charge of kidnapping as defined by section 1250 of the Penal Law (Consol.Laws c. 40) which reads: "§ 1250. Kidnapping defined. A person who willfully: 1. Seizes, confines, inveigles, or kidnaps another, with intent to cause him, without authority of law, to be secretly confined or imprisoned within this state, or to be sent out of the state or to be sold as a slave, or in any way held to service or kept or detained, against his will; * * * is guilty of kidnapping."

* * *

* * * It was sufficient to charge and prove that the defendant willfully and unlawfully seized McCarthy, against his will, and confined and kidnapped him with intent to cause him to be secretly confined, detained, or imprisoned within this state. All of those elements were established to the satisfaction of the jury. The intent was evidenced by the fact that he was secretly seized in the nighttime by use of a gun and actually imprisoned, confined, and restrained in the automobile.

* * *

* * * McCarthy was secretly seized in the night under circumstances calculated to terrify him. His captors had guns which they threatened to use

to kill him with if he moved. They forced him to take the rear seat in the car. They apparently intended to take him in the car to Long Island, as Klemmer was told to drive there. They had complete control of his person; he was confined and imprisoned in the car. That was not a mere assault or imprisonment. He was secretly confined and imprisoned because his captors were concealing their purpose from the public by compelling Klemmer and McCarthy to appear to be willing participants in the automobile ride, when in fact they were compelled upon the threat of death to act as they did.

The confinement and detention in the automobile for a short time, coupled with the intent, brings the case within the purview of the statute.

It seems clear that, under the common understanding of the term "kidnapping," the defendant is guilty of the crime charged, and the facts bring the case within the spirit and intent of the statute.

The judgment should be affirmed.

KELLOGG, J. (dissenting).

Doubtless, to "kidnap," according to popular usage, is "to carry one away by unlawful force or by fraud and against his will." Webster's International Dictionary. However, we are not now dealing with a case involving the popular use of words. * * * Our decision must be controlled by the definition of kidnapping given in the statute which makes the act a crime. * * * Self-evidently, the person accused, to be guilty, must not merely seize or kidnap, in the popular sense of these words, with intent so to do; he must so seize or kidnap with an ultimate purpose of accomplishing something more than the mere seizure. Secret confinement or imprisonment within the state; slavery or bondage or detention without the state—the accomplishment of some one of either of these two sets of purposes must have been aimed at by the seizure. Certainly slavery or bondage without the state was not intended. Nor is there proof, direct or inferential, that secret confinement within the state was the objective of the defendant. Therefore I think the crime charged was not established.

CARDOZO, C.J., and POUND, CRANE, LEHMAN, and O'BRIEN, JJ., concur with HUBBS, J.

Judgment affirmed.

People v. Kuntzsch

Kings County Court, New York, 1946.
64 N.Y.S.2d 116.

SOBEL, JUDGE.

* * *

Defendant is a member of a labor union. Complainant was an employee of a plant on strike. While outside the struck premises, she was accosted by the defendant. He told her that she ought to join the union. He took her by the arm and forced her to enter a cab which he hailed. At the same time another female employee was similarly forced to enter the same cab. The other employee protested. She screamed. She was permitted to leave the cab. The complainant did not scream. She testifies she was frightened.

The cab proceeded across the bridge to union headquarters in Manhattan. The defendant told her he wanted her to join the union. She had previously been a member.

At union headquarters she was led upstairs. Although in the Magistrates' Court she relates that she was not forced to enter the building and that she met several people she knew outside the building, she testified in the Grand Jury that she went upstairs unwillingly. In the office she was told that unless she joined the union she would be unable to remain at her job. She joined the union. She remained at union headquarters for four hours even attending a union meeting. In answer to the question "During all that time you were kept there against your will, is that right?" she answered "yes." In the Magistrates' Court she testified she remained there willingly. Some minutes after the meeting, she left for home. She testifies no one attempted forcibly to restrain her at any time after she entered the building but she was afraid.

The pertinent provisions of the kidnapping statute are as follows:

Section 1250, Penal Law. A person who wilfully seizes, confines, inveigles, or kidnaps another with intent to cause him, without authority of law, to be confined or imprisoned within this state is guilty of kidnapping.

The minimum penalty for kidnapping is imprisonment for from 20 years to life.

A literal reading of the statute makes a wilful seizure with intent to confine, against the will of the person seized, a kidnapping. Such a literal construction can be carried to absurd extremes. In People v. Camp, 139 N.Y. 87, 34 N.E. 755, the Court refers to a hypothetical situation where a defendant inflamed by religious zeal forcibly seizes his daughter and carries her to some church and compels her to sit in a pew by his side during religious services. It would be absurd to hold that such a seizure and detention was kidnapping within the legislative intent. Suppose a situation where a defendant drags a boy into an ice cream parlor against his will and forces him to drink an ice cream soda—would such action constitute the crime of kidnapping?

* * *

In People v. Hope, 257 N.Y. 147, 177 N.E. 402, 405, the Court said: "A person is guilty of kidnapping not merely if he 'seizes, confines, inveigles, or kidnaps another,' but only if he does so 'with intent to cause him, without authority of law, to be secretly confined or imprisoned within this state.' "

Of course, every seizure and intentional detention is not a kidnapping. As pointed out, such a construction would lead to absurd results.

We must give the statute a practical construction. In every seizure and intentional detention, there is an objective. The objective may be to hold for ransom or for some other unlawful purpose. Such cases offer no difficulty. The unlawful ultimate objective furnishes clear evidence that the detention was itself unlawful and within the legislative intent. The intentional detention may itself be the ultimate objective of the seizure. The defendant may have no other purpose in mind. In such a situation, the problem is more difficult. We must look to the length of the detention and the acts and conduct of the defendant to determine whether the seizure coupled with the intentional detention is within the legislative intent expressed in the kidnapping statute. This is a question of fact for a jury.

The Court in construing the Statute should keep in mind the penalty imposed for violation of the statute. The crime is most serious. I hold that where the ultimate objective of the seizure and detention is perfectly legal and the detention itself is for a short period of time and only incidental to the lawful objective, there is no jury question involved. As a matter of law, the seizure and detention cannot be said to have been wilful and accomplished "with intent to cause him, without authority of law, to be confined or imprisoned within the state." Nor is there a "confinement" or "imprisonment." There is merely a temporary detention incidental to a lawful objective. There is no violation of the kidnapping statute.

That is this case. The motion is granted and the indictment is dismissed.

Questions

1. Is the *Kuntzsch* case consistent with People v. Hope?

2. Can you reconcile these four cases from the same jurisdiction? In the first two cases, the charge was that the accused had violated statutory burglary provisions which punished intrusions with intent to steal goods of a stated value. The fourth case was a juvenile proceeding, but the issue was whether, if the child had been an adult, he would have violated such a statute. The third case was a common law burglary prosecution. In Felkner v. State, 218 Md. 300, 146 A.2d 424 (1958), the accused took a typewriter and blank check forms worth, in themselves, less than the statutory amount, pursuant to a forgery scheme designed to realize much more than the statutory amount; not guilty. In Holtman v. State, 219 Md. 512, 150 A.2d 223 (1959), the accused broke into a gas station office and made off with all the contents of value he could find; guilty, though the value of what he took was less than the statutory $100. In Clemons v. State, 228 Md. 237, 179 A.2d 418 (1962), the accused broke into a dwelling house and was captured before accomplishing whatever he may have had in mind. He never disclosed his objective, but his lawyer noted at the trial that he had a prior (misdemeanor) Peeping Tom conviction; guilty of common law burglary. In In re John A., 44 Md.App. 476, 409 A.2d 744 (1980), the accused juvenile broke into a summer home in October, smoked a cigarette, and left without taking anything. When he later saw smoke coming from the house, he called the fire department; not guilty.

3. To what extent are the *Hope* and *Kuntzsch* cases and the cases in the preceding question about interpreting statutes, and to what extent are they about interpreting human intentions?

Robinson v. United States

Supreme Court of the United States, 1945.
324 U.S. 282, 65 S.Ct. 666, 89 L.Ed. 944.

MR. JUSTICE BLACK delivered the opinion of the Court.

* * *

The Act authorizes the death sentence when recommended by a jury "provided that the sentence of death shall not be imposed by the court if, prior to its imposition, the kidnapped person has been liberated unharmed."

The indictment charged, and there was evidence before the jury, to the effect that the kidnapping victim yielded to capture only after the petitioner had twice violently struck her on the head with an iron bar; that while held in custody her lips were abrased and made swollen by repeated applications of tape on her mouth; and that wounds resulting from these assaults were not healed when she was liberated after six days' captivity. No evidence was introduced, nor did the indictment charge, that the injuries inflicted were permanent, or that the victim still suffered from them when the petitioner was sentenced, nine years after commission of the offense.[1] The trial court charged the jury that in determining whether the victim had been "liberated unharmed" they were limited to a consideration of her condition at the time she was liberated, and that they were not authorized to recommend the death penalty if at the time of her liberation she had recovered from her injuries. Petitioner took no exception to the charge, and asked no other. Its correctness is before us only to the extent that we are asked to say that the injuries inflicted must be permanent or they must be in existence at the time of sentence in order to authorize the infliction of the death sentence.

The scant legislative history of the Act is of little assistance to us in interpreting this proviso. Two possible reasons suggest themselves, however, as to the motivation of Congress in making the severity of a kidnapper's punishment depend upon whether his victim has been injured. The first reason is the old belief that the severity of the injury should measure the rigor of the punishment. If this be the reasoning implicit in the statute, it would appear that Congress intended that for a kidnapper to obtain the benefit of the proviso he must both liberate and refrain from injuring his victim. Congress may equally have intended this provision as a deterrent, on the theory that kidnappers would be less likely to inflict violence upon their victims if they knew that such abstention would save them from the death penalty. This assumption finds some slight support in the legislative history, is not contested by the government, has been accepted in one case and is the chief prop for the interpretation which the petitioner urges. He argues upon this assumption that the wider the scope of the exemption from the death penalty, the greater the inducement for the kidnapper to release the victim. To magnify the inducement, we are asked to interpret the proviso as granting immunity from the death sentence to any kidnapper who does not permanently injure his victim. We cannot expand the meaning of the statute on such a hypothesis and we turn to its language.

We accept the word "unharmed" appearing in the proviso as meaning uninjured. Neither the word "permanent" nor any other word susceptible of that meaning was used by Congress. The quality of the injury to which Congress referred is not defined. It may be possible that some types of injury would be of such trifling nature as to be excluded from the category of injuries which Congress had in mind. We need indulge in no speculation in

1. Petitioner pleaded guilty to the offense in 1936. In August, 1943, a district court held his plea of guilty invalid on the ground that he had been denied counsel. This appeal is from a trial which took place in October, 1943. See Robinson v. Johnston, 9 Cir., 118 F.2d 998; Id., 316 U.S. 649, 62 S.Ct. 1301, 86 L.Ed. 1732; Id., 10 Cir., 130 F.2d 202; Id., D.C., 50 F.Supp. 774.

regard to such a category. The injuries inflicted upon his victim were of such degree that they can not be read out of the Act's scope without contracting it to the point where almost all injuries would be excluded. We find no justification whatever for grafting the word permanent onto the language which Congress adopted.

Nor can we construe the proviso as precluding the death sentence where the kidnapped person's injuries have been healed at the time sentence is imposed. It is not to be assumed that Congress intended a matter of such grave consequence to defendants and the public to turn on the fortuitous circumstance of the length of time that a case is pending in the courts. Far too many contingencies are involved, for example, the time it takes to apprehend a criminal, the condition of the trial docket, and the uncertainties of appeals. We would long hesitate before interpreting the Act so as to make the severity of sentence turn upon the date sentence is ultimately imposed, even if the language of the Act more readily lent itself to such a construction than this one does. At the very least, the proviso's language must mean that the kidnapped person shall not be suffering from injuries when liberated; the kidnapped person here was still suffering from her injuries when liberated.

Nevertheless it is argued that the death penalty proviso should be held invalid on the ground that there is uncertainty as to the precise meaning and scope of the word "unharmed" and the phrase "liberated unharmed." In most English words and phrases there lurk uncertainties. The language Congress used in this Act presents no exception to this general truth. One thing about this Act is not uncertain, and that is the clear purpose of Congress to authorize juries to recommend and judges to inflict the death penalty, under certain circumstances, for kidnappers who harmed their victims. And we cannot doubt that a kidnaper who violently struck the head of his victim with an iron bar, as evidence showed that this petitioner did, comes within the group Congress had in mind. This purpose to authorize a death penalty is clear even though Congress did not unmistakably mark some boundary between a pin prick and a permanently mutilated body. It is for Congress and not for us to decide whether it is wise public policy to inflict the death penalty at all. We do not know what provision of law, constitutional or statutory, gives us power wholly to nullify the clearly expressed purpose of Congress to authorize the death penalty because of a doubt as to the precise congressional purpose in regard to hypothetical cases that may never arise.

The trial court committed no error of which this petitioner can complain.

Affirmed.

MR. JUSTICE RUTLEDGE, dissenting.

The penalty of death should not be imposed upon conditions defined so uncertainly that their identity cannot be ascertained or is left open to grave doubt. If words ever need to be clear, they do when they perform this function. I do not know what Congress meant when it commanded that "the sentence of death shall not be imposed by the court if, prior to its imposition, the kidnaped person has been liberated unharmed." 48 Stat. 781.

The words have the sound of certainty which simple, everyday language gives forth. The certainty is only illusion. What does "liberated unharmed" mean? The statute does not tell us. Nor does the legislative history. Neither does the Court's opinion. It rather demonstrates the statute's ambiguity. It does not say what Congress meant. It says only that Congress meant one of two things, and either would cover this case. A third possible construction, put forward by petitioner, is rejected. The statute, it is held, does not mean that the death penalty can be imposed only when the injuries inflicted are permanent or, presumably, only when they remain at the time of sentence, though not permanent. The Court does not say what "liberated" means. Nor does it define "unharmed," except that it excludes the injury inflicted in this case.

What act is pointed to by "liberated"? Does it refer only to release by the kidnapper or does it include a case of rescue overcoming his will and purpose? Does it cover his abandonment of the victim in flight, leaving him perhaps gagged and bound in some lonely spot or cell, not free but no longer in the kidnapper's power? Or must he, before the pressures become too great, change his mind, exercise discretion and set the victim free before he is forced to do so?

Similarly, what is "unharmed"? A scratch, a cut, abrasions, left by removal of tape or rope, bruises, nervous shock, disturbance of digestion, all of a kind which heals or passes before "liberation" occurs? Few kidnappings take place without harm of some kind to the victim. They may be executed by force or by mere threats. One produces traumatic injury, from minor abrasion to death, the other nervous or mental shock of momentary or lifetime duration. How much injury, and what kind, did Congress have in mind?

Is the death penalty to be imposed for the identical cut or abrasion, whether minor or serious, inflicted during the act of taking the victim, merely because in one case the kidnapper releases or abandons him quickly, perhaps because forced to do so, but forbidden in another because he holds the victim until the injury heals? Is reward thus to be given for prolonging the agony?

* * *

There are still other uncertainties. Was it the intent (1) that the kidnapper must both liberate and refrain from injuring his victim or (2) merely that he must not inflict harm, however the liberation may occur? We are not told what was Congress' purpose, whether to measure the rigor of the punishment by the severity of the injury or to induce kidnappers not to use violence at all, deterring them by the threat of death for its use in whatever degree. Neither the legislative history nor the opinion gives light on this question. If Congress wished to induce gentle kidnappings, injuries inflicted in the course of the act of kidnapping are covered, provided they remain at the time of "liberation." They would not be included, if healed before it, however grave when inflicted or however distant liberation from infliction. What if the kidnapper, knowing that time is crucial, keeps his victim until the injuries are healed? Was it Congress' purpose to induce longer detention, the more serious the injury inflicted during the original act? What if it is inflicted afterward, but during the course of the detention? Once injury has taken place, the inducement held out by the statute necessarily is either to hold the victim until cure is effected or to do away with him so that evidence, both of the injury and of the kidnapping, is destroyed. The more serious the injury the stronger these inducements. It is only upon such considerations, affecting the victim's safety, that Congress' qualification of the power to impose the sentence of death can be accounted for.

Finally, was Congress attempting to offer the maximum inducement to liberation? If this was the purpose, petitioner's construction, rejected by the Court, has more force than the other possible ones among which it declines to choose. For in that event the kidnapper would have inducement, once injury is inflicted, though serious, to surrender the victim in the hope that care after surrender might bring about cure before imposition of sentence. If the single and vague word "unharmed" is construed to mean absence of permanent injury or grave injury, though not permanent, he would have the hope, the inducement that surrender might give escape from the maximum sentence. Contrary to the Court's view that this interpretation is impossible, it goes directly to the unanswered questions, how much and what kinds of injury Congress had in mind; and to adopt it would accord with the rule that criminal statutes should be strictly construed. Moreover it would apply in this case, since there is no evidence of permanent injury or even that the injuries inflicted were critical at the time of the victim's release. She testified at the trial.

It is true this construction would make imposition of that penalty depend upon fortuitous circumstances, the length of time between release and sentence, as well as the chances of the victim to recover and their successful working out in that period. But any other construction either makes it depend upon circumstances equally fortuitous or has the inevitable effect, in many cases, of holding out inducement to the kidnapper to inflict the ultimate harm rather than to refrain from inflicting harm at all. Petitioner's construction more than any other takes into account the victim's safe surrender. Once the victim is hurt, the kidnapper's problem of what to do with him becomes inescapable and the provision for the extreme penalty can work only to defeat or defer liberation. Was this what Congress intended, knowing that few kidnappings can occur in which some substantial harm will not be done?

* * *

I think the statute turns the power to impose the death penalty upon facts so vaguely defined that only judicial legislation can remedy the defect. This is not the kind of thing courts should be left to work out case by case through the "gradual process of inclusion and exclusion." This business rather belongs to Congress, not to the courts. As the Court's opinion states, though I think in contradiction of its judgment, "It is for Congress and not for us to decide whether it is wise public policy to inflict the death penalty at all." Congress' mandate in such matters must be clear; otherwise we, not Congress, decide. In this one it is beyond understanding.

I would vacate the judgment and remand the cause for the petitioner to be resentenced.

MR. JUSTICE MURPHY joins in this opinion.

Question

Who has the better of the argument in the *Robinson* case?

Macomber v. State

Supreme Court of Nebraska, 1940.
137 Neb. 882, 291 N.W. 674.

[The statement of the facts is taken from the dissenting opinion.]

In this prosecution competent evidence proves beyond a reasonable doubt the following facts or proper inferences therefrom as found by the jury in their verdict of guilty: The three defendants named in the information, Macomber, a policeman of North Platte, Baskins, a member of the city council, and Hastings, a boss in city politics, conspired together to compel Sam I. Pappas, who had been permitted by them to operate a gambling den, to confess to a felony of which he was innocent—a confession which, if made, might subject him to imprisonment in the penitentiary for 20 years and perhaps for life. The motive for the purpose to compel the confession was to get rid of Pappas and procure profits from gambling. Macomber and Baskins drove to the home of Pappas in a police cruiser not long before midnight, Sunday, November 21, 1937. Macomber intimated that something for the good of Pappas was contemplated and the latter readily consented to leave home in the cruiser with the city officials. He had not been accused of any offense and there had been no warrant for his arrest. He was not told he was under arrest. He was taken to Macomber's room 25, in the Ritner Hotel, without knowledge of what was in store for him there. Hastings was promptly called to the hotel by telephone and while the four men, Macomber, Baskins, Hastings and Pappas, were in room 25, with the door closed and bolted on the inside, Macomber made a demand on Pappas to confess his guilt of a lawless act of degeneracy. The latter asserted his innocence and refused to confess. Threats to make him do so were loud and profane. To compel such a confession Baskins and Hastings held Pappas while Macomber beat him. Pappas tried to escape, unbolted the door and got into the hall outside, was beaten there, dragged back into the room where the beating was continued. These inhuman atrocities did not compel Pappas to confess guilt. After the beating and turmoil ceased in room 25 with the departure of the four occupants, there was blood on the walls, on the floor, on a rug in front of the bed, on the bedspread, on the drapes, on the walls in the hall and on the radiator. Physical injuries inflicted on Pappas as described by an examining physician and as related in the majority opinion were:

"Face badly bruised; eyes swollen shut; deep cut, with ragged edges, an inch long over the left eye; slighter cut over same eye; nose skinned; lip cut on right side; inside of cheek bruised on upper right side; lacerations close to the lips; right side of face puffed with air, passing under the tissues and extending over the entire side of head and face to margin of collarbone; portion of air breathed passed through torn tissues under the skin, over the side of the face and neck; lachrymal bone fractured; whites of both eyes red; bump on head back of ear; stitches required to close wounds."

Unsteady on his legs, his face smeared with gore, Pappas was denied the privilege of washing away the blood and in that condition was taken to the police station and confronted with the pervert who was asked to identify him as a companion in criminal depravity. The identification was refused. Pappas was not the guilty man. He was released, taken home and to the hospital without being accused of any violation of law.

MESSMORE, JUSTICE.

* * *

That this plaintiff in error was guilty of conduct which richly deserves the condemnation of all good people is not to be denied, but the question for us to decide, and for the state to prove beyond a reasonable doubt, is whether defendant Macomber kidnaped Sam I. Pappas, in violation of the strict terms of the statute and as charged in the information.

"In this state all public offenses are statutory; no act is criminal unless the Legislature has in express terms declared it to be so; and no person can be punished for any act or omission which is not made penal by the plain import of the written law." Lane v. State, 120 Neb. 302, 232 N.W. 96. "It is elementary that penal statutes are inelastic and must be strictly construed. They are never extended by implication." Weber v. State, 122 Neb. 369, 240 N.W. 429; Preston v. State, 106 Neb. 848, 184 N.W. 925. The foregoing Nebraska cases definitely determine the manner of construing the provisions of criminal statutes in this state.

Section 28–417, Comp.St.1929, in its entirety, contains possibly four separate divisions that may be stated as follows: * * * The second provision of this section of the statute is: "Whoever shall unlawfully carry off or decoy, entice away, secrete or imprison any person, for the purpose of extorting from such person or from his or her relatives or friends any money, * * * or for the purpose of compelling the performance of any act by such person," shall be imprisoned in the penitentiary for and during the period of his natural life. * * *

The dominating element of the offense of kidnaping is the intent with which the acts enumerated in the statute are done. The purpose of the enactment of statutes prohibiting kidnaping is to secure the personal liberty of citizens, to protect the custody of parents or guardians, or other persons having lawful custody of children, also the children. The present statute (Comp.St.1929, sec. 28–417) was passed in this state immediately after the kidnaping of young Edward Cudahy, where the kidnapers sought ransom for the return of the boy. We find no case that is of direct assistance in determining the adaptability of the facts in the instant case to section 28–417, supra. It is apparent that when the legislature enacted section 28–417 it had in mind the unlawful carrying away, decoying, enticing, or imprisoning of any person for the purpose of extorting from such person, relatives or friends any money, property or promise, and for the purpose of compelling the performance of any act by such person.

The state's contention is that the taking of Pappas in an effort to procure a confession, or in an effort to get him to confess to the crime of sodomy, was sufficient when any force was used upon him in that connection. The word "purpose" means that which one sets before him to accomplish. To "compel," within the contemplation of section 28–417, supra, means to force; and "performance" means, as the term implies, such other fulfilment of a duty as puts an end to obligation by leaving nothing to be done. While there is apparently great force in the reasoning in the state's brief, we do not believe that the legislature intended, considering the history of the enactment of this law and the reason therefor, to include a state of facts as exists in the instant case within the section of the statute herein discussed.

In Holy Trinity Church v. United States, 143 U.S. 457, 12 S.Ct. 511, 512, 36 L.Ed. 226, it was said: "It is a familiar rule that a thing may be within the letter of the statute and yet not within the statute, because not within its spirit nor within the intention of its makers. * * * This is not the substitution of the will of the judge for that of the legislator; for frequently words of general meaning are used in a statute, words broad enough to include an act in question, and yet a consideration of the whole legislation, or of the circumstances surrounding its enactment, or of the absurd results which follow from giving such broad meaning to the words, makes it unreasonable to believe that the legislator intended to include the particular act." And on page 463 of 143 U.S., on page 513 of 12 S.Ct., 36 L.Ed. 226, we find this language: "Again, another guide to the meaning of a statute is found in the evil which it is designed to remedy; and for this the court properly looks at contemporaneous events, the situation as it existed, and as it was pressed upon the attention of the legislative body." Citing United States v. Union P.R. Co., 91 U.S. 72, 79, 23 L.Ed. 224. In the latter case it was said: "But courts, in construing a statute, may with propriety recur to the history of the times when it was passed; and this is frequently necessary, in order to ascertain the reason as well as the meaning of particular provisions in it. Aldridge v. Williams, 3 How. [9], 24 [11 L.Ed. 469]; Preston v. Browder, 1 Wheat. [115] 120 [4 L.Ed. 50]."

In State v. Clark, 29 N.J.L. 96, the court said: "If a literal construction of the words of a statute be absurd, the act must be so construed as to avoid the absurdity. The court must restrain the words. The object designed to be reached by the act must limit and control the literal import of the terms and phrases employed. 1 Kent's Com. 462; Commonwealth v. Kimball, 24 Pick. [Mass., 366], 370; United States v. Fisher, 2 Cranch [358], 400 [2 L.Ed. 304]; 1 Bl.Com. 60." And in United States v. Kirby, 7 Wall. 482, 486, 19 L.Ed. 278, it was said: "All laws should receive a sensible construction. General terms should be so limited in their application as not to lead to injustice, oppression, or an absurd consequence. It will always, therefore, be presumed that the Legislature intended exceptions to its language, which would avoid results of this character. The reason of the law, in such cases, should prevail over its letter." The circumstances under which the statute in question was passed and the purposes to be accomplished by it, in its scope and effect, are inconsistent with the position taken by the state.

* * *

The judgment of the district court is reversed, and the cause remanded for further proceedings.

Reversed.

JOHNSEN, J., concurs in result.

ROSE, JUSTICE (dissenting).

* * *

When this law was enacted, contemporaneous history showed that the art of kidnapping had progressed to the point where a helpless victim was tortured by the threat his eyes would be gouged out if he failed to write and sign a letter containing the threat and address it to parent, brother, sister or other relative. The law was intended to protect the victim, his relatives and the public generally. The penalty for kidnaping was adapted to the atrocity of the crime.

* * *

* * * Macomber at the time was a police officer in uniform and was armed. He was assisted by Baskins, a member of the city council and by Hastings, a political boss who gave orders to police officers at the police station—orders that were obeyed. Pappas was known in advance to be unarmed. His eyesight was impaired and he was weakened by a disease of long standing. He was imprisoned by these enemies of law and order and was helpless in their presence. Officialdom and bossism gave them no immunity from their lawlessness. In legal conduct of public duty officers of the law are not in danger of prosecution for kidnaping. The facts narrated and the necessary inferences therefrom were clearly shown beyond reasonable doubt by competent evidence which the jury believed.

My understanding of the facts and the law is that the state in the prosecution of Macomber proved beyond a reasonable doubt every element of kidnaping as defined by statute—enticing Pappas away from home, transporting him to room 25 in the Ritner Hotel, imprisoning him therein and beating him in the manner indicated for the purpose of compelling him against his will to confess guilt of a felony. Each of these acts was unlawful and all together with criminal intent amounted to kidnaping. Such a confession, if compelled, would have been an "act" within the meaning of that word as used in the kidnaping statute. * * *

The kidnaping statute is in plain unambiguous language and needs no construction. I do not agree with the majority that enforcement of the kidnaping statute according to its literal terms led to injustice, oppression or absurdity invalidating the conviction. I examined the entire record with care and I did not find any error in the proceedings below or in the sentence of the district court to justify the acquittal of Macomber on the charge of kidnaping.

Question

Is the majority opinion in *Macomber* outrageous, or is it merely not written as persuasively as it might be?

People v. Spinks

Supreme Court of New York, Appellate Division, Third Department, 1977.
58 A.D.2d 659, 395 N.Y.S.2d 709.

Before KOREMAN, P.J., and GREENBLOTT, SWEENEY, MAIN and LARKIN, JJ.

MEMORANDUM DECISION.

Appeal from a judgment of the County Court of Warren County, rendered June 25, 1973, upon a verdict convicting defendant of the crimes of burglary in the first degree, robbery in the first degree, grand larceny in the second degree, kidnapping in the second degree and burglary in the third degree.

During the early morning hours of October 28, 1969, Audrey and Melvin Smith were awakened in the bedroom of their Queensbury home by a person holding what appeared to be a pistol. After the Smiths were tied up by the gunman and questioned about money and the safes in their home and in a store which they owned, they were ordered to leave the house and to enter their 1969 Oldsmobile Toronado. The car was halted at a wooded area and, after tying the Smiths to a tree, the gunman left with the vehicle. The Smiths eventually freed themselves and walked approximately one mile to a house from which they telephoned for medical assistance. While traveling in an ambulance, at approximately 4:00 A.M., the Smiths observed what they believed to be their automobile.

Patrolman Murphy of the Glens Falls Police Department proceeded to the Smiths' store following their report, received by the police department at approximately 3:15 to 3:30 A.M., of a possible burglary at the store. The officer observed an individual standing by the rear of the building about 200 feet away. The individual crossed the parking lot leading to the sidewalk, got into an Oldsmobile Toronado parked in a driveway and drove away. Officer Murphy testified that he observed the individual from as close a distance as 25 feet under conditions of good lighting. There was evidence that the store had been broken into that evening.

The defendant's first claim is that prior photographic identifications of him by the Smiths and Officer Murphy were so impermissibly suggestive as to give rise to a very substantial likelihood of irreparable misidentification (Simmons v. United States, 390 U.S. 377, 88 S.Ct. 967, 19 L.Ed.2d 1247). We disagree. * * *

In view of the recent affirmance by the Court of Appeals of the so-called "merger doctrine" (People v. Cassidy, 40 N.Y.2d 763, 390 N.Y.S.2d 45, 358 N.E.2d 870), we reach a different result with respect to defendant's argument that the kidnapping charge should be dismissed. In *People v. Cassidy, (supra),* the court described this doctrine, which precludes kidnapping convictions in certain situations, as "of judicial origin and was based on an aversion to prosecuting a defendant on a kidnapping charge in order to expose him to the heavier penalty thereby made available, where the period of abduction was brief, the criminal enterprise in its entirety appeared as no more than an offense of robbery or rape, and there was lacking a genuine 'kidnapping' flavor [citation omitted]" (id. at 765–766, 390 N.Y.S.2d at 47, 358 N.E.2d at 872). The court further noted that the purpose of the merger doctrine was "to preclude conviction for kidnapping based on acts which are so much the part of another substantive crime that the substantive crime could not have been committed without such acts and that independent criminal responsibility may not fairly be attributed to them" (id. at 767, 390 N.Y.S.2d at 47, 358 N.E.2d at 873).

The conclusion is inescapable in this case that the "kidnapping" was merely an element of the burglary at the store, without which, because the Smiths would most assuredly have notified the police of its possible commission, the burglary would not have been feasible. "It is a common occurrence in robbery, for example, that the victim be confined briefly at gunpoint or bound and detained, or moved into and left in another room and place" (People v. Levy, 15 N.Y.2d 159, 164, 256 N.Y.S.2d 793, 796, 204 N.E.2d 842, 844). The kidnapping charge cannot stand.

* * *

Judgment modified, on the law and the facts, by reversing the conviction for kidnapping in the second degree and dismissing the fourth count of the indictment, and, as so modified, affirmed.

Note and Question on People v. Cassidy

People v. Cassidy, 40 N.Y.2d 763, 767–768, 390 N.Y.S.2d 45, 48, 358 N.E.2d 870, 873 (1976), relied upon and quoted in the *Spinks* case, said:

> There is an exception to the doctrine, however, which in operation denies application of the rule in circumstances to which it would apply were it not for this qualification. This aspect invites attention to the manner or means employed in effectuating what would otherwise be the merged detention. "[T]he rule has no purpose of ignoring as independent crimes alternative or optional means used in committing another crime which, by the gravity and even horrendousness of the means used, constitute and should constitute a separately cognizable offense." If such be found to be the circumstance, the kidnapping aspect aggravated by the particular means or manner of the abduction may then support a separate prosecution.
>
> We turn then to the cases before us, in none of which was the means or manner of the detention such as to invoke the exception to the merger rule. In *Cassidy* a young woman was walking home in the early evening after having attended classes at Brooklyn College. Defendant grabbed her from the rear and dragged her at knifepoint some 70 feet into a garage where he sought to assault her sexually. After the victim lost consciousness, defendant left her. She did not regain consciousness until some two hours later. We agree with the Appellate Division that there was here no independent abduction; the detention of the victim was incidental to the commission of the crimes of assault and attempted sexual abuse. There was no asportation which could be the predicate for conviction of a separately cognizable offense; we cannot accept the contention that, because the assault did not take place on the street in full public view at the spot where the attack was initiated but rather occurred under cover in a garage about 70 feet away, it should be permissible to prosecute defendant for kidnapping as well.
>
> We reach a similar conclusion in *Dolan.* There the victim was also walking home in Brooklyn, in this instance shortly before midnight. After asking directions defendant grabbed the victim and pulled her into an automobile at knifepoint. He then drove around stopping briefly several times to make sexual advances until finally the victim was dropped off a

couple of blocks from her home about an hour and a half later. Again the "true" crime was the intermittent, continuing sexual assault and the confinement in the car was only the incidental means to the accomplishment of that assault.

Finally, in *Usher,* defendant grabbed a nurse as she was returning home from the hospital shortly after midnight. At knifepoint the nurse was pulled across the street to an abandoned building. Inside the vestibule defendant and an accomplice robbed their victim. The nurse was then taken through a courtyard into an adjoining building, up a flight of stairs and into a small room where she was raped at knifepoint. When defendant and his accomplice left, the nurse found her way out of the building, back onto the street and then to her home. In this instance there were two sequential but discrete crimes of violence, first robbery and then rape. As to each, however, the abduction here, too, was only the incidental means employed to facilitate the commission of the underlying crimes.

We hold therefore that the merger doctrine precludes conviction for kidnapping in the second degree in each of these cases.

Did the *Spinks* court understand and apply correctly the reasoning of the *Cassidy* case?

Compare with *Cassidy* Commonwealth v. Sumner, 18 Mass.App. 349, 465 N.E.2d 1213 (1984), finding that locking a rape victim in an apartment for two hours after the rape was not merely an incidental detention, and the later Massachusetts case of Commonwealth v. Rivera, 397 Mass. 244, 490 N.E.2d 1160 (1986), diapproving the *Cassidy* analysis where there is confinement or movement of the victim, going beyond mere restraint incidental to the other crime. State v. Amarillo, 198 Conn. 285, 503 A.2d 146 (1986), rejects a merger rule for kidnappings incidental to rape or robbery where the elements of both crimes are present. Some jurisdictions may allow conviction of either the primary crime or kidnapping, but not both. See, generally, Anno., 17 A.L.R.2d 1003.

A Note on Double Jeopardy

The provision in the Fifth Amendment to the United States Constitution that no person shall "be subject for the same offense to be twice put in jeopardy of life or limb," was originally applicable only to federal cases. It was applied generally in criminal prosecutions throughout the United States, however, on the basis of state constitutions or common law principles. The scope of the bar, though extending to all criminal punishments, varied from jurisdiction to jurisdiction until Benton v. Maryland, 395 U.S. 784, 89 S.Ct. 2056, 23 L.Ed.2d 707 (1969), when the Fifth Amendment guarantee, in the federal form, was held binding on the states.

The policy of the provision is to prevent both multiple punishments for the same offense and multiple prosecutions for the same offense. The convicted defendant is not to be punished more severely than the law provides through the device of punishing him for several offenses when he has committed only one. Nor is the accused to be harassed by a second prosecution based on the same conduct when the government is not fully satisfied by the result of the first. Such multiple prosecutions are also costly and a burden on the court calendar. Note that the constitutional bar does not prevent charging the defendant with both breaking and entering and burglary with respect to the same transaction, at the same trial, and convicting him of both, as long as he is not sentenced for both, even though, as we shall see, he could not be subjected to separate proceedings for the two offenses; he is neither punished twice nor prosecuted twice. There may be a sound reason for combining the two charges in a single proceeding, because the prosecution cannot always be certain that its proof of all of the burglary elements will be adequate.

When is a second prosecution for "the same offense" as the first? Obviously there is a bar when the facts and the offense alleged are precisely the same. But suppose two different prohibitions are applied to similar facts. If the accused is charged with several sales of drugs to the same person, each sale may be punished as a separate offense. But as to a single sale, may the accused be punished twice because two statutory prohibitions, one against a sale of drugs not in the original stamped package, and another against a sale not in pursuance of a written order, are violated? Blockburger v. United States, 284 U.S. 299, 52 S.Ct. 180, 76 L.Ed. 306 (1932), held that he could, because each prohibition requires proof of a fact which the other does not require. One requires proof about the package, not needed in the other; the other requires proof about the order, not relevant in the first. Therefore there are two separate crimes in the single sale and there may be two prosecutions and two punishments. The *Blockburger* rule continues to be followed. In Brown v. Ohio, 432 U.S. 161, 97 S.Ct. 2221, 53 L.Ed.2d 187 (1977), the Supreme Court barred prosecution for larceny of an automobile when the accused had already been convicted under the joy-riding statute. While the larceny statute required proof of a fact not required for a joy-riding conviction (intention to deprive permanently), proof of joy-riding required no fact in addition to what had to be shown for larceny. It was therefore an included offense in larceny, and the two crimes were not separate in the jeopardy sense. The test appears to turn on the actual need, in the circumstances of the second prosecution, to rely on the facts proved in the first; if the route actually used to the second conviction does not rely on the facts used in the first prosecution (even though those facts might have formed a different basis for the second charge), there is no bar. So, when the first conviction was for failure to reduce speed to avoid an accident (in which two people were killed), there was no bar to a subsequent manslaughter prosecution for the deaths if manslaughter could be established without resting on the failure to reduce speed. See Illinois v. Vitale, 447 U.S. 410, 100 S.Ct. 2260, 65 L.Ed.2d 228 (1980). The Supreme Court has held that when the issue is multiple punishments only, and not multiple prosecutions, the *Blockburger* test need not be followed if there is a clear legislative intention to punish the same conduct twice under separate statutes (intention to punish for felony committed with a deadly weapon in addition to robbery with a deadly weapon). Missouri v. Hunter, 459 U.S. 359, 103 S.Ct. 673, 74 L.Ed.2d 535 (1983).

Even if *Blockburger* does not bar the later prosecution, Grady v. Corbin, 495 U.S. ___, 110 S.Ct. 2084, 109 L.Ed.2d 548 (1990) may do so. In *Grady,* after killing one victim and injuring another, the defendant driver pleaded guilty in town court to traffic tickets charging him with driving while intoxicated and crossing a median line. His subsequent trials, based on the same conduct, for manslaughter, criminally negligent homicide, and assault were held barred, even though *Blockburger,* which protects against multiple *punishments* for the same conduct, did not reach this situation: the offenses charged originally and the newly charged offenses each have elements not found in the other. The *Grady* bar is based on prohibition of multiple *prosecutions.* In the second prosecution, the government may not prove conduct which constitutes an offense for which it has already prosecuted the accused; to do so would be to subject the accused unnecessarily to multiple trials. (The government may be allowed to pursue a second prosecution when it relies on different conduct to establish the second offense. In *Grady* the manslaughter and other charges might have been permissible if based on excessive speed, rather than on driving while intoxicated or driving on the wrong side of the road.[a])

Grady recognized that an exception may exist to the *Blockburger* prohibition where, at the time of the first prosecution, the facts would not have supported a second charge. If a change in circumstances later makes the second charge possible, *Blockburger* may not prevent a prosecution on the second charge even if the charges would ordinarily be barred. So, if after a conviction of battery, the victim dies, *Blockburger* may not bar a later manslaughter or murder prosecution. See, e.g., Hopkins v. United States, 4 App.D.C. 430 (1894).

You can see that the *Blockburger* test would not treat a burglary and the burglar's intended object crime as "the same offense," since the object crime of larceny, murder, etc., would have factual elements different from the burglary, and the burglary would have some factual elements different from the object crime. But where a crime like burglary, or more commonly, robbery or rape, also involves inherently an incidental detention which would qualify as kidnapping, a *Blockburger* issue may arise with respect to so much of the detention as is essential to the carrying out of the other crime. Where the detention goes beyond what is inherently necessary to accomplish the burglary, robbery, or rape, legal policy may still oppose double convictions, as in *Spinks* and *Cassidy,* even if there is no constitutional bar.

When we conclude that we are dealing with "the same offense" under *Blockburger,* we must be sure at the second prosecution that the accused was put in jeopardy at the first before we can decide that a bar exists. When the accused is expressly or impliedly *acquitted* of the same offense at the first trial, he has been placed in jeopardy. Implied acquittal may occur when the charge is submitted to the trier of fact and the trier of fact says nothing directly about the charge, as where it convicts of a lesser or merely different charge without reference to the one in question. Another sovereign might not be barred by an acquittal under the double jeopardy provision where the law is violated.

A prior final *conviction* of the same offense is of course also a bar to a second prosecution by the same jurisdiction, though perhaps not to a trial by another sovereign, where the same act violates the laws of two states or federal and state law. See, e.g., Bartkus v. Illinois, 359 U.S. 121, 79 S.Ct. 676, 3 L.Ed.2d 684 (1959), rehearing denied 360 U.S. 907, 79 S.Ct. 1283, 3 L.Ed.2d 1258 (1959). Heath v. Alabama, 474 U.S. 82, 106 S.Ct. 433, 88 L.Ed.2d 387 (1985), held that states may successively prosecute for the same conduct. Is there any bar to a retrial for an offense as to which a conviction has been reversed on appeal? Where the defendant obtains a reversal for error in the proceedings below, as where there has been an erroneous ruling on evidence or jury instruction, retrial is allowed, on one theory or another; e.g., the original

a. Principles of collateral estoppel may also limit successive prosecutions. Ashe v. Swenson, 397 U.S. 436, 90 S.Ct. 1189, 25 L.Ed.2d 469 (1970).

proceedings may be regarded as continuing until a judgment becomes final, and there is no jeopardy claim to the retrial. Price v. Georgia, supra. Where the reversal is based on legal insufficiency of the evidence to make out the charge, there is a constitutional bar to retrial, because there should have been an acquittal (which would bar retrial), but there is no jeopardy bar when the reversal is merely because the appellate court, sitting as a "thirteenth juror," believes the conviction was against the weight of the evidence. Tibbs v. Florida, 457 U.S. 31, 102 S.Ct. 2211, 72 L.Ed.2d 652 (1982). In such a case the Court reasoned, the prosecution did not fail to present legally sufficient evidence to support the charge; there is merely "jurors'" disagreement as to the weight of the evidence and the prosecution may try again, as it could in the case of failure to agree by the trial jurors. Jeopardy does not bar retrial after reversal for erroneous admission of testimony if the evidence actually admitted, correctly or not, could sustain the conviction. Lockhart v. Nelson, 488 U.S. 33, 109 S.Ct. 285, 102 L.Ed.2d 265 (1988).

Assuming a permissible retrial after reversal of conviction, may the sentencing judge constitutionally impose a greater sentence than was imposed at the first trial? The Court has consistently held that the jeopardy clause is no bar to such an increased sentence, although a due process claim may arise if there is a question of a State's vindictive action against the accused for pursuing a right of appeal. North Carolina v. Pearce, 395 U.S. 711, 89 S.Ct. 2072, 23 L.Ed.2d 656 (1969). This case also decided that where the accused has served part of the original sentence, he must be given credit for time served against the later sentence.

Suppose the first trial never proceeds as far as a finding by the trier of fact; does it place the accused once in jeopardy? The Supreme Court does not require that jeopardy attach until, in a jury trial, the first juror is selected and sworn, Illinois v. Somerville, 410 U.S. 458, 93 S.Ct. 1066, 35 L.Ed.2d 425 (1973), or, in a court trial or juvenile proceeding, until the judge begins to hear evidence, Breed v. Jones, 421 U.S. 519, 95 S.Ct. 1779, 44 L.Ed.2d 346 (1975). Even if jeopardy has attached, in certain cases where a mistrial is declared there may be no bar against a retrial. If there is manifest necessity for a mistrial, as where the trial judge becomes incapacitated in circumstances where another cannot continue the trial, or where the jury cannot agree, there is no bar to a second trial; even where the necessity is not quite manifest, but there is merely a sound exercise of the trial judge's discretion, there may be no bar. Arizona v. Washington, 434 U.S. 497, 98 S.Ct. 824, 54 L.Ed.2d 717 (1978). Where the defendant himself seeks and obtains a mistrial he may invoke the jeopardy bar only if the conduct giving rise to his motion was prosecutorial or judicial misconduct *intended* to provoke the defendant into moving for a mistrial. Oregon v. Kennedy, 456 U.S. 667, 102 S.Ct. 2083, 72 L.Ed.2d 416 (1982).

Question

How far is the search for legislative purpose undertaken in the cases in this section a legitimate one? How far is it merely a method of rationalizing the preference of the opinion writer?

5. Drafting Exercises OMIT 371-373

Drafting is probably a larger part of most lawyers' work than trying cases in court. Lawyers are called upon to draft letters to and for clients, memoranda about facts and law, formal documents such as wills and contracts, and briefs and legislation. Techniques vary to some extent; patent specifications and claims do not bear much surface resemblance to motions for summary judgment or opinion letters. But there are rules of broad application.

First, you must form a reasonably clear notion of what it is you are trying to do. Limits will be present in such forms as instructions from clients, procedural rules for formal presentations, or governing legal principles. When you believe you know approximately what you want to do, write out a statement of this as clearly and completely as you can. You will almost certainly expose in this process some uncertainties and problems you were unaware of at the start. Resolve these as best you can.

Next, try to carry out the work as you have defined it in a form approaching the intended finished product. More problems will surface. As you work through these, you may find that your original conception of the end undergoes subtle changes—sometimes even drastic changes—as you enrich your understanding of the practical, legal, and verbal problems.

You will eventually emerge with a draft solution which seems pretty good. Next, try to read what you have written with a fresh and critical eye. Imagine an unfriendly interpreter of your language; this villain will, if possible, read your words in the wrong way. Make appropriate thwarting amendments, but be reasonable; you cannot protect yourself against the constructions of every perverse idiot. Simplify and tighten your prose where you can do so without distorting meaning.

When you are proud of your work, show it to others. They will probably help you to see new problems to be dealt with. Drafting by committee is likely to be frustrating and wasteful, but review of the draft by others is a powerful aid. One and a half wits is better than one.

Your study of the cases on statutory construction should help you, less by acquainting you with the rule of *ejusdem generis* than by alerting you to the uncertainties which may lurk in what is seemingly a clear statement. In the exercises which follow, imagine that you are the draftsman for a legislative commission. The commission is moderately but not overwhelmingly impressed by the Model Penal Code. For the present, it doesn't want to adopt the whole Code, but wants to add a few of its provisions to the amalgam of common law and statute now existing. Note that this means that you may have to deal specifically with some matters of justification and excuse left in the Model Penal Code to general provisions.

1. The commission would like a draft of a "failure to deal with a dangerous fire" provision based on Model Penal Code § 220.1(3). It wants failure to report the fire to be the offense, and it wants to state, more fully than the Code section does, proper justifications and excuses for failure to report. You have got this far:

> A person who knows that a fire is endangering life or a substantial amount of property in which a person, not consenting thereto, other than the defendant, has a possessory or proprietary interest, and who knows (a) that he is under an official or contractual duty to report, prevent, or combat the

fire, or (b) that the fire was caused, whether lawfully or not, by him or with his assent, or on property in his custody or control, and who fails to give a prompt fire alarm is guilty of failure to report a dangerous fire.

It is a defense to a prosecution under this section that:

Take it from there. Think carefully about what ought to be said. Don't worry about the penalty provision.

2. The commission is revamping the kidnapping provisions. The basic misdemeanor is to be called unlawful detention, and punishment is provided simply for one who "detains" another person. The heart of the provision is to be in the definition of "detains," and this definition is your task:

a. The definition must include a statement of the appropriate *mens rea*. To be guilty, the accused must realize that the detention is unlawful.

b. We must give a standard definition of the *actus reus* part of "detain," and also deal with custodial interference here. This can be mentioned in the definition and then defined separately.

c. In general the detention must be without consent of the victim, but this may mean something different from the usual thing in the case of a child. We must also consider that deception, rather than force, may be used by the accused.

d. Custodial interference in general means assumption of custody by one who is not a lawful custodian or authorized by a lawful custodian. (Don't bother to define lawful custodian; the commission will work on that later.) The age of the child has a bearing here. Children 16 or over can be treated as adults. Children 13 or over but not yet 16, may become runaways; we don't want to make criminals of kindly people who take these children in and don't harm them.

You may also have some other ideas to incorporate.

3. Try your skills outside the arson—burglary—kidnapping area.

The commission is considering a general "mistake of law" provision. It regards the Model Penal Code provision in § 2.04(3)(b) as too generous to the defense. You are perhaps not entirely sympathetic with the concerns of the commission, but you want to alleviate them while retaining the heart of the provision.

Some expressed concerns of members of the commission include:

a. Can any citizen reasonably rely on what he or she thinks a statute means?

b. Casual or offhand official statements should not be the basis for reliance.

c. Get rid of any reliance on "out-of-state" law.

You may think of other helpful limitations.

4. The commission would like you to draft a cruelty to animals provision. It is generally satisfied with Model Penal Code § 250.11, as far as it goes, but it is willing to listen to suggestions for improvement. (It is a little worried about prosecution of hunters and meat packers, and it is not sure that there should be a blanket exception for all medical research.) It also wants you to attempt definitions of "animal" and possibly "cruel" as used in the

provision, despite the opinion of the Institute that such attempts would not be profitable.

6. A Final Warning: Regina v. Ojibway

The following case comes to us from Canada and is unofficially reported in 8 Criminal Law Quarterly 137 (1965).* For a reason which you may be able to fathom, it has never been officially reported. It is, however, frequently referred to in legal circles, and it may constitute the last word on the perils of statutory interpretation.

(IN THE SUPREME COURT)

Regina v. Ojibway

BLUE, J. AUGUST, 1965

BLUE, J.: This is an appeal by the Crown by way of a stated case from a decision of the magistrate acquitting the accused of a charge under the Small Birds Act, R.S.O., 1960, c. 724, s. 2. The facts are not in dispute. Fred Ojibway, an Indian, was riding his pony through Queen's Park on January 2, 1965. Being impoverished, and having been forced to pledge his saddle, he substituted a downy pillow in lieu of the said saddle. On this particular day the accused's misfortune was further heightened by the circumstance of his pony breaking its right foreleg. In accord with Indian custom, the accused then shot the pony to relieve it of its awkwardness.

The accused was then charged with having breached the Small Birds Act, s. 2 of which states:

> 2. Anyone maiming, injuring or killing small birds is guilty of an offence and subject to a fine not in excess of two hundred dollars.

The learned magistrate acquitted the accused holding, in fact, that he had killed his horse and not a small bird. With respect, I cannot agree.

In light of the definition section my course is quite clear. Section 1 defines "bird" as "a two legged animal covered with feathers". There can be no doubt that this case is covered by this section.

Counsel for the accused made several ingenious arguments to which, in fairness, I must address myself. He submitted that the evidence of the expert clearly concluded that the animal in question was a pony and not a bird, but this is not the issue. We are not interested in whether the animal in question is a bird or not in fact, but whether it is one in law. Statutory interpretation has forced many a horse to eat birdseed for the rest of its life.

Counsel also contended that the neighing noise emitted by the animal could not possibly be produced by a bird. With respect, the sounds emitted by an animal are irrelevant to its nature, for a bird is no less a bird because it is silent.

Counsel for the accused also argued that since there was evidence to show accused had ridden the animal, this pointed to the fact that it could not be a bird but was actually a pony. Obviously, this avoids the issue. The issue is not whether the animal was ridden or not, but whether it was shot or not, for to ride a pony or a bird is of no offence at all. I believe counsel now sees his mistake.

Counsel contends that the iron shoes found on the animal decisively disqualify it from being a bird. I must inform counsel, however, that how an animal dresses is of no concern to this court.

Counsel relied on the decision in *Re Chicadee,* where he contends that in similar circumstances the accused was acquitted. However, this is a horse of a different colour. A close reading of that case indicates that the animal in question there was not a small bird, but, in fact, a midget of a much larger species. Therefore, that case is inapplicable to our facts.

Counsel finally submits that the word "small" in the title Small Birds Act refers not to "Birds" but to "Act", making it The Small Act relating to Birds. With respect, counsel did not do his homework very well, for the Large Birds Act, R.S.O. 1960, c. 725, is just as small. If pressed, I need only refer to the Small Loans Act R.S.O. 1960, c. 727 which is twice as large as the Large Birds Act.

It remains then to state my reason for judgment which, simply, is as follows: Different things may take on the same meaning for different purposes. For the purpose of the Small Birds Act, all two legged, feather-covered animals are birds. This, of course, does not imply that only two-legged animals qualify, for the legislative intent is to make two legs merely the minimum requirement. The statute therefore contemplated multi-legged animals with feathers as well. Counsel submits that having regard to the purpose of the statute only small animals "naturally covered" with feathers could have been contemplated. However, had this been the intention of the legislature, I am certain that the phrase "naturally covered" would have been expressly inserted just as 'Long' was inserted in the Longshoreman's Act.

Therefore, a horse with feathers on its back must be deemed for the purposes of this Act to be a bird, and *a fortiori,* a pony with feathers on its back is a small bird.

Counsel posed the following rhetorical question: If the pillow had been removed prior to the shooting, would the animal still be a bird? To this let me answer rhetorically: Is a bird any less of a bird without its feathers?

Appeal allowed.

Reported by: H. Pomerantz
S. Breslin

Chapter V

HOMICIDE; JUSTIFICATION, EXCUSE, AND MITIGATION; THE JUSTNESS AND MORALITY OF THE CRIMINAL LAW

A. INTRODUCTORY NOTE

1. The Nature of Homicide

Homicide is a principal substantive law topic for this chapter. In the development of the law of theft, problems of *mens rea* were relatively few; the difficult distinctions had to do with the *actus reus* requirements of the various theft offenses. The opposite is true of homicide. The act—causing the death of a human being—is fairly easily described and remains the same throughout the homicide offenses. It is the differences in mental state which produce the distinctions and most of the difficulties.

At common law and under all statutory plans, homicides may be criminal or non-criminal. Even intentional killings bring no criminal liability if they are justified (e.g., done by the official executioner pursuant to proper judicial order) or excused (e.g., committed while insane). Unintentional killings may be accidental or may involve too little fault to invoke criminal penalties (e.g., killings produced by no more than ordinary tort negligence). At common law criminal killings were murder, characterized by the presence of "malice aforethought" or "malice"—the terms are used interchangeably, or manslaughter, characterized by its absence. "Malice" is a technical term which here bears only a distant resemblance to the word in a non-legal context. Its exact legal meaning varies from one crime to another and even from one type of homicide to another. You will be able to arrive at an approximate definition of malice for each type of homicide we consider; if you put these definitions together you will be able to describe the various mental states which are necessary and sufficient to constitute murder at common law (always assuming, of course, the presence of the *actus reus* as well). The term is so complex that jurisdictions following the Model Penal Code have abandoned it, preferring to describe the various appropriate mental states differently.

At common law, there were no degrees of murder or manslaughter. In the United States most jurisdictions have by statute created degrees of murder, and some have created degrees of manslaughter. These degrees permit different punishments when the legislature believes differences are warranted. We will examine the typical situation of a jurisdiction having two degrees of murder. (Manslaughter is sometimes divided into voluntary and involuntary manslaughter. If not otherwise defined, voluntary manslaughter usually refers to manslaughters placed in Class I in the following paragraph, and involuntary manslaughter to those placed in Class II or Class III.)

Homicides can be divided roughly into three classes for purposes of study. Class I consists of cases in which the killer intends to kill or injure someone (not necessarily the person killed). Class II consists of cases in which no such intention exists, but in which the killer is reckless or negligent in causing death. Class III, not present in all jurisdictions, consists of cases in which the killer need not intend injury or death and need not be negligent, but is held liable because he causes a death in the course of committing some unlawful act, such as a robbery. We will study these three classes in order in this chapter. It may be useful to use a page of your notebook to make a chart in the following form:

	Class I	Class II	Class III
First degree murder			
Second degree murder			
Manslaughter			
No crime			

Fill in the boxes in the course of your study. Some will have several alternate entries. Some may be empty.

After looking at Class I murders and manslaughters, we will look at Class I killings which are not criminal because they are justified or excused. This will be an occasion for an extended and more general study of justification and excuse, which apply throughout the criminal law. Intentional killings present the clearest and most numerous instances of these problems, which can be efficiently studied in this context.

We will then go on to Class II killings, criminal and non-criminal. Next will come a look at the *actus reus* of homicide, including a more general study of the problem of causation, which you will need to know something about before studying the third class of killings, those committed in the course of unlawful acts. We will conclude with a look at the death penalty.

2. The Justness and Morality of the Criminal Law

Throughout this chapter we will also be concerned with the justness and morality of the criminal law. Are the particular legal principles we will study unfair or contrary to moral principles? In what way and for what reason?

Law is inevitably associated with moral and political theory. Among the important functions of law is the guidance of human conduct according to principles thought proper by the lawmaker. In the field of contracts the principal form of this guidance may be to provide a framework by which people can reach enforceable agreements. In criminal law the guidance is very direct. We wish to prevent certain conduct or punish it if we fail to prevent it. As we have noted in Chapter I, what the maker of criminal law undertakes to prevent largely depends on his moral and political views. What is wrong or unjust? What is an improper interference with liberty? What are unacceptable economic, political or moral costs of enforcement? These are questions in which the legal problems are inseparable from moral and political ones.

Some theories of law hold that morality is inseparable from law, in the sense that a law ceases to be a law when it becomes bad enough. Others sharply distinguish realms of law and morals in definition, but do not deny that there are important interrelationships and matters of joint concern. For our present purposes it is not necessary to choose among such theories; we merely wish to look closely at these interrelationships and joint concerns. It would be helpful, of course, to have full-blown ethical and political theories to tell us when a statute or decision is bad or unjust or an infringement on the liberties of the citizen, or at least to provide us with guidelines for testing these questions. Some of you may be able to bring to your consideration of legal problems a sophisticated philosophical approach. But many have little or no training in ethics or political theory. It is therefore useful to have simple guidelines for the initial testing process to enable members of the class to communicate intelligibly.

Questions raised about morals or political theory in the materials will usually assume a simple ethical utilitarianism. We will assume, in other words, that the goal of society is the greatest good for the greatest number. We will equate with good the production of pleasure [a]—broadly defined to include all kinds of things which produce happiness, from ice cream to music, from doing a job well to malicious contemplation of the misfortunes of others—and the prevention of pain, its reverse. We will ask of a rule of law or a judicial decision whether it tends to maximize happiness. We must take into account its effects, not only on the immediate participants (most prominently the accused and the victim), but also the effects on those (including other legislators and judges) who learn of the decision and perhaps modify their conduct on account of it.

There is a certain hopelessness in trying to calculate all of the ripple effects of a particular action. It certainly cannot be done with much precision. But it is a task which must be an important concern for legislators, lawyers, and judges. One must try to discover the relevant concerns and assign them rough weights. Jeremy Bentham, the nineteenth century founder of utilitarianism, proposed a felicific calculus to help in problems of measurement of pleasure or pain. We should, he said, consider intensity, duration, certainty of occurrence, propinquity, fecundity (likelihood of being followed by like and not by contrary feelings), and extent (number of those experiencing pleasure or pain).

Utilitarian theory presents a number of difficulties and ambiguities, some of which will be merely mentioned here:

1. Who or what counts as the relevant population whose pleasures and pains are to be considered? Do we take into account all sentient beings, as Bentham thought, or only human beings, or only law-abiding citizens, or what?

2. What is the relationship between "greatest good" and "greatest number"? It would seem that something which produces 1000 net units of pleasure spread among 700 people is to be preferred over an alternative which produces 1000 net units of pleasure to be divided among only 20 people. But, do we necessarily believe this? If a single unit of pleasure produces only the mildest of sensations, but 50 units of good experienced by a person means intense pleasure, some might prefer the latter alternative, perhaps with a lottery to pick the lucky 20. Do we prefer something which produces 1001 units of good for 20 people to an alternative which produces

a. Some utilitarians recognize other goods than pleasure, but we will consider utilitarianism in its most common form.

1000 units of good for 100 people? Do we maximize total pleasure even at the expense of reducing the "greatest number"?

3. How do we deal with what might be categorized as problems of concealed evil? Suppose a prosecutor is considering bringing charges against X for a murderous act of terrorism. The evidence of guilt would be convincing to a jury. X suffers from partial amnesia, but believes that he must have committed the act. The prosecutor alone knows, however, that X is innocent and that the real killer has died accidentally and cannot therefore be tried. The prosecutor is convinced that the deterrent effect of convicting and punishing X will have a dramatically beneficial result in reducing terrorism and will save scores of lives, and that if X is convicted, the truth will never be discovered. According to utilitarian precepts, must the prosecutor proceed with the trial of X under his duty to maximize pleasure? If we are utilitarians and we say no, it may be because we believe that the pain to the accused and his friends of the punishment, plus the pain to the prosecutor (in terms of guilt feelings) will outweigh the pain to be saved on account of the scores of murders which will be prevented. (Of course, our predictions as to the probability of conviction and, especially, the probability of deterrence, are somewhat uncertain, but all utilitarian calculations must be based on such predictions.) Perhaps the rational utilitarian prosecutor will feel no guilt; he acts from the highest utilitarian motives and does not, it may be thought, corrupt himself in any way. He is not even harming respect for the system of justice; nobody will ever know what he has done. We might try to avoid the uncomfortable result favoring prosecution by saying that the utilitarian actor must check his proposed action against general situations; he must ask whether he would be willing that others similarly situated act in the way he proposes to do. Should prosecutors prosecute the known innocent for deterrent effect if they believe they can pretty surely get away with it? Would such general conduct produce anti-utilitarian effects? But it is doubtful that we can really resolve the problem by this approach, since a careful answer to the last question might be "no." If we allow only the sincere and careful utilitarian prosecutor of good judgment so to act, we might be willing to extend permission to all in that position.

4. One thing which probably underlies our difficulties with the problem of X is our belief or half-belief that deliberate punishment of the innocent is an evil of such magnitude that it must be considered separately from its utilitarian effects. Perhaps there are certain liberties, such as freedom of speech, which are to be treated specially. Perhaps there are some values, such as human life, which tempt us to override the utilitarian calculus. If so, we are no longer utilitarians. Accepting the goal of utility only most of the time is not enough. If we accept an alternative value to that of the greatest good for the greatest number—a value which is not to be reduced to its qualities of pleasure and pain production—we reject utilitarianism. As you go through the cases, you might search for candidates for such alternative values and consider whether you can accept any of them.

A prime candidate for such an alternative is justice. Aristotle, in Book V of the *Nichomachean Ethics,* attempted to describe just and unjust actions among human beings. Justice, he believed, is not claiming an undue share of good things or evil things. In developing his concept of corrective justice, he assumed that human relationships are in balance before the first party delivers under a contract, or a person commits a tort or crime. The balance must then be restored by payment of an equivalent by the benefitted party. (Aristotle conceded the difficulty of deciding what is an equivalent and did not attempt to resolve it.) He also considered the idea of distributive justice, which deals with the distribution of social assets and liabilities in some equivalent fashion, perhaps equally, or according to desert, or to talent, or to contributions made.

In the example of the prosecutor and the terrorist, the argument against prosecution might have been stated in terms of injustice to the accused, and we might argue that we should sacrifice the utilitarian principle for the sake of justice. The early utilitarian John Stuart Mill thought that justice was almost always consistent with utilitarian principles, but that when it was not it ought to yield to the greatest good for the greatest number. Justice, he wrote in Chapter V of his essay on *Utilitarianism,* is not a wholly consistent concept; it combines a number of ideas, such as, not depriving one of his legal rights, not depriving one of his moral rights, returning good for good or evil for evil, not disappointing expectations one has knowingly and voluntarily created, acting impartially, and treating people equally. When these ideas point to different conclusions (as where, for example, one has improvidently promised more than a "fair" share of one's estate to one of three nephews), Mill believed that only the principle of utility could mediate the conflict.

While we leave open the possibility of alternative values such as justice, it is convenient to take an initial utilitarian stance to provide a framework for argument. Alternatives may properly be put forward when the utilitarian analysis is exhausted.

[The writings of Aristotle and Mill referred to are easily available in standard editions. For Bentham's views see Bowring's edition of the *Works of Jeremy Bentham: An Introduction to the Principles of Morals and Legislation* (1 *Works* 1); *Essay on the Influence of Time and Place in Matters of Legislation* (1 *Works* 169); and *Nomography; or the Art of Instituting Laws, Appendix* (3 *Works* at 286–287).]

B. KILLINGS IN WHICH THE ACCUSED INTENDS DEATH OR BODILY HARM

1. Introduction

a. *INTENTION AND KNOWLEDGE*

We begin with the most obvious sorts of cases; the accused is charged with killing another, intending death or bodily injury. A difficulty of classification immediately appears: Suppose in Model Penal Code terms, the accused has knowledge but not purpose; does he belong in this category? A wants to cut off communication from a remote farm to a town. With this purpose, he knocks out the supports of a crude bridge, an act which effectively isolates the farm. A knows that almost certainly this will kill B, a child then crossing the bridge towards the farm. A is indifferent to B's fate. B is in fact killed.

Should this case be treated as an "intentional" case (class I), as a "recklessness" case (class II), or does it require a separate category of its own? From a theoretical point of view, knowledge is neither intention nor recklessness, but, practically, it may be right to treat knowledge as though it were purpose in cases of this sort. If one knows that the consequences of his conduct are almost certain to include the death or serious injury of another, is he not morally and should he not be legally in the position of one who intends death or serious injury? The death or injury cannot be treated as some relatively trivial consequence of a course of action directed to some other end. Of course, whether the consequence is intended or merely known, there may be circumstances which might justify or excuse it. Perhaps A is insane; perhaps he takes the only practicable way to prevent someone from sending out a message which would cause the deaths of hundreds of innocent people.

The issue becomes more difficult as the seriousness of the injury known to be caused diminishes. Suppose, in our bridge case, A, taking a reasonable view of the probabilities, knows only that B will be shaken up when the bridge collapses, but does not expect him to fall more than a few feet or receive more than a slight battery. Contrary to reasonable expectations, B is killed. Should A be treated as though he intended the minor injury (not merely as though he knew it would occur) and death unexpectedly resulted? Traditionally, in that case, as we will see, A is guilty of manslaughter. If this result seems harsh for an intentional slight injury, it is even more harsh for this case. Perhaps the answer is that A should only be guilty of battery in either case. (I have assumed in this paragraph that we are considering prosecution on a Class I theory only; of course, to the extent that A's conduct is reckless with respect to the death or serious injury of the child, we may find liability on a Class II theory. As a practical matter, it is often difficult—and perhaps unnecessary—to distinguish a recklessness theory from an intentional injury theory in cases of intentional or knowing slight injury. However, one can imagine a state of facts which would pretty well eliminate a recklessness theory. Suppose A has consulted all of the best expert advice on the dangers to the child of his proposed course of conduct. All are in convincing agreement that the child will get no more than a shaking up. If they turn out to be wrong, an intentional injury theory of prosecution seems more convincing than a recklessness theory.)

Whatever the theoretical doubts, most courts treat knowledge as purpose in these Class I cases, except in one situation; where purpose to kill is legislatively required for first degree murder.

b. THE PRESUMPTION OF MALICE

At common law and under most statutory schemes, the "intentional" injury cases are subject to the presumption of malice. Malice in Class I cases means (1) "intention" to kill or to inflict grievous bodily harm (2) without justification, excuse, or mitigating circumstances. The presumption of malice provides that if the evidence establishes the first, affirmative, element of malice and there is no evidence, or at any rate no evidence sufficient to raise a jury question, as to the second, negative, element, then that second, negative, element is presumed. Intentional killings are therefore presumptively murders, and a murder verdict is proper if there is no credible evidence of justification, excuse, or mitigation. If any such evidence does appear, the presumption disappears, and the issue is in the case to be established or disproved by the side with the burden of persuasion. The situation is summarized in Gilbert v. State, 36 Md.App. 196, 198–200, 373 A.2d 311, 314–315 (1977), where it was undisputed that the accused had purposely caused the victim's death by shooting him in the chest with a gun:

Homicide in Maryland comes in five varieties—(1) justifiable, (2) excusable, (3) manslaughter, (4) second-degree murder and (5) first-degree murder. * * * The variations are not in the *actus* but in the *mens rea* of the actor—the degree of moral blameworthiness. * * *

In ascending the ladder of culpability, the State needs to establish that the killing was (1) not justified and (2) not excused in order to climb from the non-criminal first and second rungs up to the third rung, where criminally felonious liability first attaches. It must then establish that the killing was (3) not mitigated in order to climb on from the third rung (or manslaughter level) onto the higher rungs (where the killing is not mitigated and is, therefore, murder). It must finally establish premeditation and deliberation (or some equivalent * * *) in order to climb from the fourth rung (murder in the second degree) onto the fifth and top rung (murder in the first degree). It will be perceived that only the final probandum involves an affirmative element. The probandum required for each of the first three steps up the ladder of culpability is a negative element. Because such notions as justification, excuse and mitigation are not monolithic phenomena but come rather in infinite variety, anticipatory disproof of them in the abstract becomes a practical impossibility.

An example may serve to illustrate the absurdity of requiring anticipatory disproof of every consideration that might lower a homicidal *mens rea*. Posit a bank robber, armed and wearing a ski mask, apprehended at the bank door as a teller lies dead inside. It is hypothetically conceivable that the man in the ski mask is * * * a policeman in pursuit of a fleeing felon, a soldier in time of war, a threatened victim killing the teller in self-defense, the cleaner of a gun which went off by accident, a hot-blooded victim beaten by the teller, a hot-blooded combatant involved in a mutual affray with the teller, an outraged husband cuckolded by the teller, * * * etc., *ad infinitum*. There are a number of reasons why we do not require such anticipatory disproof by the State, not the least of which is the devastating impact it would have upon judicial economy. At the most fundamental level, however, we do not require it, because to require it would be an absurdity.

The device by which this relief is accomplished is called a presumption. The presumption operates in favor of the State. Absent some legally sufficient indication to the contrary, the homicide will be presumed to be not justified, not excused and not mitigated. Under the due process clause as interpreted by In Re Winship, 397 U.S. 358, 90 S.Ct. 1068, 25 L.Ed.2d 368 (1970) * * * such a presumption in a criminal case has constitutional limitations. It may shift to the defendant the burden of producing evidence sufficient to generate a genuine jury question as to one or more of the possible defensive issues. It may never shift to the defendant the heavier burden of ultimate persuasion. In its lesser function of shifting to the defendant merely the burden of producing evidence, the presumption dissipates or totally disappears ("the bubble bursts") as soon as the defendant has met his lesser burden of producing enough evidence to generate a genuine jury question. At that point, the State no longer has the benefit of the presumption. The State then assumes the burden of disproving, beyond a reasonable doubt, the defensive issue which has been generated. * * *.

2. Grading of Intentional Criminal Homicides

Intentional homicides, that is, homicides where death or injury is intended, are presumptively murder at common law because of the presumption of malice. In a jurisdiction which has two statutory degrees of murder, an intentional homicide is presumptively murder in the second degree. The prosecution must prove something more (beyond a reasonable doubt) to establish murder in the first degree. That "something more" is established by the legislatures of the various states. Commonly, the presence of premeditation, deliberation, and purpose to kill is enough to raise second degree murder to first, and there may be alternative possibilities. The defense may establish other facts which reduce second degree murder to manslaughter, or as we shall see when we study justification and excuse, even remove criminality altogether.

We will first examine the line between first and second degree murder. We will then look at those cases which are no more than second degree murder because the intention is not to kill, but only to injure, to see which of them are second degree murder and which manslaughter. Next, we will look at what may mitigate what would otherwise be murder to manslaughter.

Finally, we will look at the question of burden of persuasion as to elements of mitigation, excuse, and justification. This will prepare us for the next section, which deals with justification and excuse: matters which serve to acquit in cases of intentional homicide.

a. *PREMEDITATION, DELIBERATION, AND PURPOSE TO KILL*

Midgett v. State

Supreme Court of Arkansas, 1987.
292 Ark. 278, 729 S.W.2d 410.

NEWBERN, JUSTICE.

This child abuse case resulted in the appellant's conviction of first degree murder. The sole issue on appeal is whether the state's evidence was sufficient to sustain the conviction. We hold there was no evidence of the "* * * premeditated and deliberated purpose of causing the death of another person * * *" required for conviction of first degree murder by Ark.Stat.Ann. § 41–1502(1)(b) (Repl.1977). However, we find the evidence was sufficient to sustain a conviction of second degree murder, described in Ark.Stat.Ann. § 41–1503(1)(c) (Repl.1977), as the appellant was shown to have caused his son's death by delivering a blow to his abdomen or chest "* * * with the purpose of causing serious physical injury * * *." The conviction is thus modified from one of first degree murder to one of second degree murder and affirmed.

The facts of this case are as heart-rending as any we are likely to see. The appellant is six feet two inches tall and weighs 300 pounds. His son, Ronnie Midgett, Jr., was eight years old and weighed between thirty-eight and forty-five pounds. The evidence showed that Ronnie Jr. had been abused by brutal beating over a substantial period of time. Typically, as in other child abuse cases, the bruises had been noticed by school personnel, and a school counselor as well as a SCAN worker had gone to the Midgett home to inquire. Ronnie Jr. would not say how he had obtained the bruises or why he was so lethargic at school except to blame it all, vaguely, on a rough playing little brother. He did not even complain to his siblings about the treatment he was receiving from the appellant. His mother, the wife of the appellant, was not living in the home. The other children apparently were not being physically abused by the appellant.

Ronnie Jr.'s sister, Sherry, aged ten, testified that on the Saturday preceding the Wednesday of Ronnie Jr.'s death their father, the appellant, was drinking whiskey (two to three quarts that day) and beating on Ronnie Jr. She testified that the appellant would "bundle up his fist" and hit Ronnie Jr. in the stomach and in the back. On direct examination she said that she had not previously seen the appellant beat Ronnie Jr., but she had seen the appellant choke him for no particular reason on Sunday nights after she and Ronnie Jr. returned from church. On cross-examination, Sherry testified that Ronnie Jr. had lied and her father was, on that Saturday, trying to get him to tell the truth. She said the bruises on Ronnie Jr.'s body noticed over the preceding six months had been caused by the appellant. She said the beating administered on the Saturday in question consisted of four blows, two to the stomach and two to the back.

On the Wednesday Ronnie Jr. died, the appellant appeared at a hospital carrying the body. He told hospital personnel something was wrong with the child. An autopsy was performed, and it showed Ronnie Jr. was a very poorly nourished and under-developed eight-year-old. There were recently caused bruises on the lips, center of the chest plate, and forehead as well as on the back part of the lateral chest wall, the soft tissue near the spine, and the buttocks. There was discoloration of the abdominal wall and prominent bruising on the palms of the hands. Older bruises were found on the right temple, under the chin, and on the left mandible. Recent as well as older, healed, rib fractures were found.

The conclusion of the medical examiner who performed the autopsy was that Ronnie Jr. died as the result of intra-abdominal hemorrhage caused by a blunt force trauma consistent with having been delivered by a human fist. The appellant argues that in spite of all this evidence of child abuse, there is no evidence that he killed Ronnie Jr. having premeditated and deliberated causing his death. We must agree.

It is true that premeditation and deliberation may be found on the basis of circumstantial evidence. That was the holding in House v. State, 230 Ark. 622, 324 S.W.2d 112 (1959), where the evidence showed a twenty-four-year-old man killed a nineteen-year-old woman with whom he was attempting to have sexual intercourse. The evidence showed a protracted fight after which the appellant dumped the body in a water-filled ditch not knowing, according to House's testimony, whether she was dead or alive. Although it is not spelled out, presumably the rationale of the opinion was that House had time to premeditate during the fight and there was substantial evidence he intended the death of the victim when he left her in the water. Our only citation of authority on the point of showing premeditation and deliberation by circumstantial evidence in that case was Weldon v. State, 168 Ark. 534, 270 S.W. 968 (1925), where we said:

> The very manner in which the deadly weapons were used was sufficient to justify the jury in finding that whoever killed Jones used the weapons with a deliberate purpose to kill. Jones' body was perforated three times through the center with bullets from a pistol or rifle, and was also horribly mutilated with a knife. The manner, therefore, in which these deadly weapons were used tended to show that the death of Jones was the result of premeditation and deliberation.

While a fist may be a deadly weapon, the evidence of the use of the fist in this case is not comparable to the evidence in House v. State, supra, and Weldon v. State, supra, where there was some substantial evidence consisting of other circumstances that the appellant who dumped the apparently immobile body in the water and walked away and the appellant who wielded the deadly weapons intended and premeditated that death occur. Nor do we have in this case evidence of any remark made or other demonstration that the appellant was abusing his son in the hope that he eventually would die.

The annotation at 89 A.L.R.2d 396 (1963) deals with the subject of crimes resulting from excessive punishment of children. While some of the cases cited are ones in which a parent or stepparent flew into a one-time rage and killed the child, others are plain child abuse syndrome cases like the one before us now. None of them, with one exception, resulted in affirmance of a first degree murder conviction. Several were decisions in which first degree murder convictions were set aside for lack of evidence of premeditation and deliberation. The case cited in the annotation in which a first degree murder conviction was affirmed is Morris v. State, 270 Ind. 245, 384 N.E.2d 1022 (1979). There the appellant was left alone for about fifteen minutes with his five-month-old baby. When the child's mother returned to their home she found the baby had been burned severely on one side. About a month later, the appellant and his wife were engaged in an argument when the baby began to whine. The appellant laid the baby on the floor, began hitting the baby in the face and then hit the baby's head on the floor, causing the baby's death. At the time of the offense, the Indiana law required malice, purpose, and premeditation to convict of first degree murder. In discussing the premeditation requirement, the court said only:

> Premeditation which also may be inferred from the facts and circumstances surrounding the killing, need not long be deliberated upon, but may occur merely an instant before the act. [Citation omitted.] It is clear from the facts adduced at trial regarding the burning and beating of the child that the jury could well have inferred that his killing was perpetrated purposely and with premeditated malice. [384 N.E.2d at 1024]

No explanation is given for the quantum leap from "the facts," horrible as they were, to the inference of premeditation. We made the same error in Burnett v. State, 287 Ark. 158, 697 S.W.2d 95 (1985), another child abuse case in which the facts were particularly repugnant, where we said:

> Premeditation, deliberation and intent may be inferred from the circumstances of the case, such as the weapon used and the nature, extent and location of the wounds inflicted * * *. [T]he weapon used was a fist

which struck the abdomen with such force as to rupture the colon. The child sustained fingernail scratches, four broken ribs, and other internal damage, as well as numerous bruises due to blows with a fist all over his body. The required mental state for first degree murder can be inferred from the evidence of abuse, which is substantial. [287 Ark. at 162–163, 697 S.W.2d at 98]

The problem with these cases is that they give no reason, like the reasons found in House v. State, supra, and Weldon v. State, supra, to make the inference of premeditation and deliberation.

* * *

* * * The appellant argues, and we must agree, that in a case of child abuse of long duration the jury could well infer that the perpetrator comes not to expect death of the child from his action, but rather that the child will live so that the abuse may be administered again and again. Had the appellant planned his son's death, he could have accomplished it in a previous beating.

In this case the evidence might possibly support the inference that the blows which proved fatal to Ronnie Jr. could have been struck with the intent to cause his death developed in a drunken, misguided, and overheated attempt at disciplining him for not having told the truth. Even if we were to conclude there was substantial evidence from which the jury could fairly have found the appellant intended to cause Ronnie Jr.'s death in a drunken disciplinary beating on that Saturday, there would still be no evidence whatever of a premeditated and deliberated killing.

In Ford v. State, 276 Ark. 98, 633 S.W.2d 3, cert. den. 459 U.S. 1022, 103 S.Ct. 389, 74 L.Ed.2d 519 (1980), we held that to show the appellant acted with a premeditated and deliberated purpose, the state must prove that he (1) had the conscious object to cause death, (2) formed that intention before acting, and (3) weighed in his mind the consequences of a course of conduct, as distinguished from acting upon sudden impulse without the exercise of reasoning power. Viewing the evidence most favorable to the appellee, the circumstances of this case are not substantial evidence the appellant did (2) and (3), as opposed to acting on impulse or with no conscious object of causing death. The jury was thus forced to resort to speculation on these important elements.

A clear exposition of the premeditation and deliberation requirement which separates first degree from second degree murder is found in 2 W. LaFave and A. Scott, Jr., *Substantive Criminal Law* § 7.7 (1986):

> Almost all American jurisdictions which divide murder into degrees include the following two murder situations in the category of first degree murder: (1) intent-to-kill murder where there exists (in addition to the intent to kill) the elements of premeditation and deliberation, and (2) felony murder where the felony in question is one of five or six listed felonies, generally including rape, robbery, kidnapping, arson and burglary. Some states instead or in addition have other kinds of first degree murder.
>
> (a) Premeditated, Deliberate, Intentional Killing. To be guilty of this form of first degree murder the defendant must not only intend to kill but

in addition he must premeditate the killing and deliberate about it. It is not easy to give a meaningful definition of the words "premeditate" and "deliberate" as they are used in connection with first degree murder. Perhaps the best that can be said of "deliberation" is that it requires a cool mind that is capable of reflection, and of "premeditation" that it requires that the one with the cool mind did in fact reflect, at least for a short period of time before his act of killing.

It is often said that premeditation and deliberation require only a "brief moment of thought" or a "matter of seconds," and convictions for first degree murder have frequently been affirmed where such short periods of time were involved. The better view, however, is that to "speak of premeditation and deliberation which are instantaneous, or which take no appreciable time, * * * destroys the statutory distinction between first and second degree murder," and * * * this view is growing in popularity. This is not to say, however, that premeditation and deliberation cannot exist when the act of killing follows immediately after the formation of the intent. The intention may be finally formed only as a conclusion of prior premeditation and deliberation, while in other cases the intention may be formed without prior thought so that premeditation and deliberation occurs only with the passage of additional time for "further thought, and a turning over in the mind." [Footnotes omitted.]

The evidence in this case supports only the conclusion that the appellant intended not to kill his son but to further abuse him or that his intent, if it was to kill the child, was developed in a drunken, heated, rage while disciplining the child. Neither of those supports a finding of premeditation or deliberation.

Perhaps because they wish to punish more severely child abusers who kill their children, other states' legislatures have created laws permitting them to go beyond second degree murder. For example, Illinois has made aggravated battery one of the felonies qualifying for "felony murder," and a child abuser can be convicted of murder if the child dies as a result of aggravated battery. See People v. Ray, 80 Ill.App.3d 151, 35 Ill.Dec. 688, 399 N.E.2d 977 (1979). * * * Idaho has made murder by torture a first degree offense, regardless of intent of the perpetrator to kill the victim, and the offense is punishable by the death penalty. See State v. Stuart, 110 Idaho 163, 715 P.2d 833 (1985). * * *

All of this goes to show that there remains a difference between first and second degree murder, not only under our statute, but generally. Unless our law is changed to permit conviction of first degree murder for something like child abuse or torture resulting in death, our duty is to give those accused of first degree murder the benefit of the requirement that they be shown by substantial evidence to have premeditated and deliberated the killing, no matter how heinous the facts may otherwise be. We understand and appreciate the state's citation of Burnett v. State, supra, but, to the extent it is inconsistent with this opinion, we must overrule it.

The dissenting opinion begins by stating the majority concludes that one who starves and beats a child to death cannot be convicted of murder. That is not so, as we are affirming the conviction of murder; we are, however, reducing it to second degree murder. The dissenting opinion's conclusion that the appellant starved Ronnie Jr., must be based solely on the child's underdeveloped condition which could, presumably, have been caused by any number of physical malfunctions. There is no evidence the appellant starved the child. The dissenting opinion says it is for the jury to determine the degree of murder of which the appellant is guilty. That is true so long as there is substantial evidence to support the jury's choice. The point of this opinion is to note that there was no evidence of premeditation or deliberation which are required elements of the crime of first degree murder. * * *

In this case we have no difficulty with reducing the sentence to the maximum for second degree murder. Dixon v. State, 260 Ark. 857, 545 S.W.2d 606 (1977). The jury gave the appellant a sentence of forty years imprisonment which was the maximum for first degree murder, and we reduce that to twenty years which is the maximum imprisonment for second degree murder. Just as walking away from the victim in the water-filled ditch in House v. State, supra, after a protracted fight, and the "overkill" and mutilation of the body in Weldon v. State, supra, were circumstances creating substantial evidence of premeditation and deliberation, the obvious effect the beatings were having on Ronnie Jr. and his emaciated condition when the final beating occurred are circumstances constituting substantial evidence that the appellant's purpose was to cause serious physical injury, and that he caused his death in the process. * * *

Affirmed as modified.

HICKMAN, HAYS and GLAZE, JJ., dissent.

HICKMAN, JUSTICE, dissenting.

* * *

Convictions for murder resulting from child abuse have become more common in our courts. That is probably because such cases are being reported more often and prosecutors are more apt to seek retribution.

* * *

In this case the majority, with clairvoyance, decides that this parent did not intend to kill his child, but rather to keep him alive for further abuse. This is not a child neglect case. The state proved Midgett starved the boy, choked him, and struck him several times in the stomach and back. The jury could easily conclude that such repeated treatment was intended to kill the child.

* * *

Note on the Standard Formula

The Origin of the Formula

At common law, all murders were subject to the death penalty. One way the states found to reduce the number of executions was to divide murder into two or (in a few jurisdictions, more than two) degrees and make the death penalty applicable only to murders in the first degree. In intentional killings, one plausible division is according to whether the killing is planned or impulsive; this distinction became the basis for most statutory classifications. Those who killed with a deliberate and premeditated design to cause death were first degree murderers and subject to the death penalty. (Later, not all first degree murders were capital.) Other common law murderers who killed while intending to kill or injure, unless perhaps they fit into some other narrowly defined statutory category which the jurisdiction might have adopted (such as killers by poison or torture), were guilty of murder in the second degree.

Problems With the Formula

One problem is really evidentiary. We may understand what the test means but not be sure how we go about establishing that the defendant does or does not meet it. Sometimes the circumstances permit us to say with confidence that the accused plainly planned to kill. A scheme to do so may have been carefully worked out and disclosed to others weeks before it was carried out. More commonly, as in *Midgett,* it may be hard to be sure (1) that the killer meant to kill rather than merely to injure, or (2) that he actually premeditated and deliberated his actions. The jury may properly use the circumstances of the killing as a guide here.

The so-called deadly weapon rule allows an almost self-evident conclusion: If the defendant intentionally uses a weapon which is likely to cause death, in a way in which its deadly potential is likely to be realized, on a vitally vulnerable part of the victim's body, and the victim dies from the wound, the jury is permitted to conclude that the defendant meant to kill the victim. So, if the defendant aims a pistol from a few feet away at the victim's heart, and the bullet kills him, the jury may find an intentional killing.

In a more general way, the jury may draw sensible conclusions from the circumstances. Suppose the jury believes that the ordinary person would have had sufficient time to premeditate and deliberate and would not have acted as the accused did unless he meant to kill. If they find that the accused is such an ordinary person, and not, for example, mentally slow, they may conclude that the accused did premeditate and deliberate and intend to kill. Note that the ultimate question is subjective: what actually went on in this defendant's mind. The reasonable person is a helpful, but not a conclusive, guide to resolution of this problem.

The major problem with the formula is more basic: How literally do we take the requirements of premeditation and deliberation? Do we give them their full meaning and require careful weighing of the choice over a substantial period of time, do we say that the slightest forethought is enough, or do we draw a line somewhere in between? The excerpts from the Royal Commission on Capital Punishment and the cases which follow explore this problem.

a. Report of the Royal Commission on Capital Punishment, 1949–1953, at p. 183: *

> 520. Although "deliberate and premeditated" killing is murder in the first degree in all the States in which murder has been graded, the meaning given to these terms is seldom that which they bear in ordinary usage. There

* Extract from Cmd 8932, Report of the Royal Commission on Capital Punishment (1949–1953). Reproduced with the permission of the Controller of Her Britannic Majesty's Stationery Office.

seems to be little doubt that in the original Pennsylvania Statute, these words, which go back to a statute introduced by William Penn in 1682, were used advisedly and were intended to have their literal meaning. This is borne out by the discussions leading to the enactment of the Act of 1794 and by the words "by poison or by lying in wait or by any other kind of wilful, deliberate and premeditated killing". Yet before the year was out a Judge had said that "if the design of killing be formed previous to the act, I am inclined to believe it is the true meaning of the law, that it is murder in the first degree"; and this view was adopted in several other Pennsylvania cases before the end of the century.[3] This interpretation, which in substance reduces the concept to no more than "intent to kill", has since been followed by the majority of States.[a] Premeditation seems nowhere to require the lapse of a substantial time between design and action. In a few States deliberation has been held to imply an element of calm reflection; in Missouri, for example, it has been said that it can be exercised only in "a cool state of the blood", not in "the heat of passion".[4] This view is, however, exceptional. * * *

b. Smith v. State, 41 Md.App. 277, 317–320, 398 A.2d 426, 448–450 (1979): [b]

* * * "Deliberation and premeditation may be instantaneous." Aldridge v. United States, 60 App.D.C. 45, 46, 47 F.2d 407, 408 (1931). "The period of time required for premeditation [and deliberation] in first-degree murder is only that which is necessary for one thought to follow another." Bradney v. People, 162 Colo. 403, 426 P.2d 765 (1967). For a killing to be premeditated there

3. Keedy, *History of the Pennsylvania Statute Creating Degrees of Murder,* 97 University of Pennsylvania Law Review 759 ff.

a. The interpretation here suggested may not be quite as drastic as it seems. See, for example the early leading case of Commonwealth v. Drum, 58 Pa. 9, 16 (1868), where the first quoted paragraph seems to support the Commission's view, but the second modifies it:

> In this case we have to deal only with that kind of murder in the first degree described as "wilful, deliberate, and premeditated." Many cases have been decided under this clause, in all of which it has been held that the *intention* to kill is the essence of the offence. Therefore, if an intention to kill exists, it is wilful; if this intention be accompanied by such circumstances as evidence a mind fully conscious of its own purpose and design, it is deliberate; and if sufficient time be afforded to enable the mind fully to frame the design to kill, and to select the instrument, or to frame the plan to carry this design into execution, it is premeditated. The law fixes upon no length of time as necessary to form the intention to kill, but leaves the existence of a fully formed intent as a fact to be determined by the jury, from all the facts and circumstances in the evidence.
>
> A learned judge (Judge Rush, in Commonwealth v. Richard Smith) has said: "It is equally true both in fact and from experience, that *no* time is too short for a wicked man to frame in his mind his scheme of murder, and to contrive the means of accomplishing it." But this expression must be qualified, lest it mislead. It is true that such is the swiftness of human thought, that no time is so short in which a wicked man may not form a design to kill, and frame the means of executing his purpose; yet this suddenness is opposed to premeditation, and a jury must be well convinced upon the evidence that there was time to deliberate and premeditate. The law regards, and the jury must find, the actual intent; that is to say, the fully formed purpose to kill, with so much time for deliberation and premeditation, as to convince them that this purpose is not the immediate offspring of rashness and impetuous temper, and that the mind has become fully conscious of its own design. If there be time to frame in the mind, fully and consciously, the intention to kill, and to select the weapon or means of death, and to think and know beforehand, though the time be short, the use to be made of it, there is time to deliberate and to premeditate.

4. State v. Kotovsky, 74 Mo. 247 [1881].

b. The Maryland Court of Appeals repudiated this view; it requires an appreciable time for premeditation and deliberation, in accordance with earlier Maryland cases, in Ferrell v. State, 304 Md. 679, 500 A.2d 1050 (1985).

"need be no appreciable space of time between the intention to kill and the killing—they may be as instantaneous as successive thoughts of the mind." Carey v. State, 91 Idaho 706, 429 P.2d 836, 840 (1967). * * * In People v. Jackson, 196 N.Y. 357, 89 N.E. 924, 925, the Court of Appeals of New York affirmed a conviction based upon the following charge:

> "But the time that elapses which shows deliberation need not be a day. It need not be a minute. It may be a second, or a fraction of it. It must be time enough so that reasons arise for not doing the act thought of, and so that the mind makes its choice and decides to do that which was done."

This diminution of the time interval virtually to the vanishing point is illustrated by the following definitions of the necessary interval: "only an instant," State v. Masato Karumai, 101 Utah 592, 600, 126 P.2d 1047, 1051 (1942); "no particular time," Bailey v. Commonwealth, 191 Va. 510, 62 S.E.2d 28, 31 (1950); "thought beforehand * * * however short," State v. Lamn, 232 N.C. 402, 406, 61 S.E.2d 188, 191 (1950) * * *.

The same process has been inexorably at work in Maryland. The evidence was found to be legally sufficient to support deliberation and premeditation in the following questionable circumstances: Houston v. State, 225 Md. 403, 171 A.2d 233 (1961) (a street fight where the defendant only turned upon the victim at the moment when the victim attempted to dissuade him from killing another); Cook v. State, 225 Md. 603, 171 A.2d 460 (1961) (an unexplained killing following a drunken quarrel); Taylor v. State, 226 Md. 561, 174 A.2d 573 (1961) (a drunken quarrel with the time interval being represented by the time necessary to walk across the room, pick up a gun, raise it and fire it). * * *

There yet may be, however, some residual function for the word "premeditated" or, at least, for the fuller phrase "wilful, deliberate and premeditated." When dealing with murder of the specific-intent-to-kill variety, it would not appear that there is any necessary content, as an absolute matter of law, to the words. Whenever there is evidence of a specific intent to kill, it follows that there is at least a permitted inference of wilfulness, deliberation and premeditation as these terms have been liberally interpreted by latter-day case law. To the extent to which there is some arguable nuance of difference between second-degree murder of the specific-intent-to-kill variety and first-degree murder of that same variety, the preciously small cargo of metaphysical difference would seem to be carried exclusively by the adjective "deliberate" rather than by its two companions. The lack of necessary additional content, however, does not preclude the *possibility* of additional content whenever a jury might wish to read in such additional content. The very ambiguity of the terms would seem to give the jurors the discretion to move upward to a first-degree verdict whenever the circumstances of heinousness and atrociousness inspire them to move upward and yet permit them to move downward to a second-degree verdict when some undifferentiated compassion persuades them to move downward. * * *

c. State v. Rutten, 13 Wash. 203, 211–213, 43 P. 30, 32 (1895):

> * * * Our statute defines murder in the first degree as follows: "Every person who shall purposely, and of deliberate and premeditated malice, * * * kill another, shall be deemed guilty of murder in the first degree. * * *" * * * The court properly instructed the jury, after reciting the statute, that the main distinction between murder in the first degree and murder in the second degree was the presence or absence of premeditation

or deliberation. * * * And in count 21 the court * * * said: "In deliberating, there need be no appreciable space of time between the intention to kill and the act of killing. That may be as instantaneous as the successive thoughts of the mind. It is only necessary that the act of killing be preceded by a concurrence of will, deliberated and premeditated, on the part of the slayer; and, if such is the case, the killing is murder in the first degree, no matter how rapidly the acts of the mind may succeed each other, or how quickly they may be followed by the act of killing." It seems to us that the language used wipes out the distinction made in the statute between murder in the first and second degree. While no great amount of time necessarily intervenes between the intention to kill and the act of killing, yet, under our statute, there must be time enough to deliberate, and no deliberation can be instantaneous. * * * [D]eliberation means to weigh in the mind, to consider the reasons for and against, and consider maturely, to reflect upon; and while it may be difficult to determine just how short a time it will require for the mind to deliberate, yet, if any effect is to be given to the statute which makes a difference between murder in the first and second degree, the language used by the learned court is too broad. * * *

d. People v. Anderson, 70 Cal.2d 15, 26–27, 73 Cal.Rptr. 550, 557, 447 P.2d 942, 949 (1968):

The type of evidence which this court has found sufficient to sustain a finding of premeditation and deliberation falls into three basic categories: (1) facts about how and what defendant did *prior* to the actual killing which show that the defendant was engaged in activity directed toward, and explicable as intended to result in, the killing—what may be characterized as "planning" activity; (2) facts about the defendant's *prior* relationship and/or conduct with the victim from which the jury could reasonably infer a "motive" to kill the victim, which inference of motive, together with facts of type (1) or (3), would in turn support an inference that the killing was the result of "a pre-existing reflection" and "careful thought and weighing of considerations" rather than "mere unconsidered or rash impulse hastily executed" (People v. Thomas, supra, 25 Cal.2d 880, at pp. 898, 900, 901, 156 P.2d 7, at p. 14); (3) facts about the nature of the killing from which the jury could infer that the *manner* of killing was so particular and exacting that the defendant must have intentionally killed according to a "preconceived design" to take his victim's life in a particular way for a "reason" which the jury can reasonably infer from facts of type (1) or (2).

Analysis of the cases will show that this court sustains verdicts of first degree murder typically when there is evidence of all three types and otherwise requires at least extremely strong evidence of (1) or evidence of (2) in conjunction with either (1) or (3).

Cases Possibly Misclassified Under the Formula

In General: Other problems have been identified. The Report of the Royal Commission on Capital Punishment, 1949–1953, at pp. 174–175,* notes:

* Extract from Cmd 8932, Report of the Royal Commission on Capital Punishment (1949–1953). Reproduced with the permission of the Controller of Her Britannic Majesty's Stationery Office.

500. If "premeditation" and "deliberation" are taken in their ordinary sense,[8] the idea that the worst murders, and those deserving of capital punishment, are "planned and cold-blooded" murders appears at first sight to accord with natural feelings; but, although such murders may indeed be among the most heinous, a little reflection serves to show that premeditation, or deliberation, or both together, are nevertheless entirely inadequate criteria. The objections to premeditation were summarised as follows in the Home Office memorandum:

> "Among the worst murders are some which are not premeditated, such as murders committed in connection with rape, or murders committed by criminals who are interrupted in some felonious enterprise and use violence without premeditation, but with a reckless disregard of the consequences to human life. Some of the murders for which the death penalty is most obviously inappropriate are premeditated, for example, so-called 'mercy' murders, suicide pacts and murders of children by mothers in pitiful circumstances not covered by the Infanticide Act. There are also many murders where the killing is clearly intentional, unlawful, and unaccompanied by any mitigating circumstances, but where there is no evidence to show whether there was or was not premeditation."

That is to say, the criterion is at once too wide and too narrow. The examples cited by the Home Office of murders which are not premeditated but are among the most heinous would, it is true, be included in the second category proposed by the Royal Commission of 1866, but there are many heinous murders committed suddenly on little or no provocation which would not be so included. We may quote the examples given by Stephen:[9]

> "As much cruelty, as much indifference to the life of others, a disposition at least as dangerous to society, probably even more dangerous, is shown by sudden as by premeditated murders. The following cases appear to me to set this in a clear light. A, passing along the road, sees a boy sitting on a bridge over a deep river and, out of mere wanton barbarity, pushes him into it and so drowns him. A man makes advances to a girl who repels him. He deliberately but instantly cuts her throat. A man civilly asked to pay a just debt pretends to get the money, loads a rifle and blows out his creditor's brains. In none of these cases is there premeditation unless the word is used in a sense as unnatural as 'aforethought' in 'malice aforethought', but each represents even more diabolical cruelty and ferocity than that which is involved in murders premeditated in the natural sense of the word."

8. "*Premeditation.* * * *. Previous deliberation upon or thinking out of something to be done; now esp. designing, planning or contrivance to do something."

"*Premeditated.* Considered, contemplated, or composed beforehand; previously contrived or planned."

"*Deliberation.* The action of deliberating, or weighing a thing in the mind; careful consideration with a view to decision."

"*Deliberate.* Well weighed or considered; carefully thought out; formed, carried out, etc. with careful consideration and full intention; done of set purpose; studied; not hasty or rash."

Oxford English Dictionary.

9. *History of the Criminal Law,* III, 94.

We should agree with the view expressed by Professor Wechsler that "an impulsive killing, resting on the slightest provocation, hardly presents a stronger case for mitigation than a homicide committed after genuine internal struggle in response to a strong provocation (in the largest sense of the extrinsic causes of the homicide). The very fact of the internal struggle may be evidence that the defendant's homicidal impulse was entirely aberrational, far more the product of extraordinary circumstances than true reflection of the actor's normal self". Thus a sudden killing may be the direct expression of an incorrigibly vicious nature, while a premeditated and deliberate murder may be among the most excusable. This would be true not only of such offences as those mentioned by the Home Office, but also in such cases as when a husband kills a wife who has persistently flaunted her infidelity or a wife kills a cruel and brutal husband.

Mercy Killings: As noted, the formula would make "mercy killings" first degree murder, and only on sentencing would the motive of the accused be taken into account. Should mercy killings be made second degree murder or be removed altogether from the murder category? Consider the Report of the Royal Commission on Capital Punishment, 1949–1953, at pp. 63–64: *

177. Murders are committed from time to time in circumstances where it is clear that there can be no question of exacting the extreme penalty, as, for example, where a mother has killed her child or a husband has killed his wife from merciful motives of pity and humanity. In cases of this kind the solemn pronouncing of the death sentence is a painful and distressing ordeal which everyone concerned would wish, if it were possible, to avoid. We therefore approached the proposal that such cases should be taken out of the category of murder with the hope that this might be found practicable. There can be no doubt, however, that it is open to very serious objections. * * *

178. The Archbishop of Canterbury considered that it would be wrong in principle to take "mercy killings" out of the category of murder. A deliberate and intentional killing, whatever the motive, was murder and nothing else. "The law ought to adjust the penalty to suit the circumstances of the act, but the law ought not to call the act something different from what it is." The word "murder" was itself a strong moral deterrent, which ought not to be lightly removed from categories of killing which are, in the proper sense of the word, murders. * * *

179. This view was reinforced by the objections of other witnesses on different grounds. They thought it would be most dangerous to provide that "mercy killings" should not be murder, because it would be impossible to define a category which could not be seriously abused. Such a definition could only be in terms of the motive of the offender, but both English and Scottish law have always eschewed definitions in terms of motive, which is notoriously difficult to establish and cannot, like intent, be inferred from a person's overt actions. Moreover it was agreed by almost all witnesses, * * * that, even if such a definition could be devised, it would in practice often prove extremely difficult to distinguish killings where the motive was

* Extract from Cmd 8932, Report of the Royal Commission on Capital Punishment (1949–1953). Reproduced with the permission of the Controller of Her Britannic Majesty's Stationery Office.

merciful from those where it was not. How, for example, were the jury to decide whether a daughter had killed her invalid father from compassion, from a desire for material gain, from a natural wish to bring to an end a trying period of her life, or from a combination of motives?

Questions

1. Are murders by poison or lying in wait in the Pennsylvania formula ["by poison or by lying in wait or by any other kind of wilful, deliberate and premeditated killing"] merely examples of the more general class of intentional, premeditated, and deliberate killings? What difference does it make?

2. Any formula for division of murder into degrees is likely to misclassify, in the minds of many, a few of the factual situations to which it is to be applied. If a division is to be made, can the premeditation, deliberation, purpose formula be improved? Compare the Model Penal Code, § 210.6, which does not propose degrees of murder, but which does suggest methods of identifying those murders eligible for capital punishment in jurisdictions which choose to retain it. We will return to the problem when we consider the death penalty at the end of the chapter.

3. How, if at all, does it affect "the greatest good for the greatest number" to divide murder into degrees according to the premeditation/deliberation/purpose to kill formula, or any other formula?

b. INTENTION TO INJURE

Director of Public Prosecutions v. Smith

House of Lords, 1961.
[1961] A.C. 290.

The facts stated by Viscount Kilmuir L.C. were as follows: At about 7:30 p.m. on March 2, 1960, the respondent, accompanied by a man named Artus, was driving a Ford Prefect motor-car through Woolwich. In the boot and the back of the car were sacks containing scaffolding clips that they had just stolen. The car was stopped in Beresford Square by the police officer on point duty in the normal course of traffic control and, while it was so stopped, P.C. Meehan, who was acquainted with the respondent, came to the driver's window and spoke to him. No doubt as a result of what P.C. Meehan saw in the back of the car he told the respondent when the traffic was released to draw in to his near-side. The respondent began to do so and P.C. Meehan walked beside the car. Suddenly, however, the respondent accelerated along Plumstead Road and P.C. Meehan began to run with the car, shouting to the officer on point duty to get on to the police station. Despite the fact that the respondent's car had no running board, P.C. Meehan succeeded in hanging on and never let go until some 130 yards up Plumstead Road when he was thrown off the car and under a bubble car coming in the opposite direction, suffering a crushed skull and other injuries from which he died.

* * *

After P.C. Meehan had been thrown off, the respondent drove his car a little further up Plumstead Road and into a side turning where he and Artus threw the sacks of clips out of the car. Artus then went off but the respondent returned to the scene. According to P.C. Weatherill the respondent first asked: "Is he dead?" and then, on being told that it was believed so, he said: "I knew the man. I wouldn't do that for the world. I only wanted to shake him off." * * *

* * *

July 28. VISCOUNT KILMUIR L.C. * * *

In his final direction to the jury the trial judge, Donovan J., said: "If you are satisfied that * * * he must as a reasonable man have contemplated that grievous bodily harm was likely to result to that officer * * * and that such harm did happen and the officer died in consequence, then the accused is guilty of capital murder. * * * On the other hand, if you are not satisfied that he intended to inflict grievous bodily harm upon the officer—in other words, if you think he could not as a reasonable man have contemplated that grievous bodily harm would result to the officer in consequence of his actions—well, then, the verdict would be guilty of manslaughter."

The respondent appealed to the Court of Criminal Appeal alleging misdirection by the trial judge, the main ground being that the direction cited above was wrong in that the question for the jury was what he, the respondent, in fact contemplated. The appeal was heard by the Court of Criminal Appeal on May 9 and 10, 1960, when the court allowed the appeal, substituted a verdict of guilty of manslaughter and imposed a sentence of 10 years' imprisonment. The court gave its reasons on May 18, 1960. They upheld the respondent's contention, holding that "there always remained the question whether the appellant" (the present respondent) "really did * * * realise what was the degree of likelihood of serious injury."

* * *

The main complaint is that the learned judge was there applying what is referred to as an objective test, namely, the test of what a reasonable man would contemplate as the probable result of his acts, and therefore would intend, whereas the question for the jury, it is said, was what the respondent himself intended. This, indeed, was the view of the Court of Criminal Appeal * * *.

* * * Unless the jury were satisfied that he in fact had such contemplation, the necessary intent to constitute malice would not in their view, have been proved. This purely subjective approach involves this, that if an accused said that he did not in fact think of the consequences, and the jury considered that that might well be true, he would be entitled to be acquitted of murder.

My Lords, the proposition has only to be stated thus to make one realise what a departure it is from that upon which the courts have always acted. The jury must, of course, in such a case as the present make up their minds on the evidence whether the accused was unlawfully and voluntarily doing something to someone. The unlawful and voluntary act must clearly be aimed at someone in order to eliminate cases of negligence or of careless or dangerous driving. Once, however, the jury are satisfied as to that, it matters not what the accused in fact contemplated as the probable result or whether he ever contemplated at all, provided he was in law responsible and accountable for his actions, that is, was a man capable of forming an intent, not insane within the M'Naghten Rules and not suffering from diminished responsibility. On the assumption that he is so accountable for his actions, the sole question is whether the unlawful and voluntary act was of such a kind that grievous bodily harm was the natural and probable result. The only test available for this is what the ordinary responsible man would, in all the circumstances of the case, have contemplated as the natural and probable result. * * *

* * *

The last criticism of the summing-up which was raised before your Lordships was in regard to the meaning which the learned judge directed the jury was to be given to the words "grievous bodily harm." The passages of which complaint is made are the following: "When one speaks of an intent to inflict grievous bodily harm upon a person, the expression grievous bodily harm does not mean for that purpose some harm which is permanent or even dangerous. It simply means some harm which is sufficient seriously to interfere with the victim's health or comfort."

* * *

The direction in these passages was clearly based on the well known direction of Willes J. in Reg. v. Ashman [17] * * *. * * *

My Lords, I confess that * * * I can find no warrant for giving the words "grievous bodily harm" a meaning other than that which the words convey in their ordinary and natural meaning. "Bodily harm" needs no explanation, and "grievous" means no more and no less than "really serious." * * *

It was, however, contended before your Lordships on behalf of the respondent that the words ought to be given a more restricted meaning in considering the intent necessary to establish malice in a murder case. It was said that the intent must be to do an act "obviously dangerous to life" or "likely to kill." It is true that in many of the cases the likelihood of death resulting has been incorporated into the definition of grievous bodily harm, but this was done, no doubt, merely to emphasise that the bodily harm must be really serious, and it is unnecessary, and I would add inadvisable, to add anything to the expression "grievous bodily harm" in its ordinary and natural meaning.

To return to the summing-up in the present case, it is true that in the two passages cited the learned judge referred to "grievous bodily harm" in the terms used by Willes J. in *Reg. v. Ashman,* but in no less than four further passages, and in particular in the vital direction given just before the jury retired, he referred to "serious hurt" or "serious harm." Read as a whole, it is, I think, clear that there was no misdirection. Further, on the facts of this case it is quite impossible to say that the harm which the respondent must be taken to have contemplated could be anything but of a very serious nature coming well within the term "grievous bodily harm."

* * *

In the result the appeal should, in my opinion, be allowed and the conviction of capital murder restored.

17. (1858) 1 F. & F. 88.

Notes

1. *Application of the Objective Standard.* In Reg. v. Ward, [1956] 1 Q.B. 351, a babysitter of subnormal intelligence accidentally strangled an eighteen month old child when he shook her to stop her crying. An objective standard was applied and the defendant was convicted of murder; the jury found that a reasonable person would have anticipated serious harm from the defendant's actions.

2. *Parliamentary Response.* Criminal Justice Act, 1967, c. 80, § 8:

> A court or jury, in determining whether a person has committed an offence,—
>
> (a) shall not be bound in law to infer that he intended or foresaw a result of his actions by reason only of its being a natural and probable consequence of those actions; but
>
> (b) shall decide whether he did intend or foresee that result by reference to all the evidence, drawing such inferences from the evidence as appear proper in the circumstances.

3. *Subsequent Case.* In Reg. v. Cunningham, [1982] A.C. 566 (H.L., 1981), the following jury instruction was approved:

> As a matter of law, the question of fact on which your verdict depends is solely this * * * "At the time when the defendant inflicted the injuries on Kim * * * did he intend to do him really serious harm?" If the answer to that question is "yes," you find him guilty of murder. If the answer to the question is "no," then you find him not guilty of murder, but guilty of manslaughter. [Quoted at p. 573.]

(It was conceded by the defendant that he was guilty at least of manslaughter.) The Lord Chancellor rejected a suggestion found in a dissenting judgment in Reg. v. Hyam, [1975] A.C. 55, that at least an intention to endanger life should be required for murder.

Question

Much modern American authority treats cases in which injury but not death is intended under the heading of reckless killing rather than, as the common law did, as cases of intentional homicide. See, e.g., Model Penal Code §§ 210.2, Comment 5, and 210.3, Comment 8 (Official Draft 1980). Does it make any practical difference which approach is taken? If so, which is more apt to lead to just results?

c. PROVOCATION AND RELATED PROBLEMS

State v. Ott

Supreme Court of Oregon, In Banc, 1984.
297 Or. 375, 686 P.2d 1001.

LENT, JUSTICE.

The primary issue is how a jury is to be instructed on "extreme emotional disturbance" for the purpose of determining whether a criminal homicide [1] is

1. ORS 163.005 in pertinent part provides:

"(1) A person commits criminal homicide if, without justification or excuse, he intentionally * * * causes the death of another human being.

"(2) 'Criminal homicide' is murder, manslaughter or criminally negligent homicide."

murder or manslaughter. The defendant was charged with murder for killing his wife in April, 1980. It is undisputed that the defendant killed her intentionally; the dispute is whether he was under the influence of extreme emotional disturbance. If he was, he would be guilty of manslaughter rather than murder.[2]

At that time[3] ORS 163.115 provided:

"(1) * * * [C]riminal homicide constitutes murder when:

"(a) It is committed intentionally by a person who is not under the influence of an extreme emotional disturbance.

"* * *

"(2) For the purposes of paragraph (a) of subsection (1) of this section, a homicide which would otherwise be murder is committed under the influence of extreme emotional disturbance when such disturbance is not the result of the person's own intentional, knowing, reckless or criminally negligent act, and for which disturbance there is a reasonable explanation. The reasonableness of the explanation for the disturbance shall be determined from the standpoint of an ordinary person in the actor's situation under the circumstances as the actor reasonably believes them to be."

* * *

The Evidence

A description of the evidence and the facts which could be found therefrom as perceived by the defendant is relevant to the question of whether he could have been found by the jury to be under the influence of extreme emotional disturbance when he committed the criminal homicide, thereby necessitating an instruction on extreme emotional disturbance. There was evidence of the following:

The defendant exhibited instability after his discharge from the Air Force in 1972. He "drifted in various parts of the United States" and put "very little order to his life." In 1975 he returned to his mother's home in Grants Pass and stayed there intermittently.

At some point after his return to Grants Pass, he began to cohabit with a woman who had three children. This lasted for a little over a year. The woman then asked the defendant to move out because of his drinking and

2. See ORS 163.115 and 163.118 prior to amendment by Oregon Laws 1981, chapter 873, sections 5 and 6.

At times during this opinion we may refer to the mitigating factor as a "defense." Where we do so, it is for convenience of expression only. We recognize that we do not deal with a defense, such as "self defense," which, when found to exist, completely exonerates a defendant of criminal responsibility. Intentionally killing while under the influence of extreme emotional disturbance does not present a true "defense," for the punishment is merely reduced through the mechanism of denominating the crime as "manslaughter" rather than "murder." It could be considered a "partial defense" in the sense that an acquittal of the charge of murder occurs when the jury finds that the defendant is guilty only of manslaughter.

3. In 1981 ORS 163.115, 163.118 and 163.135 were amended for the apparent purpose of making it an "affirmative defense" that a defendant committed criminal homicide under the influence of extreme emotional disturbance, which would reduce the crime from murder to manslaughter. Or.Laws 1981, ch. 873, §§ 5 and 6.

unannounced disappearances. She was three months' pregnant by him at the time.

The defendant then enrolled at Rogue Community College at Grants Pass. There he met the now deceased Stephanie Elaine Brinkley, whom he married three weeks after their initial meeting. Some months after their marriage, they had a fight over "money matters" and separated. They were soon together again; however, not long thereafter welfare authorities threatened to cut off Stephanie's assistance unless they separated. The defendant moved out, joined a mining operation and made a small amount of money.

Defendant attempted to return to his wife; however, she had begun seeing someone else. Defendant attempted to fight Stephanie's new lover. Stephanie intervened, sent her new lover away and promised that her conduct would not be repeated.

There were other separations, and the defendant, upon his return from each separation and his learning of more infidelities, became progressively more upset. This was especially so after the birth of their first child.

At one point, upon Stephanie's invitation to resume living together, the defendant returned home to find his wife engaged in sex with another man. A fight ensued. The police were called, and the defendant was arrested for the crime of menacing. Upon arraignment, the court in that case observed that defendant appeared to be emotionally disturbed.

After his conviction in that case, the court ordered a presentence report. The report contained a psychological evaluation which indicated the possibility that defendant could exhibit psychotic behavior under stress and recommended that the defendant be treated with therapy and medication. Defendant was given a three-year suspended sentence and was released from jail subject to the condition that he receive counseling from the county mental health department. Although he received counseling, he never received any medication.

He had been warned by the "authorities" to stay away from Stephanie. She apparently caused him to be placed under a judicial restraining order; however, despite her obtaining the order, Stephanie telephoned him regarding their divorce. They engaged in an apparently protracted series of arguments on the telephone over child custody, which eventuated in the defendant's arrest and jailing for harassment. Even though they engaged in arguments and fights, they continued to associate. Defendant could not stay away from Stephanie and Stephanie did not always discourage his attentions.

In 1980 Stephanie began to live with another man. This conduct affected the defendant, as before, with tension and "stress." The defendant's reaction was even more intense than before, and he threatened to kill Stephanie on several occasions.

In early April, 1980, Stephanie's son, Jonathan (defendant's stepson), broke his arm and was in the hospital. The defendant and Stephanie met each other at the hospital in order to visit with the child on three occasions. It was arranged that on the third occasion the defendant was to drive Stephanie home after hospital visiting hours were over. Defendant had the impression from their first two meetings at the hospital that the relationship was improving. He was thus angered and disappointed when his wife's new lover appeared at the hospital on their third meeting to take her home. Defendant left the hospital in a state of agitation. He retrieved a .22 rifle that he had stored at the home of a friend, caught up with his wife and her lover, ran their truck off the road and shot his wife three times.

* * *

History of Mitigating Factor

* * *

The defense of extreme emotional disturbance is a modification of the defense of provocation or heat of passion. The provocation defense is very old. The distinction between a slaying in cold blood and one in the heat of passion existed in Anglo–Saxon criminal law and survived the Norman conquest of 1066.[4] The "Doctrine of Provocation" became firmly established in the law in 1628 when Coke adopted the distinction between homicide committed after deliberation and homicide committed in the course of a sudden quarrel. Coke defined murder as necessitating "malice aforethought," as distinguished from manslaughter, which he understood occurs "upon a sudden occasion" and was, therefore, called "chance-medley." Then, as now, manslaughter, understood as chance-medley, depended on the presence of heat of passion caused by adequate provocation.

As originally conceived, the only adequate provocation for heat of passion was mutual combat. Hence, heat of passion was difficult to distinguish from self defense. Other provocations were gradually recognized as legally adequate, including assault and adultery. In some jurisdictions, illegal arrest, injuries to third parties, and words conveying information of the occurrence of a legally sufficient ground have also been recognized.

In the mid-nineteenth century, the judgment as to whether a provocation was adequate for the heat of passion defense was made by the judge as a determination of law; however, judges gradually began to leave borderline cases to the jury. The reasonable man standard of review for provocation was devised as a manner of instructing the jury on marginal cases. It was also a device for enabling the jury to serve as community conscience or standard of measure for reasonable behavior.

The reasonable man test for provocation contained four elements: (1) there had to be a provocation that would arouse a reasonable man to the heat of passion; (2) the defendant must actually have been aroused to the heat of passion; (3) a reasonable man would not have cooled off; and (4) the defendant did not, in fact, cool off. This has been said to be an objective test, meaning that neither the mental nor physical peculiarities of the accused are evaluated in determining whether his loss of self-control was reasonable.

Criticism of the "Ordinary" or "Reasonable" Man Test

* * *

4. For a short history of the provocation defense, see Donovan, D. and Wildman, S., *Is the Reasonable Man Obsolete? A Critical Perspective on Self–Defense and Provocation,* 14 Loyola L.Rev. 435, 446–450 (1980). (Donovan and Wildman hereafter.)

The common law heat of passion or provocation defense placed the jury in the conceptually awkward (to put it kindly) position of having to determine when it is reasonable for a reasonable man to act unreasonably. In an article on the subject, Granville Williams explained:

> "In the law of contract and tort, and elsewhere in the criminal law, the test of the reasonable man indicates an ethical standard; but it seems absurd to say that the reasonable man will commit a felony the possible punishment for which is imprisonment for life. To say that the 'ordinary' man will commit this felony is hardly less absurd. The reason why provoked homicide is punished is to deter people from committing the offence; and it is a curious confession of failure on the part of the law to suppose that, notwithstanding the possibility of heavy punishment, an ordinary person will commit it. If the assertion were correct, it would raise serious doubts whether the offence should continue to be punished."
>
> "Surely the true view of provocation is that it is a concession to 'the frailty of human nature' in those exceptional cases where the legal prohibition fails of effect. It is a compromise, neither conceding the propriety of the act nor exacting the full penalty for it. This being so, how can it be that that paragon of virtue, the reasonable man, gives way to provocation?"

Williams, *Provocation and the Reasonable Man,* 1954 Crim.L.Rev. 740, 742.

* * *

The Model Penal Code

The drafters of the Model Penal Code were aware of the anomaly and pointed out that harsh and unjust results were obtained from applying the objective test for provocation. They cited State v. Gounagias, 88 Wash. 304, 153 P. 9 (1915), as a model of an unjust result achieved through application of the objective test for provocation. That case may serve as an illustration of the test for provocation and also, by negative implication, of the object of modifying that defense.

While lying in a drunken stupor, Gounagias, a member of the "Greek community," was sodomized by another member of that community. Outraged and greatly embarrassed, he upbraided his assailant the next morning and asked him not to spread any stories among other members of the community about what had happened. The assailant, however, proved unsympathetic. From taunts, conversational innuendos and jeering signs, Gounagias realized that the story had been spread far and wide. His anger and isolation from the rest of his community increased at every embarrassing innuendo. Some weeks after the original incident, Gounagias went to a coffee house where an incident occurred which, in the words of the court, "excited and enraged" him. He went home, retrieved a pistol hidden under his mattress, and went to the home of his assailant. By the light of a match, Gounagias found him asleep in his bed and shot him five times in the head.

Charged with murder, Gounagias asked for mitigation based on the common law defense of provocation. The Supreme Court of Washington set out the standard for that defense as follows:

> "* * * if the act of killing, though intentional, be committed under the influence of sudden intense anger or heat of blood obscuring the reason, produced by an adequate or reasonable provocation, and before sufficient time has elapsed for the blood to cool and reason to reassert itself, so that the killing is the result of temporary excitement rather than of wickedness of heart or innate recklessness of disposition, then the law, recognizing the standard of human conduct as that of the ordinary or average man, regards the offense so committed as of less heinous character than premeditated or deliberate murder. Measured, as it must be, by the conduct of the average man, what constitutes adequate cause is incapable of exact definition."

88 Wash. at 311–312, 153 P. 9. * * *

With this understanding of provocation, the Washington court reached the conclusion that Gounagias waited too long after the original incident for provocation to be a reasonable explanation of his behavior. In the words of the court:

> "To say that these repeated demonstrations, coupled with the original outrage, *culminated* in a sudden passion and heat of blood when he encountered the same character of demonstration in the coffee house on the night of the killing is to say that sudden passion and heat of blood, in the mitigative sense, may be a cumulative result of repeated reminders of a single act of provocation occurring weeks before, and this, whether that provocation be regarded as the original outrage or the spreading of the story among appellant's associates, both of which he knew and fully realized for three weeks before the fatal night. This theory of the cumulative effect of reminders of former wrongs, not of new acts of provocation by the deceased, is contrary to the idea of sudden anger as understood in the doctrine of mitigation. In the nature of the thing, *sudden* anger cannot be cumulative. A provocation which does not cause instant resentment, but which is only resented after being thought upon and brooded over, is not a provocation sufficient in law to reduce intentional killing from murder to manslaughter * * *"

88 Wash. at 318, 153 P. 9.

The drafters of the Model Penal Code found it "shocking" to disregard that the passage of time served only to increase rather than diminish Gounagias' outrage as the story became known. Model Penal Code Tentative draft No. 9 § 201.3 at 48. They said:

> "Though it is difficult to state a middle ground between a standard which ignores all individual peculiarities and one which makes emotional distress decisive regardless of the nature of its cause, we think that such a statement is essential. For surely if the actor had just suffered a traumatic injury, if he were blind or were distraught with grief, if he were experiencing an unanticipated reaction to a therapeutic drug, it would be deemed atrocious to

appraise his crime for purposes of sentence without reference to any of these matters. They are material because they bear upon the inference as to the actor's character that it is fair to draw upon the basis of his act. So too in such a situation as *Gounagias,* supra, where lapse of time increased rather than diminished the extent of the outrage perpetrated on the actor, as he became aware that his disgrace was known, it was shocking in our view to hold this vital fact to be irrelevant."

* * *

Legislative Modification

The Commission presented to the legislature the following subsection:

> "(1) Criminal homicide constitutes manslaughter when:
>
> " * * *
>
> "(b) A homicide which would otherwise be murder is committed under the influence of extreme mental or emotional disturbance for which there is a reasonable explanation and excuse. The reasonableness of such explanation and excuse shall be determined from the standpoint of a person in the actor's situation under the circumstances as he believes them to be."

Early on, members of the legislature and witnesses questioned whether this approach was too subjective. * * *

By March 5, 1971, controversy over whether the test was too subjective led to amendment of the section so as to read essentially as it now does. We must conclude from this legislative history that the legislature, as distinguished from the Commission, intended to present a test to be used by court and jury that would measure the reasonableness of the explanation for the disturbance more objectively than that proposed by the Commission.

The Trial Court's Instruction

* * *

An explanation of the term "extreme emotional disturbance" which reflects the situational or relative character of the concept was given in People v. Shelton, 88 Misc.2d 136, 149, 385 N.Y.S.2d 708, 717 (1976), as follows:

> "That extreme emotional disturbance is the emotional state of an individual who: * * * (b) is exposed to an extremely unusual and overwhelming stress; and (c) has an extreme emotional reaction to it, as a result of which there is a loss of self-control and reason is overborne by intense feelings, such as passion, anger, distress, grief, excessive agitation or other similar emotions."

We find ourselves in agreement with the Court of Appeals of New York as to the meaning and place of the term "extreme emotional disturbance" in this context. In People v. Casassa, 49 N.Y.2d 668, 427 N.Y.S.2d 769, 775, 404 N.E.2d 1310, 1316 (1980), in discussing the defense that court acknowledged that its discussion and description of the defense "provides no precise guidelines and necessarily leaves room for the exercise of judgmental evaluation by the jury. This, however, appears to have been the intent of the draftsmen. 'The purpose was explicitly to give full scope to what amounts to a plea in mitigation based upon a mental or emotional trauma of significant dimensions, with the jury asked to show whatever empathy it can.' (Wechsler, Codification of Criminal Law in the United States: The Model Penal Code, 68 Col.L.Rev. 1425, 1446.)"

We conclude that in instructing a jury on the meaning of the term "extreme emotional disturbance" a trial court, after proper instruction as to the burden of persuasion, should pose the issue in terms of whether defendant was under the influence of an emotional disturbance to the extent that he lost his self-control that would have otherwise prevented his committing the homicide.

We have still to determine how a jury is to determine whether there was a reasonable explanation for the emotional disturbance. This is a sensitive task because the Oregon statute requires that the "reasonableness of the explanation for the disturbance shall be determined from the standpoint of an ordinary person," ORS 163.135(1). On the other hand, the statute requires that the reasonableness of the interpretation must be judged from the standpoint of "the actor's situation under the circumstances as the actor reasonably believes them to be." The juxtaposition of these two requirements for determining the adequacy of the explanation prevents the adequacy from being determined on either wholly objective or subjective grounds. * * *

This legislative mix of the "ordinary" person's views and the subjective belief of the defendant as to the reasonableness of his conduct in what the defendant believes the circumstances to be revives the grounds for the criticism of judicial analysis of the former adequate provocation/heat of passion defense, to which we have already referred. Under that former defense, personal characteristics of the defendant were not important. An example is found in Bedder v. Director of Public Prosecutions, W.L.R. 1119, 2 All.E.R. 801 (1954).

> "Just as mental peculiarities do not give a privileged position in the law of provocation, so neither do physical peculiarities. This was decided by the House of Lords in *Bedder* [1954] 1 W.L.R. 1119; [1954] Crim.L.R. 721. The appellant was a youth of eighteen who was sexually impotent but who attempted to have sexual intercourse with a prostitute. Discovering his impotence she jeered at him and attempted to get away; he tried still to hold her, but (according to his evidence) she slapped him in the face, punched him in the stomach, and (when he pushed her back) kicked him in the private parts. The appellant thereupon stabbed her twice with a pocket knife, causing her death. The judge directed the jury in terms of what the reasonable or ordinary person would have done, and an appeal against a conviction of murder was dismissed both by the Court of Criminal Appeal and by the House of Lords. If the provocation was insufficient for a normal man, it could not help the

accused that he was conscious of his impotence and therefore liable to be more excited if 'twitted' or attacked on the subject of that particular infirmity. In applying the test of the reasonable man, it could not be supposed that this hypothetical reasonable man in the position of the accused was himself impotent."

Williams, *Provocation and the Reasonable Man,* 1954 Criminal L.Rev. 740, 747. Similarly, Donovan and Wildman in their article, *Is the Reasonable Man Obsolete? A Critical Perspective on Self–Defense and Provocation,* hypothesize the following example:

> "An Asian–American man, Harold Sato, who had been interned in a detention camp for Japanese during World War II, faces repeated racial prejudice at his job. One day after repeated racial slurs from a co-worker he kills the co-worker."

14 Loyola L.Rev. 435, 438 (1981). The authors observe:

> "The anomaly of a purely objective standard of provocation is underlined by Mr. Sato's case * * *. A reasonable man, viewed in the abstract, is not likely to be roused to the heat of passion by a verbal insult. However, an Asian–American who had been interned in a concentration camp *is* likely to be roused to the heat of passion by racial slurs. To the extent that a jury is not allowed to consider Mr. Sato's racial background and previous experience of racial discrimination in determining his moral culpability, Mr. Sato is more likely to be convicted of murder * * * than of voluntary manslaughter."

Id. at 449.

By requiring the factfinder to focus on a person in the defendant's "situation," the drafters of the Model Penal Code sought to work change. One writer, relying upon the Model Penal Code commentary, has put it:

> "[I]t makes the test more, although not entirely, subjective, by requiring the jury to test the reasonableness of the actor's conduct, 'from the viewpoint of a person in the actor's situation.' Thus, the actor's sex, sexual preference, pregnancy, physical deformities, and similar characteristics are apt to be taken into consideration in evaluating the reasonableness of the defendant's behavior." (Footnotes omitted.)

Dressler, *Rethinking Heat of Passion: A Defense in Search of a Rationale,* 73 Journal of Criminal Law and Criminology 421, 431 (1982).

As will be recalled, the Commission proposed to the Oregon legislature the Model Penal Code concept of viewing the matter from the standpoint of a person in the actor's situation. One must conclude that the Commission envisioned that the actor's situation included the actor's personal characteristics.[20] A fair conclusion from the legislative treatment of the Commission's proposal is that the legislature was aware of this injection of subjectivity, yet

20. In its brief in the Court of Appeals, the state, apparently aware of the "legislative" history, candidly acknowledged:

> "The actor's situation may include personal characteristics such as age, sex, race, nationality, physical stature, and mental and physical handicaps."

the legislature made no change in that part of the Commission's proposal. The 1971 statute, originally and now, makes the test depend upon the actor's situation. We have found nothing to indicate that this does not include those "personal" characteristics noted by the drafters of the Model Penal Code.

In this case the trial court instructed that the jury was not to consider the defendant's "personality characteristics" but only the "personality characteristics which would be possessed by an ordinary person in our society today" in determining the reasonableness of the explanation for extreme emotional disturbance. Defendant argued that "personality characteristics" are a part of the actor's personal characteristics and thus of the actor's "situation" that must be taken into account in determining reasonableness.

The state answered that there is nothing in the legislative history, at either the Commission level or the legislative level, to suggest that personality traits are properly to be considered. As the state argues, such an interpretation would permit the acquittal of a bad-tempered person of murder and the conviction of an even-tempered person of murder in "precisely the same situation and circumstances." We agree. As we noted, the Commission did not go so far. We have no reason to believe that the legislature did so.

* * *

Conclusion

Given the hybrid approach adopted by the legislature to the weight to be accorded to subjective and objective factors in the calculus involved in this kind of case, we do not believe that any court can state a suggested jury instruction that is completely impervious to criticism of its logic. We must leave the trial courts and juries where the statute places them. Making the best of this situation, we conclude that a trial court's charge must be constructed for any particular case along the following general lines.

First, the jury's attention must be drawn to the relevant statutory text.

Second, the jury must be instructed as to the burden of persuasion on the issue.

Third, the jury should be asked to consider whether the homicide was committed under the influence of extreme emotional disturbance. * * * The jury should be instructed that if it finds that the homicide was not committed under the influence of extreme emotional disturbance, the jury need not further consider the issue of mitigation of murder to manslaughter. If the jury finds that the homicide was committed under the influence of extreme emotional disturbance, it must then consider other issues.

Fourth, the jury must determine whether the extreme emotional disturbance was the result of the defendant's intentional, knowing, reckless or criminally negligent act, and the meaning of those adjectives must be explained. If the jury finds that this causal relationship existed, it need not further consider the mitigation issue. If the jury finds this causal relationship not to exist, it must then consider the reasonableness of the explanation for the disturbance.

Fifth, the jury must determine what was the defendant's situation in the circumstances which the defendant reasonably believed to exist. The jury must then determine whether an ordinary person in that situation and those circumstances would have experienced extreme emotional disturbance.

* * *

Reversed and remanded for a new trial.

Notes

1. In Commonwealth v. Bermudez, 370 Mass. 438, 348 N.E.2d 802, 93 A.L.R.3d 920 (1976), a typical common law decision, the defendant claimed that after a three week separation, he went to see his wife [the court said that the inference was warranted that he went because the man his wife was now living with had asked him to do so to prove that they were now living together]; that he went upstairs to see their baby and came down and told her that the baby needed his diaper changed; and that, using an obscenity, she told him, "I don't need you around here, I have got another man." He repeated his request; she again used an obscenity and told him to get out; he pulled out a gun and shot and killed her. The trial judge refused to instruct on provocation, and the court approved a second degree murder verdict, on the ground that quarreling or words of insult cannot constitute provocation, and that, while words of information, such as those disclosing an immediately preceding adultery might qualify, discovery of a past adultery—and here there was no reference to a specific act of adultery—is insufficient to allow the jury to find provocation.

2. *Provocation at Common Law.* At common law, provocation first requires that the defendant have acted under the influence of passion. In most of the cases the passion is anger; some authorities accept fear and other overwhelming emotions. The test here is subjective; it is not enough that many people would have become infuriated in the circumstances. An unusually cool-headed person who manages to keep his temper cannot claim provocation. For the remainder of this note, we will assume an actually impassioned defendant.

There is also an objective part of the test, which is difficult to state because it involves some illogical assumptions. It is sometimes said that the nature of the provocation must be such as might cause a reasonable person to act as the accused did. The idea is to introduce some element of objectivity; we do not want to reward the unusually bad tempered person for his lack of self-control. But, of course, the reasonable person doesn't lose his temper and kill somebody in a flash of anger. The image of the reasonable person in a fit of passion is not an easy one to sustain. However, the idea is not without meaning. If the provocation rule is a limited concession to human imperfection, it may apply only to situations in which the acts of the defendant do not depart too far from the norm and do not reflect a generally dangerous and unstable character.

It might be enough to instruct the jury in terms which would convey some such idea, but judges commonly look closely at the sufficiency of the evidence of provocation before giving any provocation instruction at all. Many jurisdictions have developed rules that certain kinds of acts are insufficient as a matter of law to amount to provocation; words of abuse are often said to be insufficient. Minor assaults and batteries may be excluded, as may actions of the victim taken in reasonable self-defense. Alleged provocation arising out of mutual combat, most assaults, and serious threats of imminent grave injury will probably get to the jury, as will sudden discovery of a spouse in the act of adultery, or perhaps a spouse's sudden confession of adultery. Violent assaults or sexual assaults on close relatives may suffice, but generally the provoking act must reasonably appear to be directed by the victim to the accused.

Even if there is an adequate act of provocation, mitigation will not be allowed if the accused acted after there was adequate time for him to cool off—and this time is measured on the same sort of objective standard.

Note that at common law provocation is not a defense to ordinary assault, which is only a misdemeanor. It might, of course, be taken into account in sentencing. In the case of statutory assault with intent to murder, the intent to murder requirement is not met if there is provocation sufficient to reduce the crime to manslaughter, had the victim died.

3. *Model Penal Code Position.* Model Penal Code § 210.3, Comment 5 (Official Draft, 1980), at pp. 61–65: *

> 5. *Mental or Emotional Disturbance.* * * * Section 210.3(1)(b) does require that the actor's emotional distress be based on "reasonable explanation or excuse." This language preserves the essentially objective character of the inquiry and erects a barrier against debilitating individualization of the legal standard. But the statute further provides that the "reasonableness of such explanation or excuse shall be determined from the viewpoint of a person in the actor's situation under the circumstances as he believes them to be." The last clause clarifies the role of mistake. The trier of fact must evaluate the actor's conduct under the circumstances that the actor believed to exist. Thus, for example, a man who reasonably but mistakenly identifies his wife's rapist and kills the wrong person may be eligible for mitigation if his extreme emotional disturbance were otherwise subject to reasonable explanation or excuse.
>
> The critical element in the Model Code formulation is the clause requiring that reasonableness be assessed "from the viewpoint of a person in the actor's situation." The word "situation" is designedly ambiguous. On the one hand, it is clear that personal handicaps and some external circumstances must be taken into account. Thus, blindness, shock from traumatic injury, and extreme grief are all easily read into the term "situation." This result is sound, for it would be morally obtuse to appraise a crime for mitigation of punishment without reference to these factors. On the other hand, it is equally plain that idiosyncratic moral values are not part of the actor's situation. An assassin who kills a political leader because he believes it is right to do so cannot ask that he be judged by the standard of a reasonable extremist. Any other result would undermine the normative message of the criminal law. In between these two extremes, however, there are matters neither as clearly distinct from individual blameworthiness as blindness or handicap nor as integral a part of moral depravity as a belief in the rightness of killing. Perhaps the classic illustration is the unusual sensitivity to the epithet "bastard" of a person born illegitimate. An exceptionally punctilious sense of personal honor or an abnormally fearful temperament may also serve to differentiate an individual actor from the hypothetical reasonable man, yet none of these factors is wholly irrelevant to the ultimate issue of culpability. The proper role of such factors cannot be resolved satisfactorily by abstract definition of what may constitute adequate provocation. The Model Code endorses a formulation that affords sufficient flexibility to differentiate in particular cases between those special aspects of the actor's situation that should be deemed material for purpose of grading and those that should be ignored. There thus will be room for interpretation of the word "situation," and that is precisely the flexibility desired. There will be opportunity for argument about the reasonable-

ness of explanation or excuse, and that too is a ground on which argument is required. In the end, the question is whether the actor's loss of self-control can be understood in terms that arouse sympathy in the ordinary citizen. Section 210.3 faces this issue squarely and leaves the ultimate judgment to the ordinary citizen in the function of a juror assigned to resolve the specific case.

Many modern revision efforts have followed the Model Code formulation in its essential aspects, though some require the accused to prove extreme emotional distress by a preponderance of the evidence. Perhaps some additional clarification was achieved by the National Commission on Reform of Federal Criminal Laws. Its proposal provides for mitigation of punishment where the actor causes the death of another "under the influence of extreme emotional disturbance for which there is reasonable excuse." [59] After specifying that reasonableness shall be determined in a manner parallel to that of the Model Code, the National Commission further states that an emotional disturbance is excusable "if it is occasioned by any provocation, event or situation *for which the offender was not culpably responsible.*" [60] Under this formulation, extreme emotional disturbance will not reduce murder to manslaughter if the actor has intentionally, knowingly, recklessly, or negligently brought about his own mental disturbance, such as by involving himself in a crime.[61] This idea is implicit in the Model Code formulation * * *.

* * *

Note: How Objective Is the Test?

After the *Bedder* case [a], Parliament provided in § 3 of the Homicide Act of 1957:

> Where on a charge of murder there is evidence on which the jury can find that the person charged was provoked (whether by things done or by things said or by both together) to lose self-control, the question whether the provocation was enough to make a reasonable man do as he did shall be left to be determined by the jury; and in determining that question the jury shall take into account everything both done and said according to the effect which, in their opinion, it would have on a reasonable man.

In Regina v. Camplin, [1978] A.C. 705 (H.L.), the defense of the accused, a fifteen year old male, to a murder charge was that he was forcibly sodomized by the victim, who then laughed at him, and that the accused thereupon lost his self-control and killed the victim with a blow from a chapati pan, a kitchen utensil like a frying pan. The jury was instructed to apply the test of a reasonable man, not a reasonable fifteen year old. The House of Lords approved the substitution by the Court of Criminal Appeal of a verdict of manslaughter for the murder verdict. Lord Diplock said, at [1978] A.C. 716–719:

59. Brown Comm'n, Final Report § 1602(b).

60. Id. (emphasis added). The full text of the Brown Commission proposal reads:

> A person is guilty of manslaughter, a Class B felony, if he * * * (b) causes the death of another human being under circumstances which would be murder, except that he causes the death under the influence of extreme emotional disturbance for which there is reasonable excuse. The reasonableness of the excuse shall be determined from the viewpoint of a person in his situation under the circumstances as he believed them to be. An emotional disturbance is excusable, within the meaning of this paragraph, if it is occasioned by any provocation, event or situation for which the offender was not culpably responsible.

61. Id. Comment (1).

a. Discussed, supra, p. 404.

As I have already pointed out, for the purposes of the law of provocation the "reasonable man" has never been confined to the adult male. It means an ordinary person of either sex, not exceptionally excitable or pugnacious, but possessed of such powers of self-control as everyone is entitled to expect that his fellow citizens will exercise in society as it is today. A crucial factor in the defence of provocation from earliest times has been the relationship between the gravity of provocation and the way in which the accused retaliated, both being judged by the social standards of the day. When Hale was writing in the seventeenth century, pulling a man's nose was thought to justify retaliation with a sword; when Mancini v. Director of Public Prosecutions [1942] A.C. 1 was decided by this House, a blow with a fist would not justify retaliation with a deadly weapon. But so long as words unaccompanied by violence could not in law amount to provocation the relevant proportionality between provocation and retaliation was primarily one of degrees of violence. Words spoken to the accused before the violence started were not normally to be included in the proportion sum. But now that the law has been changed so as to permit of words being treated as provocation even though unaccompanied by any other acts, the gravity of verbal provocation may well depend upon the particular characteristics or circumstances of the person to whom a taunt or insult is addressed. To taunt a person because of his race, his physical infirmities or some shameful incident in his past may well be considered by the jury to be more offensive to the person addressed, however equable his temperament, if the facts on which the taunt is founded are true than it would be if they were not. It would stultify much of the mitigation of the previous harshness of the common law in ruling out verbal provocation as capable of reducing murder to manslaughter if the jury could not take into consideration all those factors which in their opinion would affect the gravity of taunts or insults when applied to the person whom they are addressed. So to this extent at any rate the unqualified proposition accepted by this House in Bedder v. Director of Public Prosecutions [1954] 1 W.L.R. 1119 that for the purposes of the "reasonable man" test any unusual physical characteristics of the accused must be ignored requires revision as a result of the passing of the Act of 1957.

That he was only 15 years of age at the time of the killing is the relevant characteristic of the accused in the instant case. It is a characteristic which may have its effects on temperament as well as physique. If the jury think that the same power of self-control is not to be expected in an ordinary, average or normal boy of 15 as in an older person, are they to treat the lesser powers of self-control possessed by an ordinary, average or normal boy of 15 as the standard of self-control with which the conduct of the accused is to be compared?

Lord Simon of Glaisdale observed, at [1978] A.C. 724–727:

* * * Subsequent discussion of *Bedder* has, however, shown that some of its implications constitute affronts to common sense and any sense of justice. By way of example only, a blow on the face might be quite insufficient to make an ordinary reasonable man lose his self-control, whereas if he had a severe abscess in his cheek the situation might be very different; but, according to *Bedder,* the abscess would have to be disregarded. And it is accepted that the phrase "reasonable man" really means "reasonable

person," so as to extend to "reasonable woman" (see, specifically, Holmes v. Director of Public Prosecutions [1946] A.C. 588, 597). So, although this has never yet been a subject of decision, a jury could arguably, consistently with *Bedder* and its precedent authorities, take the sex of the accused into account in assessing what might reasonably cause her to lose her self-control. (A "reasonable woman" with her sex eliminated is altogether too abstract a notion for my comprehension or, I am confident, for that of any jury. In any case, it hardly makes sense to say that an impotent man must be notionally endowed with virility before he ranks within the law of provocation as a reasonable man, yet that a normal woman must be notionally stripped of her femininity before she qualifies as a reasonable woman.) If so, this is already some qualification on the "reasonable person" as a pure abstraction devoid of any personal characteristics, even if such a concept were of any value to the law. This qualification might be crucial: take the insult "whore" addressed respectively to a reasonable man and a reasonable woman. Nevertheless, as counsel for the appellant sternly and cogently maintained, *Bedder* would preclude the jury from considering that the accused was, say, pregnant (Rex v. Smith (1914) 11 Cr.App.R. 36) or (presumably, undergoing menstruation or menopause).

Such refinements, anomalies and affronts to common sense invite courts to distinguish an authority. In the instant case the Court of Appeal distinguished *Bedder* [1954] 1 W.L.R. 1119 on the ground that age is a universal quality not a personal idiosyncrasy. It is certainly not a "physical infirmity or disability." This distinction is, further, arguably justified by the implications of the "reasonable woman" as a standard. It could be said that the law, in distinguishing from personal idiosyncrasy something universal like age, was doing no more than it had already done in distinguishing implicitly something universal like sex.

Nevertheless, the distinction drawn by the Court of Appeal leads to great difficulties. If youth is to be considered (and, presumably, advanced years too), what about immaturity in a person of full years or premature senility? These would seem to fall on the other, on the *Bedder,* side of the line. One calls to mind what Lord Reid said in Reg. v. National Insurance Commissioner, Ex parte Hudson [1972] A.C. 944, 966: "It is notorious that where an existing decision is disapproved but cannot be overruled courts tend to distinguish it on inadequate grounds." * * *

* * *

In the exceptional circumstances whereby the reasoning of a decision of your Lordships' House, and that of the authorities on which it was founded, has been undermined by a subsequent Act of Parliament (even though the decision has not been clearly and expressly abrogated), I think that your Lordships are justified in saying that *Bedder* should no longer be followed. I think that the law as it now stands in this country is substantially the same as that enacted in the New Zealand Crimes Act 1961, section 169(2), as explained by the Court of Appeal of New Zealand in Reg. v. McGregor [1962] N.Z.L.R. 1069.

I think that the standard of self-control which the law requires before provocation is held to reduce murder to manslaughter is still that of the reasonable person (hence his invocation in section 3); but that, in determining whether a person of reasonable self-control would lose it in the circumstances, the entire factual situation, which includes the characteristics of the accused, must be considered.

Subsequently, in Reg. v. Newell, 71 Crim.App. 331 (1980), the Court of Appeal (Criminal Division) considered the meaning of "characteristic," as used in *Camplin.* In Newell, after the woman with whom he had been living deserted him, defendant, a chronic alcoholic, attempted suicide. A few days later he was drinking with his friend, another alcoholic, and expressing his grief, when the friend unexpectedly spoke of the woman in insulting terms and suggested that he and the defendant engage in homosexual relations. Defendant then killed him by striking him repeatedly on the head with an ash tray. On appeal from his murder conviction, defendant seeks application of the *Camplin* case. The Court responded, at pp. 338–340:

> It seems to us that to ascertain the meaning of the speeches in * * * *Camplin* it is necessary to consider the meaning of the word "characteristics" as used in those speeches. To do so we find it helpful to refer, as we were invited to do by Mr. Crespi, to *McCregor* [1962] N.Z.L.R. 1069, referred to by Lord Simon of Glaisdale. First, we would read the material parts of section 169 of the New Zealand Crimes Act 1961:
>
> "(1) Culpable homicide that would otherwise be murder may be reduced to manslaughter if the person who caused the death did so under provocation. (2) Anything done or said may be provocation if— (*a*) In the circumstances of the case it was sufficient to deprive a person having the power of self-control of an ordinary person, but otherwise having the characteristics of the offender, of the power of self-control; and (*b*) It did in fact deprive the offender of the power of self-control and thereby induced him to commit the act of homicide. (3) Whether there is any evidence of provocation is a question of law. (4) Whether, if there is evidence of provocation, the provocation was sufficient as aforesaid, and whether it did in fact deprive the offender of the power of self-control and thereby induced him to commit the act of homicide, are questions of fact."
>
> In McGregor the judgment of the court was delivered by North J., and contains the following passage which appears to us to be entirely apt to the situation in the instant case:
>
> "The Legislature has given us no guide as to what limitations might be imposed, but perforce there must be adopted a construction which will ensure regard being had to the characteristics of the offender without wholly extinguishing the ordinary man. The offender must be presumed to possess in general the power of self-control of the ordinary man, save in so far as his power of self-control is weakened because of some particular characteristic possessed by him. It is not every trait or disposition of the offender that can be invoked to modify the concept of the ordinary man. The characteristic must be something definite and of sufficient significance to make the offender a different person from the ordinary run of mankind, and have also a sufficient degree of permanence to warrant its being regarded as something constituting part of the individual's character or personality. A disposition to be unduly suspicious or to lose one's temper readily will not suffice, nor will a temporary or transitory state of mind such as a mood of depression,

excitability or irascibility. These matters are either not of sufficient significance or not of sufficient permanency to be regarded as 'characteristics' which would enable the offender to be distinguished from the ordinary man. The 'unusually excitable or pugnacious individual' spoken of in *Lesbini* (1914) 11 Cr.App.R. 11; [1914] 3 K.B. 1116 is no more entitled to special consideration under the new section than he was when that case was decided. Still less can a self-induced transitory state be relied upon, as where it arises from the consumption of liquor. The word 'characteristics' in the context of this section is wide enough to apply not only to physical qualities but also to mental qualities and such more indeterminate attributes as colour, race and creed. It is to be emphasised that of whatever nature the characteristic may be, it must be such that it can fairly be said that the offender is thereby marked off or distinguished from the ordinary man of the community. Moreover, it is to be equally emphasised that there must be some real connection between the nature of the provocation and the particular characteristic of the offender by which it is sought to modify the ordinary man test. The words or conduct must have been exclusively or particularly provocative to the individual because, and only because, of the characteristic. In short, there must be some direct connection between the provocative words or conduct and the characteristic sought to be invoked as warranting some departure from the ordinary man test. Such a connection may be seen readily enough where the offender possesses some unusual physical peculiarity. Though he might in all other respects be an ordinary man, provocative words alluding for example to some infirmity or deformity from which he was suffering might well bring about a loss of self-control. So too, if the colour, race or creed of the offender be relied on as constituting a characteristic, it is to be repeated that the provocative words or conduct must be related to the particular characteristic relied upon. Thus, it would not be sufficient, for instance, for the offender to claim merely that he belongs to an excitable race, or that members of his nationality are accustomed to resort readily to the use of some lethal weapon. Here again, the provocative act or words require to be directed at the particular characteristic before it can be relied upon. Special difficulties, however, arise when it becomes necessary to consider what purely mental peculiarities may be allowed as characteristics.

"In our opinion it is not enough to constitute a characteristic that the offender should merely in some general way be mentally deficient or weak-minded. To allow this to be said would, as we have earlier indicated, deny any real operation to the reference made in the section to the ordinary man, and it would, moreover, go far towards the admission of a defence of diminished responsibility without any statutory authority in this country to sanction it. There must be something more, such as provocative words or acts directed to a particular phobia from which the offender suffers. Beyond that, we do not think it is advisable that we should attempt to go."

That passage, and the reasoning therein contained, seem to us to be impeccable. It is not only expressed in plain, easily comprehended language; it represents also, we think, the law of this country as well as that of New

Zealand. In the present case the only matter which could remotely be described as a characteristic was the appellant's condition of chronic alcoholism. Assuming that that was truly a characteristic (and we expressly make no determination as to that), nevertheless it had nothing to do with the words by which it is said that he was provoked. There was no connection between the derogatory reference to the appellant's girl friend and the suggestion of a possible homosexual act and his chronic alcoholism. It had nothing at all to do with the words by which it is said that he was provoked.

* * *

The other matters advanced by Mr. Ashe Lincoln as being characteristics which the jury should have been invited to consider, in examining what a reasonable man might or would have done, are not characteristics at all. The appellant's drunkenness, or lack of sobriety, his having taken an overdose of drugs and written a suicide note a few days previously, his grief at the defection of his girl friend, and so on, are none of them matters which can properly be described as characteristics. They were truly transitory in nature, in the light of the words and reasoning of North J., in *McGregor's* case.

In State v. Pratt, 226 N.J.Super. 307, 544 A.2d 392 (1988), the court concluded that ordinarily, and in the circumstances before the court, the defendant's age (here, also fifteen) was not relevant to provocation, but that perhaps, e.g., in a case where a child's age suggests a general inability to meet a course of ill treatment, thereby inducing a homicidal response in a person of reasonable firmness, it might be.

Questions

1. When applying the objective branch of the provocation test, how far should the peculiarities of the particular defendant be assigned to the reasonable person against whose response the defendant's is to be tested? It seems clear that matters of pure temperament cannot be allowed to help the accused if any objective standard is to be retained. To test the nature of the hot-blooded defendant's response against the probable response of a hot-blooded reasonable person would not be very illuminating, though it might point up an argument, say, that even most hot-blooded people would not have had the extreme reaction that the defendant had. On the other hand, there seems to be no threat to proper objectivity in investing the reasonable man with perceptual difficulties of the accused, if these difficulties are not produced by his own fault. If the poor vision of the defendant causes him to interpret an offered handshake as a threatening blow, why should not the jury consider a reasonable person with poor eyesight? Of course, such a person would be aware of his limitation, and would anticipate possible errors of this kind, and would guard against them with reasonable care. Other kinds of peculiarities present more difficulty, as the English cases show. *Camplin* might suggest that the defendant has the advantage of everything but temperamental excesses. *Newell* would eliminate the various circumstances which led up to the defendant's explosion except to the extent that they are "characteristics" which are directly affected by the provocation offered. Where should the line be drawn, and on what principle?

2. To what extent are the English cases in the previous note consistent with the Model Penal Code position?

3. *Policy.* At common law provocation was not an excusing or justifying circumstance, but it did reduce an intentional killing from murder to manslaughter.

One who kills in the grip of overwhelming passion brought about by circumstances which are legally sufficient for provocation is entitled to mitigation of his offense. Why should the law take what might be thought to be a compromise position as to provocation? Is one who meets the provocation requirements less reprehensible, less dangerous, less subject to deterrence, less in need of reformation, than the ordinary murderer? Is there an argument that provocation should be an aggravating, rather than a mitigating, factor?

Note on Arrest Powers

The next principal case deals with resisting unlawful arrest. Resisting lawful arrest is a common law misdemeanor; affirmative resistance would amount to an assault as well. If the arrestee, in resisting, kills the arrester, there is certainly nothing in the arrest to mitigate the homicide offense otherwise committed. In the case of an unlawful arrest, however, the circumstances are different because traditionally there has been a right to resist under some circumstances.

As background for the cases, it is useful to have some basic knowledge of the nature of the right to make an arrest. An arrest made on a warrant issued by a magistrate is rarely illegal. Most problems arise in arrests made without the formality of a warrant. While statutes often enlarge police powers in warrantless arrests, the following notes provide summaries, sufficient for our purposes, of the powers of the police and private citizens to make warrantless arrests.

1. *Police Officer Arresting for a Felony.* United States v. Watson, 423 U.S. 411, 418–419, 421–423, 96 S.Ct. 820, 825, 827–828, 46 L.Ed.2d 598, 606, 608–609 (1976):

> The cases construing the Fourth Amendment thus reflect the ancient common-law rule that a peace officer was permitted to arrest without a warrant for a misdemeanor or felony committed in his presence as well as for a felony not committed in his presence if there was reasonable ground for making the arrest. 10 Halsbury's Laws of England 344–345 (3d ed. 1955); 4 W. Blackstone, Commentaries * 292; 1 J. Stephen, A History of the Criminal Law of England 193 (1883); 2 M. Hale, Pleas of the Crown * 72–74; Wilgus, Arrest Without a Warrant, 22 Mich.L.Rev. 541, 547–550, 686–688 (1924); Samuel v. Payne, 1 Doug. 359, 99 Eng.Rep. 230 (K.B.1780); Beckwith v. Philby, 6 Barn. & Cress. 635, 108 Eng.Rep. 585 (K.B.1827). This has also been the prevailing rule under state constitutions and statutes. "The rule of the common law, that a peace officer or a private citizen may arrest a felon without a warrant, has been generally held by the courts of the several States to be in force in cases of felony punishable by the civil tribunals." Kurtz v. Moffitt, 115 U.S. 487, 504, 6 S.Ct. 148, 154, 29 L.Ed. 458 (1885).
>
> * * *
>
> The balance struck by the common law in generally authorizing felony arrests on probable cause, but without a warrant, has survived substantially intact. It appears in almost all of the States in the form of express statutory authorization. In 1963, the American Law Institute undertook the task of formulating a model statute governing police powers and practice in criminal law enforcement and related aspects of pretrial procedure. In 1975, after years of discussion, A Model Code of Pre-arraignment Procedure was proposed. Among its provisions was § 120.1 which authorizes an officer to take a person into custody if the officer has reasonable cause to believe that

the person to be arrested has committed a felony, or has committed a misdemeanor or petty misdemeanor in his presence.[11] The commentary to this section said: "The Code thus adopts the traditional and almost universal standard for arrest without a warrant."

This is the rule Congress has long directed its principal law enforcement officers to follow. Congress has plainly decided against conditioning warrantless arrest power on proof of exigent circumstances. Law enforcement officers may find it wise to seek arrest warrants where practicable to do so, and their judgments about probable cause may be more readily accepted where backed by a warrant issued by a magistrate. But we decline to transform this judicial preference into a constitutional rule when the judgment of the Nation and Congress has for so long been to authorize warrantless public arrests on probable cause rather than to encumber criminal prosecutions with endless litigation with respect to the existence of exigent circumstances, whether it was practicable to get a warrant, whether the suspect was about to flee, and the like.

2. *Police Officer Arresting for a Misdemeanor.* In re Alonzo C., 87 Cal. App.3d 707, 712–713, 151 Cal.Rptr. 192, 194–195, 197 (1978):

We do not agree with the contention of appellant that the test is whether circumstances exist that would cause a reasonable person to believe a crime had been committed. Such is the rule as to felonies, but not to misdemeanors. Rather, the correct test for misdemeanors is whether circumstances exist that would cause a reasonable person to believe a crime has been committed *in his presence.* This distinction between felonies, where the offense need not be committed in the presence of the officer to justify a warrantless arrest, and misdemeanors, where the offense must be committed in the presence of the officer, has been followed by case law in California for many years * * *. * * *

The term "in his presence" is liberally construed. The acts must become known to the officer through the sensory perceptions of the officer. The test is whether the misdemeanor is "apparent to the officer's senses." Any and all of the senses are included. (People v. Bock Leung Chew (1956) 142 Cal.App.2d 400, 403, 298 P.2d 118 (possession of narcotic, yen shee, shown by *smell*); People v. Cahill (1958) 163 Cal.App.2d 15, 328 P.2d 995, (*hearing* over the telephone a proposition to engage in prostitution); People v. Lewis (1963) 214 Cal.App.2d 799, 29 Cal.Rptr. 825 (*hearing* over a radio transmitter); Roynon v. Battin (1942) 55 Cal.App.2d 861, 132 P.2d 266 (*telescopic observation* of fish and game laws violation).) Mere suspicion is insufficient. Likewise, it is insufficient cause to arrest for a misdemeanor

11. Section 120.1 of the Model Code provides, in pertinent part:

"(1) *Authority to Arrest Without a Warrant.* A law enforcement officer may arrest a person without a warrant if the officer has reasonable cause to believe that such person has committed

"(a) a felony;

"(b) a misdemeanor, and the officer has reasonable cause to believe that such person

"(i) will not be apprehended unless immediately arrested; or

"(ii) may cause injury to himself or others or damage to property unless immediately arrested; or

"(c) a misdemeanor or petty misdemeanor in the officer's presence."

outside of the officer's presence (which is often the case). The only recourse in such event is to seek a warrant.

The question of reasonable cause to believe that a misdemeanor is taking place in the officer's presence is measured by the events observable to the officer at the time of the arrest. If the officer cannot testify, based on his or her senses, to acts which constitute every material element of the misdemeanor, it cannot be said that the officer has reasonable cause to believe that the misdemeanor was committed *in his presence.*

* * *

* * * The mere fact that Alonzo had paint on his face and an odor of paint and had dropped the sock saturated with paint only shows that at sometime in the past Alonzo had undoubtedly been sniffing, but the time of any sniffing is not established. No evidence exists in the record to show from the observable facts that anyone was ingesting the fumes at the time the officers arrived. While the officer may have had reasonable cause to believe that Alonzo had violated Penal Code section 381, the officer did not have reasonable cause to believe that that misdemeanor took place *in his presence.* * * *

3. *Private Citizen Arresting for a Felony.* United States v. Brown, 551 F.2d 639, 644–645 (5th Cir.1977), reversed en banc on other grounds 569 F.2d 236 (5th Cir.1978):

* * * Mary Brown was initially apprehended by Mr. Mitchell. Although Mitchell is a police officer in Hallandale, Florida, he acted as a private citizen since he was not within his official jurisdiction when he took Mary into custody. Florida follows common law rules regarding arrests by private citizens. At common law, when a felony has actually been committed, a private citizen, acting in good faith, may lawfully arrest a person whom he reasonably believes to have committed the felony. Since a felony had in fact been committed, the next step is to determine whether Mr. Mitchell had reasonable grounds to believe that Mary Brown committed it.

Mary Brown was at the Sears jewelry counter when Phyllis Brown was discussing the purchase of a diamond ring. Both women were observed with books of certificates in their possession. Mary left for another department as Phyllis handed Ms. Cole several unstamped certificates. While she was busy calling security to check on these certificates, Ms. Cole observed the two women hastily leave the store. They left without the ring and without the $100 in certificates Ms. Cole had taken. Mr. Mitchell, after receiving the call, followed the women to their car and asked them if they had any more certificates. Phyllis reached under the seat of the car and handed him some books of certificates. In light of these facts, it appears that Mr. Mitchell had sufficient grounds to believe that the two women had committed a felony. * * *

4. *Private Citizen Arresting for a Misdemeanor.* Baltimore & O.R. Co. v. Cain, 81 Md. 87, 100, 102–103, 31 A. 801, 803–804 (1895):

* * * But the right of a person not an officer to make an arrest is not confined to cases of felony, for he may take into custody, without a warrant, one who in his presence is guilty of an affray or a breach of the peace. "It seems agreed that any one who sees others fighting may lawfully part them, and also stay them till the heat be over, and then deliver them to the

constable, who may carry them before a justice of the peace, in order to their finding sureties for the peace." 1 *Rus. on Crimes,* 272; 1 *Arch. Crim. Prac. & Pl.,* 82; 1 *Haw.P.C.,* ch. 63, sec 11 and 17; 2 *Hale P.C.,* 90; *East P.C.,* 306; Timothy v. Simpson, 1 C.M. & R. 757. * * *

Now, if it be true that the plaintiff was guilty of the reprehensible and disorderly conduct attributed to him by the witnesses, he was incontestably engaged in a flagrant and an outrageous breach of the peace, as pronounced as if there had been an actual affray during the whole time he was in the defendant's car; and it was clearly lawful, under these conditions, for the conductor to expel him and his drunken companions from the train if he had a sufficient force to overcome their threatened resistance, or else to arrest them all without warrant and then deliver them to the first peace officer he could procure within a reasonable time. * * *

The problem of the arrester who injures or kills the arrestee in the course of an arrest will be considered in the material on justification later in the chapter.

Commonwealth v. Moreira

Supreme Judicial Court of Massachusetts, Middlesex, 1983.
338 Mass. 596, 447 N.E.2d 1224.

Before HENNESSEY, C.J., and WILKINS, LIACOS, NOLAN and LYNCH, JJ.

NOLAN, JUSTICE.

After a jury trial in the Superior Court, the defendant was convicted of assault and battery on one Joseph P. Munroe, a Somerville police officer, and he appealed. The Appeals Court reversed the judgment and ordered a new trial on the basis of the trial judge's erroneous instructions with respect to the defense of justification. We granted further appellate review to resolve the issue of a person's right to resist an unlawful arrest.

There was evidence which would allow the jury to find that the police had probable cause to stop the defendant and his companions to inquire into their possession of a handgun on a public street late at night. This would have occurred outside the defendant's home if the defendant had not pushed Officer Munroe into the house, where he assaulted the officer. This evidence was sufficient to support a conclusion that the officer's entry into the defendant's house was involuntary and, therefore, lawful, and that the defendant was without justification to resist, or aid another in resisting a police investigation. This evidence would support a conviction of assault and battery.

There was also evidence presented by the defendant which would warrant the jury in finding that * * * Officer Munroe burst into the house, striking the defendant and sending him violently to the floor. The defendant retaliated, striking Munroe twice with his fists. When Munroe kicked the defendant in the knee, the defendant punched the officer again, hit him with a wrench, and was pushed into the living room and struck with a billy club. The defendant denied striking Munroe with a wrench. The gun which the defendant allegedly had in his possession was not found. This evidence, if believed, would warrant the jury in concluding that the police made an unlawful entry into the defendant's home.

Although the defendant requested that the judge instruct the jury as to the defendant's right to resist an unlawful police intrusion into his home, the judge did not so instruct the jury. The defendant, likewise, requested that the judge instruct the jury that they should consider whether the police had a reasonable basis for believing that the defendant was engaged in the commission of a felony and, thus, whether the police officers' conduct was lawful. The judge declined to give such an instruction.

The Appeals Court concluded that the judge's instructions "had the effect of usurping the jury's fact-finding function on the issue of the lawfulness of the police conduct and, therefore, served to deprive the defendant of a substantial ground of his justification defense." Commonwealth v. Moreira, 14 Mass.App. 909, 911, 436 N.E.2d 423 (1982). On this basis, the Appeals Court reversed the conviction. We agree with that disposition.

We granted the Commonwealth's application for further appellate review to resolve the issue of a person's right to use force to resist an unlawful arrest. In Regina v. Tooley, 2 Ld. Raymond Rep. 1296, 1299–1301 (Q.B.1709), it was held that a person had the right to use force to resist an unlawful arrest. The court declared, "[I]f one be imprisoned upon an unlawful authority, it is a sufficient provocation to all people out of compassion; much more where it is done under a colour of justice, and where the liberty of the subject is invaded, it is a provocation to all the subjects of *England.*" Id. at 1301. In 1865, we held that a person had the right to resist forcibly an unlawful arrest. Upon review of this area of the law, we conclude that this rule is no longer consistent with the needs of modern society and should be abrogated.

We note that the trend in this country has been away from the old rule and toward the resolution of disputes in court.[2] Since 1709, society has

2. See Miller v. State, 462 P.2d 421, 427 (Alaska 1969); State v. Hatton, 116 Ariz. 142, 147–148, 568 P.2d 1040 (1977); State v. Richardson, 95 Idaho 446, 451, 511 P.2d 263 (1973), cert. denied, 414 U.S. 1163, 94 S.Ct. 928, 39 L.Ed.2d 117 (1974); State v. Thomas, 262 N.W.2d 607, 610–611 (Iowa 1978); State v. Austin, 381 A.2d 652, 655 (Me.1978); In the Matter of the Welfare of Burns, 284 N.W.2d 359, 360 (Minn.1979); State v. Nunes, 546 S.W.2d 759, 762 (Mo.App.1977); State v. Koonce, 89 N.J.Super. 169, 183–184, 214 A.2d 428 (App.Div.1965); State v. Doe, 92 N.M. 100, 102–103, 583 P.2d 464 (1978); Columbus v. Fraley, 41 Ohio St.2d 173, 179–180, 324 N.E.2d 735, cert. denied, 423 U.S. 872, 96 S.Ct. 138, 46 L.Ed.2d 102 (1975); State v. Blaine, 133 Vt. 345, 348 (1975). But see Brooks v. State, 144 Ga.App. 97, 100, 240 S.E.2d 593 (1977) (person may use force to resist unlawful arrest only to extent necessary to prevent arrest); State v. Goering, 193 Kan. 307, 312, 392 P.2d 930 (1964) (person may not use more force than is necessary to escape); Jenkins v. State, 232 Md. 529, 534, 194 A.2d 618 (1963) (same); People v. Krum, 374 Mich. 356, 361, 132 N.W.2d 69, cert. denied, 381 U.S. 935, 85 S.Ct. 1765, 14 L.Ed. 2d 699 (1965) (person may use such force as is necessary to resist unlawful arrest); Smith v. State, 208 So.2d 746, 747 (Miss.1968) (person has right to use reasonable force to resist unlawful arrest); State v. Sanders, 295 N.C. 361, 367, 245 S.E.2d 674 (1978) (person may resist unlawful arrest only by such force as appears to be necessary); Sandersfield v. State, 568 P.2d 313, 315 (Okl.Cr.App.1977) (within limits dictated by circumstances of case, person may reasonably resist unlawful arrest); State v. DeBerry, 250 S.C. 314, 320, 157 S.E.2d 637 (1967), cert. denied, 391 U.S. 953, 88 S.Ct. 1857, 20 L.Ed.2d 867 (1968) (person may use such force as is necessary to prevent unlawful arrest); Shelton v. State, 3 Tenn.Cr. App. 310, 460 S.W.2d 869, 874 (Tenn.Cr. App.1970) (person may use such force as is proportionate to efforts of police officer); State v. Rousseau, 40 Wash.2d 92, 94–96, 241 P.2d 447 (1952) (in resisting unlawful arrest person may use reasonable force proportionate to the injury attempted); State v. Gum, 68 W.Va. 105, 109, 69 S.E. 463 (1910) (person may use such force as is necessary to effectuate escape). We also note that some legislatures have abrogated the common law rule. See Ala.Code § 13A–3–28 (1982); Ark.Stat.Ann.

changed. In this era of constantly expanding legal protection of the rights of the accused in criminal proceedings, an arrestee may be reasonably required to submit to a possibly unlawful arrest and to take recourse in the legal processes available to restore his liberty. An arrestee has the benefit of liberal bail laws, appointed counsel, the right to remain silent and to cut off questioning, speedy arraignment, and speedy trial. As a result of these rights and procedural safeguards, the need for the common law rule disappears—self-help by an arrestee has become anachronistic. * * *

Thus, the modern view, adopted by eleven States by judicial decision, and by nineteen States by legislative enactment, emerges: a person may not resist an unlawful arrest which is accomplished without excessive force. If a police officer is making an illegal arrest, but without excessive force, the remedy is to be found in the courts. The legality of an arrest may often be a close question as to which even lawyers and judges may disagree. Such a close question is more properly decided by a detached magistrate rather than by the participants in what may well be a highly volatile imbroglio. * * *

Accordingly, we conclude that in the absence of excessive or unnecessary force by an arresting officer, a person may not use force to resist an arrest by one who he knows or has good reason to believe is an authorized police officer, engaged in the performance of his duties, regardless of whether the arrest was unlawful in the circumstances. We shall no longer follow cases in this Commonwealth to the contrary on this issue. This principle is to be applied to incidents occurring after the date of this decision. Thus, the rule that we announce today is not to be applied in a new trial of this case. * * *

Our conclusion does not apply to cases in which the police officer uses excessive force in his attempt to subdue the arrestee. In such a situation, the disposition of the case depends on the application of the rules pertaining to self-defense. Thus, we conclude that where the officer uses excessive or unnecessary force to subdue the arrestee, regardless of whether the arrest is lawful or unlawful, the arrestee may defend himself by employing such force as reasonably appears to be necessary. Moreover, once the arrestee knows or reasonably should know that if he desists from using force in self-defense, the officer will cease using force, the arrestee must desist. Otherwise, he will forfeit his defense.

The questions whether the officer used excessive force and whether the arrestee used reasonable force to resist the excessive force are questions of fact to be resolved by the jury on proper instruction by the trial judge. Application of this rule will not require that the arrestee act in a manner commensurate with such action as would follow detached and reasoned

§ 41–512 (1977); Cal.Penal Code § 834a (Deering 1971); Colo.Rev.Stat. § 18–8–103(2) (1978); Conn.Gen.Stat. § 53a–23 (1981); Del.Code Ann. tit. 11, § 464(d) (1979); Fla. Stat. § 776.051(1) (1976); Ill.Stat.Ann. ch. 38, § 7–7 (Smith–Hurd 1972); Iowa Code § 804.12 (1980); Mont.Code Ann. § 45–3–108 (1981); Neb.Rev.Stat. § 28–1409(2) (1979); N.H.Rev.Stat.Ann. § 594.5 (1974); N.Y. Penal Law § 35.27 (McKinney 1975); Or.Rev.Stat. § 161.260 (1981); 18 Pa.Cons. Stat. § 505(b)(1), (2) (Purdon 1973); R.I.Gen. Laws § 12–7–10 (1981); S.D.Comp.Laws Ann. § 22–11–5 (1978); Tex.Penal Code §§ 9.31(b)(2), 38.03 (Vernon 1974); Va.Code § 18.2–460 (1982). See also Ky.Rev.Stat. § 520.090 (1975); Model Penal Code § 3.04(2)(a)(i) (1974).

reflection. Some recognition must be given to the frailty of human nature. The rule merely requires the finder of fact to determine whether the arrestee's conduct was reasonable in light of all the circumstances.

In summary, we conclude that in the absence of excessive force by the arresting officer, an arrestee is not privileged to use force to resist an unlawful arrest if the arrestee knows or reasonably believes that the arresting officer is an authorized police officer. However, where the arresting officer uses excessive force in his attempt to subdue the arrestee, the arrestee has the right to use such force as is reasonably necessary to repel such excessive force.

* * *

Judgment of the Superior Court reversed.

Verdict set aside.

Notes

1. *Illegal arrest as provocation at common law.* Davis v. State, 204 Md. 44, 53–54, 102 A.2d 816, 820–821 (1954):

> There are two major lines of judicial reasoning in a case of a killing in resisting an illegal arrest. One says that once the illegality of the arrest is established, the degree of homicide cannot be greater than manslaughter unless express malice is proven. * * * Other courts reach the same result by a rationalization that an illegal arrest is such an affront to the ordinary citizen that it is to be conclusively presumed that there is aroused in him a passion amounting to exculpatory provocation. The fundamental reason for the result reached, either with or without rationalization, is that a wise and sound social policy requires the protection of the liberty of the citizen against the unlawful enforcement of the law * * *.
>
> The second major line of cases recognizes the wisdom and necessity of the social policy but refuses to permit a reduction of the grade of the homicide to come about automatically. These cases apply a subjective standard and hold that the accused must in fact have been filled with passion aroused by the illegal arrest sufficient to meet the usual provocation tests, if murder is to be reduced to manslaughter.

2. *Model Penal Code Position.* Model Penal Code § 3.04, Comment 3: *

3. *Limitations on Use of Force.* * * *

> (a) *Resisting Arrest.* Subsection (2)(a)(i) denies a justification for the use of force to resist an officer who is merely making an arrest, when the actor knows that it is a peace officer who is making the arrest. The lawfulness of the arrest, or the actor's belief in this regard, is immaterial.
>
> At the time the Model Code was approved, it was undoubtedly the prevailing rule in penal law as well as tort law that one might use moderate force to defend oneself against an illegal arrest. The Restatement of Torts then did, and still does, sanction the use of any means of self-defense against confinement that the actor "is privileged to use to protect himself against a harmful or offensive contact or other bodily harm"—a principle that justifies the use of moderate but not deadly force.

The Model Code reflects the Institute's view that legislative reconsideration of the issue should result in the conclusion that there ought not to be a privilege to employ force against a public officer who, to the actor's knowledge, is attempting only to arrest him and subject him to the processes of law. It should be possible to provide adequate remedies against illegal arrest without permitting the arrested person to resort to force—a course of action highly likely to result in even greater injury to himself than the detention. There is also the fact that the law of arrest is at present confused and cumbersome; there are quite likely to be instances of technical illegality where the values to be enforced by recognizing the illegality should be determined in a prompt judicial hearing, rather than on the street in a test of force. To the extent that law can encourage conduct on this point, it is believed to be entirely sound that the encouragement be in favor of judicial resolution of the legality of the arrest, rather than self-help.

Opponents of this subsection, including a substantial minority of the members of the Institute, have advanced a number of arguments for the old rule. They suggest that the Code's approach will encourage abuses of authority, eliminating one restraint on illegal police behavior and affording the police a new weapon against persons improperly arrested. They urge that alternative remedies for police misbehavior have proved ineffective. And they doubt that the criminal prohibition of resistance will much affect the actions of outraged citizens subjected to illegal arrests. The result, they fear, will be not to substantially reduce clashes of force in these situations, but to add the penalty of criminal charges for citizens who typically will come off second best in physical encounters with the police. Despite the force of those contentions, the most sensible way in which to develop the law is to make efforts to reduce such clashes of force, as this subsection seeks to do, and to strengthen other remedies for genuine abuses.

It should of course be noted, however, that the limitation forbids the use of force for the sole purpose of preventing an arrest; it has no application when the actor apprehends bodily injury, as when the arresting officer unlawfully employs or threatens deadly force, unless the actor knows that he is in no greater peril than arrest if he submits to the assertion of authority. The actor thus does not lose his justification if the officer uses more force than is necessary to effect the arrest, or otherwise constitutes a danger to the safety of the citizen.

It should be noted also that the limitation does not apply to the resistance of illegal arrest by a person not known to the actor to be a peace officer. * * *

* * *

Questions

1. Should the existence or non-existence of an arrest warrant be relevant to the existence of a privilege to resist an illegal arrest?

2. Should there ever be a privilege to resist arrest?

d. *THE BURDEN OF PERSUASION*

Introductory Note

In criminal cases the state has the burden of persuasion beyond a reasonable doubt as to the criminal act and as to the mental attitude with respect to it (purpose, knowledge, recklessness, or negligence, in Model Penal Code terms). Sometimes, however, as to particular matters of justification, excuse, or mitigation, legislation or case law may place the burden of persuasion, usually by a preponderance of the evidence, on the accused. The chart shows the difference it makes if, for example, the defendant has the burden of persuasion on the issue of self-defense.

State of the evidence	State has burden of persuasion on all issues Consequence	Accused has burden of persuasion on self-defense only Consequence
1. State proves *actus reus* and intention to kill or inflict grievous bodily harm beyond a reasonable doubt; no further evidence	Jury may convict of murder	Jury may convict of murder
2. Evidence appears which raises a reasonable doubt in the minds of the jury that the killing was not committed in self-defense	Jury should acquit	No consequence; jury may convict of murder
3. Evidence appears which persuades the jury by a preponderance of the evidence that the accused acted in self-defense	------------------	Jury should acquit

Martin v. Ohio deals with the problem of the constitutionality of shifting the burden of persuasion on such issues to the defense.

Application of the rules of proof does not work with complete smoothness. Apart from confusion about the facts, or misinterpretation of the instructions on the law, the jury may want to resist the conclusion that the law seems to compel. This raises the problem of jury nullification. On this, see, e.g., the concurring opinion of Justice Kaus in People v. Dillon, 34 Cal.3d 441, 490–492, 194 Cal. Rptr. 390, 421–422, 668 P.2d 697, 728–729 (1983):

"When the jury asked whether it was compelled to find defendant guilty of first degree murder if it found certain facts to be true, it was obviously looking for a way to avoid the harsh consequences of the felony-murder rule. The court reiterated its earlier instruction on the law, concluding that if 'this killing occurred during the attempted robbery, then it would be murder of the first degree.' When this instruction is coupled with the court's earlier standard admonition that it is the jury's duty 'to apply the rules of law that I state to you to the facts as you determine them * * *' this left the jury no choice. As far as the average lay juror is concerned, failure to follow the court's instructions invites legal sanctions of some kind and unless the juror is willing to risk a fine, jail or heaven knows what, he or she feels bound to follow the instructions. Yet the essence of the jury's power to 'nullify' a rule or result which it considers unjust is precisely that the law cannot touch a juror who joins in a legally unjustified acquittal or guilty verdict on a lesser charge than the one which the proof calls for.[1] It seems to me that when the jury practically begged the court to show it a way by which to

1. For diverse views on the subject of jury nullification, see, e.g., Scheflin & Van Dyke, *Jury Nullification: The Contours of a Controversy* (1980) 43 Law & Contemp.Probs. No. 4, p. 51; Scheflin, *Jury Nullification: The Right To Say No* (1972) 45 So.Cal.L.Rev. 168; Christie, *Lawful Departures From Legal Rules: "Jury Nullification" and Legitimated Disobedience* (Book Review 1974) 62 Cal.L.Rev. 1289 (hereafter *Christie*); Kadish & Kadish, Discretion to Disobey (Stan.U.Press 1973); Kalven & Zeisel, The American Jury (Little, Brown 1966) pp. 286–312.

avoid a first degree verdict, its immunity from legal harm if it followed its conscience was a fact of legal life on which the court was bound to instruct.[2]

* * *

"* * * To instruct on nullification at the outset of deliberations affirmatively invites the jury to consider disregarding the law. I understand the arguments against such a course and do not advocate it. What happened here, however, is that the court was faced with a jury which, after some deliberation and of its own accord, in effect asked: 'May we nullify?' The answer it was given was obviously incorrect."

* * *

Martin v. Ohio

Supreme Court of the United States, 1987.
480 U.S. 228, 107 S.Ct. 1098, 94 L.Ed.2d 267.

JUSTICE WHITE delivered the opinion of the Court.

The Ohio Code provides that "[e]very person accused of an offense is presumed innocent until proven guilty beyond a reasonable doubt, and the burden of proof for all elements of the offense is upon the prosecution. The burden of going forward with the evidence of an affirmative defense, and the burden of proof by a preponderance of the evidence, for an affirmative defense, is upon the accused." Ohio Rev.Code Ann. § 2901.05(A) (1982). An affirmative defense is one involving "an excuse or justification peculiarly within the knowledge of the accused, on which he can fairly be required to adduce supporting evidence." Ohio Rev.Code Ann. § 2901.05(C)(2) (1982). The Ohio courts have "long determined that self-defense is an affirmative defense," and that the defendant has the burden of proving it as required by § 2901.05(A).

As defined by the trial court in its instructions in this case, the elements of self-defense that the defendant must prove are (1) that the defendant was not at fault in creating the situation giving rise to the argument; (2) the defendant had an honest belief that she was in imminent danger of death or great bodily harm and that her only means of escape from such danger was in the use of such force; and (3) the defendant must not have violated any duty to retreat or avoid danger. The question before us is whether the Due Process Clause of the Fourteenth Amendment forbids placing the burden of proving self-defense on the defendant when she is charged by the State of Ohio with committing the crime of aggravated murder, which, as relevant to this case, is defined by the Revised Code of Ohio as "purposely, and with prior calculation and design, caus[ing] the death of another." Ohio Rev.Code Ann. § 2903.01 (1982).

The facts of the case, taken from the opinions of the courts below, may be succinctly stated. On July 21, 1983, petitioner Earline Martin and her husband, Walter Martin, argued over grocery money. Petitioner claimed that her husband struck her in the head during the argument. Petitioner's version of what then transpired was that she went upstairs, put on a robe, and later

2. Minimally such an instruction should have informed the jury of (1) its power to render a verdict more lenient than the facts justify, and (2) its immunity from punishment if it chooses to exercise that power.

came back down with her husband's gun which she intended to dispose of. Her husband saw something in her hand and questioned her about it. He came at her, she lost her head and fired the gun at him. Five or six shots were fired, three of them striking and killing Mr. Martin. She was charged with and tried for aggravated murder. She pleaded self-defense and testified in her own defense. The judge charged the jury with respect to the elements of the crime and of self-defense and rejected petitioner's Due Process Clause challenge to the charge placing on her the burden of proving self-defense. The jury found her guilty.

Both the Ohio Court of Appeals and the Supreme Court of Ohio affirmed the conviction. Both rejected the constitutional challenge to the instruction requiring petitioner to prove self-defense. The latter court, relying upon our opinion in Patterson v. New York, 432 U.S. 197, 97 S.Ct. 2319, 53 L.Ed.2d 281 (1977), concluded that, the State was required to prove the three elements of aggravated murder but that *Patterson* did not require it to disprove self-defense, which is a separate issue that did not require Mrs. Martin to disprove any element of the offense with which she was charged. * * *

In re Winship, 397 U.S. 358, 364, 90 S.Ct. 1068, 1072, 25 L.Ed.2d 368 (1970), declared that the Due Process Clause "protects the accused against conviction except upon proof beyond a reasonable doubt of every fact necessary to constitute the crime with which he is charged." A few years later, we held that *Winship*'s mandate was fully satisfied where the State of New York had proved beyond reasonable doubt, each of the elements of murder, but placed on the defendant the burden of proving the affirmative defense of extreme emotional disturbance, which, if proved, would have reduced the crime from murder to manslaughter. Patterson v. New York, supra. We there emphasized the preeminent role of the States in preventing and dealing with crime and the reluctance of the Court to disturb a State's decision with respect to the definition of criminal conduct and the procedures by which the criminal laws are to be enforced in the courts, including the burden of producing evidence and allocating the burden of persuasion. New York had the authority to define murder as the intentional killing of another person. It had chosen, however, to reduce the crime to manslaughter if the defendant proved by a preponderance of the evidence that he had acted under the influence of extreme emotional distress. To convict of murder, the jury was required to find beyond a reasonable doubt, based on all the evidence, including that related to the defendant's mental state at the time of the crime, each of the elements of murder and also to conclude that the defendant had not proved his affirmative defense. The jury convicted Patterson, and we held there was no violation of the Fourteenth Amendment as construed in *Winship*. * * * It was also observed that "the fact that a majority of the States have now assumed the burden of disproving affirmative defenses—for whatever reasons—[does not] mean that those States that strike a different balance are in violation of the Constitution."

As in *Patterson,* the jury was here instructed that to convict it must find, in light of all the evidence, that each of elements of the crime of aggravated murder must be proved by the State beyond reasonable doubt and that the burden of proof with respect to these elements did not shift. To find guilt, the jury had to be convinced that none of the evidence, whether offered by the State or by Martin in connection with her plea of self-defense, raised a reasonable doubt that Martin had killed her husband, that she had the specific purpose and intent to cause his death, or that she had done so with prior calculation and design. It was also told, however, that it could acquit if it found by a preponderance of the evidence that Martin had not precipitated the confrontation, that she had an honest belief that she was in imminent danger of death or great bodily harm, and that she had satisfied any duty to retreat or avoid danger. The jury convicted Martin.

We agree with the State and its Supreme Court that this conviction did not violate the Due Process Clause. * * *

It would be quite different if the jury had been instructed that self-defense evidence could not be considered in determining whether there was a reasonable doubt about the state's case, i.e., that self-defense evidence must be put aside for all purposes unless it satisfied the preponderance standard. Such instruction would relieve the state of its burden and plainly run afoul of *Winship*'s mandate. The instructions in this case could be clearer in this respect, but when read as a whole, we think they are adequate to convey to the jury that all of the evidence, including the evidence going to self-defense, must be considered in deciding whether there was a reasonable doubt about the sufficiency of the state's proof of the elements of the crime.

We are thus not moved by assertions that the elements of aggravated murder and self-defense overlap in the sense that evidence to prove the latter will often tend to negate the former. It may be that most encounters in which self-defense is claimed arise suddenly and involve no prior plan or specific purpose to take life. In those cases, evidence offered to support the defense may negate a purposeful killing by prior calculation and design, but Ohio does not shift to the defendant the burden of disproving any element of the state's case. When the prosecution has made out a *prima facie* case and survives a motion to acquit, the jury may nevertheless not convict if the evidence offered by the defendant raises any reasonable doubt about the existence of any fact necessary for the finding of guilt. Evidence creating a reasonable doubt could easily fall far short of proving self-defense by a preponderance of the evidence. Of course, if such doubt is not raised in the jury's mind and each juror is convinced that the defendant purposely and with prior calculation and design took life, the killing will still be excused if the elements of the defense are satisfactorily established. We note here, but need not rely on it, the observation of the Supreme Court of Ohio that "Appellant did not dispute the existence of [the elements of aggravated murder], but rather sought to justify her actions on grounds she acted in self-defense." 21 Ohio St.3d, at 94, 488 N.E.2d, at 168.**

** The dissent believes that the self-defense instruction might have led the jury to believe that the defendant had the burden of proving prior calculation and design. Indeed, its position is that *no* instruction could be clear enough not to mislead the jury. As is evident from the test, we disagree. We do not harbor the dissent's mistrust of the jury; and the instructions were sufficiently clear to convey to the jury that the state's burden of proving prior calculation did not shift and that self-defense evidence had to be considered in determining whether the state's burden had been discharged. We do not depart from Patterson v.

* * *

As we noted in *Patterson,* the common law rule was that affirmative defenses, including self-defense, were matters for the defendant to prove. "This was the rule when the Fifth Amendment was adopted, and it was the American rule when the Fourteenth Amendment was ratified." 432 U.S., at 202, 97 S.Ct., at 2322. Indeed, well into this century, a number of States followed the common law rule and required a defendant to shoulder the burden of proving that he acted in self-defense. We are aware that all but two of the States, Ohio and South Carolina, have abandoned the common law rule and require the prosecution to prove the absence of self-defense when it is properly raised by the defendant. But the question remains whether those States are in violation of the Constitution; and, as we observed in *Patterson,* that question is not answered by cataloging the practices of other States. * * *

The judgment of the Ohio Supreme Court is accordingly

Affirmed.

JUSTICE POWELL, with whom JUSTICE BRENNAN and JUSTICE MARSHALL join, and with whom JUSTICE BLACKMUN joins with respect to Parts I and III, dissenting.

Today the Court holds that a defendant can be convicted of aggravated murder even though the jury may have a reasonable doubt whether the accused acted in self-defense, and thus, whether he is guilty of a crime. Because I think this decision is inconsistent with both precedent and fundamental fairness, I dissent.

I

* * *

In *Patterson,* the Court upheld a state statute that shifted the burden of proof for an affirmative defense to the accused. New York law required the prosecutor to prove all of the statutorily defined elements of murder beyond a reasonable doubt, but permitted a defendant to reduce the charge to manslaughter by showing that he acted while suffering an "extreme emotional disturbance." The Court found that this burden-shifting did not violate due process, largely because the affirmative defense did "not serve to negative any facts of the crime which the State is to prove in order to convict of murder." The clear implication of this ruling is that when an affirmative defense *does* negate an element of the crime, the state may not shift the burden. In such a case, In re Winship, 397 U.S. 358, 90 S.Ct. 1068, 25 L.Ed. 2d 368 (1970), requires the state to prove the nonexistence of the defense beyond a reasonable doubt.

The reason for treating a defense that negates an element of the crime differently from other affirmative defenses is plain. If the jury is told that the prosecution has the burden of proving all the elements of a crime, but then

New York, 432 U.S. 197, 97 S.Ct. 2319, 53 L.Ed.2d 281 (1977), in this respect, or in any other.

also is instructed that the defendant has the burden of *dis* proving one of those same elements, there is a danger that the jurors will resolve the inconsistency in a way that lessens the presumption of innocence. For example, the jury might reasonably believe that by raising the defense, the accused has assumed the ultimate burden of proving that particular element. Or, it might reconcile the instructions simply by balancing the evidence that supports the prosecutor's case against the evidence supporting the affirmative defense, and conclude that the state has satisfied its burden if the prosecution's version is more persuasive. In either case, the jury is given the unmistakable but erroneous impression that the defendant shares the risk of nonpersuasion as to a fact necessary for conviction.

Given these principles, the Court's reliance on *Patterson* is puzzling. Under Ohio law, the element of "prior calculation and design" is satisfied only when the accused has engaged in a "definite process of reasoning *in advance* of the killing," *i.e.,* when he has given the plan at least some "studied consideration." In contrast, when a defendant such as Martin raises a claim of self-defense, the jury also is instructed that the accused must prove that she "had an honest belief that she was in *imminent* danger of death or great bodily harm." In many cases, a defendant who finds himself in immediate danger and reacts with deadly force will not have formed a prior intent to kill. The Court recognizes this when it states:

> "It may be that most encounters in which self-defense is claimed arise suddenly and involve no prior plan or specific purpose to take life. In those cases, evidence offered to support the defense may negate a purposeful killing by prior calculation and design. * * *"

Under *Patterson,* this conclusion should suggest that Ohio is precluded from shifting the burden as to self-defense. The Court nevertheless concludes that Martin was properly required to prove self-defense, simply because "Ohio does not shift to the defendant the burden of disproving any element of the state's case."

* * *

This reasoning is flawed in two respects. First, it simply ignores the problem that arises from inconsistent jury instructions in a criminal case. The Court's holding implicitly assumes that the jury in fact understands that the ultimate burden remains with the prosecutor at all times, despite a conflicting instruction that places the burden on the accused to disprove the same element. But as pointed out above, the *Patterson* distinction between defenses that negate an element of the crime and those that do not is based on the legitimate concern that the jury *will* mistakenly lower the state's burden. * * *

Second, the Court significantly, and without explanation, extends the deference granted to state legislatures in this area. Today's decision could be read to say that virtually all state attempts to shift the burden of proof for affirmative defenses will be upheld, regardless of the relationship between the elements of the defense and the elements of the crime. As I understand it, *Patterson* allowed burden-shifting because evidence of an extreme emotional disturbance did not negate the *mens rea* of the underlying offense. After today's decision, however, even if proof of the defense *does* negate an element of the offense, burden-shifting still may be permitted because the jury can consider the defendant's evidence when reaching its verdict.

* * * In the past we have emphasized that in some circumstances it may be necessary to look beyond the text of the State's burden-shifting laws to satisfy ourselves that the requirements of *Winship* have been satisfied. In Mullaney v. Wilbur, 421 U.S. 684, 698–699, 95 S.Ct. 1881, 1889, 44 L.Ed. 2d 508 (1975) we explicitly noted the danger of granting the State unchecked discretion to shift the burden as to any element of proof in a criminal case. * * *

* * *

II

Although I believe that this case is wrongly decided even under the principles set forth in *Patterson,* my differences with the Court's approach are more fundamental. I continue to believe that the better method for deciding when a state may shift the burden of proof is outlined in the Court's opinion in *Mullaney* and in my dissenting opinion in *Patterson.* In *Mullaney,* we emphasized that the state's obligation to prove certain facts beyond a reasonable doubt was not necessarily restricted to legislative distinctions between offenses and affirmative defenses. The boundaries of the state's authority in this respect were elaborated in the *Patterson* dissent, where I proposed a two-part inquiry:

> "The Due Process Clause requires that the prosecutor bear the burden of persuasion beyond a reasonable doubt only if the factor at issue makes a substantial difference in punishment and stigma. The requirement of course applies *a fortiori* if the factor makes the difference between guilt and innocence * * *. It also must be shown that in the Anglo–American legal tradition the factor in question historically has held that level of importance. If either branch of the test is not met, then the legislature retains its traditional authority over matters of proof." 432 U.S., at 226–227, 97 S.Ct., at 2335 (footnotes omitted).

* * *

III

In its willingness to defer to the State's legislative definitions of crimes and defenses, the Court apparently has failed to recognize the practical effect of its decision. Martin alleged that she was innocent because she acted in self-defense, a complete justification under Ohio law. Because she had the burden of proof on this issue, the jury could have believed that it was just as likely as not that Martin's conduct was justified, and yet still have voted to convict. In other words, even though the jury may have had a substantial doubt whether Martin committed a crime, she was found guilty under Ohio law. * * *

Notes

1. *Rebuttable presumptions.* In Francis v. Franklin, 471 U.S. 307, 105 S.Ct. 1965, 85 L.Ed.2d 344 (1985), the Supreme Court considered a jury instruction, as to an element of the crime charged, which stated that the acts of a person of sound mind were rebuttably presumed to be the product of his will, and that he was rebuttably presumed to intend the natural and probable consequences of his acts. The jury was also instructed that the State must prove every element of the offense beyond a reasonable doubt. A majority of the Court held that an instruction based on mandatory presumption—one which requires the jury to find the presumed fact if the State proves certain predicate facts (here, one which requires the jury to find that the act was willed or intended and that the accused intended the natural and probable consequences of his acts, if he was of sound mind)—is unconstitutional if it relieves the State of the burden of persuasion on an element of the offense (here, intent). The Court continued (at 316–318 of U.S., 1972–1973 of S.Ct., 354–356 of L.Ed.2d):

> The challenged sentences are cast in the language of command: They instruct the jury that "acts of a person of sound mind and discretion *are presumed* to be the product of the person's will," and that a person "*is presumed* to intend the natural and probable consequences of his acts,". These words carry precisely the message of the language condemned in Sandstrom [v. Montana, 442 U.S. 510, 99 S.Ct. 2450, 61 L.Ed.2d 39 (1979)] (" '[t]he law presumes that a person intends the ordinary consequences of his voluntary acts' "). The jurors "were not told that they had a choice or that they *might* infer that conclusion they were told only that the law presumed it. It is clear that a reasonable juror could easily have viewed such an instruction as mandatory." The portion of the jury charge challenged in this case directs the jury to presume an essential element of the offense—intent to kill—upon proof of other elements of the offense—the act of slaying another. In this way the instructions "undermine the factfinder's responsibility at trial, based on evidence adduced by the State, to *find* the ultimate facts beyond a reasonable doubt."
>
> The language challenged here differs from *Sandstrom,* of course, in that the jury in this case was explicitly informed that the presumptions "may be rebutted." The State makes much of this additional aspect of the instruction in seeking to differentiate the present case from *Sandstrom.* This distinction does not suffice, however, to cure the infirmity in the charge. Though the Court in *Sandstrom* acknowledged that the instructions there challenged could have been reasonably understood as creating an irrebuttable presumption, it was not on this basis alone that the instructions were invalidated. Had the jury reasonably understood the instructions as creating a mandatory *rebuttable* presumption the instructions would have been no less constitutionally infirm.
>
> An irrebuttable or conclusive presumption relieves the State of its burden of persuasion by removing the presumed element from the case entirely if the State proves the predicate facts. A mandatory rebuttable presumption does not remove the presumed element from the case if the State proves the predicate facts, but it nonetheless relieves the State of the affirmative burden of persuasion on the presumed element by instructing the jury that it must find the presumed element unless the defendant persuades the jury not to make such a finding. A mandatory rebuttable presumption is perhaps less onerous from the defendant's perspective, but it is no less unconstitutional. * * *
>
> * * * Standing alone, the challenged language undeniably created an unconstitutional burden-shifting presumption with respect to the element of intent.

The majority concluded that a reasonable juror might have thought that the burden of persuasion had shifted to the defendant, in spite of other instructions which tended to negative this, and that therefore a federal writ of *habeas corpus* (appropriate to obtain release in certain cases of unconstitutional confinement) had properly been issued.

2. *Intending Natural and Probable Consequences.* The statement that a person is presumed to intend the natural and probable consequences of his act has several possible intended meanings. (1) It might be intended to mean that he is conclusively presumed to do so. This is another way of saying that it makes no difference whether he did so or not; we will treat him as though he did in any event. So, if a natural and probable consequence of hitting V on the head with a hammer is V's death, a jury would be told in effect that if it found that D had intentionally hit V on the head with a hammer, it should also find that D intended to kill V. (2) The statement might be intended to mean less: that the jury should find the intention to kill if it found the intentional hammer blow, unless D persuaded them (usually by preponderance of the evidence) that he in fact had no such intent. These two constructions are impermissible in criminal cases, assuming intention to kill to be an element of the offense, because they would conflict with *Winship* and *Mullaney.* (3) It might be intended to mean the rebuttable presumption discussed in *Francis,* which is impermissible if a reasonable juror might think that the burden of persuasion is shifted to the defendant. (4) It might only be intended to mean that the jury is free to conclude, if it wants to do so, that if D intended the blow, he intended to kill. As such, it may be only a rule of common sense, and it may not be necessary or advisable to mention it to the jury at all. Certainly, it should not be phrased as a presumption. Any mention of the principle should be sufficiently explained so as to eliminate interpretations (1), (2), and (3).

Apart from the constitutionality question, are any of the four interpretations in the preceding paragraph unreasonable, unfair, or unjust, as applied in the hammer example?

3. *Deadly Weapon Rule.* The "deadly weapon rule" is a special case of the "natural and probable consequences principle"; see Smith v. State, 41 Md.App. 277, 281–282, 398 A.2d 426, 430 (1979):

> In this particular case, the variety of intent we are dealing with is the specific intent to kill. In this regard, we have evidence that the appellant fired a sawed-off shotgun at point-blank range into the chest of the victim. This represents, quite clearly, the directing of a dangerous and deadly weapon at a vital part of the human anatomy. It is well established that this gives rise to a permitted inference of the intent to kill. As we said in Evans v. State, at 28 Md.App. 640, 704, 349 A.2d 300, 339–340:
>
>> "The only inference of any significance in our homicide law is the permitted inference of an intent to kill or of an intent to do grievous bodily harm from the directing of a deadly weapon at a vital part of the human anatomy or from some similar use of deadly force. The earlier case law sometimes spoke of the use of a deadly weapon as giving rise to a 'presumption of malice.' In Lindsay v. State, supra (8 Md.App. 100, 258 A.2d 760), however, Chief Judge Orth stole a march on *Mullaney v. Wilbur* and strove mightily to refine the appellate vocabulary of Maryland and to bring it into the 20th century. He meticulously explained that we do not 'presume' anything from the use of deadly force; we are only permitted (but not required) to draw inferences from such use of deadly force. He further pointed out that this permitted inference of fact passes full constitutional muster under Leary v. United States, supra (395 U.S. 6, 89 S.Ct. 1532, 23

L.Ed.2d 57). We reaffirm and add that it thereby also passes constitutional muster according to *Mullaney v. Wilbur* and *Winship.*"

Sometimes, particularly in older cases, the rule is stated too broadly and carries with it in such form the constitutional objections noted in Francis v. Franklin.

Questions

1. Where should the burden of persuasion lie on the issue of self-defense? Why?

2. Is it a defensible rule to have the constitutionality of placing the burden of persuasion on self-defense on the accused turn on whether the legislature adopted a particular form of language?

C. JUSTIFICATION AND EXCUSE

1. Introductory Note

We here examine *mens rea* factors which render conduct which ordinarily is criminal non-criminal. The existence of ordinary *mens rea* for the crime is not denied. The accused may have intended to accomplish the *actus reus* of the offense, or known that he would produce it.[a] But, in a case of justification, we argue that the accused did the right thing—that he was entitled to commit the *actus reus* of an offense to preserve another value. In a case of self-defense, for example, we say that the accused was entitled to injure or kill to save himself from attack. Excuse is less persuasive. We don't claim that the defendant did the right thing; we say only that he has an explanation which makes it unfair or pointless to hold him accountable (or fully accountable). An excuse is usually complete, but it may only mitigate, as in the case of provocation.

Justification and excuse apply to all crimes, so in this section we are looking not only at intentional homicide, but at any crimes which serve to illustrate the principles.

While most of the major instances of justification and excuse are considered here, some, such as consent, appear elsewhere, and some are left to be explored in the treatises.

2. Justification

a. *SELF-DEFENSE AND DEFENSE OF OTHERS*

People v. Flannel

Supreme Court of California, En Banc, 1979.
25 Cal.3d 668, 160 Cal.Rptr. 84, 603 P.2d 1.

TOBRINER, JUSTICE.

Defendant Charles M. Flannel appeals from a judgment of conviction entered on jury verdicts finding him guilty of second degree murder (Pen. Code, § 187), and finding affirmatively on a firearm use allegation (Pen.Code, §§ 1203, subd. d(6) and 12022.5). He contends that the court erred in

a. Justification and excuse are also relevant in crimes of recklessness and negligence, but (except for insanity and infancy, which operate just as in cases of purpose and knowledge to acquit directly) there they become an actual part of the assessment of the existence of recklessness or negligence itself, rather than a separate acquitting matter.

failing to instruct the jury sua sponte that defendant's honest but unreasonable belief that he must defend himself from deadly attack negates malice so that the offense is reduced from murder to manslaughter. * * *

* * *

On June 28, 1976, about 4:15 in the afternoon, defendant shot and killed Charles Daniels. The two men had a history of hostile and violent relations. Daniels objected to defendant's treatment of Daniels' common law daughter, who was defendant's girlfriend, later his wife. Defendant resented Daniels' interference with his romance. Previously, both men had threatened each others' lives. In January 1976 defendant attacked Daniels at a friend's home, kicking Daniels in the chest and head and hitting him with a glass. Rather than prosecute defendant, the district attorney's office held a citation hearing and warned the two men to avoid one another.

On the morning of the killing defendant consumed some four tall cans of beer and a shot or two of whiskey, took his girlfriend shopping and ate lunch. He joined friends in front of a building in Oakland about 2:30 that afternoon. As he talked with friends, defendant shared some beer and whiskey.

About 4 p.m. defendant, observing Daniels approach from nearby, retrieved his gun from the trunk of his car. One friend reassured him that there was no need for a gun, that everybody was "his friend"; when Daniels came close a second time at 4:15 another friend urged defendant to leave in order to prevent trouble. Defendant walked about 12 or 14 feet away but changed his mind and returned to watch Daniels arrive.

Daniels and the group exchanged greetings. Defendant walked up to Daniels and, standing directly in front of him with his hand on the gun in his right front pocket, asked him what was "happening." Daniels graphically told defendant to "stop messing" with him, that they were not supposed to be around each other, and asked him to "get goin'."

Daniels began backing away from the car upon which he had been leaning, waiving defendant away with his left hand while his right hand remained near his back pocket where he was known to have kept his knife. Defendant followed, saying "Was you going to stick me in the side with a knife?" "Come on pull your knife." He then drew the gun from his pocket, extended his arm full length and fired one shot into Daniels' temple from a distance of approximately two feet. As Daniels fell, his switchblade knife flew into the air, landing on the ground where it spun around and popped open. No one observed the knife in Daniels' hand.

Defendant immediately told his friends not to touch Daniels but to "leave him right there." He said, "He pulled a knife on me," adding that Daniels "deserved to be dead, nobody cares." Defendant dropped his weapon and waited until the police arrived.

At trial defendant relied on a theory of self-defense. He testified that Daniels came toward him, grabbed his chest to stabilize him, that Daniels then drew his knife from his back pocket. Defendant was "surprised and scared." Seeing the knife, he pulled his gun out of his front pocket, then jerked away from Daniels and, as Daniels came at him again, he fired. * * *

* * *

To be exculpated on a theory of self-defense one must have an honest *and* reasonable belief in the need to defend. * * *

This rule is not questioned here. Rather, the issue is whether a defender has committed murder or manslaughter when his belief, although honestly held, fails to meet the standard of a "reasonable person."

In People v. Wells (1949) 33 Cal.2d 330, 202 P.2d 53, a prison inmate charged with assault on an officer, a capital offense requiring malice aforethought, sought to introduce evidence of an abnormal mental condition, not amounting to insanity, which caused him to fear for his personal safety. We stated that if defendant "acted only under the influence of fear of bodily harm, in the belief, *honest though unreasonable,* that he was defending himself from such harm by the use of a necessary amount of force, then defendant, although he would not be guiltless of crime, would not have committed that particular aggravated offense with which he is charged, for the essential element of '*malice aforethought*' would be lacking." (Emphasis added.) (33 Cal.2d at p. 345, 202 P.2d at p. 62–63.) *Wells,* then, stands for the proposition that as a mental state, malice cannot coexist with such an unreasonable belief; in finding no prejudicial error, we stated that the jury could find malice motivated the action rather than the "influence of honest, mistaken fear," (id., at p. 358, 202 P.2d 53) which could have negated malice aforethought.

* * *

This approach to unreasonable belief expresses the rule at common law. As one scholar notes, "Since manslaughter is a 'catch-all' concept, covering all homicides which are neither murder nor innocent, it logically includes some killings involving other types of mitigation, and such is the rule of the common law. For example, if one man kills another intentionally, under circumstances beyond the scope of innocent homicide, the facts may come so close to justification or excuse that the killing will be classed as voluntary manslaughter rather than murder." Perkins On Criminal Law (2d ed. 1969) pp. 69–70.)[6] Perkins goes on to add that "some legislative enactments have spoken of voluntary manslaughter in terms only of a killing in 'a sudden heat of passion caused by a provocation' and so forth. Such restriction is probably unintentional, being attributable to the fact that this is by far the most common type of mitigation; but it is very unfortunate." (Id., at p. 70.)[7]

6. A few commentators would hold that *any* honestly held but mistaken belief exculpates rather than mitigates. (See e.g., Williams, Criminal Law, The General Part (2d ed. 1961) p. 204; Keedy, Ignorance and Mistake in the Criminal Law (1908) 22 Harv.L.Rev. 75, 84–85.)

7. In some jurisdictions, such as California, the courts have given effect to the "lack of malice" requirement of otherwise restrictive manslaughter statutes to uphold the unreasonable belief principle. (See, e.g., Allison v. State (1904) 74 Ark. 444, 453–454, 86 S.W. 409; Hartfield v. State (1936) 176 Miss. 776, 784, 170 So. 531; Wood v. State (Okl.Cr.1971) 486 P.2d 750, 752; Commonwealth v. Thompson (1957) 389 Pa. 382, 133 A.2d 207.) In still other states, legislators have passed statutes specifically providing for manslaughter when an individual holds an unreasonable but honest belief in the need to defend against deadly attack. (See, e.g., Colo.Rev. Stat., § 18–3–105(1)(b) (1978); Ill.Rev.Stat. Ann. ch. 38, § 9–2(b) (1972); Wis.Stat.Ann., § 940.05(2) (1958).)

California's rule on the effect of an unreasonably held belief in the need to defend is almost universally supported by those legal commentators who have given in consideration. In the words of two scholars it is "the more humane view that, while [the defender] is not innocent of crime, he is nevertheless not guilty of murder; rather, he is guilty of the in-between crime of manslaughter." (LaFave & Scott, Handbook on Criminal Law (1972) p. 397; see also Model Pen.Code, § 201.3, coms. at pp. 40–46 (Tent.Draft No. 9, 1959); Model Pen.Code, § 3.09, coms. at p. 78 (Tent.Draft No. 8, 1958).) * * *

* * *

Questions

For acquittal on grounds of justification in self-defense the black letter law is that the accused must hold a belief in the need to act which is both honest and reasonable. Suppose that there is an actual need to act in self-defense, but the information available to the accused would not at the time have supported a reasonable, or even an honest, belief in the necessity. E.g., suppose that in *Flannel,* Daniels, unknown to Flannel, had a knife and had told friends that he was going to use it to kill Flannel the next time he saw him. Daniels was on the point of stabbing Flannel when Flannel, not sensing the attack, shot him in anger. If Flannel had not acted, he, and not Daniels, would have died. Should he have a defense?

Notes

1. *Self-defense in Assault.* The cases in this section deal with defendants who killed or who used deadly (probably death-producing) force. Self-defense, however, is applicable to ordinary assault cases as well as to homicides and aggravated assaults. If assaulted, the accused may use non-deadly force, honestly and reasonably believed to be no more than is necessary to protect himself. According to most authority, there is no obligation to retreat as long as non-deadly force is used.

2. *Honest Belief in Necessity. Flannel* expresses the view of many of the modern cases that where the defendant acts honestly but unreasonably, this, at least short of extremely unreasonable conduct, mitigates the killing and makes it manslaughter. California says that malice is absent in such circumstances. Other jurisdictions may treat the problem as analogous to one of those of the general class of reckless killings (in which, it will be remembered, the accused does not intend to injure or kill another). If one is reckless in assessing the need to defend himself, why not convict him of a homicide crime—manslaughter—for which recklessness is an appropriate state of mind? This approach may also allow a final determination of murder if the recklessness is extreme enough to qualify for the depraved heart theory (infra, p. 622), or, where the crime exists, of criminally negligent homicide, where there is negligence. This is essentially the position of the Model Penal Code; read section 3.09(2) in conjunction with section 3.04 and the other justification sections (where the same principle of mitigation applies for honest but unreasonable belief). Other authorities simply accept the result of mitigation as a reasonable compromise. The prevailing common law view was that if justification failed for any reason, the homicide was not mitigated at all.

3. *Excessive Force.* Where some force would be justified in self-defense, but the force actually used is moderately excessive, a manslaughter compromise may also be reached. Suppose A commits an assault upon B, using ordinary force. B resists by

using fatal force when only ordinary force would be justified. Manslaughter is a likely result. Of course, if B responds to a shove with machine gun fire, it will be murder.

Garcia v. State

Supreme Court of Wyoming, 1983.
667 P.2d 1148.

THOMAS, JUSTICE.

* * *

This appeal is taken from a conviction of murder in the second degree * * *. * * *

There is no question raised in this case about the fact that the victim, Cary Connelly, was killed by a stab wound and the fact that the stab wound was inflicted by the appellant. At least from the time of the first contact by law enforcement officers the appellant took the position that the homicide had been committed in self-defense by him while he was acting under a belief that his life was in danger. The appellant so testified at the trial of this case, and consequently the only question really presented in the entire case was whether the homicide was justified.

The underlying facts may be briefly stated. On the night that Cary Connelly was killed a party was being held in a house in the southern part of the City of Cheyenne, Wyoming. The imbibing of beer at this party was extensive, as is probably true at most "keggers," which is the term used to describe a party in which the refreshments consist primarily of a keg of beer. During the course of the evening the appellant and Connelly quarreled; this quarrel apparently evolved from Connelly's assertion that the appellant had taken his cigarettes. The testimony of the witnesses describes several confrontations between the two and sets forth assaults and simple batteries involving these two. These consisted of such events as the swinging of a dog chain by the appellant at Connelly; the pushing of the appellant by Connelly, even down to the ground; and one witness saw a black pot being swung by the appellant. At one point during the evening the appellant went to his own home. It appears that he wanted to get his baseball bat to defend himself. Connelly and another person apparently prevented him from entering his own home, and he returned to the party. During the course of the evening one witness saw the appellant with a knife in his hand, and at that time the appellant indicated he was going to inflict revenge upon a person he believed had called him a derogatory name while he was using the bathroom.

As we have noted, the appellant admitted the stabbing. The eye-witness who observed the most about the killing stated that Connelly was standing by the television in the living room and that the appellant went into the kitchen. He was not followed into the kitchen by Connelly. In the kitchen the appellant opened a drawer and got out a knife. He twirled it and then went back into the living room. He there went toward Connelly and stabbed him in the chest. After Connelly fell to the ground he stabbed him again in the buttocks. The same witness had described an earlier event during the course of which the appellant said to the victim, "you're dead."

While the record is somewhat incomplete with respect to the physical layout of the premises where the killing occurred, it does appear that from a porch there were entrances into the kitchen and into the living room. The living room, where the killing occurred, and the kitchen were connected by a doorway. The clear inference from the record is that the appellant was not under attack by the victim when he went into the kitchen to obtain the knife, and he could have exited the house by means of the door from the kitchen onto the porch. The record also establishes that the appellant stood only about 5 feet 3 inches and weighed about 90 pounds, while Connelly weighed about 190 pounds, which were distributed over a 6 foot 3 inch frame. The disparity in physical size was impressive to all.

It is in the context of this background that the appellant insists that he committed the homicide in self-defense. While our reading of the record leaves us skeptical as to the validity of the defense under these circumstances, we recognize that it was the duty of the district court to give an instruction on self-defense because that was the appellant's theory of the case. We previously have held that a defendant in a criminal case is entitled to an instruction as to his theory of the case if there is evidence to support it.

While the only real evidence in the record of any circumstances that would suggest self-defense comes from the testimony of the appellant, that is sufficient to raise the issue of self-defense consistent with his theory.

The instruction on self-defense which was given by the district court was taken from the Wyoming Pattern Jury Instructions Criminal, No. 5.207, and it reads as follows:

> "Even if the defendant had reasonable ground to believe and actually did believe that he was in imminent danger of death or serious bodily harm, he was justified in using deadly force to repel the danger only if he retreated as far as he safely could before doing so. The law requires a person to retreat rather than to take the life of his adversary if there was a convenient mode of retreat without increasing his peril or apparent peril. To excuse a failure to retreat, it is necessary the defendant's peril would be increased, or that it reasonably appeared that it would be increased by retreat. If you find that the defendant could have safely retreated but failed to do so, the defendant cannot rely on the justification of self defense."

This instruction was objected to by the appellant, and he proposed Instruction No. D, which reads as follows:

> "The defendant has a right to go where he will. If the defendant had reasonable grounds to believe and actually did believe that he was in imminent danger of serious bodily harm, and that deadly force was necessary to repel such danger, he was not required to retreat from a place where he is legally entitled to be. He was entitled to stand his ground and use such force as was reasonably necessary under the circumstances to save his life or protect himself from serious bodily harm.
>
> "The defendant had no duty to retreat if he had even the slightest doubt that he could retreat in complete safety. Even the slightest

doubt, if reasonable, was enough to justify his standing his ground. In determining whether the defendant's doubt was reasonable you may make every allowance for the situation in which Steve Garcia was placed by Cary Connelly."

Appellant contends that his proffered instruction represents what he urges to be a majority view in other jurisdictions in the United States. * * * In his brief the appellant quotes from Mischke, Criminal Law—Homicide—Self-Defense—Duty to Retreat, 48 Tenn.L.Rev. 1000 (1981). We are impressed with the fact that this theory seems to depend upon a person being without fault in bringing on an assault and may, according to some authorities, be restricted to his home or curtilage. While some courts have extended to other places the area within which the defendant can claim the benefit of the rule, we do not perceive the circumstances of this case as those in which the appellant can claim to be without fault.

The appellant participated fully in the prior quarreling and conflict with Connelly. When he went into the kitchen to obtain the knife he had the option of walking on out the door and going peacefully to his own home. There is nothing to indicate that his life was in imminent jeopardy at that time except his claim that it was. Instead he chose to take a knife from a kitchen drawer, return to the living room, and fatally stab Connelly. While the appellant may want to believe that those circumstances constitute self-defense, the law should not justify him in this aberrant style of thinking.

This court previously has considered the defense of self-defense in homicide cases in a number of instances. Self-defense also has been asserted in assault and battery cases.

We can identify several articulations of the rule of self-defense, and it may be that they are not definitive.

> "* * * Self-defense will justify a homicide when a reasonable person deems it necessary in order to avoid infliction of death or great bodily harm upon his or her person. To justify a homicide on this ground, it must appear that the defendant was in great peril of death or serious bodily harm, or had reasonable grounds for so believing. It must appear that the killing was a necessary and reasonable means of avoiding the threatened harm, and the facts and circumstances surrounding the event must be such as to afford such grounds for that belief." Leeper v. State, supra, 589 P.2d at 382.

* * *

> "The law of self defense is founded upon necessity. To justify a homicide, it must appear that the slayer was in great peril of death or serious bodily harm, or had reasonable ground for believing and did believe, that he was in such peril and that the killing was necessary to avert such peril, and that no other reasonable means of avoiding it was open to him. * * *" Durham v. State, 29 Wyo. [85] at 96, 210 P. [934] at 938.

* * *

This court has addressed the so-called "duty to retreat" on several occasions. In general, it can be concluded from these prior discussions that an individual who is without fault in bringing about the incident in which he kills his assailant need not restrict his freedom of movement to go where he has a right to be. The "duty to retreat," where it prevails, is applied in cases of actual assault. Under the circumstances of this case the following comment is instructive:

> "* * * [A] person who provokes or brings on the difficulty in which he kills his assailant cannot invoke the right of self-defense, unless he in good faith retreats as far as he safely can, making that fact manifest to his adversary. * * *" State v. Flory, 40 Wyo. [184] at 199, 276 P. [458] at 462.

Given these prior adjudications with respect to self-defense, the law in the State of Wyoming requires that prior to resorting to deadly force a defendant has a duty to pursue reasonable alternatives under the circumstances. Among those reasonable alternatives may be the duty to retreat. Because that opportunity was so obviously available to the appellant in this case we hold that there was no error in the form of instruction which was given by the district judge. It might not be appropriate in all other cases but it was appropriate in this case. The circumstances would not justify the instruction requested by the appellant.

* * *

Finding no prejudicial error, the conviction of the appellant is affirmed.

Notes

1. *The Model Penal Code View.* State v. Abbott, 36 N.J. 63, 69–72, 174 A.2d 881, 884–886 (1961):

> The question whether one who is neither the aggressor nor a party to a mutual combat must retreat has divided the authorities. Self-defense is measured against necessity. Brown v. State, 62 N.J.L. 666, 708, 42 A. 811 (E. & A.), affirmed, 175 U.S. 172, 20 S.Ct. 77, 44 L.Ed. 119 (1899); State v. Hipplewith, 33 N.J. 300, 316–318, 164 A.2d 481 (1960). From that premise one could readily say there was no necessity to kill in self-defense if the use of deadly force could have been avoided by retreat. The critics of the retreat rule do not quarrel with the theoretical validity of this conclusion, but rather condemn it as unrealistic. The law of course should not denounce conduct as criminal when it accords with the behavior of reasonable men. Upon this level, the advocates of no-retreat say the manly thing is to hold one's ground, and hence society should not demand what smacks of cowardice. Adherents of the retreat rule reply it is better that the assailed shall retreat than that the life of another be needlessly spent. They add that not only do right-thinking men agree, but further a rule so requiring may well induce others to adhere to that worthy standard of behavior. There is much dispute as to which view commands the support of ancient precedents, a question we think it would be profitless to explore.
>
> * * *
>
> We are not persuaded to depart from the principle of retreat. We think it salutary if reasonably limited. Much of the criticism goes not to its inherent validity but rather to unwarranted applications of the rule. For example, it is correctly observed that one can hardly retreat from a rifle shot at close range.

But if the weapon were a knife, a lead of a city block might well be enough. Again, the rule cannot be stated baldly, with indifference to the excitement of the occasion. As Mr. Justice Holmes cryptically put it, "Detached reflection cannot be demanded in the presence of an uplifted knife." Brown v. United States, 256 U.S. 335, 343, 41 S.Ct. 501, 502, 65 L.Ed. 961, 963 (1921). Such considerations, however, do not demand that a man should have the absolute right to stand his ground and kill in any and all situations. Rather they call for a fair and guarded statement of appropriate principles.

In Brown, supra, the United States Supreme Court said (256 U.S., at p. 343, 41 S.Ct. at p. 502, 65 L.Ed., at p. 963):

> "* * * Rationally the failure to retreat is a circumstance to be considered with all the others in order to determine whether the defendant went farther than he was justified in doing; not a categorical proof of guilt."

* * *

We believe the following principles are sound:

1. The issue of retreat arises only if the defendant resorted to a deadly force. It is deadly force which is not justifiable when an opportunity to retreat is at hand. Model Penal Code § 3.04(2)(b)(iii). As defined in § 3.12(2) a deadly force means "force which the actor uses with the purpose of causing or which he knows to create a substantial risk of causing death or serious bodily harm."

Hence it is not the nature of the force defended against which raises the issue of retreat, but rather the nature of the force which the accused employed in his defense. If he does not resort to a deadly force, one who is assailed may hold his ground whether the attack upon him be of a deadly or some lessor character. * * *

2. What constitutes an opportunity to retreat which will defeat the right of self-defense? As § 3.04(2)(b)(iii) of the Model Penal Code states, deadly force is not justifiable "if the actor *knows* that he can avoid the necessity of using such force *with complete safety* by retreating * * *." We emphasize "knows" and "with complete safety." One who is wrongfully attacked need not risk injury by retreating, even though he could escape with something less than serious bodily injury. It would be unreal to require nice calculations as to the amount of hurt, or to ask him to endure any at all. And the issue is not whether in retrospect it can be found the defendant could have retreated unharmed. Rather the question is whether he knew the opportunity was there, and of course in that inquiry the total circumstances including the attendant excitement must be considered. * * *

2. *Various Views of The Retreat Requirement.* There is much confusion in the cases about when the duty to retreat arises. Most agree that there is no duty unless three conditions exist:

a. The defendant is at the point of using deadly force, and

b. The defendant is not within the "castle" exception (question 4, infra), and

c. The defendant knows that he can retreat with safety.

The Model Penal Code in § 3.04 and cases like *Abbott* hold that if these three conditions are present, there is generally a duty to retreat to avoid inflicting fatal force. (No duty of retreat is placed upon a police officer in the performance of his duty or upon anyone justified in using force to make an arrest or prevent an escape.) Suppose a robber threatens fatal force unless the victim surrenders his wallet, and the victim, rather than retreat, kills the robber. The Model Penal Code, under provisions relating to the protection of property, justifies this (as it justifies fatal force to protect against arson, burglary, and some other property crimes) where the robber himself employs or threatens deadly force, or where a response by the robbery victim of less than fatal force would bring serious danger. See § 3.06(3)(d)(ii). Suppose that the robber threatens force which is painful but not "deadly"—that is, which does not cause substantial risk of death or serious bodily harm (see § 3.11(2)). It seems that the Model Penal Code would require surrender of the wallet or flight rather than the use of deadly force; neither § 3.04(2)(b), § 3.06(3)(d)(ii), nor § 3.07(5)(a)(ii) [preventing crime] would justify.

Another large group of authorities (perhaps the majority) does not require retreat unless, in addition to the three conditions earlier mentioned, a fourth is met:

d. The defendant was in some sense an aggressor in bringing on the incident. One who is in no sense an aggressor, in this view, may stand his ground. This is the position recognized in the *Garcia* opinion, immediately after the quotation from Durham v. State.

In general, actions which are candidates for "aggression" include assaults and batteries, trespasses, verbal taunts, and other conduct calculated to infuriate the opponent. It is quite possible that both participants are aggressors; in such a case neither may be justified in standing his ground.

The difference between the Model Penal Code position and the position just described can be illustrated by the following hypothetical: Two gunfighters meet by accident in the middle of the main street of town. Gunfighter A draws a line in the dust with his boot and says: "Cross this line, and I'll kill you." Gunfighter B says, "Please get out of my way so that I can attend the Sunday School picnic." A draws and aims his gun as B steps across the line, and B responds with a fatal shot. B is guilty of murder under the Model Penal Code, if he could, as he knew, have retreated safely. (See § 3.04(2)(b).) He has a valid claim of self-defense under the view which makes only aggressors retreat.

A third position is that of Mr. Justice Holmes, shown in the quotation from the *Brown* case in State v. Abbott: No flat retreat principle can be stated; failure to retreat is merely one factor in the determination of defendant's reasonableness.

Questions

1. What does sound social policy call for with respect to the retreat rule? Is it clear which rule will produce the fewest deaths and injuries? Should the rule vary with the sort of community attitudes towards standing one's ground which exist at the place of the incident, or with the effectiveness of local law enforcement and of judicial remedies for one threatened or attacked?

2. Suppose a client presents the following problem by telephone: "I'm marooned by an avalanche in my cabin in the woods; my telephone is the only link to the outside. Rescuers tell me it will take at least three days to dig me out. With me is Fred Frenzy, who I thought was my friend. He stopped by to visit me just before the avalanche. As I was hanging up his coat, a hand grenade rolled out of his pocket. He admitted that he meant to kill me with it because, he thinks, I've been having an affair with his wife. At the moment, I have the grenade, and he is in the other room. I have warned him that if he starts to come out, I will throw the grenade from behind the sofa where I am barricaded and kill him. He is much stronger that I am, and I have no other weapon or means of neutralizing him. He says that he will come in and kill me as soon as I fall asleep, and I believe him; he seems half out of his mind. I am feeling very sleepy, and I don't know how much longer I can stay awake. May I

pull the pin and throw the grenade into the other room? I think this would kill him without injuring me." What is your advice, assuming that you believe his story?

3. Should it matter if Frenzy in question 2 is not criminally responsible because of insanity? May one take the life of one known to be "innocent" in self-defense? May one endanger a bystander?

4. What is the rationale for absolving the defendant from a duty to retreat if he is in his own home? What is the "home" or "castle" for the purpose of the rule? Does it include the yard around the house? Does anything turn on whether the fight occurs in the common home of victim and defendant? On this point compare the majority and dissenting opinions in State v. Shaw, 185 Conn. 372, 441 A.2d 561 (1981); cert. denied 454 U.S. 1155, 102 S.Ct. 1027, 71 L.Ed.2d 312 (1982):

Majority (185 Conn. at 380–382, 441 A.2d at 565–566):

When faced with the problem of violence between two persons entitled to occupancy of the same dwelling, American jurisdictions have gone both ways on the issue of a duty to retreat. The majority of jurisdictions have adopted the rule that there is no difference created by the status of the assailant: there is no duty to retreat in one's dwelling whether one's assailant be an intruder or a codweller. Courts that have adopted this rule have done so for want of a reason for a distinction, and state the rule without more, e.g.: "Why, it may be inquired, should one retreat from his own house * * * when assailed by a stranger who is lawfully upon the premises? Whither shall he flee, and how far, and when may he be permitted to return? He has a lawful right to be and remain there, and the legal nature and value of this right is not abrogated by its enjoyment in connection with another * * *. It is our opinion that the doctrine of retreat, or of declining combat by retreat, has no application to cases of this character * * *." Jones v. State, 76 Ala. 8, 16 (1884).

"The rationale behind the no-retreat jurisdictions * * * was inherited from those periods when retreat from one's dwelling was necessarily attended with increased peril. In a civilized country a person's leaving his dwelling does not automatically ordain that he is forsaking a place of safety for one wrought with danger." Note, "Criminal Law—A Further Erosion of the Retreat Rule in North Carolina," 12 Wake Forest L.Rev. 1093, 1100 (1976). Yes, times have changed; the world is different. The ancient sampler that a man's house is his castle has frayed a bit under the American experience. "There are no castles in America." Comment, "Is a House a Castle?" 9 Conn.L.Rev. 110, 111 (1976). * * *

In recognition of the demise of the solitary fortress and the great value of human life the drafters of the Restatement (Second) of Torts have adopted the minority view. "The privilege [to defend oneself against another by force intended or likely to cause death or serious bodily harm] exists although the actor correctly or reasonably believes that he can safely avoid the necessity of so defending himself by (a) retreating if he is attacked within his *dwelling place, which is not also the dwelling place of the other* * * *. The privilege * * * does not exist * * * *in a place which is also the dwelling of the other* * * *." (Emphasis added.) Restatement (Second), Torts § 65 (1965).

We adopt the codweller retreat rule set forth by the Restatement. A minority of jurisdictions have long recognized it. E.g., Oney v. Commonwealth, 225 Ky. 590, 9 S.W.2d 723 (1928); Commonwealth v. Johnson, 213 Pa. 432, 62 A. 1064 (1906). This rule is in line with a policy favoring human life over the burden of retreating from the home, and the usual self-defense principles would still apply to allow defense at the wall or where retreat is impossible. In the great majority of homicides the killer and the victim are relatives or close acquaintances. Edwards,

"Murder and Gun Control," 18 Wayne L.Rev. 1335 (1972). We cannot conclude that the Connecticut legislature intended to sanction the reenactment of the climactic scene from "High Noon" in the familial kitchens of this state. The trial court did not err in not giving the defendant's requested instruction that he had no duty to retreat from his codweller even if he could safely do so.

Dissent (185 Conn. at 388–389, 441 A.2d at 568–569):

General Statutes § 53a–19(b)(1) recognizes only one exception to the rule that a person, in his dwelling, need not retreat before resorting to a deadly physical defense in a reasonable belief that another person is (1) using or about to use deadly physical force, or (2) inflicting or about to inflict great bodily harm. That exception denies the benefit of the rule to an initial aggressor. General Statutes § 53a–19(b)(1). Today the court adds a second exception to the rule and thereby makes criminal the failure to retreat in one's dwelling before resorting to deadly physical force in self-defense against the use of deadly physical force or the infliction of great bodily harm by an initial aggressor who happens to be a co-occupant of the dwelling. Such an act is not encompassed by the plain meaning of the penal code. The court justifies this addition by finding the second exception in our prior case law. An examination of the cases cited in the opinion reveals no such exception. * * * Because there is no such case law, adoption of the new exception abandons the rule of strict construction and violates the constitutional guarantee of due process by making the defendant's conduct criminal without having given him a reasonable opportunity to know that it was prohibited and to act accordingly. State v. Chetcuti, 173 Conn. 165, 167, 377 A.2d 263 (1977); State v. Cataudella, supra, 159 Conn. 556, 271 A.2d 99.

Furthermore General Statutes § 53a–19(b)(1) is based on comparable provisions of the New York Penal Code and the Model Penal Code. The commentary to the comparable section of the Model Penal Code states: "The Institute voted not to require retreat from the actor's dwelling when he is assailed by another person whose dwelling it also is * * *." Model Penal Code, § 3.04(2)(b)(ii)(1) Proposed Official Draft 1962, p. 49. In view of the plain language and the derivation of § 53a–19(b)(1), I believe that the majority usurps the legislature's authority by rejecting the statute's limitation on the retreat doctrine.

Castillo v. State

Supreme Court of Alaska, 1980.
614 P.2d 756.

BURKE, JUSTICE.

Peter Castillo was convicted of the attempted murder of Eli Sharclane * * *. In this appeal he challenges that conviction upon several grounds. We affirm.

Shortly after midnight, on September 25, 1977, Castillo was returning home from a dance when he encountered Sharclane on the Douglas side of the Juneau-Douglas Bridge. Castillo approached Sharclane to talk to him and, when Sharclane ignored Castillo's questions, Castillo struck him in the arm. A brief fight ensued; Sharclane then broke away and ran across the bridge towards Juneau with Castillo chasing him.

In a statement that Castillo now maintains was impermissibly elicited from him by the Juneau police, he stated that Sharclane stopped on the bridge, turned and faced Castillo in a fighting position and that the two once again began to struggle with one another. Castillo stated that he then threw Sharclane off the bridge.

On November 17, 1977, Eli Sharclane's grandfather filed a missing persons report. The Juneau police began an investigation shortly thereafter, and on December 8, 1977, a grand jury was convened to consider the matter. At the close of the state's evidentiary presentation, the grand jury indicted Castillo for second degree murder. Following a jury trial, Castillo was found guilty of attempted murder. This appeal followed.

Castillo first argues that the trial court erred in denying his motion to dismiss the indictment. He contends, among other things, that the indictment should have been dismissed because his confessions and admissions were improperly submitted to the grand jury since there was insufficient independent evidence to establish the *corpus delicti* of the crime charged.[2]

The function of the *corpus delicti* doctrine[3] was discussed in Armstrong v. State, 502 P.2d 440 (Alaska 1972):

> It is a settled principle of American jurisprudence that a criminal conviction must rest on firmer ground than the uncorroborated confession or admission of an accused. To avoid convicting a person solely out of his own admissions, the law requires, for a case to be submissible to the trier of fact, additional independent evidence. Thus, in a homicide case, there must be independent evidence of (1) the fact of death which (2) was caused by criminal agency of another before the question of guilt of this defendant could be submitted to the jury.

Id. at 447 (footnotes omitted). Under the test developed in *Armstrong,* to justify submission of the defendant's statement to the trier of fact there must be "substantial independent evidence which would tend to establish the trustworthiness of the statements." In the instant case, Castillo maintains that the state failed to establish by substantial independent evidence the fact of death caused by the criminal agency of another.

The state, in order to establish the necessary evidence to warrant Castillo's indictment, marshalled the following evidence. A police check indicated that Sharclane had not departed from Juneau since September 24th via any scheduled or nonscheduled airline or by the state ferry system. Similar checks with villages and other communities where Sharclane had ties were also negative, as was a nationwide listing of him as a missing person on

2. Castillo's argument assumes that proof of the *corpus delicti* is required at the indictment stage, just as it is at trial. * * * However, we need not decide this precise issue, since we have concluded that even if required, there was sufficient proof of the *corpus delicti* to support the indictment in this case.

3. For an interesting discussion of the origins of the doctrine, see R. Perkins, Criminal Law 97–100 (2d ed. 1969). Of particular interest is his summary of Perry's Case, 14 How.St.Tr. 1312 (1661), described by Professor Perkins as "the most astounding case of its kind on record." In Perry, a mother and her two sons were convicted and hanged after one of the sons gave a confession implicating all three in the supposed robbery and murder of one Harrison. Although the mother and her other son insisted that the confession was a complete fabrication, the son who had confessed steadfastly maintained that his story was true until the time of his death. A few years later the "victim," Harrison, reappeared, apparently little the worse for wear. Id. at 98–99.

the NCIC Computer system. Friends of his, including his girlfriend whom he had expressed a desire to marry, had not seen him since just prior to the incident, nor had his sister, his father, his grandfather, or his aunt. Several witnesses did, however, testify that they had seen or might have seen Sharclane after the night in question.

Conflicting evidence was presented as to whether Sharclane could swim. Sharclane's sister claimed he could swim even though she had actually never seen him do so. However, a friend of Sharclane's and Sharclane's father testified that he was unable to swim, and that he had always been afraid of the water. Testimony also indicated that on the evening of his disappearance, Sharclane was in the possession of a quart of vodka, and was "well on his way." Moreover, Sgt. Windred, who investigated the scene of the incident, testified that under tide conditions believed to have existed on the night in question there was forty-nine feet between the railing and the water.

Further evidence, independent of Castillo's statements, was introduced to show the fact of Sharclane's death and the fact that his death was caused by the criminal agency of another. While there was no eyewitness who saw the men fighting on the bridge, or saw Sharclane thrown from the bridge, a Ms. Conidi saw Sharclane running across the bridge on the night in question, and testified that she heard moaning or sobs coming from the bridge shortly after the incident occurred. Brian Cropley saw Sharclane and Castillo fighting on the Douglas side of the bridge, and then saw Castillo chasing Sharclane over the bridge towards Juneau.

Additionally, Castillo's fiancee stated that she had been raped by Sharclane about three years earlier. According to Albert Valentine, a friend of Castillo's, Castillo "didn't like" the fact that this had occurred, and stated about two weeks before the incident that he intended to throw Sharclane off the bridge. * * *

To establish the *corpus delicti* of murder the state may rely on pre-crime statements of the defendant. Perkins, *The Corpus Delicti of Murder,* 48 Va. L.Rev. 173, 178 (1962), citing Warszower v. United States, 312 U.S. 342, 61 S.Ct. 603, 85 L.Ed. 876 (1941). According to Professor Perkins, these statements contain none of the inherent weaknesses of confessions or admissions after the fact.

* * * [O]ur *corpus delicti* doctrine does not require proof that the criminal activity was that of the defendant charged. To require proof that the defendant was the killer as an essential element of the *corpus delicti* was characterized by Wigmore as "absurd." Generally, proof of the "'criminal agency of another' requires evidence which tends to show that the deceased died, not as a result of natural or accidental causes, or by his own hand, but by the hand of another." Perkins, *supra* at 193 (footnote omitted).

We conclude that the state presented sufficient independent evidence to establish the *corpus delicti* of the crime charged.

* * *

For the reasons stated, we hold that Castillo's statement was admissible and that the superior court properly denied his motion to suppress.

Claiming that there was evidence that he had acted in self-defense, Castillo submitted several instructions on that issue. All were rejected by the trial court. Castillo maintains that the court thus committed reversible error.

It is a well-established rule of law that an aggressor forfeits the right to claim self-defense except in two situations: (1) where an aggressor using non-deadly force (i.e., one who begins an encounter, using only his fists or some non-deadly weapon) is met with deadly force, the initial aggressor may justifiably defend himself against the deadly attack; (2) when an aggressor withdraws from the altercation that he has started, he may then defend himself from further attack. This, however, requires actual notice of his intent to withdraw or at least that he take reasonable steps to give such notice. W. La Fave & A. Scott, Criminal Law § 53, at 395 (1972).

The facts in the case at bar, even when viewed in the light most favorable to the defense, simply fail to support either of these exceptions. Where there is no evidentiary basis for an instruction on the law of self-defense, no such instruction need be given. Des Jardins v. State, 551 P.2d 181, 189 (Alaska 1976); Gray v. State, 463 P.2d 897, 909 n. 20 (Alaska 1970).

Affirmed.

BOOCHEVER, J., not participating.

Note: The Corpus Delicti Rule

The rule applies generally, and not merely in homicide cases. In common law arson, for example, it requires some proof, independent of the accused's confession, that a dwelling house of another has burned and that the burning was by criminal means.

Questions

1. Suppose Castillo had made a murderous attack on his visitor Sharclane in Castillo's own home, and Sharclane had temporarily gained the upper hand, threatening Castillo's life. Should Castillo be required to withdraw before his right to self-defense revives? Withdrawal, generally required only of one who is a felonious aggressor, e.g., one attempting to murder or rob, is usually said to require (a) retreat, (b) complete abandonment of the fight, at least on the present occasion, and (c) reasonable steps to make the abandonment known to the opponent. Suppose retreat is physically impossible; should one who would ordinarily be required to withdraw have a right to self-defense after he meets the other requirements of withdrawal?

2. Suppose Defendant is committing adultery with Victim's wife, and Victim, upon sudden discovery, attacks Defendant, under circumstances which would render the crime manslaughter, on account of provocation, if Victim killed Defendant. Having no other way to escape death, Defendant kills Victim and claims self-defense. What result?

State v. Allery

Supreme Court of Washington, 1984.
101 Wn.2d 591, 682 P.2d 312.

DORE, JUSTICE.

Defendant Sherry Allery appeals her conviction for the second degree murder of her husband, Wayne Allery. She assigns error to the trial court's instruction on self-defense and evidentiary rulings excluding expert testimony on the battered woman syndrome. She further contends the trial court erred in failing to instruct the jury on the defendant's duty to retreat.

We hold the trial court's instructions were defective in explaining the law of self-defense. We also hold expert testimony on the battered woman syndrome is admissible to show the defendant's fear of imminent danger at the time of the shooting. We reverse and remand for a new trial.

I

The defendant married Wayne Allery in 1975. Shortly after the marriage, she began to experience what was to become a consistent pattern of physical abuse at the hands of her husband. She suffered periodic pistol whippings, assaults with knives, and numerous beatings from her husband's fists throughout the marriage. In 1978, Mrs. Allery was hospitalized after her husband struck her on the head with a tire iron. During the last year of their marriage, the beatings increased in frequency and severity. Finally, on October 24, 1980, Mrs. Allery initiated divorce proceedings and served her husband with restraining orders.

The shooting occurred early in the morning of November 1, 1980. The defendant testified that she entered her house late at night not expecting to find her husband there because of the restraining orders. She bolted the door locked when she entered. As she moved through the house and into the kitchen, a light came on by the couch. Mr. Allery was lying there and said to her, "I guess I'm just going to have to kill you sonofabitch. Did you hear me that time?" Report of Proceedings, at 611.

The defendant went into the bedroom and tried unsuccessfully to open the window to escape. She heard a metallic noise from the kitchen and thought Mr. Allery was getting a knife. While in the bedroom, the defendant loaded one shell into a shotgun. She moved from the bedroom to the kitchen area and fired the shot that killed her husband while he remained lying on the couch.

II

* * *

The justification of self-defense must be evaluated from the defendant's point of view as conditions appeared to her at the time of the act. State v. McCullum, 98 Wash.2d 484, 656 P.2d 1064 (1983). The jurors must understand that, in considering the issue of self-defense, they must place themselves in the shoes of the defendant and judge the legitimacy of her act in light of all that she knew at the time.

> All of these facts and circumstances should have been placed before the jury, to the end that they could put themselves in the place of the appellant, get the point of view which he had at the time of the tragedy, and view the conduct of the [deceased] with all its pertinent sidelights as the appellant was warranted in viewing it. In no other way could the jury safely say what a reasonably prudent man similarly situated would have done.

State v. Wanrow, 88 Wash.2d [221,] 235–36, 559 P.2d 548, quoting from State v. Tribett, 74 Wash. 125, 130, 132 P. 875 (1913).

In the instant case, the jury was instructed to consider the self-defense issue in terms of the defendant's reasonable apprehension of danger as circumstances appeared to her at the time of the incident. On its face, the instruction adequately conveys the subjective self-defense standard. See WPIC 16.02 (1977). However, standing by itself, without additional instructions from the trial court, this instruction does not make the subjective self-defense standard " 'manifestly apparent to the average juror.' " State v. Painter, 27 Wash.App. 708, 713, 620 P.2d 1001 (1980), quoting State v. Fischer, 23 Wash.App. 756, 759, 598 P.2d 742, (1979). The instruction is inadequate because it does not instruct the jury to consider the conditions as they appeared to the slayer, taking into consideration all the facts and circumstances known to the slayer at the time and prior to the incident. State v. Wanrow, supra.

Defendant's theory of the case was that her intimate familiarity with her husband's history of violence convinced her that she was in serious danger at the time the shooting occurred. There was substantial evidence of the history of violence throughout the marriage between defendant and the victim. The jury should have been instructed to consider the self-defense issue from the defendant's perspective in light of all that she knew and had experienced with the victim. State v. Wanrow, supra.

III

At trial, defendant offered the expert testimony of Karil Klingbeil to explain the battered woman syndrome. Ms. Klingbeil was the founder of the sexual assault unit at Harborview Hospital in Seattle and has done extensive research in the areas of sexual assault and battered women. After extensive voir dire conducted out of the presence of the jury, the trial judge refused Klingbeil's testimony.

The record shows that Klingbeil would have described her professional analysis of the behavior and emotional patterns of women suffering from repeated physical abuse by their husbands and lovers. She would have testified that in her opinion defendant Allery displayed the behavioral and emotional characteristics of a battered woman. Defense counsel was very specific in explaining the purpose of Klingbeil's testimony. It was offered to (1) explain the mentality and behavior of battered women generally, (2) to provide a basis from which the jury could understand why defendant perceived herself in imminent danger at the time of the shooting, and (3) to explain why a battered woman remains in a relationship that is both psychologically and physically dangerous.

ER 702 provides:

> If scientific, technical, or other specialized knowledge will assist the trier of fact to understand the evidence or to determine a fact in issue, a witness qualified as an expert by knowledge, skill, experience, training, or education, may testify thereto in the form of an opinion or otherwise.

The admissibility of expert testimony under this rule depends upon whether (1) the witness qualifies as an expert, (2) the opinion is based upon an explanatory theory generally accepted in the scientific community, and (3) the expert testimony would be helpful to the trier of fact. State v. Canaday, 90 Wash.2d 808, 585 P.2d 1185 (1978). See generally 5A Tegland, Wash. Prac., *Evidence* § 288, at 25 (2d ed. 1982).

The qualifications of Klingbeil were well established at trial and are not an issue here. The particular issue before us is whether the scientific understanding of the battered woman syndrome is sufficiently developed so that expert testimony on the syndrome is admissible.

Klingbeil testified that the battered woman syndrome is a recognized phenomenon in the psychiatric profession and is defined as a technical term of art in professional diagnostic textbooks. The syndrome is comprised of three distinct phases. In the first phase, tension mounts between the woman and her partner and minor abuse occurs. More serious violence follows and the woman experiences a sense of powerlessness to do anything to stop her husband. Psychologists describe a phenomenon known as "learned helplessness," a condition in which the woman is psychologically locked into her situation due to economic dependence on the man, an abiding attachment to him, and the failure of the legal system to adequately respond to the problem. Finally, there is a temporary lull in the physical abuse inflicted on the battered woman, and she forgives her assailant, hoping that the abuse will not reoccur. See generally Eber, *The Battered Wife's Dilemma: To Kill or To Be Killed,* 32 Hastings L.J. 895 (1981).

We join with those courts which hold expert testimony on the battered woman syndrome admissible. Smith v. State, 247 Ga. 612, 277 S.E.2d 678 (1981); Hawthorne v. State, 408 So.2d 801 (Fla.Dist.Ct.App.1982); Ibn-Tamas v. United States, 407 A.2d 626 (D.C.1979). We find that expert testimony explaining why a person suffering from the battered woman syndrome would not leave her mate, would not inform police or friends, and would fear increased aggression against herself would be helpful to a jury in understanding a phenomenon not within the competence of an ordinary lay person. Smith v. State, supra. Where the psychologist is qualified to testify about the battered woman syndrome, and the defendant establishes her identity as a battered woman, expert testimony on the battered woman syndrome is admissible. This evidence may have a substantial bearing on the woman's perceptions and behavior at the time of the killing and is central to her claim of self-defense. State v. Anaya, 438 A.2d 892 (Me.1981).

Our holding today is in harmony with our decision in State v. Wanrow, supra. There we held that the jury must consider all the facts and circumstances known to the woman at the time of the killing in evaluating her claim of self-defense. To effectively present the situation as perceived by the defendant, and the reasonableness of her fear, the defense has the option to explain her feelings to enable the jury to overcome stereotyped impressions about women who remain in abusive relationships. It is appropriate that the jury be given a professional explanation of the battering syndrome and its effects on the woman through the use of expert testimony. See Cross, *The Expert as Educator; A Proposed Approach to the Use of Battered Woman Syndrome Expert Testimony,* 35 Vand.L.Rev. 741 (1982).

IV

Defendant also assigns error to the trial court's failure to instruct the jury that she had no duty to retreat at the time of the shooting. No duty to retreat exists when one is feloniously assaulted in a place where she has a right to be. State v. Hiatt, 187 Wash. 226, 60 P.2d 71 (1936); State v. Lewis, 6 Wash. App. 38, 491 P.2d 1062 (1971). The State argues that no instruction was required because the defendant was in no danger when she shot her husband.

A party is entitled to an instruction when there is sufficient evidence in the record to support it. State v. King, 92 Wash.2d 541, 599 P.2d 522 (1979). Defendant testified that she was afraid and thought she was in danger when she entered her home and found her husband. She testified he threatened to kill her. Her testimony was sufficient to support the proposed instruction. The trial court erred in refusing to instruct the jury that defendant had no duty to retreat.

* * *

Question

Allery relied upon the earlier Washington case of State v. Wanrow, 88 Wn.2d 221, 559 P.2d 548 (1977). That case involved a claim of self-defense in the killing of an intoxicated victim, believed on good grounds to have molested children and to have attempted sexual molestation of the female defendant's son. The victim came to the house of defendant's friend, where defendant's son was staying, "to clear up" the situation, and made what appeared to the people there to be a sexual approach to another child. He refused to leave; the defendant went to the front door to get help from those outside. She testified that when she turned around she was "gravely" startled to find defendant immediately behind her and shot and killed him in what amounted to a reflex action.

In an opinion concurred in by four of the eight justices, JUSTICE UTTER wrote that the jury instructions (1) had failed to give an adequate statement that the jury should consider all of the history and circumstances known to the defendant, and (2) had given an instruction which was too objective. He said (at 88 Wn.2d 240–241, 559 P.2d 558–559):

> The second paragraph of instruction No. 10 contains an equally erroneous and prejudicial statement of the law. That portion of the instruction reads:
>
> > However, when there is no reasonable ground for the person attacked to believe that *his* person is in imminent danger of death or great bodily harm,

> and it appears to *him* that only an ordinary battery is all that is intended, and all that *he* has reasonable grounds to fear from *his* assailant, *he* has a right to stand *his* ground and repel such threatened assault, yet *he* has no right to repel a threatened assault with naked hands, by the use of a deadly weapon in a deadly manner, unless *he* believes, and *has reasonable grounds* to believe, that *he* is in imminent danger of death or great bodily harm.

(Italics ours.) In our society women suffer from a conspicuous lack of access to training in and the means of developing those skills necessary to effectively repel a male assailant without resorting to the use of deadly weapons. Instruction No. 12 does indicate that the "relative size and strength of the persons involved" may be considered; however, it does not make clear that the defendant's actions are to be judged against her own subjective impressions and not those which a detached jury might determine to be objectively reasonable. The applicable rule of law is clearly stated in [State v.] Miller, [141 Wash. 104, 105, 250 P. 645 (1926)]:

> If the appellants, at the time of the alleged assault upon them, as reasonably and ordinarily cautious and prudent men, honestly believed that they were in danger of great bodily harm, they would have the right to resort to self-defense, and their conduct is to be judged by the condition appearing to them at the time, not by the condition as it might appear to the jury in the light of testimony before it.

The second paragraph of instruction No. 10 not only establishes an objective standard, but through the persistent use of the masculine gender leaves the jury with the impression the objective standard to be applied is that applicable to an altercation between two men. The impression created—that a 5′4″ woman with a cast on her leg and using a crutch must, under the law, somehow repel an assault by a 6′2″ intoxicated man without employing weapons in her defense, unless the jury finds her determination of the degree of danger to be objectively reasonable—constitutes a separate and distinct misstatement of the law and, in the context of this case, violates the respondent's right to equal protection of the law. The respondent was entitled to have the jury consider her actions in the light of her own perceptions of the situation, including those perceptions which were the product of our nation's "long and unfortunate history of sex discrimination." Frontiero v. Richardson, 411 U.S. 677, 684, 93 S.Ct. 1764, 1769, 36 L.Ed.2d 583 (1973). Until such time as the effects of that history are eradicated, care must be taken to assure that our self-defense instructions afford women the right to have their conduct judged in light of the individual physical handicaps which are the product of sex discrimination. To fail to do so is to deny the right of the individual woman involved to trial by the same rules which are applicable to male defendants. The portion of the instruction above quoted misstates our law in creating an objective standard of "reasonableness." It then compounds that error by utilizing language suggesting that the respondent's conduct must be measured against that of a reasonable male individual finding himself in the same circumstances.

What do you think of this criticism? Compare the consideration of gender and provocation in the opinion of Lord Simon of Glaisdale in the *Camplin* case, supra. p. 410.

Werner v. State

Court of Criminal Appeals of Texas, En Banc, 1986.
711 S.W.2d 639.

[While sitting on his friend Netterville's porch, the defendant saw the victim, previously unknown to him, negligently run into Netterville's parked car and then speed away. Netterville came out of the house, handed defendant a pistol, and urged him to take a particular direction and "get" the victim, while Netterville took a different route. Defendant found the victim inspecting his own car for damage, and, after a brief colloquy, in which the victim seems to have asked defendant why he didn't shoot, defendant shot the victim in the chest and killed him.

[Defendant offered the testimony of a police officer as to a conversation in the patrol car as it took him from the scene of the shooting and of a psychiatrist defendant consulted after the shooting. The officer would have testified that defendant talked about his family, stating that his father and grandparents were in the Holocaust; that he thought defendant said that his father had witnessed people going to the gas chamber without argument and had told defendant about it; and that defendant was sorry to present his father with this situation after all he had been through. The psychiatrist, who had been a concentration camp inmate and had specialized in problems of survivors, would have testified that defendant told him that some members of his family did not survive the concentration camp, that he grew up with family stories of seeing people beaten to death who did not fight back, and that when he pulled the trigger, he was thinking only of protecting himself. He would also have testified that defendant's knowledge of the Holocaust shaped his view of self-defense, and that it "was his state of mind to defend himself because he comes from a family that did not." He would have said that defendant displayed some of the characteristics of the Holocaust syndrome.

[A statute provided: "In all prosecutions for murder or voluntary manslaughter, the state or defendant shall be permitted to offer testimony as to all relevant facts and circumstances surrounding the killing and the previous relationship existing between the accused and the deceased, together with all relevant facts and circumstances going to show the condition of the mind of the accused at the time of the offense." V.T.C.A., Penal Code, § 19.06 (Evidence).

[The trial judge excluded the evidence, and Onion, J., wrote for the majority of the court, affirming a murder conviction, on the ground that the accused had made no insanity claim; that the evidence was not "relevant" on self-defense, which requires that a person using deadly force reasonably believe it necessary to act as he did to defend himself against the victim's use or attempted use of deadly force; and that there was no evidence of such conduct by the victim. The court also thought that even if a self-defense issue was before the jury, the psychiatrist's testimony was not sufficiently connected with the defendant's actual state of mind at the time of the offense.]

TEAGUE, J., dissenting.

[JUDGE TEAGUE was ambivalent about whether the psychiatrist's testimony would be admissible on the issue of self-defense, but he believed that the statute made the evidence admissible anyway, for whatever weight the jury chose to give it in determining what the accused's state of mind might have been.]

* * *

In the dissenting opinion that he filed in this cause, when it was pending in the Houston First Court of Appeals, JUSTICE LEVY of that court correctly observed the following: "The very purpose of 19.06's sweeping language was to distinguish the particular 'mind of the accused at the time of the offense' from the mind of the theoretical 'reasonable and prudent man,' and permit the jury, as the trier of fact—not the court—to evaluate the killing in such light." Werner v. State, 680 S.W.2d 858, 867 (Tex.App.—Houston [1st] 1984).

* * *

The subject "The Holocaust Syndrome" appears to be a new type of syndrome in psychiatric circles. Excluding a reference to one book entitled *Adolescent Psychiatry: Developmental and Clinical Studies,* at p. 66 (1982), all other references that counsel for the appellant directs us to are articles found in three newspapers. My independent research has yet to find a single reported court case which has discussed this syndrome.[1]

* * *

When a relatively large number of persons, having the same symptoms, exhibit a combination or variation of functional psychiatric disorders that leads to purely emotional stress that causes intense mental anguish or emotional trauma, i.e., trauma having no direct physical effect upon the body, psychiatrists put those persons under one or more labels. Today, we have the following labels: "The Battered Wife Syndrome," (see *post*); "The Battered Woman Syndrome;" "The Battered Child Syndrome;" "The Battered Husband Syndrome," (see Steinmetz, "The Battered Husband Syndrome, Victimology," *An International Journal* (1977–1978); Gelles, "The Myth of Battered Husbands—And Other Facts About Sanity Violence," *Ms.*

1. My independent research also reveals that the following articles have been written on the subject: Kestenberg, "Psychoanalyses of Children of Survivors From the Nazi Persecution: The Continuing Struggle of Survivor Parents," 5 *Victimology* 368–373 (Spr–Fall 1980); Danieli, "Countertransference in the Treatment and Study of Nazi Holocaust Survivors and Their Children," 5 *Victimology* 355–367 (Spr–Fall 1980); Ammon, "Symposium on the Psychodynamics of the Holocaust—Psychiatric and Psychohistorical Aspects," 17 *Dynamische Psychiatrie* (1984); Nadler, Kav–Venaki, Gleitman, "Transgenerational Effects of the Holocaust: Externalization of Aggression in Second Generation of Holocaust Survivors," 53 *Journal of Consulting & Clinical Psychology* 365–369 (1985); Krell, "Holocaust Survivors and Their Children: Comments on Psychiatric Consequences and Psychiatric Terminology," 25 *Comprehensive Psychiatry* 521–528 (1984); Virag, "Children of the Holocaust and Their Children's Children: Working Through Current Trauma in the Psychotherapeutic Process," 2 *Dynamic Psychotherapy* 47–60 (Spr–Sum 1984); Schmolling, "Human Reactions to the Nazi Concentration Camps: A Summing Up," 10 *Journal of Human Stress* 108–120 (Fall, 1984); Roden, "Children of Holocaust Survivors," 10 *Adolescent Psychiatry* 66–72 (1982); Steinitz, "Psychological–Social Effects of the Holocaust on Aging Survivors and Their Families," 4 *Journal of Gerontological Social Work* 145–152 (Spr–Sum, 1982); Ornstein, "The Effects of the Holocaust on Life–Cycle Experiences: The Creation and Recreation of Families," 14 *Journal of Geriatric Psychiatry* 135–154 (1981).

(Oct.,1979); Schultz, "The Wife Assaulter," 6 J.Soc. *Therapy* 103 (1960)); "The Battered Parent Syndrome;" "The Familial Child Sexual Abuse Syndrome," (see State v. Middleton, 294 Or. 427, 657 P.2d 1215 (1983); "The Rape Trauma Syndrome," (see "Admissibility, at Criminal Prosecution, of Expert Testimony on Rape Trauma Syndrome," 42 *A.L.R.4th,* commencing at page 879)); "The Battle Fatigue Syndrome;" "The Viet Nam Post–Traumatic Stress Syndrome," (see Miller v. State, 338 N.W.2d 673, 678 (S.D.1983) (Henderson, J., dissenting opinion); State v. Felde, 422 So.2d 370 (La.1982)); "The Policeman's Syndrome," see Binder, Psychiatry in the Everyday Practice of Law (2nd ed. 1982);" "The Post–Concussive Syndrome," (Id.); "The Whiplash Syndrome;" "The Low–Back Syndrome;" "The Lover's Syndrome;" "The Love Fear Syndrome," (People v. Terry, 2 Cal.3d 362, 85 Cal. Rptr. 409, 466 P.2d 961 (1970)); "The Organic Delusional Syndrome;" "The Chronic Brain Syndrome," (Illinois v. Reed, 8 Ill.App.3d 977, 290 N.E. 2d 612 (1972)); and "The Holocaust Syndrome." Tomorrow, there will probably be additions to the list, such as "The Appellate Court Judge Syndrome."

In this instance, there is no challenge by the State to Dr. Roden's qualifications to testify on the subject "The Holocaust Syndrome." From his impressive list of credentials, as well as his study of the subject, Dr. Roden appears to possess special knowledge upon the specific matter about which his expertise was sought.

If scientific, technical, or other specialized knowledge will assist the trier of fact to better understand the evidence or determine a fact in issue, a witness is qualified as an expert by knowledge, skill, experience, training, or education, and he should be able to testify in the form of opinion evidence.

In this instance, I find that the subject "The Holocaust Syndrome" was beyond the ken of the average lay person. The jury was entitled to know that when the appellant fired the fatal shot he believed that because of his past experiences, if his life was ever threatened, he would act to protect himself, and that is why he acted in the manner in which he did, i.e., that his state of mind at the time was affected, not only by that which he visually saw on the night in question, but also because of his belief that it was necessary for him to defend himself because he comes from a family who did not defend themselves, thus causing them to perish in the Holocaust. * * *

* * *

Although there are obvious differences between the syndrome now known as "The Battered Wife Syndrome" and the syndrome now known as "The Holocaust Syndrome," in principle they have much in common. Today, it is not unusual for our more enlightened trial courts to admit testimony of expert witnesses on "The Battered Wife Syndrome," as relevant to explain the legitimacy of a wife's reactions to threats of danger from her spouse, and to counteract prosecutorial claims that the wife's continued presence in the home means that the homicide was not necessary. It should be obvious to almost anyone that without such testimony it would be difficult, if not impossible, for persons unfamiliar with how "The Battered Wife Syndrome" manifests itself to understand what effect the actions of the former spouse had on the state or condition of the wife's mind when she shot and killed her former spouse. In any event, it simply cannot be logically argued that such testimony would not be of assistance to the trier of fact in determining what the condition of the defendant's mind might have been when the offense was committed.

All courts are not in agreement that expert testimony in "The Battered Woman Syndrome" type case is always admissible. Some courts have held that such testimony is relevant to the issue of self-defense and therefore admissible, see State v. Allery, 101 Wash.2d 591, 682 P.2d 312 (1984); State v. Kelly, 97 N.J. 178, 478 A.2d 364 (1984); State v. Leidholm, 334 N.W.2d 811 (N.D.1983); State v. Anaya, 438 A.2d 892 (Me.1981); Smith v. State, 247 Ga. 580, 277 S.E.2d 687 (1981), on remand, 159 Ga.App. 183, 283 S.E.2d 98 (1982); Hawthorne v. State, 408 So.2d 801 (Fla.Dis.Ct.App.1982); State v. Middleton, 294 Or. 427, 657 P.2d 1215 (1983); Ibn–Tamas v. United States, 407 A.2d 626 (D.C.1979), appeal after remand, 455 A.2d 893 (D.C.1983), other courts have held that such testimony is admissible for reasons other than self-defense, see People v. Minnis, 118 Ill.App.3d 345, 74 Ill.Dec. 179, 455 N.E.2d 209 (1983); State v. Baker, 120 N.H. 773, 424 A.2d 171 (1980); State v. Kelly, 102 Wash.2d 188, 685 P.2d 564 (1984); Buhrle v. State, 627 P.2d 1374 (Wyo.1981); Fultz v. State, 439 N.E.2d 659 (Ind. App.1982); Commonwealth v. McCusker, 448 Pa. 382, 292 A.2d 286 (1972), while other courts hold that such testimony is absolutely inadmissible, see State v. Thomas, 66 Ohio St.2d 518, 423 N.E.2d 137 (1981); People v. White, 90 Ill.App.3d 1067, 46 Ill.Dec. 474, 414 N.E.2d 196 (1980). Also see the annotation entitled "Admissibility of Expert or Opinion Testimony on Battered Wife or Battered Woman Syndrome," 18 *A.L.R.4th,* commencing at page 1153; *Criminal Law Defenses,* supra; Thar, "The Admissibility of Expert Testimony on Battered Wife Syndrome * * * An Evidentiary Analysis," 77 *Northwestern Law Review* 348 (1982); Jones, "When Battered Women Fight Back," 9 *Barrister* 12 (Fall, 1982); "The Battered Wife's Dilemma: To Kill or to be Killed," 32 *Hastings Law Journal* 895 (1981); Cross, "The Expert as Educator: A Proposed Approach to the Use of Battered Woman Syndrome Expert Testimony," 35 *Vanderbilt Law Review* 741 (1982); Giannelli, "The Admissibility of Novel Scientific Evidence: Frye v. United States, A Half–Century Later," 80 *Colum.Law Review* 1197 (1980); Comment, "Expert Testimony Based Upon Novel Scientific Technique: Admissibility Under Federal Rules of Evidence," 48 *George Washington Law Review* 774 (1980); Graham, "Lay Witness Opinion Testimony; Opinion on Ultimate Issue By Lay or Expert Witness," *Criminal Law Bulletin,* March–April 1986, commencing at page 144.

* * *

Notes

1. *Imminence.* People v. Aris, 215 Cal.App.3d 1178, 1189, 1192, 264 Cal. Rptr. 167, 174, 176 (1989):

> We distill from these cases the rule that a defendant should not be excused from guilt of murder when he or she kills the one who threatened death or serious bodily injury unless the defendant at least actually, if not reasonably, perceives in

the victim's behavior at the moment of the killing an indication that the victim is about to attempt, or is attempting, to fulfill the threat. In making that evaluation, the defendant is entitled to consider prior threats, assaults, and other circumstances relevant to interpreting the attacker's behavior.

This definition of imminence reflects the great value our society places on human life. The criminal law would not sentence to death a person such as the victim in this case for a murder he merely threatened to commit, even if he had committed threatened murders many times in the past and had threatened to murder the defendant; it follows that the criminal law will not even partially excuse a potential victim's slaying of his attacker unless more than merely threats and a history of past assaults is involved.

Furthermore, batterers of women, even though they deserve punishment for their acts of battery, nevertheless are entitled to the same protection of their lives by the law that is afforded to everyone. That protection is the deterrence to would be killers afforded by the knowledge that a killing with malice aforethought will be punished as a murder unless the killer actually perceived an imminent danger of death or serious bodily injury at the hands of the deceased.

* * *

* * * We hold that defendant presented no substantial evidence that a reasonable person under the same circumstances would have perceived imminent danger and a need to kill in self-defense. No "jury composed of reasonable men could have concluded that" a sleeping defendant presents an imminent danger of great bodily harm, especially when the defendant was able to, and actually did, leave the bedroom, and subsequently returned to shoot him.

2. *Insanity and "syndromes".* For the relationship of the post-traumatic stress syndrome to the issue of insanity, see Miller v. State, infra p. 549.

State v. Gelinas

Supreme Court of Rhode Island, 1980.
417 A.2d 1381.

OPINION

BEVILACQUA, CHIEF JUSTICE.

A Superior Court jury convicted the defendant of assault on a uniformed police officer engaged in the performance of his duties, the assault causing bodily injury, a violation of G.L.1956 (1969 Reenactment) § 11–5–5, as amended by P.L.1979, ch. 249, § 1. * * *

* * *

The record reveals that two Woonsocket police officers in the early evening hours of August 27, 1976, responded to a complaint that a number of juveniles were consuming alcoholic beverages on the corner of Fairmont Street and Third Avenue in that city. The youths scattered when the uniformed policemen arrived, but four of them remained to gather together their liquor. The officers confiscated the liquor and ordered the four youths into the patrol car. * * *

One of the four, defendant's younger brother Billy Gelinas, walked away from the group down Third Avenue to join approximately twenty people gathered in the parking lot of the Bourcier Brothers' warehouse. The officers put the other three juveniles into the cruiser and drove to the parking lot intending to apprehend the fourth. Officer Michael F. Magnan approached Billy, and explained to him that he would have to come to the police station. Billy refused, and when the officer placed his hand on Billy, he struck the officer. A struggle ensued. Billy testified that Officer Magnan had torn his shirt and had dragged him face down across the parking lot.

As Officer Magnan attempted to subdue Billy, the other officer, Emil LeDuc, drew his nightstick and ran in a semicircle around the combatants to fend off the crowd that had closed in on them. Billy's older brothers, Eddy Gelinas and defendant, Terrence Gelinas, joined the affray. The defendant threatened Officer LeDuc, saying, "Leave my brother alone, LeDuc, or I'm going to get you." He insisted on getting past Officer LeDuc to where Billy and Officer Magnan were struggling. He and Officer LeDuc began shoving each other.

Officer LeDuc testified that the crowd began to press in on him and to kick and shove him. He stated that the crowd then separated somewhat and he was able to run to the cruiser to radio for help.

The defendant followed Officer LeDuc to the patrol car repeatedly insisting that he leave Billy alone. After calling for assistance, Officer LeDuc turned to see his partner struggling on the ground with both Billy and Eddy Gelinas, the latter striking the officer with a piece of tar about the back and head. Officer LeDuc pushed past defendant and ran to aid Officer Magnan.

He testified that he struck Eddy Gelinas with his club [3] and then turned around to defend against an anticipated attack from defendant whom he knew to have followed close behind. Officer LeDuc stated that as he turned, he received a blow to the face and fell to the ground. He claimed that defendant then sat on him and began striking him. The officer testified that he could not get up and that he saw defendant pick up a piece of concrete and strike him in the face with it as he lay on the ground. * * *

* * *

The trial justice in his instructions stated,

* * *

"If you find that LeDuc was not using excessive force and was in the performance of his duty in attempting to arrest Edward for interfering with Magnan, and this defendant on that occasion then struck Officer LeDuc, LeDuc being engaged in the performance of his duty; and LeDuc was injured as a result, then he is guilty as charged by the State. If LeDuc used excessive force in the attempt to remove Edward Gelinas from Officer Magnan, LeDuc was not in the performance of his duty, and the defendant is not guilty."

* * *

* * * The trial justice in effect instructed the jury that they must decide that the officer in fact used excessive force against defendant's brothers at the time defendant attacked the officer before they could find that defendant committed a justifiable act. If the jury believed that excessive

3. Edward testified that Officer LeDuc had struck him with a billy-club on his arms as he covered his head with them.

force was not actually used, they had to reject defendant's alleged defense and, on satisfaction of the other elements, return a guilty verdict.

It is a well-accepted principle that in effecting an arrest an officer has the right to use such force as he may reasonably believe necessary in order to discharge properly his duty. General Laws 1956 (1969 Reenactment) § 12–7–8; see State v. Ramsdell, 109 R.I. at 326, 285 A.2d at 404; Tessier v. LeNois, 97 R.I. 414, 417, 198 A.2d 142, 143 (1964). When there is evidence tending to show the law-enforcement officer's use of excessive force, the trial justice must instruct the jury that the force used against the law-enforcement officer was justified provided the defendant limited his assault to the use of reasonable force in defending himself from excessive force. State v. Ramsdell, 109 R.I. at 327, 285 A.2d at 404.

There are two contrasting principles that control the defense of another as it exists in other jurisdictions.[5] One rule adopted by a number of states takes the position that a third-party intervenor stands in the shoes of a person whom he is aiding. Under this view it is immaterial whether the intervenor defendant acted as a reasonable person would have; the right attaches to the defendant only when the person being defended would have had the right of self-defense. See, e.g., People v. Booher, 18 Cal.App.3d 331, 95 Cal.Rptr. 857 (1971); Purdy v. United States, 210 A.2d 1 (D.C.App.1965) (dictum); State v. Anderson, 40 N.C.App. 318, 253 S.E.2d 48 (1979); State v. Wenger, 58 Ohio St.2d 336, 390 N.E.2d 801 (1979).[6] In contrast, other jurisdictions focus on the conduct of the intervenor without regard to the self-defense claim of the arrestee and hold that an intervenor may aid another if it appears to be necessary, though he acts on a mistaken belief, even in a situation in which the person who is aided would not have had the right to claim self-defense. See, e.g., United States v. Ochoa, 526 F.2d 1278 (5th Cir.1976); United States v. Grimes, 413 F.2d 1376 (7th Cir.1969); Coleman v. State, Del., 320 A.2d 740 (1974); Commonwealth v. Martin, 369 Mass. 640, 341 N.E.2d 885 (1976); State v. Andrews, 199 Neb. 60, 255 N.W.2d 875 (1977); Ky.Rev.Stat. § 503.070 (1975).

Up until now, this court has never been asked to decide under what conditions a defendant may claim justifiable use of force when intervening on

5. Some jurisdictions adhere to the somewhat antiquated view that a person may only defend others to whom he is somehow related, either by consanguinity, employment, marriage, or acquaintance. E.g., Tipton v. State, 1 Md.App. 556, 562, 232 A.2d 289, 291 (1967); Carter v. State, 507 P.2d 932, 934 (Okl.Cr.1973).

Apparently, these states believe that the relationship between the protector and his charge not only compels action but also minimizes the likelihood that the actor will misinterpret the situation and intercede on behalf of the wrongdoer. While we do not question the utility of allowing family members to protect one another, we believe that restricting the privilege only to family members ignores the important social goal of crime prevention, a duty of every citizen. See Commonwealth v. Martin, 369 Mass. 640, 650, 341 N.E.2d 885, 891 (1976). See generally Note, *Justification; The Impact of the Model Penal Code on Statutory Reform,* 75 Colum.L.Rev. 914, 932–33 (1975).

6. In New York the rule developed in case law has been modified by legislative action. Compare People v. Young, 11 N.Y.2d 274, 229 N.Y.S.2d 1, 183 N.E.2d 319 (1962), with N.Y.Penal Law § 35.15 (McKinney 1975). Opinions in Washington's Supreme Court and Court of Appeals appear at odds. Compare State v. Penn, 89 Wash.2d 63, 568 P.2d 797 (1977), with State v. Westlund, 13 Wash.App. 460, 536 P.2d 20 (1975).

behalf of a third party. Being confronted with different schools of thought, we must decide which theory of law we shall follow.

After reviewing the available authorities, we hereby adopt the rule that one who comes to the aid of an arrestee must do so at his own peril and should be excused only when the individual would himself be justified in defending himself from the use of excessive force by the arresting officer. Purdy v. United States, 210 A.2d at 2; State v. Anderson, 40 N.C.App. at 323–325, 253 S.E.2d at 52; State v. Wenger, 58 Ohio St.2d at 340–41, 390 N.E.2d at 804. A third party intervenor stands in the shoes of the person whom he is aiding. The defendant may use such force to prevent injury to the person he aids as defendant would use in self-defense. See Del.Code tit. 11, § 469 (1979), Model Penal Code § 3.05 (Tent.Draft No. 8, 1958).
* * *

The defendant before us was entitled to an instruction that presented the jury with the choice of findings that defendant was justified in interfering with the arrest of his brother if the arrestee was himself justified in resisting arrest. In reading the trial justice's instructions we are of the opinion that he adequately charged the jury as to the rights of a person who defends another against the use of excessive force. He told the jury in clear language that unless they found that Officer LeDuc has used excessive force against defendant's brother, they could not find that defendant had acted justifiably. This instruction is consistent with the rule we adopt today since if Officer LeDuc had not used excessive force, Edward could have had no right to resist the arrest, and, accordingly, defendant could not have been privileged to come to Edward's defense. The jury therefore resolved this factual issue in the light of a charge that properly set out the controlling law in this jurisdiction.

* * *

Questions

1. The court gives no reasons for its preference for one of the two theories it considers. What reasons might be advanced for each theory? Is one theory in better accord with good morals than the other?

2. Should it matter whether the person assisted is "related" to the accused?

b. PROTECTION OF PROPERTY, PREVENTION OF CRIME, AND LAW ENFORCEMENT

People v. Ceballos

Supreme Court of California, En Banc, 1974.
12 Cal.3d 470, 116 Cal.Rptr. 233, 526 P.2d 241.

BURKE, JUSTICE.

Don Ceballos was found guilty by a jury of assault with a deadly weapon (Pen.Code, § 245). Imposition of sentence was suspended and he was placed on probation. He appeals from the judgment, contending primarily that his conduct was not unlawful because the alleged victim was attempting to commit burglary when hit by a trap gun mounted in the garage of defendant's dwelling and that the court erred in instructing the jury. We have concluded that the former argument lacks merit, that the court did not commit prejudicial error in instructing the jury, and that the judgment should be affirmed.

Defendant lived alone in a home in San Anselmo. The regular living quarters were above the garage, but defendant sometimes slept in the garage and had about $2,000 worth of property there.

In March 1970 some tools were stolen from defendant's home. On May 12, 1970, he noticed the lock on his garage doors was bent and pry marks were on one of the doors. The next day he mounted a loaded .22 caliber pistol in the garage. The pistol was aimed at the center of the garage doors and was connected by a wire to one of the doors so that the pistol would discharge if the door was opened several inches.

The damage to defendant's lock had been done by a 16-year-old boy named Stephen and a 15-year-old boy named Robert. On the afternoon of May 15, 1970, the boys returned to defendant's house while he was away. Neither boy was armed with a gun or knife. After looking in the windows and seeing no one, Stephen succeeded in removing the lock on the garage doors with a crowbar, and, as he pulled the door outward, he was hit in the face with a bullet from the pistol.

Stephen testified: He intended to go into the garage "[f]or musical equipment" because he had a debt to pay to a friend. His "way of paying that debt would be to take [defendant's] property and sell it" and use the proceeds to pay the debt. He "wasn't going to do it [i.e., steal] for sure, necessarily." He was there "to look around," and "getting in, I don't know if I would have actually stolen."

Defendant, testifying in his own behalf, admitted having set up the trap gun. He stated that after noticing the pry marks on his garage door on May 12, he felt he should "set up some kind of a trap, something to keep the burglar out of my home." When asked why he was trying to keep the burglar out, he replied, " * * * Because somebody was trying to steal my property * * * and I don't want to come home some night and have the thief in there * * * usually a thief is pretty desperate * * * and * * * they just pick up a weapon * * * if they don't have one * * * and do the best they can."

When asked by the police shortly after the shooting why he assembled the trap gun, defendant stated that "he didn't have much and he wanted to protect what he did have."

* * *

Defendant contends that had he been present he would have been justified in shooting Stephen since Stephen was attempting to commit burglary (Pen.Code, § 459) * * *. * * *

* * *

In the United States, courts have concluded that a person may be held criminally liable under statutes proscribing homicides and shooting with intent to injure, or civilly liable, if he sets upon his premises a deadly mechanical device and that device kills or injures another. However, an exception to the rule that there may be criminal and civil liability for death or injuries caused by such a device has been recognized where the intrusion is, in fact, such that the person, were he present, would be justified in taking the life or inflicting the bodily harm with his own hands. The phrase "were he present" does not hypothesize the actual presence of the person (see Rest.2d Torts, § 85, coms. (a), (c) & (d)), but is used in setting forth in an indirect manner the principle that a person may do indirectly that which he is privileged to do directly.

Allowing persons, at their own risk, to employ deadly mechanical devices imperils the lives of children, firemen and policemen acting within the scope of their employment, and others. Where the actor is present, there is always the possibility he will realize that deadly force is not necessary, but deadly mechanical devices are without mercy or discretion. Such devices "are silent instrumentalities of death. They deal death and destruction to the innocent as well as the criminal intruder without the slightest warning. The taking of human life [or infliction of great bodily injury] by such means is brutally savage and inhuman." (See State v. Plumlee, supra, 149 So. 425, 430.)

It seems clear that the use of such devices should not be encouraged. Moreover, whatever may be thought in torts, the foregoing rule setting forth an exception to liability for death or injuries inflicted by such devices "is inappropriate in penal law for it is obvious that it does not prescribe a workable standard of conduct; liability depends upon fortuitous results." (See Model Penal Code (Tent.Draft No. 8), § 3.06, com. 15.) We therefore decline to adopt that rule in criminal cases.

Furthermore, even if that rule were applied here, as we shall see, defendant was not justified in shooting Stephen. Penal Code section 197 provides: "Homicide is * * * justifiable * * * 1. When resisting any attempt to murder any person, or to commit a felony, or to do some great bodily injury upon any person; or, 2. When committed in defense of habitation, property, or person, against one who manifestly intends or endeavors, by violence or surprise, to commit a felony * * *." (See also Pen.Code, § 198.) Since a homicide is justifiable under the circumstances specified in section 197, *a fortiori* an attempt to commit a violent injury upon another under those circumstances is justifiable.

By its terms subdivision 1 of Penal Code section 197 appears to permit killing to prevent any "felony," but in view of the large number of felonies today and the inclusion of many that do not involve a danger of serious bodily harm, a literal reading of the section is undesirable. * * * We must look further into the character of the crime, and the manner of its perpetration (see Storey v. State [71 Ala. 329]). *When these do not reasonably create a fear of great bodily harm,* as they could not if defendant apprehended only a misdemeanor assault, *there is no cause for the exaction of a human life."* (Italics added; see also Harper and James, The Law of Torts (1956) pp. 1441–1442, fn. 38; but see 1 Bishop's Criminal Law (9th ed.) p. 608.)

* * * [S]ubdivision 2 of that section is likewise so limited. The term "violence or surprise" in subdivision 2 is found in common law authorities and, whatever may have been the very early common law, the rule devel-

oped at common law that killing or use of deadly force to prevent a felony was justified only if the offense was a forcible and atrocious crime. * * *

Examples of forcible and atrocious crimes are murder, mayhem, rape and robbery. * * *

Burglary has been included in the list of such crimes. However, in view of the wide scope of burglary under Penal Code section 459, as compared with the common law definition of that offense, in our opinion it cannot be said that under all circumstances burglary under section 459 constitutes a forcible and atrocious crime.[2]

Where the character and manner of the burglary do not reasonably create a fear of great bodily harm, there is no cause for exaction of human life, or for the use of deadly force (see generally 13 Stan.L.Rev. 566, 577). The character and manner of the burglary could not reasonably create such a fear unless the burglary threatened, or was reasonably believed to threaten, death or serious bodily harm.

In the instant case the asserted burglary did not threaten death or serious bodily harm, since no one but Stephen and Robert was then on the premises. A defendant is not protected from liability merely by the fact that the intruder's conduct is such as would justify the defendant, were he present, in believing that the intrusion threatened death or serious bodily injury. * * *

* * *

Defendant also argues that had he been present he would have been justified in shooting Stephen under subdivision 4 of Penal Code section 197, which provides, "Homicide is * * * justifiable * * * 4. When necessarily committed in *attempting,* by lawful ways and means, *to apprehend* any person for any felony committed * * *." (Italics added.) The argument cannot be upheld. The words "attempting * * * to apprehend" contain the idea of acting for the purpose of apprehending. * * * Here no showing was made that defendant's intent in shooting was to apprehend a felon. Rather it appears from his testimony and extrajudicial statement heretofore recited that his intent was to prevent a burglary, to protect his property, and to avoid the possibility that a thief might get into defendant's house and injure him upon his return.

* * *

Defendant does not, and could not properly, contend that the intrusion was, in fact, such that were he present, he would be justified under Penal Code sections 692 and 693 in using deadly force. By its terms section 692 authorizes merely "lawful" resistance to an offense by the party about to be

2. At common law burglary was the breaking and entering of a mansion house in the night with the intent to commit a felony. (People v. Barry, 94 Cal. 481, 482, 29 P. 1026; see 1 Witkin, Cal.Crimes (1963) p. 414; 1 Cooley's Blackstone, pp. 223–228; comment, 25 So.Cal.L.Rev. 75.) Burglary under Penal Code section 459 differs from common law burglary in that the entry may be in the daytime and of numerous places other than a mansion house (see 1 Witkin, supra, pp. 416–418), and breaking is not required (see People v. Allison, 200 Cal. 404, 408, 253 P. 318). For example, under section 459 a person who enters a store with the intent of committing theft is guilty of burglary. (See People v. Corral, 60 Cal.App.2d 66, 140 P.2d 172.) It would seem absurd to hold that a store detective could kill that person if necessary to prevent him from committing that offense. (See 13 Stan.L.Rev. 566, 579.)

injured. The circumstances in which resistance by such party is lawful are set forth in Penal Code section 693, which provides, "Resistance sufficient to prevent the offense may be made by the party about to be injured: 1. To prevent an offense against his person, or his family, or some member thereof. 2. To prevent an illegal attempt by force to take or injure property in his lawful possession." Subdivision 1 of section 693 manifestly does not apply, since in the instant case there was no attempt to commit "an offense against [defendant's] person, or his family, or some member thereof." Nor does subdivision 2 of that section apply. Section 693, like Penal Code section 197, should be read in the light of the common law, and, as heretofore stated, the rule developed at common law that deadly force to prevent a felony was justified only if the offense was a forcible and atrocious crime. Here the asserted attempted larceny, like the asserted attempted burglary, was not such a crime because the offense did not threaten death or serious bodily harm.

Defendant also does not, and could not properly, contend that the intrusion was in fact such that, were he present, he would be justified under Civil Code section 50 in using deadly force. That section provides, "Any necessary force may be used to protect from wrongful injury the person or property of oneself * * *." This section also should be read in the light of the common law, and at common law in general deadly force could not be used solely for the protection of property. (See Model Penal Code, supra, § 3.06, com. 8; Perkins on Criminal Law, supra, p. 1026, fn. 6; 13 Stan.L. Rev. 566, 575–576.) * * *

* * *

At common law an exception to the foregoing principle that deadly force could not be used solely for the protection of property was recognized where the property was a dwelling house in some circumstances. (See Simpson v. State, supra, 59 Ala. 1, 14; Perkins on Criminal Law, supra, pp. 1022–1025; Model Penal Code, supra, § 3.06, com. 8, pp. 38–41.) "According to the older interpretation of the common law, even extreme force may be used to prevent dispossession [of the dwelling house]." (See Model Penal Code, supra, com. 8.) Also at common law if another attempted to burn a dwelling the owner was privileged to use deadly force if this seemed necessary to defend his "castle" against the threatened harm. (See Perkins on Criminal Law, supra, p. 1023; 1 Hale, Pleas of the Crown, supra, p. 485.) Further, deadly force was privileged if it was, or reasonably seemed, necessary to protect the dwelling against a burglar. (See Perkins on Criminal Law, supra, p. 1023.)

Here we are not concerned with dispossession or burning of a dwelling, and, as heretofore concluded, the asserted burglary in this case was not of such a character as to warrant the use of deadly force.

* * *

The judgment is affirmed.

Tennessee v. Garner

Supreme Court of the United States, 1985.
471 U.S. 1, 105 S.Ct. 1694, 85 L.Ed.2d 1.

JUSTICE WHITE delivered the opinion of the Court.

This case requires us to determine the constitutionality of the use of deadly force to prevent the escape of an apparently unarmed suspected felon. We conclude that such force may not be used unless it is necessary to prevent the escape and the officer has probable cause to believe that the suspect poses a significant threat of death or serious physical injury to the officer or others.

I

At about 10:45 p.m. on October 3, 1974, Memphis Police Officers Elton Hymon and Leslie Wright were dispatched to answer a "prowler inside call." Upon arriving at the scene they saw a woman standing on her porch and gesturing toward the adjacent house. She told them she had heard glass breaking and that "they" or "someone" was breaking in next door. While Wright radioed the dispatcher to say that they were on the scene, Hymon went behind the house. He heard a door slam and saw someone run across the back yard. The fleeing suspect, who was appellee-respondent's decedent, Edward Garner, stopped at a 6-feet-high chain link fence at the edge of the yard. With the aid of a flashlight, Hymon was able to see Garner's face and hands. He saw no sign of a weapon, and, though not certain, was "reasonably sure" and "figured" that Garner was unarmed. He thought Garner was 17 or 18 years old and about 5 '5 " or 5 '7 " tall.[2] While Garner was crouched at the base of the fence, Hymon called out "police, halt" and took a few steps toward him. Garner then began to climb over the fence. Convinced that if Garner made it over the fence he would elude capture,[3] Hymon shot him. The bullet hit Garner in the back of the head. Garner was taken by ambulance to a hospital, where he died on the operating table. Ten dollars and a purse taken from the house were found on his body.

In using deadly force to prevent the escape, Hymon was acting under the authority of a Tennessee statute and pursuant to Police Department policy. The statute provides that "[i]f, after notice of the intention to arrest the defendant, he either flee or forcibly resist, the officer may use all the

2. In fact, Garner, an eighth-grader, was 15. He was 5 ' 4 " tall and weighed somewhere around 100 or 110 pounds.

3. When asked at trial why he fired, Hymon stated:

"Well, first of all it was apparent to me from the little bit that I knew about the area at the time that he was going to get away because, number 1, I couldn't get to him. My partner then couldn't find where he was because, you know, he was late coming around. He didn't know where I was talking about. I couldn't get to him because of the fence here, I couldn't have jumped this fence and come up, consequently jumped this fence and caught him before he got away because he was already up on the fence, just one leap and he was already over the fence, and so there is no way that I could have caught him."

He also stated that the area beyond the fence was dark, that he could not have gotten over the fence easily because he was carrying a lot of equipment and wearing heavy boots, and that Garner, being younger and more energetic, could have outrun him.

necessary means to effect the arrest." Tenn.Code Ann. § 40–7–108 (1982). The Department policy was slightly more restrictive than the statute, but still allowed the use of deadly force in cases of burglary. The incident was reviewed by the Memphis Police Firearm's Review Board and presented to a grand jury. Neither took any action.

Garner's father then brought this action in the Federal District Court for the Western District of Tennessee, seeking damages under 42 U.S.C. § 1983 for asserted violations of Garner's constitutional rights. The complaint alleged that the shooting violated the Fourth, Fifth, Sixth, Eighth, and Fourteenth Amendments of the United States Constitution. It named as defendants Officer Hymon, the Police Department, its Director, and the Mayor and city of Memphis. After a 3-day bench trial, the District Court entered judgment for all defendants. It dismissed the claims against the Mayor and the Director for lack of evidence. It then concluded that Hymon's actions were authorized by the Tennessee statute, which in turn was constitutional. Hymon had employed the only reasonable and practicable means of preventing Garner's escape. * * *

The Court of Appeals for the Sixth Circuit affirmed with regard to Hymon, finding that he had acted in good-faith reliance on the Tennessee statute and was therefore within the scope of his qualified immunity. 600 F.2d 52 (1979). It remanded for reconsideration of the possible liability of the city, however, in light of Monell v. New York City Dept. of Social Services, 436 U.S. 658, 98 S.Ct. 2018, 56 L.Ed.2d 611 (1978), which had come down after the District Court's decision. The District Court was directed to consider whether a city enjoyed a qualified immunity, whether the use of deadly force and hollow point bullets in these circumstances was constitutional, and whether any unconstitutional municipal conduct flowed from a "policy or custom" as required for liability under *Monell*. 600 F.2d, at 54–55.

The District Court concluded that *Monell* did not affect its decision. While acknowledging some doubt as to the possible immunity of the city, it found that the statute, and Hymon's actions, were constitutional. * * *

The Court of Appeals reversed and remanded. 710 F.2d 240 (CA6 1983). * * *[7]

7. The Court of Appeals concluded that the rule set out in the Model Penal Code "accurately states Fourth Amendment limitations on the use of deadly force against fleeing felons." 710 F.2d, at 247. The relevant portion of the Model Penal Code provides:

"The use of deadly force is not justifiable * * * unless (i) the arrest is for a felony; and (ii) the person effecting the arrest is authorized to act as a peace officer or is assisting a person whom he believes to be authorized to act as a peace officer; and (iii) the actor believes that the force employed creates no substantial risk of injury to innocent persons; and (iv) the actor believes that (1) the crime for which the arrest is made involved conduct including the use or threatened use of deadly force; or (2) there is a substantial risk that the person to be arrested will cause death or serious bodily harm if his apprehension is delayed." American Law Institute, Model Penal Code § 3.07(2)(b) (Proposed Official Draft 1962).

The court also found that "[a]nalysis of the facts of this case under the Due Process Clause" required the same result, because the statute was not narrowly drawn to further a compelling state interest. 710 F.2d, at 246–247. The court considered the generalized interest in effective law enforcement sufficiently compelling only when the suspect is dangerous. Finally, the court held, relying on Owen v. City of Independence, 445 U.S. 622, 100

The State of Tennessee, which had intervened to defend the statute, see 28 U.S.C. § 2403(b), appealed to this Court. The city filed a petition for certiorari. We noted probable jurisdiction in the appeal and granted the petition.

II

Whenever an officer restrains the freedom of a person to walk away, he has seized that person. While it is not always clear just when minimal police interference becomes a seizure, there can be no question that apprehension by the use of deadly force is a seizure subject to the reasonableness requirement of the Fourth Amendment.

A

A police officer may arrest a person if he has probable cause to believe that person committed a crime. Petitioners and appellant argue that if this requirement is satisfied the Fourth Amendment has nothing to say about *how* that seizure is made. This submission ignores the many cases in which this Court, by balancing the extent of the intrusion against the need for it, has examined the reasonableness of the manner in which a search or seizure is conducted. * * *

* * *

B

The same balancing process * * * demonstrates that, notwithstanding probable cause to seize a suspect, an officer may not always do so by killing him. The intrusiveness of a seizure by means of deadly force is unmatched. The suspect's fundamental interest in his own life need not be elaborated upon. The use of deadly force also frustrates the interest of the individual, and of society, in judicial determination of guilt and punishment. Against these interests are ranged governmental interests in effective law enforcement.[8] It is argued that overall violence will be reduced by encouraging the peaceful submission of suspects who know that they may be shot if they flee. Effectiveness in making arrests requires the resort to deadly force, or at least

S.Ct. 1398, 63 L.Ed.2d 673 (1980), that the city was not immune.

8. The dissent emphasizes that subsequent investigation cannot replace immediate apprehension. We recognize that this is so, see infra, n. 13; indeed, that is the reason why there is any dispute. If subsequent arrest were assured, no one would argue that use of deadly force was justified. Thus, we proceed on the assumption that subsequent arrest is not likely. Nonetheless, it should be remembered that failure to apprehend at the scene does not necessarily mean that the suspect will never be caught.

In lamenting the inadequacy of later investigation, the dissent relies on the report of the President's Commission on Law Enforcement and Administration of Justice. It is worth noting that, notwithstanding its awareness of this problem, the Commission itself proposed a policy for use of deadly force arguably even more stringent than the formulation we adopt today. See President's Commission on Law Enforcement and Administration of Justice, Task Force Report: The Police 189 (1967). The Commission proposed that deadly force be used only to apprehend "perpetrators who, in the course of their crime threatened the use of deadly force, or if the officer believes there is a substantial risk that the person whose arrest is sought will cause death or serious bodily harm if his apprehension is delayed." In addition, the officer would have "to know, as a virtual certainty, that the suspect committed an offense for which the use of deadly force is permissible." Ibid.

the meaningful threat thereof. "Being able to arrest such individuals is a condition precedent to the state's entire system of law enforcement."

Without in any way disparaging the importance of these goals, we are not convinced that the use of deadly force is a sufficiently productive means of accomplishing them to justify the killing of nonviolent suspects. The use of deadly force is a self-defeating way of apprehending a suspect and so setting the criminal justice mechanism in motion. If successful, it guarantees that that mechanism will not be set in motion. And while the meaningful threat of deadly force might be thought to lead to the arrest of more live suspects by discouraging escape attempts,[9] the presently available evidence does not support this thesis.[10] The fact is that a majority of police departments in this country have forbidden the use of deadly force against nonviolent suspects. If those charged with the enforcement of the criminal law have abjured the use of deadly force in arresting nondangerous felons, there is a substantial basis for doubting that the use of such force is an essential attribute of the arrest power in all felony cases. * * *

The use of deadly force to prevent the escape of all felony suspects, whatever the circumstances, is constitutionally unreasonable. It is not better that all felony suspects die than that they escape. Where the suspect poses no immediate threat to the officer and no threat to others, the harm resulting from failing to apprehend him does not justify the use of deadly force to do so. It is no doubt unfortunate when a suspect who is in sight escapes, but the fact that the police arrive a little late or are a little slower afoot does not always justify killing the suspect. A police officer may not seize an unarmed, nondangerous suspect by shooting him dead. The Tennessee statute is unconstitutional insofar as it authorizes the use of deadly force against such fleeing suspects.

It is not, however, unconstitutional on its face. Where the officer has probable cause to believe that the suspect poses a threat of serious physical

9. We note that the usual manner of deterring illegal conduct—through punishment—has been largely ignored in connection with flight from arrest. Arkansas, for example, specifically excepts flight from arrest from the offense of "obstruction of governmental operations." The commentary notes that this "reflects the basic policy judgment that, absent the use of force or violence, a mere attempt to avoid apprehension by a law enforcement officer does not give rise to an independent offense." Ark.Stat.Ann. § 41–2802(3)(a) (1977) and commentary. In the few States that do outlaw flight from an arresting officer, the crime is only a misdemeanor. See, e.g., Ind.Code § 35–44–3–3 (1982). Even forceful resistance, though generally a separate offense, is classified as a misdemeanor. E.g., Ill.Rev.Stat., ch. 38, § 31–1 (1984); Mont.Code Ann. § 45–7–301 (1984); N.H.Rev.Stat.Ann. § 642:2 (Supp.1983); Ore.Rev.Stat. § 162.315 (1983).

This lenient approach does avoid the anomaly of automatically transforming every fleeing misdemeanant into a fleeing felon—subject, under the common-law rule, to apprehension by deadly force—solely by virtue of his flight. However, it is in real tension with the harsh consequences of flight in cases where deadly force is employed. For example, Tennessee does not outlaw fleeing from arrest. The Memphis City Code does, § 30–15, subjecting the offender to a maximum fine of $50, § 1–8. Thus, Garner's attempted escape subjected him to (a) a $50 fine, and (b) being shot.

10. See Sherman, Reducing Police Gun Use, in Control in the Police Organization 98, 120–123 (M. Punch, ed. 1983); Fyfe, Observations on Police Deadly Force, 27 Crime & Delinquency 376, 378–381 (1981); W. Geller & K. Karales, Split-Second Decisions 67 (1981); App. 84 (Affidavit of William Bracey, Chief of Patrol, New York City Police Department). See generally Brief for Police Foundation et al. as *Amici Curiae*.

harm, either to the officer or to others, it is not constitutionally unreasonable to prevent escape by using deadly force. Thus, if the suspect threatens the officer with a weapon or there is probable cause to believe that he has committed a crime involving the infliction or threatened infliction of serious physical harm, deadly force may be used if necessary to prevent escape, and if, where feasible, some warning has been given. As applied in such circumstances, the Tennessee statute would pass constitutional muster.

III

A

It is insisted that the Fourth Amendment must be construed in light of the common-law rule, which allowed the use of whatever force was necessary to effect the arrest of a fleeing felon, though not a misdemeanant. As stated in Hale's posthumously published Pleas of the Crown:

> "[I]f persons that are pursued by these officers for felony or the just suspicion thereof * * * shall not yield themselves to these officers, but shall either resist or fly before they are apprehended or being apprehended shall rescue themselves and resist or fly, so that they cannot be otherwise apprehended, and are upon necessity slain therein, because they cannot be otherwise taken, it is no felony." 2 M. Hale, Historia Placitorum Coronae 85 (1736). See also 4 W. Blackstone, Commentaries * 289.

Most American jurisdictions also imposed a flat prohibition against the use of deadly force to stop a fleeing misdemeanant, coupled with a general privilege to use such force to stop a fleeing felon.

The State and city argue that because this was the prevailing rule at the time of the adoption of the Fourth Amendment and for some time thereafter, and is still in force in some States, use of deadly force against a fleeing felon must be "reasonable." It is true that this Court has often looked to the common law in evaluating the reasonableness, for Fourth Amendment purposes, of police activity. On the other hand, it "has not simply frozen into constitutional law those law enforcement practices that existed at the time of the Fourth Amendment's passage." Because of sweeping change in the legal and technological context, reliance on the common-law rule in this case would be a mistaken literalism that ignores the purposes of a historical inquiry.

B

It has been pointed out many times that the common-law rule is best understood in light of the fact that it arose at a time when virtually all felonies were punishable by death. "Though effected without the protections and formalities of an orderly trial and conviction, the killing of a resisting or fleeing felon resulted in no greater consequences than those authorized for punishment of the felony of which the individual was charged or suspected." American Law Institute, Model Penal Code § 3.07, Comment 3, p. 56 (Tentative Draft No. 8, 1958) (hereinafter Model Penal Code Comment).

Courts have also justified the common-law rule by emphasizing the relative dangerousness of felons.

Neither of these justifications makes sense today. Almost all crimes formerly punishable by death no longer are or can be. And while in earlier times "the gulf between the felonies and the minor offences was broad and deep," 2 Pollock & Maitland, 467, n. 3; Carroll v. United States, 267 U.S. 132, 158, 45 S.Ct. 280, 287, 69 L.Ed. 543 (1925), today the distinction is minor and often arbitrary. Many crimes classified as misdemeanors, or nonexistent, at common law are now felonies. Wilgus, 22 Mich.L.Rev., at 572–573. These changes have undermined the concept, which was questionable to begin with, that use of deadly force against a fleeing felon is merely a speedier execution of someone who has already forfeited his life. They have also made the assumption that a "felon" is more dangerous than a misdemeanant untenable. Indeed, numerous misdemeanors involve conduct more dangerous than many felonies.

There is an additional reason why the common-law rule cannot be directly translated to the present day. The common-law rule developed at a time when weapons were rudimentary. Deadly force could be inflicted almost solely in a hand-to-hand struggle during which, necessarily, the safety of the arresting officer was at risk. Handguns were not carried by police officers until the latter half of the last century. L. Kennett & J. Anderson, The Gun in America 150–151 (1975). Only then did it become possible to use deadly force from a distance as a means of apprehension. As a practical matter, the use of deadly force under the standard articulation of the common-law rule has an altogether different meaning—and harsher consequences—now than in past centuries. See Wechsler & Michael, A Rationale for the Law of Homicide: I, 37 Colum.L.Rev. 701, 741 (1937).[13]

One other aspect of the common-law rule bears emphasis. It forbids the use of deadly force to apprehend a misdemeanant, condemning such action as disproportionately severe.

In short, though the common law pedigree of Tennessee's rule is pure on its face, changes in the legal and technological context mean the rule is distorted almost beyond recognition when literally applied.

[C]

In evaluating the reasonableness of police procedures under the Fourth Amendment, we have also looked to prevailing rules in individual jurisdictions. The rules in the States are varied. * * *

13. It has been argued that sophisticated techniques of apprehension and increased communication between the police in different jurisdictions have made it more likely that an escapee will be caught than was once the case, and that this change has also reduced the "reasonableness" of the use of deadly force to prevent escape. E.g., Sherman, Execution Without Trial: Police Homicide and the Constitution, 33 Vand.L.Rev. 71, 76 (1980). We are unaware of any data that would permit sensible evaluation of this claim. Current arrest rates are sufficiently low, however, that we have some doubt whether in past centuries the failure to arrest at the scene meant that the police had missed their only chance in a way that is not presently the case. In 1983, 21% of the offenses in the FBI crime index were cleared by arrest. Federal Bureau of Investigation, Uniform Crime Reports, Crime in the United States 159 (1984). The clearance rate for burglary was 15%. Ibid.

* * *

It cannot be said that there is a constant or overwhelming trend away from the common-law rule. In recent years, some States have reviewed their laws and expressly rejected abandonment of the common-law rule. Nonetheless, the long-term movement has been away from the rule that deadly force may be used against any fleeing felon, and that remains the rule in less than half the States.

This trend is more evident and impressive when viewed in light of the policies adopted by the police departments themselves. Overwhelmingly, these are more restrictive than the common-law rule. C. Milton, J. Halleck, J. Lardner, & G. Abrecht, Police Use of Deadly Force 45–46 (1977). The Federal Bureau of Investigation and the New York City Police Department, for example, both forbid the use of firearms except when necessary to prevent death or grievous bodily harm. Id., at 40–41; App. 83. For accreditation by the Commission on Accreditation for Law Enforcement Agencies, a department must restrict the use of deadly force to situations where "the officer reasonably believes that the action is in defense of human life * * * or in defense of any person in immediate danger of serious physical injury." Commission on Accreditation for Law Enforcement Agencies, Inc., Standards for Law Enforcement Agencies 1–2 (1983) (italics deleted). * * * Overall, only, 7.5% of departmental and municipal policies explicitly permit the use of deadly force against any felon; 86.8% explicitly do not. * * *

[D]

Actual departmental policies are important for an additional reason. We would hesitate to declare a police practice of long standing "unreasonable" if doing so would severely hamper effective law enforcement. But the indications are to the contrary. There has been no suggestion that crime has worsened in any way in jurisdictions that have adopted, by legislation or departmental policy, rules similar to that announced today. *Amici* noted that "[a]fter extensive research and consideration, [they] have concluded that laws permitting police officers to use deadly force to apprehend unarmed, nonviolent fleeing felony suspects actually do not protect citizens or law enforcement officers, do not deter crime or alleviate problems caused by crime, and do not improve the crime fighting ability of law enforcement agencies." Brief for Police Foundation et al. as *Amici Curiae* 11. The submission is that the obvious state interests in apprehension are not sufficiently served to warrant the use of lethal weapons against all fleeing felons.

Nor do we agree with petitioners and appellant that the rule we have adopted requires the police to make impossible, split-second evaluations of unknowable facts. See Brief for Petitioners 25; Brief for Appellant 11. We do not deny the practical difficulties of attempting to assess the suspect's dangerousness. However, similarly difficult judgments must be made by the police in equally uncertain circumstances. Nor is there any indication that in States that allow the use of deadly force only against dangerous suspects the standard has been difficult to apply or has led to a rash of litigation involving inappropriate second-guessing of police officers' split-second decisions.

Moreover, the highly technical felony/misdemeanor distinction is equally, if not more, difficult to apply in the field. * * *

IV

* * *

The dissent argues that the shooting was justified by the fact that Officer Hymon had probable cause to believe that Garner had committed a nighttime burglary. While we agree that burglary is a serious crime, we cannot agree that it is so dangerous as automatically to justify the use of deadly force. The FBI classifies burglary as a "property" rather than a "violent" crime. Although the armed burglar would present a different situation, the fact that an unarmed suspect has broken into a dwelling at night does not automatically mean he is physically dangerous. This case demonstrates as much. In fact, the available statistics demonstrate that burglaries only rarely involve physical violence. During the 10-year period from 1973–1982, only 3.8% of all burglaries involved violent crime. Bureau of Justice Statistics, Household Burglary, p. 4 (1985).[23]

V

We wish to make clear what our holding means in the context of this case. The complaint has been dismissed as to all the individual defendants. The State is a party only by virtue of 28 U.S.C. § 2403(b) and is not subject to liability. The possible liability of the remaining defendants—the Police Department and the city of Memphis—hinges on Monell v. New York City Dept. of Social Services, 436 U.S. 658, 98 S.Ct. 2018, 56 L.Ed.2d 611 (1978), and is left for remand. We hold that the statute is invalid insofar as it purported to give Hymon the authority to act as he did. As for the policy of the Police Department, the absence of any discussion of this issue by the courts below, and the uncertain state of the record, preclude any consideration of its validity.

The judgment of the Court of Appeals is affirmed, and the case is remanded for further proceedings consistent with this opinion.

So ordered.

JUSTICE O'CONNOR, with whom THE CHIEF JUSTICE and JUSTICE REHNQUIST join, dissenting.

The Court today holds that the Fourth Amendment prohibits a police officer from using deadly force as a last resort to apprehend a criminal suspect who refuses to halt when fleeing the scene of a nighttime burglary. This

23. The dissent points out that three-fifths of all rapes in the home, three-fifths of all home robberies, and about a third of home assaults are committed by burglars. These figures mean only that if one knows that a suspect committed a rape in the home, there is a good chance that the suspect is also a burglar. That has nothing to do with the question here, which is whether the fact that someone has committed a burglary indicates that he has committed, or might commit, a violent crime.

The dissent also points out that this 3.8% adds up to 2.8 million violent crimes over a 10-year period, as if to imply that today's holding will let loose 2.8 million violent burglars. The relevant universe is, of course, far smaller. At issue is only that tiny fraction of cases where violence has taken place and an officer who has no other means of apprehending the suspect is unaware of its occurrence.

conclusion rests on the majority's balancing of the interests of the suspect and the public interest in effective law enforcement. Notwithstanding the venerable common-law rule authorizing the use of deadly force if necessary to apprehend a fleeing felon, and continued acceptance of this rule by nearly half the States, the majority concludes that Tennessee's statute is unconstitutional inasmuch as it allows the use of such force to apprehend a burglary suspect who is not obviously armed or otherwise dangerous. Although the circumstances of this case are unquestionably tragic and unfortunate, our constitutional holdings must be sensitive both to the history of the Fourth Amendment and to the general implications of the Court's reasoning. By disregarding the serious and dangerous nature of residential burglaries and the longstanding practice of many States, the Court effectively creates a Fourth Amendment right allowing a burglary suspect to flee unimpeded from a police officer who has probable cause to arrest, who has ordered the suspect to halt, and who has no means short of firing his weapon to prevent escape. I do not believe that the Fourth Amendment supports such a right, and I accordingly dissent.

* * *

* * * Where a police officer has probable cause to arrest a suspected burglar, the use of deadly force as a last resort might well be the only means of apprehending the suspect. With respect to a particular burglary, subsequent investigation simply cannot represent a substitute for immediate apprehension of the criminal suspect at the scene. See Report of President's Commission on Law Enforcement and Administration of Justice, The Challenge of Crime in a Free Society 97 (1967). Indeed, the Captain of the Memphis Police Department testified that in his city, if apprehension is not immediate, it is likely that the suspect will not be caught. Although some law enforcement agencies may choose to assume the risk that a criminal will remain at large, the Tennessee statute reflects a legislative determination that the use of deadly force in prescribed circumstances will serve generally to protect the public. Such statutes assist the police in apprehending suspected perpetrators of serious crimes and provide notice that a lawful police order to stop and submit to arrest may not be ignored with impunity.

* * *

Against the strong public interests justifying the conduct at issue here must be weighed the individual interests implicated in the use of deadly force by police officers. The majority declares that "[t]he suspect's fundamental interest in his own life need not be elaborated upon." This blithe assertion hardly provides an adequate substitute for the majority's failure to acknowledge the distinctive manner in which the suspect's interest in his life is even exposed to risk. For purposes of this case, we must recall that the police officer, in the course of investigating a nighttime burglary, had reasonable cause to arrest the suspect and ordered him to halt. The officer's use of force resulted because the suspected burglar refused to heed this command and the officer reasonably believed that there was no means short of firing his weapon to apprehend the suspect. Without questioning the importance of a person's interest in his life, I do not think this interest encompasses a right to flee unimpeded from the scene of a burglary. * * *

* * *

Even if I agreed that the Fourth Amendment was violated under the circumstances of this case, I would be unable to join the Court's opinion. The Court holds that deadly force may be used only if the suspect "threatens the officer with a weapon or there is probable cause to believe that he has committed a crime involving the infliction or threatened infliction of serious physical harm." The Court ignores the more general implications of its reasoning. Relying on the Fourth Amendment, the majority asserts that it is constitutionally unreasonable to *use* deadly force against fleeing criminal suspects who do not appear to pose a threat of serious physical harm to others. By declining to limit its holding to the use of firearms, the Court unnecessarily implies that the Fourth Amendment constrains the use of any police practice that is potentially lethal, no matter how remote the risk.

* * *

* * * Police are given no guidance for determining which objects, among an array of potentially lethal weapons ranging from guns to knives to baseball bats to rope, will justify the use of deadly force. The Court also declines to outline the additional factors necessary to provide "probable cause" for believing that a suspect "poses a significant threat of death or serious physical injury," when the officer has probable cause to arrest and the suspect refuses to obey an order to halt. But even if it were appropriate in this case to limit the use of deadly force to that ambiguous class of suspects, I believe the class should include nighttime residential burglars who resist arrest by attempting to flee the scene of the crime. We can expect an escalating volume of litigation as the lower courts struggle to determine if a police officer's split-second decision to shoot was justified by the danger posed by a particular object and other facts related to the crime. Thus, the majority opinion portends a burgeoning area of Fourth Amendment doctrine concerning the circumstances in which police officers can reasonably employ deadly force.

* * *

Notes

1. Review the *Note on Arrest Powers,* supra, p. 415.

2. *The Model Penal Code Position.* Model Penal Code § 3.07, Comments 2, 3, 4, and 6: *

> 2. *Use of Force for Arrest.* Subsection (1) affirms a general justification for the use of force that the actor believes to be necessary to effect a lawful arrest. As in the other formulations in Article 3, the justifying principle is cast in terms of the actor's belief in the immediate necessity of his conduct, subject to the operation of Section 3.09(2) when the actor is reckless or negligent in forming his belief and is prosecuted for an offense for which recklessness or negligence, as the case may be, suffices to establish culpability.
>
> Recklessness or negligence apart, the justification holds regardless of the illegality of the arrest, so long as the actor believes in its legality. There is the additional qualification, however, that if the actor's mistake as to the legality of the arrest is based upon an error of law, whether a provision of the criminal law or the

law relating to the scope of his powers to arrest, he will be denied the justification under Section 3.09(1). This follows from the general policy concerning ignorance of law which has been articulated most fully in Section 2.04. * * *

* * *

3. *Limitations on Use of Force for Arrest.* * * *

* * *

(c) *Deadly Force.* Paragraph (b) of Subsection (2) is addressed to the crucial problem of the extent to which it should be justifiable to use deadly force to effect an arrest.

The problem addressed here, it should be noted, is much narrower than the question of when an officer or other person making an arrest is justified in using deadly force. As Section 3.04(2)(b)(ii)(B) recognizes, one who is justified in making an arrest is not obliged to desist because resistance is encountered. He may not only stand his ground but may also press forward to achieve his object, meeting force with force, and if he believes that deadly force is necessary to protect himself, he may employ such force. Under other provisions, one making an arrest is also privileged to use deadly force to protect the lives of others and in some circumstances to prevent successful flight from certain crimes that interfere with property interests.

* * * This problem arises primarily in cases where the person sought to be arrested flees and the actor believes it necessary that he shoot to prevent the escape. In order to understand the Model Code's formulation, it is helpful to consider the law in effect when the Code was drafted.

> (i) *Prior Law.* The common law approach to the problem of deadly force in arrest was based on the distinction between felony and misdemeanor. Deadly force was authorized where necessary to prevent the escape of one fleeing from arrest for felony, but not for misdemeanor. * * *
>
> The common law rule, whatever its virtues for the period in which the rules of justification were formulated, seems manifestly inadequate for modern law. Such rational justification for the common law as can be adduced rests largely on the fact that virtually all felonies in the common law period were punishable by death. * * *

Today, the significance of the distinction between felony and misdemeanor has wholly altered. Relatively few crimes are punishable by death. A very small percentage of arrests actually made are for offenses that are capitally punishable. Of these, the number in which capital punishment is likely to be imposed is very substantially smaller, and given recent trends the number of actual executions is comparatively miniscule. Moreover, under modern legislation, many statutory misdemeanors involve conduct more dangerous to life and limb than some felonies. * * * Even a felony that often is committed in such a way as to endanger life may in particular cases be committed in a fashion that creates no such peril. Accordingly, the felony/misdemeanor distinction is inherently incapable of separating out those persons of such dangerousness that the perils arising from failure to accomplish immediate apprehension justify resort to extreme force to effect the arrest.

In some jurisdictions, the prior law was unsatisfactory also in its definition of the mental element required to justify the use of deadly force in these cases. The extreme breadth of the privilege apparently induced some courts and legislatures to limit its application in the very worst way—by imposing a rule of strict liability. Thus, the privilege was at times said to attach only when the deceased had in fact committed a felony, apart from all considerations of good faith and reasonable belief on the part of the arresting officer. In other jurisdictions, the rule appears to have required that a felony must in fact have been committed, though the deceased need not have committed it if the officer reasonably believed that he did. Such a rule also creates the possibility of an absolute liability. Still other jurisdictions appeared to adhere to a rule of reasonable belief, but the law was in a state of considerable ambiguity and uncertainty on this vital point.

The common law rules in the arrest cases also created difficulties of another sort. The arrest rules were broader than those that evolved to justify the use of deadly force to prevent the commission of felonies. In the latter case, justification was commonly granted only where the felony was of a "violent" type or, at least, where its commission normally involved a substantial risk to life or limb. Thus, justification might be granted to a person employing deadly force where an attempt to effect an arrest was made, even though a primary motive for the apprehension was to prevent the commission or completion of a "nonviolent" felony; and yet justification might be denied in the same case where the use of deadly force is sought to be defended simply as a means to prevent the felony. The perplexities created by such inconsistencies in the doctrines of justification were serious and the Institute concluded that they should be eliminated.

* * *

(ii) *Model Penal Code Formulation and Recent Revisions.*

* * *

The approach of the provision differs in many respects from earlier attempts at reform. Like the common law rule, Paragraph (i) of Subsection (2)(b) restricts the use of extreme force to arrests for felonies. * * * But unlike the common law rule, Subsection (2)(b) imposes certain additional qualifications on the privilege.

(A) *Limitation to Peace Officers and Those Assisting Them.* First, the use of deadly force is restricted by Paragraph (ii) of Subsection (2)(b) to those who, under the law of the jurisdiction, are authorized to act as peace officers and to those who are assisting persons whom they believe are authorized to act as peace officers. Where the purpose to be served is the apprehension of persons to answer criminal charges, it has seemed important, in an age of firearms, to restrict the use of deadly force to situations where official personnel are involved, or at least are believed to be involved. * * *

* * *

(B) *Absence of Risk to Innocent Bystanders.* Another difference between the common law and these provisions is stated in Paragraph (iii) of Subsection (2). It is there recognized that the public interest is poorly served if the use of deadly force creates a substantial risk of injury to innocent bystanders. The privilege is accordingly withheld unless the actor believes that there is no such risk.

* * *

(C) *Character of Offender Determinative.* The third way in which these provisions differ from the common law is contained in Paragraph (iv) of Subsection (2)(b), which is based on the principle that the character of the offender as it can be inferred from the available information, rather than from an abstract classification of the offense he is thought to have committed, should be determinative as to the use of deadly force. Specifically, the judgment is that the use of deadly force should be sanctioned only in cases where the offender is thought to pose such a danger to life or limb that his immediate apprehension overrides competing considerations.

Paragraph (A) of Subsection (2)(b)(iv) permits deadly force in cases in which the crime for which the arrest is made is believed to involve the use or threatened use of deadly force. This provision reflects a judgment that the display of deadly force in the commission of an offense indicates the offender's potential for future violence and justifies extreme measures to assure his immediate capture. It gives peace officers a specific criterion by which to govern their conduct.

Paragraph (B) of Subsection (2)(b)(iv) states a broader, second criterion as a governing principle that can be used for other occasions when the use of deadly force might be thought appropriate. Deadly force is justified when the actor believes that there is a substantial risk that the offender will cause death or serious bodily injury if his apprehension is delayed. The offender's use or threatened use of deadly force during an attempt to resist the arrest may provide the evidential basis upon which this conclusion can be drawn, as may factors that are known about his prior record, his disposition to use force, whether he is armed, the likelihood of apprehending him with less danger on another occasion, and so on.

* * *

4. *Escape.* Subsection (3) is an effort to deal expressly with the problems of the use of force to prevent the escape of a person in custody after lawful arrest. It appeared prudent to state explicitly whether, and under what circumstances, the same or different rules regulating the use of force should apply to escape from custody and arrest.

The subsection states in effect that, contrary to a notion sometimes encountered, a peace officer or other person has no greater privilege to use force to prevent the escape of the arrested person from his custody than he had in effecting the arrest in the first instance. The observations of the Arkansas Supreme Court seem apposite:

> It is admitted that an officer cannot lawfully kill one who merely flees to avoid arrest for a misdemeanor, although it may appear that he can never be taken otherwise. If he runs, then, before the officer has laid his hands upon him with words of arrest, he may do so without danger to his life. But if, by surprise or otherwise, he be for a moment sufficiently restrained to constitute an arrest and then "break away," the officer may kill him if he cannot overtake him. Such is the effect of the argument and of the rule in support of which it is made. We can see no principle of reason or justice on which such a distinction can rest, and we therefore hold that the force or violence which an officer may lawfully use to prevent the escape of a person arrested for a misdemeanor is no greater than such as might have been rightfully employed to effect his arrest.[36]

Subsection (3) also deals, however, with a very different problem. The public interest in prevention of escape by persons lawfully in the custody of penal institutions is regarded by the provision as sufficient to warrant the use of deadly

36. Thomas v. Kinkead, 55 Ark. 502, 508–09, 18 S.W. 854, 856 (1892).

force where the custodian or guard believes that only such force can prevent the escape. Persons in institutions are in a meaningful sense in the custody of the law and not of individuals; the social and psychological significance of an escape is very different in degree from flight from an arrest.

* * *

6. *Suicide or Commission of Crime.* Subsection (5) deals with the use of force to prevent another from committing suicide, from inflicting serious bodily harm upon himself, or from committing certain types of criminal offenses. The use of force for this purpose is justified, as in other cases, when the actor believes force to be immediately necessary to effect the desired objectives. * * *

* * *

(c) *Deadly Force.* Special limitations are imposed upon the use of deadly force to prevent the commission of crime by Subsection (5)(a)(ii). The provision requires that the actor believe that there is a substantial risk that the person whom he seeks to prevent from committing a crime will cause death or serious bodily harm unless the crime is prevented, and further, that he believe that the use of such force creates no substantial risk of injury to innocent persons. These limitations do not apply, however, to the use of deadly force that is believed to be necessary to suppress a riot or a mutiny and that follows a warning that such force may be used.

(i) *Crimes Other Than Riot or Mutiny.* It will be noted that the limitation in Paragraph (A) of Subsection (5)(a)(ii) parallels in policy the qualification in Paragraph (B) of Subsection (2)(b)(iv) on the justifiable use of deadly force to effect an arrest.

It is logically possible to distinguish between the two situations, for the view may be taken that the use of extreme force is more justifiable to prevent a crime than to arrest the criminal when the crime has become an accomplished fact. But to the contrary, it may be said that the same concern for the protection of life and limb that underlies the provision on arrest applies also to the prevention of crime. This is the view that is adopted here. Subsection (5)(a)(ii)(A) differs from its prototype in the law of arrest, however, in that it is not restricted to deadly force used by peace officers and those who assist them, whereas Subsection (2)(b)(ii) is so limited with respect to arrests. In modern conditions, the arrest of suspected criminals is peculiarly the concern of the police. The prevention of crime, on the other hand, is properly the concern of everybody.

Thus, the provision does not justify the killing of a criminal merely because his identity is unknown and undiscoverable (e.g., because the crime is attempted at night), or merely because he is engaged in the theft or destruction of property of great value, or merely because the crime is being attempted in a dwelling house. In these respects, it differs from many earlier statutes that allowed the killing of criminals on broad grounds. * * *

* * *

It should be noted that Paragraph (A) of Subsection (5)(a)(ii) does not in practical effect preclude the use of deadly force in many situations where such force would be justifiable under earlier law. Such force may be employed in self-protection or the protection of others from death or serious injury, as well as to prevent dispossession from a dwelling or the successful completion of serious property offense, under the justifications formulated in Sections 3.04–3.06. Thus, deadly force may be employed to prevent a robbery provided that deadly force is used or threatened by the robber, as well as to prevent the robber from escaping with the fruits of his crime in such a case.

What the limitation contained in Paragraph (A) does is to employ as the standard for the use of extreme force the criterion of peril to life or serious injury, including, of course, sexual outrage, rather than the abstract concept of prevention of a felony. The principle is followed, moreover, in cases where Sections 3.04 and 3.05 may not be brought into play because the peril is not to a particular or identifiable person. A policeman, for example, who sees an armed burglar attempting entry into a dwelling, might be justified in killing if he thinks it necessary to prevent the burglary, in the view that there is a substantial risk that the burglar will cause death or serious bodily harm unless his entry is prevented—though the officer may not know that there is a person in the dwelling and it may in fact be empty. * * *

* * *

c. *NECESSITY AND THE GENERAL PRINCIPLE OF JUSTIFICATION*

The Queen v. Dudley and Stephens

Queen's Bench Division, 1884.
14 Q.B.D. 273.

INDICTMENT for the murder of Richard Parker on the high seas within the jurisdiction of the Admiralty.

At the trial before Huddleston, B., at the Devon and Cornwall Winter Assizes, November 7, 1884, the jury, at the suggestion of the learned judge, found the facts of the case in a special verdict which stated "that on July 5, 1884, the prisoners, Thomas Dudley and Edward Stephens, with one Brooks, all able-bodied English seamen, and the deceased also an English boy, between seventeen and eighteen years of age, the crew of an English yacht, a registered English vessel, were cast away in a storm on the high seas 1600 miles from the Cape of Good Hope, and were compelled to put into an open boat belonging to the said yacht. That in this boat they had no supply of water and no supply of food, except two 1lb. tins of turnips, and for three days they had nothing else to subsist upon. That on the fourth day they caught a small turtle, upon which they subsisted for a few days, and this was the only food they had up to the twentieth day when the act now in question was committed. That on the twelfth day the remains of the turtle were entirely consumed, and for the next eight days they had nothing to eat. That they had no fresh water, except such rain as they from time to time caught in their oilskin capes. That the boat was drifting on the ocean, and was probably more than 1000 miles away from land. That on the eighteenth day, when they had been seven days without food and five without water, the prisoners spoke to Brooks as to what should be done if no succour came, and suggested that some one should be sacrificed to save the rest, but Brooks dissented, and the boy, to whom they were understood to refer, was not consulted. That on the 24th of July, the day before the act now in question, the prisoner Dudley proposed to Stephens and Brooks that lots should be cast who should be put to death to save the rest, but Brooks refused to consent, and it was not put to the boy, and in point of fact there was no drawing of lots. That on that day the prisoners spoke of their having families, and suggested it would be better to kill the boy that their lives should be saved, and Dudley proposed that if there was no vessel in sight by the morrow morning the boy should be killed. That next day, the 25th of July, no vessel appearing, Dudley told Brooks that he had better go and have a sleep, and made signs to Stephens and Brooks that the boy had better be killed. The prisoner Stephens agreed to the act, but Brooks dissented from it. That the boy was then lying at the bottom of the boat quite helpless, and extremely weakened by famine and by drinking sea water, and unable to make any resistance, nor did he ever assent to his being killed. The prisoner Dudley offered a prayer asking forgiveness for them all if either of them should be tempted to commit a rash act, and that their souls might be saved. That Dudley, with the assent of Stephens, went to the boy, and telling him that his time was come, put a knife into his throat and killed him then and there; that the three men fed upon the body and blood of the boy for four days; that on the fourth day after the act had been committed the boat was picked up by a passing vessel, and the prisoners were rescued, still alive, but in the lowest state of prostration. That they were carried to the port of Falmouth, and committed for trial at Exeter. That if the men had not fed upon the body of the boy they would probably not have survived to be so picked up and rescued, but would within the four days have died of famine. That the boy, being in a much weaker condition, was likely to have died before them. That at the time of the act in question there was no sail in sight, nor any reasonable prospect of relief. That under these circumstances there appeared to the prisoners every probability that unless they then fed or very soon fed upon the boy or one of themselves they would die of starvation. That there was no appreciable chance of saving life except by killing some one for the others to eat. That assuming any necessity to kill anybody, there was no greater necessity for killing the boy than any of the other three men. But whether upon the whole matter by the jurors found the killing of Richard Parker by Dudley and Stephens be felony and murder the jurors are ignorant, and pray the advice of the Court thereupon, and if upon the whole matter the Court shall be of opinion that the killing of Richard Parker be felony and murder, then the jurors say that Dudley and Stephens were each guilty of felony and murder as alleged in the indictment."

The learned judge then adjourned the assizes until the 25th of November at the Royal Courts of Justice. On the application of the Crown they were again adjourned to the 4th of December, and the case ordered to be argued before a Court consisting of five judges.

* * *

LORD COLERIDGE, C.J.

* * *

* * * From these facts, stated with the cold precision of a special verdict, it appears sufficiently that the prisoners were subject to terrible temptation, to sufferings which might break down the bodily power of the strongest man, and try the conscience of the best. * * * But nevertheless this is clear, that the prisoners put to death a weak and unoffending boy upon the chance of preserving their own lives by feeding upon his flesh and blood after he was killed, and with the certainty of depriving *him* of any possible chance of survival. The verdict finds in terms that "if the men had not fed

upon the body of the boy they would *probably* not have survived," and that "the boy being in a much weaker condition was *likely* to have died before them." They might possibly have been picked up next day by a passing ship; they might possibly not have been picked up at all; in either case it is obvious that the killing of the boy would have been an unnecessary and profitless act. * * *

* * *

There remains to be considered the real question in the case—whether killing under the circumstances set forth in the verdict be or be not murder. The contention that it could be anything else was, to the minds of us all, both new and strange, and we stopped the Attorney General in his negative argument in order that we might hear what could be said in support of a proposition which appeared to us to be at once dangerous, immoral, and opposed to all legal principle and analogy. All, no doubt, that can be said has been urged before us, and we are now to consider and determine what it amounts to. First it is said that it follows from various definitions of murder in books of authority, which definitions imply, if they do not state, the doctrine, that in order to save your own life you may lawfully take away the life of another, when that other is neither attempting nor threatening yours, nor is guilty of any illegal act whatever towards you or any one else. But if these definitions be looked at they will not be found to sustain this contention. * * *

* * * [T]he doctrine contended for receives no support from the great authority of Lord Hale. It is plain that in his view the necessity which justified homicide is that only which has always been and is now considered a justification. "In all these cases of homicide by necessity," says he, "as in pursuit of a felon, in killing him that assaults to rob, or comes to burn or break a house, or the like, which are in themselves no felony" (1 Hale's Pleas of the Crown, p. 491). Again, he says that "the necessity which justifies homicide is of two kinds: (1) the necessity which is of a private nature; (2) the necessity which relates to the public justice and safety. The former is that necessity which obligeth a man to his own defence and safeguard, and this takes in these inquires:—(1.) What may be done for the safeguard of a man's own life;" and then follow three other heads not necessary to pursue. Then Lord Hale proceeds:—"As touching the first of these—viz., homicide in defence of a man's own life, which is usually styled se defendendo." It is not possible to use words more clear to show that Lord Hale regarded the private necessity which justified, and alone justified, the taking the life of another for the safeguard of one's own to be what is commonly called "self-defence." (Hale's Pleas of the Crown, i. 478.)

But if this could be even doubtful upon Lord Hale's words, Lord Hale himself has made it clear. For in the chapter in which he deals with the exemption created by compulsion or necessity he thus expresses himself:—"If a man be desperately assaulted and in peril of death, and cannot otherwise escape unless, to satisfy his assailant's fury, he will kill an innocent person then present, the fear and actual force will not acquit him of the crime and punishment of murder, if he commit the fact, for he ought rather to die himself than kill an innocent; but if he cannot otherwise save his own life the law permits him in his own defence to kill the assailant, for by the violence of the assault, and the offence committed upon him by the assailant himself, the law of nature, and necessity, hath made him his own protector cum debito moderamine inculpatae tutelae." (Hale's Pleas of the Crown, vol. i. 51.)

But, further still, Lord Hale in the following chapter deals with the position asserted by the casuists, and sanctioned, as he says, by Grotius and Puffendorf, that in a case of extreme necessity, either of hunger or clothing; "theft is no theft, or at least not punishable as theft, as some even of our own lawyers have asserted the same." "But," says Lord Hale, "I take it that here in England, that rule, at least by the laws of England, is false; and therefore, if a person, being under necessity for want of victuals or clothes, shall upon that account clandestinely and animo furandi steal another man's goods, it is felony, and a crime by the laws of England punishable with death." (Hale, Pleas of the Crown, i. 54.) If, therefore, Lord Hale is clear—as he is—that extreme necessity of hunger does not justify larceny, what would he have said to the doctrine that it justified murder?

It is satisfactory to find that another great authority, second, probably, only to Lord Hale, speaks with the same unhesitating clearness on this matter. Sir Michael Foster, in the 3rd chapter of his Discourse on Homicide, deals with the subject of "homicide founded in necessity"; and the whole chapter implies, and is insensible unless it does imply, that in the view of Sir Michael Foster "necessity and self-defence" (which he defines as "opposing force to force even to the death") are convertible terms. There is no hint, no trace, of the doctrine now contended for; the whole reasoning of the chapter is entirely inconsistent with it.

In East's Pleas of the Crown (i. 271) the whole chapter on homicide by necessity is taken up with an elaborate discussion of the limits within which necessity in Sir Michael Foster's sense (given above) of self-defence is a justification of or excuse for homicide. There is a short section at the end very generally and very doubtfully expressed, in which the only instance discussed is the well-known one of two shipwrecked men on a plank able to sustain only one of them, and the conclusion is left by Sir Edward East entirely undetermined.

* * *

Is there, then, any authority for the proposition which has been presented to us? * * * The American case cited by my Brother Stephen in his Digest, from Wharton on Homicide, in which it was decided, correctly indeed, that sailors had no right to throw passengers overboard to save themselves, but on the somewhat strange ground that the proper mode of determining who was to be sacrificed was to vote upon the subject by ballot, can hardly, as my Brother Stephen says, be an authority satisfactory to a court in this country. * * *

The one real authority of former time is Lord Bacon, who, in his commentary on the maxim, "necessitas inducit privilegium quoad jura privata," lays down the law as follows:—"Necessity carrieth a privilege in itself. Necessity is of three sorts—necessity of conservation of life, necessity of obedience, and necessity of the act of God or of a stranger. First of conservation of life; if a man steal viands to satisfy his present hunger, this is no felony nor larceny. So if divers be in danger of drowning by the casting away of some boat or barge, and one of them get to some plank, or on the boat's side to keep himself above water, and another to save his life thrust him from it, whereby he is drowned, this is neither se defendendo nor by misadventure, but justifiable." On this it is to be observed that Lord Bacon's proposition that stealing to satisfy hunger is no larceny is hardly supported by Staundforde, whom he cites for it, and is expressly contradicted by Lord Hale in the passage already cited. And for the proposition as to the plank or boat, it is said to be derived from the canonists. At any rate he cites no authority for it, and it must stand upon his own. Lord Bacon was great even as a lawyer; but it is permissible to much smaller men, relying upon principle and on the authority of others, the equals and even the superiors of Lord Bacon as lawyers, to question the soundness of his dictum. There are many conceivable states of things in which it might possibly be true, but if Lord Bacon meant to lay down the broad proposition that a man may save his life by killing, if necessary, an innocent and unoffending neighbour, it certainly is not law at the present day.

There remains the authority of my Brother Stephen, who, both in his Digest and in his History of the Criminal Law, uses language perhaps wide enough to cover this case. The language is somewhat vague in both places, but it does not in either place cover this case of necessity, and we have the best authority for saying that it was not meant to cover it. If it had been necessary, we must with true deference have differed from him, but it is satisfactory to know that we have, probably at least, arrived at no conclusion in which if he had been a member of the Court he would have been unable to agree. Neither are we in conflict with any opinion expressed upon the subject by the learned persons who formed the commission for preparing the Criminal Code. They say on this subject:

"We are certainly not prepared to suggest that necessity should in every case be a justification. We are equally unprepared to suggest that necessity should in no case be a defence; we judge it better to leave such questions to be dealt with when, if ever, they arise in practice by applying the principles of law to the circumstances of the particular case."

* * *

Now, except for the purpose of testing how far the conservation of a man's own life is in all cases and under all circumstances, an absolute, unqualified, and paramount duty, we exclude from our consideration all the incidents of war. We are dealing with a case of private homicide, not one imposed upon men in the service of their Sovereign and in the defence of their country. Now it is admitted that the deliberate killing of this unoffending and unresisting boy was clearly murder, unless the killing can be justified by some well-recognised excuse admitted by the law. It is further admitted that there was in this case no such excuse, unless the killing was justified by what has been called "necessity." But the temptation to the act which existed here was not what the law has ever called necessity. Nor is this to be regretted. Though law and morality are not the same, and many things may be immoral which are not necessarily illegal, yet the absolute divorce of law from morality would be of fatal consequence; and such divorce would follow if the temptation to murder in this case were to be held by law an absolute defence of it. It is not so. To preserve one's life is generally speaking a duty, but it may be the plainest and the highest duty to sacrifice it. War is full of instances in which it is a man's duty not to live, but to die. The duty, in case of shipwreck, of a captain to his crew, of the crew to the passengers, of soldiers to women and children, as in the noble case of the *Birkenhead;* these duties impose on men the moral necessity, not of the preservation, but of the sacrifice of their lives for others, from which in no country, least of all, it is to be hoped, in England, will men ever shrink, as indeed, they have not shrunk. It is not correct, therefore, to say that there is any absolute or unqualified necessity to preserve one's life. "Necesse est ut eam, non ut vivam," is a saying of a Roman officer quoted by Lord Bacon himself with high eulogy in the very chapter on necessity to which so much reference has been made. It would be a very easy and cheap display of commonplace learning to quote from Greek and Latin authors, from Horace, from Juvenal, from Cicero, from Euripides, passage after passage, in which the duty of dying for others has been laid down in glowing and emphatic language as resulting from the principles of heathen ethics; it is enough in a Christian country to remind ourselves of the Great Example whom we profess to follow. It is not needful to point out the awful danger of admitting the principle which has been contended for. Who is to be the judge of this sort of necessity? By what measure is the comparative value of lives to be measured? Is it to be strength, or intellect, or what? It is plain that the principle leaves to him who is to profit by it to determine the necessity which will justify him in deliberately taking another's life to save his own. In this case the weakest, the youngest, the most unresisting, was chosen. Was it more necessary to kill him than one of the grown men? The answer must be "No"—

> "So spake the Fiend, and with necessity,
> The tyrant's plea, excused his devilish deeds."

It is not suggested that in this particular case the deeds were "devilish," but it is quite plain that such a principle once admitted might be made the legal cloak for unbridled passion and atrocious crime. There is no safe path for judges to tread but to ascertain the law to the best of their ability and to declare it according to their judgment; and if in any case the law appears to be too severe on individuals, to leave it to the Sovereign to exercise that prerogative of mercy which the Constitution has intrusted to the hands fittest to dispense it.

It must not be supposed that in refusing to admit temptation to be an excuse for crime it is forgotten how terrible the temptation was; how awful the suffering; how hard in such trials to keep the judgment straight and the conduct pure. We are often compelled to set up standards we cannot reach ourselves, and to lay down rules which we could not ourselves satisfy. But a man has no right to declare temptation to be an excuse, though he might himself have yielded to it, nor allow compassion for the criminal to change or weaken in any manner the legal definition of the crime. It is therefore our duty to declare that the prisoners' act in this case was wilful murder, that the facts as stated in the verdict are no legal justification of the homicide; and to say that in our unanimous opinion the prisoners are upon this special verdict guilty of murder.[1]

THE COURT then proceeded to pass sentence of death upon the prisoners.[2]

Notes

1. *Stephen's Pre-Dudley View.* J. Stephen, *A Digest of the Criminal Law* 21–22 (1877):

> An act which would otherwise be a crime may be excused if the person accused can show that it was done only in order to avoid consequences which could not otherwise be avoided, and which, if they had followed, would have inflicted upon him or upon others whom he was bound to protect, inevitable and irreparable evil, that no more was done than was reasonably necessary for that purpose, and that the evil inflicted by it was not disproportionate to the evil avoided. *Illustrations.* * * * (2.) * A and B, swimming in the sea, after a shipwreck, get hold of a plank not large enough to support both; A pushes off B, who is drowned. This is not a crime.

After *Dudley,* Stephen commented in the fifth edition of his Digest that *Dudley* could be defended upon its peculiar facts and that he could discover no principle in the judgment. Such cases, he thought, are best decided on an ad hoc basis.

2. *The Model Penal Code View.* Model Penal Code § 3.02, Comments 1 and 3: **

> 1. *Codification of a Principle of Necessity.* This section accepts the view that a principle of necessity, properly conceived, affords a general justification for conduct that would otherwise constitute an offense. It reflects the judgment that such a qualification on criminal liability, like the general requirements of culpability, is essential to the rationality and justice of the criminal law, and is appropriately addressed in a penal code. Under this section, property may be destroyed to prevent the spread of a fire. A speed limit may be violated in pursuing a suspected criminal. An ambulance may pass a traffic light. Mountain climbers lost in a storm may take refuge in a house or may appropriate provisions. Cargo may be jettisoned or an embargo violated to preserve the vessel. An alien may violate a curfew in order to reach an air raid shelter. A druggist may dispense a drug without the requisite prescription to alleviate grave distress in an emergency.

1. My brother Grove has furnished me with the following suggestion, too late to be embodied in the judgment but well worth preserving: "If the two accused men were justified in killing Parker, then if not rescued in time, two of the three survivors would be justified in killing the third, and of the two who remained the stronger would be justified in killing the weaker, so that three men might be justifiably killed to give the fourth a chance of surviving."—C.

2. This sentence was afterwards commuted by the Crown to six months' imprisonment.

* Bacon's Maxims, No. 5. The case has actually occurred in the United States. See Commonwealth v. Holm[e]s, 1 Wall.Jr. 1 [, 26 F.Cas. 360 (C.C.E.D.Pa.1842)]. * * * In this case, shipwrecked sailors and passengers escaping in a boat which could not hold all, the sailors threw some of the passengers overboard. The Court held that the passengers ought to have been preferred to the sailors, unless the presence of all the sailors was required for the common safety, but, "under any circumstances, it was held the proper method of determining who was to be the first victim out of the particular class was by ballot." I doubt whether an English court would take this view. It would be odd to say that the two men on the raft were bound to toss up as to which should go.

A developed legal system must have better ways of dealing with such problems than to refer only to the letter of particular prohibitions, framed without reference to cases of this kind.

* * *

3. *Rejection of Limitations in Other Formulations.* The Model Code rejects any limitations on necessity cast in terms of particular evils to be avoided or particular evils to be justified * * *. * * * In contrast to that approach, this section reflects the view that the principle of necessity is one of general validity. It is widely accepted in the law of torts [11] and there is even greater need for its acceptance in the law of crime. While there may be situations, such as rape, where it is hardly possible to claim that greater evil was avoided than that sought to be prevented by the law defining the offense, this is a matter that is safely left to the determination and elaboration of the courts.

It would be particularly unfortunate to exclude homicidal conduct from the scope of the defense. For, recognizing that the sanctity of life has a supreme place in the hierarchy of values, it is nonetheless true that conduct that results in taking life may promote the very value sought to be protected by the law of homicide. Suppose, for example, that the actor makes a breach in a dike, knowing that this will inundate a farm, but taking the only course available to save a whole town. If he is charged with homicide of the inhabitants of the farm house, he can rightly point out that the object of the law of homicide is to save life, and that by his conduct he has effected a net saving of innocent lives. The life of every individual must be taken in such a case to be of equal value and the numerical preponderance in the lives saved compared to those sacrificed surely should establish legal justification for the act.[14] So too, a mountaineer, roped to a companion who has fallen over a precipice, who holds on as long as possible but eventually cuts the rope, must certainly be granted the defense that he accelerated one death slightly but avoided the only alternative, the certain death of both. Although the view is not universally held that it is ethically preferable to take one innocent life than to have many lives lost,[15] most persons probably think a net saving of lives is ethically warranted if the choice among lives to be saved is not unfair. Certainly the law should permit such a choice.

It might indeed be suggested that this section as applied to homicide is drawn too narrowly in its requirement that the evil sought to be avoided be a greater evil

11. See, e.g., Restatement (Second) of Torts §§ 197, 262 (1965).

14. See Wechsler & Michael, *A Rationale of the Law of Homicide: I,* 37 Colum.L.Rev. 701, 738–39 (1937).

15. Roman Catholic moralists have generally taken the position that one should not cause effects that are directly evil even if they are thought to be a necessary means to a greater good. See Ford, *The Morality of Obliteration Bombing,* in War and Morality 15, 26–28 (R. Wasserstrom ed. 1970); D. Callahan, Abortion: Law, Choice and Morality 422–24 (1970). Thus, it is considered wrong to terminate the life of a fetus even if that is the only way the mother can be saved and even if the fetus will die in any event. On the other hand, an ordinary operation designed directly to protect the mother's health is permissible, even if an inevitable effect is the death of the fetus, under the so-called principle of "double effect" that death is only permitted, not intended, and is not itself a means to saving the mother's life.

Many acts justifiable under this section would also be justifiable under the principle of "double effect." Diverting a flood to destroy a farmhouse instead of a town would be acceptable since the destruction of the farmhouse is not intended and is not a means of saving the town. Suppose, however, the citizens of a town receive a credible threat, say from a foreign invader, that everyone in the town will be killed unless the townspeople themselves kill their mayor, who is hiding. If the townspeople accede, they would have a substantial argument against criminal liability under this section but their act would be immoral under the double effect analysis, since they have intended to kill the mayor and it is his death that is the means to their safety.

than that sought to be prevented by the law defining the offense. For the result is that the defense would not be available to a defendant who killed *A* to save *B*, in circumstances where had he done nothing *B* would have been killed and *A* saved, assuming, of course, that there was not such aggression on either's part as to bring into play the justifications for using protective force. Nor would the defense be available to one who acted to save himself at the expense of another, as by seizing a raft when men are shipwrecked. But whatever may be thought of such cases as presenting a basis for excuse—and the problem must be faced at least in dealing with duress—they are not, in principle, cases of justification. In all ordinary circumstances lives in being must be assumed to be of equal value, equally deserving the protection of the law. If the values are equal, the case for a justification has not been made out.

Granting that it is unlikely that the law can influence the actor's choice in many situations of this kind, the only way to meet the case would be to acknowledge a justification when the evil sought to be avoided is *equal to* as well as greater than that sought to be prevented by the law defining the offense. Such a principle goes further than the common law and probably is unacceptable. In homicide the issue has at least a certain clarity, but in other cases a justification based on a choice of equal evils would draw the court unduly into value conflicts more appropriately settled by the legislature.

* * * This section does not demand that the event that triggers the choice among evils be a "natural physical force." A claim of justification is possible when an actor responds to human threats of harm. In many such situations a claim of duress can also be made, but it is proper to recognize that if *B* steals money in response to *A*'s credible threat to kill *C* immediately if *B* does not act, *B*'s conduct is not only excusable but justified.

This section does not require * * * that the evil that the actor seeks to avoid be imminent. Such a requirement unduly emphasizes one ingredient in the judgment that is called for at the expense of others just as important. It is true that genuine necessity rests on the unavailability of alternatives that would avoid both evils, and that typically when the evil is not imminent some such alternative will be available; but it is a mistake to erect imminence as an absolute requirement, since there may be situations in which an otherwise illegal act is necessary to avoid an evil that may occur in the future. If, for example, *A* and *B* have driven in *A*'s car to a remote mountain location for a month's stay and *B* learns that *A* plans to kill him near the end of the stay, *B* would be justified in escaping with *A*'s car although the threatened harm will not occur for three weeks.

3. *Further Reading.* For a hypothetical case exploring philosophical questions suggested by *Dudley,* see L. Fuller, The Case of the Speluncian Explorers, 62 Harv.L.Rev. 616 (1949). For a full study of the historical background of the principal case, see A.W. Brian Simpson, *Cannibalism and the Common Law* (U. of Chicago Press, 1984).

Questions

1. Develop arguments based on morality and legal policy for and against the *Dudley* result.

2. Is there a significant distinction to be drawn in the men-on-the-plank hypothetical according to whether the men reach the plank simultaneously or whether one is in possession before the other arrives? Would it matter that one of them, nervous about shipwreck, brought this plank along on the voyage as a life preserver, only to find that the other has reached the plank first?

3. Are the following significantly different from *Dudley:*

a. The Model Penal Code mountain climber hypothetical? (see Note 2, supra).

b. The Model Penal Code dike hypothetical?

c. The last lifeboat, which will hold no more than 75 passengers (in addition to the crew necessary for its safety), is about to leave a ship sinking in a storm. A hundred passengers remain. The ship's officer in charge of the boat chooses to put in the boat: (i) the 75 people nearest the boat; (ii) the women and children; (iii) the first class passengers; (iv) the strongest (or the weakest); or (v) a tour group of young winners of a "most likely to succeed" contest, leaving behind a group of criminals under death sentence.

State v. Warshow

Supreme Court of Vermont, 1979.
138 Vt. 22, 410 A.2d 1000.

Before BARNEY, C.J., and DALEY, LARROW, BILLINGS and HILL, JJ.

BARNEY, CHIEF JUSTICE.

The defendants were part of a group of demonstrators that travelled to Vernon, Vermont, to protest at the main gate of a nuclear power plant known as Vermont Yankee. The plant had been shut down for repairs and refueling, and these protestors had joined a rally designed to prevent workers from gaining access to the plant and placing it on-line.

They were requested to leave the private premises of the power plant by representatives of Vermont Yankee and officers of the law. The defendants were among those who refused, and they were arrested and charged with unlawful trespass.

The issue with which this appeal of their convictions is concerned relates to a doctrine referred to as the defense of necessity. At trial the defendants sought to present evidence relating to the hazards of nuclear power plant operation which, they argued, would establish that defense. After hearing the defendants' offer of proof the trial court excluded the proffered evidence and refused to grant compulsory process for the witnesses required to present the defense. The jury instruction requested on the issue of necessity was also refused, and properly preserved for appellate review.

* * *

In the various definitions and examples recited as incorporating the concept of necessity, certain fundamental requirements stand out:

(1) there must be a situation of emergency arising without fault on the part of the actor concerned;

(2) this emergency must be so imminent and compelling as to raise a reasonable expectation of harm, either directly to the actor or upon those he was protecting;

(3) this emergency must present no reasonable opportunity to avoid the injury without doing the criminal act; and

(4) the injury impending from the emergency must be of sufficient seriousness to outmeasure the criminal wrong.

See W. LaFave & A. Scott, Handbook on Criminal Law § 50 (1972).

It is the defendants' position that they made a sufficient offer of proof to establish the elements of the necessity defense to raise a jury question. The trial court rejected this contention on the ground, among others, that the offer did not sufficiently demonstrate the existence of an emergency or imminent danger.

This ruling was sound, considering the offer. The defendants wished to subpoena witnesses to testify to the dangers of nuclear accidents and the effect of low-level radiation. It was conceded that there had been no serious accident at Vermont Yankee, but defendants contended that the consequences could be so serious that the mere possibility should suffice. This is not the law.

There is no doubt that the defendants wished to call attention to the dangers of low-level radiation, nuclear waste, and nuclear accident. But low-level radiation and nuclear waste are not the types of imminent danger classified as an emergency sufficient to justify criminal activity. To be imminent, a danger must be, or must reasonably appear to be, threatening to occur immediately, near at hand, and impending. We do not understand the defendants to have taken the position in their offer of proof that the hazards of low-level radiation and nuclear waste build-up are immediate in nature. On the contrary, they cite long-range risks and dangers that do not presently threaten health and safety. Where the hazards are long term, the danger is not imminent, because the defendants have time to exercise options other than breaking the law. W. LaFave & A. Scott, supra, at 388.

Nor does the specter of nuclear accident as presented by these defendants fulfill the imminent and compelling harm element of the defense. The offer does not take the position that they acted to prevent an impending accident. Rather, they claimed that they acted to foreclose the "chance" or "possibility" of accident. This defense cannot lightly be allowed to justify acts taken to foreclose speculative and uncertain dangers. Its application must be limited to acts directed to the prevention of harm that is reasonably certain to occur. * * *

These acts may be a method of making public statements about nuclear power and its dangers, but they are not a legal basis for invoking the defense of necessity. Nor can the defendants' sincerity of purpose excuse the criminal nature of their acts.

Since the offered evidence was insufficient to support any possible defense of necessity, we need not reach any of the other issues raised by this appeal, including the effect of declared legislative policy.

Judgment affirmed.

HILL, JUSTICE, concurring.

* * *

At trial defendants sought to raise the affirmative defense of necessity, arguing that they were faced with a choice of evils—either violate the literal terms of the law or comply with the law and allow the commission of a more egregious wrong, i.e., the proliferation of nuclear power—and that they chose the course which would result in the least harm to the public, even though it meant violating the criminal law. The trial court refused to allow the defendants to present the defense, stating that it was not available "in Vermont at this time."

Necessity has long been recognized at common law as a justification for the commission of a crime. See, e.g., United States v. Ashton, 24 F.Cas. 873 (C.C.D.Mass.1834) (No. 14,470); The William Gray, 29 F.Cas. 1300 (C.C. D.N.Y.1810) (No. 17,694); Chesapeake & Ohio R.R. v. Commonwealth, 119 Ky. 519, 84 S.W. 566 (1905); State v. Jackson, 71 N.H. 552, 53 A. 1021 (1902). And, although the defense has not been explicitly recognized in Vermont in the context of a criminal prosecution, it has been accepted in the law of torts, Ploof v. Putnam, 81 Vt. 471, 71 A. 188 (1908). I see no reason why the defense should not be recognized in the criminal law context. "The principle involved is one of general validity; * * * and there is even greater need for its acceptance in the law of crime." Model Penal Code § 3.02, Comment 3 at 7 (Tent.Draft No. 8, 1958). Although this holding is implicit in the majority opinion, I would make it explicit.

The defense of necessity proceeds from the appreciation that, as a matter of public policy, there are circumstances where the value protected by the law is eclipsed by a superseding value, and that it would be inappropriate and unjust to apply the usual criminal rule. See generally W. LaFave & A. Scott, Handbook on Criminal Law § 50 (1972). The balancing of competing values cannot, of course, be committed to the private judgment of the actor, but must, in most cases, be determined at trial with due regard being given for the crime charged and the higher value sought to be achieved.

Determination of the issue of competing values and, therefore, the availability of the defense of necessity is precluded, however, when there has been a deliberate legislative choice as to the values at issue. See United States v. Kroncke, 459 F.2d 697, 701 (8th Cir.1972); State v. Dorsey, 118 N.H. 844, 846, 395 A.2d 855, 857 (1978); Model Penal Code, supra, § 3.02, Comment 1(b) at 6; W. LaFave & A. Scott, supra, at 382. * * *

Both the state of Vermont and the federal government have given their imprimatur to the development and normal operation of nuclear energy and have established mechanisms for the regulation of nuclear power. See, e.g., 18 V.S.A. §§ 1652–1658, 1700–1702; 3 V.S.A. §§ 3116a–3117; 10 V.S.A. §§ 6501–6504; 42 U.S.C. §§ 2011–2296, 5801–5891. Implicit within these statutory enactments is the policy choice that the benefits of nuclear energy outweigh its dangers.

If we were to allow defendants to present the necessity defense in this case we would, in effect, be allowing a jury to redetermine questions of policy already decided by the legislative branches of the federal and state governments. This is not how our system of government was meant to operate.

I express no opinion as to the relative merits or demerits of nuclear energy, nor do I question the sincerity of the defendants' beliefs. All that I would hold is that this Court is not the proper forum to grant defendants the relief they seek. Defendants still have the right to try to induce those forums that have made the policy choices at issue today to reconsider their decisions. But until that time I feel constrained to follow the law as it is, not as some would like it to be.

In my opinion the majority puts the cart before the horse. It measures the offer made against the requisite elements of the defense of necessity and concludes that the defendants failed to show a likelihood of imminent danger; yet it reserves judgment on the legislative policy exception to the defense. It is illogical to consider whether the necessary elements of a defense have been shown before determining whether the defense is even available in the particular situation.

The dissent, on the other hand, assumes that defendants' offer was sufficient to show not only imminent danger but also a failure of the regulatory scheme. I cannot agree with this assumption because the offer failed to show a danger not contemplated by the legislative scheme. The legislative framework was set up to deal with the very situation defendants offered to prove "might" happen. But because neither the state legislature nor Congress acted to shut down the power plant based on speculative possibilities does not, in my opinion, give rise to the questionable inference that there was an emergency which the regulatory scheme failed to avert. * * *

* * *

BILLINGS, JUSTICE, dissenting.

* * *

The defendants offered evidence on all the requisite elements of the defense of necessity. They stated as follows:

> [They had] a feeling that there was a situation of an emergency or imminent danger that would have occurred with the start up of the reactor on October 8th the time of [their] alleged crime * * * the chance * * * of the nuclear power plant having a serious accident which would cause * * * great untold damage to property and lives and health for many generations.

The defendants also stated that "there was reasonable belief that it would have been an emergency had they started that reactor up * * * there was a very good chance of an accident there for which there is no insurance coverage or very little." Specifically, the defendants offered to show by expert testimony that there were defects in the cooling system and other aspects of the power plant which they believed could and would result in a meltdown within seven seconds of failure on the start up of the plant. In addition, the defendants went to great lengths to base their defense on the imminent danger that would result from the hazardous radiation emitted from the plant and its wastes when the plant resumed operations.

While the offer made by the defendants was laced with statements about the dangers they saw in nuclear power generally, it is clear that they offered to show that the Vermont Yankee facility at which they were arrested was an imminent danger to the community on the day of the arrests; that, if it commenced operation, there was a danger of meltdown and severe radiation damage to persons and property. In support of this contention, the defendants stated that they would call experts familiar with the Vermont Yankee facility and the dangerous manner of its construction, as well as other experts who would testify on the effects of meltdown and radiation leakage, on the results of governmental testing, and on the regulation of the Vermont Yankee facility. These witnesses were highly qualified to testify about the dangers at the Vermont Yankee facility based either on personal knowledge or on conditions the defendants offered to show existed at the time of the trespass.

Furthermore, the defendants offered to show that, in light of the imminent danger of an accident, they had exhausted all alternative means of preventing the start up of the plant and the immediate catastrophe it would bring. Under the circumstances of imminent danger arising from the start up of the plant, coupled with the resistance of Vermont Yankee and government officials, which the defendants offered to prove, nothing short of preventing the workers access to start up the plant would have averted the accident that the defendants expected.

Through this offer, it cannot be said, without prejudgment, that the defendants failed to set forth specific and concrete evidence, which, if proven, would establish the existence of an imminent danger of serious proportions through no fault of the defendants which could not be averted without the trespass. Whether the defendants' expectations and opportunities were reasonable under the circumstances of this case is not for the trial court to decide without hearing the evidence. From a review of the record, I am of the opinion that the offer here measured up to the standard required and that the trial court struck too soon in excluding the offered evidence.

I would also dissent from the concurring opinion in so far as it attempts to hide behind inferences that the legislature precluded the courts from hearing the defense of necessity in the instant case on the authority of State v. Dorsey, 118 N.H. 844, 395 A.2d 855 (1978). Even assuming that such inferences can be drawn from the regulatory schemes cited, they have no bearing on this case. We were asked to infer under the facts, which the defendants offered to prove (that they were acting to avert an imminent nuclear disaster), that the legislative branch of government would not permit the courts of this state to entertain the defense of necessity because it had legislatively determined nuclear power to be safe. Were the defense raised without any offer to show an imminent danger of serious accident, it might fail both because defendants did not offer evidence on imminent danger and on the basis of legislative preclusion. But, where, as here, the defendants offer to prove an emergency which the regulatory scheme failed to avert, the inference of preclusion is unwarranted. The defendants are entitled to show that although there is a comprehensive regulatory scheme, it had failed to such an extent as to raise for them the choice between criminal trespass and the nuclear disaster which the regulatory scheme was created to prevent.

Moreover, statutory enactments in derogation of the common law are strictly construed. This Court has heretofore been of the opinion that with regard to the language of statutes, the "[r]ules of the common law are not to be changed by doubtful implication." State v. Levine, 117 Vt. 320, 322, 91 A.2d 678, 679 (1952). The concurring opinion fails to indicate any basis for its implication, and I can find none that meets this test. In fact, the statutes to which the concurring opinion directs our attention make it the duty of the Nuclear Advisory Panel "[t]o develop awareness in the state * * * of the potential liabilities * * * of a fixed nuclear facility in this state," 18 V.S.A. § 1701(a)(5), and generally secure to the people, as individuals and through their local and state representatives, the right to evaluate the dangers of depositing, storing, or reprocessing high-level radioactive waste materials, 10 V.S.A. §§ 6501–6504. Moreover, the legislature has seen fit to recognize the right of individuals to sue for damages resulting from ionizing radiation. 12 V.S.A. § 518. It cannot be said categorically that "[i]mplicit within these statutory enactments is the policy choice that the benefits of nuclear energy outweighs its dangers," as the concurring opinion states.

I am of the opinion that the defendants are entitled to present evidence on the defense of necessity as it exists at common law. To deny them this opportunity is to deny them a fair trial merely because they express unpopular political views. I would hold that they are entitled to present evidence on this defense even though they may well fail to establish a sufficient case to send the issue to the jury for deliberation, because I find the offer of proof sufficient for this purpose under the law of Vermont.

Notes

1. *Limitations.* Nelson v. State, 597 P.2d 977, 979–980 (Alaska 1979):

> * * * Nelson argues that he was entitled to wording which would explicitly allow the jury to find a necessity defense if a reasonable person at the time of acting would have believed that the necessary elements were present. Nelson is correct in stating that the necessity defense is available if a person acted in the reasonable belief that an emergency existed and there were no alternatives available even if that belief was mistaken.[5] Moreover, the person's actions should be weighed against the harm reasonably foreseeable at the time, rather than the harm that actually occurs.[6]

5. United States v. Ashton, 24 F.Cas. 873, 874 (No. 14,470) (C.C.D.Mass.1834); W. LaFave & A. Scott, supra § 50 at 384–88; Arnolds & Garland, supra at 294. See Townsend v. United States, 68 App.D.C. 223, 95 F.2d 352, 358 (1938); Hall v. State, 136 Fla. 644, 187 So. 392 (1939).

The Model Penal Code does not require that the actor's belief be reasonable. However, if he is "reckless or negligent * * * in appraising the necessity for his conduct," he has no defense to crimes in which recklessness or negligence suffice to establish culpability. ALI Model Penal Code § 3.02 (1962) and Commentary; W. LaFave & A. Scott, supra § 50 at 386 n. 32.

It appears that a few jurisdictions require a showing of an actual emergency. A reasonable belief that an emergency exists or that there are no lawful alternatives is not enough. See Tiffany & Anderson, *Legislating the Necessity Defense in Criminal Law,* 52 Den.L.J. 839, 855–56 (1975).

6. W. LaFave & A. Scott, supra § 50 at 386. But see State v. Marley, 509 P.2d 1095, 1109 (Hawaii 1973) (necessity defense available only where harm resulting from compliance with law would significantly exceed the harm *actually resulting* from the actor's violation of law).

As noted above, the defendant must also have acted in the belief that the reasonably foreseeable harm resulting from the violation would be less than the harm resulting from compliance with the law. However, here the defendant's belief is not by itself sufficient. An objective determination must be made as to whether the defendant's value judgment was correct, given the facts as he reasonably perceived them. W. LaFave & A. Scott, supra § 50 at 386–87; Tiffany & Anderson, supra note 5, at 871. The majority of jurisdictions appear to hold that this determination must be made, at least initially, by the court. Tiffany & Anderson, supra note 5, at 871–72.

Assuming that the instruction given was not worded adequately to convey these concepts to the jury, we would find the error harmless, for Nelson failed to make out a case for the necessity defense. The "emergency" situation claimed by Nelson to justify his appropriation of the construction equipment was the alleged danger that his truck, stuck in the mud, might tip over, perhaps damaging the truck top. However by the time Nelson decided to use the equipment the truck had already been stuck for several hours. The dire nature of the emergency may be judged by the fact that some twelve hours later, having unsuccessfully attempted to remove the vehicle from the mud, one of Nelson's companions fell asleep in the truck, which had still not tipped over.

Nor can it be said that Nelson had no lawful alternatives in his situation. The record shows that during the time Nelson was trying to free the vehicle people stopped on several different occasions and offered their services in the form of physical assistance, rides, or offers to telephone state troopers or a tow truck.

Finally, it cannot be said that the harm sought to be avoided in this case—potential damage to Nelson's truck—was greater than the harm caused by Nelson's illegal actions. Even disregarding the actual damage to the equipment caused by Nelson's use,[a] the seriousness of the offenses committed by Nelson were disproportionate to the situation he faced. The legislature has made this clear by making reckless destruction of personal property a crime punishable by imprisonment for up to one year and a $5,000 fine, and joyriding punishable by imprisonment for up to one year and a $1,000 fine. The equipment taken by Nelson was marked with no trespassing signs. Nelson's fears about damage to his truck roof were no justification for his appropriation of sophisticated and expensive equipment.

2. *Possession of Marijuana.* State v. Diana, 24 Wn.App. 908, 914–916, 604 P.2d 1312, 1316–1317 (1979):

Although the defense of necessity has been variously applied, only one trial court decision has been called to our attention where the defense was recognized to a charge of possession of marijuana. That case is United States v. Randall, 104 Daily Wash.L.Rptr. 2249 (D.C.Super.Ct. Nov. 24, 1976). There, a defendant grew marijuana plants and used them to treat his own glaucoma. Expert testimony revealed that conventional glaucoma medications were ineffective and that defendant's experimental use of marijuana normalized inner-ocular pressure and lessened visual distortions caused by the disease. In determining whether the evil to be avoided by the defendant's act was greater than that inherent in the possession and personal use of marijuana, the court balanced the defendant's interest in preserving his sight against the government's interest in controlling the drug. The court concluded that Mr. Randall's right to preserve his sight outweighed the government's interest in outlawing the drug. Special emphasis was placed upon the importance of an individual's right to preserve and protect his own health and body. Roe v. Wade, 410 U.S. 113, 93 S.Ct. 705, 727, 35 L.Ed. 2d 147 (1973); Doe v. Bolton, 410 U.S. 179, 93 S.Ct. 739, 35 L.Ed.2d 201 (1973) (abortion cases). See also Rutherford v. United States, 399 F.Supp. 1208 (W.D.Okl.1975), in which a federal district court decided that a cancer patient's right to treatment outweighed the government's interest in banning laetrile.

The wisdom of the *Randall* decision was recognized by the legislature in our State when it enacted the Controlled Substances Therapeutic Research Act, Laws of Washington 1979, Reg.Sess. ch. 136, effective March 27, 1979. That

a. Damage to the borrowed equipment exceeded $10,000, partly because, unknown to Nelson, a front-end loader taken was being repaired and had no transmission lubricant.

legislation recognizes marijuana as a medicinal drug and makes it available under controlled circumstances to alleviate the effects of glaucoma and cancer chemotherapy. The patient must be certified to the State Board of Pharmacy by a licensed physician. In addition, under the Act other disease groups may be included if pertinent medical data is presented to the Board.

We believe that the defendant here should be given the opportunity to demonstrate the alleged beneficial effect, if any, of marijuana on the symptoms of multiple sclerosis. Accordingly, we remand his case to the trial court, here the trier of fact, for determination of whether medical necessity exists.

In making that determination, the court should refer to the authorities cited in this opinion. To summarize, medical necessity exists in this case if the court finds that (1) the defendant reasonably believed his use of marijuana was necessary to minimize the effects of multiple sclerosis; (2) the benefits derived from its use are greater than the harm sought to be prevented by the controlled substances law; and (3) no drug is as effective in minimizing the effects of the disease. To support the defendant's assertions that he reasonably believed his actions were necessary to protect his health, corroborating medical testimony is required. In reaching its decision, the court must balance the defendant's interest in preserving his health against the State's interest in regulating the drug involved. Defendant bears the burden of proving the existence of necessity, an affirmative defense, by a preponderance of the evidence. * * *

3. *Preventing Abortion.* People v. Stiso, 93 Ill.App.3d 101, 101–104, 48 Ill. Dec. 687, 688–690, 416 N.E.2d 1209, 1210–1212 (1981):

On May 20, 1978 defendants, Nicholas Stiso and Monica Migliorino, were arrested inside the Albany Clinic in Chicago after they sought to bar access to rooms where abortions were performed. Both defendants were charged with having breached the peace in violation of * * * the State disorderly conduct statute. * * *

On appeal the defendants contend that the trial court erred in granting the State's motion *in limine* to bar defendants from raising the defense of necessity.

* * *

* * * Defendants contend that they were entitled to raise this defense by presenting evidence that they acted to prevent the death of fetuses. This identical contention was recently rejected by this court in People v. Krizka (1980), 92 Ill. App.3d 288, 416 N.E.2d 36, 48 Ill.Dec. 141. There the defendants entered a medical center and blocked access to operating rooms where abortions were to be performed. It was stipulated at trial that those defendants believed their conduct was necessary to prevent the greater injury which would result from the abortions, the death of fetuses. However the defendants were not permitted to introduce additional evidence to support this contention. On appeal this court upheld the exclusion of this evidence, finding that the necessity defense was inapplicable because the alleged injury sought to be avoided, the abortions, was not a legally recognized injury. This determination was based on the fact that the United States Supreme Court has upheld the right of women to obtain first trimester abortions without interference from the State (Roe v. Wade (1973), 410 U.S. 113, 93 S.Ct. 705, 35 L.Ed.2d 147), and without interference from spouses or parents to whom the State had sought to give an absolute veto over such a decision. Planned Parenthood of Central Missouri v. Danforth (1976), 428 U.S. 52, 96 S.Ct. 2831, 49 L.Ed.2d 788.

* * *

Defendants cite City of Chicago v. Mayer (1974), 56 Ill.2d 366, 308 N.E.2d 601, as an example of the necessity defense being applied to interference with a legal activity. In *Mayer* a medical student had sought to prevent an injured man from being moved by the police because he suspected the man had a spinal injury which would be worsened by the move. The trial judge did not allow the jury to be instructed on the defense of necessity and defendant was convicted of disorderly conduct and interference with a police officer in the performance of his duty. On appeal our Supreme Court reversed, holding that defendant was entitled to an instruction on that defense. But the crucial distinction between that case and the case at bar is that the injury sought to be avoided in *Mayer,* aggravation of a spinal injury, was not protected by law. Here the very thing which defendants allegedly sought to prevent through their actions, abortion of fetuses, has been given the legal protection we have described.

4. For some recent applications of the necessity doctrine—going beyond what the title specifies—see Note: And Forgive Them Their Trespasses: Applying the Defense of Necessity to the Criminal Conduct of the Newsgatherer, 103 Harv.L.Rev. 890, 893–899 (1990).

Question

What limitations are properly imposed upon a necessity defense?

3. Excuse

a. *DURESS*

State v. Tremulo

Supreme Court of Ohypo, 1990.
316 Ohypo 19.

Trilby Tremulo was charged with murder, and, in the alternative, manslaughter, for the death of six year old Victoria Nastie on October 12, 1988; with kidnapping in the third degree of Victoria; and with perjury on account of lying to the grand jury investigating Victoria's death. Our offense of kidnapping in the third degree is defined by the legislature as follows:

> Whoever, being a parent, or being an aider or abettor of a parent, of a child under the age of fourteen years, intentionally seizes, inveigles, or secretes such a child, contrary to the known custodial rights of the other parent or of a legal guardian of such a child, shall be guilty of the misdemeanor of kidnapping in the third degree and punishable by imprisonment for not more than three years, or a fine of not more than $5,000, or both.

Murder, manslaughter, and perjury are common law offenses.

There is little dispute as to the facts. Ten years ago, Victoria's father-to-be, Nelson Nastie, came to the town of Centerville, to take a job as a junior officer at the Centerville Bank. He is a hard-driving and shrewd businessman, and he rapidly advanced at the bank. He soon came to the attention of Medea Moore, the daughter of the bank's chairman of the board.

In Medea, he found a woman with an even stronger and more forceful character than his own. She brooked no interference with her plans and had a well-deserved reputation for toughness and violence. At the age of sixteen, she had horsewhipped a groom in her father's stable after she had fallen from a horse. At twenty she was about to be tried for arson of a newspaper reporter's house—he had published a story about her escapades; the prosecution was dropped for want of evidence when he disappeared on the eve of the trial. Her parents' influence and wealth was often used to save her from the consequences of her acts. It is fair to say that most people in Centerville were afraid of her.

Nelson and Medea fell in love, and, after a tempestuous courtship, married. Victoria was born a year later. By that time, her parents were already quarreling violently. The family skirmishes turned into a full-scale war, and spectacular divorce proceedings were soon under way. Nelson was ultimately granted a divorce and custody of Victoria. Medea Moore Nastie, who was not used to losing, began a campaign to get Victoria back. She charged that Nelson was sexually molesting the child, a charge that the courts ultimately rejected after a ferocious court battle.

One evening, a week after the decision that Nelson should retain custody, the doorbell rang at the home of defendant Tremulo, Victoria's piano teacher. The accused was a frail woman of seventy, who had lived alone with her beloved fox terrier Fido since the death of her invalid mother a year before. She was of a timid and retiring nature, with few friends. Her visitor was Medea, with Victoria held in an arm lock. Like most of the townspeople, Trilby Tremulo was aware that the courts had granted Nelson custody, knew all about Medea, and was afraid of her anger.

Medea said, "I'm sorry about this, but you're going to have to keep Vickie for a day. I snatched her after school, and she was scheduled to be flown out of here on a private plane, but the wimpy pilot says the weather is too bad, and she can't leave until tomorrow afternoon. Her pervert of a father will never think of looking for her here. Keep her quiet and out of sight until I come for her tomorrow. Just to make sure you stay in line, I'm taking the mutt with me. If Nelson finds Vickie, I'll send Fido to my taxidermist, and you'll get him back stuffed. In that case, I'm not sure about your own future prospects for good health, either." She then grabbed Fido and left.

Defendant testified at her trial that she was terrified of what Medea would do if Victoria was found. She cancelled her piano lessons for the following day, and kept the child over night. A violent storm passed through town during the evening, ending telephone service for the next twenty-four hours. In the morning the child was restless, kept looking out the windows, and wanted to go out to play. The accused said she tried everything she could think of to keep her out of sight and quiet, and finally gave her a tranquilizer pill from a bottle of Dratitol she had in her medicine cabinet. Victoria had an immediate violent allergic reaction to the pill and died within a few minutes of taking it.

The accused rushed to Medea's house and told her what had happened. Medea returned Fido, took defendant's house key, and told her to walk Fido in the park for an hour and then return home, by which time the body would be gone. She added, "You must never tell what you know. If you do, I will kill you. I've always found it easy to get somebody to kill for a few hundred dollars if I don't feel like strangling you myself."

Defendant followed instructions and went home to find the body gone. She did nothing. A few days later, Victoria's buried body was discovered, and the police, having heard from a neighbor that the child had been seen at Tremulo's window the day after her disappearance from school, questioned her. She denied that Victoria had been there, and repeated her claim under oath before a grand jury when called as a witness in the investigation of her death. Further investigation led the police to suspect Medea. A warrant for her arrest was obtained, and when the police sought to execute it, Medea was killed in a gun battle, resisting arrest.

Thereafter, Tremulo voluntarily came to the police and told the full story of the events, claiming that she had been afraid to speak while Medea was alive. She gave the same account at the trial, claiming a defense of duress as to all of the charges. The trial judge declined to give a duress instruction, and the jury brought in verdicts of guilty of manslaughter, kidnapping in the third degree, and perjury, with a strong recommendation of mercy. The trial judge departed from our sentencing guidelines and gave consecutive sentences of two months imprisonment on each charge, with a total fine of $1,000. The defendant appeals.

BLYNKEN, J.: The judgment of conviction of manslaughter is affirmed. The judgments of conviction of kidnapping in the third degree and perjury are reversed, and a new trial is awarded as to these charges.

Let us first consider the murder and manslaughter charges, upon which the jury brought in a manslaughter verdict. Duress has always been a wide-ranging defense. It may bar conviction of robbery, burglary, arson, kidnapping, theft, and a host of lesser offenses. From the beginning, however, duress has been excluded as a defense to intentional homicide, no matter how strong the compulsion exercised. One is not entitled to take the life of an innocent victim to save one's own. It is true that there is no clear rule that duress may not be a defense to a homicide charge based on felony-murder. However, this is because one committing what would otherwise be a robbery under duress is not in fact guilty of the robbery, and there is no felony upon which to hang the felony-murder charge. Treason, which may be a more serious offense even than murder, does allow the defense: treason is a continuing offense, and the person threatened is likely to be able to get away and prevent or repair the damage done. Death is final.

While there is no defense to the homicide charge, I see no reason why the jury might not accept the claim of duress as to the kidnapping charge in the circumstances disclosed here. The CHIEF JUSTICE doubts that Medea made a death threat until after the homicide. I agree that the threat was vague, but it seems to me that Tremulo and the jury could have believed that the accused's life was threatened if she did not keep Victoria quiet and out of sight.

Even if there was no death threat at the time of the kidnapping, I would allow the jury to consider the defense. I do not believe that a threat of death or great bodily harm is always necessary for duress. If the crime is very minor, I think that most people would be induced to commit it by a threat of something less than great bodily harm. "Steal that newspaper, or I will instantly run over your parked Rolls Royce with my steamroller," would induce most of us to take the newspaper. One does not have a choice of evils defense in such a case, as the CHIEF JUSTICE claims, if the necessity defense is limited to cases of an impersonal threat, as in the famous *Dudley and Stephens* case. This is a point which this court has never decided.

At the time of the perjury offense, there was a clear death threat, but the CHIEF JUSTICE complains that it was not imminent, and that Tremulo had plenty to time to seek the protection of the law. This may well have been the case, and the jury would have been free to reject the claim on this ground. However, I believe that the jury might have found that the accused was excusably afraid that the power and venom of Medea Moore Nastie were such that she could and would effect her death through an agent, even from a jail cell. It should have been left free to do so.

I would affirm only the manslaughter conviction and order a new trial on the other charges.

WYNKEN, C.J. (dissenting as to the disposition of the kidnapping and perjury charges): I believe that the judgments of conviction on all charges should be affirmed. Even if we believe all that the accused claims, no defense of duress is shown. This is no doubt a case in which one can have sympathy with the accused. I have no difficulty with the jury's recommendation of mercy or the judge's sentence, but Trilby Tremulo committed the crimes with which she was charged, and she is not entitled to be excused for her actions.

The defense of duress is the criminal law's concession to human moral frailty. Some have doubted that it should be given any status as an excuse. Stephen thought that the deterrent threat of the law was most needed "at the moment when temptation is strongest." J. Stephen, 2 History of the Criminal Law of England 107 (1883). However, it is generally accepted that the defense of duress applies to those who, in certain circumstances, under orders or threats from another, commit criminal acts because they fear that imminent death or serious bodily harm will be inflicted upon them if they do not do so. The moral suasion in duress is comparable to the involuntary act situation in which the physical power of another moves the hand which holds the lethal weapon, and there is no *actus reus* committed by the helpless person whose hand was used. We deal here, of course, with influence and intimidation, in which the accused commits the act, but may be excused.

It is essential to a defense of duress that there be a threat of great bodily harm or death to the accused or someone else. Threats of lesser harm will not suffice, no matter what the crime. The criminal law makes no concessions to those who are merely trying to preserve property or some other interest by agreeing to participate in a crime. Here, the primary threat was to kill a dog. The rest, as far as the homicide and kidnapping charges are concerned, amounted to no more than vague words, too slight to be regarded as a serious death threat.

Further, duress requires an order to commit a crime; nobody ordered the accused to give Victoria the Dratitol. Duress also requires an imminent threat, with no apparent reasonable alternative to committing the act demanded. The accused could have called in the police, and if she had, it is extremely unlikely that Medea could have or would have thought it in her best interest to carry out any threat. There was simply no threat of sufficient magnitude to excuse the action.

As to the perjury charge, there was an additional death threat to take into account, but the threat was utterly lacking in imminence. Any reasonable person would have found an opportunity to seek protection from the authorities before or at the time of the grand jury testimony.

A point made by my sister BLYNKEN requires response. She argues that threats of great bodily harm or death are not necessary to a duress defense if the crime the accused is urged to commit is very trivial, and that a reasonable person might well do the act demanded. In such a case the accused has a straightforward choice of evils justification for her acts and need not rely on the excuse of duress. Duress is needed for cases in which, out of fear, an equal or greater good is sacrificed, thus eliminating a choice of evils claim. Society can excuse such a sacrifice only under a threat of death or great bodily harm.

My sister BLYNKEN at times seems to regard the excuse as dependent on the subjective feelings of the accused, whether reasonable or not. Such an approach encourages cowardice and is too dangerous to the interests of society to be acceptable.

My brother NOD recommends what seems to be an objective test: whether a person of reasonable firmness in Tremulo's situation would have been unable to resist. However, it is not clear how objective the test in fact is. Is the jury to be told to imagine a reasonably firm "average person" in her situation, or a reasonably firm, lonely, dog-loving, woman of seventy? Incidentally, the Model Penal Code, from which this test is derived, requires a threat of bodily harm or death for duress. If it is something less than this, the defendant is allowed a defense only on a choice of evils theory, a theory upon which no instruction was requested.

In my view, the convictions were proper; there was no duress.

NOD, J. (dissenting as to the disposition of the manslaughter charge): The other members of this court find a roadblock to a duress defense in the homicide charge, but they can not agree upon its nature. One of my colleagues thinks that duress is never applicable without a threat of death or great bodily harm; the other believes that duress can never be an excuse for homicide. I contend that the defense is more flexible, and that the jury might properly have accepted it even in a homicide case, and certainly in a homicide case where there is no intention of the accused to kill.

Many—but by no means all—authorities have denied duress as a defense to intentional murder, but Tremulo had no intention to kill. She at most had intention to inflict technical bodily harm when she gave Victoria the tranquilizer. She meant only to immobilize the child. True, she had no right to do so. She knew that no authority could properly come from Medea, who had been denied custody, to do such a thing. The jury no doubt found that she intended only minor bodily harm, and hence found manslaughter rather than murder.

A policy which bars duress as a defense for intentional killings is intelligible, but there is no sound reason for extending the bar to homicide cases in which death is not intended. To tell one who is threatened with harm unless he kills that he will have no defense because the law says that he must withstand the threat may well deter some killings, but such reasoning simply does not apply to situations in which the person threatened was never commanded to kill at all, and in which she does not expect her acts to result in death.

The defense of duress is a concession to human weakness. We excuse the act because we do not think the person coerced ought to be treated as a criminal. If one only commits a crime because she is threatened with harm if she does not commit it, she may lack courage we wish she had, but she is no ordinary criminal. If left alone, she would be no danger to others. The danger is the person doing the threatening.

There is no reason why, if this argument is sound for, say, larceny, it should not also be sound for murder, even intentional killing. Suppose A awakens, locked in a concrete blockhouse. The only other occupant is B, tied to a bed. A sees the barrel of a machine gun pointing at her through a chink in the wall, and hears the voice of C, saying, "I am determined that either you or B shall die, and I don't care which. Either you strangle him at once, or I will kill you instantly." A's choice is to kill or to die. Perhaps *morality* requires that she die herself, but are we to make her a *criminal* when the choice is this stark—and when most people would kill to save their own skins?

We need an objective element in the test for duress; we can not allow unusual cowardice to provide a duress defense, when most people would have been able to resist the threat. But, the criminal law can ask no more of a person than that she respond to a situation reasonably, within the bounds of expectable human reaction. As the Model Penal Code puts it, the proper question is whether a person of reasonable firmness in Tremulo's position would be unable to resist the threat. This question should have been left to the jury in connection with the homicide charge.

The determination in a close case is for the jury, and the reasonable person, endowed with the physical characteristics of the accused, is the jury's guide in decision. A frail and isolated woman of seventy might reasonably have feared that Medea, whom she knew to be dangerous, would kill her if she allowed Victoria to be discovered. While Medea did not give specific orders to administer the tranquillizer, it was well within the scope of her more general order to keep Victoria from being noticed. Giving children tranquilizers may entail special risks, but there is nothing in the evidence to indicate that the Dratitol would have injured the health of an ordinary allergy-free child of Victoria's age.

The argument for accepting duress applies with greater force to the kidnapping and perjury charges. There were jury issues as to all charges, and there should be a new trial as to all of the crimes.

Notes

1. *Perjury.* Hourie v. State, 53 Md.App. 62, 64–66, 452 A.2d 440, 441–442 (1982):

> Common law perjury was and is the giving of a false oath in a judicial proceeding in regard to a material matter. R. Perkins, *Criminal Law* 454 (2d ed. 1969). Its dim beginnings are to be found in the ecclesiastical courts. Its essential nature was the violation of an oath sworn before God.[1] * * * The birth of the modern concept of perjury by a witness can be traced to the statute of 11 Hen. VII, c. 21 in 1495. 4 W. Holdsworth, *A History of English Law* 517–518 (1924). For the next century and a half, the high misdemeanor[2] of perjury was developed almost exclusively in the prerogative court of the Star Chamber. T. Plucknett, *A Concise History of the Common Law* 459 (5th ed. 1956). It sought to guard society's interest in the integrity of sworn statements in judicial proceedings. It was limited to the false testimony given under oath about a material matter and before a judicial tribunal.
>
> When, as an integral part of the larger Seventeenth Century struggle of Cromwell versus King, of Parliamentarian versus Royalist, and of Puritan dissent versus Established Church, the common law triumphed over and virtually obliterated its rival legal system of the prerogative courts,[3] the Court of Star Chamber was abolished in 1640. Much of the productive output of the Star Chamber, however, especially the development of the major misdemeanors, was recognized as worthy of preservation and was taken over by the common law courts. The misdemeanor of perjury was one of those legacies from the now-dead Civilian tradition. * * *
>
> It was over a century after the reception of perjury into the common law, that English judges began to recognize related problems with respect to the integrity of sworn statements that came to be required in many matters other than judicial proceedings. The common law responded to this newly perceived need by providing a penalty for wilful and corrupt false swearing in such nonjudicial settings. The name "perjury" was not employed for the new crime. It was generally known as "false swearing." R. Perkins, *Criminal Law* 454–455 (2d ed. 1969). * * *

1. The early punishment was frequently the loss of the right hand by which the false oath had been sworn. For the development of perjury generally, see 3 Sir James Fitzjames Stephen, A History of the Criminal Law of England 240–250 (1883); 2 F. Pollack and F. Maitland, The History of English Law 542 (2d ed. 1898). * * *

2. That swashbuckling phrase immediately flags an offense as a creation of the Star Chamber. Throughout the course of the 16th century, most of the development of the criminal law occurred in that prerogative court. Such innovations as the crimes of perjury, forgery, conspiracy, and attempt were made by that innovative court. Its contributions should not be forgotten, notwithstanding its badly maligned reputation during its final decades, largely at the unkind hands of Lord Coke.

The phrase "high misdemeanor" connoted a new crime that was just as grave, in terms of its social consequences and in terms of its potential punishment, as the more ancient felonies themselves. The new crimes had to be officially labeled as misdemeanors, albeit high ones, because the jurisdiction to try felonies lay exclusively in the common law courts.

3. Those courts were descended from the ecclesiastical courts and, hence, from Roman, continental law. They utilized therefore, the rules and procedures of the Civilians, which were far different from common law methods.

2. *The Model Penal Code View of Duress.* Model Penal Code, § 2.09, Comments 2 and 3: *

2. *Proper Scope of Defense.* * * *

* * *

The problem of Section 2.09, then, reduces to the question of whether there are cases where the actor cannot justify his conduct under Section 3.02, as when his choice involves an equal or greater evil than that threatened, but where he nonetheless should be excused because he was subjected to coercion. If he is so far overwhelmed by force that his behavior is involuntary, as when his arm is physically moved by someone else, Section 2.01(1) stands as a barrier to liability, following in this respect the long tradition of the penal law. The case of concern here is that in which the actor makes a choice, but claims in his defense that he was so intimidated that he was unable to choose otherwise. Should such psychological incapacity be given the same exculpative force as the physical incapacity that may afford a defense under Section 2.01? Given the other provisions of the Model Code, this is the concrete issue to be faced in judging whether and how far duress ought to be recognized as a distinct defense.

In favor of allowing the defense, it may be argued that the legal sanction cannot be effective in the case supposed and that the actor may not properly be blamed for doing what he had to choose to do. It seems clear, however, that the argument in its full force must be rejected. The crucial reason is the same as that which elsewhere leads to an unwillingness to vary legal norms with the individual's capacity to meet the standards they prescribe, absent a disability that is both gross and verifiable, such as the mental disease or defect that may establish irresponsibility. The most that it is feasible to do with lesser disabilities is to accord them proper weight in sentencing. To make liability depend upon the fortitude of any given actor would be no less impractical or otherwise impolitic than to permit it to depend upon such other variables as intelligence or clarity of judgment, suggestibility or moral insight.

Moreover, the legal standard may gain in its effectiveness by being unconditional in this respect. It cannot be known what choices might be different if the actor thought he had a chance of exculpation on the ground of his peculiar disabilities instead of knowing that he does not. No less important, legal norms and sanctions operate not only at the moment of climactic choice, but also in the fashioning of values and of character.

Though, for the foregoing reasons, the submission that the actor lacked the fortitude to make the moral choice should not be entertained as a defense, a different situation is presented if the claimed excuse is based upon the incapacity of men in general to resist the coercive pressures to which the individual succumbed. Here the essential principle is that which Henry Hart has put as follows: "Obligations of conduct fixed by a fair appraisal of the minimum requirements for the maintenance and fostering of community life will, by hypothesis, be obligations which normal members of the community will be *able* to comply with, given the necessary awareness of the circumstances of fact calling for compliance."[35] This is to say that law is ineffective in the deepest sense, indeed that it is hypocritical, if it imposes on the actor who has the misfortune to confront a dilemmatic choice, a standard that his judges are not prepared to affirm that they should and could comply with if their turn to face the

35. *The Aims of the Criminal Law,* 23 Law & Contemp.Prob. 401, 414 (1958).

problem should arise. Condemnation in such a case is bound to be an ineffective threat; what is, however, more significant is that it is divorced from any moral base and is unjust. Where it would be both "personally and socially debilitating" to accept the actor's cowardice as a defense, it would be equally debilitating to demand that heroism be the standard of legality. The proper treatment of the hero is not merely to withhold a social censure; it is to give him praise and just reward.

3. *Approach of Model Penal Code.* The Model Code accordingly provides for the defense in cases where the actor was coerced by force or threats of force "that a person of reasonable firmness in his situation would have been unable to resist." The standard is not, however, wholly external in its reference; account is taken of the actor's "situation," a term that should here be given the same scope it is accorded in appraising recklessness and negligence. Stark, tangible factors that differentiate the actor from another, like his size, strength, age, or health, would be considered in making the exculpatory judgment. Matters of temperament would not.

Given the nature of the problem and the criteria proposed for its solution, it is reasonable to confine the exculpation to the case where force against the person of the actor or another, or the threat thereof, is the instrument of coercion. Perils to property alone may sometimes justify upon a proper choice of evils and they are not excluded by the terms of Section 3.02. But when the claimed excuse is that duress was irresistible, threats to property or even reputation cannot exercise sufficient power over persons of "reasonable firmness" to warrant consideration in these terms.

Beyond this limitation to coercive force or threats against the person, no valid reason was perceived for demanding that the threat be one of death or even of great bodily harm, that the imperiled victim be the actor rather than another, or that the injury portended be immediate in point of time. It is sufficient that factors such as these be given evidential weight, along with other circumstances in the application of the statutory standard that a person of "reasonable firmness" would have succumbed to the pressure. They must be weighed, of course, together with other factors, since persons of reasonable firmness surely break at different points depending on the stakes that are involved. It is obvious that even homicide may sometimes be the product of coercion that is truly irresistible, that danger to a loved one may have greater impact on a person of reasonable firmness than a danger to himself, and, finally, that long and wasting pressure may break down resistance more effectively than a threat of immediate destruction. This section is framed on these assumptions.

* * *

Although Section 2.09 rejects a number of conventional limitations on the scope of the defense, Subsection (2) does accept the view that there should be no exculpation if the actor recklessly placed himself in a situation in which it was probable that he would be subjected to duress. Though this provision may have the effect of sanctioning conviction of a crime of purpose when the actor's culpability was limited to recklessness, the substitution is permissible in view of the exceptional nature of the defense. The provision will have its main room for operation in the case of persons who connect themselves with criminal activities, in which case it would be very difficult to assess claims of duress. On the other hand, where there is no more than negligence on the actor's part in placing himself in a situation where duress was probable, the normal pattern of the Model Code is followed. The defense is excluded only on a charge as to which negligence suffices to establish culpability. The difference between inadvertence and the conscious risk creation involved in recklessness appears to justify discriminating in this way.

* * *

3. *Duress as Mitigating in Homicide.* Wentworth v. State, 29 Md.App. 110, 120–121, 349 A.2d 421, 427–428 (1975):

> * * * As we recognized in Shuck v. State, 29 Md.App. 33, 349 A.2d 378 (1975), in dealing with mitigation by way of "imperfect" self-defense:
>
> > "Although by far the most common form of mitigation is that of a hot-blooded response to legally adequate provocation, this is not the only form of mitigation that will negate malice and will reduce what might otherwise be murder to manslaughter."
>
> It was of this very possibility that we spoke in Evans v. State, [28 Md.App. 640, 349 A.2d 300 (1975),] Part IC, at n. 4:
>
> > "This analysis presupposes that the type of mitigation fairly in issue is of the common and orthodox 'hot blood in response to legally adequate provocation' variety. The foreclosing effect of a first-degree murder conviction would not, however, apply in those very rare cases where manslaughter is predicated upon the far more esoteric extenuating circumstances, 'not yet far advanced,' of 'an "imperfect" right of self-defense or defense of others, or of crime-prevention, or of the defenses of coercion or necessity, in which the killing, though not justifiable, is not bad enough to be murder.' LaFave and Scott, *Criminal Law* (1972), § 77, 'Other-Extenuating-Circumstances Voluntary Manslaughter,' pp. 583–586. This qualification, it should be noted, is little more than an academic possibility." (For yet a second time, the qualification is more than academic.)
>
> We find highly persuasive the rationale of LaFave and Scott, op.cit., at 585:
>
> > "One who is coerced by another person, or forced by the pressure of natural physical circumstances (e.g., thirst, starvation) into committing what is otherwise a crime, may have in some circumstances a complete defense to the crime, but not if the crime in question consists of intentionally killing another human being. Thus one who, not in self-defense or defense of another, kills an innocent third person to save himself or to save another is guilty of a crime. But it is arguable that his crime should be manslaughter rather than murder, on the theory that the pressure upon him, although not enough to justify his act, should serve at least to mitigate it to something less than murder. Two of the latest state criminal codes so provide."
>
> * * *
>
> Recognizing that an "imperfect" defense of duress may not exculpate a defendant in an unlawful homicide case but may supply that mitigation necessary to lower the degree of guilt from murder to manslaughter, we conclude that the appellant here had a genuine jury issue as to mitigation. * * *

Questions

1. Is there anything to be said for a duress rule which excuses the defendant who acted unreasonably, but was really overwhelmed by terror?

2. Suppose that in the *Dudley* case, supra, p. 478, the lifeboat had been dangerously overloaded and Dudley, the only armed person aboard, had forced Stephens at gunpoint to throw the other occupants, Brooks and Parker, overboard to their deaths. Would the Model Penal Code provide a defense to Stephens? Suppose Stephens had thrown Brooks and Parker overboard to preserve the last of the

provisions for Dudley and himself. Would Stephens then have a Model Penal Code defense? If there is a difference in result, can it be justified?

b. JUSTIFICATION OR EXCUSE?; BORDERLINE PROBLEMS

Introductory Note

We have treated the material prior to duress as falling under the head of justification; if the actor reasonably believes the act is done necessarily to protect life, prevent crime, etc., and it is not disproportionate to the objective sought, we do not call the actor wrong. Although we regret the loss symbolized by the criminalization of the conduct (absent justification), we are willing to pay the price. Such cases as those in which some courts have reduced murder to manslaughter when the defendant was a little unreasonable in his reaction are really excuse cases. We don't think the defendant was justified in shooting, but we give a partial excuse because he did not depart very far from the norm and we find it unjust to exact the full consequences in the circumstances.

Apart from this problem of slight unreasonableness, it is sometimes difficult to decide whether particular conduct fits better into a justification or excuse mold, either because we are not quite sure whether we approve or only condone, or because the definitional elements of neither of a related justification and excuse—typically necessity and duress—fit the conduct exactly. Necessity suggests a reaction to avoid the consequences of an impersonal peril, such as a shipwreck. Duress normally involves the threat of another to injure or kill the accused unless what would normally be a crime is committed. The material that follows addresses this issue.

The *Lopez* case additionally raises the question of what practical difference it makes whether we classify a defense as a justification or excuse. Since the early days of the common law, it has made no practical difference as to guilt in most situations (except that partial excuses only mitigate crimes). However, in *Lopez,* we see that it can make an important difference.

United States v. Lopez

United States District Court, Northern District of California, 1987.
662 F.Supp. 1083, affirmed 885 F.2d 1428 (9th Cir.1989), cert. denied ___ U.S. ___, 110 S.Ct. 748, 107 L.Ed.2d 765 (1990).

LYNCH, DISTRICT JUDGE.

This case involves the alleged escape of two federal prisoners. Defendant Ronald McIntosh disappeared on October 28, 1986, during an unescorted transfer from F.C.I. Pleasanton to the federal prison at Lompoc. He landed a helicopter in the Pleasanton recreation yard on November 5, 1986, and flew off with defendant Samantha Lopez. Federal authorities apprehended them ten days later in a Sacramento shopping mall where they were buying a set of wedding rings.

Defendant Lopez was charged with escape from federal custody, a violation of 18 U.S.C. section 751(a). McIntosh was indicted for air piracy, 49 U.S.C. § 1472(i), use of a weapon to commit a crime, 18 U.S.C. § 924(c), and aiding and abetting Lopez' escape, 18 U.S.C. § 752. Escape charges against him are pending in a separate case.

Defendants contend that they are both entitled to raise the defense of necessity/duress to their charges. To establish a necessity/duress defense in an escape from confinement prosecution, a defendant must establish the existence of the following requirements: 1) that the threat and fear which the threat caused were immediate and involved death or serious bodily injury; 2) that the fear was well grounded, i.e., the escapee had a good faith belief in the imminence and severity of the threats and the belief was objectively reasonable; 3) that there was no reasonable opportunity to avoid or escape the threatened harm; and 4) that the defendant submitted to proper authorities after attaining a position of safety. United States v. Bailey, 444 U.S. 394, 410–13, 100 S.Ct. 624, 634–36, 62 L.Ed.2d 575 (1980); United States v. Williams, 791 F.2d 1383, 1388 (9th Cir.1986); United States v. Peltier, 693 F.2d 96, 98 (9th Cir.1982).

The government has filed a motion *in limine* for an order precluding defendants from presenting such evidence to the jury. * * * The parties agree that if Lopez makes a prima facie showing of each element of the necessity/duress defense, she will be entitled to an instruction on that defense.

The following issues are in dispute and are presently before the Court: 1) McIntosh's liability for aiding and abetting Lopez' escape if she is found not guilty by reason of necessity/duress; 2) the availability of necessity/duress as a separate defense to all of McIntosh's charges; and 3) the sufficiency of defendants' pretrial offers of proof.

I. *Aider and Abettor's Liability if the Principal is Acquitted by Reason of Necessity/Duress*

McIntosh requests the following jury instruction: "If you find defendant Samantha Lopez not guilty of escape because she acted under necessity/duress, then you must also find defendant McIntosh not guilty of aiding and abetting her alleged escape." The government contends that McIntosh can be convicted of aiding and abetting Lopez' escape even if Lopez succeeds on her necessity/duress defense.

The culpability of aiding and assisting escape under 18 U.S.C. section 752 is governed by the same principles as those of the general aiding and abetting statute, 18 U.S.C. § 2. The general rule is that a defendant can be convicted of aiding and abetting even if the principal is not identified or convicted; however, an aider and abettor may not be held liable absent proof that a criminal offense was committed by a principal. * * *

This Court must therefore determine whether Lopez committed a criminal offense if her necessity/duress defense succeeds. This determination requires an examination of the theoretical distinctions between two categories of defenses: justification and excuse. Lopez' alleged defense of necessity/duress must then be classified as either a justification or an excuse.

Justification defenses are those providing that, although the act was committed, it is not wrongful. For example, a forest fire is burning toward a town of 10,000 residents. An actor burns a field of corn located between the fire and the town in order to set up a firebreak. By setting fire to the field with the intent to destroy it, the actor satisfies all the elements of the crime of arson; however, he most likely will have a complete defense because his conduct is justified. Burning the field avoided a greater societal harm; therefore, the act is not a crime. See P. Robinson, *Criminal Law Defenses* § 24 (1984); Comment, *Necessity Defined: A New Role in the Criminal Defense System,* 29 UCLA L.Rev. 409, 413 (1981).

When a defense is categorized as an excuse, however, the result is that, although the act is wrongful, the actor will not be held accountable. "Where the actor is not blameworthy, for reasons of either incapacity or extreme pressure, there is not criminal liability." Comment, supra at 414. Thus, an insane person who robs a bank will be excused from liability.

Simply stated, when a defendant prevails on a justification defense, no wrongful act occurred; the act itself becomes lawful. If a defendant succeeds on a defense classified as an excuse, a wrongful act occurred; however, no criminal liability is attached to the actor.

The classification of a defense as a justification or an excuse has an important effect on the liability of one who aids and abets the act. A third party has the right to assist an actor in a justified act. Therefore, a third party could not be held liable for aiding and abetting the arson described in the hypothetical above. In contrast, a sane getaway driver could be convicted of aiding and abetting an insane person's bank robbery. Excuses are always personal to the actor. See G. Fletcher, *Rethinking Criminal Law* § 10.1 (1978); P. Robinson, *supra* § 37(a); Williams, *The Theory of Excuses,* Crim. L.Rev., Nov. 1982, at 414–15.

The defense of duress or coercion traditionally arises when a person unlawfully commands another to do an unlawful act using the threat of death or serious bodily injury. "The pertinent question is whether circumstances overwhelmed the actor's will so that the inability to make the 'correct' choice is excused." Comment, supra at 430. The defense of duress/coercion is generally classified as an excuse. P. Robinson, supra, § 25; Comment, supra, at 431.

The defense of necessity may be raised in a situation in which the pressure of natural physical forces compels an actor to choose between two evils. The actor may choose to violate the literal terms of the law in order to avoid a greater harm. The defense of necessity is categorized as a justification. United States v. Richardson, 588 F.2d 1235, 1239 (9th Cir.1978), cert. denied, 440 U.S. 947, 99 S.Ct. 1426, 59 L.Ed.2d 636 (1979); W. LaFave and A. Scott, *Criminal Law* § 50 (1972); Comment, supra, at 431.

In the context of prison escapes, the distinction between duress/coercion and necessity has been hopelessly blurred. In fact, courts seem to use the two terms interchangeably. See United States v. Bailey, 444 U.S. 394, 410, 100 S.Ct. 624, 634, 62 L.Ed.2d 575 (1980); United States v. Bailey, 585 F.2d 1087, 1096–98 (D.C.Cir.1978), rev'd on other grounds, 444 U.S. 394, 100 S.Ct. 624, 62 L.Ed.2d 575 (1980). The defense of duress/coercion does not precisely apply because no one has commanded the prisoner to escape. Additionally, "a prisoner who escapes because of intolerable conditions usually does not act in the panicked, overborne state associated with duress.

* * * [P]risoners threatened with physical or sexual attack generally flee not in a blind, unthinking reaction, but because escape appears preferable to risking assault." Dolinko, *Intolerable Conditions as a Defense to Prison Escapes,* 26 UCLA L.Rev. 1126, 1167–68 (1979).

The defense of necessity technically does not arise in the prison escape situation because the threat in a necessity situation traditionally emanates from physical, not human, forces. Commentators have argued that this natural forces restriction serves no useful purpose and should be abandoned. See Gardner, *The Defense of Necessity and the Right to Escape From Prison—A Step Towards Incarceration Free From Sexual Assault,* 49 S.Cal.L. Rev. 110, 132 (1975); Dolinko, *supra,* at 1170–71.

This Court believes, however, that the defense asserted by Lopez, under the facts of this case, most nearly resembles necessity, which is a justification to the alleged crime. See Dolinko, supra, at 1167–82 (concluding that "the necessity paradigm more closely approximates the prison-escape situation"). In the present case, Lopez' claim is not that the alleged threats overwhelmed her will so that her inability to make the "correct" choice should be excused. Instead, Lopez claims that she, in fact, did make the correct choice. She contends she violated the law to avoid the greater societal harm of being killed or seriously injured. The government agrees with this Court's conclusion that Lopez' defense is properly characterized as one of necessity.

Accordingly, if the jury finds Lopez not guilty of escape by reason of her necessity defense, her criminal act will be justified. A justified action is not wrongful; therefore, the prerequisite to imposing liability on McIntosh as an aider and abettor will not be satisfied. No criminal offense will have been committed by a principal. McIntosh is therefore entitled to his requested jury instruction.

II. *Defendant McIntosh's Personal Necessity Defense*

In addition to defendant McIntosh's aforementioned "derivative" necessity defense to his aiding and abetting charge, which depends entirely on whether defendant Lopez' necessity defense prevails, McIntosh also claims that he is entitled to raise his own, independent necessity defense. Essentially, McIntosh argues for a jury instruction stating that should the jury find him criminally liable for any or all of the three charges, aiding and abetting an escape, air piracy, or use of a weapon to commit a crime, he nevertheless should be acquitted because he was justified in his assistance of Lopez' escape from imminent death or serious bodily injury.

The Ninth Circuit recognizes that the defense of necessity is "available when a person is faced with a choice of two evils and then must decide whether to commit a crime or an alternative act that constitutes a greater evil." United States v. Dorrell, 758 F.2d 427, 430 (9th Cir.1985) (quoting United States v. Contento–Pachon, 723 F.2d 691, 695 (9th Cir.1984)). The defense requires a showing that the defendant "act[ed] to prevent 'an imminent harm which no available options could similarly prevent.'" *Dorrell,* 758 F.2d at 431 (quoting United States v. Nolan, 700 F.2d 479, 484 (9th Cir.1983). It is also clear that the necessity defense applies to a defendant who commits a crime in an effort to rescue or protect an unrelated third person or persons.[1] United States v. Mowat, 582 F.2d 1194, 1208 (9th Cir. 1978).

The Court has not found, nor have the parties cited, any case law setting forth the elements of a necessity defense specifically to charges of criminal acts undertaken in the aiding and abetting of a prison escape. The core elements of any necessity defense, however, are essentially those that make up the first three required showings in the necessity defense to a prison escape charge as enumerated above. Therefore, as to all three charges, McIntosh must show the following: 1) that the threats against Lopez were immediate and involved death or serious bodily injury; 2) that his fear for her safety was well grounded, i.e., he had a good faith belief in the imminence and severity of the threats against her and his belief was objectively reasonable; and 3) that there was no reasonable, legal alternative to violating the law. As to the aiding and abetting an escape charge, McIntosh, like Lopez in her necessity defense as the alleged principal in the escape, must also show that the escapee submitted to proper authorities after attaining a position of safety.[2]

III. *Offers of Proof Required of Both Defendants and the Sufficiency of These Offers*

* * *

As to defendant Lopez, the Court hereby finds that her proffered offer of proof is sufficient as a matter of law to entitle her to a jury instruction on the defense. This holding, however, is conditional upon a showing at trial that corresponds with her pretrial offer of proof on each element. If the evidence at trial on any one of the elements of Lopez' necessity defense is insufficient to sustain it even if believed, the Court will entertain a motion by the government to exclude any evidence supporting other elements of the defense.

As to defendant McIntosh, the Court analyzed whether his offer of proof was sufficient as a matter of law to entitle him to three separate necessity instructions on each of the three charges against him. The Court hereby holds that his offer of proof is sufficient for an instruction on the aiding and

1. The general rule under a duress/coercion defense, as opposed to the necessity defense at issue here, appears to be that the third person at whom the threats are directed must be a family member. *Contento–Pachon,* 723 F.2d at 694. But see United States v. Gordon, 526 F.2d 406, 408 n. 1 (9th Cir.1975) (suggesting that in exceptional circumstances there might be a possibility of a defense of duress to others not related to the accused). Despite some confusion in the briefs, at oral argument both sides seemed to agree that the issue is whether McIntosh is entitled to a necessity defense.

2. In his brief, McIntosh argued that this last element, submitting to proper authorities, does not apply to his necessity defense because the element has only been required of principals charged with escape. Given the fact that the underlying crime of escape is a continuing offense, *Bailey,* 444 U.S. at 413, 100 S.Ct. at 636, and that under the facts of this case the alleged aider and abettor was with the alleged escapee throughout her absence from confinement, we hold that he too must meet this last element in order to sustain a necessity defense to the aiding and abetting charge. At oral argument, McIntosh's counsel expressed an apparent change of position from that in his brief, agreeing with this Court's then tentative holding.

abetting an escape charge, subject to the same condition of a proper showing at trial applicable to Lopez.[4]

The Court finds, however, that McIntosh's offer is insufficient as a matter of law as to the air piracy and use of a gun to commit a crime charges. In response to these charges, McIntosh makes no showing, as he must, that there was no reasonable, legal alternative to violating both or either of these two laws.[5] *Bailey,* 444 U.S. at 410, 100 S.Ct. at 634; *Dorrell,* 758 F.2d at 431. Because his offer is insufficient on this third required element, he is not entitled to argue necessity as a defense to these charges. *Bailey,* 444 U.S. at 416, 100 S.Ct. at 638.[6]

IT IS SO ORDERED.

Notes

1. After the judgment of the District Court in *Lopez* was handed down, the Ninth Circuit held, contrary to the position it had taken earlier, as reported in footnote 2 of Judge Lynch's opinion, that *aiding* escape, unlike escape itself, is not a continuing offense. United States v. Vowiell, 869 F.2d 1264 (9th Cir.1989). "McIntosh's initial assistance to Lopez' escape does not continue as long as Lopez continues to escape, but rather only so long as he continues to assist her in escaping. * * * A more appropriate instruction would have informed the jury that the necessity defense was unavailable to McIntosh if, after Lopez reached a position of safety and failed to make bona fide efforts to surrender, he continued to aid her." United States v. Lopez, 885 F.2d 1428, 1435 (9th Cir.1989). A majority of the panel found this error harmless, given the facts.

4. Of course, given the Court's holding in the first part of this order, the jury will only reach the question of whether McIntosh was justified in aiding and abetting Lopez' alleged escape if the jury first finds that Lopez was not justified in her escape. As explained above, if the jury finds Lopez not guilty of escape by reason of her necessity defense, the government as a matter of law cannot prove an aiding and abetting charge against McIntosh.

5. We do not intend to suggest that committing either or both crimes of air piracy and using a weapon to commit a crime could never be justified in light of the imminence and severity of a real threat to life or limb. The courts have long recognized, however, that one is not justified in committing a crime under such circumstances unless, given the imminence of the threat, there was no reasonable, legal alternative. See *Bailey,* 444 U.S. at 410–11, 100 S.Ct. at 634–35. Under this third element of the necessity defense, McIntosh has made at least the minimal showing as to why there was no reasonable, legal alternative to aiding and abetting Lopez' escape. The offer of proof is silent, however, on any showing that there was no reasonable, legal alternative to air piracy and the use of a weapon to commit a crime.

6. This case was tried after this order was issued. At the close of defendants' evidence, the Court ruled that, because he introduced evidence that was not contained in his offer of proof on the issue of the existence of a reasonable, legal alternative, defendant McIntosh was also entitled to the necessity defense for the charges of air piracy and use of a weapon to commit a crime. Specifically, McIntosh demonstrated that he did not have a valid pilot's license at the time of the incident. Therefore, he could not have rented a helicopter himself. Additionally, McIntosh introduced evidence showing that security around the perimeter of the prison had been increased at the time of the incident so that it would have been impossible for McIntosh simply to cut the fence to allow Lopez to escape. The Court requested the government to suggest a reasonable, legal alternative to air piracy or committing a crime with a weapon; however, the government was unable to do so. Accordingly, the jury was instructed that the necessity defense was applicable to all charges against both defendants. The jury found the defendants guilty of all charges.

2. The criminal responsibility of those who help or encourage others to commit crimes is further considered in the section on Accomplices in Chapter VI.

Note on Defenses to an Escape Charge

State v. Miller, 313 N.W.2d 460, 462 (S.D.1981):

> Defendant Miller appeals from a jury verdict finding him guilty of escape from the South Dakota State Penitentiary. * * *
>
> * * *
>
> At trial defendant presented evidence that he had been transferred from the main prison facility to the west farm in March of 1979. In June, 1979 he was transported to the cottage facility for a medical examination and was stabbed with a knife by another inmate while waiting in the lobby. Defendant was hospitalized and returned to the west farm. He subsequently received death threats from this inmate who was housed in the main prison population. On November 13, 1979, defendant was informed by the prison personnel that he was being transferred from the west farm into the main prison facility. This transfer was made necessary because the defendant became involved in an altercation on the farm and lost his trusty status.
>
> Defendant testified that shortly after he was informed of his impending transfer, his mind snapped and he believed he was in Vietnam. He thought his fellow inmates were Vietnamese and he attempted to hide from them in a Buddha shrine. He can not recall his actions between the time his mind snapped and when he awoke four days later in a jail cell in Dodgeville, Wisconsin. On cross-examination defendant stated that he escaped because he thought he was in Vietnam and was hiding from his enemies.*
>
> * * *
>
> The jurisdictions are in conflict regarding the question of when a justification defense is properly submissible to the trier of fact. The first approach as followed in People v. Lovercamp, 43 Cal.App.3d 823, 831–832, 118 Cal.Rptr. 110, 115 (1974) (footnote omitted) limits the availability of the defense of justification to the following circumstances:
>
> > (1) The prisoner is faced with a specific threat of death, forcible sexual attack or substantial bodily injury in the immediate future;
> >
> > (2) There is no time for a complaint to the authorities or there exists a history of futile complaints which make any result from such complaints illusory;
> >
> > (3) There is no time or opportunity to resort to the courts;
> >
> > (4) There is no evidence of force or violence used towards prison personnel or other "innocent" persons in the escape; and
> >
> > (5) The prisoner immediately reports to the proper authorities when he has attained a position of safety from the immediate threat.
>
> See also Craddock v. State, 47 Md.App. 513, 424 A.2d 168 (1981); Com. v. Clark, 287 Pa.Super. 13, 429 A.2d 695 (1981).

* Defendant alleges on appeal, however, that his fear of being harmed upon return to the main prison population justified his escape.

The United States Supreme Court in construing the federal escape statute, 18 U.S.C. § 751(a), adopted a similar rigid approach recognizing that a defendant must proffer evidence of a bona fide effort to surrender or return to custody as soon as the coercive force of the claimed duress or necessity ended. United States v. Bailey, 444 U.S. 394, 100 S.Ct. 624, 62 L.Ed.2d 575 (1980).

In State v. Baker, 598 S.W.2d 540 (Mo.App.1980), the Missouri Court of Appeals rejected the rigid approach taken by the California Court in *Lovercamp* and the United States Supreme Court in *Bailey,* and held that the defense of necessity was properly raised "when the offered evidence, if believed by the jury, would support a finding by them that the offense of escape was justified by a reasonable fear of death or bodily harm so imminent or emergent that, according to ordinary standards of intelligence and morality, the desirability of avoiding the injury outweighs the desirability of avoiding the public injury arising from the offense committed to avoid injury to the prisoner." Id. at 546. The *Baker* court determined that the *Lovercamp* preconditions were only circumstances to be considered by the trier of fact regarding the weight and credibility of the defendant's testimony. See also People v. Unger, 66 Ill.2d 333, 5 Ill.Dec. 848, 362 N.E.2d 319 (1977); Com. v. Thurber, [383] Mass. [328], 418 N.E.2d 1253 (1981).

The defense of justification in South Dakota as expressed in SDCL 22–5–1 is similar to the Baker approach, for it examines the circumstances surrounding the crime based on a reasonable person standard. The statute does not limit the defense to only those situations where the five *Lovercamp* elements have been shown. We believe the *Baker* approach follows the requirements of our statute and therefore, we are inclined to follow this approach. We hold that defendant's evidence was sufficient, if believed, to properly raise the justification defense.

Questions

1. If not all of the *Lovercamp* requirements (set out in *Miller*) are essential for a successful defense to an escape charge, which are properly "only circumstances to be considered"?

2. Strict requirements like those in *Lovercamp* may be imposed in part to enable courts to dispose of most escape cases promptly and in the State's favor, on the assumption that the great majority of such cases present a frivolous defense. If the assumption is correct, are the strict requirements defensible? How much may be sacrificed to the efficient administration of justice?

United States v. Gant

United States Court of Appeals, Fifth Circuit, 1982.
691 F.2d 1159.

INGRAHAM, CIRCUIT JUDGE:

Edgar Cherry Gant was charged in the United States District Court for the Southern District of Texas with violating 18 U.S.C. app. § 1202(a)(1), which prohibits convicted felons from possessing firearms. Gant waived a jury trial and the case proceeded primarily upon an agreed stipulation of facts. Gant stipulated to a prior felony conviction and the interstate commerce jurisdictional requirement but asserted the justification defenses of duress and necessity. After considering the evidence and supplemental briefs addressing these defenses, the district court entered a general verdict of guilty and made specific findings "[t]hat at the time of the possession charged, the defendant Gant had reason to believe that he was in danger of his life or serious bodily harm or loss of property; that he did not institute that situation himself." On appeal Gant contends that the common-law defenses of duress and necessity are available against a charge of violating 18 U.S.C. app. § 1202(a)(1) and that the evidence adduced in support of these defenses entitles him to acquittal. While our recent decision in United States v. Panter, 688 F.2d 268 (5th Cir.1982), recognizes the general availability of common-law defenses to such a charge, we disagree that the evidence in the record entitles Gant to an acquittal and therefore affirm the conviction.

* * *

* * * [T]he remaining issue is whether the record contains sufficient evidence to support the conviction, Hall v. United States, 286 F.2d 676 (5th Cir.1960), cert. denied, 366 U.S. 910, 81 S.Ct. 1087, 6 L.Ed.2d 236 (1961), or whether the evidence establishes the defense of duress or necessity.[3] * * *

At 8:30 p.m. on Thursday, November 12, 1981, Officers Lewis and Byrd of the Harris County Sheriff's Department entered the business offices of Texas Transportation Company, which is owned and operated by Gant. When the officers entered the premises, they were acting in an undercover capacity and were dressed in blue jeans, sport shirts, windbreakers, and tennis shoes. The officers offered to sell Gant a .45 caliber machine gun. After he refused to purchase the gun, Gant summoned Andrews, an employee, from the storage area. Andrews inspected the gun and renewed the refusal to purchase. When the officers continued their sales efforts, Andrews and Gant excused themselves and retreated to the storage area to confer. Having been subjected to a robbery attempt a few weeks earlier, they speculated that another was in the making and decided to prevent the attempt by running the two men off the premises. Andrews felt capable of enforcing this effort since he was carrying a pistol, but Gant was unarmed. Although confident of his

3. Commentators disagree on which defense—duress or necessity—is appropriate to assert in this situation. One view would classify this as duress because the coercion had its source in the actions of other human beings, rather than in physical forces beyond the actor's control. See Bailey, 444 U.S. at 409–10, 100 S.Ct. at 634. Another approach notes that the typical duress case involves the situation in which A has ordered B to engage in criminal conduct or else suffer the threatened consequences. Necessity would be the proper classification because the threat is not direct and explicit. B would engage in a crime, not because he was ordered to do so, but because it was the lesser of two evils. See W. LaFave & A. Scott, *Criminal Law* §§ 49 n. 30, 50 n. 2, at 377, 381–82 (1972). The Model Penal Code sets forth still another approach. Under the Code, the duress defense does not preclude a choice-of-evils, or necessity, defense. Consequently, if defendant can show that "a person of reasonable firmness in his situation would have been unable to resist" engaging in the criminal conduct because of the threat of unlawful force against his person, the defense of duress is available. Model Penal Code § 2.09 (1974). If defendant can also show that the harm of the criminal conduct is less than the harm of the threat, the additional choice-of-evils (necessity) defense is available. Id. § 3.02. Thus, under the appropriate circumstances, both defenses could be asserted. Gant, however, has failed to satisfy the minimum requisites of either defense. Therefore, we analyze this case in terms of those common elements and use the general classification of justification defense.

ability to evict the men, Andrews desired a back-up and suggested that Gant retrieve a pistol from the second drawer of a filing cabinet in Gant's office. Unfortunately, Gant complied with his employee's request. Upon reentering the drivers' room with the pistol butt protruding from his pants pocket, the officers identified themselves, pulled out their revolvers, and placed everyone under arrest.

Gant contends that these facts entitle him to acquittal based upon duress or necessity. He stresses the district court's specific findings as supporting his claim. These findings alone, however, are insufficient to establish either affirmative defense. To interpose a justification defense to a charge of violating 18 U.S.C. app. § 1202(a)(1), defendant must show (1) that defendant was under an unlawful and "present, imminent, and impending [threat] of such a nature as to induce a well-grounded apprehension of death or serious bodily injury," United States v. Bailey, 585 F.2d 1087, 1110 (D.C.Cir. 1978) (Wilkey, J., dissenting), rev'd, 444 U.S. 394, 100 S.Ct. 624, 62 L.Ed.2d 575 (1980); see Model Penal Code § 3.02(1)(a) (1974);[5] (2) that defendant had not "recklessly or negligently placed himself in a situation in which it was probable that he would be [forced to choose the criminal conduct]," United States v. Agard, 605 F.2d 665, 667 (2d Cir.1979); see Model Penal Code §§ 2.09(2), 3.02(2) (1974); (3) that defendant had no "reasonable, legal alternative to violating the law, 'a chance both to refuse to do the criminal act and also to avoid the threatened harm,' " United States v. Bailey, 444 U.S. 394, 410, 100 S.Ct. 624, 634, 62 L.Ed.2d 575 (1980); and (4) "that a direct causal relationship may be reasonably anticipated between the [criminal] action taken and the avoidance of the [threatened] harm." United States v. Cassidy, 616 F.2d 101, 102 (2d Cir.1979); United States v. Simpson, 460 F.2d 515, 518 (9th Cir.1972); see Model Penal Code § 3.02(1), (2) (1974) (requiring an objective appraisal of whether criminal conduct was necessary to avoid the threatened harm).[6] Although the district court made specific findings addressing the imminent threat[7] and innocent victim[8] requisites,

5. To justify criminal conduct under the theory of choice of evil (necessity), the Code requires that "the harm or evil sought to be avoided by such conduct [must be] greater than that sought to be prevented by the law defining the offense charged." Model Penal Code § 3.02(1)(a) (1974). The legislative history provides some aid in determining what harm or evil Congress sought to avoid with the enactment of 18 U.S.C. app. § 1202. See generally Stevens v. United States, 440 F.2d 144 (6th Cir.1971) (appending the entire legislative history on the section as extracted from the Congressional Record). This section was Senator Long's amendment to the Omnibus Crime Control and Safe Streets Act of 1968, Pub.L. No. 90–351, 82 Stat. 197 (codified as amended in scattered sections of 5, 18, 18 app., 28, 42 & 47 U.S.C.) which was passed in the wake of the assassinations of Senator Robert Kennedy and Dr. Martin Luther King, Jr., and was partially motivated by President Kennedy's assassination. It was intended to prevent killings by removing firearms from persons that Congress determined would be most likely to misuse them. As Congressman Pollock explained, "[t]he overall thrust is to prohibit possession of firearms by criminals or other persons who have specific records or characteristics which raise serious doubt as to their probable use of firearms in a lawful manner." Id. at 166 (quoting 114 Cong.Rec. 61,298 (1968)). To tip the balance of harms in favor of justifying the criminal conduct, the harm sought to be avoided must be death or serious bodily injury. Any lesser justifying harm circumvents the prevention of this greater harm.

6. Some commentators argue that an explicit causal relationship is necessary for the assertion of the defense of duress. See note 3, supra.

7. The district court found that "Gant had reason to believe that he was in danger of his life or serious bodily harm or loss of property."

8. See note 8 on page 515.

there are no specific findings concerning lack of alternatives or direct causal relationship.[9] * * *

As the Supreme Court emphasized in *Bailey,* "one principle of these justification defenses remains constant: if there was a reasonable, legal alternative to violating the law, * * * the defense will fail." Bailey, 444 U.S. at 410, 100 S.Ct. at 634. In demonstrating that he had no reasonable alternative to violating § 1202, Gant must show that he had actually tried the alternative or had no time to try it, or that a history of futile attempts revealed the illusionary benefit of the alternative. The most obvious legal remedy that Gant failed to pursue was simply to call the police. Since the officers had remained in the drivers' room, Gant had a chance to call the police during the time that he was meeting with Andrews in the storage room or was retrieving the pistol from his office. Gant testified on cross examination that he did not call the police because they had been slow to respond to a call made during a previous robbery attempt. A single contact, however, does not establish a history of futile attempts that indicate an illusionary benefit. * * *

To assert either defense, Gant must also show that a direct causal relationship could be reasonably anticipated between the proscribed action and the avoidance of the threatened harm. This element is often encompassed in the lack of alternatives determination. E.g., United States v. Mauchlin, 670 F.2d 746, 748 (7th Cir.1981) ("[threatened harm] can be avoided only by commission of the crime charged"). Nevertheless, a distinct analysis is appropriate because justification defenses are based on the premise that society benefits when the lesser harm associated with the commission of the criminal activity prevents the greater harm associated with the threat. See Bailey, 585 F.2d at 1109 (Wilkey, J., dissenting); LaFave & Scott, supra note 3, §§ 49–50, at 374, 381. If the criminal act cannot abate the threatened harm, society receives no benefit from the criminal conduct because it suffers the harm from both the crime and the threatened activity.

Since the threat of loss of property without more never justifies the use of deadly force, e.g., McNabb v. United States, 123 F.2d 848, 854 (5th Cir.1941), reversed on other grounds, 318 U.S. 332, 63 S.Ct. 608, 87 L.Ed. 819 (1943), we assume that the district court would not have allowed either defense without an accompanying finding that Gant was in danger of death or serious bodily harm. See R. Perkins, *Perkins on Criminal Law* 1026 (2d ed. 1969). See also note 5, supra.

8. The district court found that Gant "did not institute that situation himself." Since the district court made limited specific findings, it could have analyzed Gant's mode of business operation as an alternative rather than under this element. Although Gant knew that the business was located in a high crime neighborhood, he chose to keep substantial amounts of cash on hand to cash his drivers' pay checks. Experience did not prove to be a good teacher for Gant because even after a robbery attempt, Gant chose to maintain his check cashing policy and chose not to extend the protection from his security guard to cover the few extra evening hours on Thursday nights when he maintained this cash. While the district court could have determined that changing his business procedures was a reasonable and legal alternative to the possession of a firearm, it could have found that Gant's choice of operating procedures placed him in a situation in which he would probably be forced to resort to the criminal possession of a firearm. We need not resolve which determination was more appropriate because Gant failed to demonstrate the other elements necessary for either defense.

9. These four requisites are merely elements common to both duress and necessity and do not define the precise contours of either. For example, continued possession beyond the time that the emergency exists will defeat the defenses. E.g., Panter, 688 F.2d at 272.

The verdict implies a finding that the causal relationship between the possession of a firearm and the abatement of the threat of death or serious bodily injury could not be reasonably anticipated. Although defendant's possession and probable use of a gun makes a robbery attempt less attractive, it does not eliminate defendant's danger. The present situation should be distinguished from the hypothetical discussed in *Panter,* in which the convicted felon disarms his assailant and holds him at bay. Panter, 688 F.2d at 271. In the hypothetical, the defendant drastically diminishes the danger to his life when he seizes the gun from his assailant. In the present setting, however, Gant's interjection of a firearm escalated the danger for everyone rather than extinguished the threat to him. When Gant reconfronted the officers, his obvious possession of the pistol precipitated the drawing of service revolvers. Fortunately, the officers' expertise prevented any shooting and no one was injured. Gant's handgun possession, however, did not provide the benefit society demands to justify such criminal behavior. Whether a causal relationship could be reasonably anticipated is an objective factual determination and we do not find the district court's implied finding clearly erroneous.

We emphasize that since the justification defenses are affirmative defenses, defendant must demonstrate each element before he may successfully raise the defense of duress or necessity. We agree with the district court that no justification defense was present in this case because defendant failed to show that he had no reasonable, legal alternatives and that the possession of the firearm could be reasonably anticipated to abate the threat of death or serious bodily injury created by the presumed robbery attempt. The conviction by the district court is therefore

Affirmed.

Note

State v. Crawford, 308 Md. 683, 695–696, 521 A.2d 1193, 1199 (1987):

> It is clear that the 1972 handgun control legislation is designed to discourage and punish the possession of handguns on the streets and public ways. The legislature determined that if a citizen is apprehensive of impending danger, his recourse is not to immediately arm himself, but instead to seek help from the State—by applying for a permit to carry a gun or, of course, by contacting the police for protection. * * *
>
> As we see it, the 1972 handgun control legislation does not address the unexpected and sudden circumstance when an individual is threatened with present, impending danger to his life or limb and as a consequence has no time to seek other protection. Furthermore, we cannot accept the contention that, in such circumstances, the General Assembly intended that the individual should succumb to his attacker and possibly forfeit his life rather than take possession of a handgun and act in self-defense. We find it entirely reasonable and consistent with * * * legislative purpose to conclude that when an individual finds himself in sudden, imminent danger of loss of life or serious bodily harm, or reasonably believes himself or others to be in such danger, and without preconceived design on his part a handgun comes into his possession,[a] he may temporarily possess the

a. Here, the accused claimed to have picked up a weapon dropped by his attacker.

weapon for a period no longer than the necessity or apparent necessity requires him to use it in self-defense. We therefore hold that necessity may be a defense to the charge of unlawful possession of a handgun.

* * *

c. INSANITY

i. Issues Other Than Criminal Responsibility

The primary issue of insanity in the criminal law is one of criminal responsibility for one's acts: should the accused be excused because mental disease or defect rendered him not fairly accountable for his conduct at the time of its commission? Before turning to this central question it is useful to contrast some other "insanity" issues. Does the accused have sufficient mental capacity to stand trial? If not, what procedures should be followed? If capacity to stand trial now exists, but the trier of fact finds that insanity rendered the accused not responsible at the time of the act, what should be done? If the accused is found not responsible, under what circumstances is confinement proper, and how do we decide upon release? Is continuing punishment appropriate for one who develops "insanity" after conviction?

We will briefly look at such problems before turning to the question of responsibility and excuse.

Note on Fitness to Stand Trial

Fitness to stand trial differs from criminal responsibility both as to time and as to the relevant issue. The mental condition at the time of the offense may be quite different from the condition, months or years later, at the time of the trial. The responsibility question is whether it is proper to excuse the defendant on account of his mental condition at the time of the act; the fitness issue is usually phrased to be whether, at the time of the trial, the accused has sufficient capacity to understand the proceedings against him and to assist in his defense.

As usually interpreted, the fitness test does not demand very much for sufficient capacity to stand trial. If he knows in some primitive sense what is going on at the trial and what he was doing at the time of the crime and can, with the help of his lawyer, do some basic planning for the trial, the accused will probably be found to have sufficient capacity to be tried. Sometimes, less may suffice.

Questions

1. Should a defendant with amnesia, who cannot recall the circumstances of the crime, be held for this reason to lack capacity to stand trial? See, e.g., People v. Francabandera, 33 N.Y.2d 429, 354 N.Y.S.2d 609, 310 N.E.2d 292 (1974).

2. Suppose the accused's lawyer believes his client lacks capacity to stand trial, but the client disagrees. May the lawyer raise the issue? May the prosecution? May the judge?

3. When the question of capacity to stand trial is raised, the accused may be sent for mental examination and report, usually at some public mental hospital. (The question of responsibility may also be put to the examining doctors at the same time, for purposes of the trial, if one follows.) If, on the basis of such a report, or otherwise, the judge finds the accused incompetent to stand trial, should he be hospitalized until

he regains capacity or allowed to go free on bail or on his own recognizance until he stands trial? Suppose the incapacity continues for a number of years, should the charges eventually be dropped?

4. Suppose the accused lacks capacity, but his attorney wants to get a trial issue like self-defense settled before the witnesses disappear or forget the circumstances; can this be done?

Note on Disposition of Those Found Not Guilty by Reason of Insanity

State procedure usually requires (unless, perhaps, it is plain to the judge that the subject no longer poses any threat) medical examination for one found not guilty by reason of insanity, to determine whether such person is dangerous to himself or others—the common test for permitting or continuing compulsory confinement of mental patients in criminal or civil matters.

Jones v. United States, 463 U.S. 354, 103 S.Ct. 3043, 77 L.Ed.2d 694 (1983), illustrates some of the problems of dealing with those found not guilty by reason of insanity.

Jones was charged in the District of Columbia with attempted petty larceny, as a would-be shoplifter. He pled not guilty by reason of insanity. There was expert testimony that he was a paranoid schizophrenic, and his insanity plea, as to which he had the burden of persuasion by a preponderance of the evidence, was upheld under the *Durham* test, then in effect in the District of Columbia. As the statute provided, he was automatically committed to a mental institution. A mandatory judicial release hearing, at which Jones had the burden of persuasion by a preponderance of the evidence to show that he was not dangerous to himself or others, was held within fifty days of commitment, and the judge found that he should be retained in hospital custody. The statute provided that thereafter he could be released either (1) on certification of recovery by the hospital, with court approval, or (2) after a judicial hearing (without jury) initiated by him, at which he established his recovery by a preponderance of the evidence; he had the right to initiate such hearings at intervals of not less than six months.

Jones initiated such a hearing after a year of hospitalization—a year being the maximum permissible sentence for the crime charged at his trial. He contended that he either ought to be released or recommitted under the civil procedures provided by statute, in the course of which his illness and dangerousness could be submitted to a jury, and in which the government would have to establish his mental illness and dangerousness by clear and convincing evidence, not a mere preponderance.

Justice Powell held for a majority of the Supreme Court that Jones was not entitled to such relief. Granting that commitment is a significant deprivation of liberty, requiring due process protection, the majority found that criminal trial and a verdict of not guilty by reason of insanity forms an adequate basis for commitment to a mental institution for an indefinite period of time. For civil commitment, due process requires that the government establish mental illness and dangerousness by clear and convincing evidence (Addington v. Texas, 441 U.S. 418, 99 S.Ct. 1804, 60 L.Ed.2d 323 (1979)); the majority found that these requirements need not be met in Jones's case. The criminal verdict established, according to the court, (1) that Jones committed the criminal act (otherwise he would have been acquitted outright), and (2) that he did so because of mental illness. Congress could and did provide that these findings constitute an adequate basis for hospitalizing Jones as mentally ill, even though it is possible that at the time of trial, conditions had changed. The fifty day hearing provided a sufficiently prompt opportunity to obtain release if Jones had recovered. The government need not relitigate the issue of a defendant's mental condition as a pre-condition of a commitment.

There is no reason, the Court thought, to require the same standard of proof as in civil commitment, where we are concerned that one may be found incompetent merely on the basis of idiosyncratic behavior. In the criminal situation, the accused advances the claim of insanity, and the criminal behavior established by the verdict is something more than mild aberration. The maximum sentence authorized upon conviction does not establish a limit on the time during which a dangerous and mentally ill person may be confined to assure safety of himself and others. Confinement is not to punish, but to protect.

Three dissenters (Justices Brennan, Marshall, and Blackmun) found no adequate reason for different standards in civil commitment and in Jones's situation. "Not guilty by reason of insanity" invokes a different standard than dangerousness, and it is applied in relation to a past situation, not to the situation at trial. Such a finding, they thought, is of little use in predicting future dangerousness. Much may depend on the circumstances of the particular case. Commitment to a mental institution involves very serious infringement of liberty, perhaps more serious infringement even than prison.

Justice Stevens agreed with the other dissenters on a further point: Even if some automatic hospitalization could be justified, there is no justification for extending it indefinitely, or beyond any maximum sentence which could be imposed upon conviction, without the safeguards present in a civil commitment.

For the federal procedure, enacted after *Jones*, requiring the person confined to establish non-dangerousness by clear and convincing evidence, see 18 U.S. C.A. § 4243 (The Insanity Defense Act of 1984).

Note on Mental Illness of Convicted Persons

People who are convicted may have been mentally ill without it affecting their guilt. They may not have been ill in a way which fits the local responsibility excuse for insanity, may have become ill later, or may simply not have raised the defense. There is no general prohibition against punishing the mentally ill, but a good corrections system will provide access to treatment for them, whether in prison or on probation or parole.

There is a constitutional prohibition, based on the Eighth Amendment, against inflicting capital punishment on the insane. Ford v. Wainwright, 477 U.S. 399, 106 S.Ct. 2595, 91 L.Ed.2d 335 (1986). It is not clear what the insanity test for eligibility for execution is.[a]

a. There is an old story, which I have been unable to trace, about a researcher, who found that the number of people on death row plus the number executed did not nearly equal the number who had been finally sentenced to death. What had happened to the missing? After investigation, he is supposed to have traced them to the state institution for the criminally insane. It seems that as the time of execution approached, many prisoners, not surprisingly, exhibited signs of mental instability. The psychiatrists were called in. Perhaps they did not like the death penalty. Perhaps they did not want to make what might be the final decision for death. Perhaps they were uncertain about the diagnosis. At any rate, the prisoners were sent to the state institution for evaluation. Upon arrival, the hardbitten war-

ii. Criminal Responsibility

Introductory Note

Traditional insanity law provides that one who meets the legal definition of an insane person at the time of committing what would otherwise be a criminal offense is for this reason to be found not guilty of the crime.

Insanity is a legal term, not a medical one. The legal term "insanity" does not, for example, correspond exactly with some medical term such as "psychosis". Rather than identifying a group with particular medical symptoms and prognoses, "insanity" points out a group of people to be excused from criminal responsibility on grounds of legal policy. Members of the group have a mental disease or mental defect, but mental disease or defect is not itself excusing. Mentally ill people may properly be found guilty of crime in some circumstances, and sent to jail. (A good penal system will provide necessary medical care for the mentally ill, as well as for the physically ill, prisoner.)

The central theoretical point was made by JUSTICE DORIS in State v. Johnson, 121 R.I. 254, 257, 399 A.2d 469, 470–471 (1979):

> Before punishing one who has invaded a protected interest, the criminal law generally requires some showing of culpability in the offender. The requirement of a mens rea, or guilty mind, is the most notable example of the concept that before punishment may be exacted, blameworthiness must be demonstrated. That some deterrent, restraint, or rehabilitative purpose may be served is alone insufficient. It has been stated that the criminal law reflects the moral sense of the community. "The fact that the law has, for centuries, regarded certain wrongdoers as improper subjects for punishment is a testament to the extent to which that moral sense has developed. Thus, society has recognized over the years that none of the three asserted purposes of the criminal law—rehabilitation, deterrence and retribution—is satisfied when the truly irresponsible, those who lack substantial capacity to control their actions, are punished." United States v. Freeman, 357 F.2d 606, 615 (2d Cir. 1966). The law appreciates that those who are substantially unable to restrain their conduct are, by definition, incapable of being deterred and their punishment in a correctional institution provides no example for others.

The law of criminal responsibility has its roots in the concept of free will. As MR. JUSTICE JACKSON stated:

> "How far one by an exercise of free will may determine his general destiny or his course in a particular matter and how far he is the toy of circumstance has been debated through the ages by theologians, philosophers, and scientists. Whatever doubts they

den told the prisoners: "You look sane to me. However, we are badly in need of help around here. If you want to stay, we have plenty for you to do while we complete your evaluation, which may take years and years. If you cause any trouble, we will find you sane and return you to death row." The missing prisoners were behaving well while cleaning floors and carrying bedpans at the institution—a troublesome, but perhaps not the worst possible, solution.

> have entertained as to the matter, the practical business of government and administration of the law is obliged to proceed on more or less rough and ready judgments based on the assumption that mature and rational persons are in control of their own conduct." Gregg Cartage & Storage Co. v. United States, 316 U.S. 74, 79–80, 62 S.Ct. 932, 935, 86 L.Ed. 1283, 1288 (1942).

Our law proceeds from this postulate and seeks to fashion a standard by which criminal offenders whose free will has been sufficiently impaired can be identified and treated in a manner that is both humane and beneficial to society at large. The problem has been aptly described as distinguishing between those cases for which a correctional-punitive disposition is appropriate and those in which a medical-custodial disposition is the only kind that is legally permissible. See Model Penal Code, § 4.01, Comment at 156 (Tent.Draft No. 4, 1955).

Note: A Short History of Responsibility Tests

THE DEVELOPMENT OF THE M'NAGHTEN TEST

State v. Johnson, 121 R.I. 254, 258–259, 399 A.2d 469, 471–472 (1979):

> The historical evolution of the law of criminal responsibility is a fascinating, complex story. For purposes of this opinion, however, an exhaustive historical discussion is unnecessary; a brief sketch will therefore suffice. The renowned "right-wrong" test had antecedents in England as early as 1582. In that year the *Eirenarcha,* written by William Lambard of the Office of the Justices of Peace, laid down as the test of criminal responsibility "knowledge of good or evil." See United States v. Currens, 290 F.2d 751, 764 (3d Cir.1961). During the 1700's the language of the test shifted its emphasis from "good or evil" to "know." See United States v. Freeman, 357 F.2d at 616. During the eighteenth century, when these tests and their progeny were evolving, psychiatry was hardly a profession, let alone a science. Belief in demonology and witchcraft was widespread and became intertwined with the law of responsibility. So eminent a legal scholar as Blackstone adamantly insisted upon the existence of witches and wizards as late as the latter half of the eighteenth century. Biggs, *The Guilty Mind* 61–62 (1955). The psychological theories of phrenology and monomania thrived and influenced the development of the "right and wrong" test.[2] Both of these compartmentalized concepts have been soundly rejected by modern medical science which views the human personality as a fully integrated system. By historical accident, however, the celebrated case of Daniel M'Naghten froze these concepts into the common law just at the time when they were beginning to come into disrepute. See generally id. at 81–107.

2. Phrenologists viewed the brain as divided into 35 distinct areas. Each area controlled a specific mental function. The sixth area, for example, was denominated "destructiveness." Monomania was a state of mind in which a single insane idea predominated while the rest of the thought processes remained normal. United States v. Freeman, 357 F.2d 606, 616 (2d Cir.1966).

Daniel M'Naghten attempted to assassinate Sir Robert Peel, Prime Minister of England, but mistakenly shot Peel's private secretary instead. This assassination had been preceded by several attempts on the lives of members of the English Royal House, including Queen Victoria herself. When M'Naghten was tried in 1843 the jury was charged with a test heavily influenced by the enlightened work of Dr. Isaac Ray who was severely critical of the "right and wrong" rule. See Ray, *Medical Jurisprudence of Insanity* (1838). After the jury acquitted M'Naghten the public indignation, spearheaded by the Queen, was so pronounced that the Judges of England were summoned before the House of Lords to justify their actions. In an extraordinary advisory opinion, issued in a pressure-charged atmosphere, Lord Chief Justice Tindal, speaking for all but one of the 15 judges, reversed the charge used at trial and articulated what has become known as the *M'Naghten* rules. * * *

M'Naghten's Case, 10 C. & F. 200, 210, 8 Eng.Rep. 718, 722 (House of Lords, 1843):

> * * * [T]o establish a defence on the ground of insanity, it must be clearly proved that, at the time of the committing of the act, the party accused was labouring under such a defect of reason, from disease of the mind, as not to know the nature and quality of the act he was doing; or, if he did know it, that he did not know he was doing what was wrong.

THE IRRESISTIBLE IMPULSE TEST

State v. Johnson, 121 R.I. 254, 263, 399 A.2d 469, 474 (1979):

Responding to criticism of *M'Naghten* as a narrow and harsh rule, several courts supplemented it with the "irresistible impulse" test. E.g., Parsons v. State, 81 Ala. 577, 2 So. 854 (1886); see Annot., *Irresistible Impulse as an Excuse for Crime,* 173 A.L.R. 391 (1948); Keedy, *Irresistible Impulse as a Defense in the Criminal Law,* 100 U.Pa.L.Rev. 956 (1952). Under this combined approach, courts inquire into both the cognitive and volitional components of the defendant's behavior. Although a theoretical advance over the stringent right and wrong test, the irresistible impulse doctrine has also been the subject of widespread criticism. Similar to *M'Naghten's* absolutist view of capacity to know, the irresistible impulse is considered in terms of a complete destruction of the governing power of the mind. See United States v. Frazier, 458 F.2d 911, 917 (8th Cir.1972); United States v. Freeman, 357 F.2d at 620. A more fundamental objection is that the test produces the misleading notion that a crime impulsively committed must have been perpetrated in a sudden and explosive fit. Thus, the irresistible impulse test excludes those "far more numerous instances of crimes committed after excessive brooding and melancholy by one who is unable to resist sustained psychic compulsion or to make any real attempt to control his conduct."

THE DURHAM TEST

United States v. Brawner, 471 F.2d 969, 976, 978 (D.C.Cir.1972):

The landmark opinion was written by Judge Bazelon in Durham v. United States, 214 F.2d 862 (1954). Prior to *Durham* the law of the District of Columbia was established by United States v. Lee, 15 D.C. (4 Mackey) 489, 496 (1886) and Smith v. United States, 36 F.2d 548 (1929), which, taken together, stated a traditional test of insanity, in terms of right and wrong and irresistible impulse. *Durham* adopted the "product rule," pioneered in State v. Pike, 49 N.H. 399, 402 (1869–70), and exculpated from criminal responsibility those whose forbidden acts were the product of a mental disease or defect.

* * *

* * * [In McDonald v. United States, 312 F.2d 847, 851 (en banc, 1962) we] provided a legal definition of mental disease or defect, and held that it included "any abnormal condition of the mind which substantially affects mental or emotional processes and substantially impairs behavior controls." (312 F.2d at 851). "Thus the jury would consider testimony concerning the development, adaptation and functioning of these processes and controls." Id.

While the *McDonald* standard of mental disease was not without an attribute of circularity, it was useful in the administration of justice because it made plain that clinical and legal definitions of mental disease were distinct, and it helped the jury to sort out its complex task and to focus on the matters given it to decide.

The *Durham* rule also required explication along other lines, notably the resolution of the ambiguity inherent in the formulation concerning actions that were the "product" of mental illness. It was supplemented in Carter v. United States, 252 F.2d 608 at 615–616 (1957):

> The simple fact that a person has a mental disease or defect is not enough to relieve him of responsibility for a crime. There must be a relationship between the disease and the criminal act; and the relationship must be such as to justify a reasonable inference that the act would not have been committed if the person had not been suffering from the disease.

Thus *Carter* clarified that the mental illness must not merely have entered into the production of the act, but must have played a necessary role. *Carter* identified the "product" element of the rule with the "but for" variety of causation.

THE MODEL PENAL CODE TEST

Model Penal Code, § 4.01, Text: *

Section 4.01. Mental Disease or Defect Excluding Responsibility

(1) A person is not responsible for criminal conduct if at the time of such conduct as a result of mental disease or defect he lacks

substantial capacity either to appreciate the criminality [wrongfulness] of his conduct or to conform his conduct to the requirements of law.

(2) As used in this Article, the terms "mental disease or defect" do not include an abnormality manifested only by repeated criminal or otherwise anti-social conduct.

THE FEDERAL TEST

The Insanity Defense Reform Act of 1984 (18 U.S.C. § 20):

§ 20. Insanity defense

(a) AFFIRMATIVE DEFENSE.—It is an affirmative defense to a prosecution under any Federal statute that, at the time of the commission of the acts constituting the offense, the defendant, as a result of a severe mental disease or defect, was unable to appreciate the nature and quality or the wrongfulness of his acts. Mental disease or defect does not otherwise constitute a defense.

(b) BURDEN OF PROOF.—The defendant has the burden of proving the defense of insanity by clear and convincing evidence.

State v. Lucifer

Supreme Court of Ohypo, 1985.
307 Ohypo 981.

PER CURIAM. The defendant appeals from a conviction of murder in the first degree, upon which he has been sentenced to imprisonment for life without possibility of parole. The victim was the Reverend Doctor Grace Good, pastor of the Community Church of Centerville, and a prominent and respected member of the community. Dr. Good was on her way to the bank with the receipts from the previous day's services when she was accosted by defendant. The incident was observed from a distance by Detective Will Watch of the Centerville police, who was on stakeout duty on another matter. Watch testified that Lucifer said something, which Watch could not hear, to Dr. Good, who shook her head in response. Lucifer then pulled a gun from his pocket and immediately shot her dead. He ran away when Watch identified himself and called out to him, but was caught by the police a few minutes later.

The prosecution's case proceeded on the theory that the facts supported either a case of premeditated and deliberate killing or a case of felony-murder based on an attempt to rob. The jury found for the state on the former theory only, apparently deciding that there was no clear indication of an attempt to rob.

The defendant did not contest Watch's account of the physical facts of the killing. He did however enter a plea of not guilty by reason of insanity. At the trial Lucifer testified that he had killed Good on command of the Devil. Merlin Mind, M.D., a psychiatrist, examined the defendant before trial. Called by the defense, he offered, out of the hearing of the jury, to testify that he diagnosed Lucifer as a paranoid schizophrenic, who suffered from a delusion that he was a servant of the Devil, who he believed had commanded Lucifer to kill any member of the clergy he encountered. In Dr. Mind's opinion, Lucifer was acting on this command when he killed Good.

The State objected to receipt of this testimony, and the following colloquy took place out of the jury's hearing:

State's Attorney:	Your honor, I don't see that this testimony is relevant to show insanity. Under our *M'Naghten* test for insanity, Mr. Darrow must show not only that his client suffered from a mental disease or defect—we of course grant that paranoid schizophrenia is a mental disease—but also that, on account of this, Lucifer either did not know the nature and quality of his act, or did not know that the act was wrong. Now, the defendant testified that he deliberately killed Dr. Good, so he knew what he was doing. And, he must have known that his act was wrong, whether "wrong" means contrary to law or morally wrong. He ran away when the detective told him to stop, which shows he knew his act was contrary to law. He knew it was morally wrong if he believed he was acting on the Devil's command.
The Court:	What about that, Mr. Darrow?
Mr. Darrow:	Dr. Mind would testify, Your Honor, first, that the mental disease prevented Mr. Lucifer from having any real understanding of the act of killing, and that he was caught up in his delusion in such a way that killing had no real meaning for him. * * *
The Court:	I will allow the jury to hear that.
Mr. Darrow:	Secondly, Dr. Mind would testify, Your Honor, that because of his disease, Mr. Lucifer lacked the will to resist what he took to be the Devil's orders. He would also testify fully as to the bizarre symptoms of Lucifer's disease and as to the various effects it had on his personality.
State's Attorney:	We would object to any such testimony, Your Honor.
The Court:	I agree. These matters go beyond anything properly proveable under *M'Naghten.* I'm not even sure about the first offer, but I'm going to receive it. You could say that *M'Naghten* doesn't require any complex understanding, only simple verbal knowledge of what he is doing and

> whether it is wrong. But, I think the test contemplates a little more. Note, for the record, that the diagnosis and opinion originally stated, together with the first offer, is accepted. The second offer, over defense objection, is rejected.

Dr. Mind testified in accordance with the ruling.

At the close of the trial, Judge Rule charged the jury in the words of the *M'Naghten* test, after giving correct instructions as to the burden of persuasion. The jury was told to consider the "Devil" evidence and Dr. Mind's testimony only insofar as it indicated that Lucifer did not know the nature or quality of his act or did not know that it was wrong. The jury rejected the insanity claim, and, as noted, it found the defendant guilty of murder in the first degree.

The judgment of conviction is reversed and the case is remanded for a new trial, in which the American Law Institute insanity test will be applied. Separate opinions of the justices follow.

BLYNKEN, J.: (concurring in the result) There is no question that, under our past decisions, which follow *M'Naghten,* the evidentiary rulings and instructions on insanity were at least as favorable to the accused as any to which he was entitled. However, I believe that we should exercise our common law authority to revise our law of insanity to bring it in line with modern medical knowledge. I favor adoption of the *Durham* rule: the accused is not guilty by reason of insanity if his otherwise criminal conduct is the product of mental disease or defect.

Modern psychiatry identifies two, or perhaps three, major groups of mental disorders. Most serious are the psychoses, in which, in the fully developed disease, the patient is unable to handle the ordinary problems of living. The personality is severely disorganized, and the subject generally does not know that he is in an abnormal state. Inability to deal with others in all spheres of activity is common. A psychosis may have organic causes, such as brain injury, arteriosclerosis, or alcohol or drug problems, or it may be functional, in which case there are no detectable structural changes in the brain. Functional psychoses include the manic-depressive type, in which there are contrasting periods of hyperactivity or elation, and passivity or depression, and the various schizophrenic disorders. In simple schizophrenia the subject withdraws from life into an apathetic state of emotional dullness, in which he may suffer delusions. In the catatonic form, there is too much or too little activity; the subject may regress to childhood or cease to engage in any voluntary activity. In the hebephrenic variety, the patient may suffer from delusions, odd mannerisms, hysteria, or speech abnormality. The paranoid schizophrenic is dominated by delusions of importance, grandeur, or persecution, which often take a religious turn. (A schizoid personality exhibits milder symptoms of a schizophrenic disorder, such as seclusiveness, regression, or inappropriate response to environment.)

Psychoneuroses are less severe mental disorders than psychoses. They are marked by phobias (e.g., fears of crowds or open spaces) or obsessions, which the subject is likely to recognize as exaggerated. There is no organic change and no severe distortion of the personality; the subject generally realizes that he is emotionally ill.

Probably most experts would recognize the sociopath (sometimes called the psychopath) as suffering from a mental disorder. If a Boy Scout is trustworthy, loyal, helpful, etc., the sociopath resembles his reverse image and is quite likely to commit crimes. He is a non-conformist, who is unlikely to exhibit any symptoms of guilt and who may be utterly indifferent to moral principles. He may lack judgment, sense of responsibility, or ability to learn from experience. Causation of the condition is uncertain; some think there is no evidence of any mental disease and that the term sociopath merely describes a group of people who tend to act and respond in certain ways. (Since there is no suggestion that Lucifer is a sociopath, it is unnecessary to decide whether sociopathy should be included in the term mental disease and thus form the basis for an insanity defense.)

Punishment is for the wicked, not for the sick. If the accused suffered from a mental disorder, and if, but for this mental disorder, he would not have killed Good, he needs sympathy for his misfortune, treatment for his illness, and confinement only to the extent necessary to protect himself and the public from harm. He does not belong in jail.

There was evidence to support a finding of the mental disease of paranoid schizophrenia in Lucifer. The jury should have been told that if it found this disease and found it to be a cause of the killing, Lucifer was entitled to a verdict of not guilty by reason of insanity. This is what the *Durham* rule provides. It also unshackles the psychiatric witness to testify fully about the scope of the accused's disorder and its relevance to what occurred. The expert is no longer limited to an artificial discussion about knowledge of nature and quality or right and wrong, terms which he is unlikely to consider for any medical purpose or to be able to form any clear understanding of. *Durham* allows him to give his testimony naturally, in a manner consistent with his own ways of professional thought and likely to be intelligible to a lay jury.

Had the jury received a *Durham* instruction, it might well have acquitted Lucifer on the evidence before it, and it perhaps would have been more ready to do so had the psychiatric evidence been allowed in full, as it would have been under *Durham.* Of course, the jury might have thought the defense a sham, but the accused is entitled to a new trial where the question can be presented properly.

My colleagues do not accept my reasoning and themselves have different views as to the proper test. In order to provide guidance for the trial judge on retrial of this case, I will cast my vote with Justice Nod, who favors the Model Penal Code test. This seems to me inadequate to take full advantage of modern medical knowledge, but I prefer it to *M'Naghten* or to the Chief Justice's modernized version of *M'Naghten.* I can accept its use in criminal trials until such time as I can persuade this court to adopt a better test.

NOD, J.: (concurring) Half of the trouble in the world is due to failure to frame issues properly. The *Durham* test, in its eagerness to embrace modern psychiatry, forgets that the proper inquiry is not whether the accused is sick, but whether he is properly held criminally responsible. Many people who have mental disorders which have some causal relationship with their criminal conduct are properly held legally responsible for that conduct. Suppose that a mental disorder entails a propensity for a certain kind of conduct, say seclusiveness, without in any sense compelling such conduct, and suppose that our seclusive schizoid personality pushes a fellow bus passenger from the seat beside him because he wants to be alone. He is guilty of battery if his mental condition does no more than tempt him to wrongful action. This is why insanity is a legal term and not a medical term. It does not correspond with any precision to a medical term such as psychosis. It identifies a person who is not to be held criminally responsible on account of mental disease or defect which operates at the time of the crime in such a way that the policy of the criminal law would not be served by punishment or condemnation.

When does such a situation exist? The answer ought to have a rational relationship to the ends of punishment. Which of the mentally ill "criminals" would it not really serve the ends of retribution, restraint, deterrence, or reformation to punish? The traditional insanity tests seek, approximately, to identify those whose condition makes it impossible or extremely difficult to avoid doing what they did. Such people belong to a non-deterrable class; the threats of the criminal law can have no effect upon them. They do not invite retribution, because they are unable to help what they did. Restraint and reform play minor theoretical roles in deciding whether to convict them of crime. Whether jailed as criminals, or (if they are dangerous) confined as mentally ill, they pose minimal risks to society. Reformation in this context means medical treatment for mental illness, which ought to be possible whether they are convicted or found not guilty by reason of insanity.

It is on this central matter of policy that the *Durham* rule fails and the *M'Naghten* rule passes, though perhaps not with the highest possible grade. The *Durham* rule is vague in application; arguably it might excuse one who has recovered from mental illness after hospitalization, but who finds his family and job gone when released and robs a bank to get funds. The robbery is in a sense a product of his mental disease. More probably the disease must operate as a disease to be a cause of the conduct, but it makes no difference under *Durham* that the accused might have been able to stop himself from committing the crime had he tried a little harder.

Under *M'Naghten,* one who, because of mental disease, carves up his wife under the impression that he is making a totem pole (and thus does not know the nature and quality of his act), or who believes he is commanded by the Almighty to kill her (and thus does not believe that he acts wrongly) is not likely to be deterred by the penal code and belongs in the insane class. *M'Naghten* also has the virtue of limiting the revenge motive for punishment to cases in which there is some argument for its acceptability. There is no argument for revenge against the *M'Naghten* insane, while there may be some such argument against the merely *Durham* insane.

As Justice Blynken points out, the *M'Naghten* test is imperfect in that it may inhibit medical testimony by limiting it to what bears clearly on "knowledge of right and wrong" or "knowledge of the nature and quality of the act."

This can make the evidence unreal and less illuminating to the jury than it ought to be. It is possible, under *M'Naghten,* to give the word "know" such a broad interpretation that there is little or no exclusion of helpful evidence, but a better formulation would compel such a result.

A *Durham* problem, of course, is that there is no real curb on psychiatric testimony, and the expert is likely to testify automatically in terms of his own views as to responsibility, which may be some distance from the legal view. Sometimes, under *Durham,* experts have even been allowed to control the definitions of mental disease and mental defect. In the District of Columbia an expert testified on Friday that a person with a sociopathic personality did not suffer from a mental disease. Over the weekend his hospital changed its view and decided that sociopathy is a mental disease; from then on physicians did an about-face and testified that sociopathy was a mental disease. See In re Rosenfield, 157 F.Supp. 18, 20–21 (D.D.C.1957) remanded sub nom. Rosenfield v. Overholser, 262 F.2d 34 (D.C.Cir.1958) (on an unrelated matter); United States v. Brawner, 471 F.2d 969, 978 (D.C.Cir. 1972).

Most of the problems with *M'Naghten* can be avoided by modifications in the formulation of the test. This is essentially what the American Law Institute has done in § 4.01 of the Model Penal Code. Instead of "know" we have "appreciate," which indicates full understanding, rather than mere glib formal knowledge. The Institute speaks in terms of "substantial capacity to conform" instead of making knowledge or appreciation a "yes" or "no" matter.

Further, the Model Penal Code adopts a modern version of the irresistible impulse test. One overwhelmed, through mental disease, by an irresistible impulse to do the act forbidden by law is no more a member of a deterrable class than one who does not know what he is doing. While "irresistible impulse" suggests that the urge must be sudden, the Institute language of "substantial capacity to conform" allows for overwhelming drives which build up over a period of time.

The facts of this case are well suited to show the advantages of the "substantial capacity" test. If the defense evidence is believed, the jury could well find that the command of the Devil, as Lucifer, because of his mental disease, believed it to be, overwhelmed his will so that he was powerless to act differently. In such a case, the jury should be instructed to acquit. Under the American Law Institute test, it could hear evidence and would receive instructions which would lead it to a proper result. We should adopt the Model Penal Code test for the retrial of this case and for all subsequent insanity cases. I agree with the test's explicit exclusion of the sociopath from the insanity defense. It is not clear whether the condition should be treated as a mental disease, or what treatment, if any, is appropriate for the condition.

WYNKEN, C.J.: (dissenting) I agree with all that my brother Nod says in criticism of *Durham* and with his argument for the "cognitive" arm of the Model Penal Code test, as an improvement on *M'Naghten.* Like the American Bar Association and the authors of the Federal Criminal Code, however, I would reject any version of the irresistible impulse test and hence the "volitional" arm of the Model Penal Code test, based upon it. Nobody knows what an irresistible impulse is or how it differs from a resistible impulse which happens not to be resisted. This branch of the test provides an easy opportunity for faked insanity claims and jury confusion.

If Lucifer really suffers from a mental disorder which so impaired him that he thought he was getting commands from the Devil to kill, his cognitive ability was impaired as well as his volitional capacity. He did not appreciate the reality of the situation before him, and he would not be convicted under the "cognitive" arm of the Model Penal Code test. A lesser impairment ought not to be a defense.

Notes on the M'Naghten Test

1. *Criticisms.* Though widely followed, the opinion produced many critics. Among the criticisms are the following:

a. The opinion is based on obsolete medical assumptions of the 1840s. These include the view that mental functions, such as knowing and willing, are so separable that, e.g., "lesions of the will" can exist without cognitive impairment. Justice Stephen argued that disturbances of the will in the nature of irresistible impulses could prevent the full consideration of a situation through consideration of "distant motives and general principles of conduct," and would thus also impair the ability to know the wrongness of the act, but most authority did not infer an irresistible impulse test as a logical correlative of the *M'Naghten* test. See Stephen, 2 History of the Criminal Law of England 169 ff. (1883).

b. Can notions of "right" and "wrong" properly form a part of an insanity test? The medical profession does not think in such terms in dealing with mental illness, and may even deny that the terms have sufficient meaning to be useful.

c. The test suggests a sharp division between the sane and the insane; the medical profession tends to think that mental health and mental disease form a continuum in which no absolute test is appropriate.

d. The meaning of the key word "know" is obscure. Does it mean merely verbal knowledge, requiring only that the accused be able to answer a kind of true-false test correctly, or does it require full mental and emotional understanding of acts and their consequences?

e. However appropriate the test may be for the delusional psychoses to which it was first applied, are there grounds for extending it to other mental diseases and defects?

State v. Johnson, 121 R.I. 254, 262–263, 399 A.2d 469, 473–474 (1979):

* * * By focusing upon total cognitive incapacity, the *M'Naghten* rule compels the psychiatrist to testify in terms of unrealistic concepts having no medical meaning. Instead of scientific opinions, the rule calls for a moral or ethical judgment from the expert which judgment contributes to usurpation of the jury's function as decision maker. See United States v. Currens, 290 F.2d at 767; Weihofen, *Mental Disorder as a Criminal Defense* 65 (1954).

Probably the most common criticism of *M'Naghten* is that it severely restricts expert testimony, thereby depriving the jury of a true picture of the defendant's mental condition. See, e.g., United States v. Freeman, 357 F.2d at 620; Hill v. State, 252 Ind. at 606, 251 N.E.2d at 432. This contention has been seriously questioned by some commentators who find no support for the argument that *M'Naghten* inhibits the flow of testimony on the responsibility issue. Goldstein, supra at 53; accord, Matthews, *Mental Disability and the Criminal Law* 44–46 (1970). As a matter of practice in this jurisdiction, expert testimony under *M'Naghten* has been unrestricted and robust. Nevertheless, we are convinced that this testimony would be more meaningful to the jury were it not for the narrow determination demanded by *M'Naghten.*

That these criticisms have had a pronounced effect is evidenced by the large and growing number of jurisdictions that have abandoned their former allegiance to *M'Naghten* in favor of the Model Penal Code formulation. We also find these criticisms persuasive and agree that *M'Naghten's* serious deficiencies necessitate a new approach.[4]

2. *An Auxiliary Test.* One largely forgotten statement in the *M'Naghten* case involved "partial insanity." It is said that there was once a college professor, sane on all other subjects, who believed that his feet were made of glass—not that he had artificial glass feet, but that the glass feet were an integral part of his body. Ask yourself how the jury ought to be instructed in a murder—self-defense case in which the professor has killed another who was attempting to hit his foot with a hammer, under the following suggested test (M'Naghten's Case, 10 C. & F. 200, 211, 8 Eng.Rep. 718, 723 (House of Lords 1843)):

> * * * [M]aking the same assumption as we did before, namely, that he labours under such partial delusion only, and is not in other respects insane, we think he must be considered in the same situation as to responsibility as if the facts with respect to which the delusion exists were real. For example, if under the influence of his delusion he supposes another man to be in the act of attempting to take away his life, and he kills that man, as he supposes, in self-defence, he would be exempt from punishment. If his delusion was that the deceased had inflicted a serious injury to his character and fortune, and he killed in revenge for such supposed injury, he would be liable to punishment. * * *

Note on the Durham Test

Development. United States v. Brawner, 471 F.2d 969, 976, 977–978, 979, 982–983, 989–990 (D.C.Cir.1972):

> Few cases have evoked as much comment as *Durham.* It has sparked widespread interest in the legal-judicial community and focused attention on the profound problems involved in defining legal responsibility in case of mental illness. It has been hailed as a guide to the difficult and problem-laden intersection of law and psychiatry, ethics and science. It has been

4. The defense of lack of criminal responsibility due to a mental illness in this jurisdiction is a judicial creation which we are free to alter. Cf. Digby v. Digby, R.I., 388 A.2d 1 (1978). Although the majority of states that have abandoned *M'Naghten* in favor of the Model Penal Code test have done so legislatively, in most of those jurisdictions the defense was statutorily derived. * * *

scored as an unwarranted loophole through which the cunning criminal might escape from the penalty of the law. We view it more modestly, as the court's effort, designed in the immemorial manner of the case method that has built the common law, to alleviate two serious problems with the previous rule.

The first of these was a problem of language which raised an important symbolic issue in the law. We felt that the language of the old right-wrong/irresistible impulse rule for insanity was antiquated, no longer reflecting the community's judgment as to who ought to be held criminally liable for socially destructive acts. We considered the rule as restated to have more fruitful, accurate and considered reflection of the sensibilities of the community as revised and expanded in the light of continued study of abnormal human behavior.

The second vexing problem that *Durham* was designed to reach related to the concern of the psychiatrists called as expert witnesses for their special knowledge of the problem of insanity, who often and typically felt that they were obliged to reach outside of their professional expertise when they were asked, under the traditional insanity rule established in 1843 by *M'Naghten's* Case, whether the defendant knew right from wrong. They further felt that the narrowness of the traditional test, which framed the issue of responsibility solely in terms of cognitive impairment, made it impossible to convey to the judge and jury the full range of information material to an assessment of defendant's responsibility.

* * *

A difficulty arose under the *Durham* rule in application. The rule was devised to facilitate the giving of testimony by medical experts in the context of a legal rule, with the jury called upon to reach a composite conclusion that had medical, legal and moral components. However the pristine statement of the *Durham* rule opened the door to "trial by label." *Durham* did distinguish between "disease," as used "in the sense of a condition which is considered capable of either improving or deteriorating," and "defect," as referring to a condition not capable of such change "and which may be either congenital or the result of injury, or the residual effect of a physical or mental disease." 214 F.2d at 875. But the court failed to explicate what abnormality of mind was an essential ingredient of these concepts. In the absence of a definition of "mental disease or defect," medical experts attached to them the meanings which would naturally occur to them—medical meanings—and gave testimony accordingly. * * *

* * *

The pivotal "product" term continued to present problems, principally that it put expert testimony on a faulty footing. Assuming that a mental disease, in the legal sense, had been established, the fate of the defendant came to be determined by what came to be referred to by the legal jargon of "productivity." On the other hand, it was obviously sensible if not imperative that the experts having pertinent knowledge should speak to the crucial question whether the mental abnormality involved is one associated with aberrant behavior. But since "productivity" was so decisive a factor in the decisional equation, a ruling permitting experts to testify expressly in language of "product" raised in a different context the concern lest the ultimate issue be in fact turned over to the experts rather than retained for the jurors representing the community.

* * *

As early as [United States v.] Carter, [252 F.2d 608 (1957)] we had warned that the function of an expert was to explain the origin, development and manifestations of mental disorders, in terms that would be coherent and meaningful to the jury. "Unexplained medical labels * * * are not enough." (252 F.2d at 617). Even after McDonald [v. United States, 312 F.2d 847 (en banc 1962)], however, we continued to see cases where the testimony of the experts was limited to the use of conclusory labels, without the explication of the underlying analysis. We do not say this was deliberated by the experts. It seems in large measure to have reflected tactical decisions of counsel, and perhaps problems of communications between the disciplines.

It was in this context that the court came to the decision in Washington v. United States, 390 F.2d 444 (1967), which forbade experts from testifying as to productivity altogether. Chief Judge Bazelon's opinion illuminates the basis of the ruling, as one intended "to help the psychiatrists understand their role in court, and thus eliminate a fundamental cause of unsatisfactory expert testimony," namely, the tendency of the expert to use "concepts [which] can become slogans, hiding facts and representing nothing more than the witness's own conclusion about the defendant's criminal responsibility." (390 F.2d at 456).

* * *

When the court used the term "product" in *Durham* it likely assumed that this was a serviceable, and indeed a natural, term for a rule defining criminal responsibility—a legal reciprocal, as it were, for the familiar term "proximate cause," used to define civil responsibility. But if concepts like "product" are, upon refinement, reasonably understood, or at least appreciated, by judges and lawyers, and perhaps philosophers, difficulties developed when it emerged that the "product" concept did not signify a reasonably identifiable common ground that was also shared by the nonlegal experts, and the laymen serving on the jury as the representatives of the community.

* * *

The expert witnesses—psychiatrists and psychologists—are called to adduce relevant information concerning what may for convenience be referred to as the "medical" component of the responsibility issue. But the difficulty—as emphasized in *Washington*—is that the medical expert comes, by testimony given in terms of a non-medical construct ("product"), to express conclusions that in essence embody ethical and legal conclusions. There is, indeed, irony in a situation under which the *Durham* rule, which was adopted in large part to permit experts to testify in their own terms concerning matters within their domain which the jury should know, resulted in testimony by the experts in terms not their own to reflect unexpressed judgments in a domain that is properly not theirs but the jury's. The irony is heightened when the jurymen, instructed under the esoteric "product" standard, are influenced significantly by "product" testimony of expert witnesses really reflecting ethical and legal judgments rather than a conclusion within the witnesses' particular expertise.

* * *

* * * The more we have pondered the problem the more convinced we have become that the sound solution lies not in further shaping of the *Durham* "product" approach in more refined molds, but in adopting the ALI's formulation as the linchpin of our jurisprudence.

* * *

Amicus Dempsey is concerned that a change by this court from *Durham-McDonald* to ALI will be taken as an indication that this court intends that the number and percentage of insanity acquittals be modified. That is not the intendment of the rule adopted today, nor do we have any basis for forecasting that effect.

Statistical data concerning the use of insanity in criminal trials in this jurisdiction were presented in the December 15, 1966, Report of the President's Commission on Crime in the District of Columbia. These data have been up-dated in Mr. Dempsey's brief, with the aid of data helpfully supplied by the United States Attorney's office. At least since *Durham* was modified by *McDonald,* insanity acquittals have run at about 2% of all cases terminated. In the seven years subsequent to *McDonald* jury verdicts of not guilty by reason of insanity averaged only 3 per annum.[32] In trials by the court, there has been an annual average of about 38 verdicts of not guilty by reason of insanity; these typically are cases where the Government psychiatrists agreed that the crime was the product of mental illness.[33] We perceive no basis in these data for any conclusion that the number of percentage of insanity acquittals has been either excessive or inadequate.

We have no way of forecasting what will be the effect on verdicts, of juries or judges, from the reduction in influence of expert testimony on "productivity" that reflects judgments outside the domain of expertise. Whatever its effect, we are confident that the rule adopted today provides a sounder relationship in terms of the giving, comprehension and application of expert testimony. Our objective is not to steer the jury's verdict but to enhance its deliberation.[35]

32. *McDonald* was decided in 1962. For fiscal years ending June 30, 1964–1970, there were 21 verdicts of not guilty by reason of insanity in trials by jury, 265 such verdicts in trials by court. These data appear in Appendix C of Mr. Dempsey's brief, as revised by submission of Sept. 21, 1971.

Mr. Dempsey provides data on all terminations for fiscal 1964–1968. The data for these five years show 7537 terminations, and 194 verdicts of not guilty by reason of insanity. The other terminations are: 3500 verdicts of guilty on plea, 1567 verdicts of guilty after trial, and 629 verdicts of not guilty.

33. These trials are discussed in the amicus submission of David Chambers, consultant, who prepared a report on the John Howard Pavilion at St. Elizabeths Hospital, submitted to the Hospital and the National Institutes of Mental Health.

Professor Chambers characterizes most insanity trials to the courts as more nearly comparable to the taking of guilty pleas—consisting of a stipulated statement of facts; a conclusory Hospital report that the crime was the product of mental illness; and brief supporting testimony from a single John Howard psychiatrist—all in a context of a "tacit or explicit understanding" that the defendant will not contest his indefinite commitment to the Hospital.

35. We do not share the cynical view that treats the instruction as devoid of consequence. In a study of the reactions of more than a thousand jurors to two experimental trials involving a defense of insanity, it was found that juries deliberated significantly longer when instructed under *Durham* than under *M'Naghten.* Yet this did not undercut consensus; there was no significant difference in the percentages of hung juries. R. Simon, The Jury and the Defense of Insanity 213 *ff.* (1967).

Notes on the Model Penal Code Test

1. Model Penal Code § 4.01, Comments 1, 3, and 4 (Tent.Draft No. 4, 1955): *

1. No problem in the drafting of a penal code presents larger intrinsic difficulty than that of determining when individuals whose conduct would otherwise be criminal ought to be exculpated on the ground that they were suffering from mental disease or defect when they acted as they did. What is involved specifically is the drawing of a line between the use of public agencies and public force to condemn the offender by conviction, with resultant sanctions in which there is inescapably a punitive ingredient (however constructive we may attempt to make the process of correction) and modes of disposition in which that ingredient is absent, even though restraint may be involved. To put the matter differently, the problem is to discriminate between the cases where a punitive-correctional disposition is appropriate and those in which a medical-custodial disposition is the only kind that the law should allow.

3. The draft accepts the view that any effort to exclude the non-deterrables from strictly penal sanctions must take account of the impairment of volitional capacity no less than of impairment of cognition; and that this result should be achieved directly in the formulation of the test, rather than left to mitigation in the application of *M'Naghten*. It also accepts the criticism of the "irresistible impulse" formulation as inept in so far as it may be impliedly restricted to sudden, spontaneous acts as distinguished from insane propulsions that are accompanied by brooding or reflection. See e.g., ROYAL COMMISSION ON CAPITAL PUNISHMENT, REPORT (1953) par. 314, p. 110.

* * *

4. One further problem must be faced. In addressing itself to impairment of the cognitive capacity, *M'Naghten* demands that impairment be complete: the actor must *not* know. So, too, the irresistible impulse criterion presupposes a complete impairment of capacity for self-control. The extremity of these conceptions is, we think, the point that poses largest difficulty to psychiatrists when called upon to aid in their administration. The schizophrenic, for example, is disoriented from reality; the disorientation is extreme; but it is rarely total. Most psychotics will respond to a command of someone in authority within the mental hospital; they thus have some capacity to conform to a norm. But this is very different from the question whether they have the capacity to conform to requirements that are not thus immediately symbolized by an attendant or policeman at the elbow. Nothing makes the inquiry into responsibility more unreal for the psychiatrist than limitation of the issue to some ultimate extreme of total incapacity, when clinical experience reveals only a graded scale with marks along the way.

We think this difficulty can and must be met. The law must recognize that when there is no black and white it must content itself with different shades of gray. The draft, accordingly, does not demand *complete* impairment of capacity. It asks instead for *substantial* impairment. This is all, we think, that candid witnesses, called on to infer the nature of the situation at a time that they did not observe, can ever confidently say, even when they know that a disorder was extreme.

* * *

2. State v. Johnson, 121 R.I. 254, 267–269, 399 A.2d 469, 476–477 (1979):

* * * The Model Penal Code test has received widespread and evergrowing acceptance. It has been adopted with varying degrees of modification in 26 states [6] and by every federal court of appeals that has addressed the issue.[7] Although no definition can be accurately described as the perfect or ultimate pronouncement, we believe that the Model Penal Code standard represents a significant, positive improvement over our existing rule. Most importantly, it acknowledges that volitional as well as cognitive impairments must be considered by the jury in its resolution of the responsibility issue. The test replaces *M'Naghten's* unrealistic all-or-nothing approach with the concept of "substantial" capacity. Additionally, the test employs vocabulary sufficiently in the common ken that its use at trial will permit a reasonable three-way dialogue between the law-trained judges and

6. The following 18 states have clearly adopted the Model Penal Code test: Alaska—Alaska Stat. § 12.45.083 (1972)—[but see § 12.47.010, adopted in 1982, which limits the insanity defense to cases in which "the defendant was unable, as a result of mental disease or defect, to appreciate the nature and quality" of his conduct.—Ed.]; California—People v. Drew, 22 Cal.3d 318, 149 Cal.Rptr. 275, 583 P.2d 1318 (1978)—[but see West's Ann.Cal.Penal Code § 25(b), which was amended in 1982 by Initiative to restore the *M'Naghten* rule.—Ed.]; Connecticut—Conn. Gen.Stat. § 53a–13 (1972); Hawaii—Haw. Rev.Stat. § 704–400 (1976); Idaho—State v. White, 93 Idaho 153, 456 P.2d 797 (1969); Illinois—Ill.Rev.Stat. ch. 38, § 6–2 (1972); Indiana—Hill v. State, 252 Ind. 601, 251 N.E.2d 429 (1969); Maine—Me.Rev.Stat. tit. 17–A, § 58 (Supp.1978); Maryland—Md.Code Ann. art. 59, § 25(a) (1972); Massachusetts—Commonwealth v. McHoul, 352 Mass. 544, 226 N.E.2d 556 (1967); Missouri—Mo.Rev.Stat. § 552.030 (1969); Oregon—Or.Rev.Stat. § 161.295 (1973); Tennessee—Graham v. State, Tenn., 547 S.W.2d 531 (1977); Utah—Utah Code Ann. § 76–2–305 (1977); Vermont—Vt.Stat.Ann. tit. 13, § 4801 (1974); West Virginia—State v. Myers, W.Va., 222 S.E.2d 300 (1976); Wisconsin—Wis.Stat. § 971.15 (1971); Wyoming—Wyo.Stat. § 7–11–304 (1977).

Additionally, eight states and the District of Columbia have adopted the Model Penal Code test with some modification: Arkansas—Ark. Stat.Ann. § 41–601 (1977) (omits "substantial"); Delaware—Del.Code tit. 11, § 401 (1975) (volitional test phrased "sufficient willpower to choose whether he would do the act or refrain from doing it"); District of Columbia—Bethea v. United States, 365 A.2d 64 (D.C.App.1976) ("recognize" rather than "appreciate"); Kentucky—Graham v. Commonwealth, 420 S.W.2d 575 (Ky.1967) (different phraseology throughout); Michigan—Mich. Stat.Ann. § 28.1044(1), M.C.L.A. § 768.21a (1978) (uses terms "mental illness" and "mental retardation" which are specifically defined); Montana—Mont.Rev.Codes Ann. § 95–501(a) (1969) ("unable either to" rather than "lacked substantial capacity"); New York—N.Y.Penal Law § 30.05 (McKinney 1975) (omits volitional test); Ohio—State v. Staten, 25 Ohio St.2d 107, 267 N.E.2d 122 (1971) (omits "substantial" and uses "know" rather than "appreciate"); Texas—Tex.Penal Code Ann. § 8.01 (Vernon 1974) ("know" rather than "appreciate").

7. United States v. Freeman, 357 F.2d 606 (2d Cir.1966); United States v. Currens, 290 F.2d 751 (3d Cir.1961); United States v. Chandler, 393 F.2d 920 (4th Cir.1968); Blake v. United States, 407 F.2d 908 (5th Cir.1969); United States v. Smith, 404 F.2d 720 (6th Cir. 1968); United States v. Shapiro, 383 F.2d 680 (7th Cir.1967); United States v. Frazier, 458 F.2d 911 (8th Cir.1972); Wade v. United States, 426 F.2d 64 (9th Cir.1970); Wion v. United States, 325 F.2d 420 (10th Cir.1963); United States v. Brawner, 153 U.S.App.D.C. 1, 471 F.2d 969 (1972).

The First Circuit court has not had recent occasion to address this issue. See Amador Beltran v. United States, 302 F.2d 48 (1st Cir. 1962). The *Currens* test is singularly distinctive because of its exclusive focus upon volitional impairments. See United States v. Currens, supra at 774.

lawyers, the medical-trained experts, and the jury. See United States v. Brawner, 471 F.2d at 983.

3. *An Alternative Formulation of the Model Penal Code Test.* State v. Johnson, 121 R.I. 254, 267–269, 399 A.2d 469, 476–477 (1979):

* * * Because of our overriding concern that the jury's function remain inviolate, we today adopt the following formulation of the Model Penal Code test:

> A person is not responsible for criminal conduct if at the time of such conduct, as a result of mental disease or defect, his capacity either to appreciate the wrongfulness of his conduct or to conform his conduct to the requirements of law is so substantially impaired that he cannot justly be held responsible.
>
> The terms "mental disease or defect" do not include an abnormality manifested only by repeated criminal or otherwise antisocial conduct.[8]

There are several important reasons why we prefer this formulation. The greatest strength of our test is that it clearly delegates the issue of criminal responsibility to the jury, thus precluding possible usurpation of the ultimate decision by the expert witnesses. Under the test we have adopted, the jury's attention is appropriately focused upon the legal and moral aspects of responsibility because it must evaluate the defendant's blameworthiness in light of prevailing community standards. Far from setting the jury at large, as in the majority Model Penal Code test the defendant must demonstrate a certain form of incapacity. That is, the jury must find that a mental disease or defect caused a substantial impairment of the defendant's capacity to appreciate the wrongfulness of his act or to conform his conduct to legal requirements. Our new test emphasizes that the degree of "substantial" impairment required is essentially a legal rather than a medical question. Where formerly under *M'Naghten* total incapacity was necessary for exculpation, the new standard allows the jury to find that incapacity less than total is sufficient. Because impairment is a matter of degree, the precise degree demanded is necessarily governed by the community sense of justice as represented by the trier of fact.

* * *

The drafters of the Model Penal Code left to each jurisdiction a choice between the terms "wrongfulness" and "criminality." We prefer the word "wrongfulness" because we believe that a person who, knowing an act to be criminal, committed it because of a delusion that the act was morally

8. This test was proposed as an alternative by the minority of the American Law Institute Council that drafted the Model Penal Code. One of its most forceful advocates was Professor Herbert Wechsler, the reporter for the Model Penal Code. See Wechsler, *The Criteria of Criminal Responsibility,* 22 U.Chi.L.Rev. 367, 372 (1955). The test is substantially similar to the tests proposed by the British Royal Commission on Capital Punishment in 1953, see United States v. Brawner, 153 U.S. App.D.C. at 18 n. 23, 471 F.2d at 986 n. 23 and by Chief Judge Bazelon in 1972, see id., 153 U.S.App.D.C. at 62–66, 471 F.2d at 1030–34 (Bazelon, C.J., concurring & dissenting). The majority of the A.L.I. Council rejected this alternative because they deemed it unwise to present questions of justice to the jury. As this opinion indicates, we believe that the jury's resolution of the responsibility issue is in the final analysis always predicated upon the community sense of justice and it is preferable to be forthright about the basis of that decision.

justified, should not be automatically foreclosed from raising the defense of lack of criminal responsibility.[9]

United States v. Brawner, 471 F.2d 969, 986, 987, 988–989 (D.C.Cir.1979):

> We have also pondered the suggestion that the jury be instructed that the defendant lacks criminal responsibility if the jury finds that the defendant's mental disease impairs his capacity or controls to such an extent that he cannot "justly be held responsible."
>
> * * *
>
> The proposal is not to be condemned out of hand as a suggestion that the jury be informed of an absolute prerogative that it can only exercise by flatly disregarding the applicable rule of law. It is rather a suggestion that the jury be informed of the matters the law contemplates it will take into account in arriving at the community judgment concerning a composite of factors. However, there is a substantial concern that an instruction overtly cast in terms of "justice" cannot feasibly be restricted to the ambit of what may properly be taken into account but will splash with unconfinable and malign consequences. * * *
>
> * * *
>
> We are impressed by the observation of Professor Abraham S. Goldstein, one of the most careful students of the problem:
>
>> [The] overly general standard may place too great a burden upon the jury. If the law provides no standard, members of the jury are placed in the difficult position of having to find a man responsible for no other reason than their personal feeling about him. Whether the psyches of individual jurors are strong enough to make that decision, or whether the "law" should put that obligation on them, is open to serious question. It is far easier for them to perform the role assigned to them by legislature and courts if they know—or are able to rationalize—that their verdicts are "required" by law.[28]
>
> Professor Goldstein was referring to the broad "justice" standard recommended by the Royal Commission. But the problems remain acute even with the modifications in the proposal of the ALI Reporter, for that still leads to "justly responsible" as the ultimate and critical term.
>
> * * *
>
> It is the sense of justice propounded by those charged with making and declaring the law—legislatures and courts—that lays down the rule that persons without substantial capacity to know or control the act shall be excused. The jury is concerned with applying the community understanding of this broad rule to particular lay and medical facts. Where the matter is unclear it naturally will call on its own sense of justice to help it determine the matter. There is wisdom in the view that a jury generally understands well enough that an instruction composed in flexible terms gives it sufficient latitude so that, without disregarding the instruction, it can provide that

9. Seventeen states have elected the term "wrongfulness": Alaska, Connecticut, Delaware, Hawaii, Idaho, Indiana, Maine, Michigan, Missouri, New York, Ohio, Tennessee, Texas, Utah, Wyoming, West Virginia, and Wisconsin. For citations see note 6 supra. The D.C., 2d, 5th, 6th, 7th, 8th and 9th Circuit Courts of Appeals have held likewise. For citations see note 7 supra.

28. A. Goldstein, The Insanity Defense 81–82 (1967).

application of the instruction which harmonizes with its sense of justice. The ALI rule generally communicates that meaning. This is recognized even by those who might prefer a more explicit statement of the matter. It is one thing, however, to tolerate and even welcome the jury's sense of equity as a force that affects its application of instructions which state the legal rules that crystallize the requirements of justice as determined by the lawmakers of the community. It is quite another to set the jury at large, without such crystallization, to evolve its own legal rules and standards of justice. It would likely be counter-productive and contrary to the larger interest of justice to become so explicit—in an effort to hammer the point home to the very occasional jury that would otherwise be too rigid—that one puts serious strains on the normal operation of the system of criminal justice.

Notes on the Sociopath

1. Model Penal Code § 4.01, Comment 6 (Tent.Draft No. 4, 1955): *

> 6. Paragraph (2) of section 4.01 is designed to exclude from the concept of "mental disease or defect" the case of so-called "psychopathic personality." The reason for the exclusion is that, as the Royal Commission put it, psychopathy "is a statistical abnormality; that is to say, the psychopath differs from a normal person only quantitatively or in degree, not qualitatively; and the diagnosis of psychopathic personality does not carry with it any explanation of the causes of the abnormality." While it may not be feasible to formulate a definition of "disease", there is much to be said for excluding a condition that is manifested only by the behavior phenomena that must, by hypothesis, be the result of disease for irresponsibility to be established. Although British psychiatrists have agreed, on the whole, that psychopathy should not be called "disease", there is considerable difference of opinion on the point in the United States. Yet it does not seem useful to contemplate the litigation of what is essentially a matter of terminology; nor is it right to have the legal result rest upon the resolution of a dispute of this kind.

2. Wade v. United States, 426 F.2d 64, 72–73 (9th Cir.1970):

> While we approve paragraph (1) of the A.L.I. test, * * * we are unable to find comparable merit in paragraph (2). The drafters of the A.L.I. test apparently intended, in framing the second paragraph, to exclude certain "psychopathic personalities," from those who might otherwise be found to suffer from a "mental disease or defect." See Model Penal Code, Comments § 4.01, at 160 (Tent.Draft No. 4, 1955). Noted medical authorities have responded that the second paragraph fails to achieve its purpose and fails to establish any meaningful test. See, e.g., Diamond, *From M'Naghten to Currens, and Beyond,* 50 Calif.L.Rev. 189, 193–94 (1962) (A.L.I. purported definition of psychopathic personalities does not make sense and discriminates against economically poor defendants who are less likely to produce expert testimony disclosing manifestations of mental illness beyond "criminal or otherwise anti-social conduct"); Overholser, *Criminal Responsibility: A Psychiatrist's Viewpoint,* 48 A.B.A.J. 527, 529–30 (1962) (no such entity as a

mental "abnormality manifested only by repeated criminal or otherwise anti-social conduct"—psychopathic personalities have numerous additional symptoms). The Sixth Circuit, noting the "great dispute over the psychiatric soundness of section 4.01(2)," has expressly refused to adopt it. United States v. Smith, 404 F.2d [720,] 727 n. 8 [(1968)].

Even more important than the need to preserve the insanity defense for those who meet the test of paragraph (1) is society's need to be protected from potential recidivists. Persons who may be labeled by experts as "psychopathic" include those who are seriously ill and who are incapable of persistent, ordered living of any kind. Although these persons might be poor subjects for successful medical treatment, they should not be sent to prison for release, after some fixed period, as likely recidivists. The inclusion of § 4.01(2) in an insanity instruction should have little or no impact on the determination of the criminal responsibility of any mentally deranged defendant, whether psychopathic or not, since it is practically inconceivable that a mental disease or defect would, in the terms of paragraph (2), be "manifested *only* by repeated criminal or otherwise anti-social conduct." (Emphasis added.)

It would be reason enough for us to refuse to approve § 4.01(2) on the grounds that it fails to accomplish the only purpose, one of debatable value, for which it was intended, and that it would burden trial courts and juries with an extra instruction which should have little, if any, impact on any necessary factual determination. There is, however, additional cause for our concern. This is the paragraph's ambiguity. It is unclear whether § 4.01(2) would require that a defendant be considered legally sane if, although the only overt acts manifesting his disease or defect were "criminal or otherwise anti-social," there arises from his acts a reasonable inference of mental derangement either because of the nature of the acts or because of credible medical or other evidence. Since § 4.01(2) is ambiguous to us, it is reasonable to believe that an instruction incorporating the section would be equally confusing and ambiguous to jurors. Therefore, as to § 4.01(2), we adopt the position of the Sixth Circuit.

3. State v. Johnson, 121 R.I. 254, 269, 399 A.2d 469, 477 (1979):

The second paragraph of our test is designed to exclude from the concept of "mental disease or defect" the so-called psychopathic or sociopathic personality. See Model Penal Code, § 4.01, Comment at 160 (Tent. Draft No. 4, 1955). We have included this language in our test to make clear that mere recidivism alone does not justify acquittal. See United States v. Freeman, 357 F.2d at 625; Bethea v. United States, 365 A.2d at 80–81. We recognize that this paragraph has been the source of considerable controversy. See, e.g., Wade v. United States, 426 F.2d 64, 72–73 (9th Cir. 1970); United States v. Smith, 404 F.2d at 727 n. 8; Diamond, *From M'Naghten to Currens, and Beyond,* 50 Calif.L.Rev. 189, 194 (1962). Nevertheless, we believe that its inclusion in our test is necessary to minimize the likelihood of the improper exculpation of defendants who are free of mental disease but who knowingly and deliberately pursue a life of crime.[10]

10. Seventeen states have included this exclusionary paragraph as part of their standard: Alaska, Arkansas, Connecticut, Hawaii, Illinois, Indiana, Maine, Maryland, Missouri, Montana, Oregon, Tennessee, Texas, Utah, Vermont, Wisconsin, and Wyoming. For citations see note 6 supra. The federal courts of appeals are nearly evenly divided on the issue.

Notes on the Federal Test

1. GEE, J., for the Court, in United States v. Lyons, 731 F.2d 243, 247–249 (5th Cir.1984):

> Because the concept of criminal responsibility in the federal courts is a congeries of judicially-made rules of decision based on common law concepts, it is usually appropriate for us to reexamine and reappraise these rules in the light of new policy considerations. Wion v. United States, 325 F.2d 420, 425 (10th Cir.1963). We last examined the insanity defense in Blake v. United States, 407 F.2d 908 (5th Cir.1969) (en banc), where we adopted the ALI Model Penal Code definition of insanity: that a person is not responsible for criminal conduct if, at the time of such conduct and as a result of mental disease or defect, he lacks substantial capacity either to appreciate the wrongfulness of his conduct or to conform his conduct to the requirements of the law. * * *
>
> Reexamining the *Blake* standard today, we conclude that the volitional prong of the insanity defense—a lack of capacity to conform one's conduct to the requirements of the law—does not comport with current medical and scientific knowledge, which has retreated from its earlier, sanguine expectations. Consequently, we now hold that a person is not responsible for criminal conduct on the grounds of insanity only if at the time of that conduct, as a result of a mental disease or defect, he is unable to appreciate the wrongfulness of that conduct.[9]
>
> We do so for several reasons. First, as we have mentioned, a majority of psychiatrists now believe that they do not possess sufficient accurate scientific bases for measuring a person's capacity for self-control or for calibrating the impairment of that capacity. Bonnie, *The Moral Basis of the Insanity Defense,* 69 ABA J. 194, 196 (1983).[10] "The line between an irresistible impulse and an impulse not resisted is probably no sharper than between twilight and dusk." *American Psychiatric Association Statement on the Insanity Defense,* 11 (1982) [APA Statement]. Indeed, Professor Bonnie states:

9. We employ the phrase "is unable" in preference to our earlier formulation "lacks substantial capacity" for reasons well stated in the Commentary of the American Bar Association Standing Committee:

> Finally, it should be pointed out that the standard employs the term "unable" in lieu of the "substantial capacity" language of the ALI test. This approach has been taken both to simplify the formulation and to reduce the risk that juries will interpret the test too loosely. By using the "substantial capacity" language, the drafters of the ALI standard were trying to avoid the rigidity implicit in the M'Naughten formulation. They correctly recognize that it is rarely possible to say that a mentally disordered person was totally unable to "know" what he was doing or to "know" that it was wrong; even a psychotic person typically retains some grasp of reality. However, the phrase "substantial capacity" is not essential to take into account these clinical realities. Sufficient flexibility is provided by the term "appreciate."

Commentary (revised November, 1983) to Standards 7–6.1(a) and 7–6.9(b), ABA Standing Committee on Association Standards for Criminal Justice (to be published).

10. See also H. Fingarette, *The Meaning of Insanity* 166 (1972); Wootton, *Book Review,* 77 Yale L.J. 1019, 1026–27 (1968); Statement of David Robinson, Jr., *The Insanity Defense,* Hearings Before the Senate Comm. on the Judiciary, 97th Cong., 2d Sess. 72–73 (1982); Testimony of Stephen Morse, *Insanity Defense in Federal Courts,* Hearings Before the Subcomm. on Criminal Justice of the House Comm. on the Judiciary, 97th Cong., 2d Sess. 211 (1982).

> There is, in short, no objective basis for distinguishing between offenders who were undeterrable and those who were merely undeterred, between the impulse that was irresistible and the impulse not resisted, or between substantial impairment of capacity and some lesser impairment.

Bonnie, supra, at 196.[11]

In addition, the risks of fabrication and "moral mistakes" in administering the insanity defense are greatest "when the experts and the jury are asked to speculate whether the defendant had the capacity to 'control' himself or whether he could have 'resisted' the criminal impulse." Bonnie, supra, at 196. Moreover, psychiatric testimony about volition is more likely to produce confusion for jurors than is psychiatric testimony concerning a defendant's appreciation of the wrongfulness of his act. APA Statement at 12. It appears, moreover, that there is considerable overlap between a psychotic person's inability to understand and his ability to control his behavior. Most psychotic persons who fail a volitional test would also fail a cognitive test, thus rendering the volitional test superfluous for them. Id.[12] Finally, Supreme Court authority requires that such proof be made by the federal prosecutor beyond a reasonable doubt, an all but impossible task in view of the present murky state of medical knowledge. Davis v. United States, 160 U.S. 469, 16 S.Ct. 353, 40 L.Ed. 499 (1895).[13]

One need not disbelieve in the existence of Angels in order to conclude that the present state of our knowledge regarding them is not such as to support confident conclusions about how many can dance on the head of a pin.[14] In like vein, it may be that some day tools will be discovered with which reliable conclusions about human volition can be fashioned. It appears to be all but a certainty, however, that despite earlier hopes they do not lie in our hands today. When and if they do, it will be time to consider again to what degree the law should adopt the sort of conclusions that they produce. But until then, we see no prudent course for the law to follow but to treat all criminal impulses—including those not resisted—as resistible. To

11. One commentator has noted that no one has ever observed the process of a person losing the capacity for self-control, and "that no one can." Fingarette, supra, at 160.

12. See also Statement of Stephen Morse, *Insanity Defense in Federal Courts,* Hearings Before the Subcomm. on Criminal Justice of the House Comm. on the Judiciary, 97th Cong., 2d Sess. 231 (1982).

13. John Hinckley is the young man who "attempted to assassinate President Reagan in order to attract attention to himself and to impress a movie actress whom he admired from a distance. The subsequent proceedings called into question not only the insanity defense but the rationality of our adversarial jury-trial system. After more than a year of expensive pretrial maneuvering and psychiatric examinations, the lawyers jousted for eight weeks of trial, examining and cross-examining expert witnesses who naturally gave conflicting and confusing testimony on whether Hinckley's obviously warped mentality amounted to legal insanity. The judge instructed the jury to return a verdict of not guilty unless they could agree 'beyond a reasonable doubt' that Hinckley was sane. If taken literally, the instruction amounted to a directed verdict of not guilty, considering the deadlock of expert opinion and the difficulty of certifying the sanity of a young man who shot the President to impress a movie star. Juries usually ignore such unpopular legal standards, but the *Hinckley* jury surprised everybody by taking the law seriously and finding him not guilty. Hinckley will now be confined to a mental hospital indefinitely because he is 'dangerous,' although there is no reliable way to predict what he would do if released and no reliable test to determine if he has been 'cured.' "

Johnson, Book Review, 50 U.Chi.L.Rev. 1534, 1536 (1983) (reviewing N. Morris, Madness and the Criminal Law (1982)).

14. "What Song the Syrens sang, or what name Achilles assumed when he hid himself among women, though puzzling questions, are not beyond all conjecture." Sir Thomas Browne, URN BURIAL, v.

do otherwise in the present state of medical knowledge would be to cast the insanity defense adrift upon a sea of unfounded scientific speculation, with the palm awarded case by case to the most convincing advocate of that which is presently unknown—and may remain so, because unknowable.

2. ALVIN B. RUBIN, J., dissenting, in United States v. Lyons, 739 F.2d 994, 944–1000 (5th Cir.1984):

The insanity defense reflects the fundamental moral principles of our criminal law. An adjudication of guilt is more than a factual determination that the defendant pulled a trigger, took a bicycle, or sold heroin. It is a moral judgment that the individual is blameworthy. * * * Central, therefore, to a verdict of guilty is the concept of responsibility. Recognition of the insanity defense rests on the conclusion that "it is unjust to punish a person who because of mental illness is without understanding of the nature or quality of his conduct and lacks the capacity to conform his behavior."[4] An acquittal by reason of insanity is a judgment that the defendant is not *guilty* because, as a result of his mental condition, he is unable to make an effective choice regarding his behavior.

The majority does not controvert these fundamental principles; indeed it accepts them as the basis for the defense when the accused suffers from a disease that impairs cognition. It rests its decision to redefine insanity and to narrow the defense on "new policy considerations." The opinion does not fully articulate these considerations, but I discuss what appear to be the principal ones.

The first is the potential threat to society created by the volitional prong of the insanity defense. Public opposition to any insanity-grounded defense is often based, either explicitly or implicitly, on the view that the plea is frequently invoked by violent criminals who fraudulently use it to evade just punishment. Some critics perceive the insanity defense as an opportunity for criminals to use psychiatric testimony to mislead juries. This perception depicts an insanity trial as a "circus" of conflicting expert testimony that confuses a naive and sympathetic jury. And it fears insanity acquittees as offenders who, after manipulating the criminal justice system, are soon set free to prey once again on the community.

Despite the prodigious volume of writing devoted to the plea, the empirical data that are available provide little or no support for these fearsome perceptions and in many respects directly refute them. Both the frequency and the success rate of insanity pleas are grossly overestimated by professionals and lay persons alike; the plea is rarely made, and even more rarely successful.[8] The number of insanity pleas based on control defects, as

4. D. Hermann, *The Insanity Defense: Philosophical, Historical, and Legal Perspectives* 128–52 (1983) (hereinafter D. Hermann, *The Insanity Defense*). See G. Morris, *Acquittal By Reason of Insanity, in Mentally Disordered Offenders* 65 (J. Monahan and H. Steadman, eds. 1983) [hereinafter, G. Morris, *Acquittal*].

* * *

8. For example, one extensive study examined the opinions held by college students, the general public, state legislators, law enforcement officers, and mental health personnel in Wyoming. Estimates of the frequency with which criminal defendants entered the plea ranged from 13% to 57%. During the time period considered, however, the actual frequency was only 0.47%: one case in 200. Similarly, although estimates of its success rate varied from 19% to 44%, during the relevant period only one of the 102 defendants who entered the plea was acquitted by reason of insanity. Pasewark, *Research Literature, supra* note 10, at 360–61. See also National

compared to those based on lack of cognition, must have been almost negligible.

The perception that the defendant who successfully pleads insanity is quickly released from custody is also based only on assumption. Although an acquittal by reason of insanity ends the criminal jurisdiction of federal courts (except in the District of Columbia), and of the courts of a few states, the acquittee is not simply set free. "The truth is that in almost every case, the acquittee is immediately hospitalized and evaluated for dangerousness. Usually, the acquittee remains hospitalized for an extended time." [9]

In sum, the available evidence belies many of the assumptions upon which much popular criticism of the insanity defense are based. The plea is rarely invoked, usually fails, and, when it is successful, the acquittees rarely go free.

Another set of objections to the plea is based on the thesis that factfinders—especially juries—are confused and manipulated by the vagueness of the legal standards of insanity and the notorious "battle of the experts" who present conclusory, superficial, and misleading testimony. These conditions, the argument runs, conspire to produce inconsistent and "inaccurate" verdicts.

Let us first put these objections in perspective. Most cases involving an insanity plea do not go to trial; instead, like most other criminal cases, they are settled by a plea bargain. In many of the cases that do go to trial, psychiatric testimony is presented by deposition, without disagreement among experts, and without opposition by the prosecution. And in the few cases in which a contest does develop, the defendant is usually convicted. Hence the stereotypic "circus tent" may be raised in only a handful of cases.

Commission, Myths & Realities, supra, note 6, at 14–15; A. Goldstein, *The Insanity Defense* 23–24 (1967).

One compendious British study, encompassing selected periods from 1740 to 1930, found the frequency of the plea to range between .29% to 1.30% with a success rate varying between 28.5% and 69.6%. 1 N. Walker, *Crime and Insanity in England* 67 (1968); 2 N. Walker and S. McCabe, Crime and Insanity in England (1973) (*Cited in* Pasewark, *Research Literature* at 361–62).

A somewhat dated survey of major metropolitan areas in the United States reported similar conclusions, finding that insanity pleas were rarely entered. [(]The highest figures were obtained in California and the District of Columbia, where the data showed the plea was invoked in 1.3% and 5.1% of all felony dispositions respectively). A. Matthews, *Mental Disability and the Law* 26–30 (1970). See also National Commission, Myths & Realities at 15 (1983).

One source estimates fewer than 100 successful insanity pleas out of 50,000 federal criminal cases brought annually. Dershowitz, *Abolishing the Insanity Defense: The Most Significant Feature of the Administration's Proposed Criminal Code—An Essay,* 9 Crim.L. Bull. 434, 436 (1973).

9. Rappeport, The Insanity Plea Scapegoating the Mentally Ill—Much Ado About Nothing?, 24 So.Tex.L.J. 687, 698 (1983). See also, National Commission, *Myths & Realities,* supra note 6 at 25 ("The Commission found that virtually all insanity acquittees spend significant time in hospitals."). See A. Goldstein, *The Insanity Defense,* 143–44 (1967). See generally, Note, *Commitment Following an Insanity Acquittal,* 94 Harv.L.Rev. 605, 605–06 & nn. 2–6 (1981) (collecting statutes); A. Brooks, *Law, Psychiatry and the Mental Health System* (1974). Other studies support this finding. Steadman and Braff found that "fully 40%" of those persons acquitted by reason of insanity in New York between 1965 and 1976 were still hospitalized in 1978. For the 1976–1978 group, almost 90% were still hospitalized at the end of the follow-up period. Steadman & Braff, *Defendants Not Guilty By Reason of Insanity, in Mentally Disordered Offenders* 109, 111, 118–19 (J. Monahan & H. Steadman eds. 1983). These investigators' results were similar to those of New Jersey and Ontario studies. Id. at 116.

The manipulated-jury argument is supported largely by declamation, not data. Although there is some evidence to support the assertion that the wording of the insanity defense has little impact on trial outcomes, one major study of jury reactions to criminal cases involving the insanity defense reached conclusions contrary to the assumption that the jury function is usurped by expert testimony. That study found that jurors responsibly and carefully consider the evidence presented, do recognize that the final responsibility for the defendant's fate rests with them, do appreciate the limits and proper use of expert testimony, and do grasp the instructions given them.[13] Although the evidence does not warrant the conclusion that juries function better in insanity trials than in other criminal cases, it certainly does not appear that they function *less* effectively. And no source has been cited to the court to support the conclusion that, as an empirical matter, pleas based upon the volitional prong present an especially problematic task for the jury.

Indeed, the majority opinion does not assert that the insanity defense, particularly the control test, *doesn't* work; it contends that the defense *can't* work. The principal basis for this contention is the belief, held by "a majority of psychiatrists," that they lack "sufficient accurate scientific bases for measuring a person's capacity for self-control or for calibrating the impairment of that capacity." This argument raises practical and important questions regarding the usefulness of expert testimony in determining whether a person has the ability to conform his conduct to law; but the absence of useful expert evidence, if indeed there is none, does not obviate the need for resolving the question whether the defendant ought to be held accountable for his criminal behavior.

Accountability for criminal conduct involves more than mere *actus reus;* it also involves the mental state with which the act is performed. Factfinders are required by law to determine the existence or non-existence of many mental states, for example, whether the defendant was mistaken; acted from necessity, duress, or coercion; acted without willfulness or knowledge or intention; or was unable to appreciate the wrongfulness of his conduct.

Our concept of responsibility in this sense is not limited to observable behavior: it embraces *meaningful* choice, and necessarily requires inferences and assumptions regarding the defendant's unobservable mental state. The accompanying external circumstances in cases such as coercion are of course observable; but their effect on the defendant's mental state is inferred, and no more tangible than the mental processes of a defendant pleading the control test. The difference between the concepts of excusing circumstances such as coercion and the insanity defense is that the former is based on objective assumptions about human behavior and is tested against hypothetical-objective standards such as "the reasonable person." "The insanity defense [on the other hand] marks the transition from the adequate man the law demands to the inadequate man he may be." [17]

13. R. Simon, *The Jury and the Defense of Insanity* 89, 175–77 (1967). Rita Simon's study re-enacted actual criminal cases before subject juries drawn from local jury pools. Another study, however, found poor comprehension rates among most juries exposed to various instructions on the insanity defense. Arens, Granfield, & Susman, *Jurors, Jury Charges and Insanity,* 14 Catholic L.Rev. 1 (1965). The significance of Arens's study is drawn into question by the authors' failure to compare juror comprehension of instructions in non-insanity cases.

17. A. Goldstein, *The Insanity Defense* 18 (1967).

The relevant inquiry under either branch of the insanity test is a subjective one that focuses on the defendant's actual state of mind. Our duty to undertake that inquiry is not based on confidence in the testimony of expert witnesses, but on the ethical precept that the defendant's mental state is a crucial aspect of his blameworthiness.[18] The competence of psychiatrists or other experts thus is not the issue. The issue is whether a defendant should be held accountable for his conduct. The availability of expert testimony and the probative value of such testimony are basically evidentiary problems that can be accommodated within the existing test.

A recent Second Circuit case demonstrates that the volitional test can be reasonably cabined to prevent abuse. In United States v. Torniero,[19] the court affirmed the trial court's refusal to allow the defendant to present evidence that his compulsive gambling disorder rendered him unable to refrain from interstate transportation of stolen jewelry. The Second Circuit established two guidelines: (1) a defendant seeking to rely on a newly recognized disorder to meet the volitional test must show "that respected authorities in the field share the view that the disorder is a disease or defect that could have impaired the defendant's ability to desist from the offense charged * * *"; and (2) the alleged disease or defect must be relevant to the crime charged. The first issue was sharply disputed at a pretrial hearing, and the trial court found in favor of the government. The circuit court upheld that finding and went on to conclude that "a compulsion to gamble, even if a mental disease or defect, is not, *ipso facto,* relevant to the issue whether the defendant was unable to restrain himself from non-gambling offenses such as transporting stolen property." [20]

Even the few cases in which the trial develops into a battle of experts provide no basis for the majority's conclusion that the prosecution faces an "all but impossible task." The prosecution appears to be able to locate experts as readily as the defense. Indeed, a defendant pleading insanity typically faces both a judge and a jury who are skeptical about psychiatry in general and the insanity plea in particular. * * *

18. Some writers further object that psychiatry, based as it is on a deterministic view of human behavior, can never profitably be reconciled with the law's premise of free will, and thus reliance on such testimony threatens to erode individual responsibility. See e.g., Statement of David Robinson, Jr., Senate Hearings, *supra* note 10, at 73. This objection is misdirected. Although the social-scientific viewpoint is undeniably deterministic, the insanity defense actually contributes to the moral authority that criminal law derives from its free-will basis. As Professor Alan Stone observed,

> [W]hat is a court to do when it confronts a case so bizarre and so incongruous that all the premises of criminal law, including free will, seem inappropriate? Should the court simply grit its teeth and go on? The court is then in that ludicruous position of the American tourist who assumes that if he speaks English loud enough, the foreigners will understand him. If so, the criminal law risks demeaning itself, risks demonstrating that its language is not universal, its moral comprehension not encompassing. How much wiser for the criminal law instead to have an escape hatch, not only to avoid embarrassment, but also because by obverse implication every other defendant does have free will. Thus, the insanity defense is in every sense the exception that proves the rule. It allows the court to treat every other defendant as someone who chose "between good and evil."

A. Stone, *Mental Health and Law: A System in Transition* 222 (1975). See also A. Goldstein, *The Insanity Defense* 224 (1967); Hermann, *Assault on the Insanity Defense: Limitations on the Effectiveness and Effect of the Insanity Defense,* 14 Rutgers L.J. 241, 252 (1983).

19. 735 F.2d 725, 730–31 (2d Cir.1984).

20. Id. at 731–32.

The majority's fear that the present test invites "moral mistakes" is difficult to understand. The majority opinion concedes that some individuals cannot conform their conduct to the law's requirements. Other writers have concluded that a strictly cognitive insanity test will overlook some individuals who would be covered by a control test. Without citing any data that verdicts in insanity cases decided under a control test are frequently inaccurate, the majority embraces a rule certain to result in the conviction of at least some who are not morally responsible and the punishment of those for whom retributive, deterrent, and rehabilitative penal goals are inappropriate. A decision that virtually ensures undeserved, and therefore unjust, punishment in the name of avoiding moral mistakes rests on a peculiar notion of morality.

I do not speak in this dissent to the merits of a new system for determining criminal responsibility that would not merely redefine the insanity plea but would reform the entire trial process and the treatment of those who are not absolved. Such a system would eliminate the concept of guilty mind or criminal intent as an element of most offenses; and it would consider such matters, including insanity, at a dispositional proceeding separate from a determination whether the defendant committed the act.[23] Unlike the majority, those who propose such reform thus make provision to take account for the mentally ill offender's condition at some point in the process. This view requires a revision of our criminal justice system from a punitive to a preventive basis, not merely a change in the definition of insanity; for it rejects the concept of such a defense. I do not address the question whether such a system would be better or worse. Adoption of the view would require legislative changes in our trial system and changes in our institutional treatment of at least some convicted persons.

This dissent is directed only at the amputation of one part of a comprehensive definition. That definition is itself an integral part of a social mechanism that begins with a prosecutorial decision about whether a particular defendant should even be charged and ends with three possible results: not guilty and free, guilty and sentenced, not guilty by reason of insanity and committed.

* * *

Judges are not, and should not be, immune to popular outrage over this nation's crime rate. Like everyone else, judges watch television, read newspapers and magazines, listen to gossip, and are sometimes themselves victims. They receive the message trenchantly described in a recent book criticizing the insanity defense: "Perhaps the bottom line of all these complaints is that *guilty people go free*—guilty people who do not have to accept judgment or responsibility for what they have done and are not held accountable for their actions. * * * These are not cases in which the defendant is *alleged* to have committed a crime. *Everyone knows he did it."* Although understandable as an expression of uninformed popular opinion, such a viewpoint ought not to serve as the basis for judicial decisionmaking; for it misapprehends the very meaning of guilt.

23. See B. Wooton, *Crime and the Criminal Law* 52–53 (1963); Wooton, *Book Review,* 77 Yale L.J. 1019, 1029–32 (1968) (applying her views specifically to the insanity defense while reviewing A. Goldstein, *The Insanity Defense*). See also Hermann, Book Review, 44 Ohio State L.J. 987, 996 (1983) (criticizing Wooton's position).

* * *

The majority opinion is a radical departure from the established jurisprudence of every federal circuit that has spoken on the issue. * * * Its effect will be felt by only two small groups: a few who otherwise might have made a case for the jury but who will be deprived of a plea that in any event would likely have been bootless, and those few unfortunate persons so afflicted by mental disease that they knew what the law forbade but couldn't control their actions sufficiently to avoid violating it. The nature of their illness makes punishment useless as a means to compel them to behave lawfully; only remission of the disease will permit change. By convicting them we will not deter others who suffer the same mental defect; they too, again by definition, have no ability to obey.

Questions

1. How far is the mutual discomfort of the criminal lawyer and the psychiatrist based on the free will assumptions of the criminal law and the deterministic assumptions of the psychiatrist? In this respect see footnote 4 in the Court's opinion in United States v. Lyons, 731 F.2d 243, 246 (5th Cir.1984):

> Speaking of the recent American Psychiatric Association Statement on the Insanity Defense, Professor Phillip E. Johnson notes:
>
> > The APA has not adopted the extreme views of Thomas Szasz, but it has definitely repudiated the ideology of Karl Menninger. The psychiatrists no longer want the criminal law to change to conform to deterministic psychiatric concepts; instead, they regard it as vital to the integrity of their own discipline that "legal or moral constructs such as free will" be understood as outside the domain of psychiatry. They emphatically affirm that most people, including those with sociopathic personality disorders, should be held accountable for what they do. They are not washing their hands of the legal problems, and they believe that the law still needs them, but they understand that legal and moral decisions are ultimately to be made by citizens, not experts. I regard this newly found modesty as evidence of the profession's increasing maturity, not as a sign of its failure.
>
> Johnson, Book Review, 50 U.Chi.L.Rev. 1534, 1548 (1983) (reviewing N. Morris, Madness and the Criminal Law (1982)).

2. How far is it relevant to the proper formulation of an insanity test that jails are easier to provide and staff than mental hospitals, and that we have no practical method in sight for dealing with a substantial increase in the "not guilty by reason of insanity" population?

3. Why is there so much opposition to excusing the insane from criminal liability, when, on the face of it, it seems barbarous to punish and brand as criminals those who are incapable, on account of mental condition, of responding to the commands of the law? Is such opposition based on the view that such people do not really exist or cannot be accurately identified?

Miller v. State

Supreme Court of South Dakota, 1983.
338 N.W.2d 673.

MORGAN, JUSTICE.

This appeal arises from a trial court's order denying appellant John Miller (Miller) post-conviction relief from a conviction for escape from the South Dakota State Penitentiary (penitentiary). Miller appeals and we affirm.

On November 13, 1979, while serving the fourth year of a twenty-five year sentence in the penitentiary, Miller escaped from the penitentiary's "west farm" near Ellis, South Dakota. Approximately four days later, Miller was arrested in Dodgeville, Wisconsin. He was subsequently convicted by a jury of escape and sentenced to two and one-half years in the penitentiary. This court affirmed that conviction in State v. Miller, 313 N.W.2d 460 (S.D.1981).[a]

Miller now brings this post-conviction proceeding under the provisions of SDCL ch. 23A–34. The trial court denied Miller's request for post-conviction relief and Miller appeals. * * *

* * *

We now turn to Miller's third contention which is that the trial court's failure to properly instruct the jury on Miller's mental illness defense denied Miller his right to a fair and impartial jury trial and to due process of law.

* * * A trial court is required to instruct on the law only when there exists evidence on the record upon which such instruction can be based. Miller *now* asserts that the heart of his defense was mental illness. As a veteran of Vietnam, Miller claims the stressful circumstances at the penitentiary caused his mind to snap and he began to hallucinate about Vietnam. Miller claims he "woke up" from the hallucinations when he was arrested in Dodgeville, Wisconsin.

According to the record, however, the heart of Miller's theory of defense was not insanity. As Pokela [Miller's trial attorney] testified at the post-conviction hearing, after receiving the psychiatric report he and Miller discussed the theory of defense and decided to drop insanity as a defense. Additionally, the record overwhelmingly indicates that Miller and Pokela pursued a theory of not guilty by reason of justification. * * *

Clearly, the record shows that Pokela and Miller decided to abandon the theory of insanity. * * *

* * *

Miller's primary claim here is that his co-counsel's failure to pursue the mental illness defense based upon "Vietnam Stress Syndrome" constitutes ineffective assistance of counsel. In support of this contention, Miller cites United States v. Baynes, 687 F.2d 659 (3rd Cir.1982), which discusses a defense attorney's duty to investigate possible defense. In *Baynes,* the court held that "a defense attorney, whether appointed or retained, is obligated to inquire thoroughly into all potentially exculpatory defenses and evidence." Id. at 668. * * *

a. Summarized supra, p. 511.

The record before us demonstrates that Pokela did not pursue the mental illness defense based upon the "Vietnam Stress Syndrome." He read the psychiatrist's report but did not seek another opinion; nor did he attempt to procure Miller's V.A. records. As Pokela testified, after the trial was in progress and Miller had testified, he had second thoughts about the mental illness defense.[6] At that time, however, it was too late since Miller and Pokela had already chosen their trial tactics.

Miller relies upon *Baynes,* supra, a recent Third Circuit Court of Appeals case. In *Baynes,* the Third Circuit Court points out that ordinarily a lawyer is not required to anticipate changes in the law or pursue novel theories of defense. The "Vietnam Stress Syndrome" is a new theory of defense. Neither party cites to a case in which this theory was utilized. The only authority cited by Miller is a 23–page pamphlet published by Disabled American Veterans in 1980. Miller escaped from the penitentiary in 1979 and this trial was held in 1980. While mental illness is an established defense, clearly this "Vietnam Stress Syndrome" is a novel theory of defense—and especially so three years ago, in 1980.

On review, it is not this court's function to second-guess tactical decisions of defense counsel at trial; this court will not substitute its own theoretical judgment for that of counsel. * * *

Accordingly, we affirm.

FOSHEIM, C.J., and WOLLMAN and DUNN, JJ., concur.

HENDERSON, J., dissents.

HENDERSON, JUSTICE (dissenting).

* * *

During the trial, defendant produced testimony that he suffered from Vietnam flashback syndrome, also termed posttraumatic stress disorder, a recognized symptom of that war. Under oath, defendant testified he hallucinated and escaped from confinement believing he was running from the Viet Cong. The jury, of course, had a right to believe or disbelieve his story. * * *

During the trial, defendant testified that when he was walking towards the milk machine in the mess hall of the Penitentiary, the inmates were no longer Americans. "It was more of the Vietnamese type thing," he told the jury. He further testified: "[T]hey were all looking at me" and "You [referring to himself] are going to get killed here." Asked by his trial counsel, who had failed to propose a critical instruction on mental illness, "What did you see in your mind as you were leaving the room?", he replied "I was back in Vietnam." Concerning leaving the work farm (escaping), he was asked: "What were your intentions when you left the farm?" His answer: "Get back to the States." After leaving the farm, defendant testified that he went downtown: "[A]nd I went to the big Buddha shrine they have there [actually it was the Cathedral Church in Sioux Falls, South Dakota], and I stayed there for a period of days, and I came out occasionally and when I did, I was still

6. Pokela later testified that Miller's testimony on the stand differed from what they discussed before trial.

surrounded by Vietnamese so I was still scared." Defendant claims he blacked out for several days and told the jury: "The last thing I remember is crossing a rice patty field and was shot at by somebody, and the next thing I remember is talking to two police officers, one was named Curley, in Wisconsin." The State vigorously cross-examined defendant on this posttraumatic stress disorder or flashback syndrome.[4] The point is: this veteran's mental illness at the time of the commission of the alleged offense was deeply in issue. Evidence having been placed before the jury on defendant's alleged mental illness during the commission of the alleged crime, the trial court was required to instruct on the law concerning this defense.

* * * In South Dakota, mental illness of short duration, referred to in the law as temporary mental illness, is as fully recognized as a defense as is mental illness of longer duration. If, at the time of alleged escape, defendant was temporarily mentally ill, he must be found not guilty by reason of mental illness in South Dakota even if he was sane at earlier or later times or at any earlier or later period. State v. Graves, 83 S.D. 600, 163 N.W.2d 542 (1968); South Dakota Pattern Jury Instructions (Criminal) § 2–14–5b. Trial counsel failed to adequately and effectively represent defendant by neglecting to request such instructions. Although expert medical testimony is lacking in this case, defendant squarely put into issue his state of mind at the time of the alleged offense.[5] * * *

Defendant was entitled to adequate and effective assistance of counsel. State v. Pieschke, 262 N.W.2d 40 (S.D.1978). Counsel should have pursued, investigated, and made himself aware of the mental problems created in Vietnam War veterans. The right of an accused to the services of an attorney envisages that his attorney will investigate and consider possible defenses. Defense counsel's representation cannot be casual and perfunctory. State v. McBride, 296 N.W.2d 551 (S.D.1980). In my opinion, it was.

The psychiatric profession has a desk manual referred to as the diagnostic and statistic manual III. "The manual was first released in unfinished form in early 1980 and was recommended to the American Psychiatric Association for use in diagnosis and treatment in July, 1981. * * * the Veteran's

4. South Dakota is rich in public education, institutions of higher learning, and public libraries. Books on the Vietnam War, and the effects on our American troops are readily found in libraries throughout this state and appreciation of this veteran's claimed mental illness could be found in public libraries in South Dakota. Such books include, but are not limited to, the following: G.I. Guinea Pigs (How the Pentagon Exposed Our Troops to Dangers More Deadly Than War: Agent Orange and Atomic Radiation), distributed by Harper & Row, copyright 1980, by Michael Uhl and Tod Ensign; Spoils of War by Charles J. Levy, Houghton Mifflin Company, Boston, 1974, copyright 1971 by Transaction, Inc.; No Victory Parades (The Return of the Vietnam Veteran) by Murray Polner published by Holt Reinhart & Winston, copyright 1971 by Murray Polner; The Discarded Army (Veterans After Vietnam), by Paul Starr, published by Charter House, New York, copyright 1973, by Center for Study of Responsive Law. Any lawyer defending a case where a Vietnam War veteran is claiming mental illness because of flashback syndrome necessarily had to understand something about the mental disorders created by that War. A book is often the key which opens the golden door of knowledge but you have to first unlock the door. An attorney owes a duty to investigate and consider possible defenses. *State v. Walker,* 287 N.W.2d 705 (S.D.1980); *State v. Erickson,* 80 S.D. 639, 129 N.W.2d 712 (1964).

5. Defense counsel sought no psychiatric evaluations for his client and made no motions to the trial court to secure expert testimony on his client's behalf. Defendant strongly urged him to do so.

Administration did not recognize posttraumatic stress disorder as a treatable disease until October, 1980." State v. Serrato, 424 So.2d 214, 223 (La. 1982). For background information to shed understanding on posttraumatic stress disorder in Vietnam veterans, this author recommends a reading of State v. Felde, 422 So.2d 370 (La.1982). Suffice it to say, these veterans uniquely feel great remorse and guilt. Sixty percent of the Vietnam War combat veterans experience posttraumatic distress. "This is because units did not stay together, there was no real war objective, the soldiers were quite young, and drugs were freely available at a low price. Vietnam soldiers averaged 19.2 years, whereas those in World War II and Korea averaged 26½. The units in World War II stayed intact and came home together whereas in Vietnam each veteran came home alone. * * * Twenty-five percent of all men in prison are Vietnam era veterans." *Felde,* 422 So.2d at 377. In my opinion, this prison population percentage is a national disgrace.

The post-conviction hearing judge openly expressed that this case created interesting and intriguing questions of particular import, especially the defense of the Vietnam stress syndrome. The post-conviction judge put it this way:

> The second question that I think is intriguing has to do with the matter concerning the Vietnam stress syndrome. I do know that has been recognized by some states as a proper defense. However, our state has repeatedly said that the test for mental illness is a right from wrong test. We don't have the irresistable [sic] impulse test in this state and I think the second question that counsel ought to address themselves to has to do with whether the Vietnam stress syndrome, you know, can somehow be reconciled with our standard and I guess I have my doubts as to whether it can, because it has to do with his conscious level and being able to distinguish right from wrong. That's just what your standard is in South Dakota.

* * * I cannot countenance the courts of this state refusing to recognize the Vietnam stress syndrome as a mental illness, albeit temporarily. The books on the Vietnam War, the American Psychiatric Association, and the United States Veterans Administration recognize it as a form of mental illness. It appears that the reviewing judge's mind was closed to the very defense that permeated the trial.

* * *

The transcript of the criminal jury trial proceedings buttresses defendant's post-conviction testimony. It reveals that defendant expressly told the trial judge in chambers that he had not abandoned his mental illness defense. Mr. Pokela admitted, on the record, during a conference immediately subsequent to the jury receiving the case for deliberation, that his client had pointed out that he wanted a mental illness instruction. Mr. Pokela told the trial judge that he had pointed out the mental illness matter earlier to the trial judge in the morning and that it was "dropped at that point." * * *

Revealingly, the trial court denied a motion for mistrial which was made by defendant and not his attorney. In so ruling, about the dropped instruction on mental illness the trial judge expressed: "But, I believe that there was a mistake made. I don't believe that the mistake, however, is prejudicial to the substantial rights of the accused." Therein, I manifestly disagree with the trial court and the entire manner in which the defense counsel pursued the mental illness defense. The truth of this record is that it glaringly reveals that although mental illness was pleaded as a defense, and mental illness was testified to as a defense, the jury was never once told about his plea or instructed concerning the law of mental illness.

* * * This defendant's Constitutional rights were violated in that he obviously did not receive a fair and impartial jury trial and effective assistance of trial counsel. His mental illness defense went to the heart of his case and although the jury deliberated at length on his innocence or guilt, no jury instruction or jury verdict form related to the very central issue of the case. By the prosecutor, trial judge, and his own defense counsel, appellant was stripped of his Sixth Amendment constitutional rights.

* * *

Commonwealth v. Trill

Superior Court of Pennsylvania, 1988.
374 Pa.Super. 549, 543 A.2d 1106.

CIRILLO, PRESIDENT JUDGE.

* * *

The charges against Trill arose out of an incident that occurred at the Riddle Ale House, Middletown Township, Delaware County, on the evening of January 8, 1984. At approximately 7:30 p.m. Trill entered the restaurant and walked behind the bar counter. He then tapped the bartender, John Naughton, on the shoulder and requested a "take out" order of beer. Mr. Naughton informed Trill that Riddle Ale House did not provide take out service for its customers, and he further explained that restaurant policy prohibited patrons from being behind the bar counter. Consequently, Mr. Naughton asked Trill to return to the area in front of the bar. Trill ignored this request and opened his overcoat to display what appeared to be a rifle. He then stated: "[T]his is a sawed-off shotgun, open that [cash register] drawer and give me the money or I'll blow your f______ brains out." Mr. Naughton indicated that he could not open the cash register drawer without the manager's assistance. Thwarted in his attempt to obtain the cash from Naughton, Trill began to search the dining room area of the restaurant, hoping to locate the manager. While Trill was gone, Naughton found his manager in the back room of the building, and told him to summon the police.

Trill exited the building without obtaining any cash and was immediately observed by State Police Trooper Joseph Karlin, who had arrived at the scene in less than thirty seconds after receiving the call. Trill was standing in the restaurant parking lot, beside a station wagon. Upon noticing the arrival of the police, Mr. Naughton vaulted out into the parking lot and struck Trill, exclaiming "That's the guy!" The police officers apprehended and arrested Trill and confiscated a toy rifle that he had allegedly represented as authentic during the attempted robbery. * * *

A jury trial was held in the Court of Common Pleas of Delaware County before the HONORABLE ANTHONY R. SEMERARO. Although Trill interposed a defense of insanity, the jury found him guilty but mentally ill * * *. * * *

* * *

Trill next asserts that the evidence was insufficient as a matter of law to sustain the finding that he was not insane at the time of the commission of his charged crimes. * * *

* * * We have examined all of the evidence involving Trill's mental state in the light most favorable to the Commonwealth. Drawing all reasonable inferences from that evidence, we have concluded that it was sufficient as a matter of law to sustain the finding of sanity. While it is true that the psychiatric testimony concerning Trill's emotional status was conflicting, it was nonetheless within the jury's province to determine which account was more credible. * * *

* * *

Trill's final claim of error surrounding the jury charge involves the assertion that the instruction of guilty but mentally ill is not mandatory, and may be waived by the defendant. He avows that by providing the jurors with the option to choose the guilty but mentally ill verdict without his consent, the court has effectively undercut his ability to present a successful insanity defense.

A common-sense reading of the Pennsylvania statutory scheme belies this allegation. Section 314 provides that when a person offers a defense of insanity, *he may be found guilty but mentally ill* if the trier of fact finds beyond a reasonable doubt that the person is guilty of an offense, was mentally ill at the time of the commission of the offense, and was not legally insane at the time of the commission of the offense. 18 Pa.C.S. § 314(a) (emphasis added). From the plain language of the statute, it logically follows that the jury *must* be charged on the guilty but mentally ill verdict whenever the insanity defense is set forth. * * *

Trill's last issue controverts the viability of Pennsylvania's guilty but mentally ill statute, 18 Pa.C.S. § 314. Trill mounts an impelling challenge to the statutory scheme implemented by our legislature; however, we conclude that his laudable effort has fallen short of its goal. The overwhelming authority generated by our sister states, many of which have been grappling with this exact issue in their appellate courts for more than a decade, coupled with our own analysis, dissuades us from invalidating a statutory scheme which we conclusively deduce passes constitutional muster.

Section 314 of our Crimes Code provides as follows:

> (a) General rule.—A person who timely offers a defense of insanity in accordance with the Rules of Criminal Procedure may be found "guilty but mentally ill" at trial if the trier of facts finds, beyond a reasonable doubt, that the person is guilty of an offense, was mentally ill at the time of the commission of the offense and was not legally insane at the time of the commission of the offense.

(b) Plea of guilty but mentally ill.—A person who waives his right to trial may plead guilty but mentally ill. No plea of guilty but mentally ill may be accepted by the trial judge until he has examined all reports prepared pursuant to the Rules of Criminal Procedure, has held a hearing on the sole issue of the defendant's mental illness at which either party may present evidence and is satisfied that the defendant was mentally ill at the time of the offense to which the plea is entered. If the trial judge refuses to accept a plea of guilty but mentally ill, the defendant shall be permitted to withdraw his plea. A defendant whose plea is not accepted by the court shall be entitled to a jury trial, except that if a defendant subsequently waives his right to a jury trial, the judge who presided at the hearing on mental illness shall not preside at the trial.

(c) Definitions.—For the purposes of this section and 42 Pa.C.S. § 9727 (relating to disposition of persons found guilty but mentally ill):

(1) "Mentally ill." One who as a result of mental disease or defect, lacks substantial capacity either to appreciate the wrongfulness of his conduct or to conform his conduct to the requirements of the law.

(2) "Legal insanity." At the time of the commission of the act, the defendant was laboring under such a defect of reason, from disease of the mind, as not to know the nature and quality of the act he was doing or, if he did know it, that he did not know he was doing what was wrong.

(d) Common Law M'Naghten's Rule preserved.—Nothing in this section shall be deemed to repeal or otherwise abrogate the common law defense of insanity (M'Naghten's Rule) in effect in this Commonwealth on the effective date of this section.

18 Pa.C.S. § 314. * * *

* * *

Trill's objection to the constitutionality of section 314 presents an unprecedented legal argument in our Pennsylvania appellate courts. Since we have not previously adjudicated the issues that appellant espouses before us today, we consider it elucidating to undertake a cursory review of the growth and implementation of the guilty but mentally ill verdict and its intended purposes.

The guilty but mentally ill verdict was first interposed into American jurisprudence by the Michigan legislature in early 1975. *See* Mich.Comp. Laws Ann. §§ 768.36, 768.29, 330.2050(1) (West Supp.1986); *see also* Mickenberg, *A Pleasant Surprise: The Guilty But Mentally Ill Verdict Has Both Succeeded In Its Own Right and Successfully Preserved The Traditional Role Of The Insanity Defense,* 55 U.Cin.L.Rev. 943, 987 (1987). This legislation propagated as a result of public outcry over the Michigan Supreme Court's holding in People v. McQuillan, 392 Mich. 511, 221 N.W.2d 569 (1974). In *McQuillan* the court had struck down Michigan's automatic commitment statutes applicable to insanity acquittees in order to bring the proceeding within civil commitment standards. A concomitant result of this ruling was the release of numerous mentally ill patients from treatment facilities into the community. Several of these individuals subsequently perpetrated highly publicized, reprehensible crimes. Less than a year later, the Michigan lawmakers became pioneers in fashioning a statutory scheme designed to avert the scenario described above.

* * *

* * * It was not until the 1982 acquittal of John W. Hinckley, Jr. for the March 30, 1981 assassination attempt of President Ronald Reagan that state lawmakers began to rapidly adopt guilty but mentally ill statutes for their respective states. See United States v. Hinckley, 672 F.2d 115 (D.C. Cir.1982); see also Kennelly & Dull, *Guilty But Mentally Ill: A New Verdict for South Dakota,* 30 S.D.L.Rev. 515 (1985). Responding to the public disdain for the alleged inequity of permitting "responsible" defendants to escape punishment for their crimes, or treatment for their disease, states' assemblies hurried to enact provisions permitting the verdict of guilty but mentally ill. Through the implementation of this verdict, jurors could effectively condemn a mentally ill defendant to incarceration for his or her deviant criminal actions while recognizing that those actions were the product of a mental aberration or illness requiring ongoing psychological therapy and treatment. See McGraw, Farthing–Capowich, Kailitz, *The Guilty But Mentally Ill Plea and Verdict: Current State of the Knowledge,* 30 Vill.L.Rev. 117, 125 (1985).

* * *

* * * Our research indicates that none of the appellate courts in the twelve states that utilize the guilty but mentally ill verdict have struck down guilty but mentally ill legislation as unconstitutional.

* * *

* * * Indeed, the Hinckley acquittal and surrounding debate generated a feeling that the common-law insanity standard was permitting culpable defendants to slip through the cracks of the criminal justice system and escape retribution. Succumbing to this national sentiment, our legislature joined the various other states who had enacted guilty but mentally ill legislation with the hope that the verdict would alleviate the incidence of insanity acquittals.[1] * * *

* * *

The legislative history of Senate Bill 171 unearths several basic concepts fundamental to our constitutional analysis of Pennsylvania's guilty but mentally ill verdict. First, we conclude that the guilty but mentally ill verdict is merely the statutory articulation of our legislature's desire to allow the finder of fact to hold responsible those mentally ill defendants who deviate from the laws of this Commonwealth, while at the same time providing them with the humane psychiatric treatment for their mental infirmities. This noble purpose emanated from two unfavorable scenarios. In the first scenario, a mentally ill defendant who is unable to meet the burden of the M'Naghten insanity standard would logically be found either guilty or not guilty. If found guilty, that person could be condemned to serve a period of incarceration for his

1. Representative Piccola, one of the sponsors of Senate Bill 171, indicated that his research disclosed sixteen insanity acquittals in 1979, seventeen acquittals in 1980, and twenty in 1981. See Pa. Legislative Journal, House, at 1627–45, 1642 (Sept. 21, 1982).

crime. One does not need to possess a medical degree with a specialty in psychiatry to realize that incarceration of a mentally ill defendant without structured psychiatric care will likely exacerbate the manifestations of his mental illness. In the second scenario, a mentally ill defendant who commits a violent crime and is adjudged to be insane under the M'Naghten standard could subsequently be released from structured psychiatric treatment into the community. Experience has shown that some chronically mentally ill patients decompensate rapidly without the structured environment, therapy, and medication that they receive in treatment facilities. Consequently, those individuals who are prone to commit violent crimes when their illness intensifies would likely revert to their prior antisocial behavior. Our legislature took these eventualities into consideration when formulating Pennsylvania's guilty but mentally ill statutory scheme and implemented a new verdict which would provide incarceration and treatment of afflicted mentally ill offenders, coupled with the protection of society from dangerously violent persons suffering from the oppression of mental illness.

The second obvious purport of the legislature was to discourage the use of the insanity defense and reform the burdens of proof required of aggrieved defendants. As experience in both Michigan case law and *Hinckley* showed, utilization of the verdict had reached alarming proportions, particularly in light of the prosecution's overwhelming burden of proving the defendant's sanity beyond a reasonable doubt. Consequently, our lawmaking body rationally sought to avert the problems encountered by other jurisdictions under the traditional "guilty," "not guilty," and "not guilty by reason of insanity" verdicts.

Lastly, we observe that our lawmakers promulgated 18 Pa.C.S. § 314 in response to the intense public pressure that surfaced in the wake of *Hinckley.* To the general public, it appeared to be incomprehensible that a man who had carefully planned to fatally injure the President, and had made an attempt to carry through with this contemptuous act, could possibly escape penal retribution for his crime. We surmise that immeasurable public contempt for the manner in which mentally ill offenders were treated in the criminal justice system was certainly a catalyst for the promotion of the new verdict. Our lawmakers responded to their constituents' grievances by statutorily enacting a verdict which had been time-tested and successful in other American jurisdictions.

* * *

[The court went on to uphold the statute against constitutional attacks based on vagueness, the equal protection clause, and the due process clause, and affirmed the judgment of conviction.]

[The concurring opinion of JUDGE BECK is omitted.]

Notes

1. *Policy. ABA Criminal Justice Mental Health Standards, Standard 7–6.10. Forms of Verdict:* *

* (B. James George, Jr., General Reporter) Copyright © 1986, 1989 by the American Bar Association. Reprinted by permission of the American Bar Association.

(a) When the defense of mental nonresponsibility [insanity] has been properly raised, the verdict returned should be in the form of either guilty, not guilty, or not guilty by reason of mental nonresponsibility [insanity]. The jury should be instructed that it may consider the verdict of not guilty by reason of mental nonresponsibility [insanity] only after finding, beyond a reasonable doubt, that the defendant committed the conduct charged.

(b) Statutes which supplant or supplement the verdict of not guilty by reason of mental nonresponsibility [insanity] with a verdict of guilty but mentally ill should not be enacted.

Commentary

As noted in the introduction to this part, the term *insanity* has been replaced by the term *mental nonresponsibility.* * * * Aside from this desirable change in nomenclature, paragraph (a) limits verdicts to the three forms traditionally provided in criminal cases: guilty, not guilty, and not guilty by reason of mental nonresponsibility [insanity].[2]

* * *

Paragraph (b) of the standard reinforces paragraph (a) by banning alternative "quasi-insanity" verdicts. It reflects policy endorsed by the Association House of Delegates in 1983 in response to a wave of guilty-but-mentally-ill statutes adopted in recent years. Since 1975, when Michigan enacted the first such statute,[4] eleven other states have enacted guilty-but-mentally-ill legislation;[5] at least ten more[6] have considered comparable laws in the wake of the *Hinckley* trial.

Under the Michigan statute, which is representative of most such formulations, defendants who file a notice of an intent to rely on the insanity defense may be found guilty, not guilty, not guilty by reason of insanity, or guilty but mentally

2. Although the Standing Committee considered a verdict form eliminating the words *not guilty* and simply stating that a defendant was "not mentally responsible," the committee rejected it because it implied a defendant who was mentally nonresponsible [insane] at the time of the offense could at the same time be "guilty" of the offense. In fact, however, a person who is found nonresponsible at the time of the act charged is not criminally culpable. Thus, the committee recommended the retention of the three traditional forms of jury verdicts, with the substitution, of course, of "mental nonresponsibility" for "insanity."

4. Mich.Comp.Laws Ann. §§ 768.29a(2), 768.36 (1982).

5. See, e.g., Alaska Stat. § 12.47.020(c) (1984); Del.Code Ann. tit. 11, §§ 401, 408 (Supp.1984); Ga.Code Ann. § 17–7–131 (Supp.1985); Ill.Ann.Stat. ch. 38, §§ 6–2, 6–4, 113–4, 113–5, 115–2, 115–3, 115–4 (as amended by 1985 PA 84–413 (approved Sept. 16, 1985) (West Supp.1986); Ind.Code Ann. § 35–36–2–5 (West 1985); Ky.Rev.Stat.Ann. § 504.130 (1985); N.M.Stat.Ann. § 31–9–3 (Supp.1985); 18 Pa.Cons.Stat.Ann. § 314 (Purdon 1983); S.D.Codified Laws Ann. §§ 23A–7–2, 23A–25–13, 23A–7–16, 23A–26–3, 23A–26–14 (Supp.1985); Utah Code Ann. §§ 77–13–1, 77–35–21.5 (Supp.1985).

See generally Hermann & Sor, *Convicting or Confining?: Alternative Directions in Insanity Law Reform: Guilty But Mentally Ill Versus New Rules for Release of Insanity Acquittees,* 1983 B.Y.U.L.Rev. 499; LaGrone & Combs, *Alternatives to the Insanity Defense,* 12 J. Psychiatry & L. 93 (1984); McGraw, Farthing–Capowich & Keilitz, *The "Guilty But Mentally Ill" Plea and Verdict: Current State of the Knowledge,* 30 Villanova L.Rev. 117 (1985); Slovenko, *Commentaries on Psychiatry and Law: "Guilty but Mentally Ill,"* 10 J. Psychiatry & L. 541 (1982); Note, *Guilty But Mentally Ill: An Impractical Alternative to the Insanity Defense,* 14 Sw.L.Rev. 544 (1984); Weiner, *Mental Disability and the Criminal Law,* in The Mentally Disabled and the Law 693, 714–716 (S. Brakel, J. Parry & B. Weiner eds., 3d ed. 1985) [hereinafter cited as Weiner]. Statutory provisions as of October 1982 are gathered in Weiner, supra, at 778–785, Table 12.6.

6. See, e.g., Florida, S. 323 (1980), H. 710 (1980); Hawaii, H. 86 (1981), S. 2073–80 (1980); Maryland, S. 806 (1980), S. 1284 (1978); New Hampshire, S. 126 (1979), S. 51 (1981); New York, S. 11765 (1980), S. 4013 (1979), S. 7185 (1978), H. 9705 (1978); Ohio, S. 297 (1979).

ill at the time of a charged offense. The latter finding is required if a factfinder concludes beyond a reasonable doubt that a defendant committed the act charged, was mentally ill at the time of the offense, and was not criminally responsible at the time of the offense. If a guilty-but-mentally-ill verdict is returned, a defendant is sentenced to any term appropriate for the offense and subjected to treatment in a mental hospital as needed. The constitutionality of the Michigan statute has been upheld by Michigan state courts on several occasions and proponents of this alternative look upon it as a successful compromise necessary for the survival of the insanity defense.

A second pattern of reform legislation, not yet legislatively adopted by any state but apparently sanctioned by one court,[9] would supplant rather than supplement the verdict of mental nonresponsibility [insanity] with a verdict of guilty but mentally ill or guilty but insane. * * *

Paragraph (b) disapproves of any type of guilty-but-mentally-ill (GBMI) verdict. This policy, adopted by the ABA House of Delegates in 1983, is also supported by the American Psychiatric Association, the National Mental Health Association Commission on the Insanity Defense, and virtually all commentators who have analyzed the subject.[12] Indeed, legislation that supplants the mental nonresponsibility [insanity] verdict arguably may be unconstitutional on its face, since it does not accord exculpatory significance to even the type of gross psychosis that would preclude requisite *mens rea*. Even if, as a result of judicial interpretation, such statutes should allow the introduction of evidence of mental abnormality relevant to *mens rea,* the fact that they abolish the defense of mental nonresponsibility [insanity] would, as discussed in the commentary to standard 7–6.1, run counter to the moral imperative of the criminal law.

Guilty-but-mentally-ill statutes that make the verdict an option in lieu of, rather than a substitute, for the nonresponsibility verdict are also unwarranted on both functional and theoretical grounds. The new verdict fails on its own terms and at the same time introduces a conceptually alien element into the criminal justice system.

Proponents of the GBMI statute argue that increasing numbers of violent crimes committed by persons prematurely released from mental institutions, after having been found not guilty by reason of mental nonresponsibility [insanity], necessitate this alternative verdict form. By offering jurors a compromise verdict between a guilty finding and a finding of mental nonresponsibility [insanity], they hope both to reduce acquittals by reason of mental nonresponsibility [insanity] and to provide greater protection to the public.

In fact, the verdict appears to accomplish neither goal. With respect to the first objective, for instance, the number of nonresponsibility acquittals in Michigan since passage of the 1975 GBMI statute has actually increased. * * *

Even assuming that a GBMI verdict effectively replaces nonresponsibility acquittals with guilty-but-mentally-ill findings, the degree of extra security it affords the public is probably negligible. A person found GBMI must be considered for parole just like any other convicted offender. Once the minimum period of confinement necessary to establish eligibility for parole has passed, the

9. See Pouncey v. State, 297 Md. 264, 465 A.2d 475 (1983).

12. See Bonnie, *The Moral Basis of the Insanity Defense,* 69 A.B.A.J. 194 (1983); Note, *The Constitutionality of Michigan's Guilty But Mentally Ill Verdict,* 12 U.Mich.J.L. Ref. 188 (1978). For a discussion of GBMI as it relates to mentally retarded defendants, see Ellis & Luckasson, *Mentally Retarded Criminal Defendants,* 53 Geo.Wash.L.Rev. 414, 442–444 (1985).

primary criterion governing the release of defendants found GBMI is the same as that ruling the release of those found not guilty by reason of mental nonresponsibility [insanity], namely, dangerousness. As a result, the duration of a given individual's confinement is likely to be roughly similar under either the traditional system or one which employs the GBMI verdict. * * *

Accepting for the sake of argument that the GBMI verdict tends both to reduce acquittals by reason of mental nonresponsibility [insanity] and to lead to longer confinement for mentally ill offenders, it is still highly debatable whether the manner in which GBMI statutes achieve this result is acceptable. Under the typical GBMI scheme, jury instructions directing when defendants should be found "insane" as opposed to merely "mentally ill" are at best confusing and at worst extremely prejudicial. There is a strong possibility that jurors, seeing little distinction between these competing terminologies, will choose the guilty-but-mentally-ill verdict solely because it appears to result in longer confinement. Persons with a valid nonresponsibility defense may, therefore, be convicted instead of acquitted on mental nonresponsibility [insanity] grounds. * * *

Finally, the GBMI verdict is deficient for an important theoretical reason: It is not a proper verdict at all. Rather it is a dispositional mechanism transferred to the guilt determination phase of the criminal process. The hybrid nature of the verdict is demonstrated by the fact that a jury determination of mental illness at the time of a charged offense is relevant not to criminal responsibility or culpability but to whether accused persons *might* receive treatment after they have been sentenced, a finding best made and acted upon after trial when information about various dispositional alternatives can be obtained and qualified experts consulted. Even if the GBMI verdict accurately identified offenders needing psychiatric treatment, which it apparently fails to do,[20] it would not be a particularly useful innovation because virtually every state already provides for the hospitalization of prisoners requiring inpatient care.

If the goal is to reduce acquittals by reason of mental nonresponsibility [insanity], attention should be deflected to the proper scope of the nonresponsibility defense. If it is instituted to prevent premature release of persons found nonresponsible, criteria for committing and releasing them should be reexamined. If, instead, the concern is the proper treatment of mentally ill or mentally retarded offenders, sentencing and prison transfer provisions should be evaluated. The guilty-but-mentally-ill verdict fails to address any of these problems adequately. Instead, it adds a confusing and conceptually unjustifiable element to the criminal justice system.

2. *Objections to Abolishing the Insanity Defense.*

a. Robinson v. California, 370 U.S. 660, 668–669, 82 S.Ct. 1417, 1421, 8 L.Ed. 2d 758, 764 (1962) (concurring opinion of DOUGLAS, J.):

In Sixteenth Century England one prescription for insanity was to beat the subject "until he had regained his reason." Deutsch, The Mentally Ill in America (1937), p. 13. In America "the violently insane went to the whipping post and into prison dungeons or, as sometimes happened, were burned at the stake or hanged"; and "the pauper insane often roamed the countryside as wild men and

20. In Michigan, 75 percent of defendants found GBMI are not mentally ill. Statement of Bill Meyer, Director of the Forensic Psychiatry Center in Ann Arbor, Michigan, at State Mental Health Forensic Directors Third Annual Conference (Sept. 1982). Of the forty-five defendants found GBMI in Illinois over a thirteen-month period, all have gone directly to the custody of the department of corrections. Statement of Terry Brelje, Coordinator for the Forensic Psychiatry Program at Chester Mental Health Center, Illinois, at Mental Health Forensic Directors Third Annual Conference (Sept. 1982).

from time to time were pilloried, whipped, and jailed." Action for Mental Health (1961), p. 26.

As stated by Dr. Isaac Ray many years ago:

> "Nothing can more strongly illustrate the popular ignorance respecting insanity than the proposition, equally objectionable in its humanity and its logic, that the insane should be punished for criminal acts, in order to deter other insane persons from doing the same thing." Treatise on the Medical Jurisprudence of Insanity (5th ed. 1871), p. 56.

Today we have our differences over the legal definition of insanity. But however insanity is defined, it is in end effect treated as a disease. While afflicted people may be confined either for treatment or for the protection of society, they are not branded as criminals.

b. State v. Johnson, 121 R.I. 254, 264–265, 399 A.2d 469, 475 (1979):

Several commentators have advocated abolition of the separate defense of lack of criminal responsibility due to a mental illness. See, e.g., Dershowitz, *Abolishing the Insanity Defense; The Most Significant Feature of the Administration's Criminal Code—An Essay,* 9 Crim.L.Bull. 434 (1973); Goldstein & Katz, *Abolish the "Insanity Defense"—Why Not?,* 72 Yale L.J. 853 (1963). Proponents contend that abolition would result in the responsibility issue being more properly considered as the existence vel non of the mens rea. Under a common proposal the criminal process would be bifurcated: first, the jury would resolve the question of guilt, and second, a panel of experts would determine the appropriate disposition. Arguably, abolition of the separate defense is subject to constitutional objections because it potentially abrogates the right to trial by jury and offends the guarantee of due process. We believe that such a drastic measure, if advisable at all, is appropriately left to the legislative process.

c. United States v. Brawner, 471 F.2d 969, 985–986 (D.C.Cir.1972):

A number of proposals in the journals recommend that the insanity defense be abolished altogether. This is advocated in the amicus brief of the National District Attorneys Association as both desirable and lawful.[17] The amicus brief of American Psychiatric Association concludes it would be desirable, with appropriate safeguards, but would require a constitutional amendment. That a constitutional amendment would be required is also the conclusion of others, generally in opposition to the proposal.

This proposal has been put forward by responsible judges for consideration, with the objective of reserving psychiatric overview for the phase of the criminal process concerned with disposition of the person determined to have been the actor.[19] However, we are convinced that the proposal cannot properly be imposed by judicial fiat.

The courts have emphasized over the centuries that "free will" is the postulate of responsibility under our jurisprudence. 4 Blackstone's Commentaries 27. The concept of "belief in freedom of the human will and a consequent ability and duty of the normal individual to choose between good and evil" is a

17. It suggests that a mental condition be exculpatory solely as it negatives mens rea.

19. See e.g., Burger, then Circuit Judge, Proceedings of the Sixth Annual Meeting of the National Conference of State Trial Judges, Chicago, Illinois, Aug. 9–11, 1963, quoted in Wion v. United States, 325 F.2d at 428, n. 10; Bazelon, Chief Judge, in Washington v. United States, 129 U.S.App.D.C. at 42, n. 33, 390 F.2d at 457 (1967); Haynesworth, Chief Judge, in en banc opinion in United States v. Chandler, 393 F.2d at 928 (1968); see also remarks of Chief Justice Weintraub (of New Jersey) in Insanity as a Defense—Panel Discussion, Annual Judicial Conference, Second Circuit, 37 F.R.D. 365, 369 (1964).

core concept that is "universal and persistent in mature systems of law." Morissette v. United States, 342 U.S. 246, 250, 72 S.Ct. 240, 243, 96 L.Ed. 288 (1952). Criminal responsibility is assessed when through "free will" a man elects to do evil. And while, as noted in *Morissette,* the legislature has dispensed with mental element in some statutory offenses, in furtherance of a paramount need of the community, these instances mark the exception and not the rule, and only in the most limited instances has the mental element been omitted by the legislature as a requisite for an offense that was a crime at common law.

The concept of lack of "free will" is both the root of origin of the insanity defense and the line of its growth. This cherished principle is not undercut by difficulties, or differences of view, as to how best to express the free will concept in the light of the expansion of medical knowledge. We do not concur in the view of the National District Attorneys Association that the insanity defense should be abandoned judicially, either because it is at too great a variance with popular conceptions of guilt [21] or fails "to show proper respect for the personality of the criminal [who] is liable to resent pathology more than punishment." [22]

These concepts may be measured along with other ingredients in a legislative re-examination of settled doctrines of criminal responsibility, root, stock and branch. Such a reassessment, one that seeks to probe and appraise the society's processes and values, is for the legislative branch, assuming no constitutional bar. The judicial role is limited, in Justice Holmes's figure, to action that is molecular, with the restraint inherent in taking relatively small steps, leaving to the other branches of government whatever progress must be made with seven-league leaps. Such judicial restraint is particularly necessary when a proposal requires, as a mandatory ingredient, the kind of devotion of resources, personnel and techniques that can be accomplished only through whole-hearted legislative commitment.

3. *Variation:* Not all of the new special pleas are alike. In Maryland, an insanity plea may produce a verdict of guilty, not guilty, or guilty but insane. Under the last verdict, the accused is found guilty of the crime, but not subject to criminal punishment and may either be set free or confined on a dangerousness standard. Langworthy v. State, 284 Md. 588, 399 A.2d 578 (1979), cert. denied 450 U.S. 960, 101 S.Ct. 1419, 67 L.Ed.2d 384 (1981). Other consequences of conviction than punishment, for example, loss of voting rights, may remain. Pouncey v. State, 297 Md. 264, 465 A.2d 475 (1983).

4. *Procedural Alternatives: Methods of Contesting.* Is it possible or desirable to improve the insanity defense by procedural changes? One possibility is the bifurcated trial, in which the first part is for determination of the facts, apart from any insanity defense; if ordinary *mens rea* and *actus reus* are found, a second part deals exclusively with the insanity defense. Another proposal would have the insanity question determined by a panel of experts, before or after trial.

5. *Procedural Alternatives: Avoiding a Contest.* It should be noted that most insanity questions are not contested at trial. Often the accused will be examined before trial by a neutral physician, whose findings will be clear enough so that both sides acquiesce. Or, all the experts may agree either that the accused is sane or that

21. Amicus argues that penal systems can only survive so long as they "accord substantially with the popular estimate of the enormity of guilt," citing 1 W. Lecky, History of the Rise and Influence of the Spirit of Rationalism in Europe 336–337 (1891).

22. Citing Harris, Respect for Persons in Ethics and Society 129–130 (R. De George ed. 1966).

he is insane. Where insanity is found and the accused is agreed to be dangerous, civil commitment may be a solution acceptable to all.

Question

Who is entitled to raise the question of the accused's sanity? Suppose the defendant's attorney wants to do so, but the defendant does not?

iii. Diminished Capacity

Johnson v. State

Court of Appeals of Maryland, 1982.
292 Md. 405, 439 A.2d 542.

Argued before MURPHY, C.J., and SMITH, DIGGES, ELDRIDGE, COLE, DAVIDSON and RODOWSKY, JJ.

DIGGES, JUDGE.

Lawrence Johnson was convicted, after removal of this criminal cause from Baltimore County, by a jury in the Circuit Court for Calvert County of first degree murder (both premeditated and in the commission of a felony), first degree rape, kidnapping, and use of a handgun during the commission of a felony or a crime of violence. The same jury subsequently sentenced Johnson to death for the murder. As is specified by the statute authorizing the sentence of death, we must, by this expedited appeal, scrutinize both the decision to execute the defendant as well as any claims of error properly presented by the parties. With the exception of the imposition of the death penalty, we sustain these convictions and sentences ordered, and remand this cause for a new hearing concerning the punishment to be given for the murder.

The sordid chronicle of this crime spree was related by the appellant, Lawrence Johnson, at trial. It began on the early morning of February 23, 1980, when he was suddenly awakened by a friend, Amos Batts, while perched on the couch at the home of his cousin, Dwayne Mayers. At the urging of Batts, Johnson followed his friend outside to a car being operated by the cousin. It soon became apparent to Johnson that Mayers and Batts had stolen the vehicle during the night and had abducted its owner, Betty Toulson, in the process. Although Johnson had earlier declined to participate when the other two decided to obtain some money through crime, the defendant this time joined them in the car with the victim. After a brief discussion, Mayers started the vehicle and drove around while the three men smoked "parsley flakes sprayed with some kind of embalming fluid." The victim remained silent throughout this journey "with her head down." Later, after driving to a remote area of Baltimore County, Mayers stopped the car and asked whether his companions "wanted to have sex" with their prisoner. Mayers and the appellant eventually raped the woman on the back seat of her car. The trio then drove the victim to another location nearby where Mayers stripped Ms. Toulson of her coat and pocketbook. After discussing the problem presented by the victim's knowledge of their identities, Mayers returned to the automobile, removed a pistol from under the seat, and presented it to appellant with instructions to kill the woman. Johnson led her into the woods and complied with the directive. Ms. Toulson's snow-covered body was recovered five days later; she had received fatal shots in the head and chest.

* * *

Johnson next asserts that the trial court erred in not admitting certain psychological evidence at trial where he sought to use this information, not to establish his legal insanity, but rather, to demonstrate that he lacked a sufficient mental capacity to form the requisite intent to commit murder in the first degree. As an aid to an understanding of this issue we set out its factual predicate.

At trial, the defense called Dr. Ernest Kamm, a clinical psychologist at the Clifton T. Perkins Hospital Center. Dr. Kamm had conducted a psychological examination of Johnson as part of the court ordered evaluation performed by the Perkins staff and had prepared a report of his findings. Counsel for Johnson proffered that he wished to use Dr. Kamm's entire report and testimony "to go to the mitigation of First Degree Murder and any specific [intent] crimes," rather than to raise the issue of defendant's sanity. The court allowed the psychologist to read to the jury only parts of his report relating to intelligence tests he had administered to Johnson and his conclusion, based on those tests, that the defendant "functions at the borderline intellectual level (I.Q. 72) * * *."[6] Appellant urges that the entire report is relevant to his defense of "diminished capacity"—that is, he did not have sufficient mental capacity to form the requisite specific intent to commit some

6. We reproduce here in full Dr. Kamm's psychological report with emphasis indicating the portions read to the jury:

TESTS ADMINISTERED:

WAIS

Bender-Gestalt

Holtsman Inkblot Technique

Color Pyramid Test

TEST BEHAVIOR:

The patient is a 19-year old youth of medium height and build who presented a neat and clean appearance. He was extremely sullen and hostile, and his cooperation for interview and test was poor. In view of this test results have to be considered tentative.

TEST RESULTS:

On the WAIS he earned a Verbal I.Q. of 78, a Performance I.Q. of 68, and a Full Scale I.Q. of 72 which places him within the borderline range of intelligence. His potential, as gauged by his abstract reasoning, is at least within the low average range. Intellectual efficiency is decreased by a combination of educational deprivation and negativism. There are some signs which point in the direction of bizarre thinking and a tenuous hold on reality. E.G. on Card 22 of the Holtzman he saw "the devil," and on Card 27 he saw "God over water." But these should be interpreted with caution, as they may also be attempts to embarrass and express contempt for the examiner by giving nonsensical answers.

The personality picture is that of an extremely deprived individual who does not expect any affection and emotional support from either parental figure. He perceives the mother figure as domineering, but distant and devoid of warmth and understanding and the father figure as hostile and threatening. Yet he has conjured up the image of an idealized, all wise and all loving father surrogate with whom he will compare any male elder. Since such a person is bound to fall short of his ideal he is apt to equate this person with the real father figure whom he sees in negative terms and reject him. As a result he not only has trouble with authority figures, but perceives the world about him as a cold inhospitable place where he does not have a chance.

CONCLUSION:

The patient functions at the borderline intellectual level (I.Q. 72), but his potential is at least within the low average range. He can be described as a severely deprived individual with a hostile and negative orientation and an [sic.] *severe authority problem.* Contract with reality is difficult to evaluate on account of his poor productivity resulting from extreme negativism.

* * *

of the crimes with which he is charged. Consequently, the argument goes, it was error to keep that information from the jury when it determines the guilt issue. In order to decide whether this ruling on the evidence was erroneous, however, we must first examine whether the criminal defense known as "diminished capacity," or as it is sometimes called, "diminished responsibility," is recognized in this State. Only if such a doctrine exists in our jurisprudence is defendant arguably entitled to produce evidence in support of it. Because we here determine, however, that this State does not recognize diminished capacity as a legal doctrine operating to negate specific criminal intent, it was not error to exclude evidence in support of it.

* * * The basic outline of diminished capacity has been summarized as follows:

> [S]ince certain crimes, by definition, require the existence of a specific intent, any evidence relevant to the existence of that intent, including evidence of an abnormal mental condition not constituting legal insanity, is competent for the purpose of [negating] that intent * * *. [T]he actual purpose of such evidence is to establish, by negating the requisite intent for a higher degree of offense, that in fact a lesser degree of the offense was committed. [Annot. 22 A.L.R.3d 1228, 1238 (1969).]

Thus, only after a defendant has been determined to be criminally accountable for his actions (legally sane) has the doctrine been applied to admit expert testimony as to a defendant's mental condition in order to determine the degree of criminality for which the accused will be held responsible.

The states are less than unanimous in their resolution of the question whether application of diminished capacity to criminal trials on the issue of guilt represents a legally sound resolution of the pressing problem of how the criminal law should treat evidence of mental abnormality that does not establish the actor's legal insanity. Compare, e.g., United States v. Brawner, 471 F.2d 969 (D.C.Cir.1972) (en banc) (expert testimony admissible to demonstrate diminished capacity) with Bethea v. United States, 365 A.2d 64, 83–92 (D.C.App.1976), cert. denied, 433 U.S. 911, 97 S.Ct. 2979, 53 L.Ed. 2d 1095 (1977) (rejection of diminished capacity doctrine). It is generally recognized, however, that adoption of the concept of diminished capacity as a separate defense involves "a fundamental change in the common law theory of [criminal] responsibility," Fisher v. United States, 328 U.S. 463, 476, 66 S.Ct. 1318, 1325, 90 L.Ed. 1382 (1946). This is true because the introduction of expert psychiatric testimony concerning the defendant's mental aberrations when the basic sanity of the accused is not at issue conflicts with the governing principle of the criminal law that all legally sane individuals are equally capable of forming and possessing the same types and degrees of intent. Consequently, an individual determined to be "sane" within the traditional constructs of the criminal law is held accountable for his action, regardless of his particular disabilities, weaknesses, poverty, religious beliefs, social deprivation or educational background. The most that is proper to do with such information is to weigh it during sentencing. This view of the relation of diminished capacity to criminal culpability is exemplified by Bethea v. United States, supra, 365 A.2d [64,] 88 [(D.C.App.1976), cert. denied 433 U.S. 911, 97 S.Ct. 2979, 53 L.Ed.2d 1095 (1977)] where the court, quoting Judge Leventhal concurring in United States v. Moore, 486 F.2d 1139, 1179–80 (D.C.Cir.1973) (en banc), cert. denied, 414 U.S. 980, 94 S.Ct. 298, 38 L.Ed.2d 224 (1973), noted that:

> [t]he legal conception of criminal capacity cannot be limited to those of unusual endowment or even average powers. A few may be recognized as so far from normal as to be entirely beyond the reach of criminal justice, but in general the criminal law is a means of social control that must be potentially capable of reaching the vast bulk of the population. Criminal responsibility is a concept that not only extends to the bulk of those below the median line of responsibility, but specifically extends to those who have a realistic problem of substantial impairment and lack of capacity * * *. The criminal law cannot "vary legal norms with the individual's capacity to meet the standards they prescribe, absent a disability that is both gross and verifiable, such as the mental disease or defect that may establish irresponsibility. The most that it is feasible to do with lesser disabilities is to accord them proper weight in sentencing."

* * *

* * * We here reaffirm our position that "the concepts of both diminished capacity and insanity involve a moral choice by the community to withhold a finding of responsibility and its consequence of punishment," Bethea v. United States, supra, 365 A.2d at 90, n. 55, and on this basis are indistinguishable.[10] Accordingly, because the legislature, reflecting communi-

10. Given the primary assumption in the criminal law concerning a defendant's criminal culpability regardless of his lesser abilities, whatever they may be, and "recognizing the unique position of the concept of insanity in the framework of criminal responsibility," Bethea v. United States, 365 A.2d 64, 86 (D.C. App.1976), we cannot agree with those courts which easily declare that evidence of a legally sane defendant's mental impairment is always probative on the factual question of whether a particular accused entertained the requisite mental state. See, e.g., State v. DiPaolo, 34 N.J. 279, 168 A.2d 401 (1961), cert. denied, 368 U.S. 880, 82 S.Ct. 130, 7 L.Ed.2d 80 (1961). There is a fundamental difference between evidence demonstrating that the defendant did not *as a fact* possess the requisite mental state, here premeditation and deliberation as opposed to evidence establishing that the defendant was *generally less capable* than a normal person of forming a requisite *mens rea*. Certainly, we recognize the basic proposition that the state must prove every element of a crime beyond a reasonable doubt including specific intent if necessary, and that an accused is entitled to rebut the state's case. Mullaney v. Wilbur, 421 U.S. 684, 95 S.Ct. 1881, 44 L.Ed.2d 508 (1975). The doctrine of diminished capacity, in our view, however, does not operate to demonstrate that, as a fact, a defendant did not entertain a requisite mental state; rather, the principle is used to establish a legally sane but mentally impaired defendant's diminished culpability for a particular criminal act.

Moreover, facile comparison of the doctrine of diminished capacity with the rule allowing certain evidence of a defendant's intoxication on the issue of *mens rea* does not withstand scrutiny. The degree of intoxication necessary to negate *mens rea* is great and is comparable with that degree of mental incapacity that will render a defendant legally insane. As noted in State v. Gover, 267 Md. 602, 608, 298 A.2d 378, 382 (1973):

> If the trier of fact determines that at the time the alleged criminal act occurred, the accused had become so inebriated that he possessed no reason or understanding, then he has reached that stage of intoxication that renders him incapable of forming the requisite *mens rea* which is a necessary element of all specific intent crimes.

Lesser degrees of incapacity, whether produced by intoxication or organic mental impairment will not relieve a defendant of full responsibility for his acts. See 267 Md. at 606–07, 298 A.2d at 381.

ty morals, has, by its definition of criminal insanity already determined which states of mental disorder ought to relieve one from criminal responsibility, this court is without authority to impose our views in this regard even if they differed.

In light of criticism of the *McNaughten* insanity test, diminished capacity has been viewed as a solution to some of the inadequacies of the traditional approach to criminal responsibility, People v. Drew, 22 Cal.3d 333, 149 Cal. Rptr. 275, 280–81, 583 P.2d 1318, 1323–1324 (1978) (en banc); People v. Henderson, 60 Cal.2d 482, 35 Cal.Rptr. 77, 82, 386 P.2d 677, 682 (1963), and many decisions allowing evidence of a sane defendant's mental abnormalities arise in jurisdictions which define criminal insanity in terms of the *McNaughten* principle. E.g., State v. Gramenz, 256 Iowa 134, 126 N.W.2d 285 (1964); State v. DiPaolo, 34 N.J. 279, 168 A.2d 401 (1961); Commonwealth v. Walzack, 468 Pa. 210, 360 A.2d 914 (1976). In fact, some assert that the judicial development of the diminished capacity defense assuaged dissatisfaction with the *McNaughten* test and actually inhibited reform of it. Arenella, *The Diminished Capacity and Diminished Responsibility Defenses: Two Children of a Doomed Marriage,* 77 Col.L.Rev. 827, 854–55 (1977). With the broadening of the concept of criminal insanity * * *, however, the arguable need for a doctrine such as diminished capacity to ameliorate the law governing criminal responsibility prescribed by the *McNaughten* rule has been eliminated to the extent the legislature has deemed it advisable to do so.

* * *

What has just been iterated does not mean, however, that evidence of a defendant's mental abnormality which does not establish his insanity has been totally precluded from the consideration of those operating the machinery of our criminal justice system. Such evidence typically constitutes part of the range of data upon which the trial judge, following establishment of guilt, focuses attention when sentencing the individual accused. Such use of this information squares with the practice prevailing in our jurisprudence of permitting the judge wide latitude in making individualized sentencing decisions after consideration of information both in aggravation and mitigation of penalty. * * *

* * *

ELDRIDGE, JUDGE, dissenting:

* * *

Turning to the merits of the majority's position, in my view the trial court correctly held that evidence of Johnson's mental condition was admissible for the purpose of showing the absence of certain elements of first degree murder and of the other specific intent crimes with which Johnson was charged. The majority's contrary holding represents an abrupt departure from prior Maryland law as well as from the prevailing view throughout the country. Moreover, it constitutes an unwarranted limitation upon a criminal defendant's constitutional right to present relevant evidence in his own defense.

* * *

The defendant Johnson, *inter alia,* was charged with murder in the first degree under Maryland Code (1957, 1976 Repl.Vol.), Art. 27, § 407. In order to constitute first degree murder under § 407, the homicide must be a "wilful, deliberate and premeditated killing." * * * The mental condition of the defendant is obviously relevant to willfulness, deliberation and premeditation. These elements of murder have been defined by this Court on numerous occasions. In Faulcon v. State, 211 Md. 249, 257, 126 A.2d 858 (1956), Judge Collins stated for the Court:

> "For a homicide to be 'wilful' there must be a specific purpose and design to kill. To be 'deliberate' there must be a full and conscious knowledge of the purpose to kill. To be 'premeditated' the design to kill must have preceded the killing by an appreciable length of time; that is, time enough to be deliberate. To justify a conviction of murder in the first degree the jury or court, sitting without a jury, must find the actual intent, the fully formed purpose to kill, with enough time for deliberation and premeditation."

Accord: Gladden v. State, 273 Md. 383, 387–388, 330 A.2d 176 (1974), and cases there cited. "Specific purpose and design to kill" and "full and conscious knowledge of the purpose to kill" certainly involve a defendant's mental state. Evidence designed to show that a particular defendant was incapable of having the requisite mental state is nothing more or less than evidence designed to show that he did not commit the crime with which he was charged.

* * *

Until today, this Court has regularly distinguished evidence of a defendant's mental state designed to negate the existence of a crime from evidence of insanity designed to show that he was not *responsible* for a crime which was in fact committed. Whenever the existence of a particular mental state is an element of a criminal offense with which the defendant has been charged, the Court has consistently held that evidence of the defendant's mental *capability* is admissible to show the absence of that element, and thus the absence of criminal conduct.

For example, in Chisley v. State, 202 Md. 87, 107–109, 95 A.2d 577 (1953), involving a conviction of first degree murder and the imposition of a death sentence, evidence of the defendant's mental capability due to drunkenness was deemed properly admissible in order for the jury to determine the degree of homicide. * * *

Later, in Beall v. State, 203 Md. 380, 385, 101 A.2d 233 (1953), the Court reiterated that mental incapability due to drunkenness may be considered by the jury in determining the degree of murder. See also Avey v. State, 249 Md. 385, 388, 240 A.2d 107 (1968), where this Court expressly approved of the statement by the Court of Special Appeals that "where intoxication exists to a degree that it deprives the accused of his *capacity* to form a specific intent, he cannot be convicted of a crime requiring that intent * * *."[4]

4. With regard to diminished mental capacity due to intoxication, the majority today states that the "degree of intoxication necessary to negate *mens rea* is great and is comparable with that degree of mental incapacity that will render a defendant legally insane" and that "[l]esser degrees of incapacity, whether produced by intoxication or organic mental impairment will not relieve a defendant of full responsibility for his acts." This state-

* * *

The majority purports to recognize that the State must prove every element of a crime, including mental elements such as specific intent, premeditation and deliberation. Nevertheless the majority asserts, without any reasoning, that "[t]here is a fundamental difference between evidence demonstrating that the defendant did not *as a fact* possess the requisite mental state, here premeditation and deliberation, as opposed to evidence establishing that the defendant was *generally less capable* than a normal person of forming a requisite *mens rea*." However, I fail to perceive this "fundamental difference" referred to by the majority. A particular individual's abnormal mental capability is a *fact*. It is part of his mental state or condition. * * *

The majority also asserts that "the governing principle of the criminal law [is] that all legally sane individuals are equally capable of forming and possessing the same types and degrees of intent." No Maryland authority is cited for this proposition. Furthermore, it directly conflicts with the principle set forth in *Armstead,* in Chisley v. State, and other cases, that a defendant's mental condition is material in determining whether he is "*capable* of deliberation and premeditation," 202 Md. at 107, 95 A.2d 577, emphasis supplied.

The error and confusion in the view adopted today by the majority, was very well described by Chief Justice Weintraub for the Supreme Court of New Jersey in State v. DiPaolo, 34 N.J. 279, 294–296, 168 A.2d 401, *cert. denied,* 368 U.S. 880, 82 S.Ct. 130, 7 L.Ed.2d 80 (1961):

> "Next defendant contends that evidence of mental illness is competent upon the issue whether the crime was murder in the first degree or murder in the second degree.
>
> * * *
>
> "The difficulty seems to be that the topic is sometimes explored under the label of 'partial responsibility' or 'diminished responsibility' or perhaps confused with some other concept intended to be so described. Both of those characterizations are misleading since they tend to connote an 'affirmative' defense designed to defeat a case the State has otherwise established and thus to suggest the intrusion of an amendment to the established basis for criminal accountability. Actually the question is simply whether there shall be excluded evidence which merely denies the existence of facts which the State must prove to establish that the murder was in the first degree.
>
> * * *
>
> "We here are concerned with the category described as a 'willful, deliberate and premeditated killing.' * * * As settled by judicial construction, the first element is premeditation, which consists of the conception of the design or plan to kill. Next comes deliberation. The statutory word 'deliberate' does not here mean 'willful' or 'intentional' as the word is frequently used in daily parlance. Rather

ment is contrary to *Chisley, Beall* and other Maryland cases.

it imports 'deliberation' and requires a reconsideration of the design to kill, a weighing of the pros and cons with respect to it. Finally, the word 'willful' signifies an intentional execution of the plan to kill which had been conceived and deliberated upon * * *.

"The three mental operations we have just described are matters of *fact*. The judiciary cannot bar evidence which rationally bears upon the factual inquiry the Legislature has ordered. The capacity of an individual to premeditate, to deliberate, or to will to execute a homicidal design, or any deficiency in that capacity, may bear upon the question whether he *in fact* did so act. Hence evidence of any defect, deficiency, trait, condition, or illness which rationally bears upon the question whether those mental operations did *in fact* occur must be accepted.

* * *

"It has long been settled that voluntary intoxication or the voluntary use of drugs may be shown for the jury's consideration with respect to whether a defendant did in fact premeditate, deliberate and willfully kill.

* * *

"Surely if voluntary intoxication or use of drugs is evidential with respect to the degree of murder, mental illness or deficiency should be accepted as a legally competent 'cause.'"

See also, e.g., United States v. Brawner, 471 F.2d 969, 999 (D.C.Cir.1972); Commonwealth v. Gould, 380 Mass. 672, 405 N.E.2d 927 (1980); Lewin, *Psychiatric Evidence in Criminal Cases for Purposes Other than the Defense of Insanity,* 26 Syracuse L.Rev. 1051, 1092, 1104 (1975).

* * *

COLE and DAVIDSON, JJ., have authorized me to state that they concur with the views expressed herein.

Notes

1. *Later developments.* For a recent case in accord with *Johnson* (divided court), reviewing authorities, see Chestnut v. State, 538 So.2d 820 (Fla.1989).

The Maryland Court of Appeals modified its position in *Johnson* in Hoey v. State, 311 Md. 473, 536 A.2d 622 (1988), and Simmons v. State, 313 Md. 33, 542 A.2d 1258 (1988). It disapproved its former statement [a] that "all legally sane individuals are equally capable of forming and possessing the same types and degrees of intent," noting that the question of *mens rea* (in the sense of having purpose, premeditation, etc.) differs from the question of responsibility considered on an insanity plea. While diminished responsibility is not a separate defense—comparable to an insanity defense—in Maryland, the accused may introduce evidence, including expert testimony, of impaired mental condition for the limited purpose of showing that the *mens rea* required by the definition of the offense is absent. The expert may not testify as to the accused's state of mind at the time of the act, but may testify as to diagnosis, characteristics of the accused's disorder, and the impact which the disorder has generally on a person's perceptions and behavior. It is doubtful that the dissent in *Johnson* was seeking more than this.

a. Reprinted, supra p. 565.

A conclusion similar to the revised Maryland position was reached in United States v. Pohlot, 827 F.2d 889 (3d Cir.1987), cert. denied 484 U.S. 1011, 108 S.Ct. 710, 98 L.Ed.2d 660 (1988), under the federal statute. The court concluded from legislative history that the statute was designed to bar a special non-insanity excuse of diminished responsibility, based on mental disorder, similar to the now repudiated California diminished responsibility defense. A representative California diminished responsibility case is People v. Wolff, 61 Cal.2d 795, 40 Cal.Rptr. 271, 394 P.2d 959 (1964), where the court found that the defendant's mental abnormality, insufficient for an insanity defense, prevented him from recognizing the enormity of the evil of his act, and that he therefore lacked the personal turpitude—not directly related to standard *mens rea* requirements—necessary for first degree murder, though not for second degree murder. The federal statute was not meant to preclude mental disorder evidence directly bearing on such mental requirements as purpose and premeditation.

2. *Partial Responsibility Compared.* Compare with the diminished responsibility theory the partial responsibility approach of the English Homicide Act of 1957, 5 & 6 Eliz. II c. 11 § 2(1) and (3):

> (1) Where a person kills or is a party to the killing of another, he shall not be convicted of murder if he was suffering from such abnormality of mind (whether arising from a condition of arrested or retarded development of mind or any inherent causes or induced by disease or injury) as substantially impaired his mental responsibility for his acts and omissions in doing or being a party to the killing.
>
> (3) A person who but for this section would be liable, whether as principal or as accessory, to be convicted of murder shall be liable instead to be convicted of manslaughter.

iv. Involuntary Conduct Compared

Regina v. Hennessy

Court of Appeal, Criminal Division, 1989.
89 Cr.App.R. 10.

THE LORD CHIEF JUSTICE: On January 15, 1988, on the second day of a trial in the Crown Court at Lewes before HIS HONOUR JUDGE BIRKS and a jury, following a ruling on the defence of non-insane automatism, this appellant, Andrew Michael Hennessy, now 27 years of age, pleaded guilty and was sentenced as follows: first of all on count 1, for taking a conveyance without authority, nine months' imprisonment suspended for two years; count 2, driving while disqualified, six months' imprisonment to run concurrently, also suspended for two years. * * *

* * *

The facts which gave rise to the charges, in so far as material, were these. On Thursday May 25, 1987, two police constables, Barnes and Grace, were on duty in St. Leonards on the Sussex coast, amongst other things looking for a Ford Granada car which had been stolen. They found the car. It was unattended. They kept it under watch. As they watched they saw the appellant get into the car, switch on the headlights and ignition, start the car and drive off. The appellant at the wheel of the car correctly stopped the car at a set of traffic lights which were showing red against him.

Constable Grace then went over to the car as it was stationary, removed the ignition keys from the ignition lock, but not before the appellant had tried to drive the motor car away and escape from the attention of the policeman. The appellant was put in the police car. On the way to the police station an informal conversation about motor vehicles took place between the appellant and the police officers, in particular about the respective merits of the new Rover motor car and the Ford Sierra. Indeed the appellant appeared to Police Constable Barnes not only to be fully in possession of his faculties but to be quite cheerful and intelligent. Indeed he went so far as to say to the police officer that if he had only got the car, which he was in the process of removing, on to the open road, he would have given the policemen a real run for their money.

However after having been at the police station for a time, he was at a later stage escorted by Police Constable Barnes to hospital. He seemed to be normal when he left the cell block at the police station, but when he arrived at the hospital he appeared to be dazed and confused. He, the appellant, complained to the sister in the casualty ward that he, the appellant, had failed to take his insulin and indeed had had no insulin since the previous Monday when he should have had regular self-injected doses. He was given insulin, with which he injected himself, and the hospital discharged him and he was taken back to the police station.

The appellant gave evidence to the effect that he had been a diabetic for about 10 years. He needed, in order to stabilise his metabolism, two insulin injections on a daily basis, morning and afternoon. The amount required would depend on factors such as stress and eating habits. He was on a strict carbohydrate diet. At the time of the offence he said he had been having marital and employment problems. His wife had submitted a divorce petition some time shortly before, and he was very upset. He had not been eating and he had not been taking his insulin. He remembered very few details of the day. He could recall being handcuffed and taken to the chargeroom at the police station. He remembered being given insulin at the hospital and injecting himself and he remembers feeling better when he got back to the police station afterwards. He said he did not recall taking the car.

When cross-examined he agreed that he had understood proceedings at the police station, and what had gone on there. Indeed he had given the name and address of his solicitor. That was a considerable time before he had had his insulin at the hospital.

His general practitioner, Dr. Higginson, was called to give evidence. He spoke as to the appellant's medical condition. He described in broad outlines the effect of diabetes: it is a deficiency in the system of the production of hormones, which should balance the sugar metabolism. The lacking hormone is of course insulin. In the absence of the hormone the blood sugar rises and that results in hyperglycaemia. If the patient does not take his insulin and does not stick to the proper diet, then hyperglycaemia will supervene. If unchecked, the liver will become affected and the increasingly high level of sugar makes the patient drowsy and he will ultimately go into a coma.

If on the other hand the balance tips the other way, if too much insulin is taken, then the blood sugar will fall and hypoglycaemia, that is to say too little sugar in the blood, will supervene.

According to the hospital notes, on the evening in question the appellant's blood sugar had been high at 22 plus millimolecules per litre, the normal being eight or nine. According to Dr. Higginson one would expect to see some physical manifestation of hyperglycaemia at that level. * * * He added—I will read a passage from his evidence in a moment—that anxiety or depression can increase the blood sugar level, a person's ability and awareness of what is going on could be impaired if there were "associated symptoms and he had other conditions and worries at the same time."

If one reads a passage from Dr. Higginson's evidence, it says this:

* * *

> "There is a great individual variability in this situation, and it is difficult to be dogmatic, but I think that would be a reasonable explanation of someone who is under a lot of stress and had a very high level of blood sugar. . . . He might not be clear about what he was doing; he might be a bit befuddled. It is well known that the reverse condition, hypoglycaemia produces these symptoms very markedly. From time to time people are arrested for being drunk."

The defence to these charges accordingly was that the appellant had failed to take his proper twice a day dose of insulin for two or three days and at the time the events in question took place he was in a state of automatism and did not know what he was doing. * * *

The judge took the view, rightly in our view, that the appellant, having put his state of mind in issue, the preliminary question which he had to decide was whether this was truly a case of automatism or whether it was a case of legal "insanity" within the McNaghten Rules. He concluded that it was the latter, and he so ruled, whereupon the appellant changed his plea to guilty and was sentenced to the terms of imprisonment suspended which we have already mentioned. The judge then certified the case fit for appeal * * *.

The McNaghten rules * * * are still relevant in so far as they may affect the defence of automatism. * * *

* * *

* * * If the defendant did not know the nature and quality of his act because of something which *did not* amount to defect of reason from disease of the mind then he will probably be entitled to be acquitted [outright] * * *. But if, on the other hand, his failure to realise the nature and quality of his act was due to a defect of reason from disease of the mind, then in the eyes of the law he is suffering from insanity * * *.

It should perhaps be added, in order to complete the picture, though it is not relevant to the present situation, that where a defendant's failure to appreciate what he was doing was wrong * * * and where that failure is due to some reason other than a defect of reason from disease of the mind he will generally have no valid defence at all.

* * *

In the present case therefore what had to be decided was whether the defendant's condition was properly described as a disease of the mind. That does not mean any disease of the brain. It means a disease which affects the proper functioning of the mind. * * *

* * *

The point was neatly raised in the case of *Quick* (1973) 57 Cr.App.R. 722, [1973] Q.B. 910, also referred to us by Mr. Owen, in which LAWTON L.J. reviews the authorities. It might perhaps help if I read a short passage from the headnote [1973] Q.B. 910:

> "The defendants, Q and P, nurses at a mental hospital, were jointly and severally charged with assaulting a patient occasioning actual bodily harm. Both pleaded not guilty. Q, a diabetic, relied on the defence of automatism. He gave evidence that he had taken insulin as prescribed on the morning of the assault, had drunk a quantity of spirits and eaten little food thereafter and had no recollection of the assault. He called medical evidence to the effect that his condition at the material time was consistent with that of hypoglycaemia. The judge ruled that that evidence could only support a defence of insanity, not automatism. Q then pleaded guilty and P was convicted of aiding and abetting Q by encouragement. The defendants appealed against that conviction."

I turn to the passage in the judgment at pp. 734, 735 and 922E, respectively, where LAWTON L.J. says:

> "A malfunctioning of the mind of transitory effect caused by the application to the body of some external factor such as violence, drugs, including anaesthetics, alcohol and hypnotic influences cannot fairly be said to be due to disease. Such malfunctioning, unlike that caused by a defect of reason from disease of the mind, will not always relieve an accused from criminal responsibility. * * * In this case Quick's alleged mental condition, if it ever existed, was not caused by his diabetes but by his use of the insulin prescribed by his doctor. Such malfunctioning of his mind as there was, was caused by an external factor and not by a bodily disorder in the nature of a disease which disturbed the working of his mind. It follows in our judgment that Quick was entitled to have his defence of automatism left to the jury and that BRIDGE J.'s ruling as to the effect of the medical evidence called by him was wrong.

Thus in *Quick* (supra) the fact that his condition was, or may have been due to the injections of insulin, meant that the malfunction was due to an external factor and not to the disease. The drug it was that caused the hypoglycaemia, the low blood sugar. As suggested in another passage of the judgment of LAWTON L.J., hyperglycaemia, high blood sugar, caused by an inherent defect, and not corrected by insulin is a disease, and if, as the defendant was asserting here, it does cause a malfunction of the mind, then the case may fall within the McNaghten Rules.

The burden of Mr. Owen's argument to us is this. It is that the appellant's depression and marital troubles were a sufficiently potent external factor in his condition to override, so to speak, the effect of the diabetic shortage of insulin upon him. He refers us not only to the passage which I have already cited in the case of *Quick,* but also to a further passage in the case of Hill v. Baxter (1958) 42 Cr.App.R. 51, [1958] 1 Q.B. 277, and the passage to which he makes reference is at p. 60 and p. 285 respectively, which is part of the judgment of DEVLIN J., sitting with LORD GODDARD C.J., and PEARSON J., in the Divisional Court of Queen's Bench.

It reads as follows:

> "I have drawn attention to the fact that the accused did not set up a defence of insanity. For the purposes of the criminal law there are two categories of mental irresponsibility, one where the disorder is due to disease and the other where it is not. The distinction is not an arbitrary one. If disease is not the cause, if there is some temporary loss of consciousness arising accidentally, it is reasonable to hope that it will not be repeated and that it is safe to let an acquitted man go entirely free. But if disease is present the same thing may happen again, and therefore, since 1800, the law has provided that persons acquitted on this ground should be subject to restraint."

That is the submission made by Mr. Owen as a basis for saying the judge's decision was wrong and that this was a matter which should have been decided by the jury.

In our judgment, stress, anxiety and depression can no doubt be the result of the operation of external factors, but they are not, it seems to us, in themselves separately or together external factors of the kind capable in law of causing or contributing to a state of automatism. They constitute a state of mind which is prone to recur. They lack the feature of novelty or accident * * *. It is contrary to the observations of Devlin J., to which we have just referred in the case of Hill v. Baxter (supra). It does not, in our judgment, come within the scope of the exception "some external physical factor such as a blow on the head or the administration of an anaesthetic."

* * *

Appeal dismissed.

Questions

1. Suppose a brain concussion produces an unconscious state, during which accused commits what would otherwise be an assault. Is this a "mental deficiency," defined as "a defect attributable to mental retardation, brain damage and learning disabilities," which by statute categorizes the defense as one of insanity? Does it matter whether the concussion has long-term effects? See the majority and dissenting opinions in Fulcher v. State, 633 P.2d 142 (Wyo.1981). Suppose the accused has a post-traumatic stress disorder, making him prone to experiencing dissassociative states, during which consciousness is altered and involuntary acts may be performed. During one such dissassociative state he kills another person. May he properly claim an automatism (involuntary act) defense? See State v. Fields, 324 N.C. 204, 376 S.E.2d 740 (1989), holding it error to preclude such a defense.

2. Should the legislative or judicial choice between automatism and insanity defenses turn on the nature of the mental condition producing the involuntary act?

the nature of the appropriate medical treatment (if any) for the condition? the continuing dangerousness of the defendant?

3. Assuming that the nature of the defendant's mental condition is undisputed, should the defendant ever have a choice of whether to claim automatism or insanity, or be allowed to claim both, in the alternative? Are there reasons for discouraging such alternative defenses, even where the nature of the condition is debatable?

4. Are there policy problems with the automatism defense, other than that of what restraints, if any, to place on one who successfully claims it?

d. INTOXICATION; THE RELEVANCE OF ADDICTION AND ALCOHOLISM

United States v. F.D.L.

United States Court of Appeals, Eighth Circuit, 1988.
836 F.2d 1113.

JOHN R. GIBSON, CIRCUIT JUDGE.

F.D.L. and R.L.R.[1] appeal from an adjudication of delinquency pursuant to 18 U.S.C. §§ 5031 and 5032 (1982) following the district court's determination that defendants were guilty of committing involuntary manslaughter on an Indian reservation in violation of 18 U.S.C. §§ 2, 1112(b) and 1153. On appeal, both F.D.L. and R.L.R. allege that the district court erred in rejecting their defense claim of temporary insanity by reason of involuntary intoxication. We affirm the judgment of the district court.

* * *

On Monday, January 27, 1986, the frozen body of Loren Lyons was discovered in the back seat of his car, which was stuck in the snow off a road in Redlake, Minnesota. Lyons had died of hypothermia.

On the previous Friday night, F.D.L., R.L.R. and Connie Lussier, R.L.R.'s fifteen-year-old half-sister, after drinking several beers, went to Robert Nadeau's gas station in the "back of town" area of Redlake. There they met Lyons, who had also been drinking, and asked him for a ride. Lyons agreed and the group went to the home of R.L.R.'s grandmother, where R.L.R. picked up a television set which they planned to pawn to get money for marijuana. * * *

Abandoning the attempt to sell the television, Lyons pulled his car to the side of the road and rolled two marijuana cigarettes. Connie Lussier saw Lyons sprinkle a white powder on the marijuana. R.L.R., who was riding in the seat next to Lyons, did not see the white powder. There was testimony that the white powder Connie Lussier saw sprinkled on the marijuana was probably phencyclidine (commonly known as PCP or angel dust). Testimony established that PCP is commonly added to marijuana cigarettes and at the time of this incident was a problem on the Red Lake Reservation. Finally, the defendants and Connie Lussier testified they felt unusually "high" after smoking the marijuana.

1. Because the appellants are juveniles, references throughout this opinion will be to their initials only.

The group drove around Red Lake for another twenty minutes or so, when Lyons stopped the car so the defendants could urinate. While the defendants were outside they heard a car door slam. Fearing that Lyons was going to drive off with Connie, leaving the two defendants stranded several miles from home, F.D.L. opened the driver's door of the car and began pulling Lyons out of the car. A fight followed. R.L.R. joined in when he thought he saw Lyons reach for a screwdriver to use as a weapon against F.D.L. Connie Lussier testified the beating lasted fifteen minutes. After the fight, Lyons was unconscious. F.D.L. and R.L.R. lifted Lyons into the car and put him in the back seat. They could hear him breathing and snoring, and didn't think they had hurt him badly. * * *

F.D.L. and R.L.R. continued to drive, with Lyons in the back seat of the car. After dropping off Connie at the home of Sheldon Bailey, R.L.R. lost control of the car as he fumbled for a cigarette. The road was icy, and the car slid into a ditch and became embedded in a snow bank.

Leaving the motor and heater running, and a door ajar to prevent carbon monoxide poisoning, the defendants abandoned the car and walked about one-half mile to the home of Sheldon Bailey. R.L.R. walked that distance without his winter coat and testified that he didn't remember feeling cold.[3] From there, Sheldon Bailey drove R.L.R., F.D.L. and Connie to the home of Charles Bolio. R.L.R. left Bolio's house and walked one mile back to his grandmother's home, again without his winter jacket.

Over the weekend several people, including F.D.L., walked past Lyons' car in the ditch. No one observed until Monday that Lyons was in it. Temperatures in the area sank from eight degrees above zero on Friday night to twenty-six degrees below on Sunday night and Lyons froze to death.

* * *

The Fifth Circuit has stated: "The concept of criminal responsibility in the federal courts is a congeries of judicially made rules of decision based on common law concepts." United States v. Lyons, 731 F.2d 243, 247 (5th Cir.) (en banc), cert. denied, 469 U.S. 930, 105 S.Ct. 323, 83 L.Ed.2d 260 (1984). The practice of relieving a defendant of criminal responsibility, because of involuntary intoxication, extends back to the earliest days of common law. See Annotation, *When Intoxication Deemed Involuntary so as to Constitute a Defense to Criminal Charge,* 73 A.L.R.3d 195 § 2 (1976).

The courts dealing with this issue, nearly all of them state courts, have defined involuntary intoxication in essentially the same terms as insanity. Like insanity, involuntary intoxication diminishes the culpability of a crime. The defendant is excused from criminality because intoxication affects the ability to distinguish between right and wrong. Thus, the mental state of an involuntarily intoxicated defendant is measured by the test of legal insanity. The Ninth Circuit has recognized involuntary intoxication as a basis for invoking the insanity defense and it has expressed the rule in the same terms. United States v. Henderson, 680 F.2d 659 (9th Cir.1982). But see *Lyons,*

3. Dr. Carroll, an expert on the effects of PCP, testified that PCP is an anesthetic, the fact that R.L.R. had no coat, yet he did not remember feeling cold is consistent with ingestion of PCP.

731 F.2d at 245 (mere drug addiction, voluntary or involuntary, raises no issue of such a mental disease or defect as can serve as a basis for the insanity defense). These cases all require a finding that there has been involuntary ingestion of an intoxicant, usually through trickery, and that the defendant was unable to appreciate the nature and quality or wrongfulness of his acts.

There are facts in this record to support a finding that R.L.R. and F.D.L. were involuntarily intoxicated because, unknown to them, PCP had been added to their marijuana cigarettes. * * * It is also true that the court could have rejected the testimony that the intoxication was involuntary. The evidence offered to establish that PCP was in the marijuana cigarettes was not indisputable. The district court made no specific finding on this issue.

The findings of the district court, however, are sufficient to dispose of the involuntary intoxication defense, as they reject its second element, namely, that the defendants were unable to appreciate the nature and quality or wrongfulness of their acts. The district court found that at the time of the acts resulting in Lyons' death, the defendants were capable of knowing and did know, that their conduct was a threat to his life and they were able to foresee the consequences of their acts. These findings establish that R.L.R. and F.D.L. were able to appreciate the nature and quality or wrongfulness of their acts. * * *

* * * The appellants do not attack the district court findings on this issue, and our review of the record convinces us that the findings are not clearly erroneous. Accordingly, we reject the argument of F.D.L. and R.L.R. that the district court erred in refusing to accept the defense of involuntary intoxication.

Additionally, even if the district court believed that PCP was added to the marijuana, it may have determined the intoxication was not involuntary, but voluntary. R.L.R. and F.D.L. had voluntarily consumed beer and smoked marijuana cigarettes. Any intoxication resulting from this activity would be no defense. Congress in recently revising the Insanity defense statute specifically rejected voluntary intoxication as a defense even if it renders the defendant unable to appreciate the nature and quality of his acts.[6]

In a factually similar case, People v. Velez, 175 Cal.App.3d 785, 221 Cal.Rptr. 631 (1985), the defendant raised the defense of involuntary intoxication after smoking a marijuana cigarette unaware it contained PCP. The Court in holding the defendant *voluntarily* intoxicated as a matter of law noted,

> [A] reasonable person has no right to assume that a marijuana cigarette furnished to him at a social gathering will not contain PCP; nor may such a person assume such a marijuana cigarette will produce any predictable intoxicating effect. Absent these assumptions, defendant cannot contend he was involuntarily intoxicated, because he has no right to expect the

6. See S.Rep. No. 225, 98th Cong., 1st Sess. 229 (1983). See also United States v. Costello, 760 F.2d 1123, 1127–28 (11th Cir. 1985); United States v. Romano, 482 F.2d 1183, 1196 (5th Cir.1973), cert. denied, sub nom., Yassen v. United States, 414 U.S. 1129, 94 S.Ct. 866, 38 L.Ed.2d 753 (1974). Involuntary manslaughter, as defined in 18 U.S.C. § 1112, is a general intent crime. Voluntary intoxication is no defense to such a crime.

> substance he consumed was other than what it was nor that it would produce an intoxicating effect different from the one it did.

Id. 221 Cal.Rptr. at 638. But cf. People v. Scott, 146 Cal.App.3d 823, 194 Cal.Rptr. 633 (1983) (accused's intoxication is considered involuntary if caused by drink that has been drugged without his knowledge).[7]

* * *

* * * The district court found that by assaulting Lyons, leaving him alone and intoxicated in an abandoned automobile in subfreezing temperatures at night, R.L.R. and F.D.R. acted with gross negligence and reckless disregard for Lyons' life. It further found that they were capable of knowing and did know that their conduct was a threat to Lyons' life and they were able to foresee the consequences of their acts. These findings are fully supported by the record at the trial. We therefore conclude that there was sufficient evidence in this case to support the convictions.

* * *

Notes

1. *Nature of Involuntary Intoxication.* Commonwealth v. Wallace, 14 Mass. App.Ct. 358, 360–365, 439 N.E.2d 848, 850–853 (1982):

> Although the circumstances of a person who drives after taking a prescription drug unaware of its possible effects differ significantly from those of a person forced to drive after having a potion rammed down his throat or after being tricked, such circumstances also differ substantially from those of a person who drives after voluntarily consuming alcohol or drugs whose effects are or should be known.[7.1] The law recognizes the differences, and authorities have characterized as "involuntary intoxication by medicine" the condition of a defendant who has taken prescribed drugs with severe unanticipated effects. See LaFave & Scott, Criminal Law § 45, at 348 (1972); Perkins, Criminal Law 897 (2d ed. 1969) ("such intoxication is involuntary, because the patient is entitled to assume that an intoxicating dose would not be prescribed").[8] See also Commonwealth v. Sheehan, 376 Mass. 765, 771 n. 6, 383 N.E.2d 1115 (1978), where the court noted that no evidence had been offered that the consumption in that case was involuntary, and pointed out that "[d]ifferent considerations may well be appropriate in determining criminal responsibility where a defendant's conduct is affected by a forced, an unknowing, or a lawful consumption of drugs."

7. The court in *Velez,* 221 Cal.Rptr. at 638, distinguishes *Scott,* supra, noting that courts have allowed the defense of involuntary intoxication based on the ingestion of an unlawful drug where the defendant reasonably believed he was consuming a lawful substance or where the unlawful drug was placed without defendant's knowledge in a *lawful* substance.

7.1 In the case of alcohol, our cases posit that "the effects of liquor upon the mind and actions of men are well known to everybody." Commonwealth v. Taylor, 263 Mass. 356, 362, 161 N.E. 245 (1928). See also Commonwealth v. Hawkins, 3 Gray 463, 466 (1855). The same assumption applies where there is a voluntary consumption (usually illicit) of statutorily defined drugs obtained other than through a physician's prescription. See Commonwealth v. Sheehan, 376 Mass. 765, 771, 383 N.E.2d 1115 (1978); Commonwealth v. Loretta, 386 Mass. 794, 799–800, 438 N.E.2d 56 (1982).

8. The Model Penal Code § 2.08(5)(b) (1962) defines self-induced intoxication as follows: "intoxication caused by substances which the actor knowingly introduces into his body, the tendency of which to cause intoxication he knows or ought to know, unless he introduces them pursuant to medical advice or under such circumstances as would afford a defense to a charge of crime."

Although there are few cases involving unanticipated effects of prescription drugs on a defendant's driving ability, and although each case depends on the specific statutory provision involved, the concept of "involuntary intoxication" has been applied to motor vehicle violations of the type under consideration in the present case. Authorities elsewhere indicate that such a nonvoluntary taking of a drug excuses certain motor vehicle offenses.

The question remains, however, whether the Massachusetts Legislature in § 24(1)(a) intended to penalize driving after such consumption, even if characterized as non-voluntary. In Commonwealth v. Kraatz, 2 Mass.App. 196, 200, 310 N.E.2d 368 (1974), we noted that the history of § 24 is "a patchwork of judicial decisions and legislative engraftments which beclouds any clear perception of legislative intent." Nevertheless, there is some indication, both in legislative material and in judicial decisions, that § 24 is not intended to impose criminal liability on unknowing defendants.

* * *

Our conclusion is strengthened by a rule of construction, followed in Massachusetts, which requires particular clarity of language before finding a legislative intent to create a "public welfare" offense punishable by a severe penalty. * * *

No such clear language appears in G.L. c. 90, § 24(1)(a). Accordingly, we hold that it was error to preclude the defendant from introducing evidence that he did not know of the possible effects of the medication on his driving ability, that he did not receive warnings as to its use, and that he had no reason to anticipate the effects which the drug induced.[15] His failure to receive warnings from his physician and pharmacist, if there is evidence of such failure, is relevant both to the charge of driving under the influence of drugs (G.L. c. 90, § 24[1][a] and to the charge of negligence (G.L. c. 90, § 24[2][a]).

2. *Addiction as a Candidate for Insanity.* United States v. Lyons, 731 F.2d 243, 245–247 (5th Cir.1984):

Today the great weight of legal authority clearly supports the view that evidence of mere narcotics addiction, standing alone and without other physiological or psychological involvement, raises no issue of such a mental defect or disease as can serve as a basis for the insanity defense. Bailey v. United States, 386 F.2d 1, 3–4 (5th Cir.1967), cert. denied, 392 U.S. 946, 88 S.Ct. 2300, 20 L.Ed.2d 1408 (1968). Accord, United States v. Moore, 486 F.2d 1139, 1181 (D.C.Cir.) (en banc), cert. denied, 414 U.S. 980, 94 S.Ct. 298, 38 L.Ed.2d 224 (1973); United States v. Freeman, 357 F.2d 606, 625 (2d Cir.1966); Cf. United States v. Romano, 482 F.2d 1183, 1196 (5th Cir.1973), cert. denied sub nom. Yassen v. United States, 414 U.S. 1129, 94 S.Ct. 866, 38 L.Ed.2d 753 (1974) (being involuntarily[a] under the influence of drugs at the time of the crime is not a legal equivalent of insanity). See also Fingarette, *Addiction and Criminal Responsibility,* 84 Yale L.J. 413, 424–25 (1975) ("there is no consensus in the medical profession that addiction is a mental disease").

There are a number of reasons why. In the first place, there is an element of reasoned choice when an addict knowingly acquires and uses drugs; he could instead have participated in an addiction treatment program. Moore, 486 F.2d at

15. We do not imply that a jury could not in some instances find that a defendant had information sufficient to place on him a duty of inquiring of his doctor as to the possible effects of a prescription drug. In such circumstances, a conviction under § 24(1)(a) would be proper if it is found that the defendant was negligent in not asking, and hence not knowing, of such possible effects on his driving.

a. [sic.] The *Romano* case said this of voluntary drug taking. See 482 F.2d at 1196.

1183 (opinion of Leventhal, J.). A person is not to be excused for offending "simply because he wanted to very, very badly." Bailey, 386 F.2d at 4. Second, since the defense of insanity is "essentially an acknowledgement on the part of society that because of mental disease or defect certain classes of wrongdoers are not properly the subjects of criminal punishment," Freeman, 357 F.2d at 625, it seems anomalous to immunize narcotics addicts from other criminal sanctions when Congress has decreed severe penalties for mere possession and sale of narcotics. Id. In addition, Congress has dealt with the problem of responsibility of narcotics addicts for their crimes by providing for civil commitment and treatment of addicts in lieu of prosecution or sentencing. Bailey, 386 F.2d at 4. See, e.g., 18 U.S.C. §§ 4251–4255 (1976); 28 U.S.C. §§ 2901–2906 (1976).

Finally, what definition of "mental disease or defect" is to be employed by courts enforcing the criminal law is, in the final analysis, a question of legal, moral and policy—not of medical—judgment. Among the most basic purposes of the criminal law is that of preventing a person from injuring others or, perhaps to a lesser degree, himself. This purpose and others appropriate to law enforcement are not necessarily served by an uncritical application of definitions developed with medical considerations of diagnosis and treatment foremost in mind. * * *

* * *

Although mere narcotics addiction is not itself to be acknowledged as a mental disease or defect, evidence of narcotics addiction has been received by some courts as evidence of such an underlying condition. Green v. United States, 383 F.2d 199, 201 (D.C.Cir.1967), cert. denied, 390 U.S. 961, 88 S.Ct. 1061, 19 L.Ed.2d 1158 (1968). In addition, if addiction has caused actual physical damage to the structures of a defendant's body, evidence of that addiction has been admitted to show any mental defect resulting from that damage. Cf. Brinkley v. United States, 498 F.2d 505, 511–12 (8th Cir.1974) (remanding to explore possible physiological and psychological effects of long term LSD use on appellant and whether these effects might amount to insanity).

We view the reasoning of such rulings as *Green* with profound misgivings. To us it seems to rest on the proposition that, assuming drug addiction itself is neither a mental disease nor a defect, yet the two are often to be found in association, so that an addicted person is more likely to suffer from some mental disorder than is one who is not addicted. By a parity of reasoning, since combat veterans as a group are self-evidently more likely to have suffered the loss of a physical member than is the populace at large, evidence of whether a party is a combat veteran should be received on the issue whether he has lost a leg. Or, to take a less extreme example, since because of light skin pigmentation persons of Scandinavian ancestry are more subject to skin cancer than are others, the family tree of a suitor should be received in evidence when his skin cancer is at legal issue. The flaw in both illustrations seems evident: where evidence bearing directly on a legal question is available, that involving tangential matters, even though perhaps logically relevant in theory, is of small practical value.

Our review of numerous records over the course of years has revealed no dearth of experts ready and willing to testify squarely on the issue of insanity in criminal trials: direct evidence on the issue seems all but too readily available. Since this is so, receiving evidence of drug addiction in addition seems to us an exercise seldom likely to prove more probative than prejudicial in practice. See Rule 403, Federal Rules of Evidence.

Nor do we see how matters are clarified by reference to the condition of addiction as one involving "psychological damage" to the addict, e.g., Brinkley v. United States, supra. As nearly as we can determine, the psychological condition so described is simply one of drug addiction to one degree or another, a condition that we have already declined to view as a mental disease or defect for legal purposes. An actual drug-induced or drug-aggravated psychosis, or physical damage to the brain or nervous system would, however, be another matter.

We do not doubt that actual physical damage to the brain itself falls within the ambit of "mental disease or defect." To refuse to recognize that a congenital microcephalic, or one who has suffered, say, extensive brain damage from a gunshot wound or other physical trauma, may be thereby rendered unable to appreciate the character of his conduct as wrongful would be presumptuous. Here, within the limits of appropriate legal and policy considerations, the medical model must have its day. The same is true of the question whether such organic brain pathology or psychosis can be caused by drugs.

3. *Mental Disorder Produced by Intoxication.* Prolonged alcohol abuse may produce a recognized mental disease or defect such as delirium tremens. The fact that the disease or defect is caused by voluntary intoxication does not prevent application of the insanity test to one who has such a disease.

Questions

1. Courts usually treat alcohol-induced and other drug-induced conduct according to the same rules. Is there any reason for not doing so?

2. Should involuntary intoxication be an excuse in an absolute liability offense?

People v. Langworthy

Supreme Court of Michigan, 1982.
416 Mich. 630, 331 N.W.2d 171.

FITZGERALD, CHIEF JUSTICE.

The common ground of these cases is that, at their trials, both defendants attempted to utilize voluntary intoxication as a defense to charges of crimes which Michigan appellate courts previously have held to be general-intent crimes. Both defendants request this Court to expand the category of specific-intent crimes to include the offenses they were convicted of, i.e., first-degree criminal sexual conduct and second-degree murder, in order to make available to them the defense of voluntary intoxication.

Facts

Defendant Lundy was found guilty but mentally ill of three counts of first-degree criminal sexual conduct, M.C.L. § 750.520b; M.S.A. § 28.788(2), and sentenced to three concurrent life terms. The convictions arose from the October 30, 1978, rape of his adult sister. The crime, carried out with the use of a knife as a threatening weapon, involved three penetrations.

At Lundy's bench trial, the major issue centered on defendant's mental state at the time of the commission of the crime. His defense was predicated upon expert testimony regarding his mental state as well as evidence that he had been sniffing glue and drinking alcohol immediately prior to the crime. The trial court rejected Lundy's insanity defense as well as his intoxication defense, ruling as to the latter that first-degree criminal sexual conduct is a general-intent crime.

The Court of Appeals affirmed in a memorandum opinion.

Defendant Langworthy was convicted of second-degree murder, M.C.L. § 750.317; M.S.A. § 28.549, and was sentenced to 60 to 90 years in prison.

After a bench trial, the trial judge found that on the night of November 5, 1976, defendant, Roy Schipani, and Alan Parker were together indulging in alcohol and drugs in a house in Ypsilanti. Parker left sometime during the early morning hours to purchase cigarettes at a gas station. There he met the decedent, William Wedge, who returned to the house with Parker.

The trial judge further found that Wedge was intoxicated and offensive and that Wedge made certain comments which irritated defendant. Wedge then passed out and the three others discussed robbing Wedge. Defendant suggested that they "blow him away" and then he turned up the stereo, went to a closet where he got a rifle and shot Wedge in the mouth and in the chest.

The trial judge determined that the defendant was not mentally ill or legally insane at the time of the commission of the crime. He found that defendant had taken at least 400 milligrams of Valium and some codeine and Nembutal and had been drinking Southern Comfort and Coke at the time of the crime. The trial judge concluded:

> "However, the Court finds that as a result of the drugs and alcohol his judgment and his appreciation of the consequence of his actions was grossly impaired.
>
> "That he committed the act knowingly with malice but 'without a real concept of the consequence of the act.' That he had a conscious intent to commit the crime but that his judgment and appreciation of the consequence of his act was grossly impaired as the result of the drugs and alcohol."

The Court of Appeals affirmed in an unpublished opinion per curiam, ruling, *inter alia,* that second-degree murder is not a specific-intent crime and that, therefore, voluntary intoxication was not a defense.

A. The Voluntary Intoxication Defense

Every jurisdiction in this country recognizes the general principle that voluntary intoxication is not any excuse for crime.[1] This is in accord with the common-law rule dating back to the sixteenth century which allowed no concession to a defendant because of his intoxication.[2] However, by the

1. Anno: *Modern status of the rules as to voluntary intoxication as defense to criminal charge,* 8 A.L.R.3d 1236; 21 Am.Jur.2d, Criminal Law, § 155, p. 295; 22 C.J.S., Criminal Law, § 66, p. 214; Perkins, Criminal Law (2d ed.), p. 898; 2 Torcia, Wharton's Criminal Law (14th ed.), § 108, p. 49; People v. Walker, 38 Mich. 156, 158 (1878); People v. Guillett, 342 Mich. 1, 5, 69 N.W.2d 140 (1955); Bishop v. United States, 71 U.S.App. D.C. 132, 136, 107 F.2d 297 (1939).

2. Hall, Criminal Law (2d ed.), p. 529; Clark & Marshall, Crimes (7th ed.), § 6.09, p. 433; Singh, *History of the Defense of Drunkenness in English Criminal Law,* 49 L.Qtr.Rev. 528 (1933).

In fact, Blackstone and Coke attempted to make drunkenness an aggravation of the offense. Hall, supra, p. 530; Singh, supra, p. 531; Miller, Criminal Law, § 42, p. 137.

early nineteenth century, the English courts began to fashion a doctrine to mitigate the harshness and rigidity of the traditional rule.[3] The doctrine, which has come to be known as the exculpatory rule, was stated by Judge Stephen as follows:

> "[A]lthough you cannot take drunkenness as any excuse for crime, yet when the crime is such that the intention of the party committing it is one of its constituent elements, you may look at the fact that a man was in drink in considering whether he formed the intention necessary to constitute the crime." [4]

It is said that the theory behind this exculpatory doctrine is that it does not hold that drunkenness will excuse crime; rather, it inquires whether the very crime which the law defines has in fact been committed. Almost every state, by statute or by common law, has adopted the exculpatory rule,[6] and Michigan is no exception.

> "While it is true that drunkenness cannot excuse crime, it is equally true that when a certain intent is a necessary element in a crime, the crime cannot have been committed when the intent did not exist." People v. Walker, 38 Mich. 156, 158 (1878). See, also, People v. Crittle, 390 Mich. 367, 212 N.W.2d 196 (1973).

The applicability of the exculpatory rule rests entirely on the determination whether the offense involved is categorized as a general- or specific-intent crime.

> "It is important in this decision to emphasize that intoxication may only negative the existence of *specific intent.* Examination of the cases reveals that where the rule was applied, it was done so in cases where the crime charged also involved a specific intent." People v. Guillett, 342 Mich. 1, 6, 69 N.W.2d 140 (1955). See, also, Roberts v. People, 19 Mich. 401 (1870).

Thus, if a crime is determined to require only a general intent, the defendant's voluntary intoxication during the commission of an offense may not be asserted as a defense to the existence of the mental element of that crime.

The general intent-specific intent dichotomy arose as a compromise between the perceived need to afford some relief to the intoxicated offender whose moral culpability was considered less than that of a sober person who committed the same offense and the view that a person who voluntarily becomes drunk and commits a crime should not escape the consequences.[8] Although the rule seems logical on the surface, it has proven to be far from

3. The doctrine was first suggested by Justice Holroyd in 1819 when he stated that voluntary drunkenness should be considered in determining the existence of premeditation. Rex v. Grindley, quoted in Rex v. Carroll, 7 C. & P. 145; 173 Eng.Rep. 64 (1835). In Regina v. Cruse, 8 C. & P. 541; 173 Eng.Rep. 610 (1838), in a case of assault with intent to murder, the jury was instructed that gross intoxication could disprove the intent element for the aggravated offense. Hall, fn 2 supra, pp 531–532; People v. Hood, 1 Cal.3d 444, 456, fn 5, 82 Cal.Rptr. 618, 462 P.2d 370 (1969); Singh, fn 2 supra, pp. 537–539.

4. Regina v. Doherty, 16 Cox.Crim.C. 306, 308 (N.P.1887).

6. See, e.g., 8 A.L.R.3d 1236, fn. 1 supra. Vermont and Missouri are the exceptions.

8. Hall, fn. 2 supra, pp. 537, 544; People v. Hood, fn. 3 supra, 377.

It is reported that Justice Coleridge first used the term "specific intention" in Regina v. Monkhouse, 4 Cox.Crim.C. 55 (1849). Yet,

logical in application. While specific intent can easily be defined as "a particular criminal intent beyond the act done" [9] (whereas general intent is the intent simply to do the physical act), the ease of stating the definition belies the difficulty of applying it in practice. In order to appreciate the problem, one need only note the divergence of opinion among the jurisdictions as to which crimes require a specific intent and, therefore, to which crimes the exculpatory rule applies.[10]

It has been noted that the law with respect to voluntary intoxication and criminal responsibility has shown little tendency to change or develop despite advances socially and medically in this area; and, we might add, despite strong criticism from treatise writers, law review commentators, case law,[14] and the drafters of the Model Penal Code.[15] My Brother Levin summarized the major criticisms of the exculpatory rule while on the Court of Appeals:

> "It has also been maintained that the availability of the intoxication defense should not depend on whether a court chooses to characterize an element of the crime charged as separate from the element of general intent. It has been observed that neither common experience nor psychology knows of any such phenomenon as 'general intent' distinguishable from 'specific intent.' It does seem incongruous to make the admissibility of mitigating evidence depend on whether the statutory definition of a crime includes a separately stated intent, and other methods of defining specific intent are highly manipulable.
>
> "The clumsiness of the exculpatory device has been criticized. A defendant who is charged with a specific intent crime may go free if he can prove he was intoxicated; this result contrasts sharply with the absolute denial of relief to the intoxicated offender charged with a crime of general intent.
>
> "If the function of the general/specific intent distinction is to eliminate the defense as to lesser included offenses, e.g., assault and

"[h]e did not mean to weave any particular magic with these words." Beck & Parker, *The Intoxicated Offender—A Problem of Responsibility,* 44 Can.Bar.Rev. 563, 578 (1966). See, also, Singh, fn. 2 supra, pp. 539–540.

9. People v. Depew, 215 Mich. 317, 320, 183 N.W. 750 (1921). See, also, Roberts v. People, 19 Mich. 401, 414 (1870); LaFave & Scott, Criminal Law, § 28, p. 202:

"[T]he most common usage of 'specific intent' is to designate a special mental element which is required above and beyond any mental state required with respect to the *actus reus* of the crime."

10. 5 Am.Jur. Proof of Facts 2d, pp. 194–196. See, e.g., 8 A.L.R.3d, fn. 1 supra, pp. 1246–1257.

14. *People v. Hood,* fn. 3 supra, Australia's High Court recently rejected the general intent—specific intent rule and held that the prosecutor must prove the mental element for each. The High Court said that the distinction between general and specific intent was unsatisfactory in that it is difficult to define, it is not based on any factual difference between various states of mind, and it does not always work rationally in that it is not always the more serious offense which requires proof of specific intent. Queen v. O'Connor, 29 Austl.L.Rpts. 449 (1980), as reported in Orchard, *Criminal Responsibility and Intoxication—The Australian Rejection of Majewski,* New Zealand L.J. 532 (1980).

15. The Model Penal Code would abolish the use of the general intent-specific intent distinction. "[W]e can see no virtue in preserving the concept of 'general intent,' which has been an abiding source of ambiguity and of confusion in the penal law." Model Penal Code (Tentative Draft No. 4, 1956), § 2.02, Comment 5, p. 128. See, also, Model Penal Code (Tentative Draft No. 9, 1958), § 2.08.

battery, but to retain it for the more serious offenses, e.g., armed robbery, and in that manner mitigate the general rule that intoxication is not a defense, then manifestly this should be done on a consistent basis. The right to interpose this defense, should depend on something more substantial than a technical distinction that was seized upon by a judge 130 years ago and adopted by other judges to reach results thought sound in the cases then before them. People v. Kelley, 21 Mich.App. 612, 628–630, 176 N.W.2d 435 (1970).

While we recognize the illogic and incongruity of the general intent-specific intent dichotomy, the remedy is not clear-cut. One solution, of course, would be to join the ranks of those few states which do not allow the voluntary intoxication defense even where a specific intent is required. We agree, however, with Professors LaFave and Scott that this view is clearly wrong.[16] It would require us to ignore basic concepts of criminal culpability as well as modern scientific views on alcoholism.

The alternative would be to allow the intoxication defense to be asserted against any charge of crime which traditionally has required general or specific intent. Although this Court has the power to so modify the common-law rule, we believe that it would be imprudent to take that step at this time. While abolishing the general intent-specific intent distinction may rid the courts of an illogical rule, it would do nothing to help solve the problem of the intoxicated offender, both from the standpoint of the offender and from the standpoint of society which suffers from the acts of the intoxicated offender. Moreover, because the parties before us did not specifically address the issue of abolishing the exculpatory rule, we do not have the benefit of an adversarial presentation of the pros and cons of such an action. This Court should be hesitant to abolish an established common-law rule without a fully developed presentation of both sides of the question.

The problem of alcoholism and crime is complex, requiring studies and policy considerations beyond the ability of any judicial body. Various solutions which have been proposed would require legislative action.[18] We urge the Legislature to consider the intoxicated-offender problem and to modernize Michigan law on this subject. Until the Legislature takes action or until we are persuaded to modify the common-law rule in an appropriate case in the future, we shall continue to struggle with applying the rule case by case.

16. LaFave and Scott, fn. 9 supra, p. 344.

18. Professor Hall has proposed that a distinction be made between inexperienced inebriates, "those who had no previous experience with intoxication that rendered them dangerous", and experienced inebriates. Hall, fn. 2 supra, p. 554.

Another commentator suggests for consideration the 1960 German *Draft* Penal Code which adopts the middle ground of holding the intoxicated offender to a diminished responsibility.

Justice Levin, in People v. Kelley, supra, 21 Mich.App. 628, fn. 23, 176 N.W.2d 435, recommends legislation defining a new crime of committing crimes under the influence of drugs or liquor. This new crime could be graded, "depending on the extent and the gravity of antisocial act(s) previously committed in a comatose condition, and on the antisocial conduct immediately involved".

B. Is First-Degree Criminal Sexual Conduct a Specific Intent Crime?

* * *

This case requires us to decide whether first-degree criminal sexual conduct is a general- or specific-intent crime. We have previously held, under the predecessor to the criminal sexual conduct statute, that rape is not a specific-intent crime. People v. Phillips, 385 Mich. 30, 187 N.W.2d 211 (1971). This comports with the overwhelming weight of authority which holds that rape is a general-intent crime.[21]

An examination of the statute convinces us that the Legislature did not intend to include specific intent as an element of first-degree criminal sexual conduct. Neither the first-degree criminal sexual conduct statute nor the corresponding statutory definition of "sexual penetration" contains any language whatsoever regarding intent. * * *

Finally, we reject defendant's argument that if an applicable lesser included offense of a criminal sexual conduct offense requires specific intent, it necessarily follows that the greater offense also requires proof of specific intent. Other courts presented with this argument have rejected it, and we reject it also. We concur with the United States Court of Appeals, writing in United States v. Thornton, 162 U.S.App.D.C. 207, 210–211, 498 F.2d 749 (1974):

> "Actually, as has been stated, '[A]ll attempts require specific intent'; so if it were to follow appellant's logic of superimposing the specific intent of an included crime upon the greater offense, a specific intent would be required for practically every crime. This could not be the law. The differing requirements for lesser offenses result principally from the differing nature of the crimes and from their historical and legislative definitions. The requirement of a specific intent for lesser crimes exists because of a desire to protect the individual against conviction on slight evidence. The same protection is unnecessary where substantial overt acts are committed and fully consummated offenses are provable. There is no rule of law that crimes which carry greater punishment require the proof of greater, or even the same, criminal intent as included or related crimes which carry lesser punishment. Each crime has its own elements and peculiarities and as we said in McGuinn v. United States, 89 U.S.App.D.C. 197, 199; 191 F.2d 477, 479 (1951), 'Rape is not a crime which requires a specific intent.' This is in accord with the great weight of authority which holds the crime of rape requires no intent other than that indicated by the commission of the acts constituting the offense."

Accordingly, we conclude that first-degree criminal sexual conduct is a general-intent crime for which the defense of voluntary intoxication is not available.

21. * * *

We have been unable to find any case which has specifically held that intoxication is a defense to a charge of rape. It appears that we are not alone. Frank v. State, 6 Md.App. 332, 335, 251 A.2d 249 (1969).

C. Is Second-Degree Murder a General or Specific Intent Crime?

Defendant Langworthy petitions this Court to extend to second-degree murder cases the rule in People v. Garcia, 398 Mich. 250, 247 N.W.2d 547 (1976), that non-felony first-degree murder is a specific-intent crime. * * *

In support of his position, defendant has cited for our consideration cases from other jurisdictions which allow murder to be reduced to manslaughter through the successful assertion of the voluntary intoxication defense. We have reviewed these cases and others, and we have concluded that they are not applicable to the situation existing in Michigan.[27] An examination of the jurisdictions which defendant relies upon demonstrates why the cases are clearly distinguishable.

Unlike that of Michigan, the statutory schemes of some states do not divide murder into degrees. To further complicate comparison, these states may require, as an element of their single crime of murder, premeditation or some other specific mental element (such as intent to kill) not required for second-degree murder in Michigan. These states do no more than Michigan already does with respect to first-degree murder, i.e., allow intoxication to negate the element of premeditation (or intent to kill) and reduce the degree of the offense. The difference is that in these states negation of premeditation, for example, means that murder has not been proven at all, whereas in Michigan it only means that first-degree murder has not been proven. This difference is due to the legislative classification of homicide, which we have no control over and, consequently, which makes these cases distinguishable.

* * *

Thus, we find that all of the jurisdictions which defendant relies upon as persuasive authority for his position are not applicable to our circumstances in Michigan. In any event, despite the existence of cases which allow a proper voluntary intoxication defense to reduce murder or second-degree murder to manslaughter, the majority rule remains as follows:

> " 'It is now generally held that intoxication may be considered where murder is divided into degrees, and in many states, may have the effect of reducing homicide from murder in the first degree to murder in the second degree. In fact, in most states the only consideration given to the fact of drunkenness or intoxication at the time of the commission of the homicide is to enable the court and jury to determine whether the prisoner may be guilty of murder in the second degree, rather than of murder in the first degree. The rule followed by most courts is that intoxication will not reduce a homicide from murder to manslaughter. 40 Am Jur 2d, Homicide,

27. The difficulty with reliance on case law from other jurisdictions in this area of law is that we are dealing with three concepts, each of which is necessary to the decision of the question involved here, and each of which is unique to the jurisdiction under consideration. Those three concepts are the definition of second-degree murder, the definition of malice, and the particular voluntary intoxication rule involved, whether statutory or common-law. The lack of identity of the three concepts makes comparison difficult. The divergence of result depending on the rule followed by a particular jurisdiction is noted in 40 Am.Jur.2d, Homicide, § 129, p. 421.

§ 129 at 420–421. See also 40 CJS, Homicide, § 5 at 831. ("Voluntary intoxication does not of itself negative the malice required to constitute murder in the second degree and thereby reduce murder in the second degree to voluntary manslaughter."); Annot. 12 ALR 861, 888 ("the great weight of authority is that intoxication will not reduce a homicide from murder to manslaughter"), 79 ALR 897, 904'."[33]

* * *

With respect to the element of malice encompassing wanton and willful disregard, we concur with the majority rule that voluntary intoxication is not a defense. We agree with the analysis of Professors LaFave and Scott:

> "The person who unconsciously creates risk because he is voluntarily drunk is perhaps morally worse than one who does so because he is sober but mentally deficient. At all events, the cases generally hold that drunkenness does not negative a depraved heart by blotting out consciousness of risk, and the Model Penal Code, which generally requires awareness of the risk for depraved-heart murder (and for recklessness manslaughter), so provides."[35]

Because second-degree murder does not require intent to kill, but rather, only wanton and willful disregard malice need be shown; and, because we have concluded that voluntary intoxication may not negate this latter category of malice, we believe that voluntary intoxication should not be a defense to a charge of second-degree murder. We are aware that there may be second-degree murder cases which involve only the intent to kill or the intent to do great bodily harm types of malice. We are further aware that these two categories of malice sound suspiciously akin to the traditional language of specific intent. However, we decline to extend the defense of voluntary intoxication to these cases on the grounds of public policy.

* * *

In short, we agree with the majority of jurisdictions which hold:

> "As between murder in the first degree and murder in the second degree, voluntary drunkenness may be a legitimate subject of inquiry, but as between murder in the second degree and manslaughter it is never material and cannot be considered."[36]

We hold that second-degree murder is not a specific-intent crime for which the defense of voluntary intoxication may be asserted.

* * *

WILLIAMS, COLEMAN and RYAN, JJ., concur.

33. State v. Hall, 214 N.W.2d 205, 208–209 (Iowa, 1974). See, also, LaFave & Scott, fn. 9 supra, pp. 345, 586; Model Penal Code (Tentative Draft No. 9, 1958), § 2.08, p. 5, Comment 2; 8 A.L.R.3d, fn. 1 supra; Hall, fn. 2 supra, p. 534; State v. Bunn, 283 N.C. 444, 196 S.E.2d 777 (1973).

35. LaFave & Scott, fn. 9 supra, p. 545. See, also, Perkins, fn. 1 supra, p. 900; Torcia, fn. 1 supra, p. 63; Rogers v. State, 196 Tenn. 263, 265 S.W.2d 559 (1954); Jones v. State, 70 Wis.2d 41, 233 N.W.2d 430 (1975); Commonwealth v. Cambric, 475 Pa. 454, 380 A.2d 1224 (1977); People v. LeGrand, 61 A.D.2d 815, 402 N.Y.S.2d 209 (1978); N.Y. Penal Law, § 15.05, N.D.Cent.Code, § 12.1–04–02.

36. Johnson v. Commonwealth, 135 Va. 524, 529, 115 S.E. 673 (1923).

RILEY, J., not participating.

COLEMAN, JUSTICE.

I have signed my colleague's opinion believing that his reasoning and conclusions are correct regarding the applicability of the voluntary intoxication defense in these cases. I write separately to note that I do not join in his recommendations to the Legislature to address the general-specific-intent analysis employed in these cases. I am not persuaded that the distinction is either illogical or unworkable.

LEVIN, JUSTICE (dissenting).

* * *

I

* * *

In People v. Garcia, 398 Mich. 250, 259, 247 N.W.2d 547 (1976), this Court recognized, in the context of first-degree murder, that intent to kill is a specific intent which voluntary intoxication can negate. Similarly, malice aforethought based upon intent to inflict great bodily harm is, by definition, a specific intent although there has not been any need to rule thereon until now. The opinion of the Court seems to agree.

The reason the Court gives for its conclusion that second-degree murder is not a specific-intent offense is that the malice requirement may be satisfied by showing "willful and wanton disregard". This ignores that it is rare for a person to be charged with second-degree murder on the theory that he acted with willful and wanton disregard. Where the evidence does not support a finding of intent to kill or to inflict great bodily harm, the charge is usually voluntary manslaughter and not second-degree murder. It is letting the tail wag the dog to classify second-degree murder as a general-intent crime because willful and wanton disregard may in a few isolated cases be the prosecution's theory.

* * *

* * * It cannot thus properly be said that second-degree murder does not include a specific intent. It can only be said that a person may—in some other case—be convicted of second-degree murder without a finding of specific intent upon a finding of wanton and willful disregard.

To be sure, the intoxication defense deserves legislative consideration. Until the Legislature acts, we should apply the judicially crafted specific-general-intent distinction on a reasoned basis. We should not ignore that where second-degree murder is charged, the people's theory is almost universally intent to kill or to inflict great bodily harm and only rarely if ever willful and wanton disregard. It is hypertechnical to classify second-degree murder, which has "intent to" elements, as a general-intent crime because in a rare case a person might be convicted on a theory of willful and wanton disregard.

In the instant case, the prosecution did not claim willful and wanton disregard. The people rather introduced evidence tending to show that Langworthy killed with premeditation, deliberation and malice. The judge found "that the defendant consciously and knowingly shot the deceased intending to kill him''. Langworthy was thus convicted on the basis of specific intent to kill, and voluntary intoxication should be a defense.

II

* * *

The general-specific-intent distinction is a formalistic one which turns on whether an ''intent to'' is an element of the offense. Specific intent crimes include larceny, because an element of the offense is felonious intent to deprive the owner permanently of his property; robbery, because it is larceny with force; first-degree murder, because the malice must be express (intent to kill or to do great bodily harm); burglary, because intent to commit a felony is an element.

The definition of common-law rape did not articulate a specific intent. Rape was the carnal knowledge of a woman by force and against her will. Because the common-law definition did not in so many words describe a particular intent, rape was generally regarded as a general-intent crime.

The Legislature has now repealed the common-law offense and substituted its own definitions in painstaking detail. The common-law definition of rape, therefore, is no longer the law of this state. We now must determine, as a matter of statutory construction, whether the *statutory* definitions encompass an element of specific intent.

We would construe the provision of the statute establishing the offense of first-degree criminal sexual conduct as requiring a specific intent because that appears to be the most reasonable construction of the statute read as a whole.

The critical words in the statute are ''sexual contact'' and ''sexual penetration''. The definition of ''sexual contact'' manifestly requires a specific intent:

> ''Sexual contact' includes the intentional touching of the victim's or actor's intimate parts or the intentional touching of the clothing covering the immediate area of the victim's or actor's intimate parts, if that intentional touching can reasonably be construed as being for the purpose of sexual arousal or gratification.'' M.C.L. § 750.520a(g); M.S.A. § 28.788(1)(g).

While the definition of ''sexual penetration'' does not explicitly state a specific intent:

> '' 'Sexual penetration' means sexual intercourse, cunnilingus, fellatio, anal intercourse, or any other intrusion, however slight, of any part of a person's body or of any object into the genital or anal openings of another person's body, but emission of semen is not required.'' M.C.L. § 750.520a(h); M.S.A. § 28.788(1)(h),

this was apparently because non-intentional penetration is unusual and it would therefore have been supererogatory to spell out ''intentional'' as part of the definition of penetration.

Given the structure of the statute, we would construe the statutory definition of ''sexual penetration'' as requiring the intent to penetrate. Not to so construe the statute would, somewhat anomalously, mean that persons who, without specific intent, "sexually penetrate" are fully criminally responsible although those who, without specific intent, "sexually contact" are free of criminal responsibility.[7] Moreover, as one author put it, speaking of the common-law offense, "the actual intention in rape is as specific as can be imagined".[8]

Because the statutory offense of first-degree criminal sexual conduct requires the specific intent to penetrate,[9] and because voluntary intoxication is a defense to specific-intent crimes, the judge erred in not considering whether Lundy was intoxicated to such an extent as to negative the mental element of intent.

* * *

We would reverse and remand for new trials.

KAVANAGH, J., concurs.

Questions

1. Would the *Langworthy* majority's difficulties have been fewer if it had defined specific intent for the purpose of the intoxication rule as the equivalent of Model Penal Code purpose or knowledge?

2. In a crime of "specific intent" what practical difference to the accused does it make whether he is found to have been voluntarily or involuntarily intoxicated?

3. Suppose involuntary intoxication prevents the deliberation required for first degree murder, but is not severe enough to acquit, applying the local insanity test. Is there a defense?

4. Is there good reason for denying the defense of voluntary intoxication to a crime of recklessness? See Model Penal Code § 2.08(2). It might be argued that the recklessness in becoming drunk counts as an equivalent to the recklessness ordinarily involved in the crime. Is voluntary intoxication always the result of (at least) the drinker's recklessness?

5. Should drunkenness aggravate crimes?

Notes

1. *Policy.* Commonwealth v. Bridge, 495 Pa. 568, 574, 435 A.2d 151, 154 (1981):

7. The effect of the distinction is to free from criminal responsibility those who sexually "contact" without specific intent, because intoxicated or narcotized, but to hold fully responsible those who sexually "penetrate" albeit in the same beclouded state of mind.

8. Hall, General Principles of Criminal Law (2d ed., 1960), 143.

9. See LaFave & Scott, Criminal Law, § 45, pp. 343, 344 (1972),

> "One is not guilty of rape, or assault with intent to rape, if he is intoxicated to such an extent that he is unable to entertain the intent to have sexual intercourse.
>
> * * *
>
> "It is sometimes stated that intoxication can negative a 'specific intent' which the crime in question may require (meaning some intent in addition to the intent to do the physical act which the crime requires), but it cannot negative a crime's 'general intent' (meaning an intent to do the physical act—or, perhaps, recklessly doing the physical act—which the crime requires). Some cases therefore have held that voluntary intoxication cannot be a defense to rape even though it blots out the intent to have intercourse, since that intent is a general intent and not a specific intent. But this is wrong on principle, for if intoxication does in fact negative an intention which is a required element of the crime (whether it be called specific intent or general intent), the crime has not been committed." (Footnotes omitted.)

* * * The difficulty arises when we reach the question as to whether or not the actor's degree of sobriety should be relevant to determine the mental state required to commit the crime charged.

At this point, the societal judgment relating to overindulgence and the concern that intoxication may be used as a device to avoid punishment comes into play. As stated where the legislature has expressly made the actor's state of sobriety relevant or where the degree of inebriation may have affected the actor's ability to perform the act required to commit the crime, the reluctance to permit evidence of intoxication to be considered by the factfinder is not present. In contrast, where the state of mind of the actor is at issue the reluctance to allow this evidence is probably reflective of the instinctive distrust of our ability to accurately ascertain the mental state of another. There is also a natural repugnance against one voluntarily depriving himself of his faculties, and then seeking to excuse errant behavior because of the absence of those faculties. Commonwealth v. McCausland, 348 Pa. 275, 35 A.2d 70 (1944); Commonwealth v. Dudash, 204 Pa. 124, 53 A. 756 (1902). Competing with these conditions is the argument that where the legislature has seen fit to define a particular state of mind as being a prerequisite of the offense then *all* factors bearing on whether that state of mind in fact existed then becomes relevant. That the legislative judgment to specifically define a particular state of mind as a prerequisite for the offense evidences an intent to make irrelevant the circumstances which brought about the state of mind of the actor when the act was committed. * * *

2. *Grounds for Punishment.* Koteles v. State, 660 P.2d 1199, 1202 (Alaska App.1983):

Koteles argues that drunks cannot be deterred, but as we noted in Wright v. State, 656 P.2d 1226 (Alaska App., 1983), those who drink knowing that they have committed crimes when drunk in the past, as well as those who drink knowing that they will be driving or handling weapons, commit a *malum in se* act by their drinking. This justifies punishment on that basis alone, when after they drink they engage in conduct harmful to others. See Hendershott v. People, 653 P.2d 385, 396–97 (Colo.1982) (self-induced intoxication is culpable conduct which constitutes *mens rea* making criminal an actor's harmful conduct when intoxicated). See also Morgan v. Municipality of Anchorage, 643 P.2d 691, 692 (Alaska App.1982) (intentionally drinking and driving establishes *mens rea* of driving while intoxicated). Cf. Model Penal Code § 2.08 commentary at 8–9 (Tent. Draft No. 9, 1959) (discussing principles of liability for intoxication). Widespread publicity that intoxication does not excuse crime in Alaska may well deter those who habitually get drunk and injure others from taking the first drink. If it does not, then isolation of those offenders will ensure that they harm no one during the period of their isolation.

Robinson v. California

Supreme Court of the United States, 1962.
370 U.S. 660, 82 S.Ct. 1417, 8 L.Ed.2d 758.

MR. JUSTICE STEWART delivered the opinion of the Court.

A California statute makes it a criminal offense for a person to "be addicted to the use of narcotics."[1] This appeal draws into question the

1. The statute is § 11721 of the California Health and Safety Code. It provides: "No person shall use, or be under the influence of, or be addicted to the use of narcotics,

constitutionality of that provision of the state law, as construed by the California courts in the present case.

The appellant was convicted after a jury trial in the Municipal Court of Los Angeles. * * *

* * *

* * * We noted probable jurisdiction of this appeal, because it squarely presents the issue whether the statute as construed by the California courts in this case is repugnant to the Fourteenth Amendment of the Constitution.

The broad power of a State to regulate the narcotic drugs traffic within its borders is not here in issue. * * *

Such regulation, it can be assumed, could take a variety of valid forms. A State might impose criminal sanctions, for example, against the unauthorized manufacture, prescription, sale, purchase, or possession of narcotics within its borders. In the interest of discouraging the violation of such laws, or in the interest of the general health or welfare of its inhabitants, a State might establish a program of compulsory treatment for those addicted to narcotics. Such a program of treatment might require periods of involuntary confinement. And penal sanctions might be imposed for failure to comply with established compulsory treatment procedures. Or a State might choose to attack the evils of narcotics traffic on broader fronts also—through public health education, for example, or by efforts to ameliorate the economic and social conditions under which those evils might be thought to flourish. In short, the range of valid choice which a State might make in this area is undoubtedly a wide one, and the wisdom of any particular choice within the allowable spectrum is not for us to decide. Upon that premise we turn to the California law in issue here.

It would be possible to construe the statute under which the appellant was convicted as one which is operative only upon proof of the actual use of narcotics within the State's jurisdiction. But the California courts have not so construed this law. Although there was evidence in the present case that the appellant had used narcotics in Los Angeles, the jury were instructed that they could convict him even if they disbelieved that evidence. The appellant could be convicted, they were told, if they found simply that the appellant's "status" or "chronic condition" was that of being "addicted to the use of narcotics." And it is impossible to know from the jury's verdict that the defendant was not convicted upon precisely such a finding.

* * *

excepting when administered by or under the direction of a person licensed by the State to prescribe and administer narcotics. It shall be the burden of the defense to show that it comes within the exception. Any person convicted of violating any provision of this section is guilty of a misdemeanor and shall be sentenced to serve a term of not less than 90 days nor more than one year in the county jail. The court may place a person convicted hereunder on probation for a period not to exceed five years and shall in all cases in which probation is granted require as a condition thereof that such person be confined in the county jail for at least 90 days. In no event does the court have the power to absolve a person who violates this section from the obligation of spending at least 90 days in confinement in the county jail."

This statute, therefore, is not one which punishes a person for the use of narcotics, for their purchase, sale or possession, or for antisocial or disorderly behavior resulting from their administration. It is not a law which even purports to provide or require medical treatment. Rather, we deal with a statute which makes the "status" of narcotic addiction a criminal offense, for which the offender may be prosecuted "at any time before he reforms." California has said that a person can be continuously guilty of this offense, whether or not he has ever used or possessed any narcotics within the State, and whether or not he has been guilty of any antisocial behavior there.

It is unlikely that any State at this moment in history would attempt to make it a criminal offense for a person to be mentally ill, or a leper, or to be afflicted with a venereal disease. A State might determine that the general health and welfare require that the victims of these and other human afflictions be dealt with by compulsory treatment, involving quarantine, confinement, or sequestration. But, in the light of contemporary human knowledge, a law which made a criminal offense of such a disease would doubtless be universally thought to be an infliction of cruel and unusual punishment in violation of the Eighth and Fourteenth Amendments.

We cannot but consider the statute before us as of the same category. In this Court counsel for the State recognized that narcotic addiction is an illness. Indeed, it is apparently an illness which may be contracted innocently or involuntarily.[9] We hold that a state law which imprisons a person thus afflicted as a criminal, even though he has never touched any narcotic drug within the State or been guilty of any irregular behavior there, inflicts a cruel and unusual punishment in violation of the Fourteenth Amendment. To be sure, imprisonment for ninety days is not, in the abstract, a punishment which is either cruel or unusual. But the question cannot be considered in the abstract. Even one day in prison would be a cruel and unusual punishment for the "crime" of having a common cold.

* * *

Reversed.

MR. JUSTICE FRANKFURTER took no part in the consideration or decision of this case.

MR. JUSTICE DOUGLAS, concurring.

* * *

Some say the addict has a disease. See Hesse, Narcotics and Drug Addiction (1946), p. 40 et seq.

Others say addiction is not a disease but "a symptom of a mental or psychiatric disorder." * * *

9. Not only may addiction innocently result from the use of medically prescribed narcotics, but a person may even be a narcotics addict from the moment of his birth. See Schneck, Narcotic Withdrawal Symptoms in the Newborn Infant Resulting from Maternal Addiction, 52 Journal of Pediatrics, 584 (1958); Roman and Middelkamp, Narcotic Addiction in a Newborn Infant, 53 Journal of Pediatrics 231 (1958); Kunstadter, Klein, Lundeen, Witz, and Morrison, Narcotic Withdrawal Symptoms in Newborn Infants, 168 Journal of the American Medical Association, 1008, (1958); Slobody and Cobrinik, Neonatal Narcotic Addiction, 14 Quarterly Review of Pediatrics, 169 (1959); Vincow and Hackel, Neonatal Narcotic Addiction, 22 General Practitioner 90 (1960); Dikshit, Narcotic Withdrawal Syndrome in Newborns, 28 Indian Journal of Pediatrics 11 (1961).

* * *

The impact that an addict has on a community causes alarm and often leads to punitive measures. Those measures are justified when they relate to acts of transgression. But I do not see how under our system *being an addict* can be punished as a crime. If addicts can be punished for their addiction, then the insane can also be punished for their insanity. Each has a disease and each must be treated as a sick person. * * *

* * *

By the time of Coke, enlightenment was coming as respects the insane. Coke said that the execution of a madman "should be a miserable spectacle, both against law, and of extreame inhumanity and cruelty, and can be no example to others." 6 Coke's Third Inst. (4th ed. 1797), p. 6. Blackstone endorsed this view of Coke. 4 Commentaries (Lewis ed. 1897), p. 25.

We should show the same discernment respecting drug addiction. The addict is a sick person. He may, of course, be confined for treatment or for the protection of society. Cruel and unusual punishment results not from confinement, but from convicting the addict of a crime. The purpose of § 11721 is not to cure, but to penalize. Were the purpose to cure, there would be no need for a mandatory jail term of not less than 90 days. * * * We would forget the teachings of the Eighth Amendment if we allowed sickness to be made a crime and permitted sick people to be punished for being sick. This age of enlightenment cannot tolerate such barbarous action.

MR. JUSTICE HARLAN, concurring.

I am not prepared to hold that on the present state of medical knowledge it is completely irrational and hence unconstitutional for a State to conclude that narcotics addiction is something other than an illness nor that it amounts to cruel and unusual punishment for the State to subject narcotics addicts to its criminal law. Insofar as addiction may be identified with the use or possession of narcotics within the State (or, I would suppose, without the State), in violation of local statutes prohibiting such acts, it may surely be reached by the State's criminal law. But in this case the trial court's instructions permitted the jury to find the appellant guilty on no more proof than that he was present in California while he was addicted to narcotics. Since addiction alone cannot reasonably be thought to amount to more than a compelling propensity to use narcotics, the effect of this instruction was to authorize criminal punishment for a bare desire to commit a criminal act.

If the California statute reaches this type of conduct, and for present purposes we must accept the trial court's construction as binding, Terminiello v. Chicago, 337 U.S. 1, 4, 69 S.Ct. 894, 895, 93 L.Ed. 1131, it is an arbitrary imposition which exceeds the power that a State may exercise in enacting its criminal law. Accordingly, I agree that the application of the California statute was unconstitutional in this case and join the judgment of reversal.

MR. JUSTICE CLARK, dissenting.

* * *

Apart from prohibiting specific acts such as the purchase, possession and sale of narcotics, California has taken certain legislative steps in regard to the status of being a narcotic addict—a condition commonly recognized as a threat to the State and to the individual. The Code deals with this problem in realistic stages. At its incipiency narcotic addiction is handled under § 11721 of the Health and Safety Code which is at issue here. It provides that a person found to be addicted to the use of narcotics shall serve a term in the county jail of not less than 90 days nor more than one year, with the minimum 90-day confinement applying in all cases without exception. Provision is made for parole with periodic tests to detect readdiction.

* * * There was no suggestion that the term "narcotic addict" as here used included a person who acted without volition or who had lost the power of self-control. Although the section is penal in appearance—perhaps a carry-over from a less sophisticated approach—its present provisions are quite similar to those for civil commitment and treatment of addicts who have lost the power of self-control * * *.

Where narcotic addiction has progressed beyond the incipient, volitional stage, California provides for commitment of three months to two years in a state hospital. California Welfare and Institutions Code, § 5355. For the purposes of this provision, a narcotic addict is defined as

> "any person who habitually takes or otherwise uses *to the extent of having lost the power of self-control* any opium, morphine, cocaine, or other narcotic drug as defined in Article 1 of Chapter 1 of Division 10 of the Health and Safety Code." California Welfare and Institutions Code, § 5350. (Emphasis supplied.)

This proceeding is clearly civil in nature with a purpose of rehabilitation and cure. Significantly, if it is found that a person committed under § 5355 will not receive substantial benefit from further hospital treatment and is not dangerous to society, he may be discharged—but only after a minimum confinement of three months. § 5355.1.

Thus, the "criminal" provision applies to the incipient narcotic addict who retains self-control, requiring confinement of three months to one year and parole with frequent tests to detect renewed use of drugs. Its overriding purpose is to cure the less seriously addicted person by preventing further use. On the other hand, the "civil" commitment provision deals with addicts who have lost the power of self-control, requiring hospitalization up to two years. Each deals with a different type of addict but with a common purpose. This is most apparent when the sections overlap: if after civil commitment of an addict it is found that hospital treatment will not be helpful, the addict is confined for a minimum period of three months in the same manner as is the volitional addict under the "criminal" provision.

In the instant case the proceedings against the petitioner were brought under the volitional-addict section. There was testimony that he had been using drugs only four months with three to four relatively mild doses a week. * * *

The majority strikes down the conviction primarily on the grounds that petitioner was denied due process by the imposition of criminal penalties for nothing more than being in a status. This view point is premised upon the theme that § 11721 is a "criminal" provision authorizing a punishment, for the majority admits that "a State might establish a program of compulsory treatment for those addicted to narcotics" which "might require periods of involuntary confinement." I submit that California has done exactly that. * * *

However, the case in support of the judgment below need not rest solely on this reading of California law. For even if the overall statutory scheme is ignored and a purpose and effect of punishment is attached to § 11721, that provision still does not violate the Fourteenth Amendment. The majority acknowledges, as it must, that a State can punish persons who purchase, possess or use narcotics. Although none of these acts are harmful to society *in themselves,* the State constitutionally may attempt to deter and prevent them through punishment because of the grave threat of future harmful conduct which they pose. Narcotics addiction—including the incipient, volitional addiction to which this provision speaks—is no different. * * *

* * *

Nor is the conjecture relevant that petitioner may have acquired his habit under lawful circumstances. There was no suggestion by him to this effect at trial, and surely the State need not rebut all possible lawful sources of addiction as part of its prima facie case.

The argument that the statute constitutes a cruel and unusual punishment is governed by the discussion above. Properly construed, the statute provides a treatment rather than a punishment. But even if interpreted as penal, the sanction of incarceration for 3 to 12 months is not unreasonable when applied to a person who has voluntarily placed himself in a condition posing a serious threat to the State. * * *

I would affirm the judgment.

MR. JUSTICE WHITE, dissenting.

* * *

* * * As defined by the trial court, addiction *is* the regular use of narcotics and can be proved only by evidence of such use. To find addiction in this case the jury had to believe that appellant had frequently used narcotics in the recent past. * * *

Nor do I find any indications in this record that California would apply § 11721 to the case of the helpless addict. I agree with my Brother CLARK that there was no evidence at all that appellant had lost the power to control his acts. There was no evidence of any use within 3 days prior to appellant's arrest. The most recent marks might have been 3 days old or they might have been 10 days old. The appellant admitted before trial that he had last used narcotics 8 days before his arrest. At the trial he denied having taken narcotics at all. The uncontroverted evidence was that appellant was not under the influence of narcotics at the time of his arrest nor did he have withdrawal symptoms. He was an incipient addict, a redeemable user, and the State chose to send him to jail for 90 days rather than to attempt to confine him by civil proceedings under another statute which requires a finding that the addict has lost the power of self-control. * * *

* * * The Fourteenth Amendment is today held to bar any prosecution for addiction regardless of the degree or frequency of use, and the

Court's opinion bristles with indications of further consequences. If it is "cruel and unusual punishment" to convict appellant for addiction, it is difficult to understand why it would be any less offensive to the Fourteenth Amendment to convict him for use on the same evidence of use which proved he was an addict. It is significant that in purporting to reaffirm the power of the States to deal with the narcotics traffic, the Court does not include among the obvious powers of the State the power to punish for the use of narcotics. I cannot think that the omission was inadvertent.

The Court has not merely tidied up California's law by removing some irritating vestige of an outmoded approach to the control of narcotics. At the very least, it has effectively removed California's power to deal effectively with the recurring case under the statute where there is ample evidence of use but no evidence of the precise location of use. Beyond this it has cast serious doubt upon the power of any State to forbid the use of narcotics under threat of criminal punishment. * * *

* * *

I respectfully dissent.

Powell v. Texas

Supreme Court of the United States, 1968.
392 U.S. 514, 88 S.Ct. 2145 (case 2), 20 L.Ed.2d 1254.

MR. JUSTICE MARSHALL announced the judgment of the Court and delivered an opinion in which THE CHIEF JUSTICE, MR. JUSTICE BLACK, and MR. JUSTICE HARLAN join.

In late December 1966, appellant was arrested and charged with being found in a state of intoxication in a public place, in violation of Vernon's Ann. Texas Penal Code, Art. 477 (1952), which reads as follows:

> "Whoever shall get drunk or be found in a state of intoxication in any public place, or at any private house except his own, shall be fined not exceeding one hundred dollars."

Appellant was tried in the Corporation Court of Austin, Texas, found guilty, and fined $20. He appealed to the County Court at Law No. 1 of Travis County, Texas, where a trial *de novo* was held. His counsel urged that appellant was "afflicted with the disease of chronic alcoholism," that "his appearance in public [while drunk was] * * * not of his own volition," and therefore that to punish him criminally for that conduct would be cruel and unusual, in violation of the Eighth and Fourteenth Amendments to the United States Constitution.

The trial judge in the county court, sitting without a jury, made certain findings of fact, but ruled as a matter of law that chronic alcoholism was not a defense to the charge. He found appellant guilty, and fined him $50. There being no further right to appeal within the Texas judicial system, appellant appealed to this Court; we noted probable jurisdiction. 389 U.S. 810, 88 S.Ct. 97, 19 L.Ed.2d 62 (1967).

I

The principal testimony was that of Dr. David Wade, a Fellow of the American Medical Association, duly certificated in psychiatry. His testimony consumed a total of 17 pages in the trial transcript. Five of those pages were taken up with a recitation of Dr. Wade's qualifications. In the next 12 pages Dr. Wade was examined by appellant's counsel, cross-examined by the State, and re-examined by the defense, and those 12 pages contain virtually all the material developed at trial which is relevant to the constitutional issue we face here. Dr. Wade sketched the outlines of the "disease" concept of alcoholism; noted that there is no generally accepted definition of "alcoholism"; alluded to the ongoing debate within the medical profession over whether alcohol is actually physically "addicting" or merely psychologically "habituating"; and concluded that in either case a "chronic alcoholic" is an "involuntary drinker," who is "powerless not to drink," and who "loses his self-control over his drinking." He testified that he had examined appellant, and that appellant is a "chronic alcoholic," who "by the time he has reached [the state of intoxication] * * * is not able to control his behavior, and [who] * * * has reached this point because he has an uncontrollable compulsion to drink." Dr. Wade also responded in the negative to the question whether appellant has "the willpower to resist the constant excessive consumption of alcohol." He added that in his opinion jailing appellant without medical attention would operate neither to rehabilitate him nor to lessen his desire for alcohol.

On cross-examination, Dr. Wade admitted that when appellant was sober he knew the difference between right and wrong, and he responded affirmatively to the question whether appellant's act in taking the first drink in any given instance when he was sober was a "voluntary exercise of his will." Qualifying his answer, Dr. Wade stated that "these individuals have a compulsion, and this compulsion, while not completely overpowering, is a very strong influence, an exceedingly strong influence, and this compulsion coupled with the firm belief in their mind that they are going to be able to handle it from now on causes their judgment to be somewhat clouded."

* * *

* * * [T]he trial court indicated its intention to disallow appellant's claimed defense of "chronic alcoholism." Thereupon defense counsel submitted, and the trial court entered, the following "findings of fact":

> "(1) That chronic alcoholism is a disease which destroys the afflicted person's will power to resist the constant, excessive consumption of alcohol.
>
> "(2) That a chronic alcoholic does not appear in public by his own volition but under a compulsion symptomatic of the disease of chronic alcoholism.
>
> "(3) That Leroy Powell, defendant herein, is a chronic alcoholic who is afflicted with the disease of chronic alcoholism."

Whatever else may be said of them, those are not findings of fact" in any recognizable, traditional sense in which that term has been used in a court of law; they are the premises of a syllogism transparently designed to bring this case within the scope of this Court's opinion in Robinson v. State of California, 370 U.S. 660, 82 S.Ct. 1417, 8 L.Ed.2d 758 (1962). Nonetheless, the dissent would have us adopt these "findings" without critical examination; it would use them as the basis for a constitutional holding that "a person may not be punished if the condition essential to constitute the defined crime is part of the pattern of his disease and is occasioned by a compulsion symptomatic of the disease."

The difficulty with that position, as we shall show, is that it goes much too far on the basis of too little knowledge. In the first place, the record in this case is utterly inadequate to permit the sort of informed and responsible adjudication which alone can support the announcement of an important and wide-ranging new constitutional principle. We know very little about the circumstances surrounding the drinking bout which resulted in this conviction, or about Leroy Powell's drinking problem, or indeed about alcoholism itself. The trial hardly reflects the sharp legal and evidentiary clash between fully prepared adversary litigants which is traditionally expected in major constitutional cases. The State put on only one witness, the arresting officer. The defense put on three—a policeman who testified to appellant's long history of arrests for public drunkenness, the psychiatrist, and appellant himself.

Furthermore, the inescapable fact is that there is no agreement among members of the medical profession about what it means to say that "alcoholism" is a "disease." One of the principal works in this field states that the major difficulty in articulating a "disease concept of alcoholism" is that "alcoholism has too many definitions and disease has practically none." [2] This same author concludes that *"a disease is what the medical profession recognizes as such."* [3] In other words, there is widespread agreement today that "alcoholism" is a "disease," for the simple reason that the medical profession has concluded that it should attempt to treat those who have drinking problems. There the agreement stops. Debate rages within the medical profession as to whether "alcoholism" is a separate "disease" in any meaningful biochemical, physiological or psychological sense, or whether it represents one peculiar manifestation in some individuals of underlying psychiatric disorders.[4]

Nor is there any substantial consensus as to the "manifestations of alcoholism." E.M. Jellinek, one of the outstanding authorities on the subject, identifies five different types of alcoholics which predominate in the United States, and these types display a broad range of different and occasionally inconsistent symptoms.[5] * * *

* * *

The trial court's "finding" that Powell "is afflicted with the disease of chronic alcoholism," which "destroys the afflicted person's will power to resist the constant, excessive consumption of alcohol" covers a multitude of

2. E. Jellinek, The Disease Concept of Alcoholism 11 (1960).

3. Id., at 12 (emphasis in original).

4. See, e.g., Joint Information Serv. of the Am. Psychiatric Assn. & the Nat. Assn. for Mental Health, The Treatment of Alcoholism—A Study of Programs and Problems 6–8 (1967) (hereafter cited as Treatment of Alcoholism).

5. Jellinek, supra, n. 2, at 35–41.

sins. Dr. Wade's testimony that appellant suffered from a compulsion which was an "exceedingly strong influence," but which was "not completely overpowering" is at least more carefully stated, if no less mystifying. Jellinek insists that conceptual clarity can only be achieved by distinguishing carefully between "loss of control" once an individual has commenced to drink and "inability to abstain" from drinking in the first place. Presumably a person would have to display both characteristics in order to make out a constitutional defense, should one be recognized. Yet the "findings" of the trial court utterly fail to make this crucial distinction, and there is serious question whether the record can be read to support a finding of either loss of control or inability to abstain.

Dr. Wade did testify that once appellant began drinking he appeared to have no control over the amount of alcohol he finally ingested. Appellant's own testimony concerning his drinking on the day of the trial would certainly appear, however, to cast doubt upon the conclusion that he was without control over his consumption of alcohol when he had sufficiently important reasons to exercise such control. * * *

* * *

It is one thing to say that if a man is deprived of alcohol his hands will begin to shake, he will suffer agonizing pains and ultimately he will have hallucinations; it is quite another to say that a man has a "compulsion" to take a drink, but that he also retains a certain amount of "free will" with which to resist. It is simply impossible, in the present state of our knowledge, to ascribe a useful meaning to the latter statement. This definitional confusion reflects, of course, not merely the undeveloped state of the psychiatric art but also the conceptual difficulties inevitably attendant upon the importation of scientific and medical models into a legal system generally predicated upon a different set of assumptions.

II

Despite the comparatively primitive state of our knowledge on the subject, it cannot be denied that the destructive use of alcoholic beverages is one of our principal social and public health problems. The lowest current informed estimate places the number of "alcoholics" in America (definitional problems aside) at 4,000,000, and most authorities are inclined to put the figure considerably higher. The problem is compounded by the fact that a very large percentage of the alcoholics in this country are "invisible"—they possess the means to keep their drinking problems secret, and the traditionally uncharitable attitude of our society toward alcoholics causes many of them to refrain from seeking treatment from any source. Nor can it be gainsaid that the legislative response to this enormous problem has in general been inadequate.

There is as yet no known generally effective method for treating the vast number of alcoholics in our society. Some individual alcoholics have responded to particular forms of therapy with remissions of their symptomatic dependence upon the drug. But just as there is no agreement among doctors and social workers with respect to the causes of alcoholism, there is no consensus as to why particular treatments have been effective in particular cases and there is no generally agreed-upon approach to the problem of treatment on a large scale. * * *

* * * It would be tragic to return large numbers of helpless, sometimes dangerous and frequently unsanitary inebriates to the streets of our cities without even the opportunity to sober up adequately which a brief jail term provides. Presumably no State or city will tolerate such a state of affairs. Yet the medical profession cannot, and does not, tell us with any assurance that, even if the buildings, equipment and trained personnel were made available, it could provide anything more than slightly higher-class jails for our indigent habitual inebriates. Thus we run the grave risk that nothing will be accomplished beyond the hanging of a new sign—reading "hospital"—over one wing of the jailhouse.

One virtue of the criminal process is, at least, that the duration of penal incarceration typically has some outside statutory limit; this is universally true in the case of petty offenses, such as public drunkenness, where jail terms are quite short on the whole. "Therapeutic civil commitment" lacks this feature; one is typically committed until one is "cured." Thus, to do otherwise than affirm might subject indigent alcoholics to the risk that they may be locked up for an indefinite period of time under the same conditions as before, with no more hope than before of receiving effective treatment and no prospect of periodic "freedom."

Faced with this unpleasant reality, we are unable to assert that the use of the criminal process as a means of dealing with the public aspects of problem drinking can never be defended as rational. The picture of the penniless drunk propelled aimlessly and endlessly through the law's "revolving door" of arrest, incarceration, release and re-arrest is not a pretty one. But before we condemn the present practice across-the-board, perhaps we ought to be able to point to some clear promise of a better world for these unfortunate people. Unfortunately, no such promise has yet been forthcoming. If, in addition to the absence of a coherent approach to the problem of treatment, we consider the almost complete absence of facilities and manpower for the implementation of a rehabilitation program, it is difficult to say in the present context that the criminal process is utterly lacking in social value. * * *

* * *

Obviously, chronic alcoholics have not been deterred from drinking to excess by the existence of criminal sanctions against public drunkenness. But all those who violate penal laws of any kind are by definition undeterred. * * *

III

* * *

Appellant, however, seeks to come within the application of the Cruel and Unusual Punishment Clause announced in Robinson v. State of California, 370 U.S. 660, 82 S.Ct. 1417, 8 L.Ed.2d 758 (1962), which involved a state statute making it a crime to "be addicted to the use of narcotics." This Court held there that "a state law which imprisons a person thus afflicted [with narcotic addiction] as a criminal, even though he has never touched any narcotic drug within the State or been guilty of any irregular behavior there, inflicts a cruel and unusual punishment * * *." Id., at 667, 82 S.Ct., at 1420–1421.

On its face the present case does not fall within that holding, since appellant was convicted, not for being a chronic alcoholic, but for being in public while drunk on a particular occasion. The State of Texas thus has not sought to punish a mere status, as California did in *Robinson;* nor has it attempted to regulate appellant's behavior in the privacy of his own home. Rather, it has imposed upon appellant a criminal sanction for public behavior which may create substantial health and safety hazards, both for appellant and for members of the general public, and which offends the moral and esthetic sensibilities of a large segment of the community. This seems a far cry from convicting one for being an addict, being a chronic alcoholic, being "mentally ill, or a leper * * *." Id., at 666, 82 S.Ct., at 1420.

* * *

It is suggested in dissent that *Robinson* stands for the "simple" but "subtle" principle that "[c]riminal penalties may not be inflicted upon a person for being in a condition he is powerless to change." Post, at 2171. In that view, appellant's "condition" of public intoxication was "occasioned by a compulsion symptomatic of the disease" of chronic alcoholism, and thus, apparently, his behavior lacked the critical element of *mens rea.* Whatever may be the merits of such a doctrine of criminal responsibility, it surely cannot be said to follow from *Robinson.* The entire thrust of *Robinson's* interpretation of the Cruel and Unusual Punishment Clause is that criminal penalties may be inflicted only if the accused has committed some act, has engaged in some behavior, which society has an interest in preventing, or perhaps in historical common law terms, has committed some *actus reus.* It thus does not deal with the question of whether certain conduct cannot constitutionally be punished because it is, in some sense, "involuntary" or "occasioned by a compulsion."

Likewise, as the dissent acknowledges, there is a substantial definitional distinction between a "status," as in *Robinson,* and a "condition," which is said to be involved in this case. * * * The only relevance of *Robinson* to this issue is that because the Court interpreted the statute there involved as making a "status" criminal, it was able to suggest that the statute would cover even a situation in which addiction had been acquired involuntarily. 370 U.S., at 667, n. 9, 82 S.Ct., at 1420. That this factor was not determinative in the case is shown by the fact that there was no indication of how Robinson himself had become an addict.

Ultimately, then, the most troubling aspects of this case, were *Robinson* to be extended to meet it, would be the scope and content of what could only be a constitutional doctrine of criminal responsibility. In dissent it is urged that the decision could be limited to conduct which is "a characteristic and involuntary part of the pattern of the disease as it afflicts" the particular individual, and that "[i]t is not foreseeable" that it would be applied "in the case of offenses such as driving a car while intoxicated, assault, theft, or robbery." Post, at 2167, n. 2. That is limitation by fiat. In the first place, nothing in the logic of the dissent would limit its application to chronic alcoholics. If Leroy Powell cannot be convicted of public intoxication, it is difficult to see how a State can convict an individual for murder, if that individual, while exhibiting normal behavior in all other respects, suffers from a "compulsion" to kill, which is an "exceedingly strong influence," but "not completely overpowering." * * *

It is not difficult to imagine a case involving psychiatric testimony to the effect that an individual suffers from some aggressive neurosis which he is able to control when sober; that very little alcohol suffices to remove the inhibitions which normally contain these aggressions, with the result that the individual engages in assaultive behavior without becoming actually intoxicated; and that the individual suffers from a very strong desire to drink, which is an "exceedingly strong influence" but "not completely overpowering." Without being untrue to the rationale of this case, should the principles advanced in dissent be accepted here, the Court could not avoid holding such an individual constitutionally unaccountable for his assaultive behavior.

Traditional common-law concepts of personal accountability and essential considerations of federalism lead us to disagree with appellant. We are unable to conclude, on the state of this record or on the current state of medical knowledge, that chronic alcoholics in general, and Leroy Powell in particular, suffer from such an irresistible compulsion to drink and to get drunk in public that they are utterly unable to control their performance of either or both of these acts and thus cannot be deterred at all from public intoxication. And in any event this Court has never articulated a general constitutional doctrine of *mens rea.*

We cannot cast aside the centuries-long evolution of the collection of interlocking and overlapping concepts which the common law has utilized to assess the moral accountability of an individual for his antisocial deeds. The doctrines of *actus reus, mens rea,* insanity, mistake, justification, and duress have historically provided the tools for a constantly shifting adjustment of the tension between the evolving aims of the criminal law and changing religious, moral, philosophical, and medical views of the nature of man. This process of adjustment has always been thought to be the province of the States.

* * *

Affirmed.

MR. JUSTICE BLACK, whom MR. JUSTICE HARLAN joins, concurring.

While I agree that the grounds set forth in MR. JUSTICE MARSHALL'S opinion are sufficient to require affirmance of the judgment here, I wish to amplify my reasons for concurring.

* * *

III

* * * The argument is made that appellant comes within the terms of our holding in *Robinson* because being drunk in public is a mere status or "condition." Despite this many-faceted use of the concept of "condition,"

this argument would require converting *Robinson* into a case protecting actual behavior, a step we explicitly refused to take in that decision.

A different question, I admit, is whether our attempt in *Robinson* to limit our holding to pure status crimes, involving no conduct whatever, was a sound one. I believe it was. Although some of our objections to the statute in *Robinson* are equally applicable to statutes that punish conduct "symptomatic" of a disease, any attempt to explain *Robinson* as based solely on the lack of voluntariness encounters a number of logical difficulties.[3] Other problems raised by status crimes are in no way involved when the State attempts to punish for conduct, and these other problems were, in my view, the controlling aspects of our decision.

Punishment for a status is particularly obnoxious, and in many instances can reasonably be called cruel and unusual, because it involves punishment for a mere propensity, a desire to commit an offense; the mental element is not simply one part of the crime but may constitute all of it. This is a situation universally sought to be avoided in our criminal law; the fundamental requirement that some action be proved is solidly established even for offenses most heavily based on propensity, such as attempt, conspiracy, and recidivist crimes.[4] * * *

* * *

IV

The rule of constitutional law urged upon us by appellant would have a revolutionary impact on the criminal law, and any possible limits proposed for the rule would be wholly illusory. If the original boundaries of *Robinson* are to be discarded, any new limits too would soon fall by the wayside and the Court would be forced to hold the States powerless to punish any conduct that could be shown to result from a "compulsion," in the complex, psychological meaning of that term. The result, to choose just one illustration, would be to require recognition of "irresistible impulse" as a complete defense to any crime; this is probably contrary to present law in most American jurisdictions.

The real reach of any such decision, however, would be broader still, for the basic premise underlying the argument is that it is cruel and unusual to punish a person who is not morally blameworthy. * * * The legislatures have always been allowed wide freedom to determine the extent to which moral culpability should be a prerequisite to conviction of a crime. The criminal law is a social tool that is employed in seeking a wide variety of

3. Although we noted in Robinson, 370 U.S., at 667, 82 S.Ct., at 1420, that narcotics addiction apparently is an illness that can be contracted innocently or involuntarily, we barred punishment for addiction even when it could be proved that the defendant had voluntarily become addicted. And we compared addiction to the status of having a common cold, a condition that most people can either avoid or quickly cure when it is important enough for them to do so.

4. As Glanville Williams puts it, "[t]hat crime requires an act is *invariably* true if the proposition be read as meaning that a private thought is not sufficient to found responsibility." Williams, Criminal Law—the General Part 1 (1961). (Emphasis added.) For the requirement of some act as an element of conspiracy and attempt, see id., at 631, 663, 668; R. Perkins, Criminal Law 482, 531–532 (1957).

goals, and I cannot say the Eighth Amendment's limits on the use of criminal sanctions extend as far as this viewpoint would inevitably carry them.

But even if we were to limit any holding in this field to "compulsions" that are "symptomatic" of a "disease," in the words of the findings of the trial court, the sweep of that holding would still be startling. Such a ruling would make it clear beyond any doubt that a narcotics addict could not be punished for "being" in possession of drugs or, for that matter, for "being" guilty of using them. A wide variety of sex offenders would be immune from punishment if they could show that their conduct was not voluntary but part of the pattern of a disease. More generally speaking, a form of the insanity defense would be made a constitutional requirement throughout the Nation, should the Court now hold it cruel and unusual to punish a person afflicted with any mental disease whenever his conduct was part of the pattern of his disease and occasioned by a compulsion symptomatic of the disease. * * *

* * *

MR. JUSTICE WHITE, concurring in the result.

If it cannot be a crime to have an irresistible compulsion to use narcotics, Robinson v. State of California, 370 U.S. 660, 82 S.Ct. 1417, 8 L.Ed.2d 758, rehearing denied, 371 U.S. 905, 83 S.Ct. 202, 9 L.Ed.2d 166 (1962), I do not see how it can constitutionally be a crime to yield to such a compulsion. Punishing an addict for using drugs convicts for addiction under a different name. Distinguishing between the two crimes is like forbidding criminal conviction for being sick with flu or epilepsy but permitting punishment for running a fever or having a convulsion. Unless *Robinson* is to be abandoned, the use of narcotics by an addict must be beyond the reach of the criminal law. Similarly, the chronic alcoholic with an irresistible urge to consume alcohol should not be punishable for drinking or for being drunk.

* * *

The trial court said that Powell was a chronic alcoholic with a compulsion not only to drink to excess but also to frequent public places when intoxicated. Nothing in the record before the trial court supports the latter conclusion, which is contrary to common sense and to common knowledge. The sober chronic alcoholic has no compulsion to be on the public streets; many chronic alcoholics drink at home and are never seen drunk in public. * * * For these reasons, I cannot say that the chronic alcoholic who proves his disease and a compulsion to drink is shielded from conviction when he has knowingly failed to take feasible precautions against committing a criminal act, here the act of going to or remaining in a public place. * * *

The fact remains that some chronic alcoholics must drink and hence must drink *somewhere*. Although many chronics have homes, many others do not. For all practical purposes the public streets may be home for these unfortunates, not because their disease compels them to be there, but because, drunk or sober, they have no place else to go and no place else to be when they are drinking. * * * For some of these alcoholics I would think a showing could be made that resisting drunkenness is impossible and that avoiding public places when intoxicated is also impossible. As applied to them this statute is in effect a law which bans a single act for which they may not be convicted under the Eighth Amendment—the act of getting drunk.

It is also possible that the chronic alcoholic who begins drinking in private at some point becomes so drunk that he loses the power to control his movements and for that reason appears in public. The Eighth Amendment might also forbid conviction in such circumstances, but only on a record satisfactorily showing that it was not feasible for him to have made arrangements to prevent his being in public when drunk and that his extreme drunkenness sufficiently deprived him of his faculties on the occasion in issue.

These prerequisites to the possible invocation of the Eighth Amendment are not satisfied on the record before us. * * *

* * *

MR. JUSTICE FORTAS, with whom MR. JUSTICE DOUGLAS, MR. JUSTICE BRENNAN, and MR. JUSTICE STEWART join, dissenting.

* * *

I

The issue posed in this case is a narrow one. There is no challenge here to the validity of public intoxication statutes in general or to the Texas public intoxication statute in particular. This case does not concern the infliction of punishment upon the "social" drinker—or upon anyone other than a "chronic alcoholic" who, as the trier of fact here found, cannot "resist the constant, excessive consumption of alcohol." Nor does it relate to any offense other than the crime of public intoxication.

The sole question presented is whether a criminal penalty may be imposed upon a person suffering the disease of "chronic alcoholism" for a condition—being "in a state of intoxication" in public—which is a characteristic part of the pattern of his disease and which, the trial court found, was not the consequence of appellant's volition but of "a compulsion symptomatic of the disease of chronic alcoholism." * * * This case does not raise any question as to the right of the police to stop and detain those who are intoxicated in public, whether as a result of the disease or otherwise; or as to the State's power to commit chronic alcoholics for treatment. Nor does it concern the responsibility of an alcoholic for criminal *acts.* We deal here with the mere *condition* of being intoxicated in public.[2]

2. It is not foreseeable that findings such as those which are decisive here—namely that the appellant's being intoxicated in public was a part of the pattern of his disease and due to a compulsion symptomatic of that disease—could or would be made in the case of offenses such as driving a car while intoxicated, assault, theft, or robbery. Such offenses require independent acts or conduct and do not typically flow from and are not part of the syndrome of the disease of chronic alcoholism. If an alcoholic should be convicted for criminal conduct which is not a characteristic and involuntary part of the pattern of the disease as it afflicts him, nothing herein would prevent his punishment.

II

* * *

It is entirely clear that the jailing of chronic alcoholics is punishment. It is not defended as therapeutic, nor is there any basis for claiming that it is therapeutic (or indeed a deterrent). The alcoholic offender is caught in a "revolving door"—leading from arrest on the street through a brief, unprofitable sojourn in jail, back to the street and, eventually, another arrest. The jails, overcrowded and put to a use for which they are not suitable, have a destructive effect upon alcoholic inmates.

Finally, most commentators, as well as experienced judges, are in agreement that "there is probably no drearier example of the futility of using penal sanctions to solve a psychiatric problem than the enforcement of the laws against drunkenness."

* * *

III

* * *

Robinson stands upon a principle which, despite its sublety, must be simply stated and respectfully applied because it is the foundation of individual liberty and the cornerstone of the relations between a civilized state and its citizens: Criminal penalties may not be inflicted upon a person for being in a condition he is powerless to change. In all probability, Robinson at some time before his conviction elected to take narcotics. But the crime as defined did not punish this conduct.[29] The statute imposed a penalty for the offense of "addiction"—a condition which Robinson could not control. Once Robinson had become an addict, he was utterly powerless to avoid criminal guilt. He was powerless to choose not to violate the law.

In the present case, appellant is charged with a crime composed of two elements—being intoxicated and being found in a public place while in that condition. The crime, so defined, differs from that in *Robinson.* The statute covers more than a mere status. But the essential constitutional defect here is the same as in *Robinson*, for in both cases the particular defendant was accused of being in a condition which he had no capacity to change or avoid. The trial judge sitting as trier of fact found upon the medical and other relevant testimony, that Powell is a "chronic alcoholic." He defined appellant's "chronic alcoholism" as "a disease which destroys the afflicted person's will power to resist the constant, excessive consumption of alcohol." He also found that "a chronic alcoholic does not appear in public by his own volition but under a compulsion symptomatic of the disease of chronic alcoholism." I read these findings to mean that appellant was powerless to avoid drinking; that having taken his first drink, he had "an uncontrollable

29. The Court noted in *Robinson* that narcotic addiction "is apparently an illness which may be contracted innocently or involuntarily." 370 U.S., at 667, 82 S.Ct., at 1420. In the case of alcoholism it is even more likely that the disease may be innocently contracted, since the drinking of alcoholic beverages is a common activity, generally accepted in our society, while the purchasing and taking of drugs are crimes. As in *Robinson,* the State has not argued here that Powell's conviction may be supported by his "voluntary" action in becoming afflicted.

compulsion to drink'' to the point of intoxication; and that, once intoxicated, he could not prevent himself from appearing in public places.

* * *

Note

See v. State, 296 Ark. 498, 757 S.W.2d 947, 950 (1988):

> Our review of the cases that have considered the involuntary intoxication defense, that the appellant argues here, generally reflects the same or similar rationale as set out in *Powell.* In general terms, most jurisdictions have held that an irresistable compulsion to consume intoxicants caused by a physiological or psychological disability does not render the ensuing intoxication involuntary. See Annot., *Involuntary Intoxication as Defense;* 73 A.L.R.3d 195 § 12(a) (1976); see, e.g., Evans v. State, 645 P.2d 155 (Alaska 1982) (all intoxication is to be regarded as voluntary unless it is unknowingly or externally compelled); People v. Morrow, 268 Cal.App.2d 939, 74 Cal.Rptr. 551 (1969) (when a person takes his first drink by choice and afterwards drinks successively and finally gets drunk, that is voluntary intoxication, even though he may be an alcoholic); State v. Palacio, 221 Kan. 394, 559 P.2d 804 (1977) (any person, including a chronic alcoholic, who is sane and rational when sober, and who becomes intoxicated by consuming alcoholic beverages is voluntarily intoxicated); State v. Johnson, 327 N.W.2d 580 (Minn.1982) (self-induced intoxication by chronic alcoholic constitutes voluntary, rather than involuntary, intoxication); Shurbet v. State, 652 S.W.2d 425 (Tex.Ct.App.1982) (alcoholism may not be the basis for the defense of involuntary intoxication).

Questions

1. Are the crimes charged in *Robinson* and *Powell* properly regarded as status crimes?

2. If addiction or alcoholism is to excuse crimes at all, should it excuse (a) being under the influence of drugs or alcohol, (b) possessing drugs or alcohol, (c) stealing drugs or alcohol for personal use (no other supply being available), (d) robbing someone to get money for alcohol or drugs, or (e) recklessly killing someone while being under the influence of alcohol or drugs?

3. Is it properly relevant to the decision whether to admit alcoholism or addiction as a defense to some crimes that we do not have adequate treatment methods or facilities to deal with the mass of alcoholics and addicts who would be acquitted under the defense and who would presumably require some treatment or supervision?

e. INFANCY

At common law there was a conclusive presumption that a child under the age of seven years could not form a criminal state of mind, and hence could not be convicted of any crime requiring *mens rea*. If the child was at least seven, but not yet fourteen, there was a rebuttable presumption of such incapacity, very strong at age seven and becoming much weaker as the child approached fourteen. Anyone fourteen years of age or older had no defense of infancy.

These presumptions provided a crude way of dealing (or refusing to deal) with juveniles. With the growth of the juvenile court systems in this century, the common law rule has become less important, and it has often been modified by statute. However, it may still apply when juvenile court jurisdiction over a particular child is waived, or, in some jurisdictions, even in juvenile proceedings. In re William A., 313 Md. 690, 548 A.2d 130 (1988).

The juvenile justice system provides material for a course in itself. Generally, it purports to treat the child, who may simply be in need of care or control, or who may have committed what in an adult would be a crime, as in need of social assistance rather than punishment. But some juvenile dispositions have strong punitive connotations, and many of the constitutional protections as to procedures available to criminal defendants are also available in juvenile court cases. See In re Gault, 387 U.S. 1, 87 S.Ct. 1428, 18 L.Ed.2d 527 (1967).

D. KILLINGS IN WHICH THE ACCUSED ACTS RECKLESSLY OR NEGLIGENTLY

1. Reckless Killings

Introductory Note

Negligence and recklessness are matters of degree. Such conduct in homicide cases may shade all the way from fault so slight that not even tort liability results, through fault sufficient for tort liability only, through fault sufficient for criminally negligent homicide or reckless manslaughter, to fault which results in murder. In the four principal cases which follow, all of the defendants were found to be in the manslaughter range. Which came nearest to murder? Try to rank them and to identify the factors which put them higher or lower on the scale of culpability.

Commonwealth v. Welansky

Supreme Judicial Court of Massachusetts, 1944.
316 Mass. 383, 55 N.E.2d 902.

LUMMUS, JUSTICE.

On November 28, 1942, and for about nine years before that day, a corporation named New Cocoanut Grove, Inc., maintained and operated a "night club" in Boston, having an entrance at 17 Piedmont Street, for the furnishing to the public for compensation of food, drink and entertainment, consisting of orchestra and band music, singing and dancing. It employed about eighty persons. The corporation, its officers and employees, and its business, were completely dominated by the defendant Barnett Welansky, who is called in this opinion simply the defendant, since his codefendants were acquitted by the jury. He owned, and held in his own name or in the names of others, all the capital stock. He leased some of the land on which the corporate business was carried on, and owned the rest, although title was held for him by his sister. He was entitled to, and took, all the profits. Internally, the corporation was operated without regard to corporate forms, as though the business were that of the defendant as an individual. It was not shown that responsibility for the number or condition of safety exits had been delegated by the defendant to any employee or other person.

The defendant was accustomed to spend his evenings at the night club, inspecting the premises and superintending the business. On November 16, 1942, he became suddenly ill, and was carried to a hospital, where he was in bed for three weeks and remained until discharged on December 11, 1942. During his stay at the hospital, although employees visited him there, he did not concern himself with the night club, because, as he testified, he "knew it would be all right" and that "the same system * * * [he] had would continue" during his absence. There is no evidence of any act, omission or condition at the night club on November 28, 1942 (apart from the lighting of a match hereinafter described), that was not within the usual and regular practice during the time before the defendant was taken ill when he was at the night club nearly every evening. * * *

[The diagram on the facing page* shows the layout of the night club.]

* Diagram by Palacios from P. Benzaquin, *Holocaust!* Copyright © 1959, Henry Holt & Co. Copyright assigned to Paul Benzaquin, the author, with whose permission it is reprinted.

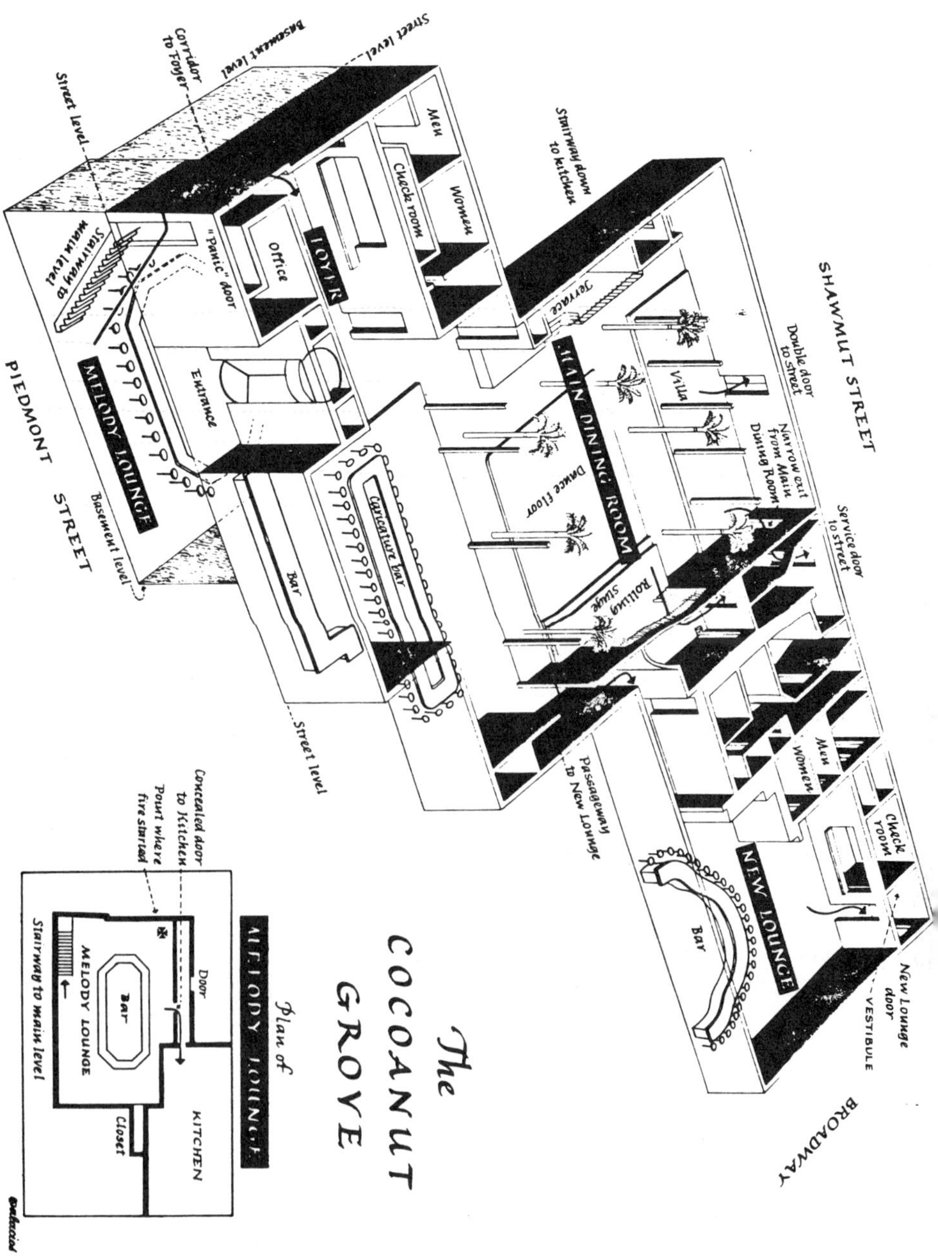

[The door from the New Lounge vestibule to Broadway] * * * and the revolving door at 17 Piedmont Street were the only entrances and exits intended for the ordinary use of patrons. Besides these doors, and the exit through the wooden partition from the Melody Lounge, already described, there were five possible emergency exits from the night club, all on the first or street floor. These will now be listed and described.

(1) A door, opening outward to Piedmont Street, two and one-half feet wide, at the head of the stairway leading to and from the basement Melody

Lounge. That door apparently was not visible from the greater part of the foyer, for it was in a passageway that ran from one end of the foyer past the office to the stairway. That door was marked "Exit" by an electric sign. It was equipped with a "panic" or "crash" bar, intended to unbolt and open the door upon pressure from within the building. But on the evidence it could have been found that the device just mentioned was regularly made ineffective by having the door locked by a separate lock operated by a key that was kept in a desk in the office. Late in the evening of November 28, 1942, firemen found that door locked and had to force it open with an axe. The jury were entitled to disbelieve the testimony of the defendant that he had instructed the head waiter, who died in the occurrence of that evening, always to keep that door unlocked. It may be observed that if that door should be left so that it could be opened by means of the panic bar, a patron might leave through that door without paying his bill. It does not appear that anyone watched that door to prevent patrons from so doing.

(2) A door [not shown on the diagram] two and one-third feet wide leading from the foyer, near the revolving door, into the small vestibule adjoining the office, already described. From that vestibule another similar door, swinging inward, gave egress to Piedmont Street, near the revolving door. The door to Piedmont Street could not be opened fully, because of a wall shelf. And that door was commonly barred in the evening, as it was on November 28, 1942, by a removable board with clothing hooks on it, and by clothing, for in the evening the office and vestibule were used for checking clothing.

(3) A door, opening outward, from the middle of the wall of the main dining room to Shawmut Street, and marked "Exit" by an electric sign. The opening was about three and two-thirds feet wide. The defendant testified that this was the principal exit provided for emergencies. From the sides of the opening hung double doors, equipped with "panic" bars intended to unbolt and open the doors upon pressure from within. But on the evening of November 28, 1942, one of the two doors did not open upon pressure, and had to be hammered with a table before it would open. Besides, the "panic" doors were hidden from the view of diners by a pair of "Venetian" wooden doors, swinging inward, and fastened by a hook, which had to be opened before one could operate the "panic" doors. In addition, dining tables were regularly placed near the Venetian doors, one of them within two feet, and these had to be moved away in order to get access to the doors. That condition prevailed on the evening of November 28, 1942.

(4) The service door, two and one-half feet wide, swinging inward, leading to Shawmut Street at 8 Shawmut Street. This door was near the stage, at the foot of a stairway leading to dressing rooms on the second floor, and was in a part of the premises to which patrons were not admitted and which they could not see. This door was known to employees, but doubtless not to patrons. It was kept locked by direction of the defendant, and the key was kept in a desk in the office.

(5) The door [not shown on the diagram], two and three-fourths feet wide, swinging inward, leading from a corridor into which patrons had no

occasion to go, to Shawmut Street at 6 Shawmut Street. No patron was likely to know of this door. It was kept locked by direction of the defendant, but he ordered the key placed in the lock at seven every evening.

We now come to the story of the fire. A little after ten o'clock on the evening of Saturday, November 28, 1942, the night club was well filled with a crowd of patrons. It was during the busiest season of the year. An important football game in the afternoon had attracted many visitors to Boston. * * * Upon the evidence it could have been found that at that time there were from two hundred fifty to four hundred persons in the Melody Lounge, from four hundred to five hundred in the main dining room and the Caricature Bar, and two hundred fifty in the Cocktail Lounge. Yet it could have been found that the crowd was no larger than it had been on other Saturday evenings before the defendant was taken ill, and that there had been larger crowds at earlier times. There were about seventy tables in the dining room, each seating from two to eight persons. There was testimony that all but two were taken. Many persons were standing in various rooms. * * *

A bartender in the Melody Lounge noticed that an electric light bulb which was in or near the cocoanut husks of an artificial palm tree in the corner had been turned off and that the corner was dark. He directed a sixteen year old bar boy who was waiting on customers at the tables to cause the bulb to be lighted. A soldier sitting with other persons near the light told the bar boy to leave it unlighted. But the bar boy got a stool, lighted a match in order to see the bulb, turned the bulb in its socket, and thus lighted it. The bar boy blew the match out, and started to walk away. Apparently the flame of the match had ignited the palm tree and that had speedily ignited the low cloth ceiling near it, for both flamed up almost instantly. The fire spread with great rapidity across the upper part of the room, causing much heat. The crowd in the Melody Lounge rushed up the stairs, but the fire preceded them. People got on fire while on the stairway. The fire spread with great speed across the foyer and into the Caricature Bar and the main dining room, and thence into the Cocktail Lounge. * * * The crowd were panic stricken, and rushed and pushed in every direction through the night club, screaming, and overturning tables and chairs in their attempts to escape.

The door at the head of the Melody Lounge stairway was not opened until firemen broke it down from outside with an axe and found it locked by a key lock, so that the panic bar could not operate. Two dead bodies were found close to it, and a pile of bodies about seven feet from it. The door in the vestibule of the office did not become open, and was barred by the clothing rack. The revolving door soon jammed, but was burst out by the pressure of the crowd. The head waiter and another waiter tried to get open the panic doors from the main dining room to Shawmut Street, and succeeded after some difficulty. The other two doors to Shawmut Street were locked, and were opened by force from outside by firemen and others. Some patrons escaped through them, but many dead bodies were piled up inside them. A considerable number of patrons escaped through the Broadway door, but many died just inside that door. Some employees, and a great number of patrons, died in the fire. Others were taken out of the building with fatal burns and injuries from smoke, and died within a few days.

* * *

[The conviction of defendant on nineteen counts of manslaughter was affirmed.]

The Commonwealth disclaimed any contention that the defendant intentionally killed or injured the persons named in the indictments as victims. It based its case on involuntary manslaughter through wanton or reckless conduct. The judge instructed the jury correctly with respect to the nature of such conduct.

Usually wanton or reckless conduct consists of an affirmative act, like driving an automobile or discharging a firearm, in disregard of probable harmful consequences to another. But where as in the present case there is a duty of care for the safety of business visitors invited to premises which the defendant controls, wanton or reckless conduct may consist of intentional failure to take such care in disregard of the probable harmful consequences to them or of their right to care.

To define wanton or reckless conduct so as to distinguish it clearly from negligence and gross negligence is not easy. Sometimes the word "wilful" is prefaced to the words "wanton" and "reckless" in expressing the concept. That only blurs it. Wilful means intentional. In the phrase "wilful, wanton or reckless conduct," if "wilful" modifies "conduct" it introduces something different from wanton or reckless conduct, even though the legal result is the same. Wilfully causing harm is a wrong, but a different wrong from wantonly or recklessly causing harm. * * * The words "wanton" and "reckless" are practically synonymous in this connection, although the word "wanton" may contain a suggestion of arrogance or insolence or heartlessness that is lacking in the word "reckless." But intentional conduct to which either word applies is followed by the same legal consequences as though both words applied.

The standard of wanton or reckless conduct is at once subjective and objective, as has been recognized ever since Commonwealth v. Pierce, 138 Mass. 165, 52 Am.Rep. 264. Knowing facts that would cause a reasonable man to know the danger is equivalent to knowing the danger. The judge charged the jury correctly when he said, "To constitute wanton or reckless conduct, as distinguished from mere negligence, grave danger to others must have been apparent and the defendant must have chosen to run the risk rather than alter his conduct so as to avoid the act or omission which caused the harm. If the grave danger was in fact realized by the defendant, his subsequent voluntary act or omission which caused the harm amounts to wanton or reckless conduct, no matter whether the ordinary man would have realized the gravity of the danger or not. But even if a particular defendant is so stupid [or] so heedless * * * that in fact he did not realize the grave danger, he cannot escape the imputation of wanton or reckless conduct in his dangerous act or omission, if an ordinary normal man under the same circumstances would have realized the gravity of the danger. A man may be reckless within the meaning of the law although he himself thought he was careful."

The essence of wanton or reckless conduct is intentional conduct, by way either of commission or of omission where there is a duty to act, which conduct involves a high degree of likelihood that substantial harm will result to another. Am.Law Inst. Restatement: Torts, § 500; LeSaint v. Weston, 301 Mass. 136, 138, 16 N.E.2d 631. Wanton or reckless conduct amounts to what has been variously described as indifference to or disregard of probable consequences to that other. * * *

The words "wanton" and "reckless" are thus not merely rhetorical or vituperative expressions used instead of negligent or grossly negligent. They express a difference in the degree of risk and in the voluntary taking of risk so marked, as compared with negligence, as to amount substantially and in the eyes of the law to a difference in kind. For many years this court has been careful to preserve the distinction between negligence and gross negligence, on the one hand, and wanton or reckless conduct on the other. * * *

Notwithstanding language used commonly in earlier cases, and occasionally in later ones,[3] it is now clear in this Commonwealth that at common law conduct does not become criminal until it passes the borders of negligence and gross negligence and enters into the domain of wanton or reckless conduct. There is in Massachusetts at common law no such thing as "criminal negligence."

Wanton or reckless conduct is the legal equivalent of intentional conduct. If by wanton or reckless conduct bodily injury is caused to another, the person guilty of such conduct is guilty of assault and battery. And since manslaughter is simply a battery that causes death if death results he is guilty of manslaughter.

To convict the defendant of manslaughter, the Commonwealth was not required to prove that he caused the fire by some wanton or reckless conduct. Fire in a place of public resort is an ever present danger. It was enough to prove that death resulted from his wanton or reckless disregard of the safety of patrons in the event of fire from any cause.

* * *

The Commonwealth was properly allowed to show that an exit from the Cocktail Lounge to Shawmut Street and fire doors in the Cocktail Lounge and between that and the older part of the premises, called for by the plans that were approved by the building department of the city of Boston under St. 1907, c. 550, § 12, as amended, had not been provided when the defendant last had knowledge of the premises on November 16, 1942, although he planned to open the Cocktail Lounge the next day; that the mode of construction of the Cocktail Lounge indicated that he did not intend to

3. In early cases what is now known as wanton or reckless conduct was variously described as wilful negligence, wanton negligence, gross negligence, and culpable negligence. So in criminal cases what was necessary to make conduct criminal was often so described. The expression "criminal negligence" was often used. But it seems that what we now know as wanton or reckless conduct was in fact required. The terminology, not the law, is what has changed. At least one statute purports to impose criminal liability for "gross negligence." G.L.(Ter.Ed.) c. 265, § 30. Whether that expression really means wanton or reckless conduct has not been decided. In other jurisdictions a variety of similar expressions has been used in describing conduct that will create criminal liability. But in many of them the substantial equivalent of wanton or reckless conduct is required.

provide either; and that they had not been provided at the time of the fire. As planned, the fire doors were to be held open by fusible plugs that would melt and allow the doors to close automatically in case of fire. They and the exits might have afforded some protection to persons in the Cocktail Lounge. The violation of such a statute is not negligence per se but sometimes is evidence of negligence. Standing by itself, it would not warrant a finding of wanton or reckless conduct. But it might be considered with other evidence. There was no error in its admission.

* * *

Regina v. Machekequonabe

Ontario Divisional Court, 1897.
28 Ont. Rep. 309.

It appeared from the evidence that the prisoner was a member of a tribe of pagan Indians who believed in the existence of an evil spirit clothed in human flesh, or in human form called a Wendigo which would eat a human being.

That it was reported that a Wendigo had been seen and it was supposed was in the neighbourhood of their camp desiring to do them harm.

That among other precautions to protect themselves, guards and sentries, the prisoner being one, were placed out in pairs armed with firearms (the prisoner having a rifle); that the prisoner saw what appeared to be a tall human being running in the distance, which he supposed was the Wendigo; that he and another Indian gave chase, and after challenging three times and receiving no answer fired and shot the object, when it was discovered to be his own foster father, who died soon afterward.

The jury found affirmative answers to the following questions:

Are you satisfied the prisoner did kill the Indian?

Did the prisoner believe the object he shot at to be a Wendigo or spirit?

Did he believe the spirit to be embodied in human flesh?

Was it the prisoner's belief that the Wendigo could be killed by a bullet shot from a rifle?

Was the prisoner sane apart from the delusion or belief in the existence of a Wendigo?

The learned trial Judge then proceeded with his charge as follows:— "Assuming these facts to be found by you, I think I must direct you as a matter of law that there is no justification here for the killing; and culpable homicide without justification is manslaughter, so that unless you can suggest to yourselves something stated in the evidence, or drawn from the evidence to warrant a different conclusion, I think it will be your duty to return a verdict of manslaughter. * * *

The jury found the prisoner guilty of manslaughter recommending him to mercy, and the learned Judge reserved a case for consideration whether upon the findings of the jury in answer to the questions he had submitted and upon his direction to them and upon the evidence the prisoner was properly found guilty of manslaughter.

The case was argued on February 8th, 1897, before a Divisional Court composed of ARMOUR, C.J., and FALCONBRIDGE, and STREET, JJ.

J.K. Kerr, Q.C., for the prisoner. The evidence shews the Indian tribe were pagans, and believed in an evil spirit clothed in human form which they called a Wendigo, and which attacked, killed and ate human beings. The man that was shot was thought to be a Wendigo, a spirit as distinguished from a human being. It is true there was a mistake, but there was no intention even to harm a human being much less to kill. The evidence shews the mistake was not unreasonable. * * *

The judgment of the Court was delivered by

ARMOUR, C.J.:

Upon the case reserved if there was evidence upon which the jury could find the prisoner guilty of manslaughter it is not open to us to reverse that finding, and the question we have to decide is whether there was such evidence.

We think there was, and therefore do not see how we can say that the prisoner was not properly convicted of manslaughter.

Regina v. Benge

Kent Assizes, 1865.
4 F. & F. 504, 176 Eng.Rep. 665.

The prosecution arose out of a fatal railway accident, which occurred on the South Eastern Railway at a place called Staplehurst, where there was a bridge, about two miles in the direction towards London from a station called Headcorn.[1] The tidal trains of that day would be due at Staplehurst at 3.15 p.m., on Friday, the 9th of June. The prisoner Benge was foreman of a gang of plate-layers, who had been employed to repair the rails within a certain distance, including the portion of the line at Staplehurst, and for that purpose it would be necessary to take up and replace the rails. * * * The time at which the work was done at any part of the line was left to the direction of the prisoner Benge, as the foreman of the gang. And he was furnished with a time book, in which the precise time of the arrival of the various trains on each day was marked; for each week in columns headed by the name of the day of the week. This book was clear in its arrangement, and printed in good, large, legible type, so that with the least care in its perusal, no mistake would be possible. The hour of arrival of the tidal train varied of course with the tide, and was different on each day. And on the day in question the prisoner Benge had looked at the column for Saturday—the next day—instead of Friday, the 9th. The time of arrival on the Saturday would be 5.20 p.m.; whereas the time for Friday, the day in question, would be 3.15. Thinking that the time would be 5.20, the prisoner Benge, when the last of the trains before the tidal train had passed, which was at 2.50 p.m., directed his gang to take up the rails at Staplehurst bridge, and they were accordingly taken up.

1. The explanation that appeared to be given by Benge was that on the day in question he had looked at the book furnished him by the company, in which the time the trains would arrive at Staplehurst was stated, but that he by accident looked at the wrong day * * *.

There was, it will be seen, barely half an hour between the time at which the 2.50 train passed, and the time—3.15—at which the tidal train would arrive; and half an hour as it turned out, and as indeed was well known would be far too short a time to allow of the rails taken up being replaced! If the prisoner had read the time of arrival of the tidal train rightly, he would not have thought of taking up the rails, but he did not expect it until 5.20, which would have allowed nearly three hours, and the job would be completed in about an hour. * * * It was usual * * * to send on one of the gang as a signal man with a flag in his hand, who was to go on at least 1000 yards in the direction in which the expected train was to come, and when he had got that distance he was to stand and raise a flag when it appeared, which would be seen at a distance of above 500 yards, and thus would give a distance of 1500 yards, or nearly a mile, between the train and the spot at which the rails were up, so as to allow of ample time to stop the train. Books of printed rules were in the hands of the foreman of plate-layers, and among others, of the prisoner; and these rules expressly provided that rails should not be taken up without these precautions. On the occasion in question one of the men of the prisoner's gang, named Wills, was sent forward as signal man, but without (as it appeared) any particular directions from the prisoner Benge, and instead of going 1000 yards he went, as he said, only 540 yards; and there he stood till he saw the advancing train, and moved his flag. He was observed, but not until the train was too near to be stopped. The engine-driver was not paying a very sharp look-out, and though so soon as he saw the signal man he gave the signal to stop, and the steam was shut off, and the breaks put on, it was too late to stop the train, which was going at the rate of 50 miles an hour, and it came on to the bridge, and then running off the line at the spot where the rails were up, it dashed on to the bridge, and the catastrophe ensued in which many lives were lost.

There was evidence that at the distance of 1000 yards, the train could easily have been stopped, at any rate of speed.

PIGOTT, B., * * * Was the accident mainly caused by the taking up of the rails at a time when an express train was about to arrive, was that the act of the prisoner, and was it owing to culpable negligence on his part? His counsel had urged that it was not so, because the flagman and engine-driver had been guilty of negligence, which had contributed to cause the catastrophe; but they, in their turn, might make the same excuse, and so, if it was valid, no one could be criminally responsible at all. This would be an absurd and unreasonable conclusion and showed that the contention of the prisoner's counsel could not be sound. * * * Now, here the primary cause was certainly the taking up of the rails at a time when the train was about to arrive, and when it would be impossible to replace them in time to avoid the accident. And this the prisoner admitted was owing to his own mistake. Was that mistake culpable negligence, and did it mainly or substantially cause the accident? The book was clearly and plainly printed, and must have been read carelessly to admit of such a mistake. Was it not the duty of the prisoner who knew the fearful consequences of a mistake to take reasonable care to be correct? And had he taken such care? * * *

Verdict—Guilty.

Historical Note

The Staplehurst accident killed ten people and injured another forty seriously. Among the survivors were Charles Dickens, his intimate friend, the actress Ellen Ternan, and her mother, all returning from a holiday in France. Dickens took a leading part in organizing the rescue which followed, helping the injured. The accident haunted him for the rest of his life. From the wreck he retrieved the manuscript of his novel-in-progress, Our Mutual Friend, at the end of which will be found the statement that he could "never be much nearer parting company with [his] readers for ever" than he was "on Friday the Ninth of June in the present year * * * until there shall be written against my life, the two words with which I have closed this book. [The End]" See F. Kaplan, Dickens, A Biography (William Morrow & Co. 1988) 458–462.

Commonwealth v. Pierce

Supreme Judicial Court of Massachusetts, 1884.
138 Mass. 165.

* * *

The evidence for the government tended to show that the defendant publicly practised as a physician; that he was called to attend Mary A. Bemis on December 29, 1882, and continued to attend her until January 7, 1883; that on that day, she being very sick and confined to her bed, he prescribed that kerosene oil should be applied to her as follows: that a flannel shirt, flannel drawers, and stockings should be saturated with it, and placed on her, and kept wet by renewing the wet flannels, &c. every three hours; that this was done, with her consent, by her husband and attendants, but not by the defendant personally; that after the defendant had gone, in about two hours, owing to the pain and distress of the patient, and upon her demand, the saturated flannels were removed, and the defendant was sent for.

* * *

The defendant prescribed that the flannels should not be taken off, but kept wet with kerosene oil by pouring it upon them from a can, and this was done as before by her nurse and attendants, and not by the doctor personally. The flannels, saturated as aforesaid, were kept upon the patient until January 9, 1883, when they were removed by the defendant's direction.

The evidence tended to show that the effect of the kerosene was to blister and burn a large part of the surface of the body, removing the scarf skin from two thirds the surface, as estimated by the witnesses, and taking off the true skin over one third the surface of the body, and causing suppurating sores.

The defendant continued to attend her until January 14, when he was discharged, and other physicians were called, who testified that she was then past recovery. She died on January 16, 1883, and evidence was introduced tending to show that the cause of death was the burning and blistering produced by the application of kerosene oil as aforesaid.

The defendant introduced evidence tending to show that he had, prior to that time, made application of kerosene oil to patients for various complaints, with beneficial results, and with slight and temporary affection of the skin.

After the close of the defendant's evidence, the government was allowed, in the exercise of the discretion of the court, against the defendant's objection, to introduce a witness, who testified that the defendant had, prior to the time referred to in the indictment, applied to her kerosene oil, and that the effect was to blister and burn her flesh on her neck and breast to the bone, and that the doctor's attention was called to this at the time.

* * *

HOLMES, J. The defendant has been found guilty of manslaughter * * *.

* * *

* * * The jury have found that it was applied as the result of foolhardy presumption or gross negligence, and that is enough. * * *

* * *

Note on the Recklessness Standard

Look again at the definition of recklessness in Model Penal Code, § 2.02(2)(c), supra, p. 138, and compare it for clarity with the language in *Welansky*. Here are two still different views, the first emphasizing the subjective element, and the second, taken from the last principal case, emphasizing objective factors:

a. State v. Bates, 65 S.D. 105, 107–109, 271 N.W. 765, 766–767 (1937):

> * * * This assignment raises the question of the meaning of the term "culpable negligence" as used in section 4024, R.C.1919. Said section 4024, so far as here material, is as follows: "Every killing of one human being by the * * * culpable negligence of another, * * * is manslaughter in the second degree." * * *
>
> * * * [T]he common law required that negligence to be sufficient to support a criminal action must be something more than mere inadvertence. There must be some action from which the jury might reasonably infer the mens rea. The statute has described this action as "culpable." To define the word "culpable" as used in the statute by substituting therefor some equally indefinite term such as "gross," "wanton," or even "reckless" does not seem to us very helpful, or to convey to a jury any meaning not already expressed by the words used in the statute.
>
> This court was confronted with a problem very similar to that with which we are now confronted in the case of Melby v. Anderson, 266 N.W. 135, 137, wherein we construed the words "gross negligence * * * [or] wilful and wanton misconduct," as used in the so-called guest statute, chapter 147, Laws of 1933. It is our opinion that the conduct which the Legislature was there attempting to describe by use of the words "gross, wilful and wanton" is the same conduct which, when brought before a jury in a criminal case under the statute here involved, is sufficient to give rise to the mens rea which, as we have said above, we believe to be necessary before a conviction might be sustained under this section 4024. * * * So it now seems to us, applying what we there said to this more general statute, that before the acts of a person come within the meaning of the term "culpable negligence" as used in the statute now under consideration, the jury must find as a fact that the defendant intentionally did something which he should not have done or intentionally failed to do something which he

should have done under such circumstances, that it can be said that he consciously realized that his conduct would in all probability (as distinguished from possibly) produce the precise result which it did produce. * * *

b. Commonwealth v. Pierce, 138 Mass. 165, 175–180 (1884):

But recklessness in a moral sense means a certain state of consciousness with reference to the consequences of one's acts. No matter whether defined as indifference to what those consequences may be, or as a failure to consider their nature or probability as fully as the party might and ought to have done, it is understood to depend on the actual condition of the individual's mind with regard to consequences, as distinguished from mere knowledge of present or past facts or circumstances from which some one or everybody else might be led to anticipate or apprehend them if the supposed act were done. We have to determine whether recklessness in this sense was necessary to make the defendant guilty of felonious homicide, or whether his acts are to be judged by the external standard of what would be morally reckless, under the circumstances known to him, in a man of reasonable prudence.

More specifically, the questions raised by the foregoing requests and rulings are whether an actual good intent and the expectation of good results are an absolute justification of acts, however foolhardy they may be if judged by the external standard supposed, and whether the defendant's ignorance of the tendencies of kerosene administered as it was will excuse the administration of it.

So far as civil liability is concerned, at least, it is very clear that what we have called the external standard would be applied, and that, if a man's conduct is such as would be reckless in a man of ordinary prudence, it is reckless in him. * * *

If this is the rule adopted in regard to the redistribution of losses, which sound policy allows to rest where they fall in the absence of a clear reason to the contrary, there would seem to be at least equal reason for adopting it in the criminal law, which has for its immediate object and task to establish a general standard, or at least general negative limits, of conduct for the community, in the interest of the safety of all.

* * *

If a physician is not less liable for reckless conduct than other people, it is clear, in the light of admitted principle and the later Massachusetts cases, that the recklessness of the criminal no less than that of the civil law must be tested by what we have called an external standard. In dealing with a man who has no special training, the question whether his act would be reckless in a man of ordinary prudence is evidently equivalent to an inquiry into the degree of danger which common experience shows to attend the act under the circumstances known to the actor. The only difference is, that the latter inquiry is still more obviously external to the estimate formed by the actor personally than the former. But it is familiar law that an act causing death may be murder, manslaughter, or misadventure, according to the degree of danger attending it. If the danger is very great, as in the case of an assault with a weapon found by the jury to be deadly, or an assault with hands and feet upon a woman known to be exhausted by illness, it is murder. * * *

The very meaning of the fiction of implied malice in such cases at common law was, that a man might have to answer with his life for consequences which he neither intended nor foresaw. To say that he was presumed to have intended them, is merely to adopt another fiction, and to disguise the truth. The truth was, that his failure or inability to predict them was immaterial, if, under the circumstances known to him, the court or jury, as the case might be, thought them obvious.

As implied malice signifies the highest degree of danger, and makes the act murder; so, if the danger is less, but still not so remote that it can be disregarded, the act will be called reckless, and will be manslaughter, as in the case of an ordinary assault with feet and hands, or a weapon not deadly, upon a well person. * * *

* * *

* * * The use of the thing must be dangerous according to common experience, at least to the extent that there is a manifest and appreciable chance of harm from what is done, in view either of the actor's knowledge or of his conscious ignorance. * * * Common experience is necessary to the man of ordinary prudence, and a man who assumes to act as the defendant did must have it at his peril. * * *

Questions

1. Some jurisdictions, by statute or by court decision, establish special manslaughter rules for deaths due to careless handling of automobiles, firearms, etc. E.g., negligence might be sufficient for liability for automobile manslaughter; pointing a gun, even if it is believed to be unloaded, at another, might when death results, produce jury instructions which would make acquittal of manslaughter unlikely. Is special treatment justified in such cases?

2. The Model Penal Code grades negligent killings as negligent homicide (§ 210.4), reckless killings as the greater offense of manslaughter (§ 210.3(1)(a)), and reckless killings committed "under circumstances manifesting extreme indifference to the value of human life" as murder (§ 210.2(1)(b)). Grading is according to *mens rea,* except to the extent that negligence need not involve any fault at all. The *actus reus* in each case is taking the "substantial and unjustifiable risk," "the disregard of which involves a gross deviation" from the proper standard of conduct. See § 2.02. How far are the cases in this section and the next consistent with this approach?

2. Depraved Heart Killings

Neitzel v. State

Court of Appeals of Alaska, 1982.
655 P.2d 325.

SINGLETON, JUDGE.

Stanley Neitzel shot his girlfriend, Irene Reedy, in the head causing her death. The undisputed evidence establishes that Neitzel fired a number of shots directly at Reedy while she sat on the ground. Many of these earlier bullets struck the ground within an inch of Ms. Reedy before the fatal shot entered her head. Eyewitnesses were unsure of whether Neitzel fired at Reedy to discipline her for drinking vodka which belonged to him, to frighten her, to demonstrate his marksmanship by seeing how close he could come without hitting her, or to just have fun with his rifle. Neitzel denied any recollection of the incident. Two hours after the shooting his blood alcohol level was .15%. The state offered expert testimony suggesting that Neitzel's blood alcohol level could have been as high as .18% at the time of the crime. Neitzel was convicted of second degree murder in violation of AS 11.41.110(a)(2), which provides in relevant part:

> *Murder in the Second Degree.* (a) A person commits the crime of murder in the second degree if
>
> * * *
>
> (2) he intentionally performs an act that results in the death of another person under circumstances manifesting an extreme indifference to the value of human life * * *.

* * *

In order to understand the legislature's intentions in enacting AS 11.41.110(a)(2), it is necessary to briefly trace the evolution of what can best be described as reckless murder through the common law, the Model Penal Code, upon which our current statutes are modeled, the tentative draft prepared by the Alaska Code Revision Commission, Subcommission on Criminal Law (hereafter referred to as the Tentative Draft), and the Alaska Revised Criminal Code ultimately enacted by the legislature (hereafter referred to as the Revised Code). When such a study is completed, we believe the legislature's intent is clear.

At common law, murder was homicide committed with "malice aforethought." R. Perkins, *Criminal Law* § 1, at 34 (2d ed. 1969). "Aforethought" suggests planning but this term fell into disuse leaving "malice" the significant term differentiating murder from other forms of culpable homicide. Id. at 34–35. Malice was primarily defined to mean an intent to kill in the absence of (1) justification, (2) excuse, or (3) mitigation. Id. at 35.

This definition was subject to an exception which is central to the issue before us. Common law courts permitted a jury to find malice in the absence of a specific intent to kill where "in the absence of any circumstance of exculpation or mitigation an act [was] done with such heedless disregard of a harmful result, foreseen as a likely possibility, that it differs little in the scale of moral blameworthiness from an actual intent to cause such harm." Id. at 768. To distinguish such a crime from intentional murder, it is useful to call it "reckless murder," and to distinguish its *mens rea* from an intent to kill by calling it "constructive malice."

Typical examples of this kind of murder are: shooting, regardless of the consequences, into a home, room, train, or automobile in which others are known to be or might be. Id. at 36. Perkins calls the mental state accompanying such an act "a man-endangering-state-of-mind." Id. at 759.

The Tentative Draft prepared by the Subcommission on Criminal Law was based on a number of recent state codifications of criminal law. These codes in turn were substantially derived from the New York Revised Penal Code of 1965 which was based on the Model Penal Code.

* * *

In this case we must review three Model Penal Code concepts: (1) culpable mental states; (2) the Model Penal Code definition of reckless murder (particularly the differences between reckless murder, as conceived by the drafters of the Model Penal Code, and manslaughter); and (3) finally, the treatment of intoxication as a defense in the Model Penal Code, the Tentative Draft, and our Revised Code. Such a review will clarify the legislature's intent in defining reckless murder and the part intoxication plays in defending against a charge of reckless murder.

* * *

The Model Penal Code and the Tentative Draft establish one offense of murder which can be committed purposefully, knowingly, or, under limited circumstances, recklessly. The Tentative Draft differs from the Model Penal Code in substituting the word "intentionally" for "purposefully." Compare Model Penal Code § 210.2 *with* Tentative Draft 11.41.110. * * *

* * *

* * * As we interpret it, AS 11.41.110(a)(2) requires that the actor must knowingly engage in conduct causing the death of another which in light of the circumstances is reckless to the point that it manifests an extreme indifference to the value of human life. This is what we understand Model Penal Code § 210.2(1)(b) to mean as well.

* * *

* * * In conclusion, applying the statutory terminology as defined in the code, to be guilty of second degree murder Neitzel had to know he was firing a gun and be reckless regarding: (1) the circumstances, i.e., the location of Ms. Reedy, her vulnerability, and the direction in which he was shooting; and (2) the result, i.e., her death. Under the Revised Code, intoxication is not relevant in evaluating the culpable mental states of "knowingly," AS 11.81.900(a)(2), or "recklessly," AS 11.81.900(a)(3).

* * *

Neitzel does not dispute his ability to know he was firing a gun. The focus of his due process attack is on the claim that he recklessly disregarded the surrounding circumstances. In this regard, the Revised Code follows the Model Penal Code in precluding evidence of intoxication on the issue of recklessness. See Model Penal Code § 2.08(2). * * *

* * *

Neitzel's equal protection argument is also unfounded. Neitzel argues that reckless murder, as we define it, is conceptually indistinguishable from reckless manslaughter. See B. Gegan, *A Case of Depraved Mind Murder*, 49 St. John's L.Rev. 417, 440–50 (1974) (criticizing the comparable New York statute on this ground). If intoxication is held to be a defense to murder but not manslaughter, Neitzel concludes the two offenses are kept separate and the equal protection problem disappears.

We reject this argument because even without allowing intoxication as a defense to murder, the two offenses are sufficiently distinct to avoid equal protection problems. The Revised Code simply follows the Model Penal Code in distinguishing reckless murder from reckless manslaughter. The drafters of the Model Penal Code suggest the following reasons:

Section 210.2(1)(b) also provides that criminal homicide constitutes murder when it is "committed recklessly under circumstances manifesting extreme indifference to the value of human life." This provision reflects the judgment that there is a kind of reckless homicide that cannot fairly be distinguished in grading terms from homicides committed purposely or knowingly.

Recklessness, as defined in Section 2.02(2)(c), presupposes an awareness of the creation of substantial homicidal risk, a risk too great to be deemed justifiable by any valid purpose that the actor's conduct serves. Since risk, however, is a matter of degree and the motives for risk creation may be infinite in variation, some formula is needed to identify the case where recklessness may be found and where it should be assimilated to purpose or knowledge for purposes of grading. Under the Model Code, this judgment must be made in terms of whether the actor's conscious disregard of the risk, given the circumstances of the case, so far departs from acceptable behavior that it constitutes a "gross deviation from the standard of conduct that a law-abiding person would observe in the actor's situation." Ordinary recklessness in this sense is made sufficient for a conviction of manslaughter under Section 210.3(1)(a). In a prosecution for murder, however, the Code calls for the further judgment whether the actor's conscious disregard of the risk, under the circumstances, manifests extreme indifference to the value of human life. The significance of purpose or knowledge as a standard of culpability is that, cases of provocation or other mitigation apart, purposeful or knowing homicide demonstrates precisely such indifference to the value of human life. Whether recklessness is so extreme that it demonstrates similar indifference is not a question, it is submitted, that can be further clarified. It must be left directly to the trier of fact under instructions which make it clear that recklessness that can fairly be assimilated to purpose or knowledge should be treated as murder and that less extreme recklessness should be punished as manslaughter.

Insofar as Subsection (1)(b) includes within the murder category cases of homicide caused by extreme recklessness, though without purpose to kill, it reflects both the common law and much preexisting statutory treatment usually cast in terms of conduct evidencing a "depraved heart regardless of human life" or some similar words. Examples usually given include shooting into a crowd or into an occupied house or automobile, though they are not, of course, exhaustive.

Some indication of the content of this concept as a means of differentiating murder and manslaughter may be afforded by prior decisional law. One case involved a game of Russian roulette, where the defendant pointed a revolver loaded with a single cartridge at his friend. The weapon fired on the third try, and the fatal wound resulted. The court affirmed the conviction for murder, despite ample evidence that the defendant had not desired to kill his

> friend, with the statement that "malice in the sense of a wicked disposition is evidenced by the intentional doing of an uncalled-for act in callous disregard of its likely harmful effects on others." In another case, the defendant's claimed intention was to shoot over his victim's head in order to scare him. The court held that, even crediting this assertion, the jury could find the defendant guilty of murder on the ground that his act showed "such a reckless disregard for human life as was the equivalent of a specific intent to kill." A third illustration involved a defendant who fired several shots into a house which he knew to be occupied by several persons. The court affirmed his conviction of murder because the defendant's conduct was "imminently dangerous" and "evinced a wicked and depraved mind regardless of human life." Other acts held to show sufficient recklessness to justify a conviction of murder include shooting into a moving automobile and throwing a heavy beer glass at a woman carrying a lighted oil lamp. The Model Code formulation would permit a jury to reach the same conclusion in each of these cases.

A.L.I., *Model Penal Code and Commentaries,* Part II § 210.2, at 21–23 (1980) (footnotes omitted). The commentator concludes:

> Given the Model Code definition of recklessness, the point involved is put adequately and succinctly by asking whether the recklessness rises to the level of "extreme indifference to the value of human life." As has been observed, it seems undesirable to suggest a more specific formulation. The variations referred to above [various formulations from modern codes discussed in the commentary] retain in some instances greater fidelity to the common-law phrasing but they do so at great cost in clarity. Equally obscure are the several attempts to depart from the common law to which reference has been made. The result of these formulations is that the method of defining reckless murder is impaired in its primary purpose of communicating to jurors in ordinary language the task expected of them. The virtue of the Model Penal Code language is that it is a simpler and more direct method by which this function can be performed.

Id. at 25–26 (footnotes omitted).

In conclusion, jurors asked to evaluate conduct resulting in death to determine whether it was negligent, reckless or malicious must weigh four factors:

> (1) The social utility of the actor's conduct,
>
> (2) the magnitude of the risk his conduct creates including both the nature of forseeable harm and the likelihood that the conduct will result in that harm;
>
> (3) the actor's knowledge of the risk; and
>
> (4) any precautions the actor takes to minimize the risk.

See G. Fletcher, *Rethinking Criminal Law* § 4.3, at 259–62 (1978) (Homicide by Excessive Risk Taking); W. LaFave and A. Scott, *Handbook on Criminal*

Law § 70, at 541–45 (1972) (Depraved-Heart Murder). Under the Revised Code, negligent homicide and reckless manslaughter are satisfied by conduct creating a significant risk of death absent justification or excuse. They differ only in the actor's knowledge of the risk. In differentiating reckless murder from reckless manslaughter, the jury is asked to determine whether the recklessness manifests an extreme indifference to human life. In so doing, it might pay particular attention to the social utility of the defendant's conduct and the precautions he takes to minimize the apparent risks. In evaluating the social utility of the actor's conduct, the jury must of course consider defenses such as provocation, necessity, the defense of self and of others, if supported by the evidence. Shooting at someone, by itself, is devoid of social utility and consequently has been used by the commentators as the paradigm of extreme indifference to human life. Where, however, a gun is fired at an attacking lion in an attempt to rescue the victim and the bullet strikes the victim, the social utility of the conduct may excuse it despite the magnitude of the risk. Cf. Lee v. State, 490 P.2d 1206 (Alaska 1971) (a civil case where the victim was shot in the course of her rescue from a lioness; jury absolved defendant of gross negligence, case remanded for trial for ordinary negligence), overruled on other grounds, Munroe v. City Council, 545 P.2d 165, 170 n. 11, modified on rehearing, 547 P.2d 839 (Alaska 1976).

In addition, the jury may evaluate any precautions taken. Thus, a person may be reckless in the sense that he knowingly engages in conduct which creates a foreseeable risk of death and amounts to a gross deviation from the standard of conduct that a reasonable person would observe in the sense that the social utility of his conduct does not warrant exposing another to the risk of death. He may, however, still not manifest an extreme indifference to the life of the person endangered if he takes substantial precautions to minimize the risk.

Finally, and most importantly, the jury must consider the nature and gravity of the risk, including the harm to be foreseen and the likelihood that it will occur. For both murder and manslaughter, the harm to be foreseen is a death. Therefore, the significant distinction is in the likelihood that a death will result from the defendant's act. Where the defendant's act has limited social utility, a very slight though significant and avoidable risk of death may make him guilty of manslaughter if his act causes death. Driving an automobile has some social utility although substantially reduced when the driver is intoxicated. The odds that a legally intoxicated person driving home after the bars close will hit and kill or seriously injure someone may be as low as one chance in a thousand and still qualify for manslaughter. Where murder is charged, however, an act must create a much greater risk that death or serious physical injury will result. This is the point, in the Model Penal Code commentary "that recklessness * * * can fairly be assimilated to purpose or knowledge * * *."

How likely death must be before murder can be charged is not susceptible to mathematical demonstration. An examination of the classic example given to distinguish murder from manslaughter—Russian roulette—gives some guidance. If a revolver had six chambers in its cylinder and only one contains a bullet and we assume no imperfection in the revolver, then the odds are one in six that a bullet will fall under the hammer when the cylinder is spun and the trigger is pulled. Stated otherwise a participant has a 16.7% chance of being killed or seriously injured and an 83.3% chance of not being killed or seriously injured in a game of Russian Roulette each time he puts the gun to his temple and pulls the trigger. The act is so dangerous and so lacking in social utility, however, that it demonstrates extreme indifference to human life and serves to distinguish murder from manslaughter.

The commentary to the Model Penal Code suggests that all of these concepts are adequately conveyed to the jury in the single phrase "extreme indifference to the value of human life." We therefore hold that the Revised Code sufficiently distinguishes between reckless murder and reckless manslaughter to satisfy equal protection.

* * *

The judgment of the superior court is Affirmed.

Note

People v. France, 57 A.D.2d 432, 433–435, 394 N.Y.S.2d 891, 892–893 (1977):

We are of the opinion that the trial court was in error in submitting to the jury that count of the indictment charging murder (Penal Law, § 125.25[2] [Depraved Mind Murder]). Section 125.25 provides: "A person is guilty of murder in the second degree when: * * * 2. Under circumstances evincing a depraved indifference to human life, he recklessly engages in conduct which creates a grave risk of death to another person, and thereby causes the death of another person."

There can be no doubt that the defendant's conduct was reckless and that such conduct caused the death of another. But it does not follow that because defendant was attempting to escape from capture by police at 3:00 A.M., at high speed in a motor car, and ignored successive traffic signals, these circumstances "evinc[ed] a depraved indifference to human life".

Although testimony concerning the condition of the streets and thoroughfares at the time involved and the defendant's rate of speed while driving is sketchy, there is no doubt that the collision at the intersection with its most tragic consequences was fortuitous; it was not as if the defendant, in an effort to elude pursuers, drove his auto into congestion deliberately disregarding other vehicles or pedestrians who happened to block his way.

* * *

* * * [T]he evidence should require, as it did in a hoary precedent, that the act must be "perpetrated with a full consciousness of the probable consequences" (Darry v. People, 10 N.Y. 120, Selden, J., at p. 148) and certainly be one which would support the observation that "the imminently dangerous act, the extreme depravity of mind and the *regardlessness of human life* properly place the crime upon the same level as the taking of life by premeditated design" (Darry, supra, Parker, J., at p. 158) (emphasis added).

* * *

Such condemned behavior is required to be "extremely dangerous and fatal conduct performed without specific homicidal intent but with a depraved kind of wantonness: for example, shooting into a crowd, placing a time bomb in a public place, or opening the door of the lions' cage in the zoo (see People v. Jernatowski, 1924, 238 N.Y. 188, 144 N.E. 497; Darry v. People, supra)."

(Practice Commentaries by Arnold D. Hechtman, McKinney's Cons.Laws of N.Y., Book 39, Penal Law, § 125.25) and not merely carelessness or recklessness in the operation of an automobile. * * *

Question

"Depraved heart killings" are usually second degree murder in jurisdictions which divide murder into two degrees, perhaps because they are relatively uncommon and may be overlooked in statutes creating first degree murders. As a matter of policy, should they be first degree murders?

E. THE ACTUS REUS OF CRIMINAL HOMICIDE

1. Causation

State v. Bangs

Supreme Court of Ohypo, 1983.
301 Ohypo 426.

NOD, J.: Jonah Jinx was crossing the street with the green light in a protected intersection when he was hit by a car driven by the defendant, Barbara Bangs. According to witnesses, Ms. Bangs had turned around almost completely in the driver's seat to adjudicate a dispute between her two children. She apparently did not see the red light or Mr. Jinx before she hit him. She stopped to render aid and saw Jinx rise to his knees, when a second car careened around the corner at high speed and hit Jinx again. The second car disappeared and has not been identified.

Jinx was rushed to the hospital where he was at first thought to be in surprisingly good condition. Both cars had apparently hit somewhat glancing blows. There was a simple fracture of the left arm and there were numerous minor cuts and bruises. None of these contributed to Jinx's subsequent death. The one serious injury was a puncture wound in the abdomen, caused by a ball point pen, which Jinx had just purchased and upon which he fell when he was hit by one of the automobiles. It was impossible to determine whether the puncture wound occurred after the first or second hit.

An operation was necessary to repair the damage caused by the pen. In preparation, Jinx was given curare, which paralyzes the chest muscles. While Jinx was under the influence of the curare, it was necessary for the anesthesiologist, Dr. Dream, to ventilate or breathe for Jinx by squeezing a bag of oxygen into his lungs. The surgeon, Dr. Slice, while repairing the puncture wound, discovered that Jinx had an incarcerated hernia. When he had finished closing the puncture wound, he turned to the hernia, which he testified he thought might endanger Jinx's life if not attended to. Had it not been repaired and had it become gangrenous, either on its own, or as a result of complications relating to the puncture wound—not unlikely possibilities—it would have at least required a second operation and it might have proved fatal. An independent medical expert, Dr. Wise, called by the trial judge, testified that it was good medical practice to correct such a condition when discovered unexpectedly in the course of another surgical procedure.

While Dr. Slice was operating on the hernia, Jinx lost his pulse and went into cardiac arrest, as a result of which he suffered massive damage to his brain and to other organs. It is common ground that as a result of the cardiac arrest, he died a month later, without ever having regained consciousness. The puncture wound had healed completely before his death. When Dr. Wise was asked what had caused the cardiac arrest, he testified that the shock or physical strain of the puncture wound or of either phase of the operation might have done so, but that a more likely cause was failure to ventilate the patient properly during the operations, if this failure had in fact occurred. He said that it was probable that Jinx would have survived without cardiac arrest if the hernia procedure had been omitted; this is because the total shock and strain would have been less and because any improper ventilation would have had a shorter time period in which to cause harm. It was his view that it was extremely unlikely that anything other than the possibilities he discussed might have brought on cardiac arrest. Slice testified that Dr. Dream had told him after the operation that he had become so absorbed in thinking about a medical paper he was preparing that he had forgotten to continue ventilating the patient.

Ms. Bangs was charged with manslaughter and released on bail pending trial. When she discovered the hernia operation and the suggestion of Dream's negligence (which Dream informally denied), she insisted that the doctors, and not she, should have been prosecuted. When no steps were taken to charge them, she prepared and packaged two bombs, one addressed to each of the physicians, and sent them for delivery via the Untied Package Delivery Service. The packages were given to route man Feckless for delivery. Feckless arrived at Dream's house near the end of the working day and discovered that he would have to climb some fifty steps to get to Dream's front door. He decided to call it a day and go home. On the way he tossed the few undelivered items, including both bombs, from which he had removed the address labels, into a trash can about five blocks from Dream's house.

Later that evening Dr. Dream was out jogging. He passed the trash can and saw a wrapped box on top of the trash, with no identification on the box. Curious, he opened the box, which coincidentally had previously been addressed to him, and was blown to bits. The second bomb was discovered unexploded in the trash can and traced to the defendant, who was charged with first degree murder in the death of Dream. The two homicide charges were consolidated for trial, and the jury found Bangs guilty of manslaughter in Jinx's death and first degree murder in Dream's.

We unanimously reverse the convictions on account of the trial court's erroneous admission of evidence for the prosecution. [The court's discussion of this point is omitted.]

Issues of causation were raised at the trial and are likely to recur if there are new trials on the two charges. A few words of guidance may be helpful. I put to one side all cases in which the alleged liability is based on causing death in the course of an unlawful act, where somewhat stricter causal requirements may apply, and limit my discussion to cases like the present one, in which the accused is charged with causing death through purpose, knowledge, recklessness, or negligence.

All authorities agree that for guilt there must be a legally adequate causal relationship between the conduct of the accused and the death of the victim. (One ancient requirement, recently abolished by our legislature, is that the death must occur within a year and a day of the infliction of the injury.) At a minimum, death must follow from the act or criminal omission of the accused. We must be able to say that but for the defendant's conduct, the death would not have happened substantially as it did. Suppose a third person had shot Jinx through the heart at the same moment he was struck by Bangs' car, and that he had died immediately, solely from the bullet wound. Or, suppose Jinx had died solely from a long-existing cancer while waiting to be wheeled into the operating room. Bangs would then have no homicidal liability; her conduct would simply have been irrelevant to the death. But here, Bangs's conduct was a necessary antecedent to the death which in fact occurred. Had Bangs not run over Jinx, he would not have been hit by the second car either. He would not have suffered the puncture wound, have been given the curare, have been operated on for either the wound or the incarcerated hernia, or (whether or not Dr. Dream had ventilated him properly) have suffered the cardiac arrest. It is similarly clear that but for the sending of the bomb, Dream would not have died substantially in the way that he did.

A little more than this may be required for legally adequate "but-for" causation. Not only some causal connection, but a "substantial" one is required for legal liability. If a victim bleeds to death from the combination of a serious stab wound and an independently administered pin prick, the pin prick is not a substantial cause. "Substantial" is relative; had the victim died from the combined effects of a thousand independently administered pin pricks, each would have been a substantial factor.

The defendant argues that she was not a but-for cause of Jinx's death because the injuries inflicted by the second car alone would be sufficient to account for all that followed, even if she had never struck the victim at all. As noted, the facts do not support this claim, because Jinx would probably never have been hit by the second car if Bangs had missed him. But even if the two cars had hit Jinx simultaneously and the proof had shown that each blow would have been mortal standing alone, the causal connection should be held adequate. It is mere verbal trickery to argue in such a case that because either blow could have been omitted with no change in result, neither is a but-for cause of death.

"But-for" causation is plainly present as to both deaths here. While this is necessary, it is not sufficient as a causal connection to allow conviction. There are millions of but-for causes for every event. Here, for example, the defendant's learning to drive a car, or for that matter her conception and birth, were but-for causes of the deaths. So were Jinx's purchase of the pen, Slice's decision to operate, and as to Dream's death, an architect's decision to build Dream's house on a hill, with a long stairway leading up to the front door. Most of this sea of but-for causes is insignificant from a criminal law point of view because no *mens rea* adequate for liability generates the causal activity leading up to the deaths. We need concern ourselves, when considering the guilt of a particular party, only with those causal paths which lead from her criminal conduct to the criminal result. Even with this focus, we demand something more than but-for causation connecting the *mens rea* with the death.

Suppose, for example, that I desire the death of my enemy and attempt to kill him by firing a gun at him. I miss, but he fears that I will try again and moves to another town to escape me. There, his new job does not work out well, his family becomes discontented, and after a run of bad luck, he throws himself in the river and is drowned. I am a but-for cause of the drowning and I meant to kill him, but the chain of events is such that it would be unjust to say that I caused his death. There are too many unexpected things and too long a time delay for me to be held responsible. I find it impossible to lay down precise rules, but I am in rough agreement with the Model Penal Code; generally there is adequate causation only when the result is within the purpose, knowledge, or risk known to the defendant (in recklessness), or risk known to the reasonable person in defendant's position (in negligence), appropriate to the crime, and when the result is not so outlandish as to make conviction unfair.

It remains only to attempt to apply the suggested test to the facts. Dream's death was a crime of purpose. In sending the bomb, Bangs meant to kill him, and she did. But the sequence of circumstances was bizarre. When Feckless abandoned the bomb package in the trash can five blocks from Dream's home, with no label present to allow a passerby to rescue it and make the intended delivery, what were the probabilities of harm? Expert testimony established that only opening the package would set off the bomb and also that moisture would destroy the effectiveness of the firing mechanisms. A heavy rain storm had been predicted and actually arrived shortly after the explosion; in fact it rendered the firing mechanism of the other bomb useless, and would certainly have done the same for the first. It would be unfair in the circumstances to hold Bangs criminally responsible for Dream's highly improbable death.

We must assume, as the jury found, that Bangs was reckless with respect to Jinx in running the red light. Injury and death to Jinx were within the risk. It is well established in the law that one causing such an injury takes hospital risks, that is, risks of delay, infection, improper diagnosis, or improper treatment by doctors or other hospital personnel. If your criminal fault puts the victim in the hospital, you (as well, of course, as any hospital personnel guilty of criminal misconduct contributing to the death) are responsible for what the hospital does. There is an exception only for outrageous misconduct in the hospital. If a doctor knowingly uses unsterilized instruments, for example, this may be outside the risk created by the defendant. But here, it was normal surgical procedure to repair the hernia in the circumstances, and, if Dream was negligent in failing to ventilate his patient properly, this is the sort of ordinary negligence which does not excuse Bangs. As for the second automobile, it is a normal risk of running over someone that he will be put in a perilous situation in which he may be hit again. I see no causal bar to a conviction of manslaughter with respect to Jinx.

BLYNKEN, J.: I do not believe that there is a sufficient causal connection to allow the conviction of Bangs for either death. I agree with what Justice Nod has to say about but-for causation and its application to these facts, except to note that there is some authority to suggest that if the forces set in motion by the accused come to rest in a position of apparent safety, only to be reactivated later by someone else, the legal causal relationship is broken by this "coming to rest." It is arguable here that, as to Dream's death, the bomb had come to rest in the trash can; as Justice Nod notes, further harm was then unlikely.

However that may be, I agree with my brother Nod that the remaining part of the causal requirement is not met as to Dream. While I believe it is possible to state the rule with more precision than he attempts to do, he correctly concludes that the connection is too remote. This is because of the conduct of Feckless, who had interrupted the forces put in motion by Bangs to use them for his own purposes—here to discard the packages to avoid work. Suppose that Bangs had planted the bomb under Dream's chair and that Feckless had found and recognized the bomb and used it to blow up someone else. It seems clear that Bangs would not be guilty of murder. Feckless would have taken Bangs's force and made it his own. In this example, as in the case, Feckless had preempted the situation and wiped out Bangs' homicide liability with respect to the bomb. Of course, Bangs may be guilty of an *attempt* to murder Dream.

The death of Jinx requires more careful examination. Where the *mens rea* is recklessness or negligence, but-for causation is enough unless there is a supervening cause. A supervening cause must first be intervening; that is, it must come into operation after the defendant has set his cause in motion and change the result in some significant way. The candidate for an intervening cause must not cooperate with the original cause so that, acting together, they produce death. In that case the causes are concurrent, and the second cause is not supervening or excusing, because it is not intervening. To illustrate, consider the second car to hit Jinx. If it had merely added to wounds already received and Jinx had died from both sets of wounds, it would be a concurrent cause and would not bar Bangs' liability. If the second hit had produced an exclusive cause of death, as would be the case if it had instantly crushed Jinx's head, it would then be an intervening cause, and, if other requirements could be met, would be supervening or excusing.

The second requirement for a supervening cause is that it be independent—that is, not traceable to the defendant's own conduct, with its own more obvious chain of causation (independent in the sense that the defendant is not one who generated, produced, motivated, or incited the other cause, as well as his more obvious one). Had Jinx, under the stress of the accident, stood up and wandered into the path of an oncoming truck, his response would have been dependent. Had the second vehicle to strike Jinx been an ambulance, called to the scene to cope with the result of defendant's act, the ambulance injury would have been a dependent cause and not a supervening one. There is no sign that the second car on the actual facts was in any way brought on the scene by what Bangs did; it was not therefore dependent.

Finally, a supervening or excusing cause must be unforeseeable; that is, a reasonable person in the defendant's position (and of course the defendant herself) must not have foreseen as a reasonable possibility that something like the second injury might occur. It is here that the second car fails as a supervening cause. It could have been foreseen that an injured pedestrian in the street might be hit again. If Bangs' injury was a but-for cause, then, the second car does not supervene to prevent her responsibility.

What happened in the hospital is another matter. Some things can be eliminated as supervening causes. The incarcerated hernia was a pre-existing physical condition. To the extent that it contributed to the cardiac arrest, it was a concurrent cause. It is well settled that the defendant takes the victim as she finds him; if he is already in poor physical condition before the injury, this is her (and of course also his) hard luck. His physical condition does not intervene.

As Justice Nod says, most hospital risks are assumed by the accused. The actions of the hospital staff are almost always dependent causes—the defendant's act has generated the need for treatment; usually foreseeable—everyone knows that medical treatment, particularly in emergency situations, may be imperfect and even negligent; and often such treatment, if harmful, merely contributes concurrently to the cause of death. Any one of these conditions would be enough to prevent the treatment from being a supervening cause.

The problem for the prosecution is that it is not entirely clear what "caused" Jinx's death, if we go back in time before the cardiac arrest. There are many possibilities. The most likely ones are:

A. Dream's negligence was non-existent or played a minor role, and the important role was played by the injuries received in the two automobile accidents. Ventilation problems and complications from the hernia operation were at most concurrent causes. Obviously, in this situation, there is no supervening cause and the defendant may be found guilty of manslaughter.

B. The negligence of the anesthesiologist was central. The operations contributed to the arrest only by bringing the anesthesiologist on the scene, and Dream's negligence would have brought on the cardiac arrest even if there had been no second phase of the operation. Here, since Dream's negligence was dependent on the automobile injuries and was foreseeable, his conduct was not a supervening cause and Bangs remains responsible.

C. Cardiac arrest was caused primarily by the hernia phase of the operation, although the decision to proceed with it may have been a perfectly proper one, from both the legal and medical points of view. Either the hernia operation itself directly brought about the cardiac arrest, or the increased time under the influence of the curare (the effect of which would have been promptly reversed by another drug at the end of the operation) allowed Dream's negligence to bring about the arrest. Here, Bangs is not causally responsible. Such a course of events is intervening, independent, and unforeseeable. There is essentially a new episode causing death. This scenario is a likely one; it was not eliminated beyond a reasonable doubt by the evidence. For this reason, the manslaughter conviction should also be reversed on causal grounds.

WYNKEN, C.J.: I see no causal bar to either conviction. Why, when we have present all of the non-causal elements of the crime, plus but-for causation, should the accused be excused? She has the *mens rea* appropriate for the crime and has "caused" the harm. Surely, penal theory favors punishment except in some highly unusual sort of situation. (Like the other members of the court, I do not attempt to deal with special problems of the felony-murder and misdemeanor-manslaughter rules.)

Where, as in the case of the killing of Dream, the defendant desires death (or knows that it will occur), the criminal law has traditionally found sweeping liability, even though events take an unexpected turn. There is free substitution of victims. Suppose A wants to kill his enemy B, but the bullet from his gun kills C instead. A is guilty of murdering C, whether he mistook C for B, or whether his aim was poor and he hit passerby C by mistake. So, in this case, had the bomb package been opened by someone other than Dream, as it might well have been, Bangs would have been guilty of murdering that person. One who criminally sets such a dangerous force in motion must accept the consequences. Of course, there are some limits. It is hard to see how an operable bomb ever reaches a position of apparent safety, but we might imagine a case in which, apparently ruined by the rain, the bomb had enjoyed the baking sun of the city dump for a week, and against the physical probabilities had again become operable when it dried. It then went off and killed a scavanger. It is arguable that Bangs should not be guilty there. And, the bomb must operate as a bomb for Bangs to be guilty. Had Dream unexpectedly eaten it and died of poisoning, Bangs would not be liable.

Again, had some third person discovered the package, recognized it as a bomb, and deliberately used it for his own criminal purpose, Bangs should not be held for the result. This is the kind of remote possibility which does excuse. But in the actual case, the bomb has not been taken over by another in this way; its action can fairly be attributed to Bangs' original plan.

As to Jinx's death, I see no need for Justice Blynken's fine distinctions, which do not really seem to help much when a difficult case like this one arises. It seems clear enough for conviction that despite possible negligence of Dream and despite the reasonable medical choice to operate on the hernia, the recklessness of Bangs led directly to the cardiac arrest and death. There is no sound reason to excuse her.

Note

There are two kinds of approaches to problems of criminal causation. Both insist on a finding of "but-for" causation. "Simple" theories, like that of the Model Penal Code's section 2.03, attempt no detailed rules beyond this requirement. Adherents of such theories look for results within contemplation or risk and provide a safety valve for complicated situations where conviction seems unreasonable. They believe it either impossible or not worth the trouble to look for clear and accurate sub-principles. "Complex" theories, like that of Professor Perkins (see Perkins & Boyce, Criminal Law

769–825 (3rd ed. 1982)) attempt detailed rules of analysis. Courts may use either kind of theory, and you should be familiar with both. Try to decide for yourself how far the detailed rules of the more complex theories really help to resolve causal problems in satisfactory fashion.

Questions

1. With purpose to kill, A pushes V off the roof of a ten story building. As V falls, he is hit by a bullet fired by B through the fifth floor window. V dies. What is the criminal liability of A and B for V's death? Does it matter whether B's shot was accidental or calculated to kill? Does it matter what the autopsy showed?

2. In a mountain gorge, X fires a rifle at his enemy Y, intending to kill him. The bullet hits a tree branch and is deflected to the ground. An eagle, perched on the branch, is startled into flight by the bullet and flies off in the direction of Y. The noise of a sudden landslide frightens the bird into dropping a rat it had caught just before the shot was fired. The rat falls on Y and bites him in fright. Y dies of rabies communicated by the rat. Is X criminally liable?

3. Here is another old hypothetical you might want to think about for review. R is about to cross the desert with water just sufficient for the journey, in two leather water bottles, carried by his camel. While R is away for a few minutes, his enemy S pours a vial of poison into one of the water bottles; one swallow of the liquid would be fatal. After S leaves, T punches a tiny hole in the bottom of the bottle holding the poison. R returns and starts across the desert, drinking by chance first from the undisturbed bottle. When he finishes this, he turns to the other bag, only to find it empty, and dies of thirst. What is the criminal responsibility of S and T? Consider that T might have known nothing of S's acts and wished to kill R, or might have tried to save R's life by getting rid of the poison, hoping that R would find enough water to survive.

State v. Petersen

Court of Appeals of Oregon, 1974.
17 Or.App. 478, 522 P.2d 912.

Before SCHWAB, C.J., and FORT and TANZER, JJ.

TANZER, JUDGE.

* * *

The issue of the criminal responsibility of one racing driver for the death of a person actually killed by another racer appears to be a matter of first impression in Oregon, but it has been the subject of appellate decisions in other jurisdictions. At least as early as 1846, it was held that where two individuals were racing their vehicles (in that case, horsedrawn carts) along a public road, and one of them ran into and killed a third person during the course of the race, both racers were guilty of manslaughter. Regina v. Swindall, 2 Car & K 230, 175 Eng.Reprint 95 (1846). Each participant engages mutually in reckless conduct which causes death. Regardless of which vehicle strikes the victim, the recklessness of both causes the death. That principle has been adhered to by most courts which have addressed the issue. See State v. Melcher, 15 Ariz.App. 157, 487 P.2d 3 (1971); People v. Kemp, 150 Cal.App.2d 654, 310 P.2d 680 (1957); Jacobs v. State, 184 So.2d 711 (Fla.App.1966); State v. Youngblut, 257 Iowa 343, 132 N.W.2d 486 (1965); Jones v. Commonwealth, 247 S.W.2d 517 (Ky.1952); State v.

Fennewald, 339 S.W.2d 769 (Mo.1960); State v. Butler, 11 Ohio St.2d 23, 40 Ohio Op.2d 43, 227 N.E.2d 627 (1967). See also Anno., Manslaughter—Person Liable, 95 A.L.R.2d 175, 195–196. Those cases which have reached a conclusion that the driver was not guilty appear to have done so not because of disagreement with the general principle, but rather because, in the particular case, a causal link between the defendant's conduct and the death was not proven. See, e.g., People v. Lemieux, 176 Misc. 305, 27 N.Y.S.2d 235 (Queens County Ct.1941); Commonwealth v. Root, 403 Pa. 571, 170 A.2d 310 (1961).

We adopt the general rule and hold that one who recklessly participates in an automobile race may be criminally responsible for a death resulting therefrom, even though his vehicle is not the direct instrument of death.

* * *

On the evening of February 19, 1973, defendant and one Mike Barlow encountered Daniel Warren (the decedent for whose death defendant was indicted) and Richard Wille at a service station, and Mr. Wille expressed an interest in racing his Chevrolet Nova against defendant's pickup truck. * * * The vehicles stopped for a moment some 100 feet south of Division Street, there was a short conversation and then both vehicles took off rapidly in the direction of Powell. The Chevrolet Nova, occupied by driver Richard Wille and passenger Daniel Warren, was in the right lane. The pickup truck, occupied by defendant, who was driving, and Mike Barlow, was in the inside lane. The distance from Division Street to Powell Boulevard on 148th Street is approximately four-tenths of a mile. Defendant's pickup was in the lead from the start and continued in the lead as the vehicles reached speeds estimated at 60–80 miles per hour. The posted speed limit was 35 miles per hour. At some point prior to coming to the intersection with Powell Boulevard, defendant began to decelerate his pickup and brought his vehicle to a stop in the left turn lane at the intersection of 148th and Powell. As defendant came to a stop, Wille passed defendant and proceeded without any apparent diminution in speed through a stop sign into the intersection where his car was struck by a truck which was travelling west on Powell. Both Wille and his passenger, Warren, were killed.

* * *

* * * The fact-finder was not required to find that the defendant's unilateral and uncommunicated act of slowing and stopping was such an act of termination as would purge his earlier initiation of the race of its quality of recklessness. The evidence authorized a finding that defendant's setting the race in motion was reckless or that there was no effective withdrawal so long as the acts which defendant helped impel had not yet ceased. The substantial and unjustifiable risk to the lives of other motorists and pedestrians created in part by his conduct could be found to have continued unabated up to and including the time of the collision.

The next issue to be considered with regard to this assignment of error is the sufficiency of the evidence of causation: Whether defendant's reckless conduct caused the death of Daniel Warren. Analysis of this issue involves a two-step approach: First, was defendant's conduct a cause in fact of the death? Second, if so, was it also a legal cause of the death in the contemplation of statutes imposing criminal liability? LaFave and Scott, Criminal Law 248, § 35 (1972).

The test for causation in fact can be stated as follows: Was the defendant's conduct a substantial factor in bringing about the forbidden result? LaFave and Scott, supra, at 250; Perkins on Criminal Law 695–696, § 9 (1969). In this case, had defendant not engaged in the unlawful race with Richard Wille, the accident would never have occurred. Defendant helped create the dangerous situation, and was a part of it. His conduct was a substantial factor in bringing about the decedent's death.

Was defendant's conduct the legal cause of the death? Defendant's argument centers on a discussion of tort concepts such as proximate cause, intervening cause, and foreseeability of harm, but tort concepts are of limited utility in criminal prosecutions since they spring from different policy considerations. LaFave and Scott, supra, at 251–252; Perkins, supra, at 693. Basically, criminal culpability exists where the result is within the area of risk which the rules of caution violated by the defendant are intended to minimize.

In this case, the decedent was clearly within the class endangered by the conduct of street-racing, i.e., motorists, pedestrians, etc., and the collision was the sort of injurious event which the prohibitions against street-racing are supposed to prevent. ORS 483.122(1). Therefore, there is a clear legal causative connection between the defendant's acts and the death.

Defendant suggests that Wille's act of accelerating his auto past defendant's pickup truck and into the intersection was an intervening cause, and that defendant was thereby relieved of responsibility, i.e., that Wille's act superseded defendant's conduct as the cause of death. However, in order to be a superseding cause, the intervening cause must be independent, that is, it must not be a consequence of defendant's antecedent conduct. Perkins on Criminal Law, supra, at 722–725. In the case at bar, Wille's conduct was within the risk of the race, particularly since no finish line had been agreed upon.

Defendant suggests that a distinction should be drawn between cases where the decedent was not a participant in the race and cases where he was a participant, and that, since the evidence showed that the decedent was a passenger in one of the racing automobiles, defendant could not be criminally liable for the death. This is also the position taken by the dissent. However, there is no indication that such an exception was intended by the legislature. The words of the statutes are inclusive. They specify no exception. One is guilty of manslaughter if he "recklessly * * * causes the death of another human being." ORS 163.005, 163.125(1)(a). Had the legislature intended that liability not attach if the victim were a participant in the events leading to the death, it could have easily so provided. It did so regarding felony murder, ORS 163.115(1)(c), and was capable of specifying a similar exception to manslaughter if it had intended to create one. In the absence of such a provision, this court ought not to amend the statute under the rubric of "policy."

Moreover, logic does not compel the carving out of such an exception. The gravamen of the offense charged in the indictment is recklessness, i.e., the conscious disregard of a substantial and unjustifiable risk that a death would occur, and a death resulting therefrom. That a participant's passenger was killed rather than an innocent third party was an immaterial matter of chance. Such tort concepts as contributory negligence and assumption of the risk are not defenses against responsibility for criminal conduct. State v. Mellenberger, 163 Or. 233, 95 P.2d 709, 128 A.L.R. 1506 (1939); see generally Perkins on Criminal Law 969–973 (2d ed. 1970). The defendant's conduct is equally reckless, equally causative and equally anti-social regardless of which person is killed in a collision of participants and non-participants or whether a car happens to hit a utility post or a pedestrian. He remains criminally liable or not regardless of how the civil law may allocate responsibility for money damages.

The dissent, to over-simplify, argues that policy requires that assumption of risk negates the element of causation. In support of that proposition it cites examples such as skydivers and race-track drivers who mutually engage in dangerous activities. We need not decide this case upon extreme examples because these facts are easily distinguishable. The activity at bar presents a substantial risk to the nonparticipating public. As noted, the chance death of a participant does not diminish the danger of the act to others. The examples cited by the dissent incur only a negligible risk to the public and speculation regarding legislative intent toward coverage of such acts has no application to the facts of this case.

There was sufficient evidence to justify the trier of fact in concluding that defendant was guilty of manslaughter. Defendant's motion for judgment of acquittal on Count I was properly denied.

* * *

Affirmed.

SCHWAB, CHIEF JUDGE (dissenting).

I would reverse the manslaughter conviction.

A person commits criminal homicide when he "causes the death of another human being." ORS 163.005(1). Criminal homicide constitutes manslaughter when it "is committed recklessly." ORS 163.125(1)(a). Reckless means "that a person is aware of and consciously disregards a substantial and unjustifiable risk that the result [death] will occur." ORS 161.085(9).

As I see it, the question is whether defendant's reckless conduct "caused" the death of the victim. The problem here is not "causation in fact," it is "legal causation." See generally LaFave and Scott, Criminal Law 246–267 (1972); Perkins, Criminal Law 685–738 (2d ed. 1969). In unusual cases like this one, whether certain conduct is deemed to be the legal cause of a certain result is ultimately a policy question. The question of legal causation thus blends into the question of whether we are willing to hold a defendant responsible for a prohibited result. Or, stated differently, the issue is not causation, it is responsibility. In my opinion, policy considerations are against imposing responsibility for the death of a *participant* [1] in a race on the surviving racer when his sole contribution to the death is the participation in the activity mutually agreed upon.

Commonwealth v. Root, 403 Pa. 571, 170 A.2d 310, 82 A.L.R.2d 452 (1961), illustrates the rule I would adopt. In that case, two persons were racing their cars on the highway. One of the racers collided with another car, resulting in that racer's death. The court reversed the surviving racer's manslaughter conviction, holding the necessary legal causation to be absent as to a fellow participant in the race, but suggesting legal causation [2] would be present had the victim not been a participant. Accord: Thacker v. State, 103 Ga.App. 36, 117 S.E.2d 913 (1961).

The facts of Commonwealth v. Atencio, 345 Mass. 627, 189 N.E.2d 223 (1963), are another illustration. In that case, three persons were playing "Russian roulette" and one of them shot and killed himself. A survivor's conviction for manslaughter, i.e., recklessly causing the death of another, was affirmed. I would vote to reverse such a conviction. Since the participants had knowingly and voluntarily joined in a reckless course of conduct, I would not impose liability for manslaughter on the survivors.

It is not unheard of for people to engage in hazardous vocations and avocations. It could be said, for example, that professional racetrack drivers earn their living by consciously disregarding a substantial risk that death will occur on the racetrack. Yet, it would probably strike most people as strange if the surviving drivers were prosecuted for manslaughter following a fatal racetrack accident. But that result could follow from the majority's analysis of legal causation; that result would not be possible under my analysis.

And some people engage in recreational activities—everything from skydiving to deep-sea diving—knowing they involve a risk of death. Suppose two fishermen knowingly and voluntarily take a small boat into the ocean even though a severe storm is predicted. Each encourages the other to do so. If one drowned in the storm, would we say the survivor "caused" his death? The majority's analysis would answer that question in the affirmative; my analysis would answer it in the negative.

My point is that people frequently join together in reckless conduct. As long as all participants do so knowingly and voluntarily, I see no point in holding the survivor(s) guilty of manslaughter if the reckless conduct results in death. Contrary to the majority, I find no expression of legislative policy on this issue in the manslaughter statute, or in any other statute. The issue here

1. Although the victim in this case was a passenger in one of the cars, rather than a driver, he was there knowingly and voluntarily. Indeed, there was evidence that he first suggested the idea of racing. Thus, I regard the victim as a participant in the race. * * *

2. The suggestion is implicit in the holding rather than contained in the language of the opinion. As pointed out by LaFave and Scott, Criminal Law at 265, in analyzing the Pennsylvania court's holding in Commonwealth v. Root, 403 Pa. 571, 170 A.2d 310, 82 A.L.R.2d 452 (1961), and in Commonwealth v. Redline, 391 Pa. 486, 137 A.2d 472 (1958):

> "It is submitted that the true reason for the holding in these two cases is the court's feeling, not clearly expressed in the two cases, that *A* should not, in all justice, be held for the death of *B* who was an equally willing and foolhardy participant in the bad conduct which caused his death * * *."

is "legal causation," an issue which has been traditionally left to the courts.[3] Of course, all participants could be prosecuted if their reckless conduct constitutes some other offense. And all participants could be prosecuted if their reckless conduct results in the death or injury of a nonparticipant. Drawing the line at that point, however, seems to be a sufficient deterrent to me. Extending the concept of legal causation beyond that point, as the majority does, can only be justified to deter people from jointly engaging in hazardous activity, knowing what the risks are and being willing to take them. I would have that a matter of choice for each individual.

* * *

[On appeal, the Supreme Court of Oregon agreed with the reasoning of Chief Judge Schwab and adopted the dissenting opinion as the opinion of the court. State v. Petersen, 270 Or. 166, 526 P.2d 1008 (1974).]

Questions

1. Are there persuasive policy reasons for choosing one of the opinions in *Petersen* rather than the other?

2. Why excuse *any* defendant who is a but-for cause of another's death and who has adequate *mens rea?*

2. The Death of a Human Being

Introductory Note

Perhaps one day a visitor from outer space or an abominable snowman will appear and be killed, and the interesting question of what "human being" means will be presented in a general way in a criminal case. But, at present, there appear to be no borderline cases as to membership in the human species.

Ordinary human beings do present issues, however, near the beginning and near the end of life. One cannot be a homicide victim before one becomes a human being or after one is dead. At what point does one first become a human being for purposes of the law of homicide? We know the common law answer from the *Keeler* case, supra, p. 84: when the child is born alive. The fetus could not be a homicide victim at common law. However, the law of abortion shows that the unborn child was of concern to the criminal law. Intentionally causing a miscarriage of a woman quick with child was a common law misdemeanor, unless done to save the mother's life. Probably, although there is some disagreement on this point, it was not a common law crime to cause a miscarriage before the child quickened or moved within the womb, if this was done with the woman's consent.

In 1959 the Model Penal Code proposed broadening the justification for abortion to extend beyond acts reasonably done to save the mother's life. Under § 230.3(2) substantial risk that there would be grave impairment of the physical or mental health of the mother if the pregnancy continued, or that a child would be born with a grave physical or mental defect, or that the pregnancy resulted

3. "* * * Since most penal codes contain no statutory provision defining causation, imputing responsibility to a defendant for having 'caused' or brought about a result requires finding a standard that fits the policy underlying the particular crime, as defined by statute * * *." Ruy, Causation in Criminal Law, U. of Pa.Law.Rev. 773, 785 (1958).

from rape, incest, or certain other forms of criminal intercourse, justified abortion with the mother's consent.

Roe v. Wade, 410 U.S. 113, 93 S.Ct. 705, 35 L.Ed.2d 147 (1973), took a different approach, removing, on right of privacy grounds, criminal sanctions from abortions agreed upon by the woman and her physician, if performed during the first trimester of pregnancy. Increasing dangers to the mother's health from abortion may permit the states to regulate abortion for the sake of her health thereafter. When the fetus becomes viable (potentially able to live outside the womb, though perhaps only with artificial support), the state may be permitted to regulate or forbid abortion to protect the life of the fetus.

Since one who is already dead cannot be killed, it becomes necessary to fix the time of death whenever the accused is charged with killing someone who might have died from other causes before the conduct charged took effect. Common law definitions centered around cessation of heartbeat. Modern medicine encourages a more sophisticated definition.

State v. Shaffer

Supreme Court of Kansas, 1977.
223 Kan. 244, 574 P.2d 205.

MCFARLAND, JUSTICE:

This is a direct appeal in a criminal action in which defendant-appellant, Ronald G. Shaffer, was convicted after a trial by jury of first degree murder (K.S.A. 21–3401), aggravated robbery (K.S.A. 21–3427), and unlawful possession of a firearm (K.S.A. 21–4204[1][*b*]).

The evidence reveals that at approximately 7:30 A.M. on February 29, 1976 a customer of the Louk Oil Station in Topeka discovered Donald Becker, a station employee, lying on the floor of the back room of the station. Mr. Becker had been shot in the head but was still breathing and had a definable pulse. * * * An ambulance arrived at 7:51 A.M. and at that time, Mr. Becker was breathing and had a pulse and blood pressure. Mr. Becker arrived at St. Francis Hospital at 8:28 A.M. The emergency room physician, Dr. Steve Roskos, made a preliminary observation and immediately called Dr. John Runnels, a neurological surgeon, who performed manual tests for signs of life. Dr. Runnels found Mr. Becker had suffered irretrievable brain damage and advised Dr. Roskos that Mr. Becker could be pronounced dead at any time.

The deceased's mother was told of her son's condition and that he could be maintained by artificial means for an indefinite period. The deceased's family made the decision not to prolong his life by a respirator and to allow the deceased's kidneys to be transplanted. At approximately 11:00 A.M. both kidneys were removed by Dr. John D. Mayer, the respirator was turned off, and all bodily functions ceased. Prior to the removal of the kidneys, Dr. Mayer examined Mr. Becker and determined he was, in fact, dead. The defendant called an expert witness, Dr. John Nichols, who testified more tests should have been given before death was pronounced.

* * *

The defendant contends K.S.A. 1976 Supp. 77–202 was never intended to apply to criminal homicide trials and that the instruction given pursuant to same was, accordingly, erroneous. K.S.A. 1976 Supp. 77–202 provides:

> "Definition of Death. A person will be considered medically and legally dead if, in the opinion of a physician, based on ordinary standards of medical practice, there is the absence of spontaneous respiratory and cardiac function and, because of the disease or condition which caused, directly or indirectly, these functions to cease, or because of the passage of time since these functions ceased, attempts at resuscitation are considered hopeless; and, in this event, death will have occurred at the time these functions ceased; or
>
> "A person will be considered medically and legally dead if, in the opinion of a physician, based on ordinary standards of medical practice, there is the absence of spontaneous brain function; and if based on ordinary standards of medical practice, during reasonable attempts to either maintain or restore spontaneous circulatory or respiratory function in the absence of aforesaid brain function, it appears that further attempts at resuscitation or supportive maintenance will not succeed, death will have occurred at the time when these conditions first coincide. Death is to be pronounced before artificial means of supporting respiratory and circulatory function are terminated and before any vital organ is removed for purposes of transplantation.
>
> "These alternative definitions of death are to be utilized for all purposes in this state, including the trials of civil and criminal cases, any laws to the contrary notwithstanding."

* * * The legislation was entitled, "AN ACT relating to and defining death" (1970 Kan.Sess.Laws, Ch. 378). The last sentence clearly states it is to be utilized "for all purposes in this state, including the trials of civil and criminal cases, any laws to the contrary notwithstanding." There is no ambiguity as to legislative intent.

* * *

The defendant's next point is that K.S.A. 1976 Supp. 77–202, when applied to murder in the first degree, as defining an essential element of the crime is unconstitutionally vague by allowing either of two separate standards to be applied to the single phenomenon of death. The two standards are essentially (1) cardiac-respiratory death and (2) brain death. Until relatively recently the standards of death were primarily based on respiratory-cardiac functions, i.e., breathing and heartbeat. Modern science has developed equipment that artificially sustains these functions after the body is unable to do so. The *Karen Ann Quinlan* case received national publicity and focused attention on the dilemma of the newly created problems in the field. Theoretically a person pronounced medically dead by all tests could be kept "alive" by artificial means indefinitely. The increasing number of organ transplant operations complicates the situation further as organs such as kidneys may become too damaged for transplant within five minutes after respiration ceases. So for kidney transplants, respiration must continue almost uninterrupted until the kidney is removed.

Kansas was the first state to enact a statutory definition of death (K.S.A. 1976 Supp. 77–202). Accordingly, the Kansas act has been widely praised and criticized. By providing the brain death alternative, it recognizes the fact that modern science has developed equipment that makes the traditional cardiac-respiratory test obsolete as the only test. The alternative test is based on practical medical considerations in keeping with advanced medical technology. This constitutional point is found to be without merit. There is not constitutional requirement that a single standard be used. In fact the cardiac-respiratory test, itself, involves two bodily functions.

The defendant's final point is that K.S.A. 1976 Supp. 77–202 is unconstitutionally vague for failure to enumerate procedures for determining when death has occurred, but leaves the determination to be based on the "ordinary standards of medical practice." There is disagreement within the medical profession as to exactly what tests should be employed to determine death. This, of course, is not unusual within that profession. Three different physicians independently examined the deceased before the transplant removal operation. The neurosurgeon and the surgeon independently concluded irretrievable brain damage had occurred and the patient was dead. The defendant argued to the jury that death was caused by the operation. An instruction was given to the jury on this theory as follows:

Instruction No. 2a

> " * * * If you find defendant's acts contributed to the death of Donald W. Becker then responsibility cannot be avoided by the fact that independent causes such as the negligence of others also contributed to the death. However, if you find the cause of death resulted solely from erroneous treatment by the physicians you must acquit defendant of the offense charged in Count I."

The defendant introduced expert evidence on his theory of insufficient testing. The instruction given is a proper statement of the applicable law. Where a person inflicts upon another a wound which is calculated to endanger or destroy life, it is not a defense to a charge of homicide that the alleged victim's death was contributed to or caused by the negligence of the attending physicians or surgeons.

"Ordinary standards of medical practice" change as medical knowledge and technology improve. Under the instructions given in this case, it was for the jury to determine whether the medical standards required by K.S.A. 1976 Supp. 77–202 had been met. Much of the testimony presented at trial went to this very point. The attack on the statute for failure to specifically enumerate criteria is held to be without merit.

The judgment is affirmed.

F. KILLINGS IN THE COURSE OF UNLAWFUL ACTS

1. The Felony-Murder Rule

Introductory Note

The felony-murder rule disregards any intention the accused may have had to kill or injure the victim and any recklessness as to causing death displayed; it places guilt of murder on the basis of accidentally causing death in the course of the commission of a felony. In the first principal case, Judge Stephen gives a broad statement of the rule and then a narrower statement which he believes more accurate and proper. Consider whether this narrower form would make murder any conduct which would not be murder anyway on a theory of intentional or reckless killing. If it would not, or whether, if only a few situations would be added to the murder category by Stephen's rule, would the rule accomplish anything of importance?

Stephen's preferred statement is even narrower than most jurisdictions which retain the rule would make it today. The later cases in the section show several ways in which various jurisdictions have limited the broad form of the rule.

Regina v. Serné

Central Criminal Court, 1887.
16 Cox Crim.Cas. 311.

The prisoners Leon Serné and John Henry Goldfinch were indicted for the murder of a boy, Sjaak Serné, the son of the prisoner Leon Serné, it being alleged that they wilfully set on fire a house and shop, No. 274, Strand, London, by which act the death of the boy had been caused.

It appeared that the prisoner Serné with his wife, two daughters and two sons, were living at the house in question; and that Serné, at the time he was living there, in Midsummer, 1887, was in a state of pecuniary embarrassment, and had put into the premises furniture and other goods of but very little value, which at the time of the fire were not of greater value than 30£. It also appeared that previously to the fire the prisoner Serné had insured the life of the boy Sjaak Serné, who was imbecile, and on the 1st day of September, 1887, had insured his stock at 274, Strand, for 500£., his furniture for 100£., and his rent for another 100£.; and that on the 17th of the same month the premises were burnt down.

Evidence was given on behalf of the prosecution that fires were seen breaking out in several parts of the premises at the same time, soon after the prisoners had been seen in the shop together; two fires being in the lower part of the house and two above, on the floor whence escape could be made on to the roof of the adjoining house, and in which part were the prisoners and the wife and two daughters of Serné, who escaped. That on the premises were a quantity of tissue transparencies for advertising purposes, which were of a most inflammable character; and that on the site of one of the fires was found a great quantity of these transparencies close to other inflammable materials. That the prisoner Serné, his wife and daughters, were rescued from the roof of the adjoining house, the other prisoner being rescued from a window in the front of the house, but that the boys were burnt to death, the body of the one being found on the floor near the window from which the prisoner Serné, his wife and daughters, had escaped, the body of the other being found at the basement of the premises.

STEPHEN, J.—* * * The definition of murder is unlawful homicide with malice aforethought; and the words malice aforethought are technical. You must not, therefore, construe them or suppose that they can be construed by ordinary rules of language. The words have to be construed according to a long series of decided cases, which have given them meanings different from those which might be supposed. One of those meanings is, the killing of another person by an act done with an intent to commit a felony. Another meaning is, an act done with the knowledge that the act will probably cause the death of some person. Now it is such an act as the last which is alleged to have been done in this case; and if you think that either or both of these men in the dock killed this boy, either by an act done with intent to commit a felony, that is to say, the setting of the house on fire in order to cheat the insurance company, or by conduct which, to their knowledge, was likely to cause death, and was therefore eminently dangerous in itself—in either of these cases the prisoners are guilty of wilful murder in the plain meaning of the word. I will say a word or two upon one part of this definition, because it is capable of being applied very harshly in certain cases, and also because, though I take the law as I find it, I very much doubt whether the definition which I have given, although it is the common definition, is not somewhat too wide. Now when it is said that murder means killing a man by an act done in the commission of a felony, the mere words cover a case like this, that is to say, a case where a man gives another a push with an intention of stealing his watch, and the person so pushed, having a weak heart, or some other internal disorder, dies. To take another very old illustration, it was said that if a man shot at a fowl with intent to steal it, and accidentally killed a man, he was to be accounted guilty of murder, because the act was done in the commission of a felony. I very much doubt, however, whether that is really the law, or whether the court for the Consideration of Crown Cases Reserved would hold it to be so. The present case, however, is not such as I have cited, nor anything like them. In my opinion the definition of the law which makes it murder to kill by an act done in the commission of a felony might and ought to be narrowed, whilst that part of the law under which the Crown in this case claim to have proved a case of murder is maintained. I think that, instead of saying that any act done with intent to commit a felony and which causes death amounts to murder, it would be reasonable to say that any act known to be dangerous to life, and likely in itself to cause death done for the purpose of committing a felony which caused death, should be murder. As an illustration of this, suppose that a man, intending to commit a rape upon a woman, but without the least wish to kill her, squeezed her by the throat to overpower her, and in so doing killed her, that would be murder. I think that everyone would say in a case like that, that when a person began doing wicked acts for his own base purposes, he risked his own life as well as that of others. That kind of crime does not differ in any serious degree from one committed by using a deadly weapon, such as a bludgeon, a pistol, or a knife.

If a man once begins attacking the human body in such a way, he must take the consequences if he goes further than he intended when he began. That I take to be the true meaning of the law on the subject. In the present case, gentlemen, you have a man sleeping in a house with his wife, his two daughters, his two sons, and a servant, and you are asked to believe that this man, with all these people under his protection, deliberately set fire to the house in three or four different places, and thereby burnt two of them to death. It is alleged that he arranged matters in such a way that any person of the most common intelligence must have known perfectly well that he was placing all those people in deadly risk. It appears to me that if that were really done, it matters very little indeed whether the prisoners hoped the people would escape or whether they did not. If a person chose, for some wicked purpose of his own to sink a boat at sea, and thereby caused the deaths of the occupants, it matters nothing whether at the time of committing the act he hoped that the people would be picked up by a passing vessel. He is as much guilty of murder, if the people are drowned, as if he had flung every person into the water with his own hand. Therefore, gentlemen, if Serné and Goldfinch set fire to this house when the family were in it, and if the boys were by that act stifled or burnt to death, then the prisoners are as much guilty of murder as if they had stabbed the children. I will also add, for my own part, that I think in so saying the law of England lays down a rule of broad, plain, common sense. Treat a murderer how you will, award him what punishment you choose, it is your duty, gentlemen, if you think him really guilty of murder, to say so. That is the law of the land, and I have no doubt in my mind with regard to it. There was a case tried in this court which you will no doubt remember, and which will illustrate my meaning. It was the Clerkenwell explosion case in 1868, when a man named Barrett was charged with causing the death of several persons by an explosion which was intended to release one or two men from custody; and I am sure that no one can say truly that Barrett was not justly hanged. With regard to the facts in the present case, the very horror of the crime, if crime it was, the abomination of it, is a reason for your taking the most extreme care in the case, and for not imputing to the prisoners anything which is not clearly proved. God forbid that I should, by what I say, produce on your minds, even in the smallest degree, any feeling against the prisoners. You must see, gentlemen, that the evidence leaves no reasonable doubt upon your minds; but you will fail in the performance of your duty if, being satisfied with the evidence, you do not convict one or both the prisoners of wilful murder, and it is wilful murder of which they are accused. [The learned Judge then proceeded to review the evidence. In the result the jury found a verdict of not guilty in respect of each of the prisoners.]

MODEL PENAL CODE § 210.2, COMMENT 6*

6. *Felony Murder.* * * * Section 210.2 advances a new approach to the problem of homicide occurring in the course of a felony. Such

homicides will only constitute murder if they are committed purposely, knowingly, or recklessly under circumstances manifesting extreme indifference to the value of human life. Subsection (1)(b) creates a presumption of the required recklessness and extreme indifference, however, if a homicide occurs during the commission or attempted commission of robbery, sexual attack, arson, burglary, kidnapping, or felonious escape. The presumption also arises if the defendant is in flight after such conduct or if he is an accomplice to the commission of one of the specified crimes when the killing takes place. Beyond the operation of this presumption, it is the submission of the Model Code that the felony-murder doctrine should be abandoned as an independent basis for establishing the criminality of homicide.

* * *

The classic formulation of the felony-murder doctrine declares that one is guilty of murder if a death results from conduct during the commission or attempted commission of any felony. Some courts have made no effort to qualify the application of this doctrine, and a number of earlier English writers also articulated an unqualified rule. At the time the Model Code was drafted, a number of American legislatures, moreover, perpetuated the original statement of the rule by statute. As thus conceived, the rule operated to impose liability for murder based on the culpability required for the underlying felony without separate proof of any culpability with regard to the death. The homicide, as distinct from the underlying felony, was thus an offense of strict liability. This rule may have made sense under the conception of *mens rea* as something approaching a general criminal disposition rather than as a specific attitude of the defendant towards each element of a specific offense. Furthermore, it was hard to claim that the doctrine worked injustice in an age that recognized only a few felonies and that punished each as a capital offense.

In modern times, however, legislatures have created a wide range of statutory felonies. Many of these crimes concern relatively minor misconduct not inherently dangerous to life and carry maximum penalties far less severe than those authorized for murder. Application of the ancient rigor of the felony-murder rule to such crimes will yield startling results. For example, a seller of liquor in violation of a statutory felony becomes a murderer if his purchaser falls asleep on the way home and dies of exposure. And a person who communicates disease during felonious sexual intercourse is guilty of murder if his partner subsequently dies of the infection.

The prospect of such consequences has led to a demand for limitations on the felony-murder rule. American legislatures had responded to these demands at the time the Model Code was drafted primarily by dividing felony-homicides into two or more grades or by lowering the degree of murder for felony homicide. Only Ohio had abandoned the rule completely.

In addition, the courts had imposed restrictions, both overt and covert, on the reach of the felony-murder doctrine. An example of covert limitation was the use of especially demanding interpretations of legal or proximate causation. The commentary to Section 2.03 discusses the problem of causation in general terms, but it is worth noting here that courts sometimes precluded liability for felony murder on the ground of insufficiently direct causal connection in circumstances where, had intent to kill been proved, the causation requirement would not have been construed to bar conviction. In other words, courts hostile to this strict liability species of murder sometimes introduced a culpability requirement through the back door of causation.

Other judicial limitations on the rule were accomplished by several different methods. First, courts required that the felony be "independent" of the homicide. Under this theory, an assault with a deadly weapon could not support a conviction for felony murder because the assault is an offense included in the charge of homicide. Since every death resulting from the use of a deadly weapon is preceded by an assault with that weapon, application of the felony-murder rule would make the defenses of provocation and diminished responsibility irrelevant and obliterate the distinction between murder and manslaughter. Other courts required that the felony be one recognized as such at common law. These offenses included arson, burglary, robbery, mayhem, larceny, rape, and sodomy. The rule was also applied by some courts only to felonies judged *mala in se* rather than *mala prohibitum.* The content of the former designation, though not entirely clear, usually includes the roster of common-law felonies. Still other courts narrowly construed the period during which the felony was in the process of commission as a method of limiting the operation of the rule. A few courts embarked on an effort to classify each felony according to whether that crime, abstractly considered, was inherently dangerous to human life. The absurdity of this approach is illustrated by People v. Williams,[89] where the court concluded that conspiracy to possess methadrine was not an inherently dangerous felony and reversed the defendant's conviction of felony murder. The court ignored evidence that the conspiracy involved gaining possession of the drug through force and violence because this focused on the facts of the particular case, not the elements of the crime of conspiracy in the abstract. More sensibly, some courts have inquired into the facts of each case to see whether the defendant's conduct in committing the felony involved a foreseeable risk to life. Finally, some courts have limited felony-murder liability to cases where the act of killing was committed by the defendant or his accomplice in the furtherance of the felony, and several modern statutes limit felony-murder liability to the killing of one other than a participant in the underlying felony.

These limitations confine the scope of the felony-murder rule, but they do not resolve its essential illogic. This doctrine aside, the criminal law does not predicate liability simply on conduct causing the death of another. Punishment for homicide obtains only when the deed is done with a state of mind that makes it reprehensible as well as unfortunate. Murder is invariably punished as a heinous offense and is the principal crime for which the death penalty is authorized. Sanctions of such gravity demand justification, and their imposition must be premised on the confluence of conduct and culpability. Thus, under the Model Code, as at common law, murder occurs if a person kills purposely, knowingly, or with extreme recklessness. Lesser

89. 63 Cal.2d 452, 406 P.2d 647, 47 Cal. Rptr. 7 (1965).

culpability yields lesser liability, and a person who inadvertently kills another under circumstances not amounting to negligence is guilty of no crime at all. The felony-murder rule contradicts this scheme. It bases conviction of murder not on any proven culpability with respect to homicide but on liability for another crime. The underlying felony carries its own penalty and the additional punishment for murder is therefore gratuitous—gratuitous, at least, in terms of what must have been proved at trial in a court of law.

It is true, of course, that the felony-murder rule is often invoked where liability for murder exists on another ground. One who kills in the course of armed robbery is almost certainly guilty of murder in the form of intentional or extremely reckless homicide without any need of special doctrine. Similarly, a man who burns another's house will scarcely be heard to complain that he lacks the culpability for murder if the blaze kills a sleeping occupant. For the vast majority of cases it is probably true that homicide occurring during the commission or attempted commission of a felony is murder independent of the felony-murder rule. At bottom, continued adherence to the doctrine may rest on assessments of this sort.

The problem is that criminal liability attaches to individuals, not generalities. It is a weak rejoinder to a complaint of unjust conviction to say that for most persons in the defendant's situation the result would have been appropriate. * * *

Principled argument in favor of the felony-murder doctrine is hard to find. The defense reduces to the explanation that Holmes gave for finding the law "intelligible as it stands":

> [I]f experience shows, or is deemed by the law-maker to show, that somehow or other deaths which the evidence makes accidental happen disproportionately often in connection with other felonies, or with resistance to officers, or if on any other ground of policy it is deemed desirable to make special efforts for the prevention of such deaths, the law-maker may consistently treat acts which, under the known circumstances, are felonious, or constitute resistance to officers, as having a sufficiently dangerous tendency to be put under a special ban. The law may, therefore, throw on the actor the peril, not only of the consequences foreseen by him, but also of consequences which, although not predicted by common experience, the legislator apprehends.[95]

The answer to such argument is twofold. First, there is no basis in experience for thinking that homicides *which the evidence makes accidental* occur with disproportionate frequency in connection with specified felonies.[96] Second, it remains indefensible in principle to use the sanctions that the law employs to deal with murder unless there is at least a finding that the actor's conduct manifested an extreme indifference to the value of human life. * * *

* * *

95. O. Holmes, The Common Law 49 (1881).

96. See note 96 on page 653.

Note

Chief Justice Bird, concurring in People v. Dillon, 34 Cal.3d 441, 495–498, 194 Cal.Rptr. 390, 424–427, 668 P.2d 697, 731–734 (1983):

> Thus, the only *actual* consequence of the first degree felony-murder rule is to mete out to certain persons who cause a death unintentionally or accidentally the punishment which society prescribes for premeditated murder. Serious questions remain as to whether the state and federal Constitutions permit the government to exact such extreme punishment in the absence of proof that an accused deliberated or harbored malice.
>
> * * *
>
> What the exact contours of this doctrine are is another matter. The two most frequently mentioned constitutional limitations on substantive criminal law are a constitutional doctrine of mens rea and the Eighth Amendment's requirement of proportionality in criminal punishment.
>
> If either source for such a theory is adopted, the doctrine of felony murder as a rule of substantive criminal law is highly vulnerable. Since the rule punishes as murder any killing in the course of a felony without a showing of a culpable mental state with respect to that result, its continued application would impermissibly conflict with a constitutional requirement of mens rea.[4]

96. In fact, the number of all homicides which occur in the commission of such crimes as robbery, burglary, or rape is lower than might be expected. For example, comparison of the figures for solved and unsolved homicides from M. Wolfgang, Criminal Homicide (1958), with statistics on basic felonies taken from the FBI Uniform Crime Reports reveals the following for Philadelphia from 1948–1952:

RELATION OF TOTAL FELONIES TO HOMICIDES OCCURRING DURING THE FELONY

PHILADELPHIA 1948–1952

Offense	No. of Crimes Reported	No. Accompanied by Homicide	%	No. per 1000
Robbery	6,432	38	0.59	5.9
Rape	1,133	4	0.35	3.5
Burglary	27,669	1	0.0036	.36[.036?]
Auto Theft	10,315	2	0.019	1.9 [.19?]

Similar figures are found in Cook County, Illinois, robbery statistics from 1926–1930. There were 71 murders committed during robberies in Cook County during 1926 and 1927. Illinois Crime Survey 610 (1929). Although robbery statistics for those years are not available, 7,196 robberies were committed in the county in 1930. Assuming this number of robberies in 1926 and 1927, it appears that only .49 per cent of the robberies in those two years resulted in homicide. More recent statistics derived from N.J. State Police, Crime in New Jersey: Uniform Crime Reports 42–45 (1975) reveal strikingly similar percentages. In 1975, 16,273 robberies were committed in New Jersey, and 66 homicides resulted from these robberies, only .41 per cent, a figure even lower than the earlier statistics from Cook County and Philadelphia. When other violent felonies are taken into account, this percentage drops even lower. In 1975, there were 1,382 forcible rapes and 111,264 forcible breaking-and-enterings in New Jersey in addition to the 16,273 robberies. These crimes resulted in 136 deaths. Thus only .10 per cent of these serious felonies resulted in homicide.

---

4. It is true that in order for a defendant to be convicted of felony murder, the state must first establish his mental culpability with respect to the underlying felony. He is not morally blameless. However, as the United States Supreme Court noted in Jackson v. Virginia (1979) 443 U.S. 307, 323–324, 99 S.Ct. 2781, 2791, 61 L.Ed.2d 560, "[t]he constitu-

Moreover, proportionality may be violated when one considers that, at least in the absence of a showing of mens rea, defendants are in reality punished for the commission of the underlying felony. Two similarly situated felons may receive grossly disproportionate punishments based on the fortuity that a totally unintended and nonnegligent death occurred in one case but not the other.

Question

Are any ends of justice served by some form of a felony-murder rule? Is the Model Penal Code proposal an improvement?

People v. Sirignano

California Court of Appeal, Second District, Division 4, 1974.
42 Cal.App.3d 794, 117 Cal.Rptr. 131.

JEFFERSON, ASSOCIATE JUSTICE.

Defendant Rea Marie Sirignano, 18 years of age, was charged with the murder of Roderick MacLeod, in violation of Penal Code section 187. Following a jury trial, she was found guilty of murder in the first degree. * * *

* * *

Defendant was arrested on August 8 and after being advised of her constitutional rights, discussed the events of the previous evening with Officer Bostard. She first told him that early in the evening on August 7, while she was at the Box Bar near the hotel, a barmaid there named Rita had told her that a pool hustler in the bar had learned that one of the customers was carrying a large amount of money, $2000. Rita had suggested to defendant that she assist in luring the proposed victim outside the bar in order to rob him. "We'll get the money and split it three ways" said Rita to defendant. Defendant told Officer Bostard that she refused to participate, went on to other bars and then home late in the evening.

A different version slowly emerged from defendant's subsequent conversations with Bostard. According to his testimony, defendant admitted that she had had drinks with the sailor, MacLeod, on the evening of August 7; that the sailor had invited Rita and her to a party on board his ship that evening; that after the bars closed at 2 a.m., Rita and defendant had brought the sailor to Room 301 so that defendant could change her clothes for the party. When they entered the hotel room, Collette had struck MacLeod down from behind. Rita had emptied the victim's pockets, and had departed

tional necessity of proof beyond a reasonable doubt is not confined to those defendants who are morally blameless. E.g., Mullaney v. Wilbur, 421 U.S. at 697–698 [95 S.Ct. at 1888–1889] (requirement of proof beyond a reasonable doubt is not 'limit[ed] to those facts which, if not proved, would wholly exonerate' the accused). Under our system of criminal justice even a thief is entitled to complain that he has been unconstitutionally convicted and imprisoned as a burglar."

Once the prosecution proves defendant's culpable mental state with respect to the underlying felony, that culpability level is punishable by the sanction attached to the felony itself. The felony-murder rule, which mandates the imposition of severe additional punishment without any showing of additional mental culpability, is properly characterized as a strict liability criminal law concept. It is a concept which is blatantly unconstitutional if the Constitution prohibits the imposition of criminal punishment without a showing of a culpable mental state with respect to the result achieved. * * *

from the room with defendant, giving her two dollars as her share of the proceeds of the robbery. Defendant had then gone to Brad's Restaurant for a cup of coffee. She returned to Room 301, however, and discovered that MacLeod had been tied up with strips torn from a red dress; he was moaning and covered with blood. She saw Collette and "Big Savage" hitting the victim; "Big Savage" was also covered with blood, and instructed her to find him some clean clothes. After a trip around the hotel area, she located some clothing for him and returned with it to Room 301. She then discovered MacLeod was dead; helped remove blood from the walls of the room; helped the others remove the body. * * *

* * *

Defendant contends that the evidence was insufficient to permit application of the felony murder rule, and that her conviction should be reversed.

Penal Code section 189 states, in pertinent part, that "All murder * * * committed in the perpetration of, or attempt to perpetrate, * * * robbery * * * is murder of the first degree." The objective of the Legislature in enacting this provision was to deter persons from killing during the commission of certain enumerated crimes, including robbery, by holding them strictly accountable for such killings "whether * * * wilful, deliberate and premeditated, or merely accidental or unintentional, and whether or not the killing is planned as a part of the commission [of the underlying offense]." (People v. Stamp, 2 Cal.App.3d 203, 209, 82 Cal.Rptr. 598, 602; People v. Johnson, 28 Cal.App.3d 653, 658, 104 Cal.Rptr. 807.)

It has long been held that the felony-murder rule may apply only where there is proof that defendant had formed the specific intent to commit the concomitant felony prior in time to the killing; that intent may be proved by circumstantial evidence.

In the instant case, there was ample evidence that defendant and others had formed a plan on the evening of August 7 to lure the victim MacLeod to Room 301 of the Deluxe Hotel and rob him of what was believed to be a substantial sum of money. The first blow, which might have been a fatal one according to the medical testimony, was struck prior to the actual robbery. Long after it was apparent that no additional money would be forthcoming from the victim, the persons involved, including defendant, continued to assault him; when he was dead, the group took steps to avoid apprehension for the robbery and death. In our view, the evidence was more than ample, indeed overwhelming, in support not only of applicability of the felony-murder rule, but in support of conviction of first degree murder without reference to Penal Code section 189. * * *

It is true, as defendant contends, that the felony-murder rule has been held inapplicable to those situations where the concomitant felony has been completed prior to the killing. It has been held inapplicable when, after the completion of a robbery, the person or persons committing the robbery have possession of the plunder and have made their way to a place of temporary safety. Whether in fact the underlying offense has been completed prior to the killing is a question of fact to be determined by the jury. Defendant contends that the evidence conclusively demonstrated that the robbery of

MacLeod was completed prior to the killing, that defendant had received her share of the proceeds of the crime and had reached a place of temporary safety before MacLeod died; thus, the felony-murder rule did not apply.

The record supports the inference that the defendant and her associates had planned to kill the victim so that he would not be able to testify against them. There was substantial evidence to support the conclusion that the events of the evening formed one "continuous transaction," and such a finding clearly results in felony-murder, in the first degree.

The jury was carefully and completely instructed that if they believed "that the robbery had been completed and terminated prior to the killing of Roderick MacLeod, then such robbery may not be used to find defendant guilty of murder in the first degree." They were also instructed that a "robbery is no longer being committed when the person or persons committing the robbery have possession of the plunder and have made their way to a place of temporary safety even if just momentarily. Failure to win one's way to a place of temporary safety means that said person is still fleeing or still trying to escape." We conclude that defendant received the benefit of every instruction to which she was entitled, based upon the evidence. Defendant's further contention, that the instructions were erroneous because the jury might have been misled as to the requirement that the events be part of a "continuous transaction," is without merit.

* * *

Judgment affirmed.

Notes

1. *Duration of the Felony.* All would agree that, for the felony-murder rule to attach, the injury causing death must occur while, in some sense, the felony is in progress. It would be possible to take a literal approach and say that one or more of the elements mentioned in the definition of the offense must be occurring at the time of the fatal injury, but no version of the rule is so narrow. For one thing, the rule applies during the attempt stage of the underlying felony: that is, from the moment the accused has done enough to be found guilty of a criminal attempt to commit the underlying crime. (For more on the nature of an attempt, see Chapter VI.) So, if striking a match with intent to apply the flame immediately to the victim's dwelling house is attempted arson, and the victim thereupon suffers a fatal heart attack at the prospect of seeing his house burned down, it may be felony-murder even if the arson is never committed.

A burglary is complete, in the sense that enough has been done for conviction, as soon as entry under appropriate circumstances has been accomplished. Suppose that the burglar, while searching the house for things to steal, accidentally causes the death of an occupant. All would agree that it is not too late in time to apply the felony-murder rule while the burglar is still on the premises. Most cases would go further, as *Sirignano* suggests, and continue to apply the rule during the *res gestae* of the underlying felony. The meaning of *res gestae* is not entirely clear; time, geography, and continuity of action play a part. When the situation has reached a state of at least temporary equilibrium, and the felon has made his getaway and eluded any hot pursuit, it is usually held to be too late to apply the rule. However, for an extreme case, see State v. Metalski, 116 N.J.L. 543, 185 A. 351 (1936), where, two hours after a bank robbery, sixty miles away, and after a half hour stop for lunch by the robbers, the felony-murder rule was applied.

2. *What Crimes are "Felonies."* The common law felony-murder rule might be construed to extend to all new statutory felonies, but few would support so great an extension. In jurisdictions retaining the rule, there are almost always significant limits as to the crimes to which it applies. The rule may be limited to common law felonies, to specified crimes, or to "dangerous" felonies, for example.

The rule is not ordinarily applied to larceny or any theft offense carrying no element of danger to the person. It is not applied where the underlying felony is the criminal homicide of the victim—based on a theory of purposeful or reckless killing; otherwise these categories would disappear as a practical matter, because all such killings would be felony-murder (probably punishable as first degree murder).

Further problems of limiting the underlying crimes to which the rule may apply are explored in the two Kansas cases which follow.

State v. Underwood

Supreme Court of Kansas, 1980.
228 Kan. 294, 615 P.2d 153.

FROMME, JUSTICE:

Curtis Leon Underwood appeals from a jury conviction of felony murder (K.S.A. 21–3401). The underlying felony which is being used to classify the homicide as a felony murder is unlawful possession of a firearm as defined in K.S.A. 21–4204(1)(*b*). This forms the basis for appeal No. 51,401 in this court.

* * *

* * * On August 2, 1974, when appellant Underwood was eighteen years old, he assisted Gus Hankins, Jr. in stealing a bicycle from the Wichita State University campus. * * * The appellant entered a plea of nolo contendere to the charge of felony theft and was sentenced for a period of from one to ten years. He was placed on probation for a two year period. His probation was terminated when fully served in September 1976.

The events leading to appellant's conviction on the felony murder charge occurred on October 28, 1978. Appellant and some friends were attending a card party at 2718 East 10th Street, Wichita, Kansas. While appellant was watching the game, one of the players, Earl Brewer, accused him of stealing a bag of marijuana. They exchanged angry words and eventually began fighting in the yard. During this altercation the bag of marijuana dropped to the ground. The fight stopped. A friend of Brewer came from the house carrying a shotgun and handed it to Brewer. Brewer brandished the shotgun. The appellant and his friends entered their cars to leave. From the car appellant announced that he would return.

* * * Appellant * * * obtained a .32 caliber pistol. The pistol had recently been purchased by appellant with funds from his live-in girl friend, ostensibly for her protection. Appellant gave the gun to his half-brother, Phil Marzett, for safekeeping before returning to the scene of the fight.

The appellant and his friends returned to the 10th Street address and Brewer was summoned to come outside the house. The fight was resumed.

Friends of both men became embroiled in the fighting. One man was stabbed. A friend of Brewer emerged from the house with the shotgun. Brewer and appellant had been fighting on the ground. Brewer stood up and ran toward his friend with the shotgun. The appellant retrieved the pistol from Marzett and shot at Brewer. Four shots were fired by appellant. One bullet struck and killed Brewer. Appellant testified he fired the shots because he saw Brewer reaching for the shotgun; he feared for the safety of his friends and himself.

Shortly after the shooting appellant telephoned the police and arranged to turn himself in. Appellant was charged with the unlawful possession of a firearm and with felony murder. The firearm charge which formed the underlying felony for the felony murder charge was based on the fact that appellant had been convicted of the 1974 bicycle theft and had possession of a firearm.

Appellant filed a motion in the trial court seeking annulment of the 1974 bicycle theft conviction. He argued that his attorney, the prosecutor, and the judge had assured him that the 1974 conviction would be cleared and annulled as soon as he finished serving his two year probationary period. Appellant further contended he entered his plea and testified against Hankins because of this assurance.

After conducting an evidentiary hearing on the motion, the trial court refused to annul the 1974 conviction. The court found that although appellant may have been aware of the possibility of annulment, the sentencing court did not discuss annulment when the plea was accepted and apparently no one explained that the annulment procedure was not automatic. The trial court, after examining the statutes providing for annulment and for expungement, held the present statutes would not permit the annulment or expungement of appellant's firearm violation in any event.

Appellant then filed the motion to withdraw his nolo contendere plea under K.S.A. 22–3210(7) "to correct manifest injustice." * * *

* * *

* * * Considering the lapse of time and the facts of this case we cannot find the trial court abused its discretion in refusing to permit the appellant to withdraw his plea.

The final issue raised by the appellant is not new to the case law of this State. This court is again confronted with the question decided in State v. Moffitt, 199 Kan. 514, Syl. ¶ 6, 431 P.2d 879 (1967), and State v. Goodseal, 220 Kan. 487, Syl. ¶¶ 3, 11, 553 P.2d 279 (1976). The question in those cases was whether the collateral felony of unlawful possession of a firearm by an ex-felon under K.S.A. 21–4204 was an inherently dangerous felony so as to support the application of the felony murder rule under K.S.A. 21–3401. This court held in *Moffitt* and *Goodseal* that this possession felony would support the charge of felony murder. Since *Moffitt* and *Goodseal* were decided this rule has been followed in State v. Guebara, 220 Kan. 520, 553 P.2d 296 (1976); and State v. Birch, 221 Kan. 122, 558 P.2d 119 (1976). Other cases of felony murder which followed *Moffitt* do not appear to rely on the collateral felony of unlawful possession of a firearm by an ex-felon.

For the reasons set forth below a majority of this court has concluded that it was prejudicial error for the trial court to instruct the jury on the theory of felony murder. Accordingly we reverse the judgment.

This court in arriving at its decision in State v. Moffitt, 199 Kan. 514, 431 P.2d 879, relied on three California cases, People v. Ford, 60 Cal.2d 772, 36 Cal.Rptr. 620, 388 P.2d 892 (1964); People v. Williams, 63 Cal.2d 452, 47 Cal.Rptr. 7, 406 P.2d 647 (1965); and People v. Robillard, 55 Cal.2d 88, 10 Cal.Rptr. 167, 358 P.2d 295, 83 A.L.R.2d 1086 (1960). In State v. Goodseal, 220 Kan. at 491, 553 P.2d 279, this court acknowledged that the California Supreme Court had receded from its former position in the foregoing cases in deciding the later case of People v. Satchell, 6 Cal.3d 28, 98 Cal.Rptr. 33, 489 P.2d 1361, 50 A.L.R.3d 383 (1971). The California court ruled in *Satchell* that the unlawful possession of a firearm by a convicted felon, when viewed in the abstract, is not a felony inherently dangerous to human life for purposes of the felony murder rule and will not support a felony murder charge. However, this court in *Goodseal* in a 4–3 decision refused to reverse its previous position taken in *Moffitt,* and continued to rely on *Moffitt* and the cases overruled by the California Supreme Court.

The difference in the result reached in *Satchell* and in *Goodseal* comes from the rules adopted by these respective courts to help determine whether a particular collateral felony could be considered inherently dangerous to human life so as to support a conviction of felony murder. In *Goodseal* the court in considering the nature of the collateral felony not only views the felony in the abstract but also considers the circumstances of its commission. So in *Goodseal* it was not the possession of the firearm but its use by the ex-felon which enabled the court to find the felony was inherently dangerous to human life. In *Satchell* the California court decided that whether a collateral felony is inherently dangerous should be determined by viewing the elements of the crime in the abstract without considering the circumstances of commission. It held the possession was passive and not inherently dangerous to human life. Use of the gun was not considered.

The Kansas felony murder statute provides:

> "Murder in the first degree is the killing of a human being committed maliciously, willfully, deliberately and with premeditation *or committed in the perpetration or attempt to perpetrate any felony."* K.S.A. 21–3401. Emphasis supplied.

Under the literal wording of this statute any felony is sufficient to support a charge of felony murder if a causal relation exists. This court in State v. Goodseal, 220 Kan. at 492, 553 P.2d 279, quoting from a Delaware case, acknowledges that the ostensible purpose of the felony murder doctrine is to deter those engaged in felonies from killing negligently or accidentally, and that the doctrine should not be extended beyond its rational function which it was designed to serve. To invoke the felony murder rule there must be proof that a homicide was committed in the perpetration of or an attempt to perpetrate a felony and that the collateral felony was one inherently dangerous to human life. This court has declared certain rules applicable to such cases. Some of these rules are summarized in State v. Smith, 225 Kan. 796, 799, 800, 594 P.2d 218 (1979), as follows:

> "In order to invoke the felony murder rule under K.S.A. 21–3401, there must be proof that the homicide was committed in the perpetration of or an attempt to perpetrate a felony. This means there must be a direct causal connection between the commission of the felony and the homicide. State v. Moffitt, 199 Kan. 514, 534, 431 P.2d 879 (1967); see also 40 Am.Jur.2d, Homicide § 73, p. 367; 40 C.J.S. Homicide § 21b. Moreover, the underlying felony must be one inherently dangerous to human life. State v. Moffitt, 199 Kan. at 534, 431 P.2d 879. Thus, the State must establish the defendant committed a felony inherently dangerous to human life and the killing took place during the commission of the felony. State v. Branch and Bussey, 223 Kan. 381, 382, 573 P.2d 1041 (1978) and cases cited therein. * * *"

An interesting discussion of the history of the felony murder rule of various states and countries, including England where it was abrogated in 1957, and the varied application of the rule in this country appears in the Model Penal Code § 201.2, Comment (Tent.Draft No. 9, 1959.) * * *

Theoretically the elements of malice, deliberation and premeditation which are required for murder in the first degree are deemed to be supplied by felonious conduct alone if a homicide results. It is not necessary for the prosecutor to prove these elements or for the jury to find such elements of the crime. They are established by proof of the collateral felony. State v. Wilson, 220 Kan. 341, Syl. ¶ 2, 552 P.2d 931 (1976). Therefore, to support a conviction for felony murder all that is required is to prove that a felony was being committed, which felony was inherently dangerous to human life, and that the homicide which followed was a direct result of the commission of that felony. State v. Bey, 217 Kan. 251, 260, 535 P.2d 881 (1975).

The felony murder rule has logic based on the theory of transferred intent. The malicious and premeditated intent of committing the inherently dangerous collateral felony is transferred to the homicide to supply the elements of malice and premeditation without further proof. Consistent with this thinking, most courts require that the collateral felony be inherently dangerous for the felony murder rule to be applicable. * * *

The collateral felony we are dealing with in the present case is defined in K.S.A. 21–4204 as follows:

> "(1) Unlawful possession of a firearm is:
>
> "(*a*) Possession of any firearm by an habitual drunkard or narcotics addict; or
>
> "(*b*) Possession of a firearm with a barrel less than twelve (12) inches long by a person who, within five (5) years preceding such violation has been convicted of a felony under the laws of Kansas or any other jurisdiction or has been released from imprisonment for a felony."

This crime is a status crime in that it is limited to drunkards, drug addicts and ex-felons. It is *malum prohibitum.* The possession of the firearm is prohibited because a firearm in the possession of a habitual drunkard, a narcotics addict or an ex-felon is against the public policy of the State as declared by the legislature. The possession of the firearm when viewed in the abstract is not inherently dangerous to human life. This is true because it seems unlikely that mere possession, which has been defined as dominion and control over an object, and not its use, could be undertaken in so dangerous a manner that the prohibited possession would result in murder in the first degree. The above meaning of the possession as contemplated in this firearm statute is taken from State v. Neal, 215 Kan. 737, 738, 529 P.2d 114 (1974). It appears quite impossible to find an intent in this collateral felony encompassing malice, deliberation and premeditation so as to transfer these elements to the homicide and relieve the prosecution from proof of the same. If these elements are present in the use of the firearm they are not present in the possession of the firearm. They should then be proven as elements of premeditated first degree murder by reason of the malicious and deliberate use of the gun.

We note that once the *use* of the firearm begins, a separate crime is committed; e.g., assault with a deadly weapon assuming the required intent is present. Aggravated assault is an integral part of the homicide and felony murder cannot be based thereon. State v. Clark, 204 Kan. 38, Syl. ¶ 1, 460 P.2d 586 (1969). It follows that unlawful possession of a firearm, when viewed in the abstract, does not harbor the malice and premeditation for the transferred intent so as to make a homicide a felony murder.

Mr. Justice Prager in the dissent in State v. Goodseal, 220 Kan. 503, beginning at page 506, 553 P.2d 279, sets forth three examples of the illogical results which can flow when a homicide is unintentional and the collateral felony is not viewed in the abstract in determining whether it is inherently dangerous to human life. These examples are as follows:

> "For example, let us assume that a defendant, having been previously convicted of felony for writing an insufficient fund check, purchases a firearm to protect himself and his family against criminal invaders of his home. He accidentally drops the gun, causing it to strike the floor and be discharged, killing a guest in his home. Since the killing occurred during commission of a felony, possession of the gun unlawfully, defendant would be precluded from interposing the defense of accident. Under the rule adopted by the majority defendant would be guilty of murder in the first degree and possibly subjected to a term of life imprisonment in the state penitentiary.
>
> "Another example—a farm lad served in the Vietnam war and at the time of his discharge obtained an automatic rifle which he took to his farm home. He wanted the gun not only for the protection of himself and his family but also for use in the killing of predators that might attack his livestock. Under the provisions of K.S.A. 21–4201(1)(*g*) it is a class E felony for any person to possess a firearm capable of discharging automatically more than once by a

single function of the trigger. An intruder comes upon the defendant's farm. The defendant points a gun at the intruder, directing him to get off his place. The gun accidentally discharges and kills the intruder. The rule adopted by the majority in this case would require the jury to convict the defendant of murder in the first degree since at the time of the killing the defendant was committing another felony—possession of an automatic weapon—at the time the killing took place.

"One more example should suffice. A defendant having been previously convicted of a felony accidentally shoots another person. At the time defendant was in possession of a firearm with a barrel eleven-inches long. Applying the felony-murder rule the defendant would be guilty of felony murder and upon conviction a life sentence would be imposed. If the firearm involved in the case had a barrel twelve-inches long the defendant would not be guilty of any criminal offense since the shooting was accidental and would fall into the category of an excusable homicide. It does not seem reasonable to impute malice to the defendant in the first situation and not to do so in the second situation; yet this absurd result would follow under the rule adopted by the majority of the court in this case." 220 Kan. at 506, 507, 553 P.2d at 295.

Further injustice may occur in felony murder cases because the charge of felony murder may strip an accused of the normal defenses possible in a murder case. In the present case, for instance, appellant had no intent to violate the law by possessing the firearm. He believed his previous bicycle theft conviction was automatically dismissed when he successfully completed his probation. He was in error and he possessed a firearm so under the felony murder charge the defenses such as accident, lack of malice and heat of passion were not open to him for the possession establishing the underlying felony could not be disputed. When proof of the underlying felony is strong no instructions on lesser degrees of murder are required. State v. Sullivan & Sullivan, 224 Kan. 110, 124, 578 P.2d 1108 (1978); State v. Reed, 214 Kan. 562, 564, 520 P.2d 1314 (1974).

In addition, filing a charge under the felony murder rule in most, if not all, cases removes any possibility of establishing the defense of self-defense. Under K.S.A. 21–3211, a person is justified in the use of force against an aggressor when and to the extent it appears to him, and he reasonably believes, that such conduct is necessary to defend himself or another against the aggressor's imminent use of unlawful force. If two men are fighting, as in this case, and one grabs a shotgun he is then the aggressor and the other may defend himself by use of a gun, if he can find one in time. However, under K.S.A. 21–3214 an instruction on self-defense permitted by K.S.A. 21–3211 is not available to a person who is committing a forcible felony. State v. Purdy, 228 Kan. 264, 615 P.2d 131, this day decided. Under K.S.A. 1979 Supp. 21–3110(8) the definition of forcible felony includes treason, murder, voluntary manslaughter, rape, robbery, burglary, arson, kidnapping, aggravated battery, aggravated sodomy and *any other felony which involves the use or threat of physical force or violence against any person.* Unlawful possession of a firearm is not included in the forcible felonies enumerated nor does it fit within the catch-all phrase at the end of the definition.

Now, where does that leave the person who is confronted with the rule in *Moffitt* and *Goodseal* holding that possession of a pistol after conviction of a felony is inherently dangerous to human life? Logically under *Goodseal* it follows that the defendant when charged with felony murder is not entitled to an instruction on self-defense. If the court considers the use of the firearm to establish that the collateral felony is inherently dangerous to human life, the use also establishes that the collateral felony is a forcible felony. This takes away from the accused the defense of self-defense.

A majority of this court now are convinced that the logic, reasoning and rule urged by Mr. Justice Prager in the dissent in State v. Goodseal, 220 Kan. at 503, 553 P.2d 279, should be adopted for Kansas. Accordingly, we hold that in determining whether a particular collateral felony is inherently dangerous to human life so as to justify a charge of felony murder under K.S.A. 21–3401, the elements of the collateral felony should be viewed in the abstract, and the circumstances of the commission of the felony should not be considered in making the determination. State v. Moffitt, 199 Kan. 514, (Syl. ¶¶ 6, 7,) 431 P.2d 879, and all cases holding to the contrary are disapproved.

The unlawful possession of a firearm proscribed by K.S.A. 21-4204(1)(*b*) when considered in the abstract is not a felony inherently dangerous to human life and will not sustain a conviction for murder in the first degree under the felony murder rule. The rule formerly stated and applied in State v. Moffitt, 199 Kan. 514, Syl. ¶¶ 6, 7, 431 P.2d 879 (1967); and its progeny, State v. Goodseal, 220 Kan. 487, 553 P.2d 279 (1976); State v. Guebara, 220 Kan. 520, 553 P.2d 296 (1976); and State v. Birch, 221 Kan. 122, 558 P.2d 119 (1976), is disapproved and overruled.

* * *

The order of the trial court denying annulment of the conviction and refusing to allow withdrawal of the plea of nolo contendere in the bicycle theft case, in Appeal No. 51,420 herein, is affirmed.

The judgment of conviction on the felony murder charge, in Appeal No. 51,401 herein, is reversed and the case is remanded for a new trial.

SCHROEDER, CHIEF JUSTICE, dissenting.

State v. Moffitt, 199 Kan. 514, 431 P.2d 879 (1967), has been the law of Kansas for thirteen years. The court now reverses its position on the law in that case regarding felony murder, where the underlying felony is the unlawful possession of a firearm proscribed by K.S.A. 21–4204(1)(*b*).

I would adhere to the law in the *Moffitt* decision.

MILLER and MCFARLAND, JJ., join in the foregoing dissenting opinion.

State v. Foy

Supreme Court of Kansas, 1978.
224 Kan. 558, 582 P.2d 281.

SCHROEDER, CHIEF JUSTICE.

This is an appeal in a criminal action from a jury verdict which found Roger D. Foy (defendant-appellant) guilty of felony murder (K.S.A. 21–3401).

Numerous trial errors are asserted on appeal for reversal of the conviction and sentence.

The appellant and Sharon Foy were married in Littleton, Colorado, in 1966. Their marriage was characterized by frequent periods of discord and violence. Sharon obtained a divorce from the appellant in 1973; however, the two continued to live together at various intervals. The appellant testified he attributed his marital problems largely to interference by Sharon's mother, Mrs. Grace Kruelhous.

The appellant and Sharon were living together with their family in the basement of Grace Kruelhous' home in Dodge City, Kansas, on January 1, 1976, when the events leading up to the shooting began. During the afternoon of New Year's Day Sharon went drinking with some girl friends. Subsequently, she accompanied the group to a private party at Marvin Schmidt's trailer where she continued to drink and smoke marijuana. When Sharon had not arrived home by 7:00 p.m. the appellant and a friend began looking for her. After finding her at Schmidt's trailer the appellant demanded she return home. When Sharon refused, the appellant slapped and kicked her in front of the others.

The following day Sharon signed a complaint charging the appellant with battery. For some reason the complaint was not filed until January 19, 1976. In any event, Sharon told the appellant she had signed the complaint at her mother's urging and asked him to live with her brother, Rex Kreie, in order to "give Mom a chance to cool off," but the appellant and Sharon continued to see one another until the night she was shot and killed.

On January 20, 1976, the appellant was served at work with a summons for the battery charge. He borrowed a truck from his employer and went to the cafe where Sharon was working to discuss the situation. Apparently, she assured him they would talk when she got off work. The appellant then began drinking, and when Sharon failed to contact him, he started calling Grace Kruelhous' home.

The appellant testified on two of these occasions he heard Grace holler to "Hang up on the son-of-a-bitch and call the Police." After informing Sharon he contemplated suicide she urged him to visit a relative of hers to talk and to pray. The appellant did visit Sharon's aunt, Elsie Sterling, and she and her husband counseled and prayed with him.

After returning home the appellant resumed his drinking and decided to walk to Grace's house in order to talk to Sharon. He testified he took a sawed-off shotgun with him thinking if Grace interfered, he would kill her. As he approached the Sonic Drive-In he saw his friend Steve Smith and asked him for a ride to Grace's house. Smith testified he asked the appellant what he was going to do with the gun and the appellant answered, "blow somebody's shit away." When Smith asked to whom he was referring, the appellant answered, "The old lady." The appellant testified he was referring to Grace. After this conversation the appellant put the gun in his pants and pulled his coat over it.

Grace Kruelhous testified at approximately 8:00 p.m. she and Sharon had been watching television when the appellant opened the front door and walked in. While the evidence is conflicting, Sharon allegedly stated, "Roger, you are not supposed to be in mamma's house." She said that she would "call the Law" if he did not leave. The two stood facing each other in the front hall at the time. As Grace arose from her chair to call the police the appellant glanced in her direction and in his anger squeezed down on the hammer. The gun discharged shooting Sharon in the face and killing her instantly.

* * *

At the trial the judge instructed the jury, over objection, on the theory of felony murder based upon aggravated burglary as the underlying felony. The jury then found the appellant guilty of first-degree murder under the felony murder provisions of the statute. * * *

* * *

The appellant * * * objects to the instruction of felony murder using aggravated burglary as the felony with the intent to commit aggravated assault on Grace Kruelhous. * * *

* * *

Of course, in Kansas, the felony-murder doctrine is not applicable in cases of felonious assault resulting in death because the assault *merges* into the homicide. (State v. Clark, 204 Kan. 38, 460 P.2d 586 [1969].) Thus, aggravated assault may *not* be the underlying felony itself. (State v. Clark, supra at 44, 460 P.2d 586; see also State v. Rueckert, 221 Kan. 727, 733, 561 P.2d 850 [1977]; and State v. Goodseal, 220 Kan. 487, 493, 553 P.2d 279 [1976].) Here, however, aggravated burglary was the underlying felony, but it was predicated upon aggravated assault.

Should the merger doctrine for assault cases be extended to limit the felony-murder instruction in burglary cases in which the burglary is based upon an assault? We think not.

While our court has never examined this issue, several states confronted with the question have held that burglary based upon the crime of assault can properly serve as the predicate for a felony-murder conviction. (Blango v. United States, 373 A.2d 885 [D.C.App.1977]; State v. Miller, 110 Ariz. 489, 520 P.2d 1113 [1974]; People v. Miller, 32 N.Y.2d 157, 344 N.Y.S.2d 342, 297 N.E.2d 85 [1973]; and State v. Tremblay, 4 Or.App. 512, 479 P.2d 507 [1971]. See also Comment, *The Merger Doctrine As A Limitation On The Felony-Murder Rule: A Balance Of Criminal Law Principles,* 13 Wake Forest L.Rev. 369, 388–94 [1977].)

We find the reasoning in People v. Miller, supra, persuasive. The court states:

> "* * * [P]ersons within domiciles are in greater peril from those entering the domicile with criminal intent, than persons on the street who are being subjected to the same criminal intent. Thus, the burglary statutes prescribe greater punishment for a criminal act committed within the domicile than for the same act committed on the street. Where, as here, the criminal act underlying the burglary is an assault with a dangerous weapon, the likelihood that the assault will culminate in a homicide is significantly increased by the situs of

the assault. When the assault takes place within the domicile, the victim may be more likely to resist the assault; the victim is also less likely to be able to avoid the consequences of the assault, since his paths of retreat and escape may be barred or severely restricted by furniture, walls and other obstructions incidental to buildings. Further, it is also more likely that when the assault occurs in the victim's domicile, there will be present family or close friends who will come to the victim's aid and be killed. * * *" (32 N.Y.2d pp. 160–161, 344 N.Y.S.2d pp. 345–346, 297 N.E.2d p. 87).

Here the evidence supports a finding that aggravated burglary was complete upon the unlawful entry by the appellant into the home of Grace Kruelhous with the prerequisite intent to commit a felony therein (aggravated assault). Thereafter the homicide was committed in the course of the burglary. Accordingly, we reject the holding of People v. Wilson, 1 Cal.3d 431, 82 Cal.Rptr. 494, 462 P.2d 22 (1969) and hold the merger doctrine does not apply in felony-murder cases where an aggravated burglary is based upon an aggravated assault.

* * *

Finally, the appellant asserts it was error for the trial court to refuse an instruction on involuntary manslaughter based upon criminal trespass as a lesser included offense of felony murder. * * *

* * * Here the evidence of the underlying felony (aggravated burglary) was inconclusive. The appellant was going to his mother-in-law's home where his wife Sharon was staying. He went for the purpose of talking with Sharon. The jury might have found from the evidence that the appellant committed a criminal trespass upon opening the front door and entering the home (K.S.A. 21–3721). On the evidence the shooting of Sharon by the appellant may have been a malicious and willful act or, according to the testimony of the defendant (that his hand slipped off the hammer), it could have been accidental. A jury question is presented. Accordingly, the trial court erred in failing to give an instruction on involuntary manslaughter which is a lesser included offense.

* * *

PRAGER, JUSTICE, concurring and dissenting:

I concur in the reversal of the case and the granting of a new trial. * * * I cannot agree with the majority that the felony-murder rule is applicable under the circumstances of this case. * * *

* * * In State v. Wilson, 220 Kan. 341, 552 P.2d 931 (1976), we stated that the purpose of the felony-murder rule is to relieve the state of the burden of proving premeditation and malice when the victim's death is caused by the killer while he is committing another felony. The rationale of the rule was said to be that the killer's malignant purpose is established by proof of intent to commit the collateral felony. The application of the felony-murder rule is subject to the limitation that the elements constituting the other felony must be so distinct from that of the homicide so as not to be ingredients of the homicide itself. In State v. Fisher, 120 Kan. 226, 243 P. 291 (1926), this court held that an aggravated assault which resulted in a

homicide could not be utilized as an independent felony to invoke the felony-murder doctrine. The rationale of *Fisher* is applicable in this case. Here the aggravated burglary, the independent felony required for invocation of the felony-murder rule, had as an essential element, the intent to commit an aggravated assault. The same intent is then used as an element of the homicide itself. I, of course, agree that in a proper case a burglary may be used to invoke the felony-murder rule. I cannot agree that an intent to commit the same assault may be used both as an element of the burglary and also as an element of the homicide so as to make the felony-murder rule applicable. For a case reaching this conclusion see People v. Wilson, 1 Cal. 3d 431, 82 Cal.Rptr. 494, 462 P.2d 22 (1969).

* * *

MILLER, J., joins in the foregoing concurring and dissenting opinion.

Questions

1. State v. Rupe, 226 Kan. 474, 601 P.2d 675 (1979), arose on facts almost identical to those of *Foy*; the only significant difference was that the mother-in-law figure was absent. Defendant, armed, broke into his former wife's house, apparently intending to assault or kill her and then commit suicide. The actual fatal shooting of the former wife may have been accidental. The court, one judge dissenting, affirmed the conviction on the basis of *Foy*. Are the cases distinguishable?

2. Suppose that it is a statutory felony to dope a race horse. D enters the stall of a race horse surreptitiously to inject a drug. The horse kicks when it feels the needle, thereby killing a stable boy, who, unknown to D, is asleep in the hay. What homicide crime, if any, has D committed?

3. In the famous Lindbergh kidnapping case, the principal prosecution theory of the crime was that the defendant Hauptmann had, on the night of the crime, climbed a home-made ladder to a second floor window of the Lindbergh house, opened the window, taken the baby, and started back down the ladder with him, when a rung broke, causing Hauptmann accidentally to drop the child, who fell to his death. Hauptmann buried the victim nearby, first removing his sleeping suit, which he sent to the parents through an intermediary with a ransom demand. Ransom was paid, and some of the bills were later found on Hauptmann's premises. If the jury found this theory proven, could it properly have found Hauptmann guilty of murder? (Kidnapping was not a felony in the jurisdiction at the time.)

4. *Underwood* suggests the question of whether self-defense should ever be justification in a homicide charge based on a felony-murder theory. What do you think? Suppose that the defendant claims he participated in a robbery only under duress, and one of the others accidentally killed the victim. Would duress be a defense to a charge of felony-murder?

5. May one properly be punished for *both* the underlying felony and for felony-murder?

King v. Commonwealth

Court of Appeals of Virginia, 1988.
6 Va.App. 351, 368 S.E.2d 704.

COLEMAN, JUDGE.

We consider whether the facts in this case constitute a violation of the felony-murder statute, Code § 18.2–33. Nelson James King appeals his conviction of second degree murder under the statute. He argues that he could not be convicted of second degree murder for the accidental death of a cofelon occurring during the commission of a felony. * * * We hold that because the death was not caused by an act of the felons in furtherance of the felony, appellant is not criminally liable for the death.

On October 17, 1984, King and his copilot, Mark Lee Bailey, were flying a Beechcraft Bonanza airplane carrying over five hundred pounds of marijuana to the New River Valley airport in Dublin, Virginia. They were flying for Wallace Thrasher, who owned the airplane and ran the drug smuggling operation. King was a licensed pilot; Bailey was not. The two encountered heavy cloud cover and fog near Mt. Airy, North Carolina and apparently became lost. In an effort to navigate through the cloud cover and fog, they flew the plane to a lower altitude in order to follow U.S. Route 52. Bailey was piloting the plane at this time. As Bailey flew, King was examining navigation maps in an attempt to determine the plane's whereabouts. The airplane crashed into Fancy Gap Mountain killing Bailey almost instantly. King was thrown from the plane and survived. King was charged with felony homicide under Code § 18.2–33 for Bailey's death. A jury convicted King of second degree murder under the statute and recommended a six-year penitentiary sentence.

Code § 18.2–33 defines second degree felony homicide: "The killing of one accidentally, contrary to the intention of the parties, while in the prosecution of some felonious act other than those specified in §§ 18.2–31 and 18.2–32, is murder of the second degree and is punishable as a Class 3 felony." This statute and its companion, § 18.2–32, defining first degree felony-murder, codify the common law doctrine of felony-murder. Heacock v. Commonwealth, 228 Va. 397, 403, 323 S.E.2d 90, 93 (1984). The doctrine was developed to elevate to murder a homicide committed during the course of a felony by imputing malice to the killing. The justification for imputing malice was the theory that the increased risk of death or serious harm occasioned by the commission of a felony demonstrated the felon's lack of concern for human life. See generally Morris, *The Felon's Responsibility for the Lethal Acts of Others,* 105 U.Pa.L.Rev. 50 (1956). The doctrine was originally limited, therefore, to felonies that were inherently or foreseeably dangerous. The purpose of the doctrine was to deter inherently dangerous felonies by holding the felons responsible for the consequences of the felony, whether intended or not. While the range of felonies which may be a predicate for the felony-murder conviction has changed, the function of the doctrine is still to elevate to murder a homicide resulting from a felony by imputing malice.

* * *

The second degree felony-murder statute in Virginia contemplates a killing with malice. *Heacock,* 228 Va. at 403, 323 S.E.2d at 93. Indeed, "the commission of *any* felonious act * * * supplies the malice which raises the incidental homicide to the level of second-degree murder." Id. It does not follow, however, that any death of any person which occurs during the period in which a felony is being committed will subject the felon to criminal liability under the felony-murder rule. To construe our statute to encompass every accidental death occurring during the commission of a felony, regardless of whether it causally relates to or results from the commission of the felony, is to make felons absolutely liable for the accidental death of another even though such death is fortuitous and the product of causes wholly unrelated to the commission of the felony. Recognizing the potentially harsh and far reaching effects of such a construction of the felony-murder doctrine, the Virginia courts, as well as others, have limited its application. In order for the incidental accidental killing to be murder, the homicide must be criminal in nature and must contain the elements or attributes of criminal homicide cognizable at common law.

One of the most significant factors in defining the scope of the felony-murder involves the causation required between the felony and the death. Previous decisions of the Virginia Supreme Court have found it unnecessary to decide whether "a mere nexus" between the death and predicate felony is sufficient to satisfy the statute or whether a more direct causal relationship is required. We must address that issue at this time.

In Virginia, it is clear when the homicide is within the *res gestae* of the initial felony and emanates therefrom, it is committed in the perpetration of that felony. Haskell v. Commonwealth, 218 Va. 1033, 1041, 243 S.E.2d 477, 482 (1978). The Court explained that "the felony-murder statute applies where the killing is so closely related to the felony in time, place, and causal connection as to make it a part of the same criminal enterprise." Thus, the court in *Haskell* affirmed first degree murder convictions when the murder of a robbery victim was within five feet of the site of the robbery, within moments of the robbery, and was to facilitate the robbers' escape without being identified. Under these circumstances, the killing was obviously causally related to the robbery and was part of the same enterprise. The Court did not elaborate on the degree of causal connection required under the statute.

In a more recent case, the Virginia Supreme Court affirmed a conviction under the felony-murder rule when a death by cocaine overdose was charged to the person who distributed the cocaine. *Heacock,* 228 Va. at 401–02, 323 S.E.2d at 92–93. In that circumstance, the court declined to address whether the felony-murder rule required a showing of causal relationship flowing from the felony to the homicide or whether a "mere nexus" would suffice because the death was a direct result of the felony of distribution of cocaine.

In a leading case involving the felony-murder doctrine, which the Virginia Supreme Court has cited with approval, the Pennsylvania Supreme Court addressed the causation problem at length. Rejecting their previous standard of proximate cause, the court stated:

> In adjudging a felony-murder, it is to be remembered at all times that the thing which is imputed to a felon for a killing incidental to his felony is *malice* and *not the act of killing.* The mere coincidence of homicide and felony is not enough to satisfy the requirements of the felony-murder doctrine * * *. "Death must be a consequence of the felony * * * and not merely coincidence."

Commonwealth v. Redline, 391 Pa. 486, 495, 137 A.2d 472, 476 (1958) (citations omitted). The court noted further: "[T]he 'causation' requirement for responsibility in a felony-murder is that the homicide stem from the commission of the felony." Id. at 505, 137 A.2d at 481. The *Redline* court noted that the malice of the underlying felony attaches to whatever else the criminal may do in connection with the felony. Therefore, "the killing must have been done by the defendant or by an accomplice or confederate or by one acting in furtherance of the felonious undertaking." Id. at 495–96, 137 A.2d at 476. (emphasis omitted).

The implications of this reasoning are threefold. First, only acts causing death which are committed by those involved in the felony can be the basis for a conviction. Second, the act causing death must result from some effort to further the felony before malice can be imputed to that act. Third, there must be some act attributable to the felons which causes death. It is not sufficient that death be only temporarily related to commission of the felony. Death must be directly related in time, place, and causal connection to the commission of the felony; the felony or acts in furtherance thereof must contribute to cause the death to constitute a "killing" within the felony-murder statute.

Adhering to this causation requirement, the Pennsylvania court reversed a murder conviction where the cofelon was killed by police bullets. The court noted two problems with affirming the conviction. First, the act causing death was not committed by any of the felons, but rather by a third party. Indeed, the killing in *Redline* was justifiable because it was committed by a police officer in the line of duty; a justifiable homicide could not rationally support a murder charge which must involve an unlawful killing. Second, the killing was inflicted not by one in furtherance of the felonious undertaking, but by one opposed to it. Thus, the act that caused the death did not occur as a result of the effort to further the felony.

The *Redline* limitation was approved and adopted by the Virginia Supreme Court in Wooden v. Commonwealth, 222 Va. 758, 763–64, 284 S.E.2d 811, 815 (1981). In *Wooden,* the defendant was convicted of two counts of felony-murder. One of the men killed was the victim of a robbery in which Wooden participated; the other was a cofelon who was killed by the victim before he died. The court held that under the reasoning of *Redline,* no malice could be imputed to the defendant for the death of her cofelon because the killing was done by a third party who was resisting, not furthering the felony. Further, because the victim of the felony killed the cofelon and such a killing was justifiable, no unlawful homicide could be attributed to the felon.

In the present case, King and Bailey were in the airplane to further the felony of possession of marijuana with the intent to distribute. They were flying over the mountains while committing the felony. The time and the place of the death were closely connected with the felony. However, no causal connection exists between the felony of drug distribution and the killing by a plane crash. Thus, no basis exists to find that the accidental death was part or a result of the criminal enterprise. In the felony-murder cases cited above, death, to be considered an "accidental killing" within the statute, has resulted from a particular act which was an integral part of the felony or an act in direct furtherance of the felony—shooting a gun, striking a match, distributing cocaine. In this case, there is no such act which caused the death. Thus, there has been no homicide, or unlawful killing by another, for which a cofelon can be held accountable. Bailey, who was flying the plane at the time of the crash, was not killed by King or by any act of King which was in furtherance of the felony. We see no "act of killing" which we can attribute to King or to the felony. The felony-murder rule does not exist to enable courts to impute "the act of killing" where an accidental death results from fortuitous circumstances and the only connection with the felony is temporal.

The cause of Bailey's death was Bailey's piloting and adverse weather conditions. The accident stemmed not from the possession or distribution of drugs, but from fog, low cloud cover, pilot error, and inexperience. Had Bailey and King been transporting drugs in an automobile when they encountered heavy fog and Bailey, not seeing a curve, had driven off the mountain, the legal consequences would be the same. The commission of the felony merely accounted for their presence at the location of the accident, and nothing directly related to the commission of the felony caused the accident. Thus, flying into the mountain was not a direct consequence of the felony. Had the plane been flying low or recklessly to avoid detection, for example, the crash would be a consequence or action which was directly intended to further the felony and a different result might obtain. See People v. Ulsh, 27 Cal.Rptr. 408, 416–17, 211 Cal.App.2d 258, 271 (1962) (death in automobile accident a consequence of high speed chase during attempted escape after felony).

We adopt the Pennsylvania Supreme Court's analysis in *Redline* that the felony-murder rule provides for imputing malice to an accidental killing; it does not impute the act of killing. Therefore, if the accidental death, in the absence of imputed malice, would not have been a criminal homicide, then the statute does not elevate it to second degree murder and impute culpability for the death to a cofelon. Moreover, we hold that a death which results not from actions of the felons nor from acts directly calculated to further the felony or necessitated by the felony, but from circumstances coincident to the felony, is not a death for which a felony-murder conviction will obtain. "To punish as a murderer, every man who, while committing a heinous offense, causes death by pure misadventure, is a course which evidently adds nothing to the security of human life." Commonwealth ex rel. Smith v. Myers, 438 Pa. 218, 226, 261 A.2d 550, 554 (1970).

The Commonwealth argues that the jury could infer that King's conduct in the commission of the underlying felony was inherently dangerous to human life and that his action of putting the plane in a dangerous position and allowing an unlicensed pilot to fly caused the crash. Accepting without comment the Commonwealth's argument that the evidence established involuntary manslaughter based on King's antecedent negligence, the evidence still establishes no causal relationship between the felony of possession of marijuana and the death by plane crash. If King and Bailey had been transporting legal cargo that day, the crash would still have occurred. It is true, of course, that but for the felony, King and Bailey probably would not have been in the plane. However, criminal liability for felony-murder requires more than a finding that "but for" the felony the parties would not have been present at the time and location of the accidental death. The act or acts causing death must have been directly calculated to further the felony or necessitated by the commission of the felony. Such a causal connection is absent in this case.

* * *

Reversed and dismissed.

Questions

1. Is there any justification for a stricter causal requirement in felony-murder? Suppose, unknown to the participants, a sidewalk grating over a shaft to a basement has so rusted that it is ready to collapse if anyone steps on it, and (a) X, intending to kill V, shoots him, but not fatally, and the wounded V staggers onto the grating and falls to his death; or (b) Y recklessly drives his car up on the sidewalk, and V steps on the grating to get out of the way and falls to his death; or (c) Z, intending to rob V, requires him to stand on the grating, where the light is good enough for Z to see what money he has, and V falls to his death. Is X, Y, or Z properly responsible criminally for V's death?

2. Even if some tightening of the causal requirement in felony-murder is proper, does it make sense to refuse to apply the rule where, in an exchange of gunfire in the course of a felony, the fatal shot is fired by a non-felon in response to the situation created by the felon? Is this a case of an illogical limitation, which is nevertheless acceptable because it mitigates the effect of a bad rule, or can you defend the limitation on its merits in terms of justice or utility?

2. The Misdemeanor-Manslaughter Rule

State v. Yowell

Supreme Court of Kansas, 1959.
184 Kan. 352, 336 P.2d 841.

PARKER, CHIEF JUSTICE.

The defendant, Ernest L. Yowell, was arrested, tried, convicted and sentenced on a charge of manslaughter in the fourth degree in violation of G.S.1949, 21–420. He appeals from the overruling of his motion for a new trial and from the judgment.

* * *

On the morning of January 4, 1958, at about 7:30 a.m., defendant, whose license to drive a motor vehicle upon the public highways had been suspended pursuant to the laws of this state, was driving his automobile in an easterly direction on U.S. Highway 54 on the outskirts, but within the legal limits of the city of Wichita. The highway at that point was unposted and daytime speed limit was limited to seventy miles per hour. Mrs. Betty J. Wise, a resident of Clearwater, was ahead of defendant and driving her automobile east on the same highway, en route to Wichita. Defendant overtook Mrs. Wise and attempted to pass her automobile. In making this attempt he struck the rear end of the Wise car, just to the left of the center of such vehicle. * * * As a result of the collision Mrs. Wise was thrown from her car and sustained a brain concussion which resulted in her immediate death.

* * * It suffices to say we have carefully reviewed the record and find ample substantial competent evidence on which the jury in reaching its verdict would have been warranted in finding that at the time of the accident the defendant was driving under the influence of intoxicating liquor, driving at a speed exceeding the lawful speed limit at the time and place in question, and driving at a rate of speed that was greater than reasonable and prudent under the circumstances. * * *

* * *

At the close of the trial the court instructed the jury in writing. Only one of the instructions is involved on appeal. It is instruction No. 3 which reads:

> "The law of Kansas provides that the killing of a human being resulting from unlawful conduct such as driving after suspension and revocation of a driver's license, or driving while under the influence of intoxicating liquor, or driving beyond the lawful speed limit, or driving at a speed greater than was reasonable and prudent under the circumstances, shall be deemed manslaughter in the fourth degree, provided that the death would not have occurred except for the unlawful conduct. It is for the jury to determine whether the defendant was engaging in any unlawful conduct and whether the death would not have occurred except for such unlawful conduct.
>
> "The law also provides that the killing of a human being resulting from conduct amounting to recklessness or a disregard of or indifference to life or the safety of others, although no harm may have been intended, shall be deemed manslaughter in the fourth degree provided that death would not have resulted except for such conduct. It is for the jury to determine whether the defendant was engaging in any such conduct and whether the death would not have occurred except for such conduct."

* * *

Limited to portions of instruction No. 3, now under consideration, contentions advanced by appellant in support of his position the instruction is erroneous may be summarized in the following manner: 1. The court in effect, in such instruction, informed the jury that they could properly find that the death of Mrs. Wise resulted from the presence of the appellant upon the highway while his driver's license had been suspended. 2. The lack of a driver's license had nothing whatsoever to do with the circumstances surrounding the accident. 3. Had appellant had a driver's license that would not have avoided the involved accident. 4. Appellant's driver's license suspension had no causal relationship whatsoever to the circumstances of the accident. 5. The fact that his license had been suspended did not and would not have constituted in and of itself actionable negligence or warranted recovery of damages in a civil action under Kansas decisions.

* * *

Turning to appellee's contentions it may be conceded that the first paragraph of instruction 3 was based on syllabus par. 4 of the landmark case of State v. Custer, 129 Kan. 381, 282 P. 1071, 67 A.L.R. 909, which reads:

> "If death results from unlawful conduct amounting to misdemeanor denounced by statute for the purpose of protecting human life and safety, and the death would not have resulted except for the unlawful conduct, the killing would be manslaughter at common law." (Syl. par. 4.)

* * * Custer was charged with driving an automobile on a public highway at an unlawful rate of speed, thus causing the death of another on the highway (The unlawful act being the direct cause of the death) whereas—as here—he was not only charged with three acts of that character but also charged with an additional act, driving after suspension and revocation of a driver's license, all four of which acts were alleged to have so caused his automobile to strike another vehicle on a public highway and result in the death of Betty J. Wise. In this connection we pause to note, that in three of our subsequent decisions (State v. Spohr, 171 Kan. 129, 132, 230 P.2d 1013; State v. Champ, 172 Kan. 737, 242 P.2d 1070; State v. Gibler, 182 Kan. 578, 322 P.2d 829), involving prosecutions for manslaughter in the fourth degree, where the above stated rule of the Custer case is followed and quoted at length, it appears the only penal infractions in question involved acts having a direct or causal bearing on the collision resulting in death. * * *

From what has been heretofore stated it becomes obvious appellant's contentions respecting the sufficiency of the instruction raises questions of first impression in this jurisdiction. In their determination, keeping in mind that this court, under facts disclosing acts consisting of penal delinquencies which have a direct bearing on death resulting therefrom, is committed to the rule announced in syllabus par. 4 of the Custer case, it may be helpful to refer to decisions of other states touching the relationship of statutory violations to the cause of death in prosecutions for manslaughter.

At the outset, it goes without saying, that throughout the years there have been many involuntary manslaughter cases where the death was accompanied by the violation of some positive law. Whether the violator is guilty of manslaughter when he has violated such a law has long presented complex problems and the courts of the land have resorted to various lines of reasoning in order to reach a just and proper result. A review of these cases reveals several rules to which we shall presently refer.

One line of cases discusses the distinction between acts *malum prohibitum* and *malum in se.*

The distinction made by the foregoing decisions is stated in Keller v. State, 155 Tenn. 633, 299 S.W. 803, 59 A.L.R. 685, where it is said:

> " * * * It was shown in Holder v. State, supra [152 Tenn. 390, 277 S.W. 900], that distinction was taken in the authorities in this connection between unlawful acts *malum prohibitum* and unlawful acts *malum in se.* Acts of the former class do not supply the criminal intent necessary to render one punishable for a homicide, unless the killing be the natural or probable result of the act. Acts of

the latter class, *malum in se,* do supply the criminal intent." (155 Tenn. at page 636, 299 S.W. at page 804.)

* * *

The rule and the reasons for its pronouncement are well-illustrated in State v. Hupf, 9 Terry 254, 48 Del. 254, 101 A.2d 355, by the following statement:

> "We agree that by no means all the American authorities are in accord with the common-law rule. Some courts have imported into the law of involuntary manslaughter a distinction, in respect of unlawful acts, between one *malum prohibitum* and one *malum in se.* Such a distinction has never been recognized in our cases, and we see no reason to adopt it. To do so would be to introduce confusion and uncertainty into a rule of law now plain and understandable. There are no doubt many regulations applicable to motor vehicles the violation of which does not evince moral turpitude; but it does not seem too much to ask that the automobile driver be held to strict accountability for violation of regulations prescribed by the law-making power in the interest of public order and safety, if that violation is the cause of the death of another. A careful application by the courts of the doctrine of proximate cause, and the common sense of the jury, should prevent any undue hardship in the enforcement of the common-law rule." (48 Del. at page 265, 101 A.2d at page 360.)

And in State v. Nichols, 34 N.M. 639, 288 P. 407, which reads:

> "It would, in our opinion, be ridiculous to say that any accidental killing resulting indirectly or remotely while committing an unlawful act is involuntary manslaughter. Our statutes make it unlawful for a person to drive an automobile without a red tail-light or without first having obtained a license. If, while committing such an unlawful act alone, a person is accidently and unavoidably run over and killed, the unlawful act could have no bearing whatsoever upon the killing. Would any one contend that the driver be guilty of involuntary manslaughter? Our statutes also make the carrying of a deadly weapon an unlawful act. What has the mere carrying of the deadly weapon to do with the unlawful killing of a person with said weapon? The mere carrying of the weapon unaccompanied by some other act or factor could not result in death. It is our opinion that our statute contemplates that the unlawful act must be the proximate cause of the homicide. In this view we are almost uniformally [sic] supported by textwriters and decisions throughout the United States." (34 N.M. at page 641, 288 P. at page 407.)

Another rule is that some causal connection and/or legal relation between the commission of the unlawful act and the death must appear and that there must be more than a mere coincidence of time and place between the wrongful act and the death. For cases from courts adhering to this rule see Thompson v. State of Florida, 108 Fla. 370, 372, 146 So. 201; Maxon v. State, 177 Wis. 379, 385, 187 N.W. 753, 21 A.L.R. 1484; Votre v. State,

192 Ind. 684, 685, 686, 138 N.E. 257; People v. Mulcahy, 318 Ill. 332, 149 N.E. 266.

The basis for this rule is well outlined in * * * the opinion of Votre v. State, 192 Ind. 684, 138 N.E. 257, which reads:

> "The court cannot say as a matter of law that death is the usual or probable result of taking a drink of intoxicating liquor. It is only for the natural or probable result of a wrongful act that a wrongdoer is liable.
>
> "To constitute the crime of manslaughter, there must be such legal relation between the commission of the unlawful act and the homicide, that it logically follows that the homicide occurred as a concomitant part of the perpetration of, or in furtherance of an attempt to commit, the unlawful act. Therefore it follows that death must be the natural result and the probable consequence of the commission of the unlawful act upon which the homicide is based. (Citing cases.)" (192 Ind. at pages 685, 686, 138 N.E. at page 257.)

For a general statement of such rule see 3 Wharton's Criminal Law and Procedure 154, § 985 which states:

> "It must be shown that the death must have been the natural and probable consequence of the negligent or unlawful act, and not the result of misadventure, or of an independent intervening cause, in which accused did not participate. There must be something more than a mere coincidence of time and place between the wrongful act and the death. * * *"

An additional rule is that if the defendant committed the unlawful act in question under conditions that were dangerous to the deceased, the criminality consisting of the two elements of the unlawfulness of the act and the unlawfulness and dangers in the mode of its execution constitute manslaughter (Estell v. State, 51 N.J.L. 182, 17 A. 118). Another decision, dealing with the same subject, is State v. DiLorenzo, 138 Conn. 281, 83 A.2d 479.

For still another rule, particularly applicable in the instant case because the opinion of the case in which it is announced deals with a prosecution for manslaughter, based on operating an automobile without an operator's license, see Commonwealth v. Piper, 183 Pa.Super. 229, 130 A.2d 195, where it is said:

> "Operating an automobile without an operator's license, or permitting another without such license to operate one's automobile, does not alone make the parties guilty of involuntary manslaughter if the car is involved in a fatal accident. The unlawful act must be something more than a remote unit in a sequence of events culminating in a fatality, or an attendant condition without which the death could not have occurred; the death must be the natural result or probable consequence of the unlawful act. If the appellant was blameless except for the violation of Section 622 of the Motor Vehicle Code [75 P.S. § 233], supra (requiring a driver's license), he

was not guilty of involuntary manslaughter. (Citing cases.)" (183 Pa.Super. at page 233, 130 A.2d at page 197.)

A decision of like import, both from the standpoint of facts and principles involved, as well as conclusions there reached, is Commonwealth v. Williams, 133 Pa.Super. 104, 1 A.2d 812.

In connection with the foregoing subject it should perhaps be stated that, in our extended review of the authorities, the two cases last above cited are the only reported appellate court decisions we have been able to find, dealing with prosecutions for manslaughter based on a statute making it unlawful to drive an automobile without an operator's and/or driver's license.

Once again directing attention to the rule in the Custer case, as directly applied to the case at bar, appellee's position, as we understand it, is that such rule must be construed as compelling a conclusion that, standing alone, the mere violation of 8–262, supra, which was conceded by appellant on cross-examination, followed by the death of Mrs. Wise as a result of the involved accident, was sufficient to convict appellant of manslaughter, as defined in 21–420; hence the trial court was warranted in instructing the jury the law of Kansas provides the killing of a human being resulting from unlawful conduct such as driving after suspension and revocation of a driver's license shall be deemed manslaughter in the fourth degree, provided that death would not have occurred except for such unlawful conduct.

Upon careful consideration and analysis of the opinion in the Custer case, the rule announced in syllabus par. 4 thereof, and the previously cited decisions from foreign jurisdictions, we are unable to agree with appellee's position on either of the two points last above mentioned.

With respect to the first of such points we believe the import to be given the rule announced in syllabus par. 4 of the Custer case, under what is there said, as well as what is held in other jurisdictions, is that, though the act, made unlawful by statute (here driving a motor vehicle on the highway after suspension and revocation of a driver's license in violation of 8–262, supra), is an act merely *malum prohibitum* and is ordinarily insufficient, still, when such an act is accompanied by negligence or further wrong, so as to be, in its nature, dangerous, or so as to manifest a reckless disregard for the safety of others, then it may be sufficient to supply the wrongful intent essential to criminal homicide, and, when such act results in the death of another, may constitute manslaughter as defined in G.S.1949, 21–420.

As to the second point, * * * the instruction * * * was objected to in such a way as to direct the trial court's attention to the fact appellant was claiming that, since he had admitted suspension and revocation of his driver's license, the legal effect of such instruction was to advise the jury it could convict him of manslaughter simply because he was driving on the highway at the time of the involved accident without a driver's license. We * * * are convinced that, under the rule announced in the preceding paragraph of this opinion, the trial court, when faced by such objection, was required to amplify the portion of the instruction now under consideration by advising the jury as to the matters, heretofore stated in the preceding paragraph, such jury was required to consider before it could find the appellant guilty of manslaughter because of his violation of 8–262, supra; and that its failure to do so resulted in reversible error.

* * *

Questions

1. It is a statutory misdemeanor to operate a multi-storied rooming house without providing an outside fire escape which is maintained in good condition. A, the owner of such a rooming house, permits the fire escape to fall into a state of serious disrepair; most of the bolts have rusted through. In a heavy storm the fire escape is blown down and a piece of it is blown across a railroad track, a half a block from the house, where the debris derails a freight train, causing the death of the engineer. Can A be held liable on a misdemeanor-manslaughter theory?

2. It is a misdemeanor for a pharmacist to sell a misbranded or mislabeled drug, whether or not he knows or should know of the misbranding or mislabeling. Pharmacist B fills a prescription calling for sodium citrate from a bottle so marked, but which in fact contains poisonous sodium nitrate, a fact which B did not know and could not reasonably be expected to know. The medicine is administered to a child, causing his death. Misdemeanor-manslaughter? See People v. Stuart, 47 Cal.2d 167, 302 P.2d 5 (1956).

3. The Model Penal Code does not have a misdemeanor-manslaughter provision. See § 210.3, comment 7. Is this sound?

G. THE DEATH PENALTY

Furman v. Georgia

Supreme Court of the United States, 1972.
408 U.S. 238, 92 S.Ct. 2726, 33 L.Ed.2d 346.

PER CURIAM.

Petitioner in No. 69–5003 was convicted of murder in Georgia and was sentenced to death pursuant to Ga.Code Ann. § 26–1005 (Supp.1971) (effective prior to July 1, 1969). 225 Ga. 253, 167 S.E.2d 628 (1969). Petitioner in No. 69–5030 was convicted of rape in Georgia and was sentenced to death pursuant to Ga.Code Ann. § 26–1302 (Supp.1971) (effective prior to July 1, 1969). 225 Ga. 790, 171 S.E.2d 501 (1969). Petitioner in No. 69–5031 was convicted of rape in Texas and was sentenced to death pursuant to Vernon's Tex.Penal Code, Art. 1189 (1961). 447 S.W.2d 932 (Ct.Crim.App.1969). Certiorari was granted limited to the following question: "Does the imposition and carrying out of the death penalty in [these cases] constitute cruel and unusual punishment in violation of the Eighth and Fourteenth Amendments?" 403 U.S. 952, 91 S.Ct. 2287, 29 L.Ed.2d 863 (1971). The Court holds that the imposition and carrying out of the death penalty in these cases constitute cruel and unusual punishment in violation of the Eighth and Fourteenth Amendments. The judgment in each case is therefore reversed insofar as it leaves undisturbed the death sentence imposed, and the cases are remanded for further proceedings. So ordered.

Judgment in each case reversed in part and cases remanded.

MR. JUSTICE DOUGLAS, MR. JUSTICE BRENNAN, MR. JUSTICE STEWART, MR. JUSTICE WHITE, and MR. JUSTICE MARSHALL have filed separate opinions in support of the judgments.

THE CHIEF JUSTICE, MR. JUSTICE BLACKMUN, MR. JUSTICE POWELL, and MR. JUSTICE REHNQUIST have filed separate dissenting opinions.

MR. JUSTICE DOUGLAS, concurring.

* * *

Jackson, a black, convicted of the rape of a white woman, was 21 years old. A court-appointed psychiatrist said that Jackson was of average education and average intelligence, that he was not an imbecile, or schizophrenic, or psychotic, that his traits were the product of environmental influences, and that he was competent to stand trial. Jackson had entered the house after the husband left for work. He held scissors against the neck of the wife, demanding money. She could find none and a struggle ensued for the scissors, a battle which she lost; and she was then raped, Jackson keeping the scissors pressed against her neck. While there did not appear to be any long-term traumatic impact on the victim, she was bruised and abrased in the struggle but was not hospitalized. Jackson was a convict who had escaped from a work gang in the area, a result of a three-year sentence for auto theft. He was at large for three days and during that time had committed several other offenses—burglary, auto theft, and assault and battery.

Furman, a black, killed a householder while seeking to enter the home at night. Furman shot the deceased through a closed door. He was 26 years old and had finished the sixth grade in school. Pending trial, he was committed to the Georgia Central State Hospital for a psychiatric examination on his plea of insanity tendered by court-appointed counsel. The superintendent reported that a unanimous staff diagnostic conference had concluded "that this patient should retain his present diagnosis of Mental Deficiency, Mild to Moderate, with Psychotic Episodes associated with Convulsive Disorder." The physicians agreed that "at present the patient is not psychotic, but he is not capable of cooperating with his counsel in the preparation of his defense"; and the staff believed "that he is in need of further psychiatric hospitalization and treatment."

Later, the superintendent reported that the staff diagnosis was Mental Deficiency, Mild to Moderate, with Psychotic Episodes associated with Convulsive Disorder. He concluded, however, that Furman was "not psychotic at present, knows right from wrong and is able to cooperate with his counsel in preparing his defense."

Branch, a black, entered the rural home of a 65-year-old widow, a white, while she slept and raped her, holding his arm against her throat. Thereupon he demanded money and for 30 minutes or more the widow searched for money, finding little. As he left, Jackson said if the widow told anyone what happened, he would return and kill her. The record is barren of any medical or psychiatric evidence showing injury to her as a result of Branch's attack.

He had previously been convicted of felony theft and found to be a borderline mental deficient and well below the average IQ of Texas prison inmates. He had the equivalent of five and a half years of grade school education. He had a "dull intelligence" and was in the lowest fourth percentile of his class.

We cannot say from facts disclosed in these records that these defendants were sentenced to death because they were black. Yet our task is not restricted to an effort to divine what motives impelled these death penalties. Rather, we deal with a system of law and of justice that leaves to the uncontrolled discretion of judges or juries the determination whether defendants committing these crimes should die or be imprisoned. Under these laws no standards govern the selection of the penalty. People live or die, dependent on the whim of one man or of 12.

* * *

In a Nation committed to equal protection of the laws there is no permissible "caste" aspect of law enforcement. Yet we know that the discretion of judges and juries in imposing the death penalty enables the penalty to be selectively applied, feeding prejudices against the accused if he is poor and despised, and lacking political clout, or if he is a member of a suspect or unpopular minority, and saving those who by social position may be in a more protected position. * * *

The high service rendered by the "cruel and unusual" punishment clause of the Eighth Amendment is to require legislatures to write penal laws that are evenhanded, nonselective, and nonarbitrary, and to require judges to see to it that general laws are not applied sparsely, selectively, and spottily to unpopular groups.

A law that stated that anyone making more than $50,000 would be exempt from the death penalty would plainly fall, as would a law that in terms said that blacks, those who never went beyond the fifth grade in school, those who made less than $3,000 a year, or those who were unpopular or unstable should be the only people executed. A law which in the overall view reaches that result in practice has no more sanctity than a law which in terms provides the same.

Thus, these discretionary statutes are unconstitutional in their operation. They are pregnant with discrimination and discrimination is an ingredient not compatible with the idea of equal protection of the laws that is implicit in the ban on "cruel and unusual" punishments.

* * *

MR. JUSTICE BRENNAN, concurring.

* * *

II

* * *

There are, then, four principles by which we may determine whether a particular punishment is "cruel and unusual." The primary principle, which I believe supplies the essential predicate for the application of the others, is that a punishment must not by its severity be degrading to human dignity. The paradigm violation of this principle would be the infliction of a torturous punishment of the type that the Clause has always prohibited. Yet "[i]t is unlikely that any State at this moment in history[,]" Robinson v. California,

370 U.S., at 666, 82 S.Ct., at 1420, would pass a law providing for the infliction of such a punishment. Indeed, no such punishment has ever been before this Court. The same may be said of the other principles. It is unlikely that this Court will confront a severe punishment that is obviously inflicted in wholly arbitrary fashion; no State would engage in a reign of blind terror. Nor is it likely that this Court will be called upon to review a severe punishment that is clearly and totally rejected throughout society; no legislature would be able even to authorize the infliction of such a punishment. Nor, finally, is it likely that this Court will have to consider a severe punishment that is patently unnecessary; no State today would inflict a severe punishment knowing that there was no reason whatever for doing so. In short, we are unlikely to have occasion to determine that a punishment is fatally offensive under any one principle.

Since the Bill of Rights was adopted, this Court has adjudged only three punishments to be within the prohibition of the Clause. See Weems v. United States, 217 U.S. 349, 30 S.Ct. 544, 54 L.Ed. 793 (1910) (12 years in chains at hard and painful labor); Trop v. Dulles, 356 U.S. 86, 78 S.Ct. 590, 2 L.Ed.2d 630 (1958) (expatriation); Robinson v. California, 370 U.S. 660, 82 S.Ct. 1417, 8 L.Ed.2d 758 (1962) (imprisonment for narcotics addiction). Each punishment, of course, was degrading to human dignity, but of none could it be said conclusively that it was fatally offensive under one or the other of the principles. Rather, these "cruel and unusual punishments" seriously implicated several of the principles, and it was the application of the principles in combination that supported the judgment. * * *

III

The punishment challenged in these cases is death. * * *

* * *

The unusual severity of death is manifested most clearly in its finality and enormity. Death, in these respects, is in a class by itself. Expatriation, for example, is a punishment that "destroys for the individual the political existence that was centuries in the development[,]" that "strips the citizen of his status in the national and international political community[,]" and that puts "[h]is very existence" in jeopardy. Expatriation thus inherently entails "the total destruction of the individual's status in organized society." Id., at 101, 78 S.Ct., at 598. "In short, the expatriate has lost the right to have rights." Id., at 102, 78 S.Ct., at 598. Yet, demonstrably, expatriation is not "a fate worse than death." Id., at 125, 78 S.Ct., at 611 (Frankfurter, J., dissenting). Although death, like expatriation, destroys the individual's "political existence" and his "status in organized society," it does more, for, unlike expatriation, death also destroys "[h]is very existence." There is, too, at least the possibility that the expatriate will in the future regain "the right to have rights." Death forecloses even that possibility.

Death is truly an awesome punishment. The calculated killing of a human being by the State involves, by its very nature, a denial of the executed person's humanity. The contrast with the plight of a person punished by imprisonment is evident. An individual in prison does not lose "the right to have rights." A prisoner retains, for example, the constitutional rights to the free exercise of religion, to be free of cruel and unusual punishments, and to treatment as a "person" for purposes of due process of law and the equal protection of the laws. A prisoner remains a member of the human family. Moreover, he retains the right of access to the courts. His punishment is not irrevocable. Apart from the common charge, grounded upon the recognition of human fallibility, that the punishment of death must inevitably be inflicted upon innocent men, we know that death has been the lot of men whose convictions were unconstitutionally secured in view of later, retroactively applied, holdings of this Court. The punishment itself may have been unconstitutionally inflicted, see Witherspoon v. Illinois, 391 U.S. 510, 88 S.Ct. 1770, 20 L.Ed.2d 776 (1968), yet the finality of death precludes relief. An executed person has indeed "lost the right to have rights." As one 19th century proponent of punishing criminals by death declared, "When a man is hung, there is an end of our relations with him. His execution is a way of saying, 'You are not fit for this world, take your chance elsewhere.' " [39]

In comparison to all other punishments today, then, the deliberate extinguishment of human life by the State is uniquely degrading to human dignity. I would not hesitate to hold, on that ground alone, that death is today a "cruel and unusual" punishment, were it not that death is a punishment of longstanding usage and acceptance in this country. I therefore turn to the second principle—that the State may not arbitrarily inflict an unusually severe punishment.

The outstanding characteristic of our present practice of punishing criminals by death is the infrequency with which we resort to it. The evidence is conclusive that death is not the ordinary punishment for any crime.

There has been a steady decline in the infliction of this punishment in every decade since the 1930's, the earliest period for which accurate statistics are available. In the 1930's, executions averaged 167 per year; in the 1940's, the average was 128; in the 1950's, it was 72; and in the years 1960–1962, it was 48. There have been a total of 46 executions since then, 36 of them in 1963–1964. Yet our population and the number of capital crimes committed have increased greatly over the past four decades. The contemporary rarity of the infliction of this punishment is thus the end result of a long-continued decline. That rarity is plainly revealed by an examination of the years 1961–1970, the last 10-year period for which statistics are available. During that time, an average of 106 death sentences was imposed each year. Not nearly that number, however, could be carried out, for many were precluded by commutations to life or a term of years, transfers to mental institutions because of insanity, resentences to life or a term of years, grants of new trials and orders for resentencing, dismissals of indictments and reversals of convictions, and deaths by suicide and natural causes. On January 1, 1961, the death row population was 219; on December 31, 1970, it was

39. Stephen, Capital Punishments, 69 Fraser's Magazine 753, 763 (1864).

608; during that span, there were 135 executions. Consequently, had the 389 additions to death row also been executed the annual average would have been 52. In short, the country might, at most, have executed one criminal each week. In fact, of course, far fewer were executed. Even before the moratorium on executions began in 1967, executions totaled only 42 in 1961 and 47 in 1962, an average of less than one per week; the number dwindled to 21 in 1963, to 15 in 1964, and to seven in 1965; in 1966, there was one execution, and in 1967, there were two.

When a country of over 200 million people inflicts an unusually severe punishment no more than 50 times a year, the inference is strong that the punishment is not being regularly and fairly applied. To dispel it would indeed require a clear showing of nonarbitrary infliction.

Although there are no exact figures available, we know that thousands of murders and rapes are committed annually in States where death is an authorized punishment for those crimes. However the rate of infliction is characterized—as "freakishly" or "spectacularly" rare, or simply as rare—it would take the purest sophistry to deny that death is inflicted in only a minute fraction of these cases. How much rarer, after all, could the infliction of death be?

* * *

* * * When the rate of infliction is at this low level, it is highly implausible that only the worst criminals or the criminals who commit the worst crimes are selected for this punishment. No one has yet suggested a rational basis that could differentiate in those terms the few who die from the many who go to prison. Crimes and criminals simply do not admit of a distinction that can be drawn so finely as to explain, on that ground, the execution of such a tiny sample of those eligible. Certainly the laws that provide for this punishment do not attempt to draw that distinction; all cases to which the laws apply are necessarily "extreme." Nor is the distinction credible in fact. If, for example, petitioner Furman or his crime illustrates the "extreme," then nearly all murderers and their murders are also "extreme." Furthermore, our procedures in death cases, rather than resulting in the selection of "extreme" cases for this punishment, actually sanction an arbitrary selection. For this Court has held that juries may, as they do, make the decision whether to impose a death sentence wholly unguided by standards governing that decision. * * *

* * *

When there is a strong probability that an unusually severe and degrading punishment is being inflicted arbitrarily, we may well expect that society will disapprove of its infliction. I turn, therefore, to the third principle. An examination of the history and present operation of the American practice of punishing criminals by death reveals that this punishment has been almost totally rejected by contemporary society.

* * *

Our practice of punishing criminals by death has changed greatly over the years. One significant change has been in our methods of inflicting death. * * *

Also significant is the drastic decrease in the crimes for which the punishment of death is actually inflicted. While esoteric capital crimes remain on the books, since 1930 murder and rape have accounted for nearly 99% of the total executions, and murder alone for about 87%. In addition, the crime of capital murder has itself been limited. As the Court noted in McGautha v. California, 402 U.S., at 198, 91 S.Ct., at 1462, 1463, there was in this country a "rebellion against the common-law rule imposing a mandatory death sentence on all convicted murderers." Initially, that rebellion resulted in legislative definitions that distinguished between degrees of murder, retaining the mandatory death sentence only for murder in the first degree. Yet "[t]his new legislative criterion for isolating crimes appropriately punishable by death soon proved as unsuccessful as the concept of 'malice aforethought[,]' " ibid., the common-law means of separating murder from manslaughter. Not only was the distinction between degrees of murder confusing and uncertain in practice, but even in clear cases of first-degree murder juries continued to take the law into their own hands: if they felt that death was an inappropriate punishment, "they simply refused to convict of the capital offense." Id., at 199, 91 S.Ct., at 1463. The phenomenon of jury nullification thus remained to counteract the rigors of mandatory death sentences. Bowing to reality, "legislatures did not try, as before, to refine further the definition of capital homicides. Instead they adopted the method of forthrightly granting juries the discretion which they had been exercising in fact." Ibid. In consequence, virtually all death sentences today are discretionarily imposed. Finally, it is significant that nine States no longer inflict the punishment of death under any circumstances, and five others have restricted it to extremely rare crimes.

* * * Juries, "express[ing] the conscience of the community on the ultimate question of life or death," Witherspoon v. Illinois, 391 U.S., at 519, 88 S.Ct., at 1775 have been able to bring themselves to vote for death in a mere 100 or so cases among the thousands tried each year where the punishment is available. Governors, elected by and acting for us, have regularly commuted a substantial number of those sentences. And it is our society that insists upon due process of law to the end that no person will be unjustly put to death, thus ensuring that many more of those sentences will not be carried out. In sum, we have made death a rare punishment today.

* * *

The final principle to be considered is that an unusually severe and degrading punishment may not be excessive in view of the purposes for which it is inflicted. This principle, too, is related to the others. When there is a strong probability that the State is arbitrarily inflicting an unusually severe punishment that is subject to grave societal doubts, it is likely also that the punishment cannot be shown to be serving any penal purpose that could not be served equally well by some less severe punishment.

The States' primary claim is that death is a necessary punishment because it prevents the commission of capital crimes more effectively than any less severe punishment. The first part of this claim is that the infliction of death is necessary to stop the individuals executed from committing further crimes. The sufficient answer to this is that if a criminal convicted of a capital crime poses a danger to society, effective administration of the State's pardon and parole laws can delay or deny his release from prison, and techniques of isolation can eliminate or minimize the danger while he remains confined.

The more significant argument is that the threat of death prevents the commission of capital crimes because it deters potential criminals who would not be deterred by the threat of imprisonment. The argument is not based upon evidence that the threat of death is a superior deterrent. Indeed, as my Brother Marshall establishes, the available evidence uniformly indicates, although it does not conclusively prove, that the threat of death has no greater deterrent effect than the threat of imprisonment. The States argue, however, that they are entitled to rely upon common human experience, and that experience, they say, supports the conclusion that death must be a more effective deterrent than any less severe punishment. Because people fear death the most, the argument runs, the threat of death must be the greatest deterrent.

* * *

* * * Proponents of this argument necessarily admit that its validity depends upon the existence of a system in which the punishment of death is invariably and swiftly imposed. Our system, of course, satisfies neither condition. A rational person contemplating a murder or rape is confronted, not with the certainty of a speedy death, but with the slightest possibility that he will be executed in the distant future. The risk of death is remote and improbable; in contrast, the risk of long-term imprisonment is near and great. In short, whatever the speculative validity of the assumption that the threat of death is a superior deterrent, there is no reason to believe that as currently administered the punishment of death is necessary to deter the commission of capital crimes. * * *

* * *

In sum, the punishment of death is inconsistent with all four principles: Death is an unusually severe and degrading punishment; there is a strong probability that it is inflicted arbitrarily; its rejection by contemporary society is virtually total; and there is no reason to believe that it serves any penal purpose more effectively than the less severe punishment of imprisonment. The function of these principles is to enable a court to determine whether a punishment comports with human dignity. Death, quite simply, does not.

* * *

MR. JUSTICE STEWART, concurring.

* * *

Legislatures—state and federal—have sometimes specified that the penalty of death shall be the mandatory punishment for every person convicted of engaging in certain designated criminal conduct. Congress, for example, has provided that anyone convicted of acting as a spy for the enemy in time of war shall be put to death. The Rhode Island Legislature has ordained the death penalty for a life term prisoner who commits murder. * * *

If we were reviewing death sentences imposed under these or similar laws, we would be faced with the need to decide whether capital punishment is unconstitutional for all crimes and under all circumstances. We would need to decide whether a legislature—state or federal—could constitutionally determine that certain criminal conduct is so atrocious that societys' interest in deterrence and retribution wholly outweighs any considerations of reform or rehabilitation of the perpetrator, and that, despite the inconclusive empirical evidence,[7] only the automatic penalty of death will provide maximum deterrence.

On that score I would say only that I cannot agree that retribution is a constitutionally impermissible ingredient in the imposition of punishment. The instinct for retribution is part of the nature of man, and channeling that instinct in the administration of criminal justice serves an important purpose in promoting the stability of a society governed by law. When people begin to believe that organized society is unwilling or unable to impose upon criminal offenders the punishment they "deserve," then there are sown the seeds of anarchy—of self-help, vigilante justice, and lynch law.

The constitutionality of capital punishment in the abstract is not, however, before us in these cases. For the Georgia and Texas Legislatures have not provided that the death penalty shall be imposed upon all those who are found guilty of forcible rape. And the Georgia Legislature has not ordained that death shall be the automatic punishment for murder. * * *

Instead, the death sentences now before us are the product of a legal system that brings them, I believe, within the very core of the Eighth Amendment's guarantee against cruel and unusual punishments, a guarantee applicable against the States through the Fourteenth Amendment. Robinson v. California, 370 U.S. 660, 82 S.Ct. 1417, 8 L.Ed.2d 758. In the first place, it is clear that these sentences are "cruel" in the sense that they excessively go beyond, not in degree but in kind, the punishments that the state legislatures have determined to be necessary. Weems v. United States, 217 U.S. 349, 30 S.Ct. 544, 54 L.Ed. 793. In the second place, it is equally clear that these sentences are "unusual" in the sense that the penalty of death is infrequently imposed for murder, and that its imposition for rape is extraordinarily rare. But I do not rest by conclusion upon these two propositions alone.

These death sentences are cruel and unusual in the same way that being struck by lightning is cruel and unusual. For, of all the people convicted of rapes and murders in 1967 and 1968, many just as reprehensible as these, the petitioners are among a capriciously selected random handful upon whom the sentence of death has in fact been imposed. My concurring Brothers have demonstrated that, if any basis can be discerned for the selection of these few to be sentenced to die, it is the constitutionally impermissible basis of race. See McLaughlin v. Florida, 379 U.S. 184, 85 S.Ct. 283, 13 L.Ed.2d 222. But racial discrimination has not been proved, and I put it to one side. I simply conclude that the Eighth and Fourteenth Amendments cannot tolerate the

7. Many statistical studies—comparing crime rates in jurisdictions with and without capital punishment and in jurisdictions before and after abolition of capital punishment—have indicated that there is little, if any, measurable deterrent effect. See II. Bedau, The Death Penalty in America 258–332 (1967 rev.ed.). There remains uncertainty, however, because of the difficulty of identifying and holding constant all other relevant variables.

infliction of a sentence of death under legal systems that permit this unique penalty to be so wantonly and so freakishly imposed.

* * *

MR. JUSTICE WHITE, concurring.

* * *

I begin with what I consider a near truism: that the death penalty could so seldom be imposed that it would cease to be a credible deterrent or measurably to contribute to any other end of punishment in the criminal justice system. It is perhaps true that no matter how infrequently those convicted of rape or murder are executed, the penalty so imposed is not disproportionate to the crime and those executed may deserve exactly what they received. It would also be clear that executed defendants are finally and completely incapacitated from again committing rape or murder or any other crime. But when imposition of the penalty reaches a certain degree of infrequency, it would be very doubtful that any existing general need for retribution would be measurably satisfied. Nor could it be said with confidence that society's need for specific deterrence justifies death for so few when for so many in like circumstances life imprisonment or shorter prison terms are judged sufficient, or that community values are measurably reinforced by authorizing a penalty so rarely invoked.

Most important, a major goal of the criminal law—to deter others by punishing the convicted criminal—would not be substantially served where the penalty is so seldom invoked that it ceases to be the credible threat essential to influence the conduct of others. For present purposes I accept the morality and utility of punishing one person to influence another. I accept also the effectiveness of punishment generally and need not reject the death penalty as a more effective deterrent than a lesser punishment. But common sense and experience tell us that seldom-enforced laws become ineffective measures for controlling human conduct and that the death penalty, unless imposed with sufficient frequency, will make little contribution to deterring those crimes for which it may be exacted.

The imposition and execution of the death penalty are obviously cruel in the dictionary sense. But the penalty has not been considered cruel and unusual punishment in the constitutional sense because it was thought justified by the social ends it was deemed to serve. At the moment that it ceases realistically to further these purposes, however, the emerging question is whether its imposition in such circumstances would violate the Eighth Amendment. It is my view that it would, for its imposition would then be the pointless and needless extinction of life with only marginal contributions to any discernible social or public purposes. A penalty with such negligible returns to the State would be patently excessive and cruel and unusual punishment violative of the Eighth Amendment.

It is also my judgment that this point has been reached with respect to capital punishment as it is presently administered under the statutes involved in these cases. * * *

* * *

MR. JUSTICE MARSHALL, concurring.

* * *

III

* * *

* * * The decisions discussed in the previous section imply that a punishment may be deemed cruel and unusual for any one of four distinct reasons.

First, there are certain punishments that inherently involve so much physical pain and suffering that civilized people cannot tolerate them—e.g., use of the rack, the thumbscrew, or other mont, 144 U.S., at 339, 12 S.Ct., at 699. (Field, J., dissenting). * * *

Second, there are punishments that are unusual, signifying that they were previously unknown as penalties for a given offense. * * * In light of the meager history that does exist, one would suppose that an innovative punishment would probably be constitutional if no more cruel than that punishment which it superseded. We need not decide this question here, however, for capital punishment is certainly not a recent phenomenon.

Third, a penalty may be cruel and unusual because it is excessive and serves no valid legislative purpose. * * *

Fourth, where a punishment is not excessive and serves a valid legislative purpose, it still may be invalid if popular sentiment abhors it. For example, if the evidence clearly demonstrated that capital punishment served valid legislative purposes, such punishment would, nevertheless, be unconstitutional if citizens found it to be morally unacceptable. A general abhorrence on the part of the public would, in effect, equate a modern punishment with those barred since the adoption of the Eighth Amendment. There are no prior cases in this Court striking down a penalty on this ground, but the very notion of changing values requires that we recognize its existence.

It is immediately obvious, then, that since capital punishment is not a recent phenomenon, if it violates the Constitution, it does so because it is excessive or unnecessary, or because it is abhorrent to currently existing moral values.

We must proceed to the history of capital punishment in the United States.

IV

* * *

By 1500, English law recognized eight major capital crimes: treason, petty treason (killing of husband by his wife), murder, larceny, robbery, burglary, rape, and arson. Tudor and Stuart kings added many more crimes to the list of those punishable by death, and by 1688 there were nearly 50. George II (1727–1760) added nearly 36 more, and George III (1760–1820) increased the number by 60.

* * *

Capital punishment was not as common a penalty in the American Colonies. * * *

* * *

During the 1830's, there was a rising tide of sentiment against capital punishment. In 1834, Pennsylvania abolished public executions, and two years later, The Report on Capital Punishment Made to the Maine Legislature was published. It led to a law that prohibited the executive from issuing a warrant for execution within one year after a criminal was sentenced by the courts. The totally discretionary character of the law was at odds with almost all prior practices. The "Maine Law" resulted in little enforcement of the death penalty, which was not surprising since the legislature's idea in passing the law was that the affirmative burden placed on the governor to issue a warrant one full year or more after a trial would be an effective deterrent to exercise of his power. The law spread throughout New England and led to Michigan's being the first State to abolish capital punishment in 1846.

* * *

By 1850, societies for abolition existed in Massachusetts, New York, Pennsylvania, Tennessee, Ohio, Alabama, Louisiana, Indiana, and Iowa. New York, Massachusetts, and Pennsylvania constantly had abolition bills before their legislatures. In 1852, Rhode Island followed in the footsteps of Michigan and partially abolished capital punishment. Wisconsin totally abolished the death penalty the following year. Those States that did not abolish the death penalty greatly reduced its scope, and "[f]ew states outside the South had more than one or two * * * capital offenses" in addition to treason and murder.

But the Civil War halted much of the abolition furor. One historian has said that "[a]fter the Civil War, men's finer sensibilities, which had once been revolted by the execution of a fellow being, seemed hardened and blunted." Some of the attention previously given to abolition was diverted to prison reform. An abolitionist movement still existed, however. * * *

One great success of the abolitionist movement in the period from 1830–1900 was almost complete elimination of mandatory capital punishment. Before the legislatures formally gave juries discretion to refrain from imposing the death penalty, the phenomenon of "jury nullification," in which juries refused to convict in cases in which they believed that death was an inappropriate penalty, was experienced. Tennessee was the first State to give juries discretion, Tenn. Laws 1837–1838, c. 29, but other States quickly followed suit. Then, Rep. Curtis of New York introduced a federal bill that ultimately became law in 1897 which reduced the number of federal capital offenses from 60 to 3 (treason, murder, and rape) and gave the jury sentencing discretion in murder and rape cases.

By 1917 12 States had become abolitionist jurisdictions. But, under the nervous tension of World War I, four of these States reinstituted capital punishment and promising movements in other States came grinding to a halt. During the period following the First World War, the abolitionist movement never regained its momentum.

* * *

At the present time, 41 States, the District of Columbia, and other federal jurisdictions authorize the death penalty for at least one crime. It would be fruitless to attempt here to categorize the approach to capital punishment taken by the various States. It is sufficient to note that murder is the crime most often punished by death, followed by kidnaping and treason. Rape is a capital offense in 16 States and the federal system.

* * *

V

In order to assess whether or not death is an excessive or unnecessary penalty, it is necessary to consider the reasons why a legislature might select it as punishment for one or more offenses, and examine whether less severe penalties would satisfy the legitimate legislative wants as well as capital punishment. If they would, then the death penalty is unnecessary cruelty, and, therefore, unconstitutional.

There are six purposes conceivably served by capital punishment: retribution, deterrence, prevention of repetitive criminal acts, encouragement of guilty pleas and confessions, eugenics, and economy. These are considered *seriatim* below.

A. The concept of retribution is one of the most misunderstood in all of our criminal jurisprudence. The principal source of confusion derives from the fact that, in dealing with the concept, most people confuse the question "why do men in fact punish?" with the question "what justifies men in punishing?" Men may punish for any number of reasons, but the one reason that punishment is morally good or morally justifiable is that someone has broken the law. * * *

* * *

Punishment as retribution has been condemned by scholars for centuries, and the Eighth Amendment itself was adopted to prevent punishment from becoming synonymous with vengeance.

* * * Retribution surely underlies the imposition of some punishment on one who commits a criminal act. But, the fact that *some* punishment may be imposed does not mean that *any* punishment is permissible. If retribution alone could serve as a justification for any particular penalty, then all penalties selected by the legislature would by definition be acceptable means for designating society's moral approbation of a particular act. The "cruel and unusual" language would thus be read out of the Constitution * * *.

* * *

The history of the Eighth Amendment supports only the conclusion that retribution for its own sake is improper.

B. The most hotly contested issue regarding capital punishment is whether it is better than life imprisonment as a deterrent to crime.

While the contrary position has been argued, it is my firm opinion that the death penalty is a more severe sanction than life imprisonment. Admittedly, there are some persons who would rather die than languish in prison for a lifetime. But, whether or not they should be able to choose death as an alternative is a far different question from that presented here—i.e., whether the State can impose death as a punishment. Death is irrevocable; life imprisonment is not. * * *

It must be kept in mind, then, that the question to be considered is not simply whether capital punishment is a deterrent, but whether it is a better deterrent than life imprisonment.

There is no more complex problem than determining the deterrent efficacy of the death penalty. "Capital punishment has obviously failed as a deterrent when a murder is committed. We can number its failures. But we cannot number its successes. No one can ever know how many people have refrained from murder because of the fear of being hanged." This is the nub of the problem and it is exacerbated by the paucity of useful data. * * *

The two strongest arguments in favor of capital punishment as a deterrent are both logical hypotheses devoid of evidentiary support, but persuasive nonetheless. The first proposition was best stated by Sir James Stephen in 1864:

> "No other punishment deters men so effectually from committing crimes as the punishment of death. This is one of those propositions which it is difficult to prove, simply because they are in themselves more obvious than any proof can make them. It is possible to display ingenuity in arguing against it, but that is all. The whole experience of mankind is in the other direction. The threat of instant death is the one to which resort has always been made when there was an absolute necessity for producing some result. * * * No one goes to certain inevitable death except by compulsion. Put the matter the other way. Was there ever yet a criminal who, when sentenced to death and brought out to die, would refuse the offer of a commutation of his sentence for the severest secondary punishment? Surely not. Why is this? It can only be because 'All that a man has will he give for his life.' In any secondary punishment, however, terrible, there is hope; but death is death; its terrors cannot be described more forcibly."

This hypothesis relates to the use of capital punishment as a deterrent for any crime. The second proposition is that "if life imprisonment is the maximum penalty for a crime such as murder, an offender who is serving a life sentence cannot then be deterred from murdering a fellow inmate or a prison officer." This hypothesis advocates a limited deterrent effect under particular circumstances.

Abolitionists attempt to disprove these hypotheses by amassing statistical evidence to demonstrate that there is no correlation between criminal activity and the existence or nonexistence of a capital sanction. Almost all of the evidence involves the crime of murder, since murder is punishable by death in more jurisdictions than are other offenses, and almost 90% of all executions since 1930 have been pursuant to murder convictions.

Thorsten Sellin, one of the leading authorities on capital punishment, has urged that if the death penalty deters prospective murderers, the following hypotheses should be true:

"(a) Murders should be less frequent in states that have the death penalty than in those that have abolished it, other factors being equal. Comparisons of this nature must be made among states that are as alike as possible in all other respects—character of population, social and economic condition, etc.—in order not to introduce factors known to influence murder rates in a serious manner but present in only one of these states.

"(b) Murders should increase when the death penalty is abolished and should decline when it is restored.

"(c) The deterrent effect should be greatest and should therefore affect murder rates most powerfully in those communities where the crime occurred and its consequences are most strongly brought home to the population.

"(d) Law enforcement officers would be safer from murderous attacks in states that have the death penalty than in those without it." (Footnote omitted.)

Sellin's evidence indicates that not one of these propositions is true. This evidence has its problems, however. One is that there are no accurate figures for capital murders; there are only figures on homicides and they, of course, include noncapital killings. A second problem is that certain murders undoubtedly are misinterpreted as accidental deaths or suicides, and there is no way of estimating the number of such undetected crimes. A third problem is that not all homicides are reported. Despite these difficulties, most authorities have assumed that the proportion of capital murders in a State's or nation's homicide statistics remains reasonably constant, and that the homicide statistics are therefore useful.

Sellin's statistics demonstrate that there is no correlation between the murder rate and the presence or absence of the capital sanction. He compares States that have similar characteristics and finds that irrespective of their position on capital punishment, they have similar murder rates. * * *

Sellin also concludes that abolition and/or reintroduction of the death penalty had no effect on the homicide rates of the various States involved. This conclusion is borne out by others who have made similar inquiries and by the experience of other countries. Despite problems with the statistics, Sellin's evidence has been relied upon in international studies of capital punishment.

Statistics also show that the deterrent effect of capital punishment is no greater in those communities where executions take place than in other communities. In fact, there is some evidence that imposition of capital punishment may actually encourage crime, rather than deter it. And, while police and law enforcement officers are the strongest advocates of capital punishment, the evidence is overwhelming that police are no safer in communities that retain the sanction than in those that have abolished it.

There is also a substantial body of data showing that the existence of the death penalty has virtually no effect on the homicide rate in prisons. Most of the persons sentenced to death are murderers, and murderers tend to be model prisoners.

In sum, the only support for the theory that capital punishment is an effective deterrent is found in the hypotheses with which we began and the occasional stories about a specific individual being deterred from doing a contemplated criminal act. These claims of specific deterrence are often spurious, however, and may be more than counterbalanced by the tendency of capital punishment to incite certain crimes.

The United Nations Committee that studied capital punishment found that "[i]t is generally agreed between the retentionists and abolitionists, whatever their opinions about the validity of comparative studies of deterrence, that the data which now exist show no correlation between the existence of capital punishment and lower rates of capital crime."

Despite the fact that abolitionists have not proved non-deterrence beyond a reasonable doubt, they have succeeded in showing by clear and convincing evidence that capital punishment is not necessary as a deterrent to crime in our society. This is all that they must do. We would shirk our judicial responsibilities if we failed to accept the presently existing statistics and demanded more proof. * * *

* * *

C. Much of what must be said about the death penalty as a device to prevent recidivism is obvious—if a murderer is executed, he cannot possibly commit another offense. The fact is, however, that murderers are extremely unlikely to commit other crimes either in prison or upon their release. For the most part, they are first offenders, and when released from prison they are known to become model citizens. Furthermore, most persons who commit capital crimes are not executed. With respect to those who are sentenced to die, it is critical to note that the jury is never asked to determine whether they are likely to be recidivists. In light of these facts, if capital punishment were justified purely on the basis of preventing recidivism, it would have to be considered to be excessive; no general need to obliterate all capital offenders could have been demonstrated, nor any specific need in individual cases.

D. The three final purposes which may underlie utilization of a capital sanction—encouraging guilty pleas and confessions, eugenics, and reducing state expenditures—may be dealt with quickly. If the death penalty is used to encourage guilty pleas and thus to deter suspects from exercising their rights under the Sixth Amendment to jury trials, it is unconstitutional. * * *

Moreover, to the extent that capital punishment is used to encourage confessions and guilty pleas, it is not being used for punishment purposes. A State that justifies capital punishment on its utility as part of the conviction process could not profess to rely on capital punishment as a deterrent. Such a State's system would be structured with twin goals only: obtaining guilty pleas and confessions and imposing *imprisonment* as the maximum sanction. Since life imprisonment is sufficient for bargaining purposes, the death penalty is excessive if used for the same purposes.

In light of the previous discussion on deterrence, any suggestions concerning the eugenic benefits of capital punishment are obviously meritless.

As I pointed out above, there is not even any attempt made to discover which capital offenders are likely to be recidivists, let alone which are positively incurable. No test or procedure presently exists by which incurables can be screened from those who would benefit from treatment. On the one hand, due process would seem to require that we have some procedure to demonstrate incurability before execution; and, on the other hand, equal protection would then seemingly require that all incurables be executed, cf. Skinner v. Oklahoma, 316 U.S. 535, 62 S.Ct. 1110, 86 L.Ed. 1655 (1942). In addition, the "cruel and unusual" language would require that life imprisonment, treatment and sterilization be inadequate for eugenic purposes. More importantly, this Nation has never formally professed eugenic goals, and the history of the world does not look kindly on them. If eugenics is one of our purposes, then the legislatures should say so forthrightly and design procedures to serve this goal. Until such time, I can only conclude, as has virtually everyone else who has looked at the problem, that capital punishment cannot be defended on the basis of any eugenic purposes.

As for the argument that it is cheaper to execute a capital offender than to imprison him for life, even assuming that such an argument, if true, would support a capital sanction, it is simply incorrect. A disproportionate amount of money spent on prisons is attributable to death row. Condemned men are not productive members of the prison community, although they could be, and executions are expensive. Appeals are often automatic, and courts admittedly spend more time with death cases.

At trial, the selection of jurors is likely to become a costly, time-consuming problem in a capital case, and defense counsel will reasonably exhaust every possible means to save his client from execution, no matter how long the trial takes.

During the period between conviction and execution, there are an inordinate number of collateral attacks on the conviction and attempts to obtain executive clemency, all of which exhaust the time, money, and effort of the State. There are also continual assertions that the condemned prisoner has gone insane. Because there is a formally established policy of not executing insane persons, great sums of money may be spent on detecting and curing mental illness in order to perform the execution. Since no one wants the responsibility for the execution, the condemned man is likely to be passed back and forth from doctors to custodial officials to courts like a ping-pong ball. The entire process is very costly.

When all is said and done, there can be no doubt that it costs more to execute a man than to keep him in prison for life.

E. There is but one conclusion that can be drawn from all of this—i.e., the death penalty is an excessive and unnecessary punishment that violates the Eighth Amendment. The statistical evidence is not convincing beyond all doubt, but it is persuasive. * * *

* * *

MR. CHIEF JUSTICE BURGER, with whom MR. JUSTICE BLACKMUN, MR. JUSTICE POWELL, and MR. JUSTICE REHNQUIST join, dissenting.

At the outset it is important to note that only two members of the Court, Mr. Justice Brennan and Mr. Justice Marshall, have concluded that the Eighth Amendment prohibits capital punishment for all crimes and under all circumstances. Mr. Justice Douglas has also determined that the death penalty contravenes the Eighth Amendment, although I do not read his opinion as necessarily requiring final abolition of the penalty. * * * I conclude that the constitutional prohibition against "cruel and unusual punishments" cannot be construed to bar the imposition of the punishment of death.

Mr. Justice Stewart and Mr. Justice White have concluded that petitioners' death sentences must be set aside because prevailing sentencing practices do not comply with the Eighth Amendment. * * * I believe this approach fundamentally misconceives the nature of the Eighth Amendment guarantee and flies directly in the face of controlling authority of extremely recent vintage.

* * *

II

Counsel for petitioners properly concede that capital punishment was not impermissibly cruel at the time of the adoption of the Eighth Amendment. Not only do the records of the debates indicate that the Founding Fathers were limited in their concern to the prevention of torture, but it is also clear from the language of the Constitution itself that there was no thought whatever of the elimination of capital punishment. * * *

In the 181 years since the enactment of the Eighth Amendment, not a single decision of this Court has cast the slightest shadow of a doubt on the constitutionality of capital punishment. In rejecting Eighth Amendment attacks on particular modes of execution, the Court has more than once implicitly denied that capital punishment is impermissibly "cruel" in the constitutional sense. Wilkerson v. Utah, 99 U.S. 130, 25 L.Ed. 345 (1879); Louisiana ex rel. Francis v. Resweber, 329 U.S., at 464, 67 S.Ct., at 376. In re Kemmler, 136 U.S. 436, 10 S.Ct. 930, 34 L.Ed. 519 (1890) (dictum). It is only 14 years since Mr. Chief Justice Warren, speaking for four members of the Court, stated without equivocation:

> "Whatever the arguments may be against capital punishment, both on moral grounds and in terms of accomplishing the purposes of punishment—and they are forceful—the death penalty has been employed throughout our history, and, in a day when it is still widely accepted, it cannot be said to violate the constitutional concept of cruelty." Trop v. Dulles, 356 U.S., at 99, 78 S.Ct., at 597.

It is only one year since Mr. Justice Black made his feelings clear on the constitutional issue:

> "The Eighth Amendment forbids 'cruel and unusual punishments.' In my view, these words cannot be read to outlaw capital punishment because that penalty was in common use and authorized by law here and in the countries from which our ancestors came at the time the Amendment was adopted. It is inconceivable to me that the framers intended to end capital punishment by the Amend-

ment." McGautha v. California, 402 U.S. 183, 226, 91 S.Ct. 1454, 1477, 28 L.Ed.2d 711 (1971) (separate opinion).

* * * Nonetheless, the Court has now been asked to hold that a punishment clearly permissible under the Constitution at the time of its adoption and accepted as such by every member of the Court until today, is suddenly so cruel as to be incompatible with the Eighth Amendment.

Before recognizing such an instant evolution in the law, it seems fair to ask what factors have changed that capital punishment should now be "cruel" in the constitutional sense as it has not been in the past. * * *

However, the inquiry cannot end here. For reasons unrelated to any change in intrinsic cruelty, the Eighth Amendment prohibition cannot fairly be limited to those punishments thought excessively cruel and barbarous at the time of the adoption of the Eighth Amendment. A punishment is inordinately cruel, in the sense we must deal with it in these cases, chiefly as perceived by the society so characterizing it. The standard of extreme cruelty is not merely descriptive, but necessarily embodies a moral judgment. The standard itself remains the same, but its applicability must change as the basic mores of society change. * * * Nevertheless, the Court up to now has never actually held that a punishment has become impermissibly cruel due to a shift in the weight of accepted social values; nor has the Court suggested judicially manageable criteria for measuring such a shift in moral consensus.

The Court's quiescence in this area can be attributed to the fact that in a democratic society legislatures, not courts, are constituted to respond to the will and consequently the moral values of the people. * * *

* * * The critical fact is that this Court has never had to hold that a mode of punishment authorized by a domestic legislature was so cruel as to be fundamentally at odds with our basic notions of decency. Judicial findings of impermissible cruelty have been limited, for the most part, to offensive punishments devised without specific authority by prison officials, not by legislatures. See, e.g., Jackson v. Bishop, 404 F.2d 571 (CA8 1968); Wright v. McMann, 387 F.2d 519 (CA2 1967). The paucity of judicial decisions invalidating legislatively prescribed punishments is powerful evidence that in this country legislatures have in fact been responsive—albeit belatedly at times—to changes in social attitudes and moral values.

I do not suggest that the validity of legislatively authorized punishments presents no justiciable issue under the Eighth Amendment, but, rather, that the primacy of the legislative role narrowly confines the scope of judicial inquiry. Whether or not provable, and whether or not true at all times, in a democracy the legislative judgment is presumed to embody the basic standards of decency prevailing in the society. This presumption can only be negated by unambiguous and compelling evidence of legislative default.

III

There are no obvious indications that capital punishment offends the conscience of society to such a degree that our traditional deference to the legislative judgment must be abandoned. It is not a punishment such as burning at the stake that everyone would ineffably find to be repugnant to all civilized standards. Nor is it a punishment so roundly condemned that only a few aberrant legislatures have retained it on the statute books. Capital punishment is authorized by statute in 40 States, the District of Columbia, and in the federal courts for the commission of certain crimes. On four occasions in the last 11 years Congress has added to the list of federal crimes punishable by death. In looking for reliable indicia of contemporary attitude, none more trustworthy has been advanced.

One conceivable source of evidence that legislatures have abdicated their essentially barometric role with respect to community values would be public opinion polls, of which there have been many in the past decade addressed to the question of capital punishment. Without assessing the reliability of such polls, or intimating that any judicial reliance could ever be placed on them, it need only be noted that the reported results have shown nothing approximating the universal condemnation of capital punishment that might lead us to suspect that the legislatures in general have lost touch with current social values.[9]

Counsel for petitioners rely on a different body of empirical evidence. They argue, in effect, that the number of cases in which the death penalty is imposed, as compared with the number of cases in which it is statutorily available, reflects a general revulsion toward the penalty that would lead to its repeal if only it were more generally and widely enforced. It cannot be gainsaid that by the choice of juries—and sometimes judges—the death penalty is imposed in far fewer than half the cases in which it is available. To go further and characterize the rate of imposition as "freakishly rare," as petitioners insist, is unwarranted hyperbole. And regardless of its characterization, the rate of imposition does not impel the conclusion that capital punishment is now regarded as intolerably cruel or uncivilized.

* * *

* * * The selectivity of juries in imposing the punishment of death is properly viewed as a refinement on, rather than a repudiation of, the statutory authorization for that penalty. Legislatures prescribe the categories of crimes for which the death penalty should be available, and, acting as "the conscience of the community," juries are entrusted to determine in individual cases that the ultimate punishment is warranted. Juries are undoubtedly influenced in this judgment by myriad factors. The motive or lack of motive of the perpetrator, the degree of injury or suffering of the victim or victims, and the degree of brutality in the commission of the crime would seem to be prominent among these factors. Given the general awareness that death is no longer a routine punishment for the crimes for which it is made available, it is hardly surprising that juries have been increasingly meticulous in their imposition of the penalty. But to assume from the mere fact of relative infrequency that only a random assortment of pariahs are sentenced to death, is to cast grave doubt on the basic integrity of our jury system.

9. A 1966 poll indicated that 42% of those polled favored capital punishment while 47% opposed it, and 11% had no opinion. A 1969 poll found 51% in favor, 40% opposed, and 9% with no opinion. See Erskine, The Polls: Capital Punishment, 34 Public Opinion Quarterly 290 (1970).

It would, of course, be unrealistic to assume that juries have been perfectly consistent in choosing the cases where the death penalty is to be imposed, for no human institution performs with perfect consistency. There are doubtless prisoners on death row who would not be there had they been tried before a different jury or in a different State. In this sense their fate has been controlled by a fortuitous circumstance. However, this element of fortuity does not stand as an indictment either of the general functioning of juries in capital cases or of the integrity of jury decisions in individual cases. * * *

* * *

IV

Capital punishment has also been attacked as violative of the Eighth Amendment on the ground that it is not needed to achieve legitimate penal aims and is thus "unnecessarily cruel." As a pure policy matter, this approach has much to recommend it, but it seeks to give a dimension to the Eighth Amendment that it was never intended to have and promotes a line of inquiry that this Court has never before pursued.

* * *

* * * Two of the several aims of punishment are generally associated with capital punishment—retribution and deterrence. It is argued that retribution can be discounted because that, after all, is what the Eighth Amendment seeks to eliminate. There is no authority suggesting that the Eighth Amendment was intended to purge the law of its retributive elements, and the Court has consistently assumed that retribution is a legitimate dimension of the punishment of crimes. See Williams v. New York, 337 U.S. 241, 248, 69 S.Ct. 1079, 1083, 93 L.Ed. 1337 (1949); United States v. Lovett, 328 U.S. 303, 324, 66 S.Ct. 1073, 1083, 90 L.Ed. 1252 (1946) (Frankfurter, J., concurring). Furthermore, responsible legal thinkers of widely varying persuasions have debated the sociological and philosophical aspects of the retribution question for generations, neither side being able to convince the other. It would be reading a great deal into the Eighth Amendment to hold that the punishments authorized by legislatures cannot constitutionally reflect a retributive purpose.

The less esoteric but no less controversial question is whether the death penalty acts as a superior deterrent. Those favoring abolition find no evidence that it does. Those favoring retention start from the intuitive notion that capital punishment should act as the most effective deterrent and note that there is no convincing evidence that it does not. Escape from this empirical stalemate is sought by placing the burden of proof on the States and concluding that they have failed to demonstrate that capital punishment is a more effective deterrent than life imprisonment. Numerous justifications have been advanced for shifting the burden, and they are not without their rhetorical appeal. However, these arguments are not descended from established constitutional principles, but are born of the urge to bypass an unresolved factual question. Comparative deterrence is not a matter that lends itself to precise measurement; to shift the burden to the States is to provide an illusory solution to an enormously complex problem. If it were proper to put the States to the test of demonstrating the deterrent value of capital punishment, we could just as well ask them to prove the need for life imprisonment or any other punishment. Yet I know of no convincing evidence that life imprisonment is a more effective deterrent than 20 years' imprisonment, or even that a $10 parking ticket is a more effective deterrent than a $5 parking ticket. In fact, there are some who go so far as to challenge the notion that any punishments deter crime. If the States are unable to adduce convincing proof rebutting such assertions, does it then follow that all punishments are suspect as being "cruel and unusual" within the meaning of the Constitution? On the contrary, I submit that the questions raised by the necessity approach are beyond the pale of judicial inquiry under the Eighth Amendment.

V

Today the Court has not ruled that capital punishment is *per se* violative of the Eighth Amendment; nor has it ruled that the punishment is barred for any particular class or classes of crimes. The substantially similar concurring opinions of Mr. Justice Stewart and Mr. Justice White, which are necessary to support the judgment setting aside petitioners' sentences, stop short of reaching the ultimate question. The actual scope of the Court's ruling, which I take to be embodied in these concurring opinions, is not entirely clear. This much, however, seems apparent: if the legislatures are to continue to authorize capital punishment for some crimes, juries and judges can no longer be permitted to make the sentencing determination in the same manner they have in the past. This approach—not urged in oral arguments or briefs—misconceives the nature of the constitutional command against "cruel and unusual punishments," disregards controlling case law, and demands a rigidity in capital cases which, if possible of achievement, cannot be regarded as a welcome change. Indeed the contrary seems to be the case.

As I have earlier stated, the Eighth Amendment forbids the imposition of punishments that are so cruel and inhumane as to violate society's standards of civilized conduct. The Amendment does not prohibit all punishments the States are unable to prove necessary to deter or control crime. The Amendment is not concerned with the process by which a State determines that a particular punishment is to be imposed in a particular case. And the Amendment most assuredly does not speak to the power of legislatures to confer sentencing discretion on juries, rather than to fix all sentences by statute.

The critical factor in the concurring opinions of both Mr. Justice Stewart and Mr. Justice White is the infrequency with which the penalty is imposed. This factor is taken not as evidence of society's abhorrence of capital punishment—the inference that petitioners would have the Court draw—but as the earmark of a deteriorated system of sentencing. It is concluded that petitioners' sentences must be set aside, not because the punishment is impermissibly cruel, but because juries and judges have failed to exercise their sentencing discretion in acceptable fashion.

* * *

* * * The decisive grievance of the opinions—not translated into Eighth Amendment terms—is that the present system of discretionary sentencing in capital cases has failed to produce evenhanded justice; the problem is not that too few have been sentenced to die, but that the selection process has followed no rational pattern. This claim of arbitrariness is not only lacking in empirical support, but also it manifestly fails to establish that the death penalty is a "cruel and unusual" punishment. The Eighth Amendment was included in the Bill of Rights to assure that certain types of punishments would never be imposed, not to channelize the sentencing process. The approach of these concurring opinions has no antecedent in the Eighth Amendment cases. It is essentially and exclusively a procedural due process argument.

* * *

While I would not undertake to make a definitive statement as to the parameters of the Court's ruling, it is clear that if state legislatures and the Congress wish to maintain the availability of capital punishment, significant statutory changes will have to be made. Since the two pivotal concurring opinions turn on the assumption that the punishment of death is now meted out in a random and unpredictable manner, legislative bodies may seek to bring their laws into compliance with the Court's ruling by providing standards for juries and judges to follow in determining the sentence in capital cases or by more narrowly defining the crimes for which the penalty is to be imposed. If such standards can be devised or the crimes more meticulously defined, the result cannot be detrimental. However, * * * all past efforts "to identify before the fact" the cases in which the penalty is to be imposed have been "uniformly unsuccessful." One problem is that "the factors which determine whether the sentence of death is the appropriate penalty in particular cases are too complex to be compressed within the limits of a simple formula * * *." Report of Royal Commission on Capital Punishment, 1949–1953, Cmd. 8932, ¶ 498, p. 174 (1953). * * * But even assuming that suitable guidelines can be established, there is no assurance that sentencing patterns will change so long as juries are possessed of the power to determine the sentence or to bring in a verdict of guilt on a charge carrying a lesser sentence; juries have not been inhibited in the exercise of these powers in the past. Thus, unless the Court in *McGautha* misjudged the experience of history, there is little reason to believe that sentencing standards in any form will substantially alter the discretionary character of the prevailing system of sentencing in capital cases. That system may fall short of perfection, but it is yet to be shown that a different system would produce more satisfactory results.

Real change could clearly be brought about if legislatures provided mandatory death sentences in such a way as to deny juries the opportunity to bring in a verdict on a lesser charge; under such a system, the death sentence could only be avoided by a verdict of acquittal. If this is the only alternative that the legislatures can safely pursue under today's ruling, I would have preferred that the Court opt for total abolition.

It seems remarkable to me that with our basic trust in lay jurors as the keystone in our system of criminal justice, it should now be suggested that we take the most sensitive and important of all decisions away from them. I could more easily be persuaded that mandatory sentences of death, without the intervening and ameliorating impact of lay jurors, are so arbitrary and doctrinaire that they violate the Constitution. The very infrequency of death penalties imposed by jurors attests their cautious and discriminating reservation of that penalty for the most extreme cases. * * *

* * *

MR. JUSTICE POWELL, with whom THE CHIEF JUSTICE, MR. JUSTICE BLACKMUN, and MR. JUSTICE REHNQUIST join, dissenting.

* * *

IV

* * *

Any attempt to discern contemporary standards of decency through the review of objective factors must take into account several overriding considerations which petitioners choose to discount or ignore. In a democracy the first indicator of the public's attitude must always be found in the legislative judgments of the people's chosen representatives. Mr. Justice Marshall's opinion today catalogues the salient statistics. Forty States, the District of Columbia, and the Federal Government still authorize the death penalty for a wide variety of crimes. That number has remained relatively static since the end of World War I. That does not mean, however, that capital punishment has become a forgotten issue in the legislative arena. As recently as January, 1971, Congress approved the death penalty for congressional assassination. 18 U.S.C. § 351. In 1965 Congress added the death penalty for presidential and vice presidential assassinations. 18 U.S.C. § 1751. Additionally, the aircraft piracy statute passed in 1961 also carries the death penalty. 49 U.S.C. § 1472(i). * * * On the converse side, a bill proposing the abolition of capital punishment for all federal crimes was introduced in 1967 but failed to reach the Senate floor.

* * *

* * * It is also worthy of note that the annual rate of death sentences has remained relatively constant over the last 10 years and that the figure for 1970—127 sentences—is the highest annual total since 1961. It is true that the sentencing rate might be expected to rise, rather than remain constant, when the number of violent crimes increases as it has in this country. And it may be conceded that the constancy in these statistics indicates the unwillingness of juries to demand the ultimate penalty in many cases where it might be imposed. But these considerations fall short of indicating that juries are imposing the death penalty with such rarity as to justify this Court in reading into this circumstance a public rejection of capital punishment.

One must conclude, contrary to petitioners' submission, that the indicators most likely to reflect the public's view—legislative bodies, state referenda and the juries which have the actual responsibility—do not support the contention that evolving standards of decency require total abolition of capital punishment. Indeed, the weight of the evidence indicates that the public generally has not accepted either the morality or the social merit of the views so passionately advocated by the articulate spokesmen for abolition. But however one may assess the amorphous ebb and flow of public opinion generally on this volatile issue, this type of inquiry lies at the periphery—not the core—of the judicial process in constitutional cases. The assessment of popular opinion is essentially a legislative, not a judicial, function.

V

* * *

Members of this Court know, from the petitions and appeals that come before us regularly, that brutish and revolting murders continue to occur with disquieting frequency. Indeed, murders are so commonplace in our society that only the most sensational receive significant and sustained publicity. It could hardly be suggested that in any of these highly publicized murder cases—the several senseless assassinations or the too numerous shocking multiple murders that have stained this country's recent history—the public has exhibited any signs of "revulsion" at the thought of executing the convicted murderers. The public outcry, as we all know, has been quite to the contrary. Furthermore, there is little reason to suspect that the public's reaction would differ significantly in response to other less publicized murders. It is certainly arguable that many such murders, because of their senselessness or barbarousness, would evoke a public demand for the death penalty rather than a public rejection of that alternative. Nor is there any rational basis for arguing that the public reaction to any of these crimes would be muted if the murderer were "rich and powerful." The demand for the ultimate sanction might well be greater, as a wealthy killer is hardly a sympathetic figure. While there might be specific cases in which capital punishment would be regarded as excessive and shocking to the conscience of the community, it can hardly be argued that the public's dissatisfaction with the penalty in particular cases would translate into a demand for absolute abolition.

* * *

Certainly the claim is justified that this criminal sanction falls more heavily on the relatively impoverished and underprivileged elements of society. The "have-nots" in every society always have been subject to greater pressure to commit crimes and to fewer constraints than their more affluent fellow citizens. This is, indeed, a tragic byproduct of social and economic deprivation, but it is not an argument of constitutional proportions under the Eighth or Fourteenth Amendment. The same discriminatory impact argument could be made with equal force and logic with respect to those sentenced to prison terms. The Due Process Clause admits of no distinction between the deprivation of "life" and the deprivation of "liberty." If discriminatory impact renders capital punishment cruel and unusual, it likewise renders invalid most of the prescribed penalties for crimes of violence. The root causes of the higher incidence of criminal penalties on "minorities and the poor" will not be cured by abolishing the system of penalties. Nor, indeed, could any society have a viable system of criminal justice if sanctions were abolished or ameliorated because most of those who commit crimes happen to be underprivileged. The basic problem results not from the penalties imposed for criminal conduct but from social and economic factors that have plagued humanity since the beginning of recorded history, frustrating all efforts to create in any country at any time the perfect society in which there are no "poor," no "minorities" and no "underprivileged." The causes underlying this problem are unrelated to the constitutional issue before the Court.

* * *

A final comment on the racial discrimination problem seems appropriate. The possibility of racial bias in the trial and sentencing process has diminished in recent years. The segregation of our society in decades past, which contributed substantially to the severity of punishment for interracial crimes, is now no longer prevalent in this country. Likewise, the day is past when juries do not represent the minority group elements of the community. The assurance of fair trials for all citizens is greater today than at any previous time in our history. Because standards of criminal justice have "evolved" in a manner favorable to the accused, discriminatory imposition of capital punishment is far less likely today than in the past.

VI

* * *

First, I find no support—in the language of the Constitution, in its history, or in the cases arising under it—for the view that this Court may invalidate a category of penalties because we deem less severe penalties adequate to serve the ends of penology. While the cases affirm our authority to prohibit punishments that are cruelly inhumane and punishments that are cruelly excessive in that they are disproportionate to particular crimes, the precedents of this Court afford no basis for striking down a particular form of punishment because we may be persuaded that means less stringent would be equally efficacious.

Secondly, if we were free to question the justifications for the use of capital punishment, a heavy burden would rest on those who attack the legislatures' judgments to prove the lack of rational justifications. * * *

I come now to consider, subject to the reservations above expressed, the two justifications most often cited for the retention of capital punishment. The concept of retribution—though popular for centuries—is now criticized as unworthy of a civilized people. Yet this Court has acknowledged the existence of a retributive element in criminal sanctions and has never heretofore found it impermissible. * * *

While retribution alone may seem an unworthy justification in a moral sense, its utility in a system of criminal justice requiring public support has long been recognized. Lord Justice Denning, now Master of the Rolls of the Court of Appeal in England, testified on this subject before the British Royal Commission on Capital Punishment:

> "Many are inclined to test the efficacy of punishment solely by its value as a deterrent: but this is too narrow a view. Punishment is the way in which society expresses its denunciation of wrong doing: and, in order to maintain respect for law, it is essential that the punishment inflicted for grave crimes should adequately reflect the

revulsion felt by the great majority of citizens for them. It is a mistake to consider the objects of punishment as being deterrent or reformative or preventive and nothing else. If this were so, we should not send to prison a man who was guilty of motor manslaughter, but only disqualify him from driving; but would public opinion be content with this? The truth is that some crimes are so outrageous that society insists on adequate punishment, because the wrong-doer deserves it, irrespective of whether it is a deterrent or not."

The view expressed by Lord Denning was cited approvingly in the Royal Commission's Report, recognizing "a strong and widespread demand for retribution." Mr. Justice Stewart makes much the same point in his opinion today when he concludes that expression of man's retributive instincts in the sentencing process "serves an important purpose in promoting the stability of a society governed by law." Ante, at 2761. The view, moreover, is not without respectable support in the jurisprudential literature in this country, despite a substantial body of opinion to the contrary. And it is conceded on all sides that, not infrequently, cases arise that are so shocking or offensive that the public demands the ultimate penalty for the transgressor.

Deterrence is a more appealing justification, although opinions again differ widely. Indeed, the deterrence issue lies at the heart of much of the debate between the abolitionists and retentionists. Statistical studies based primarily on trends in States that have abolished the penalty, tend to support the view that the death penalty has not been proved to be a superior deterrent. Some dispute the validity of this conclusion, pointing out that the studies do not show that the death penalty has no deterrent effect on any categories of crimes. On the basis of the literature and studies currently available, I find myself in agreement with the conclusions drawn by the Royal Commission following its exhaustive study of this issue:

"The general conclusion which we reach, after careful review of all the evidence we have been able to obtain as to the deterrent effect of capital punishment, may be stated as follows. *Prima facie* the penalty of death is likely to have a stronger effect as a deterrent to normal human beings than any other form of punishment, and there is some evidence (though no convincing statistical evidence) that this is in fact so. But this effect does not operate universally or uniformly, and there are many offenders on whom it is limited and may often be negligible. It is accordingly important to view this question in a just perspective and not base a penal policy in relation to murder on exaggerated estimates of the uniquely deterrent force of the death penalty."

* * *

[The dissenting opinion of MR. JUSTICE BLACKMUN, in which THE CHIEF JUSTICE, MR. JUSTICE POWELL, and MR. JUSTICE REHNQUIST joined, and the dissenting opinion of MR. JUSTICE REHNQUIST, in which THE CHIEF JUSTICE, MR. JUSTICE BLACKMUN, and MR. JUSTICE POWELL joined, are omitted.]

Note on the Death Penalty as a Deterrent

JUSTICE MARSHALL, dissenting in Gregg v. Georgia, 428 U.S. 153, 234–242, 96 S.Ct. 2909, 2974–2977, 49 L.Ed.2d 859, 908–912 (1976), wrote:

> The Solicitor General in his *amicus* brief in these cases relies heavily on a study by Isaac Ehrlich,[4] reported a year after *Furman,* to support the contention that the death penalty does deter murder. Since the Ehrlich study was not available at the time of *Furman* and since it is the first scientific study to suggest that the death penalty may have a deterrent effect, I will briefly consider its import.
>
> The Ehrlich study focused on the relationship in the Nation as a whole between the homicide rate and "execution risk"—the fraction of persons convicted of murder who were actually executed. Comparing the differences in homicide rate and execution risk for the years 1933 to 1969, Ehrlich found that increases in execution risk were associated with increases in the homicide rate. But when he employed the statistical technique of multiple regression analysis to control for the influence of other variables posited to have an impact on the homicide rate,[6] Ehrlich found a negative correlation between changes in the homicide rate and changes in execution risk. His tentative conclusion was that for the period from 1933 to 1967 each additional execution in the United States might have saved eight lives.

The methods and conclusions of the Ehrlich study have been severely criticized on a number of grounds.[8] It has been suggested, for example, that the study is defective because it compares execution and homicide rates on a nationwide, rather than a state-by-state, basis. The aggregation of data from all States—including those that have been abolished the death penalty—obscures the relationship between murder and execution rates. Under Ehrlich's methodology, a decrease in the execution risk in one State combined with an increase in the murder rate in another State would, all other things being equal, suggest a deterrent effect that quite obviously would not exist. Indeed, a deterrent effect would be suggested if, once again all other things being equal, one State abolished

4. I. Ehrlich, The Deterrent Effect of Capital Punishment: A Question of Life and Death (Working Paper No. 18, National Bureau of Economic Research, Nov. 1973); Ehrlich, The Deterrent Effect of Capital Punishment: A Question of Life and Death, 65 Am.Econ.Rev. 397 (June 1975).

6. The variables other than execution risk included probability of arrest, probability of conviction given arrest, national aggregate measures of the percentage of the population between age 14 and 24, the unemployment rate, the labor force participation rate, and estimated per capita income.

8. See Passell & Taylor, The Deterrent Effect of Capital Punishment: Another View (unpublished Columbia University Discussion Paper 74–7509, Mar. 1975), reproduced in Brief for Petitioner App. E. in Jurek v. Texas, O.T. 1975, No. 75–5844; Passell, The Deterrent Effect of the Death Penalty: A Statistical Test, 28 Stan.L.Rev. 61 (1975); Baldus & Cole, A Comparison of the Work of Thorsten Sellin & Isaac Ehrlich on the Deterrent Effect of Capital Punishment, 85 Yale L.J. 170 (1975); Bowers & Pierce, The Illusion of Deterrence in Isaac Ehrlich's Research on Capital Punishment, 85 Yale L.J. 187 (1975); Peck, The Deterrent Effect of Capital Punishment: Ehrlich and His Critics, 85 Yale L.J. 359 (1976). See also Ehrlich, Deterrence: Evidence and Inference, 85 Yale L.J. 209 (1975); Ehrlich, Rejoinder, 85 Yale L.J. 368 (1976). In addition to the items discussed in text, criticism has been directed at the quality of Ehrlich's data, his choice of explanatory variables, his failure to account for the interdependence of those variables, and his assumptions as to the mathematical form of the relationship between the homicide rate and the explanatory variables.

the death penalty and experienced no change in the murder rate, while another State experienced an increase in the murder rate.

The most compelling criticism of the Ehrlich study is that its conclusions are extremely sensitive to the choice of the time period included in the regression analysis. Analysis of Ehrlich's data reveals that all empirical support for the deterrent effect of capital punishment disappears when the five most recent years are removed from his time series—that is to say, whether a decrease in the execution risk corresponds to an increase or a decrease in the murder rate depends on the ending point of the sample period. This finding has cast severe doubts on the reliability of Ehrlich's tentative conclusions. Indeed, a recent regression study, based on Ehrlich's theoretical model but using cross-section state data for the years 1950 and 1960 found no support for the conclusion that executions act as a deterrent.

The Ehrlich study, in short, is of little, if any, assistance in assessing the deterrent impact of the death penalty. Accord, Commonwealth v. O'Neal, 369 Mass. 242, 256, 339 N.E.2d 676, 684 (1975). The evidence I reviewed in *Furman* remains convincing, in my view that "capital punishment is not necessary as a deterrent to crime in our society." 408 U.S., at 353, 92 S.Ct., at 2784. The justification for the death penalty must be found elsewhere.

* * *

* * * [O]ur recognition that retribution plays a crucial role in determining who may be punished by no means requires approval of retribution as a general justification for punishment. * * *

* * * As my Brother Brennan stated in *Furman,* "[t]here is no evidence whatever that utilization of imprisonment rather than death encourages private blood feuds and other disorders." 408 U.S., at 303, 92 S.Ct., at 2758 (concurring opinion). It simply defies belief to suggest that the death penalty is necessary to prevent the American people from taking the law into their own hands.

In a related vein, it may be suggested that the expression of moral outrage through the imposition of the death penalty serves to reinforce basic moral values—that it marks some crimes as particularly offensive and therefore to be avoided. The argument is akin to a deterrence argument, but differs in that it contemplates the individual's shrinking from antisocial conduct, not because he fears punishment, but because he has been told in the strongest possible way that the conduct is wrong. This contention, like the previous one, provides no support for the death penalty. It is inconceivable that any individual concerned about conforming his conduct to what society says is "right" would fail to realize that murder is "wrong" if the penalty were simply life imprisonment.

The foregoing contentions—that society's expression of moral outrage through the imposition of the death penalty pre-empts the citizenry from taking the law into its own hands and reinforces moral values—are not retributive in the purest sense. They are essentially utilitarian in that they portray the death penalty as valuable because of its beneficial results. These justifications for the death penalty are inadequate because the penalty is, quite clearly I think, not necessary to the accomplishment of those results.

There remains for consideration, however, what might be termed the purely retributive justification for the death penalty—that the death penalty is appropriate, not because of its beneficial effect on society, but because the taking of the murderer's life is itself morally good. * * *

* * *

* * * To be sustained under the Eighth Amendment, the death penalty must "compor[t] with the basic concept of human dignity at the core of the Amendment," the objective in imposing it must be "[consistent] with our respect for the dignity of [other] men." Under these standards, the taking of life "because the wrongdoer deserves it" surely must fall, for such a punishment has as its very basis the total denial of the wrongdoer's dignity and worth.

Note: Capital Punishment in the Supreme Court After Furman

Capital punishment cases have not grown easier for the Court after *Furman*. It has not since then produced an opinion setting forth a general theoretical position on the death penalty which has been joined in by at least five justices.

Justice Rehnquist has consistently voted to uphold death penalty statutes, adhering to the view that capital punishment questions are for the states and do not, as such, present cruel and unusual punishment issues. Justices Brennan and Marshall have never retreated from their view that the death penalty is unconstitutional *per se*.

Former Justices Stewart and Powell, with Justice Stevens, staked out a middle ground in five cases decided by the court at the same time in 1976. In Gregg v. Georgia, 428 U.S. 153, 96 S.Ct. 2909, 49 L.Ed.2d 859 (1976); Profitt v. Florida, 428 U.S. 242, 96 S.Ct. 2960, 49 L.Ed.2d 913 (1976); and Jurek v. Texas, 428 U.S. 262, 96 S.Ct. 2950, 49 L.Ed.2d 929 (1976), rehearing denied 429 U.S. 875, 97 S.Ct. 198, 50 L.Ed.2d 158 (1976), they voted with the Chief Justice and Justices White, Blackmun, and Rehnquist to sustain death penalty statutes more narrowly drawn than the statutes in *Furman*. The Georgia and Florida statutes followed the plan of Model Penal Code § 210.6, providing statutory factors of aggravation and mitigation in murder, to be considered in the sentencing proceeding where death was a possibility; they also provided for appellate review to insure against disproportionate application of the tests. Georgia further provided for a separate proceeding on punishment after guilt had been found. Texas made the death penalty applicable only in five limited categories of first degree murder, which were likened to aggravating circumstances, and allowed for consideration of mitigating circumstances. In *Gregg,* the most fully considered of the cases, the three "middle-ground" justices explained:

> *Furman* mandates that where discretion is afforded a sentencing body on a matter so grave as the determination of whether a human life should be taken or spared, that discretion must be suitably directed and limited so as to minimize the risk of wholly arbitrary and capricious action.
>
> * * *
>
> In summary, the concerns expressed in *Furman* that the penalty of death not be imposed in an arbitrary or capricious manner can be met by a carefully drafted statute that ensures that the sentencing authority is given adequate information and guidance. As a general proposition these concerns are best met by a system that provides for a bifurcated proceeding at which the sentencing authority is apprised of the information relevant to the imposition of sentence and provided with standards to guide its use of the information.

We do not intend to suggest that only the above-described procedures would be permissible under *Furman* or that any sentencing system constructed along these general lines would inevitably satisfy the concerns of *Furman,* for each distinct system must be examined on an individual basis. Rather, we have embarked upon this general exposition to make clear that it is possible to construct capital-sentencing systems capable of meeting *Furman's* constitutional concerns.

* * *

These procedures require the jury[a] to consider the circumstances of the crime and the criminal before it recommends sentence. No longer can a Georgia jury do as *Furman's* jury did: reach a finding of the defendant's guilt and then, without guidance or direction, decide whether he should live or die. Instead, the jury's attention is directed to the specific circumstances of the crime: Was it committed in the course of another capital felony? Was it committed for money? Was it committed upon a peace officer or judicial officer? Was it committed in a particularly heinous way or in a manner that endangered the lives of many persons? In addition, the jury's attention is focused on the characteristics of the person who committed the crime: Does he have a record of prior convictions for capital offenses? Are there any special facts about this defendant that mitigate against imposing capital punishment (e.g., his youth, the extent of his cooperation with the police, his emotional state at the time of the crime). As a result, while some jury discretion still exists, "the discretion to be exercised is controlled by clear and objective standards so as to produce non-discriminatory application." Coley v. State, 231 Ga. 829, 834, 204 S.E.2d 612, 615 (1974).

As an important additional safeguard against arbitrariness and caprice, the Georgia statutory scheme provides for automatic appeal of all death sentences to the State's Supreme Court. That court is required by statute to review each sentence of death and determine whether it was imposed under the influence of passion or prejudice, whether the evidence supports the jury's finding of a statutory aggravating circumstance, and whether the sentence is disproportionate compared to those sentences imposed in similar cases. § 27–2537(c) (Supp.1975).

In short, Georgia's new sentencing procedures require as a prerequisite to the imposition of the death penalty, specific jury findings as to the circumstances of the crime or the character of the defendant. Moreover, to guard further against a situation comparable to that presented in *Furman,* the Supreme Court of Georgia compares each death sentence with the sentences imposed on similarly situated defendants to ensure that the sentence of death in a particular case is not disproportionate. * * *

(428 U.S. 189, 195–198, 96 S.Ct. 2932, 2935–2937, 49 L.Ed.2d 883, 887–888). Justice White, writing also for the Chief Justice and Justice Rehnquist, also found the Georgia statute acceptable, in that there was no evidence that the penalty was imposed discriminatorily, wantonly and freakishly, or so infrequently as to be inconsistent with *Furman*.

a. State law may constitutionally assign to a judge rather than a jury the weighing of aggravating and mitigating circumstances and the determination of the sentence. Walton v. Arizona, 496 U.S. ___, 110 S.Ct. 3047, 111 L.Ed.2d 511 (1990).

In the remaining two cases, Woodson v. North Carolina, 428 U.S. 280, 96 S.Ct. 2978, 49 L.Ed.2d 944 (1976), and (Stanislaus) Roberts v. Louisiana, 428 U.S. 325, 96 S.Ct. 3001, 49 L.Ed.2d 974 (1976), the three "middle ground" justices joined with Justices Brennan and Marshall to strike down statutes which, respectively, made the death penalty mandatory for all first degree murder, and for all cases in which a purpose to kill or inflict grievous bodily harm was proved in five categories of first degree murder (certain felony-murders, killing of a policeman or fireman performing his duties, murder for hire, murder with the intent to harm more than one person, and killing by one previously convicted of murder or under a current life sentence), as failing to provide, *inter alia,* for sufficiently particularized consideration for each case.[b]

In Coker v. Georgia, 433 U.S. 584, 97 S.Ct. 2861, 53 L.Ed.2d 982 (1977), Justices Brennan and Marshall were joined by Justices Stewart, White, Blackmun, and Stevens, who found the death penalty for rape to be disproportionate and excessive. The case suggests that the death penalty for other common law felonies than murder is impermissible. Justice Powell agreed that the death penalty for rape is improper when the victim is an adult who does not sustain serious or lasting injuries, and the crime is not committed with excessive brutality. The Chief Justice and Justice Rehnquist dissented.

Only Justice Rehnquist dissented in a case in which the Chief Justice agreed with Justices Stewart, Powell, and Stevens that a death penalty statute could not limit the kinds of mitigating circumstances to be considered in sentencing (except perhaps in rare situations in which a prisoner serving a life sentence or a prison escapee murders). Justice Brennan did not sit. Justice Marshall concurred because of his view that the death penalty is unconstitutional *per se*. Justice White concurred on the ground that the statute permitted the death penalty without a finding of the defendant's purpose to kill. Justice Blackmun believed that the statute was unconstitutional in not permitting the sentencing authority to take into account the extent of the particular defendant's involvement or the degree of her *mens rea,* and also in allowing the sentencing judge to bar the death penalty "in the interests of justice" if, but only if, the defendant pled guilty or no contest. Lockett v. Ohio, 438 U.S. 586, 98 S.Ct. 2954, 57 L.Ed.2d 973 (1978).

In Godfrey v. Georgia, 446 U.S. 420, 100 S.Ct. 1759, 64 L.Ed.2d 398 (1980), the Court found that the legislature, in making it an aggravating factor that a first degree murder was "outrageously or wantonly vile, horrible, or inhuman," had provided too broad and vague a standard to be constitutionally acceptable. (Per Justices Stewart, Blackmun, Powell, and Stevens; Justices Brennan and Marshall concurred; the Chief Justice and Justices White and Rehnquist dissented.) The Court reached the same conclusion as to the characterization "especially heinous, atrocious, or cruel." Maynard v. Cartwright, 486 U.S. 356, 108 S.Ct. 1853, 100 L.Ed.2d 372 (1988), but a majority found acceptable the phrase "especially heinous, cruel or depraved," when the state supreme court had

b. The Louisiana statute came before the Court again in the following year, in connection with another one of the five capital categories discussed in the *(Stanislaus) Roberts* case. The Court divided five to four as before in overturning the sentence; it indicated that mandatory death categories, with no opportunity to consider mitigating circumstances, were, with the possible exception of murders by prisoners serving life sentences, too broad. (Harry) Roberts v. Louisiana, 431 U.S. 633, 97 S.Ct. 1993, 52 L.Ed.2d 637 (1977). This possible exception for life prisoners was removed in Sumner v. Shuman, 483 U.S. 66, 107 S.Ct. 2716, 97 L.Ed.2d 56 (1987).

previously further explained the meaning of the term. Walton v. Arizona, 497 U.S. ___, 110 S.Ct. 3047, 111 L.Ed.2d 511 (1990).

The Court has continued to work out the problems presented by the use of aggravating and mitigating circumstances. Recent illustrative cases are Blystone v. Pennsylvania, 494 U.S. ___, 110 S.Ct. 1078, 108 L.Ed.2d 255 (1990) (Eighth Amendment satisfied by allowing jury to consider all relevant mitigating circumstances, but requiring death sentence if jury unanimously found at least one aggravating factor which outweighed any mitigating circumstances); Clemons v. Mississippi, 494 U.S. ___, 110 S.Ct. 1441, 108 L.Ed.2d 725 (1990) (state appellate court may uphold death sentence based in part on an invalid or improperly defined aggravating circumstance if it reweighs aggravating and mitigating factors or finds harmless error); and McKoy v. North Carolina, 494 U.S. ___, 110 S.Ct. 1227, 108 L.Ed. 369 (1990) (individual jurors can not be limited to consideration of those mitigating factors which the jury unanimously finds to exist).

While the Eighth Amendment bars the execution of one who is then "insane," Ford v. Wainwright, 477 U.S. 399, 106 S.Ct. 2595, 91 L.Ed.2d 335 (1986), it does not necessarily bar imposition of a capital sentence on one who is to some degree mentally retarded, Penry v. Lynaugh, 492 U.S. ___, 109 S.Ct. 2934, 106 L.Ed.2d 256 (1989). In Thompson v. Oklahoma, 487 U.S. 815, 108 S.Ct. 2687, 101 L.Ed.2d 702 (1988), Justice Kennedy did not sit; all the other members of the court took seriously the proposition that the cruel and unusual punishment provision might, in the light of evolving standards of decency, bar the execution of a defendant who was under the age of sixteen—in this case, fifteen—at the time of commission of the crime. The plurality (Justice Stevens, with Justices Brennan, Marshall, and Blackmun) concluded that there was such a bar. The dissent (Justice Scalia, with Chief Justice Rehnquist and Justice White) disagreed, but conceded that a cut-off at some lower age might be appropriate. Justice O'Connor thought the plurality was likely to be right about the consensus, but chose to decide on the narrow ground that since the jurisdiction did not specify any minimum age for imposition of the penalty, it might have overlooked the possibility that a fifteen year old could be executed; she thought that without such a specification the penalty could not be imposed. Later, in Stanford v. Kentucky, 492 U.S. ___, 109 S.Ct. 2969, 106 L.Ed.2d 306 (1989), the Court found no bar to the imposition of the death sentence on one who committed the offense at age sixteen.

The appointments of Justice Scalia to the Court in 1986, when Justice Rehnquist was elevated to Chief Justice upon the retirement of Chief Justice Burger, and of Justice Kennedy in 1988, to replace Justice Powell, who retired, have strengthened the wing of the Court which is inclined to uphold imposition of the death penalty by the states.

In Enmund v. Florida, 458 U.S. 782, 102 S.Ct. 3368, 73 L.Ed.2d 1140 (1982), the majority of the Court saw the issue before it to be whether the Eighth Amendment permitted Florida to impose the death penalty upon one convicted of felony-murder, solely on the basis of his being a principal in the second degree—as the driver of the getaway car. It decided that execution "in the absence of proof that Enmund killed or attempted to kill, and regardless of whether Enmund intended or contemplated that life would be taken" was impermissible. It noted that death is not a common incident of robbery—one which any robber ought to contemplate as likely—and that the most recent crime statistics suggest that less than one half of one per cent of robberies result in homicide. Justice O'Connor (with the Chief Justice and Justice Rehnquist) thought that the majority should not have made an intention to kill requirement a part of constitutional law. The dissenters believed that the record supported a finding that Enmund had planned the robbery (though not the death), as well as driven the getaway car, and that there was nothing constitutionally impermissible in Florida's deciding that such participation in the robbery might warrant the death penalty.

In Tison v. Arizona, 481 U.S. 137, 107 S.Ct. 1676, 95 L.Ed.2d 127 (1987), defendants, two brothers, aged 20 and 19, with another brother, brought weapons to their father and another prison inmate, and helped in their escape, knowing that the father had killed in an earlier escape attempt. They participated in the kidnapping and robbery of a family in a passing car, watched without attempting to interfere when the escapees murdered the family, and continued to assist the escapees. The Court held that imposition of the death penalty was consistent with *Enmund.* Justice O'Connor, writing for a majority of the Court, depicted *Enmund* as standing for the proposition that, for proportionality reasons, one who was *a minor participant* in an armed robbery, was not on the scene, and did not kill, attempt to kill, or have a culpable mental state with respect to the death, might not be executed, while, at the other extreme, one who actually killed, intended to kill, or attempted to kill in the course of a felony, might be. Defendants fit into neither of these groups; *Enmund* therefore does not foreclose the result. Arizona could, and did, find that they were major participants, and such, consistent with the views of most states imposing the death penalty and with the constitution, may be sentenced to death, when they exhibit a "reckless disregard for human life," even if they do not kill, attempt to kill, or intend to kill. The case was remanded for more findings on this point.

McCleskey v. Kemp, 481 U.S. 279, 107 S.Ct. 1756, 95 L.Ed.2d 262 (1987), rejected an Eighth Amendment attack on a death sentence, made solely on the ground that, in Georgia, black defendants and killers of white victims were sentenced to death more frequently than others, after factors other than race had been accounted for; no attempt was made to prove the particular impact of racial bias on McCleskey himself. Four dissenters argued that it had been shown that murder cases in Georgia having white victims are more than four times as likely to produce death sentences as cases involving black victims, and that a different *risk* of the penalty is enough to show unconstitutional irrationality in the sentencing scheme, without need to prove the impact on McCleskey. The majority, while expressing some reservations about the statistical studies, ultimately accepted them, but maintained that the defendant must show that there was purposeful discrimination which had an impact on him, and that the statistics did not establish this.

Booth v. Maryland, 482 U.S. 496, 107 S.Ct. 2529, 96 L.Ed.2d 440 (1987), decided that victim impact statements were barred as evidence on the issue of capital punishment, as irrelevant and as an invitation to arbitrary and capricious action by the jury.

In Pulley v. Harris, 465 U.S. 37, 104 S.Ct. 871, 79 L.Ed.2d 29 (1984), the Court decided, per Justice White, that the proportionality requirements of Solem v. Helm, supra, p. 39, do not extend to compelling State appellate courts to compare the sentence imposed in the case before it with sentences given others convicted of the same crime. It noted that while capital sentencing plans approved by the Supreme Court had often included provisions for proportionality review, this had not been required. See, e.g., Jurek v. Texas, supra p. 707. It approved the following California scheme:

> * * * Under this scheme, a person convicted of first degree murder is sentenced to life imprisonment unless one or more "special circumstances" are found, in which case the punishment is either death or life imprisonment without parole. Cal.Penal Code Ann. §§ 190, 190.2 (West 1977).[13] Special circumstances are alleged in the charging paper and tried with the issue of guilt at the initial phase of the trial. At the close of evidence, the jury decides guilt or innocence and determines whether the special circumstances alleged are present. Each special circumstance must be proved beyond a reasonable doubt. § 190.4(a). If the jury finds the defendant guilty of first degree murder and finds at least one special circumstance, the trial proceeds to a second phase to determine the appropriate penalty. Additional evidence may be offered and the jury is given a list of relevant factors. § 190.3.[14] "After having heard all the evidence, the trier of fact shall consider, take into account and be guided by the aggravating and mitigating circumstances referred to in this section, and shall determine whether the penalty shall be death or life imprisonment without the possibility of parole." Ibid. If the jury returns a verdict of death, the defendant is deemed to move to modify the verdict. § 190.4(e). The trial judge then reviews the evidence and, in light of the statutory factors, makes an "independent determi-

13. Briefly, the statutory special circumstances are: (1) the murder was for profit; (2) the murder was perpetrated by an explosive; (3) the victim was a police officer killed in the line of duty; (4) the victim was a witness to a crime, killed to prevent his testifying in a criminal proceeding; (5) the murder was committed during the commission of robbery, kidnapping, rape, performance of a lewd or lascivious act on someone under 14, or burglary; (6) the murder involved torture; (7) the defendant had been previously convicted of first or second degree murder, or was convicted of more than one murder in the first or second degree in this proceeding. Cal.Penal Code Ann. § 190.2 (West 1977). These are greatly expanded in the current statute. See Cal.Penal Code Ann. § 190.2 (West Supp.1983).

14. The statute does not separate aggravating and mitigating circumstances. § 190.3 provides:

"In determining the penalty the trier of fact shall take into account any of the following factors if relevant:

(a) The circumstances of the crime of which the defendant was convicted in the present proceeding and the existence of any special circumstances found to be true pursuant to § 190.1.

(b) The presence or absence of criminal activity by the defendant which involved the use or attempted use of force or violence or the expressed or implied threat to use force or violence.

(c) Whether or not the offense was committed while the defendant was under the influence of extreme mental or emotional disturbance.

(d) Whether or not the victim was a participant in the defendant's homicidal conduct or consented to the homicidal act.

(e) Whether or not the offense was committed under circumstances which the defendant reasonably believed to be a moral justification or extenuation for his conduct.

(f) Whether or not the defendant acted under extreme duress or under the substantial domination of another person.

(g) Whether or not at the time of the offense the capacity of the defendant to appreciate the criminality of his conduct or to conform his conduct to the requirements of law was impaired as a result of mental disease or the effects of intoxication.

(h) The age of the defendant at the time of the crime.

(i) Whether or not the defendant was an accomplice to the offense and his participation in the commission of the offense was relatively minor.

(j) Any other circumstance which extenuates the gravity of the crime even though it is not a legal excuse for the crime."

> nation as to whether the weight of the evidence supports the jury's findings and verdicts." Ibid. The judge is required to state on the record the reasons for his findings. Ibid. If the trial judge denies the motion for modification, there is an automatic appeal. §§ 190.4(e), 1239(b). The statute does not require comparative proportionality review or otherwise describe the nature of the appeal. It does state that the trial judge's refusal to modify the sentence "shall be reviewed." § 190.4(e). This would seem to include review of the evidence relied on by the judge. As the California Supreme Court has said, "the statutory requirements that the jury specify the special circumstances which permit imposition of the death penalty, and that the trial judge specify his reasons for denying modification of the death penalty, serve to assure thoughtful and effective appellate review, focusing upon the circumstances present in each particular case." People v. Frierson, 25 Cal.3d 142, 179, 158 Cal.Rptr. 281, 302, 599 P.2d 587, 609 (1979). That court has reduced a death sentence to life imprisonment because the evidence did not support the findings of special circumstances. People v. Thompson, 27 Cal. 3d 303, 165 Cal.Rptr. 289, 611 P.2d 883 (1980).
>
> By requiring the jury to find at least one special circumstance beyond a reasonable doubt, the statute limits the death sentence to a small sub-class of capital-eligible cases. The statutory list of relevant factors, applied to defendants within this sub-class, "provide[s] jury guidance and lessen[s] the chance of arbitrary application of the death penalty," Harris v. Pulley, 692 F.2d, at 1194, "guarantee[ing] that the jury's discretion will be guided and its consideration deliberate," id., at 1195. The jury's "discretion is suitably directed and limited so as to minimize the risk of wholly arbitrary and capricious action." Gregg, 428 U.S., at 189, 96 S.Ct., at 2932. Its decision is reviewed by the trial judge and the State Supreme Court. * * *

(at 880–881 of S.Ct., 1043–1045 of L.Ed.2d). Justice Stevens concurred, stressing that some meaningful State appellate review in capital cases is essential. Justices Brennan and Marshall dissented, believing that, as long as capital punishment is to be permitted, comparative proportionality review is essential to reduce what they regard as the arbitrary and capricious imposition of the penalty.

Death penalty cases frequently raise procedural issues. An example is Caldwell v. Mississippi, 472 U.S. 320, 105 S.Ct. 2633, 86 L.Ed.2d 231 (1985), in which the Court overturned a death sentence after the prosecutor had urged the jury not to view itself as having the final say in whether defendant would die, because any death sentence would be reviewed by the State Supreme Court. A majority of the justices thought that the argument invited abdication of jury responsibility for the initial determination. Justice Rehnquist, for three dissenting justices, noted:

> This Court should avoid turning every perceived departure from what it conceives to be optimum procedure in a capital case into a ground for constitutional reversal. In this case the State of Mississippi proved four aggravating factors, including that petitioner previously had been convicted of four crimes involving threat of violence to a person. The jury was instructed to find the facts based upon the evidence and to apply those facts to the law as charged; at the sentencing proceeding it was told that it must find that the aggravating factors outweighed the mitigating factors, and the prosecutor's argument stressed these aspects of the jury's singular duty. There is no

> indication in the record that the jury returned the death sentence on any basis other than the evidence adduced, nor is there any reason to question the jury's conclusion. Under those circumstances I do not think that the Eighth Amendment or any other provision of the Constitution requires that petitioner's death sentence be overturned.

(at 2651 of S.Ct., 887–888 of L.Ed.2d).

This attitude often prevails in the current Court.

Questions

1. If the arguments of the justices were made entirely on grounds of utility or justice, rather than being based on constitutional principles, how would they differ from their present forms?

2. If we assume that the death penalty is proper for some, but not for all murders, and the murders for which it is proper are characterized by the presence of certain aggravating factors, what are some of the appropriate aggravating factors? Should they be selected with an eye to such goals of punishment as retribution or deterrence, or on some other basis?

3. If there is to be a death penalty, how much discretion should be allowed and who should exercise it? Should it be applied to all who meet narrow, previously defined criteria, should all decisions be made ad hoc, or what?

Chapter VI

ACCOMPLICES AND VICARIOUS AND CORPORATE LIABILITY; ATTEMPTS AND CONSPIRACY; LIVING WITH INTRACTABLE LEGAL PROBLEMS

A. INTRODUCTORY NOTE

This chapter deals with fringe areas of crime. The material on accomplices presents the question of the responsibility of those who encourage or assist the principal criminal actor. The bank employee who intentionally furthers the bank robbery plan by giving advance information and the driver of the getaway car should be punished for their parts in the robbery. What about the financier who launders the securities stolen, the arms dealer who sells the guns to the robbers as well-suited for bank robberies, and the mechanic who fine-tunes the getaway car to enable it to outrun the police? Is the human or corporate employer liable for crimes committed by employees?

The law of attempt deals with the chronological beginning of a criminal offense. At what stage in the conduct leading up to the commission of an offense does it first become criminal? This is the central problem of the attempt section. Where there is more than one person involved in the enterprise, there may be a criminal conspiracy, and criminal liability may appear at an even earlier stage than would ordinarily be the case with an attempt. Attempt and conspiracy are sometimes called inchoate crimes. The term aptly suggests both the undeveloped nature of the criminal activity and the state of the law. In the inchoate offenses and in the area of accomplices are a number of legal questions which have been seeking good answers for many years.

A beginning law student is very likely to think of the law as a coherent body of rules, changing slowly (if at all) and furnishing rather clear answers if approached with sufficient application and learning. (It is particularly important in criminal law, as we have seen, that the law give fair warning to the citizen of its prohibitions.) There is certainly much truth in this picture; there are a lot of reasonably clear answers in the law. But the new lawyer's first surprise is likely to be the discovery of the vast number of unresolved questions which confront him in his practice. Some are questions of first impression; others are recurring problems which simply do not seem to be resolved consistently or satisfactorily in practice. At least five reasons for this phenomenon can be suggested:

1. Perhaps the most significant factor was noted by Aristotle in Book V of the Nichomachean Ethics: Rules are general statements, and it is somehow impossible, in human affairs, to make proper provision for some particular things in any universal statement. Life has a way of being slightly incongruent with the

best drafted rules. This is a part of the secret of the ease with which a Socratic questioner can confound a group of beginning law students trying to formulate a legal principle. It is possible to think of fact situations which show the need for at least slight reformulation of almost any stated principle.

2. Sometimes, we fail to get good answers because we have not yet learned to put the right questions. The centuries of agonized hair-splitting in the field of theft over such issues as whether the accused had committed a trespass now seem to be over. Why? Because we have slowly come to realize that we were asking an unnecessary question. We do not really care whether a technical trespass has occurred, although this seemed to be an important question in earlier times, when it seemed to identify the serious wrongdoer. The questioning has moved on to more promising terrain. There is no reason to think that we are any smarter than our legal ancestors. We are certainly asking some questions today which our legal descendants will find foolish. Changing policy views, to be considered shortly, may help us to see issues more clearly, but much of our problem is simply due to easy acceptance of rules as they are, without pausing to inquire as to why they are as they are. Learning to entertain new questions is a difficult but important skill for lawyers to develop.

3. Sometimes, the faulty question asked is not so much based on inertia and insufficiently explored policy grounds as it is simply too broadly or too narrowly posed. Consider "the problem" of the effect of the victim's consent in criminal law. To try to deal with this as a single problem for which rules might be developed might be a tactical error. It might assume a unity where there is none. On the other hand, if we looked at consent only in connection with each particular crime, we might be overlooking a forest (to which at least some of our trees belonged) for the trees.

4. Where there is much policy conflict, rules are apt to be unstable or unclear. The agonizing reappraisals of the death penalty by the Supreme Court illustrate this in a situation where there are strongly felt differences on important issues. Sometimes the conflict is more subtle. In areas which are somewhat remote from the central concerns of a legal policy, the policy operates with less force and may be more easily overcome by different sets of policies. In fringe areas between galaxies of legal principles bits of matter may be drawn to one or another of the systems in apparently random fashion. The punitive policy of the criminal law is relatively weak in its application to one on the fringes of criminal activities. Principles of economic freedom and efficiency may protect one who knowingly furnishes some minor product or service to be used in criminal activity, for example.

5. As public perception and policies change, the common law may begin to follow. Shifts in the law are apt to produce at least short run doctrinal confusion. Something of this sort may be occurring now in response to recent increased concern about various forms of sexual imposition. Some of the principles of the law of rape and evidence concerning rape may be changing in response to this.

By now, you are aware that few legal principles are graven in stone, even though most have a large measure of stability. You are also beginning to be aware of areas in which legal principles seem inadequate or incomplete. There are many such spots in the material in this chapter. Some of the inadequately resolved questions may be listed here:

1. Should a purpose to advance the criminal enterprise be required for accomplice and conspirator liability? Should the two situations get identical treatment?

2. To what extent must an accomplice or conspirator have objectives entirely congruent with the others involved in the undertaking?

3. How, if at all, should the criminal law punish corporations?

4. How should the line between preparation and attempt be drawn?

5. To what extent is it proper to punish conduct before it reaches the stage of attempt?

6. To what extent, if at all, should impossibility of achieving the criminal objective be a defense to a charge of attempt or conspiracy?

7. What is the nature of the crime of conspiracy? (Almost all questions about this puzzling crime are difficult to answer in any intelligible way.)

As you reach these questions, and others of the same nature you may identify, try to decide why they have proved so hard to resolve. Most are problems of long standing; lawyers have lived with the difficulties for many years. You will have to learn to do so as well, but occasionally in your career you will see a solution and assist in improving the law, whether by advancing an argument in a brief, by proposing legislation, or by writing a judicial opinion.

B. ACCOMPLICES

1. Introduction

State v. Tally

Supreme Court of Alabama, 1894.
102 Ala. 25, 15 So. 722.

[Impeachment proceedings against Judge John B. Tally, grounded on his alleged complicity in the murder of Robert C. Ross. Ross had seduced Annie Skelton, Tally's wife's sister, in Scottsboro, and had then left town, in fear of murderous attack by Robert, James, and Walter Skelton, Annie's brothers, and John Skelton, a cousin. Ross returned several weeks later on account of his wife's illness, and, a few days later, still in fear, fled again early one morning by horse and wagon for Stevenson, eighteen miles away, intending to catch a train for Chattanooga.

[The Skeltons pursued, as soon as they learned of Ross's flight. Tally knew nothing of the pursuit until after they had left Scottsboro. He then went to the telegraph office to prevent Ross from being warned of the pursuit. He observed Ed Ross sending a telegram to his kinsman Robert and got a look at the message: "Four men on horseback with guns following. Look out." Tally then had the Scottsboro telegraph operator, Whitner, send a message to Huddleston, the Stevenson telegraph operator, and a friend of Tally's: "Do not let the party warned get away. Say nothing." The second message reached Huddleston five or ten minutes before Robert Ross arrived in Stevenson, and Huddleston did not deliver the first message or pass a warning to him because of Tally's request. As Ross was unloading baggage, the Skeltons arrived and murdered him in the street.]

McCLELLAN, J.

* * *

The second count of the information charges that "John B. Tally, judge of the ninth judicial circuit of the state of Alabama, unmindful of the duties of his said office, was, before the filing of said report of said grand jury, and while in such office, guilty of an offense involving moral turpitude, to wit, the offense of murder." * * *

This narrows the issues to three inquiries—two of fact and one of law: First (a question of fact), did Judge Tally, on Sunday, February 4, 1894, knowing the intention of the Skeltons to take the life of Ross, and after they had gone in pursuit of him, do any act intended to further their design, and aid them in the taking of his life? If he did, then, second (a question of law), is it essential to his guilt that his act should have contributed to the effectuation of their design—to the death of Ross? And, if so, third (another inquiry of fact), did his act contribute to the death of Ross? There can be no reasonable doubt that Judge Tally knew, soon after the Skeltons had departed, that they had gone in pursuit of Ross, and that they intended to take his life. * * * This was the situation: Ross was in what he supposed to be secret flight from the Skeltons. He was unaware that his early departure had been seen by one of them. He did not know they were all in full pursuit to take his life. * * * Judge Tally might well feel satisfied with the posture of affairs; he might well feel assured that his folks would take care of themselves, as they did. All he wanted was that this situation, which portended the death of Ross and the safety of his folks, should not be changed. * * * It would not do * * * to stop the warning by threatening or overpowering * * * the operator. The young man was a newcomer, and a stranger there, and a resort to moral suasion with him was therefore unpromising and hazardous. Not so with the operator at the other end of the line. He was Judge Tally's friend of long standing. He, through whose hands Ed Ross' message of warning was intended to pass, could be approached, and to him Tally addressed himself. * * * We therefore find and hold that John B. Tally, with full knowledge that the Skeltons were in pursuit of Ross with the intent to take his life, committed acts, * * * with the intent to aid, the said Skeltons to take the life of Ross under the circumstances which rendered them guilty of murder.

* * * Our statute has abolished the common law distinctions between accessories before the fact and principals, and between principals, in the first and second degrees in cases of felony, and provided that "all persons concerned in the commission of a felony, whether they directly commit the act constituting the offense, or aid or abet in its commission, though not present, must hereafter be indicted, tried and punished as principals, as in the case of misdemeanors." Code, § 3704. And, though the respondent here is proceeded against by virtue of this statute as a principal in the first degree, the evidence, it being confessed that he did not personally, or in such other way as to make him a principal in the first degree at common law, take the life of Ross, must present him in the light either of an accessory before the fact or as a principal in the second degree, as those distinctions obtained before the enactment of the statute to which we have adverted, or he cannot be

convicted. We have already stated our conclusion, and the considerations which led us to it, that Judge Tally did not command, direct, incite, counsel, or encourage the Skeltons to the murder of Ross. We have failed to find, and have so stated, that he knew of their felonious purpose before their departure from Scottsboro in pursuit of Ross. Up to that time there was no instigation or incitement by him to the commission of the crime by them until after the death of Ross, and hence, pending the pursuit, he could not have encouraged or instigated them to kill Ross. Judge Tally was therefore not, on the view we take of the evidence, an accessory before the fact to the killing of Ross. To be guilty of murder, therefore, not being a common-law principal, and not being an accessory before the fact,—to be concerned in the commission of the offense within the meaning of our statute,—he must be found to have aided or abetted the Skeltons in the commission of the offense in such sort as to constitute him at common law a principal in the second degree. A principal in this degree is one who is present at the commission of a felony by the hand of the principal in the first degree, and who, being thus present, aids or abets, or aids and abets, the latter therein. The presence which this definition requires need not be actual, physical juxtaposition in respect of the personal perpetrator of the crime. It is enough, so far as presence is concerned, for the principal in the second degree to be in a position to aid the commission of the crime by others. It is enough if he stands guard while the act is being perpetrated by others to prevent interference with them, or to warn them of the approach of danger; and it is immaterial how distant from the scene of the crime his vigil is maintained, provided it gives some promise of protection to those engaged in its active commission. At whatever distance he may be, he is present in legal contemplation if he is at the time performing any act in furtherance of the crime, or is in a position to give information to the principal which would be helpful to the end in view, or to prevent others from doing any act, by way of warning the intended victim or otherwise, which would be but an obstacle in the way of the consummation of the crime, or render its accomplishment more difficult. This is well illustrated by the case of State v. Hamilton, 13 Nev. 386, in which a plan was arranged between Laurie and others to rob the treasure of Wells, Fargo & Co. on the road between Eureka and some point in Nye county. Laurie was to ascertain when the treasure left Eureka, and signal his confederates by building a fire on the top of a mountain in Eureka county, which could be seen by them in Nye county, 30 or 40 miles distant. This signal was given by him, and his confederates, advised by it, met the stage, attacked and attempted to rob it, and in the attempt killed one of the guards. * * * He was constructively present though 30 or 40 miles away, and he was guilty as a principal in the second degree in that from and across this distance he aided and abetted his confederates by the beacon lights which he set upon a hill. * * *

So far, therefore, as presence goes, Judge Tally, on guard at Scottsboro, to prevent warning being sent to Ross, or intercepting, or attempting to intercept, messages of warning which had started on their flight, was in legal contemplation present at Stevenson,—the scene of the homicide,—standing over Huddleston, to stay him in the performance of his duty of delivering warnings to Ross. He was constructively there, and hence, for all practical legal purposes, actually there. Being thus present, did he aid or abet the killing of Ross? * * * The legal definition of "aid" is not different from its meaning in common parlance. It means "to assist," "to supplement the efforts of another." Rap. & L. Law Dict. p. 43. "Abet" is a French word, compounded of the two words "a" and "beter,"—"to bait or excite an animal;" and Rapalje and Lawrence thus define it: "To abet is to incite or encourage a person to commit a crime. An abettor is a person who, being present or in the neighborhood, incites another to commit a crime, and thus becomes a principal in the offense." Id. p. 4. * * * The definition must go further. It should appear by it that, to be an aider or abettor when no assistance is given or word uttered, the person so charged must have been present by preconcert, special or general, or at least to the knowledge of the principal, with the intent to aid him. This view is very clearly stated by Mr. Wharton. He says: "It is not necessary, therefore, to prove that the party actually aided in the commission of the offense. If he watched for his companions in order to prevent surprise, or remained at a convenient distance in order to favor their escape, if necessary, or was in such a situation as to be able readily to come to their assistance, the knowledge of which was calculated to give additional confidence to his companions, in contemplation of law he was aiding and abetting." 1 Whart. Cr.Law, § 210. * * * And Mr. Wharton further says: "Something must be shown in the conduct of the bystander which indicates [to the perpetrator, manifestly] a design to encourage, incite, or in some manner afford aid or consent to the particular act, though when the bystander is a friend of the perpetrator, and knows that his presence will be regarded by the perpetrator as an encouragement and protection, presence alone will be regarded as an encouragement. * * * The confederacy must be real. * * * Mere consent to a crime, when no aid is given and no encouragement rendered, does not amount to participation." 1 Whart. Cr. Law, §§ 211a, 211c, 211d. * * *

We are therefore clear to the conclusion that, before Judge Tally can be found guilty of aiding and abetting the Skeltons to kill Ross, it must appear that his vigil at Scottsboro to prevent Ross from being warned of his danger was by preconcert with them, or at least known to them, whereby they would naturally be incited, encouraged, and emboldened—"given confidence"—to the deed, or that he aided them to kill Ross, contributed to Ross' death, in point of physical fact, by means of the telegram he sent to Huddleston. The assistance given, however, need not contribute to the criminal result in the sense that but for it the result would not have ensued. It is quite sufficient if it facilitated a result that would have transpired without it. It is quite enough if the aid merely rendered it easier for the principal actor to accomplish the end intended by him and the aider and abettor, though in all human probability the end would have been attained without it. If the aid in homicide can be shown to have put the deceased at a disadvantage, to have deprived him of a single chance of life which but for it he would have had, he who furnishes such aid is guilty, though it cannot be known or shown that the dead man, in the absence thereof, would have availed himself of that chance; as, where one counsels murder, he is guilty as an accessory before the fact, though it appears to be probable that murder would have been done without his counsel; and as, where one being present by concert to aid if necessary is guilty as a principal in the second degree, though, had he been absent murder would have been committed * * *.

We have already said enough to indicate the grounds of the conclusion which we now announce that Tally's standing guard at the telegraph office in Scottsboro to prevent Ross being warned of the pursuit of the Skeltons was not by preconcert with them, and was not known to them. It is even clear and more certain that they knew neither of the occasion nor the fact of the sending of the message by him to Huddleston; and hence they were not, and could not have been, aided in the execution of their purpose to kill by the keeping of this vigil, or by the mere fact of the forwarding of the message to Stevenson, since these facts in and of themselves could not have given them any actual, substantial help, as distinguished from incitement and encouragement, and they could not have aided them by way of incitement and encouragement, because they were ignorant of them; and so we are come to a consideration of the effect, if any, produced upon the situation at Stevenson by the message of Judge Tally to Huddleston. Its effect upon the situation could only have been through Huddleston, and upon his action in respect of the delivery to Ross of the message of warning sent by Ed Ross. This latter message reached Huddleston for Ross, we suppose, about five minutes—certainly not more than ten minutes—before Ross arrived at Stevenson. * * * Upon receiving the two messages, he went at once without waiting, to copy them, to the Stevenson Hotel, which is located very near the telegraph office, in quest of Ross, upon the idea that he might have already arrived. * * * Not finding him there (for he had not yet reached Stevenson), Huddleston returned to the door of the depot, upstairs, in which was the telegraph office. By this time the command which Judge Tally had laid upon him had overmastered his sense of duty, and diverted him from his purpose to deliver Ed Ross' message * * *. He did not warn Ross, because he did not want Ross to get away, and this because Judge Tally had asked him not to let Ross get away * * *.

It remains to be determined whether the unwarranted delay in the delivery of the message to Ross, or in advising him of its contents, thus caused by Judge Tally, with intent thereby to aid the Skeltons to kill Ross, did, in fact, aid them or contribute to the death of Ross, by making it easier than it would otherwise have been for the Skeltons to kill him, by depriving him of some advantage he would have had had he been advised of its contents when his carriage stopped, or immediately upon his alighting from it, or by leaving him without some chance of life which would have been his had Huddleston done his duty. * * * The knowledge that he would have had if the telegram of Ed Ross had been delivered to him, when it could and should have been delivered, of the pursuit of the Skeltons, together with the knowledge which would have been imparted to him by the report of the first gun in connection with the contents of the message, would instantly have advised him of the extent of his danger,—a danger which he could not combat, which was deadly in character, and from which he would naturally have been at once impressed the only hope of escape lay in immediate flight.

That was a chance for his life that this knowledge would have given him. That was a chance of which the withholding of this knowledge deprived him. Tally's telegram to Huddleston deprived him of that knowledge. * * * It is inconceivable to us after the maturest consideration, reflection, and discussion, but that Ross' predicament was rendered infinitely more desperate, his escape more difficult, and his death of much more easy and certain accomplishment by the withholding from him of the message of Ed Ross. This withholding was the work of Judge Tally. * * * And we are impelled to find that John B. Tally aided and abetted the murder of Robert C. Ross, as alleged in the second specification of the second count of the information, and to adjudge that he is guilty as charged in that specification, and guilty of murder as charged in said second count; and judgment deposing him from office will be entered on the records of this court.

No consideration or conclusion of fact in this opinion must be allowed to exert any influence upon the trials of the Skeltons and Judge Tally on the indictments for murder now pending against them.

[The dissenting opinion of HEAD, J., is omitted.]

Notes

1. *Parties at Common Law.* At common law, in the case of felonies, the law identified principals in the first degree, principals in the second degree, accessories before the fact, and (treated more leniently) accessories after the fact. As State v. Small, 301 N.C. 407, 412–413, 272 S.E.2d 128, 132 (1980), puts it:

> * * * A principal is one who is present at and participates in the commission of the crime charged. He who actually perpetrates the crime either by his own hand or through an innocent agent, or who acts in concert with the principal perpetrator, is a principal in the first degree. Any other person who is actually or constructively present at the place and time of the crime and who aids, abets, assists, or advises in its commission, is a principal in the second degree. Principals in the first degree and those in the second degree are equally guilty of the offense committed and may be punished with equal vigor.
>
> An accessory before the fact is one who is absent from the scene when the crime was committed but who participated in the planning or contemplation of the crime in such a way as to "counsel, procure, or command" the principal(s) to commit it. Thus, the primary distinction between a principal in the second degree and an accessory before the fact is that the latter was not actually or constructively present when the crime was in fact committed.
>
> At common law principals in the first degree, principals in the second degree, and accessories before the fact were all guilty of the same felony; they were all parties to the same crime. "This merely gave recognition to the legal theory that one is considered to have done what he has caused to be done." R. Perkins, *The Act of One Conspirator,* 26 Hastings L.J. 337, 349 (1974). There were nevertheless important procedural differences in the prosecution of principals and accessories before the fact, one of which was that accessories before the fact must have been indicted as such in order for a conviction to stand. Virtually all states have by now avoided such procedural limitations by legislative reform. See Model Penal Code § 2.04, Appendix (Tent.Draft No. 1, 1953) and the statutes cited therein. * * *

In the case of treason, the offense was so serious that those whose actions would have made them accessories before or after the fact in felonies were principals. In the case of misdemeanors, those whose actions would have made them accessories before the fact in felonies were treated as principals and there was no criminal liability based on accessoryship after the fact to misdemeanors.

At common law the guilt of an accessory was dependent on the established guilt of at least one principal (in either degree). This produced several procedural problems, the most important of which was that no accessory could be tried and convicted, without his consent, until a principal had been convicted. The accessory could escape if the only principal fled the jurisdiction and could not be recovered, or died before trial, or was acquitted. These rules have almost entirely disappeared today.

2. *Accessories After the Fact; Conduct.* United States v. Barlow, 470 F.2d 1245, 1249–1253 (D.C.Cir.1972):

> * * * It has been held that where the defendant merely provided assistance to the perpetrator of the actual crime *after its completion*—and nothing more—a conviction for aiding and abetting the principal regarding that crime cannot stand. * * *
>
> The evidence against Barlow, which on appeal is to be given the most favorable interpretation to support the convictions, disclosed the following facts: (1) that he had known Brown (the thief) since 1959; (2) that he had talked with Brown immediately after Brown returned to the Rhode Island Avenue lot from the Labor Department with the stolen goods in the panel truck; (3) when Brown entered the room in the office at Rhode Island Avenue, Barlow and Proctor were there and Brown at that time said, "I think they got me"; (4) almost immediately thereafter Barlow "hurried" to his Pontiac car which was parked near the panel truck, and opened the left rear door of the car so that Brown could place two boxes containing the stolen typewriter and tape recorder in the back seat; (5) after the boxes were placed in Barlow's car, he closed the car door; (6) Barlow then argued with Brown for several minutes before he (Barlow) got in his car and drove off with the stolen typewriter and tape recorder in the back seat of his car; (7) he then drove out Rhode Island Avenue toward the Maryland state line but apparently soon noticed that he was being followed and began to drive in what could be considered an attempt to evade his followers; (8) at one place he made a left-hand turn without giving any signal and turned closely in front of an oncoming dump truck; (9) thereafter he turned back toward the Rhode Island Avenue lot, drove through a red light and returned to the lot at a high rate of speed, parked his car and went into the office building and asked Brown to remove the boxes from his car and refused to be associated with such removal.
>
> From these facts it is obvious that Barlow drove off with the stolen goods within a few minutes after Brown brought them to the lot. * * *
>
> The nature and timing of Barlow's acts could also be considered by the jury as indicating that the asportation of the stolen goods, which was an essential part of the theft, was still in progress. The theft had been committed when Brown took the articles and removed them the slightest distance from their location at the Labor Building, but, since larceny is a continuing offense, the asportation element of the offense was still in progress when Brown arrived at the lot with the stolen goods. At that juncture his transfer of the stolen goods to Barlow's car, and the act of Barlow in driving away with them, could well have been considered by the jury as a continuation of the asportation rather than a receipt of stolen property by Barlow. * * *

* * *

* * * Thus, we recognize that all the elements necessary for an indictable crime had been committed when the articles were moved from their location at the Labor Building, but the asportation feature of the crime was still in progress when Brown drove into the lot and quickly transferred the stolen goods to Barlow's car. It was this continuation of the crime by Barlow that permitted him to be charged and convicted as an aider and abettor.

* * *

Barlow is not an accessory after the fact because that is an offense where one "knowing that an offense * * * has been committed, receives, relieves, comforts or assists *the offender* in order to hinder his apprehension, trial or punishment. * * *" (Emphasis added.) The gist of being an accessory after the fact lies essentially in obstructing justice by rendering assistance to hinder or prevent the arrest of the offender after he has committed the crime. Evidence of this offense is most frequently found in acts which harbor, protect and conceal the individual criminal such as by driving him away after he commits a murder. The very definition of the crime also requires that the felony not be in progress when the assistance is rendered because then he who renders assistance would aid in the commission of the offense and be guilty as a principal. That is precisely the situation we have here and the jury was fully justified in so concluding. The crime of larceny obviously continues as long as the asportation continues and the original asportation continues at least so long as the perpetrator of the crime indicates by his actions that he is dissatisfied with the location of the stolen goods immediately after the crime and with no more than a few minutes delay causes another to continue the asportation.

* * *

3. *Accessories After the Fact; Mens Rea.* Reg. v. Andrews, 47 Crim.App. 32, 34–35 (1962):

The point taken here is that the learned Chairman did not properly direct the jury as to what constituted the offence of being an accessory after the fact. That he did not do so fully is clear, because a full direction entails telling the jury that they must be satisfied that the defendant did the acts complained of for the purpose of assisting the principal felon to escape apprehension or conviction. * * * Lord Denning, in Sykes v. D.P.P. (1961) 45 Cr.App.R. 230; [1961] A.C. 528, refers to the definition of an accessory after the fact, and he said (at pp. 247 and 561 of the respective reports): "So that if the assistance was not given the felon personally, but only indirectly by persuading witnesses not to give evidence against him (see Roberts' Case (1569) 3 Coke's Inst. 139); or if the acts of assistance were done, not to hinder the arrest of the felon, but with another motive, such as to avoid arrest himself (see Jones (1948) 33 Cr.App.R. 33; [1949] 1 K.B. 194), or to make money for himself without regard to what happened to the felon (as in the present case) he would not be guilty as an accessory after the fact." In other words, Lord Denning is saying that if the acts done by the accused were to make money for himself without regard to what happened to the felon, he could not be guilty of the offence of being an accessory after the fact.
* * *

Questions

1. How does the Model Penal Code deal with the accessory after the fact?

2. A, B, and C are dragging V through the woods with the idea of lynching him. D, who is hidden behind a bush, overhears A say that he forgot to bring a rope and

thereupon, unobserved, tosses a piece of rope into the pathway where A finds it. When A, B, and C arrive at a clearing there is a large crowd assembled. E, a member of the crowd calls out "String him up," but is not heard by A, B, or C. The other observers merely stand by and watch the lynching. Who are parties to the crime?

3. In statutes punishing such crimes as statutory rape, sale of lottery tickets, or prostitution, it is sometimes suggested that the other willing party to the transaction be punished as a principal in the second degree. Such prosecutions usually fail. Is there a good reason why they should?

Note on Suicide and Related Offenses

At early common law suicide was a felony (punishable by forfeiture of goods). It is not clear whether it was a separate crime or a branch of criminal homicide. Absent statute, it may still be a crime today, although no modern form of punishment is applicable. Attempted suicide was a common law misdemeanor.

Where suicide remains a crime, those who aid or abet a suicide or an attempted suicide are punishable according to ordinary accomplice rules. Where suicide is not any longer a crime, the courts disagree as to the effects on the law of attempts and accomplices, absent clear statutory guidelines. Retaining attempted suicide as a crime does have the virtue of giving the police a clear ground to intervene and stop a suicide in progress, but it is not retained as a crime by states following the Model Penal Code.

The Model Penal Code does punish in section 210.5: (a) one who causes the suicide of another under given circumstances and (b) one who purposely aids another to commit suicide, or who solicits another to commit suicide, whether or not a suicide or attempted suicide follows.

2. *Mens Rea* Problems

State v. Weeks

Supreme Court of New Jersey, 1987.
107 N.J. 396, 526 A.2d 1077.

O'HERN, J.

* * *

The defendant was charged as an accomplice to the robbery of a bakery. The alleged principal, Godfrey, was tried separately at about the same time defendant was tried. Defendant had been seen driving, with a passenger in his car, away from the area where the robbery occurred. When defendant was arrested soon after the robbery, he was alone and had only $12 in his possession. He maintained that both he and his wife were steadily employed, and hence he would have no reason to commit a robbery. But despite his claim that he did not know that his passenger planned a robbery, much less one with a weapon, defendant was convicted of first degree robbery because the evidence showed that he was an accomplice to a robbery committed with a gun. * * *

* * *

In this case, defendant was found guilty of robbery, which was elevated to the first degree under N.J.S.A. 2C:15–1b because "in the course of committing the theft the [principal] * * * [was] armed with * * * a deadly weapon." Because of the serious consequences of this conviction as an accomplice, a clearer understanding of the scope of accomplice liability under the Code of Criminal Justice, N.J.S.A. 2C:2–6, must be imparted to the jury.

> Accomplice law deviates from traditional legal rules in the sense that crimes are defined as if the accomplice actually committed the acts that constitute the offense. For example, the murderer "kills" and the rapist "intentionally has sexual intercourse with" or "carnally knows" the victim. The accomplice does none of these things, yet * * * is convicted of murder or rape, not of "aiding a murder" or "aiding a rapist."
>
> > [Dressler, "Reassessing the Theoretical Underpinnings of Accomplice Liability: New Solutions to an Old Problem," 37 Hastings L.J. 91, 92 n. 3 (1985).]

The author notes that early common law of accomplice liability was intricate and frequently illogical. * * *

Legislative reform sought to clarify the distinctions between principals and all accessory or accomplice liability, with the result that accomplices are judged and punished as if they were the actual criminal offenders. Because of a moral intuition about holding one accountable for the wrongdoing of another, id. at 108, the extent of accomplice liability has been defined carefully in our Code of Criminal Justice. We restate the summary made by JUSTICE SCHREIBER in State v. White, supra:

> Under the New Jersey Code of Criminal Justice (Code), a person is guilty of an offense if it is committed "by the conduct of another person for which he is legally accountable * * *." N.J.S.A. 2C:2–6a. Legal accountability exists when a person "is an accomplice of such other person in the commission of an offense." N.J.S.A. 2C:2–6b(3). The Code defines a person as the accomplice of another when:
>
> > [w]ith the purpose of promoting or facilitating the commission of *the* offense; he
> >
> > (a) Solicits such other person to commit it;
> >
> > (b) Aids or agrees or attempts to aid such other person in planning or committing it; or
> >
> > (c) Having a legal duty to prevent the commission of the offense, fails to make proper effort so to do. [N.J.S.A. 2C:2–6c(1) (emphasis supplied).]

By definition an accomplice must be a person who acts with the *purpose* of promoting or facilitating the commission of the substantive offense for which he is charged as an accomplice. II The New Jersey Penal Code: Final Report of the New Jersey Criminal Law Revision Commission 57 (1971) observes that "one is 'legally accountable' for the conduct of another when he is an 'accomplice' of the other person 'in *the* offense.' By 'the offense' is meant that offense charged for which guilt is in question under § 2C:2–6a." [Emphasis in original.]

The Code defines purposely as follows:

> A person acts purposely with respect to the nature of his conduct or a result thereof if it is his conscious object to engage in conduct of that nature or to cause such a result. [98 N.J. at 128–29, 484 A.2d 122.]

Justice Schreiber's exposition focuses on the word "purpose." The use of the word in the statute evidences a careful legislative judgment, concerning the degree of an accomplice liability, arrived at after extended debate. The drafters of the Model Penal Code (MPC) originally presented a tentative formulation of accomplice liability premised on the culpable mental state of knowledge [1] as the sufficient predicate for establishing the liability of the accessory. This tentative formulation was rejected, and the MPC now specifically requires that the accomplice have the "purpose of promoting or facilitating the commission of the offense" of which the principal was convicted. *Model Penal Code and Commentaries* (Official Draft and Revised Comments) § 2.06(3)(a) (1985) (hereinafter *Model Penal Code and Commentaries*). The language in N.J.S.A. 2C:2–6c(1) is identical.

"[T]he Institute rejected th[e] position [of broadened liability], principally on the argument that the need for stating a general principle in this section pointed toward a narrow formulation in order not to include situations where liability was inappropriate."[2] *Model Penal Code and Commentaries,* supra, at 318 (comment to § 2.06). The drafters of our Code adopted this same policy * * *.

This narrow but important distinction between the culpable mental states of purpose and knowledge, set forth in the Code to establish the degree of accomplice liability, was effectuated inadequately in the trial of this case in two respects: (1) the instructions failed to convey to the jury that in order to convict the defendant as an accomplice to robbery in the first degree, an armed robbery, it had to find that the defendant had the *purpose* to participate in the crime defined in the Code, i.e., an armed robbery; and (2) the excessive cross-examination of the defendant about his *knowledge* of other alleged crimes of the principal combined with this erroneous instruction to create a clear capacity to lead the jury to conclude that "dealing with known criminals" would suffice as the mental state of culpability sufficient to convict.[3]

1. Knowledge can be equated with substantial certainty that a result will follow. N.J.S.A. 2C:2–2b(2).

2. Examples were given by the MPC commentators of situations where guilty knowledge was deemed insufficient to warrant congruent liability: Farm boy clears the ground for setting up a still, knowing that the venture is illicit; a landlord rents with knowledge that the premises will be used to establish a house of ill repute. *Model Penal Code and Commentaries* (Official Draft and Revised Comments) 316 (comment to § 2.06) (1985).

3. Not to be confused is the distinction between one's purpose to engage in the criminal offense and one's purpose to bring about the result of the perpetrator's conduct. See Robinson, "Imputed Criminal Liability," 93 *Yale L.J.* 609, 637 (1984).

> One may want to assist the perpetrator, but also wish that a possible harmful result not occur. For example, if A and B are engaged in a robbery, A may desire to assist B in the robbery even though A realizes that his assistance will increase the chance of B's wounding the robbery victim. [Id. at 637 n. 99.]

Under such circumstances, it has been held that A may be convicted for felony murder. But see N.J.S.A. 2C:11–3a(3) qualifying the felony murder rule in New Jersey.

* * *

The court's instruction * * * recited the statutory premise of N.J.S.A. 2C:2–6c(1)(b) that a person is an accomplice of another in the commission of an offense if, with the purpose of promoting or facilitating the commission of the offense, he aids or agrees or attempts to aid the other person, and if he is found to "share the same intent required to be proven against the person who actually committed the act." The charge did not, however, equally relate those principles to the degrees of robbery involved. The jury was told:

> If you find that the defendant William Weeks willfully and knowingly aided, agreed to aid or attempted to aid another person in the commission of a robbery, then you must consider him a principal and equally guilty.

Hence, the instruction did not clearly require the jury to find that defendant had shared the purpose to commit a robbery *with a weapon.*

* * *

For the reasons stated, the judgment of the Appellate Division is reversed and the cause remanded.

Note

Model Penal Code, § 2.04(3), Text and Comment 3 (Tent. Draft No. 1, 1953):*

Section 2.04. Liability based on behavior; Liability for behavior of another; Complicity

* * *

(3) A person is an accomplice of another person in commission of a crime if:

(a) with the purpose of promoting or facilitating the commission of the crime, he

(1) commanded, requested, encouraged or provoked such other person to commit it; or

(2) aided, agreed to aid or attempted to aid such other person in planning or committing it; or

(3) having a legal duty to prevent the crime, failed to make proper effort so to do; or

(b) acting with knowledge that such other person was committing or had the purpose of committing the crime, he knowingly, substantially facilitated its commission; or

* * *

(c) his behavior is expressly declared by law to establish his complicity.

* * *

The issue is whether knowingly facilitating the commission of a crime ought to be sufficient for complicity, absent a true purpose to advance the criminal end. The problem, to be sure, is narrow in its focus: often, if not usually, aid rendered with guilty knowledge implies purpose since it has no other motivation. But there

* Copyright © 1953 by The American Law Institute. Reprinted with the permission of The American Law Institute. (Section 2.04 has been renumbered and now appears as § 2.06. Paragraph (3)(b) was deleted by vote of the Institute.)

are many and important cases where this is the central question in determining a liability. A lessor rents with knowledge that the premises will be used to establish a bordello. A vendor sells with knowledge that the subject of the sale will be used in commission of a crime. * * * A utility provides telephone or telegraph service, knowing it is used for book-making. An employee puts through a shipment in the course of his employment though he knows the shipment is illegal. A farm boy clears the ground for setting up a still, knowing that the venture is illicit. Such cases can be multiplied indefinitely; they have given courts much difficulty when they have been brought, whether as prosecutions for conspiracy or for the substantive offense involved.

The problem has had most attention in the federal courts where there is division of opinion as to the criterion that measures liability. The Second Circuit, speaking through Judge Learned Hand, has taken the position that the traditional definitions of complicity (aiding, abetting, counseling, procuring, etc.) "have nothing whatever to do with the probability that the forbidden result would follow upon the accessory's conduct; and that they all demand that he in some sort associate himself with the venture, that he participate in it as in something that he wishes to bring about, that he seek by his action to make it succeed. All the words used—even the most colorless, 'abet'—carry an implication of purposive attitude towards it."[31] Restating the principle in a case where vendors of sugar and malt were charged as conspirators with their vendees to distill illegally, Judge Hand said: "There are indeed instances of criminal liability * * * where the law imposes punishment merely because the accused did not forbear to do that from which the wrong was likely to follow; but in prosecutions for conspiracy or abetting, his attitude towards the forbidden undertaking must be more positive. It is not enough that he does not forgo a normally lawful activity, of the fruits of which he knows that others will make an unlawful use; he must in some sense promote their venture himself, make it his own, have a stake in its outcome. The distinction is especially important today when so many prosecutors seek to sweep within the dragnet of conspiracy all those who have been associated in any degree whatever with the main offenders."[32]

The Supreme Court has quoted the *Peoni* formulation with approval and it has had some influence on other Circuits. Strong disagreement has, however, been expressed. Judge Parker, for example, has declared that guilt "as an accessory depends, not on 'having a stake' in the outcome of the crime * * * but on aiding and assisting the perpetrators * * * The seller may not ignore the purpose for which the purchase is made if he is advised of that purpose, or wash his hands of the aid that he has given the perpetrator of a felony by the plea that he has merely made a sale of merchandise. One who sells a gun to another knowing that he is buying it to commit a murder, would hardly escape conviction as an accessory to the murder by showing that he received full price for the gun * * *."[35] * * *

31. United States v. Peoni, 100 F.(2d) 401, 402 (1938). * * *

32. United States v. Falcone, 109 F.(2d) 579, 581 (1940), aff'd. without passing on the issue 311 U.S. 205 (1940). See generally Falcone Revisited: The Criminality of Sales to an Illegal Enterprise, 53 Col.L.Rev. 228 (1953).

35. Backun v. United States, 112 F.(2d) 635, 637 (4th Cir.1940). See also e.g., Bacon v. United States, 127 F.(2d) 985, 987 (10th Cir.1942) (sale of liquor to illegal state importer); Malatakofski v. United States, 179 F.(2d) 905, 916 (1st Cir.1950) (providing bribe money with knowledge of intended use). Earlier decisions generally held that aid with knowledge was enough. See e.g., Vukich v. United States, 28 F.(2d) 666 (9th Cir.1928); Jindra v. United States, 69 F.(2d) 429 (5th Cir.1934).

The draft, it is submitted, should not embrace the *Peoni* limitation. Conduct which knowingly facilitates the commission of crimes is by hypothesis a proper object of preventive effort by the penal law, unless, of course, it is affirmatively justifiable. It is important in that effort to safeguard the innocent but the requirement of guilty knowledge adequately serves this end—knowledge both that there is a purpose to commit a crime and that one's own behavior renders aid. There are, however, infinite degrees of aid to be considered. This is the point, we think, at which distinctions should be drawn. Accordingly, when a true purpose to further the crime is lacking, the draft requires that the accessorial behavior substantially facilitate commission of the crime and that it do so to the knowledge of the actor. This qualification provides a basis for discrimination that should satisfy the common sense of justice. A vendor who supplies materials readily available upon the market arguably does not make substantial contribution to commission of the crime since the materials could have as easily been gotten elsewhere. The minor employee may win exemption on this ground, though he minded his own business to preserve his job. What is required is to give the courts and juries a criterion for drawing lines that must be drawn. The formula proposed accomplishes this purpose by a standard that is relevant, it is submitted, to all the legal ends involved. There will, of course, be arguable cases; they should, we think, be argued in these terms.

* * *

Questions

1. An American jazz musician entered England, subject as he and the defendant knew, to a condition, designed to protect English workers from competition, that he not perform for profit while there. The defendant, proprietor of a jazz magazine, was in the party meeting the musician at the airport and reported his arrival for the magazine. The defendant subsequently purchased a ticket to a concert, where, as he knew, the musician was to perform illegally, so that he could attend and report the occasion favorably in his magazine. Was the defendant a party to the illegal performance?

2. The defendant was a weighmaster at a coal yard, entitled, as he knew, to refuse to sell the coal if the departing truck was overloaded. As he knew, driving an overloaded truck on the public highways was a crime (made so to protect the roads from undue wear). He found a particular truck to be four tons too heavy, but when the driver said he would risk it, the defendant allowed the sale to go through and the truck to depart. Was the defendant a party to the road offense? Would a finding of guilt be a greater or lesser extension of criminal liability than a finding of guilt in problem two?

Wilson v. People

Supreme Court of Colorado, 1939.
103 Colo. 441, 87 P.2d 5.

OTTO BOCK, JUSTICE.

Plaintiff in error was charged and convicted under two counts of having unlawfully and feloniously aided, abetted and assisted one Dwight J. Pierce in the commission of a burglary and larceny. One of his defenses was the absence of felonious intent on his part to commit the crimes in question, because he acted solely as a decoy to detect the commission of the crime and to report it to the proper officers, so that Pierce might be apprehended. Plaintiff in error will hereinafter be referred to as Wilson.

The facts, substantially, are as follows:

On the night of February 19, 1938, Wilson, son of the deputy district attorney of the thirteenth judicial district, and employed by him for several months prior thereto, was in Johnson's Cafe in Sterling, Colorado. Some time after 10 o'clock p.m. Pierce entered. Pierce had been drinking and was looking for a place where he could purchase more liquor. Without previous arrangement, Pierce approached Wilson and prevailed upon him to make an effort to find such a place. The two left the cafe and went to the Commercial Hotel, where Pierce borrowed some money. Wilson left and came back to report to Pierce that no whiskey could be had, but he could get a pint of sloe gin. This was satisfactory to Pierce, and Wilson procured a bottle of the gin which he delivered to Pierce, and both returned to the Johnson Cafe, where they drank some of the liquor. During that time a wrist watch which Wilson had been wearing disappeared while he was in the company of Pierce. When Wilson missed his watch he immediately accused Pierce of taking it. He continued to make the accusation through the evening, and at one time threatened to fight Pierce because of the alleged theft. Pierce denied the theft. * * *

* * * Wilson did not first propose the burglarizing, the idea originating with Pierce, and after the latter had told Wilson that he had burglarized the Wheat Growers Cafe several days before. There is some conflict in the evidence as to who first suggested breaking into Hecker Brothers' Drugstore, but they proceeded to the building in which it was located, tried several doors, finally going outside, and effecting an entry through the front transom. After Wilson had boosted Pierce up so that he could break the glass in the transom, and after looking around to see if anyone had heard them, Wilson again lifted Pierce and the latter handed the broken glass to Wilson, who dropped it on the cement. Thereupon Wilson again lifted Pierce up so that he could crawl through the transom. Pierce then proceeded to the cash register. Immediately after Pierce was inside the store Wilson ran to his father's office and telephoned the police to come to Hecker Brothers' Drugstore. He then returned to where the entry had been effected, and a few moments before the police arrived, Pierce handed to Wilson, through the transom, two or three bottles of liquor which he placed on the cement. Pierce noticed after he entered the store that Wilson had disappeared. Immediately after arrival of the police Wilson told them that Pierce was inside, designating him as "that guy from the Commercial Hotel." The police officer asked him how he knew, and he replied, "I boosted him in." Pierce escaped through the back door and Wilson immediately volunteered to track him down, and did so by going to Pierce's room at the Commercial Hotel, where he identified Pierce as the burglar in the presence of the police authorities. Wilson told the police, shortly after the apprehension of Pierce, that his connection with the burglary was for the purpose of getting even with Pierce for taking his watch, and that that was the only way he hoped to recover it. * * *

* * *

Instruction No. 10, to the giving of which defendant assigns error, reads as follows:

"One may not participate in the commission of a felony and then obtain immunity from punishment on the ground that he was a mere detective or spy.

"One who attempts to detect the commission of crime in others must himself stop short of lending assistance, or participation in the commission of the crime."

Defendant contends that this instruction is erroneous because it left no question of fact for the determination of the jury on his defense of decoy and detection. Wilson did assist Pierce in entering the drugstore. This he never denied and immediately revealed to the police his part in the transaction when they arrived in response to his call. The instruction inferentially placed guilt upon Wilson, because he did not "stop short of lending assistance," but actually gave assistance.

We find the following language in 16 Corpus Juris at page 128, section 115:

"For one to be guilty as principal in the second degree, it is essential that he share in the criminal intent of the principal in the first degree; the same criminal intent must exist in the minds of both."

And on page 129:

"One who participates in a felony as a feigned accomplice, in order to entrap the other, is not criminally liable, and he need not take an officer of the law into his confidence to avoid an imputation of criminal intent."

* * *

In this connection we cite also Wharton's Criminal Law (12th Ed.), volume 1, section 271, which reads in part as follows: "A detective entering apparently into a criminal conspiracy already formed for the purpose of exploding it is not an accessory before the fact. For it should be remembered that while detectives, when acting as decoys, may apparently provoke the crime, the essential element of dolus, or malicious determination to violate the law, is wanting in their case. And it is only the formal, and not the substantive, part of the crime that they provoke. They provoke, for instance, in larceny, the asportation of the goods, but not the ultimate loss by the owner. They may be actuated by the most unworthy of motives, but the animus furandi in larceny is not imputable to them; and it is in larcenous cases or cheats that they are chiefly employed."

It may be that the jury in the instant case placed more stress on the motives that actuated Wilson in his participation in the transaction than they did on the necessity of determining his felonious intent under the circumstances.

Reverting to Instruction No. 10, by judicial fiat this instruction makes any assistance in the perpetration of an offense criminal, whether felonious or not. The determination of whether the assistance by Wilson under the evidence in this case was given with felonious intent was solely the province of the jury, and this instruction erroneously invaded that province. There may be offenses and circumstances when any assistance rendered may make a participant guilty of a criminal offense; but here we are concerned only with the facts, circumstances and defenses in this case. Forfeiture of individual liberty through criminal procedure, by courts, must on our part meet all the demands of impartial justice. The giving of Instruction No. 10 constituted prejudicial error.

The judgment is reversed and the cause remanded for new trial.

Questions

1. Suppose that in the principal case, it had been Wilson instead of Pierce who had entered the store, Wilson acting only to secure Pierce's conviction, as in the actual case. Would this affect the criminal liability of either?

2. Suppose Pierce had entered the store, believing Wilson's story that it belonged to Wilson, in order, as he thought, to retrieve Wilson's property for him after Wilson had lost his key. What is the criminal liability of each?

Note

United States v. Beck, 615 F.2d 441, 448–453 (7th Cir.1980):

* * *

18 U.S.C. § 2(a) provides:

> Whoever commits an offense against the United States or aids, abets, counsels, commands, induces or procures its commission, is punishable as a principal.

The most well-accepted formulation of the standard of proof for aiding and abetting is that expressed by Judge Learned Hand in United States v. Peoni, 100 F.2d 401 (2d Cir.1938). He wrote that the prosecution must show that the defendant "in some sort associate himself with the venture, that he participate in it as in something he wishes to bring about, [and] that he seek by his action to make it succeed." Id. at 402.

The standard has two prongs—association and participation. United States v. Greer, 467 F.2d 1064 (7th Cir.1972), cert. denied, 410 U.S. 929, 93 S.Ct. 1364, 35 L.Ed.2d 590 (1973). To prove association, there must be evidence to establish that the defendant shared in the criminal intent of the principal, United States v. Smith, 546 F.2d 1275 (5th Cir.1977), that is, the state of mind required for the statutory offense must be shown for conviction as an aider and abettor. The defendant, however, need not have the exact intent as the principal. The "community of unlawful intent" does not rise to the level of agreement.[9] United States v. Lozano, 511 F.2d 1 (7th Cir.), cert. denied, 423 U.S. 850, 96 S.Ct. 94, 46 L.Ed.2d 74 (1975).

Criminal intent is often difficult to demonstrate by direct proof; it may be inferred from the attendant facts and circumstances. United States v. Groomer, 596 F.2d 356, 358 (9th Cir.1979).

9. It is this fact, indeed, that distinguishes aid and abet liability from conspiracy. Conspiracy requires proof of agreement, aiding and abetting does not. United States v. Cowart, 595 F.2d 1023 (5th Cir.1979). "Aiding and abetting has a broader application [than conspiracy]. It makes a defendant a principal when he consciously shares in any criminal act whether or not there is a conspiracy." Nye & Nissen v. United States, 336 U.S. 613, 620, 69 S.Ct. 766, 770, 93 L.Ed. 919 (1949).

A high level of activity need not be shown to prove participation, the second prong. "The defendant need not have participated in every phase of the criminal venture." United States v. Diecidue, 603 F.2d 535, 557 (5th Cir.1979). Instead, "there must be evidence to establish that the defendant engaged in some affirmative conduct; that is, there must be evidence that [the] defendant committed an overt act designed to aid in the success of the venture." United States v. Longoria, 569 F.2d 422, 425 (5th Cir.1978).

* * *

Conviction under 22 U.S.C. § 2778(a) and (c) and 22 C.F.R. § 127.01 [10] requires proof that the defendant (1) exported or attempted to export (2) goods that are on the United States Munitions List (3) without first having obtained a license for the export (4) willfully. The trial court found the evidence insufficient to prove Beck's participation in the attempted export. In ruling on the motion for acquittal, the trial court said Beck did nothing more than order and buy the merchandise.

* * * A purchaser of stolen goods is not liable as an aider and abettor of the theft because of his status as a buyer, but because he enters the plan too late. United States v. Varelli, 407 F.2d 735 (7th Cir.1969). See also United States v. Gallagher, 565 F.2d 981 (7th Cir.1977) (willing buyer not an aider and abettor of possession of stolen securities). The gravamen of the offense is the theft, not what happens to the goods afterwards. If the defendant does not aid the theft itself, he does not commit an act that aids the commission of the offense.

The illegal act required in a § 2778 prosecution is an export or attempted export—that is, the movement of goods across the international border. Beck did not merely purchase guns in South Africa which had already been exported. He worked actively with Freilich in developing the export plan. He gave specific packaging instructions so that there would be less chance of confiscation and said the goods should be shipped via direct South African flights for the same reason. He later arranged for a different freight forwarding company to call Freilich; Freilich changed shippers. He sent Freilich a copy of his import permits so that Freilich could tailor his invoices to Beck's needs. Beck consciously assisted the transportation of the goods across the international border. He did not enter the plan too late, but did so right on time.

10. 22 U.S.C. § 2778 provides in part:

(a)(1) In furtherance of world peace and the security and foreign policy of the United States, the President is authorized to control the import and export of defense articles and defense services and to provide foreign policy guidance to persons of the United States involved in the export and import of such articles and services. The President is authorized to designate those items which shall be considered as defense articles and defense services for the purposes of this section and to promulgate regulations for the import and export of such articles and services. The items so designated shall constitute the United States Munitions List.

(2) Decisions on issuing export licenses under this section shall be made in coordination with the Director of the United States Arms Control and Disarmament Agency and shall take into account the Director's opinion as to whether the export of an article will contribute to an arms race, increase the possibility of outbreak or escalation of conflict, or prejudice the development of bilateral or multilateral arms control arrangements.

* * *

(c) Any person who willfully violates any provision of this section or section 2779 of this title, or any rule or regulation issued under either section * * * shall upon conviction be fined not more than $100,000, or imprisoned not more than two years, or both.

22 C.F.R. § 127.01 provides in part:

(a) It is unlawful to export or attempt to export from the United States any article * * * for which a license or approval is required by this subchapter without first obtaining the required license or written approval from the Department of State.

* * *

Beck next asserts that even if he assisted the export, he lacked the requisite intent. Beck testified at trial that he did not know that Freilich lacked an export license; he further testified that he thought the export of the guns, which he characterized as sporting goods, was perfectly legal in the United States.

Beck's first contention has already been rejected as a basis for overturning a guilty verdict. In United States v. Lizarraga-Lizarraga, 541 F.2d 826 (9th Cir. 1976), the Ninth Circuit held that the defendant need not know that he is specifically required to have an export license. Rather, "the 'willfully' requirement of § 1934 [the predecessor statute to § 2778] indicates that the defendant must know that his conduct in exporting from the United States articles proscribed by the statute is violative of the law." Id. at 828–29. The government must "prove that the defendant voluntarily and intentionally violated a known legal duty not to export the proscribed articles." Id. Since the aider and abettor must have the same state of mind as the principal, an aider and abettor need not know that the principal needs or lacks an export license. The prosecution must only show that the defendant was aware of a legal duty not to export the articles.

Evidence adduced at trial showed that Beck had been in the arms business since 1972 and that he was a well-educated, knowledgeable businessman. Beck admitted that he knew about the arms embargo on South Africa but said he thought it was "on military weapons, military hardware and not directly on sporting rifles and sporting handguns."

The jury could have easily disbelieved Beck's story that the guns were sporting goods. * * *

* * *

Conviction under 18 U.S.C. § 1001 and 22 C.F.R. § 127.02 requires proof that the defendant made (1) an export document (2) containing a false statement (3) knowingly and willfully. * * *

* * * As in all cases of aiding and abetting, it is not necessary that the defendant have knowledge of the particular means the principal in the crime uses to carry out the criminal activity. United States v. Diecidue, 603 F.2d 535, 557 (5th Cir.1979). In a prosecution for violation of § 1001, the defendant is not required to be the actual preparer of the documents. United States v. Glantzman, 447 F.2d 199 (3d Cir.1971); Nye & Nissen v. United States, 336 U.S. 613, 69 S.Ct. 766, 93 L.Ed. 919 (1949). An aider and abettor of a § 1001 violation need not even know the particular document charged in the indictment will be filed. For example, in United States v. Lozano, 511 F.2d 1 (7th Cir.), cert. denied, 423 U.S. 850, 96 S.Ct. 94, 46 L.Ed.2d 74 (1975), the defendant was convicted of aiding and abetting the making of false statements to the Immigration and Naturalization Service (INS). The principal sought to improve an alien's immigration status by going through a fake marriage. The court upheld Lozano's conviction, although he was not present when the principal "filled in the petition form, and there is no direct proof that he was aware of the specific information called for or the exact responses she would make." Id. at 5. The court found that Lozano had committed acts which aided the making of the false statements because he actively and intentionally participated in the earlier steps of the transaction. The alien lived at a boarding house owned by Lozano, and there was evidence that Lozano put the alien in touch with someone else who helped arrange the marriage.

* * * [T]he evidence demonstrates that Beck was an active participant in the earlier steps of the export scheme. His failure to participate in the actual

preparation of the export declarations alone does not bar his conviction as an aider and abettor.

Section 1001 requires a knowing and willful intent in making a false statement. The intent requirement is satisfied when the defendant knows that misrepresentations to and concealment from a government agency are essential in order for a scheme to succeed. Lozano, 511 F.2d at 5. Although the defendant in *Lozano* did not order the statement to be made, it was "easily foreseeable" that the principal would "affirmatively inform the INS of the marriage and conceal its limited nature." Id. Personal knowledge of the false information also satisfies the intent requirement.

Taken together, aiding and abetting is proven if a defendant voluntarily gives false information or participates in a plan such that it is foreseeable that false information will be used in statements made to a government agency in order to further the plan. * * *

State v. McVay

Supreme Court of Rhode Island, 1926.
47 R.I. 292, 132 A. 436 (case 2), 44 A.L.R. 572.

BARROWS, J. Heard on a certification of a question of law before trial. Three indictments for manslaughter, each containing four counts, were brought against the captain and engineer of the steamer Mackinac, as principals, and against Kelley, as accessory before the fact. The steamer carried several hundred passengers from Pawtucket to Newport via Narragansett Bay. The boiler producing the steam by which the vessel was propelled burst near Newport and many lives were lost. The present indictments are for causing the deaths of three persons killed by escaping steam after the explosion of the boiler.

* * *

That the indictment charges manslaughter against the captain and engineer as a result of criminal negligence connected with the operation of the ship's boiler for present purposes is not disputed. * * *

* * * Because the manslaughter charge is "without malice" and "involuntary," Kelley contends that he cannot be indicted legally as an accessory before the fact. The argument is that manslaughter, being a sudden and unpremeditated crime, inadvertent and unintentional by its very nature, cannot be "maliciously" incited before the crime is committed. * * *

While every one must agree that there can be no accessory before the fact when a killing results from a sudden and unpremeditated blow, we do not think it can be broadly stated that premeditation is inconsistent with every charge of manslaughter. Manslaughter may consist, among other things, of doing an unlawful act resulting in unintentional killing, such as violation of motor vehicle laws or administration of drugs to procure an abortion. 29 C.J. § 136, p. 1149. Manslaughter is likewise committed if an unintentional killing is occasioned by gross negligence in the doing of an act lawful in itself. 29 C.J. § 141, p. 1154. There is no inherent reason why, prior to the commission of such a crime, one may not aid, abet, counsel, command, or procure the doing of the unlawful act or of the lawful act in a negligent manner. A premeditated act may be involved in such unlawful homicides. * * *

* * *

We have been referred to no case of an accessory before the fact on an indictment charging negligent manslaughter. The absence of such cases may be due to the fact that, by statute, in many jurisdictions accessories before the fact are treated as principals. Our statute relates only to their punishment and not to the nature of the offense. Gen. Laws 1923, c. 402, § 2 (6251). The case of United States v. Van Schaick (C.C.) 134 F. 592, treated all defendants as principals, holding the directors of a steamboat company negligent in failing to provide life preservers, as a result of which many passengers were drowned. The negligence was held to be a continuing cause actually operating to produce the deaths, though the directors personally were not present at the moment of death. The negligence charged against Kelley is not of this type.

We are convinced that in some types of manslaughter there may be an accessory before the fact and, from our study of the present indictments, we believe they aver such cases. Specific duties are stated to have been laid upon the captain and engineer. Defendant is charged with full knowledge of those duties and of the fact that the boiler was unsafe. He is charged with counseling and procuring the principals at Pawtucket to disregard their duties and negligently create steam. Until the explosion no crime was committed. Defendant was not present when the negligence resulted in a criminal act. The advice at Pawtucket was not continuing negligence on Kelley's part. The facts set forth in these indictments, if existent, are such that a jury might find that defendant Kelley, with full knowledge of the possible danger to human life, recklessly and willfully advised, counseled, and commanded the captain and engineer to take a chance by negligent action or failure to act.

* * *

Note

State v. Diorio, 12 Conn.App. 74, 75–76, 79–80, 529 A.2d 1320, 1321, 1323 (1987), cert. denied 484 U.S. 1065, 108 S.Ct. 1025, 98 L.Ed.2d 990 (1988):

> * * * The defendant's daughter was a member of the graduating class of a junior high school. Prior to graduation, the dean of students at the school had disciplined the defendant's daughter. Seeking revenge, the defendant hired and paid one Robert Fuller to dress as a clown at graduation and throw a pie in the face of the dean of students. The dean was hit with a cream pie in front of between one thousand and two thousand people.
>
> * * *
>
> General Statutes § 53a–8 requires that a defendant have the *mental state required for the commission of a crime* while intentionally aiding another. "[A]n accessory may be liable in aiding another if he acts intentionally, knowingly, recklessly or with criminal negligence toward the result, depending on the mental state required by the substantive crime." State v. Foster, 202 Conn. 520, 531, 522 A.2d 277 (1987). One may be an accessory to a crime without having a conscious objective to cause the result described by a statute defining the crime. Id. Thus, a person may be held liable as an accessory to a reckless act—in this instance, breach of the peace—if he has the requisite culpable mental state—

recklessness—for the commission of the substantive offense, and he intentionally aids another in the crime. Therefore, we find that being an accessory to a breach of the peace is a cognizable crime under Connecticut law. * * *

State v. Etzweiler

Supreme Court of New Hampshire, 1984.
125 N.H. 57, 480 A.2d 870.

BATCHELDER, JUSTICE, with whom BROCK, JUSTICE, concurs.

The issues raised in these consolidated cases involve the applicability of New Hampshire's motor vehicle laws and Criminal Code to a simple fact situation. The State and Mark A. Etzweiler, one of the defendants, have stipulated to the following facts. On July 30, 1982, the defendants, Mark Etzweiler and Ralph Bailey, arrived in Etzweiler's automobile at the plant where both were employed. Bailey had been drinking alcoholic beverages and was, allegedly, intoxicated. Etzweiler, allegedly knowing that Bailey was intoxicated, loaned his car to Bailey and proceeded into the plant to begin work. Bailey drove Etzweiler's car away. Approximately ten minutes later, Bailey, driving recklessly, collided with a car driven by Susan Beaulieu. As a result of the accident, two passengers in the Beaulieu car, Kathryn and Nathan Beaulieu, were killed.

On August 26, 1982, the grand jury handed down two indictments charging Etzweiler with negligent homicide, RSA 630:3, I, and two indictments charging Bailey with manslaughter, RSA 630:2, I(b) (Supp.1983). Subsequently, on April 6, 1983, the grand jury issued two additional indictments charging Etzweiler with negligent homicide as an accomplice.

Etzweiler filed motions to quash all indictments against him, and the Superior Court (PAPPAGIANIS, J.) transferred to this court the questions of law raised by the motions. * * *

* * * We dismiss all indictments against Etzweiler * * *

* * *

The First Indictments

The first indictments charge Etzweiler with negligent homicide, RSA 630:3, I.

> "[He] negligently entrusted his motor vehicle to one, Ralph Bailey, knowing that Mr. Bailey was drunk and was going to operate said motor vehicle * * * that Mr. Bailey while so operating said motor vehicle while drunk * * * did cross into the opposite lane and collide with a motor vehicle in which [decedents were passengers] * * * thereby causing decedent[s'] death[s]."

The requisites of the negligent homicide statute are met if a defendant negligently causes death. RSA 630:3, I. The State must establish that the defendant failed to become aware of a substantial and unjustifiable risk that his or her conduct may cause the death of another human being. RSA 626:2, II(d). "The risk must be of such a nature and degree that his [or her] failure to become aware of it constitutes a gross deviation from the conduct that a reasonable person would observe in the situation." Id.

In this case, however, death resulted not from the conduct of Etzweiler but from the conduct of Bailey, and the accountability of Etzweiler therefore must rest on the complicity of Etzweiler in Bailey's conduct.

At common law, an individual, who did not actually engage in the felonious conduct, could be held criminally liable as a principal if he or she were present during the commission of the crime, aiding and abetting the perpetrator. Thus, the owner of an automobile who lent his or her car to an intoxicated individual, sat by that individual and permitted him to operate the vehicle, may be convicted as a principal to manslaughter if death results from the operation of the vehicle.

At common law, Etzweiler could not have been guilty as a principal. He was not actually or constructively present during the commission of the offense, a necessary prerequisite. If he aided and abetted Bailey, although not present at the commission of the crime, Etzweiler, at common law, may have been guilty as an accessory before the fact to involuntary manslaughter. However, at common law, the crimes of principals and accessories before the fact were distinct and separate.

In 1973, the legislature enacted the Criminal Code and created RSA 626:8, the accomplice liability statute. That statute abrogated the common-law distinction between principals and accessories and narrowly defined those situations in which an individual could be held criminally liable for the conduct of another. Etzweiler's conduct, in lending his automobile to Bailey, must be measured against the standards set forth in the statute.

Etzweiler's conduct *may* fall within the statutory language defining negligent homicide. However, whether to impose criminal liability on Etzweiler involves an important policy decision of broad social consequences. The awesome deliberative task of making such a judgment should not, in the first instance, be thrust upon the juries in our trial courts but should be resolved through the legislative process to determine in what manner society seeks to deal with the criminal liability of those who permit unqualified operators to wreak havoc upon our public ways. This is a matter for legislative concern and is not a matter for judicial innovation.

The Second Indictments

The second indictments charge Etzweiler with the offense of negligent homicide as an accomplice. RSA 626:8; RSA 630:3, I.

RSA 626:8 delineates all situations in which an individual may be held criminally liable for the conduct of another. One situation is when an individual "is an accomplice of [another] in the commission of the offense." RSA 626:8, II(c). Accomplice liability under RSA 626:8, II(c) is defined in two parts, RSA 626:8, III and IV. Section III sets forth the elements which must be present above, beyond, and regardless of the substantive offense. Section IV sets forth the elements of the substantive offense that must be present in order to charge the accomplice.

RSA 626:8, III provides:

> "A person is an accomplice of another person in the commission of an offense if: (a) with the purpose of promoting or facilitating the commission of the offense, he aids * * * such other person in planning or committing it * * *."

* * *

Under section III, the State has the burden of establishing that the accomplice acted with the purpose of promoting or facilitating the commission of the substantive offense. * * *

Section IV sets forth the elements of the substantive offense that the State has the burden of establishing against the accomplice. "When causing a particular result is an element of an offense," the accomplice must act "with the kind of culpability, if any, with respect to that result that is sufficient for the commission of the offense." RSA 626:8, IV.

Our interpretation of the accomplice liability statute effectuates the policy that an accomplice's liability ought not to extend beyond the criminal purposes that he or she shares. Because accomplice liability holds an individual criminally liable for actions done by another, it is important that the prosecution fall squarely within the statute.

Applying these statutory prerequisites, we turn to the indictments charging Etzweiler as an accomplice to negligent homicide. * * * The State has alleged that, with the purpose of promoting or facilitating the offense of driving under the influence of alcohol, Etzweiler aided Bailey in the commission of that offense. However, under our statute, the accomplice must aid the primary actor in the substantive offense with the purpose of facilitating the substantive offense—in this case, negligent homicide. Therefore, the indictments against Etzweiler must be quashed.

Even if the indictments tracked the statutory language of RSA 626:8, III and IV, Etzweiler, as a matter of law, could not be an accomplice to negligent homicide. To satisfy the requirements of RSA 626:8, III, the State must establish that Etzweiler's acts were designed to aid Bailey in committing negligent homicide. Yet under the negligent homicide statute, Bailey must be unaware of the risk of death that his conduct created. We cannot see how Etzweiler could intentionally aid Bailey in a crime that Bailey was unaware that he was committing. Thus, we hold, as a matter of law, that, in the present context of the Criminal Code, an individual may not be an accomplice to negligent homicide. We need not reach the question of whether the statute provides for accomplices to manslaughter or murder.

* * *

SOUTER, JUSTICE, concurring specially:

* * * Although there would be no value in an extended analysis at this point, I do not read RSA 626:8, IV as my brother does. That section provides that

> "[w]hen causing a particular result is an element of an offense, an accomplice in the conduct causing such result is an accomplice in the commission of that offense, if he acts with the kind of culpability, if any,

> with respect to that result that is sufficient for the commission of the offense."

I read this language as an attempt to provide that a person may be criminally liable as an accomplice even if he does not act "with the purpose of promoting or facilitating the commission of an offense." RSA 626:8, III(a).

The attempt fails because the meaning of "accomplice" in section IV is unclear. * * * Whatever the explanation, section IV fails to give any comprehensible, let alone fair, notice of its intended effect and is thus unenforceable. * * *

* * *

KING, CHIEF JUSTICE, dissenting * * * (with whom DOUGLAS, JUSTICE, joins in Part I) * * *:

For the reasons that follow, I would affirm both sets of indictments against Etzweiler, as a principal to negligent homicide and as an accessory to negligent homicide. * * *

* * *

I. The Original Indictments

The original set of indictments charge that Etzweiler violated RSA 630:3, I by negligently causing the deaths of Kathryn and Nathan Beaulieu. RSA 626:2, II(d) states:

> "A person acts negligently with respect to a material element of an offense when he fails to become aware of a substantial and unjustifiable risk that the material element exists *or will result from his conduct.* The risk must be of such a nature and degree that his failure to become aware of it constitutes a gross deviation from the conduct that a reasonable person would observe in the situation." (Emphasis added.)

The questions transferred by the superior court pose, in effect, a single question: whether it is foreseeable that the act of knowingly lending an automobile to an intoxicated driver will result in a fatal accident. *See* RSA 626:2, II(d). This question of criminal foreseeability is a question of fact for the trier of fact to resolve. Therefore, the original set of indictments should be upheld.

* * *

If the State can establish that a person's purposeful conduct in lending his automobile to an intoxicated driver is itself a gross deviation from reasonable conduct and as such criminally negligent, the State must then demonstrate that the lender's conduct was a legal cause of the deaths. That is, the State must prove that the lender's criminally negligent conduct was a cause-in-fact of the deaths and also that the victims were members of the class of persons foreseeably endangered by the lender's criminally negligent conduct.

The court asserts that the deaths in this case "resulted not from the conduct of Etzweiler but from the conduct of Bailey." This conclusion, made without benefit of a trial court record or a finding by the trier of fact, begs the fundamental question in this case which should be reserved for the trier of fact: that is, who caused the deaths, how were they caused, and were the deaths foreseeable. It should be noted that the case law cited herein suggests that there can be more than one legal cause of a death.

* * *

Today, as the majority opinion concedes, Etzweiler's conduct must be measured against the standards set forth in the Criminal Code. The enactment of the Criminal Code effectively abrogated the common-law requirement that a principal must be, at a minimum, constructively present during the commission of the offense. In fact, the statutory language defining criminal negligence makes no mention of the constructive presence requirement.

* * *

Courts in other jurisdictions have upheld both the convictions and the indictments of persons charged as principals to criminal homicide although those persons were not present at the scene of the offenses when the deaths occurred. These cases appear to rest on the rationale that despite the defendants' absence when the homicides were committed, their gross negligence or unlawful conduct was a legal cause—although not the only legal cause—of the deaths. That is, the defendants' *own conduct* provided an instrumentality which caused the deaths.

In the cases in which a defendant loaned his car to an intoxicated driver and was present in the automobile sitting on the front seat beside the intoxicated driver when a fatal accident occurred, some courts have not relied upon the presence of the defendant at the moment of death as an element in assigning liability to the lender of the car as a principal. Freeman v. State, 211 Tenn. 27, 362 S.W.2d 251 (1962) (lending car to an intoxicated driver was a criminally negligent act and a legal cause of the resulting death, regardless of lender's presence or absence in car); State v. Hopkins, 147 Wash. 198, 265 P. 481 (1928) (presence of lender of car during fatal accident was not a material element in lender's conviction of manslaughter).

* * *

Finally, the court today holds that the question whether to impose criminal liability on Etzweiler should be resolved by the legislature and not by the juries in our trial courts. The court chooses to defer to the legislature despite conceding that "Etzweiler's conduct *may* fall within the statutory language defining negligent homicide." The court reasons that the imposition of criminal liability on Etzweiler is such an "awesome deliberative task" that "judicial innovation" should give way to the "legislative process."

The court's rationale, even though limited to a very specific fact pattern, is nevertheless troubling in its implications. That is, whenever cases arise involving exceptional conduct defined by the language of the negligent homicide statute, the court will wait until the legislature specifically proscribes that conduct by amendment to the Criminal Code before the court allows these cases to reach juries. The merit of such an approach is undiscernible when conduct such as Etzweiler's is already fully contemplated by our existing criminal laws. Further, such an approach may render the negligent homicide statute ineffective.

* * *

II. The Second Indictments

* * *

While the statutory phrase "accomplice in the conduct causing [a particular] result" provided by RSA 626:8, IV is not explicitly defined in the statute, when viewed as part of a totality it is implicitly defined by RSA 626:8, III(a). Under section III(a), a person is an accomplice in the principal's criminal conduct causing a particular result if, with the purpose of promoting or facilitating the principal's criminal conduct, the person solicits that conduct, or aids or agrees or attempts to aid that conduct. Section III also assigns liability in those situations in which the accomplice actively seeks the criminal *result* by aiding and abetting the principal without caring precisely how the principal achieves that result.

Therefore, for a person to be criminally liable under RSA 626:8, IV for the crime of a principal, that person must act *purposefully* with respect to the principal's criminal *conduct*. However, with respect to the *result* of the principal's criminal conduct, section IV requires a showing that the person acted with the same state of mind required of the principal. * * *

* * *

* * * The statutory analysis herein satisfies the rule of statutory construction that all parts of a statute be read as meaningful and consistent parts of a whole. This analysis also fulfills the court's duty to interpret a statute so as to effectuate its legislative intent: here, to inculpate persons who purposely further the criminal conduct of others while grossly unaware of the substantial and unjustifiable risks attending that criminal conduct.

The court's holding that as a matter of law "a person may not have a purpose of having another commit negligent homicide" is problematic. First, this holding is not supported by the language of RSA 626:8. Second, the court's holding requiring purposeful conduct with respect to the result of the principal's offense, effectively precludes criminal liability for aiding any homicide other than intentional homicide. The justification, theoretical or otherwise, for such an approach to accomplice liability is imperceptible.

A pattern of case law in other jurisdictions supports the view that the State properly indicted Etzweiler as an accomplice to Bailey's negligent homicide even though Etzweiler was absent from the car, and neither he nor Bailey acted "purposely" with respect to the resulting deaths.

* * *

Note: **Mens Rea** *of Accessory When Principal Acts Recklessly or Negligently*

Model Penal Code, § 2.06, Comment 3:*

3. *Innocent or Irresponsible Agent.* * * *

* * *

When crimes call for no more than recklessness or negligence for their commission, it should suffice that one with such recklessness or negligence causes the required overt conduct by an innocent or irresponsible person; there is no reason for demanding that such conduct be caused purposely. A reckless motorist who runs down a pedestrian is no less guilty of manslaughter because a carefully performed emergency operation is the immediate cause of death. One who recklessly leaves his car keys with an irresponsible agent known to have a penchant for mad driving should, by the same token, be accountable for a homicide due to such driving if the irresponsible agent uses the car in that way. So too an aggressor who provokes his victim to fire in reasonable self-defense ought to be guilty, at the least, of manslaughter if a bystander is hit, even though he does not mean to cause the shot in self-defense. Analytically, these are situations where liability rests on causing conduct of another, even though they are not always thought of in this way.

The Code formulation meets the difficulties described. A defendant is accountable for the behavior of an innocent or irresponsible person when he has caused such behavior to occur, provided he has caused it with the purpose, knowledge, recklessness or negligence that the law requires for commission of the crime with which he has been charged. One who directs a child to kill is guilty of intentional homicide if death results, because he meant the death to occur. If recklessly endangering life is a crime, one may commit it by causing a madman to perform the dangerous action, whether one does so purposely or recklessly. So too, if the defendant recklessly caused a child to kill intentionally, the child's intent to kill is not imputed to him; he may be guilty of manslaughter for his recklessness but he is accountable for nothing more. But if obtaining property by false pretenses is a crime only if the false pretenses are made purposely, one does not commit it by negligently causing an innocent agent to make statements that are false; one must do so purposely. In short, the section proposes to determine liability by the culpability and state of mind of the defendant, coupled with his own overt conduct and the conduct in which he has caused another to engage. This probably has been the law; even more clearly, it should be the law, and most of the recent revisions so provide.

Question

Does the propriety of McVay's criminal liability seem clearer than that of Etzweiler? If so, why?

Note: **Mens Rea** *of Accessory in Absolute Liability Offense*

In Johnson v. Youden, [1950] 1 K.B. 544, the defendant solicitors were charged with aiding and abetting a builder in the absolute liability offense of selling of a house for a greater price than the law permitted. The trial court was held properly to have dismissed the charges against the solicitors when it found that they did not know that the extra money had been paid. Lord Goddard, C.J., held that while, for liability, an accessory need not know that an offense is being committed—the accessory need not know the law—he must know that the essential facts constituting the offense exist.

3. The Effect of Diverging Purposes

Parker v. Commonwealth

Court of Appeals of Kentucky, 1918.
180 Ky. 102, 201 S.W. 475.

SAMPSON, J. * * * The defendant, Clarkie Parker, was a candidate for re-election as constable in his district, and was electioneering. The defendant, Shepherd, while a stranger in that neighborhood, was riding with Parker as he canvassed the neighborhood where the homicide occurred. Parker also claims that he held a warrant for the arrest of Roscoe Farris upon a charge of affray, and was then in search of Farris, and that he had summoned Shepherd to help in making the arrest. The deceased, Sams, lived at the forks of the road near a schoolhouse and in a fairly thickly populated community. * * * Parker and Shepherd, who were riding mules, passed by the Sams home, apparently under the influence of liquor, and holloed and sang. No one seems to know exactly what was said by the men on the mules, although some of the witnesses state that Parker called for the deceased to come out. At any rate Sams did not go out to the road. * * * The travelers did not go very far past the house until they returned and called for the deceased to come out to the road, and he and his neighbor, Wisen, went out to where Shepherd and Parker were on their mules. Some conversation ensued, and finally Parker asked Sams to vote for him in the election, and this Sams declined to do, giving as his reason that Parker and another had upon a former occasion treated him badly. This angered Parker, who told Sams that he would not stand for any bulldozing. Parker at the time had a 38-caliber pistol in his saddle pockets. Some of the witnesses state that Sams then turned to go to his house when Parker rode his mule around in front of Sams and cut him off from his home. About this time Shepherd, who was some little distance up the hill, rode his mule rapidly down the slope in the direction of Parker and Sams, dismounted quickly behind his mule and drew a pistol. Parker dismounted about the same time on the side next to Sams. Meanwhile there were threats and curses exchanged between the parties. Instantly Shepherd began to fire at Sams, one bullet taking effect in the leg of Sams and the other in his abdomen. He then turned quickly on an old man named Wise, an entirely innocent bystander, and fired at him, killing him instantly, then fired at and wounded another onlooker named John Alex Sams, inflicting only a slight injury in the left arm. Before any one could realize what had happened both Shepherd and Parker ran away, leaving their mules as well as the dead and dying. There is no evidence that Parker fired a shot, or that he exhibited a pistol. The evidence further shows that the deceased, Sams, was unarmed except he had in his pocket an ordinary pocketknife. * * *

* * *

The point is further made that the third paragraph of instruction No. 1 directs the jury to find the defendant Parker guilty of willful murder if the jury believe from the evidence beyond a reasonable doubt that the shooting by Shepherd was done in sudden heat of passion or sudden affray, and that the aiding and abetting by Parker was done with malice aforethought. To thoroughly understand this instruction one must be acquainted with the facts of the case. It will be remembered that Parker and another man named Baker had some time before the killing imposed upon and abused the deceased, Sams, and that there was bad feeling existing between Parker and Sams. The commonwealth asserted that this was on Parker's mind at the time he passed the house the first time on the day of the killing and caused him to return, and that all this is fully proven by his acts, conduct, and manner described by the witnesses in the evidence. While Shepherd may not have entertained malice against the deceased, Sams, the evidence sufficiently sustains the conclusion reached by the jury that Parker did entertain such feeling towards Sams, and this feeling in his breast, after passing the house of the deceased, induced this desperate man, Shepherd, to return to the house of the deceased for the purpose, as the jury no doubt concluded from the evidence, of precipitating a difficulty and thus giving Shepherd an opportunity, under the excitement of the moment to shoot and kill the deceased, Sams. Under such facts the shooting and killing by Shepherd may have been in sudden heat or passion so far as Shepherd was concerned, but the aiding, abetting, encouraging, inciting, and commanding on the part of Parker was with malice aforethought, and Parker, under such facts, is guilty of willful murder. This court has several times recognized the principle that where the person who fires the shot which produces the death acts in sudden heat and passion or sudden affray, and is guilty only of manslaughter, the aider and abettor who incites the killing may be guilty of willful murder if he at the time aids, abets, and incites the killing, entertains malice aforethought, and his actions are controlled by such malice. Mickey v. Commonwealth, 9 Bush, 596; Dorsey v. Commonwealth, 17 S.W. 183; Arnold v. Commonwealth, 55 S.W. 894. The rule is stated as follows: If several persons are present at the death of a man, they may be guilty of different degrees of homicide, as one of murder and another of manslaughter; for if there be no malice in the party striking, and malice in the abettor, it will be murder in the latter, though only manslaughter in the former. 1 East, P.C. c. 5, § 121, p. 121. So, likewise, it may be murder in the party striking the fatal blow and only manslaughter on the part of the abettor. 1 Hale, 446; Russell on Crimes, 510; Roberson's Kentucky Criminal Law, vol. 1, p. 93.

* * *

Note: Convicting Accessory of Greater Offense Than Principal

State v. Ward, 284 Md. 189, 201–204, 396 A.2d 1041, 1049–1050 (1978):

At the common law the principal in the second degree may be tried and convicted prior to the trial of the principal in the first degree, or even after the latter has been tried and acquitted. 1 Hale P.C. *437. Furthermore, a principal in the second degree may be convicted of a higher crime or a lower crime than the principal in the first degree. Clark & Marshall § 8.05, p. 521; Perkins at 670–671.[15] With respect to accessories, however, the common

15. Perkins gives examples. "[The principal in the second degree] may be convicted of first-degree murder, for example, although the [principal in the first degree] has been convicted of second-degree murder. Similarly, the former may be convicted of murder although the latter has been convicted of manslaughter, since an abettor may counsel with malice aforethought what the other perpetrates in the sudden heat of passion. An abettor may be convicted of felony even though the perpetrator has been convicted of misdemeanor only.

law took a different path. An accessory cannot be tried, without his consent, before the principal.[16] State v. Williamson, 282 Md. at 112, 382 A.2d 588 (concurring opinion by Levine, J.); Clark & Marshall § 8.05, p. 523; Perkins at 672–673. And an accessory could not be convicted of a higher crime than his principal. Blackstone declares flatly:

> "It is a maxim, that *accessorius sequitur naturam sui principalis*: and therefore an accessory cannot be guilty of a higher crime than his principal; being only punished as a partaker of his guilt." Blackstone at *36.

See Clark & Marshall § 8.03, p. 514; Hochheimer § 38; Perkins at 675; Wharton § 276. The rule that an accessory before the fact may not be convicted of a higher crime than the principal has not been altered by statute or judicial decision in Maryland and is the law of this State at the present time.[a]

In arguing to the trial court that a person could be convicted of murder in the first degree as an accessory, although the principal has been convicted of that murder in the second degree, the State declared that "Wharton says we can do it." We think that the State misinterpreted Wharton. It is correct that Wharton says:

> "The instigator may act in hot blood, in which case he will be guilty only of manslaughter, while the perpetrator may act coolly, and thus be guilty of murder. The converse, also, may be true: the instigation may be cool and deliberate, the execution in hot blood by a person whom the instigator finds in a condition of unreasoning frenzy. A person desiring coolly to get rid of an enemy, for instance, may employ as a tool someone whom that enemy has aggrieved, and who is infuriated by his grievance. Hence an accessory before the fact (or, to adopt the terms of recent codes, an instigator) may be guilty of murder, while the principal (or perpetrator) may be guilty of manslaughter; or the accessory before the fact (instigator), acting in hot blood, may be guilty of manslaughter, while the perpetrator (principal), acting with deliberate malice, may be guilty of murder." Wharton § 276, pp. 363–364.

Immediately preceding this statement, however, is a recognition of the common law rule and a qualification regarding the view expressed:

Needless to say, the abettor may be convicted of a lower degree of crime than the perpetrator." Id. at 671 (footnotes omitted).

16. Even when the accessory waives the right, and may be tried before the principal, if he is convicted it is necessary to respite judgment until the trial of the principal because a subsequent acquittal of the latter would annul this conviction. 1 Hale P.C. *623.

The principal and the accessory may be tried jointly, unless the accessory is entitled to a severance, but if they are tried together the trier of fact must first inquire into the guilt of the principal, and, if it finds him not guilty, the accessory must be acquitted. Only upon finding the principal guilty may the trier of fact consider whether the accessory is guilty. An acquittal of the principal, of course, bars a subsequent trial of the accessory. Perkins at 672–673. Professor Perkins finds this aspect of the principal-accessory concept to be "quite absurd." He points out: "Anything which prevents conviction of the principal makes impossible the conviction of the accessory. Hence, if the principal is never apprehended, or if before the moment of conviction he should die or be pardoned, the accessory must go free although his guilt may be well known and easy to prove. Furthermore, if both are convicted in due course, but the conviction of the principal is thereafter reversed, the conviction of the accessory cannot stand." Id. at 673.

a. This is no longer true in Maryland. Jones v. State, 302 Md. 153, 486 A.2d 184 (1985).

> "Under the old law, the defendant was first convicted, and then the accessory was charged with being accessory to the offense which the conviction covered. *But now that instigation is a substantive offense,* it must be remembered that the offense of the instigator is not necessarily of the same grade as that of the perpetrator." Id. § 276, p. 363 (emphasis added).

Before us the State also quotes Williams § 130, pp. 390–391. Professor Williams refers to the rule that a principal in the first degree may be convicted of murder and a principal in the second degree of manslaughter, and asserts: "There is no reason why a similar result should not be reached for accessories before." Id. § 130, p. 390 (§ 62, p. 210 (1st ed. 1953)). He gives examples whereby an accessory before the fact could be guilty of manslaughter and the principal of murder, and the converse where the guilt of the secondary party is the greater. He concludes: "To put the matter generally, a secondary party can be convicted of a crime of a higher degree than the principal." Id. § 130, p. 391 (§ 62, p. 211 (1st ed. 1953)). But he relies heavily on Wharton, and we are constrained to conclude that his view, like that of Wharton, depends upon the status of the law whereby accessoryship before the fact has been made a substantive offense by statute.

Accessoryship before the fact was not a substantive offense under common law, and there being neither statute nor judicial decision in this jurisdiction making it so, it is not a substantive offense in Maryland. * * *

Note

For the effect of the principal's justification or excuse upon the liability of the accomplice, see United States v. Lopez, supra p. 505.

State v. Craft

Supreme Court of Missouri, 1936.
338 Mo. 831, 92 S.W.2d 626.

COOLEY, COMMISSIONER.

By information filed in the circuit court of Dunklin county, defendant was charged with robbery in the first degree alleged to have been committed by means of a dangerous and deadly weapon, a pistol. The cause was sent on change of venue to the circuit court of Stoddard county, where it was tried, resulting in defendant's conviction and sentence to 10 years' imprisonment in the penitentiary. He appeals.

The robbery occurred on October 28, 1933, on a highway between Kennett and Senath, in Dunklin county. There was then no bank at Senath, and Jones Brothers, a partnership, operated at that place a business called Jones Brothers' Exchange, where checks were cashed and money advanced for cotton picking, etc. This exchange was managed by one Dee McMunn, who each morning would take from a bank at Kennett to Senath a sufficient sum for the expected needs of the day. There was another similar exchange at Senath operated by a Mr. Caneer, the money for which was brought from Paragould, Ark., and which exchange is generally referred to in the evidence as the Paragould Exchange.

About 7:30 on the morning of October 28, 1933, McMunn started from Kennett to Senath, alone and unarmed, in an automobile, having in his possession about $4,200, belonging to Jones Brothers. On the way, according to his testimony, he was stopped and robbed of the money, at the point of a pistol, by two men whom he met, driving a Chrysler automobile, and who, after passing him, turned and followed him a short distance and then forced him to the side of the road and compelled him to stop. Those two men were subsequently arrested and were identified as Elmer Craft, a cousin of defendant, and Jap Brooks. Both were eventually tried and convicted.

Defendant was not present at the actual robbery. * * *

* * *

* * * His testimony, however, and that of one of his witnesses, * * * tended to prove that * * * it was the messenger of the Paragould Exchange and not McMunn or a messenger or agent of the Jones Brothers' Exchange whom it was contemplated to rob. Defendant denied having participated in a conspiracy to rob anybody, but he contended and offered evidence tending to prove that there had been no proposition or talk of robbing any one but the messenger of the Paragould Exchange. * * *

* * *

* * * It is true that defendant at all times *said* he would not have anything to do with the robbery. But there was evidence from which the jury could find that he was present at all, or practically all, of the conferences held among the conspirators, and especially with the instigating and moving spirit, Doherty, preceding the robbery, and at the meeting at which all were present and at which definite plans were made for the commission of the robbery. He recommended, or at least suggested, a man to commit the overt act; first Nicholson, and when Nicholson "got cold feet," and refused to participate in the actual robbery, Elmer Craft, who, with Brooks, did do it. He took Doherty to see Elmer Craft for the purpose of getting the latter to commit the robbery, helped arrange for those two to get together, and was present at the subsequent conference when all the conspirators were together and the definite plans were made. He went with Nicholson, one of the conspirators (and who was subsequently convicted), to purchase an automobile to be used in the robbery. * * *

Defendant requested an instruction, 8–D, as follows: "The Court further instructs the jury that even though you may find and believe from the evidence in this case that the defendant Tom J. Craft did conspire or agree with Delmar G. Doherty and others to rob some person or persons other than D. McMunn or other messenger or employee in the service or employment of Irl Jones, Byron Jones and L.R. Jones, doing business under the style of Jones Brothers Exchange, yet you cannot convict the said Tom J. Craft in this case for having such agreement or entering into such conspiracy if you should find that he had such agreement or entered into such conspiracy, but you must convict the said Tom J. Craft, if you convict him at all, for having agreed or conspired to rob the said D. McMunn or other person or persons in the employment of said Irl Jones, Byron Jones and L.R. Jones, doing business as Jones Brothers Exchange, as set forth in other instructions, and for not having conspired to rob some other exchange, person or persons whomsoever."

The court refused that instruction in the form requested, but modified it by adding thereto, "provided you find that he had not conspired with said persons to commit robbery generally," and gave it as thus modified. Complaint is made of such action of the court. We think that complaint well founded. The last part of the instruction as requested, viz., "and for not having conspired to rob some other exchange, person or persons whomsoever," seems somewhat confusing. Perhaps the writer thereof meant to say, "and *not for* having conspired," etc. That part of the instruction might well have been omitted entirely. But the purport of the instruction as a whole, in the form requested, is plain, viz., that defendant could be convicted only if the jury found that he had conspired to rob McMunn or other messenger or employee of Jones Brothers' Exchange. Under the evidence we think defendant was entitled to an instruction to that effect, and that the modification made by the court was improper, as was also a similar modification of defendant's requested instruction 12–D.

Defendant is charged with a specific crime, the robbery of Dee McMunn. He did not participate in the overt act, and is guilty, if at all, only by reason of having conspired with the actual perpetrators to commit that crime, thus making himself an accessory before the fact and under the rule in this state liable as a principal. In 16 C.J. p. 135, § 128, it is said:

> "* * * An accessory is liable for any criminal act which in the ordinary course of things was the natural or probable consequence of the crime that he advised or commanded, although such consequence may not have been intended by him. So also the fact that the crime is not committed in the particular way designated by the procurer or conspirator does not prevent him from being liable as an accessory before the fact. *But for crimes which are the outcome of a total or substantial departure from his counsel, agreement, directions, or instructions he is not liable.* Where a particular intent is requisite to constitute a crime, an accessory before the fact must have participated in that particular intent." (Italics ours.)

The same principle is announced in 1 Wharton on Crim. Law (7th Ed.) § 134, p. 143, thus:

> "So, if the accessory order or advise one crime, and the principal intentionally commit another; as, for instance, to burn a house, and instead of that he commit a larceny, or, to commit a crime against A., instead of so doing he commit the same crime against B., the accessory will not be answerable; but if the principal commit the same offense against B., by mistake, instead of A., it seems it would be otherwise."

In State v. Lucas, 55 Iowa, 321, 7 N.W. 583, 584, the defendant and one Wood conspired to rob a mill. They assaulted and tied the watchman (Edwards) and while the defendant went for a sledge with which to open the safe in the mill Wood robbed Edwards. In condemning a certain instruction and reversing the conviction, the court quoted and applied 1 Wharton Crim. Law, § 134, supra, and said: "It follows that the defendant cannot be convicted of a robbery of Edwards, from the mere fact that he abetted his associates in the robbery of Barclay and Hemmingway's safe. If the intention of Lucas was to abet and share in the proceeds of any robbery that his associates might commit, a different rule would apply. But this is not the thought of the instruction under consideration." That decision is in point on the facts of the instant case.

The same principle was applied in Watts v. State, 5 W.Va. 532. It was there charged that Randolph and Pleasants had feloniously and burglariously entered the house of one Perry with intent to assault, shoot, stab, and wound one Saunders therein, and that the defendant, Watts, had counseled, procured, aided, and abetted them so to do. Watts was not present when the entry was made. The trial court admitted evidence that, after forcibly entering Perry's house, one of the intruders ravished Perry's wife. The Supreme Court held that such evidence should not have been admitted, being evidence of another and different offense than that for which the defendant was on trial, one which he had not contemplated, and not "in the ordinary course of things a probable consequence" of the felony planned. The court said: "If the principal totally and substantially departs from his instructions, as if, being solicited to burn a barn, he moreover commits a robbery while so doing, he stands single in the latter crime, and the other is not held responsible for it as accessory"—citing 3 Greenleaf Evid. § 44.

* * *

Similar in principle to the foregoing authorities, this court said in State v. May, 142 Mo. 135, 153, 43 S.W. 637, 642, quoting from 1 Bishop, New Crim.Law, § 637: "Where two combine to fight a third with fists, if death accidentally results from a blow inflicted by one, the other also is answerable for the homicide. But if the one resorts to a deadly weapon without the other's knowledge or consent, he only is thus liable."

In the instant case there was no evidence of a conspiracy to commit robbery generally. Had there been such evidence we would have a different question with which to deal. But here, as we have stated, all of the state's evidence was to the effect that the conspiracy was to rob the agent of the Jones Brothers' Exchange, who carried their money, a specific robbery, and none other. From defendant's side, while he disclaimed having conspired to rob anybody, there was evidence to the effect that the only robbery proposed or talked about was the robbery of the messenger of the Paragould Exchange, a separate and distinct, but single, offense; one not charged in the information, and which, moreover, was not committed. But even if it could be found under the evidence that the conspirators planned and authorized the two they selected to do the overt act to rob the messenger of either one or the other of said two exchanges, that cannot, we think, be held to constitute a conspiracy to *commit robbery generally.* The said modification of instructions 8–D and 12–D was therefore erroneous, and we think prejudicially so.

Defendant was on friendly terms with the Jones brothers. * * * It is conceivable that even if defendant had been willing to rob the Paragould Exchange he would not have been willing to participate in the robbery of the

Jones Brothers' Exchange. At least he had the right to have the jury pass upon that question. * * *

* * *

PER CURIAM.

The foregoing opinion by COOLEY, C., is adopted as the opinion of the court.

All of the Judges concur.

Question

Arm, Plott, Wheel, Madd, and Twitch plan to rob the Bellyup Bank the next day, the understanding being that Arm and Plott will not go to the site. Arm leaves the meeting early, and the other four then decide that, if the Bellyup Bank seems too crowded, they will find another bank to rob.

The next day, Wheel drives Madd and Twitch to the Bellyup Bank, where they decide that the bank is too crowded for the robbery, and Wheel then drives them two blocks away to the Defaulters' Bank for the robbery. Wheel remains in the car as the getaway driver, while Madd and Twitch go in to reconnoiter the bank and commit the robbery. Before the robbery takes place, Wheel is spotted, arrested, and carried off to jail by a passing policeman on an outstanding burglary warrant.

Madd and Twitch force the employees and customers to lie down on the floor and Madd keeps them covered with his gun while Twitch, also armed, goes through the cash drawers. Madd notices that one of the customers on the floor is his former neighbor Fence, with whom he had a dispute, and he angrily rapes her. Twitch is unnerved by this unexpected incident and accidentally fires his gun, killing a teller, Count.

What is the criminal liability of Arm, Plott, Wheel, Madd and Twitch?

C. VICARIOUS LIABILITY AND THE SPECIAL CASE OF CORPORATE LIABILITY

Introductory Note

To what extent is one who engages another to carry out a task criminally responsible for acts committed by the agent in the course of the work, perhaps not contemplated by the principal? This is the problem of vicarious liability. The general form of the answer has been anticipated in our study of the liability of accomplices. Generally, one is not absolved because the *actus reus* of a crime is committed by another. However, if the crime requires *mens rea,* fault in some sense must be brought home to each of those to be found guilty. For criminal responsibility, one might expect usually to find that the principal had encouraged or approved the act.

This reasoning originally suggested a theory that a corporation (an artificial legal construct, having no mind, much less a guilty one) could not be guilty of any offense requiring *mens rea.* The troublesome nature of this theory is apparent; consider a case in which the corporate board of directors hires thugs to beat up or kill employees of competitors. Apart from punishment of thugs and board members, it may be important to fine the corporation. The cases which follow explore the principles upon which corporate liability should be imposed.

In absolute liability offenses,[a] there is no theoretical bar to holding an individual or corporate employer, free of any fault, vicariously liable for acts of the employee. If the sale of adulterated butter is an absolute liability offense and A's employee B sells adulterated butter without any fault on the part of either, A can be found guilty though he had no *mens rea* and committed personally no *actus reus*. Is this wrong?

Vicarious liability normally goes all the way to the top without stopping to impose liability along the way. That is, it does not impose any liability upon intermediate managers (who, of course may be otherwise liable on account of their own fault), but only upon the individual or corporate proprietors. Why should this be?

People v. Jackson

Court of Appeals of Michigan, 1989.
176 Mich.App. 620, 440 N.W.2d 39.

Before HOOD, P.J., and WAHLS and NEFF, JJ. PER CURIAM.

* * *

The record reveals that defendant, Philip C. Jackson, a certified commercial applicator of pesticides under the Pesticide Control Act, is the branch manager of the Kalamazoo outlet of the Orkin Company, a nationwide pest control service. In May, 1987, James A. Gregart, who happens to be the prosecuting attorney for Kalamazoo County, contracted with the Orkin Company to treat his home with chlordane, a pesticide regulated under the Pesticide Control Act. Defendant dispatched Andrew Price, a noncertified applicator of pesticides, to the Gregart home to apply the chlordane. Price's failure to follow the recommended and accepted procedures for use of the chemical prompted a complaint. Apparently, Price sprayed chlordane on the lawn of the Gregart home. When the complaint was verified, defendant discharged Price and, with an associate, properly applied the pesticide at the Gregart household. In addition, the Orkin Company refunded the downpayment of $167, cancelled the remaining balance of $930, added one year to the warranty period, paid $1321 to replace carpeting in the downstairs area of the Gregart home, and paid $807 for medical examinations and testing for Gregart, his wife and his children.

Gregart subsequently applied for the appointment of a special prosecutor who would seek to impose criminal sanctions against defendant under the Pesticide Control Act. As a result, a misdemeanor warrant was issued against defendant naming Gregart as the victim and a representative of the Michigan Department of Agriculture as the complaining witness. A preliminary motion to dismiss the charge was denied by the district court, and a plea of nolo contendere was entered pursuant to a plea bargain under the terms of which the issue of defendant's vicarious liability under the Pesticide Control Act was preserved for appeal. A fine of $100, costs of $50, and a fee of $5 were levied and, by stipulation, were to remain unpaid pending appeal. The circuit court reversed defendant's misdemeanor conviction and the present appeal by the people ensued.

a. See supra, pp. 151–165.

The sections of the Pesticide Control Act pertinent to this appeal, being §§ 12(5) and (6), 26(1), and 29(1), provide as follows:

> "(5) A pesticide applicator shall follow recommended and accepted good practices in the use of pesticides including use of a pesticide in a manner consistent with its labeling.
>
> "(6) A certified applicator shall be responsible for the application of a pesticide by a noncertified applicator under his instruction and control even though the certified applicator is not physically present. * * *." M.C.L. § 286.562(5) and (6); M.S.A. § 12.340(12)(5) and (6).
>
> "(1) A person who violates this act is guilty of a misdemeanor and shall be fined not more than $500.00 for each offense." M.C.L. § 286.576(1); M.S.A. § 12.340(26)(1).
>
> "(1) This act shall not terminate or in any way modify any liability, civil or criminal, which is in existence on the effective date of this act." M.C.L. § 286.579(1); M.S.A. § 12.340(29)(1).

* * *

The circuit court, in reversing the district court, concluded that § 12(6) of the act does not subject certified applicators to vicarious criminal responsibility for the acts of noncertified applicators because such responsibility would be in derogation of the common law and was not specifically provided for in § 12(6). * * *

* * *

In the Pesticide Control Act the Legislature provided that any person who violates a provision of the act is guilty of a misdemeanor. Since no level of intent is mentioned, strict liability is applicable. One provision of the act, § 12(5), requires a pesticide applicator to follow the recommended and accepted good practices in the use of pesticides, and another provision of the act, § 12(6), makes a certified applicator "responsible" for the application of a pesticide by a noncertified applicator under his instruction and control. While, as the circuit court stressed, the Legislature did not insert the modifier "criminally" before the operative word "responsible" in § 12(6), neither did it insert the word "civilly." The effect of the circuit court's ruling, however, is to limit the plain meaning of the term used by the Legislature so that the unlimited term "responsible" may mean only civilly, not criminally, responsible. We see no need to so qualify, circumscribe or restrict the plain meaning of the word chosen by the Legislature in drafting § 12(6) of the Pesticide Control Act. * * *

Nor is this plain meaning of the word "responsible" restricted or narrowed, as suggested by the circuit court, by the language in § 29(1). That section, as noted above, provides that the act does not terminate or modify any liability, civil or criminal, which was in existence on the act's effective date. We believe that the language of § 29(1) merely preserves any liability, civil or criminal, which preexisted the Pesticide Control Act. * * * We believe that § 29(1) simply reflects the intent to ensure the continued viability of the common law in this area wherever the common law does not conflict with a provision of the Pesticide Control Act. In the case at bar, regarding the vicarious criminal responsibility of a certified applicator for the acts of a noncertified applicator under his instruction and control, the common law conflicts with § 12(6). Thus, the latter controls.

Our analysis and conclusion in this case are consistent with the comments of other legal authorities. For example, in 21 Am.Jur.2d, Criminal Law, § 181, pp. 336–337, it is stated:

> "Unless he in some way participates in, counsels, or approves of what the servant does, or, as it is sometimes put, unless he counsels, commands, aids, or abets, or procures the commission of, an act, an employer or principal is not, in the absence of a statute, criminally liable for the acts of his employee or agent. * * *
>
> "A statute may in certain instances fix criminal responsibility on an employer or principal for an act committed by his employee or agent."

In addition, in LaFave & Scott, supra, pp. 224–225, it is stated:

> "Some criminal statutes, generally containing no language of fault, specifically impose criminal liability upon the employer for the bad conduct of his employee—e.g., 'whoever, by himself or by his agent, sells articles at short weight shall be punished by * * *,' or 'whoever sells liquor to a minor is punishable by * * * and any sale by an employee shall be deemed the act of the employer as well as the act of the employee.' Such statutes (generally carrying a misdemeanor penalty) are naturally construed to impose vicarious liability upon the employer though he expressly forbade his employee to engage in the forbidden conduct.
>
> "Often statutes are not that specific as to whether or not they impose vicarious liability. In such a case, if the statutory crime is worded in language requiring some type of fault ('knowingly,' 'wilfully,' 'with intent to,' etc.), then it is the rule that the employer must personally know or be wilful or have the requisite intention to be liable for the criminal conduct of his employee; even though the latter is acting to further his employer's business, the employer is not criminally liable unless he knew of or authorized that action. That is, if the statute requires mental fault, it will not be presumed that the legislature intended that the fault of the employee should suffice for conviction of the employer.
>
> "In between the statutes which specifically require fault and those which specifically impose criminal liability on the employer for his employee's conduct fall those statutes which neither contain fault-words nor contain any expression that the conduct of the employee makes the employer liable. Thus a statute may simply state that 'whoever employs children under 14 in a factory is guilty of a misdemeanor.' The factory owner instructs his manager not to employ children under 14, but the manager disregards the instruction and does so. Is the owner liable? The question is one of construction of the statute, and is likely to be approached in much the same way as the question of whether statutes empty of language of fault are to be construed to impose strict liability. If the authorized punishment is light—a fine or perhaps a short imprisonment—the statute is likely to be construed to impose vicarious liability on

a faultless employer. But if the permitted punishment is severe—a felony or a serious misdemeanor—the statute is not apt to be so construed in the absence of an express provision for vicarious responsibility."

Even if we were to agree with defendant that the language in the Pesticide Control Act regarding the vicarious criminal responsibility of certified applicators is ambiguous and, thus, requires construction, we believe that the intent of the Legislature is to impose such responsibility. The authorized punishment is light, a fine of not more than $500 for each offense. * * * Moreover, only by imposing vicarious criminal responsibility can the full intent of the legislation, to protect the public health and safety from deliberate as well as negligent environmental degradation, effectively be carried out. The Pesticide Control Act allows the hiring of uncertified applicators to apply pesticides, but places on the certified applicators the responsibility for selecting, training, and instructing such uncertified applicators. To allow the certified applicator to escape vicarious criminal responsibility under these circumstances would be to preclude employment of the law's most puissant implement of public protection and to diminish the statute's deterrent effect. * * *

It is obvious that the relationship between the environment and public health is synergistic in nature. * * * The illicit use of pesticides, of course, might well release into the environment poisons to which a person cannot adapt. A major purpose of the Pesticide Control Act is to regulate the release of such poisons so as to reduce the possibility of deleterious effects on the public health. We believe that our holding in this case is consistent with that purpose and is mandated under the language of the Pesticide Control Act.

Reversed.

Waste Conversion, Inc. v. Commonwealth

Commonwealth Court of Pennsylvania, 1990.
130 Pa.Cmwlth. 443, 568 A.2d 738.

PALLADINO, JUDGE.

Waste Conversion, Inc., (Appellant) appeals from an order of the Lycoming County Court of Common Pleas which denied Appellant's post-verdict motions and imposed a fine for Appellant's violation of section 610(8)(i) of the Solid Waste Management Act (Act).[1] We affirm.

Appellant was convicted of violating the Act following a non-jury trial based upon stipulated facts. The pertinent facts are as follows. Appellant operates a hazardous and residual waste treatment, storage and disposal facility in Montgomery County, Pennsylvania under a Department of Environmental Resources (DER) license. Appellant hired Wills Trucking Company of Ohio (Wills) to transport processed waste to disposal facilities. Appellant's employees loaded non-hazardous waste into a truck owned and driven by Al Cullenen (Driver) who was an independent hauler hired by Wills. Driver was to transport the waste to a disposal site in Michigan.

1. Section 610(8)(i) of the Solid Waste Management Act, Act of July 7, 1980, P.L. 380, *as amended*, 35 P.S. § 6018.610(8)(i).

Appellant's employees loaded Driver's truck to 83,500 pounds.[2] Driver was traveling on Route 80 when he became aware that state police were operating a weigh station ahead. To avoid detection of the excessive weight, Driver re-routed the truck to a back road. Unable to negotiate the hill, Driver backed down the road to a more level position. While attempting to redistribute the load by raising the bed of the trailer, a substantial amount of waste slid out of the truck and onto the side of the road. With a lighter load, Driver was able to negotiate the hill.

After an investigation by the Toxic Waste Investigation and Prosecution Section of the Office of Attorney General, the waste was traced to Appellant. Appellant, Driver and Wills were charged with violations of the Act. Only Appellant's case is before us.

Appellant filed a motion to quash the information and a petition to declare section 610(8)(i) of the Act unconstitutional. The trial court denied the motion and the petition. At a non-jury trial Appellant was found guilty of violating the Act. Appellant filed post-trial motions again questioning the constitutionality of section 610(8)(i) of the Act. These motions were denied. At sentencing, Appellant was fined $10,000. Appellant has filed this appeal.

* * *

Section 610(8)(i) of the act provides in pertinent part as follows:

> It shall be unlawful for any person or municipality to:
>
> * * *
>
> (8) Consign, assign, sell, entrust, give or in any way transfer residual or hazardous waste which is at any time subsequently, by any such person or any other person;
>
> (i) dumped or deposited or discharged in any manner into the surface of the earth or underground or into the waters of the Commonwealth unless a permit for the dumping or depositing or discharging of such residual or hazardous waste has first been obtained from the department.

The criminal penalties section of the Act under which Appellant was convicted and sentenced, section 606, 35 P.S. § 6018.606, states in pertinent part as follows:

> (b) Any person other than a municipal official exercising his official duties who violates any provision of this act, any rule or regulation of the department, any order of the department, or any term or condition of any permit, shall be guilty of a misdemeanor of the third degree and, upon conviction, shall be sentenced to pay a fine of not less than $1,000 but not more than $25,000 per day for each violation or to imprisonment for a period of not more than one year, or both.
>
> * * *
>
> (i) With respect to the offenses specified in subsections (a), (b), (c) and (f), it is the legislative purpose to impose absolute liability for such offenses. * * *

2. This is 3,500 pounds more than the allowable weight limit under Pennsylvania law.

(j) With respect to the offenses specified in subsections (a), (b), (c), (d), (e), (f) and (g), it is the legislative purpose to impose liability on corporations.

* * *

Appellant argues the ultimate waste dumper was an independent contractor whose actions were beyond Appellant's control. Without the ability to control the Driver's conduct, Appellant argues that the Act violates Appellant's right to substantive due process.

* * *

Appellant relies upon Commonwealth v. Koczwara, 397 Pa. 575, 155 A.2d 825 (1959), cert. denied, 363 U.S. 848, 80 S.Ct. 1624, 4 L.Ed.2d 1731 (1960). In *Koczwara,* the supreme court vacated the jail sentence of a tavern operator who was held vicariously liable for the liquor code violations of an employee. However, the court upheld a $500 fine imposed upon the tavern owner despite his due process arguments. The court noted that the actual violations were committed without the personal knowledge, participation or presence of the defendant. Appellant relies upon the following court language "[o]ur own courts have stepped in time and again to protect a defendant from being held criminally responsible for acts about which he had no knowledge and over which he had little control." Id. at 586, 155 A.2d at 830. Appellant asserts that this language requires that a defendant must have at least some degree of control over the actual perpetrator to be held vicariously liable for his actions.

An examination of the Act reveals that Appellant can be deemed to have such control. * * *

The Act is a comprehensive scheme designed to protect the public from health and environmental hazards caused by inadequate solid waste practices. Appellant, as a corporation licensed to operate in this hazardous business, owes the highest duty of responsibility to insure that the citizens of this state are protected from the dangers necessarily a part of waste disposal. This was a * * * [principal] reason for the legislature's imposition of strict vicarious liability. By undertaking the responsibility to dispose of waste, Appellant has assumed the duty to ensure that it is completed as required by the Act. Appellant cannot absolve itself of this responsibility by transferring it to independent contractors and claiming that it has no control over them. We hold that, because Appellant has assumed responsibility in the waste disposal process, Appellant maintains control of the independent contractors it hires for the purpose of its waste disposal duties. Appellant's failure to maintain control cannot be used as a defense to avoid liability.

* * *

Appellant next asserts that the $10,000 fine imposed is too high for absolute vicarious liability. Appellant, citing *Koczwara,* argues that only "light monetary fines" are permissible for vicarious liability under the doctrine of due process. In *Koczwara,* the court struck a jail sentence but upheld a $500 fine for vicarious liability of an individual tavern owner. Appellant argues that vicarious liability penalties are therefore limited to the $300 to $500 range.

Koczwara was decided in 1959. The fine was levied upon an individual. Here, trial court levied a $10,000 fine upon a corporation consistent with the Act. Certainly, we cannot be locked into the $500 fine imposed in *Koczwara* for all time in all cases. Under the circumstances of this case, we hold that Appellant's fine does not clearly and palpably violate the due process clause.

Accordingly, we hold that, under the circumstances of this case, Appellant's right of due process was not violated by the Act.

* * *

Accordingly, the trial court is affirmed.

COLINS, J., dissents.

Notes

1. *Corporate liability for crimes against the person.* Granite Construction Co. v. Superior Court of Fresno County, 149 Cal.App.3d 465, 467, 469–470, 197 Cal. Rptr. 3, 5, 6, 45 A.L.R.4th 1011, 1013, 1015–1016 (1983):

> Petitioner claims surprise at the prosecution of a corporation for manslaughter, asserting that the indictment was "totally unforeseeable," and that a corporation may be charged with crimes against "property," but "not against the person." This attempt to distinguish crimes against property from crimes against the person relies on the corporation's nature as an economically motivated entity. While a corporation may directly benefit from a crime against property, crimes against persons are not as directly linked to the profit motive. This argument is unsuccessful. It overlooks the substantial *indirect* economic benefits that may accrue to the corporation through crimes against the person. To get these economic benefits, corporate management may shortcut expensive safety precautions, respond forcibly to strikes, or engage in criminal anticompetitive behavior. If any such risk-taking is a corporate action, the corporation becomes a proper criminal defendant.
>
> * * *
>
> California Penal Code section 193 prescribes imprisonment as the ordinary punishment for manslaughter, but does not impose a fine. Petitioner argues that absence of an appropriate punishment for corporations at this juncture indicates that section 192 does not reach corporate defendants.
>
> Section 672 provides appropriate punishment for corporate crimes.[1] * * * When construing a statute with several provisions, constructions that give effect to all are preferred. (Code Civ.Proc., § 1858.)[2]

1. Penal Code section 672: "Upon a conviction for any crime punishable by imprisonment in any jail or prison, in relation to which no fine is herein prescribed, the court may impose a fine on the offender not exceeding five hundred dollars ($500) in cases of misdemeanors or five thousand dollars ($5,000) in cases of felonies, in addition to the imprisonment prescribed."

2. Courts in other states have also imposed fines on corporations where both fines and imprisonment would be imposed on natural persons. (See generally, Annot., Corporations Liability to Criminal Prosecution As Affected By Punishment or Penalty Imposed (1977) 80 A.L.R.3d 1220, and cases cited therein.)

The academic literature has discussed the adequacy of fines as the penalty for corporate misconduct in several articles and notes. (See, e.g., Corporate Criminal Liability for Employee Endangering Activities (Winter 1983) 18 Colum.J. of L. and Soc.Prob. 39–75; Developments in the Law, Corporate Crime: Regulating Corporate Behavior Through Criminal Sanction (1979) 92 Harv.L.Rev. 1227, 1251–1257; Geis, Criminal Penalties for Corporate Criminals (1972) 8 Crim.L.Bull. 377; Note Corporate Homicide: The Stark Realities of Artificial Beings and Legal Fictions (1981) 8 Pepperdine L.Rev. 367, 409–417). The inadequacy of the penalty provided by section 672 is a legislative problem irrelevant to this case.

2. *Liability of superior employees.* In United States v. Park, 421 U.S. 658, 95 S.Ct. 1903, 44 L.Ed.2d 489 (1975), the Supreme Court construed the Federal Food, Drug and Cosmetic Act § 301(k), which states no *mens rea* requirement and forbids storing of food in buildings exposed to rodent contamination, to permit conviction of the president of the corporation operating the warehouse, when he had delegated correction of the problem to a subordinate, who had failed, unknown to the defendant, to correct it, and where the defendant did not suggest that he was powerless to prevent the violation. The Court thought a negligence standard appropriate, with the burden of going forward with evidence of powerlessness on the accused and the ultimate burden of persuasion on the prosecution. The Court states (at pp. 670–671 of U.S., 1910–1911 of S.Ct., 499–500 of L.Ed.2d):

> The rule that corporate employees who have "a responsible share in the furtherance of the transaction which the statute outlaws" are subject to the criminal provisions of the Act was not formulated in a vacuum. Cf. Morissette v. United States, 342 U.S. 246, 258, 72 S.Ct. 240, 96 L.Ed. 288 (1952). Cases under the Federal Food and Drugs Act of 1906 reflected the view both that knowledge or intent were not required to be proved in prosecutions under its criminal provisions, and that responsible corporate agents could be subjected to the liability thereby imposed. See, e.g., United States v. Mayfield, 177 F. 765 (ND Ala.1910). Moreover, the principle had been recognized that a corporate agent, through whose act, default, or omission the corporation committed a crime, was himself guilty individually of that crime. The principle had been applied whether or not the crime required "consciousness of wrongdoing," and it had been applied not only to those corporate agents who themselves committed the criminal act, but also to those who by virtue of their managerial positions or other similar relation to the actor could be deemed responsible for its commission.
>
> In the latter class of cases, the liability of managerial officers did not depend on their knowledge of, or personal participation in, the act made criminal by the statute. Rather, where the statute under which they were prosecuted dispensed with "consciousness of wrongdoing," an omission or failure to act was deemed a sufficient basis for a responsible corporate agent's liability. It was enough in such cases that, by virtue of the relationship he bore to the corporation, the agent had the power to prevent the act complained of.

Commonwealth v. Beneficial Finance Co.

Supreme Judicial Court of Massachusetts, Suffolk, 1971.
360 Mass. 188, 275 N.E.2d 33, 52 A.L.R.3d 1143, cert. denied 407 U.S. 914, 92 S.Ct. 2433, 32 L.Ed.2d 689 (1972).

SPIEGEL, JUSTICE.

We have before us appeals emanating from 2 separate series of indictments and 2 separate jury trials of various individual and corporate defendants.

All of these appeals were taken under G.L. c. 278, §§ 33A–33G, and are before us because of the convictions of a number of individuals and corporations. The corporations convicted in the first trial were Beneficial Finance

The existence of a penalty applicable to corporations makes this prosecution more than "waste motion." Regardless of the penalty, the corporation has reason to defend itself against the charge, because of damage to its reputation, the standing of management in the eyes of its stockholders, and the like.

Company (Beneficial), Household Finance Corporation (Household) and Liberty Loan Corporation (Liberty). The individuals convicted in the first trial were John M. Farrell, Francis T. Glynn, Nathaniel W. Barber, James S. Pratt, Lyle S. Woodcock, Morris Garfinkle and Martin J. Hanley. * * *

These cases have become generally known as the "small loans" cases. In each case the defendants were charged with various offences under numerous indictments returned in 1964 by a special grand jury. The offences charged were offering or paying, or soliciting or receiving, bribes, or conspiring to do so. * * *

* * *

The evidence in the first trial * * * is here synopsized. This evidence tends to show that during the year 1962, several licensed small loans companies (corporate defendants), together with certain of their officers and employees (some of whom are defendants), conspired to bribe Hanley and Garfinkle in their capacities as public officials. The purpose of the alleged conspiracy and the payment of the bribe money was to insure the maintenance of a maximum interest rate which companies licensed to do business in the Commonwealth were permitted to charge. Hearings on this matter were conducted by the Small Loans Regulatory Board (Rate Board) in 1962 and the bribe money allegedly paid to Hanley was intended to "fix" the results of these hearings.

* * *

Having concluded that the evidence was sufficient to establish that the defendants Pratt and Woodcock were part of a conspiracy joined in by Farrell, Glynn and Barber to bribe Hanley and Garfinkle, we turn to the question of whether there was sufficient evidence to support a finding that Beneficial, Household, and Liberty were parties to the conspiracy. * * *

* * *

The defendants and the Commonwealth have proposed differing standards upon which the criminal responsibility of a corporation should be predicated. The defendants argue that a corporation should not be held criminally liable for the conduct of its servants or agents unless such conduct was performed, authorized, ratified, adopted or tolerated by the corporations' directors, officers or other "high managerial agents" who are sufficiently high in the corporate hierarchy to warrant the assumption that their acts in some substantial sense reflect corporate policy. This standard is that adopted by the American Law Institute Model Penal Code, approved in May, 1962. Section 2:07 of the Code provides that, except in the case of regulatory offences and offences consisting of the omission of a duty imposed on corporations by law, a corporation may be convicted of a crime if "the commission of the offence was authorized, requested, commanded, performed or recklessly tolerated by the board of directors or by a high managerial agent acting in behalf of the corporation within the scope of his office or employment." The section proceeds to define "high managerial agent" as "an officer of a corporation * * * or any other agent * * * having duties of such responsibility that his conduct may fairly be assumed to represent the policy of the corporation." [55]

The Commonwealth, on the other hand, argues that the standard applied by the judge in his instructions to the jury was correct. These instructions, which prescribe a somewhat more flexible standard than that delineated in the Model Penal Code, state in part, as follows: "[T]he Commonwealth must prove beyond a reasonable doubt that there existed between the guilty individual or individuals and the corporation which is being charged with the conduct of the individuals, such *a relationship that the acts and the intent of the individuals were the acts and intent of the corporation.* Or, to put it differently, the Commonwealth must prove beyond a reasonable doubt that when the individuals were acting criminally in committing the acts which constitute the crime, and in having the intent required for the crime, *the corporation was actually so acting and intending,* and therefore is criminally liable. The Commonwealth must prove that.

"How is that to be shown? * * * The Commonwealth must prove that the individual for whose conduct it seeks to charge *the corporation criminally was placed in a position by the corporation where he had enough power, duty, responsibility and authority to act for and in behalf of the corporation to handle the particular business or operation or project of the corporation in which he was engaged at the time that he committed the criminal act, with power of decision as to what he would or would not do while acting for the corporation, and that he was acting for and in behalf of the corporation in the accomplishment of that particular business or operation or project, and that he committed a criminal act while so acting.*

* * *

"Now, this test doesn't depend upon the power, duty, the responsibility, or the authority which the individual has with reference to the entire corporation business. The test should be applied to his position with relation to the particular operation or project in which he is serving the corporation." (emphasis supplied).

The difference between the judge's instructions to the jury and the Model Penal Code lies largely in the latter's reference to a "high managerial agent" and in the Code requirement that to impose corporate criminal liability, it at least must appear that its directors or high managerial agent "authorized * * * or recklessly tolerated" the allegedly criminal acts. The judge's instructions focus on the authority of the corporate agent in relation to the *particular* corporate business in which the agent was engaged. * * *

55. Section 2.07 of the Model Penal Code was materially amended between 1955 (Tentative Draft No. 4, p. 22; see pp. 146–155, for the comments on the unamended section) and its adoption in 1962 (Proposed Final Draft, pp. 35, 38) by adding the italicized words "or recklessly tolerated." These words seem to expand corporate criminal liability to include at least cases where high managerial officers shut their eyes to (or try to remain aloof from and apparently unaware of) criminal activity by subordinates undertaken for the corporation's benefit. Cf. Restatement 2d: Agency, § 217D, comment d (1957): "Apart from statute, an employer is not subject to a penalty for an unauthorized act constituting a crime committed by an ordinary servant in the scope of employment if the basis for liability is a specific criminal intent. However, * * * an employer may be penalized for the act of an advisory or managerial person acting in the scope of employment."

Close examination of the judge's instructions reveals that they preserve the underlying "corporate policy rationale of the Code by allowing the jury to infer "corporate policy" from the *position* in which the corporation placed the agent in commissioning him to handle the particular corporate affairs in which he was engaged at the time of the criminal act. * * * It is not clear (see fn. 55, supra) that if the Code had been in effect in Massachusetts, when the acts alleged and proved were committed, the corporate defendants would have been in a better situation, in view of the proof here of concerted criminal conduct (in a "program" designed to be of benefit to finance companies) by plainly significant representatives of three or more competing financing companies and the sums involved. We do not consider whether the circumstances would permit inferences of facts constituting a violation of the Code. The judge correctly charged the jury on the basis of decided cases, rather than on the basis of a proposed model code.

It may also be observed that the judge's standard is somewhat similar to the traditional common law rule of respondeat superior. However, in applying this rule to a criminal case, the judge added certain requirements not generally associated with that common law doctrine. He further qualified the rule of respondeat superior by requiring that the conduct for which the corporation is being held accountable be performed *on behalf of the corporation.* This factor is noted as important in the commentary to § 2.07(1) of the Model Penal Code. It may well be that there is often little distinction between an act done *on behalf of a principal* and an act done *within the scope of employment,* which is the traditional requirement of the doctrine of respondeat superior. Nevertheless, in the circumstances of this case it might reasonably be concluded that the explicit instruction of the judge that the jury look to the authority vested in the agent by the corporation to act within the particular sphere of corporate affairs relating to the criminal act, together with the explicit instruction that such act be performed on behalf of the corporation, required, in effect, the type of evidence which would support an inference that the criminal act was done as a matter of corporate policy. We deem this to be a valid conclusion, especially in view of the quantum of proof required in a criminal case in order to prove guilt beyond a reasonable doubt.

* * *

The thrust of each of the cases cited above involving a human principal is that it is fundamental to our criminal jurisprudence that for more serious offences guilt is personal and not vicarious. "One is punished for his own blameworthy conduct, not that of others." Commonwealth v. Stasiun, 349 Mass. 38, 48, 206 N.E.2d 672, 679, citing Perkins, Criminal Law, 550, and Sayre, Criminal Responsibility for the Acts of Another, 43 Harv.L.Rev. 689. Professor Sayre's article is heavily relied on by Beneficial for the proposition that the considerations proposed by Sayre apply with equal weight to corporations. However, we do not think that the Sayre article, or the rule in the master-servant cases, is helpful to these corporations. The essence of Sayre's discussion is that, as to certain crimes, a theory of vicarious liability is an inadequate basis for imposing criminal liability on a natural person who can suffer imprisonment or ignominy for the acts of his agents. Id. at 722–723. * * *

* * * [T]he very nature of a corporation as a "person" before the law renders it impossible to equate the imposition of vicarious liability on a human principal with the imposition of vicarious liability on a corporate principal. "A corporation can act only through its agents. * * * [C]orporate criminal liability is necessarily vicarious." Note, Criminal Liability of Corporations for Acts of Their Agents, 60 Harv.L.Rev. 283. Since a corporation is a legal fiction, comprised only of individuals, it has no existence separate and distinct from those whom it has clothed with authority and commissioned to act for it whether such individuals are directors, officers, shareholders or employees. Thus, the issue is not whether vicarious liability should be imposed on a corporation under the "direct participation and assent rule" of the master-servant cases * * *, but rather, whether the acts and intent of natural persons, be they officers, directors or employees, can be treated as the acts and intent of the corporation itself. For the foregoing reasons, despite the strenuous urging of the defendants, we are unconvinced that the standard for imposing criminal responsibility on a human principal adequately deals with the evidentiary problems which are inherent in ascribing the acts of individuals to a corporate entity.

* * *

It is obvious that criminal conspiratorial acts are not performed within the glare of publicity, nor would we expect a board of directors to meet officially and record on the corporate records a delegation of authority to initiate, conduct or conclude proceedings for the purpose of bribing a public official. Of necessity, the proof authority to so act must rest on all the circumstances and conduct in a given situation and the reasonable inferences to be drawn therefrom.

Additional factors of importance are the size and complexity of many large modern corporations which necessitate the delegation of more authority to lesser corporate agents and employees. As the judge pointed out: "There are not enough seats on the Board of Directors, nor enough offices in a corporation, to permit the corporation engaged in widespread operations to give such a title or office to every person in whom it places the power, authority, and responsibility for decision and action." This latter consideration lends credence to the view that the title or position of an individual in a corporation should not be conclusively determinative in ascribing criminal responsibility. In a large corporation, with many numerous and distinct departments, a high ranking corporate officer or agent may have no authority or involvement in a particular sphere of corporate activity, whereas a lower ranking corporate executive might have much broader power in dealing with a matter peculiarly within the scope of his authority. Employees who are in the lower echelon of the corporate hierarchy often exercise more responsibility in the *everyday operations* of the corporation than the directors or officers. Assuredly, the title or office that the person holds may be considered, but it should not be the decisive criterion upon which to predicate corporate responsibility.

* * *

To permit corporations to conceal the nefarious acts of their underlings by using the shield of corporate armor to deflect corporate responsibility, and to separate the subordinate from the executive, would be to permit "endocratic" corporations to inflict widespread public harm without hope of redress. It would merely serve to ignore the scramble and realities of the market place.[58] This we decline to do. We believe that stringent standards must be adopted to discourage any attempt by "endocratic" corporations' executives to place the sole responsibility for criminal acts on the shoulders of their subordinates.

We believe that our decision is supported by basic considerations of public policy. The President's Commission on Law Enforcement and Administration of Justice, Task Force Report—Crime and Its Impact—An Assessment (1967) provides a sound rationale for imputing criminal responsibility to the corporation for the acts of lower echelon corporate officials who have the authority to act on behalf of the corporation. * * * The President's Commission concluded, at p. 108, that: "where corporate misconduct is involved, the offenders—and particularly the offenders against whom evidence of guilt can be obtained—act as part of a corporate hierarchy and, ordinarily, follow a pattern of corporate behavior. Individual responsibility is therefore reduced—the offenders are often following orders from above, either explicit or implicit. Moreover, the fact that acts are performed to further the interests of the corporation, and not merely the offenders' personal interests, helps to rationalize misconduct. * * *

* * *

Considering everything we have said above, we are of opinion that the quantum of proof necessary to sustain the conviction of a corporation for the acts of its agents is sufficiently met if it is shown that the corporation has placed the agent in a position where he has enough authority and responsibility to act for and in behalf of the corporation in handling the *particular* corporate business, operation or project in which he was engaged at the time he committed the criminal act. The judge properly instructed the jury to this effect and correctly stated that this standard does not depend upon the responsibility or authority which the agent has with respect to the entire corporate business, but only to his position with relation to the particular business in which he was serving the corporation. Some of the factors that the jury were entitled to consider in applying the above test, although perhaps not in themselves decisive, are the following: (1) the extent of control and authority exercised by the individual over and within the corporation; (2) the extent and manner to which corporate funds were used in the crime; (3) a repeated pattern of criminal conduct tending to indicate corporate toleration or ratification of the agent's acts. * * *

* * *

All judgments affirmed.

58. The term "endocratic" was coined by Dean Rostow and means a "large, publicly-held corporation, whose stock is scattered in small fractions among thousands of stockholders." Note, Increasing Community Control Over Corporate Crime—A Problem in the Law of Sanctions, 71 Yale L.J. 280, 281, n. 3.

Note

Model Penal Code, § 2.07, Comments 2, 3, 6, and 7: *

2. *Corporate Liability.* Subsections (1)(a), (1)(b) and (1)(c) deal with three different situations in which the corporation can be held criminally liable. Subsection (1)(a) indicates that corporations can be liable for violations and for offenses for which a legislative purpose to impose such liability appears if the conduct is performed by an agent of the corporation acting on the corporation's behalf within the scope of his employment. Subsection (1)(b) affirmatively recognizes the responsibility of corporations for the commission of offenses consisting of the omission of a duty imposed by law on such bodies. Subsection (1)(c) states a general principle of corporate liability that is designed to govern any situation not included in (1)(a) or (1)(b).

* * *

The provisions of the Model Penal Code dealing with the criminal liability of corporations must be considered both in connection with offenses defined in the Code and offenses defined by other statutes. Subsection (1)(a) deals, in part, with the latter. During the last ninety years a great mass of regulatory legislation imposing criminal liability on corporations for the offenses there defined has been added to the laws of American jurisdictions. Often, perhaps typically, criminal penalties added to such regulatory legislation have been hastily and inadequately considered. In many cases, however, such penal provisions form an integral part of the regulatory policy and are based on considerable pragmatic experience indicating their usefulness. The provisions of Subsection (1)(a) are based on the theory that the criminal code ought not to attempt a pro tanto repeal of such legislation by denying corporate criminal liability under statutes in which it is plainly recognized. The consequences of a general repeal of these provisions could hardly be anticipated and, in an indeterminate number of situations, might produce serious effects on the enforcement of regulatory policy. * * *

Subsection (1)(a) also recognizes corporate responsibility for the commission of violations, whether defined by the Code or by other statutes. The term "violation," defined in Section 1.04(5) refers generally to those minor offenses that are not classified as crimes and that are punishable only by fine. Subsection (1)(a) is thus a reflection of the judgment that liability for the more serious offenses defined by a criminal code—misdemeanors and felonies—should be ascribed to corporations only after the satisfaction of a more rigorous standard than the one it sets forth. * * *

* * *

Finally, Subsection (1)(a) specifically saves any special limitations contained in regulatory legislation designed to restrict the types of agents or employees for whose conduct the corporation should be liable in a particular context or to qualify the circumstances under which the corporation should be liable. The purpose of the language is simply to assure that the specific regulatory statutes will control such matters rather than the general principles here set forth.

(b) *Omissions.* Subsection (1)(b) deals with a situation where the criminal law speaks explicitly to corporations, and thus like Subsection (1)(a) leaves the question of more general liability to Subsection (1)(c). The reference to a "specific" duty imposed on corporations by law is designed to make it clear that the provision does not govern in such a case as negligent homicide, where the duty violated is one that the law imposes generally. Rather, the section will apply when there is a failure, for example, to file a report of a kind that the corporation is specifically required to file, or to maintain records that the corporation is required by law to keep. * * *

(c) *Other Cases.* Subsection (1)(c) governs the general liability of corporations for crimes defined by the criminal code. In essence, it defines the types of conduct engaged in by corporate officials that will result in charging the offense to the entity.

In approaching the analysis of corporate criminal capacity, it will be observed initially that the imposing of criminal penalties on corporate bodies results in a species of vicarious liability. The direct burden of a corporate fine is visited upon the shareholders of the corporation. In most cases, the shareholders have not participated in the criminal conduct and lack the practical means of supervision of corporate management to prevent misconduct by corporate agents. This is not to say, of course, that all the policy considerations at issue in imposing vicarious responsibility on a human principal are present to the same degree in the corporate cases. Two fundamental distinctions should be noted. First, the fact that the corporation is the party nominally convicted means that the individual shareholders escape the opprobrium and incidental disabilities that normally follow a personal conviction or even indictment. Second, the shareholder's loss is limited to his equity in the corporation. His personal assets are not ordinarily subject to levy and the conviction of the corporation will not result in loss of liberty to the stockholders. Nevertheless, the fact that the direct impact of corporate fines is felt by a group ordinarily innocent of criminal conduct underscores the point that such fines ought not to be authorized except where they clearly may be expected to accomplish desirable social purposes. To the extent that shareholders participate in criminal conduct, or to the extent that there are unlawful transactions involving the shareholders' holdings, they may be reached directly through application of the ordinary principles of criminal liability.

It would seem that the ultimate justification of corporate criminal responsibility must rest in large measure on an evaluation of the deterrent effects of corporate fines on the conduct of corporate agents. Is there a reason for anticipating a substantially higher degree of deterrence from fines levied on corporate bodies than can fairly be anticipated from proceeding directly against the guilty officer or agent or from other feasible sanctions of a noncriminal character?

It may be assumed that ordinarily a corporate agent is not likely to be deterred from criminal conduct by the prospect of corporate liability when, in any event, he faces the prospect of individually suffering serious criminal penalties for his own act. If the agent cannot be prevented from committing an offense by the prospect of personal liability, he ordinarily will not be prevented by the prospect of corporate liability.

Yet the problem cannot be resolved so simply. For there are probably cases in which the economic pressures within the corporate body are sufficiently potent to tempt individuals to hazard personal liability for the sake of company gain, especially where the penalties threatened are moderate and where the offense does not involve behavior condemned as highly immoral by the individual's associates. This tendency may be particularly strong where the individual knows that his guilt may be difficult to prove or where a favorable reaction to his position by a jury may be anticipated even where proof of guilt is strong. A number of appellate opinions reveal situations in which juries have held the corporate defendant criminally liable while acquitting the obviously guilty agents who committed the criminal acts.[9]

This may reflect more than faulty or capricious judgment on the part of the juries. It may represent a recognition that the social consequences of a criminal conviction may fall with a disproportionately heavy impact on the individual defendants where the conduct involved is not of a highly immoral character. It may also reflect a shrewd belief that the violation may have been produced by pressures on the subordinates created by corporate managerial officials even though the latter may not have intended or desired the criminal behavior and even though the pressures can only be sensed rather than demonstrated. Furthermore, the great mass of legislation calling for corporate criminal liability suggests a widespread belief on the part of legislators that such liability is necessary to effectuate regulatory policy. * * *

The case so made out, however, does not demonstrate the wisdom of corporate fines generally. Rather, it tends to suggest that such liability can best be justified in cases in which penalties directed to the individual are moderate and where the criminal conviction is least likely to be interpreted as a form of social moral condemnation. This indicates a general line of distinction between the "malum prohibitum" regulatory offenses, on the one hand, and more serious offenses on the other. The same distinction is suggested in dealing with the problem of jury behavior. The cases cited above involving situations in which individual defendants were acquitted are all cases of economic regulations. It may be doubted that such results would have followed had the offenses involved a more obvious moral element. In any event, it is not clear just what conclusions are to be drawn from the cited cases. In each, the jury had corporate liability available as an alternative to acquittal of all of the defendants. Conceivably, if that alternative had not been available, verdicts against the individuals in some of the cases might have been returned. Thus, it is at least possible that corporate liability encourages erratic jury behavior. It may be true that the complexities of organization characteristic of large corporate enterprise at times present real problems of identifying the guilty individual and establishing his criminal liability. It would be hoped, however, that more could be pointed to in justification of placing the pecuniary burdens of criminal fines on the innocent than the difficulties of proving the guilt of the culpable individual. Where there is concrete evidence that the difficulties are real, however, the effectuation of regulatory policy may be thought to justify the means.

In surveying the case law on the subject of corporate criminal liability one may be struck at how few are the types of common law offenses that have actually resulted in corporate criminal responsibility. They are restricted for the most part to thefts (including frauds) and involuntary manslaughter. Conspiracy might also be included, but generally the cases have involved conspiracies to violate regulatory statutes (such as the antitrust laws), and often these statutes include specific conspiracy provisions made applicable to corporate bodies. No cases have been found in which a corporation was sought to be held criminally liable for such crimes as murder, treason, rape and bigamy. In general, such offenses may be effectively punished and deterred by prosecutions directed against the guilty individuals. One would not anticipate the same reluctance on the part of juries to convict individuals that seems sometimes to be present where

9. See, e.g., United States v. General Motors Corp., 121 F.2d 376, 411 (7th Cir.), cert. denied, 314 U.S. 618 (1941); United States v. Austin Bagley Corp., 31 F.2d 229, 233 (2d Cir.), cert. denied, 279 U.S. 863 (1929). See also I Brown Comm'n Working Papers 172–73.

the offense is a regulatory crime. Moreover, in many of the situations, such as those involving involuntary manslaughter, there is a strong possibility that the shareholders will be called upon to bear the burden of tort recoveries, a prospect that may also be expected to encourage supervision of subordinate employees by executive personnel.

The burden of this analysis may suggest the conclusion that corporate criminal responsibility should be withheld from serious crimes defined by the criminal code. There are considerations, however, that indicate the prudence of retaining responsibility on a more restricted basis for these crimes. As noted above, the acquisitive offenses, both common law crimes and those defined by special legislation such as the Federal Mail Fraud Act, traditionally have constituted one of the major categories of corporate crime. In a rough way, also, corporate fines in these cases may be employed to deprive a corporation of an unjust enrichment resulting from the commission of offenses by its agents. Moreover, there may be situations in which it is highly desirable to retain a degree of corporate responsibility for the criminal code offenses as when the crime is committed in the state by a foreign corporation but where the guilty individual agent is outside the jurisdiction and hence not amenable to prosecution in the state.

The approach of Subsection (1)(c) is to provide for a more restricted basis of liability for all cases not included within the terms of Subsections (1)(a) and (1)(b). The general *respondeat superior* approach of Subsection (1)(a) is rejected for these cases, and corporate liability is confined to situations in which the criminal conduct is performed, participated in or recklessly tolerated by the board of directors or by corporate officers or agents sufficiently high in the hierarchy to make it reasonable to assume that their acts are in some substantial sense reflective of the policy of the corporate body. The agents having such power to make the corporation criminally liable are described by the terms of Subsection (1)(c) as the board of directors or any "high managerial agent acting in behalf of the corporation within the scope of his office or employment." The phrase "high managerial agent" is defined in Subsection (4)(c). Given the wide variations in corporate structure, these criteria are necessarily very general. But taken with Subsection (4)(c), they are considerably more precise than those enunciated by many courts as a matter of decisional law.

* * *

In practical effect, Subsection (1)(c) would result in corporate liability for the conduct of the corporate president or general manager but not for conduct of a foreman in a large plant or of an insignificant branch manager in the absence of participation at higher levels of corporate authority. The provision thus works a substantial limitation on corporate responsibility in cases in which the deterrent effects of corporate fines are most dubious but preserves it in cases in which the shareholders are most likely to be in a position to bring pressures to bear to prevent corporate crime.

* * *

3. *Absolute Liability.* Subsection (2) states a rule of interpretation that has the effect of making corporations liable to prosecution for all offenses that carry absolute liability, unless a contrary legislative intent plainly appears. The kinds of offenses that typically preclude culpability defenses are those in which the activity sought to be prevented is frequently engaged in through the corporate mold. It is thus sensible to assume a legislative intent to impose liability on corporations in the absence of explicit indications to the contrary. To impose such liability on corporations, moreover, results in no greater inequities to the corporation or to

the innocent shareholder than to the individual who is held criminally liable despite the absence of the normal requisites of culpability. * * *

6. *Defense of Due Diligence.* Subsection (5) makes an important contribution to the rationalization of corporate criminal responsibility. It is based on the assumption that a primary purpose of the corporate fine is to encourage diligent supervision of corporate personnel by managerial employees in those cases in which the corporation is bound by the conduct of lower echelon employees. Where that diligence can be shown by a preponderance of the evidence, exculpation should follow in all but those cases where such a defense is clearly inconsistent with the legislative purpose manifested in defining the particular offense. * * *

* * *

7. *Individual Liability.* Subsection (6) is designed to overcome certain difficulties in the direct imposition of criminal sanctions on guilty corporate agents. It supplements the provisions of Section 2.06.

Subsection (6)(a) makes certain that the corporate agent will not escape liability because all or part of his conduct is performed through or in the name of the corporation. The difficulties are illustrated by the case of People v. Strong.[41] Officers and directors were individually indicted for embezzlement because of the failure of the corporation to turn over to the state certain taxes collected by the company. The state statute provided only imprisonment as a penalty for the embezzlement. The officers, said the Illinois Supreme Court, "were not principals, because they neither received nor possessed the tax money, and they cannot be accessories, because no one can aid or abet a corporation in the commission of a crime of which the corporation is incapable. Without a principal there are no accessories." The provisions of Subsection (6)(a) avoid such substantial failures of justice. * * *

Subsection (6)(b) deals with the case in which the offense consists of an omission by the corporation or association to perform a duty imposed on it by law. Under the antecedent law of accessorial liability, the corporate officer, even though under affirmative obligation to perform the duty on behalf of the corporation, might escape individual liability if his conduct consisted of non-action. The subsection provides for individual liability of the corporate officer having the primary responsibility for performance of the duty on behalf of the corporation. * * *

Subsection (6)(c) avoids the difficulties suggested by People v. Duncan.[46] In that case, the defendant, a corporate officer, was convicted as an accomplice of the corporation and was fined on certain counts and sentenced to imprisonment on others. The court, in setting aside the defendant's sentence, ruled that since the principal (the corporation) could not be imprisoned, such a penalty could not properly be imposed on the accessory. More than that, even if the individual accessory was fined, the statutory provisions calling for imprisonment to compel payment of the fine would be inapplicable since such sanctions could not be imposed on the corporate principal. This result seems clearly unjustifiable as a matter of policy, and in precluding such a holding the provisions of this subsection are consistent with the objectives of Section 2.06.

* * *

41. 363 Ill. 602, 2 N.E.2d 942 (1936).

46. 363 Ill. 495, 2 N.E.2d 705 (1936).

D. ATTEMPTS

1. *Mens Rea*

People v. Hall

Court of Appeals of Michigan, 1989.
174 Mich.App. 686, 436 N.W.2d 446.

Before MACKENZIE, P.J., and MCDONALD and ROBINSON, JJ.

PER CURIAM.

Defendant appeals as of right from her jury trial convictions of arson of a dwelling house, M.C.L. § 750.72; M.S.A. § 28.267, attempted murder, M.C.L. § 750.91; M.S.A. § 28.286, and attempted manslaughter, M.C.L. § 750.321; M.S.A. § 28.553. We reverse.

Defendant's convictions arise out of the July 27, 1985, burning of a duplex in which the victims, Dennis Reed and Robert Mapes, were sleeping. Defendant, also a resident of the duplex, allegedly started the fire in an attempt to kill Reed. Although defendant and Mapes were romantically involved, Reed and defendant apparently did not get along. The night before the fire, Reed had struck defendant, blackening her eye.

Defendant made two statements to the police in which she admitted setting the fire in an attempt to kill Reed. Although defendant was not angry with Mapes, she stated he was in the wrong place at the wrong time. * * * Both Mapes and Reed escaped and survived the fire. Defendant was charged with arson of a dwelling and two counts of attempted murder.

On appeal defendant claims the trial court erred when instructing the jury on the elements required for a finding of attempted murder. We agree.

* * *

When instructing the jury on attempted murder, the trial court not only read CJI 16:2:01, first-degree premeditated murder, but also CJI 16:3:01, second degree murder. We believe the reading of 16:3:01 in its entirety constituted error requiring reversal. CJI 16:3:01 states in relevant part:

> "(7) Fourth, for second-degree murder you must find that the defendant acted with a certain state of mind in causing the death. You must find that the defendant had one of the following states of mind at the time of the killing:
>
> "(8) That the defendant intended to kill [name deceased], or
>
> "(9) That the defendant intended to do great bodily harm to [name deceased], or
>
> "(10) That the defendant intended to create a very high risk of death or great bodily harm with knowledge that death or great bodily harm was the probable result of [his/her] act."

The problem with CJI 16:3:01 as it applies to the instant case is, here, defendant was not charged with murder but with attempted murder, there being no death. An essential element of the crime of attempt is an attempt to commit the substantive crime, thus rendering attempt a specific intent crime.

The application of the specific intent crime of attempt to a general intent crime, such as second-degree murder, People v. Langworthy, 416 Mich. 630, 331 N.W.2d 171 (1982), was discussed in [People v. Genes, 58 Mich.App. 108, 227 N.W.2d 241 (1975),] where this Court addressed the requirements necessary to support a conviction of attempted manslaughter. The *Genes* Court cited with approval the following comments to § 1001 of the Michigan Revised Criminal Code, page 82:

> "The proposed definition of attempt follows the conventional pattern of limiting this inchoate crime to purposeful conduct, i.e., the actor must have an 'intent to commit a specific offense.' Thus, where criminal liability rests on the causation of a prohibited result, the actor must have an intent to achieve the result even though violation of the substantive offense may require some lesser *mens rea*. Reckless driving, for example, does not constitute attempted manslaughter. A person charged with the substantive crime of manslaughter may be liable as a result of negligence or recklessness causing death, but the same recklessness would not be sufficient if the victim did not die and the actor were only charged with attempt; here, the state would have to show an intent to achieve the prohibited end result, death of the victim. In this area, as in others if the substantive crime requires only recklessness, the *mens rea* requirement for an attempt is substantially higher than that for the substantive crime."

Just as there can be no conviction of attempted manslaughter based on defendant's negligent or reckless behavior, there cannot be a conviction of attempted second-degree murder based on any state of mind less than a defendant's intent to bring about the prohibited result, death. Thus, in the instant case the trial court erred in instructing the jury that defendant could be found guilty of attempted murder if they found defendant intended to do great bodily harm or intended to create a very high risk of death or bodily harm with knowledge that death or great bodily harm would be the probable result of the act.

To summarize, although a defendant may be charged with and convicted of attempted manslaughter or attempted second-degree murder, both crimes require a showing that the defendant intended to bring about a death, and may not be based on a defendant's negligent or reckless actions.

* * *

REVERSED AND REMANDED.

Note

Model Penal Code, § 5.01, comment 2: *

2. *Requirement of Purpose.* A closer analysis of Subsection (1) must begin with a discussion of the mens rea of attempt. As will be seen, all three of the subdivisions of Subsection (1), with two exceptions to be noted, are designed to follow the conventional pattern of limiting the crime of attempt to purposive

conduct. The general principle is thus that the actor must affirmatively desire to engage in the conduct or to cause the result that will constitute the principal offense.

The first exception relates to the circumstances under which the offense must be committed. The requirement of purpose extends to the conduct of the actor and to the results that his conduct causes, but his purpose need not encompass all of the circumstances included in the formal definition of the substantive offense.[9] As to them, it is sufficient that he acts with the culpability that is required for commission of the completed crime.

Several illustrations may serve to clarify the point. Assume, for example, a statute that provides that sexual intercourse with a female under a prescribed age is an offense, and that a mistake as to age will not afford a defense no matter how reasonable its foundation. The policy of the substantive offense as to age, therefore, is one of strict liability, and if the actor has sexual intercourse with a female, he is guilty or not, depending upon her age and irrespective of his views as to her age. Suppose, however, that he is arrested before he engages in the proscribed conduct, and that the charge is an attempt to commit the offense. Should he then be entitled to rely on a mistake as to age as a defense? Or should the policy of the substantive crime on this issue carry over to the attempt as well? Or, assume a statute that makes it a federal offense to murder an FBI agent and treats the agent's status as a member of the FBI as a jurisdictional ingredient, with no culpability required in respect to that element. The question again is whether the policy of the substantive crime should control the same issue when it arises on a charge of attempt, or whether there is a special policy that the law of attempt should embrace to change the result on this point.

Under the formulation in Subsection (1)(c),[11] the proffered defense would not succeed in either case. In the statutory rape example, the actor must have a purpose to engage in sexual intercourse with a female in order to be charged with the attempt, and must engage in a substantial step in a course of conduct planned to culminate in his commission of that act. With respect to the age of the victim, however, it is sufficient if he acts "with the kind of culpability otherwise required for the commission of the crime," which in the case supposed is none at all. Since, therefore, mistake as to age is irrelevant with respect to the substantive offense, it is likewise irrelevant with respect to the attempt. The same result would obtain in the murder illustration. The actor must, in the case supposed, engage in a substantial step in a course of conduct planned to culminate in the

9. The "circumstances" of the offense refer to the objective situation that the law requires to exist, in addition to the defendant's act or any results that the act may cause. The elements of "nighttime" in burglary, "property of another" in theft, "female not his wife" in rape, and "dwelling" in arson are illustrations. "Conduct" refers to "breaking and entering" in burglary, "taking" in theft, "sexual intercourse" in rape and "burning" in arson. Results, of course, include "death" in homicide. While these terms are not airtight categories, they have served as a helpful analytical device in the development of the Code. *See* Section 2.02 and its Comment for a further elaboration.

11. Subsection (1)(a) would not apply to either illustration, because in both instances the defendant would have committed the substantive offense if he had successfully completed his conduct. If he did not complete his planned course of conduct, Subsection (1)(c) would apply. Subsection (1)(b) could apply to the FBI illustration if the actor shot at the agent with the intent to kill and missed. Then he would have done all that he intended to do, and thus would be liable to prosecution under Subsection (1)(b). If he were stopped before he pulled the trigger, Subsection (1)(c) would apply. The analysis on the point under discussion would be the same, however, whether the actor completed his proposed conduct and was prosecuted under Subsection (1)(b) or whether he did not and was prosecuted under Subsection (1)(c).

death of his victim. But with respect to his awareness of the status of his victim as an FBI agent, a mistake would not be relevant since the policy of the substantive offense controls on such matters and that policy is one of strict liability.[13]

The judgment is thus that if the defendant manifests a purpose to engage in the type of conduct or to cause the type of result that is forbidden by the criminal law, he has sufficiently exhibited his dangerousness to justify the imposition of criminal sanctions, so long as he otherwise acts with the kind of culpability that is sufficient for the completed offense. * * *

* * * Cases will arise where the defendant engaged in conduct that recklessly or negligently created a risk of death, but where the death did not result. Should the law of attempts encompass such cases?

The approach of the Model Code is not to treat such behavior as an attempt. * * * The Institute's judgment was that the scope of the criminal law would be unduly extended if one could be liable for an attempt whenever he recklessly or negligently created a risk of any result whose actual occurrence would lead to criminal responsibility. * * *

When, on the other hand, a person actually believes that his behavior will produce the proscribed result, it is appropriate to treat him as attempting to cause the result, whether or not that is his purpose.

Subsection (1)(b) provides that when causing a particular result is an element of the crime, as in homicide offenses or criminally obtaining property, an actor commits an attempt when he does or omits to do anything with the purpose of causing "or with the belief that it will cause" such result without further conduct on his part. Thus, a belief that death will ensue from the actor's conduct, or that property will be obtained, will suffice, as well as would a purpose to bring about those results. If, for example, the actor's purpose were to demolish a building and, knowing that persons were in the building and that they would be killed by the explosion, he nevertheless detonated a bomb that turned out to be defective, he could be prosecuted for attempted murder even though it was no part of his purpose that the inhabitants of the building would be killed.

It is difficult to say what the decision would be under prevailing attempt principles in a case of this kind. It might be held that the actor did not specifically intend to kill the inhabitants of the building; on the other hand, the concept of "intent" has always been an ambiguous one and might be thought to include results that the actor believed to be the inevitable consequence of his conduct. In any event, the inclusion of such conduct as the basis for liability under Subsection (1)(b) is based on the conclusion that the manifestation of the actor's dangerousness is just as great—or very nearly as great—as in the case of purposive conduct. In both instances a deliberate choice is made to bring about the consequence forbidden by the criminal laws, and the actor has done all within his power to cause this result to occur. The absence of any desire that the result occur is not, under these circumstances, a sufficient basis for differentiating between the two types of conduct involved. * * *

* * *

13. It should be noted that while offenses involving strict liability were chosen for clarity of illustration, the analysis would be the same for circumstance elements where the culpability level is set at recklessness or negligence. For example, if negligence as to age or the status of the FBI agent were required and sufficient for the substantive offense, the same would hold true for the attempt.

Questions

1. Suppose a jurisdiction which defines robbery to require knowledge, but not purpose, as to all of its *actus reus* elements. Attempt requires that the accused act "with the kind of culpability otherwise required for commission of" the offense attempted and engage "in conduct constituting a substantial step toward the commission of the offense. A substantial step is any conduct * * * which is strongly corroborative of the firmness of the actor's purpose to complete the commission of the offense."

On the morning of the day on which he allegedly committed attempted robbery, the accused, in a depressed and suicidal state of mind, had been released from a halfway house after being a patient in a mental hospital. He put a putty knife to the throat of a store clerk and demanded money, only to be disarmed by a customer before any money was handed over. The accused intended to perform the acts he did and was aware that he thereby placed the clerk in reasonable fear of injury and that he would almost certainly obtain money. He did not, however, desire either the fear or the money; he only hoped that he would be returned to the mental hospital for help as a result of his conduct.

Does he have an appropriate mental state for attempted robbery, either under the law of the jurisdiction or under Model Penal Code, § 5.01?

2. Do the crimes of attempted manslaughter and attempted felony-murder exist?

2. *Actus Reus*

a. *PREPARATION AND ATTEMPT*

State v. Verge

Supreme Court of Ohypo, 1980.
288 Ohypo 593.

Verna Verge appeals from convictions of attempted theft and attempt to defraud an insurance company. As to each offense, the conviction is affirmed by a divided court.

WYNKEN, C.J.: The relevant portion of our theft statute provides:

> Whoever takes moveable property in which another person has an interest which the taker is not entitled to infringe, intending to deprive him of his interest therein, is guilty of theft. * * * (27 Ohypo Rev.Code § 409)

The relevant portion of our insurance fraud statute reads:

> Whoever, being insured against loss by fire or theft of property in which he has an interest, obtains any money from such insurer on the basis of any knowingly false claim of loss is guilty of insurance fraud. * * * (27 Ohypo Rev.Code § 788)

Our legislature has not defined the crime of attempt; we are governed by the common law.

The prosecution evidence showed that Verge, who had inherited substantial wealth from her grandfather, was the owner of a valuable country home, Giltacres. One of her prized possessions was a letter purportedly written by Abraham Lincoln and obtained by way of her grandfather from a distant cousin who had been a friend of Lincoln's. The letter contains material of great historical interest and it was independently appraised for insurance purposes in 1972 at $65,000. The letter was displayed on a stand in a glass case on a table in the Giltacres entrance hall.

Since 1972 Verge has carried a policy of insurance with the Nadir Insurance Company, covering all of her personal property, including the Lincoln letter, against loss by theft or fire (excluding, of course, any fire deliberately set by Verge). In September, 1979, Verge decided to spend the winter in her town house in the city, and she rented Giltacres, together with the house furnishings and the Lincoln letter, to old friends of hers, Mr. and Mrs. Bertram Bailey, for the period of December 1, 1979, through February 28, 1980. Verge's butler Jukes and other members of the staff were temporarily employed by the Baileys during the rental period. The Baileys invited Verge to join a Christmas house party at Giltacres for the Christmas, 1979, season, and she accepted.

A few days before she left for Christmas at Giltacres, Verge learned that distinguished experts had cast doubts on the authenticity of her Lincoln letter and that they were about to request her to permit them to examine it. When she arrived at Giltacres on the morning of December 23rd, she privately told Jukes that she planned to play a joke on the Baileys and asked him to shut off the house's main electrical switch (located in a closet under the grand staircase in the entrance hall) during the dessert course at Christmas Eve dinner. Jukes, who believed her, agreed to do so.

On the afternoon of Christmas Eve, Verge began a handwritten letter to the Nadir Insurance Company, postdated December 25, 1979. This was discovered on a subsequent police search. The text of the uncompleted letter reads:

> I hereby claim a loss under the terms of your renewal policy # 2,308,401, covering the period of August 1, 1979, through July 31, 1980. The item for which the claim is made is the letter from Abraham Lincoln, referred to in Schedule B, attached to the policy application. This was valued at $65,000 by an appraiser approved by you in 1972. The loss occurred last night under the following circumstances: * * *

As she wrote the letter, Verge was interrupted to go downstairs for cocktails and dinner. During the cocktail hour the Baileys and their 22 guests removed the top of the glass case, which was not replaced, and examined the Lincoln letter, without removing it from its stand. At dinner, Jukes, as instructed, shut off the electricity. Verge then immediately said, "It's that old trouble with the fuse box. Jukes never can fix it, but I know how. Just wait here, and I'll be back in a minute." She then picked up a candle from the dining table and went off in the direction of the entrance hall.

Mr. Bailey noticed that she seemed to be behaving in an unnatural manner, and, after a moment, he followed her. As he came into the hall, he saw her, still holding the candle, standing at the glass case and reaching in the direction of the letter. He heard her whisper to herself, "I can't afford to leave you for the experts." At this point he shouted for her to stop, and she did. The police were called. After proper *Miranda* warnings Verge confessed that she had planned to take and hide the letter and later, after obtaining the theft insurance money, find an unscrupulous purchaser for the letter. The front door was unlocked; she said that she did not anticipate being suspected of the theft herself.

The question for determination on this appeal is whether there is sufficient evidence to sustain the convictions. Attempt requires, first, a purpose to do acts which, if carried out, would constitute the crime as to which the attempt is charged. There is ample evidence in the confession, corroborated by Verge's conduct, that she intended to steal the Lincoln letter and to defraud Nadir. (It is of course possible for the "owner" of personal property to steal it from one who, as in this case, is a bailee or lessee for a term, entitled to its possession during the term.)

But an attempt requires more than *mens rea*. It requires an act taken as a substantial step in the direction of accomplishing the end. The conduct must pass beyond mere preparation to commit the crime, but the exact nature of the conduct which crosses the line between non-criminal preparation and criminal attempt has plagued judges and scholars for many years. It is reasonably clear that, in the ordinary case, when the accused has done what, from her point of view, is the last necessary act to complete the crime, she has gone far enough to be guilty of an attempt. So, for example, one who plans to kill by a massive dose of poison and who has placed the poison in the victim's cereal as the victim heads downstairs for breakfast is guilty of attempted murder. If things go as expected, the killer will need to do nothing more. That stage had not been reached in Verge's case, of course. Verge still had to pick up the letter to be guilty of theft, and she still had to complete and mail the insurance claim (and receive the money) to be guilty of defrauding Nadir.

Fortunately for the safety of the public, while commission of the last necessary act is sufficient for attempt, it is not required. Attempt may exist before this point. In a case of slow poisoning, with daily doses contemplated over a period of weeks, for example, at attempt clearly exists by the time the first dose, in itself inadequate to kill, is administered. According to most traditional authority the test turns on how far along the path to completion the accused has gone and how much remains to be done, in other words, on proximity to success. This involves difficult matters of degree.

Where the accused must obtain the cooperation of another person (other than the victim) to succeed, there is probably no attempt before that person cooperates, or at least agrees to cooperate. Here, only the innocent cooperation of Jukes was necessary, and Jukes performed his role.

In general, the question of proximity focuses on how much is yet to be done before the completed crime will be committed. There is always a difficulty in evaluating the significance of conduct in the stages which may lead up to a crime. Even assuming that the purpose of the defendant is articulated and seems clear, how firm is it? Would it become qualified or diverted if normal obstacles are met? Perhaps, as time passes, the planner might repent and abandon his plan. A few would say that there should be no guilt of attempt until all chance for effective repentence has passed, but this would surely be an unworkable test. In many cases repentence is possible until the very last moment, and, if there were no attempt until such time, there would be almost no room for attempt law to operate at all. Of course, one can say that when the accused approaches fairly closely, it is relatively unlikely that he will repent. But this is not really of much help in deciding particular cases. (In any event, if we are interested in the possibility of repentence at all, we are interested only in voluntary repentence, due to change of heart, not to abandonment of the plan when the accused finds himself at the point of capture.)

We should wait until the accused's conduct exhibits firm purpose and is seriously close to commission of a crime before imposing liability for an attempt.

Admittedly, this test is general and furnishes no certain answers in particular fact situations. Several ideas have been advanced to help sharpen focus. Mr. Justice Holmes believed that the element of danger was to be considered along with physical proximity, so that the point of attempt might be reached sooner with more serious crimes. See Hyde v. United States, 225 U.S. 347, 32 S.Ct. 793, 56 L.Ed. 1114 (1912), Commonwealth v. Kennedy, 170 Mass. 18, 48 N.E. 770 (1897). A distinction between gathering forces (preparation) and discharging forces (attempt) has been suggested. See Hall, General Principles of Criminal Law 583 (2d ed.1947). Perhaps an attempt occurs at the point when the law first recognizes some slight invasion of a protected legal interest, as where an assault or trespass is committed. See, e.g., Strahorn, *Preparation for Crime as Criminal Attempt,* 1 Wash. & Lee L.Rev. 1 (1939).

If we try to apply a proximity test to the charges before us, the result is fairly easy to see. As to the attempted theft charge, Verge had done everything short of grasping the letter when she was stopped, and the taking itself would have been enough for the completed crime. Obviously she was dangerously proximate to success and was properly found guilty of attempted theft. As to the attempted fraud charge, however, she had not even finished writing out her claim. I do not see how she could be regarded as close to success before she mailed the claim. There was time for repentence; she was still preparing materials for the crime and had not yet begun to discharge her forces, and she had not yet come close to violating any legal right of Nadir's. Her conviction should be reversed as a matter of law on the attempted fraud charge.

BLYNKEN, J.: The Chief Justice follows the approach of most of the common law cases in seeking to settle this case on the basis of Verge's proximity to success. But, why should proximity be the test? The real issue is whether the offender has convincingly shown that he is dangerous, not whether he has almost committed a dangerous act. As the Chief Justice rightly notes, it is often difficult to see where a particular course of conduct is leading. When is the importunate and aggressive lover a would-be rapist, and when is he not? When is the insistent demander of funds about to rob, and when is he merely a zealous beggar? If we are allowed to see the end of the scene, we find out, but when the action is interrupted before completion, as it often is in attempt cases, it may be difficult or impossible to be sure. Sometimes in these ambiguous situations, statements of the accused before or after the event as to his intention are used to settle the matter, but this can be very dangerous. The time of the physically or psychologically coerced confession (or the merely false one) is not over. Casual or boastful statements before the event may seem damning to a jury, although they may be of no significance in determining the true state of mind of the accused at the crucial moment.

Criminal purpose must of course be proved, and the accused's statements, within the rules of evidence, are admissible to prove such purpose. But the *actus reus* of attempt should be independently established. In this phase of the case, one should disregard the accused's own declarations as to his intentions and ask whether his conduct, considered in isolation, unequivocally demonstrates his particular, clear, and settled criminal intention. This *res ipsa loquitur* test is explained in The King v. Barker, [1924] N.Z.L.R. 865, and Salmond, Jurisprudence 404 (7th ed.1924). This is the only safe way to make sure we can identify the dangerous offender. (Where the attempt involves the use of some material which has no reasonably possible innocent purpose, as, for example, a die to counterfeit coins, it may be easy to be sure of criminality very early in the proceedings.)

In the attempted fraud charge, there can be no reasonable question as to what Verge was doing, even if we disregard her confession. She began a draft of her post-dated claim before anything had been lost, and she wrote it as if the loss had already occurred. She arranged for the blackout and was found as she was about to reach for the letter, identified in her claim as the subject of the loss. It is clear from this conduct that she was well embarked on a scheme to make a fraudulent claim, and her attempted fraud conviction should be upheld.

It is otherwise as to the attempted theft conviction. If we disregard her confession (and perhaps we must disregard also her ambiguous words, "I can't afford to leave you for the experts," which, while not a direct statement of criminal intention, should perhaps be regarded as coming very close to such a statement), we cannot be sure that it was theft and not a form of statutory arson that she was about to commit. The policy covered accidental fire loss as well as theft loss. She had a candle with her, and perhaps she could have made a more plausible claim of accidental burning in the circumstances than of mysterious theft by a person unknown. Since her acts do not in themselves make clear her purpose, the conviction of attempted theft should be reversed.

The test proposed by my brother Nod in the opinion which follows is an exceedingly dangerous one, though based on the usually admirable work of the American Law Institute. Model Penal Code §§ 5.01(1)(c) and 5.01(2) permit conviction of attempt when the accused purposely does anything which is a substantial step toward the commission of the crime attempted, if the conduct is strongly corroborative of the accused's criminal purpose. This test allows reliance on the accused's statements of intention and requires very little to be done. When it is combined with the provisions of § 5.05, which in most cases punish attempt as severely as the completed crime (a result which is similar to what is permitted under our common law decisions, though usually in practice not produced in actual sentencing), frightening possibilities of miscarriage of justice are presented.

NOD, J.: Both convictions should be affirmed. My vote will combine with Chief Justice Wynken's to uphold the attempted theft conviction and with Justice Blynken's to uphold the attempted fraud conviction. I am satisfied that no miscarriage of justice thereby occurs.

On what grounds do we punish attempts? Deterrence can hardly be a significant factor; would-be criminals are generally optimistic and are deterred, if they are going to be deterred at all, by the equal or more severe penalty for the completed crime. Revenge, generally regarded as an inappropriate ground, does not apply; the attempter has not caused significant harm by his abortive conduct. We must then punish either for reasons of incapacitation or of reform. As to these points it really makes no important difference whether the accused succeeds or fails (except perhaps that, having once failed, he may have learned more efficient methods without having spent his original motive for the act, and be even more dangerous than, and as much in need of reform as, one who has succeeded). This is why the Model Penal Code punishes attempts about as severely as completed offenses. As soon as the accused has demonstrated the will to act out his criminal plan, we should, for the protection of the public, find him guilty of an attempt.

The criminal purpose cannot here really be in question. Verge's confession is persuasive, particularly in context. I doubt that even Justice Blynken really doubts the aims of theft and fraud. It is only for the purpose of an artificial analysis that she chooses to disregard what she knows.

In each case, as the Model Penal Code requires, the accused has taken at least a substantial step, strongly corroborative of criminal purpose, towards her objective. These steps do not quite fit the specific examples suggested in § 5.01(2). She did not lie in wait for a victim, entice a victim to the place of crime, reconnoiter the place of crime, effect an unlawful entry, or possess any specially designed materials, or materials incapable of innocent use. Nor, I think, did she possess or fabricate materials to be employed in committing the crime at or near the place of commission, where this serves no lawful purpose. The claim letter was not fabricated near the office of Nadir, where the crime was to be committed, and the candle perhaps served the lawful purpose of enabling her to see where she was going as she restored electric power. Finally, she did not solicit an innocent agent to engage in conduct constituting an element of the crime. Jukes was an innocent agent, but what he did formed no "element" of the theft or fraud. However, these factors are only illustrative, and Verge engaged in fully equivalent conduct with respect to both offenses. She was plainly embarked fully on her criminal schemes, and her convictions of attempt should stand.

Question

What should be the guiding principle or principles in dividing non-criminal preparation from criminal attempt? Why? Should there be a separate attempt rule for each crime attempted?

Notes

1. *Policy.* Model Penal Code, § 5.01, Comment 1 (Tent.Draft No. 10, 1960): *

1. *The Definition of Attempt.* * * * The question is what conduct, when engaged in with a purpose to commit a crime or to advance towards the attainment of a criminal objective, should suffice to constitute a criminal attempt?

In fashioning an answer we must keep in mind that in attempt, as distinct from solicitation and conspiracy, it is not intrinsic to the actor's conduct that he has disclosed his criminal design to someone else; nor is there any natural line that is suggested by the situation—like utterance or agreement. The law must deal with the problem presented by a single individual and must address itself to conduct that may fall anywhere upon a graded scale from early preparation to the final effort to commit the crime.

We think, therefore, that it is useful to begin with any conduct designed to effect or to advance towards the attainment of the criminal objective and to ask when it ought *not* to be regarded as a crime, either because it does not adequately manifest the dangerousness of the actor or on other overriding grounds of social policy. * * *

2. *Substantial Step.* Model Penal Code, § 5.01, Comment 6: **

6. *Model Penal Code Approach to Preparation Problem.* Subsections (1)(c) and (2) set forth the Code's proposed solution of the problem of framing criteria to determine when the actor has progressed sufficiently toward his criminal objective to have committed an attempt. Subsection (1)(c) provides that the actor must have engaged in conduct that constitutes "a substantial step" in a course of conduct planned to culminate in his commission of the crime. Subsection (2) elaborates what is meant by "a substantial step" in two ways. It provides that conduct shall not be held to be a substantial step unless "it is strongly corroborative of the actor's criminal purpose." It also specifies a number of situations that, without negativing the sufficiency of other conduct, should not be held insufficient as a matter of law if they are strongly corroborative of the actor's criminal purpose.

(a) *Requirements of "Substantial Step" and Corroboration of Purpose.* Whether a particular act is a substantial step is obviously a matter of degree. To this extent, the Code retains the element of imprecision found in most of the other approaches to the preparation-attempt problem. There are, however, several differences to be noted:

First, this formulation shifts the emphasis from what remains to be done, the chief concern of the proximity tests, to what the actor has already done. That further major steps must be taken before the crime can be completed does not preclude a finding that the steps already undertaken are substantial. It is expected, in the normal case, that this approach will broaden the scope of attempt liability.

Second, although it is intended that the requirement of a substantial step will result in the imposition of attempt liability only in those instances in which some firmness of criminal purpose is shown, no finding is required as to whether the actor would probably have desisted prior to completing the crime. Potentially the probable desistance test could reach very early steps toward crime, depending on how one assesses the probabilities of desistance; but since in practice this test follows closely the proximity approaches, rejection of a test of probable desistance will not narrow the scope of attempt liability.

Finally, the requirement of proving a substantial step generally will prove less of a hurdle for the prosecution than the res ipsa loquitur approach, which requires that the actor's conduct itself have manifested the criminal purpose. The basic rationale of the requirement that the actor's conduct shall strongly corroborate his purpose to commit a crime is, of course, the same as that underlying the res ipsa loquitur view. But framed in terms of corroboration, the present formulation does not so narrowly circumscribe the scope of attempt liability. Rigorously applied, the res ipsa loquitur doctrine would provide immunity in many instances in which the actor had gone far toward the commission of an offense and had strongly indicated a criminal purpose. * * *

* * *

Despite their weaknesses, confessions play an important role in the apprehension and conviction of criminals. The res ipsa loquitur test unduly restricts their value in an attempt case. The objectives of the res ipsa loquitur test will be met if it is required that the actor's conduct, considered in the light of all the circumstances, adds significant evidential force to any proof of criminal purpose based solely on the actor's statements. The actor's conduct would then be "strongly corroborative" of his purpose to commit the crime.

Under the Model Code formulation, the two purposes to be served by the res ipsa loquitur test are, to a large extent, treated separately. Firmness of criminal purpose is intended to be shown by requiring a substantial step, while problems of proof are dealt with by the requirement of corroboration—although under the reasoning previously expressed the latter will also tend to establish firmness of purpose.

In addition to assuring firmness of purpose, the requirement of a substantial step will remove very remote preparatory acts from the ambit of attempt liability and the relatively stringent sanctions imposed for attempts. On the other hand, by broadening liability to the extent suggested, apprehension of dangerous persons will be facilitated and law enforcement officials and others will be able to stop the criminal effort at an earlier stage, thereby minimizing the risk of substantive harm, but without providing immunity for the offender.

* * *

3. *Failure.* Originally failure was a necessary element of attempt. If the accused could show that he succeeded, the attempt had "merged" into the completed offense and disappeared and there could be no attempt conviction. Today, most jurisdictions allow an attempt conviction, even if the proof turns out to show the completed offense.

4. *Sentencing.* Model Penal Code, § 5.05, Comment 2: *

2. *Grading.* Subsection (1) of 5.05 departs from the law that preceded promulgation of the Model Code by treating attempt, solicitation and conspiracy on a parity for purposes of sentence and by determining the grade or degree of

the inchoate crime by the gravity of the most serious offense that is its object. Only when the object is a capital crime or a felony of the first degree does the Code deviate from this solution, grading the inchoate offense in that case as a felony of the second degree.

The theory of this grading system may be stated simply. To the extent that sentencing depends upon the antisocial disposition of the actor and the demonstrated need for a corrective sanction, there is likely to be little difference in the gravity of the required measures depending on the consummation or the failure of the plan. It is only when and insofar as the severity of sentence is designed for general deterrent purposes that a distinction on this ground is likely to have reasonable force. It is doubtful, however, that the threat of punishment for the inchoate crime can add significantly to the net deterrent efficacy of the sanction threatened for the substantive offense that is the actor's object, which he, by hypothesis, ignores. Hence, there is a basis for economizing in use of the heaviest and most afflictive sanctions by removing them from the inchoate crimes. The sentencing provisions for second degree felonies, including the provision for extended terms, should certainly suffice to meet whatever danger is presented by the actor.

On the other side of the equation, it is clear that the inchoate crime should not be graded higher than the substantive offense; it is the danger that the actor's conduct may culminate in its commission that justifies creating the inchoate crime. * * *

5. *Punishing Preparatory Conduct.* Sometimes the criminal law punishes specific preparatory conduct at a stage earlier than the local law of attempt would reach it. Recall, for example, the discussion of vagrancy and loitering problems, supra, pp. 97–106. And consider such crimes as possessing burglar's tools. Is such a particularized approach better or worse than the American Law Institute's early intervention in attempt law across the board?

State v. Otto

Supreme Court of Idaho, 1981.
102 Idaho 250, 629 P.2d 646.

McFadden, Justice.

The appellant appeals his conviction of attempted first degree murder based on his hiring of an undercover police officer to kill Captain Ailor of the Lewiston Police Department. Appellant had been under investigation by Captain Ailor concerning the disappearance of the appellant's wife in August, 1976.

On October 24, 1976, appellant was in the Long Branch Saloon owned by Stan Kuykendall. Mr. Kuykendall testified that during a conversation appellant expressed a desire to find a "hit-man" to kill Captain Ailor because Ailor had been harassing him over Mrs. Otto's disappearance. Mr. Kuykendall reported this to the Lewiston Police Department. Following this report an officer telephoned appellant and said he was a "hit-man." This officer later testified that appellant stated he was willing to spend $500 to have the killing done, but after dickering a price of $1,000 was agreed upon.

The Lewiston police called in members of the Idaho State Police to assist them in investigating the matter. It was decided that Officer Watts of the Idaho State Police would wear a "bug" and attempt to record his conversations with appellant. On the afternoon of October 26, 1976, Officer Watts, wearing the transmitter, met with appellant at the Long Branch as prearranged earlier in the day. During this conversation, Watts agreed to kill Captain Ailor for $250 "up front" if he were to receive an additional $750 after the killing. It was agreed that appellant would place the $250 in a cup in Watts pickup, which appellant was seen to do later in the day. Appellant was arrested on October 27 and charged with attempted murder in the first degree, I.C. §§ 18–4001, 4003 and 306.

The essential question before this court is whether the appellant's conduct amounted to more than solicitation of another to murder and reached the extent or degree of an attempt under accepted principles of criminal law. We hold it did not and thus the conviction must be reversed.

The concern of the criminal law is to determine at which points along a continuum of activity criminal liability of differing degrees will attach. There can be no doubt that what the appellant did in this case was criminal as well as reprehensible. But the task facing this court is not merely to pass judgment; we must strive to correctly determine under the accepted precepts of the law whether the appellant's conviction can stand. The sincere desire to protect society from acts such as the appellant's here cannot lead us to slight this duty.

It is recognized, of course, that a close relationship exists between solicitation and attempt. In the early stages of criminal activity, the two offenses may run parallel courses. However, there exists an accepted and distinct difference between them in law, the strength of which cannot be muted by a few courts erroneously treating the terms and concepts as interchangeable.

It is supported beyond contradiction that, regardless how heinous, no man can be convicted for having criminal intent alone. An *actus reus* is essential. And in the sphere of inchoate criminal offenses, it is clear that not every act will, when combined with criminal intent, suffice to establish the basis for an attempt. In the voluminous jurisprudence on attempts in the criminal law, some well supported tenets have been established in regard to the act required.

LaFave and Scott state in their treatise, Criminal Law (1972):

> "The crime of attempt * * * consists of: (1) an intent to do an act or to bring about certain consequences which would in law amount to a crime; and (2) an act in furtherance of that intent *which, as it is most commonly put, goes beyond mere preparation.*" (Emphasis supplied.) LaFave at 423.

* * *

While the distinction between acts of preparation and those of commission (or as is more commonly phrased "perpetration") may be difficult to make in many situations, courts have widely adopted the differentiation.[2]

2. The essential focus in regard to this distinction is upon the proximity of the act, both spatially and temporally, to the completion of the criminal design.

"It is often said, with variations in the exact wording, that for a criminal attempt there 'must be a dangerous proximity to success.'

* * *

The general rule in regard to solicitations within the context of the preparatory-perpetratory acts sufficient for an attempt[4] is well stated by the Tennessee Supreme Court in Gervin v. State, 212 Tenn. 653, 371 S.W.2d 449 (1963):

> "The weight of American authority holds, as a general proposition, that mere criminal solicitation of another to commit a crime does not constitute an attempt. 1 Wharton, Criminal Law and Procedure, Sec. 81 at 168 (1957); 1 Burdick, Law of Crime, Sec. 106 at 117 (1946); Perkins, Criminal Law, 505, 508 (1957); Clark and Marshall, Crimes, Sec. 4.05 at 200 (6th ed. 1958); Model Penal Code, Sec. 5.02, comment at 86 (Tent.Draft No. 10, 1960); 14 Am. Jur., Criminal Law, Sec. 66 at 814 (1938) and 22 C.J.S. Criminal Law § 73 at 225 (1961). The one significant exception to this position is 1 Bishop, Criminal Law, Secs. 767, 768 at 543–546 (9th ed. 1923).
>
> The weight of authority is, of course, not determinative, but the reasons for that position are compelling." 371 S.W.2d at 450–1.

* * * A few courts, however, have held that solicitation can be sufficient predicate for an attempt to commit the crime solicited. Braham v. State, 571 P.2d 631 (Alaska 1977) cert. den. 436 U.S. 910, 98 S.Ct. 2246, 56 L.Ed.2d 410 (1978); State v. Gay, 4 Wash.App. 834, 486 P.2d 341 (1971); State v. Mandel, 78 Ariz. 226, 278 P.2d 413 (1954). Since the state relies primarily on the minority view expressed in these last cited cases to support appellant's conviction, a brief discussion of this line of authority is called for.

These decisions rely heavily upon the proposition that when the intent that a crime be committed is clearly shown, "slight acts" on the part of the solicitor will make him liable for an attempt to commit that target crime. * * *

* * *

We disagree with the reasoning in the case of State v. Gay, 4 Wash.App. 834, 486 P.2d 341 (1971). While that court noted that a "mere" solicitation is not an attempt, the court there held that the transfer of "consideration,"

> "This does not involve an additional requirement but is included within the preparation-perpetration concept. While the measures taken with criminal intent are obviously remote they remain under the label 'preparation,' and only when apparent proximity is reached has there been the beginning of 'perpetration.'" Perkins, supra, at p. 572. See also LaFave, supra, at pp. 432–434; 22 C.J.S. Criminal Law, § 75(2), pp. 230–33.

The "dangerous proximity" language probably had its genesis in the often cited dissent of Justice Holmes in Hyde v. United States, 225 U.S. 347, 387–8, 32 S.Ct. 793, 810, 56 L.Ed. 1114 (1911), where he stated, comparing the overt act requirement necessary to support a charge of conspiracy with that necessary for an attempt to commit the conspired crime:

> "* * * combination, intention, and overt act may all be present without amounting to a criminal attempt,—as if all that were done should be an agreement to murder a man 50 miles away, and the purchase of a pistol for the purpose. There must be dangerous proximity to success. But when that exists the overt act is the essence of the offense."

The application of this analysis to the area of solicitation—i.e.—preparation, as well as to the facts of the instant case, is manifest.

4. The prerequisite to an understanding of the general rule is the recognition that solicitation is in the nature of the incitement or encouragement of another to commit a crime in the future. Thus it is essentially preparatory to the commission of the targeted offense. See, e.g., Black's Law Dictionary (5th ed. 1979) p. 1249; Clark & Marshall, supra, § 4.02, pp. 219–20; 22 C.J.S. Criminal Law, § 78; Bassiouni, Substantive Criminal Law (1978) p. 224.

i.e., the partial payment for the contracted killing, was a "slight" yet sufficient act upon which an attempt could be found. (This is the same "slight act" relied on in part by the *Mandel* court, supra 278 P.2d at 415.)

Facially there would appear to be no persuasive reason why a request to kill, however phrased or whatever enticement offered, should be treated differently under the law merely because part of the agreed upon fee has passed hands. There is no greater proximity, no significantly greater likelihood of consummation, and no act of a nature other than the incitement or preparation inherent in the solicitation itself. * * *

In State v. Braham, supra, 571 P.2d 631 (1977), the most recent adoption of the minority position, the Alaska court also recognized that there must be an overt act beyond mere preparation. Yet, after noting the disparate lines of authority, that court elected to join with the Arizona and Washington courts. In the factual context of the *Braham* case, the court found the requisite overt act in the solicitee's visit to the intended victim at the urging of the solicitor for the purpose of gaining the victim's confidence. At that time, the solicitee was still committed to the planned murder; it was only upon later realizing that the police were well informed of the circumstances of the planned murder that the solicitee became an informer. There thus appears to be a valid basis for the Alaska decision holding the solicitor guilty of an attempt. While on the face of the case the citation to the *Gay* and *Mandel* precedent would indicate that the solicitor's consummation of the contract to kill or the finding of other "slight acts" on his part supported his conviction of an attempt, the act actually relied upon by the court as satisfying the overt act element was the solicitee's visit with the intended victim pursuant to the plan. It is well accepted that when the parties are acting in furtherance of a plan, the solicitor shares any attempt liability that accrues due to the actions of his agent. Citation to *Gay* and *Mandel* is unnecessary.

While the concept of "slight acts" is doubtlessly appealing in some respects, especially to those seeking to punish reprehensible acts when criminal intent is clear, use of this phrase in the manner of the *Gay* and *Mandel* decisions is improper. The solicitor of another, assuming neither solicitor nor solicitee proximately acts toward the crime's commission, cannot be held for an attempt. He does not by his incitement of another to criminal activity commit a dangerously proximate act of perpetration. The extension of attempt liability back to the solicitor destroys the distinction between preparation and perpetration. As stated by Clark and Marshall:

> "[W]hen that course of action is followed it would seem that the zone of perpetration is pushed back into what is virtually the preparation stage, e.g., the accused inciting his prospective actor or partner." Clark and Marshall, supra, § 4.05 at p. 227.

It is foreseeable that jurisdictions faced with a general attempt statute and no means of severely punishing a solicitation to commit a felony might resort to the device of transforming the solicitor's urgings into a proximate attempted commission of the crime urged but doing so violates the very essence of the requirement that a sufficient *actus reus* be proven before criminal liability will attach.

In light of the foregoing discussion, the facts in appellant's situation take on additional clarity. Here appellant desired to have Captain Ailor murdered. In structuring his plan, he solicited an agent to commit the actual act, and in this regard he paid $250 and promised him a larger sum after the crime had been committed. Neither appellant nor the agent ever took any steps of perpetration in dangerous proximity to the commission of the offense planned. The conversation in the Long Branch at which appellant solicited the undercover policeman, and the payment of part of the agreed upon fee, are not acts of perpetration at all but are clearly the preparatory acts of incitement of another to commit a crime, i.e., of mere solicitation. These acts are not sufficient under the law above discussed to support a conviction on the charge of attempted murder.

* * *

Appellant's conviction on the charge of attempted first degree murder is reversed.

DONALDSON and SHEPARD, JJ., concur.

BAKES, CHIEF JUSTICE, dissenting:

* * *

* * * The defendant's intent to murder Captain Ailor was clear and, under the circumstances, the acts of the defendant were more than sufficient to support a conviction for attempted murder under our statute. The defendant had in fact done everything necessary on his part to kill Captain Ailor. All that he had to do was wait for the result. Such a state of events clearly establishes an attempt.

Under I.C. § 18–306, it does not matter that at common law the same conduct may only have been the crime of solicitation. What does matter is whether the conduct is or is not included within the ambit of I.C. § 18–306. * * * ["Every person who attempts to commit any crime, but fails, or is prevented or intercepted in the perpetration thereof, is punishable * * *."] * * *

The majority also attempts to distinguish between acts of preparation and acts of perpetration. Although this type of analysis has been accepted by some courts, the distinction is in fact highly artificial, since all acts leading up to the ultimate consummation of a crime are by their very nature preparatory. The real question is whether acts of preparation when coupled with intent have reached a point at which they pose a danger to the public so as to be worthy of law's notice. See Strahorn, Preparation For Crime as a Criminal Attempt, 1 Wash. & Lee L.R. 1, 4, 21 (1939). In the present case, the jury determined that the defendant's conduct had reached such a point, and I.C. § 18–306 certainly supports that conclusion.

Although it is not necessarily contended that every solicitation will constitute an attempt, the broad sweep of I.C. § 18–306 indicates that an attempt often may include solicitation within its bounds. This is certainly the case where, as here, the solicitor has done all that he needs to do in accomplishing the target crime. It may even be, under particular fact situations, that intent and danger to the public are so evident that mere solicitation itself might constitute a sufficient overt act to support an attempt conviction. * * *

* * *

Had the defendant been arrested and charged based only on an offer to employ a "hit man," the common law crime of solicitation might be applicable, as the majority urges. However, the acts here went far beyond an offer of "employment." As discussed previously, the type of weapon to be utilized and the manner in which the hit was to be made were discussed, an agreement was reached, payment was made, and the defendant completed all the necessary steps preliminary to the "hit" being made. In view of these facts, it appears that the majority would not find an attempt under our statute until the bullet was sailing through the air. That our legislature intended such a result is inconceivable. For the reasons stated above, I would affirm the conviction.

[The dissenting opinion of JUSTICE BISTLINE is omitted.]

Note

History of Solicitation. Huffman v. Commonwealth, 222 Va. 823, 826–828, 284 S.E.2d 837, 839–840 (1981):

> Code § 18.2–29 [1] is a product of the 1975 revision of the general laws of Virginia relating to crimes and offenses generally.
>
> This court recognized solicitation as a common law offense more than a century ago. In Womack v. Circle, 70 Va. (29 Gratt.) 192, 198 (1877), a civil case, we said: "To solicit another to commit a felony, although the felony be not afterwards committed, is a misdemeanor at common law, indictable and punishable." (Citations omitted.) This court addressed the subject again in Wiseman v. Commonwealth, 143 Va. 631, 637–38, 130 S.E. 249, 251 (1925), stating:
>
>> [S]ome discussion has arisen as to whether solicitation is an attempt, but it seems well established that to invite or solicit one to commit crime, where no attempt is actually made to commit it, at least in some cases, is indictable at common law as solicitation. Solicitation, or inciting to crime, does not proceed to the point of some overt act in the commission of crime. When it proceeds to this point it becomes an attempt to commit crime and is indictable as such.
>
> * * *
>
> * * * In Cherry [v. State, 18 Md.App. 252, 306 A.2d 634 (1973)], the Maryland court contributes this background discussion on solicitation:
>
>> The inchoate crimes generally are of recent vintage in the history of the common law. The latest and the least of these is solicitation. Its first formulation, as something distinct from a mere aspect in the law of attempts, was in Rex v. Higgins, in 1801, 2 East 5, 102 Eng.Rep. 269 * * *. Solicitation is now universally recognized in the United States as a part of

1. Code § 18.2–29. *Criminal solicitation; penalty.*—Any person who commands, entreats, or otherwise attempts to persuade another person to commit a felony, shall be guilty of a Class 6 felony. Acts 1975, pp. 21 and 105, effective October 1, 1975.

Anglo-American common law. In Clark and Marshall, Law of Crimes (7th ed. 1967), its characteristics are well set out, at 219–223:

> "Solicitation is a distinct common-law misdemeanor in which the act forbidden consists of the accused person's parol or written efforts to activate another to commit a criminal offense. It is immaterial whether the solicitation is of any effect and whether the crime solicited is in fact committed * * *.
>
> "The gist of this offense is incitement. In brief, the gravamen of this common-law misdemeanor lay in counselling, enticing, or inducing another to commit a crime * * *.
>
> "Inciting or soliciting another to commit a crime is the act of the least magnitude which is punishable by the common law. In such offenses the actor does nothing himself but he urges others to violate the law. The necessity for punishing such persons is obvious, and such conduct is generally punished as a substantive crime, notwithstanding the solicitation does not move the party solicited to commit the offense."

18 Md.App. at 257–58, 306 A.2d at 637–38. See also W. LaFave and A. Scott, Jr., *Criminal Law* § 58 (1972); Note, *Reforming the Law of Inchoate Crimes,* 59 Va.L.Rev. 1235, 1260 *et seq.* (1973); and Wechsler, Jones and Korn, *The Treatment of Inchoate Crimes in the Model Penal Code of the American Law Institute: Attempt, Solicitation, and Conspiracy,* 60 Colum. L.Rev. 957 (1961).

Questions

1. D is stopped by a police officer for speeding and offers him money from his wallet to forget the incident. Is this attempted bribery? Is it solicitation to bribe-receiving? (Both bribery and bribe-receiving are usually criminal.)

2. The crime of solicitation traditionally requires that the agent solicited not be innocent—that is, that the agent understand the nature of the act he is to perform (though he need not know the criminal law). So, if A asks B to pick up "A's" car and bring it to a certain spot, there is no solicitation if B believes the car is A's, though there is if B correctly believes the car is not A's. Is there any good reason for this distinction? Solicitation, particularly solicitation to commit a misdemeanor, is not always recognized as a crime.

Thomas v. State

Court of Criminal Appeals of Texas, En Banc, 1986.
708 S.W.2d 861.

W.C. DAVIS, JUDGE.

* * *

Edna Trosclair testified that at about 6:30 p.m., on July 5, 1982, she saw appellant and another man knocking on doors and looking in windows in her neighborhood. She saw them walk around the side of a neighbor's house into the back yard. The neighbor, Catherine Coates, was not at home. Trosclair called the police.

Officer Hayden Meredith arrived at the house and walked into Coates's back yard. He saw appellant and another man "walking towards the back fence of the residence looking over their shoulders, * * *" Meredith ordered them to stop and arrested them. Appellant had a pair of cloth gloves stuffed into the front of his pants; a buck knife in his front pocket, and a plastic bag containing change in his back pocket. Appellant's companion also had gloves stuffed into the front of his pants. Meredith noticed that the molding from one of the windows near the place appellant had walked from had been removed and was lying on the ground beneath the window. Meredith saw fresh scratches in the dust around the window and smudges on the glass.

In his confession appellant stated:

> After ringing the bell at 2714 Wallis St. and finding no one home, I decided to break in (sic) the house and get some money. I went to the side window and took off some weather stripping from around the window with my knife. Then I changed my mind and decided to leave. That's when the police came and arrested us.

V.T.C.A. Penal Code, § 15.04 provides in pertinent part for a renunciation defense:

> (a) It is an affirmative defense to prosecution under Section 15.01 of this code that under circumstances manifesting a voluntary and complete renunciation of his criminal objective the actor avoided commission of the offense attempted by abandoning his criminal conduct or, if abandonment was insufficient to avoid commission of the offense, by taking further affirmative action that prevented the commission.

In the instant case appellant was charged with and convicted of attempted burglary. See V.T.C.A. Penal Code, § 15.01. The evidence is sufficient to show attempted burglary. However, we agree with appellant that the Court of Appeals incorrectly interpreted § 15.04(a) by holding that "[A]ppellant's renunciation argument is irrelevant because the crime of attempted burglary of a habitation had already been committed when he allegedly renounced his intent." The Court of Appeals' interpretation renders § 15.04(a) meaningless because it equates "criminal objective" and "offense attempted" with the attempt itself, rather than with the completed "object" crime, i.e., burglary. Therefore, it would be impossible, under the Court of Appeals' interpretation, to renounce intent when an actor has completed an attempt by doing "an act amounting to more than mere preparation" but has not completed the object crime. The Court of Appeals' interpretation would permit a renunciation defense only *prior* to commission of an *attempt.* Conduct that has not yet reached the stage of an attempt is not even criminal and § 15.04(a) would thus be useless.

The Court of Appeals' interpretation would defeat the twofold purpose for permitting the defense of renunciation. First, the defense tends to negative dangerousness; second, it provides actors with motive for desisting in criminal objective, thus, diminishing the risk that the substantive crime will be committed. See Model Penal Code, § 5.01.

> And, because of the importance of encouraging desistance in the final stages of the attempt, the defense is allowed even when the last proximate act has occurred but the criminal result can be avoided, as for example when the fuse has been lit but can still be stamped out. If,

> however, the actor has put in motion forces that he is powerless to stop, then the attempt has been completed and cannot be abandoned.

Model Penal Code, § 5.01, at p. 360 (1985).

* * *

Appellant contends that the evidence reflects that he voluntarily and completely renounced his criminal objective (burglary of a habitation) and proved the affirmative defense of renunciation under § 15.04(a). The State disagrees, arguing that the evidence does not show, by a preponderance, that the renunciation was voluntary under § 15.04(c)(1).

* * * In the instant case the evidence pertaining to voluntary and complete renunciation consists of appellant's statement in his confession that he changed his mind and decided to leave. Appellant's conduct of walking toward the back fence can support such change of mind as well as contradict it. The State argues that the evidence that Officer Meredith "* * * first observed them, * * * walking toward the back fence of the residence looking over their shoulders * * *" rebuts appellant's statement. The State points out that evidence showed that appellant entered the back yard by going through an open gate on the side of the yard. Yet, when Officer Meredith entered the back yard, appellant was walking toward the fence in the back, which was a redwood privacy fence which did not have a gate or opening through which a person could exit. Appellant was looking over his shoulder, indicating or permitting the inference that he heard someone coming and decided to leave a different way than he had entered and a different way from the way the police officer that he heard was coming. Because the evidence can be interpreted to show that appellant's abandonment of the attempt to commit burglary was due to the arrival of the police, it is not voluntary under § 15.04(c) which states:

> (c) Renunciation is not voluntary if it is motivated in whole or in part:
>
> (1) by circumstances not present or apparent at the inception of the actor's course of conduct that increase the probability of detection or apprehension or that make more difficult the accomplishment of the objective; * * *.

Viewing the evidence that pertains to the affirmative defense in a light most favorable to the verdict, we hold that the abandonment was not voluntary under § 15.04(c)(1) but was due to "circumstances not present or apparent at the inception of the actor's course of conduct that increase[d] the probability of detection or apprehension," namely, the arrival of the police. A rational trier of fact could have disbelieved appellant's statement of a change of heart in light of his conduct of walking toward the solid back fence, a different way than he had entered, and looking over his shoulder as if he heard someone approaching. A rational trier of fact could have found that this evidence did not prove voluntary and complete renunciation by a preponderance.

Because we find the evidence sufficient to support the conviction for attempted burglary, we likewise find it sufficient under the lesser standard necessary for revocation of probation, to support the revocation of appellant's probation in Cause No. F–81–11091–MP. The judgment of the Court of Appeals is affirmed.

ONION, P.J., and CLINTON and MCCORMICK, JJ., concur in result.

[The dissenting opinion of JUDGE TEAGUE joined by JUDGE CAMPBELL, is omitted.]

Notes

1. *Attempted burglary.* DeGidio v. State, 289 N.W.2d 135, 136–137 (Minn. 1980):

* * *

Petitioner's * * * contention is that since burglary is defined in terms of doing an act with intent to commit some other crime, it is a form of attempt, and that it is illogical therefore to permit the conviction of a person for attempted burglary since to do so would be to convict someone of attempted attempt.

This argument is discussed in Model Penal Code § 5.01, Comments (Tent. Draft No. 10, 1960):

> One of the questions frequently litigated is whether there can be an attempt to attempt. As an abstract proposition of law the construction has been condemned by the majority of cases considering the issue, and it seems as a matter of sound analysis that the construction is not necessary. An attempt to attempt can always be considered as a more remote attempt to commit the same substantive crime, so long, of course, as it goes far enough to meet the basic test of liability. Thus, if an assault is an attempt to commit a battery, an attempt to assault can more properly be charged as itself an attempt to commit a battery and its sufficiency determined on that basis. In any case, convictions have been sustained for attempts to assault.
>
> A more complicated problem arises where the attempt is not described as such, but is defined as an act done with intent to commit some other crime. Among the traditional offenses burglary is such an attempt, a breaking and entering under certain circumstances with intent to commit a felony. But there has been no difficulty in sustaining charges of attempted burglary. Nor has there been difficulty generally in finding attempt liability where the "substantive offense" is even more clearly an attempt: possessing burglar's tools with intent to commit burglary; conveying tools into prison with intent to facilitate an escape; offering a bribe; exploding a substance with intent to cause personal injury; employing a drug or instrument with intent to procure a miscarriage; procuring a noxious drug with intent to supply it to another for use in committing abortion. In each case attempt liability has been sustained. It would be possible to treat each of these acts as an attempt to commit the more remote substantive crime but this is unduly cumbersome; the existing approach seems preferable. If a preliminary act is prominent enough to serve as the basis of substantive liability, it should also provide a sufficient foundation for attempt liability. (*Footnotes omitted.*) Id. at 74–75.

Moreover, as the postconviction court pointed out, while burglary is in a sense an inchoate crime, the legislature clearly has determined that the conduct covered by the burglary statute merits separate treatment as a substantive offense. Because the legislature in enacting the attempt statute gave no indication that some substantive crimes could not serve as a foundation for attempt convictions and because burglary is a separate substantive offense, it seems clear to us that the legislature intended to permit prosecutions and convictions for attempted burglary or attempted burglary with tools.

2. *Attempted assault.* Courts disagree as to whether an attempted assault is possible. If assault is an attempt, and if attempts are supposed to identify the earliest punishable stages of a crime, how can an attempted attempt be allowed? One problem with this argument is that assault law became fixed along fairly conservative lines while attempt law has sometimes expanded to reach earlier conduct. A consequence of this is seen in the following case.

State v. Hetzel

Supreme Court of Ohio, 1953.
159 Ohio St. 350, 112 N.E.2d 369.

Defendant was indicted for assault with intent to rape, and, after pleading "not guilty," was found guilty of that crime and sentenced to the penitentiary.

* * *

TAFT, JUDGE.

In his charge to the jury the trial judge stated in part:

> "In order *to constitute the crime of attempt to have carnal knowledge,* as hereinbefore explained to you, there must be proved not only the existence of a criminal intent, or, in other words, a criminal purpose, but *there must have been coupled with* such *criminal intention to have sexual intercourse an overt, substantive act apparently adapted to perfect that intent,* that is, *some concomitant act or movement toward the execution of that purpose or intention, some physical action or movement adapted to and approximating a gratification of sexual passion* of the defendant to have carnal knowledge of the said Vera Kohut, as herein defined, forcibly and against her will. * * *
>
> "The terms 'rape' and *'attempted rape'* have been used * * *
>
> "Now, members of the jury, in connection with an *attempt to rape under the statute* as given to you in relation thereto, said term may be *defined to be a physical effort toward the accomplishment of the object of sexual intercourse.* * * *

* * *

Section 12421, General Code, under which defendant was indicted, reads:

> "Whoever assaults another with intent to kill, or to commit robbery or rape upon the person so assaulted, shall be imprisoned in the penitentiary not less than one year nor more than fifteen years."

From the words of the charge, as hereinbefore quoted, it is apparent that the jury was told that defendant could be convicted for acts which might not have amounted to an assault.

In the court's opinion in Fox v. State, 34 Ohio St. 377, 379, it is said:

> "Under our statute, an attempt to commit rape is not an offense, unless the intent to commit it is accompanied with some act or movement toward its accomplishment which constitutes an 'assault.' The question, therefore, is: Are the words 'attempt to

commit rape,' in their ordinary meaning, the exact equivalent of the words 'assault with intent to commit rape?' We think not, but that the former phrase may describe a state of facts which does not constitute an assault with intent to ravish.

* * *

"The distinction may be thus defined: An assault is an act done toward the commission of a battery; it must precede the battery, but it does so immediately. The next movement would, at least at all appearance, complete the battery. While an act constituting an attempt to commit a felony may be more remote * * * 'the overt act done in the attempt to commit an offense need not be the last proximate act prior to the consummation of the felony intended to be perpetrated.' " See, also, State v. Farmer, 156 Ohio St. 214, 216, 102 N.E.2d 11.

It is apparent, therefore, that a charge is erroneous if it is such as to permit the jury to believe that it may find a defendant guilty of an assault with intent to rape if it merely finds the defendant guilty of an attempt to rape. The charge of the court as quoted above did just that. There may be an attempt to commit rape without an assault with intent to commit rape.

* * *

The judgment of the Court of Appeals is reversed and the cause is remanded to the Common Pleas Court for further proceedings.

Judgment reversed.

b. IMPOSSIBILITY

State v. Roundsquare

Supreme Court of Ohypo, 1981.
290 Ohypo 772.

BLYNKEN, J.: Defendant Roundsquare, at the time of the alleged crime, was a thirteen year old male. He was dating a school classmate whom he believed reasonably to be thirteen years of age. She had told him so, and her appearance was consistent with her statement. In fact, she was fifteen; she had been held back in school for two years because of a serious illness in her childhood, and she preferred her classmates to think that she was their own age. An adolescent romance developed. Apparently both had had some prior sexual experience, and they decided to have sexual intercourse. However, at the crucial moment, Roundsquare discovered himself to be temporarily sexually impotent. Her parents found them in bed together and turned him over to the juvenile authorities. The juvenile court waived jurisdiction, and a criminal information was filed against Roundsquare, charging him with attempted statutory rape. We have common law rules as to attempt law. Our statutory rape statute provides:

> Whoever shall have sexual intercourse with a female under the age of fifteen years shall be guilty of statutory rape. * * * (27 Ohypo Rev.Code § 600)

The trial judge overruled various motions for a directed verdict of acquittal and the jury convicted of attempted statutory rape. Roundsquare raises the following points on appeal:

1. Infancy. He claims to be entitled to a presumption of incapacity to entertain criminal intention because of his age.

2. Impotence. He claims that his physical condition was such that he could not in fact have had sexual intercourse, and therefore that he cannot be guilty of attempting such an act.

3. The victim's age. Since the victim was not under the age of fifteen, as required by the statute, nobody could have been guilty of statutory rape of her, and therefore nobody should be guilty of an attempt.

4. The defendant's own age. There was at common law a conclusive presumption that a male under the age of fourteen was physically incapable of sexual intercourse. Since the defendant was only thirteen, he could not be guilty of any offense requiring intercourse and should not be guilty of an attempt to commit any such offense.

As to the first point, the presumption of incapacity to entertain criminal intention, the trial judge correctly instructed the jury that, in a child over the age of six, the presumption is rebuttable. There was ample evidence to permit the jury to find that in Roundsquare's case, the presumption was in fact rebutted.

The remaining points for appeal raise the troublesome defense of impossibility. Points two and three raise respectively questions of intrinsic and extrinsic factual impossibility.

Intrinsic factual impossibility exists when the means adopted by the accused are inherently incapable of accomplishing the criminal end. If a gun is loaded with shot which is incapable of carrying the distance necessary to hit the intended victim, or, as in the famous case of Commonwealth v. Kennedy, 170 Mass. 18, 48 N.E. 770 (1897), a poison, "Rough-on-Rats," not proved to be potentially fatal to human beings, is placed, with murderous intent, on the underside of the crossbar of the victim's mustache cup, a claim of impossibility may be raised. Unfortunately for the defendant, intrinsic factual impossibility is not a defense to a charge of attempt. If the accused intends to commit the crime, and only through some error as to the means adopted fails to commit it, he has demonstrated the criminal character and dangerousness for criminality, and there is no reason to excuse him.

There may perhaps be rare *de minimis* situations where a defense would be recognized. Suppose that the accused believes that sugar is a deadly poison and sprinkles a spoonful on the victim's food, intending to kill him. The law might see so little danger here that the defense would be recognized. But defendant's acts were hardly of so trivial a nature, and his impotence, not known to him, is no defense. (Of course, if he had been aware of it, he could not have intended to commit the crime.)

The victim's age would prevent her from being a victim of statutory rape. Where the accused fails because of a mistaken belief that the object is one upon which it would be possible to commit the crime, we have a case of extrinsic factual impossibility. Where an intended rape victim is a man masquerading as a woman, where an accused attempts to purchase talcum powder believing it to be narcotics, where a pickpocket has the bad luck to try his art on a pocket which turns out to be empty, we find other examples in this class. This kind of factual impossibility is not usually recognized as a defense. Again, the elements of criminal character and dangerousness are present. Next time, it is likely that a suitable object will be found and the crime will be committed. As in the case of intrinsic impossibility, there may be a few cases so trivial as not to merit conviction.

Factual impossibility, then, except perhaps in very rare instances, is no defense to a charge of criminal attempt. Legal impossibility, however, is a defense. Where an accused might carry out his plan, succeeding entirely in his own view in what he wished to do, and still would commit no crime, he is not guilty of an attempt. Had Roundsquare had the physical ability, and had the victim been under the age of fifteen, and had sexual intercourse taken place, there would have been no statutory rape; the common law conclusive presumption of physical incapacity remains in force in this state. It is not appropriate, as the trial judge thought it was, for judges to abolish it. This is a legislative matter. The policy, perhaps resting in part on the view that the very young ought not be convicted of rape—until they have time to learn to control sexual passion—may well be unsound, but the legislature must settle the debate.

There is no reason to punish one who attempts to do what the law says is no crime. Even if the accused thinks he is committing a crime, he shows no more than a generalized willingness to violate the criminal law, not an intention to act in a way in which in fact he might commit a crime. Because Roundsquare was under the age of fourteen years, he was legally incapable of committing or attempting statutory rape, and his conviction must be reversed.

WYNKEN, C.J.: I concur in the result reached by Justice Blynken. I agree that factual impossibility is no defense to an attempt charge, that legal impossibility is a defense, and that because of the conclusive presumption of physical incapacity in one of Roundsquare's age, his conviction must be reversed.

But I do not agree fully with her analysis. I think that the victim's age presents another instance of legal impossibility, and not, as Justice Blynken believes, extrinsic factual impossibility, and that this independently requires reversal of the judgment of conviction. It is often not easy to distinguish the case of legal impossibility from the seemingly similar case of extrinsic factual impossibility. The well-known case of People v. Jaffe, 185 N.Y. 497, 78 N.E. 169 (1906), is instructive. Jaffe was charged with the offense of attempting to receive stolen goods. The police had recovered stolen goods from a thief, and, suspecting that Jaffe would be willing to receive stolen goods, they offered him the property as stolen property, and he sought to buy it. In reversing his conviction, the court pointed out that the crime of receiving required knowledge that the goods were stolen, and that the particular act which Jaffe set out to perform was not the knowing receipt of stolen goods, because the goods were no longer technically stolen goods once they were recovered by the police for the owner. Had Jaffe purchased them, no matter what his belief, he could not have received stolen goods knowingly; he could not know what was not true. The act which Jaffe set out to do was not made a crime by the law, and, as Justice Blynken says, an attempt to do such an act is not a crime, either, because of legal impossibility.

Where the act that one sets out to do is no crime, it is legally impossible to be guilty of an attempt to commit the crime. In the case before us, the victim's age would prevent any intercourse with her from being the crime of statutory rape; there can be no attempt to commit statutory rape with her as a victim, either. Such a case must be distinguished from true cases of factual impossibility, such as the pickpocket cases. The pickpocket, when he reaches into the empty pocket, sets out to commit larceny. If there were money there, he could commit the crime. There is no reason why he cannot be guilty of attempting larceny.

I might add a note on my sister Blynken's attempt to deal with the rare cases of extreme factual impossibility, where she suggests that she might allow a defense. I would not do so. I think that those who commit such acts are always dangerous. The "sugar poisoner" may turn to arsenic when he sees that sugar does not work. And, suppose his mistake is not that sugar is a poison, but rather that the sugar bowl contains arsenic. Surely he should be guilty when he adds a spoon full of sugar to the food of his enemy.

NOD, J.: I dissent. I believe that the conviction should be affirmed. The members of this court are in agreement that factual impossibility, at least in all but the most extraordinary circumstances (not here present), is not a defense. (As to the extraordinary cases, I prefer the approach of Model Penal Code § 5.05.) My colleagues, however, accept a defense of legal impossibility. I would follow the Model Penal Code in rejecting the defense of legal impossibility also. See § 5.01, Comment 4 (Tent.Draft No. 10, 1960).

First, I would like to express agreement with Justice Blynken in her conclusion that the victim's age presents a factual, not a legal, impossibility issue. Assuming for the moment that there is no other possible bar to the conviction than the victim's age, Roundsquare would have committed statutory rape had the facts been as he supposed and had he carried out his purpose. This is factual impossibility; his conduct shows a dangerous inclination to do what the criminal law prohibits, and his mistake certainly ought not to acquit him, any more than Jaffe ought to have been acquitted of attempting to receive stolen goods.

The Chief Justice's statement, "When the act that one sets out to do is no crime, it is legally impossible to be guilty of an attempt to commit the crime," reflects the views of some older cases like *Jaffe.* But the test is generally rejected by modern cases because it does not reflect sound policy, or because it is so ambiguous as to be impossible of application. What is meant by "the act one sets out to do"? Jaffe meant (a) to buy the particular goods offered, and (b) to buy (as he thought) stolen goods. Roundsquare meant (a) to have intercourse with the particular female victim, and (b) to have intercourse (as he thought) with a female under the statutory age. The pickpocket meant (a) to steal goods from the particular pocket, and (b) to steal from (as he thought) a full pocket. They are all in precisely the same position. They all set out to commit a crime; they all failed only because they mistook the situation before them. They all exhibited determined dangerousness. They all should be convicted.

There is a narrow class of cases in which conviction is improper. Where the result sought, in the factual circumstances as the accused believes them to be, is not criminal, he violates no policy and should not be convicted of an attempt. Suppose the accused sets out to violate a prohibition law. He believes he is purchasing gin from a bootlegger. All that is missing from the prosecution's case is a prohibition law; it has just been repealed by the legislature, unknown to the accused. The accused is trying to commit what is not a crime at all. He should not be convicted, as the Model Penal Code recognizes. While one might label this a case of legal impossibility, it is much better to avoid this confusing term and simply to note that there is no attempt to do anything prohibited by the criminal law.

As the facts have been presented, Roundsquare's being under the age of fourteen and therefore conclusively presumed to be sexually impotent—a presumption which I hope the legislature will see fit to abolish—qualifies as a defense. Simply put, it is not a criminal offense for a male under the age of fourteen to have sexual intercourse under any circumstances. Roundsquare therefore appears to have attempted nothing prohibited by the criminal law.

However, there is an additional fact, previously unmentioned, which casts a different light on the case. Roundsquare is an orphan who has lived in a succession of foster homes. He did not know his exact age and obtained a copy of his birth certificate from the State Department of Vital Statistics. This copy reproduced a typographical error in the original physician's return, which showed his birth as having occurred exactly one year earlier than the true date, easily established by other Department records. Unquestionably, Roundsquare reasonably relied on the copy and believed himself to be fourteen, not thirteen, at the time of the act. If, therefore, the facts and circumstances had been as he believed, he would have committed a crime. He would have been a fourteen year old having intercourse with a thirteen year old, and this is statutory rape. The words of the American Law Institute: "If, according to his beliefs as to facts and legal relationships, the result desired or intended is not a crime, the actor will not be guilty of an attempt even though he firmly believes that his goal is criminal," expressing the only "impossibility" situation in which the Institute would acquit, do not apply. Model Penal Code § 5.01, Comment 4 (Tent.Draft No. 10, 1960).

The conviction should therefore be affirmed.

Notes

1. *The View of the House of Lords.* In Haughton v. Smith, [1975] A.C. 476 (1973), the House of Lords overturned the conviction of Smith of attempting to receive stolen goods, when it turned out that the goods had lost their character as stolen goods at the time of the attempt. An elaborate analysis of impossibility situations was attempted, in the course of which answers were suggested to a number of hypothetical problems; one such answer was that an accused could not be guilty of an attempt to

steal from an empty pocket. After much critical discussion of *Smith,* Parliament passed the Criminal Attempts Act of 1981, which provided:

> 1.—(1) If, with intent to commit an offence to which this section applies, a person does an act which is more than merely preparatory to the commission of the offence, he is guilty of attempting to commit the offence.
>
> (2) A person may be guilty of attempting to commit an offence to which this section applies even though the facts are such that the commission of the offence is impossible.
>
> (3) In any case where—(*a*) apart from this subsection a person's intention would not be regarded as having amounted to an intent to commit an offence; but (*b*) if the facts of the case had been as he believed them to be, his intention would be so regarded, then, for the purposes of subsection (1) above, he shall be regarded as having had an intent to commit that offence.
>
> (4) This section applies to any offence which, if it were completed, would be triable in England and Wales as an indictable offence, other than [the ensuing exceptions are irrelevant for present purposes] * * *.
>
> * * *
>
> 6.—(1) The offence of attempt at common law and any offence at common law of procuring materials for crime are hereby abolished for all purposes not relating to acts done before the commencement of this Act * * *.

In Anderton v. Ryan, [1985] A.C. 560, [1985] 2 All E.R. 355, the House of Lords, by a vote of four to one, approved dismissal of charges of receiving when the prosecution proved that the accused believed that she was receiving stolen goods, but could not prove that the goods were in fact stolen. LORD BRIDGE OF HARWICH reasoned as follows ([1985] A.C. 582–583, [1985] 2 All E.R. 365–367):

> The question may be stated in abstract terms as follows. Does s 1 of the 1981 Act create a new offence of attempt where a person embarks on and completes a course of conduct, which is objectively innocent, solely on the ground that the person mistakenly believes facts which, if true, would make that course of conduct a complete crime? If the question must be answered affirmatively it requires convictions in a number of surprising cases: the classic case, put by Bramwell B in R v Collins (1864) 9 Cox CC 497 at 498, of the man who takes away his own umbrella from a stand, believing it not to be his own with intent to steal it; the case of the man who has consensual intercourse with a girl over 16 believing her to be under that age; the case of the art dealer who sells a picture which he represents to be and which is in fact a genuine Picasso, but which the dealer mistakenly believes to be a fake.
>
> The common feature of all these cases, including that under appeal, is that the mind alone is guilty, the act is innocent. I should find it surprising that Parliament, if intending to make this purely subjective guilt criminally punishable, should have done so by anything less than the clearest express language, and, in particular, should have done so in a section aimed specifically at inchoate offences.
>
> I agree with my noble and learned friend Lord Roskill that sub-ss (1) and (4) of s 1 of the 1981 Act provide a statutory substitute for the common law offence of attempt abolished by s 6. It seems to me possible to find ample substance and content in sub-ss (2) and (3), reversing aspects of the law of attempt which emerge from *Smith's* case, without straining them to make the present appellant guilty of any offence. It is sufficient to say of sub-s (2) that it is plainly intended to reverse the law * * * that the pickpocket who puts his hand in an empty

pocket commits no offence. Putting the hand in the pocket is the guilty act, the intent to steal is the guilty mind, the offence is appropriately dealt with as an attempt, and the impossibility of committing the full offence for want of anything in the pocket to steal is declared by the subsection to be no obstacle to conviction. The precise scope of sub-s (3) is more difficult to delineate and I will not be so rash as to attempt to identify to which of the numerous hypothetical cases discussed in *Smith's* case it would apply; but I have no difficulty in giving an example of my own to which it certainly would. A wages clerk collects £10,000 in cash from the bank every Friday in a suitcase. An informer tells the police that a thief plans on a particular Friday to snatch the case and steal the money. The police set a trap, but, in case the thief should escape, arrange that the bank will fill the suitcase with torn strips of newspaper. The thief snatches the suitcase intending to throw it away and take the money which he believes it contains. At common law his only offence is stealing the torn pieces of newspaper. The effect of s 1(1) and (3) of the 1981 Act is that he is guilty of attempting to steal £10,000. Here again there is a guilty act 'more than merely preparatory to the commission of the offence' under sub-s (1). Apart from sub-s (3) his intention would not be regarded as an intention to steal £10,000. By sub-s (3) his erroneous belief requires that his intention should be so regarded. It follows that the section enables him to be convicted of attempting to steal £10,000.

The distinction attempted by Lord Bridge, based on whether or not the accused's conduct is "objectively innocent," was soon abandoned by the House of Lords in Regina v. Shivpuri, [1987] A.C. 1 (1986). The English position now seems to be in agreement with the prevailing American view that, except perhaps in extraordinary cases, extrinsic factual impossibility is no defense to a charge of attempt.

2. *The Model Penal Code and the Impossibility Defense.* Model Penal Code, § 5.01, Comment 3: *

3. *Impossibility.* Subsection (1) is also designed to reject the defense of impossibility, which has sometimes been successful in attempt prosecutions. It does so, as is explained below, by providing that the defendant's conduct should be measured according to the circumstances as he believes them to be, rather than the circumstances as they may have existed in fact. Before the formulation is elaborated, however, it may be helpful to review what courts have done and said about the problem.

(a) *Background.* There are decisions on the books holding that a person accepting goods that he believed to have been stolen, but that were not then "stolen" goods, was not guilty of an attempt to receive stolen goods; [28] that an actor who offered a bribe to a person whom he believed to be a juror, but who was not a juror, could not be said to have attempted to bribe a juror; [29] that an official who contracted a debt that was unauthorized and a nullity, but that he believed to be valid, could not be convicted for an

28. People v. Jaffe, 185 N.Y. 497, 78 N.E. 169 (1906). * * * For decisions rejecting the *Jaffe* approach, *see* People v. Rojas, 55 Cal.2d 252, 358 P.2d 921, 10 Cal.Rptr. 465 (1961) (citing the MPC) * * *.

29. State v. Taylor, 345 Mo. 325, 133 S.W.2d 366 (1939); State v. Porter, 125 Mont. 503, 242 P.2d 984 (1952). Similarly, it has been held that attempted bribery may not be based on the offer of a bribe to an official who cannot render the requested service. State v. Butler, 178 Mo. 272, 77 S.W. 560 (1903). * * *

attempt illegally to contract a valid debt;[30] and that a hunter who shot a stuffed deer believing it to be alive had not attempted to take a deer out of season.[31]

The primary rationale of these decisions is that, judging the actor's conduct in the light of the actual facts, what he intended to do did not amount to a crime.[32] This approach, however, is unsound in that it seeks to evaluate a mental attitude—"intent" or "purpose"—not by looking to the actor's mental frame of reference, but to a situation wholly at variance with the actor's beliefs. In so doing, the courts exonerate defendants in situations where attempt liability most certainly should be imposed. In all of these cases the actor's criminal purpose has been clearly demonstrated; he went as far as he could in implementing that purpose; and, as a result, his "dangerousness' is plainly manifested.

Apart from these decisions, however, the claim of impossibility has proven to be a poor shield against a charge of criminal attempt. One of the most common examples of claimed impossibility has arisen in charges of attempt to steal where there is nothing to be stolen. After a few early English decisions to the contrary,[33] it has uniformly been held that one is liable if he attempts to steal from an empty pocket,[34] an empty receptacle,[35] or an empty house.[36] The rule has been the same whether the attempt is to commit burglary,[37] robbery,[38] extortion,[39] obtaining by false pretenses[40] or ordinary larceny. * * *

Similarly, it has been held that one can attempt to receive stolen property[47] or attempt to transport illegal whiskey[48] or attempt to possess narcotics[49] even though the commodity is not present when the offender seeks to take it into custody. There can be an attempt to corrupt a juror although the juror is not at home when the actor calls to make his proposition,[50] and there can be an attempt to murder though the intended

30. Marley v. State, 58 N.J.L. 207, 33 A. 208 (Sup.Ct.1895). * * *

31. State v. Guffey, 262 S.W.2d 152 (Mo. Ct.App.1953).

32. See, e.g., United States v. Berrigan, 482 F.2d 171 (3d Cir.1973), in which the defendants were charged with attempting to violate 18 U.S.C. § 1791, prohibiting the smuggling of objects into or out of a federal correctional institution. Since the evidence established that the warden had knowledge of the smuggling plan, and since his lack of knowledge was a necessary element of the offense, the defendants could not be found guilty of violating the statute. The court held that such knowledge by the warden would also preclude conviction for the attempt, since "attempting to do that which is not a crime is not attempting to commit a crime." 482 F.2d at 190.

33. Regina v. Collins, 169 Eng.Rep. 1477 (C.C.R.1864); Regina v. M'Pherson, 169 Eng. Rep. 975 (C.C.R.1857); see also Regina v. Taylor, 25 L.T.R. (n.s.) 75 (Middx.Sess.1871).

34. People v. Twiggs, 223 Cal.App.2d 455, 35 Cal.Rptr. 859 (1963) * * *.

35. State v. Meisch, 86 N.J.Super. 279, 206 A.2d 763 (App.Div.1965); Clark v. State, 86 Tenn. 511, 8 S.W. 145 (1888).

36. State v. Utley, 82 N.C. 556 (1880).

37. People v. Dogoda, 9 Ill.2d 198, 137 N.E.2d 386 (1956) * * *.

38. State v. Scarlett, 291 S.W.2d 138 (Mo. 1956) * * *.

39. People v. Fratianno, 132 Cal.App.2d 610, 627, 282 P.2d 1002, 1011 (1955) (no defense that person threatened might not be able to convey the property desired by defendant).

40. People v. Arberry, 13 Cal.App. 749, 114 P. 411 (1910).

47. In re Magidson, 32 Cal.App. 566, 163 P. 689 (1917). Compare note 28 supra.

48. Collins v. City of Radford, 134 Va. 518, 113 S.E. 735 (1922).

49. People v. Siu, 126 Cal.App.2d 41, 271 P.2d 575 (1954) (defendant obtained possession of talcum believing it to be narcotics) * * *.

50. Summers v. State ex rel. Boykin, 66 Ga.App. 648, 19 S.E.2d 28 (1942).

victim is not where the assailant believes him to be.[51] Attempt liability sometimes has been rejected in instances where, instead of assailing a person not present, the actor searched or waited for a person who was never contacted,[52] such decisions resting in part on the fact that the actor had not yet proceeded far enough toward his criminal goal.

While a missing victim is no defense in the case of an actual assault, it has been said that there is no attempt to murder if the actor shoots at a corpse[53] or a tree stump[54] believing it to be a living person. It has been argued to the contrary that it is no less an attempt to try to take life from a lifeless object than to seek money in an empty pocket.[55] It has been held that sexual intercourse with one who is believed to be an unconscious and unwilling female, but one who is in fact a lifeless female is attempted rape.[56] * * *

Another broad category of impossibility cases embraces instances in which the instrumentality chosen by the actor is incapable of producing the criminal result desired. Some early decisions exculpated the actor of attempted murder if the instrumentality selected was not adequate for committing the crime contemplated, but the general rule today is that one can be guilty of an attempt to murder although the gun[59] or poison[60] or bomb[61] is incapable of producing death. * * * And despite statements by commentators to the contrary, recent cases have held that impotency is no defense to a charge of attempted rape.[65] Earlier decisions had reached the same result where the charge was assault with intent to rape.[66] * * *

An analogous line of cases concerns verbal actions that do not produce the result desired. While lack of response is generally held to prevent consummation of the crime in these cases, it does not afford immunity from an attempt charge. Thus an attempt to extort is possible although the victim

51. People v. Lee Kong, 95 Cal. 666, 30 P. 800 (1892); State v. Mitchell, 170 Mo. 633, 71 S.W. 175 (1902); cf. The King v. White, [1910] 2 K.B. 124 (Crim.App.) (intended victim died before taking poison) * * *.

52. People v. Rizzo, 246 N.Y. 334, 158 N.E. 888 (1927) * * *. *Contra,* Stokes v. State, 94 Miss. 415, 46 So. 627 (1908); *see* People v. Gormley, 222 App.Div. 256, 225 N.Y.S. 653 (1927), aff'd mem., 248 N.Y. 583, 162 N.E. 533 (1928) (distinguishing People v. Rizzo, supra).

53. See State v. Taylor, 345 Mo. 325, 333, 133 S.W.2d 336, 341 (1939) (dictum); State v. Guffey, 262 S.W.2d 152, 156 (Mo.Ct.App. 1953) (dictum).

54. Rex v. Osborn, 84 J.P. 63 (Central Crim.Ct.1919) * * *.

55. See 1 W. Russell, Crime 187 (12th ed. J. Turner 1964).

56. United States v. Thomas, 13 C.M.A. 278, 32 C.M.R. 278 (1962) (citing MPC Section 5.01 in support).

59. State v. Damms, 9 Wis.2d 183, 100 N.W.2d 592 (1960); Rex v. Jones, 18 T.L.R. 156 (Assizes 1901) * * *. But see In re Magidson, 32 Cal.App. 566, 570, 163 P. 689, 691 (1917) (dictum) * * *.

60. Commonwealth v. Kennedy, 170 Mass. 18, 48 N.E. 770 (1897) * * *.

61. See People v. Grant, 105 Cal.App.2d 347, 233 P.2d 660 (1951) (premature explosion of bomb no bar to liability for attempted murder).

65. People v. Peckham, 249 Cal.App.2d 941, 57 Cal.Rptr. 922 (1967) * * *.

66. Hunt v. State, 114 Ark. 239, 169 S.W. 773 (1914); * * *.

The foregoing decisions are to be contrasted with rulings that a boy under 14 is incapable of attempting rape because he is conclusively presumed to be incapable of committing the completed offense. Foster v. Commonwealth, 96 Va. 306, 31 S.E. 503 (1898); see The Queen v. Williams, [1893] 1 Q.B. 320, 321 (C.C.R.); State v. Handy, 4 Del. (4 Harr.) 566, 567 (1845) (assault with intent to rape). Although sometimes couched in terms of impotency, such decisions are explicable on the ground that the policy precluding conviction for the completed offense applied no less to conviction of an attempt. But cf. Commonwealth v. Green, 19 Mass. 380 (1823) (sustaining conviction of boy under 14 for assault with intent to rape).

is not put in fear; [68] an attempt to bribe may be charged although the actor's offer meets with an unsympathetic attitude; [69] an attempt to obtain by false pretenses may be found even though the contemplated victim is not deceived.[70] * * *

* * *

(b) *Policy Considerations.* Insofar as it has not rested on conceptual tangles that have been largely independent of policy considerations, the defense of impossibility seems to have been employed to serve a number of functions. First, it has been used to verify criminal purpose; if the means selected were absurd, there is good ground for doubting that the actor really planned to commit a crime. Similarly, if the defendant's conduct, objectively viewed, is ambiguous, there may be ground for doubting the firmness of his purpose to commit a criminal offense. A general defense of impossibility is, however, an inappropriate way of assuring that the actor has a true criminal purpose.

A second function that the defense of impossibility seems to have served in some cases is to supplement the defense of entrapment. In situations in which the technical entrapment rules do not exonerate the defendant, there is a temptation to find that the presence of traps and decoys makes the actor's endeavor impossible. The Model Code has a separate formulation on entrapment which is believed to state the appropriate considerations for a defense on this ground.

A third consideration that has been advanced in support of an impossibility defense is the view that the criminal law need not take notice of conduct that is innocuous, the element of impossibility preventing any dangerous proximity to the completed crime. The law of attempts, however, should be concerned with manifestations of dangerous character as well as with preventive arrests; the fact that particular conduct may not create an actual risk of harmful consequences, though it would if the circumstances were as the defendant believed them to be, should not therefore be conclusive. The innocuous character of the particular conduct becomes relevant only if the futile endeavor itself indicates a harmless personality, so that immunizing the conduct from liability would not result in exposing society to a dangerous person.

Using impossibility as a guide to dangerousness of personality presents serious difficulties.[88] What is needed is a guideline that can inform judgment in particular cases, so that those that involve a danger to society can be successfully prosecuted while those that do not can be dismissed. Such a vehicle is provided in Section 5.05(2), which authorizes the court to reduce

68. People v. Camodeca, 52 Cal.2d 142, 338 P.2d 903 (1959); People v. Robinson, 130 Cal.App. 664, 20 P.2d 369 (1933); People v. Lavine, 115 Cal.App. 289, 1 P.2d 496 (1931), appeal dismissed, 286 U.S. 528 (1932); People v. Gardner, 144 N.Y. 119, 38 N.E. 1003 (1894). But cf. Queen Empress v. Mangesh Jivaji, 11 Indian L.R. Bombay 376 (App.Crim.1887).

69. People v. Bennett, 182 App.Div. 871, 170 N.Y. 718, aff'd mem., 224 N.Y. 594, 120 N.E. 871 (1918).

70. People v. Hickman, 31 Cal.App.2d 4, 87 P.2d 80 (1939) * * *.

88. Cases can be imagined in which it might well be accurate to say that the nature of the means selected, say black magic, substantially negates dangerousness of character. On the other hand, there are many cases as well where one who tries to commit a crime by what he later learns to be inadequate methods will recognize the futility of his course of action and seek more efficacious means. There are, in other words, many instances of dangerous character revealed by "impossible" attempts, and to develop a theory around highly exceptional situations ignores the propriety of convictions in these.

* * *

the grade of the offense, or dismiss the prosecution, in situations where the conduct charged to constitute an attempt is "so inherently unlikely to result or culminate in the commission of a crime that neither such conduct nor the actor presents a public danger warranting" the normal grading of the offense as an attempt. Section 5.05(2) thus takes account of those cases where neither the offender nor his conduct presents a serious threat to the public. There is also, of course, prosecutorial discretion, which seems to have eliminated most such cases from litigation in the past.

The course of eliminating impossibility as a defense has commended itself to legislative efforts. Indeed, there is very little modern authority that supports a retention of the impossibility defense as such.

(c) *Model Penal Code Formulation.* It may be helpful to consider how the Code would be applied to some of the situations noted above. Subsection (1)(a) would deal with many of the problems. The *Jaffe* case,[90] for example, would result in a conviction under the Code, because the defendant would have purposely engaged in conduct that would constitute the crime "if the attendant circumstances were as he believes them to be." Since the defendant believed the property to be stolen, he could be convicted even though at the time the property was technically classified as non-stolen. The same resolution would be reached in the pickpocket case, as well as in many other situations discussed above where the attendant circumstances were different from those that the actor believed to exist.

* * *

It should also be noted that, in order to constitute an attempt under any of the subdivisions of Subsection (1), it is of course necessary that the result desired or intended by the actor constitute a crime. If, according to his beliefs as to relevant facts and legal relationships, the result desired or intended is not a crime, the actor will not be guilty of an attempt, even though he firmly believes that his goal is criminal. This is in accord with present authority, and follows, as Professor Williams has pointed out, from "the principle of legality; in effect [under a contrary rule] the law of attempt would be used to manufacture a new crime, when the legislature has left the situation outside of the ambit of the law." [93]

* * *

Question

Do you believe the American Law Institute would agree with the conclusion of Justice Nod in *Roundsquare?*

90. See supra note 28.

93. G. Williams, Criminal Law: The General Part 634 (2d ed. 1961). * * *

E. CONSPIRACY

1. Introduction

Commonwealth v. Nighelli

Appeals Court of Massachusetts, Plymouth, 1982.
13 Mass.App.Ct. 590, 435 N.E.2d 1058.

CUTTER, JUSTICE.

The defendants Nighelli and Melanson were found guilty, after a six-day trial before a Superior Court judge and a jury, on indictments charging that each conspired with the other on July 3 and 12, 1979, and on other occasions between July 3 and 24, 1979, to murder Vincent Ferrara. Each defendant has appealed. At trial, each defendant rested at the close of the Commonwealth's case, and filed a motion for a required finding of not guilty. These motions were denied.

1. The evidence most favorable to the Commonwealth was that one or both defendants had been having discussions in June, 1979, with Flemming Budual. Beginning in early July, 1979, further conferences took place.

(a) By arrangement, Budual met both defendants at a Howard Johnson restaurant in Kingston on July 3. After discussion of a separate enterprise, Nighelli asked Budual if he "knew somebody that could make two persons disappear." When asked what he meant, Nighelli said * * * "some big shot in the M.B.T.A. wanted * * * it because" his son had been killed, "someone had killed his son." Budual said he would "see if * * * [he could] find somebody." Budual was told by Nighelli that a proposed victim was "living in New Hampshire * * * that * * * [Nighelli] knew what kind of car he was driving every day, [and] which way he was going back to his home," and that the victim was not "related to organized crime." When asked the cost, Budual said he "didn't know, but * * * [estimated] three to five thousand dollars." Melanson (known to Budual only as "Mel") assured Budual that "everything Nighelli told * * * [him] was true."

(b) On July 12, 1979, Budual went to Friendly's Restaurant in Plymouth to meet Nighelli but found Melanson there. Melanson told Budual that Nighelli was in Lowell and asked Budual "if * * * [he] ever got a * * * hit man to kill the persons from New Hampshire." Budual told Melanson that he would call and arrange for Melanson and Nighelli to meet the hit man at the Howard Johnson Restaurant in South Boston the next day. The appointment apparently was not kept by Melanson and Nighelli.

(c) On July 20, 1979, Budual met Nighelli at Friendly's Restaurant at Plymouth. Nighelli told Budual "that Mel screwed up and * * * was out of it now," but that "the hit was still on, was still going on."

(d) On July 24, Budual, "in the midday hours" met with Nighelli and one Don Cuccinelli (known to Nighelli only as "Pauly") at the Howard Johnson Restaurant in Kingston. Cuccinelli asked Nighelli for "information about the person that has to be hit." Nighelli gave Cuccinelli a paper which contained the intended victim's motor vehicle license plate number, make of automobile, and road address. Cuccinelli, as the supposed "hit man," then "asked for some money up front for expenses." Nighelli said he would go to Boston, "speak with the person [who] wanted the job done and get the money from him." Nighelli said that the job could not be done as "an accident," but must be carried out in some manner that would make the victim "an example" so that other people involved would know "that the guy died for a good reason." They met again at the same place later that day about 5:30 P.M. Nighelli had not obtained any money, but said, "[Y]ou go ahead and do the hit, anyway, because he [Nighelli's friend] will be good for the money." Nighelli disclosed the name of the proposed victim as Vincent Ferrara.

(e) On July 27, Nighelli called Budual by telephone to report that Ferrara "was in prison." He asked if it could be arranged to "get him hit inside the prison."

Nighelli and Melanson were unfortunate in their confidants. Budual was an undercover informer for the Drug Enforcement Administration of the Department of Justice, who "knew an awful lot about illegal trafficking in drugs" and had become an informer because he did not like people who used and sold drugs. Cuccinelli was a State police officer, working under cover in the narcotics unit and posing as a "hit man" in respect of the proposal to kill Ferrara. Budual and Officer Cuccinelli each testified. Their testimony, already described, was sufficient to warrant a rational jury in finding beyond a reasonable doubt that the defendants, as early as July 3, were guilty of the offense of conspiracy to murder one and possibly two unnamed New Hampshire residents. Ferrara's name was not mentioned to Budual until after Nighelli had told Budual on July 20 that Melanson "screwed up and was out of it now." Evidence that Ferrara was a resident of New Hampshire was produced in the form of Ferrara's motor vehicle registration and a Massachusetts house of correction record (each showing him to be a resident of Nashua, New Hampshire). Melanson had shown continuing participation in the venture by his inquiry of Budual on July 12 about the "hit man." Nighelli's pursuit of the objective was indicated by his later talks with Budual on July 20 and 24, at which he met Officer Cuccinelli.

The crime, at least in this simple two-participant type of conspiracy, under Massachusetts law is complete upon the formation of an agreement and a combination to commit, or cause to be committed, a crime or an unlawful act. * * * There is in Massachusetts no requirement that an overt act be committed.

* * * The jury could infer from the conversation of July 3, at which both defendants were present, that each defendant then had in mind the same victim or victims, although no victim was then identified to Budual. The testimony about what each said and did when together on July 3, if believed, constituted proof of participation in a combination "directed toward the accomplishment of the same object," viz. the death of two New Hampshire residents not then named to Budual. * * * Even if these defendants did not intend to participate directly and personally in killing the

victim or victims they could be found to have conspired to bring about the result. The motions for required findings of not guilty were denied properly.

* * *

3. There was no error in the action of the trial judge in charging that Melanson's possible withdrawal from the conspiracy (as reported by Nighelli to Budual at their conference of July 20, 1979; see part 1[c] of this opinion, supra) was "not a defense * * * as the crime of conspiracy is complete upon the making of the agreement" and the "combination." * * * Whatever weight may be given to withdrawal from a continuing conspiracy in Federal anti-trust proceedings, withdrawal from a conspiracy has not been shown to have any effect upon the commission of the common law offense of conspiracy to commit a crime under Massachusetts law. See Nolan, Criminal Law, § 452, at 289.[5] This is a logical extension of cases, already cited in part 1 of this opinion, applying the "traditional rule" (referred to in the comments to Model Penal Code, § 5.03[6], at 143 [Tent.Draft No. 10 [1960]) that "the crime is complete with the agreement" so that "no subsequent action can exonerate the conspirator of that crime." [6]

* * *

Notes

1. *Policy Considerations.* Model Penal Code, § 5.03, Comment 1: *

5. In LaFave & Scott, supra, § 62, at 486–488, some respects are pointed out in which withdrawal from the conspiracy may be significant, e.g. (a) relief from liability for substantive crimes committed, pursuant to the conspiracy, after the date of withdrawal by a conspirator; (b) running of the statute of limitations (see United States v. Panebianco, 543 F.2d 447, 453–454 [2d Cir.1976], cert. denied, 429 U.S. 1103, 97 S.Ct. 1128, 51 L.Ed.2d 553 [1977]), after the withdrawal; (c) period when statements of one coconspirator may bind other conspirators, and similar matters. On the record before us, we need not consider to what extent in Massachusetts, these exceptions to the general rule may be of importance.

6. On this meager record, even if the Model Penal Code had been applicable, it would seem that Melanson's action as described by Nighelli on July 20 would not have provided him a defense, for it was not shown that Melanson "thwarted" the conspiracy by whatever he did. The 1962 Proposed Official Draft of the Model Penal Code, § 5.03(6) reads "(6) *Renunciation of Criminal Purpose.* It is an affirmative defense that the actor, after conspiring to commit a crime, *thwarted the success of the conspiracy,* under circumstances manifesting a complete and voluntary renunciation of his criminal purpose" (emphasis in text supplied). See comments on subsection (6), Model Penal Code (Tent.Draft No. 10) at 142–144. See also comments upon renunciation of other inchoate crimes, at 71–73. Subsection (7) of § 5.03 (Proposed Official Draft, at 85–86) reads in part "For purposes of Section 1.06(4) * * * (c) if an individual abandons the agreement, the conspiracy is terminated as to him only if and when he advises those with whom he conspired of his abandonment or he informs the law enforcement authorities of the existence of the conspiracy and of his participation therein." This language does not purport to deal with renunciation as a *defense* to a charge of conspiracy but only with "abandonment" of the conspiracy, as it affects the date when the crime occurs and when time starts to run. See for § 1.06(4), Proposed Official Draft at 9–10, and comments on subsection (7) in Tentative Draft No. 10, at 144–155. A proposed revision (somewhat based on the Model Penal Code) of our statutes on criminal conspiracy was set out in the "Proposed Criminal Code of Massachusetts," c. 263, §§ 48 & 49(3), prepared in 1971 for the Governor's Committee on Law Enforcement and the Administration of Criminal Justice and the Criminal Law Revision Commission, 1972 Senate Doc. No. 200, reprinted by Lawyers Cooperative Publishing Co. and The Michie Co. in 1972. These provisions have not been enacted.

1. *Introduction.* * * *

* * *

It is worthwhile to note preliminarily that conspiracy as an offense has two different aspects, reflecting the different functions it serves in the legal system. In the first place, conspiracy is an inchoate crime, complementing the provisions dealing with attempt and solicitation in reaching preparatory conduct before it has matured into commission of a substantive offense. Second, it is a means of striking against the special danger incident to group activity, facilitating prosecution of the group, and yielding a basis for imposing added penalties when combination is involved.

As an inchoate crime, conspiracy fixes the point of legal intervention at agreement to commit a crime, or at agreement coupled with an overt act which may, however, be of very small significance. Conspiracy thus reaches further back into preparatory conduct than attempt, raising the question of whether this extension is desirable. The Institute believed it was, for the following reasons:

> *First:* The act of agreeing with another to commit a crime, like the act of soliciting, is concrete and unambiguous; it does not present the infinite degrees and variations possible in the general category of attempts. The danger that truly equivocal behavior may be misinterpreted as preparation to commit a crime is minimized; purpose must be relatively firm before the commitment involved in agreement is assumed.
>
> *Second:* If the agreement was to aid another to commit a crime or if it otherwise encouraged the crime's commission, complicity would be established in the commission of the substantive offense. * * *
>
> *Third:* In the course of preparation to commit a crime, the act of combining with another is significant both psychologically and practically, the former because it crosses a clear threshold in arousing expectations, the latter because it increases the likelihood that the offense will be committed. Sharing lends fortitude to purpose. The actor knows, moreover, that the future is no longer governed by his will alone; others may complete what he has had a hand in starting, even if he has a change of heart.

* * *

In its aspect as a sanction against group activity, conspiracy presents quite different problems.

> *First:* One function to be noted in this area is the use of conspiracy to proscribe agreements having objectives that would not be criminal if pursued or achieved by single individuals, on the ground that combination towards such ends presents a danger a lone actor could not create on his own. There are, of course, important areas of conduct in which such a delineation of the scope of criminality may be appropriate; it is a commonplace, for instance, in the field of antitrust. But judgments of this kind must be made sparingly and in the context of the specific conduct that is involved, taking into consideration other weapons in the legal arsenal that may be brought to bear upon these acts. It is not a matter to be dealt with in a general provision on conspiracy and it is not so dealt with in the Model Code.
>
> To the extent that earlier decisional and statutory law performed this function by defining conspiracy to embody condemnation of all combinations with objectives that are "unlawful," "malicious," "oppressive," or "injurious," as distinct from criminal, the approach was regarded as too vague for penal prohibitions and was rejected in the Code.
>
> *Second:* Group prosecution is undoubtedly made easier by the procedural advantages enjoyed by the prosecution when conspiracy is charged. Acts

and declarations of participants may be admissible against each other under an exception to the hearsay rule, and ordinarily will be received, subject to later ruling, even before the required basis has been laid. Vicarious responsibility may relax venue rules and the conception of conspiracy as a continuous offense extends the period of limitations. The presentation in the case of a full picture of the workings of a large and complex network of related criminal activities will often help the jury to grasp the part played by individuals who otherwise might be forgotten, but a strong case against some defendants may unduly blacken all; the need to work a root and branch extermination of the organized activity may overcome doubts that would otherwise prevail.

* * *

Third: The older common law rule that conspiracy, like attempt, merges in the completed crime that is its object, with the result that conviction and sentence on both grounds are barred, has been superseded on the whole in modern law. The act of combination is regarded as "an independent crime condemned by the statute for the primary purpose of discouraging organized and concerted efforts by two or more people to violate the law." Indeed, the conspiracy is often said to be more dangerous than "the mere commission of the contemplated crime."

The Code embraces this conception in part and rejects it in part. When a conspiracy is declared criminal because its object is a crime, it is entirely meaningless to say that the preliminary combination is more dangerous than the forbidden consummation; the measure of its danger is the risk of such a culmination. On the other hand, the combination may and often does have criminal objectives that transcend any particular offenses that have been committed in pursuance of its goals. In the latter case, cumulative sentences for conspiracy and substantive offenses ought to be permissible, subject to the general limits on cumulation that the Code prescribes. * * *

* * *

2. *Overt act.* As *Nighelli* says, at common law the agreement completes the conspiracy, and no action need be taken upon the agreement. Statutes often add an overt act requirement. Any conspirator may perform the act on behalf of all. As to the nature of an overt act, see infra, p. 828.

3. *Withdrawal.* Withdrawal after the offense is complete has the effects mentioned in the *Nighelli* footnote, but does not at common law constitute a defense to the conspiracy charge.

4. *Impossibility.* Historically, impossibility is a defense to a conspiracy charge to the same extent that it is a defense to attempt. It has played a smaller theoretical and practical role in conspiracy law; for one thing, most factual impossibilities do not arise until a stage in the proceedings after the crime of conspiracy is complete.

2. Agreement

Commonwealth v. Cook

Appeals Court of Massachusetts, Hampden, 1980.
10 Mass.App.Ct. 668, 411 N.E.2d 1326.

GREANEY, JUSTICE.

The defendant was tried before a jury in the Superior Court on an indictment charging conspiracy to commit rape. His motion for a required finding of not guilty was filed and denied at the conclusion of the Commonwealth's case, and he was subsequently convicted and sentenced on the indictment. * * * We hold that the evidence introduced up to the time the Commonwealth rested was insufficient to warrant his conviction of conspiracy and that, as a result, the judgment must be reversed. A summary of the Commonwealth's evidence follows.

At approximately 8:00 P.M. on the evening of July 16, 1977, the victim, age seventeen, went to Chicopee to visit some friends and to see her boyfriend. Upon discovering that her friends were not at home, she proceeded to the housing project where her boyfriend resided. As she passed the area of the project office, the defendant and his brother Maurice Cook attempted to engage her in conversation. Not knowing the Cooks, she spurned an invitation to join them and instead walked to her boyfriend's residence. After ascertaining that he was not at home, she reversed her route, intending to stay at her friends' home to await their return. As she passed the office area for the second time, she accepted the Cooks' renewed invitation to socialize, and she sat with the two brothers on a platform talking for approximately forty-five minutes. * * *

About 9:00 P.M. Maurice Cook indicated that he was out of cigarettes and suggested that the three walk to a convenience store located about a minute and a half away. The victim agreed. To reach the store, the trio proceeded along the street to a narrow path or trail located behind the project office. This path led down a hill through a wooded area to the rear of a well-lit service station adjacent to the convenience store. As they "walk[ed] towards the path" single file (with Maurice in front, the victim in the middle and the defendant in the rear), the victim "slipped * * * fell or something." She sat on the ground for a few seconds laughing when "Maurice turned around and jumped on me * * * and told me I was going to love it." After she screamed, Maurice covered her mouth with his hand, took off his belt and gave it to the defendant seated nearby. Maurice then scratched her with a stick or blunt object and said, "No blood, no blood." The defendant was overheard laughing and saying, "The bitch doesn't want to bleed, we'll make her bleed." Maurice then forcibly raped her. * * *

1. A combination of two or more persons who seek by some concerted action to accomplish a criminal act may be punished as a conspiracy. It is essential to a conviction that the Commonwealth prove the existence of an agreement, because "[t]he gravamen of * * * conspiracy * * * is the unlawful agreement." * * * Proof of a conspiracy may rest entirely or mainly on circumstantial evidence but "some record evidence" is not enough and an acquittal must be ordered if any essential element of the crime is left to surmise, conjecture or guesswork.

We are of the opinion that the evidence, tested against the foregoing principles, was insufficient to establish a conspiracy. The circumstances under which the victim and the Cooks met and socialized were not indicative of a preconceived plan between the defendant and his brother to commit a sexual assault. Rather, the meeting and subsequent engagement were consistent with a chance social encounter common between young persons. The area where the group stayed prior to setting out for the store was used frequently as a gathering spot, and there was no evidence either that the

Cooks attempted to conceal from others the fact that they were with the victim or that they consciously attempted to mislead her as to their identities. The evidence cuts directly against any such inference because of the special efforts made by the defendant and his brother to identify themselves by disclosing their names and places of employment, and by showing the victim their photographs. We do not think it plausible to infer that this conduct was an attempt by the Cooks to lull the victim into a false sense of security. Moreover, since all the conversation at the platform occurred in the victim's presence, the jury could not have properly inferred that a clandestine plan to commit an assault had been formulated during that period. While openness will not automatically sanitize a conspiracy, highly visible conduct has to be considered inconsistent with the shadowy environment which usually shrouds the crime. The purpose for leaving the area was on its face innocuous and was suggested by Maurice, not the defendant. While the route chosen was arguably suspicious, the evidence established that it also was selected by Maurice, not the defendant. There was evidence that the path provided a short, reasonably direct route to a gasoline station which was nearby, well-lighted, and visible from the crest of the hill. We do not think that the events up to the time the victim fell were sufficient to establish a criminal agreement or to warrant the jury in inferring the state of facts that the Commonwealth claims to have existed.

Nor was the prosecution's case strengthened by the circumstances surrounding the assault itself. There was no evidence that the defendant (or his brother for that matter) had anything to do with the victim's falling to the ground. The fact that Maurice's attack began immediately after the victim found herself in a compromising situation suggests spontaneity of action on his part rather than the purposeful execution of a predetermined plan. From that point on, the defendant's conduct fits the classic paradigm of an accomplice adding encouragement to a crime in progress. The fact that the defendant may have aided and abetted the crime does not, as will be discussed more fully in part 2 of this opinion, establish a conspiracy, particularly where the evidence shows that prior planning is not an inherent facet of the crime. * * *

In reaching our conclusion, we are mindful of the principle that proof of a tacit agreement to commit a crime may be enough to establish a conspiracy. See Perkins, Criminal Law 615 (2d ed. 1969). But in this case it is just as reasonable to conclude that the defendant became implicated in the crime as an accomplice after it had commenced without any advance knowledge that it was to occur, as it is to infer that the minds of the parties had met in advance "understandingly, so as to bring about an intelligent and deliberate agreement to * * * commit the offense charged." * * *

2. The remaining question raised by the Commonwealth's argument is whether the defendant can be convicted of conspiracy *solely* on the evidence tending to show his complicity as an accomplice in the commission of the substantive crime. We think on the evidence in this case such a conclusion would be unjustified.

Accomplice and conspiratorial liability are not synonymous, and one can be an accomplice aiding in the commission of a substantive offense without necessarily conspiring to commit it. The holdings which conceptually and practically separate the two types of criminal activity do so because of fundamental distinctions between them. As has already been discussed, the gist of conspiracy rests in the "agree[ment] [between the conspirators] to work in concert for the criminal or corrupt or unlawful purpose" and it is that agreement which constitutes the criminal act and which generally serves to manifest the requisite criminal intent. On the other hand, accomplice liability has a "broader application, making the defendant a principal when he consciously shares in a criminal act, regardless of the existence of a conspiracy." * * * Absent from the formulation of accomplice liability is the necessity of establishing an agreement or consensus in the same sense as those terms are used in describing the agreement or combination which hallmarks a conspiracy. When a defendant is convicted of conspiring with others to commit a crime, the conviction stems from, and is designed to punish, the unlawful agreement which preexists commission of the substantive offense. This is why proof of the conspiracy typically involves circumstantial evidence aimed at establishing a consensus prior to the commission of the target offense. Execution of the crime thus represents performance of the agreement. But because the conspiracy for practical purposes is at least one step removed from the substantive offense, the offense does not substitute for the agreement and the factfinder's analysis of the conspiracy evidence is logically directed at ascertaining whether an underlying agreement exists. * * * Implicit support for our conclusion is also contained in the following statement from Commonwealth v. Stasiun, 349 Mass. 38, 48, 206 N.E.2d 672 (1965): "[P]unishment [for conspiracy] is imposed for entering into the combination. This is not the same thing as participating in the substantive offense which was the object of the conspiracy." A contrary holding on the facts we are considering would confuse certain settled aspects of the law of conspiracy [6] and would tend unnecessarily to expand its already elastic and pervasive definition by "blur[ring] the demarcation line between a conspiracy to commit an offense and the substantive offense which is the object of the conspiracy." Ramirez v. State, 371 So.2d 1063, 1066 (Fla.Dist.Ct.App. 1979). "[A]cts of aiding and abetting clearly make each actor a principal in

6. It is established law that conspiracy to commit an offense and the subsequent commission of the crime normally do not merge into a single punishable act. Iannelli v. United States, 420 U.S. 770, 777, 95 S.Ct. 1284, 1289, 43 L.Ed.2d 616 (1975). Perkins, Criminal Law 618–619 (2d ed. 1969). The necessity of proving a separate agreement underlies the merger rule and supports the settled rule that commission of a substantive offense and a conspiracy to commit it are distinct and "a plea of double jeopardy is no defense to a conviction for both * * * [unless] the substantive offense and the conspiracy are identical * * *." Pereira v. United States, 347 U.S. 1, 11, 74 S.Ct. 358, 364, 98 L.Ed. 435 (1954). Finding the conspiratorial agreement solely in the consensus existing between accomplice and perpetrator would raise serious questions whether the offender is being exposed to jeopardy or, at the very least, would create sentencing problems under the principles of Kuklis v. Commonwealth, 361 Mass. 302, 280 N.E.2d 155 (1972), based on the notion that the "realities of the offenses and the circumstances within which they occur" (Costarelli v. Commonwealth, 374 Mass. 677, 684, 373 N.E.2d 1183 [1978]), were identical. See also concurring opinion of Justice Kaplan in Commonwealth v. Gallarelli, 372 Mass. 573, 580–582, 362 N.E.2d 923 (1977).

the substantive offense * * * but cannot, without more,[8] also make each other actor a principal in the crime of conspiracy to commit such offense * * *." Ibid. We conclude that in this case the evidence of the confederation at the scene was insufficient to warrant the defendant's conviction of conspiracy.

The judgment is reversed, the verdict is set aside, and judgment is to be entered for the defendant.

So ordered.

Note

Agreement. United States v. James, 528 F.2d 999, 1011 (5th Cir.1976):

> * * * To establish the common plan element of a conspiracy, it is not necessary for the government to prove an express agreement between the alleged conspirators to go forth and violate the law. The "common purpose and plan may be inferred from a 'development and collocation of circumstances'." "A conspiracy is seldom born of 'open covenants openly arrived at.'" "The proof, by the very nature of the crime, must be circumstantial and therefore inferential to an extent varying with the conditions under which the crime may be committed." Knowledge by a defendant of all details or phases of a conspiracy is not required. It is enough that he knows the essential nature of it. "And, it is black letter law that all participants in a conspiracy need not know each other; all that is necessary is that each know that it has a 'scope' and that for its success it requires an organization wider than may be disclosed by his personal participation."

Questions

1. Construct fact situations in which one is:

   a. guilty as an accessory before the fact but not as a conspirator.

   b. guilty as a principal in the second degree but not as a conspirator.

   c. guilty as a conspirator but not as a principal or accessory before the fact.

2. Suppose it is a crime knowingly to block a traffic intersection. A and B meet in the middle of an intersection at rush hour. Traffic cannot proceed unless one of them backs up. They sit there for five minutes, blowing horns at each other; neither moves, though either could do so. Are they guilty of conspiracy?

8. Of course, a factfinder can consider and permissibly infer the existence of a conspiracy from the circumstances surrounding the commission of the crime. For example, the sophistication surrounding the execution of the Brinks' robbery (Commonwealth v. Geagan, 339 Mass. 487, 159 N.E.2d 870 [1959]), would warrant a conclusion that its perpetrators had conspired and prepared in advance to commit it. But there the facts establishing the "more" necessary to convict the accomplices of conspiracy consisted of the numerous incidental circumstances manifested at the scene of the crime and elsewhere which demonstrated planning and pursuit of a prearranged systematic course of action. Cf. Commonwealth v. Dellinger, [10] Mass.App. [549], 409 N.E.2d 1337 [(1980)] discussing difficulties in a prosecution for conspiracy when the substantive crime has been abandoned and the Commonwealth cannot reverse engineer the conspiracy from the commission of the target offense.

People v. Carter

Supreme Court of Michigan, 1982.
415 Mich. 558, 330 N.W.2d 314.

FITZGERALD, CHIEF JUSTICE, and WILLIAMS, COLEMAN and RYAN, JUSTICES.

This opinion was written by JUSTICE BLAIR MOODY, JR., prior to his death on November 26, 1982. We concur in this opinion and adopt it as our own.

* * *

Alvin D. Carter was charged with aiding and abetting another to commit both unarmed robbery, M.C.L. § 750.530; M.S.A. § 28.798, and extortion, M.C.L. § 750.213; M.S.A. § 28.410, and with conspiracy to commit both offenses, M.C.L. § 750.157a; M.S.A. § 28.354(1).

The charges against the defendant arose out of the taking of $1,365.00 from an employee of the Consumers Power Company customer service office in Jackson around noon on December 19, 1975. The employee, Mrs. Peggie Johnson, was approached by a man, subsequently identified as Edward Kimble, who handed her a note threatening her three sons unless she gave him money. According to her testimony at defendant's trial, she complied with the demand because she feared for her own safety and that of her children.

* * *

Edward Kimble pled guilty to unarmed robbery and received a 5½– to 15–year sentence. Testifying for the prosecution at defendant's trial, he indicated that he first met Carter, who he knew only as "Hank", at Jackson Prison, where he was serving a sentence for armed robbery and Carter was employed as a prison guard. According to Kimble, he again came into contact with the defendant in November of 1975 at Leake's Lounge, a Jackson bar they both frequented. Kimble testified further that he and Carter discussed the "Consumers Power job" on the afternoon of December 18, the day before the robbery; that on that same evening Carter came to see him at the Sewell Hotel, where he lived with Diane Potter; that during that visit Carter wrote the threatening note that was to be presented to Peggie Johnson; and that Potter copied the note because Carter was afraid the victim would recognize his handwriting.

* * *

The jury, after deliberating for seven and one-half hours, returned a verdict of guilty on all four counts. * * *

In a published per curiam opinion, the Court of Appeals affirmed defendant's convictions of extortion and conspiracy to commit extortion, but reversed, as violative of the proscription against double jeopardy, the convictions of unarmed robbery and conspiracy to commit unarmed robbery. This Court granted defendant's application for leave to appeal his remaining convictions. 409 Mich. 867 (1980). The people do not contest the reversal by the Court of Appeals of defendant's robbery-related convictions.

* * *

It is a settled principle of black-letter law that conspiracy is a crime that is separate and distinct from the substantive crime that is its object. The guilt or innocence of a conspirator does not depend upon the accomplishment of the goals of the conspiracy. More importantly in the context of the instant case, a conviction of conspiracy does not merge with a conviction of the completed offense.[5] Thus, a defendant may be convicted and punished for both the conspiracy and the substantive crime. Pinkerton v. United States, 328 U.S. 640, 66 S.Ct. 1180, 90 L.Ed. 1489 (1946).

The cited justification for the prosecution of conspiracy as a crime independent of, and often in addition to, the prosecution of the object offense is the alleged increased and special danger to society presented by group as opposed to individual activity.[6] The "greater threat" rationale was detailed in Callanan v. United States, 364 U.S. 587, 593–594, 81 S.Ct. 321, 5 L.Ed.2d 312 (1961):

> "[C]ollective criminal agreement—partnership in crime—presents a greater potential threat to the public than individual delicts. Concerted action both increases the likelihood that the criminal object will be successfully attained and decreases the probability that the individuals involved will depart from their path of criminality. Group association for criminal purposes often, if not normally, makes possible the attainment of ends more complex than those which one criminal could accomplish. Nor is the danger of a conspiratorial group limited to the particular end toward which it has embarked. Combination in crime makes more likely the commission of crimes unrelated to the original purpose for which the group was formed. In sum, the danger which a conspiracy generates is not confined to the substantive offense which is the immediate aim of the enterprise." [7]

One of the major exceptions to the general principle that conspiracy and its target offense are separately punishable is known as Wharton's Rule. This rule, which operates as a substantive limitation upon the scope of the crime of conspiracy, states that an agreement by two persons to commit a substantive crime cannot be prosecuted as a conspiracy where the crime itself necessarily requires the participation and cooperation of two persons. Thus, where concerted activity and a plurality of agents are essential elements of a substantive offense, Wharton's Rule bars a prosecution for conspiracy to commit that crime. Defendant asserts that, given the offenses at issue in this case, Wharton's Rule precludes his conviction of conspiracy to commit extortion.

The classic Wharton's Rule offenses—adultery, bigamy, dueling, and incest—are those crimes where "the conspiracy to commit them is in such

5. At early common law, all conspiracies were misdemeanors, which merged into any felony committed in furtherance thereof because of the procedural differences between felony and misdemeanor trials. Under this merger doctrine, only the felony was punishable. Since the procedural differences which justified the doctrine no longer exist, it has not been largely abrogated. * * *

6. Another aspect of conspiracy as an offense in our legal system is that it allows prosecution for preparatory conduct which even precedes attempt and thus functions as a means of crime prevention. Of course, this rationale loses force when, as in this case, the substantive offense has been completed.

7. Perhaps reflecting these "greater dangers", the statute allows conspiracy to be punished more severely than the substantive offense in certain instances. See M.C.L. § 750.157a; M.S.A. § 28.354(1).

close connection with the objective offense[s] as to be inseparable from them". In re Vickers, 371 Mich. 114, 117, 123 N.W.2d 253 (1963). Additionally, the crimes are such that "[t]he parties to the agreement are the only persons who participate in [the] commission of the substantive offense, and the immediate consequences of the crime rest on the parties themselves rather than on society at large". Iannelli v. United States, 420 U.S. 770, 782–783, 95 S.Ct. 1284, 1292, 43 L.Ed.2d 616 (1975).[9]

The rationale for the rule is based on two different analyses. The primary justification relates to legislative intent; where cooperative action is a necessary component of the substantive offense, it is presumed that the Legislature took that element into account when setting forth the penalty for the offense. Recent Developments, *Criminal Law—Multiple Punishment Under The Organized Crime Control Act—A Need for Re-examination of Wharton's Rule and Double Jeopardy,* 52 Wash.L.Rev. 142 (1976). In addition, because the target offense itself requires concerted action, the combination constituting the conspiracy creates no added danger, "because nothing is involved which will not [also] be present whenever the offense is committed." Perkins, Criminal Law (2d ed.), ch. 6, § 5, p. 620.

In practice, Wharton's Rule generally operates as a judicial presumption to proscribe a conspiracy charge in the absence of legislative intent to the contrary. Iannelli v. United States, supra, 420 U.S. at 782, 95 S.Ct. at 1292. The applicability of the rule depends on the nature of the target offense that constitutes the object of the conspiracy. Specifically, the focus is upon the elements of the crime rather than upon the factual circumstances of the particular case. Thus, the test is satisfied when, by definition, the object crime necessarily requires the participation of two people. If the offense could logically be accomplished by a single individual, Wharton's Rule does not apply. The fact that in a particular case cooperation between the offenders was a practical necessity, *i.e.,* the crime could not have been committed without concerted action or would have been made much more difficult without it, is not sufficient to invoke the rule.

Thus, to determine the applicability of Wharton's Rule, "accurate identification of [the] target offense is essential". People v. Davis, p. 280, 290 N.W.2d 366 (Levin, J., concurring). The controversy in the instant case arises because the defendant and the prosecution focus on different aspects of the

9. This "victimless crime" limitation has not been strictly applied by the courts. In a recent case, this Court applied Wharton's Rule to reverse a police officer's conviction of conspiracy to obstruct justice. People v. Davis, 408 Mich. 255, 290 N.W.2d 366 (1980). Wharton's Rule has also been applied in bribery cases. See, e.g., United States v. Dietrich, 126 F. 664 (D.Neb.,1904). It has also been applied to offenses such as buying, selling or delivery of contraband, and receiving stolen goods.

For additional discussion of Wharton's Rule, see, generally, Westen & Drubel, *Toward a General Theory of Double Jeopardy,* 1978 Supreme Court Review 81; Recent Cases, *Criminal Law—Criminal Conspiracy—"Wharton's Rule" as Exception from Charge of Criminal Conspiracy,* 8 U.Ch.L.Rev. 138 (1940); Comment, *An Analysis of Wharton's Rule:* Iannelli v. United States and One Step Beyond, 71 Nw.U.L.Rev. 547 (1976); Recent Developments, *Criminal Law—Multiple Punishment Under the Organized Crime Control Act—A Need for Re-examination of Wharton's Rule and Double Jeopardy,* 52 Wash.L. Rev. 142 (1976).

target crime in their analyses, which leads them to different conclusions regarding the applicability of Wharton's Rule.

The defendant focuses upon the aiding and abetting aspect of the extortion offense. He argues that aiding and abetting necessarily requires concerted action among a plurality of agents. * * * Therefore, the agreement embodied in the conspiracy has no element of added danger that is not already present upon commission of the substantive crime. Further, when aiding and abetting occurs, no additional persons are involved in the conspiracy than are required to commit the object offense. Defendant adds that both the aiding and abetting and conspiracy statutes are directed at the same evil, namely, cooperation between perpetrators of crime. Thus, Wharton's Rule applies, and his conspiracy conviction should be vacated.

The prosecutor, in contrast, focuses on the criminal act of extortion in his Wharton's Rule analysis. The elements of extortion are: a malicious threat of violence or criminal accusation, and an intent to extort money. M.C.L. § 750.213; M.S.A. § 28.410. No agreement is required to complete the crime; further, the crime may logically be committed by one person. Therefore, Wharton's Rule is inapposite in this case.

We agree with the prosecutor. Defendant's emphasis upon the aiding and abetting aspect of the offense is misplaced under these circumstances. The purpose of the aiding and abetting statute, M.C.L. § 767.39; M.S.A. § 28.979, is to ensure that any person who participates in a substantive offense is held liable as if he had directly committed the offense. The statute declares that one who "procures, counsels, aids or abets" in the commission of a crime may be "prosecuted, indicted, tried and on conviction shall be punished" as a principal. Aiding and abetting is not in and of itself a substantive offense. It is, rather, a means of connecting a person with a completed criminal act, whether that act be extortion, as in the instant case, or any other action defined as unlawful. It takes on criminal characteristics only because of its link to that illegal action.

Reduced to its bare essentials, the basic charge against a defendant is not aiding and abetting, but rather the substantive crime that results from the aiding and abetting. In assessing the applicability of Wharton's Rule, the target offense to be evaluated is, therefore, the underlying substantive crime itself, not the means developed to hold a person liable for that crime.

In the instant case, of course, the substantive crime is extortion. Extortion is not a crime of such a nature as to necessarily require the participation of two persons.[14] Therefore, defendant's prosecution and conviction for conspiracy to commit extortion does not violate Wharton's Rule.[15]

* * *

14. In People v. Davis, fn. 9 supra, the target crime at issue, loosely termed "obstruction of justice", is not a "traditional" Wharton's Rule offense. However, a majority of the justices found that the essence of the crime in *Davis* was an agreement not to arrest another in exchange for money. Thus, since agreement was a necessary element of the offense, Wharton's Rule precluded a conspiracy conviction. Unlike the crime in Davis, the crime in the instant case cannot be construed to require the element of agreement.

15. Other courts that have addressed the issue of the applicability of Wharton's Rule to the relationship between conspiracy to commit a substantive crime and aiding and abetting the commission of the offense have reached the

The Court of Appeals is affirmed.

FITZGERALD, C.J., and WILLIAMS, COLEMAN and RYAN, JJ., concur.

RILEY, J., not participating.

KAVANAGH, JUSTICE (for reversal of conspiracy conviction).

I would affirm defendant's conviction of extortion, but would set aside his conviction of conspiracy to perpetrate extortion.

Nothing was added to the extortion by the "conspiracy" to effect it. When the extortion was carried out the charged conspiracy merged into the completed act.

LEVIN, J., concurs.

Notes

1. *Wharton's Rule in the Supreme Court.* Iannelli v. United States, 420 U.S. 770, 781–786, 95 S.Ct. 1284, 1291–1294, 43 L.Ed.2d 616, 625–628 (1975):

> Wharton's Rule first emerged at a time when the contours of the law of conspiracy were in the process of active formulation. The general question whether the conspiracy merged into the completed felony offense remained for some time a matter of uncertain resolution.[13] That issue is now settled, however, and the Rule currently stands as an exception to the general principle that a conspiracy and the substantive offense that is its immediate end do not merge upon proof of the latter. * * *
>
> This Court's prior decisions indicate that the broadly formulated Wharton's Rule does not rest on principles of double jeopardy. Instead, it has current vitality only as a judicial presumption, to be applied in the absence of legislative intent to the contrary. The classic Wharton's Rule offenses—adultery, incest, bigamy, duelling—are crimes that are characterized by the general congruence of the agreement and the completed substantive offense. The parties to the agreement are the only persons who participate in commission of the substantive offense,[15] and the immediate consequences of the crime rest on the parties themselves rather than on society at large. See United States v. Bobo, 477 F.2d, at 987. Finally, the agreement that attends the substantive offense does not appear likely to pose the distinct kinds of threats to society that the law of conspiracy seeks to avert. It cannot, for example, readily be assumed that an

same result with respect to a variety of crimes. See, e.g., State v. Williams, 395 A.2d 1158 (Me., 1978) (murder); State v. Campbell, 217 Kan. 756, 539 P.2d 329 (1975); State v. Johns, [184] Conn. [369], 439 A.2d 1049 (1981) (burglary). In Michigan, at least one panel of the Court of Appeals has arrived at the same conclusion. See People v. Hamp, 110 Mich.App. 92, 312 N.W.2d 175 (1981) (first-degree murder).

13. As previously noted, the general rule in the early common law was that the conspiracy merged with the felony upon consummation of the latter. * * *

* * *

15. An exception to the Rule generally is thought to apply in the case in which the conspiracy involves more persons than are required for commission of the substantive offense. For example, while the two persons who commit adultery cannot normally be prosecuted both for that offense and for conspiracy to commit it, the third-party exception would permit the conspiracy charge where a "matchmaker"—the third party—had conspired with the principals to encourage commission of the substantive offense. See 1 R. Anderson, Wharton's Criminal Law and Procedure § 89, p. 193 (1957); State v. Clemenson, 123 Iowa 524, 526, 99 N.W. 139 (1904). The rationale supporting this exception appears to be that the addition of a third party enhances the dangers presented by the crime. * * *

* * *

agreement to commit an offense of this nature will produce agreements to engage in a more general pattern of criminal conduct.

The conduct proscribed by § 1955 is significantly different from the offenses to which the Rule traditionally has been applied. Unlike the consequences of the classic Wharton's Rule offenses, the harm attendant upon the commission of the substantive offense is not restricted to the parties to the agreement. Large-scale gambling activities seek to elicit the participation of additional persons—the bettors—who are parties neither to the conspiracy nor to the substantive offense that results from it. Moreover, the parties prosecuted for the conspiracy need not be the same persons who are prosecuted for commission of the substantive offense. An endeavor as complex as a large-scale gambling enterprise might involve persons who have played appreciably different roles, and whose level of culpability varies significantly. It might, therefore, be appropriate to prosecute the owners and organizers of large-scale gambling operations both for the conspiracy and for the substantive offense but to prosecute the lesser participants only for the substantive offense. Nor can it fairly be maintained that agreements to enter into large-scale gambling activities are not likely to generate additional agreements to engage in other criminal endeavors. * * *

Wharton's Rule applies only to offenses that *require* concerted criminal activity, a plurality of criminal agents. In such cases, a closer relationship exists between the conspiracy and the substantive offense because *both* require collective criminal activity. The substantive offense therefore presents some of the same threats that the law of conspiracy normally is thought to guard against, and it cannot automatically be assumed that the Legislature intended the conspiracy and the substantive offense to remain as discrete crimes upon consummation of the latter. Thus, absent legislative intent to the contrary, the Rule supports a presumption that the two merge when the substantive offense is proved.

But a legal principle commands less respect when extended beyond the logic that supports it. In this case, the significant differences in characteristics and consequences of the kinds of offenses that gave rise to Wharton's Rule and the activities proscribed by § 1955 counsel against attributing significant weight to the presumption the Rule erects. More important, as the Rule is essentially an aid to the determination of legislative intent, it must defer to a discernible legislative judgment. * * *

2. *The Model Penal Code and Wharton's Rule.* Model Penal Code, § 5.04, Comment 4: *

4. *Immunity as an Accomplice.* Subsection (2) reflects the same policies that are embodied in the complicity provisions of the Model Code, in Sections 2.06(5) and 2.06(6)(a) and (6)(b). The commentary to Section 2.06 explains that to hold the victim of a crime guilty of conspiring to commit it would confound legislative purpose. Concerning crimes as to which the behavior of more than one person is "inevitably incident," such as unlawful intercourse, bribery, or unlawful sales, it is pointed out that varying and conflicting policies are often involved—for example, ambivalence in public attitudes toward the crime and the requirement of corroboration of accomplice testimony. The position taken in the complicity provision, and now adopted for conspiracy and solicitation, is to leave to the legislature in defining each particular offense the selective judgment that must be made as to whether more than one participant ought to be subject to

liability. Since the exception is confined to behavior "inevitably incident" to the commission of the crime, the problem inescapably presents itself in defining the crime.

The law prior to the drafting of the Model Code was confused, chiefly because of the doctrine commonly known as "Wharton's rule." [18] As formulated by the author whose name it bears, the doctrine holds that "when to the idea of an offense plurality of agents is logically necessary, conspiracy, which assumes the voluntary accession of a person to a crime of such a character that it is aggravated by a plurality of agents cannot be maintained." [19] The classic Wharton's rule cases involve crimes such as dueling, bigamy, adultery, and incest, but it has also been said to apply to gambling, the giving and receiving of bribes, and the buying and selling of contraband goods. The rule has been unevenly applied and has been subject to a number of exceptions and limitations.

It seems clear that Wharton's rule as generally stated and the rationale that conspiracy "assumes * * * a crime of such a nature that it is aggravated by a plurality of agents" completely overlook the functions of conspiracy as an inchoate crime. That an offense inevitably requires concert is no reason to immunize criminal preparation to commit it. Further, the rule operates to immunize from a conspiracy prosecution *both* parties to *any* offense that inevitably requires concert, thus disregarding the legislative judgment that at least one should be punishable and taking no account of the varying policies that ought to determine whether the other should be. The rule is supportable only insofar as it avoids cumulative punishment for conspiracy and the completed substantive crime, for it is clear that the legislature would have taken the factor of concert into account in grading a crime that inevitably requires concert. This consideration is of course irrelevant under the Model Code, which precludes cumulative punishment in any case for a conspiracy with a single criminal objective and the completed substantive crime.

Subsection (2) consequently goes no further than to provide that a person who may not be convicted of the substantive offense under the complicity provision may not be convicted of the inchoate crime under the general conspiracy and solicitation sections. On the other hand, the party who would be guilty of the substantive offense if it should be committed, may equally be convicted of soliciting or conspiring for its commission, since the immunity of the other party gives him no defense under Subsection (1)(b).

* * *

Lythgoe v. State

Supreme Court of Alaska, 1980.
626 P.2d 1082.

BOOCHEVER, JUSTICE.

The issue raised in this appeal is whether the parental exemption contained in Alaska's former kidnapping statute, AS 11.15.260, by implication, prevents prosecution under the former conspiracy to kidnap statute, AS 11.15.270. We conclude that the exemption does apply, and reverse the judgment of the superior court, which denied Lythgoe's motion for acquittal.

18. The so-called "Wharton's rule" was apparently first enunciated in Shannon v. Commonwealth, 14 Pa. 226 (1850).

19. 2 F. Wharton, Criminal Law § 1604 (12th ed. 1932). See also Developments in the Law, *Criminal Conspiracy,* 72 Harv.L.Rev. 920, 953–56 (1959); Note, 62 Harv.L.Rev. 1226 (1949); Note, 23 S.Cal.L.Rev. 262 (1950); Note, 8 U.Chi.L.Rev. 138 (1940).

The facts of this case need only be briefly summarized. After several reports of child abuse, S.L., the daughter of Janice Lythgoe, was removed from her mother's custody to a licensed child care facility by the State of Alaska Division of Social Services. A court order gave the state temporary custody for a thirty-day period. On the morning of July 24, 1978, during the time S.L. was in the state's custody, a man later identified as Jack Dropulich allegedly took S.L. from the facility at gunpoint. After running several blocks, Dropulich allegedly met Kenneth Crump, who was the driver of the getaway car. At the time, Crump was living with Janice Lythgoe. S.L. was recovered later in the day and Dropulich, Crump and Lythgoe were arrested.

Lythgoe was subsequently indicted and convicted of conspiracy to kidnap, AS 11.15.270, and was sentenced to ten years with five suspended.

The crime of conspiracy is generally regarded as a separate offense from the substantive crime that is the object of the conspiracy. Unlike the other preliminary offenses of attempt and solicitation, conspiracy does not merge into a conviction for the substantive crime. * * *

As a corollary to the rule that conspiracy is a separate offense, a number of courts have held that a defendant can be convicted of conspiracy even though the defendant could not commit the substantive crime. For example, a prison inmate can be convicted of escape, but one not in custody who assists an inmate in acquiring hacksaw blades can be guilty of conspiracy to escape.[1] The state urges that we follow this line of cases, reasoning that Lythgoe could be guilty of conspiracy to kidnap even though the parental exemption would bar prosecution for the substantive offense of kidnapping.

Despite authority for the state's position, there is an equally well recognized exception to the above rule where the legislature has immunized a certain group of people from prosecution for the substantive offense or provided for a lesser punishment. In these cases, the courts have generally concluded that to allow a conspiracy conviction would circumvent the legislature's intent in providing the exemption from the substantive crime.

The leading case discussing this legislative exemption is Gebardi v. United States, 287 U.S. 112, 53 S.Ct. 35, 77 L.Ed. 206 (1932). In *Gebardi,* the court concluded that Congress did not intend to punish a woman under the Mann Act (prohibiting the interstate transportation of women for prostitution or illicit sex) where a woman's only active involvement was to give her consent to be transported. The Court then concluded that it would not be possible to punish the woman for conspiracy to violate the Act, reasoning that

> [i]t would contravene that policy [to have the woman's consensual conduct unpunished] to hold that the very passage of the Mann Act effected a withdrawal by the conspiracy statute of that immunity which the Mann Act itself confers.

287 U.S. at 123, 53 S.Ct. at 38, 77 L.Ed. at 212.

1. People v. Edwards, 74 Ill.App.2d 225, 219 N.E.2d 382 (1966). See United States v. Rabinowich, 238 U.S. 78, 35 S.Ct. 682, 59 L.Ed. 1211 (1915); Cox v. State, 367 So.2d 535, 541 (Ala.Cr.App.1978); State v. Martin, 199 Iowa 643, 200 N.W. 213 (1924).

In People v. Buffum, 40 Cal.2d 709, 256 P.2d 317 (1953), the California Supreme Court followed *Gebardi* in determining whether one who could not be convicted of the substantive offense, but could be guilty of a lesser offense, could nevertheless be guilty of conspiracy to commit the greater offense. Under a then effective California statute, a woman who submitted to an illegal abortion was subject to a minimum sentence of one year, but the person who performed the abortion was subject to a minimum sentence of two years. In considering whether a woman who submitted to an abortion could be guilty of conspiracy to violate the statute prohibiting performance of abortions, the court concluded that to allow such a construction of the conspiracy statute

> would mean that the conspiracy law could be used as a device for defeating the legislative intention of imposing a lessor penalty on a woman who violates section 275 [with a one-year minimum sentence] than is prescribed for a person convicted under section 274 [providing for a two-year minimum sentence].

Id. 256 P.2d at 324. Further, the court noted that the general rule, that a person can be punished for conspiracy to commit a crime when it would not be possible for that person to commit the substantive offense, should not be applied when

> the Legislature singles out one of the parties for special treatment by enacting a statute which deals only with the conduct of that person and provides for a lesser punishment than is given to the other party.

The state recognizes the exception, but urges that it should not be applied in the case of a parent accused of conspiracy to kidnap his or her own child. The state argues that the exception has only been applied in cases where the person exempted from a conspiracy charge has also been the victim of the substantive offense, such as the woman who consents to have an illegal abortion. The state notes that S.L. was the victim of the kidnapping, not Janice Lythgoe. We are not persuaded, however, that there is any logical reason for giving the legislative exemption the very limited construction urged by the state. In our opinion, and as the cases suggest, the resolution hinges on whether it would frustrate the legislature's intent to exempt a certain class of persons if those persons could then be punished under a conspiracy statute.

The Alaska kidnapping statute in effect at the time of this offense, AS 11.15.260, provided for a maximum penalty of life imprisonment. Parents were exempted from prosecution for kidnapping, but could be convicted of child stealing under AS 11.15.290, which provided for a maximum penalty of ten years. Conspiracy to kidnap, AS 11.15.270, like kidnapping, also allowed a maximum sentence of life imprisonment.[6]

We think it is clear that the legislature viewed the abduction of a child by a parent as a far less serious offense than kidnapping, and accordingly

6. * * * We view it of some significance that the legislature provided for the parental exemption in the kidnapping statute in the same section of the act that created the crime of conspiracy to kidnap. This is some indication that the legislature intended the parental exemption of subsection (a) to apply to the conspiracy definition of subsection (b) as well.

established the lesser offense of child stealing. It seems plain that to allow a parent to be convicted of conspiracy to kidnap his or her own child would expose the parent to the same measure of liability which the legislature specifically sought to remove in the case of the kidnapping statute. It does not seem logical to suppose that the legislature would have specifically provided for a lesser penalty in one section only to reinstate it, indirectly, by another.

Alaska's new criminal code provides, in AS 11.41.300(b)(1), for exemption from prosecution for kidnapping if the person is a "relative of the victim." In commentary on the section, the code drafters explained:

> The justification for preferential treatment accorded relatives is the view that relatives who take a child or incompetent person from their lawful custodian or [sic] acting in response to understandable, if misguided, domestic passion and have a genuine interest or affection for the victim. Their conduct is neither as culpable as that of the stranger who takes the child nor are they as likely to endanger the victim's welfare or sense of security as would the stranger.

Commentary on the Alaska Revised Criminal Code, Senate Journal Supplement 19–20 (June 12, 1978).

The state argues that this rationale is not applicable to a parent that does not participate directly in the kidnapping, because the actual perpetrators may not have the same degree of affection for the child. Again, we are not persuaded that there is merit to this contention.

It seems apparent that if other persons help a parent regain custody of a child, that although they might not be responding to the same "misguided, domestic passion," they would also be careful not to harm the child. The threat of harm to the victim is in sharp contrast to a kidnapping by strangers to extort a ransom or to engage in sexual assaults or other acts of terrorism and violence. We believe the legislature, by exempting parents from the operation of the kidnapping statute, intended, by implication, to exempt parents from conspiracy to kidnap as well.

Consequently, Janice Lythgoe cannot be convicted of conspiracy to kidnap, and the decision of the superior court denying her motion for acquittal is REVERSED. Because of the decision we reach in this case, it is not necessary to consider other arguments raised by the parties.

Notes

1. *Incapacity to Commit Substantive Crime.* Model Penal Code, § 5.04, Comment 2: *

> 2. *Incapacity of Actor.* Many crimes are so defined that only a person who occupies a particular position or has a particular characteristic can be guilty of the crime. Only when a married person is involved, for example, can the crime of adultery be committed. Subsection (1)(a) accords with the settled rule that a person who is incapable of committing a particular substantive crime

because he lacks such position or characteristic may nevertheless be guilty of a conspiracy to commit it. The decisions offer numerous examples of this doctrine: the giver of a bribe has been convicted of conspiring with a public officer to commit the crime of receiving a bribe, which only the public officer could commit;[4] a person who is not a bankrupt may be convicted of conspiring with a bankrupt to conceal the latter's property from the trustee, although only the bankrupt could be guilty of the substantive crime;[5] and an unmarried man may be convicted of conspiring with a married man that the latter commit adultery.[6] The doctrine is clear on principle, for an agreement to aid another to commit a crime is not rendered less dangerous than any other conspiracy by virtue of the fact that one party is unable to commit the substantive crime so long as the other party is capable.

The cases covered by Subsection (1)(a) should be distinguished, however, from others that involve a party who has no capacity to commit the substantive offense but who also is a "victim" or engages in behavior that is "inevitably incident" to its commission. In these cases the party who is the victim or whose behavior is inevitably incident to commission of the offense may have a defense to the charge of conspiracy or solicitation under Subsection (2), but this would be immaterial to the liability of the other person for conspiracy by virtue of Subsection (1)(b).

* * *

2. *Failure to Convict Co-conspirators.* Commonwealth v. Byrd, 490 Pa. 544, 550–553, 417 A.2d 173, 176–177 (1980):

Appellant next maintains that his conspiracy conviction cannot stand because Smith, his only alleged co-conspirator, was subsequently acquitted of conspiracy at a separate trial. We reject this claim. There is no doubt that the crime of conspiracy requires proof of more than a single participant. 18 Pa.C.S. § 903(a). As Justice Cardozo once noted: "It is impossible in the nature of things for a man to conspire with himself." Morrison v. California, 291 U.S. 82, 92, 54 S.Ct. 281, 285, 78 L.Ed. 664 (1934). Nevertheless, such generalizations do not require that a valid conviction for conspiracy against one defendant must be held in limbo pending the outcome of the separate trial or trials of all alleged co-conspirators. Nor do they require that a valid conspiracy conviction must subsequently be nullified by the acquittal of the other or others charged.

At the outset it is important to emphasize certain already well-established principles in this area. There is no doubt, for example, that one convicted of conspiracy is not entitled to relief simply because others charged have not yet been tried. United States v. Shipp, 359 F.2d 185 (6th Cir.1966); DeCamp v. United States, 10 F.2d 984 (D.C.Cir.1926). That the prosecution has nolle prossed charges against one or all of the others indicted is equally insufficient to afford a single convicted conspirator any relief. United States v. Koritan, 283 F.2d 516 (3rd Cir.1960) aff'g 182 F.Supp. 143 (E.D.Pa.); United States v. Fox, 130 F.2d 56 (3rd Cir.), cert. denied, 317 U.S. 666, 63 S.Ct. 74, 87 L.Ed. 535 (1942); State v. Goldman, 95 N.J.Super. 50, 229 A.2d 818 (1967). So too, that the only other co-conspirators have been granted immunity and so cannot be

4. E.g., Downs v. United States, 3 F.2d 855, 857 (3d Cir.), cert. denied, 268 U.S. 689 (1925); State v. Myers, 36 Idaho 396, 211 P. 440 (1922); cf. Chadwick v. United States, 141 F. 225 (6th Cir.1905).

5. E.g., Jollit v. United States, 285 F. 209 (5th Cir.1922); Tapack v. United States, 220 F. 445 (3d Cir.), cert. denied, 238 U.S. 627 (1915); cf. United States v. Rabinowich, 238 U.S. 78 (1915).

6. State v. Martin, 199 Iowa 643, 200 N.W. 213 (1924).

tried does not bar conviction of the remaining defendant. Hurwitz v. State, 200 Md. 578, 92 A.2d 575 (1952); Berry v. State, 202 Ind. 294, 165 N.E. 61 (1929), 173 N.E. 705 (1930); see Farnsworth v. Zerbst, 98 F.2d 541 (5th Cir.1938) (diplomatic immunity). And, indeed, it is established that where the other alleged co-conspirators are unapprehended, Rosenthal v. United States, 45 F.2d 1000 (8th Cir.1930), unindicted, United States v. Monroe, 164 F.2d 471 (2d Cir.1947), cert. denied, 333 U.S. 828, 68 S.Ct. 452, 92 L.Ed.2d 1113 (1948), dead, People v. Nall, 242 Ill. 284, 89 N.E. 1012 (1909), or even, in some instances, unknown, United States v. General Motors Corp., 121 F.2d 376, 411 (7th Cir.), cert. denied, 314 U.S. 618, 62 S.Ct. 105, 86 L.Ed. 497 (1941), there is no basis to disturb a valid conviction for conspiracy. See generally Gardner v. State, 286 Md. 520, 524, 408 A.2d 1317, 1320 (1979); Developments in the Law—Criminal Conspiracy, 72 Harv.L.Rev. 922, 973 (1959). The only question still apparently open to any debate, see e.g., People v. Kuland, 266 N.Y. 1, 193 N.E. 439 (1934) (question is "arguable"), is whether an acquittal of all alleged co-conspirators should produce a different result. At least in the case, such as this, of a subsequent acquittal, we do not believe that it should.

Admittedly, some authority, including certain decisions of our own Superior Court, does assert that the acquittal of all but one conspirator requires the discharge of the remaining defendant. E.g., Commonwealth v. Campbell, 57 Pa. Super. 160, 390 A.2d 761 (1978); Commonwealth v. Avrach, 110 Pa.Super. 438, 168 A. 531 (1933). This rule, however, had its origins at a time when co-conspirators were jointly tried. In that circumstance a single jury would hear the evidence of conspiracy and, rightly, would not be permitted to find the evidence sufficient to prove a conspiracy involving only one of those charged. The acquittal rule that developed was thus clearly a rule of verdict consistency. Gardner, supra 286 Md. at 522–524, 408 A.2d at 1319–20 * * *. * * *

An acquittal at any trial is never a guarantee that no crime has been committed. Rather it signifies only that the Commonwealth has not proved its case to the satisfaction of the jury. Thus in the present case, different verdicts may well have been due solely to the different composition of the two juries. Alternatively, the difference may have been due to a variety of other circumstances, including a difference in the proof offered at trial. As the Fifth Circuit Court of Appeals has recently explained, "acquittal [of one of the conspirators] could have resulted from a multiplicity of factors completely unrelated to the actual existence of a conspiracy." United States v. Strother, 458 F.2d 424, 426 (5th Cir.1972). It is error to assume that the failure of a jury to convict one conspirator necessarily invalidates the Commonwealth's verdict, won from a different jury, at a separate trial. * * *

State v. John

Supreme Court of Nebraska, 1982.
213 Neb. 76, 328 N.W.2d 181.

CLINTON, JUSTICE.

The defendant was charged with the crime of criminal conspiracy as defined by Neb.Rev.Stat. § 28–202 (Reissue 1979), found guilty by a jury, and sentenced to a term of 1 to 5 years' imprisonment. * * *

* * *

Section 28–202 provides in part: "(1) A person shall be guilty of criminal conspiracy if, with intent to promote or facilitate the commission of a felony:

"(a) He agrees with one or more persons that they or one or more of them shall engage in or solicit the conduct or shall cause or solicit the result specified by the definition of the offense; and

"(b) He or another person with whom he conspired commits an overt act in pursuance of the conspiracy."

* * *

The State introduced evidence which tended to establish the following facts. On June 4, 1981, the defendant John and his wife, Barbara, were separated and an action for divorce was pending. John operated a business in Grand Island, Nebraska, and at that time lived at his place of business in an office which he had converted into a bedroom. On about June 3, 1981, the defendant John had dinner with an acquaintance from Minnesota, one Hanauer * * *. * * *

* * * According to Hanauer, John asked him if he knew where he could get an unregistered gun and where he could find someone to dispose of his wife. To the latter question Hanauer answered "No." At that time John said, "This conversation is now ended." Hanauer stated that as they walked to the door he became nervous and frightened. His thought, as indicated by inference from later testimony, apparently was that, since John had disclosed a possible intention to murder his wife, he (Hanauer) might himself be in danger if the plan were actually carried out. At that time he turned to John and said, "Well, maybe I do know somebody." He then asked for John's card, and John gave him two. Hanauer testified that the more he thought about the matter the more concerned he became. He returned to Minnesota that day. When he reached home he called the sheriff's department, made an appointment for the following day, and disclosed the nature of his conversations with John.

* * *

* * * The deputy to whom Hanauer spoke then, with Hanauer's knowledge, contacted the Hall County sheriff's office, told the sheriff's deputy of the information he had received, and later transmitted, with a memo, one of the business cards which Hanauer stated he received from John.

Upon receipt of this information the Hall County sheriff's department contacted a sergeant at the criminal investigation division of the Nebraska State Patrol. Between them it was decided that an undercover agent of the State Patrol should play the part of a hit man who had been contacted by Hanauer and get in touch with John. This was done immediately and a telephone conversation between John and the undercover agent Zeleski, a regular employee of the State Patrol, took place. There were subsequent telephone conversations and meetings between the two. * * * These conversations and meetings constitute the basis of the various overt acts (with the exception of the first, i.e., John's handing the business cards to Hanauer) charged in the information. * * *

We summarize and/or quote the contents of the conversations that took place at the various meetings between John and Zeleski. * * *

* * *

John * * * explained he could not get a picture of his wife as he never carried one, but he would furnish a picture of the two children. He then furnished Zeleski with an itinerary of the vacation which his wife and children were about to take * * *. * * *

* * *

John then gave Zeleski a general description of Mrs. John and wrote it on the back of the itinerary. He then gave Zeleski pictures of the children, stating he did not want either of them involved and that he wanted the pictures back eventually. The conversation continued:

"Inv. Zeleski: Is there anything in particular you had in mind, ah, that, ah.

"Mr. John: Well when you, when you say—like had in mind.

"Inv. Zeleski: Well, to, like you know.

"Mr. John: Well, if it could be made to look like an accident, fine. So much the better is all I'm getting at.

"Inv. Zeleski: What do, ya, a traffic accident, you mean.

"Mr. John: Traffic accident, a holdup in a store, ah, somebody shot by mistake, etc. etc. If you see what I am getting at.

* * *

Then followed a recital by John of his marital troubles, including what he referred to as his wife's unreasonable financial demands and John's expression of opinion that the judge might yield to them. The conversation then turned to charges for Zeleski's services.

* * *

After a rather meandering conversation they concluded that Zeleski would contact John in 30 days, with Zeleski saying, "if you want to call it quits," it was OK, but that he would want to get his expense money. To this John replied, "OK." * * *

When John, at trial, took the stand on his own behalf he did not deny the various meetings with Zeleski or challenge the contents of their various conversations. He explained that he was astounded when he received the first call from Zeleski. He explained his consenting to and his participation in the meetings with Zeleski by stating that he was curious to find out what a hit man was like.

It is apparent, however, the jury did not accept John's explanation * * *. * * *

The defendant's first assignment of error contains two contentions, namely, (1) there was insufficient evidence to establish the agreement and (2) no conspiracy can exist when one of the parties is feigning the agreement. The basis for the State's charge of conspiracy is clearly founded upon the conversation between the defendant and Hanauer on June 4, for that is the date stated in the information.

* * *

Disregarding for the moment the fact that Hanauer was feigning the agreement, the jury was entitled * * * to consider John's subsequent conduct in determining whether an agreement existed and the nature thereof.

We hold that the evidence was sufficient for the jury to determine beyond a reasonable doubt that John and Hanauer entered into an agreement which John understood was an agreement by Hanauer to "solicit" a hit man for the purpose of carrying out the first degree murder of Barbara John. * * * Hanauer's version of the conversation and John's subsequent conversations and transactions with the "hit" man, if believed by the jury, do establish that John agreed to have Hanauer solicit someone to murder his wife.

We now turn to the second question of whether, under the provisions of § 28–202, two people must actually agree to the criminal conduct necessary to constitute the first element of a conspiracy, or whether agreement by the defendant and a feigned agreement by the alleged coconspirator is sufficient. Prior to the adoption of § 28–202 in 1977, the Nebraska statute defining a conspiracy read: "If *two* or more persons conspire to commit any felony * * * and one or more of such parties do any act to effect the object of the conspiracy * * *." (Emphasis supplied.) Neb.Rev.Stat. § 28–301 (Reissue 1975). It is not controverted that under the former statute the conspiracy or agreement must be actual and made by two or more people. The State takes the position in this case that under the provision of § 28–202, which was adopted from Model Penal Code § 5.03 (Tentative Draft No. 10, 1960), the unilateral approach of the agreement element of conspiracy has been adopted, and under that approach only the defendant need agree with another; the second party can feign the agreement and the conspiracy may exist.

There are significant differences in the language of the two statutes. The former provided, "If two or more persons conspire * * *." The present statute says, "A person shall be guilty * * * if, with intent * * * (a) He agrees * * *." * * *

* * *

We believe it is clear that § 28–202 adopts the unilateral approach.

* * *

In determining the merits of the defendant's third assignment, it becomes necessary to discuss the nature of an overt act. An overt act is such as tends to show the preexisting conspiracy. Platt v. State, 143 Neb. 131, 8 N.W.2d 849 (1943). It is an outward act done in pursuance of the conspiracy and manifests an intent or design looking toward the accomplishment of the crime. Chavez v. United States, 275 F.2d 813 (9th Cir.1960). It need not of itself have a tendency to accomplish the object of the conspiracy. Hall v. United States, 109 F.2d 976 (10th Cir.1940). It need not be an act which is criminal in itself.

* * *

Affirmed.

Notes

1. *The Unilateral View of the Model Penal Code.* Model Penal Code, § 5.03, Comment 2: *

2. *Definition of Conspiracy.* * * *

(b) *Unilateral Approach to Conspiratorial Relationship.* As previously noted, Subsection (1) departs from the traditional view of conspiracy as an entirely bilateral or multilateral relationship, the view inherent in the standard formulation cast in terms of "two or more persons" agreeing or combining to commit a crime. Attention is directed instead to each individual's culpability by framing the definition in terms of the conduct that suffices to establish the liability of any given actor, rather than the conduct of a group of which he is charged to be a part. This approach has been designated "unilateral," and it has apparently been followed in all but a few of the recently revised codes and proposals, though some of the revisions do not accept every consequence of that approach.

The unilateral approach makes it immaterial to the guilt of a conspirator whose culpability has been established that the person or all of the persons with whom he conspired have not been or cannot be convicted. Traditional law frequently has held otherwise, reasoning from the definition of conspiracy as an agreement between two or more persons that there must be at least two guilty conspirators or none. The problem arises in a number of contexts.

First: When the person with whom the defendant conspired is irresponsible or has an immunity to prosecution or conviction for the crime, Section 5.04 explicitly provides that this is no defense for the responsible actor, a result that is already implicit in the basic formulation.

Second: When the person with whom the defendant conspired secretly intends not to go through with the plan, it is generally held that neither party can be convicted because there was no "agreement" between two persons. Under the unilateral approach of the Code, the culpable party's guilt would not be affected by the fact that the other party's agreement was feigned. He has conspired, within the meaning of the definition, in the belief that the other party was with him; apart from the issue of entrapment often presented in such cases, his culpability is not decreased by the other's secret intention. True, the project's chances of success have not been increased by the agreement; indeed, its doom may have been sealed by this turn of events. But the major basis of conspiratorial liability, the unequivocal evidence of a firm purpose to commit a crime, remains the same. * * *

Third: When the person with whom the defendant conspired has not been apprehended or tried, or his case has been disposed of in a manner that would raise questions of consistency about a conviction of the defendant, the cases have reached varying results. It is well settled that a sole defendant may be convicted of conspiracy if it is proved that he conspired with a person who has not been apprehended or is unknown to the grand jurors. The result is generally the same when the other conspirator is known and amenable to justice but has not been indicted, or has been granted immunity. The courts reason that this situation raises no questions of consistency and emphasize the importance to the state of the grant of immunity as a means of obtaining testimony. The cases differ, however, about the effect of a dismissal of charges or nolle prosequi, and when the defendant's only alleged co-conspirator has been acquitted, the prevailing view has been that his own conviction cannot stand. Under the Model Code, failure to prosecute the only co-conspirator or his acquittal in the same or in a different trial would not affect a defendant's liability. * * *

* * *

2. *Favoring the Unilateral View.* People v. Lanni, 95 Misc.2d 4, 7–9, 406 N.Y.S.2d 1011, 1013 (Sup.Ct.1978):

> The rationale of public policy, decreeing as punishable conspiratorial arrangements, was predicated upon the fear that group action is often more dangerous than individual endeavors at crime. It was believed that there is a greater likelihood of accomplishing the crime if more than one set their mind to it. * * *
>
> If the ultimate goal is essentially crime prevention, then should not the danger to society be measured by the individual criminal disposition, rather than by reference to the effect or result such would-be criminal may have after others are recruited by or voluntarily join him in a criminal combine? Additionally, the perceived danger is that, if the efforts of the criminally intentioned to conspire with others are not aborted and the conspirator is not isolated, the guilty will continue to find solace in the law's inability to appropriately deal with him. There is sure logic in the view that the law should "focus inquiry on the culpability of the actor whose liability is in issue, rather than the group of which he is alleged to be a part." (Wechsler, Jones and Korn, Treatment of Inchoate Crimes in the Model Penal Code of the American Law Institute: Attempt, Solicitation, and Conspiracy, 61 Col.L.Rev. 957, 963.)
>
> Experience has demonstrated that when conviction of any one defendant in conspiracy prosecutions requires a mutual agreement and a common intent by two or more, societal goals of crime prevention have been and would continue to be frustrated in many cases. Logic and experience dictate a new approach and old "rules, however well established, must be revised when they are found after fair trial to be inconsistent in their workings with an attainment of the ends which law is meant to serve." (Cardozo, The Growth of the Law, p. 120 [1924].) * * *

3. *Opposing the Unilateral View.* People v. Foster, 99 Ill.2d 48, 51–54, 75 Ill. Dec. 411, 412–414, 457 N.E.2d 405, 406–408 (1983):

> * * * The relevant portion of the former statute is as follows:
>
> > "If any *two or more persons* conspire or *agree together* * * * to do any illegal act * * * they shall be deemed guilty of a conspiracy." (Emphasis added.) (Ill.Rev.Stat.1961, ch. 38, par. 139.)
>
> The amended version of the statute provides:
>
> > "*A person* commits conspiracy when, with intent that an offense be committed, *he agrees* with another to the commission of that offense." (Emphasis added.) Ill.Rev.Stat.1981, ch. 38, par. 8–2(a).
>
> Since the statute is presently worded in terms of "a person" rather than "two or more persons" it is urged by the State that only one person need intend to agree to the commission of an offense. * * *

* * *

* * * Similar reasoning was employed in State v. Marian (1980), 62 Ohio St.2d 250, 405 N.E.2d 267, and State v. St. Christopher (1975), 305 Minn. 226, 232 N.W.2d 798, where the courts were asked to interpret statutory provisions analogous to section 8–2(a). In each of those decisions it was determined that deletion of the words "two or more persons" from the State's conspiracy statute reflected a legislative intent to abandon the bilateral theory. The Ohio court, however, also relied to a considerable degree upon the absence from Ohio criminal law of a statute making solicitation to commit a crime an offense. Illinois does have such a statute. Ill.Rev.Stat.1981, ch. 38, par. 8–1.

* * *

As earlier noted, Illinois does have a solicitation statute which embraces virtually every situation in which one could be convicted of conspiracy under the unilateral theory. Moreover, the penalties for solicitation and conspiracy are substantially similar. There would appear to have been little need for the legislature to adopt the unilateral theory of conspiracy in light of the existence of the solicitation statute. Even though the Model Penal Code also contains a separate solicitation offense (Model Penal Code sec. 5.02 (Tent.Draft No. 10, 1960)) and still provides for the unilateral theory, its commentary makes explicit its intent to do so. The absence of similar comments upon our statute seems difficult to explain if the intent was the same.

3. Objective

Commonwealth v. Bessette

Supreme Judicial Court of Massachusetts, 1966.
351 Mass. 148, 217 N.E.2d 893.

CUTTER, JUSTICE.

Bessette, one LeBlanc, and one Paquette were charged in indictments,[1] returned in November, 1961, with conspiracy to violate art. 65 of the "Standard Specifications" [2] of the Division of Waterways (the division) of the

1. The indictments were essentially the same in form except that indictment No. 8175 referred to contract No. 2063 between the Commonwealth and two men named Chace who were copartners doing business as Marine Development Co. and indictment No. 8176 referred to contract No. 2074 between the Commonwealth and Marine Dredging Corp. Indictment No. 8174, which related to contract No. 2038, charges, in part that on or about January 1, 1960, "and on divers other days * * * between that day and the day of the presenting of this indictment [the defendants] did conspire together and with Arnold B. Chace and Malcolm G. Chace * * * [Jr.] to assign the work under [c]ontract Number 2038, dated the first day of June * * * [1960] made by and between the Commonwealth * * * by its Department of Public Works, and * * * [the Chaces], copartners, doing business as Marine Development Co., without the previous written consent of the said Department of Public Works * * * such assignment of work being unlawful * * * and in violation [of] the provisions of Article Sixty-five of the Standard Specifications of the Division of Waterways of the Department of Public Works * * * as they, the said * * * Bessette * * * LeBlanc * * * Paquette * * * and * * * [the Chaces] well knew." * * *

2. Article 65 of the "Standard Specifications" reads, in part, "Subletting or Assignment of Contract. The Contractor shall give his personal attention constantly to the faithful prosecution of the work, shall keep the same under his personal control, and *shall not assign* by power of attorney or otherwise, *or sublet, the work or any part thereof without the previous written consent of the* * * * [*Commonwealth*] and shall not * * * assign any of the moneys payable under this agreement, or his claim thereto, unless by and with the like consent of the * * * [Commonwealth]. He shall be responsible for the acts and omissions of his sub-Contractors, if any, and of all persons directly or indirectly employed by him or them in connection with the work * * *" (emphasis supplied).

Department of Public Works (the department) in connection with certain dredging contracts. * * * Bessette, who in 1959 and 1960 was the head of the division, was found guilty on each indictment. Our discussion of the motions to quash the indictments will be clarified by a brief summary of the background of the case shown by the evidence.

The commissioners of the department on June 1, 1960, after a considerable delay voted to award, upon three sets of bids, dredging contracts to the low bidders, as follows: contract No. 2074 (Popponesset Bay and Creek, Mashpee) to Marine Dredging Corp. (Dredging); contract No. 2038 (Buttermilk Bay, Wareham) to Marine Development Company (Development); and contract No. 2063 (Parker's River, Yarmouth) also to Development. The contracts were thereafter executed.

Contract No. 2074 was the culmination of a long effort to have the Popponesset area dredged. Interests controlled by the Chaces had planned a real estate development on land surrounding Popponesset Creek. * * *

Sometime in February, 1960, one Buswell, an employee of the Chaces, partners in Development, told Bessette that Development wanted to exchange contracts Nos. 2038 (Buttermilk Bay) and 2063 (Parker's River), both later awarded to Development, for No. 2074 (Popponesset) which was later awarded to Dredging. Bessette made suggestions with respect to this exchange.

* * *

* * * [T]he trial judge would have been warranted in concluding (a) that Bessette delayed recommending award of the contracts until the low bidders agreed to assign and "swap" them; (b) that the awards followed promptly upon the "swap" arrangement; (c) that Bessette was fully informed about that arrangement; (d) that Bessette never told the commissioners of the actual arrangement but instead took precautions to conceal it in the face of the commissioners' specific refusal to allow the "swap"; (e) that Bessette, for reasons not wholly plain from the evidence, was actively supporting Development's efforts to do the dredging at Popponesset in which the Chaces had a special interest because of their land ownership; and (f) that these actions were in some degree pursuant to an understanding with representatives of Development. It could have been found that art. 65 had been employed steadily for the protection of the Commonwealth's interests as a part of the division's contracting policy for many years. There was other evidence which tended to cast doubt on the propriety of the transactions.

* * *

1. The three identical motions to quash assert principally that each indictment sets forth no offence. They also assert that there is no averment of any "prejudice to the general public or oppression of any individual."

In Commonwealth v. Dyer, 243 Mass. 472, 485, 138 N.E. 296, 303, it was said, "It is the consensus of opinion that conspiracy as a criminal offence is established when the object of the combination is either a crime, or if not a crime, is unlawful,[5] or when the means contemplated are either criminal, or if

5. There has been adverse criticism of the general principle that a criminal conspiracy may exist where neither the means nor the purpose of an alleged conspiracy, although

not criminal, are illegal, provided that, where no crime is contemplated either as the end or the means, the illegal but noncriminal element involves prejudice to the general welfare or oppression of the individual of sufficient gravity to be injurious to the public interest." See Commonwealth v. Hunt, 4 Metc. 111, 123 (see, however, pp. 127–136); Commonwealth v. Waterman, 122 Mass. 43, 56–57 (holding sufficient an indictment for conspiracy "to cause it falsely to appear" that a marriage has taken place by false personations and representations).[6] Bessette argues that these general principles have not been broadly applied in Massachusetts in recent years. He in effect would have us interpret the term "unlawful" as meaning "criminal." * * *

The recent decisions undoubtedly have tended to apply the principles of criminal conspiracy primarily to group arrangements which have a criminal purpose or contemplate the use of criminal methods. Nevertheless, in view of the *Dyer* case, we are not prepared to say that criminal conspiracy has been completely restricted to this extent. The later discussion in the *Dyer* case, 243 Mass. 472, 489, 138 N.E. 296, 305 (conspiracy for a monopoly) shows that the term "unlawful," in relation to a conspiracy, was thought to include situations where the purpose of a group plan or the proposed means of accomplishing that plan, even if not criminal, involve "an evil intent to oppress and injure the public" (or, perhaps, third persons) by activity, which is "illegal, void and against public policy."

In view of the conclusion which we reach, it is not now necessary to determine precisely when, in situations comparable to that presented in the *Dyer* case, joint action may create additional dangers and risks sufficient to make criminal as a conspiracy an agreement upon a plan for unlawful acts which would not be criminal when done by individuals separately. We think it plain, however, that the term "unlawful," as used in the criminal conspiracy cases (where neither a criminal object nor criminal means are in contemplation), is limited in any event to a narrow range of situations, (a) where there is strong probability (as in the monopolistic plans involved in the *Dyer* case) that the execution of the plan by group action will cause such significant harm to an individual or to the general public, as to be seriously contrary to the public interest, and (b) where the unlawfulness of objective or contemplated means

unlawful, would be criminal if done by an individual. See Perkins, Criminal Law, 531, 538–544; Williams, Criminal Law. The General Part (2d ed.) §§ 221–226; Anderson, Wharton's Criminal Law and Procedure, §§ 82, 93–101; Sayre, Criminal Conspiracy, 35 Harv.L.Rev. 393, 420–427; notes, 62 Harv.L.Rev. 276; 68 Harv.L.Rev. 1056, 1059–1067; 72 Harv.L.Rev. 920, 940–945. See also Krulewitch v. United States, 336 U.S. 440, 445, 449–450, 69 S.Ct. 716, 93 L.Ed. 790; Shaw v. Director of Pub. Prosecutions, [1962] A.C. 220, 269, 276–282, 283, 291, 292–294. Cf. Am.Law Inst., Model Penal Code (Tent. draft No. 10, May 6, 1960), § 5.03, and comments, pp. 96, 102–104. The code confines criminal conspiracy "to cases where the conspiratorial objective is a crime."

6. This court there said, "It is not always essential that the acts contemplated should constitute a criminal offence, for which, without the element of conspiracy, one alone could be indicted. It is the combination of two or more to do something unlawful, either as a means or as an ultimate end, which constitutes the crime; and many acts not punishable by indictment have been held to come within this definition. It is said to be sufficient if the end proposed, or the means to be employed, are *by reason of the power of the combination, particularly dangerous to the public interests,* or particularly injurious to some individual, although not criminal" (emphasis supplied).

is substantial and clear. There is sound reason for such limitation. As Perkins, Criminal Law, 544, points out, a more inclusive definition of "unlawful" might "be held void for vagueness under the Due Process Clause [of the Federal and Massachusetts Constitutions] unless what is * * * proscribed is spelled out with sufficient clearness to guide those who would be law-abiding and to advise defendants of the offense with which they are charged." Even as limited by this opinion, the rule of the *Dyer* case is necessarily indefinite and its application in a particular instance may present serious problems. This circumstance suggests strongly that certainty of statement of the criminal law would be greatly promoted by legislative definition of the types of unlawful, but not criminal, objectives and proposed means which may constitute elements of criminal conspiracy. See e.g. the discussion, infra, of 18 U.S.C. § 371 (1964).

2. The Commonwealth contends that the indictments in effect allege a conspiracy to defraud the Commonwealth by depriving it of the protection of art. 65 of the Standard Specifications. It is argued that at common law a conspiracy to perpetrate a fraud on the government was a crime. See L. Hand, J., in Falter v. United States, 23 F.2d 420, 423 (2d Cir.), and cases discussing forms of "public" fraud, e.g. Rex v. Wheatly, 2 Burr. 1125, 1127. See also Vertue v. Lord Clive, 4 Burr. 2472, 2475–2477. These indictments, however, do not in terms allege a conspiracy to defraud. Thus various Federal cases dealing with the statutory crime of conspiracy to defraud the United States are not controlling. * * *

3. Where there is alleged a conspiracy to commit a criminal offence, an indictment for criminal conspiracy generally in accord with the forms suggested in G.L. (Ter.Ed.) c. 277, § 79 (see p. 3250), will suffice. Commonwealth v. Kiernan, 348 Mass. 29, 33–34, 201 N.E.2d 504. The indictments before us, however, are not for conspiracy to commit a crime. They do not in terms aver (cf. Commonwealth v. Judd, 2 Mass. 329, 335–336) a purpose to defraud or harm seriously the Commonwealth, the general public, or any person. Cf. the Dyer case, 243 Mass. 472, 480, 138 N.E. 296, 301, where the indictments charged a conspiracy to create a monopoly "to cheat and defraud the public." Cf. also the Hunt case, 4 Metc. 111, 121–123. There is no allegation of other facts tending to show that the violation of art. 65 was likely to be of serious or substantial consequence or to cause loss to the Commonwealth, to the public or any stated portion of it, or to any individual. So far as appears from the indictments, the violation was merely a breach of contract and not necessarily a material breach.

In a case where the Commonwealth does not contend that an alleged conspiracy has a crime as its object or contemplates the use of criminal means to accomplish a lawful object, there should be precise averments of facts showing that the alleged agreement is very clearly within the principles stated in the *Dyer* case. The express allegations here fall short of such a showing.

From the very general allegations it could be inferred that Bessette knowingly violated, by agreement with others, whatever department policy lay behind the use of art. 65 in the contracts. No allegations, however, tend to show the significance of that policy or that its violation by combined action (a) would cause loss to the Commonwealth, or any material interference with, or obstruction of, departmental operations, or (b) would be "particularly dangerous to the public interests" (see fn. 6).

* * *

Exceptions sustained.

Notes

1. State v. Buchanan, 5 H. & J. 317, 351, 352 (Md.1821):

> * * * And such is the character of conspiracy, so ramified is it in its nature, the object and tendency of it being that, from which it derives its criminality, that it would be exceedingly difficult to give a single specific definition of the offence. But by a course of decisions running through a space of more than four hundred years, from the reign of Edward III, to the 59 of George III, without a single conflicting adjudication, these points are clearly settled:—
>
> 1st. That the offence of conspiracy is of common law origin, and not restricted or abridged by the Statute 33 Edward I.
>
> 2d. That a conspiracy to do any act that is criminal *per se,* is an indictable offence at common law, for which it can scarcely be necessary to offer any authority.
>
> 3d. That an indictment will lie at common law—1st. For a conspiracy to do an act not illegal, nor punishable if done by an individual, but immoral only. 2d. For a conspiracy to do an act neither illegal nor immoral in an individual, but to effect a purpose, which has a tendency to prejudice the public. * * * 3d. For a conspiracy to extort money from another, or to injure his reputation by means not indictable if practised by an individual, as by verbal defamation, and that, whether it be to charge him with an indictable offence or not. 4th. For a conspiracy to cheat and defraud a third person, accomplished by means of an act which would not in law amount to an indictable cheat, if effected by an individual. 5th. For a malicious conspiracy, to impoverish or ruin a third person in his * trade or profession. 6th. For a conspiracy to defraud a third person by means of an act not per se unlawful, and though no person be thereby injured. 7th. For a bare conspiracy to cheat or defraud a third person, though the means of effecting it should not be determined on at the time * * *. * * *
>
> From all which it results, that every conspiracy to do an unlawful act, or to do a lawful act for an illegal, fraudulent, malicious or corrupt purpose, or for a purpose which has a tendency to prejudice the public in general, is at common law an indictable offence, though nothing be done in execution of it, and no matter by what means the conspiracy was intended to be effected; which may be perfectly indifferent, and makes no ingredient of the crime, and therefore need not be stated in the indictment. * * *

2. In Commonwealth v. Donoghue, 250 Ky. 343, 63 S.W.2d 3 (1933), a conspiracy to exact usurious rates of interest from poor and necessitous wage earners was held indictable, though usury itself was not a crime.

3. Most modern statutory schemes require that the object of a conspiracy be itself a crime, or that criminal methods be contemplated to achieve a lawful result.

4. *Mens Rea*

United States v. Feola

Supreme Court of the United States, 1975.
420 U.S. 671, 95 S.Ct. 1255, 43 L.Ed.2d 541.

MR. JUSTICE BLACKMUN delivered the opinion of the Court.

This case presents the issue whether knowledge that the intended victim is a federal officer is a requisite for the crime of conspiracy, under 18 U.S.C. § 371, to commit an offense violative of 18 U.S.C. § 111,[1] that is, an assault upon a federal officer while engaged in the performance of his official duties.

Respondent Feola and three others (Alsondo, Rosa, and Farr) were indicted for violations of §§ 371 and 111. A jury found all four defendants guilty of both charges. * * *

I

The facts reveal a classic narcotics "rip-off." The details are not particularly important for our present purposes. We need note only that the evidence shows that Feola and his confederates arranged for a sale of heroin to buyers who turned out to be undercover agents for the Bureau of Narcotics and Dangerous Drugs. The group planned to palm off on the purchasers, for a substantial sum, a form of sugar in place of heroin and, should that ruse fail, simply to surprise their unwitting buyers and relieve them of the cash they had brought along for payment. The plan failed when one agent, his suspicions being aroused, drew his revolver in time to counter an assault upon another agent from the rear. Instead of enjoying the rich benefits of a successful swindle, Feola and his associates found themselves charged, to their undoubted surprise, with conspiring to assault, and with assaulting, federal officers.

* * *

The Court of Appeals reversed the conspiracy convictions * * *. The court perceived itself bound by a line of cases, commencing with Judge Learned Hand's opinion in United States v. Crimmins, 123 F.2d 271 (CA2 1941), all holding that scienter of a factual element that confers federal jurisdiction, while unnecessary for conviction of the substantive offense, is required in order to sustain a conviction for conspiracy to commit the substantive offense. * * *

1. "§ 111. Assaulting, resisting, or impeding certain officers or employees.

"Whoever forcibly assaults, resists, opposes, impedes, intimidates, or interferes with any person designated in section 1114 of this title while engaged in or on account of the performance of his official duties, shall be fined not more than $5,000 or imprisoned not more than three years, or both.

"Whoever, in the commission of any such acts uses a deadly or dangerous weapon, shall be fined not more than $10,000 or imprisoned not more than ten years, or both."

Among the persons "designated in section 1114" of 18 U.S.C. is "any officer or employee * * * of the Bureau of Narcotics and Dangerous Drugs."

II

* * *

We conclude, from all this, that in order to effectuate the congressional purpose of according maximum protection to federal officers by making prosecution for assaults upon them cognizable in the federal courts, § 111 cannot be construed as embodying an unexpressed requirement that an assailant be aware that his victim is a federal officer. All the statute requires is an intent to assault, not an intent to assault a federal officer. * * *

* * *

III

Our decisions establish that in order to sustain a judgment of conviction on a charge of conspiracy to violate a federal statute, the Government must prove at least the degree of criminal intent necessary for the substantive offense itself. Respondent Feola urges upon us the proposition that the Government must show a degree of criminal intent in the conspiracy count greater than is necessary to convict for the substantive offense; he urges that even though it is not necessary to show that he was aware of the official identity of his assaulted victims in order to find him guilty of assaulting federal officers, in violation of 18 U.S.C. § 111, the Government nonetheless must show that he was aware that his intended victims were undercover agents, if it is successfully to prosecute him for conspiring to assault federal agents. And the Court of Appeals held that the trial court's failure to charge the jury to this effect constituted plain error.

The general conspiracy statute, 18 U.S.C. § 371, offers no textual support for the proposition that to be guilty of conspiracy a defendant in effect must have known that his conduct violated federal law. The statute makes it unlawful simply to "conspire * * * to commit any offense against the United States." A natural reading of these words would be that since one can violate a criminal statute simply by engaging in the forbidden conduct, a conspiracy to commit that offense is nothing more than an agreement to engage in the prohibited conduct. Then where, as here, the substantive statute does not require that an assailant know the official status of his victim, there is nothing on the face of the conspiracy statute that would seem to require that those agreeing to the assault have a greater degree of knowledge.

* * *

With no support on the face of the general conspiracy statute or in this Court's decisions, respondent relies solely on the line of cases commencing with United States v. Crimmins, 123 F.2d 271 (CA2 1941), for the principle that the Government must prove "antifederal" intent in order to establish liability under § 371. In *Crimmins,* the defendant had been found guilty of conspiring to receive stolen bonds that had been transported in interstate commerce. Upon review, the Court of Appeals pointed out that the evidence failed to establish that Crimmins actually knew the stolen bonds had moved into the State. Accepting for the sake of argument the assumption that such knowledge was not necessary to sustain a conviction on the substantive offense, Judge Learned Hand nevertheless concluded that to permit conspiratorial liability where the conspirators were ignorant of the federal implications of their acts would be to enlarge their agreement beyond its terms as they understood them. He capsulized the distinction in what has become well known as his "traffic light" analogy:

> "While one may, for instance, be guilty of running past a traffic light of whose existence one is ignorant, one cannot be guilty of conspiring to run past such a light, for one cannot agree to run past a light unless one supposes that there is a light to run past." Id., at 273.

* * *

The question posed by the traffic light analogy is not before us, just as it was not before the Second Circuit in *Crimmins.* Criminal liability, of course, may be imposed on one who runs a traffic light regardless of whether he harbored the "evil intent" of disobeying the light's command; whether he drove so recklessly as to be unable to perceive the light; whether, thinking he was observing all traffic rules, he simply failed to notice the light; or whether, having been reared elsewhere, he thought that the light was only an ornament. Traffic violations generally fall into that category of offenses that dispense with a *mens rea* requirement. See United States v. Dotterweich, 320 U.S. 277, 64 S.Ct. 134, 88 L.Ed. 48 (1943). These laws embody the social judgment that it is fair to punish one who intentionally engages in conduct that creates a risk to others, even though no risk is intended or the actor, through no fault of his own, is completely unaware of the existence of any risk. The traffic light analogy poses the question whether it is fair to punish parties to an agreement to engage intentionally in apparently innocent conduct where the unintended result of engaging in that conduct is the violation of a criminal statute.

But this case does not call upon us to answer this question, and we decline to do so * * *. * * *

* * * In *Crimmins,* the substantive offense, namely, the receipt of stolen securities that had been in interstate commerce, proscribed clearly wrongful conduct. Such conduct could not be engaged in without an intent to accomplish the forbidden result. So, too, it is with assault, the conduct forbidden by the substantive statute, § 111, presently before us. One may run a traffic light "of whose existence one is ignorant," but assaulting another "of whose existence one is ignorant," probably would require unearthly intervention. Thus, the traffic light analogy, even if it were a correct statement of the law, is inapt, for the conduct proscribed by the substantive offense, here assault, is not of the type outlawed without regard to the intent of the actor to accomplish the result that is made criminal. If the analogy has any vitality at all, it is to conduct of the latter variety; that, however, is a question we save for another day. We hold here only that where a substantive offense embodies only a requirement of *mens rea* as to each of its elements, the general federal conspiracy statute requires no more.

The *Crimmins* rule rests upon another foundation: that it is improper to find conspiratorial liability where the parties to the illicit agreement were not aware of the fact giving rise to federal jurisdiction, because the essence of conspiracy is agreement and persons cannot be punished for acts beyond the scope of their agreement. 123 F.2d, at 273. This "reason" states little more than a conclusion, for it is clear that one may be guilty as a conspirator for acts the precise details of which one does not know at the time of the agreement. * * *

Our analysis of the substantive offense in Part II, supra, is sufficient to convince us that for the purpose of individual guilt or innocence, awareness of the official identity of the assault victim is irrelevant. We would expect the same to obtain with respect to the conspiracy offense unless one of the policies behind the imposition of conspiratorial liability is not served where the parties to the agreement are unaware that the intended target is a federal law enforcement official.

It is well settled that the law of conspiracy serves ends different from, and complementary to, those served by criminal prohibitions of the substantive offense. Because of this, consecutive sentences may be imposed for the conspiracy and for the underlying crime. Our decisions have identified two independent values served by the law of conspiracy. The first is protection of society from the dangers of concerted criminal activity. That individuals know that their planned joint venture violates federal as well as state law seems totally irrelevant to that purpose of conspiracy law which seeks to protect society from the dangers of concerted criminal activity. Given the level of criminal intent necessary to sustain conviction for the substantive offense, the act of agreement to commit the crime is no less opprobrious and no less dangerous because of the absence of knowledge of a fact unnecessary to the formation of criminal intent. Indeed, unless imposition of an "anti-federal" knowledge requirement serves social purposes external to the law of conspiracy of which we are unaware, its imposition here would serve only to make it more difficult to obtain convictions on charges of conspiracy, a policy with no apparent purpose.

The second aspect is that conspiracy is an inchoate crime. This is to say, that, although the law generally makes criminal only antisocial conduct, at some point in the continuum between preparation and consummation, the likelihood of a commission of an act is sufficiently great and the criminal intent sufficiently well formed to justify the intervention of the criminal law. * * *

Again, we do not see how imposition of a strict "anti-federal" scienter requirement would relate to this purpose of conspiracy law. Given the level of intent needed to carry out the substantive offense, we fail to see how the agreement is any less blameworthy or constitutes less of a danger to society solely because the participants are unaware which body of law they intend to violate. Therefore, we again conclude that imposition of a requirement of knowledge of those facts that serve only to establish federal jurisdiction would render it more difficult to serve the policy behind the law of conspiracy without serving any other apparent social policy.

We hold, then, that assault of a federal officer pursuant to an agreement to assault is not, even in the words of Judge Hand, "beyond the reasonable intendment of the common understanding," United States v. Crimmins, 123 F.2d, at 273. The agreement is not thereby enlarged, for knowledge of the official identity of the victim is irrelevant to the essential nature of the agreement, entrance into which is made criminal by the law of conspiracy.

* * *

To summarize, with the exception of the infrequent situation in which reference to the knowledge of the parties to an illegal agreement is necessary to establish the existence of federal jurisdiction, we hold that where knowledge of the facts giving rise to federal jurisdiction is not necessary for conviction of a substantive offense embodying a *mens rea* requirement, such knowledge is equally irrelevant to questions of responsibility for conspiracy to commit that offense.

The judgment of the Court of Appeals with respect to the respondent's conspiracy conviction is reversed.

* * *

MR. JUSTICE STEWART, with whom MR. JUSTICE DOUGLAS joins, dissenting.

* * *

For the reasons stated, I believe that before there can be a violation of 18 U.S.C. § 111, an assailant must know or have reason to know that the person he assaults is an officer. It follows *a fortiori* that there can be no criminal conspiracy to violate the statute in the absence of at least equivalent knowledge. Accordingly, I respectfully dissent from the opinion and judgment of the Court.

People v. Lauria

California Court of Appeal, Second District, 1967.
251 Cal.App.2d 471, 59 Cal.Rptr. 628.

FLEMING, ASSOCIATE JUSTICE.

In an investigation of call-girl activity the police focused their attention on three prostitutes actively plying their trade on call, each of whom was using Lauria's telephone answering service, presumably for business purposes.

On January 8, 1965, Stella Weeks, a policewoman, signed up for telephone service with Lauria's answering service. Mrs. Weeks, in the course of her conversation with Lauria's office manager, hinted broadly that she was a prostitute concerned with the secrecy of her activities and their concealment from the police. She was assured that the operation of the service was discreet and "about as safe as you can get." It was arranged that Mrs. Weeks need not leave her address with the answering service, but could pick up her calls and pay her bills in person.

On February 11, Mrs. Weeks talked to Lauria on the telephone and told him her business was modelling and she had been referred to the answering service by Terry, one of the three prostitutes under investigation. She complained that because of the operation of the service she had lost two valuable customers, referred to as tricks. Lauria defended his service and said that her friends had probably lied to her about having left calls for her. But he did not respond to Mrs. Weeks' hints that she needed customers in order to make money, other than to invite her to his house for a personal visit in order to get better acquainted. In the course of his talk he said "his business was taking messages."

On February 15, Mrs. Weeks talked on the telephone to Lauria's office manager and again complained of two lost calls, which she described as a $50 and a $100 trick. On investigation the office manager could find nothing wrong, but she said she would alert the switchboard operators about slip-ups on calls.

On April 1 Lauria and the three prostitutes were arrested. Lauria complained to the police that this attention was undeserved, stating that Hollywood Call Board had 60 to 70 prostitutes on its board while his own service had only 9 or 10, that he kept separate records for known or suspected prostitutes for the convenience of himself and the police. When asked if his records were available to police who might come to the office to investigate call girls, Lauria replied that they were whenever the police had a specific name. However, his service didn't "arbitrarily tell the police about prostitutes on our board. As long as they pay their bills we tolerate them." In a subsequent voluntary appearance before the Grand Jury Lauria testified he had always cooperated with the police. But he admitted he knew some of his customers were prostitutes, and he knew Terry was a prostitute because he had personally used her services, and he knew she was paying for 500 calls a month.

Lauria and the three prostitutes were indicted for conspiracy to commit prostitution, and nine overt acts were specified. Subsequently the trial court set aside the indictment as having been brought without reasonable or probable cause. (Pen.Code, § 995.) The People have appealed, claiming that a sufficient showing of an unlawful agreement to further prostitution was made.

* * * Here the People attempted to establish a conspiracy by showing that Lauria, well aware that his codefendants were prostitutes who received business calls from customers through his telephone answering service, continued to furnish them with such service. This approach attempts to equate knowledge of another's criminal activity with conspiracy to further such criminal activity, and poses the question of the criminal responsibility of a furnisher of goods or services who knows his product is being used to assist the operation of an illegal business. Under what circumstances does a supplier become a part of a conspiracy to further an illegal enterprise by furnishing goods or services which he knows are to be used by the buyer for criminal purposes?

The two leading cases on this point face in opposite directions. In United States v. Falcone, 311 U.S. 205, 61 S.Ct. 204, 85 L.Ed. 128, the sellers of large quantities of sugar, yeast, and cans were absolved from participation in a moonshining conspiracy among distillers who bought from them, while in Direct Sales Co. v. United States, 319 U.S. 703, 63 S.Ct. 1265, 87 L.Ed. 1674, a wholesaler of drugs was convicted of conspiracy to violate the federal narcotic laws by selling drugs in quantity to a codefendant physician who was supplying them to addicts. The distinction between these two cases appears primarily based on the proposition that distributors of such dangerous products as drugs are required to exercise greater discrimination in the conduct of their business than are distributors of innocuous substances like sugar and yeast.

In the earlier case, *Falcone,* the sellers' knowledge of the illegal use of the goods was insufficient by itself to make the sellers participants in a conspiracy with the distillers who bought from them. Such knowledge fell short of proof of a conspiracy, and evidence on the volume of sales was too vague to support a jury finding that respondents knew of the conspiracy from the size of the sales alone.

In the later case of *Direct Sales,* the conviction of a drug wholesaler for conspiracy to violate federal narcotic laws was affirmed on a showing that it had actively promoted the sale of morphine sulphate in quantity and had sold codefendant physician, who practiced in a small town in South Carolina, more than 300 times his normal requirements of the drug, even though it had been repeatedly warned of the dangers of unrestricted sales of the drug. The court contrasted the restricted goods involved in *Direct Sales* with the articles of free commerce involved in *Falcone:* "All articles of commerce may be put to illegal ends," said the court. "But all do not have inherently the same susceptibility to harmful and illegal use. * * * This difference is important for two purposes. One is for making certain that the seller knows the buyer's intended illegal use. The other is to show that by the sale he intends to further, promote and cooperate in it. This intent, when given effect by overt act, is the gist of conspiracy. While it is not identical with mere knowledge that another purposes unlawful action, it is not unrelated to such knowledge. * * * The step from knowledge to intent and agreement may be taken. There is more than suspicion, more than knowledge, acquiescence, carelessness, indifference, lack of concern. There is informed and interested cooperation, stimulation, instigation. And there is also a 'stake in the venture' which, even if it may not be essential, is not irrelevant to the question of conspiracy." (319 U.S. at 710–713, 63 S.Ct. at 1269–1270.)

While *Falcone* and *Direct Sales* may not be entirely consistent with each other in their full implications, they do provide us with a framework for the criminal liability of a supplier of lawful goods or services put to unlawful use. Both the element of *knowledge* of the illegal use of the goods or services and the element of *intent* to further that use must be present in order to make the supplier a participant in a criminal conspiracy.

* * * On this record we think the prosecution is entitled to claim positive knowledge by Lauria of the use of his service to facilitate the business of prostitution.

The more perplexing issue in the case is the sufficiency of proof of *intent* to further the criminal enterprise. The element of intent may be proved either by direct evidence, or by evidence of circumstances from which an intent to further a criminal enterprise by supplying lawful goods or services may be inferred. * * *

In the case at bench the prosecution argues that since Lauria knew his customers were using his service for illegal purposes but nevertheless continued to furnish it to them, he must have intended to assist them in carrying out their illegal activities. * * *

In examining precedents in this field we find that sometimes, but not always, the criminal intent of the supplier may be inferred from his knowledge of the unlawful use made of the product he supplies. Some consideration of characteristic patterns may be helpful.

1. Intent may be inferred from knowledge, when the purveyor of legal goods for illegal use has acquired a stake in the venture. (United States v. Falcone, 2 Cir., 109 F.2d 579, 581.) For example, in Regina v. Thomas, (1957), 2 All.E.R. 181, 342, a prosecution for living off the earnings of prostitution, the evidence showed that the accused, knowing the woman to be a convicted prostitute, agreed to let her have the use of his room between the hours of 9 p.m. and 2 a.m. for a charge of £3 a night. The Court of Criminal Appeal refused an appeal from the conviction, holding that when the accused rented a room at a grossly inflated rent to a prostitute for the purpose of carrying on her trade, a jury could find he was living on the earnings of prostitution.

In the present case, no proof was offered of inflated charges for the telephone answering services furnished the codefendants.

2. Intent may be inferred from knowledge, when no legitimate use for the goods or services exists. The leading California case is People v. McLaughlin, 111 Cal.App.2d 781, 245 P.2d 1076, in which the court upheld a conviction of the suppliers of horse-racing information by wire for conspiracy to promote bookmaking, when it had been established that wireservice information had no other use than to supply information needed by bookmakers to conduct illegal gambling operations.

In Rex v. Delaval (1763) 3 Burr. 1434, 97 E.R. 913, the charge was unlawful conspiracy to remove a girl from the control of Bates, a musician to whom she was bound as an apprentice, and place her in the hands of Sir Francis Delaval for the purpose of prostitution. Lord Mansfield not only upheld the charges against Bates and Sir Francis, but also against Fraine, the attorney who drew up the indentures of apprenticeship transferring custody of the girl from Bates to Sir Francis. Fraine, said Lord Mansfield, must have known that Sir Francis had no facilities for teaching music to apprentices so that it was impossible for him to have been ignorant of the real intent of the transaction.

In Shaw v. Director of Public Prosecutions, [1962] A.C. 220, the defendant was convicted of conspiracy to corrupt public morals and of living on the earnings of prostitution, when he published a directory consisting almost entirely of advertisements of the names, addresses, and specialized talents of prostitutes. Publication of such a directory, said the court, could have no legitimate use and serve no other purpose than to advertise the professional services of the prostitutes whose advertisements appeared in the directory. The publisher could be deemed a participant in the profits from the business activities of his principal advertisers.

Other services of a comparable nature came to mind: the manufacturer of crooked dice and marked cards who sells his product to gambling casinos; the tipster who furnishes information on the movement of law enforcement officers to known lawbreakers. (Cf. Jackson v. State of Texas, 164 Tex.Cr.R.

276, 298 S.W.2d 837 (1957), where the furnisher of signaling equipment used to warn gamblers of the police was convicted of aiding the equipping of a gambling place.) In such cases the supplier must necessarily have an intent to further the illegal enterprise since there is no known honest use for his goods.

However, there is nothing in the furnishing of telephone answering service which would necessarily imply assistance in the performance of illegal activities. Nor is any inference to be derived from the use of an answering service by women, either in any particular volume of calls, or outside normal working hours. Night-club entertainers, registered nurses, faith healers, public stenographers, photographic models, and free lance substitute employees, provide examples of women in legitimate occupations whose employment might cause them to receive a volume of telephone calls at irregular hours.

3. Intent may be inferred from knowledge, when the volume of business with the buyer is grossly disproportionate to any legitimate demand, or when sales for illegal use amount to a high proportion of the seller's total business. In such cases an intent to participate in the illegal enterprise may be inferred from the quantity of the business done. For example, in *Direct Sales,* supra, the sale of narcotics to a rural physician in quantities 300 times greater than he would have normal use for provided potent evidence of an intent to further the illegal activity. In the same case the court also found significant the fact that the wholesaler had attracted as customers a disproportionately large group of physicians who had been convicted of violating the Harrison Act. In Shaw v. Director of Public Prosecutions, [1962] A.C. 220, almost the entire business of the directory came from prostitutes.

No evidence of any unusual volume of business with prostitutes was presented by the prosecution against Lauria.

* * *

Yet there are cases in which it cannot reasonably be said that the supplier has a stake in the venture or has acquired a special interest in the enterprise, but in which he has been held liable as a participant on the basis of knowledge alone. * * * In Regina v. Bainbridge (1959), 3 W.L.R. 656 (CCA 6), a supplier of oxygen-cutting equipment to one known to intend to use it to break into a bank was convicted as an accessory to the crime. In Sykes v. Director of Public Prosecutions [1962] A.C. 528, one having knowledge of the theft of 100 pistols, 4 submachine guns, and 1960 rounds of ammunition was convicted of misprision of felony for failure to disclose the theft to the public authorities. It seems apparent from these cases that a supplier who furnishes equipment which he *knows* will be used to commit a serious crime may be deemed from that knowledge alone to have intended to produce the result. Such proof may justify an inference that the furnisher intended to aid the execution of the crime and that he thereby became a participant. For instance, we think the operator of a telephone answering service with positive knowledge that his service was being used to facilitate the extortion of ransom, the distribution of heroin, or the passing of counterfeit money who continued to furnish the service with knowledge of its use, might be chargeable on knowledge alone with participation in a scheme to extort money, to distribute narcotics, or to pass counterfeit money. The same result would follow the seller of gasoline who knew the buyer was using his product to make Molotov cocktails for terroristic use.

Logically, the same reasoning could be extended to crimes of every description. Yet we do not believe an inference of intent drawn from knowledge of criminal use properly applies to the less serious crimes classified as misdemeanors. The duty to take positive action to dissociate oneself from activities helpful to violations of the criminal law as far stronger and more compelling for felonies than it is for misdemeanors or petty offenses. In this respect, as in others, the distinction between felonies and misdemeanors, between more serious and less serious crime, retains continuing vitality. * * *

* * *

With respect to misdemeanors, we conclude that positive knowledge of the supplier that his products or services are being used for criminal purposes does not, without more, establish an intent of the supplier to participate in the misdemeanors. With respect to felonies, we do not decide the converse, viz. that in all cases of felony knowledge of criminal use alone may justify an inference of the supplier's intent to participate in the crime. The implications of *Falcone* make the matter uncertain with respect to those felonies which are merely prohibited wrongs. See also Holman v. Johnson, 98 E.R. 1120, (1775) (sale and delivery of tea at Dunkirk known to be destined for smuggling into England not an illegal contract). But decision on this point is not compelled, and we leave the matter open.

From this analysis of precedent we deduce the following rule: the intent of a supplier who knows of the criminal use to which his supplies are put to participate in the criminal activity connected with the use of his supplies may be established by (1) direct evidence that he intends to participate, or (2) through an inference that he intends to participate based on, (a) his special interest in the activity, or (b) the aggravated nature of the crime itself.

When we review Lauria's activities in the light of this analysis, we find no proof that Lauria took any direct action to further, encourage, or direct the call-girl activities of his codefendants and we find an absence of circumstances from which his special interest in their activities could be inferred. Neither excessive charges for standardized services, nor the furnishing of services without a legitimate use, nor an unusual quantity of business with call girls, are present. The offense which he is charged with furthering is a misdemeanor, a category of crime which has never been made a required subject of positive disclosure to public authority. Under these circumstances, although proof of Lauria's knowledge of the criminal activities of his patrons was sufficient to charge him with that fact, there was insufficient evidence that he intended to further their criminal activities, and hence insufficient proof of his participation in a criminal conspiracy with his codefendants to further prostitution. * * *

In absolving Lauria of complicity in a criminal conspiracy we do not wish to imply that the public authorities are without remedies to combat modern manifestations of the world's oldest profession. Licensing of telephone answering services under the police power, together with the revocation of licenses for the toleration of prostitution, is a possible civil remedy. The furnishing of telephone answering service in aid of prostitution could be made a crime. (Cf. Pen.Code, § 316, which makes it a misdemeanor to let an apartment with knowledge of its use for prostitution.) Other solutions will doubtless occur to vigilant public authorities if the problem of call-girl activity needs further suppression.

The order is affirmed.

HERNDON, J., concurs.

ROTH, P.J., concurs in the judgment.

Note

Model Penal Code, § 5.03, Comment 2: *

2. *Definition of Conspiracy.* * * *

* * *

(c) *Requirements of Culpability.* * * *

Ordinarily a crime is defined in terms of proscribed conduct or a proscribed result under specified attendant circumstances, and the actor's state of mind—whether he must act purposely, knowingly, recklessly, or negligently—with respect to each of these elements. One difficulty common to the definition of all inchoate crimes is that the definition must be expressed in terms of preparation to commit another crime that is the object of the preparation; the definition must take account of both the policy of the inchoate crime and the policies, varying elements, and culpability requirements of all substantive crimes. This problem is particularly difficult in conspiracy. The traditional definition said nothing about the actor's state of mind except insofar as the concept of agreement itself carries certain implications about his attitude toward the crime. It was left to the cases to determine the standards of culpability required by the inchoate nature of the crime of conspiracy and by the fact that it involves much accessorial behavior, and to relate these standards to the concept of agreement and the culpability requirements of substantive crimes.

Subsection (1) endeavors to provide more precise standards for meeting these problems. It requires in all cases a "purpose to promote or facilitate" commission of the crime. In addition it requires that the actor agree either that he or one or more of the persons with whom he conspires will engage in conduct that constitutes the crime or that he will aid in the planning or commission of the crime. The operation of these provisions is best illustrated by viewing them against the specific problems that have arisen in the decisions.

(i) *Requirement of Purpose.* The purpose requirement is crucial to the resolution of the difficult problems presented when a charge of conspiracy is levelled against a person whose relationship to a criminal plan is essentially peripheral. Typical is the case of the person who sells sugar to the producers of illicit whiskey. He may have little interest in the success of the distilling operation and be motivated mainly by the desire to make the normal profit from an otherwise lawful sale. To be criminally liable, of course, he must at least have knowledge of the use to which the materials are being put, but the difficult issue presented is whether knowingly facilitating the commission of a crime ought to be sufficient, absent a true purpose to advance the criminal end. In this case conflicting interests are involved: that of the vendors in freedom to engage in gainful and otherwise lawful activities without policing their vendees, and that of the community in preventing behavior that facilitates the commission of crimes. The decisions are in conflict although many of those requiring purpose properly emphasize that it can be inferred from such circumstances as, for example, quantity sales, the seller's initiative or encouragement, continuity of the relationship, and the contraband nature of the materials sold. The considerations are the same whether the charge be conspiracy or complicity in the substantive crime; and in the complicity provision of the Code the Institute resolved them in favor of requiring a purpose to advance the criminal end. Under the conspiracy provision, the same purpose requirement that governs complicity is essential for conspiracy; the actor must have "the purpose of promoting or facilitating" the commission of the crime.

* * *

It is worth noting, further, that in relation to those elements of substantive crimes that consist of proscribed conduct or undesirable results of conduct, the Code requires purposeful behavior for guilt of conspiracy, regardless of the state of mind required by the definition of the substantive crime. If the crime is defined in terms of prohibited conduct, such as the sale of narcotics, the actor's purpose must be to promote or facilitate the engaging in of such conduct by himself or another. If it is defined in terms of a result of conduct, such as homicide, his purpose must be to promote or facilitate the production of that result. Thus, it would not be sufficient, as it is under the attempt provision of the Code, if the actor only believed that the result would be produced but did not consciously plan or desire to produce it. For example, if two persons plan to destroy a building by detonating a bomb, though they know and believe that there are inhabitants in the building who will be killed by the explosion, they are nevertheless guilty only of a conspiracy to destroy the building and not of a conspiracy to kill the inhabitants. While this result may seem unduly restrictive from the viewpoint of the completed crime, it is necessitated by the extremely preparatory behavior that may be involved in conspiracy. Had the crime been completed or had the preparation progressed even to the stage of an attempt, the result would be otherwise. As to the attempt, knowledge or belief that the inhabitants would be killed would suffice. As to the liability of one who renders aid for the completed crime, a special provision in Section 2.06 covers the matter, despite the general complicity requirement of a purpose to promote or facilitate the commission of the crime. Under that provision, when causing a particular result is an element of a crime, a person is an accomplice in the crime if he was an accomplice in the behavior that caused the result and shared the same purpose or knowledge with respect to the result that is required by the definition of the crime.

A fortiori, when recklessness or negligence suffices for the actor's culpability with respect to a result element of a substantive crime, as for example when homicide through negligence is made criminal, there could not be a conspiracy to commit that crime. This should be distinguished, however, from a crime defined in terms of conduct that creates a risk of harm, such as reckless driving or driving above a certain speed limit. In this situation the conduct rather than any result it may produce is the element of the crime, and it would suffice for guilt of conspiracy that the actor's purpose was to promote or facilitate such conduct—for example, if he urged the driver of the car to go faster and faster.

The culpability requirements of conspiracy with respect to the third class of elements of substantive crimes, those involving the attendant circumstances, have proven resistant to judicial resolution. The following discussion addresses these problems in terms of the Model Code formulation.

(ii) *Culpability with Respect to Circumstance Elements.* The attempt definition requires that, as to attendant circumstance elements of the substantive crime, the actor have the same kind of culpability that is required for commission of the substantive crime. Thus, if it is a federal offense to kill an FBI agent and negligence as to the identity of the victim suffices for commission of the substantive crime, an actor who attempts to kill such an agent with negligence as to his identity would be guilty of an attempt to commit the crime.

This rule is consonant with the theories underlying inchoate criminality. If something less than knowledge—for example, recklessness, negligence, or strict liability—concerning certain circumstances suffices for a given crime, it represents a judgment that the actor's lesser awareness concerning those circumstances does not decrease his culpability or the offensiveness of his behavior below the point where criminality should be declared. * * * If an actor sets out with the purpose of engaging in the proscribed conduct or producing the undesirable result with the lesser culpability concerning attendant circumstances that suffices for commission of the crime, and his preparation progresses to the point of a conspiracy or attempt, the reasons for reaching his behavior as an inchoate crime are in no way decreased by such lesser culpability concerning the circumstances.

The fact that conspiracy is defined in terms of an agreement produces difficulties, however, with respect to the requisite awareness by the conspirator of those circumstance elements regarding which something less than knowledge suffices for the substantive crime. The problem has arisen most often in federal cases in which some circumstance that affords a basis for federal jurisdiction, such as use of the mails or crossing state lines, is made an element of the crime. Prior to the Supreme Court's apparent adoption in 1975 in United States v. Feola[90] of the Model Code's approach, most decisions involving such offenses held that although knowledge of the jurisdictional element is unnecessary for guilt of the substantive crime, it is necessary for guilt of conspiracy to commit that crime.[91] In a prosecution for use of the mails to defraud, for example, it is sufficient if the mails were in fact used for the purpose of furthering the scheme, while for conspiracy to commit

90. 420 U.S. 671.

91. E.g., United States v. Cimini, 427 F.2d 129 (6th Cir.), cert. denied, 400 U.S. 911 (1970) (stealing goods in interstate commerce) * * *.

that crime it was said that the defendants must have contemplated that the mails would be so used.[92] * * *

* * *

The conspiracy provision in the Code does not attempt to solve the problem by explicit formulation, nor have the recent legislative revisions. Here, as in the section on complicity, it was believed that the matter is best left to judicial resolution as cases that present the question may arise, and that the formulations proposed afford sufficient flexibility for satisfactory decision. Under Subsection (1) of Section 5.03 it is enough that the object of the agreement is "conduct that constitutes the crime," which can be held to import no more than the mental state required for the substantive offense into the agreement to commit it. Although the agreement must be made "with the purpose of promoting or facilitating the commission of the crime," it is arguable, though by no means certain, that such a purpose may be proved although the actor did not know of the existence of a circumstance, which did exist in fact, when knowledge of the circumstance is not required for the substantive offense. Rather than press the matter further in this section, the Institute deliberately left the matter to interpretation in the context in which the issue is presented. Too many variations, many of which cannot be foreseen with any confidence, could otherwise be expected to arise and undermine any more rigid formula.

* * *

5. Liability for Acts of Others

State v. Small

Supreme Court of North Carolina, 1980.
301 N.C. 407, 272 S.E.2d 128.

EXUM, JUSTICE.

The state's evidence tends to show that defendant hired another to murder defendant's estranged wife and that she was murdered by the one so hired. Defendant has been convicted of the murder and sentenced to death. The most important question, therefore, raised by defendant's appeal is whether one who is an accessory before the fact to a felony within the meaning of G.S. 14–5 may be convicted and punished as a principal perpetrator, once the crime is committed, on the theory that he participated in a conspiracy to commit the offense charged. We hold that he may not.

* * *

I

Defendant argues that since there was no evidence adduced at trial that he was actually or constructively present during the killing of his wife, he was criminally liable at most as an accessory before the fact to her murder. Since G.S. 14–6 provides for the punishment of life imprisonment for an accessory before the fact to murder, defendant contends that the sentence of death imposed upon him cannot stand. We agree.

* * *

92. Burns v. United States, 279 F. 982, 986–87 (8th Cir.1922) * * *.

* * * We focus not upon the crime of conspiracy *per se* but rather upon the scope of a conspirator's substantive liability for a criminal offense committed by his fellow coconspirators in his absence within the scope of, or in furtherance of, the original agreement.

One need not go far to find such familiar statements as the following:

> "A conspirator is criminally responsible for the acts of his co-conspirators which are committed in furtherance of the common design and follow incidentally as the natural and probable consequences of such design, even though he was not present when the acts were committed * * *." 15A C.J.S. *Conspiracy* § 74 (1967).

* * *

When interpreted as rules of substantive liability, statements such as these would seem to render immaterial any inquiry into whether a criminal defendant who has conspired with others to commit a completed offense should be viewed as a principal or accessory. Instead, the quoted "black letter" appears to stand for the proposition that any defendant, having once agreed with others to further an unlawful enterprise, *ipso facto* becomes liable as a principal to any crimes committed thereafter by his partners so long as the criminal acts are "in the furtherance" of or reasonably "incidental" to the original illegal design. Such a broad reading leads to the rather startling result that a conspirator's criminal liability for the act of another may be based less upon the circumstances of his personal participation than upon his presumed status as "partner" in all actions which proximately result from the venture originally agreed upon. Fictions and presumptions derived from the civil law of agency and partnership thus commingle with tort law notions of foreseeability and proximate cause to provide a stew of expanded criminal liability. We recognize that the rule adopted for federal prosecutions in Pinkerton v. United States, 328 U.S. 640, 66 S.Ct. 1180, 90 L.Ed. 1489 (1946), appears to sanction such a result. Defendant there was convicted both of conspiring with his brother to evade federal taxes and for the subsequent acts of evasion committed by his brother while defendant was in jail. The trial court had instructed the jury that they could convict defendant of the offenses committed by his brother upon a finding that the offenses were committed in the furtherance of the original conspiracy. The Supreme Court affirmed. Writing for the majority, Mr. Justice Douglas first noted that it was well settled in federal case law of conspiracy that the overt act of one conspirator may be deemed the act of all. 328 U.S. at 646–47, 66 S.Ct. at 1183–84. By analogy, then, it seemed reasonable to hold all conspirators liable for the substantive offenses committed by one of them:

> "The rule which holds responsible one who counsels, procures, or commands another to commit a crime is founded on the same principle. That principle is recognized in the law of conspiracy when the overt act of one partner is attributable to all. An overt act is an essential ingredient of the crime of conspiracy under [the Federal Criminal Code]. If that can be supplied by the act of one conspirator, we fail to see why the same or other acts in furtherance

of the conspiracy are likewise not attributable to the others for the purpose of holding them responsible for the substantive offense." Id. at 647, 66 S.Ct. at 1184.

By holding in effect that membership in a conspiracy is sufficient for criminal liability as a principal for all offenses committed in furtherance of the conspiracy, the *Pinkerton* decision obviates application of common law or statutory distinctions among the various parties to a criminal offense.

We are not so free to do the same with the law of this state. As earlier noted, the distinction between an accessory before the fact and a principal to a criminal offense is well maintained both in our cases and in our legislation. The distinction is of more than academic importance. Our General Assembly has mandated that an accessory before the fact to a felony be indicted and convicted as such, G.S. 14–5.1, and, upon conviction, be punished as such. G.S. 14–6. * * * Accordingly, we join the ranks of those who reject the rule in *Pinkerton.*[7] We hold that a defendant who was not actually or constructively present at the commission of a crime may not be convicted as a principal to that crime solely upon the basis that he participated in a conspiracy by counseling, procuring, or commanding some other person to bring it about. To hold otherwise would be to expand the scope of accessorial liability beyond the legislative design.

* * *

* * * The coconspirator rule—the well established proposition that the acts and declarations of one conspirator, made or done in the furtherance of or within the scope of the original conspiracy, may be imputed to other conspirators who were not present at the time—is a valid and useful *evidentiary* rule when it is used to establish the existence and extent of the conspiracy itself or the nature and extent of the accomplishment of the conspiracy's object. It means, in essence, that such acts and declarations of one coconspirator are *admissible* against all. Thus applied *as a rule of evidence,* it does no more than permit the jury the logical inference that one who conspires to bring about a result intends the accomplishment of that result, or of anything which naturally flows from its attempted accomplishment. When one who so conspires is shown to have been present at the commission of the crime, contemplated by or a natural consequence of the original conspiracy, evidence of the conspiracy, including the conspiratorial acts and declarations of all the conspirators, may then be relevant to show his intent and participatory presence, i.e., that he aided and abetted in the

7. Despite its force in the federal courts, the *Pinkerton* rule has never gained broad acceptance. It has been heavily criticized by legal commentators. See, e.g., 56 Yale L.J. 371 (1947); 16 Fordham L.Rev. 275 (1947); Developments in the Law, *Criminal Conspiracy,* 72 Harv.L.Rev. 920, 994–1000 (1959). It was rejected by the draftsmen of the Model Penal Code and of the proposed new Federal Criminal Code. See LaFave and Scott, Criminal Law § 65 at p. 515, notes 15 and 16. Finally, it has been flatly rejected by the highest courts of both Massachusetts, Commonwealth v. Stasiun, 349 Mass. 38, 206 N.E.2d 672 (1965), and New York, People v. McGee, 49 N.Y.2d 48, 424 N.Y.S.2d 157, 399 N.E.2d 1177 (1979). It is true that under the Model Penal Code, § 2.06 (Proposed Official Draft, 1962), § 2.04 (Tent. Draft No. 1, 1953) persons who solicit, command, request, or provoke another to commit a crime may be found guilty of the crime itself. Our statutes, however, G.S. 14–5 and G.S. 14–6, make such persons guilty and punishable only as accessories before the fact to the crime.

commission of the crime, or acted in concert with those who did, in which event he is substantively liable as a principal. Likewise, when the defendant-conspirator is shown to have been absent from the scene of the crime, evidence of the conspiracy may nevertheless be relevant to support the state's theory that the defendant participated as an accessory before the fact. In either case the coconspirator rule is a rule of evidence, the fruits of which may be accepted or rejected by the jury in determining whether a defendant's participation in the criminal acts of another rises to the level of establishing his guilt as a principal *or* an accessory before the fact.[9]

In sum, a defendant's conspiratorial involvement may often be strong evidence of his liability *as a party* to a crime which arose out of the conspiracy. His status as a party—whether he is to be deemed a principal or an accessory before the fact—will nevertheless turn upon his presence at or absence from the place of the crime's commission.[10] His involvement in the conspiracy itself will not *alone* make him a principal, or, for that matter, an accessory either. People v. McGee, 49 N.Y.2d 48, 424 N.Y.S.2d 157, 399 N.E.2d 1177 (1979).[11] * * *

* * *

As noted above, each of the decisions which have apparently predicated liability as a principal upon no more than a showing of defendant's involvement in a conspiracy to effect the substantive crime (or one related to it) drew precedential support from language in prior cases involving defendants who were in fact present at the criminal act. An analysis of these earlier cases, and of *their* cited precedents, reveals two conceptually distinct statements of

9. This is the approach sanctioned by the drafters of the Model Penal Code:

> "Conspiracy may prove command, encouragement, assistance or agreement to assist, etc.; it is evidentially important and may be sufficient for that purpose. But whether it suffices ought to be decided by the jury; they should not be told that it establishes complicity as a matter of law.
>
> "This disposition is * * * faithful to the present American statutes, none of which declares the doctrine that conspirators are liable as such; the statutes on their face require 'inference that the offender has counseled or induced or encouraged the crime' (Cardozo, J., in People v. Swersky, 216 N.Y. [471] at 476 [111 N.E. 212]). However proper it may be to draw that inference from proof of a conspiracy, the jury ought to face in concrete cases whether or not, on the evidence, the inference is one that should be drawn." American Law Institute, *Model Penal Code* § 2.04(3) Comment, pp. 23–24 (Tent.Draft No. 1, 1953).

Early cases applied the coconspirator rule only as a rule of evidence but sometimes stated it so broadly that it sounded like a rule imposing substantive liability. * * *

10. "The law of conspiracy determines who is guilty, and of what, where a conspiracy is involved, but whether one found guilty under this law is a principal or accessory depends, at common law, on the law of parties * * *. The notion that, even where unchanged by statute, all parties to a felony are principals if they are conspirators, is clearly refuted by the cases. Thus although the felony is committed in pursuance of a concerted plan, those who are not present, or so near as to be able to render assistance at the time of perpetration, are not principals, but accessories before the fact." R. Perkins, "The Act of One Conspirator," 26 Hastings L.J. 337, 346, 347 (1974). (Citations omitted.)

11. Conspiracy or preconcert, plus presence, does not automatically establish guilt as a principal in the second degree. It is possible, for example, that A and B agree (conspire) to commit a crime. A and B later visit the scene of the intended crime, but without the shared intent to commit it at the time. B nevertheless then commits the crime without A's approval or support, but in A's presence. A would not be a party to the crime. Similarly, conspiracy alone does not automatically trigger guilt as an accessory before the fact to a later substantive offense. The circumstances of the illegal agreement must also reveal that defendant procured, counseled, or commanded the subsequent offense. In most cases they will, but the matter is for the jury to decide.

rules which were ultimately taken out of context of the cases which generated them and read literally to support the notion that conspiratorial involvement itself opens a route to liability as principal.

The first, an agency rationale of the coconspirator rule of evidence, was itself derived from notions of civil accountability. Although the rule was consistently *applied* to sustain the admissibility of the acts and declarations of one conspirator against other coconspirators as *evidence* of the guilt of all, it was often *stated* in extraordinarily broad terms. It is not surprising, then, that its use in the criminal context could be misleading. * * *

The second line of statements which eventually caused confusion conceptually had nothing to do with the agency basis of the coconspirator rule, but rested upon established common law principles of accomplice liability. * * *

* * *

From the foregoing, it can be seen that the erroneous idea that a conspirator automatically becomes liable as a *principal* to all crimes committed as a result of or in furtherance of the illegal agreement has largely resulted from too broad a reading of case law statements which either (1) discussed the application of the coconspirator rule as a rule of evidence, or (2) applied established principles of accomplice liability to evidence of conspiracy and preconcert. It is likely moreover, that the more general notion expressed in Pinkerton v. United States, supra, 328 U.S. 640, 66 S.Ct. 1180, 90 L.Ed. 1489, that a defendant's involvement in a conspiracy *ipso facto* makes him *liable as a party* to all substantive offenses committed by others in furtherance of the conspiracy, likewise derives from a misreading of similar sources.[13] "But it is repugnant to our system of jurisprudence, where guilt is generally personal to the defendant * * * to impose punishment, not for the socially harmful agreement to which the defendant is a party, but for substantive offenses in which he did not participate." People v. McGee, supra, 49 N.Y.2d 48, 58, 424 N.Y.S.2d 157, 162, 399 N.E.2d 1177, 1182 (rejecting the *Pinkerton* approach); see also Commonwealth v. Stasiun, supra, n. 7, 349 Mass. 38, 206 N.E.2d 672 (also rejecting the *Pinkerton* analysis).

We have seen that, as a matter of evidence, the acts and declarations of one conspirator, made in furtherance of the conspiracy, are regarded as the acts and declarations of all. But that rule, derived from the civil law of agency, should not be extended beyond the limits of its logic to impose substantive liability solely on the basis of participation in a prior criminal agreement. Otherwise, the distinction between conspiracy and the substantive offense which results from it would disappear.[14] Evidence of a defen-

13. It has been noted that, prior to *Pinkerton,* the federal courts applied the dogma that the act of one conspirator is the act of all when committed within the scope of the conspiracy only (1) to establish as the act of all the "overt act" of one; (2) to show the extent and duration of the conspiracy, or (3) to connect all the defendants with the crime charged. Prior to *Pinkerton,* "the doctrine had not, by its own force, supported an imposition of vicarious liability for substantive offenses committed by co conspirators." 56 Yale L.J. 371, 375–76 (1947). * * *

14. We have consistently held that the crime of conspiracy is a separate offense from the accomplishment or attempt to accomplish the intended result. Thus, the offense of conspiracy does not merge into the substantive offense which results from the conspiracy's furtherance. A defendant may be properly sentenced for both offenses. See, e.g., State v.

dant's involvement in a conspiracy may well be sufficient, in a proper case, to enable the jury to infer the elements of defendant's guilt as a party to the later substantive offense. But participation in an illegal agreement does not itself establish, as a matter of law, criminal liability for crimes which result from furtherance of the agreement.

To summarize our holding today:

(1) Evidence sufficient to show defendant's involvement in a criminal conspiracy does not itself establish defendant's liability as a party to the substantive felony committed as a result of the conspiracy; it is reversible error for the court to so instruct the jury.

(2) Such evidence will nevertheless always be *relevant* to submit to the jury as proof of defendant's complicity in the substantive felony charged, in that it tends to show either (a) defendant, though absent at the felony's commission, nevertheless counseled, procured, or commanded its commission, or (b) that defendant, present at the scene of the felony, shared in the criminal intent of the actual perpetrators and thus aided and abetted in the felony's occurrence or acted in concert with those who committed it. What the evidence does in fact show, however, is for the jury to decide.

* * *

In the case before us, there is plenary evidence that the brutal murder of the deceased was committed at defendant's direction. From all the evidence, however, defendant was not present, actually or constructively, during the homicide's commission. Defendant's status as a party to the crime is at most, therefore, that of an accessory before the fact. He may not be punished as a principal.

* * *

BROCK, J., did not participate in the consideration and decision of this case.

HUSKINS, J., dissents from this opinion.

Notes

1. *Favoring Broad Liability.* United States v. Alvarez, 755 F.2d 830 (11th Cir. 1985):

> The three appellants also contend that, even if the murder was reasonably foreseeable, their murder convictions nevertheless should be reversed. The appellants argue that the murder was sufficiently distinct from the intended purposes of the drug conspiracy, and that their individual roles in the conspiracy were sufficiently minor, that they should not be held responsible for the murder. We are not persuaded.
>
> It is well established that, under the *Pinkerton* doctrine, "[a] co-conspirator is vicariously liable for the acts of another co-conspirator even though he may not have directly participated in those acts, his role in the crime was minor, or the

Goldberg, 261 N.C. 181, 134 S.E.2d 334 (1964); State v. Brewer, 258 N.C. 533, 129 S.E.2d 262 (1963). It would be otherwise, however, were a defendant convicted of the substantive offense solely on the basis of his participation in the conspiracy. In such a case, proof of guilt of the substantive offense would necessarily include (indeed, would be equivalent to) proof of involvement in the conspiracy, and the defendant could not be properly punished both for conspiracy and the separate offense. * * *

evidence against a co-defendant more damaging." United States v. Gagnon, 721 F.2d 672, 676 (9th Cir.1983); see United States v. Monaco, 702 F.2d 860, 881 n. 38 (11th Cir.1983); United States v. Poitier, 623 F.2d 1017, 1023 (5th Cir. 1980). Thus, in a typical *Pinkerton* case, the court need not inquire into the individual culpability of a particular conspirator, so long as the substantive crime was a reasonably foreseeable consequence of the conspiracy.[24]

We acknowledge that the instant case is not a typical *Pinkerton* case. Here, the murder of Agent Rios was not within the originally intended scope of the conspiracy, but instead occurred as a result of an unintended turn of events. We have not found, nor has the government cited, any authority for the proposition that all conspirators, regardless of individual culpability, may be held responsible under *Pinkerton* for reasonably foreseeable but originally unintended substantive crimes.[25] Furthermore, we are mindful of the potential due process limitations on the *Pinkerton* doctrine in cases involving attenuated relationships between the conspirator and the substantive crime.

Nevertheless, these considerations do not require us to reverse the murder convictions of Portal, Concepcion, and Hernandez, for we cannot accept the three appellants' assessment of their individual culpability. All three were more than "minor" participants in the drug conspiracy. Portal served as a look-out in front of the Hurricane Motel during part of the negotiations that led to the shoot-out, and the evidence indicated that he was armed. Concepcion introduced the agents to Alvarez, the apparent leader of the conspiracy, and was present when the shoot-out started. Finally, Hernandez, the manager of the motel, allowed the

24. A typical *Pinkerton* case falls into one of two categories. The first and most common category includes cases in which the substantive crime that is the subject of the *Pinkerton* charge is also one of the primary goals of the alleged conspiracy. See, e.g., United States v. Luis-Gonzalez, 719 F.2d 1539, 1545 n. 4 (11th Cir.1983) (conspiracy to possess with intent to distribute marijuana; substantive crime of possession of marijuana); United States v. Harris, 713 F.2d 623, 626 (11th Cir.1983) (conspiracy to distribute cocaine; substantive crimes of possession and distribution of cocaine); United States v. Tilton, 610 F.2d 302, 309 (5th Cir.1980) (conspiracy to commit mail fraud; substantive crime of mail fraud).

The second category includes cases in which the substantive crime is not a primary goal of the alleged conspiracy, but directly facilitates the achievement of one of the primary goals. See, e.g., Shockley v. United States, 166 F.2d 704, 715 (9th Cir.) (conspiracy to escape by violent means from federal penitentiary; substantive crime of first degree murder of prison guard), cert. denied, 334 U.S. 850, 68 S.Ct. 1502, 92 L.Ed. 1773 (1948); United States v. Brant, 448 F.Supp. 781, 782 (W.D.Pa.1978) (narcotics conspiracy; substantive crime of possession of a firearm during commission of a felony).

In either of these two categories, *Pinkerton* liability can be imposed on all conspirators because the substantive crime is squarely within the intended scope of the conspiracy.

25. The imposition of *Pinkerton* liability for such crimes is not wholly unprecedented. See, e.g., Government of Virgin Islands v. Dowling, 633 F.2d 660, 666 (3d Cir.) (conspiracy to commit bank robbery; substantive crime of assault with deadly weapons against police officers, committed during escape attempt), cert. denied, 449 U.S. 960, 101 S.Ct. 374, 66 L.Ed.2d 228 (1980); Park v. Huff, 506 F.2d 849, 859 (5th Cir.) (liquor conspiracy; substantive crime of first degree murder of local district attorney, committed in attempt to stop investigation of illegal liquor sales), cert. denied, 423 U.S. 824, 96 S.Ct. 38, 46 L.Ed.2d 40 (1975). In each of the aforementioned cases, however, vicarious liability was imposed only on "major" participants in the conspiracy.

At trial in the instant case, the government's attorney argued that *Pinkerton* liability for Agent Rios' murder properly could be imposed on all of the conspirators, and expressed the view that prosecutorial discretion would protect truly "minor" participants, such as appellants Rios and Raymond, from liability for the far more serious crimes committed by their coconspirators. We do not find this argument persuasive. In our view, the liability of such "minor" participants must rest on a more substantial foundation than the mere whim of the prosecutor.

drug transactions to take place on the premises and acted as a translator during part of the negotiations that led to the shoot-out.

In addition, all three appellants had actual knowledge of at least some of the circumstances and events leading up to the murder. The evidence that Portal was carrying a weapon demonstrated that he anticipated the possible use of deadly force to protect the conspirators' interests. Moreover, both Concepcion and Hernandez were present when Alvarez stated that he would rather be dead than go back to prison, indicating that they, too, were aware that deadly force might be used to prevent apprehension by Federal agents.

We find the individual culpability of Portal, Concepcion, and Hernandez sufficient to support their murder convictions under *Pinkerton,* despite the fact that the murder was not within the originally intended scope of the conspiracy. In addition, based on the same evidence, we conclude that the relationship between the three appellants and the murder was not so attenuated as to run afoul of the potential due process limitations on the *Pinkerton* doctrine. We therefore hold that *Pinkerton* liability for the murder of Agent Rios properly was imposed on the three appellants, and we decline to reverse their murder convictions on this ground.[27]

2. *The Model Penal Code Approach.* Model Penal Code, § 2.06, Comment 6: *

6. *Liability of Accomplices.* * * *

(a) *Conspiracy.* The most important point at which the Model Code formulation diverges from the language of many courts is that it does not make "conspiracy" as such a basis of complicity in substantive offenses committed in furtherance of its aims. It asks, instead, more specific questions about the behavior charged to constitute complicity, such as whether the defendant solicited commission of the particular offense or whether he aided, or agreed or attempted to aid, in its commission.

The reason for this treatment is that there appears to be no better way to confine within reasonable limits the scope of liability to which conspiracy may theoretically give rise. In People v. Luciano,[25] for example, Luciano and others were convicted of sixty-two counts of compulsory prostitution, each count involving a specific instance of placing a girl in a house of prostitution, receiving money for so doing or receiving money from the earnings of a prostitute—acts proved to have been committed pursuant to a combination to control commercialized vice in New York City.

Liability was properly imposed with respect to these defendants, who directed and controlled the combination. They solicited and aided the commission of numberless specific crimes, including the ones for which they were held. But would so extensive a liability be just for each of the prostitutes or runners involved in the plan? They have, of course, committed their own crimes; they may actually have assisted in others but they exerted no substantial influence on the behavior of a hundred other prostitutes or

27. Although our decision today extends the *Pinkerton* doctrine to cases involving reasonably foreseeable but originally unintended substantive crimes, we emphasize that we do so only within narrow confines. Our holding is limited to conspirators who played more than a "minor" role in the conspiracy, or who had actual knowledge of at least some of the circumstances and events culminating in the reasonably foreseeable but originally unintended substantive crime.

25. 277 N.Y. 348, 14 N.E.2d 433, cert. denied, 305 U.S. 620 (1938).

runners, each pursuing his own ends within the shelter of the combination. A court would and should hold that they are parties to a conspiracy; this is itself a crime, under this Code as well as most others. And they should also be held for those crimes they actually committed, or within the principle of this section for those to which they were accomplices. However, law would lose all sense of just proportion if simply because of the conspiracy itself each were held accountable for thousands of additional offenses of which he was completely unaware and which he did not influence at all.

* * *

No decision has been found in which the liability of co-conspirators for acts of one another has been pressed to limits such as these, though the limits have been approached. The cases that declare the doctrine normally involve defendants who have had a hand in planning, directing, or executing the crimes charged. When that is so, the other principles of accessorial liability establish guilt, and under this section the defendant has "solicited," "aided," "agreed to aid," or "attempted to aid" in planning or committing the crime. * * *

* * *

6. Number of Conspiracies

United States v. Glenn

United States Court of Appeals, First Circuit, 1987.
828 F.2d 855.

BREYER, CIRCUIT JUDGE.

The federal government charged Kenneth Glenn and Manuel Benevides with four drug crimes, and a jury convicted them. For present purposes, we can group the charges into two basic offenses: (1) conspiring to import and to possess "marijuana and hashish" and (2) actually importing and possessing marijuana. See 18 U.S.C. § 2; 21 U.S.C. §§ 841(a)(1), 846, 952, 960(a)(1), 963. Glenn and Benevides appeal their convictions, basically claiming that the government failed to prove that they were part of the grand marijuana and hashish smuggling scheme that the indictment described. They argue that the evidence introduced at trial showed that, as to them, the charged conspiracy was in fact two separate conspiracies, one dealing with marijuana from Thailand and the other dealing with hashish from Pakistan. Glenn says that he had nothing to do with smuggling marijuana, and Benevides says he had nothing to do with smuggling hashish. After reviewing the record, we have found that they are right. In Glenn's case, the variance between indictment and proof requires reversal, but in Benevides' case, it does not.

I.

We approach this classical "single/multiple" conspiracy problem with several well-established points in mind. First, we recognize that conspiracy law, like most criminal law, focuses upon the activities of an individual defendant. It is therefore dangerous to think of a conspiracy as a kind of "club" that one joins or a "business" in which one works. See Developments in the Law—Criminal Conspiracy, 72 *Harv.L.Rev.* 922, 934 (1959) (criticizing courts that deal with conspiracy "as though it were a group").

Those metaphors falsely suggest that the "member" or "employee" *automatically* becomes legally responsible for the entire enterprise. Instead, "the gist of the [conspiracy] offense remains the agreement, and it is therefore essential to determine what kind of agreement or understanding existed *as to each defendant*." United States v. Borelli, 336 F.2d 376, 384 (2d Cir.1964) (emphasis added).

We also recognize that an agreement or understanding may be tacit. A defendant drug distributor may *expressly* agree with his immediate supplier that he will sell any drugs provided to him, but he may *tacitly* agree with a more distant supplier, say a smuggler, that each will work for the success of the whole drug operation. A jury may find a tacit agreement at least when the distributor knows that the smuggler probably exists, that distributing drugs tends to help the smuggler, and that the smuggler's contribution to the success of the entire enterprise is likely needed if the distributor is to achieve his own more immediate objective. See United States v. Bruno, 105 F.2d 921 (2d Cir.), rev'd on other grounds, 308 U.S. 287, 60 S.Ct. 198, 84 L.Ed. 257 (1939). The known interdependence of the linked activities in such a case makes it reasonable to speak of a tacit understanding between the distributor and others upon whose unlawful acts the distributor knows his own success likely depends. Cf. Blumenthal v. United States, 332 U.S. 539, 558, 68 S.Ct. 248, 257, 92 L.Ed. 154 (1947) (finding that whiskey salesmen conspired with the original, but unknown, owner of the whiskey when they knew themselves to be aiding "a single over-all comprehensive plan"). When such interdependence is missing, when the distributor is indifferent to the purposes of others in the enterprise—say, other distributors—the tacit understanding does not exist. See Kotteakos v. United States, 328 U.S. 750, 66 S.Ct. 1239, 90 L.Ed. 1557 (1946); *Borelli,* 336 F.2d at 383 n. 2.

* * *

Finally, we are aware that a defendant cannot upset a conviction by showing that the government proved understandings or agreements different from those charged unless the "variance" between the evidence and the charges prejudiced the defendant, unless it " 'affect[ed] the substantial rights' of the accused." Berger v. United States, 295 U.S. 78, 82, 55 S.Ct. 629, 630, 79 L.Ed. 1314 (1935). As long as administrative convenience leads the government to prosecute many, or all, members of a large criminal enterprise at a single trial, variances between the scope of the conspiracy charged and that proved may, at least as to some defendants, be fairly common. The risks of prejudice in such trials are serious and warrant reversal when they materialize; but when substantial rights are not affected, the error is "harmless."

These principles of law suggest that an appellate court, reviewing the type of alleged variance here at issue, should ask the following questions. (1) Is the evidence sufficient to permit a jury to find the (express or tacit) agreement that the indictment charges? (2) If not, is it sufficient to permit a jury, under a proper set of instructions, to convict the defendant of a related, similar conspiracy? (3) If so, does the variance affect the defendant's substantial rights or does the difference between the charged conspiracy and the conspiracy proved amount to "harmless error?"

A.

The answers to these questions require us to reverse Glenn's convictions. First, we do not see how a jury could convict Glenn of the conspiracy that the indictment charged, namely, the conspiracy to import and possess both marijuana from Thailand *and* hashish from Pakistan. The evidence shows several core conspirators who met repeatedly in New York City in the fall of 1980 and in the summer and fall of 1981; who developed plans to smuggle marijuana from Thailand and hashish from Pakistan; who fraudulently borrowed $10 million from the First National Bank of Chicago to finance their plans; who bought a boat called the Adeline C, which they originally planned to use for smuggling Pakistani hashish but which they actually used for importing the Thai marijuana; who bought a landing area in Rhode Island in 1981; and who unloaded eight tons of marijuana smuggled from Thailand in that area. The evidence also shows, however, that both Glenn and the other conspirators considered Glenn to be a subsidiary figure, that Glenn's duties involved only the smuggling of hashish, and that, for the most part, Glenn attended meetings where the subject of discussion was Pakistani hashish, not Thai marijuana. The record does not show how the hashish venture could have helped the marijuana venture, or vice versa.

The government, in arguing that Glenn belonged to a single, unified conspiracy to smuggle both marijuana and hashish, points only to the following five facts: (1) three "core" conspirators (Bryon, Murray and Warden) fraudulently borrowed ten million dollars from the First National Bank to finance the smuggling of marijuana *and* hashish, (2) two other core conspirators (Cooper and Lynn) planned to distribute both marijuana *and* hashish, (3) Bryon testified that Warden bought property in Rhode Island as a site for unloading both marijuana *and* hashish, (4) Bryon changed the destination of the Adeline C from Pakistan to Thailand, and Glenn became upset when he found out, and (5) Glenn attended one meeting where the core conspirators discussed the smuggling of both marijuana *and* hashish, and was present at one or two other meetings where they discussed marijuana only. The first three of these facts may show the existence of a conspiracy to smuggle both marijuana *and* hashish among the core group; they may show that the core conspirators had that dual objective. But they do not show that *Glenn* had that dual objective or that Glenn intended to, or did, take actions that likely would help the marijuana venture. The fourth fact shows that Glenn actively opposed the core group's plans for marijuana smuggling, not that he tried to help them. And the fifth fact shows at most that Glenn *knew* about the marijuana venture; it does not show that he agreed to take, intended to take or actually took any action that he knew would likely further that smuggling. * * * The evidence is therefore insufficient to show that Glenn expressly or tacitly agreed to do more than to import and possess Pakistani hashish. See, *Blumenthal,* 332 U.S. at 558, 68 S.Ct. at 257 (noting that separate conspiracies may be found when defendants have distinct ends, when they have no interest in others' unlawful activities and when they do not aid others in conducting those activities); United States v. Melchor–Lopez, 627 F.2d 886, 891 (9th Cir.1980) ("[M]ere association with members of a conspiracy, the existence of an opportunity to join a conspiracy, or simple knowledge, approval of, or acquiescence in the object or purpose of the conspiracy * * * is not sufficient to make one a conspirator.")

* * * A properly instructed jury could have convicted Glenn of conspiring to import and possess hashish.

[T]he variance between the single conspiracy charged and the conspiracy that the evidence proved significantly prejudiced Glenn. The judge instructed the jury that even though there was no evidence that Glenn himself imported or physically possessed any marijuana, the jury could convict him on the substantive charges if they found him guilty of the charged conspiracy. The jury then convicted Glenn of *actually* importing and possessing in excess of one thousand pounds of marijuana. Glenn was sentenced to eight years in prison on the possession charge—three years more than the statutory maximum punishment for conspiring to import the hashish alone. See 21 U.S.C. § 841(b)(1)(A). As we have pointed out, however, the evidence is insufficient to connect Glenn with the charged conspiracy. Thus, Glenn's convictions on the substantive charges and his sentence depended upon an improper jury instruction—an instruction that would not have been given if Glenn had been indicted properly. * * *

B.

We turn next to Benevides. First, in our view, there is almost no evidence that Benevides conspired to import *both* marijuana and hashish. The record does not reveal any relevant contact between Benevides and the other conspirators until mid–1981, some months after the initial planning meetings. It shows that Benevides helped the core members find an off-load site for the marijuana, that he helped to find offloaders for the marijuana, that he assisted with renovations to a quonset hut used to store the marijuana, that he picked up a truck used to transport marijuana, and that he helped move some conveyor belts intended to be used in offloading. The only evidence tying him to Pakistani hashish consists of (1) his attendance at a meeting at which Warden and Bryon discussed both smuggling ventures and got into an argument, and where Benevides' only reported words were: "Let's let everybody part as friends," and (2) later testimony by Bryon that the Rhode Island property was purchased "as a base to unload marijuana and hashish from." * * * Thus, the evidence fails to show beyond a reasonable doubt that Benevides conspired, as the indictment charges, to import and possess marijuana from Thailand *and* hashish from Pakistan.

Second, the evidence is more than sufficient to permit the jury to convict Benevides, under proper instructions, of conspiring to import and possess marijuana from Thailand. Benevides does not seriously dispute this point.

Third, the variance between the conspiracies charged and the conspiracies proved did not prejudice Benevides substantially. We have found no testimony or other evidence relating to the hashish conspiracy that could have affected the jury's judgment regarding Benevides' guilt on the marijuana charges. There is therefore no possibility of "spillover" here. The substantive charges of actual importation and possession related directly to the marijuana conspiracies of which Benevides could properly have been convicted. Had Benevides been charged properly, the *Pinkerton* charge would have enabled the jury lawfully to convict Benevides of the substantive offenses charged. * * * Finally, Benevides' punishment was no greater than the lawful punishment for the marijuana conspiracy alone, and he does not claim that he was sentenced for anything he did not do. Thus, in our view, any variance from the indictment amounted to no more than harmless error.

* * *

Notes

1. *Long Term or Multiple Object Plans.* Braverman v. United States, 317 U.S. 49, 52–53, 63 S.Ct. 99, 101–102, 87 L.Ed. 23, 27–28 (1942):

> Both courts below recognized that a single agreement to commit an offense does not become several conspiracies because it continues over a period of time, and that there may be such a single continuing agreement to commit several offenses. But they thought that in the latter case each contemplated offense renders the agreement punishable as a separate conspiracy.
>
> * * *
>
> * * * [W]hen a single agreement to commit one or more substantive crimes is evidenced by an overt act, as the statute requires, the precise nature and extent of the conspiracy must be determined by reference to the agreement which embraces and defines its objects. Whether the object of a single agreement is to commit one or many crimes, it is in either case that agreement which constitutes the conspiracy which the statute punishes. The one agreement cannot be taken to be several agreements and hence several conspiracies because it envisages the violation of several statutes rather than one.

2. *Knowledge of Existence of Other Conspirators.* United States v. Kearney, 560 F.2d 1358, 1362 (9th Cir.1977), cert. denied 434 U.S. 971, 98 S.Ct. 522, 54 L.Ed.2d 460 (1977):

> Appellants assert that the Government swept several discrete conspiracies into a single conspiracy count, and that this was a misjoinder which worked to their prejudice, effecting "guilt transference" by associating them with co-defendants involved in other criminal acts. In so contending, appellants confuse *separate acts at separate times* with *separate conspiracies.* Almost any venture, criminal or legitimate, is analyzable into a series of bits, each of which, in turn, is characterizable as an independent plan or goal. The standard for determining the existence of a single conspiracy, however,
>
> > "* * * is whether there was one overall agreement among the various parties to perform various functions in order to carry out the objectives of the conspiracy * * *."
>
> Here, the evidence is clearly sufficient to show one overall scheme. The Government proved that each defendant knew, or had reason to know, that others were involved in a broad project for the illegal transportation and distribution of narcotics, and that his benefits were probably dependent upon the success of the entire operation. Proof that an alleged co-conspirator knew that he was plotting in concert with others to violate the law is sufficient to raise the necessary inference that he joined in the overall agreement. It need not even be shown that an alleged co-conspirator knew all of the purposes of and all of the participants in the conspiracy. Once the existence of a conspiracy is independently shown, only slight evidence is necessary to connect a defendant to it.

3. *Model Penal Code Guidelines.* Model Penal Code, § 5.03, Comment 3: *

3. *Unity and Scope of a Conspiracy.* * * *

* * *

The combined operation of Subsections (1), (2) and (3) is relied upon to delineate the identity and scope of a conspiracy. All three provisions focus on the culpability of the individual actor. Subsections (1) and (2) limit the scope of his conspiracy both in terms of its criminal objectives, to those crimes that he had the purpose of promoting or facilitating, and in terms of parties, to those with whom he agreed, except when the same crime that he conspired to commit is, to his knowledge, also the object of a conspiracy between one of his co-conspirators and another person or persons. Subsection (3) provides that his conspiracy is a single one despite a multiplicity of criminal objectives, as long as such crimes are the object of the same agreement or continuous conspiratorial relationship.

* * *

4. *Chains and Wheels.* There are two common fact patterns which present difficulties in determining whether there is a single large conspiracy or a group of smaller ones.

a. The chain pattern. An art museum has sent a valuable painting to Restorer for cleaning. Restorer lends the painting briefly to Artist for the making of an unauthorized copy, in criminal violation of the copyright law. Artist prepares the copy and sells it to Dealer as a copy. This unauthorized sale of an unauthorized copy is also a criminal copyright violation. Dealer gets Expert to authenticate the copy falsely so that it can be sold to Customer, in violation of a theft statute. This might be viewed as three separate conspiracies, the first between Restorer and Artist, the second between Artist and Dealer, and the third between Dealer and Expert. It might be that Restorer believes that Artist wants to make a copy for his private use, that Artist believes that Dealer will sell the copy as a copy, that Dealer and Expert do not know the history of the copy, etc. There may be successive discrete conspiracies involving the same property. On the other hand, there might be enough to weld these links into a single chain, as the court thought there was in *Glenn.*

b. The wheel pattern. Suppose our art dealer approached a second artist and a third, getting them to make copies of various paintings for sale as originals. Each copy might involve a separate conspiracy, with the dealer merely appearing as a common figure in each. But, if there was an ongoing copy factory, with the dealer as the hub, and cooperating artists and experts, aware of the whole enterprise and offering mutual assistance in the various transactions—acting like the spokes of a wheel to move the business along, we would have a single wheel conspiracy.

Question

What practical difference does it make whether a fact situation is viewed as presenting one or several conspiracies?

7. "RICO" SUAVE

RACKETEER INFLUENCED AND CORRUPT ORGANIZATIONS ACT

18 U.S.C.A. §§ 1961 ff. (1988).

§ 1961. Definitions

As used in this chapter—

(1) "racketeering activity" means (A) any act or threat involving murder, kidnaping, gambling, arson, robbery, bribery, extortion, dealing in obscene matter, or dealing in narcotic or other dangerous drugs, which is chargeable under State law and punishable by imprisonment for more than one year; (B) any act which is indictable under any of the following provisions of title 18, United States Code: Section 201 (relating to bribery), section 224 (relating to sports bribery), sections 471, 472, and 473 (relating to counterfeiting), section 659 (relating to theft from interstate shipment) if the act indictable under section 659 is felonious, section 664 (relating to embezzlement from pension and welfare funds), sections 891–894 (relating to extortionate credit transactions), section 1029 (relative to fraud and related activity in connection with access devices), section 1084 (relating to the transmission of gambling information), section 1341 (relating to mail fraud), section 1343 (relating to wire fraud), sections 1461–1465 (relating to obscene matter), section 1503 (relating to obstruction of justice), section 1510 (relating to obstruction of criminal investigations), section 1511 (relating to the obstruction of State or local law enforcement), section 1512 (relating to tampering with a witness, victim, or an informant), section 1513 (relating to retaliating against a witness, victim, or an informant), section 1951 (relating to interference with commerce, robbery, or extortion), section 1952 (relating to racketeering), section 1953 (relating to interstate transportation of wagering paraphernalia), section 1954 (relating to unlawful welfare fund payments), section 1955 (relating to the prohibition of illegal gambling businesses), section 1956 (relating to the laundering of monetary instruments), section 1957 (relating to engaging in monetary transactions in property derived from specified unlawful activity), section 1958 (relating to use of interstate commerce facilities in the commission of murder-for-hire), sections 2251–2252 (relating to sexual exploitation of children), sections 2312 and 2313 (relating to interstate transportation of stolen motor vehicles), sections 2314 and 2315 (relating to interstate transportation of stolen property), section 2321 (relating to trafficking in certain motor vehicles or motor vehicle parts), sections 2341–2346 (relating to trafficking in contraband cigarettes), sections 2421–24 (relating to white slave traffic), (C) any act which is indictable under title 29, United States Code, section 186 (dealing with restrictions on payments and loans to labor organizations) or section 501(c) (relating to embezzlement from union funds), (D) any offense

involving fraud connected with a case under title 11, fraud in the sale of securities, or the felonious manufacture, importation, receiving, concealment, buying, selling, or otherwise dealing in narcotic or other dangerous drugs, punishable under any law of the United States, or (E) any act which is indictable under the Currency and Foreign Transactions Reporting Act;

(2) "State" means any State of the United States, the District of Columbia, the Commonwealth of Puerto Rico, any territory or possession of the United States, any political subdivision, or any department, agency, or instrumentality thereof;

(3) "person" includes any individual or entity capable of holding a legal or beneficial interest in property;

(4) "enterprise" includes any individual, partnership, corporation, association, or other legal entity, and any union or group of individuals associated in fact although not a legal entity;

(5) "pattern of racketeering activity" requires at least two acts of racketeering activity, one of which occurred after the effective date of this chapter and the last of which occurred within ten years (excluding any period of imprisonment) after the commission of a prior act of racketeering activity;

(6) "unlawful debt" means a debt (A) incurred or contracted in gambling activity which was in violation of the law of the United States, a State or political subdivision thereof, or which is unenforceable under State or Federal law in whole or in part as to principal or interest because of the laws relating to usury, and (B) which was incurred in connection with the business of gambling in violation of the law of the United States, a State or political subdivision thereof, or the business of lending money or a thing of value at a rate usurious under State or Federal law, where the usurious rate is at least twice the enforceable rate;

* * *

§ 1962. Prohibited activities

(a) It shall be unlawful for any person who has received any income derived, directly or indirectly, from a pattern of racketeering activity or through collection of an unlawful debt in which such person has participated as a principal within the meaning of section 2, title 18, United States Code, to use or invest, directly or indirectly, any part of such income, or the proceeds of such income, in acquisition of any interest in, or the establishment or operation of, any enterprise which is engaged in, or the activities of which affect, interstate or foreign commerce. A purchase of securities on the open market for purposes of investment, and without the intention of controlling or participating in the control of the issuer, or of assisting another to do so, shall not be unlawful under this subsection if the securities of the issuer held by the purchaser, the members of his immediate family, and his or their accomplices in any pattern * * * [of] racketeering activity or the collection of an unlawful debt after such purchase do not amount in the aggregate to one percent of the outstanding securities of any one class, and do not confer, either in law or in fact, the power to elect one or more directors of the issuer.

(b) It shall be unlawful for any person through a pattern of racketeering activity or through collection of an unlawful debt to acquire or maintain, directly or indirectly, any interest in or control of any enterprise which is engaged in, or the activities of which affect, interstate or foreign commerce.

(c) It shall be unlawful for any person employed by or associated with any enterprise engaged in, or the activities of which affect, interstate or foreign commerce, to conduct or participate, directly or indirectly, in the conduct of such enterprise's affairs through a pattern of racketeering activity or collection of unlawful debt.

(d) It shall be unlawful for any person to conspire to violate any of the provisions of subsection (a), (b), or (c) of this section.

§ 1963. Criminal penalties

(a) Whoever violates any provision of section 1962 of this chapter shall be fined under this title or imprisoned not more than 20 years (or for life if the violation is based on a racketeering activity for which the maximum penalty includes life imprisonment), or both, and shall forfeit to the United States, irrespective of any provision of State law—

(1) any interest the person has acquired or maintained in violation of section 1962;

(2) any—

(A) interest in;

(B) security of;

(C) claim against; or

(D) property or contractual right of any kind affording a source of influence over;

Any enterprise which the person has established, operated, controlled, conducted, or participated in the conduct of, in violation of section 1962; and

(3) any property constituting, or derived from, any proceeds which the person obtained, directly or indirectly, from racketeering activity or unlawful debt collection in violation of section 1962.

The court, in imposing sentence on such person shall order, in addition to any other sentence imposed pursuant to this section, that the person forfeit to the United States all property described in this subsection. In lieu of a fine otherwise authorized by this section, a defendant who derives profits or other proceeds from an offense may be fined not more than twice the gross profits or other proceeds.

(b) Property subject to criminal forfeiture under this section includes—

(1) real property, including things growing on, affixed to, and found in land; and

(2) tangible and intangible personal property, including rights, privileges, interests, claims, and securities.

(c) All right, title, and interest in property described in subsection (a) vests in the United States upon the commission of the act giving rise to forfeiture under this section. Any such property that is subsequently transferred to a person other than the defendant may be the subject of a special verdict of forfeiture and thereafter shall be ordered forfeited to the United States, unless the transferee establishes in a hearing pursuant to subsection *(l)* that he is a bona fide purchaser for value of such property who at the time of purchase was reasonably without cause to believe that the property was subject to forfeiture under this section.

* * *

§ 1964. Civil remedies

(a) The district courts of the United States shall have jurisdiction to prevent and restrain violations of section 1962 of this chapter by issuing appropriate orders, including, but not limited to: ordering any person to divest himself of any interest, direct or indirect, in any enterprise; imposing reasonable restrictions on the future activities or investments of any person, including, but not limited to, prohibiting any person from engaging in the same type of endeavor as the enterprise engaged in, the activities of which affect interstate or foreign commerce; or ordering dissolution or reorganization of any enterprise, making due provision for the rights of innocent persons.

(b) The Attorney General may institute proceedings under this section. Pending final determination thereof, the court may at any time enter such restraining orders or prohibitions, or take such other actions, including the acceptance of satisfactory performance bonds, as it shall deem proper.

(c) Any person injured in his business or property by reason of a violation of section 1962 of this chapter may sue therefor in any appropriate United States district court and shall recover threefold the damages he sustains and the cost of the suit, including a reasonable attorney's fee.

(d) A final judgment or decree rendered in favor of the United States in any criminal proceeding brought by the United States under this chapter shall estop the defendant from denying the essential allegations of the criminal offense in any subsequent civil proceeding brought by the United States.

United States v. Pryba

United States District Court, E.D. Virginia, 1987.
674 F.Supp. 1504.

ELLIS, DISTRICT JUDGE.

Introduction

This twelve count RICO-obscenity prosecution is the latest chapter in the continuing First Amendment-pornography saga. The new twist here is the use of RICO,[2] indeed apparently the first federal prosecutorial use of RICO against purveyors of allegedly obscene materials. Until 1984, federal prosecutors targetting smut had an arsenal limited chiefly to 18 U.S.C. §§ 1461 *et seq.* Then, in 1984, Congress expanded RICO to cover obscene materials. It did so based on a concern that organized crime was contributing to and profiting from an "explosion in the volume and availability of pornography in our society." As a result, federal prosecutors may now use RICO's stiffer penalties and forfeiture provisions [5] against sellers and distributors of allegedly obscene materials. This case is just such an attempted prosecution and this Memorandum considers and decides several dispositive threshold motions made by defendants.

Roth v. United States, 354 U.S. 476, 77 S.Ct. 1304, 1 L.Ed.2d 1498 (1957), and Miller v. California, 413 U.S. 15, 93 S.Ct. 2607, 37 L.Ed.2d 419 (1973), are perhaps the most important of the earlier chapters in the First Amendment-pornography saga. *Roth* made unmistakably clear that obscenity was not constitutionally protected speech and provided a standard by which to discern obscenity, namely whether the average person,[6] applying contemporary community standards,[7] would find that the work, taken as a whole, appeals to the prurient interest.[8] This test predictably spawned more than a decade of spirited and confusing decisions.

2. Racketeer Influenced & Corrupt Organizations Act, 18 U.S.C. §§ 1961–68 (1984).

5. RICO's criminal penalties provide that whoever violates any provisions of RICO "shall be fined not more than $25,000 or imprisoned not more than twenty years, or both." 18 U.S.C. § 1963(a) (1982 & Supp. 1984).

* * *

6. In deciding whether the material appeals to a prurient interest, the jury must avoid subjective personal or private views. The average person is the *judge* and not the object of the test. The jury must evaluate what judgment will be made by a hypothetical average person applying the collective view of the adult community. Pinkus v. United States, 436 U.S. 293, 300–01, 98 S.Ct. 1808, 1813, 56 L.Ed.2d 293 (1978). The Court in *Pinkus* held that "children are not to be included * * * as part of the 'community.'" Id. at 297, 98 S.Ct. at 1811; see also Brockett v. Spokane Arcades, 472 U.S. 491, 105 S.Ct. 2794, 86 L.Ed.2d 394 (1985). * * *

7. The "contemporary community standard" is to be applied by the jury *only* when examining the first two prongs of *Miller,* namely the "prurient appeal" and "patent offensiveness" prongs. See infra note 22 (discussing the three-prong *Miller* test). The third prong of *Miller,* the "serious literary, artistic, political, or scientific value" prong, is determined not by the application of the contemporary community standard, but rather by the traditional "reasonable man" standard. See Pope v. Illinois, [481] U.S. [497], 107 S.Ct. 1918, 95 L.Ed.2d 439 (1987).

8. In Roth v. United States, 354 U.S. 476, 77 S.Ct. 1304, 1 L.Ed.2d 1498 (1957), the Court defined "prurient interest" as follows:

> A thing is obscene if, considered as a whole, its predominant appeal is to prurient interest, i.e., a shameful or morbid interest in nudity,

In 1973, in an effort to redirect the course of the law in this area, the Court, in Miller v. California, rephrased and expanded the *Roth* test.[9] Justice Brennan, who as the author of *Roth* had arguably initiated this judicial odyssey, was so disillusioned by the 15 or so years of judicial wanderings under *Roth* that at length, he dissented in *Miller* and its companion case, preferring instead an absolutist, "anything goes" approach to obscenity. Chief Justice Burger, on the other hand, persuaded a majority in *Miller* to carry on and refine the *Roth* effort to draw a line between obscenity and protected speech. Given that the instant case is the latest chapter in this saga, it is perhaps only fitting that the juxtaposed views of Justice Brennan and Chief Justice Burger serve here as a preface.

Thus, in dissenting in Paris Adult Theatre I v. Slaton, 413 U.S. 49, 93 S.Ct. 2628, 37 L.Ed.2d 446 (1973), a *Miller* companion, Justice Brennan noted that the effort to distinguish between protected and unprotected sexually oriented material, born of *Roth,* had proved so vexing, so time-consuming, and so divisive and had generated such disharmony of views[11] that the effort should be abandoned. As he put it, even after all this effort, the subject stubbornly "remained * * * resistant to the formation of stable and manageable standards." 413 U.S. at 73, 93 S.Ct. at 2665. Chief Justice Burger disagreed, noting in *Miller* that the convenient, anything goes, absolutist approach is not the law and that the "Court must face up to the tough problem of constitutional judgment involved in every obscenity case." 413 U.S. at 29–30, 93 S.Ct. at 2618 (quoting *Roth,* 354 U.S. at 498, 77 S.Ct. at 1316). So in the spirit of the former Chief Justice's words, this court now faces up to "the tough problems of constitutional judgment" raised in this novel obscenity case.

The Indictment

The indictment consists of twelve counts plus a number of RICO forfeiture allegations. Of the twelve counts, three allege RICO obscenity violations. The motions considered in this Memorandum Opinion focus solely on the three RICO counts and the accompanying forfeiture allegations.

Count I charges defendants, Dennis E. Pryba, Barbara A. Pryba, Jennifer G. Williams and Educational Books, Inc., with participating as principals in a "pattern of racketeering" involving the sale and distribution of allegedly obscene materials and with investing the proceeds of such activities in an

sex, or excretion, and if it goes substantially beyond customary limits of candor in description or representation of such matters. * * *

9. *Miller* clarified the law in several respects, including principally (a) the abandonment of the "utterly without redeeming value" standard announced in Memoirs v. Massachusetts, 383 U.S. 413, 86 S.Ct. 975, 16 L.Ed.2d 1 (1966), and (b) the rejection of a national standard for the community. The former imposed an unrealistic burden on the prosecutor, while the latter simply made the common sense point that citizens of Virginia or Wisconsin may well not be willing to find acceptable depictions of sexual conduct that would be acceptable to citizens of Las Vegas or New York.

11. The best known, most memorable, and arguably, most candid comment made on the post-*Roth* * * * line-drawing difficulties in obscenity cases was Justice Stewart's in a concurring opinion in Jacobellis v. Ohio, 378 U.S. 184, 84 S.Ct. 1676, 12 L.Ed.2d 793 (1964). He noted that the hard core pornography that was unprotected under the Constitution might be impossible to define but, he said, "I know it when I see it." Id. at 197, 84 S.Ct. at 1683.

"enterprise" engaged in interstate commerce, in violation of 18 U.S.C. § 1962(a). The enterprise is said to consist of the Prybas, Williams, Educational Books and seven unindicted corporations.

Count II alleges that Pryba and Williams, as persons employed by and associated with the enterprise, violated 18 U.S.C. § 1962(c) by conducting the affairs of the enterprise through a pattern of racketeering activity. And in Count III, the Prybas, Williams and Educational Books are charged with a Section 1962(c) conspiracy to violate section 1962(a).

Defendants mount a two-pronged attack on the RICO counts in the indictment. First, defendants argue three pleading points. Defendants assert that Counts I, II and III do not properly plead an "enterprise", as required by RICO. Next, the defendants claim that the government has not sufficiently alleged a pattern of racketeering activity. Finally, one defendant, Educational Books, asserts that it must be dismissed from Count III because a corporation cannot be guilty of conspiring with its agents when the agents are alleged to have used the corporation to carry out their own purposes. Second, they contend these counts should be dismissed because RICO's forfeiture provisions run afoul of the Constitution when applied to allegedly obscene materials.[13] Specifically, defendants allege that RICO's forfeiture provisions: (1) have a "chilling" effect upon the distribution of protected speech; (2) act as a prior restraint on protected speech; (3) are unduly harsh and thus violate the Eighth Amendment; (4) violate due process principles; and (5) violate the *ex post facto* clause of the Constitution. Each of these contentions is separately treated.

Facts and Proceedings to Date

Defendants, Dennis E. Pryba, Barbara A. Pryba, Jennifer G. Williams, and Educational Books, Inc., own and operate or assist in operating a number of retail video stores that sell allegedly obscene material. On August 13, 1987, defendants were indicted on various counts under federal RICO alleging, *inter alia,* a pattern of racketeering activity involving dealing in obscene matter.[14]

On August 13, 1987, an *ex parte* restraining order was issued that enjoined defendants from selling, encumbering, or in any other way disposing of certain property that might be forfeitable under RICO's forfeiture provisions.[15] In addition, the August 13 restraining order prohibited defendants from selling all video tapes, magazines, and other printed material. This order, however, was modified on August 25, 1987. The modified order

13. This court is not faced with the question of whether the restraining order is unconstitutional. This matter was addressed and decided by another Judge of this Division when defendants moved to dismiss the restraining order on September 4, 1987.

14. RICO was amended in 1984 to include "dealing in obscene matter" as a racketeering activity. * * *

15. The restraining order provided, in part, that defendants were prohibited from disposing of certain real property, automobiles, bank accounts, stocks, and other personal property that might be forfeitable under RICO. Title 18 U.S.C. § 1963(a) provides for three types of forfeiture: (1) any interest acquired or maintained in violation of § 1962; (2) any property affording a source of influence over the enterprise; and (3) any property derived from the proceeds of racketeering activity. If defendants are found to be guilty of dealing in obscene matter, then the real and personal property described in the restraining order might be forfeitable under section 1963(a).

permitted defendants to continue to conduct their business as normal "without substantially dissipating or diminishing the value of the assets" of their business or property.

The Pleading Issues

A. *The RICO "Enterprise"*

Defendants argue that the enterprise alleged in the indictment does not meet the statutory definition. The alleged enterprise consists of individuals and corporations. In defendant's view, the statutory definition of "enterprise" precludes lumping together individuals and corporations. * * *

Section 1961(4) states that " 'enterprise' *includes* any individual, partnership, corporation, association, or other legal entity, and any union or group of individuals associated in fact although not a legal entity" (emphasis added). This is sweeping language; there is no reason to give it a strained, restricted scope. Legislative history confirms this. The House RICO report stated that "enterprise" included

> associations in fact, as well as legally recognized associative entities. Thus infiltration of any associative group by *any individual or group capable of holding a property interest* can be reached.

House Rep.No. 91–1549, 91st Cong., 2d Sess., 1970 U.S.Code Cong. & Ad. News 4007, 4032 (emphasis added).[17] The Supreme Court, in another context, has also recognized the expansiveness of the term "enterprise". In United States v. Turkette, 452 U.S. 576, 101 S.Ct. 2524, 69 L.Ed.2d 246 (1981), the Court rejected an argument that "enterprises" should be limited to legitimate business. In reaching this conclusion, the Court noted, "Congress opted for a far broader definition of the word 'enterprise.' " It also stated that "[t]here is no restriction upon the associations embraced by the definition [in § 1961(4)]." [19]

* * *

B. *Pattern of Racketeering Activity*

Defendants argue that the three RICO counts do not sufficiently allege the requisite "pattern of racketeering activity." [21] In essence, defendants argue that the activity alleged in the indictment constitutes a single scheme, not separate acts. This indictment, they claim, is analogous to the one at issue in International Data Bank, Ltd. v. Zepkin, 812 F.2d 149 (4th Cir.1987). There the issuance of a fraudulent prospectus was held to be a single, unitary scheme, not a RICO pattern of racketeering.

Defendants' argument is unpersuasive. *Zepkin* is not in point. In contrast to the issuance of a prospectus, this indictment alleges a series of

17. For further discussion of RICO's legislative history and purpose, see United States v. Turkette, 452 U.S. 576, 588–93, 101 S.Ct. 2524, 2531–33, 69 L.Ed.2d 246 (1981) (confirming that Congress intended to give broad scope to the term "enterprise").

19. Id. at 580, 101 S.Ct. at 2527. This may be a modest overstatement as it appears unlikely that a state or municipality itself may not be a member of an enterprise. See United States v. Mandel, 415 F.Supp. 997 (D.Md.), supplemented, 415 F.Supp. 1025 (D.Md. 1976).

21. See 18 U.S.C. § 1961(1), (5), 1962(a), (c).

separate but related acts dealing with the sale and distribution of obscene material. The allegations fit squarely within RICO, which defines a "pattern" as "at least two acts" and "racketeering activity" as including "dealing in obscene matter." 18 U.S.C. § 1961(5), (1)(A). The following legislative history from the RICO Senate Report dispels any doubt that this indictment properly pleads a pattern of racketeering:

> The target of [RICO] is * * * not sporadic activity. The infiltration of legitimate business normally requires more than one "racketeering activity" to be effective. It is this factor of *continuity plus relationship* which combines to produce a pattern.

S.Rep.No. 617, 91st Cong., 1st Sess. 158, U.S.Code Cong. & Admin.News 1970, p. 4007 (emphasis added), quoted in Sedima, S.P.R.L. v. IMREX Co., Inc., 473 U.S. 479, 496 n. 14, 105 S.Ct. 3275, 3285 n. 14, 87 L.Ed.2d 346 (1985). The Fourth Circuit interprets this language to require that "the predicate acts must be related and must be a part of a continuous criminal endeavor." *Zepkin,* 812 F.2d at 154. This indictment, therefore, properly pleads a "pattern of racketeering activity."

C. *Conspiracy*

The corporate defendant, Educational Books, Inc., asserts that Count III deserves dismissal because, contrary to the indictment's allegations, the corporation cannot conspire with its own agents. In essence, this defendant urges the application in this context of the civil intracorporate conspiracy rule. See McIntyre's Mini Computer Sales Group, Inc. v. Creative Synergy Corp., 644 F.Supp. 580, 585 (E.D.Mich.1986). Dispositive of this claim is that an exception to the intracorporate conspiracy exists in the criminal arena. See, e.g., United States v. Peters, 732 F.2d 1004, 1008 (1st Cir.1984).

The Constitutional Issues

A. *Chilling Effect of RICO*

Defendants claim that RICO chills protected speech for two reasons: first, it is said that purveyors will be deterred from dealing in non-obscene erotic literature given the breadth and vagueness of the underlying criminal offense, *i.e.,* obscenity. Second, it is urged that RICO's forfeiture provisions are so draconian as to deter dealers from dealing in protected speech at the margin. In other words, vague definitions of obscenity force purveyors to guess about the status of some "speech" at the margins, and they will be deterred from such guessing by the risk of criminal prosecution and the severity of potential sanctions. The victim, defendants contend, will be protected speech at the margins, presumably erotic works that skirt the boundary but do not cross over into the realm of obscenity.[22]

22. The existing border demarcating the line between protected speech and obscenity is given by Miller v. California, 413 U.S. 15, 93 S.Ct. 2607, 37 L.Ed.2d 419 (1973). Speech may be banned as obscene where:

(a) the average person, applying contemporary community standards would find that the work, taken as a whole, appeals to the prurient interest;

(b) the work describes, in a patently offensive way, sexual conduct defined by the applicable state law; and

(c) the work, taken as a whole, lacks serious literary, political, or scientific value.

The gravamen of both prongs of this attack is the alleged excessive vagueness and breadth of the statutory proscriptions, one state (Va.Code Ann. § 18.2–372), one federal (18 U.S.C. § 1461 *et seq.*), that are the predicates for a RICO violation. The short answer is that both statutes have already passed constitutional muster. They have been found to give "adequate warning of the conduct proscribed" so as to permit the law to be fairly administered. See Roth v. United States, 354 U.S. 476, 491, 77 S.Ct. 1304, 1312, 1 L.Ed.2d 1498 (1957).

* * * To be sure, there may be some fuzziness at the boundaries, but absolute precision is neither practical nor constitutionally required.

> That there may be marginal cases in which it is difficult to determine the side of the line on which a particular fact situation falls is no sufficient reason to hold the language too ambiguous to define a criminal offense. * * *

Roth, 354 U.S. at 491–92, 77 S.Ct. at 1313. * * *

A somewhat different question is presented by the application of RICO forfeiture remedies in obscenity prosecutions. So draconian are they, the defendants claim, that the unconstitutional chilling that occurs is tantamount to a prior restraint.[25] The court turns next to this argument.

B. *Prior Restraint*

Defendants argue that RICO's forfeiture provisions (18 U.S.C. § 1963) operate in alleged obscenity cases, as here, as impermissible prior restraints. Heavy reliance is placed on Near v. Minnesota, 283 U.S. 697, 51 S.Ct. 625, 75 L.Ed. 1357 (1931), and its progeny which make unmistakably clear the courts' hostility toward prior restraints.

The flaw in this argument is the recognized distinction between prior restraints and subsequent punishment. The evil of a prior restraint is that speech is suppressed before its status is judicially determined. Such restraints are far more likely to chill, indeed to suppress, free speech than subsequent punishment, which can be imposed only after there is the procedural safeguard of a disinterested judicial determination concerning the alleged illegality. A person is punished for speech-related conduct only after he is given the opportunity to litigate, *inter alia,* the constitutionality of the statute, either facially or as applied to him. In obscenity cases, he is also permitted to present the material to a jury and attempt to persuade it, under *Miller,* that

413 U.S. at 24, 93 S.Ct. at 2615. Thus, as J.R. Distributors, Inc. v. Eikenberry, 725 F.2d 482 (9th Cir.1984), rev'd on other grounds sub nom. Brockett v. Spokane Arcades, 472 U.S. 491, 105 S.Ct. 2794, 86 L.Ed.2d 394 (1985) indicates, works that merely arouse normal sexual responses (in contrast to shameful or morbid sexual responses) may be constitutionally protected even if they contain an isolated example of a patently offensive description of sexual conduct and even if the works lack the redeeming value defined in *Miller, Eikenberry,* 725 F.2d at 490–92. It is, presumably, this speech that is at risk at the margin.

25. A "prior restraint" is defined as "the imposition of a restraint on a publication before it is published." Black's Law Dictionary 1074 (5th ed. 1979). Courts often use the terms "prior restraint" and "chilling effect" interchangeably. See, e.g., Arizona v. Feld, 745 P.2d 146 (Ariz.Ct.App.1987). Yet "chilling effect" refers to the distribution of material, not publication. Although a statute may not amount to a prior restraint on publication, it may cause a chilling effect on distribution. See United States v. John Doe (Model Magazine), 829 F.2d 1291 (4th Cir.1987).

the material deserves constitutional protection. Prior restraints deprive "speakers" of these important safeguards. * * *

This is not to say that subsequent punishment schemes such as RICO's forfeiture scheme have no chilling effect whatever. Surely it has some; indeed, it is designed to accomplish just that end. But this "chilling" is a wholly legitimate consequence of the RICO forfeiture provisions or any other criminal penalty.[27] Deterrence (or chilling) through the threat of prosecution and punishment is a legitimate goal of the criminal law. Once it is decided that obscenity does not merit First Amendment protection and indeed, once it is decided that obscenity is so pernicious that it should be criminally proscribed, then a subsequent punishment, like RICO's forfeiture scheme, is a sensible and wholly legitimate law enforcement weapon. It is specially designed to chill or deter proscribed, unprotected speech; unconstitutional chilling occurs only if the definition of obscenity is excessively broad or vague so that some protected speech is unintentionally ensnared in the imprecise net that is cast.

Nor is it significant that the forfeiture penalty may impact adversely on defendants' future speech. That fact alone does not mean that the First Amendment is implicated. The Constitution does not forbid punishment for a crime simply because that punishment might affect free expression. As the Court in Arcara v. Cloud Books, 478 U.S. 697, 106 S.Ct. 3172, 3178, 92 L.Ed.2d 568 (1986) pointed out,

> book selling in an establishment used for prostitution [or distribution of obscene materials] does not confer First Amendment coverage to defeat a valid statute aimed at penalizing and terminating illegal uses of premises.

* * *

In summary, this Court concludes that principle and authority confirm that RICO's forfeiture provisions, construed to reach the ill-gotten gains of racketeering activity, are not facially invalid prior restraints on protected speech.

The heart of this matter is that Congress has found that organized crime uses and exploits obscenity to further its pernicious aims and, therefore, that a pattern of racketeering activity deserves the forfeiture sanction. The fact that the racketeering activity involves expressive conduct is irrelevant. The First Amendment cannot be a shield for illegal activity. RICO's forfeiture provisions are not more of a restraint on free speech than is any felony conviction or prison sentence. Both of the latter are provisions that in some respect restrain speech but neither can be coherently termed a First Amendment violation. * * *

[The remaining constitutional claims were found to be without merit.]

* * *

27. One commentator argues the contrary. *See* Mayton, *Toward A Theory of First Amendment Process: Injunction of Speech, Subsequent Punishment, and the Costs of the Prior Restraint Doctrine,* 67 Cornell L.Rev. 245 (1982). *But see* Redish, *The Proper Role of the Prior Restraint Doctrine in First Amendment Theory,* 70 Va.L.Rev. 53 (1983).

* * * This court concludes, at length, that Congress' decision to use RICO as a weapon against purveyors of obscenity does not offend the Constitution. This is so because the RICO criminal forfeiture provisions, as applied to obscenity, require that there be a nexus between the obscenity purveyor's ill-gotten racketeering gains and any protected material seized. Post conviction seizure of arguably protected materials and assets is constitutionally permissible where there is proper proof that they were acquired or maintained with the ill-gotten gains from racketeering activity, including dealing in obscenity. Therefore, RICO and its forfeiture provisions do not unconstitutionally chill protected speech or act as prior restraints. To be sure, RICO's sanctions are severe, but severity alone does not cause unconstitutional chilling or convert these sanctions into prior restraints. In adding obscenity to RICO, Congress has stayed within constitutional bounds.

* * *

Notes

1. *RICO and obscenity.* See also another phase of the principal case, United States v. Pryba, 674 F.Supp. 1518 (E.D.Va.1987), dealing with the burden of persuasion in RICO forfeitures and with the use of expert testimony. In Fort Wayne Books, Inc. v. Indiana, 489 U.S. 46, 109 S.Ct. 916, 103 L.Ed.2d 34 (1989), the Supreme Court upheld a state RICO statute, as applied to an obscenity prosecution.

2. *"Enterprise".* United States v. Ivic, 700 F.2d 51, 60–63 (2d Cir.1983):

> The Government's argument is simplicity itself. Section 1962(c) makes it unlawful "for any person employed by or associated with any enterprise engaged in, or the activities of which affect, interstate or foreign commerce, to conduct or participate, directly or indirectly, in the conduct of such enterprise's affairs through a pattern of racketeering activity or collection of unlawful debt," and § 1962(d) makes it unlawful for any person to conspire to violate subsections (a), (b), or (c) of § 1962. The group of Croatian nationalists to which defendants belonged fit the definition of "enterprise" in § 1961(4) inasmuch as they comprised a "group of individuals associated in fact although not a legal entity". A conspiracy to participate in the conduct of this enterprise's affairs through a "pattern of racketeering activity" would be established by showing, as to each defendant, that he agreed to further the enterprise by committing two of the State law crimes listed in § 1961(1)(A), in this case, murder and arson. That is all.
>
> * * *
>
> When the same word is used in the same section of an act more than once, and the meaning is clear in one place, it will be assumed to have the same meaning in other places. See United States v. Nunez, 573 F.2d 769, 771 (2 Cir.), cert. denied, 436 U.S. 930, 98 S.Ct. 2828, 56 L.Ed.2d 774 (1978), and cases cited there. As it appears in subsections (a) and (b), the term "enterprise" quite clearly refers to the sort of entity in which funds can be invested and a property interest of some sort acquired, and hence the sort of entity which one joins to make money. Although perhaps somewhat wider in its reach than "business", an "enterprise", as used in these subsections, is evidently an organized profit-seeking venture. There was no charge or proof of that in this case. Defendants joined together not to make money but, as the indictment itself stated, to advance the goal of Croatian independence. They undertook to murder Badurina and to bomb the dance studio and the travel agency not to obtain money, but rather to eliminate political opponents, win publicity, or otherwise further their chosen

cause. If "enterprise" in subsection (c) is given the same meaning which that term clearly has in subsections (a) and (b), then the group to which the indictment charged and the proof showed that defendants belonged is outside its scope.

* * * The words used by Congress have a familiar connotation to ordinary people as describing money-making activities about which they read in the newspaper every day. It would be stretching such words beyond permissible bounds to apply them to the terrorist activities of misguided patriots which, although likewise subject to condemnation, are worlds removed from that of such venal organizations as gambling, narcotics, or prostitution rings. * * *

* * *

In sum, RICO is the lineal descendant of a pair of 1967 Senate bills designed to apply antitrust-type measures to the problem of "black money". Although the bill ultimately enacted as RICO went somewhat beyond this initial conception, preventing and reversing the infiltration of legitimate businesses by organized crime elements remained its core purpose. * * *

*

APPENDIX A

MODEL PENAL CODE *

TABLE OF CONTENTS

PART I. GENERAL PROVISIONS

ARTICLE 1. PRELIMINARY

ARTICLE 2. GENERAL PRINCIPLES OF LIABILITY

ARTICLE 3. GENERAL PRINCIPLES OF JUSTIFICATION

ARTICLE 4. RESPONSIBILITY

ARTICLE 5. INCHOATE CRIMES

ARTICLE 6. AUTHORIZED DISPOSITION OF OFFENDERS

[omitted]

ARTICLE 7. AUTHORITY OF COURT IN SENTENCING

[omitted]

PART II. DEFINITION OF SPECIFIC CRIMES

OFFENSES INVOLVING DANGER TO THE PERSON

ARTICLE 210. CRIMINAL HOMICIDE

ARTICLE 211. ASSAULT; RECKLESS ENDANGERING; THREATS

ARTICLE 212. KIDNAPPING AND RELATED OFFENSES; COERCION

ARTICLE 213. SEXUAL OFFENSES

OFFENSES AGAINST PROPERTY

ARTICLE 220. ARSON, CRIMINAL MISCHIEF, AND OTHER PROPERTY DESTRUCTION

ARTICLE 221. BURGLARY AND OTHER CRIMINAL INTRUSION

ARTICLE 222. ROBBERY

ARTICLE 223. THEFT AND RELATED OFFENSES

ARTICLE 224. FORGERY AND FRAUDULENT PRACTICES

OFFENSES AGAINST THE FAMILY

ARTICLE 230. OFFENSES AGAINST THE FAMILY

OFFENSES AGAINST PUBLIC ADMINISTRATION

ARTICLE 240. BRIBERY AND CORRUPT INFLUENCE

ARTICLE 241. PERJURY AND OTHER FALSIFICATION IN OFFICIAL MATTERS

ARTICLE 242. OBSTRUCTING GOVERNMENTAL OPERATIONS; ESCAPES

ARTICLE 243. ABUSE OF OFFICE

[omitted]

OFFENSES AGAINST PUBLIC ORDER AND DECENCY

ARTICLE 250. RIOT, DISORDERLY CONDUCT, AND RELATED OFFENSES

ARTICLE 251. PUBLIC INDECENCY

PART III. TREATMENT AND CORRECTION

[omitted]

PART IV. ORGANIZATION OF CORRECTION

[omitted]

PART I. GENERAL PROVISIONS

ARTICLE 1. PRELIMINARY

Section 1.02 Purposes; Principles of Construction

(1) The general purposes of the provisions governing the definition of offenses are:

(a) to forbid and prevent conduct that unjustifiably and inexcusably inflicts or threatens substantial harm to individual or public interests;

(b) to subject to public control persons whose conduct indicates that they are disposed to commit crimes;

(c) to safeguard conduct that is without fault from condemnation as criminal;

(d) to give fair warning of the nature of the conduct declared to constitute an offense;

(e) to differentiate on reasonable grounds between serious and minor offenses.

(2) The general purposes of the provisions governing the sentencing and treatment of offenders are:

(a) to prevent the commission of offenses;

(b) to promote the correction and rehabilitation of offenders;

(c) to safeguard offenders against excessive, disproportionate or arbitrary punishment;

(d) to give fair warning of the nature of the sentences that may be imposed on conviction of an offense;

(e) to differentiate among offenders with a view to a just individualization in their treatment;

(f) to define, coordinate and harmonize the powers, duties and functions of the courts and of administrative officers and agencies responsible for dealing with offenders;

(g) to advance the use of generally accepted scientific methods and knowledge in the sentencing and treatment of offenders;

(h) to integrate responsibility for the administration of the correctional system in a State Department of Correction [or other single department or agency].

(3) The provisions of the Code shall be construed according to the fair import of their terms but when the language is susceptible of differing constructions it shall be interpreted to further the general purposes stated in this Section and the special purposes of the particular provision involved. The discretionary powers conferred by the Code shall be exercised in accordance with the criteria stated in the Code and, insofar as such criteria are not decisive, to further the general purposes stated in this Section.

Section 1.03 Territorial Applicability

(1) Except as otherwise provided in this Section, a person may be convicted under the law of this State of an offense committed by his own conduct or the conduct of another for which he is legally accountable if:

(a) either the conduct which is an element of the offense or the result which is such an element occurs within this State; or

(b) conduct occurring outside the State is sufficient under the law of this State to constitute an attempt to commit an offense within the State; or

(c) conduct occurring outside the State is sufficient under the law of this State to constitute a conspiracy to commit an offense within the State and an overt act in furtherance of such conspiracy occurs within the State; or

(d) conduct occurring within the State establishes complicity in the commission of, or an attempt, solicitation or conspiracy to commit, an offense in another jurisdiction which also is an offense under the law of this State; or

(e) the offense consists of the omission to perform a legal duty imposed by the law of this State with respect to domicile, residence or a relationship to a person, thing or transaction in the State; or

(f) the offense is based on a statute of this State which expressly prohibits conduct outside the State, when the conduct bears a reasonable relation to a legitimate interest of this State and the actor knows or should know that his conduct is likely to affect that interest.

(2) Subsection (1)(a) does not apply when either causing a specified result or a purpose to cause or danger of causing such a result is an element of an offense and the result occurs or is designed or likely to occur only in another jurisdiction where the conduct charged would not constitute an offense, unless a legislative purpose plainly appears to declare the conduct criminal regardless of the place of the result.

(3) Subsection (1)(a) does not apply when causing a particular result is an element of an offense and the result is caused by conduct occurring outside the State which would not constitute an offense if the result had occurred there, unless the actor purposely or knowingly caused the result within the State.

(4) When the offense is homicide, either the death of the victim or the bodily impact causing death constitutes a "result," within the meaning of Subsection (1)(a) and if the body of a homicide victim is found within the State, it is presumed that such result occurred within the State.

(5) This State includes the land and water and the air space above such land and water with respect to which the State has legislative jurisdiction.

Section 1.04 Classes of Crimes; Violations

(1) An offense defined by this Code or by any other statute of this State, for which a sentence of [death or of] imprisonment is authorized, constitutes a crime. Crimes are classified as felonies, misdemeanors or petty misdemeanors.

(2) A crime is a felony if it is so designated in this Code or if persons convicted thereof may be sentenced [to death or] to imprisonment for a term which, apart from an extended term, is in excess of one year.

(3) A crime is a misdemeanor if it is so designated in this Code or in a statute other than this Code enacted subsequent thereto.

(4) A crime is a petty misdemeanor if it is so designated in this Code or in a statute other than this Code enacted subsequent thereto or if it is defined by a statute other than this Code which now provides that persons convicted thereof may be sentenced to imprisonment for a term of which the maximum is less than one year.

(5) An offense defined by this Code or by any other statute of this State constitutes a violation if it is so designated in this Code or in the law defining the offense or if no other sentence than a fine, or fine and forfeiture or other civil penalty is authorized upon conviction or if it is defined by a statute other than this Code which now provides that the offense shall not constitute a crime. A violation does not constitute a crime and conviction of a violation shall not give rise to any disability or legal disadvantage based on conviction of a criminal offense.

(6) Any offense declared by law to constitute a crime, without specification of the grade thereof or of the sentence authorized upon conviction, is a misdemeanor.

(7) An offense defined by any statute of this State other than this Code shall be classified as provided in this Section and the sentence that may be imposed upon conviction thereof shall hereafter be governed by this Code.

Section 1.05 All Offenses Defined by Statute; Application of General Provisions of the Code

(1) No conduct constitutes an offense unless it is a crime or violation under this Code or another statute of this State.

(2) The provisions of Part I of the Code are applicable to offenses defined by other statutes, unless the Code otherwise provides.

(3) This Section does not affect the power of a court to punish for contempt or to employ any sanction authorized by law for the enforcement of an order or a civil judgment or decree.

Section 1.06 Time Limitations

(1) A prosecution for murder may be commenced at any time.

(2) Except as otherwise provided in this Section, prosecutions for other offenses are subject to the following periods of limitation:

(a) a prosecution for a felony of the first degree must be commenced within six years after it is committed;

(b) a prosecution for any other felony must be commenced within three years after it is committed;

(c) a prosecution for a misdemeanor must be commenced within two years after it is committed;

(d) a prosecution for a petty misdemeanor or a violation must be commenced within six months after it is committed.

(3) If the period prescribed in Subsection (2) has expired, a prosecution may nevertheless be commenced for:

(a) any offense a material element of which is either fraud or a breach of fiduciary obligation within one year after discovery of the offense by an aggrieved party or by a person who has legal duty to represent an aggrieved party and who is himself not a party to the offense, but in no case shall this provision extend the period of limitation otherwise applicable by more than three years; and

(b) any offense based upon misconduct in office by a public officer or employee at any time when the defendant is in public office or employment or within two years thereafter, but in no case shall this provision extend the period of limitation otherwise applicable by more than three years.

(4) An offense is committed either when every element occurs, or, if a legislative purpose to prohibit a continuing course of conduct plainly appears, at the time when the course of conduct or the defendant's complicity therein is terminated. Time starts to run on the day after the offense is committed.

(5) A prosecution is commenced either when an indictment is found [or an information filed] or when a warrant or other process is issued, provided that such warrant or process is executed without unreasonable delay.

(6) The period of limitation does not run:

(a) during any time when the accused is continuously absent from the State or has no reasonably ascertainable place of abode or work within the State, but in no case shall this provision extend the period of limitation otherwise applicable by more than three years; or

(b) during any time when a prosecution against the accused for the same conduct is pending in this State.

Section 1.12 Proof Beyond a Reasonable Doubt; Affirmative Defenses; Burden of Proving Fact When Not an Element of an Offense; Presumptions

(1) No person may be convicted of an offense unless each element of such offense is proved beyond a reasonable doubt. In the absence of such proof, the innocence of the defendant is assumed.

(2) Subsection (1) of this Section does not:

(a) require the disproof of an affirmative defense unless and until there is evidence supporting such defense; or

(b) apply to any defense which the Code or another statute plainly requires the defendant to prove by a preponderance of evidence.

(3) A ground of defense is affirmative, within the meaning of Subsection (2)(a) of this Section, when:

(a) it arises under a section of the Code which so provides; or

(b) it relates to an offense defined by a statute other than the Code and such statute so provides; or

(c) it involves a matter of excuse or justification peculiarly within the knowledge of the defendant on which he can fairly be required to adduce supporting evidence.

(4) When the application of the Code depends upon the finding of a fact which is not an element of an offense, unless the Code otherwise provides:

(a) the burden of proving the fact is on the prosecution or defendant, depending on whose interest or contention will be furthered if the finding should be made; and

(b) the fact must be proved to the satisfaction of the Court or jury, as the case may be.

(5) When the Code establishes a presumption with respect to any fact which is an element of an offense, it has the following consequences:

(a) when there is evidence of the facts which give rise to the presumption, the issue of the existence of the presumed fact must be submitted to the jury, unless the Court is satisfied that the evidence as a whole clearly negatives the presumed fact; and

(b) when the issue of the existence of the presumed fact is submitted to the jury, the Court shall charge that while the presumed fact must, on all the evidence, be proved beyond a reasonable doubt, the law declares that the jury may regard the facts giving rise to the presumption as sufficient evidence of the presumed fact.

(6) A presumption not established by the Code or inconsistent with it has the consequences otherwise accorded it by law.

Section 1.13 General Definitions

In this Code, unless a different meaning plainly is required:

(1) "statute" includes the Constitution and a local law or ordinance of a political subdivision of the State;

(2) "act" or "action" means a bodily movement whether voluntary or involuntary;

(3) "voluntary" has the meaning specified in Section 2.01;

(4) "omission" means a failure to act;

(5) "conduct" means an action or omission and its accompanying state of mind, or, where relevant, a series of acts and omissions;

(6) "actor" includes, where relevant, a person guilty of an omission;

(7) "acted" includes, where relevant, "omitted to act";

(8) "person," "he" and "actor" include any natural person and, where relevant, a corporation or an unincorporated association;

(9) "element of an offense" means (i) such conduct or (ii) such attendant circumstances or (iii) such a result of conduct as

(a) is included in the description of the forbidden conduct in the definition of the offense; or

(b) establishes the required kind of culpability; or

(c) negatives an excuse or justification for such conduct; or

(d) negatives a defense under the statute of limitations; or

(e) establishes jurisdiction or venue;

(10) "material element of an offense" means an element that does not relate exclusively to the statute of limitations, jurisdiction, venue or to any other matter similarly unconnected with (i) the harm or evil, incident to conduct, sought to be prevented by the law defining the offense, or (ii) the existence of a justification or excuse for such conduct;

(11) "purposely" has the meaning specified in Section 2.02 and equivalent terms such as "with purpose," "designed" or "with design" have the same meaning;

(12) "intentionally" or "with intent" means purposely;

(13) "knowingly" has the meaning specified in Section 2.02 and equivalent terms such as "knowing" or "with knowledge" have the same meaning;

(14) "recklessly" has the meaning specified in Section 2.02 and equivalent terms such as "recklessness" or "with recklessness" have the same meaning;

(15) "negligently" has the meaning specified in Section 2.02 and equivalent terms such as "negligence" or "with negligence" have the same meaning;

(16) "reasonably believes" or "reasonable belief" designates a belief which the actor is not reckless or negligent in holding.

ARTICLE 2. GENERAL PRINCIPLES OF LIABILITY

Section 2.01 Requirement of Voluntary Act; Omission as Basis of Liability; Possession as an Act

(1) A person is not guilty of an offense unless his liability is based on conduct which includes a voluntary act or the omission to perform an act of which he is physically capable.

(2) The following are not voluntary acts within the meaning of this Section:

(a) a reflex or convulsion;

(b) a bodily movement during unconsciousness or sleep;

(c) conduct during hypnosis or resulting from hypnotic suggestion;

(d) a bodily movement that otherwise is not a product of the effort or determination of the actor, either conscious or habitual.

(3) Liability for the commission of an offense may not be based on an omission unaccompanied by action unless:

(a) the omission is expressly made sufficient by the law defining the offense; or

(b) a duty to perform the omitted act is otherwise imposed by law.

(4) Possession is an act, within the meaning of this Section, if the possessor knowingly procured or received the thing possessed or was aware of his control thereof for a sufficient period to have been able to terminate his possession.

Section 2.02 General Requirements of Culpability

(1) *Minimum Requirements of Culpability.* Except as provided in Section 2.05, a person is not guilty of an offense unless he acted purposely, knowingly, recklessly or negligently, as the law may require, with respect to each material element of the offense.

(2) *Kinds of Culpability Defined.*

(a) *Purposely.*

A person acts purposely with respect to a material element of an offense when:

(i) if the element involves the nature of his conduct or a result thereof, it is his conscious object to engage in conduct of that nature or to cause such a result; and

(ii) if the element involves the attendant circumstances, he is aware of the existence of such circumstances or he believes or hopes that they exist.

(b) *Knowingly.*

A person acts knowingly with respect to a material element of an offense when:

(i) if the element involves the nature of his conduct or the attendant circumstances, he is aware that his conduct is of that nature or that such circumstances exist; and

(ii) if the element involves a result of his conduct, he is aware that it is practically certain that his conduct will cause such a result.

(c) *Recklessly.*

A person acts recklessly with respect to a material element of an offense when he consciously disregards a substantial and unjustifiable risk that the material element exists or will result from his conduct. The risk must be of such a nature and degree that, considering the nature and purpose of the actor's conduct and the circumstances known to him, its disregard involves a gross deviation from the standard of conduct that a law-abiding person would observe in the actor's situation.

(d) *Negligently.*

A person acts negligently with respect to a material element of an offense when he should be aware of a substantial and unjustifiable risk that the material element exists or will result from his conduct. The risk must be of such a nature and degree that the actor's failure to perceive it, considering the nature and purpose of his conduct and the circumstances known to him, involves a gross deviation from the standard of care that a reasonable person would observe in the actor's situation.

(3) *Culpability Required Unless Otherwise Provided.* When the culpability sufficient to establish a material element of an offense is not prescribed by law,

such element is established if a person acts purposely, knowingly or recklessly with respect thereto.

(4) *Prescribed Culpability Requirement Applies to All Material Elements.* When the law defining an offense prescribes the kind of culpability that is sufficient for the commission of an offense, without distinguishing among the material elements thereof, such provision shall apply to all the material elements of the offense, unless a contrary purpose plainly appears.

(5) *Substitutes for Negligence, Recklessness and Knowledge.* When the law provides that negligence suffices to establish an element of an offense, such element also is established if a person acts purposely, knowingly or recklessly. When recklessness suffices to establish an element, such element also is established if a person acts purposely or knowingly. When acting knowingly suffices to establish an element, such element also is established if a person acts purposely.

(6) *Requirement of Purpose Satisfied if Purpose Is Conditional.* When a particular purpose is an element of an offense, the element is established although such purpose is conditional, unless the condition negatives the harm or evil sought to be prevented by the law defining the offense.

(7) *Requirement of Knowledge Satisfied by Knowledge of High Probability.* When knowledge of the existence of a particular fact is an element of an offense, such knowledge is established if a person is aware of a high probability of its existence, unless he actually believes that it does not exist.

(8) *Requirement of Wilfulness Satisfied by Acting Knowingly.* A requirement that an offense be committed wilfully is satisfied if a person acts knowingly with respect to the material elements of the offense, unless a purpose to impose further requirements appears.

(9) *Culpability as to Illegality of Conduct.* Neither knowledge nor recklessness or negligence as to whether conduct constitutes an offense or as to the existence, meaning or application of the law determining the elements of an offense is an element of such offense, unless the definition of the offense or the Code so provides.

(10) *Culpability as Determinant of Grade of Offense.* When the grade or degree of an offense depends on whether the offense is committed purposely, knowingly, recklessly or negligently, its grade or degree shall be the lowest for which the determinative kind of culpability is established with respect to any material element of the offense.

Section 2.03 Causal Relationship Between Conduct and Result; Divergence Between Result Designed or Contemplated and Actual Result or Between Probable and Actual Result

(1) Conduct is the cause of a result when:

(a) it is an antecedent but for which the result in question would not have occurred; and

(b) the relationship between the conduct and result satisfies any additional causal requirements imposed by the Code or by the law defining the offense.

(2) When purposely or knowingly causing a particular result is an element of an offense, the element is not established if the actual result is not within the purpose or the contemplation of the actor unless:

(a) the actual result differs from that designed or contemplated, as the case may be, only in the respect that a different person or different property is injured or affected or that the injury or harm designed or contemplated would have been more serious or more extensive than that caused; or

(b) the actual result involves the same kind of injury or harm as that designed or contemplated and is not too remote or accidental in its occurrence to have a [just] bearing on the actor's liability or on the gravity of his offense.

(3) When recklessly or negligently causing a particular result is an element of an offense, the element is not established if the actual result is not within the risk of which the actor is aware or, in the case of negligence, of which he should be aware unless:

(a) the actual result differs from the probable result only in the respect that a different person or different property is injured or affected or that the probable injury or harm would have been more serious or more extensive than that caused; or

(b) the actual result involves the same kind of injury or harm as the probable result and is not too remote or accidental in its occurrence to have a [just] bearing on the actor's liability or on the gravity of his offense.

(4) When causing a particular result is a material element of an offense for which absolute liability is imposed by law, the element is not established unless the actual result is a probable consequence of the actor's conduct.

Section 2.04 Ignorance or Mistake

(1) Ignorance or mistake as to a matter of fact or law is a defense if:

(a) the ignorance or mistake negatives the purpose, knowledge, belief, recklessness or negligence required to establish a material element of the offense; or

(b) the law provides that the state of mind established by such ignorance or mistake constitutes a defense.

(2) Although ignorance or mistake would otherwise afford a defense to the offense charged, the defense is not available if the defendant would be guilty of another offense had the situation been as he supposed. In such case, however, the ignorance or mistake of the defendant shall reduce the grade and degree of the offense of which he may be convicted to those of the offense of which he would be guilty had the situation been as he supposed.

(3) A belief that conduct does not legally constitute an offense is a defense to a prosecution for that offense based upon such conduct when:

(a) the statute or other enactment defining the offense is not known to the actor and has not been published or otherwise reasonably made available prior to the conduct alleged; or

(b) he acts in reasonable reliance upon an official statement of the law, afterward determined to be invalid or erroneous, contained in (i) a statute or other enactment; (ii) a judicial decision, opinion or judgment; (iii) an administrative order or grant of permission; or (iv) an official interpretation of the public officer or body charged by law with responsibility for the interpretation, administration or enforcement of the law defining the offense.

(4) The defendant must prove a defense arising under Subsection (3) of this Section by a preponderance of evidence.

Section 2.05 When Culpability Requirements Are Inapplicable to Violations and to Offenses Defined by Other Statutes; Effect of Absolute Liability in Reducing Grade of Offense to Violation

(1) The requirements of culpability prescribed by Sections 2.01 and 2.02 do not apply to:

(a) offenses which constitute violations, unless the requirement involved is included in the definition of the offense or the Court determines that its application is consistent with effective enforcement of the law defining the offense; or

(b) offenses defined by statutes other than the Code, insofar as a legislative purpose to impose absolute liability for such offenses or with respect to any material element thereof plainly appears.

(2) Notwithstanding any other provision of existing law and unless a subsequent statute otherwise provides:

(a) when absolute liability is imposed with respect to any material element of an offense defined by a statute other than the Code and a conviction is based upon such liability, the offense constitutes a violation; and

(b) although absolute liability is imposed by law with respect to one or more of the material elements of an offense defined by a statute other than the Code, the culpable commission of the offense may be charged and proved, in which event negligence with respect to such elements constitutes sufficient culpability and the classification of the offense and the sentence that may be imposed therefor upon conviction are determined by Section 1.04 and Article 6 of the Code.

Section 2.06 Liability for Conduct of Another; Complicity

(1) A person is guilty of an offense if it is committed by his own conduct or by the conduct of another person for which he is legally accountable, or both.

(2) A person is legally accountable for the conduct of another person when:

(a) acting with the kind of culpability that is sufficient for the commission of the offense, he causes an innocent or irresponsible person to engage in such conduct; or

(b) he is made accountable for the conduct of such other person by the Code or by the law defining the offense; or

(c) he is an accomplice of such other person in the commission of the offense.

(3) A person is an accomplice of another person in the commission of an offense if:

(a) with the purpose of promoting or facilitating the commission of the offense, he

(i) solicits such other person to commit it; or

(ii) aids or agrees or attempts to aid such other person in planning or committing it; or

(iii) having a legal duty to prevent the commission of the offense, fails to make proper effort so to do; or

(b) his conduct is expressly declared by law to establish his complicity.

(4) When causing a particular result is an element of an offense, an accomplice in the conduct causing such result is an accomplice in the commission of that offense, if he acts with the kind of culpability, if any, with respect to that result that is sufficient for the commission of the offense.

(5) A person who is legally incapable of committing a particular offense himself may be guilty thereof if it is committed by the conduct of another person for which he is legally accountable, unless such liability is inconsistent with the purpose of the provision establishing his incapacity.

(6) Unless otherwise provided by the Code or by the law defining the offense, a person is not an accomplice in an offense committed by another person if:

(a) he is a victim of that offense; or

(b) the offense is so defined that his conduct is inevitably incident to its commission; or

(c) he terminates his complicity prior to the commission of the offense and

(i) wholly deprives it of effectiveness in the commission of the offense; or

(ii) gives timely warning to the law enforcement authorities or otherwise makes proper effort to prevent the commission of the offense.

(7) An accomplice may be convicted on proof of the commission of the offense and of his complicity therein, though the person claimed to have committed the offense has not been prosecuted or convicted or has been convicted of a different offense or degree of offense or has an immunity to prosecution or conviction or has been acquitted.

Section 2.07 Liability of Corporations, Unincorporated Associations and Persons Acting, or Under a Duty to Act, in Their Behalf

(1) A corporation may be convicted of the commission of an offense if:

(a) the offense is a violation or the offense is defined by a statute other than the Code in which a legislative purpose to impose liability on corporations plainly appears and the conduct is performed by an agent of the corporation acting in behalf of the corporation within the scope of his office or employment, except that if the law defining the offense designates the agents for whose conduct the corporation is accountable or the circumstances under which it is accountable, such provisions shall apply; or

(b) the offense consists of an omission to discharge a specific duty of affirmative performance imposed on corporations by law; or

(c) the commission of the offense was authorized, requested, commanded, performed or recklessly tolerated by the board of directors or by a high managerial agent acting in behalf of the corporation within the scope of his office or employment.

(2) When absolute liability is imposed for the commission of an offense, a legislative purpose to impose liability on a corporation shall be assumed, unless the contrary plainly appears.

(3) An unincorporated association may be convicted of the commission of an offense if:

(a) the offense is defined by a statute other than the Code which expressly provides for the liability of such an association and the conduct is performed by an agent of the association acting in behalf of the association within the scope of his office or employment, except that if the law defining the offense designates the agents for whose conduct the association is accountable or the circumstances under which it is accountable, such provisions shall apply; or

(b) the offense consists of an omission to discharge a specific duty of affirmative performance imposed on associations by law.

(4) As used in this Section:

(a) "corporation" does not include an entity organized as or by a governmental agency for the execution of a governmental program;

(b) "agent" means any director, officer, servant, employee or other person authorized to act in behalf of the corporation or association and, in the case of an unincorporated association, a member of such association;

(c) "high managerial agent" means an officer of a corporation or an unincorporated association, or, in the case of a partnership, a partner, or any other agent of a corporation or association having duties of such responsibility that his conduct may fairly be assumed to represent the policy of the corporation or association.

(5) In any prosecution of a corporation or an unincorporated association for the commission of an offense included within the terms of Subsection (1)(a) or Subsection (3)(a) of this Section, other than an offense for which absolute liability has been imposed, it shall be a defense if the defendant proves by a preponderance of evidence that the high managerial agent having supervisory responsibility over the subject matter of the offense employed due diligence to prevent its commission. This paragraph shall not apply if it is plainly inconsistent with the legislative purpose in defining the particular offense.

(6)(a) A person is legally accountable for any conduct he performs or causes to be performed in the name of the corporation or an unincorporated association or in its behalf to the same extent as if it were performed in his own name or behalf.

(b) Whenever a duty to act is imposed by law upon a corporation or an unincorporated association, any agent of the corporation or association having primary responsibility for the discharge of the duty is legally accountable for a reckless omission to perform the required act to the same extent as if the duty were imposed by law directly upon himself.

(c) When a person is convicted of an offense by reason of his legal accountability for the conduct of a corporation or an unincorporated association, he is subject to the sentence authorized by law when a natural person is convicted of an offense of the grade and the degree involved.

Section 2.08 Intoxication

(1) Except as provided in Subsection (4) of this Section, intoxication of the actor is not a defense unless it negatives an element of the offense.

(2) When recklessness establishes an element of the offense, if the actor, due to self-induced intoxication, is unaware of a risk of which he would have been aware had he been sober, such unawareness is immaterial.

(3) Intoxication does not, in itself, constitute mental disease within the meaning of Section 4.01.

(4) Intoxication which (a) is not self-induced or (b) is pathological is an affirmative defense if by reason of such intoxication the actor at the time of his conduct lacks substantial capacity either to appreciate its criminality [wrongfulness] or to conform his conduct to the requirements of law.

(5) *Definitions.* In this Section unless a different meaning plainly is required:

(a) "intoxication" means a disturbance of mental or physical capacities resulting from the introduction of substances into the body;

(b) "self-induced intoxication" means intoxication caused by substances which the actor knowingly introduces into his body, the tendency of which to cause intoxication he knows or ought to know, unless he introduces them pursuant to medical advice or under such circumstances as would afford a defense to a charge of crime;

(c) "pathological intoxication" means intoxication grossly excessive in degree, given the amount of the intoxicant, to which the actor does not know he is susceptible.

Section 2.09 Duress

(1) It is an affirmative defense that the actor engaged in the conduct charged to constitute an offense because he was coerced to do so by the use of, or a threat to use, unlawful force against his person or the person of another, which a person of reasonable firmness in his situation would have been unable to resist.

(2) The defense provided by this Section is unavailable if the actor recklessly placed himself in a situation in which it was probable that he would be subjected to duress. The defense is also unavailable if he was negligent in placing himself in such a situation, whenever negligence suffices to establish culpability for the offense charged.

(3) It is not a defense that a woman acted on the command of her husband, unless she acted under such coercion as would establish a defense under this

Section. [The presumption that a woman, acting in the presence of her husband, is coerced is abolished.]

(4) When the conduct of the actor would otherwise be justifiable under Section 3.02, this Section does not preclude such defense.

Section 2.10 Military Orders

It is an affirmative defense that the actor, in engaging in the conduct charged to constitute an offense, does no more than execute an order of his superior in the armed services which he does not know to be unlawful.

Section 2.11 Consent

(1) *In General.* The consent of the victim to conduct charged to constitute an offense or to the result thereof is a defense if such consent negatives an element of the offense or precludes the infliction of the harm or evil sought to be prevented by the law defining the offense.

(2) *Consent to Bodily Harm.* When conduct is charged to constitute an offense because it causes or threatens bodily harm, consent to such conduct or to the infliction of such harm is a defense if:

(a) the bodily harm consented to or threatened by the conduct consented to is not serious; or

(b) the conduct and the harm are reasonably foreseeable hazards of joint participation in a lawful athletic contest or competitive sport; or

(c) the consent establishes a justification for the conduct under Article 3 of the Code.

(3) *Ineffective Consent.* Unless otherwise provided by the Code or by the law defining the offense, assent does not constitute consent if:

(a) it is given by a person who is legally incompetent to authorize the conduct charged to constitute the offense; or

(b) it is given by a person who by reason of youth, mental disease or defect or intoxication is manifestly unable or known by the actor to be unable to make a reasonable judgment as to the nature or harmfulness of the conduct charged to constitute the offense; or

(c) it is given by a person whose improvident consent is sought to be prevented by the law defining the offense; or

(d) it is induced by force, duress or deception of a kind sought to be prevented by the law defining the offense.

Section 2.12 De Minimis Infractions

The Court shall dismiss a prosecution if, having regard to the nature of the conduct charged to constitute an offense and the nature of the attendant circumstances, it finds that the defendant's conduct:

(1) was within a customary license or tolerance, neither expressly negatived by the person whose interest was infringed nor inconsistent with the purpose of the law defining the offense; or

(2) did not actually cause or threaten the harm or evil sought to be prevented by the law defining the offense or did so only to an extent too trivial to warrant the condemnation of conviction; or

(3) presents such other extenuations that it cannot reasonably be regarded as envisaged by the legislature in forbidding the offense.

The Court shall not dismiss a prosecution under Subsection (3) of this Section without filing a written statement of its reasons.

Section 2.13 Entrapment

(1) A public law enforcement official or a person acting in cooperation with such an official perpetrates an entrapment if for the purpose of obtaining evidence of the commission of an offense, he induces or encourages another person to engage in conduct constituting such offense by either:

(a) making knowingly false representations designed to induce the belief that such conduct is not prohibited; or

(b) employing methods of persuasion or inducement which create a substantial risk that such an offense will be committed by persons other than those who are ready to commit it.

(2) Except as provided in Subsection (3) of this Section, a person prosecuted for an offense shall be acquitted if he proves by a preponderance of evidence that his conduct occurred in response to an entrapment. The issue of entrapment shall be tried by the Court in the absence of the jury.

(3) The defense afforded by this Section is unavailable when causing or threatening bodily injury is an element of the offense charged and the prosecution is based on conduct causing or threatening such injury to a person other than the person perpetrating the entrapment.

ARTICLE 3. GENERAL PRINCIPLES OF JUSTIFICATION

Section 3.01 Justification an Affirmative Defense; Civil Remedies Unaffected

(1) In any prosecution based on conduct which is justifiable under this Article, justification is an affirmative defense.

(2) The fact that conduct is justifiable under this Article does not abolish or impair any remedy for such conduct which is available in any civil action.

Section 3.02 Justification Generally: Choice of Evils

(1) Conduct which the actor believes to be necessary to avoid a harm or evil to himself or to another is justifiable, provided that:

(a) the harm or evil sought to be avoided by such conduct is greater than that sought to be prevented by the law defining the offense charged; and

(b) neither the Code nor other law defining the offense provides exceptions or defenses dealing with the specific situation involved; and

(c) a legislative purpose to exclude the justification claimed does not otherwise plainly appear.

(2) When the actor was reckless or negligent in bringing about the situation requiring a choice of harms or evils or in appraising the necessity for his conduct, the justification afforded by this Section is unavailable in a prosecution for any offense for which recklessness or negligence, as the case may be, suffices to establish culpability.

Section 3.03 Execution of Public Duty

(1) Except as provided in Subsection (2) of this Section, conduct is justifiable when it is required or authorized by:

(a) the law defining the duties or functions of a public officer or the assistance to be rendered to such officer in the performance of his duties; or

(b) the law governing the execution of legal process; or

(c) the judgment or order of a competent court or tribunal; or

(d) the law governing the armed services or the lawful conduct of war; or

(e) any other provision of law imposing a public duty.

(2) The other sections of this Article apply to:

(a) the use of force upon or toward the person of another for any of the purposes dealt with in such sections; and

(b) the use of deadly force for any purpose, unless the use of such force is otherwise expressly authorized by law or occurs in the lawful conduct of war.

(3) The justification afforded by Subsection (1) of this Section applies:

(a) when the actor believes his conduct to be required or authorized by the judgment or direction of a competent court or tribunal or in the lawful execution of legal process, notwithstanding lack of jurisdiction of the court or defect in the legal process; and

(b) when the actor believes his conduct to be required or authorized to assist a public officer in the performance of his duties, notwithstanding that the officer exceeded his legal authority.

Section 3.04 Use of Force in Self-Protection

(1) *Use of Force Justifiable for Protection of the Person.* Subject to the provisions of this Section and of Section 3.09, the use of force upon or toward another person is justifiable when the actor believes that such force is immediately necessary for the purpose of protecting himself against the use of unlawful force by such other person on the present occasion.

(2) *Limitations on Justifying Necessity for Use of Force.*

(a) The use of force is not justifiable under this Section:

(i) to resist an arrest which the actor knows is being made by a peace officer, although the arrest is unlawful; or

(ii) to resist force used by the occupier or possessor of property or by another person on his behalf, where the actor knows that the person using the force is doing so under a claim of right to protect the property, except that this limitation shall not apply if:

(1) the actor is a public officer acting in the performance of his duties or a person lawfully assisting him therein or a person making or assisting in a lawful arrest; or

(2) the actor has been unlawfully dispossessed of the property and is making a re-entry or recaption justified by Section 3.06; or

(3) the actor believes that such force is necessary to protect himself against death or serious bodily harm.

(b) The use of deadly force is not justifiable under this Section unless the actor believes that such force is necessary to protect himself against death, serious bodily harm, kidnapping or sexual intercourse compelled by force or threat; nor is it justifiable if:

(i) the actor, with the purpose of causing death or serious bodily harm, provoked the use of force against himself in the same encounter; or

(ii) the actor knows that he can avoid the necessity of using such force with complete safety by retreating or by surrendering possession of a thing to a person asserting a claim of right thereto or by complying with a demand that he abstain from any action which he has no duty to take, except that:

(1) the actor is not obliged to retreat from his dwelling or place of work, unless he was the initial aggressor or is assailed in his place of work by another person whose place of work the actor knows it to be; and

(2) a public officer justified in using force in the performance of his duties or a person justified in using force in his assistance or a person justified in using force in making an arrest or preventing an escape is not obliged to desist from efforts to perform such duty, effect such arrest or prevent such escape because of resistance or threatened resistance by or on behalf of the person against whom such action is directed.

(c) Except as required by paragraphs (a) and (b) of this Subsection, a person employing protective force may estimate the necessity thereof under the circumstances as he believes them to be when the force is used, without retreating, surrendering possession, doing any other act which he has no legal duty to do or abstaining from any lawful action.

(3) *Use of Confinement as Protective Force.* The justification afforded by this Section extends to the use of confinement as protective force only if the actor takes all reasonable measures to terminate the confinement as soon as he knows that he safely can, unless the person confined has been arrested on a charge of crime.

Section 3.05 Use of Force for the Protection of Other Persons

(1) Subject to the provisions of this Section and of Section 3.09, the use of force upon or toward the person of another is justifiable to protect a third person when:

(a) the actor would be justified under Section 3.04 in using such force to protect himself against the injury he believes to be threatened to the person whom he seeks to protect; and

(b) under the circumstances as the actor believes them to be, the person whom he seeks to protect would be justified in using such protective force; and

(c) the actor believes that his intervention is necessary for the protection of such other person.

(2) Notwithstanding Subsection (1) of this Section:

(a) when the actor would be obliged under Section 3.04 to retreat, to surrender the possession of a thing or to comply with a demand before using force in self-protection, he is not obliged to do so before using force for the protection of another person, unless he knows that he can thereby secure the complete safety of such other person; and

(b) when the person whom the actor seeks to protect would be obliged under Section 3.04 to retreat, to surrender the possession of a thing or to comply with a demand if he knew that he could obtain complete safety by so doing, the actor is obliged to try to cause him to do so before using force in his protection if the actor knows that he can obtain complete safety in that way; and

(c) neither the actor nor the person whom he seeks to protect is obliged to retreat when in the other's dwelling or place of work to any greater extent than in his own.

Section 3.06 Use of Force for the Protection of Property

(1) *Use of Force Justifiable for Protection of Property.* Subject to the provisions of this Section and of Section 3.09, the use of force upon or toward the person of another is justifiable when the actor believes that such force is immediately necessary:

(a) to prevent or terminate an unlawful entry or other trespass upon land or a trespass against or the unlawful carrying away of tangible, movable property, provided that such land or movable property is, or is believed by the actor to be, in his possession or in the possession of another person for whose protection he acts; or

(b) to effect an entry or re-entry upon land or to retake tangible movable property, provided that the actor believes that he or the person by whose authority he acts or a person from whom he or such other person derives title was unlawfully dispossessed of such land or movable property and is entitled to possession, and provided, further, that:

(i) the force is used immediately or on fresh pursuit after such dispossession; or

(ii) the actor believes that the person against whom he uses force has no claim of right to the possession of the property and, in the case of land, the circumstances, as the actor believes them to be, are of such urgency that it would be an exceptional hardship to postpone the entry or re-entry until a court order is obtained.

(2) *Meaning of Possession.* For the purposes of Subsection (1) of this Section:

(a) a person who has parted with the custody of property to another who refuses to restore it to him is no longer in possession, unless the property is movable and was and still is located on land in his possession;

(b) a person who has been dispossessed of land does not regain possession thereof merely by setting foot thereon;

(c) a person who has a license to use or occupy real property is deemed to be in possession thereof except against the licensor acting under claim of right.

(3) *Limitations on Justifiable Use of Force.*

(a) *Request to Desist.* The use of force is justifiable under this Section only if the actor first requests the person against whom such force is used to desist from his interference with the property, unless the actor believes that:

(i) such request would be useless; or

(ii) it would be dangerous to himself or another person to make the request; or

(iii) substantial harm will be done to the physical condition of the property which is sought to be protected before the request can effectively be made.

(b) *Exclusion of Trespasser.* The use of force to prevent or terminate a trespass is not justifiable under this Section if the actor knows that the exclusion of the trespasser will expose him to substantial danger of serious bodily harm.

(c) *Resistance of Lawful Re-entry or Recaption.* The use of force to prevent an entry or re-entry upon land or the recaption of movable property is not justifiable under this Section, although the actor believes that such re-entry or recaption is unlawful, if:

(i) the re-entry or recaption is made by or on behalf of a person who was actually dispossessed of the property; and

(ii) it is otherwise justifiable under paragraph (1)(b) of this Section.

(d) *Use of Deadly Force.* The use of deadly force is not justifiable under this Section unless the actor believes that:

(i) the person against whom the force is used is attempting to dispossess him of his dwelling otherwise than under a claim of right to its possession; or

(ii) the person against whom the force is used is attempting to commit or consummate arson, burglary, robbery or other felonious theft or property destruction and either:

(1) has employed or threatened deadly force against or in the presence of the actor; or

(2) the use of force other than deadly force to prevent the commission or the consummation of the crime would expose the actor or another in his presence to substantial danger of serious bodily harm.

(4) *Use of Confinement as Protective Force.* The justification afforded by this Section extends to the use of confinement as protective force only if the actor takes all reasonable measures to terminate the confinement as soon as he knows that he can do so with safety to the property, unless the person confined has been arrested on a charge of crime.

(5) *Use of Device to Protect Property.* The justification afforded by this Section extends to the use of a device for the purpose of protecting property only if:

(a) the device is not designed to cause or known to create a substantial risk of causing death or serious bodily harm; and

(b) the use of the particular device to protect the property from entry or trespass is reasonable under the circumstances, as the actor believes them to be; and

(c) the device is one customarily used for such a purpose or reasonable care is taken to make known to probable intruders the fact that it is used.

(6) *Use of Force to Pass Wrongful Obstructor.* The use of force to pass a person whom the actor believes to be purposely or knowingly and unjustifiably obstructing the actor from going to a place to which he may lawfully go is justifiable, provided that:

(a) the actor believes that the person against whom he uses force has no claim of right to obstruct the actor; and

(b) the actor is not being obstructed from entry or movement on land which he knows to be in the possession or custody of the person obstructing him, or in the possession or custody of another person by whose authority the obstructor acts, unless the circumstances, as the actor believes them to be, are of such urgency that it would not be reasonable to postpone the entry or movement on such land until a court order is obtained; and

(c) the force used is not greater than would be justifiable if the person obstructing the actor were using force against him to prevent his passage.

Section 3.07 Use of Force in Law Enforcement

(1) *Use of Force Justifiable to Effect an Arrest.* Subject to the provisions of this Section and of Section 3.09, the use of force upon or toward the person of another is justifiable when the actor is making or assisting in making an arrest and the actor believes that such force is immediately necessary to effect a lawful arrest.

(2) *Limitations on the Use of Force.*

(a) The use of force is not justifiable under this Section unless:

(i) the actor makes known the purpose of the arrest or believes that it is otherwise known by or cannot reasonably be made known to the person to be arrested; and

(ii) when the arrest is made under a warrant, the warrant is valid or believed by the actor to be valid.

(b) The use of deadly force is not justifiable under this Section unless:

(i) the arrest is for a felony; and

(ii) the person effecting the arrest is authorized to act as a peace officer or is assisting a person whom he believes to be authorized to act as a peace officer; and

(iii) the actor believes that the force employed creates no substantial risk of injury to innocent persons; and

(iv) the actor believes that:

(1) the crime for which the arrest is made involved conduct including the use or threatened use of deadly force; or

(2) there is a substantial risk that the person to be arrested will cause death or serious bodily harm if his apprehension is delayed.

(3) *Use of Force to Prevent Escape from Custody.* The use of force to prevent the escape of an arrested person from custody is justifiable when the force could justifiably have been employed to effect the arrest under which the person is in custody, except that a guard or other person authorized to act as a peace officer is justified in using any force, including deadly force, which he believes to be immediately necessary to prevent the escape of a person from a jail, prison, or other institution for the detention of persons charged with or convicted of a crime.

(4) *Use of Force by Private Person Assisting an Unlawful Arrest.*

(a) A private person who is summoned by a peace officer to assist in effecting an unlawful arrest, is justified in using any force which he would be justified in using if the arrest were lawful, provided that he does not believe the arrest is unlawful.

(b) A private person who assists another private person in effecting an unlawful arrest, or who, not being summoned, assists a peace officer in effecting an unlawful arrest, is justified in using any force which he would be justified in using if the arrest were lawful, provided that (i) he believes the arrest is lawful, and (ii) the arrest would be lawful if the facts were as he believes them to be.

(5) *Use of Force to Prevent Suicide or the Commission of a Crime.*

(a) The use of force upon or toward the person of another is justifiable when the actor believes that such force is immediately necessary to prevent such other person from committing suicide, inflicting serious bodily harm upon himself, committing or consummating the commission of a crime involving or threatening bodily harm, damage to or loss of property or a breach of the peace, except that:

(i) any limitations imposed by the other provisions of this Article on the justifiable use of force in self-protection, for the protection of others, the protection of property, the effectuation of an arrest or the prevention of an escape from custody shall apply notwithstanding the criminality of the conduct against which such force is used; and

(ii) the use of deadly force is not in any event justifiable under this Subsection unless:

(1) the actor believes that there is a substantial risk that the person whom he seeks to prevent from committing a crime will cause death or serious bodily harm to another unless the commis-

sion or the consummation of the crime is prevented and that the use of such force presents no substantial risk of injury to innocent persons; or

(2) the actor believes that the use of such force is necessary to suppress a riot or mutiny after the rioters or mutineers have been ordered to disperse and warned, in any particular manner that the law may require, that such force will be used if they do not obey.

(b) The justification afforded by this Subsection extends to the use of confinement as preventive force only if the actor takes all reasonable measures to terminate the confinement as soon as he knows that he safely can, unless the person confined has been arrested on a charge of crime.

Section 3.08 Use of Force by Persons With Special Responsibility for Care, Discipline or Safety of Others

The use of force upon or toward the person of another is justifiable if:

(1) the actor is the parent or guardian or other person similarly responsible for the general care and supervision of a minor or a person acting at the request of such parent, guardian or other responsible person and:

(a) the force is used for the purpose of safeguarding or promoting the welfare of the minor, including the prevention or punishment of his misconduct; and

(b) the force used is not designed to cause or known to create a substantial risk of causing death, serious bodily harm, disfigurement, extreme pain or mental distress or gross degradation; or

(2) the actor is a teacher or a person otherwise entrusted with the care or supervision for a special purpose of a minor and:

(a) the actor believes that the force used is necessary to further such special purpose, including the maintenance of reasonable discipline in a school, class or other group, and that the use of such force is consistent with the welfare of the minor; and

(b) the degree of force, if it had been used by the parent or guardian of the minor, would not be unjustifiable under Subsection (1)(b) of this Section; or

(3) the actor is the guardian or other person similarly responsible for the general care and supervision of an incompetent person; and:

(a) the force is used for the purpose of safeguarding or promoting the welfare of the incompetent person, including the prevention of his misconduct, or, when such incompetent person is in a hospital or other institution for his care and custody, for the maintenance of reasonable discipline in such institution; and

(b) the force used is not designed to cause or known to create a substantial risk of causing death, serious bodily harm, disfigurement, extreme or unnecessary pain, mental distress, or humiliation; or

(4) the actor is a doctor or other therapist or a person assisting him at his direction, and:

(a) the force is used for the purpose of administering a recognized form of treatment which the actor believes to be adapted to promoting the physical or mental health of the patient; and

(b) the treatment is administered with the consent of the patient or, if the patient is a minor or an incompetent person, with the consent of his parent or guardian or other person legally competent to consent in his behalf, or the treatment is administered in an emergency when the actor believes that no one competent to consent can be consulted and that a reasonable person, wishing to safeguard the welfare of the patient, would consent; or

(5) the actor is a warden or other authorized official of a correctional institution, and:

(a) he believes that the force used is necessary for the purpose of enforcing the lawful rules or procedures of the institution, unless his belief in the lawfulness of the rule or procedure sought to be enforced is erroneous and his error is due to ignorance or mistake as to the provisions of the Code, any other provision of the criminal law or the law governing the administration of the institution; and

(b) the nature or degree of force used is not forbidden by Article 303 or 304 of the Code; and

(c) if deadly force is used, its use is otherwise justifiable under this Article; or

(6) the actor is a person responsible for the safety of a vessel or an aircraft or a person acting at his direction, and

(a) he believes that the force used is necessary to prevent interference with the operation of the vessel or aircraft or obstruction of the execution of a lawful order, unless his belief in the lawfulness of the order is erroneous and his error is due to ignorance or mistake as to the law defining his authority; and

(b) if deadly force is used, its use is otherwise justifiable under this Article; or

(7) the actor is a person who is authorized or required by law to maintain order or decorum in a vehicle, train or other carrier or in a place where others are assembled, and:

(a) he believes that the force used is necessary for such purpose; and

(b) the force used is not designed to cause or known to create a substantial risk of causing death, bodily harm, or extreme mental distress.

Section 3.09 Mistake of Law as to Unlawfulness of Force or Legality of Arrest; Reckless or Negligent Use of Otherwise Justifiable Force; Reckless or Negligent Injury or Risk of Injury to Innocent Persons

(1) The justification afforded by Sections 3.04 to 3.07, inclusive, is unavailable when:

(a) the actor's belief in the unlawfulness of the force or conduct against which he employs protective force or his belief in the lawfulness of an arrest which he endeavors to effect by force is erroneous; and

(b) his error is due to ignorance or mistake as to the provisions of the Code, any other provision of the criminal law or the law governing the legality of an arrest or search.

(2) When the actor believes that the use of force upon or toward the person of another is necessary for any of the purposes for which such belief would establish a justification under Sections 3.03 to 3.08 but the actor is reckless or negligent in having such belief or in acquiring or failing to acquire any knowledge or belief which is material to the justifiability of his use of force, the justification afforded by those Sections is unavailable in a prosecution for an offense for which recklessness or negligence, as the case may be, suffices to establish culpability.

(3) When the actor is justified under Sections 3.03 to 3.08 in using force upon or toward the person of another but he recklessly or negligently injures or creates a risk of injury to innocent persons, the justification afforded by those Sections is unavailable in a prosecution for such recklessness or negligence towards innocent persons.

Section 3.10 Justification in Property Crimes

Conduct involving the appropriation, seizure or destruction of, damage to, intrusion on or interference with property is justifiable under circumstances which would establish a defense of privilege in a civil action based thereon, unless:

(1) the Code or the law defining the offense deals with the specific situation involved; or

(2) a legislative purpose to exclude the justification claimed otherwise plainly appears.

Section 3.11 Definitions

In this Article, unless a different meaning plainly is required:

(1) "unlawful force" means force, including confinement, which is employed without the consent of the person against whom it is directed and the employment of which constitutes an offense or actionable tort or would constitute such offense or tort except for a defense (such as the absence of intent, negligence, or mental capacity; duress; youth; or diplomatic status) not amounting to a privilege to use the force. Assent constitutes consent, within the meaning of this Section, whether or not it otherwise is legally effective, except assent to the infliction of death or serious bodily harm.

(2) "deadly force" means force which the actor uses with the purpose of causing or which he knows to create a substantial risk of causing death or serious bodily harm. Purposely firing a firearm in the direction of another person or at a vehicle in which another person is believed to be constitutes deadly force. A threat to cause death or serious bodily harm, by the production of a weapon or otherwise, so long as the actor's purpose is limited to creating an apprehension that he will use deadly force if necessary, does not constitute deadly force;

(3) "dwelling" means any building or structure, though movable or temporary, or a portion thereof, which is for the time being the actor's home or place of lodging.

ARTICLE 4. RESPONSIBILITY

Section 4.01 Mental Disease or Defect Excluding Responsibility

(1) A person is not responsible for criminal conduct if at the time of such conduct as a result of mental disease or defect he lacks substantial capacity either to appreciate the criminality [wrongfulness] of his conduct or to conform his conduct to the requirements of law.

(2) As used in this Article, the terms "mental disease or defect" do not include an abnormality manifested only by repeated criminal or otherwise anti-social conduct.

Section 4.02 Evidence of Mental Disease or Defect Admissible When Relevant to Element of the Offense; [Mental Disease or Defect Impairing Capacity as Ground for Mitigation of Punishment in Capital Cases]

(1) Evidence that the defendant suffered from a mental disease or defect is admissible whenever it is relevant to prove that the defendant did or did not have a state of mind which is an element of the offense.

[(2) Whenever the jury or the Court is authorized to determine or to recommend whether or not the defendant shall be sentenced to death or imprisonment upon conviction, evidence that the capacity of the defendant to appreciate the criminality [wrongfulness] of his conduct or to conform his conduct to the requirements of law was impaired as a result of mental disease or defect is admissible in favor of sentence of imprisonment.]

Section 4.03 Mental Disease or Defect Excluding Responsibility Is Affirmative Defense; Requirement of Notice; Form of Verdict and Judgment When Finding of Irresponsibility Is Made

(1) Mental disease or defect excluding responsibility is an affirmative defense.

(2) Evidence of mental disease or defect excluding responsibility is not admissible unless the defendant, at the time of entering his plea of not guilty or within ten days thereafter or at such later time as the Court may for good cause permit, files a written notice of his purpose to rely on such defense.

(3) When the defendant is acquitted on the ground of mental disease or defect excluding responsibility, the verdict and the judgment shall so state.

Section 4.04 Mental Disease or Defect Excluding Fitness to Proceed

No person who as a result of mental disease or defect lacks capacity to understand the proceedings against him or to assist in his own defense shall be tried, convicted or sentenced for the commission of an offense so long as such incapacity endures.

Section 4.10 Immaturity Excluding Criminal Conviction; Transfer of Proceedings to Juvenile Court

(1) A person shall not be tried for or convicted of an offense if:

(a) at the time of the conduct charged to constitute the offense he was less than sixteen years of age [, in which case the Juvenile Court shall have exclusive jurisdiction *]; or

(b) at the time of the conduct charged to constitute the offense he was sixteen or seventeen years of age, unless:

(i) the Juvenile Court has no jurisdiction over him, or,

(ii) the Juvenile Court has entered an order waiving jurisdiction and consenting to the institution of criminal proceedings against him.

(2) No court shall have jurisdiction to try or convict a person of an offense if criminal proceedings against him are barred by Subsection (1) of this Section. When it appears that a person charged with the commission of an offense may be of such an age that criminal proceedings may be barred under Subsection (1) of this Section, the Court shall hold a hearing thereon, and the burden shall be on the prosecution to establish to the satisfaction of the Court that the criminal proceeding is not barred upon such grounds. If the Court determines that the proceeding is barred, custody of the person charged shall be surrendered to the Juvenile Court, and the case, including all papers and processes relating thereto, shall be transferred.

ARTICLE 5. INCHOATE CRIMES

Section 5.01 Criminal Attempt

(1) *Definition of Attempt.* A person is guilty of an attempt to commit a crime if, acting with the kind of culpability otherwise required for commission of the crime, he:

(a) purposely engages in conduct which would constitute the crime if the attendant circumstances were as he believes them to be; or

(b) when causing a particular result is an element of the crime, does or omits to do anything with the purpose of causing or with the belief that it will cause such result without further conduct on his part; or

(c) purposely does or omits to do anything which, under the circumstances as he believes them to be, is an act or omission constituting a substantial step in a course of conduct planned to culminate in his commission of the crime.

(2) *Conduct Which May Be Held Substantial Step Under Subsection (1)(c).* Conduct shall not be held to constitute a substantial step under Subsection (1)(c) of this Section unless it is strongly corroborative of the actor's criminal purpose. Without negativing the sufficiency of other conduct, the following, if strongly corroborative of the actor's criminal purpose, shall not be held insufficient as a matter of law:

(a) lying in wait, searching for or following the contemplated victim of the crime;

* The bracketed words are unnecessary if the Juvenile Court Act so provides or is amended accordingly.

(b) enticing or seeking to entice the contemplated victim of the crime to go to the place contemplated for its commission;

(c) reconnoitering the place contemplated for the commission of the crime;

(d) unlawful entry of a structure, vehicle or enclosure in which it is contemplated that the crime will be committed;

(e) possession of materials to be employed in the commission of the crime, which are specially designed for such unlawful use or which can serve no lawful purpose of the actor under the circumstances;

(f) possession, collection or fabrication of materials to be employed in the commission of the crime, at or near the place contemplated for its commission, where such possession, collection or fabrication serves no lawful purpose of the actor under the circumstances;

(g) soliciting an innocent agent to engage in conduct constituting an element of the crime.

(3) *Conduct Designed to Aid Another in Commission of a Crime.* A person who engages in conduct designed to aid another to commit a crime which would establish his complicity under Section 2.06 if the crime were committed by such other person, is guilty of an attempt to commit the crime, although the crime is not committed or attempted by such other person.

(4) *Renunciation of Criminal Purpose.* When the actor's conduct would otherwise constitute an attempt under Subsection (1)(b) or (1)(c) of this Section, it is an affirmative defense that he abandoned his effort to commit the crime or otherwise prevented its commission, under circumstances manifesting a complete and voluntary renunciation of his criminal purpose. The establishment of such defense does not, however, affect the liability of an accomplice who did not join in such abandonment or prevention.

Within the meaning of this Article, renunciation of criminal purpose is not voluntary if it is motivated, in whole or in part, by circumstances, not present or apparent at the inception of the actor's course of conduct, which increase the probability of detection or apprehension or which make more difficult the accomplishment of the criminal purpose. Renunciation is not complete if it is motivated by a decision to postpone the criminal conduct until a more advantageous time or to transfer the criminal effort to another but similar objective or victim.

Section 5.02 Criminal Solicitation

(1) *Definition of Solicitation.* A person is guilty of solicitation to commit a crime if with the purpose of promoting or facilitating its commission he commands, encourages or requests another person to engage in specific conduct which would constitute such crime or an attempt to commit such crime or which would establish his complicity in its commission or attempted commission.

(2) *Uncommunicated Solicitation.* It is immaterial under Subsection (1) of this Section that the actor fails to communicate with the person he solicits to commit a crime if his conduct was designed to effect such communication.

(3) *Renunciation of Criminal Purpose.* It is an affirmative defense that the actor, after soliciting another person to commit a crime, persuaded him not to do so or otherwise prevented the commission of the crime, under circumstances manifesting a complete and voluntary renunciation of his criminal purpose.

Section 5.03 Criminal Conspiracy

(1) *Definition of Conspiracy.* A person is guilty of conspiracy with another person or persons to commit a crime if with the purpose of promoting or facilitating its commission he:

(a) agrees with such other person or persons that they or one or more of them will engage in conduct which constitutes such crime or an attempt or solicitation to commit such crime; or

(b) agrees to aid such other person or persons in the planning or commission of such crime or of an attempt or solicitation to commit such crime.

(2) *Scope of Conspiratorial Relationship.* If a person guilty of conspiracy, as defined by Subsection (1) of this Section, knows that a person with whom he conspires to commit a crime has conspired with another person or persons to commit the same crime, he is guilty of conspiring with such other person or persons, whether or not he knows their identity, to commit such crime.

(3) *Conspiracy With Multiple Criminal Objectives.* If a person conspires to commit a number of crimes, he is guilty of only one conspiracy so long as such multiple crimes are the object of the same agreement or continuous conspiratorial relationship.

(4) *Joinder and Venue in Conspiracy Prosecutions.*

(a) Subject to the provisions of paragraph (b) of this Subsection, two or more persons charged with criminal conspiracy may be prosecuted jointly if:

(i) they are charged with conspiring with one another; or

(ii) the conspiracies alleged, whether they have the same or different parties, are so related that they constitute different aspects of a scheme of organized criminal conduct.

(b) In any joint prosecution under paragraph (a) of this Subsection:

(i) no defendant shall be charged with a conspiracy in any county [parish or district] other than one in which he entered into such conspiracy or in which an overt act pursuant to such conspiracy was done by him or by a person with whom he conspired; and

(ii) neither the liability of any defendant nor the admissibility against him of evidence of acts or declarations of another shall be enlarged by such joinder; and

(iii) the Court shall order a severance or take a special verdict as to any defendant who so requests, if it deems it necessary or appropriate to promote the fair determination of his guilt or innocence, and shall take any other proper measures to protect the fairness of the trial.

(5) *Overt Act.* No person may be convicted of conspiracy to commit a crime, other than a felony of the first or second degree, unless an overt act in

pursuance of such conspiracy is alleged and proved to have been done by him or by a person with whom he conspired.

(6) *Renunciation of Criminal Purpose.* It is an affirmative defense that the actor, after conspiring to commit a crime, thwarted the success of the conspiracy, under circumstances manifesting a complete and voluntary renunciation of his criminal purpose.

(7) *Duration of Conspiracy.* For purposes of Section 1.06(4):

(a) conspiracy is a continuing course of conduct which terminates when the crime or crimes which are its object are committed or the agreement that they be committed is abandoned by the defendant and by those with whom he conspired; and

(b) such abandonment is presumed if neither the defendant nor anyone with whom he conspired does any overt act in pursuance of the conspiracy during the applicable period of limitation; and

(c) if an individual abandons the agreement, the conspiracy is terminated as to him only if and when he advises those with whom he conspired of his abandonment or he informs the law enforcement authorities of the existence of the conspiracy and of his participation therein.

Section 5.04 Incapacity, Irresponsibility or Immunity of Party to Solicitation or Conspiracy

(1) Except as provided in Subsection (2) of this Section, it is immaterial to the liability of a person who solicits or conspires with another to commit a crime that:

(a) he or the person whom he solicits or with whom he conspires does not occupy a particular position or have a particular characteristic which is an element of such crime, if he believes that one of them does; or

(b) the person whom he solicits or with whom he conspires is irresponsible or has an immunity to prosecution or conviction for the commission of the crime.

(2) It is a defense to a charge of solicitation or conspiracy to commit a crime that if the criminal object were achieved, the actor would not be guilty of a crime under the law defining the offense or as an accomplice under Section 2.06(5) or 2.06(6)(a) or (b).

Section 5.05 Grading of Criminal Attempt, Solicitation and Conspiracy; Mitigation in Cases of Lesser Danger; Multiple Convictions Barred

(1) *Grading.* Except as otherwise provided in this Section, attempt, solicitation and conspiracy are crimes of the same grade and degree as the most serious offense which is attempted or solicited or is an object of the conspiracy. An attempt, solicitation or conspiracy to commit a [capital crime or a] felony of the first degree is a felony of the second degree.

(2) *Mitigation.* If the particular conduct charged to constitute a criminal attempt, solicitation or conspiracy is so inherently unlikely to result or culminate in the commission of a crime that neither such conduct nor the actor presents a public danger warranting the grading of such offense under this Section, the Court

shall exercise its power under Section 6.12 to enter judgment and impose sentence for a crime of lower grade or degree or, in extreme cases, may dismiss the prosecution.

(3) *Multiple Convictions.* A person may not be convicted of more than one offense defined by this Article for conduct designed to commit or to culminate in the commission of the same crime.

Section 5.06 Possessing Instruments of Crime; Weapons

(1) *Criminal Instruments Generally.* A person commits a misdemeanor if he possesses any instrument of crime with purpose to employ it criminally. "Instrument of crime" means:

(a) anything specially made or specially adapted for criminal use; or

(b) anything commonly used for criminal purposes and possessed by the actor under circumstances which do not negative unlawful purpose.

(2) *Presumption of Criminal Purpose from Possession of Weapon.* If a person possesses a firearm or other weapon on or about his person, in a vehicle occupied by him, or otherwise readily available for use, it shall be presumed that he had the purpose to employ it criminally, unless:

(a) the weapon is possessed in the actor's home or place of business;

(b) the actor is licensed or otherwise authorized by law to possess such weapon; or

(c) the weapon is a type commonly used in lawful sport.

"Weapon" means anything readily capable of lethal use and possessed under circumstances not manifestly appropriate for lawful uses which it may have; the term includes a firearm which is not loaded or lacks a clip or other component to render it immediately operable, and components which can readily be assembled into a weapon.

(3) *Presumptions as to Possession of Criminal Instruments in Automobiles.* Where a weapon or other instrument of crime is found in an automobile, it shall be presumed to be in the possession of the occupant if there is but one. If there is more than one occupant, it shall be presumed to be in the possession of all, except under the following circumstances:

(a) where it is found upon the person of one of the occupants;

(b) where the automobile is not a stolen one and the weapon or instrument is found out of view in a glove compartment, car trunk, or other enclosed customary depository, in which case it shall be presumed to be in the possession of the occupant or occupants who own or have authority to operate the automobile;

(c) in the case of a taxicab, a weapon or instrument found in the passengers' portion of the vehicle shall be presumed to be in the possession of all the passengers, if there are any, and, if not, in the possession of the driver.

Section 5.07 Prohibited Offensive Weapons

A person commits a misdemeanor if, except as authorized by law, he makes, repairs, sells, or otherwise deals in, uses, or possesses any offensive weapon.

"Offensive weapon" means any bomb, machine gun, sawed-off shotgun, firearm specially made or specially adapted for concealment or silent discharge, any blackjack, sandbag, metal knuckles, dagger, or other implement for the infliction of serious bodily harm which serves no common lawful purpose. It is a defense under this Section for the defendant to prove by a preponderance of evidence that he possessed or dealt with the weapon solely as a curio or in a dramatic performance, or that he possessed it briefly in consequence of having found it or taken it from an aggressor, or under circumstances similarly negativing any purpose or likelihood that the weapon would be used unlawfully. The presumptions provided in Section 5.06(3) are applicable to prosecutions under this Section.

PART II. DEFINITION OF SPECIFIC CRIMES

OFFENSES INVOLVING DANGER TO THE PERSON

ARTICLE 210. CRIMINAL HOMICIDE

Section 210.0 Definitions

In Articles 210–213, unless a different meaning plainly is required:

(1) "human being" means a person who has been born and is alive;

(2) "bodily injury" means physical pain, illness or any impairment of physical condition;

(3) "serious bodily injury" means bodily injury which creates a substantial risk of death or which causes serious, permanent disfigurement, or protracted loss or impairment of the function of any bodily member or organ;

(4) "deadly weapon" means any firearm, or other weapon, device, instrument, material or substance, whether animate or inanimate, which in the manner it is used or is intended to be used is known to be capable of producing death or serious bodily injury.

Section 210.1 Criminal Homicide

(1) A person is guilty of criminal homicide if he purposely, knowingly, recklessly or negligently causes the death of another human being.

(2) Criminal homicide is murder, manslaughter or negligent homicide.

Section 210.2 Murder

(1) Except as provided in Section 210.3(1)(b), criminal homicide constitutes murder when:

(a) it is committed purposely or knowingly; or

(b) it is committed recklessly under circumstances manifesting extreme indifference to the value of human life. Such recklessness and indifference are presumed if the actor is engaged or is an accomplice in the commission of, or an attempt to commit, or flight after committing or attempting to commit robbery, rape or deviate sexual intercourse by force or threat of force, arson, burglary, kidnapping or felonious escape.

(2) Murder is a felony of the first degree [but a person convicted of murder may be sentenced to death, as provided in Section 210.6].

Section 210.3 Manslaughter

(1) Criminal homicide constitutes manslaughter when:

(a) it is committed recklessly; or

(b) a homicide which would otherwise be murder is committed under the influence of extreme mental or emotional disturbance for which there is reasonable explanation or excuse. The reasonableness of such explanation or excuse shall be determined from the viewpoint of a person in the actor's situation under the circumstances as he believes them to be.

(2) Manslaughter is a felony of the second degree.

Section 210.4 Negligent Homicide

(1) Criminal homicide constitutes negligent homicide when it is committed negligently.

(2) Negligent homicide is a felony of the third degree.

Section 210.5 Causing or Aiding Suicide

(1) *Causing Suicide as Criminal Homicide.* A person may be convicted of criminal homicide for causing another to commit suicide only if he purposely causes such suicide by force, duress or deception.

(2) *Aiding or Soliciting Suicide as an Independent Offense.* A person who purposely aids or solicits another to commit suicide is guilty of a felony of the second degree if his conduct causes such suicide or an attempted suicide, and otherwise of a misdemeanor.

Section 210.6 Sentence of Death for Murder; Further Proceedings to Determine Sentence

(1) *Death Sentence Excluded.* When a defendant is found guilty of murder, the Court shall impose sentence for a felony of the first degree if it is satisfied that:

(a) none of the aggravating circumstances enumerated in Subsection (3) of this Section was established by the evidence at the trial or will be established if further proceedings are initiated under Subsection (2) of this Section; or

(b) substantial mitigating circumstances, established by the evidence at the trial, call for leniency; or

(c) the defendant, with the consent of the prosecuting attorney and the approval of the Court, pleaded guilty to murder as a felony of the first degree; or

(d) the defendant was under 18 years of age at the time of the commission of the crime; or

(e) the defendant's physical or mental condition calls for leniency; or

(f) although the evidence suffices to sustain the verdict, it does not foreclose all doubt respecting the defendant's guilt.

(2) *Determination by Court or by Court and Jury.* Unless the Court imposes sentence under Subsection (1) of this Section, it shall conduct a separate proceeding to determine whether the defendant should be sentenced for a felony of the first degree or sentenced to death. The proceeding shall be conducted before the Court alone if the defendant was convicted by a Court sitting without a jury or upon his plea of guilty or if the prosecuting attorney and the defendant waive a jury with respect to sentence. In other cases it shall be conducted before the Court sitting with the jury which determined the defendant's guilt or, if the Court for good cause shown discharges that jury, with a new jury empanelled for the purpose.

In the proceeding, evidence may be presented as to any matter that the Court deems relevant to sentence, including but not limited to the nature and circumstances of the crime, the defendant's character, background, history, mental and physical condition and any of the aggravating or mitigating circumstances enumerated in Subsections (3) and (4) of this Section. Any such evidence which the Court deems to have probative force may be received, regardless of its admissibility under the exclusionary rules of evidence, provided that the defendant's counsel is accorded a fair opportunity to rebut any hearsay statements. The prosecuting attorney and the defendant or his counsel shall be permitted to present argument for or against sentence of death.

The determination whether sentence of death shall be imposed shall be in the discretion of the Court, except that when the proceeding is conducted before the Court sitting with a jury, the Court shall not impose sentence of death unless it submits to the jury the issue whether the defendant should be sentenced to death or to imprisonment and the jury returns a verdict that the sentence should be death. If the jury is unable to reach a unanimous verdict, the Court shall dismiss the jury and impose sentence for a felony of the first degree.

The Court, in exercising its discretion as to sentence, and the jury, in determining upon its verdict, shall take into account the aggravating and mitigating circumstances enumerated in Subsections (3) and (4) and any other facts that it deems relevant, but it shall not impose or recommend sentence of death unless it finds one of the aggravating circumstances enumerated in Subsection (3) and further finds that there are no mitigating circumstances sufficiently substantial to call for leniency. When the issue is submitted to the jury, the Court shall so instruct and also shall inform the jury of the nature of the sentence of imprisonment that may be imposed, including its implication with respect to possible release upon parole, if the jury verdict is against sentence of death.

Alternative formulation of Subsection (2):

(2) *Determination by Court.* Unless the Court imposes sentence under Subsection (1) of this Section, it shall conduct a separate proceeding to determine whether the defendant should be sentenced for a felony of the first degree or sentenced to death. In the proceeding, the Court, in accordance with Section 7.07, shall consider the report of the pre-sentence investigation and, if a psychiatric examination has been ordered, the report of such examination. In addition, evidence may be presented as to any matter that the Court deems relevant to

sentence, including but not limited to the nature and circumstances of the crime, the defendant's character, background, history, mental and physical condition and any of the aggravating or mitigating circumstances enumerated in Subsections (3) and (4) of this Section. Any such evidence which the Court deems to have probative force may be received, regardless of its admissibility under the exclusionary rules of evidence, provided that the defendant's counsel is accorded a fair opportunity to rebut any hearsay statements. The prosecuting attorney and the defendant or his counsel shall be permitted to present argument for or against sentence of death.

The determination whether sentence of death shall be imposed shall be in the discretion of the Court. In exercising such discretion, the Court shall take into account the aggravating and mitigating circumstances enumerated in Subsections (3) and (4) and any other facts that it deems relevant but shall not impose sentence of death unless it finds one of the aggravating circumstances enumerated in Subsection (3) and further finds that there are no mitigating circumstances sufficiently substantial to call for leniency.

(3) *Aggravating Circumstances.*

(a) The murder was committed by a convict under sentence of imprisonment.

(b) The defendant was previously convicted of another murder or of a felony involving the use or threat of violence to the person.

(c) At the time the murder was committed the defendant also committed another murder.

(d) The defendant knowingly created a great risk of death to many persons.

(e) The murder was committed while the defendant was engaged or was an accomplice in the commission of, or an attempt to commit, or flight after committing or attempting to commit robbery, rape or deviate sexual intercourse by force or threat of force, arson, burglary or kidnapping.

(f) The murder was committed for the purpose of avoiding or preventing a lawful arrest or effecting an escape from lawful custody.

(g) The murder was committed for pecuniary gain.

(h) The murder was especially heinous, atrocious or cruel, manifesting exceptional depravity.

(4) *Mitigating Circumstances.*

(a) The defendant has no significant history of prior criminal activity.

(b) The murder was committed while the defendant was under the influence of extreme mental or emotional disturbance.

(c) The victim was a participant in the defendant's homicidal conduct or consented to the homicidal act.

(d) The murder was committed under circumstances which the defendant believed to provide a moral justification or extenuation for his conduct.

(e) The defendant was an accomplice in a murder committed by another person and his participation in the homicidal act was relatively minor.

(f) The defendant acted under duress or under the domination of another person.

(g) At the time of the murder, the capacity of the defendant to appreciate the criminality [wrongfulness] of his conduct or to conform his conduct to the requirements of law was impaired as a result of mental disease or defect or intoxication.

(h) The youth of the defendant at the time of the crime.

ARTICLE 211. ASSAULT; RECKLESS ENDANGERING; THREATS

Section 211.0 Definitions

In this Article, the definitions given in Section 210.0 apply unless a different meaning plainly is required.

Section 211.1 Assault

(1) *Simple Assault.* A person is guilty of assault if he:

(a) attempts to cause or purposely, knowingly or recklessly causes bodily injury to another; or

(b) negligently causes bodily injury to another with a deadly weapon; or

(c) attempts by physical menace to put another in fear of imminent serious bodily harm.

Simple assault is a misdemeanor unless committed in a fight or scuffle entered into by mutual consent, in which case it is a petty misdemeanor.

(2) *Aggravated Assault.* A person is guilty of aggravated assault if he:

(a) attempts to cause serious bodily injury to another, or causes such injury purposely, knowingly or recklessly under circumstances manifesting extreme indifference to the value of human life; or

(b) attempts to cause or purposely or knowingly causes bodily injury to another with a deadly weapon.

Aggravated assault under paragraph (a) is a felony of the second degree; aggravated assault under paragraph (b) is a felony of the third degree.

Section 211.2 Recklessly Endangering Another Person

A person commits a misdemeanor if he recklessly engages in conduct which places or may place another person in danger of death or serious bodily injury. Recklessness and danger shall be presumed where a person knowingly points a firearm at or in the direction of another, whether or not the actor believed the firearm to be loaded.

Section 211.3 Terroristic Threats

A person is guilty of a felony of the third degree if he threatens to commit any crime of violence with purpose to terrorize another or to cause evacuation of a building, place of assembly, or facility of public transportation, or otherwise to cause serious public inconvenience, or in reckless disregard of the risk of causing such terror or inconvenience.

ARTICLE 212. KIDNAPPING AND RELATED OFFENSES; COERCION

Section 212.0 Definitions

In this Article, the definitions given in Section 210.0 apply unless a different meaning plainly is required.

Section 212.1 Kidnapping

A person is guilty of kidnapping if he unlawfully removes another from his place of residence or business, or a substantial distance from the vicinity where he is found, or if he unlawfully confines another for a substantial period in a place of isolation, with any of the following purposes:

(a) to hold for ransom or reward, or as a shield or hostage; or

(b) to facilitate commission of any felony or flight thereafter; or

(c) to inflict bodily injury on or to terrorize the victim or another; or

(d) to interfere with the performance of any governmental or political function.

Kidnapping is a felony of the first degree unless the actor voluntarily releases the victim alive and in a safe place prior to trial, in which case it is a felony of the second degree. A removal or confinement is unlawful within the meaning of this Section if it is accomplished by force, threat or deception, or, in the case of a person who is under the age of 14 or incompetent, if it is accomplished without the consent of a parent, guardian or other person responsible for general supervision of his welfare.

Section 212.2 Felonious Restraint

A person commits a felony of the third degree if he knowingly:

(a) restrains another unlawfully in circumstances exposing him to risk of serious bodily injury; or

(b) holds another in a condition of involuntary servitude.

Section 212.3 False Imprisonment

A person commits a misdemeanor if he knowingly restrains another unlawfully so as to interfere substantially with his liberty.

Section 212.4 Interference With Custody

(1) *Custody of Children.* A person commits an offense if he knowingly or recklessly takes or entices any child under the age of 18 from the custody of its parent, guardian or other lawful custodian, when he has no privilege to do so. It is an affirmative defense that:

(a) the actor believed that his action was necessary to preserve the child from danger to its welfare; or

(b) the child, being at the time not less than 14 years old, was taken away at its own instigation without enticement and without purpose to commit a criminal offense with or against the child.

Proof that the child was below the critical age gives rise to a presumption that the actor knew the child's age or acted in reckless disregard thereof. The offense is a misdemeanor unless the actor, not being a parent or person in equivalent relation to the child, acted with knowledge that his conduct would cause serious alarm for the child's safety, or in reckless disregard of a likelihood of causing such alarm, in which case the offense is a felony of the third degree.

(2) *Custody of Committed Persons.* A person is guilty of a misdemeanor if he knowingly or recklessly takes or entices any committed person away from lawful custody when he is not privileged to do so. "Committed person" means, in addition to anyone committed under judicial warrant, any orphan, neglected or delinquent child, mentally defective or insane person, or other dependent or incompetent person entrusted to another's custody by or through a recognized social agency or otherwise by authority of law.

Section 212.5 Criminal Coercion

(1) *Offense Defined.* A person is guilty of criminal coercion if, with purpose unlawfully to restrict another's freedom of action to his detriment, he threatens to:

(a) commit any criminal offense; or

(b) accuse anyone of a criminal offense; or

(c) expose any secret tending to subject any person to hatred, contempt or ridicule, or to impair his credit or business repute; or

(d) take or withhold action as an official, or cause an official to take or withhold action.

It is an affirmative defense to prosecution based on paragraphs (b), (c) or (d) that the actor believed the accusation or secret to be true or the proposed official action justified and that his purpose was limited to compelling the other to behave in a way reasonably related to the circumstances which were the subject of the accusation, exposure or proposed official action, as by desisting from further misbehavior, making good a wrong done, refraining from taking any action or responsibility for which the actor believes the other disqualified.

(2) *Grading.* Criminal coercion is a misdemeanor unless the threat is to commit a felony or the actor's purpose is felonious, in which cases the offense is a felony of the third degree.

ARTICLE 213. SEXUAL OFFENSES

Section 213.0 Definitions

In this Article, the definitions given in Section 210.0 apply unless a different meaning plainly is required.

Section 213.1 Rape and Related Offenses

(1) *Rape.* A male who has sexual intercourse with a female not his wife is guilty of rape if:

(a) he compels her to submit by force or by threat of imminent death, serious bodily injury, extreme pain or kidnapping, to be inflicted on anyone; or

(b) he has substantially impaired her power to appraise or control her conduct by administering or employing without her knowledge drugs, intoxicants or other means for the purpose of preventing resistance; or

(c) the female is unconscious; or

(d) the female is less than 10 years old.

Rape is a felony of the second degree unless (i) in the course thereof the actor inflicts serious bodily injury upon anyone, or (ii) the victim was not a voluntary social companion of the actor upon the occasion of the crime and had not previously permitted him sexual liberties, in which cases the offense is a felony of the first degree. Sexual intercourse includes intercourse per os or per anum, with some penetration however slight; emission is not required.

(2) *Gross Sexual Imposition.* A male who has sexual intercourse with a female not his wife commits a felony of the third degree if:

(a) he compels her to submit by any threat that would prevent resistance by a woman of ordinary resolution; or

(b) he knows that she suffers from a mental disease or defect which renders her incapable of appraising the nature of her conduct; or

(c) he knows that she is unaware that a sexual act is being committed upon her or that she submits because she falsely supposes that he is her husband.

Section 213.2 Deviate Sexual Intercourse by Force or Imposition

(1) *By Force or Its Equivalent.* A person who engages in deviate sexual intercourse with another person, or who causes another to engage in deviate sexual intercourse, commits a felony of the second degree if:

(a) he compels the other person to participate by force or by threat of imminent death, serious bodily injury, extreme pain or kidnapping, to be inflicted on anyone; or

(b) he has substantially impaired the other person's power to appraise or control his conduct, by administering or employing without the knowledge of the other person drugs, intoxicants or other means for the purpose of preventing resistance; or

(c) the other person is unconscious; or

(d) the other person is less than 10 years old.

Deviate sexual intercourse means sexual intercourse per os or per anum between human beings who are not husband and wife, and any form of sexual intercourse with an animal.

(2) *By Other Imposition.* A person who engages in deviate sexual intercourse with another person, or who causes another to engage in deviate sexual intercourse, commits a felony of the third degree if:

(a) he compels the other person to participate by any threat that would prevent resistance by a person of ordinary resolution; or

(b) he knows that the other person suffers from a mental disease or defect which renders him incapable of appraising the nature of his conduct; or

(c) he knows that the other person submits because he is unaware that a sexual act is being committed upon him.

Section 213.3 Corruption of Minors and Seduction

(1) *Offense Defined.* A male who has sexual intercourse with a female not his wife, or any person who engages in deviate sexual intercourse or causes another to engage in deviate sexual intercourse, is guilty of an offense if:

(a) the other person is less than [16] years old and the actor is at least [4] years older than the other person; or

(b) the other person is less than 21 years old and the actor is his guardian or otherwise responsible for general supervision of his welfare; or

(c) the other person is in custody of law or detained in a hospital or other institution and the actor has supervisory or disciplinary authority over him; or

(d) the other person is a female who is induced to participate by a promise of marriage which the actor does not mean to perform.

(2) *Grading.* An offense under paragraph (a) of Subsection (1) is a felony of the third degree. Otherwise an offense under this section is a misdemeanor.

Section 213.4 Sexual Assault

A person who subjects another not his spouse to any sexual contact is guilty of sexual assault, a misdemeanor, if:

(1) he knows that the contact is offensive to the other person; or

(2) he knows that the other person suffers from a mental disease or defect which renders him or her incapable of appraising the nature of his or her conduct; or

(3) he knows that the other person is unaware that a sexual act is being committed; or

(4) the other person is less than 10 years old; or

(5) he has substantially impaired the other person's power to appraise or control his or her conduct, by administering or employing without the other's knowledge drugs, intoxicants or other means for the purpose of preventing resistance; or

(6) the other person is less than [16] years old and the actor is at least [four] years older than the other person; or

(7) the other person is less than 21 years old and the actor is his guardian or otherwise responsible for general supervision of his welfare; or

(8) the other person is in custody of law or detained in a hospital or other institution and the actor has supervisory or disciplinary authority over him.

Sexual contact is any touching of the sexual or other intimate parts of the person of another for the purpose of arousing or gratifying sexual desire of either party.

Section 213.5 Indecent Exposure

A person commits a misdemeanor if, for the purpose of arousing or gratifying sexual desire of himself or of any person other than his spouse, he exposes his genitals under circumstances in which he knows his conduct is likely to cause affront or alarm.

Section 213.6 Provisions Generally Applicable to Article 213

(1) *Mistake as to Age.* Whenever in this Article the criminality of conduct depends on a child's being below the age of 10, it is no defense that the actor did not know the child's age, or reasonably believed the child to be older than 10. When criminality depends on the child's being below a critical age other than 10, it is a defense for the actor to prove that he reasonably believed the child to be above the critical age.

(2) *Spouse Relationships.* Whenever in this Article the definition of an offense excludes conduct with a spouse, the exclusion shall be deemed to extend to persons living as man and wife, regardless of the legal status of their relationship. The exclusion shall be inoperative as respects spouses living apart under a decree of judicial separation. Where the definition of an offense excludes conduct with a spouse or conduct by a woman, this shall not preclude conviction of a spouse or woman as accomplice in a sexual act which he or she causes another person, not within the exclusion, to perform.

(4) *Sexually Promiscuous Complainants.* It is a defense to prosecution under Section 213.3. and paragraphs (6), (7) and (8) of Section 213.4 for the actor to prove by a preponderance of the evidence that the alleged victim had, prior to the time of the offense charged, engaged promiscuously in sexual relations with others.

(5) *Prompt Complaint.* No prosecution may be instituted or maintained under this Article unless the alleged offense was brought to the notice of public authority within [3] months of its occurrence or, where the alleged victim was less than [16] years old or otherwise incompetent to make complaint, within [3] months after a parent, guardian or other competent person specially interested in the victim learns of the offense.

(6) *Testimony of Complainants.* No person shall be convicted of any felony under this Article upon the uncorroborated testimony of the alleged victim. Corroboration may be circumstantial. In any prosecution before a jury for an offense under this Article, the jury shall be instructed to evaluate the testimony of a victim or complaining witness with special care in view of the emotional involvement of the witness and the difficulty of determining the truth with respect to alleged sexual activities carried out in private.

OFFENSES AGAINST PROPERTY

ARTICLE 220. ARSON, CRIMINAL MISCHIEF, AND OTHER PROPERTY DESTRUCTION

Section 220.1 Arson and Related Offenses

(1) *Arson.* A person is guilty of arson, a felony of the second degree, if he starts a fire or causes an explosion with the purpose of:

(a) destroying a building or occupied structure of another; or

(b) destroying or damaging any property, whether his own or another's, to collect insurance for such loss. It shall be an affirmative defense to prosecution under this paragraph that the actor's conduct did not recklessly endanger any building or occupied structure of another or place any other person in danger of death or bodily injury.

(2) *Reckless Burning or Exploding.* A person commits a felony of the third degree if he purposely starts a fire or causes an explosion, whether on his own property or another's, and thereby recklessly:

(a) places another person in danger of death or bodily injury; or

(b) places a building or occupied structure of another in danger of damage or destruction.

(3) *Failure to Control or Report Dangerous Fire.* A person who knows that a fire is endangering life or a substantial amount of property of another and fails to take reasonable measures to put out or control the fire, when he can do so without substantial risk to himself, or to give a prompt fire alarm, commits a misdemeanor if:

(a) he knows that he is under an official, contractual, or other legal duty to prevent or combat the fire; or

(b) the fire was started, albeit lawfully, by him or with his assent, or on property in his custody or control.

(4) *Definitions.* "Occupied structure" includes a ship, trailer, sleeping car, airplane, or other vehicle, structure or place adapted for overnight accommodation of persons or for carrying on business therein, whether or not a person is actually present. Property is that of another, for the purposes of this section, if anyone other than the actor has a possessory or proprietory interest therein. If a building or structure is divided into separately occupied units, any unit not occupied by the actor is an occupied structure of another.

Section 220.2 Causing or Risking Catastrophe

(1) *Causing Catastrophe.* A person who causes a catastrophe by explosion, fire, flood, avalanche, collapse of building, release of poison gas, radioactive material or other harmful or destructive force or substance, or by any other means of causing potentially widespread injury or damage, commits a felony of the second degree if he does so purposely or knowingly, or a felony of the third degree if he does so recklessly.

(2) *Risking Catastrophe.* A person is guilty of a misdemeanor if he recklessly creates a risk of catastrophe in the employment of fire, explosives or other dangerous means listed in Subsection (1).

(3) *Failure to Prevent Catastrophe.* A person who knowingly or recklessly fails to take reasonable measures to prevent or mitigate a catastrophe commits a misdemeanor if:

(a) he knows that he is under an official, contractual or other legal duty to take such measures; or

(b) he did or assented to the act causing or threatening the catastrophe.

Section 220.3 Criminal Mischief

(1) *Offense Defined.* A person is guilty of criminal mischief if he:

(a) damages tangible property of another purposely, recklessly, or by negligence in the employment of fire, explosives, or other dangerous means listed in Section 220.2(1); or

(b) purposely or recklessly tampers with tangible property of another so as to endanger person or property; or

(c) purposely or recklessly causes another to suffer pecuniary loss by deception or threat.

(2) *Grading.* Criminal mischief is a felony of the third degree if the actor purposely causes pecuniary loss in excess of $5,000, or a substantial interruption or impairment of public communication, transportation, supply of water, gas or power, or other public service. It is a misdemeanor if the actor purposely causes pecuniary loss in excess of $100, or a petty misdemeanor if he purposely or recklessly causes pecuniary loss in excess of $25. Otherwise criminal mischief is a violation.

ARTICLE 221. BURGLARY AND OTHER CRIMINAL INTRUSION

Section 221.0 Definitions

In this Article, unless a different meaning plainly is required:

(1) "occupied structure" means any structure, vehicle or place adapted for overnight accommodation of persons, or for carrying on business therein, whether or not a person is actually present.

(2) "night" means the period between thirty minutes past sunset and thirty minutes before sunrise.

Section 221.1 Burglary

(1) *Burglary Defined.* A person is guilty of burglary if he enters a building or occupied structure, or separately secured or occupied portion thereof, with purpose to commit a crime therein, unless the premises are at the time open to the public or the actor is licensed or privileged to enter. It is an affirmative defense to prosecution for burglary that the building or structure was abandoned.

(2) *Grading.* Burglary is a felony of the second degree if it is perpetrated in the dwelling of another at night, or if, in the course of committing the offense, the actor:

(a) purposely, knowingly or recklessly inflicts or attempts to inflict bodily injury on anyone; or

(b) is armed with explosives or a deadly weapon.

Otherwise, burglary is a felony of the third degree. An act shall be deemed "in the course of committing" an offense if it occurs in an attempt to commit the offense or in flight after the attempt or commission.

(3) *Multiple Convictions.* A person may not be convicted both for burglary and for the offense which it was his purpose to commit after the burglarious entry or for an attempt to commit that offense, unless the additional offense constitutes a felony of the first or second degree.

Section 221.2 Criminal Trespass

(1) *Buildings and Occupied Structures.* A person commits an offense if, knowing that he is not licensed or privileged to do so, he enters or surreptitiously remains in any building or occupied structure, or separately secured or occupied portion thereof. An offense under this Subsection is a misdemeanor if it is committed in a dwelling at night. Otherwise it is a petty misdemeanor.

(2) *Defiant Trespasser.* A person commits an offense if, knowing that he is not licensed or privileged to do so, he enters or remains in any place as to which notice against trespass is given by:

(a) actual communication to the actor; or

(b) posting in a manner prescribed by law or reasonably likely to come to the attention of intruders; or

(c) fencing or other enclosure manifestly designed to exclude intruders.

An offense under this Subsection constitutes a petty misdemeanor if the offender defies an order to leave personally communicated to him by the owner of the premises or other authorized person. Otherwise it is a violation.

(3) *Defenses.* It is an affirmative defense to prosecution under this Section that:

(a) a building or occupied structure involved in an offense under Subsection (1) was abandoned; or

(b) the premises were at the time open to members of the public and the actor complied with all lawful conditions imposed on access to or remaining in the premises; or

(c) the actor reasonably believed that the owner of the premises, or other person empowered to license access thereto, would have licensed him to enter or remain.

ARTICLE 222. ROBBERY

Section 222.1 Robbery

(1) *Robbery Defined.* A person is guilty of robbery if, in the course of committing a theft, he:

(a) inflicts serious bodily injury upon another; or

(b) threatens another with or purposely puts him in fear of immediate serious bodily injury; or

(c) commits or threatens immediately to commit any felony of the first or second degree.

An act shall be deemed "in the course of committing a theft" if it occurs in an attempt to commit theft or in flight after the attempt or commission.

(2) *Grading.* Robbery is a felony of the second degree, except that it is a felony of the first degree if in the course of committing the theft the actor attempts to kill anyone, or purposely inflicts or attempts to inflict serious bodily injury.

ARTICLE 223. THEFT AND RELATED OFFENSES

Section 223.0 Definitions

In this Article, unless a different meaning plainly is required:

(1) "deprive" means: (a) to withhold property of another permanently or for so extended a period as to appropriate a major portion of its economic value, or with intent to restore only upon payment of reward or other compensation; or (b) to dispose of the property so as to make it unlikely that the owner will recover it.

(2) "financial institution" means a bank, insurance company, credit union, building and loan association, investment trust or other organization held out to the public as a place of deposit of funds or medium of savings or collective investment.

(3) "government" means the United States, any State, county, municipality, or other political unit, or any department, agency or subdivision of any of the foregoing, or any corporation or other association carrying out the functions of government.

(4) "movable property" means property the location of which can be changed, including things growing on, affixed to, or found in land, and documents although the rights represented thereby have no physical location. "Immovable property" is all other property.

(5) "obtain" means: (a) in relation to property, to bring about a transfer or purported transfer of a legal interest in the property, whether to the obtainer or another; or (b) in relation to labor or service, to secure performance thereof.

(6) "property" means anything of value, including real estate, tangible and intangible personal property, contract rights, choses-in-action and other interests in or claims to wealth, admission or transportation tickets, captured or domestic animals, food and drink, electric or other power.

(7) "property of another" includes property in which any person other than the actor has an interest which the actor is not privileged to infringe, regardless of the fact that the actor also has an interest in the property and regardless of the fact that the other person might be precluded from civil recovery because the property was used in an unlawful transaction or was subject to forfeiture as contraband. Property in possession of the actor shall not be deemed property of another who has only a security interest therein, even if legal title is in the creditor pursuant to a conditional sales contract or other security agreement.

Section 223.1 Consolidation of Theft Offenses; Grading; Provisions Applicable to Theft Generally

(1) *Consolidation of Theft Offenses.* Conduct denominated theft in this Article constitutes a single offense embracing the separate offenses heretofore known as larceny, embezzlement, false pretense, extortion, blackmail, fraudulent conversion, receiving stolen property, and the like. An accusation of theft may be supported by evidence that it was committed in any manner that would be theft under this Article, notwithstanding the specification of a different manner in the indictment or information, subject only to the power of the Court to ensure fair trial by granting a continuance or other appropriate relief where the conduct of the defense would be prejudiced by lack of fair notice or by surprise.

(2) *Grading of Theft Offenses.*

(a) Theft constitutes a felony of the third degree if the amount involved exceeds $500, or if the property stolen is a firearm, automobile, or other motor-propelled vehicle, or in the case of theft by receiving stolen property, if the receiver is in the business of buying or selling stolen property.

(b) Theft not within the preceding paragraph constitutes a misdemeanor, except that if the property was not taken from the person or by threat, or in breach of a fiduciary obligation, and the actor proves by a preponderance of the evidence that the amount involved was less than $50, the offense constitutes a petty misdemeanor.

(c) The amount involved in a theft shall be deemed to be the highest value, by any reasonable standard, of the property or services which the actor stole or attempted to steal. Amounts involved in thefts committed pursuant to one scheme or course of conduct, whether from the same person or several persons, may be aggregated in determining the grade of the offense.

(3) *Claim of Right.* It is an affirmative defense to prosecution for theft that the actor:

(a) was unaware that the property or service was that of another; or

(b) acted under an honest claim of right to the property or service involved or that he had a right to acquire or dispose of it as he did; or

(c) took property exposed for sale, intending to purchase and pay for it promptly, or reasonably believing that the owner, if present, would have consented.

(4) *Theft from Spouse.* It is no defense that theft was from the actor's spouse, except that misappropriation of household and personal effects, or other property normally accessible to both spouses, is theft only if it occurs after the parties have ceased living together.

Section 223.2 Theft by Unlawful Taking or Disposition

(1) *Movable Property.* A person is guilty of theft if he takes, or exercises unlawful control over, movable property of another with purpose to deprive him thereof.

(2) *Immovable Property.* A person is guilty of theft if he unlawfully transfers immovable property of another or any interest therein with purpose to benefit himself or another not entitled thereto.

Section 223.3 Theft by Deception

A person is guilty of theft if he obtains property of another by deception. A person deceives if he purposely:

(a) creates or reinforces a false impression, including false impressions as to law, value, intention or other state of mind; but deception as to a person's intention to perform a promise shall not be inferred from the fact alone that he did not subsequently perform the promise; or

(b) prevents another from acquiring information which would affect his judgment of a transaction; or

(c) fails to correct a false impression which the deceiver previously created or reinforced, or which the deceiver knows to be influencing another to whom he stands in a fiduciary or confidential relationship; or

(d) fails to disclose a known lien, adverse claim or other legal impediment to the enjoyment of property which he transfers or encumbers in consideration for the property obtained, whether such impediment is or is not valid, or is or is not a matter of official record.

The term "deceive" does not, however, include falsity as to matters having no pecuniary significance, or puffing by statements unlikely to deceive ordinary persons in the group addressed.

Section 223.4 Theft by Extortion

A person is guilty of theft if he obtains property of another by threatening to:

(a) inflict bodily injury on anyone or commit any other criminal offense; or

(b) accuse anyone of a criminal offense; or

(c) expose any secret tending to subject any person to hatred, contempt or ridicule, or to impair his credit or business repute; or

(d) take or withhold action as an official, or cause an official to take or withhold action; or

(e) bring about or continue a strike, boycott or other collective unofficial action, if the property is not demanded or received for the benefit of the group in whose interest the actor purports to act; or

(f) testify or provide information or withhold testimony or information with respect to another's legal claim or defense; or

(g) inflict any other harm which would not benefit the actor.

It is an affirmative defense to prosecution based on paragraphs (b), (c) or (d) that the property obtained by threat of accusation, exposure, lawsuit or other invocation of official action was honestly claimed as restitution or indemnification for harm done in the circumstances to which such accusation, exposure, lawsuit or other official action relates, or as compensation for property or lawful services.

Section 223.5 Theft of Property Lost, Mislaid, or Delivered by Mistake

A person who comes into control of property of another that he knows to have been lost, mislaid, or delivered under a mistake as to the nature or amount of the property or the identity of the recipient is guilty of theft if, with purpose to deprive the owner thereof, he fails to take reasonable measures to restore the property to a person entitled to have it.

Section 223.6 Receiving Stolen Property

(1) *Receiving.* A person is guilty of theft if he receives, retains, or disposes of movable property of another knowing that it has been stolen, or believing that it has probably been stolen, unless the property is received, retained, or disposed with purpose to restore it to the owner. "Receiving" means acquiring possession, control or title, or lending on the security of the property.

(2) *Presumption of Knowledge.* The requisite knowledge or belief is presumed in the case of a dealer who:

(a) is found in possession or control of property stolen from two or more persons on separate occasions; or

(b) has received stolen property in another transaction within the year preceding the transaction charged; or

(c) being a dealer in property of the sort received, acquires it for a consideration which he knows is far below its reasonable value.

"Dealer" means a person in the business of buying or selling goods.

Section 223.7 Theft of Services

(1) A person is guilty of theft if he obtains services which he knows are available only for compensation, by deception or threat, or by false token or other means to avoid payment for the service. "Services" includes labor, professional service, telephone or other public service, accommodation in hotels, restaurants or elsewhere, admission to exhibitions, use of vehicles or other movable property. Where compensation for service is ordinarily paid immediately upon the rendering of such service, as in the case of hotels and restaurants, refusal to pay or absconding without payment or offer to pay gives rise to a presumption that the service was obtained by deception as to intention to pay.

(2) A person commits theft if, having control over the disposition of services of others, to which he is not entitled, he diverts such services to his own benefit or to the benefit of another not entitled thereto.

Section 223.8 Theft by Failure to Make Required Disposition of Funds Received

A person who obtains property upon agreement, or subject to a known legal obligation, to make specified payment or other disposition, whether from such property or its proceeds or from his own property in equivalent amount, is guilty of theft if he deals with the property obtained as his own and fails to make the required payment or disposition. The foregoing applies notwithstanding that it may be impossible to identify particular property as belonging to the victim at the time of the actor's failure to make the required payment or disposition. An officer or employee of the government or of a financial institution is presumed: (i) to know any legal obligation relevant to his criminal liability under this Section, and (ii) to have dealt with the property as his own if he fails to pay or account upon lawful demand, or if an audit reveals a shortage or falsification of accounts.

Section 223.9 Unauthorized Use of Automobiles and Other Vehicles

A person commits a misdemeanor if he operates another's automobile, airplane, motorcycle, motorboat, or other motor-propelled vehicle without consent of the owner. It is an affirmative defense to prosecution under this Section that the actor reasonably believed that the owner would have consented to the operation had he known of it.

ARTICLE 224. FORGERY AND FRAUDULENT PRACTICES

Section 224.0 Definitions

In this Article, the definitions given in Section 223.0 apply unless a different meaning plainly is required.

Section 224.1 Forgery

(1) *Definition.* A person is guilty of forgery if, with purpose to defraud or injure anyone, or with knowledge that he is facilitating a fraud or injury to be perpetrated by anyone, the actor:

(a) alters any writing of another without his authority; or

(b) makes, completes, executes, authenticates, issues or transfers any writing so that it purports to be the act of another who did not authorize that act, or to have been executed at a time or place or in a numbered sequence other than was in fact the case, or to be a copy of an original when no such original existed; or

(c) utters any writing which he knows to be forged in a manner specified in paragraphs (a) or (b).

"Writing" includes printing or any other method of recording information, money, coins, tokens, stamps, seals, credit cards, badges, trade-marks, and other symbols of value, right, privilege, or identification.

(2) *Grading.* Forgery is a felony of the second degree if the writing is or purports to be part of an issue of money, securities, postage or revenue stamps, or other instruments issued by the government, or part of an issue of stock, bonds or other instruments representing interests in or claims against any property or enterprise. Forgery is a felony of the third degree if the writing is or purports to be a will, deed, contract, release, commercial instrument, or other document evidencing, creating, transferring, altering, terminating, or otherwise affecting legal relations. Otherwise forgery is a misdemeanor.

Section 224.2 Simulating Objects of Antiquity, Rarity, Etc.

A person commits a misdemeanor if, with purpose to defraud anyone or with knowledge that he is facilitating a fraud to be perpetrated by anyone, he makes, alters or utters any object so that it appears to have value because of antiquity, rarity, source, or authorship which it does not possess.

Section 224.3 Fraudulent Destruction, Removal or Concealment of Recordable Instruments

A person commits a felony of the third degree if, with purpose to deceive or injure anyone, he destroys, removes or conceals any will, deed, mortgage, security instrument or other writing for which the law provides public recording.

Section 224.4 Tampering With Records

A person commits a misdemeanor if, knowing that he has no privilege to do so, he falsifies, destroys, removes or conceals any writing or record, with purpose to deceive or injure anyone or to conceal any wrongdoing.

Section 224.5 Bad Checks

A person who issues or passes a check or similar sight order for the payment of money, knowing that it will not be honored by the drawee, commits a misdemeanor. For the purposes of this Section as well as in any prosecution for theft committed by means of a bad check, an issuer is presumed to know that the check or order (other than a postdated check or order) would not be paid, if:

(a) the issuer had no account with the drawee at the time the check or order was issued; or

(b) payment was refused by the drawee for lack of funds, upon presentation within 30 days after issue, and the issuer failed to make good within 10 days after receiving notice of that refusal.

Section 224.6 Credit Cards

A person commits an offense if he uses a credit card for the purpose of obtaining property or services with knowledge that:

(a) the card is stolen or forged; or

(b) the card has been revoked or cancelled; or

(c) for any other reason his use of the card is unauthorized.

It is an affirmative defense to prosecution under paragraph (c) if the actor proves by a preponderance of the evidence that he had the purpose and ability to meet all obligations to the issuer arising out of his use of the card. "Credit card" means a writing purporting to evidence an undertaking to pay for property or services delivered or rendered to or upon the order of a designated person or bearer. An offense under this Section is a felony of the third degree if the value of the property or services secured or sought to be secured by means of the credit card exceeds $500; otherwise it is a misdemeanor.

Section 224.7 Deceptive Business Practices

A person commits a misdemeanor if in the course of business he:

(a) uses or possesses for use a false weight or measure, or any other device for falsely determining or recording any quality or quantity; or

(b) sells, offers or exposes for sale, or delivers less than the represented quantity of any commodity or service; or

(c) takes or attempts to take more than the represented quantity of any commodity or service when as buyer he furnishes the weight or measure; or

(d) sells, offers or exposes for sale adulterated or mislabeled commodities. "Adulterated" means varying from the standard of composition or quality prescribed by or pursuant to any statute providing criminal penalties for such variance, or set by established commercial usage. "Mislabeled" means varying from the standard of truth or disclosure in labeling prescribed by or pursuant to any statute providing criminal penalties for such variance, or set by established commercial usage; or

(e) makes a false or misleading statement in any advertisement addressed to the public or to a substantial segment thereof for the purpose of promoting the purchase or sale of property or services; or

(f) makes a false or misleading written statement for the purpose of obtaining property or credit; or

(g) makes a false or misleading written statement for the purpose of promoting the sale of securities, or omits information required by law to be disclosed in written documents relating to securities.

It is an affirmative defense to prosecution under this Section if the defendant proves by a preponderance of the evidence that his conduct was not knowingly or recklessly deceptive.

Section 224.8 Commercial Bribery and Breach of Duty to Act Disinterestedly

(1) A person commits a misdemeanor if he solicits, accepts or agrees to accept any benefit as consideration for knowingly violating or agreeing to violate a duty of fidelity to which he is subject as:

(a) agent or employee of another;

(b) trustee, guardian, or other fiduciary;

(c) lawyer, physician, accountant, appraiser, or other professional adviser or informant;

(d) officer, director, partner, manager or other participant in the direction of the affairs of an incorporated or unincorporated association; or

(e) arbitrator or other purportedly disinterested adjudicator or referee.

(2) A person who holds himself out to the public as being engaged in the business of making disinterested selection, appraisal, or criticism of commodities or services commits a misdemeanor if he solicits, accepts or agrees to accept any benefit to influence his selection, appraisal or criticism.

(3) A person commits a misdemeanor if he confers, or offers or agrees to confer, any benefit the acceptance of which would be criminal under this Section.

Section 224.9 Rigging Publicly Exhibited Contest

(1) A person commits a misdemeanor if, with purpose to prevent a publicly exhibited contest from being conducted in accordance with the rules and usages purporting to govern it, he:

(a) confers or offers or agrees to confer any benefit upon, or threatens any injury to a participant, official or other person associated with the contest or exhibition; or

(b) tampers with any person, animal or thing.

(2) *Soliciting or Accepting Benefit for Rigging.* A person commits a misdemeanor if he knowingly solicits, accepts or agrees to accept any benefit the giving of which would be criminal under Subsection (1).

(3) *Participation in Rigged Contest.* A person commits a misdemeanor if he knowingly engages in, sponsors, produces, judges, or otherwise participates in a publicly exhibited contest knowing that the contest is not being conducted in compliance with the rules and usages purporting to govern it, by reason of conduct which would be criminal under this Section.

Section 224.10 Defrauding Secured Creditors

A person commits a misdemeanor if he destroys, removes, conceals, encumbers, transfers or otherwise deals with property subject to a security interest with purpose to hinder enforcement of that interest.

OFFENSES AGAINST THE FAMILY

ARTICLE 230. OFFENSES AGAINST THE FAMILY

Section 230.1 Bigamy and Polygamy

(1) *Bigamy.* A married person is guilty of bigamy, a misdemeanor, if he contracts or purports to contract another marriage, unless at the time of the subsequent marriage:

(a) the actor believes that the prior spouse is dead; or

(b) the actor and the prior spouse have been living apart for five consecutive years throughout which the prior spouse was not known by the actor to be alive; or

(c) a Court has entered a judgment purporting to terminate or annul any prior disqualifying marriage, and the actor does not know that judgment to be invalid; or

(d) the actor reasonably believes that he is legally eligible to remarry.

(2) *Polygamy.* A person is guilty of polygamy, a felony of the third degree, if he marries or cohabits with more than one spouse at a time in purported exercise of the right of plural marriage. The offense is a continuing one until all cohabitation and claim of marriage with more than one spouse terminates. This section does not apply to parties to a polygamous marriage, lawful in the country of which they are residents or nationals, while they are in transit through or temporarily visiting this State.

(3) *Other Party to Bigamous or Polygamous Marriage.* A person is guilty of bigamy or polygamy, as the case may be, if he contracts or purports to contract marriage with another knowing that the other is thereby committing bigamy or polygamy.

Section 230.2 Incest

A person is guilty of incest, a felony of the third degree, if he knowingly marries or cohabits or has sexual intercourse with an ancestor or descendant, a brother or sister of the whole or half blood [or an uncle, aunt, nephew or niece of the whole blood]. "Cohabit" means to live together under the representation or appearance of being married. The relationships referred to herein include blood relationships without regard to legitimacy, and relationship of parent and child by adoption.

Section 230.3 Abortion

(1) *Unjustified Abortion.* A person who purposely and unjustifiably terminates the pregnancy of another otherwise than by a live birth commits a felony of the third degree or, where the pregnancy has continued beyond the twenty-sixth week, a felony of the second degree.

(2) *Justifiable Abortion.* A licensed physician is justified in terminating a pregnancy if he believes there is substantial risk that continuance of the pregnancy would gravely impair the physical or mental health of the mother or that the child would be born with grave physical or mental defect, or that the pregnancy resulted from rape, incest, or other felonious intercourse. All illicit intercourse with a girl below the age of 16 shall be deemed felonious for purposes of this subsection. Justifiable abortions shall be performed only in a licensed hospital except in case of emergency when hospital facilities are unavailable. [Additional exceptions from the requirement of hospitalization may be incorporated here to take account of situations in sparsely settled areas where hospitals are not generally accessible.]

(3) *Physicians' Certificates; Presumption from Non–Compliance.* No abortion shall be performed unless two physicians, one of whom may be the person performing the abortion, shall have certified in writing the circumstances which they believe to justify the abortion. Such certificate shall be submitted before the abortion to the hospital where it is to be performed and, in the case of abortion following felonious intercourse, to the prosecuting attorney or the police. Failure to comply with any of the requirements of this Subsection gives rise to a presumption that the abortion was unjustified.

(4) *Self–Abortion.* A woman whose pregnancy has continued beyond the twenty-sixth week commits a felony of the third degree if she purposely terminates her own pregnancy otherwise than by a live birth, or if she uses instruments, drugs or violence upon herself for that purpose. Except as justified under Subsection (2), a person who induces or knowingly aids a woman to use instruments, drugs or violence upon herself for the purpose of terminating her pregnancy otherwise than by a live birth commits a felony of the third degree whether or not the pregnancy has continued beyond the twenty-sixth week.

(5) *Pretended Abortion.* A person commits a felony of the third degree if, representing that it is his purpose to perform an abortion, he does an act adapted to cause abortion in a pregnant woman although the woman is in fact not pregnant, or the actor does not believe she is. A person charged with unjustified abortion under Subsection (1) or an attempt to commit that offense may be convicted thereof upon proof of conduct prohibited by this Subsection.

(6) *Distribution of Abortifacients.* A person who sells, offers to sell, possesses with intent to sell, advertises, or displays for sale anything specially designed to terminate a pregnancy, or held out by the actor as useful for that purpose, commits a misdemeanor, unless:

(a) the sale, offer or display is to a physician or druggist or to an intermediary in a chain of distribution to physicians or druggists; or

(b) the sale is made upon prescription or order of a physician; or

(c) the possession is with intent to sell as authorized in paragraphs (a) and (b); or

(d) the advertising is addressed to persons named in paragraph (a) and confined to trade or professional channels not likely to reach the general public.

(7) *Section Inapplicable to Prevention of Pregnancy.* Nothing in this Section shall be deemed applicable to the prescription, administration or distribution of drugs or other substances for avoiding pregnancy, whether by preventing implantation of a fertilized ovum or by any other method that operates before, at or immediately after fertilization.

OFFENSES AGAINST PUBLIC ADMINISTRATION

ARTICLE 240. BRIBERY AND CORRUPT INFLUENCE

Section 240.0 Definitions

In Articles 240–243, unless a different meaning plainly is required:

(1) "benefit" means gain or advantage, or anything regarded by the beneficiary as gain or advantage, including benefit to any other person or entity in whose welfare he is interested, but not an advantage promised generally to a group or class of voters as a consequence of public measures which a candidate engages to support or oppose;

(2) "government" includes any branch, subdivision or agency of the government of the State or any locality within it;

(3) "harm" means loss, disadvantage or injury, or anything so regarded by the person affected, including loss, disadvantage or injury to any other person or entity in whose welfare he is interested;

(4) "official proceeding" means a proceeding heard or which may be heard before any legislative, judicial, administrative or other governmental agency or official authorized to take evidence under oath, including any referee, hearing examiner, commissioner, notary or other person taking testimony or deposition in connection with any such proceeding;

(5) "party official" means a person who holds an elective or appointive post in a political party in the United States by virtue of which he directs or conducts, or participates in directing or conducting party affairs at any level of responsibility;

(6) "pecuniary benefit" is benefit in the form of money, property, commercial interests or anything else the primary significance of which is economic gain;

(7) "public servant" means any officer or employee of government, including legislators and judges, and any person participating as juror, advisor, consultant or otherwise, in performing a governmental function; but the term does not include witnesses;

(8) "administrative proceeding" means any proceeding the outcome of which is required to be based on a record or documentation prescribed by law, or in which law or regulation is particularized in application to individuals.

Section 240.1 Bribery in Official and Political Matters

A person is guilty of bribery, a felony of the third degree, if he offers, confers or agrees to confer upon another, or solicits, accepts or agrees to accept from another:

(1) any pecuniary benefit as consideration for the recipient's decision, opinion, recommendation, vote or other exercise of discretion as a public servant, party official or voter; or

(2) any benefit as consideration for the recipient's decision, vote, recommendation or other exercise of official discretion in a judicial or administrative proceeding; or

(3) any benefit as consideration for a violation of a known duty as public servant or party official.

It is no defense to prosecution under this section that a person whom the actor sought to influence was not qualified to act in the desired way whether because he had not yet assumed office, or lacked jurisdiction, or for any other reason.

ARTICLE 241. PERJURY AND OTHER FALSIFICATION IN OFFICIAL MATTERS

Section 241.0 Definitions

In this Article, unless a different meaning plainly is required:

(1) the definitions given in Section 240.0 apply; and

(2) "statement" means any representation, but includes a representation of opinion, belief or other state of mind only if the representation clearly relates to state of mind apart from or in addition to any facts which are the subject of the representation.

Section 241.1 Perjury

(1) *Offense Defined.* A person is guilty of perjury, a felony of the third degree, if in any official proceeding he makes a false statement under oath or equivalent affirmation, or swears or affirms the truth of a statement previously made, when the statement is material and he does not believe it to be true.

(2) *Materiality.* Falsification is material, regardless of the admissibility of the statement under rules of evidence, if it could have affected the course or outcome of the proceeding. It is no defense that the declarant mistakenly believed the falsification to be immaterial. Whether a falsification is material in a given factual situation is a question of law.

(3) *Irregularities No Defense.* It is not a defense to prosecution under this Section that the oath or affirmation was administered or taken in an irregular manner or that the declarant was not competent to make the statement. A document purporting to be made upon oath or affirmation at any time when the actor presents it as being so verified shall be deemed to have been duly sworn or affirmed.

(4) *Retraction.* No person shall be guilty of an offense under this Section if he retracted the falsification in the course of the proceeding in which it was made before it became manifest that the falsification was or would be exposed and before the falsification substantially affected the proceeding.

(5) *Inconsistent Statements.* Where the defendant made inconsistent statements under oath or equivalent affirmation, both having been made within the period of the statute of limitations, the prosecution may proceed by setting forth the inconsistent statements in a single count alleging in the alternative that one or the other was false and not believed by the defendant. In such case it shall not be necessary for the prosecution to prove which statement was false but only that one or the other was false and not believed by the defendant to be true.

(6) *Corroboration.* No person shall be convicted of an offense under this Section where proof of falsity rests solely upon contradiction by testimony of a single person other than the defendant.

Section 241.2 False Swearing

(1) *False Swearing in Official Matters.* A person who makes a false statement under oath or equivalent affirmation, or swears or affirms the truth of such a statement previously made, when he does not believe the statement to be true, is guilty of a misdemeanor if:

(a) the falsification occurs in an official proceeding; or

(b) the falsification is intended to mislead a public servant in performing his official function.

(2) *Other False Swearing.* A person who makes a false statement under oath or equivalent affirmation, or swears or affirms the truth of such a statement previously made, when he does not believe the statement to be true, is guilty of a petty misdemeanor, if the statement is one which is required by law to be sworn or affirmed before a notary or other person authorized to administer oaths.

(3) *Perjury Provisions Applicable.* Subsections (3) to (6) of Section 241.1 apply to the present Section.

Section 241.3 Unsworn Falsification to Authorities

(1) *In General.* A person commits a misdemeanor if, with purpose to mislead a public servant in performing his official function, he:

(a) makes any written false statement which he does not believe to be true; or

(b) purposely creates a false impression in a written application for any pecuniary or other benefit, by omitting information necessary to prevent statements therein from being misleading; or

(c) submits or invites reliance on any writing which he knows to be forged, altered or otherwise lacking in authenticity; or

(d) submits or invites reliance on any sample, specimen, map, boundary-mark, or other object which he knows to be false.

(2) *Statements "Under Penalty."* A person commits a petty misdemeanor if he makes a written false statement which he does not believe to be true, on or pursuant to a form bearing notice, authorized by law, to the effect that false statements made therein are punishable.

(3) *Perjury Provisions Applicable.* Subsections (3) to (6) of Section 241.1 apply to the present section.

Section 241.4 False Alarms to Agencies of Public Safety

A person who knowingly causes a false alarm of fire or other emergency to be transmitted to or within any organization, official or volunteer, for dealing with emergencies involving danger to life or property commits a misdemeanor.

Section 241.5 False Reports to Law Enforcement Authorities

(1) *Falsely Incriminating Another.* A person who knowingly gives false information to any law enforcement officer with purpose to implicate another commits a misdemeanor.

(2) *Fictitious Reports.* A person commits a petty misdemeanor if he:

(a) reports to law enforcement authorities an offense or other incident within their concern knowing that it did not occur; or

(b) pretends to furnish such authorities with information relating to an offense or incident when he knows he has no information relating to such offense or incident.

Section 241.6 Tampering With Witnesses and Informants; Retaliation Against Them

(1) *Tampering.* A person commits an offense if, believing that an official proceeding or investigation is pending or about to be instituted, he attempts to induce or otherwise cause a witness or informant to:

(a) testify or inform falsely; or

(b) withhold any testimony, information, document or thing; or

(c) elude legal process summoning him to testify or supply evidence; or

(d) absent himself from any proceeding or investigation to which he has been legally summoned.

The offense is a felony of the third degree if the actor employs force, deception, threat or offer of pecuniary benefit. Otherwise it is a misdemeanor.

(2) *Retaliation Against Witness or Informant.* A person commits a misdemeanor if he harms another by any unlawful act in retaliation for anything lawfully done in the capacity of witness or informant.

(3) *Witness or Informant Taking Bribe.* A person commits a felony of the third degree if he solicits, accepts or agrees to accept any benefit in consideration of his doing any of the things specified in clauses (a) to (d) of Subsection (1).

Section 241.7 Tampering With or Fabricating Physical Evidence

A person commits a misdemeanor if, believing that an official proceeding or investigation is pending or about to be instituted, he:

(a) alters, destroys, conceals or removes any record, document or thing with purpose to impair its verity or availability in such proceeding or investigation; or

(b) makes, presents or uses any record, document or thing knowing it to be false and with purpose to mislead a public servant who is or may be engaged in such proceeding or investigation.

Section 241.8 Tampering With Public Records or Information

(1) *Offense Defined.* A person commits an offense if he:

(a) knowingly makes a false entry in, or false alteration of, any record, document or thing belonging to, or received or kept by, the government for information or record, or required by law to be kept by others for information of the government; or

(b) makes, presents or uses any record, document or thing knowing it to be false, and with purpose that it be taken as a genuine part of information or records referred to in paragraph (a); or

(c) purposely and unlawfully destroys, conceals, removes or otherwise impairs the verity or availability of any such record, document or thing.

(2) *Grading.* An offense under this Section is a misdemeanor unless the actor's purpose is to defraud or injure anyone, in which case the offense is a felony of the third degree.

Section 241.9 Impersonating a Public Servant

A person commits a misdemeanor if he falsely pretends to hold a position in the public service with purpose to induce another to submit to such pretended official authority or otherwise to act in reliance upon that pretense to his prejudice.

ARTICLE 242. OBSTRUCTING GOVERNMENTAL OPERATIONS; ESCAPES

Section 242.0 Definitions

In this Article, unless another meaning plainly is required, the definitions given in Section 240.0 apply.

Section 242.1 Obstructing Administration of Law or Other Governmental Function

A person commits a misdemeanor if he purposely obstructs, impairs or perverts the administration of law or other governmental function by force, violence, physical interference or obstacle, breach of official duty, or any other unlawful act, except that this Section does not apply to flight by a person charged with crime, refusal to submit to arrest, failure to perform a legal duty other than an official duty, or any other means of avoiding compliance with law without affirmative interference with governmental functions.

Section 242.2 Resisting Arrest or Other Law Enforcement

A person commits a misdemeanor if, for the purpose of preventing a public servant from effecting a lawful arrest or discharging any other duty, the person creates a substantial risk of bodily harm to the public servant or anyone else, or employs means justifying or requiring substantial force to overcome the resistance.

Section 242.3 Hindering Apprehension or Prosecution

A person commits an offense if, with purpose to hinder the apprehension, prosecution, conviction or punishment of another for crime, he:

(a) harbors or conceals the other; or

(b) provides or aids in providing a weapon, transportation, disguise or other means of avoiding apprehension or effecting escape; or

(c) conceals or destroys evidence of the crime, or tampers with a witness, informant, document or other source of information, regardless of its admissibility in evidence; or

(d) warns the other of impending discovery or apprehension, except that this paragraph does not apply to a warning given in connection with an effort to bring another into compliance with law; or

(e) volunteers false information to a law enforcement officer.

The offense is a felony of the third degree if the conduct which the actor knows has been charged or is liable to be charged against the person aided would constitute a felony of the first or second degree. Otherwise it is a misdemeanor.

Section 242.4 Aiding Consummation of Crime

A person commits an offense if he purposely aids another to accomplish an unlawful object of a crime, as by safeguarding the proceeds thereof or converting the proceeds into negotiable funds. The offense is a felony of the third degree if the principal offense was a felony of the first or second degree. Otherwise it is a misdemeanor.

Section 242.5 Compounding

A person commits a misdemeanor if he accepts or agrees to accept any pecuniary benefit in consideration of refraining from reporting to law enforcement authorities the commission or suspected commission of any offense or information relating to an offense. It is an affirmative defense to prosecution under this Section that the pecuniary benefit did not exceed an amount which the actor believed to be due as restitution or indemnification for harm caused by the offense.

Section 242.6 Escape

(1) *Escape.* A person commits an offense if he unlawfully removes himself from official detention or fails to return to official detention following temporary leave granted for a specific purpose or limited period. "Official detention" means arrest, detention in any facility for custody of persons under charge or conviction of crime or alleged or found to be delinquent, detention for extradition or deportation, or any other detention for law enforcement purposes; but "official detention" does not include supervision of probation or parole, or constraint incidental to release on bail.

(2) *Permitting or Facilitating Escape.* A public servant concerned in detention commits an offense if he knowingly or recklessly permits an escape. Any person who knowingly causes or facilitates an escape commits an offense.

(3) *Effect of Legal Irregularity in Detention.* Irregularity in bringing about or maintaining detention, or lack of jurisdiction of the committing or detaining authority, shall not be a defense to prosecution under this Section if the escape is from a prison or other custodial facility or from detention pursuant to commitment by official proceedings. In the case of other detentions, irregularity or lack of jurisdiction shall be a defense only if:

(a) the escape involved no substantial risk of harm to the person or property of anyone other than the detainee; or

(b) the detaining authority did not act in good faith under color of law.

(4) *Grading of Offenses.* An offense under this Section is a felony of the third degree where:

(a) the detainee was under arrest for or detained on a charge of felony or following conviction of crime; or

(b) the actor employs force, threat, deadly weapon or other dangerous instrumentality to effect the escape; or

(c) a public servant concerned in detention of persons convicted of crime purposely facilitates or permits an escape from a detention facility.

Otherwise an offense under this section is a misdemeanor.

OFFENSES AGAINST PUBLIC ORDER AND DECENCY

ARTICLE 250. RIOT, DISORDERLY CONDUCT, AND RELATED OFFENSES

Section 250.1 Riot; Failure to Disperse

(1) *Riot.* A person is guilty of riot, a felony of the third degree, if he participates with [two] or more others in a course of disorderly conduct:

(a) with purpose to commit or facilitate the commission of a felony or misdemeanor;

(b) with purpose to prevent or coerce official action; or

(c) when the actor or any other participant to the knowledge of the actor uses or plans to use a firearm or other deadly weapon.

(2) *Failure of Disorderly Persons to Disperse Upon Official Order.* Where [three] or more persons are participating in a course of disorderly conduct likely to cause substantial harm or serious inconvenience, annoyance or alarm, a peace officer or other public servant engaged in executing or enforcing the law may order the participants and others in the immediate vicinity to disperse. A person who refuses or knowingly fails to obey such an order commits a misdemeanor.

Section 250.2 Disorderly Conduct

(1) *Offense Defined.* A person is guilty of disorderly conduct if, with purpose to cause public inconvenience, annoyance or alarm, or recklessly creating a risk thereof, he:

(a) engages in fighting or threatening, or in violent or tumultuous behavior; or

(b) makes unreasonable noise or offensively coarse utterance, gesture or display, or addresses abusive language to any person present; or

(c) creates a hazardous or physically offensive condition by any act which serves no legitimate purpose of the actor.

"Public" means affecting or likely to affect persons in a place to which the public or a substantial group has access; among the places included are highways, transport facilities, schools, prisons, apartment houses, places of business or amusement, or any neighborhood.

(2) *Grading.* An offense under this section is a petty misdemeanor if the actor's purpose is to cause substantial harm or serious inconvenience, or if he persists in disorderly conduct after reasonable warning or request to desist. Otherwise disorderly conduct is a violation.

Section 250.3 False Public Alarms

A person is guilty of a misdemeanor if he initiates or circulates a report or warning of an impending bombing or other crime or catastrophe, knowing that the report or warning is false or baseless and that it is likely to cause evacuation of a building, place of assembly, or facility of public transport, or to cause public inconvenience or alarm.

Section 250.4 Harassment

A person commits a petty misdemeanor if, with purpose to harass another, he:

(a) makes a telephone call without purpose of legitimate communication; or

(b) insults, taunts or challenges another in a manner likely to provoke violent or disorderly response; or

(c) makes repeated communications anonymously or at extremely inconvenient hours, or in offensively coarse language; or

(d) engages in any other course of harmful conduct serving no legitimate purpose of the actor.

Section 250.5 Public Drunkenness; Drug Incapacitation

A person is guilty of an offense if he appears in any public place manifestly under the influence of alcohol, narcotics or other drug, not therapeutically administered, to the degree that he may endanger himself or other persons or property, or annoy persons in his vicinity. An offense under this Section constitutes a petty misdemeanor if the actor has been convicted hereunder twice before within a period of one year. Otherwise the offense constitutes a violation.

Section 250.6 Loitering or Prowling

A person commits a violation if he loiters or prowls in a place, at a time, or in a manner not usual for law-abiding individuals under circumstances that warrant alarm for the safety of persons or property in the vicinity. Among the circumstances which may be considered in determining whether such alarm is warranted is the fact that the actor takes flight upon appearance of a peace officer, refuses to identify himself, or manifestly endeavors to conceal himself or any object. Unless flight by the actor or other circumstances makes it impracticable, a peace officer shall prior to any arrest for an offense under this section afford the actor an opportunity to dispel any alarm which would otherwise be warranted, by requesting him to identify himself and explain his presence and conduct. No person shall be convicted of an offense under this Section if the peace officer did not comply with the preceding sentence, or if it appears at trial that the explanation given by the actor was true and, if believed by the peace officer at the time, would have dispelled the alarm.

Section 250.7 Obstructing Highways and Other Public Passages

(1) A person, who, having no legal privilege to do so, purposely or recklessly obstructs any highway or other public passage, whether alone or with others, commits a violation, or, in case he persists after warning by a law officer, a petty misdemeanor. "Obstructs" means renders impassable without unreasonable inconvenience or hazard. No person shall be deemed guilty of recklessly obstructing in violation of this Subsection solely because of a gathering of persons to hear him speak or otherwise communicate, or solely because of being a member of such a gathering.

(2) A person in a gathering commits a violation if he refuses to obey a reasonable official request or order to move:

(a) to prevent obstruction of a highway or other public passage; or

(b) to maintain public safety by dispersing those gathered in dangerous proximity to a fire or other hazard.

An order to move, addressed to a person whose speech or other lawful behavior attracts an obstructing audience, shall not be deemed reasonable if the obstruction can be readily remedied by police control of the size or location of the gathering.

Section 250.8 Disrupting Meetings and Processions

A person commits a misdemeanor if, with purpose to prevent or disrupt a lawful meeting, procession or gathering, he does any act tending to obstruct or interfere with it physically, or makes any utterance, gesture or display designed to outrage the sensibilities of the group.

Section 250.11 Cruelty to Animals

A person commits a petty misdemeanor if he purposely or recklessly:

(1) subjects any animal to cruel mistreatment; or

(2) subjects any animal in his custody to cruel neglect; or

(3) kills or injures any animal belonging to another without legal privilege or consent of the owner.

Subsections (1) and (2) shall not be deemed applicable to accepted veterinary practices and activities carried on for scientific research.

ARTICLE 251. PUBLIC INDECENCY

Section 251.1 Open Lewdness

A person commits a petty misdemeanor if he does any lewd act which he knows is likely to be observed by others who would be affronted or alarmed.

Section 251.2 Prostitution and Related Offenses

(1) *Prostitution.* A person is guilty of prostitution, a petty misdemeanor, if he or she:

(a) is an inmate of a house of prostitution or otherwise engages in sexual activity as a business; or

(b) loiters in or within view of any public place for the purpose of being hired to engage in sexual activity.

"Sexual activity" includes homosexual and other deviate sexual relations. A "house of prostitution" is any place where prostitution or promotion of prostitution is regularly carried on by one person under the control, management or supervision of another. An "inmate" is a person who engages in prostitution in or through the agency of a house of prostitution. "Public place" means any place to which the public or any substantial group thereof has access.

(2) *Promoting Prostitution.* A person who knowingly promotes prostitution of another commits a misdemeanor or felony as provided in Subsection (3). The following acts shall, without limitation of the foregoing, constitute promoting prostitution:

(a) owning, controlling, managing, supervising or otherwise keeping, alone or in association with others, a house of prostitution or a prostitution business; or

(b) procuring an inmate for a house of prostitution or a place in a house of prostitution for one who would be an inmate; or

(c) encouraging, inducing, or otherwise purposely causing another to become or remain a prostitute; or

(d) soliciting a person to patronize a prostitute; or

(e) procuring a prostitute for a patron; or

(f) transporting a person into or within this state with purpose to promote that person's engaging in prostitution, or procuring or paying for transportation with that purpose; or

(g) leasing or otherwise permitting a place controlled by the actor, alone or in association with others, to be regularly used for prostitution or the promotion of prostitution, or failure to make reasonable effort to abate such use by ejecting the tenant, notifying law enforcement authorities, or other legally available means; or

(h) soliciting, receiving, or agreeing to receive any benefit for doing or agreeing to do anything forbidden by this Subsection.

(3) *Grading of Offenses Under Subsection (2).* An offense under Subsection (2) constitutes a felony of the third degree if:

(a) the offense falls within paragraph (a), (b) or (c) of Subsection (2); or

(b) the actor compels another to engage in or promote prostitution; or

(c) the actor promotes prostitution of a child under 16, whether or not he is aware of the child's age; or

(d) the actor promotes prostitution of his wife, child, ward or any person for whose care, protection or support he is responsible.

Otherwise the offense is a misdemeanor.

(4) *Presumption from Living off Prostitutes.* A person, other than the prostitute or the prostitute's minor child or other legal dependent incapable of self-support, who is supported in whole or substantial part by the proceeds of prostitution is presumed to be knowingly promoting prostitution in violation of Subsection (2).

(5) *Patronizing Prostitutes.* A person commits a violation if he hires a prostitute to engage in sexual activity with him, or if he enters or remains in a house of prostitution for the purpose of engaging in sexual activity.

(6) *Evidence.* On the issue whether a place is a house of prostitution the following shall be admissible evidence: its general repute; the repute of the persons who reside in or frequent the place; the frequency, timing and duration of visits by non-residents. Testimony of a person against his spouse shall be admissible to prove offenses under this Section.

Section 251.3 Loitering to Solicit Deviate Sexual Relations

A person is guilty of a petty misdemeanor if he loiters in or near any public place for the purpose of soliciting or being solicited to engage in deviate sexual relations.

Section 251.4 Obscenity

(1) *Obscene Defined.* Material is obscene if, considered as a whole, its predominant appeal is to prurient interest, that is, a shameful or morbid interest, in nudity, sex or excretion, and if in addition it goes substantially beyond customary limits of candor in describing or representing such matters. Predominant appeal

shall be judged with reference to ordinary adults unless it appears from the character of the material or the circumstances of its dissemination to be designed for children or other specially susceptible audience. Undeveloped photographs, molds, printing plates, and the like, shall be deemed obscene notwithstanding that processing or other acts may be required to make the obscenity patent or to disseminate it.

(2) *Offenses.* Subject to the affirmative defense provided in Subsection (3), a person commits a misdemeanor if he knowingly or recklessly:

(a) sells, delivers or provides, or offers or agrees to sell, deliver or provide, any obscene writing, picture, record or other representation or embodiment of the obscene; or

(b) presents or directs an obscene play, dance or performance, or participates in that portion thereof which makes it obscene; or

(c) publishes, exhibits or otherwise makes available any obscene material; or

(d) possesses any obscene material for purposes of sale or other commercial dissemination; or

(e) sells, advertises or otherwise commercially disseminates material, whether or not obscene, by representing or suggesting that it is obscene.

A person who disseminates or possesses obscene material in the course of his business is presumed to do so knowingly or recklessly.

(3) *Justifiable and Non-Commercial Private Dissemination.* It is an affirmative defense to prosecution under this Section that dissemination was restricted to:

(a) institutions or persons having scientific, educational, governmental or other similar justification for possessing obscene material; or

(b) non-commercial dissemination to personal associates of the actor.

(4) *Evidence; Adjudication of Obscenity.* In any prosecution under this Section evidence shall be admissible to show:

(a) the character of the audience for which the material was designed or to which it was directed;

(b) what the predominant appeal of the material would be for ordinary adults or any special audience to which it was directed, and what effect, if any, it would probably have on conduct of such people;

(c) artistic, literary, scientific, educational or other merits of the material;

(d) the degree of public acceptance of the material in the United States;

(e) appeal to prurient interest, or absence thereof, in advertising or other promotion of the material; and

(f) the good repute of the author, creator, publisher or other person from whom the material originated.

Expert testimony and testimony of the author, creator, publisher or other person from whom the material originated, relating to factors entering into the determination of the issue of obscenity, shall be admissible. The Court shall dismiss a prosecution for obscenity if it is satisfied that the material is not obscene.

APPENDIX B

SELECTIONS FROM FEDERAL SENTENCING GUIDELINES

UNITED STATES SENTENCING COMMISSION

Effective November 1, 1987

Including

November 1, 1989 Amendments

CHAPTER ONE—INTRODUCTION AND GENERAL APPLICATION PRINCIPLES

PART A—INTRODUCTION

* * *

2. The Statutory Mission

The Comprehensive Crime Control Act of 1984 foresees guidelines that will further the basic purposes of criminal punishment, i.e., deterring crime, incapacitating the offender, providing just punishment, and rehabilitating the offender. It delegates to the Commission broad authority to review and rationalize the federal sentencing process.

The statute contains many detailed instructions as to how this determination should be made, but the most important of them instructs the Commission to create categories of offense behavior and offender characteristics. An offense behavior category might consist, for example, of "bank robbery/committed with a gun/$2500 taken." An offender characteristic category might be "offender with one prior conviction who was not sentenced to imprisonment." The Commission is required to prescribe guideline ranges that specify an appropriate sentence for each class of convicted persons, to be determined by coordinating the offense behavior categories with the offender characteristic categories. The statute contemplates the guidelines will establish a range of sentences for every coordination of categories. Where the guidelines call for imprisonment, the range must be narrow: the maximum imprisonment cannot exceed the minimum by more than the greater of 25 percent or six months. 28 U.S.C. § 994(b)(2).

The sentencing judge must select a sentence from within the guideline range. If, however, a particular case presents atypical features, the Act allows the judge to depart from the guidelines and sentence outside the range. In that case, the judge must specify reasons for departure. 18 U.S.C. § 3553(b). If the court sentences within the guideline range, an appellate court may review the sentence to see if the guideline was correctly applied. If the judge departs from the guideline range, an appellate court may review the reasonableness of the departure. 18 U.S.C. § 3742. The Act requires the offender to serve virtually all of any prison sentence imposed, for it abolishes parole and substantially restructures good behavior adjustments.

* * *

The Commission, with the aid of its legal and research staff, considerable public testimony, and written commentary, has developed an initial set of guidelines which it now transmits to Congress. The Commission emphasizes, however, that it views the guideline-writing process as evolutionary. It expects, and the governing statute anticipates, that continuing research, experience, and analysis will result in modifications and revisions to the guidelines by submission of amendments to Congress. To this end, the Commission is established as a permanent agency to monitor sentencing practices in the federal courts throughout the nation.

3. The Basic Approach (Policy Statement)

To understand these guidelines and the rationale that underlies them, one must begin with the three objectives that Congress, in enacting the new sentencing law, sought to achieve. Its basic objective was to enhance the ability of the criminal justice system to reduce crime through an effective, fair sentencing system. To achieve this objective, Congress first sought <u>honesty</u> in sentencing. It sought to avoid the confusion and implicit deception that arises out of the present sentencing system which requires a judge to impose an indeterminate sentence that is automatically reduced in most cases by "good time" credits. In addition, the parole commission is permitted to determine how much of the remainder of any prison sentence an offender actually will serve. This usually results in a substantial reduction in the effective length of the sentence imposed, with defendants often serving only about one-third of the sentence handed down by the court.

Second, Congress sought <u>uniformity</u> in sentencing by narrowing the wide disparity in sentences imposed by different federal courts for similar criminal conduct by similar offenders. Third, Congress sought <u>proportionality</u> in sentencing through a system that imposes appropriately different sentences for criminal conduct of different severity.

Honesty is easy to achieve: The abolition of parole makes the sentence imposed by the court the sentence the offender will serve. There is a tension, however, between the mandate of uniformity (treat similar cases alike) and the mandate of proportionality (treat different cases differently) which, like the historical tension between law and equity, makes it difficult to achieve both goals simultaneously. Perfect uniformity—sentencing every offender to five years—destroys proportionality. Having only a few simple categories of crimes would make the guidelines uniform and easy to administer, but might lump together offenses that are different in important respects. For example, a single category for robbery that lumps together armed and unarmed robberies, robberies with and without injuries, robberies of a few dollars and robberies of millions, is far too broad.

At the same time, a sentencing system tailored to fit every conceivable wrinkle of each case can become unworkable and seriously compromise the certainty of punishment and its deterrent effect. A bank robber with (or without) a gun, which the robber kept hidden (or brandished), might have frightened (or merely warned), injured seriously (or less seriously), tied up (or simply pushed) a guard, a teller or a customer, at night (or at noon), for a bad (or arguably less bad) motive, in an effort to obtain money for other crimes (or for other purposes), in the company of a few (or many) other robbers, for the first (or fourth) time that day, while sober (or under the influence of drugs or alcohol), and so forth.

* * *

In the end, there is no completely satisfying solution to this practical stalemate. The Commission has had to simply balance the comparative virtues and vices of broad, simple categorization and detailed, complex subcategorization, and within the constraints established by that balance, minimize the discretionary powers of the sentencing court. Any ultimate system will, to a degree, enjoy the benefits and suffer from the drawbacks of each approach.

A philosophical problem arose when the Commission attempted to reconcile the differing perceptions of the purposes of criminal punishment. Most observers of the criminal law agree that the ultimate aim of the law itself, and of punishment in particular, is the control of crime. Beyond this point, however, the consensus seems to break down. Some argue that appropriate punishment should be defined primarily on the basis of the moral principle of "just deserts." Under this principle, punishment should be scaled to the offender's culpability and the resulting harms. Thus, if a defendant is less culpable, the defendant deserves less punishment. Others argue that punishment should be imposed primarily on the basis of practical "crime control" considerations. Defendants sentenced under this scheme should receive the punishment that most effectively lessens the likelihood of future crime, either by deterring others or incapacitating the defendant.

Adherents of these points of view have urged the Commission to choose between them, to accord one primacy over the other. Such a choice would be profoundly difficult. The relevant literature is vast, the arguments deep, and each point of view has much to be said in its favor. A clear-cut Commission decision in favor of one of these approaches would diminish the chance that the guidelines would find the widespread acceptance they need for effective implementation. As a practical matter, in most sentencing decisions both philosophies may prove consistent with the same result.

For now, the Commission has sought to solve both the practical and philosophical problems of developing a coherent sentencing system by taking an empirical approach that uses data estimating the existing sentencing, system as a starting point. It has analyzed data drawn from 10,000 presentence investigations, crimes as distinguished in substantive criminal statutes, the United States Parole Commission's guidelines and resulting statistics, and data from other relevant sources, in order to determine which distinctions are important in present practice. After examination, the Commission has accepted, modified, or rationalized the more important of these distinctions.

This empirical approach has helped the Commission resolve its practical problem by defining a list of relevant distinctions that, although of considerable length, is short enough to create a manageable set of guidelines. Existing categories are relatively broad and omit many distinctions that some may believe important, yet they include most of the major distinctions that statutes and presentence data suggest make a significant difference in sentencing decisions. Important distinctions that are ignored in existing practice probably occur rarely. A sentencing judge may take this unusual case into account by departing from the guidelines.

* * *

4. The Guidelines' Resolution of Major Issues (Policy Statement)

The guideline-writing process has required the Commission to resolve a host of important policy questions, typically involving rather evenly balanced sets of competing considerations. As an aid to understanding the guidelines, this introduction will briefly discuss several of those issues. Commentary in the guidelines explains others.

* * *

(b) Departures.

The new sentencing statute permits a court to depart from a guideline-specified sentence only when it finds "an aggravating or mitigating circumstance of a kind, or to a degree, not adequately taken into consideration by the Sentencing Commission * * *". 18 U.S.C. § 3553(b). Thus, in principle, the Commission, by specifying that it had adequately considered a particular factor, could prevent a court from using it as grounds for departure. In this initial set of guidelines, however, the Commission does not so limit the courts' departure powers. The Commission intends the sentencing courts to treat each guideline as carving out a "heartland," a set of typical cases embodying the conduct that each guideline describes. When a court finds an atypical case, one to which a particular guideline linguistically applies but where conduct significantly differs from the norm, the court may consider whether a departure is warranted. Section 5H1.10 (Race, Sex, National Origin, Creed, Religion, Socio–Economic Status), the third sentence of § 5H1.4, and the last sentence of § 5K2.12, list a few factors that the court cannot take into account as grounds for departure. With those specific exceptions, however, the Commission does not intend to limit the kinds of factors (whether or not mentioned anywhere else in the guidelines) that could constitute grounds for departure in an unusual case.

* * *

(h) The Sentencing Table.

The Commission has established a sentencing table. For technical and practical reasons it has 43 levels. Each row in the table contains levels that overlap with the levels in the preceding and succeeding rows. By overlapping the levels, the table should discourage unnecessary litigation. Both prosecutor and defendant will realize that the difference between one level and another will not necessarily make a difference in the sentence that the judge imposes. Thus, little purpose will be served in protracted litigation trying to determine, for example, whether $10,000 or $11,000 was obtained as a result of a fraud. At the same time, the rows work to increase a sentence proportionately. A change of 6 levels roughly doubles the sentence irrespective of the level at which one starts. The Commission, aware of the legal requirement that the maximum of any range cannot exceed the minimum by more than the greater of 25 percent or six months, also wishes to permit courts the greatest possible range for exercising discretion. The table overlaps offense levels meaningfully, works proportionately, and at the same time preserves the maximum degree of allowable discretion for the judge within each level.

* * *

PART B—GENERAL APPLICATION PRINCIPLES

§ 1B1.1 Application Instructions

(a) Determine the applicable offense guideline section from Chapter Two.

* * *

(b) Determine the base offense level and apply any appropriate specific offense characteristics contained in the particular guideline in Chapter Two in the order listed.

(c) Apply the adjustments as appropriate related to victim, role, and obstruction of justice from Parts A, B, and C of Chapter Three.

(d) If there are multiple counts of conviction, repeat steps (a) through (c) for each count. Apply Part D of Chapter Three to group the various counts and adjust the offense level accordingly.

(e) Apply the adjustment as appropriate for the defendant's acceptance of responsibility from Part E of Chapter Three.

(f) Determine the defendant's criminal history category as specified in Part A of Chapter Four. Determine from Part B of Chapter Four any other applicable adjustments.

(g) Determine the guideline range in Part A of Chapter Five that corresponds to the offense level and criminal history category determined above.

(h) For the particular guideline range, determine from Parts B through G of Chapter Five the sentencing requirements and options related to probation, imprisonment, supervision conditions, fines, and restitution.

(i) Refer to Parts H and K of Chapter Five, Specific Offender Characteristics and Departures, and to any other policy statements or commentary in the guidelines that might warrant consideration in imposing sentence.

Commentary

Application Notes:

1. The following are definitions of terms that are used frequently in the guidelines:

* * *

(b) "Bodily injury" means any significant injury; e.g., an injury that is painful and obvious, or is of a type for which medical attention ordinarily would be sought. As used in the guidelines, the definition of this term is somewhat different than that used in various statutes.

(c) "Brandished" with reference to a dangerous weapon (including a firearm) means that the weapon was pointed or waved about, or displayed in a threatening manner.

(d) "Dangerous weapon" means an instrument capable of inflicting death or serious bodily injury. Where an object that appeared to be a dangerous weapon was brandished, displayed, or possessed, treat the object as a dangerous weapon.

(e) "Firearm" means any weapon which is designed to or may readily be converted to expel any projectile by the action of an explosive. A weapon, commonly known as "BB" or pellet gun, that uses air or carbon dioxide pressure to expel a projectile is a dangerous weapon but not a firearm.

(f) "More than minimal planning" means more planning than is typical for commission of the offense in a simple form. "More than minimal planning" also exists if significant affirmative steps were taken to conceal the offense.

"More than minimal planning" is deemed present in any case involving repeated acts over a period of time, unless it is clear that each instance was purely opportune. Consequently, this adjustment will apply especially frequently in property offenses.

In an assault, for example, waiting to commit the offense when no witnesses were present would not alone constitute more than minimal planning. By contrast, luring the victim to a specific location, or wearing a ski mask to prevent identification, would constitute more than minimal planning.

In a commercial burglary, for example, checking the area to make sure no witnesses were present would not alone constitute more than minimal planning. By contrast, obtaining building plans to plot a particular course of entry, or disabling an alarm system, would constitute more than minimal planning.

In a theft, going to a secluded area of a store to conceal the stolen item in one's pocket would not alone constitute more than minimal planning. However, repeated instances of such thefts on several occasions would constitute more than minimal planning. Similarly, fashioning a special device to conceal the property, or obtaining information on delivery dates so that an especially valuable item could be obtained, would constitute more than minimal planning.

In an embezzlement, a single taking accomplished by a false book entry would constitute only minimal planning. On the other hand, creating purchase orders to, and invoices from, a dummy corporation for merchandise that was never delivered would constitute more than minimal planning, as would several instances of taking money, each accompanied by false entries.

(g) "Otherwise used" with reference to a dangerous weapon (including a firearm) means that the conduct did not amount to the discharge of a firearm but was more than brandishing, displaying, or possessing a firearm or other dangerous weapon.

* * *

4. The offense level adjustments from more than one specific offense characteristic within an offense guideline are cumulative (added together) unless the guideline specifies that only the greater (or greatest) is to be used. Within each specific offense characteristic subsection, however, the offense level adjustments are alternative; only the one that best describes the conduct is to be used. E.g., in § 2A2.2(b)(3), pertaining to degree of bodily injury, the subdivision that best describes the level of bodily injury is used; the adjustments for different degrees of bodily injury (subdivisions (A)–(E)) are not added together.

5. Where two or more guideline provisions appear equally applicable, but the guidelines authorize the application of only one such provision, use the provision that results in the greater offense level. E.g., in § 2A2.2(b)(2), if a firearm is both discharged and brandished, the provision applicable to the discharge of the firearm would be used.

* * *

CHAPTER TWO—OFFENSE CONDUCT

Introductory Commentary

Chapter Two pertains to offense conduct. The chapter is organized by offenses and divided into parts and related sections that may cover one statute or many. Each offense has a corresponding base offense level and may have one or more specific offense characteristics that adjust the offense level upward or downward. Certain factors relevant to the offense that are not covered in specific guidelines in Chapter Two are set forth in Chapter Three, Parts A (Victim–Related Adjustments), B (Role in the Offense), and C (Obstruction); Chapter Four, Part B (Career Offenders and Criminal Livelihood); and Chapter Five, Part K (Departures).

PART A—OFFENSES AGAINST THE PERSON

* * *

3. CRIMINAL SEXUAL ABUSE

§ 2A3.1 Criminal Sexual Abuse; Attempt or Assault With the Intent to Commit Criminal Sexual Abuse

(a) Base Offense Level: 27

(b) Specific Offense Characteristics

(1) If the offense was committed by the means set forth in 18 U.S.C. § 2241(a) or (b) (including, but not limited to, the use or display of any dangerous weapon), increase by 4 levels.

(2) (A) If the victim had not attained the age of twelve years, increase by 4 levels; otherwise, (B) if the victim was under the age of sixteen, increase by 2 levels.

(3) If the victim was in the custody, care, or supervisory control of the defendant, was a corrections employee, or a person held in the custody of a correctional facility, increase by 2 levels.

(4) (A) If the victim sustained permanent or life-threatening bodily injury, increase by 4 levels; (B) if the victim sustained serious bodily injury, increase by 2 levels; or (C) if the degree of injury is between that specified in subdivisions (A) and (B), increase by 3 levels.

(5) If the victim was abducted, increase by 4 levels.

Commentary

Application Notes:

* * *

2. "The means set forth in 18 U.S.C. § 2241(a) or (b)" are: by using force against the victim; by threatening or placing the victim in fear that any person will be subject to death, serious bodily injury, or kidnapping; by rendering the victim unconscious; or by administering by force or threat of force, or without the knowledge or permission of the victim, a drug, intoxicant, or other similar substance and thereby substantially impairing the ability of the victim to appraise or control conduct. This provision would apply, for example, where any dangerous weapon was used, brandished, or displayed to intimidate the victim.

Background: Sexual offenses addressed in this section are crimes of violence. Because of their dangerousness, attempts are treated the same as completed acts of criminal sexual abuse. The maximum term of imprisonment authorized by statute is life imprisonment. The base offense level represents sexual abuse as set forth in 18 U.S.C. § 2242. An enhancement is provided for use of force; threat of death, serious bodily injury, or kidnapping; or certain other means as defined in 18 U.S.C. § 2241. This includes any use or threatened use of a dangerous weapon.

An enhancement is provided when the victim is less than sixteen years of age. An additional enhancement is provided where the victim is less than twelve years of age. Any criminal sexual abuse with a child less than twelve years of age, regardless of "consent," is governed by § 2A3.1.

An enhancement for a custodial relationship between defendant and victim is also provided. Whether the custodial relationship is temporary or permanent, the defendant in such a case is a person the victim trusts or to whom the victim is entrusted. This represents the potential for greater and prolonged psychological damage. Also, an enhancement is provided where the victim was an inmate of, or a person employed in, a correctional facility. Finally, enhancements are provided for permanent, life-threatening, or serious bodily injury and abduction.

* * *

PART B—OFFENSES INVOLVING PROPERTY

* * *

3. ROBBERY, EXTORTION, AND BLACKMAIL

§ 2B3.1. Robbery

(a) Base Offense Level: 20

(b) Specific Offense Characteristics

(1) If the offense involved robbery or attempted robbery of the property of a financial institution or post office, increase by 2 levels.

(2) (A) If a firearm was discharged, increase by 5 levels; (B) if a dangerous weapon (including a firearm) was otherwise used, increase by 4 levels; (C) if a dangerous weapon (including a firearm) was brandished, displayed, or possessed, increase by 3 levels; or (D) if an express threat of death was made, increase by 2 levels.

* * *

(6) If the loss exceeded $10,000, increase the offense level as follows:

	Loss (Apply the Greatest)	Increase in Level
(A)	$10,000 or less	no increase
(B)	More than $10,000	add 1
(C)	More than $50,000	add 2
(D)	More than $250,000	add 3
(E)	More than $800,000	add 4
(F)	More than $1,500,000	add 5
(G)	More than $2,500,000	add 6
(H)	More than $5,000,000	add 7.

Commentary

Application Notes:

1. "Firearm," "dangerous weapon," "otherwise used," "brandished," "abducted," and "physically restrained" are defined in the Commentary to § 1B1.1 (Application Instructions).

* * *

PART F—OFFENSES INVOLVING FRAUD OR DECEIT

§ 2F1.1. Fraud and Deceit

(a) Base Offense Level: 6

(b) Specific Offense Characteristics

(1) If the loss exceeded $2,000, increase the offense level as follows:

	Loss (Apply the Greatest)	Increase in Level
(A)	$2,000 or less	no increase
(B)	More than $2,000	add 1
(C)	More than $5,000	add 2
(D)	More than $10,000	add 3
(E)	More than $20,000	add 4
(F)	More than $40,000	add 5
(G)	More than $70,000	add 6
(H)	More than $120,000	add 7
(I)	More than $200,000	add 8

	Loss (Apply the Greatest)	Increase in Level
(J)	More than $350,000	add 9
(K)	More than $500,000	add 10
(L)	More than $800,000	add 11
(M)	More than $1,500,000	add 12
(N)	More than $2,500,000	add 13
(O)	More than $5,000,000	add 14
(P)	More than $10,000,000	add 15
(Q)	More than $20,000,000	add 16
(R)	More than $40,000,000	add 17
(S)	More than $80,000,000	add 18.

(2) If the offense involved (A) more than minimal planning, or (B) a scheme to defraud more than one victim, increase by 2 levels.

(3) If the offense involved (A) a misrepresentation that the defendant was acting on behalf of a charitable, educational, religious or political organization, or a government agency, or (B) violation of any judicial or administrative order, injunction, decree or process, increase by 2 levels. If the resulting offense level is less than level 10, increase to level 10.

(4) If the offense involved the conscious or reckless risk of serious bodily injury, increase by 2 levels. If the resulting offense level is less than level 13, increase to level 13.

(5) If the offense involved the use of foreign bank accounts or transactions to conceal the true nature or extent of the fraudulent conduct, and the offense level as determined above is less than level 12, increase to level 12.

Commentary

Application Notes:

1. The adjustments in § 2F1.1(b)(3) are alternative rather than cumulative. If in a particular case, however, both of the enumerated factors applied, an upward departure might be warranted.

2. "More than minimal planning" (subsection (b)(2)(A)) is defined in the Commentary to § 1B1.1 (Application Instructions).

3. "Scheme to defraud more than one victim," as used in subsection (b)(2)(B), refers to a design or plan to obtain something of value from more than one person. In this context, "victim" refers to the person or entity from which the funds are to come directly. Thus, a wire fraud in which a single telephone call was made to three distinct individuals to get each of them to invest in a pyramid scheme would involve a scheme to defraud more than one victim, but passing a fraudulently endorsed check would not, even though the maker, payee and/or payor all might be considered victims for other purposes, such as restitution.

* * *

8. The amount of loss need not be precise. The court is not expected to identify each victim and the loss he suffered to arrive at an exact figure. The court need only make a reasonable estimate of the range of loss, given the available information. The estimate may be based on the approximate number of victims

and an estimate of the average loss to each victim, or on more general factors, such as the nature and duration of the fraud and the revenues generated by similar operations. Estimates based upon aggregate "market loss" (e.g., the aggregate decline in market value of a stock resulting from disclosure of information that was wrongfully withheld or misrepresented) are especially appropriate for securities cases. The offender's gross gain from committing the fraud is an alternative estimate that ordinarily will understate the loss.

9. Dollar loss often does not fully capture the harmfulness and seriousness of the conduct. In such instances, an upward departure may be warranted. Examples may include the following:

   (a) the primary objective of the fraud was non-monetary;

   (b) false statements were made for the purpose of facilitating some other crime;

   (c) the offense caused physical or psychological harm;

   (d) the offense endangered national security or military readiness;

   (e) the offense caused a loss of confidence in an important institution;

   (f) completion of the offense was prevented, or the offense was interrupted before it caused serious harm.

* * *

Background: This guideline is designed to apply to a wide variety of fraud cases. The statutory maximum term of imprisonment for most such offenses is five years. The guideline does not link offense characteristics to specific code sections. Because federal fraud statutes are so broadly written, a single pattern of offense conduct usually can be prosecuted under several code sections, as a result of which the offense of conviction may be somewhat arbitrary. Furthermore, most fraud statutes cover a broad range of conduct with extreme variation in severity.

Empirical analyses of current practices show that the most important factors that determine sentence length are the amount of loss and whether the offense is an isolated crime of opportunity or is sophisticated or repeated. Accordingly, although they are imperfect, these are the primary factors upon which the guideline has been based.

The extent to which an offense is planned or sophisticated is important in assessing its potential harmfulness and the dangerousness of the offender, independent of the actual harm. A complex scheme or repeated incidents of fraud are indicative of an intention and potential to do considerable harm. In current practice, this factor has a significant impact, especially in frauds involving small losses. Accordingly, the guideline specifies a 2–level enhancement when this factor is present.

* * *

PART X—OTHER OFFENSES

1. CONSPIRACIES, ATTEMPTS, SOLICITATIONS

§ 2X1.1 Attempt, Solicitation, or Conspiracy (Not Covered by a Specific Offense Guideline)

(a) Base Offense Level: The base offense level from the guideline for the object offense, plus any adjustments from such guideline for any intended offense conduct that can be established with reasonable certainty.

(b) Specific Offense Characteristics

(1) If an attempt, decrease by 3 levels, unless the defendant completed all the acts the defendant believed necessary for successful completion of the offense or the circumstances demonstrate that the defendant was about to complete all such acts but for apprehension or interruption by some similar event beyond the defendant's control.

* * *

Commentary

Application Notes:

1. Certain attempts, conspiracies, and solicitations are expressly covered by other offense guidelines.

   Offense guidelines that expressly cover attempts include: § 2A2.1 (Assault With Intent to Commit Murder; Conspiracy or Solicitation to Commit Murder; Attempted Murder); § 2A3.1 (Criminal Sexual Abuse; Attempt or Assault with the Intent to Commit Criminal Sexual Abuse); § 2A3.3 (Criminal Sexual Abuse of a Minor (Statutory Rape) or Attempt to Commit Such Acts); § 2A3.3 (Criminal Sexual Abuse of a Ward or Attempt to Commit Such Acts); § 2A3.4 (Abusive Sexual Contact or Attempt to Commit Abusive Sexual Contact); § 2A4.2 (Demanding or Receiving Ransom Money); § 2A5.1 (Aircraft Piracy or Attempted Aircraft Piracy); § 2C1.1 (Offering, Giving, Soliciting, or Receiving a Bribe; Extortion Under Color of Official Right); § 2C1.2 (Offering, Giving, Soliciting, or Receiving a Gratuity); § 2D1.4 (Attempts and Conspiracies); § 2E5.1 (Offering, Accepting, or Soliciting a Bribe or Gratuity Affecting the Operation of an Employee Welfare or Pension Benefit Plan); § 2N1.1 (Tampering or Attempting to Tamper Involving Risk of Death or Serious Injury); § 2Q1.4 (Tampering or Attempted Tampering with Public Water System).

   * * *

2. Under § 2X1.1(a) the base offense level will be the same as that for the object offense which the defendant solicited, or conspired or attempted to commit. But the only specific offense characteristics from the guideline for the object offense that apply are those that are determined to have been specifically intended or actually occurred. Speculative specific offense characteristics will not be applied. For example, if two defendants are arrested during the conspiratorial stage of planning an armed bank robbery, the offense level ordinarily would not include aggravating factors regarding possible injury to others, hostage taking, discharge of a weapon, or obtaining a large sum of money, because such factors would be speculative. The offense level would simply reflect the level applicable to robbery of a financial institution, with the enhancement for possession of a weapon. If it was established that the defendants actually intended to physically restrain the teller, the specific offense characteristic for physical restraint would be added. In an attempted theft, the value of the items that the defendant attempted to steal would be considered.

3. If the object offense is not covered by a specific guideline, see § 2X5.1 (Other Offenses).

4. In certain cases, the participants may have completed (or have been about to complete but for apprehension or interruption) all of the acts necessary for the successful completion of part, but not all, of the intended offense. In such cases,

the offense level for the count (or group of closely-related multiple counts) is whichever of the following is greater: the offense level for the intended offense minus 3 levels (under § 2X1.1(b)(1), (b)(2), or (b)(3)(A)), or the offense level for the part of the offense for which the necessary acts were completed (or about to be completed but for apprehension or interruption). For example, where the intended offense was the theft of $800,000 but the participants completed (or were about to complete) only the acts necessary to steal $30,000, the offense level is the offense level for the theft of $800,000 minus 3 levels, or the offense level for the theft of $30,000, whichever is greater.

In the case of multiple counts that are not closely-related counts, whether the 3–level reduction under § 2X1.1(b)(1) or (2) applies is determined separately for each count.

Background: In most prosecutions for conspiracies or attempts, the object offense was substantially completed or was interrupted or prevented on the verge of completion by the intercession of law enforcement authorities or the victim. In such cases, no reduction of the offense level is warranted. Sometimes, however, the arrest occurs well before the defendant or any co-conspirator has completed the necessary acts of the object offense. Under such circumstances, a reduction of 3 levels is provided under § 2X1.1(b)(1) or (2).

* * *

5. ALL OTHER OFFENSES

§ 2X5.1 Other Offenses

If the offense is a felony or Class A misdemeanor for which no guideline expressly has been promulgated, apply the most analogous offense guideline. If there is not a sufficiently analogous guideline, the provisions of 18 U.S.C. § 3553(b) shall control.

Commentary

Background: Many offenses, especially assimilative crimes, are not listed in the Statutory Index or in any of the lists of Statutory Provisions that follow each offense guideline. Nonetheless, the specific guidelines that have been promulgated cover the type of criminal behavior that most such offenses proscribe. The court is required to determine if there is a sufficiently analogous offense guideline, and, if so, to apply the guideline that is most analogous. Where there is no sufficiently analogous guideline, the provisions of 18 U.S.C. § 3553(b) control. That statute provides in relevant part as follows: "In the absence of an applicable sentencing guideline, the court shall impose an appropriate sentence, having due regard for the purposes set forth in [18 U.S.C. § 3553] subsection (a)(2). In the absence of an applicable sentencing guideline in the case of an offense other than a petty offense, the court shall also have due regard for the relationship of the sentence imposed to sentences prescribed by guidelines applicable to similar offenses and offenders, and to the applicable policy statements of the Sentencing Commission."

CHAPTER THREE—ADJUSTMENTS

PART A—VICTIM-RELATED ADJUSTMENTS

1. VICTIM-RELATED ADJUSTMENTS

Introductory Commentary

The following adjustments are included in this Part because they may apply to a wide variety of offenses. They are to be treated as specific offense characteristics.

§ 3A1.1 Vulnerable Victim

If the defendant knew or should have known that a victim of the offense was unusually vulnerable due to age, physical or mental condition, or that a victim was otherwise particularly susceptible to the criminal conduct, increase by 2 levels.

Commentary

Application Notes:

1. This adjustment applies to offenses where an unusually vulnerable victim is made a target of criminal activity by the defendant. The adjustment would apply, for example, in a fraud case where the defendant marketed an ineffective cancer cure or in a robbery where the defendant selected a handicapped victim. But it would not apply in a case where the defendant sold fraudulent securities by mail to the general public and one of the victims happened to be senile.
2. Do not apply this adjustment if the offense guideline specifically incorporates this factor.

§ 3A1.2 Official Victim

If—

(a) the victim was a law enforcement or corrections officer; a former law enforcement or corrections officer; an officer or employee included in 18 U.S.C. § 1114; a former officer or employee included in 18 U.S.C. § 1114; or a member of the immediate family of any of the above, and the offense of conviction was motivated by such status; or

(b) during the course of the offense or immediate flight therefrom, the defendant or a person for whose conduct the defendant is otherwise accountable, knowing or having reasonable cause to believe that a person was a law enforcement or corrections officer, assaulted such officer in a manner creating a substantial risk of serious bodily injury,

increase by 3 levels.

* * *

§ 3A1.3 Restraint of Victim

If a victim was physically restrained in the course of the offense, increase by 2 levels.

Commentary

Application Notes:

1. "Physically restrained" is defined in the Commentary to § 1B1.1 (Application Instructions).
2. This adjustment applies to any offense in which a victim was physically restrained in the course of the offense, except where such restraint is an element of the offense, specifically incorporated into the base offense level, or listed as a specific offense characteristic.
3. If the restraint was sufficiently egregious, an upward departure may be warranted. See § 5K2.4 (Abduction or Unlawful Restraint).

PART B—ROLE IN THE OFFENSE

Introductory Commentary

This Part provides adjustments to the offense level based upon the role the defendant played in committing the offense. When an offense is committed by more than one participant, § 3B1.1 or § 3B1.2 (or neither) may apply. Section 3B1.3 may apply to offenses committed by any number of participants.

§ 3B1.1 Aggravating Role

Based on the defendant's role in the offense, increase the offense level as follows:

(a) If the defendant was an organizer or leader of a criminal activity that involved five or more participants or was otherwise extensive, increase by 4 levels.

(b) If the defendant was a manager or supervisor (but not an organizer or leader) and the criminal activity involved five or more participants or was otherwise extensive, increase by 3 levels.

(c) If the defendant was an organizer, leader, manager, or supervisor in any criminal activity other than described in (a) or (b), increase by 2 levels.

* * *

§ 3B1.2 Mitigating Role

Based on the defendant's role in the offense, decrease the offense level as follows:

(a) If the defendant was a minimal participant in any criminal activity, decrease by 4 levels.

(b) If the defendant was a minor participant in any criminal activity, decrease by 2 levels.

In cases falling between (a) and (b), decrease by 3 levels.

* * *

§ 3B1.3 Abuse of Position of Trust or Use of Special Skill

If the defendant abused a position of public or private trust, or used a special skill, in a manner that significantly facilitated the commission or concealment of the offense, increase by 2 levels. This adjustment may not be employed in addition to that provided for in § 3B1.1, nor may it be employed if an abuse of trust or skill is included in the base offense level or specific offense characteristic.

Commentary

Application Notes:

1. The position of trust must have contributed in some substantial way to facilitating the crime and not merely have provided an opportunity that could as easily have been afforded to other persons. This adjustment, for example, would not apply to an embezzlement by an ordinary bank teller.

2. "Special skill" refers to a skill not possessed by members of the general public and usually requiring substantial education, training or licensing. Examples would include pilots, lawyers, doctors, accountants, chemists, and demolition experts.

Background: This adjustment applies to persons who abuse their positions of trust or their special skills to facilitate significantly the commission or concealment of a crime. Such persons generally are viewed as more culpable.

§ 3B1.4 In any other case, no adjustment is made for role in the offense

Commentary

Many offenses are committed by a single individual or by individuals of roughly equal culpability so that none of them will receive an adjustment under this Part. In addition, some participants in a criminal organization may receive increases under § 3B1.1 (Aggravating Role) while others receive decreases under § 3B1.2 (Mitigating Role) and still other participants receive no adjustment.

PART C—OBSTRUCTION

§ 3C1.1 Willfully Obstructing or Impeding Proceedings

If the defendant willfully impeded or obstructed, or attempted to impede or obstruct the administration of justice during the investigation or prosecution of the instant offense, increase the offense level by 2 levels.

Commentary

This section provides a sentence enhancement for a defendant who engages in conduct calculated to mislead or deceive authorities or those involved in a judicial proceeding, or otherwise to willfully interfere with the disposition of criminal charges, in respect to the instant offense.

Application Notes:

1. The following conduct, while not exclusive, may provide a basis for applying this adjustment:

   (a) destroying or concealing material evidence, or attempting to do so;

   (b) directing or procuring another person to destroy or conceal material evidence, or attempting to do so;

   (c) testifying untruthfully or suborning untruthful testimony concerning a material fact, or producing or attempting to produce an altered, forged, or counterfeit document or record during a preliminary or grand jury proceeding, trial, sentencing proceeding, or any other judicial proceeding;

(d) threatening, intimidating, or otherwise unlawfully attempting to influence a co-defendant, witness, or juror, directly or indirectly;

(e) furnishing material falsehoods to a probation officer in the course of a presentence or other investigation for the court.

2. In applying this provision, suspect testimony and statements should be evaluated in a light most favorable to the defendant.

3. This provision is not intended to punish a defendant for the exercise of a constitutional right. A defendant's denial of guilt is not a basis for application of this provision.

* * *

PART E—ACCEPTANCE OF RESPONSIBILITY

§ 3E1.1 Acceptance of Responsibility

(a) If the defendant clearly demonstrates a recognition and affirmative acceptance of personal responsibility for his criminal conduct, reduce the offense level by 2 levels.

(b) A defendant may be given consideration under this section without regard to whether his conviction is based upon a guilty plea or a finding of guilt by the court or jury or the practical certainty of conviction at trial.

(c) A defendant who enters a guilty plea is not entitled to a sentencing reduction under this section as a matter of right.

Commentary

Application Notes:

1. In determining whether a defendant qualifies for this provision, appropriate considerations include, but are not limited to, the following:

   (a) voluntary termination or withdrawal from criminal conduct or associations;

   (b) voluntary payment of restitution prior to adjudication of guilt;

   (c) voluntary and truthful admission to authorities of involvement in the offense and related conduct;

   (d) voluntary surrender to authorities promptly after commission of the offense;

   (e) voluntary assistance to authorities in the recovery of the fruits and instrumentalities of the offense;

   (f) voluntary resignation from the office or position held during the commission of the offense; and

   (g) the timeliness of the defendant's conduct in manifesting the acceptance of responsibility.

2. Conviction by trial does not preclude a defendant from consideration under this section. A defendant may manifest sincere contrition even if he exercises his constitutional right to a trial. This may occur, for example, where a defendant goes to trial to assert and preserve issues that do not relate to factual guilt (e.g., to

make a constitutional challenge to a statute or a challenge to the applicability of a statute to his conduct).

3. A guilty plea may provide some evidence of the defendant's acceptance of responsibility. However, it does not, by itself, entitle a defendant to a reduced sentence under this section.

4. Conduct resulting in an enhancement under § 3C1.1 (Willfully Obstructing or Impeding Proceedings) ordinarily indicates that the defendant has not accepted responsibility for his criminal conduct. There may, however, be extraordinary cases in which adjustments under both §§ 3C1.1 and 3E1.1 may apply.

5. The sentencing judge is in a unique position to evaluate a defendant's acceptance of responsibility. For this reason, the determination of the sentencing judge is entitled to great deference on review and should not be disturbed unless it is without foundation.

Background: The reduction of offense level provided by this section recognizes legitimate societal interests. For several reasons, a defendant who clearly demonstrates a recognition and affirmative acceptance of personal responsibility for the offense by taking, in a timely fashion, one or more of the actions listed above (or some equivalent action) is appropriately given a lesser sentence than a defendant who has not demonstrated sincere remorse.

The availability of a reduction under § 3E1.1 is not controlled by whether the conviction was by trial or plea of guilty. Although a guilty plea may show some evidence of acceptance of responsibility, it does not automatically entitle the defendant to a sentencing adjustment.

CHAPTER FOUR—CRIMINAL HISTORY AND CRIMINAL LIVELIHOOD

PART A—CRIMINAL HISTORY

Introductory Commentary

The Comprehensive Crime Control Act sets forth four purposes of sentencing. (See 18 U.S.C. § 3553(a)(2).) A defendant's record of past criminal conduct is directly relevant to those purposes. A defendant with a record of prior criminal behavior is more culpable than a first offender and thus deserving of greater punishment. General deterrence of criminal conduct dictates that a clear message be sent to society that repeated criminal behavior will aggravate the need for punishment with each recurrence. To protect the public from further crimes of the particular defendant, the likelihood of recidivism and future criminal behavior must be considered. Repeated criminal behavior is an indicator of a limited likelihood of successful rehabilitation.

The specific factors included in § 4A1.1 and § 4A1.3 are consistent with the extant empirical research assessing correlates of recidivism and patterns of career criminal behavior. While empirical research has shown that other factors are correlated highly with the likelihood of recidivism, e.g., age and drug abuse, for policy reasons they were not included here at this time. The Commission has made no definitive judgment as to the reliability of the existing data. However, the Commission will review additional data insofar as they become available in the future.

§ 4A1.1 Criminal History Category

The total points from items (a) through (e) determine the criminal history category in the Sentencing Table in Chapter Five, Part A.

(a) Add 3 points for each prior sentence of imprisonment exceeding one year and one month.

(b) Add 2 points for each prior sentence of imprisonment of at least sixty days not counted in (a).

(c) Add 1 point for each prior sentence not included in (a) or (b), up to a total of 4 points for this item.

(d) Add 2 points if the defendant committed the instant offense while under any criminal justice sentence, including probation, parole, supervised release, imprisonment, work release, or escape status.

(e) Add 2 points if the defendant committed the instant offense less than two years after release from imprisonment on a sentence counted under (a) or (b) or while in imprisonment or escape status on such a sentence. If 2 points are added for item (d), add only 1 point for this item.

Commentary

The total criminal history points from § 4A1.1 determine the criminal history category (I–VI) in the Sentencing Table in Chapter Five, Part A. The definitions and instructions in § 4A1.2 govern the computation of the criminal history points. Therefore, §§ 4A1.1 and 4A1.2 must be read together. The following notes highlight the interaction of §§ 4A1.1 and 4A1.2.

Application Notes:

1. <u>§ 4A1.1(a).</u> Three points are added for each prior sentence of imprisonment exceeding one year and one month. There is no limit to the number of points that may be counted under this item. The term "prior sentence" is defined at § 4A1.2(a). The term "sentence of imprisonment" is defined at § 4A1.2(b). Where a prior sentence of imprisonment resulted from a revocation of probation, parole, or a similar form of release, see § 4A1.2(k).

   Certain prior sentences are not counted or are counted only under certain conditions:

   A sentence imposed more than fifteen years prior to the defendant's commencement of the instant offense is not counted unless the defendant's incarceration extended into this fifteen year period. See § 4A1.2(e).

   A sentence imposed for an offense committed prior to the defendant's eighteenth birthday is counted under this item only if it resulted from an adult conviction. See § 4A1.2(d).

   A sentence for a foreign conviction, a conviction that has been expunged, or an invalid conviction is not counted. See § 4A1.2(h) and (j) and the Commentary to § 4A1.2.

2. <u>§ 4A1.1(b).</u> Two points are added for each prior sentence of imprisonment of at least sixty days not counted in § 4A1.1(a). There is no limit to the number of points that may be counted under this item. The term "prior sentence" is defined at § 4A1.2(a). The term "sentence of imprisonment" is defined at § 4A1.2(b).

Where a prior sentence of imprisonment resulted from a revocation of probation, parole, or a similar form of release, see § 4A1.2(k).

Certain prior sentences are not counted or are counted only under certain conditions:

A sentence imposed more than ten years prior to the defendant's commencement of the instant offense is not counted. See § 4A1.2(e).

An adult or juvenile sentence imposed for an offense committed prior to the defendant's eighteenth birthday is counted only if confinement resulting from such sentence extended into the five year period preceding the defendant's commencement of the instant offense. See § 4A1.2(d).

Sentences for certain specified non-felony offenses are never counted. See § 4A1.2(c)(2).

A sentence for a foreign conviction or a tribal court conviction, an expunged conviction, or an invalid conviction, is not counted. See § 4A1.2(h), (i), (j), and the Commentary to § 4A1.2.

A military sentence is counted only if imposed by a general or special court martial. See § 4A1.2(g).

3. § 4A1.1(c). One point is added for each prior sentence not counted under § 4A1.1(a) or (b). A maximum of four points may be counted under this item. The term "prior sentence" is defined at § 4A1.2(a).

Certain prior sentences are not counted or are counted only under certain conditions:

A sentence imposed more than ten years prior to the defendant's commencement of the instant offense is not counted. See § 4A1.2(e).

An adult or juvenile sentence imposed for an offense committed prior to the defendant's eighteenth birthday is counted only if imposed within five years of the defendant's commencement of the current offense. See § 4A1.2(d).

Sentences for certain specified non-felony offenses are counted only if they meet certain requirements. See § 4A1.2(c)(1).

Sentences for certain specified non-felony offenses are never counted. See § 4A1.2(c)(2).

A diversionary disposition is counted only where there is a finding or admission of guilt in a judicial proceeding. See § 4A1.2(f).

A sentence for a foreign conviction, a tribal court conviction, an expunged conviction, or an invalid conviction, is not counted. See § 4A1.2(h), (i), (j), and the Commentary to § 4A1.2.

A military sentence is counted only if imposed by a general or special court martial. See § 4A1.2(g).

4. § 4A1.1(d). Two points are added if the defendant committed any part of the instant offense (i.e., any relevant conduct) while under any criminal justice sentence, including probation, parole, supervised release, imprisonment, work release, or escape status. For the purposes of this item, a "criminal justice sentence" means a sentence countable under § 4A1.2 (Definitions and Instructions for Computing Criminal History).

5. § 4A1.1(e). Two points are added if the defendant committed any part of the instant offense (i.e., any relevant conduct) less than two years following release from confinement on a sentence counted under § 4A1.1(a) or (b). This also

applies if the defendant committed the instant offense while in imprisonment or escape status on such a sentence. However, if two points are added under § 4A1.1(d), only one point is added under § 4A1.1(e).

Background: Prior convictions may represent convictions in the federal system, fifty state systems, the District of Columbia, territories, and foreign, tribal, and military courts. There are jurisdictional variations in offense definitions, sentencing structures, and manner of sentence pronouncement. To minimize problems with imperfect measures of past crime seriousness, criminal history categories are based on the maximum term imposed in previous sentences rather than on other measures, such as whether the conviction was designated a felony or misdemeanor. In recognition of the imperfection of this measure however, § 4A1.3 permits information about the significance or similarity of past conduct underlying prior convictions to be used as a basis for imposing a sentence outside the applicable guideline range.

Subdivisions (a), (b), and (c) of § 4A1.1 distinguish confinement sentences longer than one year and one month, shorter confinement sentences of at least sixty days, and all other sentences, such as confinement sentences of less than sixty days, probation, fines, and residency in a halfway house.

Section 4A1.1(d) implements one measure of recency by adding two points if the defendant was under a criminal justice sentence during any part of the instant offense.

Section 4A1.1(e) implements another measure of recency by adding two points if the defendant committed any part of the instant offense less than two years immediately following his release from confinement on a sentence counted under § 4A1.1(a) or (b). Because of the potential overlap of (d) and (e), their combined impact is limited to three points. However, a defendant who falls within both (d) and (e) is more likely to commit additional crimes; thus, (d) and (e) are not completely combined.

* * *

§ 4A1.3 Adequacy of Criminal History Category (Policy Statement)

If reliable information indicates that the criminal history category does not adequately reflect the seriousness of the defendant's past criminal conduct or the likelihood that the defendant will commit other crimes, the court may consider imposing a sentence departing from the otherwise applicable guideline range. * * *

* * *

PART B—CAREER OFFENDERS AND CRIMINAL LIVELIHOOD

§ 4B1.1. Career Offender

A defendant is a career offender if (1) the defendant was at least eighteen years old at the time of the instant offense, (2) the instant offense of conviction is a felony that is either a crime of violence or a controlled substance offense, and (3) the defendant has at least two prior felony convictions of either a crime of violence or a controlled substance offense. If the offense level for a career criminal from the table below is greater than the offense level otherwise applicable, the offense level from the table below shall apply. A career offender's criminal history category in every case shall be Category VI.

	Offense Statutory Maximum	Offense Level*
(A)	Life	37
(B)	25 years or more	34
(C)	20 years or more, but less than 25 years	32
(D)	15 years or more, but less than 20 years	29
(E)	10 years or more, but less than 15 years	24
(F)	5 years or more, but less than 10 years	17
(G)	More than 1 year, but less than 5 years	12

*If an adjustment from § 3E1.1 (Acceptance of Responsibility) applies, decrease the offense level by 2 levels.

* * *

CHAPTER FIVE—DETERMINING THE SENTENCE

Introductory Commentary

For certain categories of offenses and offenders, the guidelines permit the court to impose either imprisonment or some other sanction or combination of sanctions. In determining the type of sentence to impose, the sentencing judge should consider the nature and seriousness of the conduct, the statutory purposes of sentencing, and the pertinent offender characteristics. A sentence is within the guidelines if it complies with each applicable section of this chapter. The court should impose a sentence sufficient, but not greater than necessary, to comply with the statutory purposes of sentencing. 18 U.S.C. § 3553(a).

APPENDIX B

PART A—SENTENCING TABLE

The Sentencing Table used to determine the guideline range follows:

SENTENCING TABLE (in months of imprisonment)

Criminal History Category (Criminal History Points)

Offense Level	I (0 or 1)	II (2 or 3)	III (4, 5, 6)	IV (7, 8, 9)	V (10, 11, 12)	VI (13 or more)
1	0–6	0–6	0–6	0–6	0–6	0–6
2	0–6	0–6	0–6	0–6	0–6	1–7
3	0–6	0–6	0–6	0–6	2–8	3–9
4	0–6	0–6	0–6	2–8	4–10	6–12
5	0–6	0–6	1–7	4–10	6–12	9–15
6	0–6	1–7	2–8	6–12	9–15	12–18
7	1–7	2–8	4–10	8–14	12–18	15–21
8	2–8	4–10	6–12	10–16	15–21	18–24
9	4–10	6–12	8–14	12–18	18–24	21–27
10	6–12	8–14	10–16	15–21	21–27	24–30
11	8–14	10–16	12–18	18–24	24–30	27–33
12	10–16	12–18	15–21	21–27	27–33	30–37
13	12–18	15–21	18–24	24–30	30–37	33–41
14	15–21	18–24	21–27	27–33	33–41	37–46
15	18–24	21–27	24–30	30–37	37–46	41–51
16	21–27	24–30	27–33	33–41	41–51	46–57
17	24–30	27–33	30–37	37–46	46–57	51–63
18	27–33	30–37	33–41	41–51	51–63	57–71
19	30–37	33–41	37–46	46–57	57–71	63–78
20	33–41	37–46	41–51	51–63	63–78	70–87
21	37–46	41–51	46–57	57–71	70–87	77–96
22	41–51	46–57	51–63	63–78	77–96	84–105
23	46–57	51–63	57–71	70–87	84–105	92–115
24	51–63	57–71	63–78	77–96	92–115	100–125
25	57–71	63–78	70–87	84–105	100–125	110–137
26	63–78	70–87	78–97	92–115	110–137	120–150
27	70–87	78–97	87–108	100–125	120–150	130–162
28	78–97	87–108	97–121	110–137	130–162	140–175
29	87–108	97–121	108–135	121–151	140–175	151–188
30	97–121	108–135	121–151	135–168	151–188	168–210
31	108–135	121–151	135–168	151–188	168–210	188–235
32	121–151	135–168	151–188	168–210	188–235	210–262
33	135–168	151–188	168–210	188–265	210–262	235–293
34	151–188	168–210	188–235	210–262	235–293	262–327
35	168–210	188–235	210–262	235–293	262–327	292–365
36	188–235	210–262	235–293	262–327	292–365	324–405
37	210–262	235–293	262–327	292–365	324–405	360–life
38	235–293	262–327	292–365	324–405	360–life	360–life
39	262–327	292–365	324–405	360–life	360–life	360–life
40	292–365	324–405	360–life	360–life	360–life	360–life
41	324–405	360–life	360–life	360–life	360–life	360–life
42	360–life	360–life	360–life	360–life	360–life	360–life
43	life	life	life	life	life	life

Commentary to Sentencing Table

Application Notes:

1. The Offense Level (1–43) forms the vertical axis of the Sentencing Table. The Criminal History Category (I–VI) forms the horizontal axis of the Table. The intersection of the Offense Level and Criminal History Category displays the Guideline Range in months of imprisonment. "Life" means life imprisonment. For example, the guideline range applicable to a defendant with an Offense Level of 15 and a Criminal History Category of III is 24–30 months of imprisonment.

2. In rare cases, a total offense level of less than 1 or more than 43 may result from application of the guidelines. A total offense level of less than 1 is to be treated as an offense level of 1. An offense level of more than 43 is to be treated as an offense level of 43.

3. The Criminal History Category is determined by the total criminal history points from Chapter Four, Part A. The total criminal history points associated with each Criminal History Category are shown under each Criminal History Category in the Sentencing Table.

PART B—PROBATION

Introductory Commentary

The Comprehensive Crime Control Act of 1984 makes probation a sentence in and of itself. 18 U.S.C. § 3561. Probation may be used as an alternative to incarceration, provided that the terms and conditions of probation can be fashioned so as to meet fully the statutory purposes of sentencing, including promoting respect for law, providing just punishment for the offense, achieving general deterrence, and protecting the public from further crimes by the defendant.

§ 5B1.1 Imposition of a Term of Probation

(a) Subject to the statutory restrictions in subsection (b) below, sentence of probation is authorized:

(1) if the minimum term of imprisonment in the range specified by the Sentencing Table in Part A, is zero months;

(2) if the minimum term of imprisonment specified by the Sentencing Table is at least one but not more than six months, provided that the court imposes a condition or combination of conditions requiring intermittent confinement, community confinement, or home detention as provided in § 5C1.1(c)(2) (Imposition of a Term of Imprisonment).

(b) A sentence of probation may not be imposed in the event:

(1) the offense of conviction is a Class A or B felony, 18 U.S.C. § 3561(a)(1);

(2) the offense of conviction expressly precludes probation as a sentence, 18 U.S.C. § 3561(a)(2);

(3) the defendant is sentenced at the same time to a sentence of imprisonment for the same or a different offense, 18 U.S.C. § 3561(a)(3).

* * *

§ 5B1.2 Term of Probation

(a) When probation is imposed, the term shall be:

(1) at least one year but not more than five years if the offense level is 6 or greater;

(2) no more than three years in any other case.

* * *

§ 5B1.3 Conditions of Probation

(a) If a term of probation is imposed, the court shall impose a condition that the defendant shall not commit another federal, state, or local crime during the term of probation. 18 U.S.C. § 3563(a)(1). The court shall also impose a condition that the defendant not possess illegal controlled substances. 18 U.S.C. § 3563(a)(3).

(b) The court may impose other conditions that (1) are reasonably related to the nature and circumstances of the offense, the history and characteristics of the defendant, and the purposes of sentencing and (2) involve only such deprivations of liberty or property as are reasonably necessary to effect the purposes of sentencing. 18 U.S.C. § 3563(b). Recommended conditions are set forth in § 5B1.4.

(c) If a term of probation is imposed for a felony, the court shall impose at least one of the following as a condition of probation: a fine, an order of restitution, or community service, unless the court finds on the record that extraordinary circumstances exist that would make such a condition plainly unreasonable, in which event the court shall impose one or more of the other conditions set forth under 18 U.S.C. § 3563(b). 18 U.S.C. § 3563(a)(2).

(d) Intermittent confinement (custody for intervals of time) may be ordered as a condition of probation during the first year of probation. 18 U.S.C. § 3563(b)(11). Intermittent confinement shall be credited toward the guideline term of imprisonment at § 5C1.1 as provided in the schedule at § 5C1.1(e).

* * *

§ 5B1.4 Recommended Conditions of Probation and Supervised Release (Policy Statement)

(a) The following "standard" conditions (1–13) are generally recommended for both probation and supervised release:

(1) the defendant shall not leave the judicial district or other specified geographic area without the permission of the court or probation officer;

(2) the defendant shall report to the probation officer as directed by the court or probation officer and shall submit a truthful and complete written report within the first five days of each month;

(3) the defendant shall answer truthfully all inquiries by the probation officer and follow the instructions of the probation officer;

(4) the defendant shall support his dependents and meet other family responsibilities;

(5) the defendant shall work regularly at a lawful occupation unless excused by the probation officer for schooling, training, or other acceptable reasons;

(6) the defendant shall notify the probation officer within seventy-two hours of any change in residence or employment;

(7) the defendant shall refrain from excessive use of alcohol and shall not purchase, possess, use, distribute, or administer any narcotic or other controlled substance, or any paraphernalia related to such substances, except as prescribed by a physician;

(8) the defendant shall not frequent places where controlled substances are illegally sold, used, distributed, or administered, or other places specified by the court;

(9) the defendant shall not associate with any persons engaged in criminal activity, and shall not associate with any person convicted of a felony unless granted permission to do so by the probation officer;

(10) the defendant shall permit a probation officer to visit him at any time at home or elsewhere and shall permit confiscation of any contraband observed in plain view by the probation officer;

(11) the defendant shall notify the probation officer within seventy-two hours of being arrested or questioned by a law enforcement officer;

(12) the defendant shall not enter into any agreement to act as an informer or a special agent of a law enforcement agency without the permission of the court;

(13) as directed by the probation officer, the defendant shall notify third parties of risks that may be occasioned by the defendant's criminal record or personal history or characteristics, and shall permit the probation officer to make such notifications and to confirm the defendant's compliance with such notification requirement.

(b) The following "special" conditions of probation and supervised release (14–24) are either recommended or required by law under the circumstances described, or may be appropriate in a particular case:

(14) Possession of Weapons

If the instant conviction is for a felony, or if the defendant was previously convicted of a felony or used a firearm or other dangerous weapon in the course of the instant offense, it is recommended that the court impose a condition prohibiting the defendant from possessing a firearm or other dangerous weapon.

(15) Restitution

If the court imposes an order of restitution, it is recommended that the court impose a condition requiring the defendant to make payment of restitution or adhere to a court ordered installment schedule for payment of restitution. See § 5E1.1 (Restitution).

(16) Fines

If the court imposes a fine, it is recommended that the court impose a condition requiring the defendant to pay the fine or adhere to a court ordered installment schedule for payment of the fine.

(17) Debt Obligations

If an installment schedule of payment of restitution or fines is imposed, it is recommended that the court impose a condition prohibiting the defendant from incurring new credit charges or opening additional lines of credit without approval of the probation officer unless the defendant is in compliance with the payment schedule.

(18) Access to Financial Information

If the court imposes an order of restitution, forfeiture, or notice to victims, or orders the defendant to pay a fine, it is recommended that the court impose a condition requiring the defendant to provide the probation officer access to any requested financial information.

(19) Community Confinement

Residence in a community treatment center, halfway house or similar facility may be imposed as a condition of probation or supervised release. See § 5F1.1 (Community Confinement).

(20) Home Detention

Home detention may be imposed as a condition of probation or supervised release, but only as a substitute for imprisonment. See § 5F1.2 (Home Detention).

(21) Community Service

Community service may be imposed as a condition of probation or supervised release. See § 5F1.3 (Community Service).

(22) Occupational Restrictions

Occupational restrictions may be imposed as a condition of probation or supervised release. See § 5F1.5 (Occupational Restrictions).

(23) Substance Abuse Program Participation

If the court has reason to believe that the defendant is an abuser of narcotics, other controlled substances or alcohol, it is recommended that the court impose a condition requiring the defendant to participate in a program approved by the United States Probation Office for substance abuse, which program may include testing to determine whether the defendant has reverted to the use of drugs or alcohol.

(24) Mental Health Program Participation

If the court has reason to believe that the defendant is in need of psychological or psychiatric treatment, it is recommended that the court impose a condition requiring that the defendant participate in a mental health program approved by the United States Probation Office.

(25) Curfew

If the court concludes that restricting the defendant to his place of residence during evening and nighttime hours is necessary to provide just punishment for the offense, to protect the public from crimes that the defendant might commit during those hours, or to assist in the rehabilitation of the defendant, a condition of curfew is recommended. Electronic monitoring may be used as a means of surveillance to ensure compliance with a curfew order.

* * *

PART C—IMPRISONMENT

§ 5C1.1 Imposition of a Term of Imprisonment

(a) A sentence conforms with the guidelines for imprisonment if it is within the minimum and maximum terms of the guideline range.

(b) If the minimum term of imprisonment in the applicable guideline range in the Sentencing Table is zero months, a sentence of imprisonment is not required, unless the applicable guideline in Chapter Two expressly requires such a term.

(c) If the minimum term of imprisonment in the applicable guideline range in the Sentencing Table is at least one but not more than six months, the minimum term may be satisfied by (1) a sentence of imprisonment; (2) a sentence of probation that includes a condition or combination of conditions that substitute intermittent confinement, community confinement, or home detention for imprisonment according to the schedule in § 5C1.1(e); or (3) a sentence of imprisonment that includes a term of supervised release with a condition that substitutes community confinement or home detention according to the schedule in § 5C1.1(e), provided that at least one-half of the minimum term, but in no event less than one month, is satisfied by imprisonment.

(d) If the minimum term of imprisonment in the applicable guideline range in the Sentencing Table is more than six months but not more than ten months, the minimum term may be satisfied by (1) a sentence of imprisonment; or (2) a sentence of imprisonment that includes a term of supervised release with a condition that substitutes community confinement or home detention according to the schedule in § 5C1.1(e), provided that at least one-half of the minimum term is satisfied by imprisonment.

(e) Schedule of Substitute Punishments:

(1) One day of intermittent confinement in prison or jail for one day of imprisonment (each 24 hours of confinement is credited as one day

of intermittent confinement, provided, however, that one day shall be credited for any calendar day during which the defendant is employed in the community and confined during all remaining hours);

(2) One day of community confinement (residence in a community treatment center, halfway house, or similar residential facility) for one day of imprisonment;

(3) One day of home detention for one day of imprisonment.

(f) If the minimum term of imprisonment in the applicable guideline range in the Sentencing Table is more than ten months, the guidelines require that the minimum term be satisfied by a sentence of imprisonment.

* * *

PART E—RESTITUTION, FINES, ASSESSMENTS, FORFEITURES

§ 5E1.1 Restitution

(a) Restitution shall be ordered for convictions under Title 18 of the United States Code or under 49 U.S.C. § 1472(h), (i), (j) or (n) in accordance with 18 U.S.C. § 3663(d), and may be ordered as a condition of probation or supervised release in any other case.

(b) If a defendant is ordered to make restitution and to pay a fine, the court shall order that any money paid by the defendant shall first be applied to satisfy the order of restitution.

(c) With the consent of the victim of the offense, the court may order a defendant to perform services for the benefit of the victim in lieu of monetary restitution or in conjunction therewith. 18 U.S.C. § 3663(b)(4).

Commentary

Background: Section 3553(a)(7) of Title 18 requires the court, "in determining the particular sentence to be imposed," to consider "the need to provide restitution to any victims of the offense." Section 3556 of Title 18 authorizes the court to impose restitution in accordance with 18 U.S.C. §§ 3663 and 3664, which authorize restitution for violations of Title 18 and of designated subdivisions of 49 U.S.C. § 1472. For other offenses, restitution may be imposed as a condition of probation or supervised release. See 18 U.S.C. § 3563(b)(3) as amended by Section 7110 of Pub.L. No. 100–690 (1988). An order of restitution may be appropriate in offenses not specifically referenced in 18 U.S.C. § 3663 where victims require relief more promptly than the civil justice system provides.

Subsection 5E1.1 requires the court to order restitution for offenses under Title 18 or 49 U.S.C. § 1472(h), (i), (j), or (n), unless "the court determines that the complication and prolongation of the sentencing process resulting from the fashioning of an order of restitution . . . outweighs the need to provide restitution to any victims." 18 U.S.C. § 3663(d). If the court does not order restitution, or orders only partial restitution, it must state its reasons for doing so. 18 U.S.C. § 3553(c).

In determining whether to impose an order of restitution, and the amount of restitution, the court shall consider the amount of loss the victim suffered as a result of the offense, the financial resources of the defendant, the financial needs of the defendant and his dependents, and other factors the court deems appropriate. 18 U.S.C. § 3664(a).

Pursuant to Rule 32(c)(2)(D), Federal Rules of Criminal Procedure, the probation officer's presentence investigation report must contain a victim impact statement. That report must contain information about the financial impact on the victim and the defendant's financial condition. The sentencing judge may base findings on the presentence report or other testimony or evidence supported by a preponderance of the evidence. 18 U.S.C. § 3664(d).

A court's authority to deny restitution is limited. Even "in those unusual cases where the precise amount owed is difficult to determine, section 3579(d) authorizes the court to reach an expeditious, reasonable determination of appropriate restitution by resolving uncertainties with a view toward achieving fairness to the victim." S.Rep. No. 532, 97th Cong., 2d Sess. 31, reprinted in 1982 U.S.Code Cong. & Ad.News 2515, 2537.

Unless the court orders otherwise, restitution must be made immediately. 18 U.S.C. § 3663(f)(3). The court may permit the defendant to make restitution within a specified period or in specified installments, provided that the last installment is paid not later than the expiration of probation, five years after the end of the defendant's term of imprisonment, or in any other case five years after the date of sentencing. 18 U.S.C. § 3663(f)(1) and (2). The restitution order should specify how and to whom payment is to be made.

§ 5E1.2 Fines for Individual Defendants

(a) Except as provided in subsection (f) below, the court shall impose a fine in all cases.

(b) Except as provided in subsections (f) and (i) below, or otherwise required by statute, the fine imposed shall be within the range specified in subsection (c) below. If, however, the guideline for the offense in Chapter Two provides a specific rule for imposing a fine, that rule takes precedence over subsection (c) of this section.

(c) (1) The minimum of the fine range is the greater of:

(A) the amount shown in column A of the table below; or

(B) the pecuniary gain to the defendant, less restitution made or ordered.

(2) Except as specified in (4) below, the maximum of the fine range is the greater of:

(A) the amount shown in column B of the table below;

(B) twice the gross pecuniary loss caused by the offense; or

(C) three times the gross pecuniary gain to all participants in the offense.

(3) **Fine Table**

Offense Level	**A Minimum**	**B Maximum**
3 and below	$100	$5,000
4–5	$250	$5,000

Offense Level	A Minimum	B Maximum
6–7	$500	$5,000
8–9	$1,000	$10,000
10–11	$2,000	$20,000
12–13	$3,000	$30,000
14–15	$4,000	$40,000
16–17	$5,000	$50,000
18–19	$6,000	$60,000
20–22	$7,500	$75,000
23–25	$10,000	$100,000
26–28	$12,500	$125,000
29–31	$15,000	$150,000
32–34	$17,500	$175,000
35–37	$20,000	$200,000
38 and above	$25,000	$250,000.

(4) Subsection (c)(2), limiting the maximum fine, does not apply if the defendant is convicted under a statute authorizing (A) a maximum fine greater than $250,000, or (B) a fine for each day of violation. In such cases, the court may impose a fine up to the maximum authorized by the statute.

(d) In determining the amount of the fine, the court shall consider:

(1) the need for the combined sentence to reflect the seriousness of the offense (including the harm or loss to the victim and the gain to the defendant), to promote respect for the law, to provide just punishment and to afford adequate deterrence;

(2) the ability of the defendant to pay the fine (including the ability to pay over a period of time) in light of his earning capacity and financial resources;

(3) the burden that the fine places on the defendant and his dependents relative to alternative punishments;

(4) any restitution or reparation that the defendant has made or is obligated to make;

(5) any collateral consequences of conviction, including civil obligations arising from the defendant's conduct;

(6) whether the defendant previously has been fined for a similar offense; and

(7) any other pertinent equitable considerations.

(e) The amount of the fine should always be sufficient to ensure that the fine, taken together with other sanctions imposed, is punitive.

(f) If the defendant establishes that (1) he is not able and, even with the use of a reasonable installment schedule, is not likely to become able to pay all or part of the fine required by the preceding provisions, or (2) imposition of a fine would unduly burden the defendant's dependents, the court may impose a lesser fine or waive the fine. In these circumstances, the court shall consider alternative sanctions in lieu of all or a portion of the fine, and must still impose a total combined sanction that is punitive. Although any additional sanction not proscribed by the guidelines is permissible, community service is the generally preferable alternative in such instances.

(g) If the defendant establishes that payment of the fine in a lump sum would have an unduly severe impact on him or his dependents, the court should establish an installment schedule for payment of the fine. The length of the installment schedule generally should not exceed twelve months, and shall not exceed the maximum term of probation authorized for the offense. The defendant should be required to pay a substantial installment at the time of sentencing. If the court authorizes a defendant sentenced to probation or supervised release to pay a fine on an installment schedule, the court shall require as a condition of probation or supervised release that the defendant pay the fine according to the schedule. The court also may impose a condition prohibiting the defendant from incurring new credit charges or opening additional lines of credit unless he is in compliance with the payment schedule.

(h) If the defendant knowingly fails to pay a delinquent fine, the court shall resentence him in accordance with 18 U.S.C. § 3614.

(i) Notwithstanding * * * the provisions of subsection (c) of this section, but subject to the provisions of subsection (f) herein, the court shall impose an additional fine amount that is at least sufficient to pay the costs to the government of any imprisonment, probation, or supervised release ordered.

* * *

§ 5E1.3 Special Assessments

A special assessment must be imposed on a convicted defendant in the amount prescribed by statute.

Commentary

Background: The Victims of Crime Act of 1984, Pub.L. No. 98–473, Title II, Chap. XIV, requires the courts to impose special assessments on convicted defendants for the purpose of funding the Crime Victims Fund established by the same legislation. Monies deposited in the fund are awarded to the states by the Attorney General for victim assistance and compensation programs. Under the Victims of Crime Act, as amended by Section 7085 of the Anti–Drug Abuse Act of 1988, the court is required to impose assessments in the following amounts with respect to offenses committed on or after November 18, 1988:

Individuals:

$5, if the defendant is an individual convicted of an infraction or a Class C misdemeanor;

$10, if the defendant is an individual convicted of a Class B misdemeanor;

$25, if the defendant is an individual convicted of a Class A misdemeanor; and

$50, if the defendant is an individual convicted of a felony.

Organizations:

$50, if the defendant is an organization convicted of a Class B misdemeanor;

$125, if the defendant is an organization convicted of a Class A misdemeanor; and

$200, if the defendant is an organization convicted of a felony. 18 U.S.C. § 3013.

With respect to offenses committed prior to November 18, 1988, the court is required to impose assessments in the following amounts:

$25, if the defendant is an individual convicted of a misdemeanor;

$50, if the defendant is an individual convicted of a felony;

$100, if the defendant is an organization convicted of a misdemeanor; and

$200, if the defendant is an organization convicted of a felony. 18 U.S.C. § 3013.

The Act does not authorize the court to waive imposition of the assessment.

§ 5E1.4 Forfeiture

Forfeiture is to be imposed upon a convicted defendant as provided by statute.

* * *

PART F—SENTENCING OPTIONS

§ 5F1.1 Community Confinement

Community confinement may be imposed as a condition of probation or supervised release.

Commentary

Application Notes:

1. "Community confinement" means residence in a community treatment center, halfway house, restitution center, mental health facility, alcohol or drug rehabilitation center, or other community facility; and participation in gainful employment, employment search efforts, community service, vocational training, treatment, educational programs, or similar facility-approved programs during non-residential hours.

2. Community confinement generally should not be imposed for a period in excess of six months. A longer period may be imposed to accomplish the objectives of a specific rehabilitative program, such as drug rehabilitation. The sentencing judge may impose other discretionary conditions of probation or supervised release appropriate to effectuate community confinement.

§ 5F1.2 Home Detention

Home detention may be imposed as a condition of probation or supervised release, but only as a substitute for imprisonment.

Commentary

Application Notes:

1. "Home detention" means a program of confinement and supervision that restricts the defendant to his place of residence continuously, except for authorized absences, enforced by appropriate means of surveillance by the probation office. When an order of home detention is imposed, the defendant is required to be in

his place of residence at all times except for approved absences for gainful employment, community service, religious services, medical care, educational or training programs, and such other times as may be specifically authorized. Electronic monitoring is an appropriate means of surveillance and ordinarily should be used in connection with home detention. However, alternative means of surveillance may be used so long as they are as effective as electronic monitoring.

2. The court may impose other conditions of probation or supervised release appropriate to effectuate home detention. If the court concludes that the amenities available in the residence of a defendant would cause home detention not to be sufficiently punitive, the court may limit the amenities available.

3. The defendant's place of residence, for purposes of home detention, need not be the place where the defendant previously resided. It may be any place of residence, so long as the owner of the residence (and any other person(s) from whom consent is necessary) agrees to any conditions that may be imposed by the court, e.g., conditions that a monitoring system be installed, that there will be no "call forwarding" or "call waiting" services, or that there will be no cordless telephones or answering machines.

Background: The Commission has concluded that the surveillance necessary for effective use of home detention ordinarily requires electronic monitoring. However, in some cases home detention may effectively be enforced without electronic monitoring, e.g., when the defendant is physically incapacitated, or where some other effective means of surveillance is available. Accordingly, the Commission has not required that electronic monitoring be a necessary condition for home detention. Nevertheless, before ordering home detention without electronic monitoring, the court should be confident that an alternative form of surveillance will be equally effective.

In the usual case, the Commission assumes that a condition requiring that the defendant seek and maintain gainful employment will be imposed when home detention is ordered.

§ 5F1.3 Community Service

Community service may be ordered as a condition of probation or supervised release. If the defendant was convicted of a felony and sentenced to probation, the court must order one or more of the following sanctions: a fine, restitution, or community service. 18 U.S.C. § 3563(a)(2).

Commentary

Application Note:

1. Community service generally should not be imposed in excess of 400 hours. Longer terms of community service impose heavy administrative burdens relating to the selection of suitable placements and the monitoring of attendance.

§ 5F1.4. Order of Notice to Victims

The court may order the defendant to pay the cost of giving notice to victims pursuant to 18 U.S.C. § 3555. This cost may be set off against any fine imposed if the court determines that the imposition of both sanctions would be excessive.

Commentary

Background: In cases where a defendant has been convicted of an offense involving fraud or "other intentionally deceptive practices," the court may order the defendant to "give reasonable notice and explanation of the conviction, in such form as the court may approve" to the victims of the offense. 18 U.S.C. § 3555. The court may order the notice to be given by mail, by advertising in specific areas or through specific media, or by other appropriate means. In determining whether a notice is appropriate, the court must consider the generally applicable sentencing factors listed in 18 U.S.C. § 3553(a) and the cost involved in giving the notice as it relates to the loss caused by the crime. The court may not require the defendant to pay more than $20,000 to give notice.

If an order of notice to victims is under consideration, the court must notify the government and the defendant. 18 U.S.C. § 3553(d). Upon motion of either party, or on its own motion, the court must: (1) permit the parties to submit affidavits and memoranda relevant to the imposition of such an order; (2) provide counsel for both parties the opportunity to address orally, in open court, the appropriateness of such an order; and (3) if it issues such an order, state its reasons for doing so. The court may also order any additional procedures that will not unduly complicate or prolong the sentencing process.

§ 5F1.5. Occupational Restrictions

(a) The court may impose a condition of probation or supervised release prohibiting the defendant from engaging in a specified occupation, business, or profession, or limiting the terms on which the defendant may do so, only if it determines that:

(1) a reasonably direct relationship existed between the defendant's occupation, business, or profession and the conduct relevant to the offense of conviction; and

(2) imposition of such a restriction is reasonably necessary to protect the public because there is reason to believe that, absent such restriction, the defendant will continue to engage in unlawful conduct similar to that for which the defendant was convicted.

(b) If the court decides to impose a condition of probation or supervised release restricting a defendant's engagement in a specified occupation, business, or profession, the court shall impose the condition for the minimum time and to the minimum extent necessary to protect the public.

* * *

PART H—SPECIFIC OFFENDER CHARACTERISTICS

Introductory Commentary

Congress has directed the Commission to consider whether certain specific offender characteristics "have any relevance to the nature, extent, place of service, or other incidents of an appropriate sentence" and to take them into account only to the extent they are determined relevant by the Commission. 28 U.S.C. § 994(d).

§ 5H1.1 Age (Policy Statement)

Age is not ordinarily relevant in determining whether a sentence should be outside the guidelines. Neither is it ordinarily relevant in determining the type of sentence to be imposed when the guidelines provide sentencing options. Age may be a reason to go below the guidelines when the offender is elderly and infirm and where a form of punishment (e.g., home confinement) might be equally efficient as and less costly than incarceration. If, independent of the consideration of age, a defendant is sentenced to probation or supervised release, age may be relevant in the determination of the length and conditions of supervision.

§ 5H1.2 Education and Vocational Skills (Policy Statement)

Education and vocational skills are not ordinarily relevant in determining whether a sentence should be outside the guidelines, but the extent to which a defendant may have misused special training or education to facilitate criminal activity is an express guideline factor. See § 3B1.3 (Abuse of Position of Trust or Use of Special Skill). Neither are education and vocational skills relevant in determining the type of sentence to be imposed when the guidelines provide sentencing options. If, independent of consideration of education and vocational skills, a defendant is sentenced to probation or supervised release, these considerations may be relevant in the determination of the length and conditions of supervision for rehabilitative purposes, for public protection by restricting activities that allow for the utilization of a certain skill, or in determining the type or length of community service.

§ 5H1.3 Mental and Emotional Conditions (Policy Statement)

Mental and emotional conditions are not ordinarily relevant in determining whether a sentence should be outside the guidelines, except as provided in the general provisions in Chapter Five. Mental and emotional conditions, whether mitigating or aggravating, may be relevant in determining the length and conditions of probation or supervised release.

§ 5H1.4 Physical Condition, Including Drug Dependence and Alcohol Abuse (Policy Statement)

Physical condition is not ordinarily relevant in determining whether a sentence should be outside the guidelines or where within the guidelines a sentence should fall. However, an extraordinary physical impairment may be a reason to impose a sentence other than imprisonment.

Drug dependence or alcohol abuse is not a reason for imposing a sentence below the guidelines. Substance abuse is highly correlated to an increased propensity to commit crime. Due to this increased risk, it is highly recommended that a defendant who is incarcerated also be sentenced to supervised release with a requirement that the defendant participate in an appropriate substance abuse program. If participation in a substance abuse program is required, the length of supervised release should take into account the length of time necessary for the supervisory body to judge the success of the program.

This provision would also apply in cases where the defendant received a sentence of probation. The substance abuse condition is strongly recommended and the length of probation should be adjusted accordingly. Failure to comply would normally result in revocation of probation.

§ 5H1.5 Previous Employment Record (Policy Statement)

Employment record is not ordinarily relevant in determining whether a sentence should be outside the guidelines or where within the guidelines a sentence should fall. Employment record may be relevant in determining the type of sentence to be imposed when the guidelines provide for sentencing options. If, independent of the consideration of employment record, a defendant is sentenced to probation or supervised release, considerations of employment record may be relevant in the determination of the length and conditions of supervision.

§ 5H1.6 Family Ties and Responsibilities, and Community Ties (Policy Statement)

Family ties and responsibilities and community ties are not ordinarily relevant in determining whether a sentence should be outside the guidelines. Family responsibilities that are complied with are relevant in determining whether to impose restitution and fines. Where the guidelines provide probation as an option, these factors may be relevant in this determination. If a defendant is sentenced to probation or supervised release, family ties and responsibilities that are met may be relevant in the determination of the length and conditions of supervision.

§ 5H1.7 Role in the Offense (Policy Statement)

A defendant's role in the offense is relevant in determining the appropriate sentence. See Chapter Three, Part B (Role in the Offense).

§ 5H1.8 Criminal History (Policy Statement)

A defendant's criminal history is relevant in determining the appropriate sentence. See Chapter Four (Criminal History and Criminal Livelihood).

§ 5H1.9 Dependence upon Criminal Activity for a Livelihood (Policy Statement)

The degree to which a defendant depends upon criminal activity for a livelihood is relevant in determining the appropriate sentence. See Chapter Four, Part B (Career Offenders and Criminal Livelihood).

§ 5H1.10 Race, Sex, National Origin, Creed, Religion and Socio–Economic Status (Policy Statement)

These factors are not relevant in the determination of a sentence.

PART K—DEPARTURES

1. SUBSTANTIAL ASSISTANCE TO AUTHORITIES

§ 5K1.1 Substantial Assistance to Authorities (Policy Statement)

Upon motion of the government stating that the defendant has provided substantial assistance in the investigation or prosecution of another person who has committed an offense, the court may depart from the guidelines.

(a) The appropriate reduction shall be determined by the court for reasons stated that may include, but are not limited to, consideration of the following:

(1) the court's evaluation of the significance and usefulness of the defendant's assistance, taking into consideration the government's evaluation of the assistance rendered;

(2) the truthfulness, completeness, and reliability of any information or testimony provided by the defendant;

(3) the nature and extent of the defendant's assistance;

(4) any injury suffered, or any danger or risk of injury to the defendant or his family resulting from his assistance;

(5) the timeliness of the defendant's assistance.

Commentary

Application Notes:

1. Under circumstances set forth in 18 U.S.C. § 3553(e) and 28 U.S.C. § 994(n), as amended, substantial assistance in the investigation or prosecution of another person who has committed an offense may justify a sentence below a statutorily required minimum sentence.

2. The sentencing reduction for assistance to authorities shall be considered independently of any reduction for acceptance of responsibility. Substantial assistance is directed to the investigation and prosecution of criminal activities by persons other than the defendant, while acceptance of responsibility is directed to the defendant's affirmative recognition of responsibility for his own conduct.

3. Substantial weight should be given to the government's evaluation of the extent of the defendant's assistance, particularly where the extent and value of the assistance are difficult to ascertain.

Background: A defendant's assistance to authorities in the investigation of criminal activities has been recognized in practice and by statute as a mitigating sentencing factor. The nature, extent, and significance of assistance can involve a broad spectrum of conduct that must be evaluated by the court on an individual basis. Latitude is, therefore, afforded the sentencing judge to reduce a sentence based upon variable relevant factors, including those listed above. The sentencing judge must, however, state the reasons for reducing a sentence under this section. 18 U.S.C. § 3553(c). The court may elect to provide its reasons to the defendant in camera and in writing under seal for the safety of the defendant or to avoid disclosure of an ongoing investigation.

§ 5K1.2 Refusal to Assist (Policy Statement)

A defendant's refusal to assist authorities in the investigation of other persons may not be considered as an aggravating sentencing factor.

* * *

2. GENERAL PROVISIONS

§ 5K2.0 Grounds for Departure (Policy Statement)

Under 18 U.S.C. § 3553(b) the sentencing court may impose a sentence outside the range established by the applicable guideline, if the court finds "that there exists an aggravating or mitigating circumstance of a kind, or to a degree not adequately taken into consideration by the Sentencing Commission in formulating the guidelines." Circumstances that may warrant departure from the guidelines pursuant to this provision cannot, by their very nature, be comprehensively listed and analyzed in advance. The controlling decision as to whether and to what extent departure is warranted can only be made by the court at the time of sentencing. Nonetheless, the present section seeks to aid the court by identifying some of the factors that the Commission has not been able to fully take into account in formulating precise guidelines. Any case may involve factors in addition to those identified that have not been given adequate consideration by the Commission. Presence of any such factor may warrant departure from the guidelines, under some circumstances, in the discretion of the sentencing judge. Similarly, the court may depart from the guidelines, even though the reason for departure is listed elsewhere in the guidelines (e.g., as an adjustment or specific offense characteristic), if the court determines that, in light of unusual circumstances, the guideline level attached to that factor is inadequate.

Where the applicable guidelines, specific offense characteristics, and adjustments do take into consideration a factor listed in this part, departure from the guideline is warranted only if the factor is present to a degree substantially in excess of that which ordinarily is involved in the offense of conviction. Thus, disruption of a governmental function, § 5K2.7, would have to be quite serious to warrant departure from the guidelines when the offense of conviction is bribery or obstruction of justice. When the offense of conviction is theft, however, and when the theft caused disruption of a governmental function, departure from the applicable guideline more readily would be appropriate. Similarly, physical injury would not warrant departure from the guidelines when the offense of conviction is robbery because the robbery guideline includes a specific sentence adjustment based on the extent of any injury. However, because the robbery guideline does not deal with injury to more than one victim, departure would be warranted if several persons were injured.

Also, a factor may be listed as a specific offense characteristic under one guideline but not under all guidelines. Simply because it was not listed does not mean that there may not be circumstances when that factor would be relevant to sentencing. For example, the use of a weapon has been listed as a specific offense characteristic under many guidelines, but not under immigration violations. Therefore, if a weapon is a relevant factor to sentencing for an immigration violation, the court may depart for this reason.

Harms identified as a possible basis for departure from the guidelines should be taken into account only when they are relevant to the offense of conviction, within the limitations set forth in § 1B1.3.

§ 5K2.1 Death (Policy Statement)

If death resulted, the court may increase the sentence above the authorized guideline range.

Loss of life does not automatically suggest a sentence at or near the statutory maximum. The sentencing judge must give consideration to matters that would normally distinguish among levels of homicide, such as the defendant's state of mind and the degree of planning or preparation. Other appropriate factors are whether multiple deaths resulted, and the means by which life was taken. The extent of the increase should depend on the dangerousness of the defendant's conduct, the extent to which death or serious injury was intended or knowingly risked, and the extent to which the offense level for the offense of conviction, as determined by the other Chapter Two guidelines, already reflects the risk of personal injury. For example, a substantial increase may be appropriate if the death was intended or knowingly risked or if the underlying offense was one for which base offense levels do not reflect an allowance for the risk of personal injury, such as fraud.

§ 5K2.2 Physical Injury (Policy Statement)

If significant physical injury resulted, the court may increase the sentence above the authorized guideline range. The extent of the increase ordinarily should depend on the extent of the injury, the degree to which it may prove permanent, and the extent to which the injury was intended or knowingly risked. When the victim suffers a major, permanent disability and when such injury was intentionally inflicted, a substantial departure may be appropriate. If the injury is less serious or if the defendant (though criminally negligent) did not knowingly create the risk of harm, a less substantial departure would be indicated. In general, the same considerations apply as in § 5K2.1.

§ 5K2.3 Extreme Psychological Injury (Policy Statement)

If a victim or victims suffered psychological injury much more serious than that normally resulting from commission of the offense, the court may increase the sentence above the authorized guideline range. The extent of the increase ordinarily should depend on the severity of the psychological injury and the extent to which the injury was intended or knowingly risked.

Normally, psychological injury would be sufficiently severe to warrant application of this adjustment only when there is a substantial impairment of the intellectual, psychological, emotional, or behavioral functioning of a victim, when the impairment is likely to be of an extended or continuous duration, and when the impairment manifests itself by physical or psychological symptoms or by changes in behavior patterns. The court should consider the extent to which such harm was likely, given the nature of the defendant's conduct.

§ 5K2.4 Abduction or Unlawful Restraint (Policy Statement)

If a person was abducted, taken hostage, or unlawfully restrained to facilitate commission of the offense or to facilitate the escape from the scene of the crime, the court may increase the sentence above the authorized guideline range.

§ 5K2.5 Property Damage or Loss (Policy Statement)

If the offense caused property damage or loss not taken into account within the guidelines, the court may increase the sentence above the authorized guideline range. The extent of the increase ordinarily should depend on the extent to which the harm was intended or knowingly risked and on the extent to which the harm to property is more serious than other harm caused or risked by the conduct relevant to the offense of conviction.

§ 5K2.6 Weapons and Dangerous Instrumentalities (Policy Statement)

If a weapon or dangerous instrumentality was used or possessed in the commission of the offense the court may increase the sentence above the authorized guideline range. The extent of the increase ordinarily should depend on the dangerousness of the weapon, the manner in which it was used, and the extent to which its use endangered others. The discharge of a firearm might warrant a substantial sentence increase.

§ 5K2.7 Disruption of Governmental Function (Policy Statement)

If the defendant's conduct resulted in a significant disruption of a governmental function, the court may increase the sentence above the authorized guideline range to reflect the nature and extent of the disruption and the importance of the governmental function affected. Departure from the guidelines ordinarily would not be justified when the offense of conviction is an offense such as bribery or obstruction of justice; in such cases interference with a governmental function is inherent in the offense, and unless the circumstances are unusual the guidelines will reflect the appropriate punishment for such interference.

§ 5K2.8 Extreme Conduct (Policy Statement)

If the defendant's conduct was unusually heinous, cruel, brutal, or degrading to the victim, the court may increase the sentence above the guideline range to reflect the nature of the conduct. Examples of extreme conduct include torture of a victim, gratuitous infliction of injury, or prolonging of pain or humiliation.

§ 5K2.9 Criminal Purpose (Policy Statement)

If the defendant committed the offense in order to facilitate or conceal the commission of another offense, the court may increase the sentence above the guideline range to reflect the actual seriousness of the defendant's conduct.

§ 5K2.10 Victim's Conduct (Policy Statement)

If the victim's wrongful conduct contributed significantly to provoking the offense behavior, the court may reduce the sentence below the guideline range to reflect the nature and circumstances of the offense. In deciding the extent of a sentence reduction, the court should consider:

(a) the size and strength of the victim, or other relevant physical characteristics, in comparison with those of the defendant;

(b) the persistence of the victim's conduct and any efforts by the defendant to prevent confrontation;

(c) the danger reasonably perceived by the defendant, including the victim's reputation for violence;

(d) the danger actually presented to the defendant by the victim; and

(e) any other relevant conduct by the victim that substantially contributed to the danger presented.

Victim misconduct ordinarily would not be sufficient to warrant application of this provision in the context of offenses under Chapter Two, Part A.3 (Criminal Sexual Abuse). In addition, this provision usually would not be relevant in the context of non-violent offenses. There may, however, be unusual circumstances in which substantial victim misconduct would warrant a reduced penalty in the case of a non-violent offense. For example, an extended course of provocation and harassment might lead a defendant to steal or destroy property in retaliation.

§ 5K2.11 Lesser Harms (Policy Statement)

Sometimes, a defendant may commit a crime in order to avoid a perceived greater harm. In such instances, a reduced sentence may be appropriate, provided that the circumstances significantly diminish society's interest in punishing the conduct, for example, in the case of a mercy killing. Where the interest in punishment or deterrence is not reduced, a reduction in sentence is not warranted. For example, providing defense secrets to a hostile power should receive no lesser punishment simply because the defendant believed that the government's policies were misdirected.

In other instances, conduct may not cause or threaten the harm or evil sought to be prevented by the law proscribing the offense at issue. For example, where a war veteran possessed a machine gun or grenade as a trophy, or a school teacher possessed controlled substances for display in a drug education program, a reduced sentence might be warranted.

§ 5K2.12 Coercion and Duress (Policy Statement)

If the defendant committed the offense because of serious coercion, blackmail or duress, under circumstances not amounting to a complete defense, the court may decrease the sentence below the applicable guideline range. The extent of the decrease ordinarily should depend on the reasonableness of the defendant's actions and on the extent to which the conduct would have been less harmful under the circumstances as the defendant believed them to be. Ordinarily coercion will be sufficiently serious to warrant departure only when it involves a threat of physical injury, substantial damage to property or similar injury resulting from the unlawful action of a third party or from a natural emergency. The Commission considered the relevance of economic hardship and determined that personal financial difficulties and economic pressures upon a trade or business do not warrant a decrease in sentence.

§ 5K2.13 Diminished Capacity (Policy Statement)

If the defendant committed a non-violent offense while suffering from significantly reduced mental capacity not resulting from voluntary use of drugs or other intoxicants, a lower sentence may be warranted to reflect the extent to which reduced mental capacity contributed to the commission of the offense, provided that the defendant's criminal history does not indicate a need for incarceration to protect the public.

§ 5K2.14 Public Welfare (Policy Statement)

If national security, public health, or safety was significantly endangered, the court may increase the sentence above the guideline range to reflect the nature and circumstances of the offense.

§ 5K2.15 Terrorism (Policy Statement)

If the defendant committed the offense in furtherance of a terroristic action, the court may increase the sentence above the authorized guideline range.

* * *

INDEX

References are to Pages

†